THE OXFORD HAND

MATERI

CULTURE

STUDIES

The *Oxford Handbook of Material Culture Studies* introduces and reviews current thinking in the interdisciplinary field of material culture studies. Drawing together approaches from archaeology, anthropology, geography, and Science and Technology Studies, through twenty-eight specially commissioned essays by leading international researchers, the volume explores contemporary issues and debates in a series of themed sections—Disciplinary Perspectives, Material Practices, Objects and Humans, Landscapes and the Built Environment, and Studying Particular Things. Ranging from Coca-Cola, chimpanzees, artworks, and ceramics, to museums, cities, human bodies, and magical objects, the Handbook is an essential resource for anyone with an interest in materiality and the place of material things in human life, both past and present. A comprehensive bibliography enhances its usefulness both as a research tool and as a classroom text.

Dan Hicks is Associate Professor and Curator in Archaeology, School of Archaeology and Pitt Rivers Museum, University of Oxford.

Mary C. Beaudry is Professor of Archaeology and Anthropology, Boston University.

THE OXFORD HANDBOOK OF

MATERIAL CULTURE STUDIES

Edited by
DAN HICKS
and
MARY C. BEAUDRY

OXFORD
UNIVERSITY PRESS

OXFORD
UNIVERSITY PRESS

Great Clarendon Street, Oxford, OX2 6DP,
United Kingdom

Oxford University Press is a department of the University of Oxford.
It furthers the University's objective of excellence in research, scholarship,
and education by publishing worldwide. Oxford is a registered trade mark of
Oxford University Press in the UK and in certain other countries

© Oxford University Press 2010

The moral rights of the authors have been asserted

First published 2010
First published in paperback 2018

Published in the United States of America by Oxford University Press
198 Madison Avenue, New York, NY 10016, United States of America

British Library Cataloguing in Publication Data
Data available

Library of Congress Cataloging in Publication Data
Data available

ISBN 978–0–19–921871–4 (Hbk.)
ISBN 978–0–19–882255–4 (Pbk.)

Printed and bound by
CPI Group (UK) Ltd, Croydon, CRO 4YY

for Mike O'Hanlon
DH

In memory of my late advisor James Deetz, whose enthusiasm for studying
things, large and small, inspired me and many others
MCB

CONTENTS

PART I DISCIPLINARY PERSPECTIVES

PART II MATERIAL PRACTICES

PART III OBJECTS AND HUMANS

PART IV LANDSCAPES AND THE BUILT ENVIRONMENT

PART V STUDYING PARTICULAR THINGS

* * *

LIST OF FIGURES

LIST OF TABLES

LIST OF CONTRIBUTORS

Douglass Bailey is Professor of Anthropology at San Francisco State University

Mary C. Beaudry is Professor of Archaeology, Anthropology, and Gastronomy at Boston University

Nicole Boivin is Director of the Department of Archaeology at the Max Planck Institute for the Science of Human History, Jena

Victor Buchli is Professor of Material Culture, Department of Anthropology, University College London

Ian Cook is Professor of Cultural Geography at Exeter University

Zoë Crossland is Associate Professor of Anthropology at Columbia University

Michael Dietler is Professor of Anthropology at the University of Chicago

Roland Fletcher is Professor of Theoretical and World Archaeology at the University of Sydney

Chris Fowler is Senior Lecturer in Later Prehistoric Archaeology at Newcastle University

Rodney Harrison is Professor of Heritage Studies at University College London

Lesley Head is Professor of Geography at the University of Melbourne

Dan Hicks is Associate Professor and Curator in the School of Archaeology and Pitt Rivers Museum, Oxford University

Steve Hinchliffe is Professor in Human Geography at the University of Exeter

Kacy L. Hollenback is Assistant Professor of Anthropology at Southern Methodist University

Tatyana Humle is Senior Lecturer in Conservation and Primate Behaviour at the University of Kent

Andrew M. Jones is Reader in Archaeology at Southampton University

Rosemary Joyce is Professor of Anthropology at University of California, Berkeley

Carl Knappett is Professor of Aegean Prehistory at the University of Toronto

John Law is Emeritus Professor in Sociology at Open University

Carl R. Lounsbury is Adjunct Associate Professor of History at the College of William and Mary

Gavin Lucas is Professor in Archaeology at the University of Iceland and a member of the Board of Directors of the Institute of Archaeology, Reykjavik

Lesley McFadyen is Lecturer in Archaeology at Birkbeck, University of London

Lambros Malafouris is Research Fellow in Creativity, Cognition and Material Culture at Oxford University

Hirokazu Miyazaki is Professor of Anthropology at Cornell University

Howard Morphy is Distinguished Professor of Anthropology at Australian National University

Chandra Mukerji is Professor of Communication and Science Studies at the University of California, San Diego

Peter J. Pels is Professor of the Anthropology and Sociology of Africa at Leiden University

Andrew Pickering is Emeritus Professor of Sociology, Philosophy, and Anthropology at Exeter University

Joshua Pollard is Reader in Archaeology at Southampton University

Robert Saint George is Associate Professor of History at the University of Pennsylvania

Michael Brian Schiffer is Emeritus Professor of Anthropology at the University of Arizona

Ann Brower Stahl is Professor of Anthropology at the University of Victoria, Canada

Divya Tolia-Kelly is Professor of Geography and Heritage Studies at the University of Sussex

Nigel Thrift is the Executive Director of Schwarzman Scholars

Peter Tomkins teaches Archaeology at the Catholic University of Leuven

Sarah Whatmore is Professor of Environment and Public Policy at Oxford University

PREFACE

Upon its initial publication in 2010 our hope for this Handbook was that it would shatter the notion that material culture studies has only one or relatively few gravitational centres. In 2018, with publication of its first paperback edition, we are pleased to observe that the field has more regional, institutional and disciplinary niches than ever. As this diversity expands, the coherence of the idea of 'material culture studies', which we problematize in our introduction and in the account of the "material-cultural turn", is no longer a safe assumption: it is a research problem in its own right.

As new materialisms, speculative turns, posthumanisms, object-oriented ontologies, perspectival multinaturalisms, Cthulucenes, digital ecologies, transcendental nihilisms and capitalist realisms proliferate, this volume is an object to be taken in the hand. (A geographer's roadmap, an anthropologist's pencil, an archaeologist's trowel—the choice is yours.) This object (*obiectum*—the etymology suggests that the book might hurl ideas towards its reader), takes as its subject how material culture studies have emerged and developed, and what the themes introduced across the 28 chapters mean for the humanities and social sciences today.

A handful of examples make the point. A sustained discomfort with the ur-category of 'materiality', and the focus of material culture studies on solidity and presence, offer perspectives on the problem of immateriality. Explorations beyond standard accounts of different social contexts or worldviews set the modish idea of studying multiple ontologies in cross-disciplinary context. Discussions of the built environment address pressing questions of infrastructure, cultural ecology, atmosphere, the natural histories of human cultures, and the study of the Anthropocene. Alongside immateriality, ontology or ecology, classic themes such as skill, exchange, debt, art, deposition, collecting, technology, households, animal artefacts, personhood, and the idea of the magical fetish remain vital areas of study. Among the many emerging challenges are questions of how to apply this knowledge to the study of visual and digital culture, to the politics of museums and heritage, or to the archaeology of the contemporary world.

Like any thing, material culture studies transforms, decomposes, fragments, endures. The critical importance of the field remains its ability to move beyond the documented, the spoken, the present, the institutionalized, operating between the archaeological and the anthropological, the material and the human. The reader will, we hope, use what this volume contains of the history of the study of material culture, as it has emerged over the past 150 years or so, and about its contemporary challenges, to take forward the project of reimagining what material culture studies can mean for us today. Not as an unhuman theory of materiality, but as a mode of thought and practice that eschews anthropocentrism in the name of humanism.

Dan Hicks (Oxford) and Mary Beaudry (Boston),
April 2018

Acknowledgements

Any scholarly endeavour is a collaborative effort, but this is even more the case with a volume such as this. First in any acknowledgements for this book must come our 34 contributing authors, to whom we are indebted for their excellent chapters, their accommodation of our comments and requests, and their speedy replies that kept up the momentum of the editorial process for such a large book.

We are also grateful to our commissioning editor at OUP, Hilary O'Shea, for the initial idea for this book, and for her patience as we delivered it. Lisa Hill and Sefryn Penrose played an invaluable role in assisting with the proof reading of the manuscript.

As the volume took shape and developed, we benefited greatly from discussions with and comments from a range of colleagues. Sometimes these were in relation to specific issues that arose during the editorial process, while sometimes they had a more oblique connection to the project, but in all cases they played a central role in forming the end product. Special thanks here, in addition to our contributors, are due to Michael Archer, Jeremy Coote, Inge Daniels, Paul Dresch, Matt Edgeworth, Duncan Garrow, Roberta Gilchrist, Henry Glassie, Chris Gosden, Tim Ingold, Kristian Kristiansen, Danny Miller, Simon Naylor, Mike Pearson, Richard Wentworth, Laurie Wilkie, Chris Wingfield, and Tom Yarrow.

The volume is dedicated to Mike O'Hanlon (DH) and to the memory of James Deetz (MCB), for their hastening towards what matters, and thus into the midst of things: *semper ad eventum festinat, et in medias res.*

Finally, thanks are also due to the undergraduate and postgraduate students in Archaeology, Anthropology, and Art History who took the Material Culture Studies option paper at Oxford University in 2007–8 and 2008–9, for enduring earlier drafts of the arguments put forward in Chapters 1 and 2.

Dan Hicks, Pitt Rivers Museum, May 2009

CHAPTER 1

INTRODUCTION

MATERIAL CULTURE STUDIES: A REACTIONARY VIEW

DAN HICKS

MARY C. BEAUDRY

Four years ago, we worked together on another editorial project—*The Cambridge Companion to Historical Archaeology* (Hicks and Beaudry 2006a). At the time, historical archaeology was emerging as an area of anthropological archaeology that was witnessing new discussion, energy, and innovation; it is still more vibrant today. Researchers using archaeological methods to study the modern and contemporary world have found themselves in the middle of a broader current of cross-disciplinary interest in the material dimensions of the world. In assembling that book, therefore, we started to think through why the archaeology of the modern and contemporary world—a long-standing backwater of anthropological theory and practice—might have been experiencing such resurgence. In our introduction to that book, we suggested that historical archaeology might represent one place in which anthropology could contribute to current interdisciplinary debates about material things. We were particularly interested in the idea that these debates and currents might develop into a broader 'material turn' in the humanities and social sciences, and in whether such a material turn would shift beyond an earlier 'cultural', 'linguistic', 'literary', or 'textual' turn associated with the scholarship of the 1980s, or else constitute simply an extension of its representational logic (Hicks and Beaudry 2006b: 6–7; see for example Preda 1999; Pickett 2003: 5). Without doubt, the period since the late 1980s had witnessed a fast-expanding literature in 'material culture studies' in which archaeology and anthropology have played a central role. But increasingly this literature was characterized by a dissatisfaction with what we might term purely culturalist studies of material culture, which served simply to reduce things to meanings, or else to social relations (Pinney 2005). As anthropology archaeologists, we were bothered by the idea of material culture studies as representing a new cross-disciplinary field of enquiry, rather than a place for conversation in which archaeology and anthropology might make more distinctive, more situated, and more modest, contributions. So, when we decided to work together again on a *Handbook of Material Culture Studies*, it was for two reasons. One was to explore, to gather together, and to celebrate a diversity of approaches to 'material culture studies' in anthropology, archaeology, and the related fields of cultural geography and science and technology studies (STS). The other was to try to pin down where our reservations about the idea of such a 'material turn' came from.

Material culture, objects, materiality, materials, things, stuff: a rock-solid, firmly grounded field for interdisciplinary enquiry is provided, it appears, by research that considers (to use the obligatory pun) what 'matters'. The idea of material culture studies represents, then, for many a prototype for post-disciplinarity (e.g. Miller and Tilley 1996; Tilley 2006b). The purpose of this volume is to call that idea into question. In doing so, we set out what is perhaps a reactionary view of material culture studies, which involves unpicking the culturalist uses of materials that developed during the 1980s and 1990s. In this introduction, we want to explore this argument and to explain the editorial direction of the volume by reviewing some of the key arguments put forward in the five sections of the book: (1) disciplinary perspectives; (2) material practices; (3) objects and humans; (4) landscapes and the built environment; and (5) studying particular things.

DISCIPLINARY PERSPECTIVES

The sentiment that a turn to the material represents a viable alternative to a pure culturalism, which still allows for an avoidance of the grand narratives of structuralism or traditional Marxism, has become increasingly common over the past decade. But does 'letting things in' to research mean the same for different disciplinary traditions and practices? Do different disciplines let the same things in?

Today, things are everywhere in the social sciences and humanities: from history and geography to literature studies, philosophy, and sociology. In the bookshops and libraries, accounts of particular commodities crowd the shelves of the modern history section: studies of cod (Kurlansky 1997) and salt (Kurlansky 2002) to chocolate (Coe and Coe 1996), opium (Booth 1996), tea (Moxham 2003), or tobacco (Burns 2007) proliferate. In their academic journals, geographers are embracing new vocabularies: cultural geographies of 'a more-than-human world' (Whatmore 2006), human geographies that accommodate 'nonhuman social partners' (Murdoch 1997: 328), and calls for a more general 're-materialization' of geographical thought and practice (Jackson 2000; Lees 2002). In literature studies, Bill Brown (2001, 2003) proposes 'thing theory'. In philosophy, Jane Bennett (2001: 92) develops the idea of 'enchanted materialism' to critique Weberian narratives of modern disenchantment. In sociology, Momin Rahman and Anne Witz (2003) interrogate the 'elusive quality of the material in feminist thought'.

The intellectual points of reference in the study of things in different disciplines are always, to a greater or lesser extent, overlapping. But key texts are read through disciplinary traditions, and their reception diverges as particular disciplinary methods are put into practice. Things are therefore less straightforward than they might seem.

Consider what the idea of material culture studies in the five disciplines that we gave as examples above involves. Historians have worked in intellectual traditions that include a range of forms of material histories—whether Marx's 'materialist conception of history' (Engels 1999: 79), or the historical materialism of Ferdinand Braudel (1973), or Asa Briggs' (1988) attendance to 'Victorian Things'. These are generally united in an understanding of objects as 'alternative sources' that can complement documentary materials in answering the questions posed by economic history and social history (Harvey 2009). Geographers' interests in things have related to long-standing efforts to understand the constitution of lived space. These interests have been polarized perhaps more strongly between on the one hand the use of particular forms of Marxism to focus on 'material and social conditions' (Harvey 1989: 327) and consumption and commodity chains (Jackson 2000), and on the other the more recent extension of 'human' geographies into the study of non-human animals, or new technologies, or ecologies: in 'hybrid' studies populated by cyborgs and 'companion species' and 'the implosion of trope and flesh' evoked by Donna Haraway (1991a, 2008: 383n11; see Whatmore 2002), in the heady mix of ideas about materials, space, politics, and affect drawn from Gilles Deleuze, Michel de Certeau, Baruch Spinoza, and Alfred North Whitehead in non-representational theory (Thrift 2007), or in geographical discussions of 'material imagination' (Anderson and Wylie 2009: 318). Sociological accounts, it comes as no surprise, have focused on the involvement of objects in social relations. They have similarly taken a range of forms: ranging from constructivist studies of scientific knowledge (SSK) (Latour and Woolgar 1979; Knorr-Cetina 1981; see Preda 1999), to Michel Foucault's (1977a) model of material constraint, to Anthony Giddens' (1981) critique of historical materialism, and to the consumption studies of the 1980s (Campbell 1987). In cultural studies, these interests have run from Raymond Williams' 'cultural materialism' (1958) to the idea of 'doing cultural studies' by studying the Sony Walkman (du Gay *et al.* 1997). Brown's 'thing theory' requires a reading of Martin Heidegger's (1971 [1949]) essay on 'The Thing'. Bennett's account of modern enchantments draws now from Henry Thoreau's 'attachment to the Wild', now from Ilya Prigogine and Isabelle Stengers' description of the instability of physical systems (Bennett 2001: 14, 101; cf. Prigogine and Stengers 1984). Rahman and Witz use Judith Butler to make a connection between 'the performativity of gender' with 'the question of the materiality of the body' (Butler 1993: 1).

Marx, Braudel, Deleuze, Giddens, Haraway, de Certeau, Spinoza, Williams, Heidegger, Foucault, Stengers, Butler. These overlapping points of theoretical departure for different disciplines' studies of material culture are, of course, within each discipline the subject of debate and argument (Buchli 2002a). But in practice, in the intellectual triangulations through which historians, sociologists, and others locate their enquiries into material culture—in the different ways that social theory or philosophy is put to work—disciplinarity still holds a strong influence. Drawing attention at the outset to the different disciplines that are drawn into dialogue with each other in this volume about 'material culture studies' is therefore particularly important.

This book gathers together a range of different perspectives upon material things that emerge from archaeology and socio-cultural anthropology, and from complementary work in geography and STS. The chapters have been assembled to provide a snapshot of the wide range of approaches to material things that emerge from putting distinctive methods into practice, and working within particular traditions of practice and enquiry. These range from archaeological methods for examining material culture—in the laboratory (Jones 2002a) or the museum (Edwards *et al.* 2006), through landscape survey (Hicks and McAtackney 2007), or through excavation (Edgeworth 2003)—to qualitative and quantitative approaches in socio-cultural anthropology (Epstein 2002; Bernard 2005) and the methodological challenges of postcolonial museum ethnography (Henare 2005a), the range of research methods used in human geography (Cloke *et al.* 2004), and what Annemarie Mol calls the 'praxiography' of STS (Mol 2002; also see Law 2004). For each of these four disciplines, the idea of material culture is both understood within particular intellectual trajectories, concerns, and debates, and as emerging through the answering of particular research questions, in the *mise-en-scène* of field practice. As field sciences, archaeology, anthropology, geography, and STS can bring a particular awareness of how research performs objects: how things emerge through research practice, rather than simply being bound up in social relations or webs of meaning. The status of objects as the provisional effects of contingent practices is, we suggest, precisely the same for other disciplines, and also for the vernacular material practices studied by anthropologists and others: these contingencies are, however, particularly clear in the practices of *fieldwork.* An awareness of disciplinary methods, and disciplinary histories, is a crucial first step in any adequate account of contemporary material culture studies.

***

Part I of this volume explores a number of different disciplinary perspectives upon the idea of material culture studies. In conducting an 'excavation' of the idea of material culture in British archaeology and social anthropology, Dan Hicks (Chapter 2) argues that the field has developed in two main phases: the emergence of the idea of 'material culture' in the second quarter of the twentieth century, especially in museums, as a counterpoint to Durkheimian social anthropology; and the emergence of the idea of 'material culture studies' as a way of bringing together structuralism and interpretive/semiotic approaches in the 1970s and 1980s. This second process, which he terms the 'Material-Cultural Turn', provided a provisional solution to the critiques of a purely cultural turn in these fields by apparently reconciling relativism and realism, especially through the use of the practice theories in Bourdieu and Giddens. However, more recently a number of critiques from within material culture studies, especially relating to the limitations of the textual analogy of material culture, and arguments about the extension of 'agency' from humans to material things, have led to an unfolding of the idea of 'material culture'. Hicks argues that recent thinking in archaeology and historical anthropology provides a basis for retaining the coherence of the idea of material culture studies by understanding things, and also the knowledge that is generated by studying them, as *events* and *effects*. As well as studying the involvement of things in historical processes or their effects upon human life, such a perspective breaks down the distinction between the researcher as subject and the object of scholarship. The implications of such a move, which Hicks describes as moving from the idea of 'the humility of things' to that of acts of modest witnessing (after Haraway 1997), are to call into question the idea of material culture studies as a post-disciplinary field. Instead, Hicks argues that an awareness of the contingency and partiality of our knowledge of the world is not a limitation of studying things through particular methods or disciplinary lenses: instead, this is precisely its strength. We shall return to this argument in the conclusion of this chapter, in relation to the relationships between actor-network theory (ANT) and material culture studies.

As well as archaeology and social anthropology, Part I of the book also draws together disciplinary histories and perspectives from cultural geography, folklife studies, historical anthropology, and STS. In their account of 'material geographies', Ian Cook and Divya Tolia-Kelly (Chapter 3) take stock of recent calls for the 'rematerialization' of cultural geography. They find that the idea of materiality in geography encompasses a very wide variety of concerns and theoretical approaches. Cook and Tolia-Kelly therefore choose to focus their discussion around a particular contemporary event: the wrecking of the container ship MSC *Napoli* off England's south-west coast and the subsequent arguments over the fate of the commodities washed up on the shore: a sequence of events that was unfolding as they were writing the chapter. Through three themes—landscape, commodities, and creativity—the authors demonstrate the complexity that is revealed as soon as abstract concerns with materiality are put into situated practice.

In Chapter 4, Robert Saint George traces the development of an often neglected field in material culture studies: folklife studies. This historical account traces nineteenth-century studies of 'folk' artefacts, early twentieth-century studies of geographical distributions of customs and archetypical forms of houses or crafts, the rise of open-air museums, and the emergence of folklife studies as a 'transatlantic intellectual formation' after its practice was introduced in the United States, often as means of detailing the transfer and adaptation of European traditional cultures in new settings: such as Pennsylvania German, Pennsylvania Dutch, etc. Reviewing the work on material culture in folklife studies since the 1970s, and drawing especially on the writing of Henry Glassie, Saint George provides a new account of the emergence of a distinctive tradition of ethnographic material culture studies on the American East Coast.

In Chapter 5, Ann Stahl considers the place of material culture in historical anthropology. Reviewing the idea of material histories, she begins with James Deetz's demonstration that material culture studies can bring much more than simply a new range of sources, to complement historical documents, to our understanding of the past (Deetz 1977). Stahl explores how anthropologists are building on studies by Sidney Mintz (1985), Igor Kopytoff (1986), and Anne Stoler (2001), especially through ideas of biography, deposition, and genealogy. Using examples from the history of West Africa, she demonstrates how material histories can provide distinctive accounts of 'global entanglements' that move beyond conventional concerns with the meaning of things. By following objects, over time and across, often wide, geographical spaces, Stahl argues that historical archaeology and historical anthropology reveal 'material moments': both in the past and, in her example of a fragmented Vaseline jar, the disciplinary present.

The field of STS, as it has emerged from the social constructivist approaches of the Sociology of Scientific Knowledge (SSK) since the early 1990s, has sought to accommodate non-human things within sociological studies. Bruno Latour has famously compared the relationship between sociology and STS to that between socio-cultural anthropology and physical anthropology, or between human geography and physical geography: as a kind of 'physical sociology', 'which forces colleagues immersed in the "social" and the "symbolic" to take seriously the enormous difficulty of accounting for objects, which oblige them to take up the radical hybridity of their topics' (Latour 2000a: 121). In Chapter 6, John Law reviews how STS treats materials. Focusing on how matter comes to 'matter', he contrasts SSK approaches with what he calls an awareness of 'material semiotics' and 'the patterning of practices'. This shift involves moving from understanding objects as stable, and understanding objects (as in social constructivism) as created purely by human subjects, to a sense of the unstable and shifting nature of materials. Using Annemarie Mol's arguments about multiplicities (Mol 2002), Law works through issues of 'ontological difference' and complexity (see Law 2004), and introduces the idea of an 'ontological politics'. Law concludes that the understanding of material culture that emerges from STS turns on the idea of objects as 'relational effects', and an engagement with the multiplicities and complexities of both practices and materials.

The chapters in Part I demonstrate how material things emerge in different ways from different disciplinary concerns and traditions of thought. This encourages us to move away from understanding research practices as ontologically distinct from the vernacular practices studied. Part II explores in more detail the different approaches to 'material practices': both those of the researcher, and those ongoing in the world.

MATERIAL PRACTICES

Part II reviews six kinds of 'material practice': agency, consumption, fieldwork/collecting, gift exchange, art (as a form of action), and deposition. In Chapter 7, Andy Pickering reviews the implications of the focus on practice and performance in STS literature. Building on his earlier conception of 'the mangle of practice' (Pickering 1995; Pickering and Guzik 2008), Pickering uses the idea of 'the dance of human and nonhuman agency' as a way of revealing that this focus on doing leads to an undoing of the 'linguistic turn' in sociology, since agency is no longer the sole preserve of humans. More radically than Law (Chapter 6), Pickering understands the performative focus of STS as leading away from humanistic concerns with meaning or semiotics. In a shift from epistemology to ontology, Pickering uses a series of examples—the environment, animals, buildings, and technologies of the self—as places to identify such dances of agency. He is concerned, like Law, with the new political formations that emerge from moving away from a purely humanistic focus to 'ground level' studies that can reveal alternative ways for organizing the world that offer alternatives to the subject–object distinction of modernist epistemologies.

In Chapter 8, the volume turns to a classic theme in material culture studies: that of consumption and consumerism (see Miller 1987). The turn to consumption, Michael Dietler shows, was part of a critique of production-focused studies that failed to take account of the ways in which people enrol things in everyday social practices. Reviewing the changing approaches to consumption in archaeology and socio-cultural anthropology, Dietler notes that while early studies stressed the symbolic qualities of goods, more recent work acknowledges that material culture does more than simply symbolize. Using examples drawn from the study of colonialism and of food, alcohol, and drugs, Dietler makes a strong case for the importance of methods in consumption studies. An awareness of method means that a number of distinct lessons for consumption studies from archaeology and anthropology can be identified, first among which is a critique of assumptions of the uniqueness of modern or Western consumption practices. Dietler concludes that archaeology and anthropology have made a distinct contribution to a more general shift away from an interest in consumption as purely a domain of symbolic expression or meaning into its role as a practice with particular consequences.

Issues of method and practice also form the focus of Chapter 9, in which Gavin Lucas presents an overview of the history of changing practices of collecting and doing fieldwork among anthropologists and archaeologists. Reviewing the development of studies of the history of collecting in museum studies (Pearce 1995) and ethnography (O'Hanlon and Welsch 2000), and of fieldwork in archaeology (Lucas 2001a), Lucas notes a growing awareness of the importance of field methods in defining the place of material culture studies in archaeology and anthropology— and especially an awareness of the shift of focus away from collecting with the invention of modern ethnographic fieldwork that accompanied the rise of functionalist anthropology in the early twentieth century. Lucas shows how most recently, a self-awareness of the contingency of archaeological and anthropological knowledge upon field practices has developed, often through the idea of 'reflexivity' (Hodder 1997, 1999). Such awareness has led in anthropology to the problematization of the definition of the ethnographic field as non-Western in location, while in archaeology it has led to new kinds of field methods, including phenomenology. Lucas concludes by considering the development of 'ethnographies of archaeological practice' (Edgeworth 2006a), but strongly resists suggestions, such as that by Chris Gosden, of an elision of archaeological and anthropological field practices, for example in a focus on material culture. Instead, Lucas defines archaeological fieldwork as distinct in its interventionist and transformative nature, and in the centrality of scientific techniques in the analysis of material culture, which are united in the reconstitution of past material worlds in the present. Thus, Lucas argues, the different treatment of objects in fieldwork draws a line between archaeological and anthropological material culture studies.

The classic anthropological theme of practices of gift exchange is explored by Hiro Miyazaki in Chapter 10. Tracing the long history of debate in anthropology over Marcel Mauss' classic essay *The Gift: the form and reason for exchange in archaic societies* (1923–4), Miyazaki explores the implications of Mauss' proposition, that things exchanged as gifts come to contain within themselves some part of the giver, especially through the obligation to reciprocate. The problem of reciprocity—what power it is within the gift that requires repayment—is traced through debates, from Lévi-Strauss' critique that Mauss mistook an indigenous concept (the 'spirit' (*hau*) of the gift) for a general theory of exchange, through the perspectives of Pierre Bourdieu, Marshall Sahlins, Annette Weiner, Jonathan Parry, Nancy Munn, and Webb Keane. Seeking to move beyond the framing of these debates in terms of 'problem and solution', Miyazaki then examines the feminist critique of Mauss' model of gift exchange, set out in Marilyn Strathern's *The Gender of the Gift* (1988), which, he argues, understands the relationships between people and things as 'neither a problem nor a solution'. Instead, Miyazaki argues, Strathern's account of relational personhood offers new ways of framing discussions of gift exchange, which move beyond bilateral distinctions between subjects and objects.

The inclusion of a chapter on the anthropology of art in a section on 'material practices' may at first appear a strange editorial decision. However, the study of artworks in anthropology has shifted in recent years from semiotic studies (e.g. Layton 1981) to interests in the practical involvement of artworks in social relationships, especially through Alfred Gell's (1998) model of *Art and Agency*, which argued that artworks were enrolled as secondary agents in social life. Taking a very different approach to that of Gell, in Chapter 11 Howard Morphy argues that the cross-cultural anthropological study of artworks should involve understanding them not as objects in a conventional sense, but as 'a form of intentional human action'. Critiquing Gell's dismissal of the utility of the idea of aesthetics, and seeking to move beyond the idea of objects having 'social lives' (Appadurai 1986a), Morphy stresses the need to attend to 'the cognitive and expressive dimensions of objects' in order to comprehend 'how they are seen and how they mean'. Morphy affirms that social actors sometimes believe that objects possess agency and that they have effects in the world, but is emphatic on the point that the goal of the anthropologist is not to conclude that objects *do* have agency but to achieve an understanding of how belief in the agency of objects comes about. To accomplish this, the anthropologist must first determine how an object functions in context, then attempt to explain why objects take the particular forms that they do. Offering a case study of Yolngu circumcision painting in Australia, Morphy calls for ethnographically situated and nuanced studies that retain the distinctive category of art (as action), rather than understanding artworks as simply another form of material culture and unpicking their uses in human social life.

The final contribution to Part II examines archaeological studies of practices of deposition (Chapter 12). Rosemary Joyce and Josh Pollard trace the development of the archaeological concept of the assemblage, and the different ways in which archaeologists have interpreted deposits that are the result of purposeful deposition. Joyce and Pollard work through Mike Schiffer's processual model of deposition, the post-processual idea of reading assemblages as 'structured deposition', and more recent studies of depositional practice as the evidence of human actions (both ceremonial and everyday). Through a case study drawn from fieldwork at Mantecales, Honduras, they show how in the study of assemblage and deposition archaeologists have increasingly moved from the interpretation of meaning or social structure to interests in the role of materials in everyday practice, performance, and memory.

OBJECTS AND HUMANS

As will be clear already, the contributions in this volume question the a priori distinctions between material objects and human subjects in a variety of different ways. In Part III, such distinctions are explored through five themed chapters: exploring technology, material agency, personhood, embodiment, and the use of materials by non-human primates.

Kacy Hollenback and Mike Schiffer open the section with an essay on the current state of behavioural archaeology, a programme of archaeological research developed by Schiffer since the 1970s (Schiffer 1976, 1995a, 2008a). For Hollenback and Schiffer, a reliance upon material culture and technology is what distinguishes humans from other animals. Reviewing the study of technology in archaeology and anthropology before and after the invention of the idea of 'material culture', the authors introduce a series of concepts—'performance characteristics', the study of the 'life histories' of artefacts, and 'behavioural chains'—that are central to their behavioural approach to material culture. The interest in long-term change and the 'senescence' (death) of technologies distinguishes this archaeological approach from sociological STS studies. Through two case studies— concerned with the failure of the early electric car in the 1920s, and with the relationship between the spread of smallpox and the decline of traditional pottery technology among the Mandan and Hidatsa of the Northern Plains of North America—the authors argue that behavioural archaeology offers distinctive perspectives on how human life is always indistinguishable from 'material life'.

In Chapter 14, Andy Jones and Nicky Boivin take stock of current debates over the idea of 'material agency'. One recent approach to the study of objects and humans through material culture has been to extend social agency to material things: whether understanding objects as fully agentive (Latour 1993a) or as the 'indexes' of human agency (Gell 1998). For Jones and Boivin, such arguments represent a central element of archaeology's moving beyond the concerns with material culture as holding meaning, and the idea that material culture is analogous with a 'text' (Hodder 1986). However, quite distinct from the extension of purely social agency to objects, Jones and Boivin focus on how things' actions can fall outside the constraint of human agency, or the extension of human intentionality. Through a discussion of ethnographic ideas of animism and fetishism, and drawing from work in STS and ANT, the authors show how many archaeologists are moving beyond a distinction between relativism and realism that characterizes conventional 'material culture studies'. Using examples from Late Neolithic Orkney and from Rajasthan, India, they conclude that ideas of material agency move beyond a concern with the social, and that ideas from ANT can be used in archaeology to trace 'courses of action [that] are mediated and articulated over time' by both humans and materials.

Another way in which distinctions between humans and objects have been critiqued in archaeology and anthropology is through a shift from concerns with 'identity' to the idea that material things are implicated in the emergence of 'personhood'. In Chapter 15, Chris Fowler provides an overview of the history of the study of material culture as either reflective or actively involved in the expression of identity in archaeology as background to his discussion of more recent critiques of the assumption that 'persons' exist as universal, bounded entities. Drawing especially upon Melanesian ethnography (e.g. Strathern 1988), Fowler uses ideas of distributed and relational personhood, and the idea of the 'dividual', to show how a focus on material culture can be used to critique Western notions of the strictly bounded and indivisible self. Fowler argues that ethnographic observations about the diversity of understandings of the person are of particular importance for archaeologists studying past societies, especially since they do so through material remains that may have been involved in the creation of personhood. Using examples from both prehistoric and historical archaeology, Fowler shows how recent work in archaeology focuses not simply on the relationships between objects and humans, but upon the permeabilities between them, and the historical and ethnographic contingencies of ideas of persons and objects.

Another key area of research in which the permeabilities between humans and materials have been explored is in the archaeology of embodiment. In Chapter 16, Zoë Crossland traces the rising interest in archaeologies of gender and sexuality alongside concerns with the archaeology of the body and performance of identity, for example through studies of dress and personal adornment, since the late 1980s. Through two case studies, Crossland shows how archaeologists have increasingly shown the intimate connections between the body and material culture through the idea of embodiment, and how artefacts can represent extensions of the body. Considering how seventeenth-century 'witches bottles' as apotropaic devices acted as anthropomorphic bodily metaphors, she shows how these objects are suggestive of the body as a bounded and fragile vessel, but also represent through 'an extraordinary redundancy of symbolism' both witch and victim as 'entwined and dependent biographies'. Then, through a discussion of forensic archaeology as a contemporary expression of changing ideas about the body and about perceptions of separation between the dead and the living, Crossland argues that forensic archaeology is a practice that attributes agency to the dead in ways that render an ostensibly empirical endeavour as a discourse that is as much about emotion and subjectivity as it is about science. In conclusion, Crossland argues that archaeological material culture studies can provide 'alternate narratives of the coming into being of the bounded body', in which materials and humans are studied together through objects.

The questioning of the limits of the person in relation to materials is taken one step further by a consideration of the distinctiveness of human manipulation of materials and uses of tools, as compared with non-human primates (cf. Strum and Latour 1987). Tanya Humle (Chapter 17) argues that certain non-human primates—capuchin monkeys, orangutans, and chimpanzees, and perhaps also gorillas and bonobos—can usefully be seen as having 'material cultures', and perhaps also more generally 'culture' if we apply an anthropological definition of culture as 'a system of socially transmitted behaviour(s)'. In an overview of current thinking about primate use of material culture, Humle distinguishes between innate tool use and the reordering of the material environment beyond primates (in which we could include the use of cactus spines to remove arthropods from bark by woodpecker finches, or birds nests and beehives), from physical objects used as a means to achieve an end, which includes the use of stones as hammers and anvils, the construction of shelters, and the use of sticks to extract insects or honey from trees by primates. A central issue here is the social dimension of primate material culture, which includes learnt behaviour, through observation, imitation and teaching; the importance of studying primate use of material culture in the wild rather than in laboratories is therefore underlined by Humle. Through these discussions, she demonstrates the limitations of conventional divisions between biological anthropology from cultural anthropology. The chapter calls for the development of 'cultural primatology' as fusing elements drawn from a range of disciplines—anthropology, biology, archaeology, behavioural ecology, and psychology—and underlines the urgency of studying fragile and threatened primate cultures. Humle also eloquently argues for the importance of moving beyond studying the idea of 'material culture' in non-human primates in isolation from the idea of the existence of 'culture' among them.

LANDSCAPES AND THE BUILT ENVIRONMENT

Part IV of the volume explores how the idea of material culture studies can be used to examine large entities, rather than discrete or portable objects. The chapters in this section draw together geographical approaches to 'cultural landscapes' and 'ecological landscapes' with the study of long-term change in the urban built environment, and two contrasting traditions of studying architecture and 'home cultures'.

The idea of 'cultural landscapes', Lesley Head notes in Chapter 18, derives from the work of geographer Carl Sauer in the 1920s, which has led over several generations of scholarship to a conventional division of labour in geography between the 'human' or 'cultural' and the 'physical'. Head traces how the 'cultural turn' in geography encouraged a strongly active understanding of the human cultural and meaningful shaping of landscapes, but then how more recently geographers have moved to an acknowledgement of the complexities and hybrid nature of cultural and natural landscapes, especially in the extension of the idea of 'agency' to plants, animals, and other elements of the 'natural' world. In this context, Head critically examines how the idea of 'cultural landscapes' has been put into practice in recent years, with particular reference to the 'cultural landscape' category of the World Heritage Convention, using examples of land and heritage management in Australia. Drawing on the arguments of feminist philosopher Val Plumwood, Head assesses whether the idea of cultural landscapes is 'irretrievably anthropocentric'. Rather than an a priori discrediting of the idea of cultural landscapes, in favour of a blurring of distinctions between the natural and the cultural, Head argues that in certain situations the idea of cultural landscapes can have positive outcomes, especially in relation to the politics of indigenous heritage. This argument reminds us of the importance of our conception of human and material landscapes as historically contingent, and that the uses of such conceptions, but also any attempt to overcome them, are always situated and political.

In contrast with Chapter 18, Sarah Whatmore and Steve Hinchliffe (Chapter 19) use the idea of 'ecological landscapes' to seek to dispose of any distinction between cultural and material geographies. By understanding the materials of which landscapes are made as 'energetic constituents in their fabrication', they work through arguments in phenomenology, affect, and biophilosophy to craft a reconfiguration of ideas about landscape and ecology that allows for a sense of landscape as process, as affective materiality, and as an 'enlivened', more-than-spatial entity. Whatmore and Hinchliffe see landscapes as 'complex assemblages' in which people are situated on the basis of their relationships with human and non-human others. Examining two public spaces in the contemporary urban ecology of Bristol—Thingwall Park Allotments and the Royate Hill viaduct-reserve—Whatmore and Hinchliffe call for the study of 'living cities' (rather than 'built environments'). Using concepts of vernacular ecologies and conviviality, they call for a rethinking of landscapes as 'more-than-human achievements' that are lived in before they are made, that arise not from pre-existing human vision and design but from relational engagements between human, non-human, and more-than-human agents. Such approaches, they argue, raise the potential for a 'more-than-human politics of landscap-ing', which could inform different approaches to urban policy and planning.

Urban spaces and urban materialities are also the focus of Roland Fletcher's contribution (Chapter 20), but Fletcher's concerns are centred around the effects of the accretion of the materialities of urban environments across time and space.

Building on his previous studies of urban materiality (especially Fletcher 1995), he begins by discussing the ways in which scholars across a range of disciplines have approached materiality, in order to situate his own treatment of urban materialities in terms of cross-cultural generalizations about the role of urban places in human experience throughout history. His aim is to address matters of words and representation, magnitude, and materials through time. Fletcher argues that text-based approaches to materiality have failed to engage with the sheer weight and power of urban materials. The very size of cities, Fletcher suggests, leads to what he refers to as 'self-inflicted damage' as a result of overcrowding and lack of investment in infrastructure, while warfare, especially in industrialized cities, has led to the large-scale, asymmetrical destruction of urban places. Through wide-ranging examples drawn from ancient, early modern, and modern urban contexts, he argues that archaeologists must engage more adequately with the material duration and persistence of urban places as a central element of any understanding of the contingencies and effects of urban history. Fletcher's perspective is distinctly humanistic in that he raises the ethical dimensions of urban growth, florescence, decay, and destruction to human agents in all instances: even urban destruction by natural forces Fletcher sees as the 'fault' of improvident humans. In this way, his approach differs from the presentism of some geographical calls for non-human geographies of urban landscapes, and from the local contexts of such work that contrast with his sense of 'the mega-scale' to which he argues archaeology can provide particular access. Thus, Fletcher re-thinks urban landscapes as sources of an understanding of 'the macro-scale of familiar public milieu' as well as 'the micro-scale of personal life'.

The final contributions to this section introduce two contrasting traditions of thought about the built environment. In Chapter 21, Carl Lounsbury moves us from the grand scale of cities across time and space to the smaller scale of buildings. Lounsbury's perspective as an architectural historian is steeped in ideas drawn from social history and the decorative arts and strongly influenced by material in Americanist traditions of culture studies. He focuses on the study of buildings as sources of design and as cultural artefacts, using examples drawn chiefly from North America, tracing architectural history from design-oriented and antiquarian approaches through its transformation into a social science, with greater attention to issues of environment, resources, and indigenous and non-Western architecture. In contrast with studies of the aesthetics and style of architecture, or of the work of particular architects, Lounsbury draws on traditions in American anthropology and folklife studies that examine vernacular and polite buildings as evidence for the study of power, class, gender, and race in the past. Giving examples of studies of plantation landscapes and housing for enslaved Africans, of post-colonial architectural forms, and of 'cultural landscapes' centred around commemoration and public memory, Lounsbury provides an integrated overview of the study of architecture as material culture in traditions that have developed in the eastern United States.

In Chapter 22, Victor Buchli explores how material culture studies have contributed to anthropological studies of houses and households. Building on his previous work on the idea of 'home cultures', and his observation that houses represent 'the context in which most other material culture is used, placed and understood' (Buchli 2002b: 207), Buchli reviews a wide range of anthropological and archaeological studies of the domestic sphere. Drawing upon a range of social anthropological studies of households, and upon the tradition of material culture studies developed at University College London, Buchli provides an overview of the anthropology of the domestic sphere, tracing the emergence of interests in houses as processes, rather than as types or physical forms. Buchli explains how these developments have influenced archaeologists' considerations of home life and how archaeology and anthropology can use houses and homes as places to study gender, sexuality, and consumption; techniques of governance; the impact of new technologies; and new conceptions of the body and the experience of personhood. Rather than fetishizing the dwelling as an object of enquiry, Buchli demonstrates that houses and homes represent dynamic, fluid, and lively environments in which to undertake material culture studies.

Studying particular things

One thing shared by many of the contributions to this volume is a commitment to the value of situated, extended studies of particular items or bodies of material culture: something that is all too often lost in theoretical debates about material culture or materiality. Just as Part IV introduced a range of situations in which material culture studies can be undertaken (from urban ecology to the domestic sphere), so our final section aims to show some of the analytical power that such studies of things have: allowing theoretical positions to emerge in particular material engagements—with stone tools, landscape gardens, ceramics, buildings, and 'magical things'.

In Chapter 23, Rodney Harrison addresses one of the most venerable of archaeological objects: stone tools. However, the particular object studied by Harrison is a copy of a stone point rendered in glass by indigenous people in the Kimberley region of western Australia during the nineteenth century, and collected and accessioned into the Pitt Rivers Museum in Oxford. Reviewing alternative approaches to artefact manufacture, and reviewing the history of stone tool studies in archaeology, Harrison discusses the need to account for the social agency of indigenous people by understanding the Kimberley point as an artefact of colonial encounter. He also uses Alfred Gell's discussions of the enchanting qualities of material culture in social life (Gell 1998) to introduce the idea of material agency. The brilliance of the glass Kimberley point, and the skill involved in its manufacture, contribute for Harrison to its status as a 'captivating object', the agentive qualities of which influenced the history of its being collected. But Harrison acknowledges that any account of the persistence of the object into the contemporary world involves more than an acknowledgement of its enrolment in human social agency. This is particularly clear, he argues, in accounting for the politics of indigenous heritage in Australia in debates over the repatriation of cultural remains, such as the kind of stone tools of which the Kimberley points were copies. Through ethnographic interviews with Aboriginal people working in the field of archaeological heritage management, Harrison discusses the use of material culture by people to express 'a rather conservative or old-fashioned association between race, culture and material artefacts'. This 'strategic essentialism' involves the use of material culture for purely cultural ends by minority groups. In this nuanced argument, which deals with many of the same issues as those addressed by Lesley Head in Chapter 18, Harrison shows how in accounting for the material agency of objects we must also accommodate their contemporary political power. Such uses of material culture for culturalist ends are powerful, and challenge the archaeologist to account for those forms of contemporary politics that involve things as well as people.

In Chapter 24, Chandra Mukerji provides a detailed account of the study of French landscape gardens as material culture. She argues that the value in studying early modern designed landscapes lies in their role as sites of 'ongoing experiments' in relation to the human governance of things and the demonstration of the control of nature, and as part of political life. Mukerji discusses Louis XIV's seventeenth-century gardens at Versailles, which were designed as a microcosm of the kingdom of France. She explains how the *circulades* of south-western France operated as utopian expressions of hope against the threat of potential loss of farm surplus. Recognizing the links between landscape management, politics, and religion provides a means of understanding how in France the symbolic aspects of landscape gardens were transformed over time into a far broader tradition of land use and land management: accomplished through particular material techniques and according to specific moral rationales, these landscapes served to demonstrate, validate, and underscore the 'material order' of French political and social regimes. Unlike many objects examined by material culture studies, like a silver spoon for example, gardens never hold the illusion that they are 'wholly a product of human design'. Thus, Mukerji shows, studying designed landscapes reveal the implication of both the natural and the cultural in early modern hope and ambition, models of moral reform, and ideas of territorial governance. In this way, their study demonstrates how social regimes are always both 'material and political orders'—enacted through the non-human, as well as purely the human, world.

Chapter 25 presents a dialogue between two archaeologists studying architectural construction during the European Neolithic. From four case studies, Doug Bailey and Lesley McFadyen develop four propositions about the archaeological study of the construction of 'built objects'. First, they use the study of the practical and material dimensions of the construction of long barrows in southern England to argue that archaeologists should consider building as practice and avoid thinking about buildings as crystallizations of ideas, as fixed entities. The construction of such monuments was a process that McFadyen describes as 'quick architecture', referring both to the differential speed at which phases of building take place and to the ways in which building techniques and materials affect the builder. This approach emphasizes the dynamic nature of building over the notion of interpreting architectural evidence in terms of a completed form. Secondly, in a discussion of Neolithic pit-houses from south-eastern Europe they argue that conventional distinctions between above-ground, durable dwellings, and smaller dwellings constructed by digging a pit in the ground are unhelpful. Using ideas from the American Land Art movement, they consider the transformative aspects of creating and enclosing negative spaces. Thirdly, informed by architectural theorist Bernard Tschumi's idea of *Architecture and Disjunction* (1996), Bailey and McFadyen question whether conventional distinctions of discrete construction phases for English Neolithic monuments is either helpful or possible. The idea of a construction sequence implies a continuity and regularity in construction activity, and treats the structure as fixed and constant. Neolithic constructions were nothing of the sort, the authors argue, but instead resulted from discontinuous and episodic activities and were often 'mobile' in ways that suited how Neolithic people lived their lives. Finally, returning to south-eastern Europe and to houses, a fourth proposition calls for the forms of houses to be studied at different scales from the conventional fine-grained detail of archaeological excavation. Here, the focus is on houses as objects that position people in space and create specific intellectual and physical engagements because, in ways suggested through the philosophy of Minimalist art, they become 'environmental' in the broadest sense. Developing these four propositions from four distinct archaeological contexts, Bailey and McFadyen disrupt conventional archaeological thinking about prehistoric structures. Through ideas of the pace and discontinuities of construction, and through a focus on digging as well as building and on houses as part of broader lived environments, they call for an 'unlearning of how we look at the archaeological evidence of houses, building and architecture'. This approach moves far beyond conventional interpretive archaeology into new kinds of accounts of materials and practice.

The study of ceramics is the archetypal archaeological theme when the question of 'studying particular things' is raised. However, the study by Carl Knappett,

Lambros Malafouris, and Peter Tomkins (Chapter 26) of a *pithos* (storage vessel) and *rhyton* (ceremonial vessel) from the early Bronze Age in the Aegean raises issues that go far beyond conventional ceramic studies, which focus on artefacts as evidence of economy or changing ceramic technology. Their focus is instead firmly upon what these objects do, rather than what they mean: they argue that their functions as containers means that they should be considered as part of broader technologies of containing, including baskets, gourds, or metal vessels, rather than simply within a sequence of ceramic typology. In this new approach to typology, based on items of material culture as 'action possibilities', the authors combine Jean-Pierre Warnier's study of 'containers and surfaces' (Warnier 2006) with ideas of the 'embodied mind' and 'conceptual metaphor theory' drawn from cognitive psychology (Lakoff and Johnson 1999). Their attention to categories of practice, while attending to the materiality of ceramics, builds in innovative ways upon Colin Renfrew's (2001) idea of 'material engagement'. They situate their discussion in relation to the long-term development of ceramic containers in Europe from their initial appearance in the Mesolithic, through the Neolithic and Bronze Age. The implication of this study of two Bronze Age artefacts is that archaeology can make distinctive interdisciplinary contributions by moving beyond 'artefacts as categories' (Miller 1985) towards a new appreciation of the form and type of artefacts that is grounded in the implication of particular material technologies of practice in both the cognitive and material dimensions of human life.

The final chapter in this section takes on these two overlapping dimensions of human life in a very different manner. Through his anthropological study of fetishes, commodities, and modern technologies, in Chapter 27 Peter Pels engages with categories of objects that are bound up with notions of magic. Magical objects lie at the heart of ethnographic concerns with the idea of material agency. Pels shows how the anthropological encounter with beliefs that things can 'do something' to humans led to an emphasis in scholarship on magic on the irrational and impossible, upon seemingly mistaken beliefs, psychological shortcomings, and misplaced subjectivities. He explores how over the course of the nineteenth century, ideas about magic and materiality were pulled apart from one another. But by juxtaposing William Pietz's studies of the emergence of the fetish in early modern West Africa with the anthropological study of commodities, Pels elegantly situates the Marxian idea of commodity fetishism in broader historical context. He argues that anthropological material culture studies have increasingly downplayed the importance of fetishism. Anthropocentric models of the material culture of consumerism have not allowed for the more radical attribution of agency to commodities. Through a series of case studies about twentieth-century and contemporary advertising, Pels builds an argument that bears some similarities to the 'enchanted materialism' of modern life evoked by Jane Bennett (2001), but is more explicit in how Western capitalism employs 'magic' and enchantment to construct and capture its markets. Pels sees these elements as bound up with technologies, with the prime example of the late twentieth and early twenty-first centuries being that of computer technophilia and the emergence within the hacker subculture of an overdetermined trope of programming as a magical activity performed by practitioners referred to as 'wizards' and 'master magicians'. Computer technology, then, is an area in which fetishism is not rejected but embraced; the technology magically transforms the modern commodity into a highly materialized, magical thing. Pels argues in conclusion that the Western denial of distributed or material agency is precisely the source of the magical nature of certain technological objects in the modern world: an argument that compels us to rethink the historical and ethnographic contingencies and complexities in which ideas of material agency are debated or dismissed.

MATERIAL CULTURE STUDIES:
A REACTIONARY VIEW

Together, the chapters of this volume demonstrate what the four disciplines assembled here—archaeology, anthropology, geography, and STS—have in common. Each chapter works in different ways within particular intellectual traditions, to answer particular disciplinary questions, through approaches that engage with, and sometimes immerse themselves in, complex environments of humans and non-humans, from gardens to ceramics to chimpanzees. Issues of method are more or less formalized depending on the discipline. As methods are put into practice, these studies regularly encounter, and must account for, the lives of non-humans as well as purely humans. In all four fields, these experiences are increasingly pressing researchers to move beyond the priorities of the linguistic or cultural turn, which were focused on an anthropocentric concern with the meanings or significance of material culture to people, and simultaneously beyond concerns with simply the use by people of objects in social relations. All four disciplines are seeking to retool themselves to accommodate the role of non-humans. This need is perhaps especially clear when analyses move beyond the ethnographic present and deal with transformation and change over time.

Why, then, after the editorial work that has gone into assembling these studies would we hold back from calling for a material turn that would replace the anthropocentric linguistic or cultural turn of the 1980s? The studies collected here hold many insights for the study of material culture—from ontological politics, to debates over material agency, to the implications of moving beyond literary and textual analogies for material culture, to the risks of reducing materials to anthropocentric accounts of the social. Without doubt, through editing this collection our firm belief in the importance of the study of material things in the humanities and social sciences, and our commitment to interdisciplinary collaboration, has become even stronger. But on what terms? The studies collected in this volume lead towards an appreciation not only of the effects of things, but also of *things as the effects* of material practices (both vernacular and academic). Material culture does not represent a straightforward object of enquiry, simply requiring new vocabularies for interpretation or abstract theorization. Instead, if we take seriously the critique of any a priori distinction between subject and object, then this must also encompass the academic researcher and her object of enquiry. Like any thing, for the disciplines gathered here knowledge is emergent and contingent upon material practice. This, we suggest, must be the point of departure for any interdisciplinary discussion of material culture.

Here, the distinction between material culture studies and ANT becomes clear. As a 'symmetrical anthropology' (Latour 1993a) that can present 'the sociology of a few mundane artefacts' (Latour 1992), ANT has provided a powerful model for how anthropological thinking about the place of material things in social life might achieve cross-disciplinary impact. It is above all in the transdisciplinary reception of ANT, we might suggest, that the strongest possible model for what a 'material turn' would look like is developing. But such a material turn would simply extend, through a rhetorical inversion, the cultural turn of the 1980s. While we share a sense of what we are leaving behind, the contributions assembled here (including our own) represent a series of crossroads rather than a new series of 'turns': turn upon turn, which would add up only to academic spin.

Anthropology has been here before: with the Durkheimian model of the social, and with structuralism. The transdisciplinary reception of the representational impulse in ANT—its status as a third twentieth-century theory ripe for application in diverse situations—makes it the rightful successor to the Durkheimian and structuralist models of anthropological thinking. But while we learn much from ANT, the contributions assembled here do not add up to a new interdisciplinary space in which to reconcile or inter-relate the cultural and the material, the human and non-human. Instead, they inspire us to foreground the partiality of the knowledge of the world that emerges from 'field sciences' such as archaeology, anthropology, geography, and STS as they are enacted. Unlike the idea of reflexivity, in which the situatedness of the human researcher in interpreting and representing the world is foregrounded to relate method and theory, we want to suggest that approaches to the study of things in these field sciences can provide distinctive resources for an ontological, rather than epistemological, retooling in practice.

And so we return to disciplinarity. A reactionary argument indeed: the continued relevance of modernist models of disciplinary purity. But that is not what we are after. Instead, our resistance to the idea of a postdisciplinary material turn emerges from our own deep sense, from the perspective of anthropological archaeology, of the complexity, mess, and diversity of the practices from which our knowledge emerges. Interdisciplinary collaborations are central to the future of material culture studies. But we must not forget that the things that we study are the effects of our practice, which is always historically contingent. When Bruno Latour talks of flat ontologies, these must extend between researcher and object of enquiry, as well as simply between humans and non-humans. Otherwise, we will simply continue to play back and forth across the categories of the cultural and the material: critiquing, collapsing, relating. Imagining that we *represent* a world, which we can hold at arm's length, rather than *enacting* our knowledge of things. It is in this sense—a sense of the radical partiality of our knowledge of the world, which we might celebrate rather than shy away from—that material culture studies will, as Nigel Thrift suggests in his afterword that it has, come of age.

PART I

DISCIPLINARY PERSPECTIVES

CHAPTER 2

....

THE MATERIAL-CULTURAL TURN

EVENT AND EFFECT

....

DAN HICKS

INTRODUCTION: EXCAVATING 'MATERIAL CULTURE'

....

The terms 'material culture' and 'material culture studies' emerged, one after another, during the twentieth century in the disciplines of archaeology and socio-cultural anthropology, and especially in the place of intersection between the two: anthropological archaeology. Today, 'material culture studies' is taught in most undergraduate and postgraduate programmes in archaeology and anthropology. In Britain and North America, four distinct traditions of material culture studies in archaeology and anthropology might be discerned. In the eastern United States, one tradition, associated especially with the work of Henry Glassie and his students, including Robert Saint George, Bernard Herman, and Gerald Pocius (e.g. Glassie 1975, 1999; Pocius 1991; Herman 1992, 2005; Saint George 1998), has developed from American folklife studies and cultural geography (see Saint George

I am grateful to Mary Beaudry, Victor Buchli, Jeremy Coote, Inge Daniels, Jonathan Friedman, Chris Gosden, Tim Ingold, Andy Jones, Danny Miller, Josh Pollard, Gisa Weszkalnys, Sarah Whatmore, Laurie Wilkie, Chris Wingfield, and Steve Woolgar for discussions and comments that have informed the argument set out in this chapter.

this volume, Chapter 4). This field has developed to include studies in architecture, landscape, and historical archaeology, especially through the work of Dell Upton and James Deetz (e.g. Deetz 1996; Upton 1998, 2008). Secondly, a parallel tradition of thought, which might be termed the 'decorative arts' approach, has been closely associated with the graduate programme at the Winterthur Program in Early American Culture in Delaware. Including scholars such as Barbara Carson, Jane Nylander, and Arlene Palmer Schwind (Carson 1990; Nylander 1990; Palmer 1993), this tradition has worked more with art historians and historians of the domestic interior, and also with the commercial antiques trade. Thirdly, during the 1990s a group of British archaeologists and anthropologists at University College London (UCL), including Danny Miller, Chris Tilley, and Mike Rowlands, developed, especially through the *Journal of Material Culture* and a popular graduate programme, an influential model for material culture studies, grounded in anthropology but self-consciously interdisciplinary in outlook (Tilley *et al.* 2006). Fourthly, a much looser, more widespread, and less often explicitly discussed body of material culture work ranges from the physical examination and scientific analysis of objects in laboratories and museums, to the material engagements of archaeological and anthropological fieldwork (including collecting and fieldwork, see Lucas this volume chapter 9).

Given the currency of the idea of material culture in these fields over the past three decades, it is to be expected that archaeologists and anthropologists might have a clear and distinctive contribution to make to the interdisciplinary study of material things in the social sciences, and especially to a *Handbook of Material Culture Studies*. This chapter considers the potential nature of that contribution. This is not, however, a straightforward task. The varieties of 'material culture studies' that developed in the 1980s built upon the emergence of 'material culture' as an object of enquiry for twentieth-century archaeology and anthropology, which in turn developed from museum-based studies of 'technology' and 'primitive art' during the late nineteenth century. The idea of 'material culture studies' gained a sense of coherence and significance because it was deployed to solve a number of quite specific, long-standing archaeological and anthropological problems. These related to the idea of *relationships* between the 'social'/'cultural' and the 'material'. It is in relation to these problems that the field came to acquire during the 1990s a kind of paradigmatic status: falling across, but never quite integrating, archaeological and anthropological thinking. Moreover, it is against the continued relevance of these problems—the idea of *relating* human and non-human worlds—that the contemporary value of the idea of 'material culture studies' must be considered, especially at a time in which there are so many reasons for turning away from the very idea of studying something called 'material culture'. Central here is the question recently posed by Amiria Henare, Martin Holbraad, and Sari Wastell: 'What would an artefact-oriented anthropology look like if it were not about material culture?' (Henare *et al.* 2007a: 1).

The contemporary discomfort with the idea of 'material culture' in archaeology and anthropology has three dimensions. First is the idea of culture. The past two decades have seen a range of postcolonial, feminist, and historical critiques of the essentialist, static, synchronic, and normative tendencies of the 'culture concept', and its place within the discipline's colonial legacies (Clifford 1988; Abu Lughod 1991a; Daniel 1998; Trouillot 2003). Secondly, there are the long-standing arguments over the utility of a separate category of the 'material': whether it is helpful, or even possible, to define some form of 'culture' that is *not* materially enacted (Olsen 2006, 2007; Ingold 2007a). Thirdly—a complement to these tendencies to reduce explanation to the human, or to the non-human— is the nature of the connection, relationship, or boundary between the two halves of this unhyphenated term—'material culture' (Miller 2007: 24; see Pinney 2005). Or, of course, the very idea of the existence of such a fundamental boundary in the first place, apart from in certain modernist discourses that beyond their textual accounts could only ever be partially enacted, rather than fully realized (Latour 1993a).

The purpose of this chapter, however, is to excavate the idea of 'material culture studies', rather than to bury it (cf. Miller 2005a: 37). Excavation examines the remains of the past in the present and for the present. It proceeds down from the surface, but the archaeological convention is to reverse this sequence in writing: from the past to the present. In the discussion of the history of ideas and theories, a major risk of such a chronological framework is that new ideas are narrated progressively, as paradigm shifts: imagined as gradual steps forward that have constantly improved social scientific knowledge (Darnell 1977: 407; Trigger 2006: 5–17). Noting this risk, nevertheless archaeologists and anthropologists cannot divorce the kind of histories that they write of their own disciplines from the conceptions of time that characterize their own work. As an anthropological archaeologist, my focus here is upon the taphonomic processes of residuality, durability, and sedimentation of the remains of past events. Such processes con-stantly shape the intellectual landscapes of archaeology and anthropology. In seeking to generate knowledge of the world we encounter these processes, just as we do any chunk of the landscapes in which we live our everyday lives, in the present as a 'palimpsest' of layered scratches (Hoskins 1955: 271). Archaeological accounts of historical processes operate by slowly working through, documenting, and making sense of the assemblage, rather than standing back and explaining the whole (Hicks and Beaudry 2006b). By undertaking such an iterative process, the chapter explores how the ideas of 'material culture' and 'material culture studies' are themselves artefacts of particular disciplinary conceptions of 'the social'. In conclusion, discussing the current reception of actor-network theory (ANT) in archaeology and anthropology, the chapter explores the limitations of the ideas of the 'actor-network' and of 'material culture' for archaeology and anthropology, especially in relation to their interdisciplinary contribution.

The process of excavation is, however, a time-consuming one. The reader will forgive, I hope, the length and the pace of this chapter. The purpose of working back over disciplinary histories will, I also hope, become apparent as the chapter proceeds.

***

Virtually no historical overviews of this very recent episode in archaeological and anthropological disciplinary histories have been previously attempted (but see Buchli 2002a, 2004 and Schlereth 1981 for North America). Nevertheless, anthropological archaeology routinely explores the very recent and contemporary past, rather than waiting until 'after the dust settles' (Rathje 2001: 67; Hicks and Beaudry 2006b: 4). The chapter is written in the conviction that such excavation of recent disciplinary histories is not only possible, but is an essential first step in thinking through the contribution of archaeological and anthropological thinking about things beyond these two disciplines. My focus is explicitly upon British debates where the emergence of material culture studies from archaeological and anthropological thought has been particularly strong, and upon Cambridge-, London-, and Oxford-based researchers because of their central role in the emergence of the idea of 'material culture studies'; however, the international dimensions of the shifting debates over the study of things will be considered along the way. Like all anthropological writing, it is both a situated and a 'partial' account in the sense evoked by Marilyn Strathern (2004a): neither total, nor impartial (cf. Haraway 1988).

The main argument of the chapter relates to the distinctive form taken by the 'cultural turn' in British archaeology and social anthropology during the 1980s and 1990s. For both fields, *the cultural turn was a material turn*. An explicit and rhetorical use of the study of 'the solid domain of material culture' (Tilley 1990a: 35) was deployed in order to shelter research into humanistic themes such as consumption, identity, experience, and cultural heritage from the accusations of relativism or scholasticism that accompanied the cultural turn during the late twentieth-century science wars between 'relativism' and 'realism'. In other words, whereas in many disciplines the cultural turn was characterized by a shift from objectivity to subjectivity, the situation was more entangled in British archaeology and anthropology, because considerable intellectual effort was focused on the idea of relationships between cultural subjects and cultural objects. The legacy of this epistemological move, which I shall call the 'Material-Cultural Turn', has in practice reinforced earlier divisions between archaeological and anthropological thinking—between the 'material' and 'cultural'. I shall argue that these distinctions derived in turn from a still earlier set of debates, which had led to the emergence of the idea of 'material culture' during the second quarter of the twentieth century. Thus, the chapter seeks to document what remains after this Material-Cultural Turn, and how these remains might be put to work today.

A longer-term perspective reveals that the contested place of material objects in the study of human cultures or societies has represented a fault-line running throughout interactions between British archaeological and anthropological thought and practice. By working back and forth across this fault-line, rather than down towards any solid bedrock, I shall argue that the idea of distinguishing between the material and the cultural, and of distinguishing relationships between them, was a distinctive artefact of modernist anthropology and archaeology. The challenges for the two disciplines today, therefore, lie neither in sketching out such dualisms, nor in seeking to overcome them, but more fundamentally in shaking off those modernist representational impulses of which the very concept of 'material culture' is an effect.

The rest of this chapter falls across five broadly chronological sections, and a concluding discussion. The first section (pp. 30–44) considers the development of the idea of 'object lessons' during the late nineteenth century, and traces the subsequent terminological shift from 'primitive art' and 'technology' to 'material culture' during the second quarter of the twentieth century in British anthropology and archaeology. It examines the relationships of this shift with the emergence of structural-functionalist anthropology and (later) the 'New' or processual archaeology. I shall argue that, counterintuitively, the idea of 'material culture' emerged at precisely the same moment as a very significant hiatus in the anthropological and, to a lesser extent, the archaeological study of objects and collections took place. Thus, the emergence of the idea of 'material culture' was from the outset intimately bound up with a radical shift away from the study of things. The legacies of these debates continue to shape discussion of the idea of 'material culture' today.

The second section (pp. 44–64) considers how the development of structuralist and semiotic approaches in both fields brought a new attention upon the study of material culture. I shall argue that the emergence from the 1970s of the idea of 'material culture studies' developed especially from a desire to reconcile structuralism and semiotics. Tracing the alternative influences upon British archaeology and anthropology, this section a shift from the late nineteenth-century idea of 'object-lessons' to the new conception, derived especially from practice theory, of 'object domains'. Just as practice theory emerged from two principal thinkers— Pierre Bourdieu and Anthony Giddens—so its reception in British archaeology and anthropology was mapped out through the work of two scholars and their students: Ian Hodder at Cambridge and Daniel Miller at UCL. This body of work used the idea of 'material culture studies' to craft the cultural turn in British archaeology and anthropology as a Material-Cultural Turn.

A shorter third section (pp. 64–68) outlines the 'high period' of British material culture studies since the early 1990s, sketching the principal themes in this field during that period. It also explores alternative conceptions of disciplinarity in this period, and especially the idea of material culture studies as a kind of post-disciplinary field. The fourth section (pp. 68–79) traces the gradual unfolding of the idea of 'material culture' as a fixed and coherent object of enquiry: in debates over the idea of objects as texts, various uses of phenomenology, and the idea of 'material agency'. Discussing the critique of the idea of 'materiality' by Tim Ingold, a fifth section (pp. 79–94) explores how two themes in his recent work—formation and skill—might be reoriented in the light of recent work in historical anthropology and historical archaeology, to account for the place of the researcher in the practice of material culture studies. Central here is an understanding of both things and theories as simultaneously *events* and *effects*: rather than as passive objects, active subjects, or caught up somehow in the spectral webs of networks (Latour 2005a), meshworks (Ingold 2007c), or dialectical relations (Miller 2005a). In this light, a concluding section (pp. 94–98) takes stock of prospects for the idea of material culture studies in anthropological archaeology after the Material-Cultural Turn.

I: From 'technology' to 'material culture'

The idea of studying technology in archaeology and anthropology crystallized during the two disciplines' 'Museum Period' in the last third of the nineteenth century from earlier Western colonial and antiquarian collecting practices (Sturtevant 1969: 622; Stocking 1985: 7). Between c.1865 and c.1900, when firm boundaries between the two disciplines had not yet emerged, material things—especially human 'technology'—came to be central to attempts to order cultures across time and space in a scientific manner: in self-conscious contrast with earlier antiquarian collecting practices. However, although it has often been used with reference to nineteenth-century museum anthropology or ethnographic collecting, the term 'material culture'—the definition of a 'super-category of objects' (Buchli 2002a: 3)—was not current in British archaeology and anthropology until the inter-war period of the early twentieth century. This section traces the emergence of evolutionary, diffusionist, and culture-historical models of technology, and the intellectual contexts in which gradual replacement of the term of 'technology' with that of 'material culture' took place, especially as part of the critique presented by structural-functionalist and early processualist approaches between the 1920s and 1950s.

Evolutionary, diffusionist, and culture-historical studies of technology

During the mid-nineteenth century, the 'Three Age' system, in which the technological use of different materials (stone, bronze, iron) defined changing time periods of Old World prehistory, gave structure to the earliest integrative accounts of European prehistory (Worsaae 1849; Lubbock 1865). During the 1870s and 1880s ideas of artefact typology (the analysis of archaeological and ethnographic objects according to type) emerged. These new ideas came to be used as the basis for new progressivist schemes of technological change, most famously in Augustus Lane Fox Pitt Rivers' account of 'the evolution of culture', which presented a gradualist, linear model of cultural change (Pitt Rivers 1875) in which, unlike Henry Lewis Morgan's (1877) similar contemporary scheme of social evolution, material things were central (Figure 2.1). The application of evolutionary thinking to human technologies such as that exemplified by Pitt Rivers' approach was paralleled by Marx's slightly earlier suggestion about studying 'the history of human technology', highlighted by Tim Ingold, in *Capital*:

Darwin has aroused our interest in the history of natural technology, that is to say in the origin of the organs of plants and animals as productive instruments utilised for the life purposes of those creatures. Does not the history of the origin of the production of men in society, the organs which form the material basis of every kind of social organisation, deserve equal attention? Since, as Vico says, the essence of the distinction between human history and natural history is that the former is the work of man and the latter is not, would not the history of human technology be easier to write than the history of natural technology?

Marx (1930 [1867]: 392–393, footnote 2; quoted by Ingold 2000a: 362)

As a classificatory project, Pitt Rivers' scheme was tangibly realized in the organization of his first museum collection. Opened in 1884, the Pitt Rivers Museum at Oxford University was originally organized by both evolutionary and typological principles (Pitt Rivers 1891), and was constructed as an extension to the University's Museum of Natural History (Gosden and Larson 2007). The museum made a connection between human technology and Edward Tylor's notion of 'culture', as set out in his book *Primitive Culture* (1871). Such thinking was expanded in Oxford by Henry Balfour in his study of *The Evolution of Decorative Art* (Balfour 1893) and in Cambridge by Alfred Cort Haddon in his *Evolution in Art* (1895), for both of whom the idea of the development of artefact sequences or 'series' over time, rather than a rigid theory of evolutionary change as we might understand it today, was important (Morphy and Perkins 2006a: 5).

The publication in 1896 of the English translation of Friedrich Ratzel's *The History of Mankind* (the German edition of which had been published in 1885–1888) was an important milestone in the developing use of ethnographic and archaeological collections to study human cultures. Echoing earlier developments in geology, and then evolutionary natural history, Ratzel argued that such studies could go beyond written histories:

We can conceive a universal history of civilization, which should assume a point of view commanding the whole earth, in the sense of surveying the history of the extension of civilization throughout mankind . . . At no distant future, no one will write a history of the world without touching upon those peoples which have not hitherto been regarded as possessing a history because they have left no records written or graven in stone. History consists of action; and how unimportant beside this is the question of writing or not writing, how wholly immaterial, beside the facts of doing and making, is the word that describes them.

Ratzel (1896: 5)

PLATE III.

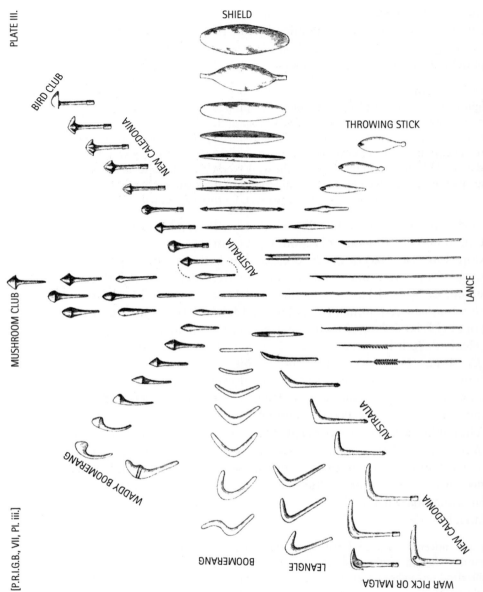

SHIELD

THROWING STICK

BIRD CLUB

NEW CALEDONIA

MUSHROOM CLUB

AUSTRALIA

LANCE

WADDY BOOMERANG

BOOMERANG

LEANGLE

AUSTRALIA

NEW CALEDONIA

WAR PICK OR MALGA

Fig. 2.1 'Clubs, Boomerangs, Shields and Lances': Pitt Rivers' scheme for Australian weapons showing forms emerging in series from the centre outwards, from a hypothetical single form (from Pitt Rivers 1875).

Fig. 2.2 'Zulu wooden vessels from the Museum of the Berlin Mission', from Ratzel 1897 (vol. 2), p. 413.

The introduction by Tylor to Ratzel's very richly illustrated volume—containing some 1,160 illustrations—captured the confidence of this late nineteenth-century conception of the study of artefacts (Figure 2.2). Describing the richness of these illustrations, Tylor argued that they

are no mere book-decorations, but a most important part of the apparatus for realising civilisation in its successive stages. They offer, in a way which no verbal description can attain to, an introduction and guide to the use of museum collections on which the Science of Man comes more and more to depend in working out the theory of human development. Works which combine the material presentation of culture with the best descriptions by observant travellers, promote the most great object of displaying mankind as related together in Nature through its very variation.

Tylor (1896: v)

Tylor contrasted biological and linguistic approaches to 'the classification of peoples' with the 'fuller though less technical treatment of the culture-side of human life': 'the material arts of war, subsistence, pleasure, the stages of knowledge, morals, religion, may be so brought to view that a compendium of them, as found among the ruder peoples, may serve not only as a lesson-book for the learner, but as a reference-book for the learned' (Tylor 1896: vi). The centrality of the classification of technological objects (e.g. Haddon 1900), combined with the curator's sense of the distinctive knowledge that can emerge from the study of material things, was captured in Tylor's coining of his famous phrase 'object-lessons':

In our time there has come to the front a special study of human life through such *object-lessons* as are furnished by the specimens in museums. These things used to be little more than curiosities belonging to the life of barbarous tribes, itself beginning to be recognised as curious and never suspected as being instructive. Nowadays it is better understood that they are material for the student 'looking before and after'.

Tylor (1896: vi, my emphasis)

Tylor's *fin-de-siècle* argument about 'looking before and after' represented a remarkably confident statement of the potential of the curation and study of objects: as not only documenting the past or understanding the present, but also envisioning the future: 'not only as interpreting the past history of mankind, but as even laying down the first stages of curves of movement which will describe and affect the courses of future opinions and institutions' (Tylor 1896: xi).

In the study of European prehistory, the idea of 'seriation' (the identification of a series or sequence through typological analysis) was during the 1880s and 1890s combined with a diffusionist approach to cultural change by Oscar Montelius, based at the Museum of National Antiquities in Stockholm (Montelius 1903). Such work inspired what came to be known as 'culture-historical archaeology', providing very different perspectives from earlier evolutionary studies of technological change that now led to the first overall accounts of the sequence of Old World prehistory by archaeologists such as John Myres (1911) and Gordon Childe (1925). These new culture-historical accounts of the prehistoric past were, however, associated especially with the identification of particular artefactual types with particular normative ethnic or cultural groups, in order to trace their migration or diffusion through detailed typological study (Figure 2.3). They also focused upon the socially determining role of technology: for example, in Childe's combination of Marxist notions of technology and production with a distinctive use of the idea of 'revolution' to underline the significance of the emergence of metallurgy in the long-term developments of European prehistory (Sherratt 1989: 179).

However, such confidence in the study of technology did not continue in British social anthropology. The early twentieth century saw the emergence of radical new forms of integrative, book-length writing in British archaeology and anthropology. These were associated with the professionalization of the disciplines as academic subjects, new models of fieldwork, and new distinctions between ethnographic and archaeological knowledge. Such distinctions were centred to a large extent on the place of the study of technology. The changing conceptions of 'technology' and 'material culture' are considered in the next section.

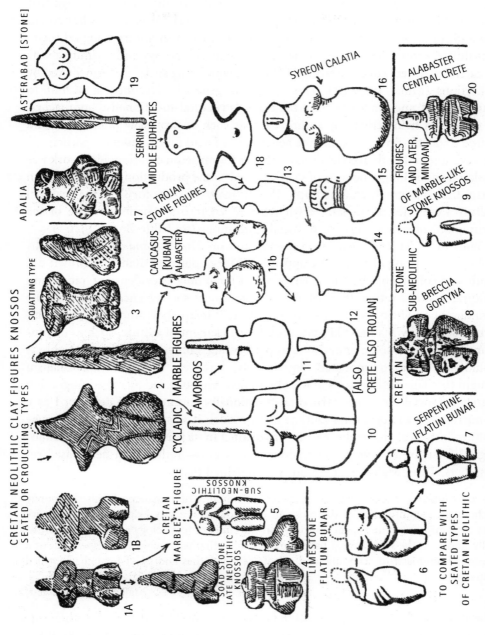

Fig. 2.3 Illustration of 'Neolithic figurines from Crete and their relatives, after [Arthur] Evans' from Gordon Childe's *The Dawn of European Civilization* (Childe 1925: 18, figure 8).

Social anthropology or material culture

In the early twentieth century a fundamental change in ethnographic field practices, which had over the previous two centuries shifted through 'the voyage [to]
the collection of curios [to] the field trip' (Defert 1982: 12), formed a new horizon in
the anthropological study of artefacts. Mainstream British anthropological interests shifted from museums and objects (especially technology and 'primitive' art)
to extended, direct contact through fieldwork with living societies, unmediated by
collections (Miller 1987: 111). This change is generally described as a shift to
'functionalist' and gradually, from the 1940s, 'structural-functionalist' approaches.
The focus of field activity by anthropologists such as Bronislaw Malinowski and
Alfred Radcliffe-Brown became the generation of field notes, based on participant
observation, rather than collections of objects for museum curation. Fieldwork was
undertaken for longer periods of time, and led to the production of a new written
form: the ethnographic monograph. Evolutionary schemes for studying material
culture were rejected as part of what developed into a broader critique of the
writing of 'conjectural history' of social institutions (Radcliffe-Brown 1941: 1).

Thus in Radcliffe-Brown's 1922 monograph on *The Andaman Islanders*, 'technology' was simply listed in the appendix (Tilley 2006a: 2). Radcliffe-Brown did
study and collect objects, but he wrote about them only as evidence of 'racial' and
cultural history, rather than of the contemporary society encountered by the
ethnographer. The presence of such appendices is instructive: since the functionalism as set out by Malinowski understood each element of culture, such as institutions or practices, to be understood as performing a function, the study of objects
could still be accommodated. Increasingly, however, structural-functionalism
sought to relate the functions of the phenomena encountered by the ethnographer
purely to social structure. Structural-functionalist anthropology developed as a
comparative sociology, on a Durkheimian model. It was integrative like the new
culture-historical archaeologies, but was distinct in its frustration with the technological focus of a previous generation of museums—rather than field-based researchers. Thus, Malinowski famously complained that:

As a sociologist, I have always had a certain amount of impatience with the purely
technological enthusiasms of the museum ethnologist. In a way I do not want to move
one inch from my intransigent position that the study of technology alone is . . . scientifically sterile. At the same time, I have come to realise that technology is indispensable as a
means of approach to economic and sociological activities and to what might be called
native science.

Malinowski (1935: 460)

The accommodation of objects within such writing was by understanding their role
in social institutions: most influentially in the study of exchange in Malinowski's
Argonauts of the Western Pacific (1922). This engendered a gradual dematerialization of social anthropology, which was closely bound up with a move away from

concerns with historical process, towards the study of 'social facts' (e.g. Mauss 1990 [1922]). In Britain, this gradual rise of a Durkheimian model for social anthropology witnessed a change in terminology, from 'technology' to a new compound term: 'material culture'. This change in the vocabulary of British anthropology between the 1920s and 1940s was very little discussed at the time.

The shift from 'technology' to 'material culture' was a desirable one for both museum- and fieldwork-focused anthropologists. On the one hand, for social anthropologists working in a structural-functionalist mode the idea of museum-based anthropology as studying 'material culture' allowed a separation off of collections, as a legacy of earlier times, from the emerging modern field of British social anthropology. In this respect, the terminological shift from 'technology' to 'material culture' was comparable with a broader shift in modes of 'objectivity' identified by Lorraine Daston and Peter Galison (1992, 2007), from the 'mechanical objectivity' of the late nineteenth century to the 'trained judgement' of the twentieth century. Such a move distinguished a modernist social anthropology from earlier technological determinism, such as that found in one of the earliest volumes to use the term 'material culture': Leonard Hobhouse, Gerald Wheeler, and Morris Ginsberg's combination of evolutionary and early functionalist approaches with statistical analysis to examine *The Material Culture and Social Institutions of the Simpler Peoples*, which focused on how 'material culture, the control of man over nature in the arts of life' might 'roughly, but no more than roughly, reflect the general level of intellectual attainment' in the society in question (Hobhouse *et al.* 1915: 6; Penniman 1965: 133n1).

On the other hand, the new term 'material culture' was equally attractive to museum-based anthropologists wishing to underline that their collections were more than simply assemblages of objects—the legacy of a previous intellectual tradition—and to revive Tylor's conception of culture in order to do so. In this view, it provided a curatorial refuge from that other compound term of the period, 'structural-functionalism'. Thus, J. H. Hutton writing in 1944 on the theme of 'The Place of Material Culture in the Study of Anthropology' expressed his 'dissent most emphatically from the functionalist point of view that the study of "material culture" is of value only, or even primarily, as an approach to the study of economic and social activity' (Hutton 1944: 3). As Mike Rowlands has put it, the idea of material culture came to represent a place of retreat for museum anthropology during the mid-twentieth century:

Material culture in an anthropological context is scarcely ever about artefacts *per se*. The term connotes instead the ambivalent feelings that anthropologists have had towards their evolutionist and diffusionist origins and towards museum studies, reflecting also their concern that the subject, in an age of specialization, should still aspire to be a totalizing and integrative approach to the study of man. The term is therefore metaphorical rather than sub-disciplinary and survived as a conceptual category to allow certain kinds of study to be practised that would not fit any of the canons established during the hegemony of British social anthropology in the inter-war years.

Rowlands (1983: 15)

The creation of the new category of 'material culture' was thus closely bound up with the emergence of British social anthropology, which increasingly comprehended object-based research as 'clearly subordinated to sociology', and defined itself as fundamentally distinct from archaeology (Stocking 2001: 187, 192–193). British anthropology was concerned with difference in the contemporary world across space (between Western and non-Western situations), rather than with change over time (Rowlands 2004: 474). In a shift often lamented by the increasingly peripheral voices of museum anthropologists (Sturtevant 1969; Reynolds 1983; see Stocking 1985: 9), British social anthropology sought to move its subject matter entirely past objects, to people.

New archaeology and material culture

The implications for archaeology of this shift away from objects in structural-functionalist social anthropology were at first felt less sharply in Britain than in North America. But in the United States similar ideas of lifting the archaeology out of purely descriptive and antiquarian accounts of the past came to be developed by two key thinkers: Walter Taylor (in the 1940s) and Lewis Binford (from the 1960s). Both Taylor and Binford presented critiques of culture-historical archaeology as privileging the study of typology above that of human behaviour in the past, in which new approaches to the study of archaeological material culture were set out. The work of these two archaeologists formed an important context for the reception of structural-functionalism, especially in relation to its implications for the study of 'material culture', in British archaeology during the 1950s and 1960s.

Walter Taylor's *A Study of Archaeology* (1948), was based on a Ph.D. written at Harvard between 1938 and 1942. It was strongly influenced by the emerging cultural-ecological models of Clyde Kluckhohn and Julian Steward, and especially by Talcott Parsons' (1937) vision of structural-functionalist sociology as a science of human action. Taylor presented a 'conjunctive approach', which foregrounded archaeological methods to argue that archaeological research leads not to 'reconstructions' but active, scientific 'constructions' of the past (Taylor 1948: 35–36): it had

as its primary goal the elucidation of cultural conjunctives, the associations and relationships, the 'affinities', *within* the manifestation under investigation. It aims at drawing the completest possible picture of past human life in terms of human and geographic environment. It is chiefly interested in the relation of item to item, trait to trait, complex to complex... *within* the culture-unit represented and only subsequently in the taxonomic relation of these phenomena to similar ones outside of it.

Taylor (1948: 95–96; original emphasis)

The distinctive identity of archaeology as a discipline was a crucial element of Taylor's argument: 'Archaeology is neither history or anthropology. As an autonomous discipline it consists of a method and a set of specialized techniques for the gathering or "production" of cultural information' (Taylor 1948: 44). Thus, Taylor criticized Alfred Kidder's study of archaeological objects in his study of *The Artifacts of Pecos* (1932):

there is neither any provenience given for the vast majority of artifacts, nor any consistent correlation of these specimens with the ceramic periods. The description of the artefacts seems to be for its own sake and for the sake of comparative study on a purely descriptive level with similar artefacts from other sites. It may well be asked whether the meaning of the artefacts for the culture of Pecos is thought to lie in their form and classification of form, or whether it lies in their relations to one another and to the broad cultural and natural environment of Pecos.

Taylor (1948: 48)

While Taylor's study concluded with a lengthy 'Outline of Procedures for the Conjunctive Approach', which argued that 'an archaeological find is only as good as the notes upon it' (Taylor 1948: 154), the outspoken attacks in *A Study of Archaeology* upon many of the most senior figures in American archaeology at the time severely limited its impact for a generation (Leone 1972): a fact later of considerable regret to Taylor himself (Taylor 1972; Maca *et al.* 2010).

During the 1960s Lewis Binford developed the line of thought begun by Taylor into a more direct critique of culture-historical archaeology. Binford's work inspired the development of 'processual' or 'New' archaeology during the 1970s. But where Taylor had argued for a strong archaeological disciplinarity, Binford's commitment (which he shared with Taylor) to a focus on behaviour rather than typology led him instead to define 'Archaeology as Anthropology': repeating Gordon Willey and Philip Phillips' contention that 'archaeology is anthropology or it is nothing' (Willey and Phillips 1958: 2; Binford 1962: 217), and extending Leslie White's neo-cultural evolutionary argument that 'culture is the extra-somatic means of adaptation for the human organism' to view 'material culture' as an 'extra-somatic means of adaptation' (White 1959: 8; Binford 1962: 217–218).

Binford distinguished between 'three major functional sub-classes of material culture': *technomic* ('those artifacts having their primary functional context in coping directly with the physical environment', *socio-technic* ('the extra-somatic means of articulating individuals one with an-other into cohesive groups capable of efficiently maintaining themselves and of manipulating the technology', such as 'a king's crown'), and *ideo-technic* ('items which signify and symbolize the ideological rationalizations for the social system and further provide the symbolic milieu in which individuals are enculturated', such as 'figures of deities') (Binford 1962: 217, 219–220). He argued that such distinctions would allow archaeologists to develop distinctive theoretical perspectives on the significance of certain material items in social life, and to distinguish alternative methods for the study of past environmental adaptation, social relations, and ideas or beliefs through material culture:

We should not equate 'material culture' with technology. Similarly we should not seek explanations for observed differences and similarities in 'material culture' within a single interpretative frame of reference. It has often been suggested that we cannot dig up a social system or ideology. Granted we cannot excavate a kinship terminology or a philosophy, but we can and do excavate the material items which functioned together with these more behavioral elements within the appropriate cultural sub-systems. The formal structure of artifact assemblages together with the between element contextual relationships should and do present a systematic and understandable picture of the *total extinct* cultural system.

Binford (1962: 218–219)

Thus, Binford argued that archaeological material culture should be understood as evidence of human behaviour and adaptation, operating in different cultural registers from the practical to the social to the ideational, rather than more general reflections of particular culture-historical traits (Figure 2.4). He developed this positivist view through the use of ethnographic analogy and a method of making general statements about the systematic relationships between human behaviour and material culture, which he termed 'middle range theory' (Binford 1983). In his classic critique of culture-historical archaeology, Binford argued that an analysis of the stone tools associated with the Middle-Upper Palaeolithic transition in Europe, in which François Bordes suggested that difference in tools represented could be understood as different traditions that he labelled 'Mousterian', 'Acheulian', etc., should instead be understood as the evidence of different behavioural adaptations rather than different cultural groups (Binford 1973; Bordes 1973). The materialism of the New Archaeology drew from the contrasting ecological perspectives of Julian Steward and the technological focus of Leslie White: both of which tended, under the banner of neo-evolutionism, towards a materialist determinism for social structure (Trigger 1984: 279).

In Britain, a similar direction to that of the Americanist New Archaeology had begun to be explored by Grahame Clark at Cambridge. Clark's transitional approach, which has been described as 'functional-processual' (Trigger 2006), made use of 'systems' approaches and an emphasis upon ecological adaptation in the reconstruction of past societies, as set out in his *Archaeology and Society* (1939). However, the reception of structural-functionalist social anthropology among British archaeologists did not lead in the same way to the development of the positivist scientific models that came to characterize the Americanist processual archaeology. This was for two principal reasons: contemporary debates in British social anthropology about historical change, and the early response to Walter Taylor's arguments from the perspectives of British culture-historical archaeology.

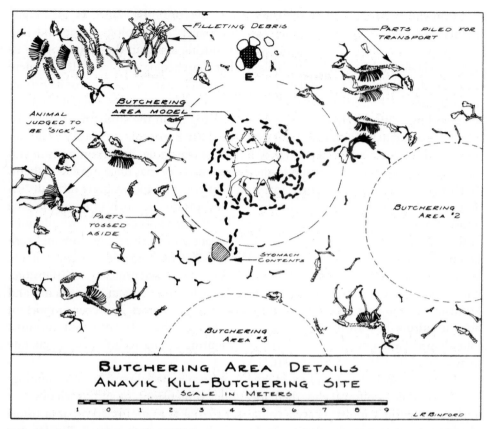

Fig. 2.4 'Close up of the butchering area at the Anavik Springs site [Alaska] showing the circular areas in which the caribou were dismembered and the location of the waste by-products', from Lewis Binford's *In Pursuit of the Past* (Binford 1983: 123, figure 61).

In British social anthropology, the shift in the structural-functionalist anthropology away from interests in change over time, which had accompanied its shift from earlier evolutionary and diffusionist approaches, came to be critiqued. A seminal contribution to this critique was Evans-Pritchard's Marrett Lecture of 1950, which described the anthropology of Malinowski and (by implication) Radcliffe-Brown as characterized by an 'insistence that a society can be understood satisfactorily without reference to its past' (Evans-Pritchard 1950: 120). Evans-Pritchard suggested that social anthropologists write 'cross-sections of history, integrative descriptive accounts of primitive peoples at a moment of time', arguing that anthropology should be located within the humanities rather than the sciences (Evans-Pritchard 1950: 122, 123–124).

Meanwhile, in archaeology the transatlantic reception of Walter Taylor's arguments was framed by Christopher Hawkes' paper 'Archaeological method and theory: a view from the Old World', written during a stay in the United States in 1953–4. Hawkes addressed 'Taylor's claim that if archeology limits itself to a mere external chronicling of material culture traits, it will be stopping short of its proper anthropological objective, and will be simply compiling statistics when it ought to be revealing culture' (Hawkes 1954: 156). Focusing upon the study of a period for which documentary sources are not available (later European prehistory), Hawkes described the archaeological process of inductive reasoning, 'from comparison and analysis of observed phenomena to the human activity that once produced them'. Such reasoning, Hawkes argued, involved four levels of increasingly difficult 'inferences': from understanding the 'techniques' producing such phenomena (the most straightforward) to information about 'subsistence-economics', 'social/political institutions', and finally 'religious institutions and spiritual life'. Moving from inference to narrative, Hawkes echoed Evans-Pritchard in his criticism of the ahistorical approach of structural-functionalism as 'scientifically indefensible', but also argued for the importance of acknowledging human movements and diffusion in the past (Hawkes 1954: 163). These last themes had been important for the culture-historical archaeology of Childe and others (Hawkes 1954: 161–165), but shaped Grahame Clark's later use of scientific dating techniques to generate new accounts of *World Prehistory* (Clark 1961).

Hawkes' model of archaeological inference from material remains to technological, economic, political and then ideational dimensions of past societies was critiqued by the 'contextual archaeology' of the 1980s as grounded on an a priori distinction between technological and symbolic objects (see below). But for our present purposes it is sufficient to note that Hawkes' reception of Taylor's arguments led him to two positions. First, he foregrounded archaeological methodology, and especially its engagement with the material remains of the past, as a central problem: a position quite possibly inspired by his early professional experiences as Assistant, and then Assistant Keeper, at the British Museum (1928–1946). Secondly, Hawkes retained earlier geographical and historical interests that contrasted with synchronic structural-functionalist approaches: echoing Evans-Pritchard in his criticism of the ahistorical approach of structural-functionalism (Hawkes 1954: 163).

While at Oxford the arguments of Hawkes (from archaeology) and Evans-Pritchard (from social anthropology) both resisted the model of social structure presented by structural-functionalism, at Cambridge from the late 1960s the Binfordian model of the New Archaeology was taken up and reworked by David Clarke. In contrast with Binford's approach, Clarke's *Analytical Archaeology* (1968) strongly restated Taylor's commitment to archaeology as a discipline distinct from both history and social anthropology. Clarke developed an account of how archaeological knowledge develops from archaeological methods as applied to archaeological materials. Central to his model was a concern about a division of disciplinary labour between the material practices of fieldwork or lab-based research and the scholarly writing of integrative accounts of the past:

> There is currently a tendency to take the term prehistorian as meaning 'a writer of history covering periods without written records', with the implication that the 'prehistorian' is an armchair synthesiser of the analytical work of the 'archaeologist'. Here the term archaeologist is warped to mean the unintelligent 'excavator' or the narrow-minded 'specialist'—the term prehistorian thus acquiring a rosy flush of dilettante value at the expense of the devalued archaeologist. The danger of historical narrative as a vehicle for archaeological results is that it pleases by virtue of its smooth coverage and apparent finality, whilst the data on which it is based are never comprehensive . . . Archaeological data are not historical data and consequently archaeology is not history. The view taken in this work is that archaeology is archaeology is archaeology (with apologies to Gertrude Stein).
>
> Clarke (1968: 11)

In presenting a vision of archaeology as 'a discipline in its own right'—'concerned with the recovery, systematic description and study of material culture in the past' (1968: 12)—Clarke sought to move forward the line of enquiry begun by Taylor by calling not only for a shift from the 'common sense' description of material culture to a disciplinary 'self-consciousness', but further to the development of a distinctive body of archaeological theory that would shift the field from a 'self-consciousness' of materials and methods to 'critical self-consciousness'. Clarke (1973) described this process as archaeology's 'loss of innocence'. With reference to the radical revisions of prehistoric chronologies that resulted from the scientific use of radiocarbon dating (Renfrew 1973a), Clarke argued for the contingency of archaeological knowledge upon materially-situated scientific practice, suggesting that 'a new environment develops new materials and new methods with new consequences, which demand new philosophies, new solutions and new perspectives' (Clarke 1973: 8–9). The continuing significance of these arguments for archaeological conceptions of material culture and fieldwork will be seen towards the end of this chapter.

***

This section has traced the layered sequence through which the sociological model of British anthropology that emerged during the early twentieth century led to a shift in terminology from 'technology' through the invention of the idea of 'material culture'. This change was a central part of a division of disciplinary labour (and disciplinary influence) between the museum and the collection on one hand, and the field site and the ethnographic monograph on the other. Thus, the idea of 'material culture' emerged at precisely the moment in anthropology's history in which a particular focus upon social structure as the object of ethnographic enquiry 'effectively banned artifact study to the comparative isolation of the anthropological museum and relegated its practitioners to a peripheral position within the discipline' (van Beek 1989: 91). However, the influence of these sociological approaches upon archaeology was mitigated by a continued focus upon the engagement with both artefacts and sites or landscapes in the study of the past. Unlike the positivist models that developed in the work of Binford and his students in the United States, the reception of the New Archaeology and the development of 'systems' approaches in the UK built, particularly through the work of David Clarke, on Taylor's focus upon the development of archaeological knowledge from the rigorous application of archaeo-logical methods: methods that involved 'inference' as well as excavation.

The sociological and humanistic critique of the excessively descriptive focus of previous materially-focused approaches was thus mediated in Clarke's work by an awareness of the active role of the archaeologist and the contingent nature of our knowledge of the past. In this sense, the New Archaeology in Britain held much in common not only with the historical focus of Evans-Pritchard, but also with the Manchester School's call for social anthropology to be grounded in detailed case studies (e.g. Gluckman 1961). This sense of importance of fieldwork in which contingent, material conditions were implicated did not, however, characterize the manner in which the new ideas of structuralism, semiotics, and practice theory were received during the 1970s and early 1980s in British archaeology and anthro-pology. This Material-Cultural Turn is considered in Section II of this chapter.

II: The Material-Cultural Turn: from 'object-lessons' to 'object domains'

In the discussion of excavated sequences, archaeologists commonly group series of layers, cuts, and fills into a broader chronological sequence of 'phases'. The second phase that we can identify in this excavation of 'material culture studies' begins with the strong influence upon social anthropology, from the 1960s, of two new, inter-related bodies of thought. The first of these was the application of structural-ist analysis, developed by Claude Lévi-Strauss from Saussurean linguistics (de Saussure 1959 [1916]), to the study of social structure (Leach 1961; Lévi-Strauss 1963). The second was a focus upon interpretation and the study of meaning and social practice, developed especially by Clifford Geertz (1973), which represented the development of a Parsonian, and ultimately Weberian, hermeneutic model for social science, but also paralleled by new Durkheimian accounts of the anthropol-ogy of ritual performance and 'symbolic action' (Turner 1975: 159; see Turner 1967). The focus in both the structuralist and interpretive anthropologies on themes such as ritual practice, symbolism, and myth provided space for a gradual refocusing of anthropological research interests upon objects. As will become clear, however, this focus on objects was concerned quite specifically with the identification and comparative study of abstract schemes of form, style, and design, and with the relationships of such phenomena with meaning and use in practice.

The publication in 1963 of the English translation of the first volume of Lévi-Strauss' *Structural Anthropology* was a watershed for anthropologists studying material culture. Lévi-Strauss presented analyses of the underlying 'grammars' of artefact designs, as part of a more general account of the structures that he understood as lying behind all manifestations of culture: from ritual masks to kinship proscriptions (cf. Lévi-Strauss 1982). For example, in his study of 'Split Representation in the Art of Asia and America', Lévi-Strauss applied approaches from structuralist linguistics to ethnographic objects in order to develop new kinds of comparative studies of 'primitive art' (Lévi-Strauss 1963: 245). In doing so, he built upon the sociological study of *Primitive Classification* that had been established by Emile Durkheim and Marcel Mauss at the start of the twentieth century (Durkheim and Mauss 1963 [1903]). The reception of French structuralism work alongside American interpretive anthropology in British anthropology inspired a range of structuralist and semiotic anthropological studies of style and form in artworks and the built environment (e.g. Munn 1973; Humphrey 1974), and the beginnings of studies of material culture as a kind of communicative system, analogous to, but not reducible to, language (Rowlands 2004: 475–476). This was also developed in New Archaeology through Martin Wobst's idea of 'stylistic behaviour' concerned with 'information exchange' (Wobst 1977).

It was in this context that British archaeology and anthropology witnessed a second major shift in the study of material things, which culminated during the 1980s as what I want to call the 'Material-Cultural Turn'. Where the various responses to the sociological model of structural-functionalism had been united in a terminological shift from 'technology' to 'material culture', the responses to structuralist and interpretive approaches led to the emergence of the idea of 'material culture studies'. The idea of material culture studies emerged from the desire to bring the structural and the meaningful together in a single analysis in archaeology and anthropology. For this reason, it can be understood to be closely associated with the reception of the 'practice theories' of Pierre Bourdieu and Anthony Giddens in archaeology and anthropology. However, French structural Marxism, American historical archaeology and 'modern material culture studies', and the 'ethnoarchaeology' that developed in American New Archaeology also represented important influences.

Structural Marxism and 'vulgar materialism' approaches

The first attempts to reconcile grand narratives of structuralism with the more fine-grained account of interpretive and symbolic anthropology developed through the reception of French structural Marxist anthropology (Meillassoux 1972; Terray 1972, 1975; Godelier 1977) by British anthropologists, and especially those such as Jonathan Friedman and Mike Rowlands who were associated with UCL (Bloch 1975; Friedman 1974, 1975; Rowlands and Gledhill 1976). As Sherry Ortner (1984: 140) has argued, the British structural Marxist anthropology of the 1970s represented 'an explicit mediation between the "materialist" and "idealist" camps of sixties anthropology': a mediation later captured by Maurice Godelier's study *The Mental and the Material* (1986).

Structural Marxists such as Friedman and Rowlands critiqued 'functional ecology' and the 'cultural materialism' of American neo-evolutionist anthropology (Harris 1968; see Patterson 2003: 102–112) as a 'simple programmatic materialism': a 'vulgar materialism' that represented an 'empiricist ideology' based on 'the *a priori* reduction of relatively autonomous phenomena . . . to a single phenomenon'. Instead, Friedman sought to offer a more ethnographic account of materialism, using Marx but grounded in the anthropological study of social relations: beginning 'with the assumption of disjunction between structures in order to establish the true relationships that unite them' (Friedman 1974: 466; Rowlands and Gledhill 1976: 31). British structural Marxist anthropology argued that, especially through its sense of historical process, distinctions between the material and the ideational could be overcome through a focus on social relations, rather than the static conception of 'social structure' that had characterized both structural-functionalism and structuralism. Similar arguments developed in American Marxist anthropology, especially the final chapter of Marshall Sahlins' book *Culture and Practical Reason* (1976), which moved radically beyond the historical materialism of his earlier *Stone Age Economics* (1972). In Sahlins' new argument,

One evident matter—for bourgeois society as much as for the so-called primitive—is that material aspects are not usefully separated from the social, as if the first were referable to the satisfaction of needs by the exploitation of nature, and the second to problems of the relations between men . . . [M]aterial effects depend on their cultural encompassment. The very form of social existence of material force is determined by its integration in the cultural system. The force may be significant—but significance, precisely, is a symbolic quality.

Sahlins (1976: 205–206)

British structural Marxist anthropology led to a distinctive way of envisaging the relationship between archaeology and social anthropology:

The material culture record in archaeology has been interpreted as a hierarchical set of entities to be ordered taxonomically. In the last analysis, archaeologists have not so much neglected the socio-historical meaning of material culture assemblages (since, in general, it has always been assumed that the ordering of material would lead to inferences about people) as displayed a timidity towards it which has much in common with that displayed by the Boasian school in ethnography. Implicit is the faith that 'understanding' will arise out of its own motion from the accumulation of fact upon fact with increasing refinement of detail . . . [But] even the development of ways of making truly 'objective' statements about the intrinsic properties of artefacts, through for instance the use of geophysical techniques, has simply underlined the need for systematic social interpretation. The more patterns archaeologists discern in their data, the more questions will be forced upon their attention.

Rowlands and Gledhill (1976: 25)

Here, the idea of a 'relation between archaeology and anthropology' mapped directly on to a conviction in 'the linkage of the material culture record to the socio-cultural system' (Rowlands and Gledhill 1976: 23, 26). In this view, just as archaeology and anthropology were complementary rather than distinct disciplines, so the idea of relationships between artefacts and social structure represented a central research question (Rowlands and Gledhill 1976: 37).

Historical archaeology and 'modern material culture studies'

As with the development of the New Archaeology in the 1960s, in the 1970s transatlantic exchanges were critical in the development of archaeological material culture studies. The reception of structuralism in American historical archaeology, especially in James Deetz's discussion in his *Invitation to Archaeology* (1967) of the 'analysis of form', was based on the idea of the 'mental template':

Artefacts are man-made objects; they are also fossilized ideas . . . [T]he making of a proper form of an object exists in the mind of the maker, and when this idea is expressed in tangible form in raw material, an artifact results . . . [T]he form of an artifact is a close approximation of this template.

Deetz (1967: 45)

Deetz sought, for example in his discussion of the making of a Chumash basket, to combine the structuralist analysis of artefacts with the study of long-term change: a focus on the making of artefact forms as influenced by tradition, but also other factors such as 'technology, function, innovation', and the importance of the idea of context in the study of material culture (Deetz 1967: 47, 67–74).

The new term 'material culture studies' came to be used to define a set of research practices rather than just the object of enquiry defined by the term 'material culture'. During the late 1970s, this new term emerged from American historical archaeology through the idea of 'modern material culture studies' (but see Fenton 1974), and a more general interest in 'the importance of material things' in historical archaeology (Ferguson 1977). This American literature was significant for British archaeology and anthropology because of how two of its characteristics were refracted into debates over the relationships between archaeology and anthropology at Cambridge during the 1970s.

First, the term 'modern material culture studies' was used to describe the archaeological study of the contemporary Western world, whether as part of ethnoarchaeology (South 1979: 213), or more commonly to describe projects such as William Rathje's 'garbology', which undertook an archaeology of the contemporary world—'the archaeology of us' (Gould and Schiffer 1981), which in Rathje's case involved the excavation of contemporary landfills in order to learn about the environmental dimensions of modern life (Rathje 1979). While such approaches were often characterized by the scientific field approaches of the New Archaeology, they also included a range of alternative interpretive or 'behavioural' views (Ascher 1974a, 1974b; Schiffer 1976).

Secondly, work such as Rathje's and Gould's extended perspectives from a new wave of interpretive Americanist historical archaeology, in particular, as developed by James Deetz (1977) in the study of early modern America, which had during the previous decade developed anthropological approaches to material culture studies that contrasted with the use of the term 'material culture' in folklife studies, decorative arts traditions, and historical archaeology in the United States (Quimby 1978). Defining 'archaeology as a social science', Deetz (1972) crucially used the study of material culture as a way of reconciling structuralist and semiotic approaches in anthropology. Deetz's definition of material culture, set out in his studies *Invitation to Archaeology* (1967) and *In Small Things Forgotten: an archaeology of early American life* (1977), was famously very broad:

Material culture is usually considered to be roughly synonymous with artifacts, the vast universe of objects used by mankind to cope with the physical world, to facilitate social intercourse, and to benefit our state of mind. A somewhat broader definition of material culture is useful in emphasising how profoundly our world is the product of our thoughts, as that sector of our physical environment that we modify through culturally determined behavior. This definition includes all artifacts, from the simplest, such as a common pin, to the most complex, such as an interplanetary space vehicle. But the physical environment includes more than what most definitions of material culture recognise. We can also consider cuts of meat as material culture, since there are many ways to dress an animal; likewise plowed fields and even the horse that pulls the plow, since scientific breeding of livestock involves the conscious modification of an animal's form according to culturally derived ideals. Our body itself is part of our physical environment, so that such things as parades, dancing, and all aspects of kinesics—human motion—fit within our definition. Nor is the definition limited only to matter in the solid state. Fountains are liquid examples, as are lily ponds, and material that is partly gas includes hot air balloons and neon signs. I have suggested in *Invitation to Archaeology* that even language is part of material culture, a prime example of it in its gaseous state. Words, after all, are air masses shaped by the speech apparatus according to culturally acquired rules.

Deetz (1977: 24–25)

Deetz's work combined structuralist and semiotic analyses of this very wide range of 'material culture' in order to gain a sense of the 'world views' of people in the past through the apparently inconsequential modern fragments studied by historical archaeology. It sought to introduce a historical dimension into structuralist analyses by studying changing world views over time. This interpretive approach bore some resemblance to the *Annales* historians' study of French material culture in relation to *mentalité*, and was directly inspired by Deetz's colleague Henry Glassie's (1975) structuralist study of vernacular buildings in Virginia in relation to the emergence of the 'Georgian Order' as a historically situated structuring principle for late eighteenth-century material culture. But Deetz also used part-fictional interpretive tableaux to evoke a kind of Geertzian 'thick description' of the material dimensions of human life in relation to significance and meaning (Geertz 1973). This similarity possibly derived from the common training received by Deetz and Geertz at Harvard during the mid-1950s, where the influence of Talcott Parsons was still strongly felt, along with more recent influences, such as Dell Hymes' nascent socio-linguistics (Hymes 1964). In the influence upon British archaeology and anthropology of Geertz's approach to interpretive anthropology, and of Deetz's combination of structuralism with a focus on historical change, their shared commitment to understanding 'human behavior [as] . . . symbolic *action*' (Geertz 1973: 10; my emphasis) laid the foundations for the later reception of practice theory (discussed below).

The emergence of material culture studies: Cambridge and UCL

It was in this intellectual context that the Material-Cultural Turn in British archaeology and anthropology emerged during the late 1970s and early 1980s at the two centres for the development of British material culture studies in the 1980s: the Department of Archaeology at Cambridge and the Department of Anthropology at University College London (UCL). The arguments of both structural Marxism and Deetzian historical archaeology/modern material culture studies, which were united by a desire to reintegrate in a single analysis of structuralist and interpretive anthropology, the material and meaningful aspects of social life— 'to connect people and things' (Deetz 1967: 138)—were received in different ways in these two departments.

In London they dovetailed with an emergent body of thinking about 'material culture studies' that developed at UCL through the work and teaching of Peter Ucko and Daryll Forde (e.g. Ucko 1969; see Rowlands 1983: 16; Buchli 2002a: 11). Especially important here was the development of teaching on material culture and 'primitive art' by Peter Ucko after his appointment in 1962 (Layton *et al.* 2006: 1–3), the influence of British symbolic-structuralist anthropologist Mary Douglas (1966; Douglas and Isherwood 1979), and the influence of Anthony Forge at the London School of Economics. The desire among this group to combine structuralist and semiotic approaches was exemplified by Forge's discussion of the study of 'Primitive Art and Society' (Forge 1973a, 1973b). Forge drew upon approaches in American archaeology to the study of 'iconics' and the 'grammar' of 'classes of objects or graphic signs', 'the analogy being with rules for sentence production in a language' (citing the work of Dell Hymes), arguing that such 'descriptive models' should be combined with the study of meaning and aesthetics (Forge 1973a: xvi–xvii): 'to concentrate on the aspect of style as a system, a visual system, but also a system of meaning' (Forge 1973b: 191). Such work provided the basis for Robert Layton's semiotic approach to *The Anthropology of Art* (1981).

At Cambridge, the idea of 'material culture studies' provided one way of answering two strong challenges: from Edmund Leach's structuralist anthropology (discussed further below) and from archaeologist Colin Renfrew's (1973b) conception of 'social archaeology', to a new generation of Cambridge archaeologists, to build an archaeology that could account for the place of the meaning of objects in social life.

In the early 1980s two responses to these challenges to accommodate both structuralist and interpretive approaches in British archaeology and anthropology made particular use of a new body of sociological thinking about the relationships between 'agency' and 'structure': the practice theories of Pierre Bourdieu (1977) and Anthony Giddens (1979). First, at Cambridge, Ian Hodder and his students developed a new 'contextual archaeology', informed by Bourdieu's notion of *habitus* (Hodder 1982a, 1982b, 1986). Secondly, leaving Cambridge for UCL, and gradually framing their work as anthropological rather than archaeological, Daniel Miller and his students developed a model of 'material culture studies' as the anthropology of consumption, which drew strongly from Giddens' notion of 'structuration'. Giddens' (1979, 1981, 1984) arguments presented a model of the 'duality of structure' involving a mutually constitutive relationship between 'agency' and 'structure'. In new studies in anthropological archaeology, Hodder and Miller sought to use what Giddens had described as 'object domains' (Miller 1987: 158) and what Bourdieu had termed *habitus* to explore the idea of relationships between cultural and material worlds.

***

Archaeological excavation often encounters horizons, caused for example through the ploughing of a field, in which earlier features are truncated, mixed, and redeposited. Such processes bring a levelling-out of surfaces. They draw a line in the sequence of formation, but walking across them the archaeologist will always encounter the abraded residual materials from earlier periods. In our excavation of material culture studies, it is this kind of reordering and persistence that characterizes the second phase of our stratigraphic sequence. Together, two bodies of thinking—Hodder's contextual archaeology and Miller's archaeological anthropology of mass consumption—constituted the Material-Cultural Turn in British archaeology and anthropology. Its emergence through works that combined ethnoarchaeological with structuralist and semiotic perspectives is considered below.

The Material-Cultural Turn: Ethnoarchaeology

The idea of 'ethnoarchaeology'—the comparative archaeological study of contemporary human societies to inform the archaeological explanation of the past—emerged during the 1970s from the desire in Binfordian New Archaeology to develop testable correlations between material remains and human behaviour (Binford 1978; Gould 1978; Kramer 1979; but see the earlier arguments of Ascher 1961, 1962). Developing the idea of 'the archaeology of a contemporary community' (Ascher 1968) as a kind of 'living archaeology' (Gould 1980), ethnoarchaeology contributed to the development of a principal theme of New Archaeology: the challenges of relating patterns in the material record to patterns of human behaviour in the past, read through the alternative cultural and natural processes that lead to the formation of the archaeological record (Schiffer 1972). Such 'archaeologically oriented ethnographic work', focused on the material dimensions of human actions, from the manufacture and use of objects to their being discarded, in the present, such as the production of ceramics (Kramer 1985: 77), and was used to contribute to the New Archaeology's aim of generating universal models for 'material correlates' of human behaviour (Lane 2006: 404).

In the early 1980s, two contributions to the Cambridge University Press series 'New Studies in Archaeology', by Ian Hodder (1982a) and Daniel Miller (1985), laid the foundations for the Material-Cultural Turn in British archaeology and anthropology. These works combined the idea of ethnoarchaeology from New Archaeology in the United States with structuralist approaches to the interpretation of symbols and categories. The choice of ethnoarchaeology—'a processual subdiscipline *par excellence*'—as a place from which to develop a critique of the New Archaeology, was as David van Reybrouck has observed, at first glance a strange one (van Reybrouck 2000: 40). However, the field provided an opportunity for archaeologists to seek to link structuralist studies of material culture with interpretive ethnographic accounts of living populations: developing case studies that explored further Hodder's early critiques, in his reorientation of David Clarke's model of 'spatial archaeology', of 'simple correlations between material culture and society' (Hodder 1978a; cf. 1978b). In this respect, the British ethnoarchaeology of the early 1980s was closer to the sociological idea of 'ethnomethodology' (Garfinkel 1967) than it was to processual ethnoarchaeology.

In *Symbols in Action: ethnoarchaeological studies of material culture* Ian Hodder (1982a) described the results of fieldwork that focused on the relationships between ethnic identity and stylistic variations in the design of items of material culture. His fieldwork was conducted among a range of groups in various locations in eastern Africa: in Kenya (among Tugen, Pokot, and Njemps groups in the Baringo district, and among Samburu agriculturalists and Dorobo hunter-gatherers on the Leroghi Plateau); western Zambia (in the Lozi kingdom); and in two Nuba communities in central Sudan. Discussing decorative symbolism in a wide range of objects from carved calabash milk containers to stools, spears, and cooking pots

Fig. 2.5 'Artefacts from the Lozi Area [western Zambia]. Wooden bowls (*mukeke wa kota*), spatula (foreground) and spoon (centre), knife, "A" basket and "B" pot', from Ian Hodder's *Symbols in Action* (Hodder 1982: 112, figure 50).

(Figure 2.5), and inspired in particular by the social anthropology of Mary Douglas (1966), Hodder argued that rather than *reflecting* cultures (as a passive by-product of social life), variability in the symbolic aspects of material culture should be interpreted from the perspective that objects are actively and meaningfully used in social life. He was particularly interested here in the role of material culture in the establishment and maintenance of ethnic boundaries. Hodder argued, in contrast with the processual archaeology of Binford, that 'culture is not man's extrasomatic means of adaptation but that it is meaningfully constituted' (1982a: 13), and that 'material culture transforms, rather than reflects, social organization according to the strategies of groups, their beliefs, concepts and ideologies' (1982a: 212):

Material culture is meaningfully constituted. Material culture patterning transforms structurally rather than reflects behaviourally social relations. Interpretation must integrate the different categories of evidence from different subsystems into the 'whole' . . . Each particular historical context must be studied as a unique combination of general principles of meaning and symbolism, negotiated and manipulated in specific ways.

Hodder (1982a: 218)

In keeping with its ethnoarchaeological aims, *Symbols in Action* concluded with an attempt to apply Hodder's perspective to late Neolithic material from Orkney, Scotland (Hodder 1982a: 218–228): a direction that was more fully explored in his development of 'symbolic and structural archaeology' into the 'contextual archaeology' that was to radicalize British archaeological engagements with material culture (discussed below).

In contrast, Daniel Miller's ethnoarchaeological study of ceramics in a rural village in the Malwa region of central India, *Artefacts as Categories*, was focused not on the identification of meaning and human identity in material culture, but on the more cognitive idea of 'categorization', and how it related to social practice. But like Hodder, Miller (1985: 5) sought to work between structuralist and semiotic approaches, moving beyond their tendency towards an 'extreme reduction' of 'social structure and cultural forms' to abstract classificatory schemes. For this reason, Miller's use of ethnoarchaeology was based on the argument that 'material culture sets reflect the organizational principles of human categorization processes, and that it is through the understanding of such processes that we may best be able to interpret changes in material culture sets over time' (Miller 1982a: 17).

In his account of fieldwork in a rural village, Miller (1985: 197) argued that the study of 'artefact variability' across technological and cultural categories could reveal how social competition between castes was expressed through ceramics. By treating 'material objects [as] a concrete lasting form of human categorisation', he sought to connect structure with material practice, to 'link *langue* with *parole* and provide explanations in a "realist" mould', since 'categorisation processes mediate and organise the social construction of reality' (Miller 1982a: 17, 23). In doing so, *Artefacts as Categories* was a transitional work that started to move beyond the normative behavioural studies of artefact style that had characterized the New Archaeology (e.g. Wiessner 1984; see Boast 1996). By undertaking 'the micro-analysis of the material world . . . in conjunction with archaeology', Miller (1985: 205) focused not on meaning and symbols, but instead began to use social theory to extend the scope of what Colin Renfrew (1973b) had, a decade earlier, termed 'social archaeology'.

However, a certain frustration not only with the aims of processual ethnoarchaeology, but also with archaeology's methods for studying material culture more generally, emerged in Miller's study. The focus was not on artefacts *per se*, but on 'artefacts as categories', and on the identification of 'a pottery code' the structure of which could be related to 'the various structural positions held by individuals in society' (Miller 1985: 201–202). In an editorial decision that recalled Radcliffe-Brown's treatment of technology in his study of *The Andaman Islanders* (see p. 36 above), a 'Detailed Description of Pottery Manufacture' was provided as an appendix (Miller 1985: 207–232; Figure 2.6). In a reversal of Hawkes' hierarchical metaphor, the attraction of ethnoarchaeology had been that 'it was usually impossible to ignore the *social basis* of material culture' (Miller 1987: 112; my emphasis). Accordingly, Miller's subsequent contributions to archaeological theory related to the uses of social theory, and especially the potential of critical theory to reveal ideology and power (Miller and Tilley 1984; Miller 1989), rather than further studies of ceramic manufacture.

Fig. 2.6 'A complete set of paddles and anvils': from the 'Detailed description of pottery manufacture' in the Malwa region of central India in the Appendix to Daniel Miller's *Artefacts as Categories* (Miller 1985, figure 55).

The suggestion by Hodder and Miller that ethnoarchaeology was particularly well-positioned to combine structuralist and symbolic approaches through a 'materialist' focus was shared elsewhere in the field, especially in African archaeology (Schmidt 1983). But British archaeology and social anthropology both shifted away from ethnoarchaeology from the mid-1980s (van Reybrouck 2000). Ian Hodder came to suggest that ethnoarchaeology should 'disappear, to be replaced by or integrated with the anthropology of material culture and social change' (1986: 108). Nevertheless, the influence of ethnoarchaeology was fundamental to the emergence of contextual archaeology, offering a field (both human and material) from which to critique the focus in processual archaeology upon methodology. This led to a long-standing debate over theory and practice in British archaeology (Hodder 1992), and to an active turning away from archaeological methods in the anthropological material culture studies conducted by those trained in archaeology (but see Hodder 1999). Distancing himself explicitly from the perspectives of David Clarke, Miller expressed discomfort with what he saw as the fetishizing of the archaeological object:

Stone tools and ceramic sequences were increasingly studied in themselves. This resulted in a kind of fetishism that archaeology is always prone to. Objects start by standing for prehistoric peoples, who are the intended subject of study, but the symbolic process is easily inverted, and peoples under terms such as 'cultures' become viewed principally as labels for groups of artefacts, which are the immediate subjects of analysis. The focus is then on the relationship between the objects themselves, which in the 1960's became the centre of interest (e.g. Clarke 1968).

Miller (1983: 5–6)

The long-term influence of this early 1980s British ethnoarchaeological work relates also, however, to the different directions in which contextual archaeology and anthropological material culture studies developed thereafter. One factor here is the significance of area studies. Richard Fardon has highlighted the dependence of the shift from structural-functionalism to structuralism in British social anthropology upon the hegemonic shift from regional schools of ethnography in eastern Africa, to India and South-east Asia (Fardon 1990; see discussions in Dresch 1992; Hicks 2003: 325). It is notable that this geographical distinction was precisely reproduced between the ethnoarchaeological studies of Hodder and Miller respectively. As Hodder developed contextual and interpretive archaeology and Miller combined structuralism and practice theory in anthropological material culture studies from the late 1980s, a parallel distinction emerged in their alternative approaches to the relationships between the social and the material. Although, both fields moved strongly away from the idea of ethnoarchaeology, the subsequent replacement of the field of enquiry with prehistoric archaeology on the one hand and modern consumption on the other allowed the distinction between these two visions of material culture studies (one apparently archaeological, one avowedly anthropological) to persist.

The Material-Cultural Turn: Contextual archaeology

The development of a body of new thinking in British archaeology, which came to be known as 'contextual archaeology', and later 'post-processual archaeology' (due to its critique of the New or processual archaeology of Binford and others), took place from about 1978 in Cambridge, principally through the work of Ian Hodder and his students. The publication of the proceedings of a conference at Cambridge, held in April 1980, on the theme of 'Symbolism and Structuralism in Archaeology' (Hodder 1982b) was a landmark in the emergence of this critique (Hodder et al. 2007). The diverse contributions to the volume were united in aiming to move beyond what they identified as a persistent functionalist approach in the New Archaeology towards society and culture, including material culture (Hodder 1982c: 2). As David van Reybrouck has argued, during the mid-1980s very much of the thinking that came to characterize British contextual archaeology developed

Fig. 2.7 Examples of 1980s British and Swedish beer cans, from Michael Shanks and Christopher Tilley's archaeological study of 'the design of contemporary beer cans' (Shanks and Tilley 1987a: 178, figure 8.4).

through applying 'an archaeological approach to the present', in Western (and, specifically, British) as well as non-Western field locations (Figure 2.7):

[Henrietta] Moore worked on settlement layout and refuse disposal with the Marakwet in Kenya (Moore 1986). Furthermore, [Ian] Hodder [1982a, 215–216] drew attention to the material culture items appropriated by punks, [Mike] Parker Pearson (1982) researched contemporary mortuary behaviour in Britain, [Michael] Shanks and [Chris] Tilley [1987a: 172–240] studied differences in design between Swedish and British beer cans, and [Daniel] Miller (1984) analysed contemporary suburban architecture in Britain. The industrialized world was considered an equally promising field for material culture studies. On top of that, the volumes edited by Hodder [1982b, 1987a and 1987b] and Miller and Tilley (1984) all contained parts devoted to studies in ethnoarchaeology, ethnohistory and modern material culture.

van Reybrouck (2000: 40)

Such 'contextual ethnoarchaeology' provided the impetus for a shift that Ian Hodder described as a more general disciplinary move beyond archaeology's 'loss of innocence' (Clarke 1973) 'towards a mature archaeology' (Hodder 1981), which he set out in his book *Reading the Past* (Hodder 1986). The definition of material culture as 'meaningfully constituted' (Hodder 1986: 4), rather than passively reflective of behaviour, was the central argument of contextual archaeology. This emergence of material culture studies at the core of archaeological debates can be understood as a response to an explicit challenge set for archaeology by structuralist anthropologist Edmund Leach in a series of papers during the 1970s (Leach 1973,

1977, 1978). In 1973, Leach's concluding remarks for *The Explanation of Culture Change: Models in Archaeology* (Renfrew 1973c) had called for archaeology to embrace structuralism, and thus to move beyond what Leach had defined as a residual functionalism in the New Archaeology:

> Do not misunderstand me. Functionalism is 'old hat' in social anthropology; it is 'new hat' in archaeology ... [T]he paradigm which is currently in high fashion among the social anthropologists, namely that of structuralism, has not yet caught up with the archaeologists at all. Don't worry, it will! But meanwhile interdisciplinary communication is rather difficult.
>
> (Leach 1973: 762)

In Leach's view, a shift to structuralism in archaeology would involve a new set of approaches to material culture, since 'functionalist proto-man is a tool-maker whereas structuralist proto-man is a user of language' (Leach 1973: 762):

> Am I making my point? Ideas are more important than things; ... archaeologists need to appreciate that the material objects revealed by their excavations are not 'things in themselves', nor are they just artifacts—things made by man—they are representations of ideas.
>
> (Leach 1977: 167)

Leach's challenge for archaeology was for the field to reconcile structuralist and symbolic approaches to material culture. In undertaking the task set by Leach— critiquing the New Archaeology as retaining many of the characteristics of functionalism (Leach 1973), and seeking to accommodate both structuralist and symbolic approaches (Leach 1977)—contextual archaeology came to use a wide range of theoretical arguments. It aimed to 'superced[e], while simultaneously integrating, structuralism', in studies undertaken by archaeologists that were 'not concerned with the abstract principles of mind, as they would be if literal structuralists', but were 'concerned with context, meaning and particular historical circumstances, as well as with the generative principles which unify particular cultures': with 'particular structures but within their historical, i.e. material, context' (Leone 1982: 179). Thus, Ian Hodder's key statement of the aims and approaches of a contextual archaeology, *Reading the Past*, identified 'four general issues of post-processual archaeology' which were expressed in terms of bilateral relationships (Hodder 1986: 188). These relationships were between 'norm and individual' (and an interest in individual agency rather than behaviour); 'process and structure' (a focus on historical change rather than static models); 'ideal and material' (and a critique of Hawkes' model of inference as a 'ladder of inference' that distinguished between the ideational and technological dimensions of the material remains of the past); and 'subject and object' (a focus on the cultural meaning rather than the social function of objects, and the idea that 'both material items and their deposition are actively involved in social relations') (Hodder 1982a: 6).

Hodder addressed these relationships through an archaeological process that was defined as 'interpretation'—an idea read through R. G. Collingwood (1946)— rather than 'explanation' (Renfrew 1973a) or a positivist philosophy of science (which

Hodder associated with Binford 1983). Hodder argued that interpreting material culture was analogous to reading texts, and distinct from straightforwardly 'reading off' from evidence through middle range theory. The contextual focus on material culture as text was, Hodder argued, distinct from a conventional structuralist focus on language (Hodder 1989). Thus, while contextual archaeology moved strongly away from the idea of ethnoarchaeology, it retained a strong sense of the contemporary nature of archaeological practice: interpreting what remains of the past in the present, working in a different sense from ethnoarchaeology on 'the present past' (Hodder 1982a).

Contextual archaeology's critique of the ahistorical character of the New Archaeology (Hodder 1991a: 12) did not extend to its own reception of structuralism, despite the static nature of structuralist models (Ucko 1995: 14). Instead, contextual archaeology sought to accommodate historical change—clearly so necessary for any meaningful study of the past—through the use of the work of Pierre Bourdieu. The English translation of Bourdieu's *Outline of a Theory of Practice* had been published in 1977, and called for 'a debate in archaeology concerning structuralism . . . and its various critiques' (1982a: 229). Bourdieu's theory of practice attempted to reconcile structuralist and phenomenological perspectives, and was grounded in the idea of the *habitus*. Bourdieu's term *habitus* referred to human dispositions gained through living in the material environment, which he understood as central to the reproduction of social structures. This work led Hodder to his definition of the inadequacy of structuralism as a failure to accommodate agency and meaning—'to develop an adequate theory of practice' (Hodder 1982a: 8)—rather than only a failure to accommodate historical change. Hodder's use of Bourdieu provided one solution to a perceived inability 'of both functionalism and structuralism . . . to explain particular historical contexts and the meaningful actions of individuals constructing social change within those contexts' (Hodder 1982a: 8–9). Historical process was thus accommodated, and 'long-term change' read through *Annales* historians' ideas of 'the structures of everyday life' (Braudel 1981), in terms of a changing of contexts, which both shaped and resulted from practice itself (Hodder 1987b).

Accordingly, the first book-length study that applied the principles of contextual archaeology, Ian Hodder's account of *The Domestication of Europe* (1990), set out a series of changing structures in Neolithic Europe, which he termed *domus*, *agrios*, and *foris*. This approach directly echoed (but did not cite) Bourdieu's conceptions *habitus* and unconscious *doxa* (Bourdieu 1977), and explored relationships between cultural and natural material environments. This focus on practice (as generating changing social contexts and new material culture), theories of long-term change, and the analogy of archaeological interpretation with the reading of texts, allowed the contextual archaeology to work with both symbolic and structuralist approaches—but also allowed the persistence of the structuralist analysis of particular artefacts and sites within an overarching chronological narrative, most vividly through the dualistic model of *domus* and *agrios* (Figure 2.8).

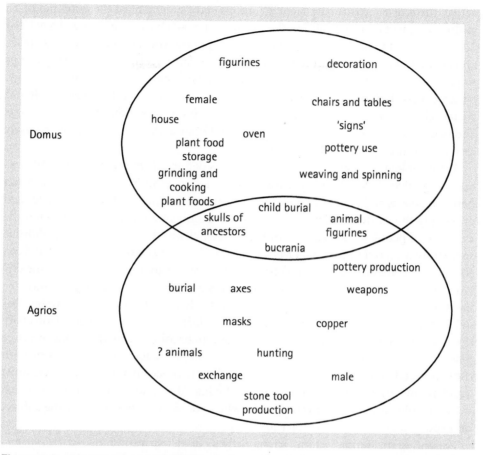

Fig. 2.8 Ian Hodder's model of 'Associations of the domus and agrios in [Neolithic] SE Europe' (from Hodder 1990: 68, figure 3.5).

The Material-Cultural Turn: the anthropology of mass consumption

A third trajectory of thought within the Material-Cultural Turn, which emerged from ethnoarchaeology and the 'symbolic and structural archaeology' of early 1980s Cambridge, was Daniel Miller's conception of 'material culture studies' as a social anthropology of consumption. This focus on consumption was an active inversion of the focus upon production in structural Marxist anthropology, and a complement to the focus on exchange in economic anthropology. It was centred on a Hegelian notion of self-creation. Miller's work in contextual archaeology (1982a, 1982b, 1982c, 1984) and ethnoarchaeology (1985) was now extended into the study of material things in the contemporary West, and was characterized by a gradual, but active, turning away from archaeology. In his early statement of the potential of an anthropology of material culture, the title of which—'Things Ain't What They Used To Be'—indicated how the study of the contemporary world might move away from archaeological studies of past material culture, Miller suggested that studying things might complement the structuralist study of language: 'Even in anthropology, which prides itself on the subtlety of its enquiry, the basic construction of self and social relations as they are mediated by images in clothes, household furnishings and such like, may be relatively neglected because they are relatively coarsely articulated in language' (Miller 1983: 6–7).

Anthropological material culture studies was defined from the outset by Miller as an 'integrative' field, drawing across disciplines to examine 'a core relationship between objects and people' (Miller 1983: 7). The study of material culture was defined as 'simply the study of human social and environmental relationships through the evidence of people's construction of their material world' (Miller 1983: 5). With his 1987 study *Material Culture and Mass Consumption*, Miller used ideas 'adapted from social archaeology', which he 'redefined and theorised to apply to modern society' (Attfield 2000: 35). The book was read by many as a kind of 'archaeology of modern life' (Weatherill 1989: 439). It was published in the Blackwell series 'Social Archaeology', just as *Artefacts as Categories* had been published in the Cambridge University Press series 'New Studies in Archaeology'. But archaeological methods and practice played no role in *Material Culture and Mass Consumption*, due to a dissatisfaction with the continued influence of processual archaeology that had characterized Americanist 'modern material culture studies': exemplifying 'the kind of fetishism to which material culture studies is always prone, when people are superseded as the subject of investigation by objects' (Miller 1987: 143).

Presenting an alternative to such materially focused 'fetishism', *Material Culture and Mass Consumption* was instead a highly abstract and theoretical study that responded to the growing literature on the consumption of everyday objects in the modern world, which had developed through the structuralist and semiotic treatment by Roland Barthes (1972 [1957], 1977) and Jean Baudrillard (1983), and especially the anthropological consumption studies developed in Mary Douglas and Baron Isherwood's *The World of Goods* (1979). The study of objects and commodities had, during the 1970s, represented a central theme for the new discipline of 'cultural studies': later inspiring studies such as *Doing Cultural Studies*, which focused on the study of the Sony Walkman (Du Gay *et al.* 1997). In such work, the conventional sociological (especially Marxist) focus upon objects only in relation to production and exchange was reversed through an interest in the active reception of mass-produced items by consumers. In this view, regardless of the intention or purpose of material goods as manufactured, the world was filled with ongoing, local, and vernacular processes of reinterpretation and appropriation. Miller's idea was that the archaeological sense of the significance of objects in social life could be developed through a social anthropology that concentrated on 'the social symbolism of the material world' (Miller 1987: viii).

The argument of *Material Culture and Mass Consumption* fell across three sections, which related to theories of 'objectification', the idea of 'material culture', and the anthropological study of 'mass consumption'.

Miller's conception of objectification adapted a Hegelian model of the dialectical relationships between subjects and objects. Working through elements of Hegel, Marx, and Simmel, along with anthropologist Nancy Munn's structuralist study of *Walbiri Iconography* (1973), Miller defined his own concept of objectification as referring to 'a process of externalization and sublation essential to the development of a given subject', in which 'the concrete material object' was 'one particular potential medium or vehicle' (Miller 1987: 85). Through what he described as a 'violent abstraction' of the Hegelian theory of the subject, Miller's theory of objectification was used to make a more general contribution to anthropological theory, based on the idea that 'the human subject cannot be considered outside of the material world within which and through which it is constructed' (Millers 1987: 86, 214).

Miller's discussion of material culture, which formed the central section of the book, considered 'the social implications of things' (1987: 85). It did so through discussion of the communicative dimensions of objects, rather than simply of language (drawing from Piaget's and Melanie Klein's stucturalist–psychological and psychoanalytical theories of child development; Miller 1987: 85–98) and through a call for the study of 'artefacts in their contexts' (drawing from Gombrich's studies of design, Erving Goffman's idea of 'frame analysis', and the practice theories of Giddens and Bourdieu; Miller 1987: 98–127) and for the structuralist analysis of form and style (Miller 1987: 127–129). Such material culture studies would be distinct from linguistic models, since 'the physicality of objects makes them much harder than language to extricate from the particular social context in which they operate, and for that reason they pose a particular problem for academic study' (Miller 1987: 109).

The concluding section of the book was a programmatic statement for the anthropological study of mass consumption, combining ideas drawn from Baudrillard, Hebdige, and especially Bourdieu and Giddens to aim to achieve a 'balance between objectivist approaches, such as those found in archaeology, and subjectivist approaches, the most extreme of which would be design history' (Miller 1987: 157). In developing an anthropological 'theory of consumption' (Miller 1987: 178), Miller used practice theory to seek to achieve 'a balance between objectivism and subjectivism' (1987: 167). He introduced the ideas of 'object domains' and the idea of the 'object world' (Miller 1987: 158, 166), both of which were terms drawn from Giddens (1984) and which echoed Bourdieu's description of 'domains of practice' created through the *habitus* (Bourdieu 1977: 20).

***

While the uses of psychology and a dialectical model of objectification drawn from Hegel were idiosyncratic and their implications for understanding the world were sometimes hard to grasp (Mukerji 1989), *Material Culture and Mass Consumption* made three arguments that were central to British social anthropology's Material-Cultural Turn.

First was Miller's idea of 'the humility of things': the recognition of the influence of apparently banal everyday items, those things 'usually regarded as trivial', upon social life (Miller 1987: 5). Directly echoing James Deetz's evocation of 'small things forgotten' a decade earlier, Miller argued that such objects mediate social relations silently, in a kind of 'ordering of the unconscious world' (Deetz 1977; Miller 1987: 99). The reception of *Artefacts as Categories* in social anthropology had seen some criticism of a lack of ethnographic detail, and concerns over the idea of an archaeological focus on the modern world as simply obsessed with irrelevant detail (Moeran 1987). But Miller's earlier discussions of the 'trivial nature of pottery' (Miller 1985: 204) led him to use an archaeological metaphor—'to excavate certain areas of investigation formerly branded as "trivial" or "inauthentic"' (Miller 1987: viii)—to explain the distinct challenges and potentials of the study of 'objects in everyday interaction', especially when compared with the study of language (Miller 1987: 98).

Secondly, there was the idea of context in the study of material culture. Here Miller's arguments were developed directly from contextual archaeology, but unlike the cultural focus upon 'text' in the work of Ian Hodder, Miller's perspectives here were closer to Giddens than Bourdieu. Miller used Gombrich's (1979) evocation of the 'anonymous and modest presence' of a picture frame (Miller 1987: 101) and Goffman's (1974) 'frame analysis' to argue that processes of objectification *constituted* contexts: so the 'pervasive presence' of 'artefacts as objects' could be understood 'as the context for modern life' (Miller 1987: 85). This change in Miller's focus from that of the contextual ethnoarchaeology might be compared with a longer-term shift in anthropological thinking about museum objects: 'from categorical thinking to relational thinking' (Gosden and Larson 2007: 242). In this respect, Miller's approach was much closer to the long-standing focus since structural-functionalism upon the analysis of social relations, rather than types and categories in their own right.

Thirdly, there was the extension of anthropological studies of objects from pre-industrial and non-Western situations into the world of modern industrial capitalism. During the 1960s and 1970s, debates in economic anthropology had been dominated by discussion of the differences between Western and non-Western economies. Arguments over the applicability of Western conceptions of economics to non-Western or precapitalist societies had raised distinction between 'formalist' and 'substantivist' economies, in which material goods were understood to be 'disembedded' from, or 'embedded' in, social structure respectively (Polanyi *et al.* 1957; see Wilk and Cliggett 2007: 3–15). These debates used a long-standing distinction in economic anthropology between 'gifts' and 'commodities', which had underpinned Marcel Mauss' comparative study of *The Gift* (Mauss 1990 [1922]), and which was grounded in an account of the modern world as engendering a schism between society and economy, *Gemeinschaft* and *Gesellschaft*. In contrast, Miller's (1987: 17) use of anthropological perspectives to study the modern world was based on the idea that consumption could 'produce an inalienable culture': in other words modern consumers were constantly transforming commodities into things that they used in their own social lives, and were thus breaking down any firm distinctions between gifts and commodities.

Here, in contrast with conventional Leftist accounts of the rise of capitalism as alienating, and their focus on production, Daniel Miller's decision 'to investigate, and to assess the consequences of the enormous increase in industrial production over the last century' (1987: 1) led him to highlight the productive nature of consumption, as it were. Critiques of capitalism, he argued, should not lead to 'a critique of mass industrial culture *per se*, since this has had the effect of stifling any positive advocacy of a potential popular alternative which remains within the context of industrial culture' (Miller 1987: 176). Thus, *Material Culture and Mass Consumption* made an important contribution to conceptions of the modern that did not use grand narratives of disenchantment (via Weber) or alienation (via Marx).

Material Culture and Mass Consumption's call for a new social anthropology of consumption contributed to a general rise in consumption studies in sociology, geography, history, and cultural studies during the late 1980s and early 1990s (McKendrick *et al.* 1983; Mintz 1985; Campbell 1987; Brewer and Porter 1993). In his edited volume *Acknowledging Consumption* (Miller 1995a), Miller presented his perspectives as shifting away from the study of 'the category of "material culture"', which links anthropology 'with archaeological concerns', towards a new 'category of consumption studies'. He argued that this development represented a 'transformation of anthropology' because it extended anthropological ideas into the modern world, as an 'authentic' object of study (1995b: 263, 268).

Miller's suggestion that the extension of anthropological perspectives into the modern world was radically new was overstated. The ethnoarchaeology of early 1980s Britain had represented the extension of two long-standing traditions of 'auto-anthropology'. One was the folklife studies that developed, especially in museums, during the 1880s (Jackson 1985), at precisely the same time as the emergence of new studies of technology described at the start of this chapter, which continued throughout the first half of the twentieth century. The other was a subsequent post-war 'sociological rediscovery of British society from the 1950s', much of which 'was made by people trained in social anthropology' (Hawthorn 1972), and which built to some degree upon the establishment in 1937 of 'Mass Observation' as a kind of anthropology of modern life undertaken by amateur researchers, combining surrealism with popular anthropology (MacClancy 1995; cf. Miller 1988: 356). UCL-based anthropologists had played a significant role in these post-war developments (e.g. Firth *et al.* 1970), which related especially to a conception of 'applied' anthropology as a relevant part of the discipline (Goody 1995: 74).

In the structural Marxist anthropology of the 1970s, Maurice Godelier's (1975) critique of empiricism was grounded in a commitment to a historical perspective that used a common set of ethnographic approaches to non-Western and to Western situations, and the different forms that 'production' might take. Meanwhile, despite the continuing use of the gift/commodity distinction in some Marxist anthropology (Gregory 1982), anthropological studies of exchange increasingly questioned the firm distinction between gifts and commodities (Strathern 1988; Gell 1992a). As will be seen below, this work led to the questioning of the a priori differences between subjects and objects in social anthropological research.

However, the focus of anthropological material culture studies as it developed after *Material Culture and Mass Consumption*, especially through the radical shift away from archaeological approaches, came to be upon 'ideas about what people do with objects, essentially as a theory of culture rather than material culture' (Rowlands 2004: 477). This focus on the meaningful use of material things in social relationships, rather than upon their detailed empirical examination, was characterized by a latent structuralism that anthropological material culture studies shared with the contextual archaeology. This Material-Cultural Turn framed the development of the 'high period' of British material culture studies during the 1990s.

III: THE 'HIGH PERIOD' OF MATERIAL CULTURE STUDIES

The third phase of the archaeological sequence identified here is one of rapid and self-confident construction, built on foundations laid in earlier periods: the 'high period' of 'material culture studies' in British archaeology and anthropology. With the publication of *Interpreting Archaeology: finding meaning in the past* in 1995 (based on a conference held at Cambridge in 1991) and the launch of the *Journal of Material Culture*, edited from UCL, in 1996, the ideas that had emerged in the Material-Cultural Turn were put into practice (Hodder *et al.* 1995a; Miller and Tilley 1996). Both interpretive archaeology and material culture studies witnessed the emergence of book-length studies: works by Ian Hodder (1990), Julian Thomas (1991a) and John Barrett (1994) in archaeology; and in anthropology Daniel Miller's (1994, 1997, 1998a) studies in Trinidad and North London and a growing number of contributions to the 'Materializing Culture' series published by Berg since 1998. By understanding objects as 'cultural forms' (Miller 1987: 110), this work built upon the identification of the different contextual uses of material culture in social life that had been highlighted by the contributions to Arjun Appadurai's seminal collection *The Social Life of Things* (Appadurai 1986a; Kopytoff 1986).

The use of detailed case studies in these works, based on ethnographic and archaeological fieldwork, contrasted with older concerns with style and design that derived from the study of objects in isolation from their social uses (Conkey 2006: 356–359). However, the exchanges between archaeology and anthropology in ethnoarchaeology that led of a common adoption of elements of practice theory and the bringing together of structuralist and semiotic approaches, gave way during the early 1990s to a radical difference between anthropological and archaeological material culture studies in Britain.

Having shifted away from the New Archaeology's concerns with method, and disillusioned with the results of ethnoarchaeology, British archaeologists and anthropologists who identified themselves as working on 'material culture studies' came to define their field by its object of enquiry: 'material culture'. However, their fieldwork was conducted in different spheres: the material dimensions of the contemporary world on the one side, and the remains of the prehistoric past on the other. A model of radical alterity emerged in archaeological discussions of 'theory and practice' (Hodder 1992): in the definition of archaeology as a kind of distanced *interpretation*. For example, the extension of interpretive archaeology into the modern period was understood as requiring the making of the familiar unfamiliar, to allow interpretation to take place (Tarlow and West 1999). Meanwhile anthropological material culture studies worked in the opposite direction: bringing ethnographic methods developed for the study of non-Western societies to bear upon the modern Western world: problematizing any general distinction between the modern and the premodern/non-Western, but dispensing with earlier discussions of method; using anthropology to work with the shock of the mundane.

During the 1990s, British post-processual archaeology developed a series of new studies informed by the idea that 'material culture is actively involved in the social world' (Shanks and Tilley 1987b: 116–117). Michael Shanks and Chris Tilley sought to shift back and forth between 'cultural' and 'social' approaches. In their 1987 study *Social Theory and Archaeology*, the chapter about 'material culture' asked 'two basic questions' about objects: 'First, how do we interpret material culture; what meaning, if any, does it possess? Secondly, how does material culture patterning relate to the social?' (Shanks and Tilley 1987b: 79).

The idea of interpretation was used to define archaeology as a process of revealing the implication of material culture in human meaning and social relations. Thus, the title of the introduction to *Interpreting Archaeology* was 'Archaeology and the interpretation of material culture: a report on the state of the discipline' (Hodder *et al.* 1995b: 1). The empirical focus was, however, almost exclusively upon the study of prehistory, especially Neolithic and Bronze Age Europe (and especially Britain). The rural locations of the sites and landscapes studied were just like the periods of time that were focused upon: as far away as possible from the modern world, and thus from the material studied by anthropological material culture studies. The purpose of interpretive archaeology was thus to 'attend to difference' (Shanks and Hodder 1995: 9). On those occasions on which the modern period was studied by post-processual archaeologists (e.g. Johnson 1996), no connections with socio-cultural anthropology were made.

In British anthropology, the effect of associating the movement of anthropological perspectives into the modern western world with a simultaneous movement away from archaeological perspectives was an isolation of the study of modern material culture from the potential archaeological contribution to the study of the modern period and the contemporary world (Hicks and Beaudry 2006b): despite the influence of James Deetz's historical archaeology upon the development of British anthropological material culture studies (Miller 1982c: 96; 1987: 140–142). The concerns with the empiricism or fetishism of archaeology were, however, concerns quite specifically with the New Archaeology, which had dominated both ethnoarchaeology and Americanist modern material culture studies in the early 1980s. Despite the archaeological training of those who developed anthropological material culture studies (Miller 1980; Tilley 1981), the twin directions that led from the Material-Cultural Turn— post-processual/interpretive archaeology and the anthropology of consumption— were parallel, rather than overlapping. This meant that the potential for exchanges between archaeological and anthropological perspectives in the study of the material dimensions of the modern world were hardly explored (Cochran and Beaudry 2006).

The significance of practice theory for both fields remained considerable. But the anthropological material culture studies played Giddens to interpretive archaeology's Bourdieu: echoing Giddens' critique of the 'concern with "meaning" to the exclusion of the practical involvements of human life in material activity' in interpretive sociology and ethnomethodology (Giddens 1976a: 155; see Giddens 1976b). This distinction between 'cultural' and 'social' models of practice theory formed the basis of John Barrett's critique of Ian Hodder's conception of contextual archaeology from a structuration perspective:

Archaeologists do not enter into a dialogue with the people they study, but our obligations to those people do remain. Can we really claim to be able to understand how they saw their world? This seems both dubious and unnecessary. Instead we can learn something, through the surviving evidence, of how their knowledge was gained in the routine practices by which they lived their lives.

Barrett (1987a: 472)

Barrett (1987b) called for a shift from a focus on archaeological material culture as text to the idea of 'fields of discourse'. He argued for a distinctive archaeological reorientation of the nature of 'structure' in Giddens' model of agency and structure, which more adequately accounted for 'material conditions':

Giddens has stated that 'structure exists only as memory traces' meaning, I take it, that action draws initially upon, and is guided in anticipation by, the subject's memory of previous experience. Important although this point is, an equal, if not greater, emphasis must be placed upon the particular material conditions within which social practices are situated.

Barrett (1987b: 8)

Meanwhile Bourdieu's focus on the lived domestic environment, most famously explored in his 1970 structuralist study of the Algerian Kabyle house, which described the lived environment as structured by a series of binary oppositions experienced through domestic life (Bourdieu 1990), was significant in the particular range of field sites or 'artefactual domains' (Miller 1998b: 10) chosen for the new anthropological material culture studies. The domestic home was pre-eminent among these (Miller 1988, 2001b, 2006a: 348–349, 2008), as 'the context in which most other material culture is used, placed and understood' (Buchli 2002b: 207; cf. Humphrey 1988). Alongside the home, anthropological material culture studies in this period focused especially upon supermarkets (Miller 1998c; Miller *et al.* 1998), domestic gardens, catalogue shopping (Clarke 1998), party selling, car boot sales, private cars, and clothing as well as the consumption of heritage at museums and historic sites (Rowlands 1998). In a related body of work, the anthropological study of artworks was increasingly understood as focusing on 'visual culture' (Pinney 2006: 131), building on studies such as Howard Morphy's engagement with Yolngu (Australian aboriginal) art, which used ethnography to examine the social contexts in which artworks were created, used, and understood: an approach that he argued could highlight the ambiguity consciously brought about through non-representational art forms (Morphy 1991; cf. Layton 1991: 1).

   The attraction of material culture studies to such themes has been criticized as providing uncritical accounts of '[Western] teenagers, home-makers and shoppers', in which anthropologists operate 'like flâneurs or tourists . . . not in the world, [but] only gazing out at it', while readers find themselves 'drifting through a symbolic forest or watching an exhibition of signs and messages' (Löfgren 1997: 102–103). Tim Ingold (2007b: 316) has argued that these choices of field sites, and especially the 'twin obsession with museums and department stores', limited material culture studies to places in which things are ordered in quite specific ways: where 'we confront things as objects'. This, however, was precisely the point that these works were making: that anthropology can examine contemporary processes of objectification, the social processes through which people come to define and understand things as objects. The narrative here usually concerned the enrolment of commodities into social relationships: most clearly stated in Miller's (1998c) 'theory of shopping' in which the idea of 'sacrifice' was seen as a creative rather than a destructive process. Here, Miller followed Alfred Gell's observation that

Very recognizable forms of consumption . . . may mislead us into making the false equation 'consumption equals destruction' because on these occasions meat, liquor and other valued substances are made to vanish. But consumption as a general phenomenon really has nothing to do with the destruction of goods and wealth but their reincorporation into the social system that produced them in some other guise.

Gell (1986: 112)

Miller's work on shopping also involved a collaboration between anthropology and cultural geography in a study of the Brent Cross shopping centre in North London to identify 'the investment in social relationships that takes place during the apparently mundane work of shopping' (Miller *et al.* 1998: 23). In such views, the consumer's decision to purchase one item of grocery rather than another could represent evidence of quite intimate social relationships: 'making love in supermarkets' by transforming the can of soup, purchased to be shared at home, into part of a loving relationship (Miller 1998b, 1998c), viewing consumption as a 'technology of love' (Miller 2006a: 350), and studying the anthropology of 'thrift' in which 'the desire to save money arise principally out of the moral imperative which dominates ordinary shopping, where the shopper stands for the interests of family and household' (Miller 2003: 362).

Similarly, global processes involving apparently homogenized cultures of commodities were shown to involve quite distinctive local enactments: as with Daniel Miller's identification of Coca-Cola as 'a black sweet drink made in Trinidad' (Miller 1998a). This focus on the place that mass-produced commodities can play in particular social relations facilitated, Miller argued, a 'transformation of anthropology' in that it broke down 'an explicit, or even implicit, culture concept as a definitional premise of anthropology' (Miller 1995b: 264) through an awareness of the active role of material culture in social life (cf. Lucas 2001a: 121–122). These were powerful and important arguments that moved away from an anthropological conception of society as purified of everyday things. However, as is explored in the next section, more recently this breaking down of the culture concept has spilled over into the material culture concept itself.

IV: The unfolding of material culture studies

The process of excavation often identifies moments of recurrence and similarity in the ways in which particular landscapes have been inhabited and reconfigured in different periods. In this sequence of disciplinary thinking and practice from the 1970s to the 1990s, we might suggest that the *fin-de-siècle* optimism over the study of 'object domains' during the 'high period' of material culture studies echoed the confidence of Tylor's arguments about 'object lessons' a century before. This time, however, it sought to fulfil the long-standing modernist ambition of British anthropology to become a comparative sociology. This was precisely the ambition that had replaced the museum collection with ethnographic participant observation as the subject of enquiry 80 years previously. Material culture studies' model of objectivism—for example, in the aspiration for 'a theory of consumption' (Miller 1987: 178–217)—involved a critique of the culture concept 'as a definitional premise of anthropology' (Miller 1995b: 265): focusing instead upon vernacular practices in which people enrolled objects in social relations. Gradually, however, the responses to calls for a focus upon material culture as 'the least understood of all the central phenomena of the modern age' (Miller 1987: 217) started to reveal the programme of material culture studies as itself an artefact of modernist thought (*sensu* Ardener 1985). Central here has been the emergence of the strangely abstract, dematerialized quality of many material culture studies, in which things appear to disappear into spectral fields of social relations or meanings, and the complexities of materials and their change over time are not accounted for. While material culture studies had turned away from archaeology, and had been isolated from historical anthropology, it was in these fields that the narratives told by material culture studies started to unfold.

Humanism and positionality

The lasting successes of the 'high period' of material culture studies lay for anthropology in the acknowledgement of the potential significance of objects in human social relations, especially those objects that appear banal or inconsequential: providing a sense of the unspoken things that constitute the everyday dimensions of social life that became important in sociology through the work of writers such as Michel de Certeau (1984; cf. Highmore 2002). Such an approach placed the everyday—or 'the blindingly obvious'—at the centre of the analysis (Miller and Woodward 2007: 337–339). For archaeology, these successes involved new contributions to a long-standing humanistic perspective in archaeology: the desire to get past things to people that had been expressed throughout the second half of the twentieth century, even, for example, in the words of Mortimer Wheeler (1954: v): 'The archaeologist is digging up not *things* but people ... In a simple direct sense, archaeology is a science that must be lived, must be "seasoned with humanity". Dead archaeology is the driest stuff that blows.'

The Material-Cultural Turn problematized the study of the socio-cultural and the material in isolation from each other. Its solution was to document how they were 'related', so as 'to transcend subject–object dualities' (Miller and Tilley 1996: 7) created by the modern world. Material culture studies documented, to use the standard parlance, 'relational' processes (Miller 2007: 25): that is, it was concerned with the relationships between objects and people. The physical form of things was thus reduced to a distinctive kind of conduit for social relations, which were the proper object of enquiry:

An analysis of an artefact must begin with its most obvious characteristic, which is that it exists as a physically concrete form independent of any individual's mental image of it. This factor may provide the key to understanding its power and significance in cultural construction. The importance of this physicality of the artefact derives from its ability thereby to act as a bridge, not only between the mental and physical worlds, but also, more unexpectedly, between consciousness and the unconscious.

Miller (1987: 99)

The heuristic distinction between materials and culture implied by the use of the term 'material culture' was justified through the idea of objectification (Miller 1987): the argument that under the conditions of capitalism and/or modernity, distinctions between objects and people are made. In this view, 'capitalism splits culture and person apart into commodities separated from their intrinsic person-making capacities, and the illusion of pure humanism outside of materiality' (Miller 2005a: 17). Similarly, Julian Thomas argued that archaeology needed actively to reconnect across a Newtonian 'separation between the human and non-human worlds, culture and nature [which has] provided the principal basis for ordering collections of material things' (Thomas 2004: 26). In practice, a focus on relatedness or 'relationality' sought to avoid what was understood as a long-standing tendency, identified especially in archaeology and museum studies, to become 'obsessed with objects as such, . . . treating them as having an independent behaviour in a manner which separated them from any social context and which amounted to a genuine fetishism of the artefact' (Miller 1987: 111–112; cf. Miller 1990).

But a further problem—that of the distinctions between the researcher as subject and the object of enquiry—has called into question the sure-footedness of material culture studies as a modernist, representational project, working with the remnants of comparative sociology, and applied structuralism. A gradual unfolding of the idea of 'material culture studies' took place. The humanism of the Material-Cultural Turn—anthropology's 'translating objects into people' (Miller 1985: ix) or archaeology's 'fleshing out in cultural terms of the basic data' (Deetz 1967: 138)—came to form the basis for critiques of normative conceptions of human identity, especially in relation to gender (Gilchrist 1994), sexuality (Voss 2008a), ethnicity (Jones 1997), and life-course (Gilchrist 2004), and the slow development of third-wave feminist perspectives in archaeology (Gilchrist 1999). The political engagement of feminist and gender archaeology, and of movements such as the World Archaeological Congress (Ucko 1987) and developments in indigenous archaeology, African-American historical archaeology and museum anthropology, meant that in interpretive archaeology issues of the *positionality* of the researcher studying material culture were interrogated. At first this was worked out through the ideas of 'critical reflexivity' or 'self-reflexive archaeology' (Shanks and Tilley 1992: 62; Hodder 1997), but increasingly it has developed into critiques of the way in which the Material-Cultural Turn in both archaeology and anthropology sought to stand upon that non-existent hyphen in 'material culture studies', so as to document traffic between two different domains, the material and the socio-cultural, while remaining detached from them both.

The risk was ever-present that detailed ethnographies of consumption (e.g. Miller 1994) or large-scale studies of the use of material culture over the long term (Hodder 1990) would give way to the uncritical presentation of appropriate case studies in what Max Gluckman would have called the 'apt illustration' of particular models of social relations (Gluckman 1961: 7). This is what George Marcus has identified as a tendency to allow social theory to 'stand in for the macro-social', with which 'micro-cultural analysis' might then be related (Marcus 2000: 17), as if these two scales of analysis operated in different worlds. Material culture studies narrated objects in particular ways. In social anthropology, the emplotment often involved the appropriation of modern, apparently 'alienable' goods through consumption to transform them into 'inalienable' items, for instance through household DIY (Miller 1988). In archaeology, the story usually involved the identification of artefact patterning as evidence of human social relations and 'traditions of practice' in which, it was asserted, a meaningful material world played a significant role, through 'ritual practice' for example (Thomas 1991a: 80–84, 187). Clearly in both cases, the focus upon human practices in relation to the material world was a long way from the identification of normative cultures or cultural behaviours reflected in artefacts. But what was at stake here was the uses to which social theory and linguistic analogy are put in archaeology and anthropology. Through a residual structuralism, the richness and complexity of the knowledge that derives from fieldwork was often reduced to the illustration of particular models of 'the material constitution of social relations' (Miller and Tilley 1996: 5; see Pinney 2005): looking from an impossible vantage-point between materials and culture, erasing any trace of standpoint (which includes not only the researcher, but the complex human and material practices that all fieldwork involves). Knowledge of material culture appeared to emerge from somewhere outside of the ethnographic situation.

Hermeneutic phenomenology

One solution to this problem of standpoint and positionality has been the distinctive kind of hermeneutic phenomenology developed in archaeological and anthropological material culture studies. Such approaches have sought to locate the lived, bodily experience of the world at the centre of the interpretation of the material world, and to relocate the focus of material culture studies upon concrete human experience. Chris Tilley and Julian Thomas have, since the early 1990s, led the way in this field, through studies of the monumental landscapes of British and Scandinavian Neolithic and Bronze Age. Using ideas from Heidegger, Merleau-Ponty, and Lefebvre, Thomas (1993, 1996, 2000a, 2000b, 2006) and Tilley (1994, 1996, 2006b) have tried to account for the bodily, meaningful, thoughtful, and reflective encounters between humans and the non-human world.

Tilley has sought to build upon the literary and linguistic analogy of material culture studies that lay at the heart of the contextual archaeology, and which he explored through studies such as *Reading Material Culture* (1990a), *Material Culture and Text* (1991), and *Material Culture and Metaphor* (1999), and his definition of interpretive archaeology as a kind of 'poetics of the past' (1993). He has continued to explore the idea that emerged in the 1970s of material culture studies as analogous, but not reducible, to the study of language: the idea that 'artefacts perform active metaphorical work in the world in a manner that words cannot' (Tilley 2002: 25). In contrast to the use of abstract models that New Archaeology's conception of 'spatial archaeology' had borrowed from 1960s New Geography (Clarke 1977), Tilley has developed 'a phenomenological perspective linked to a concept of materiality' (Tilley 2007a: 19) that seeks to account for the embodied experience of landscapes as material culture:

From a phenomenological perspective landscape is 'platial' rather than 'spatial'. It is not something defined by space as an abstract container but by the places that constitute it and make it what it is. Landscape thus sits in places, is a reflexive 'gathering' and set of relations between those places, background and foreground, figure and frame, here and there, near and far. Landscape is thus always both objective physical place and a subjective cognized image of that place.

Tilley (2006b: 20)

For Thomas, the significance of phenomenological approaches lies in their ability to move beyond modern distinctions between nature and culture in archaeology (Thomas 1996: 3). By studying barrows, cairns, megalithic tombs, and other sites and monuments from British prehistory, this branch of material culture studies has been 'concerned with the human encounter, experience and understanding of worldly things, and with how these happenings come to be possible' (Thomas 2006: 43).

In practice, however, it is very difficult to comprehend what these accounts have added to our understanding of the prehistoric past or contemporary heritage landscapes. The two-way encounter between the human body and the landscape, focused on interpretation and the representation of meaning, has retained much of what Tilley (1982: 26) described as the 'dialectical structuralism' of contextual archaeology. Too often, hermeneutic phenomenology has descended into a hyper-interpretive romanticism, most vividly in the study of the Bronze Age landscape of Leskernick in Cornwall, which combined photo-essays with fragments of diary entries, snatches of conversation, poetry writing, and the creation of 'archaeological artworks' (Bender *et al.* 2007; see Hicks 2009).

Despite privileging of human experience and cognition these texts have been oddly dematerialized, reflective accounts of the world, resorting to the human body as a stable point of reference in precisely the same way as the idea of 'material culture' has been used: to stand impossibly between alternative domains in order to represent the world. Human bodies, of course, are just as diverse as material things: and the principal critiques of phenomenological perspectives have come from feminist studies of embodiment (see Crossland this volume, Chapter 16). The positionality and perspective of the researcher remains an unresolved problem because the purpose of archaeology and anthropology remains defined in hermeneutic phenomenology as *interpreting and representing* the socio-cultural dimensions of the material world. But in the politics of archaeology and anthropology, objects are not straightforwardly involved in social relations or contested meanings: the actions of the researcher or curator, working within particular disciplinary, institutional, or historical circumstances or accidents, are always involved (Hodder 2004). The same, of course, is true for vernacular practice as for academic practice. Here two broader problems with British archaeological and anthropological material culture studies are made clear: a disregard for the significance of method, and a strong presentism, even in relation to the prehistoric past.

Meanwhile, more successful alternatives to the definition of the purpose of material culture studies as representing meaning or social relations have developed, which have been central to the process of unfolding, especially in relation to discussions of materiality and material agency, as the next section shows.

Meaning, materiality, and material agency

The shift beyond contextual and interpretive archaeology has increasingly led to a reconsideration of the limitations of the analogy of things with texts, which had allowed for the persistence of the structuralist definition of material culture studies as a complementary field of enquiry to the study of language. The textual metaphor in contextual archaeology, and the focus on human meaning as the ultimate object of enquiry in interpretive archaeology, built on a long-standing sense that the material evidence of the past was for British prehistory an equivalent of a historical text (Lucas 2001a: 111), which could be used to generate accounts of the human past. The idea of the landscape as a text had in the mid-twentieth century been associated especially with the explicitly counter-modern model of 'local history' developed by writers, such as W. G. Hoskins (1955) in his idea of the English landscape as a vulnerable 'palimpsest' wrought through centuries of human life (Hicks 2008a). The romanticism of these approaches, grounded in a sense of the past as radically different from the present, informed many British models of 'interpretive archaeology', particularly that of hermeneutic phenomenology (Hodder 2004).

The textual analogy, and the idea of archaeology following a broader interdisciplinary 'linguistic turn' (Thomas 1991b: 9), led to an increasing dematerialization as contextual archaeology developed into interpretive archaeology. Such approaches were informed by particular bodies of literary theory (Tilley 1990a), the logic of which was that 'there is nothing outside the text' (Thomas 1990: 19), since 'space is like a page on which human action writes' (Thomas 1991b: 9) and the study of material culture involved the same critical awareness as any kind of reading (Hodder 1986). In such work, material culture studies became, as Evans-Pritchard wrote of functionalist anthropology, 'little more than a literary device' (1950: 120). But a number of archaeologists have argued that the physical form of things, and in particular their durability, presents particular problems for the textual analogy: paralleling the observation from cultural geography that 'objects do far more than represent' (Thrift 2007: 239). These arguments have often been developed in terms of a shift from the study of 'material culture' to that of 'materiality'— a word that attempts to move away from the idea of a separation between different material and cultural domains, and to accommodate the material form of things.

As Ian Hodder argued two decades ago, 'perhaps because material culture is often more practical and less immediately concerned with abstract meaning, the meanings it does have are often non-discursive' (1991b: 73). Victor Buchli took this argument forward in his suggestion that 'the trouble with text' in contextual archaeology lay in the 'constituted and evocative physicality' of material culture (1995: 191). Buchli's argument was paralleled by Webb Keane's (1997) discussion of semiotics, representation, and material culture in relation to Indonesian ethnography, which demonstrated how any account of meaning must account for the refraction that occurs through material things. This growing awareness of the importance of 'the very physicality of objects' (Rowlands 2004: 478), has led to an increased interest in the physical properties and effects of materials.

For some, this has inspired the use of Peircean semiotics to highlight the contingency of how certain objects come to hold certain meanings (see discussion by Jones 2009: 95–96), an idea that develops earlier recognitions of the 'resistance' of material culture to being freighted with meaning (Shanks and Tilley 1989: 5). This moves beyond the observation that the passing of an object between different 'regimes of value' means that meanings are contingent upon social contexts (Appadurai 1986b), by suggesting that certain physical or functional properties of objects also define how they are understood, and how they operate in social life (see Gell 1996b). Equally, however, such arguments highlight how such properties of things might be understood as non-discursive: falling outside of a focus upon 'reading' material culture, and beyond the limits of a purely 'interpretive' archaeology, concerned *only* with 'finding meaning in the past' (Hodder *et al.* 1995a) or the idea that material culture represents a form of metaphor (Tilley 1999).

More radically, others have pointed to the many materials in the world that require archaeological and anthropological attention, but which are not just those things that 'matter' to humans that are highlighted by mainstream material culture studies (e.g. Miller 2001a) or a reflexive interpretive archaeology (e.g. Hodder 1999). Things can matter, we might suggest, even when people do not say that they matter. The human significance of meaningful 'material culture' is, of course, a crucial element of accounting for the material world: but the physicality of things calls into question the idea of 'material culture' as an excessively anthropocentric definition of the field of enquiry: delimited by those moments in which things are meaningful or filled with cultural significance. At the same time, the idea of materiality risks slipping into the idea of kind of universal quality of material-ness that becomes even more abstract than the idea of material culture (Ingold 2007a).

Approaches to what material things 'do', rather than just what they mean or how they are 'entangled' in social relationships (Thomas 1991) require a more adequate account of the role of the material dimensions of the world in social life than, for example, a Foucauldian notion of the 'material constraint' of architecture would provide (Foucault 1977b: 67; Foucault and Rabinow 1984). The effects of things clearly require us to move beyond imagining social life as worked out in an isomorphic world of stuff. The efficacy of things relates to material durability, as explored above, but also to the effects of residuality (Lucas 2008; Miller 2001a: 109–111; Olivier 2001), decay (Küchler 2002b; DeSilvey 2006), destruction (Collorado-Mansfeld 2003), rarity (Pels 1998), fragmentation (Chapman 2000a), and the situations in which the enchantment or dazzling effects of the material world lead to 'stoppages' (Gosden 2006: 430; Gell 1992b; cf. Coote 1992; Saunders 1999) or particular engagements of the human senses (Jones and MacGregor 2002; Edwards *et al.* 2006) and the affective charge of things. Daniel Miller (2001a: 119–120) has expressed similar effects through the term 'possession'—how owner-ship of objects can also lead to the 'possession' of humans by objects in social situations that exist within 'networks of agents that include both animate and inanimate forms'. Following Miller we could term such effects 'the consequences of materiality' (Miller 2005a: 3): foregrounding 'a concern with how the material world is manifest' and 'the transformative processes that shape the material world' (Buchli 2004: 183).

The awareness of the limitations of the textual analogy that developed from a new attention to the physicality of things might at first glance appear to be in keeping with Giddens' critique of hermeneutics, as expressed in archaeology by the papers by John Barrett (1987a, 1987b) discussed above. This would lead us back to a consideration of the relationships between 'structure' and 'agency', which has stood for so long in the background of the dialectical model of 'material culture studies'. But deeper questioning of the idea of material culture has emerged from a loose body of thought that has sought to combine elements of the hermeneutic phe-nomenology described above with perspectives from Bruno Latour's conception of ANT, as it has emerged since the early 1990s after social constructivism (Latour 2005a; see Law this volume, Chapter 6).

These arguments have typically begun with the assertion that material culture studies have somehow 'forgotten' about things: 'moved away from things' materiality and subsumed themselves to hegemonic antimaterial and social constructivist theories' (Olsen 2003: 88). Several writers, especially from an archaeological perspective, have called for a new focusing upon things, asserting that the discipline of archaeology represents 'the discipline of things *par excellence*' (Olsen 2003: 89). Most recently such arguments have taken place under the banner of a 'symmetrical archeology', a term inspired by Bruno Latour's early accounts of ANT (Olsen 2007; Witmore 2007; Webmoor and Witmore 2008; see Latour 1993a). They have also, however, led to Daniel Miller and others responding to the work of ANT by replacing the term 'material culture' with 'materiality' (Miller 2005a), and to Tim Ingold arguing for a focus upon 'materials' rather than some generalized essence of 'materiality' (Ingold 2007b).

The significance of ANT for material culture studies lies mainly in its theory of agency, which it suggests—in an extension of this concept beyond the human actors that we would encounter in structuration theory for example—is a property of 'non-humans' as well as humans. This is a different argument from the more light-touch ethnographic sense of the use of objects in human social relations, and it involves a questioning of conventional Durkheimian models of the social (as excessively anthropocentric). Latour has famously suggested that the most important part of the name 'ANT' is the hyphen between the 'actor' and the 'network' (Latour 1999a). In its reception of ANT, the unhyphenated field of material culture studies has been pressed, therefore, to examine quite what it might mean when it refers to the existence of 'relations' between the material and cultural worlds: since ANT seems to some to be effectively 'reinventing the very subject [of anthropological material culture studies]' (Miller 2005b: 3), through 'an extension . . . of approaches to objectification that arise out of dialectical theory' (Miller 2001a: 119, 2005a: 12). But for ANT, relations are not simply bilateral: they are much more far-ranging networks that emerge through the actions of both humans and non-humans.

The reception of ANT thinking was slow in anthropological material culture studies (Miller 2005a; but see Boast 1996; Miller 2002), but aspects of it were clearly directly developed (although never cited) in Alfred Gell's (1998) study *Art and Agency: an anthropological theory*, perhaps read through the arguments of Marilyn Strathern (1996) and Robin Boast (1996). Gell (1992b) developed an argument about the social use, rather than the aesthetic content, of artworks as distinctive items of 'technology', the powers of which served to 'enchant'. He likened his approach to the 'methodological atheisim' adopted by sociologists studying religion (Berger 1967: 100): in the same way, anthropologists studying artworks required a 'methodological philistinism' (Gell 1992b), focused on the work that artworks *do* in social life, rather than what they *mean*. In an account of the use of artworks by social actors ('art as a system of action'; Gell 1998: 6), Gell argued that artworks, and by extension other items of material culture, could be used to extend or distribute human social agency: a model that also drew from Peircian ideas of 'abduction' and Strathernian ideas of 'distributed personhood' (Strathern 1988; Jones 2009: 95–97). This shift in emphasis from what artworks mean to what they do wove a Latourian sense of the powers of things together with an anthropological account of social relations in a tradition that drew from Mauss' study of the gift (Küchler 2002a: 59 see Mauss 1990 [1922]). Unlike ANT, Gell's argument did not extend agency to non-humans, but instead suggested that objects could be deployed by social actors as secondary agents: 'indexes' of human agency.

While Gell's argument has been critiqued from a number of perspectives (Layton 2003; Leach 2007; Morphy 2009), the influence of his book and of ANT has combined in archaeology with the extension of the discussion of the idea of 'agency' as it is theorized in practice theory (e.g. Dobres and Robb 2000a) away from 'a human-centred view of agents and artefacts' through the idea of 'material agency' (Knappett and Malafouris 2008a: ix). Using the more radical extension of agency beyond humans presented by Latour, and presenting a critique of archaeo-logical uses of practice theory as failing to acknowledge the influence of material things, this work argues that 'no distinctions between human and non-human entities can be sustained in terms of agency' (Knappett and Malafouris 2008a: xii; cf. Knappett 2002). In a similar approach, Nicole Boivin (2008) has built on the discussions of the physicality of things outlined above to combine the shift away from the textual analogy of contextual archaeology towards a Gellian model of 'material agency'.

The idea of material agency has been criticized by anthropologist Tim Ingold, as part of his concerns about the ideas of material culture and 'materiality'. In the 'materiality debate' between Ingold and Miller (Ingold 2007a, 2007b, 2007d; D. Miller 2007), Ingold has built on his earlier complaints that the very idea of material culture studies relied upon 'the Cartesian ontology ... that divorces the activity of the mind from that of the body in the world' (2000a: 165):

In the extensive archaeological and anthropological literature on material culture ... [t]he emphasis is almost entirely upon issues of meaning and form—that is, on culture as *opposed* to materiality. Understood as a realm of discourse, meaning and value inhabiting the collective consciousness, culture is conceived to hover above the material world but not to permeate it.

Ingold (2000a: 341)

Ingold has argued that the idea of 'materiality' (e.g. Miller 2005a) has tried to do in one word what material culture did in two—to express relationships between two different worlds or domains, the social world and the object world—while material agency simply reorients these anthropocentric relationships. Ingold's alternative to models of material agency is to see 'things in life' rather than 'life in things', to avoid anthropological archaeology 'turning to stone' by understanding material culture in purely abstract, sociological, or material terms (Ingold 2005: 122).

Ingold (2007b, 2007d) argues that the ideas of 'materiality' and 'objectness' only emerge as a question or a problem from an academic practice that

in its isolation of the object, necessarily ruptures the flows of materials by which it came into being. It is as though the world came ready-made, already precipitated out of the currents, mixtures and transmutations of materials through which it was formed. To follow the materials, by contrast, is to enter a world-in-formation. In this work, things do not appear, in the first instance, as bounded objects, set over against their surroundings, but rather as specific confluences of materials that, for a moment at least, have mixed and melded together into recognisable forms.

Ingold (2007b: 314–315)

Ingold's alternative, however, is another account of networks and relations, which he calls a 'meshwork of interwoven substances' (2007c: 35). Ingold's approach, which we might call, for lack of a better term, 'meshwork studies', maintains the integrity of those elements that interact across this 'meshwork' through his resistance to the idea of 'hybridity', since such a concept presupposes the existence of two distinct forms prior to mixing, or hybridization (2008: 211). Ingold's critique of the uses of ANT in material culture studies is grounded in his concept of 'meshwork', which inspires an alternative and contrapuntal acronym—the web-weaving SPIDER ('Skilled Practice Involves Developmentally Embodied Responsiveness'). Ingold's focus is not upon social relations that constitute a network of humans and non-humans, but upon what he calls 'the *lines* along which [humans, animals and others] live and conduct [their] perception and action in the world' (Ingold 2008: 211; see Ingold 2007c). Ingold's interest is in phenomena such as 'skill' rather than 'agency' is required, since 'to attribute agency to objects that do not grow or develop that consequently develop no skill and whose movement is not therefore coupled to their perception, is ludicrous' (2008: 215).

Meanwhile, the direction in which archaeologists such as Jones, Boivin, Knappett, and Fowler are travelling leads to doing more than (or, perhaps better, less than) arguing that objects can count as subjects, or to illustrate how material things can be involved in the 'distribution of personhood'. Rather it leads towards doing more than simply continuing the impulse in modernist anthropology now to relate across, now to refuse distinctions between 'the material' and 'the socio-cultural'. After all, why is 'agency' a problem at all? Because what is meant is social agency: the Giddensian counterpoint to structure. Agency only emerges as a problem to be solved if we hold on to a particular model of society in which, in the terms of dialectical material culture studies, the question of locating the human actions that generate, and are shaped by, social structure is significant. Like the textual analogy, the debates about agency remain too often solidly anthropocentric: Alfred Gell's *Art and Agency* moved from the meaningful to the social, but retained humans as the proper object of enquiry for anthropology. One alternative might be to turn completely away from the idea of material culture studies, since as Tim Ingold asks, 'Are there contexts that are *not* social, or worlds that are *not* material?' (2007c: 32). Or to turn from anthropology itself, which we might suggest should properly study only humans. Questions about 'meaning' and agency have persisted because of the assumption that the alternative is simply incoherence. Daniel Miller once gave the example of a gas cloud that emerges 'as an unpredicted by-product of a technological process'. For Miller, this was 'only marginally an artefact' and therefore of little concern to social anthropology or social archaeology, despite being a 'product of human labour' (1987: 112–113). The logic here is a belief that 'objects are *made of* social ties' (Latour 2005a: 248–249). How then to account for the much messier and fragmented materials with which archaeologists routinely work? But while 'anthropology' and 'material culture studies', like 'archaeology', are awkward terms, there is no need to dispense with them because of what they are called, since what they actually do is far more nuanced. We might suggest that together archaeology and anthropology accommodate the majority of the world, which is, as John Law puts it, neither coherent nor incoherent but 'indefinite or noncoherent' (2004: 14). Archaeology's slow, descriptive techniques attend precisely to such otherwise unspoken fragments. Research practices in archaeology and anthropology routinely do more (or less) than focus upon accounting for human understanding: 'the understanding of the meaningful relationship between persons and things' (Tilley 2007a: 18–19). This is especially true when things are analysed over time, rather than in the ethnographic present. Theorizing agency and meaning provides solutions only to the sociological and literary problems of representing the world: documenting 'relations' between different domains. Two complementary approaches, which involve moving beyond the representational approaches that characterized the Material-Cultural Turn, its critique by Ingold, and conventional accounts of ANT, are explored in the next section. Central here is the observation that archaeology and anthropology *enact*, rather than purely *represent*, the world.

V: THINGS AS EVENTS, THINGS AS EFFECTS

While writing this chapter, I shared a draft with a number of archaeologists and anthropologists involved in current debates over the idea of material culture. The comments of one colleague were especially informative:

This chapter portrays the history of material culture studies as an elaborate academic game in which renowned contestants play off their positions vis-à-vis one another. The reader, offered a spectator's seat in the back row, is afforded the dubious privilege of listening in on the contest, as words like structuralism, semiotics, practice theory and agency get batted around. The game is punctuated by 'Turns', after each of which the words get reshuffled (sometimes with prefixes such as 'neo' and 'post' attached) and play starts all over again.

From time to time, the players refer to a mysterious planet called 'the material world', which all claim to have visited at one time or another. But if they have any knowledge of this world they take care not to reveal it to uninitiated spectators, lest by doing to they would expose the game as the charade it really is.

Tim Ingold pers. comm. (23 March 2009)

The aim of this excavation has been to reimagine George Marcus' vision of an itinerant ethnography of 'complex objects of study' in the practice of disciplinary historiography: to 'follow the metaphor' (Marcus 1995: 95, 108–109). But the archaeological trench can never map fully onto past realities, whole cultures of thought (Canolea 2007: 181). As Tim Ingold rightly observes, the sequence that is revealed is one of a constant reshuffling and re-articulation of the boundaries or connections between the 'material' and the 'cultural' or the 'social' (cf. Ingold 2000a). This reshuffling began (with the invention of the term 'material culture') in precisely the period in which the Durkheimian idea of anthropology as comparative sociology emerged in the 'structural-functionalist' approaches of Radcliffe-Brown and others. 'The material', thus, became a problem because of a particular model of 'the social'. And the term 'material culture', as opposed to the 'social' in social anthropology, represented a useful compromise. Then, since the mid-1980s the most recent layers of this sequence are characterized by another critique of the distinction between the 'material' and the 'cultural' that is implied by the idea of material culture, most commonly using practice theory to reconcile semiotic analysis with structuralism. While the idea of a distinction between the material and the human has often been criticized as a modern Western imposition, beyond which anthropology must seek to move, the rhetoric of counter-modernism has in practice been a central characteristic of modernist thinking, especially in narratives of loss or erasure seen for example in the conservation movement, rather than an alternative to it (Hicks 2008a; *pace* Thomas 2004). In long-term perspective, modernist anthropology has traced and re-traced the idea of reconciling the material with the socio-cultural as its central question.

Ingold's arguments raise serious concerns about the place of material culture in social anthropology. But, informed to a large extent by a hermeneutic phenomenology similar to that outlined above, meshwork theory itself too often simply repeats the familiar complaints about the segregation of the social/cultural from the natural/material. The practical distinction between ANT and SPIDER is obscure, especially since both distinguish between theory and practice, ethnography and anthropology, positionality, and knowledge (*pace* Ingold 2007e). This distancing effect, between scholar and object, is reinforced by the fact that without exception Ingold's case studies remain as far away as possible from the contemporary world: leading to the strange situation where modern or non-modern objects, like cell phones or woven baskets, have themselves gained a kind of rhetorical power in the 'materiality debate' between Ingold and Miller. Unlike the wide range of ethnographic fieldwork that has been carried out by those working in material culture studies, Ingold's arguments have been developed theoretically, in isolation from fieldwork. In doing so, they reproduce precisely the tendency to seek to explain the world by holding it at a sufficient distance, despite the pressing logic of his arguments to move away from such approaches.

In this section, I want to use two of Ingold's principal ideas—formation and skill—as ways of thinking about how archaeologists and anthropologists have started to focus upon objects (including objects of enquiry) as emergent through time, and as the effects of enactment, rather than bound up in webs of representation and meaningful social action. Through this discussion, I want to consider what the critique of material culture studies, from the perspective of meshwork studies but also from more general concerns about the reduction of things to meanings, or to the social, might mean in practice for archaeologists and anthropologists who continue to see value in the field that has come to be known as material culture studies (however flawed that term might be).

Formation and material histories: things as events

One central element of Ingold's contributions to debates about 'materiality' is his call for anthropologists to understand things *in formation* (Ingold 2007c). The sociological processes through which things are formed as objects were, of course, a central element of the Material-Cultural Turn (Miller 1987). A counterpoint to this discussion of objectification was provided a year after Miller's study by Marilyn Strathern's book *The Gender of the Gift* (1988), which was concerned with the *production of subjects*: specifically, upon ideas of 'personhood' in the classic 'gift societies' of Melanesia. Strathern argued that through exchange and the creation of analogies between different objects in 'inter-artefactual domains', human subjects and objects were not in this ethnographic situation understood as distinct. The exchange of objects led two simultaneous processes: the 'distribution' of person-hood, and a change in the ontological status of humans as 'dividuals' rather than 'individuals'. This argument has more general implications not just for how we comprehend personhood but also, as Donna Haraway would have it, 'what counts as an object' (Haraway 1988: 588): and, of course, what counts as a subject. At stake here is much more than the social construction of identities, or the contextual construction of meaning, but the contingent permeabilities of boundaries between humans and non-humans: how subjects and objects emerge. One way of addres-sing this is to understand things as events.

The representational impulse in material culture studies has resulted from efforts to fix the meaning or social use of objects in particular moments in time. This is an old complaint about ethnographic and archaeological museums, but is also one that can be extended to mainstream material culture studies, which have been characterized by a deep-rooted ethnographic presentism, usually justified through a belief of the exceptionalism of the contemporary material world. It is also a characteristic of the strong tendency in interpretive archaeological thinking to ascribe particular social functions to objects, and to privilege moments at which social relations or particular meanings can be identified.

The idea of 'life histories' in archaeology and anthropology is significant here. Conventional interpretive archaeologies that focus on change over time (e.g. Hodder 1990) are more accurately described as 'agency histories' or 'meaningful histories' rather than 'life histories': since life, as Tim Ingold (2000a) reminds us, involves much more than simply humans and their concerns. Life also, of course, involves constant change and flux. This includes not only social change, or the shift in the meaning of an object but the 'transformation of substance': through decay, fragmentation, residuality, etc. (Pollard 2004). As we have seen, it is conventional for material culture studies to focus only on those moments when things (even banal, everyday things such as soup cans or sherds of pottery) become important for humans: involved in social relationships, or charged with meaning. Sometimes, the field accounts for material restriction and restraint (e.g. Foucault 1977a). More recently, as we have seen, in some studies it posits the existense of 'material agency' (Knappett and Malafouris 2008b). These ideas, however, do not allow for what we might call 'the humility of change': the kind of apparently obscure and inconsequential changes in the fill of a pit, or the silting-up of a ditch, which archaeologists spend large periods of time documenting. Life histories of things at any scale, however, routinely accommodate what we might term material histories, rather than purely social histories.

This disciplinary excavation has reminded us of how the rise of contextual archaeology coincided with a range of parallel interests in the 'social life of things' in social anthropology. In the 1980s the renewed study of exchange, and especially the publication of a new English translation of Marcel Mauss' comparative study of gift exchange in 1990, brought new life to debates in economic anthropology. This atmosphere was captured in Arjun Appadurai's influential edited collection *The Social Life of Things: commodities in cultural perspective*, which examined how anthropological perspectives could be used to study the ways in which objects move between social contexts, gaining new meanings through successive recontextualizations (Appadurai 1986a). Igor Kopytoff's idea of the 'cultural biography of objects' set out in that volume has been influential in both archaeology and anthropology (Hoskins 1998; Gosden and Marshall 1999). But, the idea of studying things through the idiom of life histories has a much more complex life history of its own, which stretches back to Haddon's evolutionary idea of 'the life histories of designs' (Haddon 1895). One particularly influential use of the idea of the life histories of things was developed in the New Archaeology in Michael

Schiffer's account of the idea of tracing an artefact's 'life history' from production, through use, to deposition, in order to comprehend the formation of the archaeological record (Schiffer 1972). Like many other archaeological methods, from landscape survey to excavation recording, if you were to place your finger at any point on Schiffer's drawing of this sequence (reproduced by Harrison this volume, chapter 23, Figure 23.1), it would be difficult uniformly to assign meaning or involvement in social agency: and yet the thing would be 'doing' something. Passing from one form to another as it decayed, or simply lying below the ground or on the surface of a ploughed field. Tracing such life histories is always the product of the slow and painstaking putting of archaeological methods into practice, for apparently inconsequential materials. As Appadurai argued, the idea of 'the social lives of things' requires a degree of 'methodological fetishism':

Even if our own approach to things is conditioned necessarily by the view that things have no meanings apart from those that human transactions, attributions and motivations endow them with, the anthropological problem is that this formal truth does not illuminate the concrete, historical circulation of things. For that we have to follow the things themselves, for their meanings are inscribed in their forms, their uses, their trajectories. It is only through the analysis of these trajectories that we can interpret the human transactions and calculations that enliven things. Thus, even though from a *theoretical* point of view human actors encode things with meaning, from a *methodological* point of view it is the things-in-motion that illuminate their human and social context. No social analysis of things (whether the analyst is an economist, an art historian, or an anthropologist) can avoid a minimum level of what might be called methodological fetishism. This methodological fetishism, returning our attention to the things themselves, is in part a corrective to the tendency to excessively socialize transactions in things, a tendency we owe to Mauss.

Appadurai (1986b: 5)

The discussion above might encourage us to extend Appadurai's argument to suggest that it is not only 'human and social contexts' that are visible by tracing things-in-motion. This argument about objects' life histories would have implications for ethnographic, as well as archaeological, fieldwork. The reduction of objects' life histories to their enrolment in the lives of humans must clearly be questioned (Schiffer 1972, Gosden 2006). Human and material lives are routinely intertwined. In many archaeological and ethnographic studies, the intertwined nature of human and material life—whether through the extension of life courses through mementoes (Hallam and Hockey 2001), the role of things in human memory (Jones 2007) the intimacy of ownership and 'possession' of things that persist over time (Miller 2001b)—have been a central contribution of archaeological and anthropological material culture studies.

In these cases, things themselves can come to constitute contexts, which are by no means purely human or social contexts. The work of museum ethnographers such as Nicholas Thomas and Amiria Henare in extending material culture studies into historical anthropology has been particularly important here (N. Thomas 1999, 2000; Henare 2005a, 2005b; cf. Haas 1996; Colchester 2003). Such work builds on Marilyn Strathern's (1990) seminal study of 'artefacts of history', in which the material enactment of history was foregrounded. In practice, this means that historical anthropology cannot understand artefacts as the illustrations of social history, from which they are separated. Both objectification and subjectification require work; such processes must be made to happen and maintained. In this sense, things are always events—more or less visible depending on the constant changes in the human and non-human world. Thomas' study of the changing uses of indigenous and introduced textiles in the history of the conversion to Christianity in nineteenth-century Polynesia is of significance here. Tracing the adoption of the Tahitian practice of wearing barkcloth ponchos (*tiputa*) more widely in Polynesia, he suggests that artefacts of this kind 'were much more than mere markers of identity'. Instead, he demonstrates 'how adapted and introduced types of cloth perhaps worked as a technology that made religious change, that is, conversion to Christianity, visible as a feature of people's behaviour and domestic life' (N. Thomas 1999: 16, 6). By focusing on the effects of the physical properties of *tiputa*—which allowed for parts of the body to be covered—Thomas suggests that in such situations, 'the interpretative strategy of regarding things essentially as expressions of cultural, subcultural, religious, or political identities, depends on too static and literal an approach to their meanings' (N. Thomas 1999: 16). Thus, the Polynesian ponchos to some extent 'made' contexts themselves, rather than simply being received within particular socio-cultural (human) contexts. The implications for the writing of colonial history are significant, since alternatives to conventional social or cultural histories of colonial histories are made possible through a kind of material history:

This way of seeing things perhaps also helps us move beyond the long-standing dilemma of historical anthropology in Oceania, which has lurched between emphasis on continuity and discontinuity, between affirmation of the enduring resilience of local cultures, and critique of the effects of colonial history. Artifacts such as *tiputa* are neither inventions of tradition nor wholly unprecedented forms. They are at once implicated in the material history of Polynesian societies and departures from that history . . . More often than we have acknowledged, the indigenous peoples of the region have been concerned not to 'contextualize' things, but to use things to change contexts.

N. Thomas (1999: 18–19)

Thomas hints at how things can contribute to the formation of contexts, as well as simply fitting into contexts in which they can be used or understood, that this formation is contingent, and that this contingency includes the physical affordances of things and even the materials they are made from. As Chris Pinney has argued, this leads a long way away from the understanding of things as infinitely malleable for human ends (Pinney 2005: 268).

These developments in historical anthropology are taken a step further by new developments in British archaeology (see discussions by Pollard 2001, 2004). In historical archaeology, for example, 'material histories' involve not simply under-standing the changing social uses or meanings of artefacts, but also those aspects of the life histories of things, buildings, or landscapes that are more accurately described as non-coherent, rather than socially significant or culturally meaningful (Hicks 2003, 2005, 2007a, 2007b; Hicks and Beaudry 2006a; Hicks and McAtackney 2007; cf. Shanks 1998; Holtorf 2002; Holtorf and Williams 2006). The very idea of historical archaeology becomes meaningless if it is not grounded in the sense that so much happens that is unspoken and undocumented, but that is far from insignificant and that leaves material traces. But more than that, ideas and dis-courses are revealed from an archaeological perspective to require material enact-ment: to be fitted, usually quite awkwardly, into the world.

The point can be made by returning to the idea of capitalist processes of objectification (Miller 1987). The justification for setting up research between the 'material' and the 'cultural' was that large-scale forces (modernity, capitalism, etc.) create subjects and objects, and so anthropology should study the processes through which this takes place. But the implication of Bruno Latour's contention that *We Have Never Been Modern* (Latour 1993a) is that modernity was an idea that was never totally and coherently enacted. For the archaeologist, for instance studying the decaying concrete and steel of modernist architecture (Buchli 1999), theories of objectification serve to overdetermine the power of the modern, of capitalism, etc. (cf. Buchli and Lucas 2001a, 2001b; Hicks 2008a). Thus, one of the principal contributions of the archaeology of the modern period, as it has emerged since the early 1980s, has been to demonstrate that there was no sudden or fundamental transformation of the material world at any point in the emergence of the modern. Any model of radical difference between the premodern and the modern, and between anthropological and archaeological studies of material culture, is thus unhelpful (Hicks and Beaudry 2006b). Instead, a distinctive kind of historiography, which relates to material change, is involved (Hicks 2003, 2008b). Such material histories do not deny or critique social histories. They are perhaps best understood as 'less-than-social' histories. We could equally call them material culture studies.

Historical archaeology and historical anthropology have often studied situations in which particular understandings of a distinction between persons and objects have been held, most clearly perhaps in the treatment of people as objects in the archaeology of slavery (e.g. Kopytoff 1986). But at its best the contribution is considerably more nuanced: describing how such ideas are worked out in particular places and particular lives, rather than illustrating social history (Wilkie 2003). And it is from the intimate depictions of human and material situations in the archaeology of the recent past that the most effective alternatives to sociological studies of material culture informed by practice theory have emerged (Buchli 1999, 2002c): undertaking, as the strongest contributions in material culture studies do, a kind of 'archaeology of modern life' (Weatherill 1989: 439).

Taken together, recent research in historical anthropology and historical and prehistoric archaeology suggests that the longstanding concern with overcoming overarching dualisms between subjects and objects has derived to a considerable extent from the synchronic nature of British material culture studies: both in the ethnographic present, and in the tendency in interpretive archaeology to privilege particular moments of social agency or meaning. Human and material lives are not ontologically different: they exist in the same world. They might, however, operate at a variety of paces. Imagine screwing a manual camera to a tripod in a dimly lit room. The longer the exposure, the more will be visible in the photograph. But equally, the more blurred human actions will be, as walls and windows stand out, unmoving. It is not, of course, that buildings are not undergoing constant change. Rather, they are moving at a different pace: all buildings will fall down eventually. Moreover, the pace of change in materials is contingent upon not only their maintenance by humans—for a building, repointing a wall, or keeping a roof intact—but also upon the materials involved. Constructions out of timber decay faster than stone. As I have argued with Audrey Horning in relation to the archaeology of buildings, such perspectives require a distribution of analysis across time that parallels the distribution of intentionality, thought, or agency over time that appeared in study of the Maori meeting house in the final chapter of Alfred Gell's study *Art and Agency* (Gell 1998: 221–258; Hicks and Horning 2006). Unravelling the arguments about artworks and social agency set out in the earlier chapters of his book, Gell considered how particular material forms emerge from traditions of practice. The logic of this argument is to suggest that a diachronic approach, which understands things as involved (as well as humans) in the making of time and of contexts, must allow that 'material culture has a dangerous potentiality that it has never acquired in social theory' (N. Thomas 1999: 7). But it also means that we must allow for the time spent in the camera exposure: which implicates the researcher within the event, rather than being distanced from it, as I shall explore in the next section.

Skill and disciplinarity: things as effects

Having made this argument about things as events in what would usually be understood as the object of enquiry—the archaeological site, or the Maori meeting hut studied by the ethnographer—I now want to use Tim Ingold's arguments about skilled practice to extend precisely the same argument to theories. Theories, we might suggest, emerge in precisely the same manner as things. Things and theories are not simply events, however; they are also effects. This suggestion requires us to move anthropological interests in practice beyond human and material practices as an object of enquiry, to incorporate our own material practices as researchers. It requires more than a purely reflexive awareness of fixed and timeless positionality, since positions emerge as events in precisely the same manner as things. The conceptual and practical tools for going beyond reflexivity already exist within material culture studies, and might be freed up by the unfolding of the idea of material culture studies to include the academic subject, as well as the academic object (and thus to move beyond the 'science wars' of the 1980s between subject-ivity and object-ivity, relativism and realism). In this section, I want to suggest that an understanding of things (and theories) as events can be complemented by an understanding of things (and theories) as the effects of material practice. This line of enquiry is inspired especially by current thinking in historical archaeology. Here, the extension of archaeological research into the recent past and the contemporary world means that archaeology can no longer be defined by its object. Where archaeology used to be a discipline that examined particular key sites or objects, the 'canon' of archaeological material is broken down by the extension of the field into the nineteenth, twentieth, and twenty-first centuries: there is simply too much for any such definition to have coherence (Hicks 2003). Either archaeology is no longer a useful idea, or we must look at archaeological practices—how archaeology enacts things—to understand what archaeology is. This raises much broader issues of the aspiration of material culture studies to be a post-disciplinary field. Before discussing interdisciplinarity, however, I want to make the case for understanding things and theories as effects, as well as events. So how to account for things as events.

There is a strong line of enquiry in material culture studies that relates to the skilled use of things. This runs from Marcel Mauss' (1973) account of 'techniques of the body', through Leroi-Gourhan's (1993) account of *chaînes opératoires* (operational sequences) and his classification of techniques and gestures 'derived from the kinds of action on materials which they employ' (Lemonnier 1986: 150), to Pierre Lemonnier's vision of an anthropology of technology, moving away from 'the study of lifeless objects' (1986: 147). Attention to 'the peeling of sweet potatoes, the washing of children, or the sharpening of stone axes', to 'the observation and the transcription of operational sequences, in particular, is an indispensable part of any fieldwork. Not to do so is to treat objects as hardly less isolated and lifeless as those in a museum' (Lemonnier 1986: 181). We might locate aspects of Bruno Latour's thinking in this tradition (e.g. Latour 2000b), and certainly Tim Ingold's focus on the idea of 'skill', which is so central to his ideas of meshwork and weaving (Ingold 2000a: 289–293) and his distinction between 'building' and 'dwelling'. By extending such ideas to field practice, as Ingold (1993) did to some degree in his examination of 'the temporality of the landscape', we might underline the performative and situated dimensions of our understanding of the contemporary world, and of how we enact the past in the present (cf. Strathern 1990).

One of the distinctive characteristics of interpretive archaeology, especially as it was developed by Ian Hodder, was a self-awareness of archaeology as a contemporary practice, in which field methods should be thought through (Shanks and McGuire 1996; Hodder 1999). For the archaeologist, however, the contemporary must be an event, emergent, and contingent (Buchli and Lucas 2001b). In American cultural anthropology, the reflexive awareness of ethnographic monographs as written texts (Marcus and Cushman 1982) was summarized in the influential collection *Writing Culture* (Clifford and Marcus 1986). In contrast, the publication in the same year of *Reading the Past* described the reverse process: a passive reading from the material record, rather than the practices of writing from fieldwork (Hodder 1986). However, in the 1990s, an increasing desire to think through the processes of uniting 'theory' and 'practice' (Hodder 1999) came to generate a distinctive alternative from the turning away from method and fieldwork that characterized some other approaches in interpretive archaeology, such as Julian Thomas' argument that discussions of methods were of limited significance because 'New Archaeology *was methodology*' and a scepticism that knowledge might emerge quite precisely from method rather than the abstractions of interpretation (Thomas 2000c: 3). While much of this discussion related to the idea of 'reflexivity', which often simply reinforced the interpretive concept of a distance between scholar and object (Hicks 2005), a new body of writing about archaeological practice emerged (Edgeworth 1990, 2003, 2006a; Lucas 2001a; Yarrow 2003, 2008), especially in relation to the situated and iterative processes through which archaeological knowledge comes about (Hicks 2005). The distinction here with conventional models of social science is clear: where structuration theory suggested that 'all social actors . . . are social theorists', a focus on *field* practice involves awareness of 'the specificity of techniques, as far as "knowledge" is concerned' is crucial (Giddens 1984: 335; Strathern 1987: 30).

Such perspectives have not been applied to anthropological material culture studies, despite the important acknowledgement that 'anthropology, which grew up in cousinhood with archaeology, takes to the analysis of the minutiae of practice in a manner akin to that of an excavation' (Miller and Woodward 2007: 337), and the call from archaeologists working on the 'contemporary past' for a kind of 'critical empiricism' (Buchli and Lucas 2001a: 14; Buchli 2002b: 16). Indeed the Manchester School's arguments about the particular perspectives provided by extended case method and situational analysis were not important to anthropology's Material-Cultural Turn. But just as in archaeology, the potential in the anthropology of things for a foregrounding of the empirical work of fieldwork to bring about, in practice rather than in theory, a collapsing of object and subject, is directly related to avoiding the choice between 'objectivity' and 'subjectivity', which the Material-Cultural Turn was trying to do from the outset. As Tom Yarrow has recently argued, 'whilst archaeologists frequently assert and demonstrate the objectivity of the artefacts and contexts they unearth as distinct from their own subjective interpretations, the work required to achieve this distinction is not reducible to the distinction itself' (Yarrow 2008: 135–136).

In this conception, fieldwork is not usefully understood as purely 'relational', but as constituted by moments of permeability between fieldworker, place, things, and people. Field sciences, such as archaeology, anthropology, geography, and science and technology studies (STS), *enact* knowledge. We cannot, therefore, fail to theorize methodology (Henare *et al.* 2007a: 27). That is why Mary and I wanted to gather these four particular disciplines together in the present volume about studying things. This implication of the fieldworker in the emergence of the material studied, and the definition of material culture studies as a series of practices for enacting knowledge about things, requires an extension of that argument, from material culture studies, about the humility of things to the potential of the apparently banal to the apparently tedious work of post-excavation or museum ethnography. After all, 'knowing' as Chris Gosden and Frances Larson have recently argued, 'takes time and effort and people and things' (2007: 239). Rather than reflexivity, an awareness of the emergent situatedness of knowledge can achieve what Marilyn Strathern has described as 'a certain brand of empiricism, making the data so presented apparently outrun the theoretical effort to comprehend it' (1999: 199).

The difference from previous conceptions of material culture studies is critical: a foregrounding of disciplinarity, rather than undertaking 'an anthropology of' this object or that. Such a move is close to what Annemarie Mol has termed a shift from 'ethnography' to 'praxiography'—in which the practices of the fieldworker are implicated too, since 'praxiographic stories have composite objects' (2002: 156). Where the cultural turn across the social sciences is in so many places 'still dominated by tired constructivist themes' (Thrift 2000: 2), and since the Material-Cultural Turn in British archaeology and anthropology too often used objects to argue that its research was not, to borrow Judith Butler's phrase, 'merely cultural' (Butler 1998), the challenge lies in collapsing the gap between anthropological archaeology's acknowledgement of 'the humility of objects' and Donna Haraway's conception of knowledge practices as acts of 'modest witnessing' (Miller 1987: 85–86; Haraway 1997: 24–25).

If we understand things as events and effects, rather than fixed and solid, then 'material culture' has unfolded to the point that material culture studies can no longer be defined *by its object*. The 'materiality debate' sketched above demonstrates that the idea that material culture might represent 'the concrete counterpoint to the abstractions of culture' (Yarrow 2008: 122) is long behind us. Along with it, however, any unifying model of networks and relations between bounded entities is also lost. The material effects highlighted above demonstrate how permeabilities, as well as just relations, constitute the emergence of the world as assemblage. And they indicate that the Durkheimian conception of social agency, revived in material culture studies through practice theory in order to reconcile the structural and the semiotic, is no longer adequate: simply extending it to objects will not do (*pace* Gell 1998). Life, both human and non-human, as it is encountered in archaeology and anthropology involves not relations between fixed entities, but life as the ongoing flow of permeabilities, and the emergence of worlds. These issues have begun to be addressed in material culture studies in examinations of immateriality (Buchli 2004: 187–191), in the consumption of apparently intangible media such as the internet (Miller and Slater 2000) or radio (Tacchi 1998) and to some extent in Miller's account of 'virtualism' (Carrier and Miller 1998; D. Miller 2000). But there are ontological, rather than purely epistemological, ramifications of the unfolding of material culture as a coherent object of enquiry: as fieldworkers we do not mediate between two ontological domains.

The implications for material culture studies' ambitions to create a kind of post-disciplinary field are profound. Since the 1970s, many have observed that the study of material culture might unite 'archaeologists with certain kinds of cultural anthropologists' (Appadurai 1986b: 5). However, despite the regular inclusion of literature surveys in the relatively high number of many closely argued, programmatic statements of what 'material culture studies' might represent or aspire to be (e.g. Miller 1983, 1987, 1998b, 2005a; Miller and Tilley 1996), the 1990s was rarely characterized by genuine collaboration and exchange between British anthropology and archaeology. Where collaboration did occur, as in Chris Tilley's idea of *An Ethnography of the Neolithic* (1996), they were restricted to a particular vision of archaeology: as distant as possible from the present, and as method-less phenomenology rather than employing archaeological techniques. Similarly, in North America the development by Mike Schiffer of a 'behavioural archaeology', using the techniques of New Archaeology to study modern material culture such as radios and cars, has had little impact on socio-cultural anthropology. The diversity of methods involved in what Appadurai termed, as we saw above, the 'methodological fetishism' required to write life histories of things has rarely been considered. Instead, material culture studies developed in Britain as a self-consciously post-disciplinary field. Unlike in interpretive archaeology, there has been virtually no interest in discussions of field practice, apart from in the eclecticism of hermeneutic phenomenology sketched above. Thus, in the first editorial for the *Journal of Material Culture* Daniel Miller and Chris Tilley argued that:

The study of material culture may be most broadly defined as the investigation of the relationship between people and things irrespective of time and space. The perspective adopted may be global or local, concerned with the past or the present, or the mediation between the two . . . [T]he potential range of contemporary disciplines involved in some way or other in studying material culture is effectively as wide as the human and cultural sciences themselves.

Miller and Tilley (1996: 5)

Material culture studies in this period witnessed regular expressions of 'the advantages of being undisciplined' and celebrations of an 'eclecticism [which would in the past] have been frowned upon as diluting and undisciplined' (Miller and Tilley 1996: 12; Attfield 2000: 1). At the same time, the potential of the field becoming a discipline in its own right became a concern: there was a sense of the 'many disadvantages and constraints imposed by trying to claim disciplinary status' led to calls for 'remaining undisciplined and pursuing a field of study without respect to prior claims of disciplinary antecedents' (Miller 1998b: 4; Tilley 2006b: 12–13). As Peter Van Dommelen observed in a study of contributions to the *Journal of Material Culture*, 'the lack of a "home base" for material culture studies' was also 'a point repeatedly made and frequently emphasised' (2000: 409).

With a division of disciplinary labour between the prehistoric and the modern world, a *relational* conception of the potential connections between archaeology and anthropology, and between materials and culture, which had characterized the debates in structural Marxist anthropology two decades earlier, was effectively reinforced. This relational model of interdisciplinary exchanges had been part of a call for collaboration between archaeology and anthropology:

> Although disciplinary specialization is a necessary response to the complexity of knowledge, the institutionalization of disciplines in a pedagogic context naturally leads their members to be over-conscious of the uniqueness of their subject-matter and the rigour of their techniques to elucidate and critically examine their objects of analysis, which become too often badges of corporate identity. This tends to obscure the fact that at a higher and more abstract level it may be more pertinent to be involved in a unifying dialogue so as to share equally in the resolution of theoretical problems and to avoid a reaction to what is perceived to be a one-sided theoretical indebtedness to other disciplines.
>
> Rowlands and Gledhill (1976: 37)

This position was in contrast with the continued strength in contextual archaeology of David Clarke's vision of the distinctiveness of archaeological perspectives:

> Archaeology is neither 'historical' nor 'anthropological'. It is not even science or art. Archaeology's increasing maturity allows it to claim an independent personality with distinctive qualities to contribute.
>
> Hodder (1986: x)

In this context, the suggestion in 1998 by Chris Tilley, one of the few archaeologists working in both traditions of interpretive archaeology and anthropological material culture studies, that a loss of 'disciplinary isolation' had led to the end of archaeology as a coherent discipline at all, is informative (cf. Hicks 2003):

> there could be nothing distinctive about archaeological theory when it went beyond a concern with appropriate methodologies for excavation, fieldwork and conceptualization of factors affecting the physical survival of archaeological evidence . . . The irony [in Clarke's work] is that the death of archaeology could only result from the conceit of distinctiveness . . . How could an archaeological theory of society or human action be produced that would

not simultaneously be a social and anthropological theory?... A loss of innocence is dependent on the end of disciplinary isolation and, in this sense, archaeology no longer continues to exist.

Tilley (1998: 691–692)

This is the editorial direction of the recent Sage *Handbook of Material Culture* (Tilley *et al.* 2006). It builds within social anthropology on earlier complaints about the idea of disciplinarity in archaeology:

Why is teaching so much bound up with promoting disciplinary allegiance and asserting distinctiveness? Why are courses in archaeological institutions labelled as being archaeological theory, rather than social theory? Why should archaeologists think they can learn more from each other in their conferences, seminars, workshops, lectures and publications rather than by talking with outsiders (so-called inter-disciplinary interactions being the exception rather than the norm)? Is this anything much more than a kind of ancestor- and hero-worship... and part of a struggle for resources between competing disciplines in universities with artificial boundaries? Leaving to one side the politics and pragmatism inevitably required for the disciplinary survival of archaeology, is it any longer intellectually necessary, or sufficient, for us to be *disciplined*?

Tilley (1998: 692, original emphasis)

This post-disciplinary conception of material culture studies led to very little consideration of disciplinary histories, allegiances, and intellectual debts, creating

the impression that material culture studies is now, as it were, independently re-invented by the same theoretical discussions that earlier have tended to regard them as irrelevant. The picture created in this way is essentially a-historical, in that it reconstitutes the study of the artifact in its new domain as apparently separated from its historical roots.

van Beek (1989: 95)

It is this gap in self-awareness of disciplinary historiography that this chapter has been working to plug. Archaeological and anthropological research requires events, (like fieldwork) in which objects of enquiry emerge as effects rather than prior entities in any straightforward manner. The contingencies of these events must therefore be accounted for. And such contingencies include disciplinary traditions as well as methods: the questions that we ask of things, from which objects emerge. An awareness of disciplinary histories must therefore be a central concern. As we have seen, material culture studies were the principal element of 'postmodern anthropology' (Rowlands 2004: 474) and archaeology in Britain, but they retained very many of the elements of structuralism. The few attempts to build post-structuralist archaeologies in Britain (Baker and Thomas 1990; Bapty and Yates 1990) comprised second-hand reviews of the literature of other fields rather than genuine contributions to archaeological thinking (Shanks 1990), while the anthropology of consumption actively distanced itself from the perceived 'nihilism' of post-structuralist thinking (Miller 1987: 165, 176). The Material-Cultural Turn thus operated by 'placing the object squarely in the centre of culture theory' (van Beek 1989: 94), forming part of a broader process in which post-processual archaeology sought a kind of 'compression' of structuralist and post-structuralist approaches (Olsen 2006: 86).

While material culture studies was forged in British archaeology and anthropology as a kind of post-disciplinary field, in the 'materiality debate' this approach to disciplinarity has become more complex. For example, in his response to Tim Ingold's critique of the idea of 'materiality', Daniel Miller has underlined diversity by suggesting that the idea of 'a fixed object like a genre called "material-culture studies" is unsustainable' (Miller 2007: 24), but has at the same time suggested that a distinctive contribution of material culture studies is ethnographic:

> [W]e are not philosophers...Instead we are anthropologists constantly engaged in ethnography...Most of those working in material-culture studies, including almost everyone I work with at UCL, come from a tradition more aligned with the ethnographic study of practice—that is, the actual use of materials by people—but above all study of the way the specific character of people emerges from their interaction with the material world through practice...[O]ur profession demands an encounter with the world as we find it. My heart is in contemporary ethnography, and I do not feel the need to apologize for a material culture that has changed in recent decades largely because today it is, while a few decades ago it manifestly was not, central to this contemporary ethnography.
>
> Miller (2007: 24–27)

This perspective contrasted markedly with earlier contentions that 'material culture studies is not constituted by ethnography, but remains eclectic in its methods' (Miller 1998b: 19).

Miller's new argument inspires two responses. The first is that when material culture studies was defined by its object, a false division between past and present, formed especially after the abandonment of ethnoarchaeology, bounded off archaeology from anthropology. British archaeology has throughout the majority of literature in British material culture studies been understood in relation to prehistory rather than the archaeology of historical periods or the contemporary world (e.g. Miller 1987: 124–125). This has restricted the contributions from archaeology and anthropology to what is perceived as a current interdisciplinary 'return to things' in social scientific research (Witmore 2007: 559), and are characterized by a pressing desire to make a contribution from the perspective of material culture studies, or from archaeology to broader debates.

But secondly, the particular ways in which interdisciplinarity was envisaged in material culture studies might be reoriented. As Andrew Barry, Georgiana Born, and Gisa Weszkalnys have argued, working across disciplines need not lead to a loss of coherence, but can allow a form of 'interdisciplinary autonomy' to emerge (Barry et al. 2008), which can 'attend to the specificity of interdisciplinary fields, their genealogies and multiplicity' (Barry et al. 2008: 42). The Material-Cultural Turn associated 'disciplines' with constraint (perhaps even, subconsciously, with punishment, since Foucault 1977a). But as Marilyn Strathern has argued, 'disciplinary awareness—that is, a sense of the regional and intellectual histories within which our research is conducted, and upon the putting of particular methods into practice—is a crucial element in achieving a clarity in the contingency of the knowledge that we create upon materially-situated practices' (Strathearn 2004b: 5). Moreover, these situations emerge through practice.

The tendency to define archaeology and anthropological material culture studies by its object led to a particular conception of post-disciplinarity (e.g. Fahlander and Oestigaard 2004). Rather than the distinctions between archaeology and anthropology as defined by their objects of enquiry—the science of things or the science of people—a sensitivity to field practice (rather than just the use of practice theory) could allow new kinds of cross-disciplinary work in 'material culture studies' to develop. In this sense, the field of material culture studies holds in its hands the toolkits required to move beyond not only the representational impulse in the Material-Cultural Turn, but that in ANT as well, which too often in its interdisciplinary reception operates as an abstract theory distanced from the world just like the Durkheimian model of the social, and like structuralism. Insofar as ANT represents a third major interdisciplinary contribution from anthropology, this time involving the accommodation of 'non-humans', its transdisciplinary reception as a new representational model could be reoriented from the perspective of material culture studies.

CONCLUSIONS: FROM THE HUMILITY OF THINGS TO MODEST WITNESSING

The social sciences become devoted to the study of all phenomena that stand for what we now call society, social relations, or indeed simply the subject. By whichever name, these are the terms that describe the contents of the coffin we are about to bury.

Miller (2005a: 36)

It is conventional in British field archaeology, after the layers are drawn and recorded, recording sheets completed, artefacts gathered, bagged, and labelled, and the stratigraphic sequence constructed, to sit on the side of the evaluation trench with a cup of tea, to light a cigarette and, staring at the spoil heap, think the foregoing process through for a final time before filling the hole back in. A similar process seems appropriate after this exercise in disciplinary excavation: a counterpoint to Daniel Miller's 'rites of burial' for 'the twin terms *society* and *social relations*' (Miller 2005a: 37). The excavation has, after all, encountered only fragments of 'culture', of 'materials', and of any clear set of relationships between them. But archaeology is different from grave digging, and this evaluative trench is not a grave for material culture studies, but a glimpse of its stratigraphy.

The archaeological process yields not just fragments of abraded and residual ceramic sherds, but mud on the boots and dirt under the fingernails. It is generally conducted outside, and so involves experience of the wind, rain, or heat. It is itinerant, in that the site must be chosen, arrived at, and time spent there. It is iterative in that it involves the repeated application of a particular bundle of methods and, in Britain at least, a distinctive range of tools (pointing trowels, coal shovels, marker pens, manual cameras, biros, ring-binders, permatrace, hazard tape, hard hats, masking tape, zip lock bags, large plywood boards, 4H pencils, line levels, high visibility jackets, string, etc.). In other words, the practice of archaeology reminds us of something that is more generally true of field sciences such as anthropology, geography, STS, and archaeology: that *we enact* knowledge of the world, rather than straightforwardly *represent* it. These enactments are just like the enactment of any thing. At their best, these fields collapse any division between this enactment—the status of the knowledge that emerges from them as event and effect—and the humans and materials studied. But this requires a leaving behind of the representational impulses that continue to characterize the diverse work of Miller, Ingold, and Latour. No new grand theory of material culture is required: instead, a more modest acknowledgement of how our knowledge is formed through material practices, which are always historically contingent.

It is not the purpose of this chapter to critique the assertion that 'material culture studies may be claimed to be in the vanguard of creative theory and debate in the social sciences today' (Tilley 2006c: 5). But the coherence of the field defined according to its object is hard to perceive today: given the questioning of ideas of cultures, materials, and especially of the relationships between the two, which have emerged from material culture studies itself (cf. D. Miller 2007: 24). This, I believe, is the point that Amiria Henare, Martin Holbraad, and Sari Wastell are trying to make in their rather abstract answer to the pressing contemporary question: 'What would an artefact-oriented anthropology look like if it were not about material culture?' (Henare *et al.* 2007a: 1).

In his discussion of Pierre Bourdieu's (1984) study *Distinction*, Daniel Miller once argued that while it represented 'surely the most significant contribution to the study of consumption made by any anthropologist' to date, its principal weaknesses related to the methodology employed (which involved the sociological use of a questionnaire rather than ethnographic participant observation) and the failure to situate mass consumption 'as an historical phenomenon' (Miller 1987: 154–155). Re-reading these lines, it is difficult, especially from the vantage point offered by the side of this trench on which I am sitting, to comprehend the discomfort in anthropology's Material-Cultural Turn with issues of historical contingency and research practice since that time:

the possibility of material culture studies lies not in method, but rather in an acknowledgement of the nature of culture . . . We as academics can strive for understanding and empathy through the study of what people do with objects, because that is the way that the people that we study create a world of practice.

Miller (1998b: 19)

At the same time, the very idea of 'interpretive archaeology' presented the material and the past as distant: in different worlds from the contemporary researcher. The 'soft focus' that such imagined distance creates has led to the false impression that the dirt on my hands is somehow ontologically different from my hands themselves. We do not need to return to Mary Douglas (1966) to realize that such perspectives are the legacies of structuralism (and are concerned with a kind of epistemological purity).

Such views limit practice to those whom we observe. They distance the researcher as subject from the object of enquiry (even when that object is defined as processes of objectification). They conceive of the fieldworker as a 'participant observer', on the model of structural-functionalism and its particular Durkheimian view of the social, rather than as what folklorist John Messenger (1989) once called an 'observant participator'. This holds back the potential, which I take to be the central contribution of archaeology and anthropology to the social scientific study of material things, of the description and discussion of how alternative ontologies emerge, in a contingent manner, as particular sites and situations are enacted (Hicks and McAtackney 2007): whether in everyday life, or in academic research. The implications of such a view is to allow the metaphysics to emerge from the material as it is studied: a position that demands a theoretical eclecticism, but also a clarity about the nature of disciplinary and material positionality.

In 1985 geographer Nigel Thrift concluded his assessment of Giddens' model of practice theory, after the publication of *The Constitution of Society* (Giddens 1984), by imagining the next book that he would have liked to see Giddens write:

one for which *The Constitution of Society* would serve as a prolegomenon. It would consist of the development of structuration 'theory' in the arena of a particular place in a particular historical period of time, showing structuration in process, contextualising in context. The book would have to show how structuration 'theory' can act as a basis for challenging existing interpretations of historical events. It would therefore show whether structuration 'theory' was viable. Of course, this may sound like a plea for Giddens to do some 'empirical work'. But it seems to me that, more than most other social theories, that *is* the import of structuration theory. After all, it is not possible to expose the importance of context and then ignore it. At some point conceptual salvoes must hit particular places or disappear back into the thin air of high theory.

Thrift (1985: 621)

Giddens never wrote that book. However, this precise task was, we might suggest, taken up with considerable energy in the 'high period' of British material culture studies. Material culture studies, as an interdisciplinary project defined by a common object of enquiry, emerged from particular efforts to solve a series of quite specific disciplinary problems in anthropology and archaeology. It came to be an effect of those problems: which led to fieldwork both in modern shopping centres and in Neolithic monumental landscapes. With the unfolding of that object, as both event and effect, we can no longer continue simply to resort to using practice theory to reconcile structuralism and semiotics, through case study after anthropological case study. By understanding itself as theory rather than effect, the Material-Cultural Turn has simply made the transition, as Edwin Ardener (1985) explained all modernist theories must do, from 'life' to 'genre'.

What the development of practice theory in material culture studies has shown, however, is that the dialectical model of agency and structure, and the literary model of *langue* and *parole*, have allowed a further distinction between subjects and objects to be reinforced: the difference between researchers and their materials. I must underline that I undestand this to be the central contribution of the 'field sciences' of archaeology, anthropology, geography, and STS. We are united in having distinctive ways of putting methods into practice in order to enact the world. That is how we make knowledge: things emerge from our practices in precisely the same way they do through the vernacular practices of humans, or lives of things, that we study. As Daniel Miller has recently argued in his account of material culture on a south London street, material culture studies lead away from a Durkheimian model of social anthropology (Miller 2008: 282–297). But they also lead away from the latent structuralism in mainstream dialectical and 'relational' models of our strangely unhyphenated term, 'material culture', and more generally from modernist definition of academic practice as distanced representation. This shift, which we could describe as from epistemology to ontology (Henare *et al.* 2007a), is a reminder that an archaeologist gets dirt under the fingernails. That dirt and my fingers exist, after all, in the same world; the traces of practice until the fingers are scrubbed.

So just like any thing, the Material-Cultural Turn was both an event and an effect. As all archaeological material culture studies reveal, we build the future with the remains of the past, often the very recent past. Where, then, is the idea of 'material culture studies' left? I have tried to offer some provisional answers. The argument takes unfolding of the idea of 'material culture' in precisely the opposite direction from the phenomenological critique, which seeks to avoid 'a tendency to ontologise the status of material evidence' by comprehending 'culture as a practice' (J. S. Thomas 2007: 11), towards acknowledging the contingency of our knowledge of the world upon situated material practices that derive from distinctive disciplinary methods and traditions, rather than representing a particular brand of social theory. As an anthropological archaeologist, I know that I have distinctive ways of talking, listening, photographing, drawing, excavating, curating, etc. I put these into practice in certain landscapes, with certain artefacts, in particular museum and other institutional contexts, in particular human and political situations. That is how, as an archaeologist, with colleagues and collaborators I make knowledge of the world: in precisely the same manner in which any thing is formed. Archaeology is 'a way of *doing*' rather than just 'a way of *thinking*' (Edgeworth 2006b: xii). The same can be said of anthropology. In this sense, methodology and disciplinarity can be emancipatory, rather than restricting: allowing a kind of shifting, always messy positionality to emerge around which the idea of material culture studies can cohere. Aware that, while we are stuck with an awkward phrase, the idea of 'material culture studies' can highlight how both things and theories are always both events and effects: collapsing the idea of the 'humility of things' to encompass our own practices of witnessing, which must always be modest and provisional as they work from particular situations (both human and non-human). That sense of emergent positionality is precisely the contribution that studying things, whether small or large, in the first place can make.

CHAPTER 3

....

MATERIAL
GEOGRAPHIES

....

IAN COOK
DIVYA P. TOLIA-KELLY

INTRODUCTION

....

Geographers' engagements with materiality over the past decade have become the topic of widespread and sometimes heated debate. A steady trickle of articles has appeared critiquing the 'dematerialization' (Philo 2000) and advocating the 're-materialization' (Jackson 2000) of social and cultural geography, and claims have been made that wider 'materialist *returns*' are under way across the discipline (Whatmore 2006). Chris Philo's concerns about 'dematerialization' emerged through his reflections on the impact of geography's 'cultural turn' in the early 1990s. Too much of the work produced in its wake was too 'cultural', too 'immaterial', and too bound up in signs, symbols, texts, and discourses. It wasn't that he disliked this work, rather that its popularity had meant that too little attention was being paid to 'more "thingy", bump-into-able, stubbornly there-in-the-world kinds of "matter" (the material) with which earlier geographers tended to be more familiar' (Philo 2000: 33). In a similar vein, Peter Jackson (2000) expressed

This chapter has benefited from a number of readings, and we would like to thank the following for their comments on earlier drafts: Anjana Ford, Dan Hicks, Melanie Jackson, Barbara Bender, Jude Hill, Nicola Thomas, David Harvey, and Exeter University's Historical-Cultural Geography Research Group en masse.

his concern about a cultural geography too concerned with textual, cultural studies type work. He argued that research needed to be 'more firmly grounded' or, as he preferred to put it, 're-materialized' through a renewed emphasis on material culture (Jackson 2000: 9). Philo and Jackson discussed a number of long-standing material traditions in human geography. They referred both to studies relying on 'real world' data whose 'reality' the cultural turn had brought into question (Philo 2000) and, more specifically, to the discipline's material culture tradition based on 'Sauerian studies of landscape evolution or Kniffen's careful charting of the transformation of natural objects into regionally distinctive groupings of cultural artefacts and vernacular building styles' (Jackson 2000: 9–10; Crang 2005). Both also highlighted ongoing material work, including studies of: the 'fleshy' geographies of human bodies, actor networks, and human/non-human relations; material cultural geographies of consumption, cyberspace, and globalization; and the inhabitation of building spaces. Despite this talk of 'its' de- and re-materialization, it is important to emphasize that there never has been, nor is there now, a coherent approach to materiality in geography. Rather, as Sarah Whatmore argues, contemporary material geographies comprise a 'rich variety of analytical impulses, philosophical resources and political projects' that are 'a product of repetition turning seemingly familiar matters over and over, like the pebbles on a beach' (2006: 601).

Putting together a review of these geographies is therefore a difficult task. Others have struggled because 'materiality' is a term whose 'plasticity . . . can elide different and even incompatible ontological commitments' (Bakker and Bridge 2006: 6) and because 'geographers tend to use the material and immaterial as a shorthand for tensions between empirical and theoretical, applied and academic, concrete and abstract, reality and representation, quantitative and qualitative, objective and subjective, political economy and cultural studies, and so on' (Lees 2002: 102). We suspected that we might struggle, too, after exchanging the outlines of our 'material geographies' undergraduate modules, which had virtually nothing in common. This was perhaps because arguments about 'materiality' have become central to a disparate variety of geographical studies, including those that have attempted to (1) articulate 'culture' and 'economy', and 'postcolonialism' and 'global capitalism' (Cook and Harrison 2003: 298); (2) focus on the 'material realities and lived experience of oppression and injustice' (Pain and Bailey 2004: 320); (3) examine the 'material capacities of objects' as 'active mediator[s] of social relations' (Hoskins 2007: 437, 452); (4) think through 'the specificities of what matter does to bodies and the ways in which bodies materialise' (Colls 2007: 364); (5) reclaim 'the material' through the 'more sensuous "doing" of research exploring "bodies, performances and practices"' (Pain and Bailey 2004: 322); (6) 're-animate the missing "matter" of landscape . . . [as] co-fabricated between more-than-human bodies and a lively earth' (Whatmore 2006: 603); and (7) examine 'new viruses, climatic change, volcanoes, earthquakes and tsunamis' to remind us that 'humans are not the only actors on the planet' (Rose and Brook 2008: viii).

Attempts have been made to lend coherence to this work through identifying 'its' commitments to practice, affect, 'more-than-human modes of enquiry' and the politics of knowledge (Whatmore 2006: 604), and 'its' inadequate theorization of 'the material' as an 'unmediated, static, physicality' and/or an 'ostensive social structure that over-determines "the cultural"' (Kearnes 2003; Anderson and Tolia-Kelly 2004: 670; Anderson and Wylie 2009). Attempts have also been made to extend its remit to reassemble geography—often divided neatly down the middle into the 'physical' and the 'human'—into a more materially interconnected discipline (see Harrison *et al.* 2004a, 2004b, 2006). So, where do we start?

In the introduction to his edited collection on *Materiality*, anthropologist Daniel Miller (2005a) discusses how ethnographers constantly encounter the contradictory, juxtaposed, and incommensurable in their work. Cultural geographer Sarah Whatmore points out how new theorizations of materiality have often been provoked by 'public controversies . . . in which the practices of social, as well as natural, scientists have been caught up' (2006: 601). And archaeologist Duncan Garrow and sociologist Elizabeth Shove argue that getting scholars of materiality to analyse the same artefacts—in their case an unfinished stone axe and a toothbrush—can be an 'intriguing, surprising and intellectually rewarding' task (2007: 131). So, we thought that an event, encounter, or controversy might help us to better organize and think through our appreciations of material geographies.

Just before we began to work on this chapter, a cargo ship called the *MSC Napoli* ran aground off a stretch of coastline in south-west England and some of its containers washed up on local beaches (Figure 3.1). This quickly turned into an international controversy partly because of environmental consequences of the oil-spill that followed, but mainly because thousands of people rushed to the beach and helped themselves to the contents of the containers. The unexpected, controversial and incommensurable elements reported in the media, we thought, seemed somehow to mirror geographers' disparate engagements with materiality. So we decided to work with this '*Napoli* event'. Turning academic practice on its head, we wondered how this example could help us to understand this literature.

The *Napoli* was a 62,000-tonne container ship on its way from the English port of Felixstowe via Antwerp, Le Havre, and Las Palmas to Cape Town. On board were 26 crew and 2,394 forty-foot containers. Half of the containers were to be unloaded in South Africa. Inside them was a strange assortment of cargoes from motorbikes to flip flops (Table 3.1). The *Napoli* was due to dock in Cape Town on 29 January 2007. But on 18 January it was caught up in a violent storm in the English Channel, its hull was breached and it had to be abandoned. It subsequently developed severe structural failure as it was being towed east through continuing storms for repairs. So on 20 January it was beached along the south-west coast in the sheltered waters of Lyme Bay to prevent it breaking up at sea, causing an environmental catastrophe (BBC News 2007a).

Fig. 3.1 The container ship *MSC Napoli* grounded off the Devon coast, January 2007 (photo: Leon Neal/AFP/Getty Images).

Table 3.1 Cargo washed ashore at Branscombe, Devon after the shipwreck of the MSC Napoli, January 2007.

17 motorcycles marked 'BMW'	Organophosphate weedkillers and pesticides
Steering wheels	Methyl bromide
4X4 vehicles (mark unknown)	Beauty cream marked 'L'Oreal Revitalift'
Exhaust pipes	Beauty cream marked 'L'Oreal Men Expert
Sun visors	Revitalift'
A tractor	Shampoo marked 'Pantene Pro V'
A toy tractor	A refridgeration unit
Several hundred oak casks	Chocolate biscuits marked 'Troy' and 'Dance'
3,600 African language bibles	Hypodermic syringes
marked 'Izibhazo Ezingcweze'	Morphine
An oil painting picturing a Mediterranean villa	Dolls
with 2 large cypress trees to the left	Doll's houses
Sunglasses	Rolls of carpet
Leather jackets	Used office supplies (including a swivel chair)
Dog food marked 'Science Plan'	Games marked 'Nintendo X Box'
Cat food marked 'Science Plan'	Training shoes marked 'Reebok'
An Iraqi 50 dinar note	Training shoes marked 'Nike'
Large bales of woolen thread	A china tea set
Camera film marked 'Fuji'	Family photographs
Jeans	Battery acid
Nappies	Flip flops
Baby food	7 Ogden cigarette cards featuring pigeons
Bottles of vodka	

According to newspaper reports, for centuries Lyme Bay has been 'a place where mariners know you go for refuge when there is a storm' (*Sidmouth Herald* 2007a, 2007b). Its shallow, sandy waters are ideal beaching grounds as they can keep a stricken ship intact. Soon, however, a 200-tonne, 5-mile long oil slick from the wreck was threatening rare marine species. Reports emerged of the slick causing the deaths of three dolphins and over 1,000 seabirds that were unable to fly, dive for food, or float properly because they were covered in oil, or poisoned because they had ingested it (*Sidmouth Herald* 2007c; Morris 2007). The *Napoli* event began to gain international media coverage, albeit only after the stormy seas caused the ship to list by 35 degrees and to lose 103 containers overboard, 50 of which washed up on the beach of a tiny village called Branscombe. Initially, local people helped themselves to their contents. But, after reports of people wheeling away brand new BMW motorbikes reached the national media, thousands more joined them from as far away as Belgium in what became a 'big self-service party' (Kazim 2007). The legality of this mass 'salvage', 'beachcombing', 'treasure-hunting', 'scavenging', or 'looting' quickly became an issue. Goods removed from the beach, it transpired, were required by law to be reported to the official Receiver of the Wreck. Perhaps the most widely reported story in the international press ran as follows:

Anita Bokdal, 60, and husband Jan, 58, run a landscaping business near native Stockholm and a winery in South Africa and were shipping personal belongings to South Africa on MSC *Napoli* 'to make it feel like home'. Instead, she watched in horror as her container was broken open and paintings, embroideries, a Rosenthal tea set and carpets were removed.... Mrs Bokdal appealed to anyone who took two embroidered pictures made by her father-in-law to return them as they have great sentimental value. 'There was also a hand-made copper table, like a tray, which came from Jan's grandmother'.

> *Sidmouth Herald* (2007c; see also CNN 2007; ABC 2007; Malan 2007)

In the weeks and months that followed, the containers remaining on board were removed, while others washed up on the beach during fresh storms. A large-scale clean-up operation was mounted, and a salvage company was hired to break the *Napoli* into pieces, to be towed to a shipyard in Belfast, Northern Ireland, for 'recycling' (*Exmouth Journal* 2007a; *Exmouth Herald* 2007). Alongside, and bound up in these events, a '*Napoli* story' took shape, was told and retold. The unfolding event had been documented by a local history group called the *Branscombe Project*, headed by retired heritage anthropologist Barbara Bender. In October 2007, they staged a *Napoli* exhibition in Branscombe's Village Hall (*Express and Echo* 2007; Joint 2007; Roberts 2008). And, a month later, the *Napoli* event was the basis of an installation by artist Melanie Jackson in an exhibition called *Human Cargo: The Transatlantic Slave Trade, its Abolition and Contemporary Legacies in Plymouth and Devon*, in the City Museum and Art Gallery of the nearby port city, Plymouth (Human Cargo 2007a).

For us, the *Napoli* event and its aftermath illustrate some of the complexities of the work that we should be covering here. The *Napoli's* multiple materialities became the subject of widespread attention, excitement, debate, concern, and manipulation. Others may recognize other material geographies in this event but for us, it both showcases and questions work in three principal areas: landscape, commodity, and creative geographies. Below, then, we first discuss issues raised by *this* wreck disgorging its cargo in *this* place. We look at Lyme Bay in general and Branscombe beach in particular as landscapes where, in cultural geographical terms, the lives of people living there are intrinsically linked to the shape and heritage of this site. Secondly, we discuss issues raised by commodities on their way to South Africa being washed up on, and 'scavenged' from, this beach. We look at stories of ruptures in the 'traffic in things' (Jackson 1999) and the insights they provide about the relations between people, places, and commodities. Thirdly, we look at issues raised by the *Branscombe Project* and Melanie Jackson who creatively engaged with the *Napoli* event and story, well after the 'scavenging' had ended and the beaches had been cleaned. Here, we look at ways in which materials can be worked *with* to appreciate and express events in ways that words alone cannot convey. And, finally, we conclude by offering our thoughts on what writing such an event-based review has taught us about the 'material geographical' work (not) featured in this chapter.

LANDSCAPE

The site of the *Napoli* disaster contributed much to the reasons why it held the front pages and press interest for well over 12 months. The heritage identity of this stretch of coastline was pivotal to the stories told. The despoiling of a national treasure—a heritage landscape—drew attention and evoked emotionally charged reactions. Just as pivotal was the fact that commercial actions had resulted in the beaching of a ship here. Lyme Bay is part of a 95-mile stretch of Devon and Dorset coastline known as the *Jurassic Coast*. This 'beautiful wild landscape' (Kazim 2007), historically renowned by fossil hunters and 'made famous by Thomas Hardy as *Dead Man's Bay* in his fictional Wessex' (Roberts 2008) is a UNESCO World Heritage Site (Jurassic Coast nd; UNESCO nd). UNESCO had recognized the 'natural heritage' of this coastline, whose exposures provide 'an almost continuous sequence of Triassic, Jurassic, and Cretaceous rock formations spanning the Mesozoic Era and document approximately 185 million years of Earth history' (UNESCO nd). The *Jurassic Coast* website boasts that its footpath 'offers the walker stunning views, with a bird's eye view of many coastal features...the drama of sheer cliff faces,...the strangely eroded rock formations and above all,...the geology' (Jurassic Coast nd). The beaching of a stricken cargo vessel on this stretch of coastline confronted established constructions of its official, 'natural' heritage, with a more raucous, popular, 'cultural' heritage in which 'salvage has always been part of life on this rugged Devon coast' (Savill 2007a).

Newspapers reported that only seven of the containers that initially washed on to the beach broke open on their own. The rest were 'smashed open' as 'gangs descended', 'scattering the containers' contents across the pebble beach' (Morris 2007), 'litter[ing] the World Heritage Site' (*Sidmouth Herald* 2007d) and allegedly increasing the wreck's 'damage to the environment by 800%' (Morris 2007) (Figure 3.2). This turned Branscombe residents' 'whole world...upside down' (*Exmouth Journal* 2007b). Many 'scavengers' reported getting caught up in the excitement of this 'free-for-all'. One recalled, 'We don't make a habit of doing things like this' (*Sidmouth Herald* 2007c), while another said, 'I took a jelly shoe and [some] photos, and saw people taking personal things away, it was horrifying' (*Sidmouth Herald* 2007e). The local coastguard office described this behaviour as 'crass greed' (Morris 2007). Local journalists likened those who took things from the beach to 'a plague of locusts sweeping through the village' or 'vultures picking over the entrails of Branscombe' (*Sidmouth Herald* 2007f). Anita Bokdal said that the people who took her possessions had behaved 'like a lot of savages' (BBC News 2007b), and a local man described what he had witnessed as 'human nature at its worst' (Roberts 2008). In the future, local politicians argued, one aspect of this landscape's 'heritage' needed to be protected from the other. As one put it, 'This is a World Heritage site. We don't want every sinking ship brought in here' (Sturcke and Morris 2007).

Fig. 3.2 Thousands of people arrive on Branscombe beach to search through the containers (photo: Leon Neal/AFP/Getty Images).

These kinds of claims and discourses bring to light the types of practices that are acceptable and unacceptable from citizens in particular places. Notions of who or what is appropriate where resonate throughout these responses to the materials washed up on Branscombe beach, the reflections on the economies and flows of stuff and capital, and the moral geographies of landscape, nature, and folk that make up local society and culture. According to cultural geographer Doreen Massey (2006), landscapes—although touchable and seemingly permanent—should be appreciated as 'liquid', as in constant formation and flow. Here, she argues, 'a landscape, these hills, are the (temporary) product of a meeting up of trajectories out of which mobile uncertainty a future is—has to be—negotiated' (Massey 2006: 48). This is how geographers are now tending to interrogate matter in place and space: as mobile, and converging at points of encounter. The American cultural geographer Carl Sauer (1965 [1925]) treated the morphology of landscape as evidence of the material lives, material cultures, social rhythms, and cultural heritage of the people who had lived upon it. For cultural theorist Stuart Hall this view of heritage 'becomes the material embodiment of the spirit of nation, a collective representation of the British version of tradition, a concept pivotal to the lexicon of [national] virtues' (1999: 4). The material of land, soil, and nature can become woven into the national identity and history of Britain. Yet, as historical geographers such as David Harvey (2003) have argued, we can learn a great deal more about national identities through critically examining the heritage of heritage, unravelling the seemingly benign and 'natural' embeddedness of its values, and questioning the ways in which 'heritage' can politically exclude 'others' from the national story (see also Johnson 2000).

Understandings of the physical materialities of landscapes have served as blurry subtexts to mythologies materializing nationality via notions of bounded senses of belonging, of a 'natural' flora, fauna species, architecture, peoples, languages, and races (Tolia-Kelly 2007). Physical bodies, cells, blood groups, and DNA, for example, have become the material tools for evidencing 'proper' national citizens, in the case of 'proper women' (Colls 2004) or a 'British race' (Holloway 2003, 2004, 2005; Nash 2005) belonging to a national landscape (Young 2007). The collision between the material bodies of 'other' cultures and of a native 'national' culture have been shown to be present in modern-day tourism. Here the biology of the tourist or plant species re-emerges as significant in questions of whether they are accepted, belong, and can engage (Johnson 2004; Saldanha 2007). The materialities of race, of the racialized body, and the racialized cultures of that body have been seen as concretized through exclusion from certain landscapes, especially those of the countryside (Agyeman and Neal 2006), the national cultures of landscape (Daniels 1993) and Englishness (Matless 1998; Darby 2000). Landscapes are *nationalized*, and the nation *naturalized* (Kaufmann 1998; Jazeel 2005).

As part of this push to understand the heritage of heritage, geographers and others have argued that it is part of a nation's economy as much as it is of its history. Thus Stuart Hall (1999) argues that who is catered for, which transport routes are funded, and what facilities are provided shape and re-shape access to the landscape, but also perpetuate questions of whose heritage is reproduced. Heritage landscapes can therefore be seen as encountered both through branding and through embodied experience. Stories of a past that can be unlocked through walking, fossil hunting, imagining, and gazing, and recreated through embodied encounters with it, have evolved in relation to films, toys, and the currency of dinosaurs in their natural world, 185 million years ago. In this respect, the popular success of Steven Spielberg's *Jurassic Park* film in the 1990s and the naming of the *Jurassic Coast* World Heritage Site were not unrelated (Rocksborough-Smith 2001). Physical nature and landscape can serve as a site for textual practice, upon and through which narratives are written, where the texture, natures, forms and feel of the landscape become tools for the narrator as opposed to being felt, experienced, or encountered before or beyond narrative. Here, narratives of 'heritage' site and 'Jurassic' time combine to form an alternative 'real', a narration that abstracts the material space of this stretch of Devon and Dorset coastline to serve a discourse of the gigantic (Stewart 1993), its scale of excess and enormity making it more than the sum of its parts.

But what of those writers who argue that matter is always fluid, in the process of *becoming*, and cannot be experienced as a known material? Political theorist Jane Bennett (2001) for example, urges us to consider the animatedness, liveliness, and enchantment in people's encounters with landscapes and other things. The call to engage with memories of other times and spaces embedded within the experience of these encounters as landscapes and other things refract, emanate, and, some-times, 'magically' transport us to other sites has recently been taken up by a number of British cultural geographers (see Tolia-Kelly 2004a, 2004b; Hill 2007). For example, John Wylie (2005: 236), walking along this very coast path sets out a phenomenology of landscape experience that 'aims to spotlight tones, texts and topographies from which distinctive articulations of self and landscape [can] arise'. Here, the coastal pathway is inhabited by the silent traveller who is aware of his/her embodied encounters between feet and path, meteorology and emotion. As well as immediate phenomena, then, our engagements with land and materials are shaped ontologically, through various knowledge, memories, histories, and discourses that come before such encounters. For writers on material geographies, however, different elements of these encounters are privileged (e.g. Kearnes 2003).

Returning to that stretch of the Devon and Dorset coastline, we can see how the wrecking of the *Napoli* and the 'scavenging' of its goods exposed a number of these landscape relations: of memory and walking, consumption and commodity routes, and historical and modern identity. In time, this event will no doubt become a *naturalized* story of this landscape. Yet, throughout 2007, media stories emphasized the stark contrasts between a *Jurassic Coast* characterized by natural beauty and leisure and the *Napoli* wreck. The contents of its containers were represented as vile detritus, disengaged from the human architecture of its being. The wreck was positioned as jarring with the sites of a heritage story. Yet, it also attracted more out of season visitors to the area both to 'scavenge' and to see the spectacle. Along with a number of locals, many were seen to have exhibited behaviours, attitudes, and interests that were not welcome in this place. (Im)moral geographies took shape on Branscombe's beach as the containers were plundered. In media accounts, this was contrasted to an acceptable face of local and visitor culture, motivation, and conduct. The bands of 'scavengers' were deemed uncivilized and unworthy of a Devon welcome. Calling them 'savages' or 'locusts' positioned them as 'non-people', as bodies that were 'other', both to this landscape and to the nation (see Holloway 2005, 2007).

The *Napoli* wreck left Branscombe vulnerable to this kind of invasion. The way in which these visitors valued and appropriated the washed up goods jarred with the values of regional citizenship and 'national civility' that these media accounts celebrated (see Gilroy 1991; Daniels 1993). These values often assume a state of stable immobility (Sheller and Urry 2006), but the mobility of the *Napoli*, its debris, and its 'scavengers' threatened them. Where matter is suddenly displaced, suddenly 'out of place', it can be defiling and contaminating, disrupting to the status quo, even if it does not change in form or aesthetics (Bickerstaff and Walker 2003). Visitors' bodies were equalized with the oil, rubbish, commodities, and debris of the *Napoli*. All were material equals in the narration of the beaching as unwelcome in, and inappropriate to, this place.

COMMODITIES

These weren't the only stories about people, places, and things that emerged in the wake of the *Napoli* wreck. Other material geographies came to the surface as questions were asked about where these commodities had come from, where they were going to, where they ended up, and to whom they belonged. As well as landscape, heritage, and citizenship, the wrecking of the *Napoli* was a story of trade. The English Channel is the busiest shipping lane in the world. Container ships pass by this stretch of England's coast every day. Their cargoes are often mysterious, even for those working on board (Sekula 2003). So when one runs aground, its containers wash up on the beach, and its various cargoes spill out, we have a fascinating, momentary insight into world trade. What was being taken to South Africa from these European ports? What connections, which might not ordinarily be questioned, became known through this disaster?

All kinds of commodities, in all stages of their life histories, were washed up: brand new motorcycles, car parts, flip-flops, empty oak wine barrels, nappies, packets of biscuits, bibles, personal possessions, second-hand clothes, and much more (see Table 3.1). They were for sale to the public or to other companies, or were for distribution, exchange or (re)use in other ways. But their hidden travels were disrupted, and this disruption affected people. For example, because of its just-in-time production process, a South African Volkswagen factory expecting parts being shipped on the *Napoli* from Germany had to slow down production for 2 weeks (SABC News 2007). Similarly, the South African vineyards expecting a delivery of oak barrels had their wine production disrupted as they had to wait several weeks for a new shipment (Styles 2007). And individuals, like the Bokdals, who had shipped their possessions in one of these containers, had lost not only unique things—like photographs, tea-sets, furniture, and embroidered pictures— but also memories of people, relationships, and life events that they embodied. Newspaper stories reported that many were desperate to recover their personal possessions (see Bowerman 2007; G. Roberts 2007; Savill 2007b).

For people 'scavenging' that beach, however, these things had no such histories and connections (Figure 3.3). This was a 'treasure chest' (Savill 2007a). The containers and their contents had appeared unexpectedly, as if from nowhere, and their contents were taken, given new lives, and sometimes returned (Plymouth City Council 2007; *Sidmouth Herald* 2007c). Meanwhile the wrecked *Napoli*, itself a massive commodity produced in South Korea and 'consumed' (through its use and travels) all around the world, had to be salvaged. It was to be

Fig. 3.3 A woman collects cosmetic products washed up on Branscombe beach, Devon, January 2007.

broken up at sea and its parts towed to a Belfast shipyard for 'recycling' (see *Sidmouth Herald* 2007g, 2007h, 2007i, 2007j; *Exmouth Journal* 2007c).

This is the sort of event that brings to life, and can help to question, work that has been undertaken on the (material) geographies of commodities. These geographies are, in many ways, nothing new. Socio-cultural anthropologist Daniel Miller, for instance, recalls a school geography class in which he 'watched well-meaning videos of smiling plantation workers followed by the arrival of cocoa by ship to Britain where it was turned into bars of chocolate' (2003: 368). But, after lying low for 'a generation or more in...the dusty backrooms of economic geography', the late 1990s saw these geographies making a 'striking resurgence' in the discipline (Jackson 1999, 2002; Bridge and Smith 2003: 257). This resurgence has involved two related areas of research. First, there are studies of the material cultural geographies of consumption (Jackson and Thrift 1995). Here, for example, ethnographic studies of the acquisition, wearing, tidying, sorting, and divestment of clothes has provided a lens through which to make wider senses of relations between emotional and embodied experiences, memories, and individual/collective identities within and between the spaces, places, and times of people's lives (Gregson and Crewe 1997, 2003; Colls 2004, 2006; Gregson and Beale 2004; Gregson *et al.* 2007a, 2007b). Secondly, there are cultural-economic studies of commodity chains, circuits or networks, grounded in multisited ethnographic research and informed by the idea of the 'social lives of things' (Appadurai 1986a; G.E. Marcus 1995; P. Jackson 1999). Here, geographers have used the movements of commodities such as cut flowers, food, and clothes to research everyday exploitations, inequalities, value-contestations and consumers' reliance on countless unseen others around the world to enable them to live the lives they live every day (e.g. Hughes 2000; Cook *et al.* 2004; Cook and Harrison 2007; P. Benson and Fischer 2007; Crewe 2008).

Much of this work has drawn upon arguments that material culture studies serve as lenses through which to appreciate complex relations between wider, deeper, and more abstract processes, and, thereby, as means to critique the 'application' of abstract theoretical arguments (Marcus 1995; D. Miller 1998b; Jackson 2000; Leyshon *et al.* 2003). Yet theoretical approaches and concepts (e.g. Marxian concepts of 'alienation' and 'commodity fetishism', post-structural understandings of the liveliness and excess of 'matter' and the co-agency of humans and non-humans, and the political 'edges' that such approaches possess) continually clash and work together through this work (see Leslie and Reimer 1999; Hartwick 2000; Jackson 2000, 2002; Bakker and Bridge 2006). The effects that different forms of academic production (e.g. theorizing, fieldwork, 'story-telling', dissemination, collaboration) can have on students and other publics have also been the subject of much conjecture and some experimentation as authors consider how, when, where, and if the materialities and connective aesthetics of these commodity geographies can inspire audiences, confuse them, spark them into action, overwhelm them, encourage senses of connection, responsibility and care, recognize differences already being made, and so on (see Hartwick 1998, 2000; Cook *et al.* 2000, 2007; Friedberg 2003; Castree 2004; Barnes 2006; Barnett and Land 2007).

While these material geographies have arguably made considerable headway within and beyond the discipline (Miller 2003; Slater and Miller 2006; Foster 2006), four principal limitations have also been pointed out. First, treating commodities as entities that have 'biographies' has been deemed problematic because of the impression that can be given that they are discrete, stable, bounded entities with simple, identifiable 'origins' and destinations, rather than entities that are more complex assemblages (Cook and Crang 1996; Cook *et al.* 2004; Latham and McCormack 2004). For some, a focus on consumption has been at the expense of an acknowledgement of the roles that commodities play in other aspects of (other) people's lives, producers in particular. Yet, critics wanting to complicate the figure of the simple, linear commodity chain linking consumers and producers have added to this the lack of attention paid not only to the lives of their designers, distributors, retailers, repairers, disposers, collectors, re-sellers, thieves, counterfeiters, and others (Gregson and Crewe 1997; Crewe and Gregson 2003; Pratt 2004; Hetherington 2004), but also to the companies and other organizations that act as the 'consumers' of commodities (e.g. car parts and wine barrels made for factories and wineries), which are often not available on the 'open' market (Rusten and Bryson 2007). Secondly, critics have pointed out a tendency for researchers to study heavily advertised or fetishized 'cultural' or 'discretionary' commodities (Bridge and Smith 2003; Bakker and Bridge 2006; Goss 2006)—primarily food and/or clothing (often 'fairly' traded) but also furniture (Reimer and Leslie 2008), gold (Hartwick 1998), and diamonds (Le Billon 2006)—and to ignore the material geographies of 'hidden' and/or more 'industrial' commodities such as steel, oil, rubber, spark plugs, etc. (although see Hollander 2003 on sugar; Mansfield 2003 on surimi; Page 2005 on water). Thirdly, there is a tendency for researchers to study consumption by relatively wealthy people in the global North and production by relatively poor people in the global South, leaving this body of work open to accusations of Eurocentrism, of neglecting the material geographies of poorer people, and of neglecting North–North, South–South, and North–South trade (Jaffee *et al.* 2004; although see Miller 1998a on Coca-Cola in Trinidad; Friedberg 2005 on French beans in Burkina Faso; Kothari and Laurie 2005 and Edensor and Kothari 2006 on 'Western' clothing in Bolivia and Mauritius; and Horst and Miller 2006 on mobile phones in Jamaica). Fourthly, the commodities chosen by geographers of material culture and of the 'social life of things' have usually been tangible, solid, stable, touchable, everyday, popular, harmless, small, human-oriented commodities. Those that are, for example, gaseous, unstable, dangerous, massive, minuscule, illegal, or not for *human* consumption, have tended to be neglected (although see Jacobs 2006 and Jenkins 2002 on buildings; Anderson *et al.* 2007, Anderson 2007, Kearnes 2007, Doubleday 2007 on nanotechnology; and Gregson *et al.* (nd) on ships).

If we return to the beach at Branscombe, we can now ask how the commodity stories that emerged from the *Napoli* event echo and question what has been researched by commodity geographers. The *Napoli* was a container ship taking goods produced in the north for consumption in the south, and powerful stories emerged in the media about the ways in which these were, and became, involved in numerous identities, places, and relationships. First, they showed how the 'social lives of things' unfold both before and beyond their sites of purchase and consumption. The loss of commodities highlighted vital relationships between things and memories in the process of place making. The Bokdals, for instance, were shipping well-worn possessions, gifts, family heirlooms, and other items to their new home in South Africa in order to make it 'feel like home' (*Sidmouth Herald* 2007k). Yet most of the commodities salvaged had not yet had the chance to develop such lives and roles. Here were brand new flip-flops, nappies, bibles, motorbikes, and barrels that weren't being sold through any official channels and weren't part of a neat display in a shop or dealership. They were dumped on a beach and became part of their consumers' lives through 'scavenging' and via eBay or car boot sales (Beckford 2007; Kazim 2007; Savill 2007a; Williams 2007). Although work on second-hand markets is well developed (see Crewe and Gregson 2003; Hetherington 2004), and a literature on commodities taking unconventional routes between places of manufacture and sale (via the so-called 'grey' or 'parallel' market) is developing (see Kothari and Laurie 2005; Edensor and Kothari 2006; Yeung and Mok 2006), these stories suggest that commodity geographies involving spaces of questionable legal provision and consumption are missing from the current literature.

Secondly, these stories vividly reveal the limited range of commodities that geographers (and others) have tended to study. While studies of new and second-hand clothes (see Crewe and Gregson 2003; Miller and Woodward 2007), nickel (see Bakker and Bridge 2006), and container ships (see Gregson *et al.* nd) have been undertaken, the *Napoli* was carrying little else that commodity geographers have been interested in. There are no studies of 'cultural' or 'discretionary' commodities such as bibles, nappies, sunglasses, 'L'Oreal Revitalift' cream, or bottles of Vodka. The neglect of 'hidden' or 'industrial' commodities is starkly revealed by the *Napoli* event: where, for example, are the material geographical studies of exhaust pipes, battery acid, large balls of woollen thread, methyl bromide, or hypodermic syringes? The narrow range of commodities chosen for study raises additional questions about how and why certain commodities end up 'mattering' enough for researchers to want to study them, and what the politics and ethics of these choices might be. These issues are rarely, if ever, discussed (although see Crang and Cook 2007).

Finally, these media stories—local, national, and international—were themselves commodities with their own, quite different social lives (B. Bender, pers. comm., 2008). They not only reported but also very clearly contributed to the ways in which the *Napoli* event unfolded. As a result of a series of attention-grabbing news stories, Branscombe was unexpectedly put on the map. Local businesses cashed in on this: boat owners charged tourists for trips around the remains of the wreck, Branscombe's post office sold souvenir DVDs of the *Napoli* drama (Malone 2008); hoteliers reported increased bookings (*Sidmouth Herald* 2007l); a local brewery produced a *Napoli* ale (*Sidmouth Herald* 2007k); another company produced a cider brandy called 'Shipwrecked', which had been matured in 'salvaged' oak barrels bound for that South African winery (Usbourne 2008); and a pub in nearby Sidmouth changed its name to the 'Swag Inn' and the names of some of its beers to 'pirate' or 'booty' 'as a tribute to the media frenzy over the grounding of the *MSC Napoli*—with the regular pub sign replaced by one of the cargo ship's containers lying half submerged underwater' (*Sidmouth Herald* 2007m). Geographers have rarely researched multiple, mediated, and conjoined materialities like these (although see Ateljevic and Doorne 2004; Goss 2004; Latham and McCormack 2004). But materializations of the *Napoli* event have proliferated, gradually becoming naturalized in the Jurassic Coast's changing landscape narrative.

CREATIVITY

It was not only through the media that accounts of the *Napoli* event were put together and disseminated. There was more to this story than was, or could be, conveyed through words, photos, sound, and video. The material geographies of the event were also expressed by curators and artists working—like that brandy manufacturer—*with* the wreck's materials. The *Napoli* was the subject of an exhibition in Branscombe village hall in October 2007 that was put together by a local history group called the Branscombe Project. Its curator, retired heritage anthropologist and village resident Barbara Bender, explained to journalists, 'We camcorded things right from the start, it's a view from the bottom up' (Joint 2007). Visitors to the exhibition encountered hundreds of photos, newspaper reports, paintings, songs, and transcribed and filmed interviews with Branscombe residents. The village hall was also home to an art installation made from the wreck's debris, to which villagers unexpectedly added debris that they had collected (*Express and Echo* 2007; B. Bender, pers. comm.). Other examples of debris art were also reported in the local papers (*Sidmouth Herald* 2007e). A month later, and 60 miles away, the *Napoli* became part of an art exhibition in Plymouth. *Human Cargo* was one of many commemorations of the bicentenary of the British government's 1807 *Act for the Abolition of the Slave Trade* (Bressey 2009). Melanie Jackson's *The Undesirables* was installed in the museum's Maritime Collection Gallery and consisted of a three-dimensional paper model of the *Napoli* wreck set on the parquet floor and a 'flimsy panorama of etchings' or 'paper sculptures' depicting that Jurassic Coast landscape, those containers and commodities, the people 'scavenging' them, and the media reporting of that 'scavenging' all seemingly 'washed up' in a corner (Hoad 2007; Jaya 2007). Fascinated by the extraordinary juxtaposition of goods usually hidden from view by containerization, Jackson carefully researched those that were washed up on the beach, interviewed cargo workers, and included the list of washed-up commodities (reproduced in Table 3.1) and the eyewitness accounts collected by Bender and her colleagues for the Branscombe Project (Human Cargo 2007a, 2007b; Hoad 2007) (Figures 3.4 and 3.5). Writing about the creative process, Jackson explained how this was inspired by the content and scale of media reports of the event:

Etching was the traditional means of reproduction for circulating scenes of shipwreck. The satellite TV vans and film crews incited and were as much a part of this story as the cargo and the crowd. Every identified media image of the scavengers, the cargo, the loping ship and the media itself was produced as a drypoint etching at the scale of the newspaper image or the TV screen. It was the (impossible) attempt to piece together the scene in its entirety . . . from fragments of reportage and TV coverage, and the transcripts of eyewitness accounts. Out of the context of the newspaper and the screen the scale of the imagery operates very differently. It is a serious attempt to reconstruct and map out a story, but it is also a playful theatre of the absurd.

M. Jackson (pers. comm., 2008)

Promotional materials emphasized *The Undesirables'* associations with nineteenth-century models, panoramas, and paper theatres (Human Cargo 2007a, 2007b), and the text on the gallery wall stated that it:

recall[s] Hogarth's satirical commentaries on the excesses of 18th century society, and 19th century images of shipwrecks. Installed in the South Gallery, this work connects with the maritime history of Plymouth, in particular to the adjacent painting, *A Stormy Evening*, by Hely Smith (1862–1941). Bequeathed by a local ship owner, it depicts a cargo liner thought to be of the Castle Line, which worked routes to South Africa.

One reviewer likened *The Undesirables* to the 'bizarre juxtapositions of Dadaist poetry' and argued that siting it in this maritime gallery space took advantage of 'the opportunity an old museum offers for making connections between incongruous objects which, in the present context, becomes a political act that is akin to Walter Benjamin's study of the remains of the first shopping centres, the Parisian Arcades, in the 30s, which was intended to reveal the underlying economic structures and history of capitalism' (Glen 2007).

These exhibitions comprise a small but fascinating selection of the material geographical afterlives of the *Napoli* wreck. They tie together the arguments in this chapter's previous sections as geographies, landscapes, commodities, memories, and identities are tightly interwoven in both. However, they also point towards the third area of literature that we want to highlight: where geographers have studied,

Fig. 3.4 Melanie Jackson's *The Undesirables*: the *MSC Napoli* grounded on the gallery floor (photo: John Melville).

Fig. 3.5 Melanie Jackson's *The Undesirables*: paper sculptures of a child, some debris, and Branscombe beach (photo: Melanie Jackson).

collaborated with, been, and/or sought to become museum curators and artists. This work is important because it shows how geographers are beginning to *work with and through*—rather than just write about—the materialities they are interested in. There is a long history of geographical interest in art (Cant and Morris 2006) but, as Foster and Lorimer (2007: 425–426) explain,

geographers [now] look to artists to help their research 'outreach' to communities; geographers have been curators of art exhibitions; artists exhibit and perform at geography conferences, as well as offer papers; university departments host artists' residencies; artists contribute to geographers' research projects; artists employ a spatialised vocabulary to label, describe and explain their work that geographers recognise as their own.

In the United Kingdom, for example, new crossover work has emerged from geography Ph.D. students co-funded by research councils and museums (e.g. Butler 2006, 2007; Geoghegan in press); from geographers who were previously—and continue to work as—curators and/or artists (e.g. Paglen 2006; Scalway 2006; DeSilvey 2006, 2007); from geographers and artists working together through 'artist in residence' schemes (e.g. Driver *et al.* 2002; University of Sussex 2005, Prudames 2005; Foster and Lorimer 2007); and from geographers working with artists and curators in other ways (e.g. Cook *et al.* 2000; Anderson *et al.* 2001; Griffiths 2004; Hoskins 2007; N. J. Thomas 2007; Tolia-Kelly 2007). Such work often focuses attention on the materialities of geographic and artistic/curatorial practice, and the ways in which these can differently shape, for want of a better word, to 'capture' and draw others into research projects.

From the limited number of examples that have made it into print, it is possible to identify three kinds of work in this vein. First, like the *Napoli* artwork made from the wreck's debris, a number of geographers have collaborated with people who have much more experience of 'working practically *with* materials' to engage their audiences (Ingold 2007a: 3). Here, for instance, cartographer Edward Kinman and ceramic artist John Williams (2007) have collaborated in a project 'mapping' the lived histories of the land on which their university now stands. They talk about the significance of using clay tiles as the 'canvas' for their maps. While Williams 'was fascinated with clay's innate ability to record flame patterns in the kiln, the marks of the maker, and the patina of use. Clay had memory' (Kinman and Williams 2007: 435); for Kinman, 'clay tiles [were] one of the earliest cartographic mediums' and, given the focus on landscape, 'we wanted to use a material representative of our subject in the artwork.... we took material from the ground and altered it' (Kinman and Williams 2007: 441). Physical geographers, who are often more professionally attuned to physical materials than their human geography colleagues, have also contributed their expertise to art collaborations. Take, for example, the artificial pebbles created by coastal erosion specialist Uwe Dornbusch and artist Johanna Berger. Made from clear, tinted resin so they can be easily seen, and with a copper core so they can be found using a metal detector, these are used to track the movement of real pebbles along shorelines through processes of coastal erosion (see Williams *et al.* 2005). They are left in one location and after a specified period of time are collected from others where they have washed up. Working with Dornbusch as an 'artist in residence', Berger made 11 new pebbles, wrapping romantic messages typed on pieces of paper around the copper cores. Placed on and followed from a French beach, it was hoped that these 'romantic rocks'—like messages in bottles—would capture the public imagination and draw attention to coastal erosion and to academic work helping to make sense of it (University of Sussex 2005; Prudames 2005). For these collaborators, the properties of their materials, the ways in which they could be worked, and the ways in which they had a liveliness of their own, was essential for provoking imaginations and senses of appreciation.

Secondly, the way in which Jackson's work was sited in that Plymouth gallery—and perhaps also the way in which the various elements of the *Napoli* exhibition were arranged in Branscombe's village hall—echoes observations made by geographers of the ways in which artists have created 'spaces for imagination' through appropriate arrangements of found and crafted materials. For example, in their work with theatre group London Bubble, geographers Alison Blunt *et al.* (2007) describe what was added to a play about migration by its taking place in a 'real' domestic space. London Bubble's *My Home* was performed in a house whose 'rich material layering . . . suggested the presence of the past in ways which mirrored a central theme of the monologues: memory and the interaction of homes past and present, particularly the relationship between places left behind and current homes' (Blunt *et al.* 2007: 315; cf. Tolia-Kelly 2004a, 2004b). Similarly, in his discussion of a social sculpture called *Exchange Values: images of invisible lives* by artist Shelley Sacks, geographer Ian Cook *et al.* (2000) describes the way in which its component parts—banana skins, dried, cured, and stitched into panels hung around the walls of a gallery, headphones beneath each panel allowing visitors to hear recordings of the farmers who grew them talking about their lives, and tens of thousands of loose, dried, and cured skins neatly arranged in a rectangle on the floor—were arranged to have a visceral as well as thought-provoking effect on gallery visitors. Staring at those panels, looking closely at those skins, smelling those bananas, listening to those voices in their heads, then turning around to see those loose and mute skins on the floor, Sacks (quoted in Cook *et al.* 2000: 342) explained how she had worked with these materials to create a 'reflective space. A space of possibility. Where connections can be seen. Felt. Thought through'. In all three examples, we argue, the properties of materials and spaces, and the ways in which they were drawn upon, (re)worked, (re)arranged, and juxtaposed to include participants' bodies, memories, and imaginations were essential for provoking vivid more-than-textual appreciations.

Thirdly, if we contend that this chapter, like the exhibitions, is also a materialization of the *Napoli* event, our attention is drawn to geographer's work on and with more traditional practices of drawing and writing. Drawing, particularly in the form of field sketching, is an important but dying art in the discipline (Cloke *et al.* 2004). The embodied micro-geographic materialities of drawing have, however, been recently reflected upon by Helen Scalway, an artist who has moved into geography:

Drawing, like other embodied practices, is a form of corporeal knowing. What I had not foreseen was what it would reveal. At one moment I would find my pen whisking sharply along a steel rule as I sought to re-enact the lines of a rack of metal shelves or lighting unit, the next, the pen went whisping and wandering at an entirely different speed and pressure among the tendrils of a flowery boteh.

Scalway (2006: 456)

Writing has also been the subject of attention for material geographers. Caitlin DeSilvey's (2006, 2007) curatorial/Ph.D. work on a neglected Montana homestead, which involved working with the lively but decaying materialities of found (and archived) items, is a case in point. Here she writes, for example, about an 'over-stuffed bushel basket in the homestead's harness shed', which she tipped out to find 'scraps of printed matter mixed with a mass of pits and seeds, woolly fibre and feathers, long johns and holey socks, a 1928 license plate and a few delicate mouse spines' (DeSilvey 2006: 333). Working with these materials, DeSilvey wanted to make 'an intervention in the homestead's histories' through 'an interpretive practice willing to engage in serious play with artefacts that might otherwise be overlooked entirely' (DeSilvey 2006: 334). She did this through writing, assembling a poem from the words visible on those scraps of paper. This, she argued, was co-authored with the writers of the original magazine articles and the mice who chewed them up to leave her with the words on those scraps of paper with which to work. These examples add to our understandings of creative processes by highlighting the ways in which the ordinary materialities and practices of academic work (see for example Ogborn 2004) are, and can be developed differently as and through, creative processes.

What we are describing here, perhaps, are parts of an emerging field of 'creative geographies' (Wylie in press) that combine established and innovative research practices in work that aims to reach out beyond the text and/or beyond the academy. The Branscombe exhibition and *The Undesirables* both worked *with* old and *created* new materializations in ways that echo geographers' contemporary appreciations of materiality. Both also used these materializations to engage local and gallery-going publics in the significance of the *Napoli* event in ways that echo recent developments in participatory, public, and pedagogic geographies (see Kindon *et al.* 2008). In Branscombe village hall, the exhibition materialized the memories of locals, and exhibited the pieces of a heritage story for the nation. It was a means through which the geography, history, and local memories of this site could be made, re-made, and reflected upon (Hoeschler and Alderman 2004). While the exhibition drew upon conventional practices of heritage writing and political ideology (Hewison 1987), the wreck and its debris called for alternative hierarchies and localized conventions that could incorporate radical cultural accounts in tune with rhythms of nature, culture, and international trade. The hall was home to plural accounts that were not shackled by bounded senses of national identity linked to blood, soil, nature, and sensibilities (Schama 1995). These accounts emerged out of Bender's combined roles as Branscombe resident, head of the Branscombe Project and heritage anthropologist, and the expertise of her fellow villagers who *together* created and transformed the exhibition. This was the kind of public, participatory, affective, and connective approach that has been advocated within and beyond geography as a means to undertake research projects that use more touching, multisensory, collaborative, creative practices (see Carolan 2007; Cook *et al.* 2007; Paterson 2009).

In Plymouth, *The Undesirables* aimed to reflect and/or create an experience of abhorrence that so many commodities travel around the world on container ships, whose contents are unknown even to dock workers. Jackson (Human Cargo 2007b) drew upon the *Napoli* event to show the sheer scale and excess of the consumption and production of goods and the ways in which it defetishized those goods as stories of their origins and destinations became mainstream news. *The Undesirables* showed how these *out-of-place* goods become active pollutants endangering the living nature and consensual culture of this heritage coastline. But it also reflected upon the cavernous distance between visual representation and the material extents of the event. Its social and cultural geographies were more-than-national, -knowable and -translatable, and more than here and now. In the maritime gallery as much as on Branscombe beach, the *Napoli* story attained the proportions of the gigantic, denuding the effectiveness of art, culture, and narration. Jackson showed that the material geographies of the *Napoli* and its aftermath could not be separated from the tools at hand to recall, record, and retell them. Finally, *The Undesirables* exemplifies an approach to public engagement in which materials are created, worked with, arranged, and sited in order to create 'spaces for imagination' whose multisensory, juxtapositional aesthetic can draw visitors into collaborative sense-making processes, shaped but not determined by their material forms.

Conclusions

Writing, as sociologist Laurel Richardson (2000) has argued, is not simply a matter of setting down on paper what you already know. It is, rather, a method of enquiry.

As she puts it, 'I write because I want to find something out. I write in order to learn something that I did not know before I wrote it' (Richardson 2000: 924). We therefore want to conclude by reflecting on what we have learned about material geographies by writing about them here. First, as we noted in the introduction, we have become convinced that there never has been, nor is there now, a coherent approach to materiality in geography. Although a large number of publications have responded to Philo's and Jackson's calls for 're-materialisation', an identifiable 'material geographies' literature has not developed in social and cultural geography, or more widely. Rather, while geographers' long-standing interests in material culture have been revised and expanded, an attention to—and language of— 'liveliness', 'corporeality', 'affect', 'material capacities', 'animation', 'co-fabrication', and 'practice' has emerged via a 'rich variety of analytical impulses, philosophical resources and political projects' (Whatmore 2006: 601). Secondly, we have been able to make sense of some of the tensions between material geographers as being the result of key terms being used in both academic and everyday senses. Echoing Daniel Miller's (2005a) observations in anthropology, geographers preferring to develop careful and detailed theoretical appreciations of key terms before using them, have been critical of those using them in looser, more everyday ways. Philo's, Jackson's, and others' use of words like 'de-materialization' and 're-materialization' has attracted sometimes scornful critique in this sense (see Kearnes 2003; Anderson and Wylie 2009). But the geographies we have described in this chapter—with their language of 'liveliness', 'corporeality', and so on—require approaches to research that are theoretically *and* empirically rich, which work through abstract *and* empathetic appreciations of diverse topics that come into being through creative combinations of established and novel research practices, which should therefore work carefully through and with the multiple meanings of key terms. Thirdly, we have reflected on the advantages and disadvantages of using an event to help to interpret a literature.

The *Napoli* event did enable us to give a coherence to this chapter that the literature did not seem to possess, while also providing a vivid sense of its disparate nature. We hoped that the excess of detail provided would more easily allow missing perspectives to be read into the chapter by those with other (inter) disciplinary expertise, and that doing things this way would avoid the policing of borders and making of judgements, to instead, in the spirit of Peter Jackson's original argument, 'build bridges and . . . move discussion forward' (2000: 9). On the minus side, doing things this way did not allow us to develop in detail geographers' different theoretical appreciations of materiality, nor did it enable us to touch on the full range of material geographical research. Perhaps most notable by their absence are geographers' contributions to science and society and nature and society debates (but see Whatmore and Hinchliffe this volume, Chapter 19). This oversight can be explained not only by what was and was not part of the *Napoli* story, but also—inevitably—by the limitations of our own locations, understandings, interests, experiences, politics, and practices (which also explain our concentration on debates primarily in British geography and our reliance on work written in English). Finally, given on the one hand the exciting and important work emerging from collaborations between artists, curators, and geographers, and by interdisciplinary artist- and/or curator-geographers, and, on the other, the apparent importance of debates about, and appreciations of, 'materiality' across human and physical geography, we are excited by the prospect of new work on geography's materialities by physical and human and/or physical–human colleagues.

CHAPTER 4

MATERIAL CULTURE IN FOLKLIFE STUDIES

ROBERT SAINT GEORGE

The meaning of 'material culture' seems clear. According to archaeologist James Deetz, it included 'that sector of our physical environment that we modify through culturally determined behavior' (Deetz 1977: 24). Folklorist Henry H. Glassie has written numerous definitions of material culture, but his most recent one agrees with Deetz's idea of environmental modification, even as it swells to grander visions. According to Glassie, 'history and art connect in the study of material culture. Material culture reveals human intrusion into the environment. It is the way we imagine', he continues, 'a distinction between nature and culture, and then rebuild nature to our desire, shaping, reshaping, and arranging things during life' (Glassie 1999: 1). Such transformations of 'environment' (a term with as culturally striated a meaning as 'nature'), if even possible, do at least offer a way of imagining the 'material' of material culture. But its materiality—in exchange relations, as arbiters of taste, as a way of making visible the invisibility of quotidian existence— these, too, may be signalled by the second phrase in Glassie's definition: 'We live in material culture, depend upon it, take it for granted, and realize through it our grandest aspirations' (Glassie 1999: 1). The sweep of history, from mundane daily domestic regimes to the struggles of consciousness that define great art: material culture encloses them all. But how to anchor them in any social milieu demands we consider the history and methods of folklife studies.

The anthropological study of folklife has had a long series of connections with, and influences upon, the investigation of material culture. Folklife has brought to the analysis of landscapes, archaeology, and vernacular objects an integrative methodology. On the one hand, the integrative mandate may mean interpreting one set of material things in the context of other artefacts; thus, imagine that the private dwellings of a maritime community, say, in Cornwall can only make sense when integrated with the study of its boats and wharves. On the other hand, folklife emphasizes the utter contingency of any one expressive genre on social structure and local politics, as well as on such oral forms as myth, legend, or gossip. Thus one cannot explore that same community's built forms (dwellings, boats, wharves) without also exploring how fishing crews are related to kinship, or the myriad heightened speech registers fishermen employ to tell tall tales about the ones that got away.

As well as a series of interconnected methods for researching the material world, the term 'folklife' brings an intellectual genealogy to the study of material culture. The English word stands in debt to two earlier European terms: most directly, to the Swedish *folkliv* and then to its close but older cousin, the German *volksleben*. When Don Yoder offered a history of the terms in 1963, he observed that the earliest usage of *folkliv* came in the title of Sven Ludwig Loven's *Folklivet I Skytts harad* (*The Folklife of the Jurisdictional District of Skytt*) of 1847. In 1878, the term again found use in the title of a new journal on linguistic dialect and *folkliv*. And in 1909, Sven Loren began lecturing on *Svensk Folklivsforskning* (Swedish Folklife Research) at the University of Lund. The German *Volksleben* ('folklife') along with *Volkskunde* ('folk art') has even earlier nineteenth-century roots; the latter term was already current by 1806 (Yoder 1963: 43n1, 44n2).

In the discussion that follows, key features of the folklife studies movement warrant investigation, including the ways it differed from 'folklore', *per se*, and the importance of regional or national archives of material folk culture that were based in universities, museums, and research institutes in Sweden, Norway, Ireland, Germany, and Switzerland. The archive idea, along with the open-air museum, was one element that was also transferred to Pennsylvania in the post-World War (WW) II years. Finally, this next section addresses the emergence of folklife studies in Wales, Scotland, and Northern Ireland by examining the lives of Iorworth C. Peate, Isabel Francis Grant, and Emir Estyn Evans.

THE FOLKLIFE STUDIES MOVEMENT

The pioneer of American folklife studies, Don Yoder, presented a chronology of key terms in his overview in a 1963 essay of the 'The Folklife Studies Movement' (Yoder

1963). As a discussion of where the study of folklife originated, Yoder still provides the best compressed summary. In a series of arguments, he commented first on the tense relationship of folklife to the existing paradigm of folklore in Scandinavia, England, Germany, and Switzerland. For Yoder, while folklore studies were partial in their attention to such oral genres as legend, fairy tale, myth, proverb, and riddle, 'folklife' was more closely related to Cultural Anthropology or European Ethnology in its 'total scholarly concentration on the folk-levels of a national or regional culture'. Thus, 'folklife studies involves the analysis of a folk-culture in its entirety', he observed, continuing with a clarification of the latter term: 'By folk culture is meant in this case the lower (traditional or "folk" levels) of a literate Western (European or American) society... and is basically (although not entirely) rural and pre-industrial. Obviously it is the opposite of the mass-produced, mechanized, popular culture of the twentieth century' (Yoder 1963: 43). All fields of folklore, such as studies of field systems, house forms, costume, food recipes and cookery, or music and dance, could be folded within the idea of 'folklife'. Yoder then discussed the institutional bases of folklife in European research. Besides the national academic organization, independent research institute, and university department that offered them both a home and related curricula, Yoder identified the significance of folklife archives, often located at national or regional organizations. Archives, such as those long operated at the *Folklivsarkivet* in Lund, the *Institutet for Folkelivsgransking* in Oslo, the Irish Folklore Commission in Dublin, and the *Schweizerisches Institut für Volkskunde* in Basel, gathered interviews, photographs, and drawings from field research, and used these in order to develop more precise mapping for each 'folk atlas' or *Volkeskundeatlas* they undertook.

As they plotted the geographic diffusion of house forms or chair types, of customs and cart-types, such atlases were themselves based on the questionnaires, field work and publication of linguistic atlases, or maps made to show the geographic variation of dialect within standard, national languages. These cartographic projects or dialect maps had roots deep in the nineteenth century, with the very first use of maps coming with the publication of Johann Andrea Schmeller's *Bayerisches Wörterbuch*, a four-volume survey of Bavarian dialectal variation, published in Munich between 1827 and 1837. Schmeller's lead was followed in Germany by George Wenker, a schoolteacher from Dusseldorf. Wenker, however, took advantage of his own educational connections, and sent questionnaires to every village school in north Germany; he drew upon the responses in his 1876 *Sprachatlas der Deutchen Reiches*. This precise mapping of dialects revealed local variation, but equally for Wenker it demonstrated the distribution of German as a language, and so could be marshalled to support the integrity of the idea of the German nation-state. Even as *Sprachatlassen* were underway, however, fieldwork for similar Francophone projects advanced. The Swiss scholar Jules Gilliéron initiated research for the *Atlas Linguistique de la France* between 1897 and 1901, assisted by the formidable field investigations of Edmond Edmont, who managed to visit almost 640 villages in France and in the French-speaking parts of Italy, Belgium, and in Gilliéron's native Switzerland; along the way he interviewed male inhabitants between the ages of 15 and 83, people he termed 'local intellectuals' and 'folk speakers'. Between 1902 and 1910, Gilliéron and Edmont published 13 volumes containing 1920 maps (Mitzka 1950: 14–44; Lauwers *et al.* 2002).

Other countries fell in line with atlasing projects at a point in time that made contextual sense to their participants. In North America efforts were led by Hans Kurath, a scholar born in Villach, Austria, but educated in the United States. In 1930, the Linguistic Atlas of the United States and Canada was established, and nine fieldworkers began areal reconnaissance the following year. Kurath's *Handbook of the Linguistic Geography of New England* appeared in 1939 and included 734 maps in the course of its three volumes (Kurath 1939); in this instance, Kurath interviewed older residents, hoping his collection would thereby include dialect terms and pronunciations that were not being used by the region's younger people. Kurath's more general *A Word Geography of the Eastern United States* was published a decade later (Kurath 1949). In the United States, as in Canada, the atlas projects were both timed and designed to help articulate regional identities undercut by the national depressions that afflicted both nations between 1930 and 1938 (Kurath 1939, 1949). In England, dialect atlas projects did not begin until 1948, when Eugen Dieth from Zurich and Harold Orton of Leeds started the Survey of English Dialects initiative in 1948 at Leeds University. It was followed four years later by Angus McIntosh's *An Introduction to a Survey of Scottish Dialects*, for which McIntosh sent out questionnaires through the postal system (McIntosh 1952). Then, in 1974 and modelled on Kurath's study of 1949, Harold Orton and Nathalia Wright published *A Word Geography of England* (Orton and Wright 1974). Unlike the American case, linked to regional identity formation in the midst of the Great Depression in the 1930s, the cartographic projects undertaken by Orton and his colleagues seem to have been tied to Great Britain's attempt at unified cultural recovery from WWII, and a means of showing those 'citizens in reconstruction' (to use David Matless' phrase) that a shared national culture could be transcribed on to the regular squares of the Ordnance Survey. A post-war national, consumer-citizenry was not just a promise but a new reality that could be mapped on to the land itself (Matless 1998: 234–246).

Following the efforts of such *Sprachatlas* and *Volkeskuneatlas* authors as Wenker and Gilliéron, and such British dialectal experts as McIntosh, the staff at various folklife archives also made extensive use of questionnaires, so that a specific set of inquiries might be made across disparate communities within a region. Yoder provided one example: 'the Irish Folklife Commission has used reports on folk-tales written down on their request by school children in the Gaeltacht' (Yoder 1963: 49). Folklife archives were often operated by open-air folk museums, beginning with Artur Hazelius' establishment of Skansen in 1891 outside Stockholm. It was developed as a concept based upon his earlier experience, in 1873, of creating the Nordiska Museet, or Museum of Swedish Ethnology (a museum of local Swedish peasant life). Skansen provided a public institution where visitors could encounter typical barns, outbuildings, farmhouses, and structures representing rural as well as town life from different ecologies and regional economies of Sweden, each with its own ecological and regional economic base (Rehnberg 1957; Alexander 1983).

Skansen's representation of a geographic localism or regionalism exerted a formative influence in the 1930s and early 1940s on Lund folklorist Carl Wilhelm von Sydow's concept of the *oicotype*, a term that referred to 'local forms of a tale type, folksong, or proverb, with "local" defined in either geographic or cultural terms . . . on the village, state, regional, or national level' (Dundes 1965: 220; Von Sydow 1977 [1948]). Skansen's long shadow also sparked Stockholm ethnologist Sigurd Erixon's abiding faith from the late 1930s through the 1950s in regional analysis in the study of buildings, food, and costume; his founding of the journal *Folkliv* in 1930 may have set his entire career in motion (Erixon 1937, 1945, 1953, 1999).

The final segment of Yoder's 1963 essay revealed his underlying purpose in writing: to argue that an American version of the European regional or ethic folklife approach was both necessary and, in fact, was already under way in the activities of the Pennsylvania Folklife Society. The society had its origins in the Pennsylvania Dutch Folklore Center, formed in 1949 by Alfred Shoemaker and William Frey (faculty members at Franklin and Marshall College), and Don Yoder (then on the faculty at Muhlenberg College in Allentown). The centre was established as a research institute with its own library and folklife archive, with each modelled on the Irish Folklore Commission (founded 1935) and on the folklore archives at the Universities of Uppsala (The Institute for Dialect and Folklore Research, established 1914) and Lund (Archive for Folklife, founded 1913) in Sweden (Hedblom 1961: 1; Båsk 1990: 143). The centre, then located at Franklin and Marshall College, embarked promptly on the publication of a new journal, *The Pennsylvania Dutchman*, with the first issue appearing on 5 May 1949 (Figure 4.1). A sample of any issue of the journal reveals its great topical range. A 1956 issue, for example, contained articles on 'The Summer House', 'Diaper Lore', 'Witchcraft in Cow and Horse', and 'Dialect Folksay' (*Pennsylvania Dutchman* 1956), among others. Small wonder, then, that Yoder expressed pleasure in revealing that its subscription list had grown to over 3,500 in less than a decade (Yoder 1963: 52). As the centre grew, however, it wanted to explore additional ethnic groups that had historically defined Pennsylvania; it wished to augment its base in Germanic cultures by including Scotch-Irish, Welsh, Quaker, and later nineteenth-century emigrant groups from eastern and central Europe that played such central roles in Allegheny coal mining and the steel mills of western Pennsylvania. With such ambitious and inclusive social and historical agendas, in 1956 the centre changed both the name of its journal to *Pennsylvania Folklife*, and shifted its own title to the

Vol. IV, No. 3
July, 1952

Devoted to Pennsylvania Dutch Folk-Culture

FOLK FESTIVAL SQUARE DANCERS   Photo by Heilman

Fig. 4.1 Title page, *Pennsylvania Dutchman* IV, no. 3. July 1952, showing square dancers at the Kutztown Folk Festival in June of that year (photo: Courtesy of University of Pennsylvania Libraries).

Pennsylvania Folklife Society. Between the late 1940s and mid 1950s, then, what began as the loosely linked interests of Shoemaker, Frey, and Yoder in Pennsylvania German speech dialect and religious sectarianism, had developed into an organization that drew upon strengths in two areas.

First, the Pennsylvania Folklife Society aimed, as reflected in its name and journal title, to build upon both European studies of *folkliv* or *Volksleben* as a way of studying folk culture in its entirety. While Swedish museums and such figures as von Sydow and Erixon supplied the *folkliv* tradition, the work of German and Swiss scholars on *Volkskunde* was of perhaps greater importance to Yoder's Pennsylvania German field of expertise. He drew his own working definition of the subject from folklorist Richard Weiss's monumental study *Volkskunde der Schweiz* (1946). In many respects, Weiss' book offered a highly detailed examination of Swiss cultures, both rural and urban, ranging from hair styles, costumes, house plans and wall types to cheese production, speech patterns, among many other topics. Other than this one synthetic text, however, Weiss, along with colleague Paul Geiger, embarked in 1950 (65 years after Wenker's *Sprachatlas* first appeared) on the *Atlas der schweizerische Volkskunde* ('Atlas of Swiss Folk Arts'). Geiger passed away early in the project, in March 1952, after only two volumes of maps and one corresponding volume of *Kommantaren* had been published, but Weiss continued to supervise an additional 15 sets of maps and 13 more detailed *Kommentaren* before his own death in July 1962. Weiss' assistants continued the work until the later 1970s, and an index to the entire atlas was finally completed in 1995 (Weiss and Geiger 1950–1979; Escher *et al.* 1995).

The second aspect of the new Pennsylvania Folklife Society was its commitment to the archiving of all materials collected for study and to making the results of its research available in books, journals, lectures, and other forms of public education. In August 1952, for example, the then Pennsylvania Dutch Folklore Center sponsored a week-long series of 'Seminars on the Folk-Culture of the Pennsylvania Dutch Country', held at Bynden Wood—'a palatial mountain-top vacation spot' (Anon 1952: 2). Shoemaker, Frey, and Yoder were joined by other leading scholars on every conceivable aspect of the topic. Academic lectures on issues such as powwowing, folk cookery, and storytelling were followed by a dinner and 'a folktale fest'—and a talk about songs and hymnity was followed by a formal programme on 'Pennsylvania Dutch folksongs; evening open to general public' (Anon 1952: 2).

A final component of the centre's work was the establishment in 1950 of the Pennsylvania Dutch Folk Festival, held on the old Kutztown Fairgrounds. The festival was by no means the first such gathering to focus on folklife; Yoder himself noted the German *volksfesten* of the early twentieth century as one source (Yoder 1963: 53n37). While many of them had been functioning at a high level by that date, local *volksfesten* in fact had origins much earlier in the nineteenth century. Consider, for example, the Cannstatt festival, which many current tourists connect with beer and the city of Stuttgart. The festival, however, was only taken over by that city in 1909, and before that year it had been the principal agricultural fair of Württemberg. The festival began in 1818, when King Wilhelm I of Württemberg established the fair in order to bring people from surrounding villages together to hold horse races with prize money, and in so doing help to rebuild a local economy ravaged by the Napoleonic wars. In the centre of the fairgrounds, awards were given out at a central spot marked by a large column made of fruit. Throughout the 1840s and 1850s, the number of individuals and community social clubs going to Württemberg increased dramatically; in 1841 a parade to the fairgrounds included more than 10,000 participants. In 1882, the festival moved to a biannual schedule. By 1920, the original 1-day fair had grown to a 5-day event (Cannstatter Volksfest 2008). The *volksfest* made the Atlantic crossing to North America as a custom familiar to German immigrants who arrived in the 1860s and 1870s. Bavarians in Philadelphia started their own *Bayerischer Volksfest*. They first met in December 1878, and an initial forty members agreed to pay annual dues of two dollars. The next year a group of men met to write a constitution for the group, and soon thereafter, they were granted room to have annual meetings. They held their first four-day long *summerfest* in August 1880 (Bayerischer Volksfest 2008). In 1874 a number of German clubs in New York City and adjacent parts of northern New Jersey joined forces to establish the *Plattdeutsche Volksfest Verein* (PVV), a name that derived from members' common origins in the *Platte* or flatlands in northern Germany. In August 1874, the PVV held its first *Volksfest* in North Bergen, New Jersey, and in 1894 acquired the parkland in Bergen on which the annual summer festival was then held (Plattdeutche Volksfest 2008).

Thus, the German *Volksfest* had a double significance for the seminar programme at the Kutztown festival. Yoder made clear that it helped to anchor the Pennsylvania event in the German tradition of festivals held on old agricultural fairgrounds. And by stressing festive events using German foods (sauerkraut, roast pork, schnitzel), crafts (blacksmithing, buggy production, steam-engine power) and entertainment (singing, storytelling, hymnity), he was drawing to Kutztown members of American *Volksfest* groups such as those in Philadelphia and the New York–New Jersey area. So the festival provided one means to extend academic concerns to a general public seeking a total and enjoyable immersion in Pennsylvania German regional *Volksleben*. Immensely popular due to its use of live demonstrations, the Kutztown folk festival was drawing crowds well in excess of 100,000 by 1960. What they came to see included, in the summer of 1963, 'Dutch-English humor', 'Amish documentary film', and a 'water-witching demonstration' among others (*Pennsylvania Folklife* 1963: 28). The proceeds from the gate alone provided vital revenue for other programmes (Yoder 1963: 53).

Even as Yoder's 1963 essay consolidated the new field of folklife studies as a transatlantic intellectual formation, he nonetheless made two omissions. On the one hand his essay failed to offer detailed biographies of key intellectual figures as a means of showing how the distinct roles of museum curator, university professor, and archivist could be brought together within single working lives. Outside of continental Europe, the folklife approach also found zealous adherents in Wales, Scotland, and Northern Ireland. In these countries, a similar emphasis on regional approaches to material culture could be found in the 1930s. During this period, the growing strength of material culture study within folklife was due to the sustained labour of Iorwerth C. Peate, Isabel Francis Grant, and E. Estyn Evans. The chronological terrain charted by these scholars begins in the 1920s and 1930s and stretches through the 1950s and 1960s; they thus helped both to constitute and to symbolically reveal shifts in British society and culture in the inter-war years as well as after WWII. Perhaps in the first period, landscape and the preservation and study of old houses merged into a countryside ethos in which national interests were implicit and infrequently contested. In the years following WWII, however, regional identities within 'Britishness' seem to have broken free of country life ideology. As sectional politics and cultures took on greater force in the years from 1945 to 1965, they were countered by English planners eager to build new, cross-class 'communities', ineffable fictional settlements of consumer-citizens, living in neighbourhoods that could subsume regional affiliations as well as assuage the endless class tension of urban terrace housing (Matless 1998: 62–78, 234–235). It may be possible to describe these broad changes, but their periodization was often not so neat. As we shall see, Peate and Grant, at least, were unflinching regionalists in the 1930s.

THREE LIVES

The Welsh scholar Iorwerth C. Peate (born in Powys in 1901) undertook during the 1930s a programme of fieldwork and historical research that led to the publication of *The Welsh House: A Study in Folk Culture* (Peate 1944). This careful exploration of how house plan types and interior furnishings varied across the Welsh landscape built upon his training in human geography and museum curation. Peate had studied under H. J. Fleure (1877–1969), the French human geographer who taught at University College of Wales in Aberystwyth from 1910 to 1930; Fleure advised Peate's undergraduate work in Celtic archaeology. In 1927, Peate was appointed as Assistant Keeper in the Archaeology Department in the National Museum of Wales and learned the collection well. In 1929, he published a *Guide to the Collection of Bygones, a Descriptive Account of Old-Fashioned Life in Wales*. In 1932, Peate was appointed to care for the folk culture and industries in the museum, and the following year published *Y Crefftwr yng Nghymru*, a study of traditional craftsmen and their tools (Peate 1933).

It was during research between 1936 and 1940 for *The Welsh House* that he also began to develop ideas for a Welsh open-air museum based on the Swedish Folk Museum at Skansen. By 1948, Peate's vision, The Welsh Folk Museum, was opened at St Fagan's on the outskirts of Cardiff. During this same period of productivity, Peate also founded The Society for Folk Life Studies, and served as the founding editor of its journal, *Gwerin*, first published in late 1956. In his 'Editorial Notes' for the June 1957 issue, Peate credited Cyril Fox, the third Director of the National Museum of Wales, with establishing a Department of Folk Life, which was in turn 'merged into the newly-created Welsh Folk Museum'. It is difficult to position Cyril Fox in the cultural politics of Wales in the 1950s. Along with his co-author Lord Raglan, Fox released the three-volume study of *Monmouthshire Houses* (Fox and Raglan 1951, 1953, 1954). Published under the joint imprimatur of the National Museum of Wales and the Welsh Folk Museum, the work stands as a model of vernacular architecture study in its integration of attention to both materials and plan types, the analysis of which resulted from extensive field study between 1941 and 1948 (Fox and Raglan 1951: 10).

Both Fox and Raglan were Englishmen with an ambivalent view of immediate post-WWII politics. When doing the field research for the book, Fox was also Director of the National Museum of Wales. Raglan was a past president of a section of the British Association, a prominent member of the museum's council, and in 1950 the Chairman of the museum's Art and Archaeology Department. In a preface written for the first volume of *Monmouthshire Houses*, D. Dilwyn Jones, then the Director of the National Museum, stated that their book owed a singular debt to Peate: 'In Wales it has been stimulated', he observed, 'by the publication of *The Welsh House*.' But Jones, a Welshman himself, also noted why the Monmouth region bounded on the south by the Severn River and on the east by England, mattered. 'We want ultimately to know', he commented, 'the exact geographical boundaries in Wales and in Britain generally of particular styles and of individual craft-techniques' (Jones 1951: 3). On one hand, Jones noticed that unlike Peate's earlier study, in which his house plans are drawn with furniture in place and his photographs include living people as they used the building—Fox and Raglan included varieties of cruck joints, discussed craftsmanship without speaking to any craftsmen, and drew plans of houses as if no one lived in them. In the early 1950s, then, the representation of the Welsh landscape and its houses were linked to the emergence of Welsh nationalist political agendas and the Plaid Cymru party's maturation, from the election of Gwynfor Evans as President in 1951 to its claim of a majority of Welsh seats in Parliament in 1959. The party's emphasis on home rule served as a divisive issue within the then dominant Liberal party, which had long been seeking accommodation with English rule in Wales. The discord within the Liberal camp came from industrialists in southern Wales, who as a group chose to remain within English parliamentary control (Jones and Fowler 2008: 52–56). Monmouthshire was one area the southern Welsh captains of industry conceived of as their own territory. Thus the particular section of Wales Fox and Raglan chose to study was politically engaged in the 1950s; their choice implicitly ratified the accommodationist Liberal stance of unionist economics.

Fox, after all, was a native Hampshire man whose rise in the museum system in Wales had been nothing short of meteoric. According to a short biography written about him by Peate, Fox had been in and out of public schools in England, and schemed to become an assistant in the university museum of Cambridge. He finally earned his Ph.D. in 1922 and published his thesis as *The Archaeology of the Cambridge Region* in 1923 (Fox 1923). Even as this first work was in press, however, Fox was contacted by R. E. Mortimer Wheeler, who in 1922 had been elevated from his job as Keeper of Archaeology to Director of the National Museum of Wales. Although there was heavy pressure to name a Welsh scholar to the position he had vacated, Wheeler knew through his Cambridge contacts of Fox's work, and offered the Keeper's post to him. Fox began his work in Cardiff in late 1922. In 1926, Wheeler left the museum, and Fox became Director of the museum, a position he kept until 1948. While Director he kept up his work in archaeology, and published *The Personality of Britain*, an archaeological survey that manages to consider Welsh materials as among those Celtic fringe societies that were consistently pushed back by invading Anglo-Saxon tribes (Fox 1932). As Director, Fox was also called upon to give advice to local museums about their collections and buildings. When he visited the museum in Wrexham in Denbighshire, he was surprised to learn that its curator 'expected us to *fill the building* with loans to give them a start. When he was at Cardiff in *the* summer', Fox continued, 'someone who showed him round said we would & had "enough Holt stuff to fill two galleries". I repudiated any intention of doing this sort of thing' (quoted in Hill and Matthews 2004: 31, emphasis in original). In another instance, he visited the Powysland Museum, located in the village where Peate was born. Here, Fox merely ticked off a number of factors that bothered him: '*No heat* . . . no blinds—great extremes of temperature damaging the exhibits. *Strong sunlight* very bad. *The* Roof is *not* watertight . . . Interior *Shabby*.' The lesson that Fox drew from these failings was not merely that the museum's overseers were inadequate. Instead, he noted that 'No local museum can possibly be properly managed without a permanent paid curator. *It is* Unjust', he noted emphatically, 'and lays a heavy burden on the generosity of unpaid workers, who cannot *manage* adequately' (quoted in Hill and Matthews 2004: 85, emphasis in original).

Fox was replaced as Director of the National Museum of Wales by D. Dilwyn Jones, the man who penned the prefaces to the three volumes of *Monmouthshire Houses*. In the preface to volume two, Jones thanked Peate 'for reading the proofs of this Part'. He also stated that the Fox and Raglan survey 'is related to one of the activities of the Welsh Folk Museum: the study, and re-erection at St. Fagan's, of old Welsh buildings' (Jones 1953: 3).

The founding collections at St Fagan's, on the outskirts of Cardiff, a 100-acre site acquired by the National Museum of Wales in 1948 for an open-air museum, were drawn from key departmental holdings formerly part of the museum. St Fagan's had only a few buildings by 1957; according to Peate, it 'now exhibits a sixteenth-century manor house and its gardens and grounds, a sixteenth-century barn, a rural woollen factory, two farmhouses and a Nonconformist chapel. Two other farmhouses and a Caernarvonshire cottage are about to be re-erected.' With pride he listed the presence in 1957 of galleries, craft demonstrations, classrooms, and libraries. But 'the Welsh Folk Collection', Peate observed with regret, 'is in store awaiting the completion of the Exhibition Block, for which unfortunately there are no funds' (Peate 1957: 97–98). *Gwerin* was renamed *Folk Life* in 1963. Peate remained editor. His brief statement on the renaming reveals several pressing issues, each of which touched on considering the newly re-entitled journal as a 'clearing-house' (Peate 1963: 4) for the field of folklife studies. One concern was the arbitrary and counter-productive splitting during the inter-war years of archaeological research and anthropological work into different, highly segregated scholarly journals; the two fields found it difficult to address one another and share critical readers. As Peate put it, 'the literature of folklife research in Britain . . . was therefore fractionated throughout a wide range of journals' (Peate 1963: 3). A second problem was the total disruption caused by WWII of international folklife conferences and publication. While Erixon had founded the journal *Folk-liv* in the 1930s, Peate argued, 'the outbreak of war forced Dr. Erixon to limit the range of the journal principally to Scandinavian scholarship' (Peate 1963: 3). International conferences, some with UNESCO funding, helped overcome the journal's resulting parochialism and, as Peate lamented, 'this did not solve our British problem' (Peate 1963: 3). The British 'problem' was how to imagine a folklife scene that would effectively cut across the material cultures of Wales, Scotland, the North of Ireland, and England. The mixture of academic and museum research had become more common in 1963 than it had been in the 1930s, but at the same time it was now being used to claim regional cultural autonomy rather than advance any pan-British identity. From the 1950s to the present, the preferred use of material culture has been to insist upon the legitimacy of political strategies on local and regional levels.

The School of Scottish Studies at the University of Edinburgh began in the early 1950s. Its house journal, *Scottish Studies*, has always been a mixture of topics ranging from linguistic dialect to literature to folklife (Dalglish 2003: 23–27). The material culture of Scotland was explored and presented in a museum setting much earlier, however. On a tour of Scandinavia in the late 1920s, Isabel Frances Grant first learned of Skansen and of the corresponding open-air museum founded at Maihaugen near Lillehammer, Norway, by Anders Sandvig in 1904. Born in Edinburgh, Grant had in 1924 written her first book on an eighteenth-century ancestor of highland origins; using surviving account books, she reconstructed the economic life of William Mackintosh. As *Every-day Life on a Highland Farm* made clear, he lived in a small village near Kingussie, a picturesque town at the foot of Scotland's

Monadliath mountains that would claim Grant's attention until her death at age 96 in 1983. After seeing both Skansen and Maihaugen, she realized that material artefacts came alive in a museum setting. Beginning in the early 1930s, she conceived the idea of establishing a Highland folk museum to better insure that 'the old setting of our daily life' could be 'saved' and used to educate the public about aspects of Highland existence that were fast disappearing—a romantic, eleventh-hour rescue of reified 'tradition' (Highland Folk Museum 2008). Motoring through the countryside in her automobile, Grant gathered a wide range of domestic artefacts: pots, old stoves, chairs, ploughs, as well as things of more transient, organic materials such as horn vessels, leather, and wood harnesses for livestock. Grant travelled to different parts of the Highlands, and thus she understood the cultural diversity of the region rather than reducing it to any single identity for convenience. In 1935, she purchased a deconsecrated church on Iona, an island in the Inner Hebrides. She named the small museum-in-a-church Am Fasdagh (Scots Gaelic for 'the shelter'). In less than 5 years, the collection had outgrown the church, so Grant moved it all to another church, about 12 miles from Kingussie. In 1943 she finally secured a site in Kingussie proper, and the Highland Folk Museum officially opened on 1 June 1944, 4 years earlier than Iorwerth Peate's Welsh Folk Museum at St Fagan's.

The folklife approach to material culture that informed Grant's development of the Highland Folk Museum was set out in her book *Highland Folk Ways* (1961). The title of the work appears to draw from American scholar William Graham Sumner's influential *Folkways: A Study of the Sociological Importance of Manners, Customs, Mores and Morals* (1906). When she began her earliest research in the 1920s, the term 'folkways' may have seemed thematically precise and useful in its argument that folk customs (or 'ways') had at base a unifying sociological function: they held the moral fibre of groups together. By the time her book was actually being written (1959–1960), however, Grant had also been influenced by the ascendant paradigm of folklife, an intellectual formation that valued many functions (historical, political, economic, spiritual), and witnessed fragmentation as well as unity of purpose (hence the vagaries of 'folk*life*' and not the moral claims of 'folk*ways*'). Indeed, as she stated at the outset of the book's first chapter, 'the study of Highland Folk Life [note the change] is not merely an account of how the people managed to live in an inhospitable northern land but how they adapted this environment to their particular social ideas' (Grant 1961: 1). For Grant, a sociological lens may have been consistent with Sumner's earlier scheme, but hers remained focused on a precise, historical investigation of clan and run-rig land tenure.

The structure of *Highland Folk Ways* captured the centrality of material culture to Grant's conception of 'folk life'. The book moved from a broad, geographic and archaeological account ('The Lie of the Land and Shape of Human Settlement'), followed by chapters on farm animals and arable land ('The People's Foothold'), to ever narrowing discussions of house structure and form. Her descriptions of thatching and the difficulties of roof maintenance are convincing (Figure 4.2),

Fig. 4.2 Thatched house and south-western Scottish Highlands roping techniques for thatch: (a) general view of thatched house; (b) detail of chimney in middle of roof, showing rope encircling stack; (c) fastening of thatch to square gable end; (d) Mull type house; (e) detail of chimney at end of house, showing wrapping and pegging techniques (from Grant 1961: 152).

and her treatment of form included numerous floor plans (although neither orientation nor scales are provided). Following house form, she included a chapter on furnishing and 'plenishing' (the latter meaning such movables as pots, dishes, or stave vessels), 'The People's Daily Round and Common Tasks', and the production and use of highland fabrics. Perhaps the last quarter of the volume contained highly detailed chapters that appear as residual categories, seeming to fill out a sense of folklife genres: craftsmen, sea fishing and boats, communication and transport, sports and festivals. Throughout, Grant insisted that this wide array of material culture—from fields to fences, creepies to *chrogans*, from boats to festivals—could be integrated within the historical and ethnographic framework on folklife (Dalglish 2003: 24).

While Grant may have drawn some early inspiration from Sumner's conception of *Folkways*, a more immediate scholarly influence was E. Estyn Evans' *Irish Folk Ways* (Evans 1957). In a few respects, Evans was similar to Peate: he was a student of the human geography taught by Fleure at Aberystwyth at the same time as Peate in the mid-1920s. Evans remained a geographer throughout his long and active career. Indeed, one of Evans's earliest essays was included in the festschrift for Fleure edited by Peate (Evans 1930). Soon thereafter, Evans moved to Northern Ireland where he accepted a Lectureship in Geography at Queen's University in Belfast. Although his continuing field research in Europe was undercut by the Nazi occupation, in 1942 he published *Irish Heritage: The Landscape, The People, and Their Work*, a volume that introduced a new way to look at the Irish landscape that academics, citizens, and politicians alike found compelling (Evans 1942). In a land already divided, Evans argued that the history that came from material culture on the land—the people's greatest artwork—had the power to bring Catholics and Protestants together, as inhabitants of an older landscape, one that knew no sectarian distinctions. For Evans, this was one political power of archaeology; before the arrival of the first English planters in the twelfth century, there was only one Ireland. New bonds were immanent in heritage. He also argued in that book, as he did in earlier university and public lectures, that an open-air museum, again modelled on Skansen, should be established in Northern Ireland. The Ulster Folk Museum opened in 1958; Evans' earlier involvement with local government's Committee on Ulster Folklife helped bring the new journal *Ulster Folklife* into being in 1955; the museum commenced its publication a decade later. Evans served as one of the very first Trustees of the museum, and remained on its board until 1982 (Gailey 1990: 231–232), long after the museum had acquired its new location at Cultra, County Down, merged with the Ulster Transport Museum to form the Ulster Folk and Transport Museum in 1961, and formally reopened at the new site in 1964 (Figure 4.3).

Evans' study of *Irish Folk Ways* was published in 1957, as the museum was being developed to bring material culture to the centre of folklife interpretation (Evans 1957). In a structure that influenced Grant's later *Highland Folk Ways*, discussed

Fig. 4.3 Early nineteenth-century row housing from Sandy Row, Belfast, Northern Ireland (built in 1826, later reinstalled at the Ulster Folk and Transport Museum, Cultra, County Down; photo: Robert Saint George).

above, Evans began the work with three chapters on the formation of the land, and then moved into sequenced discussions of the 'thatched house' (Figure 4.4), 'hearth and home', 'pots and pans', and 'furniture and fittings'. Thus, Evans merged the study of human geography with that of vernacular architecture and what William Morris once called 'the lesser arts', or decorative arts (Morris 1973 [1878]: 11–30). Evans then moved through farmyards, kilns, gardens, the gathering of turf and additional 'home-made things' (Evans 1957: 100–199). Finally, Evans rounded out his discussion by addressing arenas of popular custom: 'boats and fishing', 'fairs and gatherings', 'fixed festivals', and concluded the book with a meditation on 'weddings and wakes'. The result was a staggeringly detailed portrait of ordinary people at work, finding both art and pleasure in the production of their lives.

Early contributions to *Ulster Folklife* displayed the clear imprint of Evans' keen interest in using the idea of folklife as a strategy for linking academic research to museum interpretation. Exhibition, curatorial precision, acquisition, and catalogue publication were all in Evan's purview as the Ulster Folk Museum developed. As Fleure had been to his own training, Evans now became the mentor for a new generation of scholars, such as Alan Gailey, whose *Rural Houses of the North of Ireland* (1984) was dedicated to Evans.

Evans opened the eyes of others because his own were so critical and always searching for new connections to observe and describe. In 1959, for example, he was

Fig. 4.4 Irish houses with rope thatching, western seaboard: (1) Dingle, County Kerry; (2) Achill Island, County Mayo; (3) Teeling, County Donegal (from Evans 1957: 53).

the first international guest invited to lecture on folklife approaches at the Kutz-town folk festival. In the short essay that Evans published concerning his visit, he complimented Alfred Shoemaker and Don Yoder for their intellectual energy. He addressed eighteenth-century Scots-Irish migrations from Ulster to Pennsylvania and the folklife traditions they contributed, even as presentations about Pennsyl-vania German culture dominated the festival programming (Evans 1959). Evans noted similarities between the two cultures, commenting on the forms of barns and types of ploughs, but he also marvelled at the local customs presented at the event; 'Other topics discussed', Evans observed, 'were water witching or dowsing (in which I successfully participated), ballads, broadsides, superstitious beliefs and powwowing (witchcraft or sympathetic healing).' When he turned his attention to activities under cover, the catalogue increased to include 'a similar [open-sided] tent staged a practical demonstration of traditional farming ways: wood-fence building (one of the simpler varieties was described as an Irish fence), the use and lore of hook and scythe, flailing, horse-harnessing, grain-shocking (stoking), animal calls and so on' (Evans 1959: 15).

Evans reserved his amazement, however, for other items of material culture:

The permanent buildings on the site housed a bewildering variety of exhibits and demon-strations. A large hall was occupied by stands displaying Pennsylvanian 'antiques', such as redware pottery and illuminated manuscripts (fraktur). Another hall housed craftmen demonstrating their skills in making e.g., straw-mobiles, 'cookie-cutters' of soldered tin, hand thrown pottery, baskets, quilts, and decorated Easter eggs (using pigments, resist-dyeing and rush-pith wrapping—this a recent import from the Ukraine). Young members of the Plain minorities—Amish, Mennonite, and Dunkard—displayed their costumes and their characteristic products such as Swiss cheeses.

Evans (1959: 15)

Thus, Evans sensed the irony of 'tradition' when presented in a festival context, when the relative value of a local custom shifts under the pressure of being transformed into a commodified form, as when presentations on a cultural 'stage' both de-contextualize and reify the ploughs, the water-witching, or the endless offerings of kraut served to tourists eager to eat their way to an assimilated authenticity. What is presented is less folklife in any nostalgic sense, but what were once integrated customs have been packaged as 'exhibits', endlessly reproduced as 'demonstrations', and put on static 'display'; Evans (1959: 15) uses these three words in sequence. These costumes, these tin cookie-cutters, these cheeses: they were instances of what was even then known as *folklorismus* (English: folklorism), although Evans did not use the word in his writings. This approach engaged directly the uses Shoemaker and Yoder were making of folklife's objects (its foods, domestic architecture, folk costume) and of its subjects (living history interpreters, storytellers, and healers at folk festivals).

FROM FOLKLIFE TO FOLKLORISM

When culture and its associated forms are put on view, questions arise concerning the relative authenticity of what visitors encounter. This section addresses the origins of the *folklorismus* ('folklorism') concept, and how it marked an addition to the ways in which material culture could be examined within the folklife studies approach.

In 1962 German folklorist Hans Moser penned the first critical assessment of folklorism, separating it from such terms as folklore and folkloristics (which in Germany had been associated with antiquarian collectors since the 1890s) and 'applied folkoristics'—and from its close cousin 'applied *Volkskunde*'. Applied *Volkskunde* had been established in German-speaking countries by the early twentieth century, and in its repeated invocation by regional and national groups working to legitimize *heimat*, found occasional use in support of the Third Reich. Indeed, as historian Karl Ritt has demonstrated in his discussion of the use made of the 'culture region' concept by the German archaeologist and geographer Franz Petri, he argues that Petri developed a method for determining the 'Germanness' of such territories as Belgium and parts of northern France. Although Petri never intended his work to be used for political ends, his claims about the cultural origins of Belgium and northern France provided a justification for the Third Reich to annex those areas (Ritt 2001: 246–249). National Socialist writers such as Otto Schmidt, who in 1937 wrote *Volkskunde als politischeafter Volkskunde* (*Folk Art as a Political Tool*) or Max Hildebert Boehm, whose *Volkskunde* (*Folk Art*) was published during the same year, drew on the name of the university discipline, *Volkskunde*, in order to support their Nordic-Germanic racist ideology and their faith in establishing a thousand-year *Volk* (Kamenetsky 1972: 223–226). Moreover, not just reading lists fell under the Third Reich's agenda. Smaller festival occasions felt its imprint as well; at Cannstatt, for example, during the 1935 celebration a swastika adorned the capital of the decorative fruit column that had long stood at the symbolic centre of the event (Cannstatter Volksfest 2008: 2).

As a result of the Third Reich's appropriation and outright invention of a new *Volkskunde* to its own ends—including Hitler's introduction of the 1934 commodity-wonder, the *Volkswagen*—later German scholars distanced themselves from the term, but were uncertain what might stand in its place. Hans Moser preferred folklorism. Although the precise meaning of his new word remained ambiguous, he argued its significance:

It is a term of great breadth which draws on two strands: the increased cultural leveling which leads to a growing interest in things 'folk' and the practice of satisfying, strengthening, or awakening this interest. Through various tactics, the audience is offered an impressive mixture of genuine and falsified materials from folk culture, particularly in cultural enclaves where life still seems to breathe originality, strength, and colour.

Moser (1962: 179–180, translation by Bendix 1988: 6)

According to Regina Bendix (1988: 6), Moser specified three particular forms of folklorism in his 1962 essay:

1. Performance of traditionally and functionally determined elements of folk culture outside that culture's local or class community.
2. Playful imitation of folk motifs in another social stratum.
3. The purposeful invention and creation of 'folk-like' elements outside any traditions.

Moser's understanding of folklorism thus drew obliquely on recent political uses of *Volkskunde* but used the term as well in order to represent all types of second-order folklife experiences from museum installations to mass-mediated shows of 'traditional' peoples. Still, looking over these three points it is possible to consider how dramatically many aspects of material culture and folklife studies would be redefined by Moser's way of reconceiving the new estranged role of 'tradition' in human experience. Or as sociologist Hermann Bausinger (1990: 126–127) summarized it in 1961:

The concept of folklorism was introduced to folkloristic discussion primarily by Hans Moser. Never strictly defined, the concept indicates not so much clearly circumscribed attributes as a certain process: the process of a folk culture experienced at second hand. The concept addresses the widespread fact that folklore—in the widest sense, not limited to oral tradition—appears in contexts to which it originally did not belong.

Of course, Moser's new frame of reference *mattered* precisely because he proved a keen observer of those ways in which both academics and museum curators—those material culture and folklife specialists so valued by Yoder—bore some responsibility for the analytical viewpoint that members of folk communities could provide about the origins and changing social lives of their own traditions (Bendix 1988: 6).

In 1978, the Hungarian folklorist Vilmos Voigt provided an updated survey of the intellectual history of the folklorism concept. On the one hand, he broadened the international emergence of the term itself, noting its appearance in Belgium in 1931, in Italy in 1961, and in the literatures of Greece, Russia, and Hungary itself (Voigt 1980: 421–422, 424). On the other hand, Voigt suggested that folklorism may be considered as opposed (and in many instances linked) to the process of 'folklorisation'. In the latter instance, materials from outside the small social group are moved into legitimate artistic communication near the 'innermost life' of the people. In the former case, folklore moves in the direction of cultural display, a move toward essentialized significance. Voigt's paper was published in a collection of essays edited by the English folklorist Venetia J. Newall. In order to clarify Voigt's use of the term *folklorism*, Newall added this explanatory editorial comment:

Folklorism may be used for commercial, patriotic, romantic propagandistic, and genuinely artistic purposes. It is a growing, world-wide phenomenon and is not unique to our time.

Examples of folklorism, and they are legion, would include: television displays of 'pictur-esque' folklore; the conscious wearing of national dress—for instance, at political demon-strations; the use of folk melodies by composers like Chopin, Vaughan Williams, and Bartok; the use of ethnic ornamentation in architecture; folklore and myth in the work of T.S. Eliot, Thomas Mann, Bertold Brecht, and James Joyce; the 'ethnic' souvenir industry; intellectuals who decorate their homes with examples of folk art, and so on.

Newall, in Voigt (1980: 419n)

Each of these phrases I have used—cultural display, essentialized significance—comes from a consideration of folklorism, and points toward the unfamiliar domain of a 'poetics of commodities', a term I have employed to reference objects of material culture when they are in a 'commodity situation' (Appadurai 1986b: 13–14) and when the particular strategies of indirect meaning they assume—metaphor, implication, contingency—are salient markers of that commodity's poetic qualities (Saint George 1998: 393). The ways in which such a position maps on to existing approaches to folklife studies is discussed in the section that follows.

POETICS OF COMMODITIES

The idea of folklorism, underlining the socio-political dimensions of the defini-tions of folk tradition, has informed the development of folklife studies during the past 30 years. Former students of Don Yoder have played an important role, especially Henry H. Glassie, Gerald L. Pocius, and John D. Dorst. Glassie's many, diverse writings honour and extend the folklife paradigm as outlined by Yoder. Yoder was the director of Glassie's doctoral dissertation at the University of Pennsylvania, which was published as *Pattern in the Material Folk Culture of the Eastern United States* (Glassie 1969). This study used maps in order to define both areal diffusion and regional patterns of material folk culture east of the Mississippi River. Using everything from barns and house types to settin' chairs and slingshots, Glassie argued that the influence of the Chesapeake or Tidewater region on the material culture of the inland southern region had previously been overlooked and warranted great scholarly attention (Glassie 1969: 34n, 88–89). In undertaking a critical mapping exercise, one that had a direct antecedent in the comparable mapping of linguistic dialect (Glassie 1969: 34n; Kniffen 1986 [1965]: 19, 21 [fig. 31]), he was perhaps responding to Don Yoder's wistful observation that 'the linguistic atlas technique has been applied to America by Hans Kurath, although so far the *Volkskundeatlas*, while it has spread to Switzerland, Holland, and Scandinavia, has no progeny in the United States' (Yoder 1963: 49n19).

In the mid-1970s Glassie published two further significant studies. *Folk Housing in Middle Virginia: a structural analysis of historic artifacts* was based on a close examination of about a dozen houses in Louisa and Goochland counties in Virginia. The book made one important cultural argument: that a 'revolution' in house design—and in the social life of the family behind its changing facades—happened before, and thus was a precondition of, the American revolution against British imperial control (Glassie 1975: 185–187). The book cast a long shadow for its methodological rigour. Glassie himself, looking back several years later, stated that *Folk Housing in Middle Virginia* was 'an application of structural method to artefacts designed to display the utility of material culture and structuralism for writing history' (Glassie 1982: 728n1). It also could be considered as an extended essay on the efficacy and limitations of the linguistic analogy for material culture study. The impact of the book was immediate. It awakened some historians from their insensitivity to material culture, and, when combined with another essay he published in 1977, it provided historical archaeologists with a model of establishing artefact competence and situated social performance (Glassie 1977; Johnson 1993: 35–38). The study stimulated debate and was criticized both for its avoidance of written records, and for the apparent invisibility of Glassie among the homeowners of Middle Virginia. Indeed, one reviewer went so far as to suggest that Glassie worked on the particular houses he did because they were deserted, and thus presented no social demands as he conceptually dismantled them for his own needs. Local residents, had Glassie made himself known to them, could have led him to other houses, including ones that might have challenged or confirmed his findings (McDaniel 1978: 853).

Around the same time, Glassie published his first sustained engagement with field ethnography in Northern Ireland, *All Silver and No Brass: an Irish Christmas mumming* (Glassie 1976). The story is an exploration of how elderly people in the district of Ballymenone, in the Parish of Cleenish, south-east of Enniskillin in County Fermanagh, remembered their own experiences of playing a part on a mumming team, hosting their raucous entry and entertainment, and then using the combined monies they 'begged' to put on a ball or public dance during the Christmas season (Glassie 1976). Glassie continued to interview elder residents of the district, publishing the results in *Passing the Time in Ballymenone: culture and history of an Ulster community* (1982), a work he introduced as 'an ethnography strong enough to cause disquiet in my world' (Glassie 1982: 13). It could also be described as an attempt to present an integrated cross-section of the expressive genres of a single community, especially in its commitment to fusing the study of narrative legends to material culture and the layout of local landscape. His close attention to material things—fields, the rooking or 'winning' of hay, fences, streets, barns, houses (Figure 4.5), or kitchen dressers—culminated in his analysis of the serving of tea, with its symbolic diffusion inward to metaphorically invoke communion.

Fig. 4.5 Irish house with axial alignment of house and service structures added at right, Inishowen Peninsula, County Donegal, c.1800–1920 (photo: Robert Saint George).

After his sustained work in Fermanagh, Glassie turned his attention to the production and marketing of crafts—from rugs to pottery to metalware, from things for the mosque to things for the home—in contemporary Istanbul. He began, too, to examine these productions as artefacts at once art and commodity in a competitive economy. To survive in business one needs to become a master of skill and simultaneously master the marketplace; the context of exchange is a constituent element of all things made by human hands (Glassie 1993). From Istanbul, Glassie's pursuit of comparative craftsmanship took him to Dhaka, where he concentrated on the ways in which artefacts both humble and exalted were connected by mass production and by artistic obligation. Pots fresh from the kiln were stacked in dizzying towers for sale; mass-produced rickshaws or tri-wheeled cycles were almost encrusted with painted designs, as if the attractiveness of any particular taxi were dependent on the sweepstakes of its painted virtuosity (Glassie 1997; Glassie and Mahmud 2000). These latter works, especially, marked a change in Glassie's scholarly method. Instead of seeing the tradition of folklife studies as informing his work, he initiated a new kind of material ethnography. This new ethnographic agenda, borrowing perhaps from the cross-cultural study of aesthetics developed by his friend Robert Plant Armstrong during the 1970s (Armstrong 1971), placed a heightened emphasis on the cross-cultural vitality and virtuosity of craftsmanship (in pottery, metal-working, and painted ornament) that appeared wherever he looked. In *Material Culture* (1999) he drew upon decades of previous fieldwork to offer a chapter on 'The Potter's Art' that works comparatively and develops a sequence distilled from earlier publications on Bangladesh, Turkey, and America, and then includes a new meditation on the pottery made by Norio Agawa in Japan (Glassie 1999: 198–221). The value of these investigations emerges in the final paragraph of the book: 'Examined closely, analyzed formally on the grounds of compassion', Glassie maintains, and 'then *manipulated into comparative array*, material culture breaks open to reveal the complexity of time, its simultaneous urges to progress, revitalization, and stability' (Glassie 1999: 353, emphasis added). It is the comparative juxtaposition that makes possible the productive, shattering moment of material culture.

Gerald L. Pocius' ethnographic study, *A Place to Belong: community order and everyday space in Calvert, Newfoundland* (1991), used a folklife approach to combine the results of historical and ethnographic research into a single work. As Pocius continued to work on households in Calvert, he increasingly documented how technology coexisted with tradition, most strikingly in his discussion of the provision of small, traditional Newfoundland houses with satellite dishes to better pick up mainland television broadcasts, even though such devices remain 'subservient to the continued use of spaces' and 'maintaining constant and continued social contact is paramount' (Pocius 1991: 285–287, fig. 155). People in Newfoundland thus commonly defy the neat dichotomies of outsiders (Figure 4.6), of planners from Toronto, or of tourists from the mainland and from the United States. Neither 'traditionalists' nor enthusiasts of an outright consumer culture, individuals in Calvert, Pocius showed, lived not only between such imagined poles: their sharing of space and attitudes to commodities challenge social scientific accounts of material culture and modernization (Pocius 1991: 282–285).

John D. Dorst's *The Written Suburb: an American site, an ethnographic dilemma* (1989) explored the relationships between folklorism and consumption in suburban Chadds Ford, Pennsylvania. Dorst focused attention on a series of linked phenomena in which material culture and local history map on to nostalgia and commerce. Local collector Chris Sanderson assembled a small museum in his house, and constructed an alternate temporality from the abstract order of his classification technique. Only miles from a Revolutionary War battle ground (with its own reductionist interpretation), the radical reshaping of history at Chadds Ford Days, the annual local festival (folklorism in the extreme) drew upon legend, folklore, and the town's own cultivation of Andrew Wyeth-who-is-now-a-God mythology. Considering that Dorst was trained in folklore and folklife, his choice of doing an ethnographic study of landscape and material life in deep suburbia was unusual at the time, when postmodernism endowed many projects with an appreciable irony. His study revealed clearly the ways in which doing a field study of folklorism proved an 'ethnographic dilemma', to be sure. According to Dorst 'the culture of advanced consumer capitalism . . . consists largely in the processes of

Fig. 4.6 A 1970s bungalow at Plate Cove, Newfoundland, Canada. Constructed c.1978, this house retains a direct and informal entry through the side kitchen door via a small set of steps and platform called locally the 'bridge', but combines this traditional element with a formal plan of a catalogue-ordered bungalow, the font door of which is never used (photo: Robert Saint George).

self-inscription, indigenous self-documentation and endlessly reflexive simulation' (Dorst 1989: 2). Thus, the constant production of self-referential 'texts' (in an expansive sense) marks the suburb of Chadds Ford as a tourist site and as a 'postmodern' place (a text-driven and simulacra-obsessed zone); 'what makes the contemporary suburb a privileged Site of postmodernity', Dorst observes, 'is the way it foregrounds in everyday life the pervasiveness of the commodity form, of the simulacrum, of spectacle and an economy of sign exchange' (Dorst 1989: 3). But that carries a still darker message. 'The suburb', Dorst asserts, 'is the emblem in social life not of some cultural core with an identifiable content, but of the de-centered condition of postmodernity in general' (Dorst 1989: 3). As these comments suggest, Dorst's ethnographic dilemma came in part from the suburb and its cultural qualities. At the same time, however, Dorst found the suburb fascinating precisely because no amount of training in folklife studies under Yoder had prepared him for it. The older model of 'folk culture' had a 'cultural core', the specific small town or rural area with a deep history packed into its fields, fences, and houses. But the suburban scene that confronted Dorst presented questions on every front: What if the 'community' chosen for an ethnographic study was neither old nor rural and had a built landscape in part developed by speculative builders during the past decade? Yet, the 'suburban way of life' is a commonplace in the Western world, surrounding every city. With the exception of Dorst's book, we have no equally subtle ethnographic work on the material culture and folklife of these commuter enclaves.

While Dorst's project reminds us that conditions of late consumer capitalism and the auto-ethnographic and reflexive sign-work it engenders are defining features of the deep suburban landscape, field anthropologists are discovering similar semiotics at work in a variety of west European locales. As the intellectual centre of an updated, commodity-poetics approach to folklife must necessarily shift, it is not surprising that contemporary cultural anthropologists interested in the production and marketing of representations would find in folklife a new and vital ethnographic subject. The work of cultural anthropologist Andrea Klimt stands out in this recent body of ethnographic field studies of folklorism, or of the effect of commodity poetics on European ethnology. In a recent essay she co-authored with João Leal, Klimt pauses to consider the ethnographic interest in folklore studies, how 'folk culture'—or ethnology or *volkskunde*—became, 'in the last decades of the 20th century, a major object of reflexive interrogation in contemporary anthropological research' (Klimt and Leal 2005: 5). Her interest concentrates on the 'thematization of folk culture in diverse national traditions of European (and Western) anthropology', and, in particular, 'in the political aspects of the appropriation of folklore, stressing its contemporary uses by cultural activists and policy makers, and by nationalist, regionalist and ethnic movements' (Klimt and Leal 2005: 5–6). While the different refractions of folk culture through-out the Lusophone world is the nominal topic of inquiry, the various pragmatic uses of folklorism connect their communities in Lisbon, Cape Verde, Brazil, and New Jersey, to Klimt's own previous work on Portuguese transnational migrants in Hamburg, Germany (Klimt 1989, 2000). Along the way, Klimt and Leal cite familiar figures: Hermann Bausinger, Regina Bendix, and through them both Hans Moser, as well as William Wilson's examination of folklore and nationalism in Finland (Wilson 1976).

CONCLUSIONS: WINDS OF CHANGE

The study of material culture in folklife studies has undergone a remarkable shift since the early twentieth century. What began as a unified and total method for exploring the tightly integrated expressive genres of a single folk culture—usually regional or ethnic—has developed into a field focused on the historical and ethnographic study of the roles that material things and geographic places have played in regional, nationalist, and transnational political movements. When Don Yoder surveyed the international state of the field in 1963 and used it to organize and empower Swedish, Swiss, Scottish, Welsh, Northern Irish, German, and Pennsylvania German traditions of material culture, museums, archives, and research institutes, he was in fact already adopting the pragmatics of folklife studies discourse for particular institutional ends and in local ethnic and regional politics. Even when one accounts for the rise of folklorism in Germany and in such other places as Belgium and Italy, it has never totally eclipsed the reality of those poetics to which it was so effectively moored. After all, even Yoder has long been fascinated by the 'kitchification' of tradition. Since the 1960s, at least, he has patiently amassed a collection of Pennsylvania Dutch decorative placemats, napkins embossed with horse and buggy designs, and gaudy Dutch matchbooks. Any scholar interested in traditions will appreciate how such traditions can become valuable; but folklife studies represents a distinctive kind of investment in the culture futures market. Consider this: along with his earlier studies of Pennsylvania spirituals and folksongs (Yoder *et al.* 1951; Yoder 1961), Yoder has also co-authored a study on the commercialization of the hex sign or barn star (Yoder and Graves 1989), written a foreword for a study of a West Virginia tattoo artist (Yoder 1981), and finished a recent independent study of Groundhog day, full of astute comments on its growth from a small regional occurrence to its present, highly mediatized national significance (Yoder 2003).

When he first outlined the heuristic promise of the folklife studies approach over 40 years ago and effectively pushed it to include material culture as a central concern of method and such related issues as collection, interpretation, and conservation, Don Yoder caused the winds of intellectual change to shift. In part because of his example, and in part because of the work of many other scholars working in his slipstream, those winds are blowing still.

CHAPTER 5

....

MATERIAL HISTORIES

....

ANN BROWER STAHL

INTRODUCTION

....

If human life worlds are made as much of matter as ideas—consisting of 'bundles' or 'gatherings' of people, things, and thoughts (Latour 1993a, 2004a; Ingold 2000a, 2000b; Keane 2003; Meskell 2005a)—then the study of history should be significantly enhanced by incorporating material evidence. Historical archaeologists have laboured to make this point since the 1960s, at the same time as they have struggled to move beyond James Deetz's tongue-in-cheek definition of historical archaeology as 'the most expensive way in the world to learn something we already know' (Deetz 1991: 1). Deetz's quip reflected the priority that standard history placed on words over objects, a priority that assumed a more general ontological privileging of the mental over the material. Objects, in this view, reflected ideas impressed upon the world. Words—written or oral—were seen to provide a more direct conduit to the past than material remains (artefacts, buildings, landscapes), which were perceived as sources to be consulted when these more reliable sources ran cold. For example, Marc Bloch, a founder of the French 'Annales school' argued the particular value of material sources in the study of invisible or under-represented groups in European society (commoners and peasants, Bloch 1953), a view that also informed American historical archaeology's focus on marginalized populations (e.g. Singleton 1985; Ferguson 1992; see Hall and Silliman 2006; Hicks and Beaudry

2006a). In other world areas, the availability of documentary evidence marked a boundary between 'prehistory' and 'history' that allowed the past of non-literate colonized peoples to be investigated separately from that of the literate colonizers with whom they interacted (Lightfoot 1995; Reid and Lane 2004; Wilkie 2005). But recent theoretical retoolings in the social sciences have questioned this prioritization of language (Bourdieu 1977; Latour 1993a; Pinney 2005) and underscored the significance of 'materiality' (Miller 2005a; cf. Ingold 2007a, 2007b), suggesting that we are fashioned as much by our material worlds as we fashion them (Pinney 2005). In this view, objects and people transform one another (Ingold 2000b, 2007a: 13). Contexts are produced through things that condition practices that actively fashion continuities and discontinuities with the past (Strathern 1990; N. Thomas 1999). If material configurations 'matter' in the operation of social life (Miller 1998b), it follows that our historical understandings will be enriched by taking inter-relationships between humans and materials into account. It is these configurations and inter-relationships that are a focus of what are here termed 'material histories'.

The idea of 'material histories' explored in this chapter has a dual sense (cf. Trouillot 1995: 2, 29). First, it underscores the ways in which material culture was bound up in how history as socio-historical process was lived, thus revealing how its study can provide insights into past practices and processes. Secondly, it reminds us that historical accounts—our insights into socio-historical processes—are material (i.e. germane or pertinent) to the present, thus underscoring the need to consider how those accounts are shaped by and simultaneously shape contemporary perceptions and practices (Hall 2001). Although there is value in studying the material histories of wide ranging contexts, this chapter focuses particularly on the value of material sources for deepening and extending our understanding of the effects of historical global connections on daily life as argued by a number of archaeologists, historical anthropologists, and historians (Thomas 1991; Comaroff and Comaroff 1997; Ulrich 2001; Lyons and Papadopoulos 2002; Lawrence 2003; Silliman 2005; Lightfoot 2006; Brook 2007; Ogundiran and Falola 2007). Although Marxist perspectives have inspired some of the authors drawn on in this chapter, the material histories explored here should not be confused with historical materialism or a materialist conception of history that privileges production and economy.

Whereas scholars today increasingly value material things as sources of historical insight (Brumfiel 2003), producing material histories that bring into view the bundling of people, things, and ideas past and present requires changes in academic practice (Joyce and Lopiparo 2005) if we are to produce more than simply *histories of materials*. Accordingly, this chapter begins by clarifying the distinction between 'material histories' and 'histories of materials', and explores analytical strategies that have proved valuable in generating material histories. Case studies from Africa are used to exemplify these strategies and to explore how studies of world history are enriched by the study of material culture. Building especially upon the insights of historical anthropologists such as Sidney Mintz (1985), Igor Kopytoff (1986), and Ann Stoler (2001), this chapter examines how material flows—circulations of people and objects—offer a productive and powerful pathway for analysing the mutually determining connections between an interconnected 'West' and 'the rest' (Hall 1996) with implications for how we apprehend contemporary world processes (Stoler 2006a, 2006b).

MATERIAL MOMENTS AND HISTORIES

One afternoon in the late 1990s Krista Feichtinger, an undergraduate who was inventorying bottle glass from archaeological excavations at the nineteenth-/early twentieth-century site of Makala Kataa in west-central Ghana, poked her head through my office door. She had been painstakingly piecing together fragments of glass recovered from archaeological deposits associated with a domestic structure and had reconstructed portions of an embossed jar bearing the letters:

V
CHE[partial S]
NEW YOR[partial K]

Krista was excited, and wondered aloud what the jar might have contained. Her imagination was captured by the fact that, working in an archaeology lab in upstate New York, she was piecing together a bottle that had originated in New York, but had been recovered from a village site in West Africa. Here was a material moment—one in which an artefact and its context brought into view historical connections between industrial America and rural Africa. Krista later identified the object as a 1908 container used by the Chesebrough Company of New York for retail sale of Vaseline. This petroleum jelly product was first distilled by Robert Chesebrough who, on an 1859 visit to the oil fields of Titusville, Pennsylvania, observed men in the oil fields using the 'rod wax' that built up on their drilling rigs as an ointment to treat wounds. By 1870, Chesebrough was marketing a distillate inspired by rod wax from his Brooklyn factory under the registered trademark Vaseline in a manufacturing process for which he received a US Patent in 1872 (Vaseline 2008). Sold as a protective skin ointment and first aid remedy, it had become a household product in the United States by the final decades of the nineteenth century. Among all the objects recovered from Makala Kataa, the reconstructed jar conjured the changing social and political-economic fields of early twentieth-century Banda villagers, implying as it did a ramifying web of productive relations, merchant connections, and consumer tastes, desires, and practices. In this sense, it prompted a material moment in the present at the same time as it evoked a material moment in the past, one in which a village consumer experimented with a novel product that bore superficial resemblance to locally available emollients (e.g. shea butter). Assuming the bottle arrived with its contents intact, it may have been put to familiar uses, for example as a substitute for local body rubs in a practice that simultaneously produced continuities (a familiar practice) and discontinuities (a novel product) with the past, perhaps with unanticipated consequences. The jar thus prompted material moments both past and present that informed on broader socio-historical processes of production, exchange, and consumption.

The Vaseline jar fragments are a quintessential example of what James Deetz (1977: 4) famously referred to as historical archaeology's focus upon 'small things forgotten'. Deetz borrowed this term from a seventeenth-century appraiser's entry to refer to objects that may have been overlooked in an estate inventory despite their value. Deetz argued that such 'small things'—whether gravestones, ceramics, tools, or house facades—'carry messages from their makers and users' (Deetz 1977: 4), and that it is the job of the historical archaeologist to decode those messages as an aid to better understand the human past.

Deetz's vision of historical archaeology inspired considerable work in the closing decades of the twentieth century at the same time as it became the focus of critique. For some, studies such as *In Small Things Forgotten* provided insights into everyday life that could augment historical studies in new ways, enabling archaeology to serve as more than simply a tool for verification or a material footnote to the rich documentary record of American history. Inspired by Henry Glassie's (1975) structuralist interpretation of how changes in vernacular architecture reflected changes in the eighteenth-century world view, Deetz offered compelling evidence of shifts in early American material culture ranging from head stones to table settings that expressed a new emphasis on balance, symmetry, and individuation in artefacts. In this formulation, historical archaeology augmented history by delineating how everyday material worlds were reconfigured with a shift to a Georgian world view.

Inspiring as Deetz's perspectives were, they were circumscribed by the notion that material culture is 'not culture but its product' and, therefore, reflects 'how profoundly our world is the product of our thoughts' (Deetz 1977: 24). Glassie (1999: 41–42) succinctly captured this approach when he observed that 'material culture is culture made material; it is the inner wit at work in the world . . . the study of material culture uses objects to approach human thought and action. . . . Artifacts set the mind in the body, the body in the world.'

For Deetz and Glassie, then, the study of material culture provides access to the workings of the mind, enabling them to witness a history of mentalities through a history of materials. Yet in practice, the insights derived from such an approach in historical archaeology appeared thin in relation to the 'thick' detail of textually based historical accounts.

The ontological premise that underwrote this approach to historical archaeology restricted the development of 'material histories'. Material culture was understood to *reflect* culture, and culture was imagined as an ethereal phenomenon that preceded its material existence (Pinney 2005: 257; cf. Latour 1993a; Ingold 2000b: 53). The archaeologist's fragments—such as the remains of bottles, beads, metal objects, or animal bones—represented a glass through which to view past culture darkly. The implication was that archaeology provided only a history of material culture: a narrative of how objects and material settings were transformed through changes initiated in the social or ideational realm.

An alternative ontological premise refuses to assign priority to mind and mental processes, but instead considers the bodily engagement with material worlds in which humans are constantly enmeshed as equally productive of cultural process (Latour 1993a; Ingold 2000a, 2007a). In this view it is important to consider how objects affect people, attending, for example, to how durable material culture shapes childhood socialization (Gosden 2005: 193–197), and more fundamentally how our immersion in a world of diverse materials generates and regenerates social worlds (Ingold 2007a: 4–9). By recognizing the central role of material practice in cultural process, historical studies can simultaneously engage phenomena that we analytically parse as landscapes, objects, bodies, and minds, in a manner similar to Pierre Bourdieu's idea of the *habitus* (Bourdieu 1977; see Gosden 1994: 11; Meskell 2005a: 3). From this perspective the material things that have so often been treated as ancillary to historical studies are instead viewed as sources of insight into the practices through which culture was—and is—actively produced.

Such an approach enhances the significance of Deetz's 'small things'. Though our understandings of past cultural process will always be partial, a focus on material practices helps us to move beyond histories of material to produce material histories of past life worlds that can in turn help us to apprehend the relational processes that condition contemporary life worlds. As such, material histories contribute to a broader 'emerging attempt to take the material world seriously in terms of how it affects human relations' (Gosden 2005: 196). Moreover, material histories have proved particularly effective in investigating the connections among societies formerly perceived as 'in' or 'outside' of history—in other words, between literate peoples who were perceived to have 'history' and were therefore proper objects of historical investigation and non-literate peoples who supposedly did not (Wolf 1982). The circulation of 'small things' brings the connections among so-called 'historic' and 'prehistoric' societies into view, enriching our apprehension of the relational processes through which the modern world emerged.

STUDYING MATERIAL PRACTICES: BIOGRAPHY, DEPOSITION, AND GENEALOGY

Three complementary analytical approaches in archaeology and anthropology have proved significant in helping us to develop insights into material histories: 'biographical' approaches to material culture inspired by the view that things both have and shape social lives; studies of deposition that provide important contextual insights into material practice; and genealogical perspectives on the replication and transformation of practices over time.

Biographical approaches to material practices draw our attention to the varied associations of objects as they circulate within and between contexts across a range of spatial scales (Schiffer 1972, 1976; Appadurai 1986b; Kopytoff 1986; Thomas 1991; Walker and Schiffer 2006). Objects are altered and may be put to varying uses through the course of their life history, with varied effects on those who use them. An object's life history can affect how people interact with it, classically illustrated by the fame acquired by specific shell armbands and necklaces as they circulated through the Trobriand kula exchange cycle (Leach and Leach 1983). Biographical approaches study the multiple phases of an object's life history by analysing commonalities and differences in the forms and associations of specific object classes and the 'paths and diversions' that characterize their circulations (Appadurai 1986b: 16–29). Interest has focused particularly on how objects produced in one cultural context are recontextualized as they are put to use in another (Kopytoff 1986: 67; see also Thomas 1991; Sahlins 1994). While biographical approaches have enhanced our appreciation of the active role of objects in shaping human experience, they do not in and of themselves overcome the tendency to privilege mind over embodied action if objects are seen primarily as carriers of meanings (e.g. Kopytoff 1986: 67; Gosden and Marshall 1999). But these approaches hold considerable promise for helping us to move beyond a view of objects as sources of *either* continuity *or* discontinuity by recognizing that objects simultaneously mobilize familiarity, and therefore connections with past practice, at the same time as they present novelty and transform contexts. The complex ways in which object biographies are transformed through this process is illustrated by Nicholas Thomas' (1999) exploration of Samoan adoption of Tahitian-style bark cloth capes in a period of Christian conversion. These capes reconfigured bodily practices of exposure and display in ways understood by Christian missionaries in relation to decency but which Thomas (1999: 18) suggests Christian Samoans understood as productive of forms of power consistent with previous practice. The objects were thus recontextualized at the same time as they reconfigured the context in which Christian Samoans operated. To date, biographical approaches have privileged consumption over production (Ingold 2007a: 9; though cf. Schiffer

1976), but as Ingold (2000b) stresses, there is considerable scope for deepening our appreciation of how our life worlds emerge through interactions of people and materials in the making of objects as well.

A focus on deposition draws attention to the practices and effects of drawing together—'bundling' or 'gathering'—of objects in specific contexts (Walker and Lucero 2000; Pollard 2001, 2008; Mills and Walker 2008a; Joyce with Pollard this volume, Chapter 12). This approach pays close attention to the ways in which objects and substances of diverse origins and histories may be combined to produce substantive connections and relationships, their co-presence producing networks and effects that shape human experience (Meskell 2005a: 4). Whereas some have argued that deposition and resulting object configurations were akin to messages that communicated prefigured meanings (Hodder 1991c), recent literature informed by a focus on materiality underscores the active role of depositional practice in configuring social process and constituting people as social beings (Pollard 2008: 45–46). These depositional acts can range from symbolically charged ritualized performances, as for example burial practices that simultaneously shape the identities of the living (e.g. Brück 2004), to habitual, unreflective practices of refuse disposal. Whereas the former seems to be more obviously symbolically charged, recent literature stresses that culture emerges as much through mundane, embodied action in the world as through formalized moments. Comparative studies of depositional practice that analyse the varied contexts and combinations in which specific objects occur help archaeologists to construct object biographies that in turn help us to envision how object circulations produced, maintained, or disrupted social relations (Stahl 2008a). Similarities in depositional practices through time may point to referential or citational practices that shaped social memory at the same time as they forged networks of relations among people and things (Joyce 2008a; Pollard 2008: 58–59). When augmented by a genealogical approach to materiality, attention to depositional practice provides insight into the processes through which continuities in social worlds were forged and changes took form.

Genealogical approaches focus attention on the reproduction and transformation of practice in time (Joyce and Lopiparo 2005; Joyce 2008a). Architectural forms, for example, condition human action, and a genealogical approach encourages us to consider the ways in which these forms shape continuities and foster change in social practice through time (Gosden 2005: 199; Nielsen 2008). Practices of modifying the earth and depositing soil (as in the filling of pits or the construction of earthen monuments) can create connections with past practice at the same time as they actively produce social relations through the process of building, as for example has been argued in relation to Mississippian societies of the American Midwest (Pauketat and Alt 2005; Pauketat 2008). Genealogies of practice are constructed through a comparative approach that systematically explores commonalities and differences in practices at sites in a region through time, referred to as a 'direct historical approach' when sites can be historically linked to living populations (for a methodological discussion, see Stahl 2001: 19–40).

In combination, a focus on object biographies, depositional practices, and their genealogies can yield rich insights into the contextually specific forms of 'bundling' through which worlds were woven (Ingold 2000b). The empirically rich and contextually attuned material histories that result from these analytical approaches provide robust insight into the processes through which cultural continuities and change—past and present—are forged.

MATERIAL HISTORIES OF GLOBAL ENTANGLEMENTS

The study of material histories is refiguring our understanding of a wide range of time periods in many world areas (e.g. J. S. Thomas 1999; Gosden 2005; Pauketat 2008; Pollard 2008); however, the remainder of this chapter focuses on the material histories of global entanglements associated with the emergence of a 'modern world system' over the last five centuries (Wallerstein 1974). This provides a particularly rich—if complex—site for exploring dynamic processes of 'bundling' in relation to changing political economic conditions. Until recently this process has been understood primarily through an economic lens (stressing either progress or dependency), but today we appreciate the extent to which it involved a relational discourse of self and other, 'us' and 'them' (Hall 1996) in a mutually constitutive process of nation- and empire-building (Stoler and Cooper 1997: 21; see also Wolf 1982; Thomas 1991; Cohn 1996). Whereas earlier literature highlighted the discursive dimension of this process, exploring the imagery and terminology through which social distinctions were produced (e.g. Said 1978; Mudimbe 1988, 1994), recent literature underscores the importance of material practices (e.g. Steiner 1994). These ranged in form and scale from the officially sanctioned and public to the quotidian and intimate. Europeans and 'others' were mutually constituted at international expositions and world fairs that showcased technological progress by juxtaposing artefacts drawn from both metropole and colony (Breckenridge 1989; Rydell 1993; McGowan 2005). England's 1851 Crystal Palace Exhibition was experienced by the thronging crowds who arrived on newly completed rail lines linking provinces to the capital as a 'precipice in time' (Stocking 1987: 1–6) where past and future were on display. The material lesson inscribed by exhibits of non-industrial and industrial technologies was that, although all humans perhaps shared a capacity for innovation, not all had progressed to the same level. Social distinction was also produced more intimately

(Stoler 2006a) through foodways, practices of home furnishing (Chattopadhyay 2002), and dress (Callaway 1992) among other mundane activities (see Comaroff and Comaroff 1997). Whereas material practices such as nineteenth-century British colonial preoccupations with dressing for dinner in the bush (Callaway 1992) reproduced social distinctions between colonizer and colonized, a key insight that has emerged from studies of domestic practice in colonial contexts in a variety of world areas is that distinctions upheld in public discourse were often blurred by domestic material practice. For example, archaeological remains from eighteenth-century contexts in Cape Town, South Africa reveal that masters and slaves consumed the same low-quality food resources (Hall 1993: 188) at the same time as practices of dress blurred officially sanctioned social distinctions in eighteenth-century Louisiana (Loren 2001).

A general insight to emerge from studies of material histories is that circulations of goods and people refigured processes of identification, as for example when consumers embraced goods to distinguish themselves from their neighbours (Prestholdt 2004: 761). While examples highlighted in this paper are drawn from case studies that analyse the emergence of the modern world system, other studies demonstrate the value of material histories in apprehending these processes in other contexts as well, as for example in reference to ancient Rome (Woolf 1997, 1998) or Iron Age Europe (Dietler 1990a, 1998a). The circulations of people that accompanied the emergence of a modern world system—missionaries, colonists, colonial officials, merchants, social outcasts, indentured and enslaved labourers—contributed to new material practices of inclusion and exclusion (Stoler 1989). Importantly, these circulations of goods and people were not confined to the metropolitan-colony flows that are so often the focus of analytical attention in historical studies of imports and exports. As detailed in examples below, personnel, ideas, and objects circulated from one colony to another (Gupta 2001: 46). At the same time goods crossed the national and imperial boundaries that often circumscribe our analytical units. Following these circulations provides an analytical pathway for overcoming the 'archived grooves' (Stoler 2001: 863) of conventional histories that presume the boundaries of future nations.

A key insight that has emerged from studies that follow the biographies of objects as they cross cultural boundaries is that goods are not stable entities, fixed by their production and retaining essential qualities wherever they were traded; rather, indigenous peoples were selectively interested in specific goods which they put to their own uses (Sahlins 1994). As anthropologist Nicholas Thomas noted,

To say that black bottles were given does not tell us what was received. This is so partly because the uses to which things were put were not inscribed in them by their metropolitan producers, and partly because gifts and commodities could be variously recontextualized as commodities or gifts, as unique articles for display, as artifacts of history, or as a new category of prestige valuable, the manipulation of which sustained the construction of political inequalities.

Thomas (1991: 208)

But as Thomas (N. Thomas 1999: 18) later observed, recontextualization should not be understood as a conservative strategy that merely assimilates the unfamiliar to the familiar; rather, he underscored the 'doubleness' of objects in that they 'mobilised certain precedents, certain prior values' at the same time as they 'possessed novelty and distinctiveness'. In this sense, new goods remake the contexts of human actors and thereby condition their subsequent performances (Strathern 1990; see also Pinney 2005). Equally as important, recontextualization is a reciprocal process; just as goods from the metropole were recontextualized by non-metropolitan consumers, so too were goods from the colonies recontextualized by metropolitan consumers (Thomas 1991: 125–184).

Many anthropologists have approached the recontextualization of material goods as primarily a question of meaning and linguistic signification. Inspired by this view, expressed for example by Mary Douglas and Baron Isherwood in their classic study of 'the world of goods' as 'good for thinking' and 'shor[ing] up conceptual categories' (Douglas and Isherwood 1979: 61, 66), concern has focused on how objects are endowed with new meanings as they cross cultural boundaries (McCracken 1988; Howes 1996a). But approaches centred upon 'the meanings of things' (Hodder 1989) are increasingly challenged, both theoretically and methodologically (Stahl 2002; see Strathern 1990).

One problem is that Sausurrian-inspired semiotic approaches privilege language and mind as sites of meaning-making, assuming an ontological priority of language over bodily practice, an assumption that is today widely questioned by scholars who emphasize the role of embodied practice and practical knowledge in cultural production (Lefebvre 1991; Jackson 1996; Stoller 1997; Bloch 1998: 32–35). Secondly, a scholarly preoccupation with meaning privileges a reflective and retrospective form of inquiry that obscures the practical domain of human action (Giddens 1976a: 28, 53; Bloch 1995; Jackson 1996: 42). In other words, it misconstrues the way scholars approach the world (through reflective contemplation) for the way in which humans engage in practical social action (Bourdieu 1977: 1–4; 1998: 127–140). Thirdly, meanings vary in time, space, and in relation to social parameters such as gender, class, or status. Thus social actors and analysts (e.g. anthropologists and historians) alike are confronted by polysemy (Barthes 1967a; Riggins 1994). These challenges are compounded when we work in contexts where material remains from archaeological contexts are our primary source of insight into past life worlds. Careful attention to context can provide insight into meaningful relations among objects (e.g. Hodder 1991c: 143–146), but the attribution of specific meanings generally relies on the illustrative use of analogical models that merely project a select meaning from the present into the past (Stahl 2002: 831).

More promisingly, the analytical strategies outlined above—biographical, depositional, and genealogical approaches—help us to develop robust insights into how objects were recontextualized as they moved across cultural contexts and to their effects on subsequent cultural practice. Insights into what constituted familiar practice can be discerned from temporally seriated studies of genealogically linked contexts (Stahl 2002). These material configurations can help us to discern what appear to be 'customary paths' (Appadurai 1986b: 29) and material patterns that suggest diversions from them. In an approach that combined biographical and genealogical analyses of European Iron Age contexts, Dietler (1990a, 1998) discerned variation in the way that Roman drinking paraphernalia were adopted by Iron Age societies in relation to their previous practices. Contextual analyses of depositional practice can provide insight into whether new objects were the focus of novel practices or were incorporated in ways that suggest they substituted for familiar ones. In short, these strategies enable us to move beyond meaning-centred approaches to infer sequences of action (Joyce and Lopiparo 2005: 369) from artefacts, contexts, and depositional practices that provide the evidential basis for inferring compositional processes—the 'bundling' or 'gathering' that comprise culture-making in specific locales and temporal contexts. When viewed genealogically (Gosden 2005; Pauketat and Alt 2005), objects permit us to discern diversions from and continuities with previous practice (Stahl 2002), and thereby gain insight into the trajectories of culture-making practices as they unfolded in relation to global entanglements that reshaped the object worlds of recent centuries.

I turn now to explore how the analytical approaches described above and detailed elsewhere in this volume can help us to develop material histories of African global entanglements.

MATERIAL HISTORIES OF WEST AFRICAN GLOBAL ENTANGLEMENTS

West Africa's long history of global connections extends from at least the first millennium AD when Saharan trade forged intercontinental links between sub-Saharan West Africa and the Mediterranean world. These networks were transformed after the fifteenth century by the emergence of Atlantic connections that profoundly altered West Africa's political economic landscapes. Goods and people circulated widely through processes that refigured life in areas linked by the triangular trade that moved finished goods from Europe to Africa, the enslaved from Africa to the western hemisphere, and agricultural commodities from there to Europe. Through the course of the Atlantic trade, Europeans imported a variety of goods to West Africa, which were selectively adopted by West African peoples and put to both familiar and novel purposes. Formal colonization occurred late—in many areas not until the end of the nineteenth century—but resulted nonetheless in transformations of daily practices wrought by colonial policies. Recent archaeological research demonstrates the value of material sources in studying the processes through which West Africans negotiated the changing landscape of these global entanglements. This work exemplifies the analytical strategies outlined above and has resulted in material histories that enrich our appreciation of West African cultural dynamics in an era in which profound changes were accompanied by equally as important continuities in material practice.

Akin Ogundiran's (2002) study of how cowries were recontextualized in Yorubaland through the course of Atlantic trade exemplifies the analytical value of biographical and genealogical perspectives in developing material histories of West African global entanglements. During the early modern period, Europeans imported vast quantities of cowrie shells (*Cypraea moneta*) from the Indian Ocean to West Africa where they served as a form of currency in the context of the Atlantic slave trade (Hogendorn and Johnson 1986; Mitchell 2005: 118). Whereas attention has long focused on their use as a monetary instrument, Ogundiran analysed how cowries were used, and therefore valued, in relation to extant practice and how these uses simultaneously built upon and transformed ritual practice and the materiality of social distinction. Whereas beads of various kinds had long circulated in West Africa and operated as objects of political capital in Yorubaland from the late first millennium AD, cowries were rare before the sixteenth century and used primarily in divination and propitiatory practice. With increased circulation in the context of Atlantic trade, cowries were put to novel purposes. Informed by Igor Kopytoff's (1986) biographical approach to material culture, Ogundiran explored the relationship between novel and extant practices by comparatively analysing the contexts and associations of beads and cowries to generate insight into their respective social valuation. He demonstrates how extant practices of social distinction involving beads provided a context for the reception of cowries, at the same time as their expanding circulation opened the way for transformations in ritual practice and wealth accumulation. The proliferating use of cowries in commoner shrines where elites used beads underscores the extent to which 'cowries became the value register for harnessing the spiritual and temporal powers of successful men and women after the sixteenth century' (Ogundiran 2002: 448). Through the course of the Atlantic era, cowrie accumulation was democratized as cowries became more available to a wider array of people. At the same time, cowries became a powerful ritual mediator between temporal and spiritual forces, an insight that derives from 'following the archaeological trail of cowries' function in ritual contexts' (Ogundiran 2002: 454).

By 'following the object' over time within a specific geographical context, Ogundiran convincingly illuminates the way that cowries were 'bundled' in relation to deities and shrines and were associated with practices to ensure personal well-being. By focusing his study upon material things, he reveals both the dynamism of ritual practice and how novelty emerged from previous practice in a context of political economic transformation (Figure 5.1). In light of recent historical and anthropological literature that underscores the mediating role of ritual in West African negotiations of the predatory landscapes produced by the Atlantic slave trade (Brown 1996; Baum 1999; Ferme 2001: 37; Shaw 2002; Lovejoy and Richardson 2003: 105–106; Parker 2004, 2006), biographical and genealogical approaches attuned to the dynamics of shrines and ritual practice (Bell 1992) provide a promising avenue for investigating the dynamics of Atlantic era societies (Stahl 2008b), as illustrated by recent research in Ghana. Specifically, by illuminating the material practices through which people negotiated the changing circumstances of their daily lives, object-focused histories enrich our understanding of the processes through which the modern world system emerged.

The Banda area of west central Ghana has been the focus of long-term research on the effects of global entanglements on daily life (Stahl 2001). Archaeological excavations at a series of adjacent sites have sampled different moments in Banda's complex history of inter-regional connections, beginning with sites abandoned

Fig. 5.1 Imported beads acquired through Atlantic connections play a central role in ritual practice in the Banda area, Ghana. Curated by elder women and stored in large calabashes, they are used in female rites of passage. The manacles pictured here are also used in contemporary ritual practice (photo: Alex Caton 1995).

early in the period of formal colonial rule in the late nineteenth century, extending through the period of the Atlantic trade when Banda was subject to the expansionist state of Asante during the late eighteenth and nineteenth centuries, and into the period when Saharan connections gave way to early Atlantic trade between the fourteenth and mid-seventeenth centuries (Stahl 2007). A comparative analysis of depositional practice informed by biographical and genealogical approaches illuminates the dynamics of shrines and sacrificial practices in relation to these shifting inter-regional entanglements (Stahl 2008a).

Contemporary ritual practice in the Banda area includes the deposition of objects—many drawn from mundane contexts—in shrine bundles that are secreted in ceramic vessels drawn from the repertoire of mundane pottery (Cruz 2003: 247, 265, 284) (Figure 5.2). These shrines are the focal point for animal sacrifice— typically of domestic animals whose blood is disgorged on or near the shrines— but their meat is consumed elsewhere with socially valued body parts (e.g. hind limbs) the prerogative of particular elders or chiefs. Thus, the flow of sacrificed animals is one among a number of practices that produces social hierarchy (Stahl 2008a: 169–170).

Archaeological evidence suggests continuity of this practice from nineteenth-century contexts in which we have documented bundles of objects linked to production (iron hoes), locally produced ornaments (iron bangles) and imported objects (glass beads) in shrine compositions. But this practice is discontinuous with sixteenth- to seventeenth-century contexts of an earlier Atlantic exchange in which, to date, we have no evidence for ceramic shrine bundles. Rather, ritualized practice appears to have centred on configurations of animal bones (dogs, pythons) and grinding stones (Stahl 2008a: 180–181) (Figure 5.3). These ritualized clusters of dog mandibles in sixteenth- and seventeenth-century contexts prompted an investigation of spatial patterning among dog bones more generally. An analytical strategy of 'following the bones' through the varied depositional contexts from which dog body parts were recovered provided insight into the biography of sacrificed animals (Stahl 2008a: 171–180), providing in turn insight into the materiality of social relations in this period. Mandibles of sacrificed dogs were bundled with other objects and incorporated into formalized shrines. Teeth were drilled and likely used as ornaments. Lower limb and cranial elements were deposited as part of generalized refuse on the site, while body and upper limb elements were more likely to be deposited in pits, in one instance in association with disarticulated human remains. The absence of upper hind limbs in archaeological context is not entirely accounted for by density mediated survivorship of bone, and their absence resonates with the common ethnographic practice of reserving upper hind limbs for chiefs or specific elders, underscoring the ways in which the flow of body parts produces social distinctions. Notably, our evidence suggests that the practice of dog sacrifice dropped from the practical repertoire of later settlements at which ceramic shrine bundles are documented while it

Fig. 5.2 A household shrine in the Banda area, Ghana. A variety of objects are incorporated into bundles secreted within ceramic vessels that are a focal point for offerings. This shrine remains active despite 'abandonment' of the associated dwelling (photo: Ann Stahl 1986).

Fig. 5.3 A household shrine incorporating grinding stones, Sameed, Tongo–Tengzug, Ghana (photo: Tim Insoll; from Insoll 2006, figure 3).

persisted at others, suggesting multiple communities of practice and underscoring the complexity of material histories (Stahl 2008a: 185).

Whereas the above described examples illustrate the value of genealogical approaches for investigating the dynamics of ritualization, they hold promise in studying a wide array of practices, relating to craft production, subsistence, or settlement, in relation to the exigencies of the Atlantic and internal slave trades (Stahl 2008b). For example, de Barros (2001) has explored the effects of refuging on technological practice in the Bassar region of northern Togo. Under pressure of slaving, Bassar people were forced to retreat to refuge zones where their access to ceramic trade wares was diminished. De Barros argues that the disruption of trade by unrelenting slave raiding prompted experimentation, as potters pioneered new clay sources and worked out new fabric recipes. In another example, variable approaches to forming and shaping pottery among potters in southern Mali led Barbara Frank (1993) to suggest that the distinctive technological style of Kadiolo potters—masked though it was by commonalities of vessel shape and decoration—was a legacy of their enslaved origins. She bases this insight on the conservatism of embodied practice in which habitual ways of moulding pots (e.g. through coiling or drawing and pulling) linked to motor habits acquired through a learning or apprenticeship process have been shown to be more resistant to change than other aspects of ceramic style (Gosselain 2000). Frank argues that these Kadiolo women, 'forced by circumstance to lose their social identity, chose to keep their skills as potters and to continue making pottery in the distinctive way their mothers taught them' (Frank 1993: 396).

In light of historical evidence that enslaved craft specialists were often put to work producing goods for their masters, Frank's approach holds promise for investigating the effects of incorporating slaves on an array of technological practices. Comparative genealogical study of operational sequences and techno-logical styles (Gosselain 1998, 2000) may help us to discern instances in which captives maintained distinctive approaches to craft production despite superficial accommodation to the stylistic requirements of their masters.

Ogundiran's (2002) study of cowrie shells, discussed above, demonstrates the analytical power of following objects in contexts of consumption, while Frank's (1993) underscores the value of paying careful attention to practices of production. But expanding the lens of this strategy highlights the relational quality of produc-tion and consumption. Taking Mintz's (1985) lead, extending the scope and scale of a biographical approach enhances our appreciation of how metropolitan produc-tion and non-metropolitan consumption conditioned one another. Following objects from their sources through contexts of consumption can help us to surmount the 'archived grooves' against which Stoler (2001: 863) warns. This is amply illustrated by studies that consider how consumption in the colonized regions conditioned metropolitan production.

Whereas the power of the 'core' to determine the path of the 'periphery' was assumed by earlier world systems theorists (see Ortner 1984 for a discussion), material histories of global entanglements underscore how consumer preferences in areas considered marginal to the emergence of global economies shaped metro-politan production (Inikori 2002). Traders ignorant of African tastes in textiles, beads, and metal products found themselves burdened with unsaleable goods and quickly adjusted their inventories (Richardson 1979; Steiner 1985; Alpern 1995). But only recently are we coming to appreciate the effects of these preferences on European production (e.g. Inikori 2002). Steiner (1985), for example, explored how the aesthetic and practical demands of West African consumers shaped nineteenth-century textile production in Manchester and Rouen. Similarly, Roberts (1996) demonstrated how West African demand fuelled early nineteenth-century French industrialization of cloth production in Pondicherry, India. Here, so-called guinée cloth was produced specifically for sale in Senegal where it was crucial to French efforts to extract Senegalese gum (from the southern margins of the Sahara), which was in turn crucial to the success of metropolitan textile printing in Europe. In East Africa the temporally and spatially varied demands of consumers forced traders and ultimately manufacturers to supply goods that were 'calibrated for the market' (Prestholdt 2004: 763). Nineteenth-century American merchants and manufacturers struggled to produce brass wire to conform to the width, coil, and weight desired by East Africans. Consumer preferences in beads were particularly specific, as were those for cloth, benefiting manufacturing concerns whose products were desired and creating a crisis for others (Prestholdt 2004: 769–773). At the same time, African preferences were reconfigured through a 'dialectic that reshaped extra-African locales at the same time that foreign interests, ideas, and strategies were transforming East Africa' (Prestholdt 2004: 780) In a contemporary example, Sylvanus adopts a biographical approach to the circulation of wax-print textiles and explores their shifting role in negotiations of African 'authenticity' both within and outside Africa today (Sylvanus 2007: 202). She explores the processes through which textiles manufactured first by Europeans and more recently by Chinese manufacturers for the African market, become African through localized consumption practices in parallel fashion to the way that imported Chinese porcelain became central to the perception of 'Englishness' from the eighteenth century. Once localized, wax prints in turn shape Western perceptions of 'Africanness' and circulate in Europe and North America as quintessential African products.

We understand less about how early modern metropolitan tastes and practices were recast through these material entanglements. Though we know something of the uses to which imports, such as ivory, ostrich feathers, or furs, and commodities such as sugar, coffee, and tobacco were put, we have much to learn about the processes through which these commodities were recontextualized in the metropole and how, through their consumption, they were bound up in novel 'bundlings' that conditioned metropolitan life worlds. Mintz's (1985) exemplary study of the changing uses of sugar—as a medicament and spice, as a luxury commodity, and later a staple that stretched the meagre resources of industrial workers—provides a model for the questions to be posed and the insights to be developed for other commodities. For example, it is apparent that consumption of ivory objects such as toilet sets, billiard balls, and pianos was intimately linked to the production of social distinction and gentility in the metropole (Burback 1984). But we lack detailed contextual studies that explore the effects of ivory circulations on practices and configurations of daily life in the metropole. As in Mintz's study of sugar, the growing metropolitan demand for products such as ivory should, of necessity, draw our attention yet again to the practices and implications of production in the 'peripheries' from which these products originated (see Stahl and Stahl 2004 for a discussion of how ivory production and consumption in Ghana may have been reconfigured in relation to metropolitan demand). But considerable research is required if we are to gain a detailed understanding of these material historical practices in metropolitan contexts (see Weatherill 1996 for a promising example).

As Mintz's (1985) masterful study of sugar demonstrated, following objects from contexts of production to consumption can bring into focus cross-wise linkages, for example, between colonies (e.g. French colonies in India and Africa; Roberts 1996: 168) or between regions belonging to separate colonial spheres (see also Pels 1997: 175). Prestholdt's (2004) analysis of the close ties between the interests of manufacturers and merchants in Salem, Massachusetts and East African traders and consumers underscores how the circulations of goods and people forged connections that diverged from the imperial 'grooves' that often structure academic inquiry. His discussion of how Bombay manufacturers succeeded in cultivating nineteenth-century East African markets at the same time as Indian textile production was being undermined by English colonial policy similarly underscores how, by following material circulations, we deepen our understanding of the complex and profoundly relational quality of global entanglements. Importantly, this sort of material history informs on practices that diverged from the vertically encompassing rhetorics and practices of colonial rule, thereby deepening our understanding of the reach of colonial governmentality (Scott 1995) and how people experienced the colonial state (cf. Ferguson and Gupta 2002).

Recent studies in the historical anthropology of colonialism have emphasized the relational processes through which technologies of state-craft and domination emerged (Stoler 1989; Comaroff and Comaroff 1991, 1997; Thomas 1994; Cohn 1996; Cooper and Stoler 1997; Dirks 2001). For example, practices of enumeration (e.g. census taking), surveillance (e.g. policing), hygiene (e.g. regulating sexual practice), and state ritual in the metropole were shaped by emergent practices in the colonies, which were in turn conditioned by debates over these practices in the metropole. Colonial forms of governmentality (Foucault 1991; Scott 1995; Pels 1997) were pervasive, extending into the most intimate spheres of domestic life. Documentary sources have proved valuable in investigating the links between discourses regarding domesticity and good governance in the European metropole and the colonies. Chakrabarty (1994), for example, explored how notions of domesticity in Britain were conditioned by debates over domesticity in British India. But by exploring the material practices, such as the furnishing and physical configurations of British Indian households (Chattopadhyay 2002; see also Comaroff and Comaroff 1997), we deepen our understanding of how material practices of domesticity in colonial contexts—practices of 'bundling' that materially distinguished colonial citizenry—simultaneously conditioned metropolitan practice. As Chattopadhyay (2002) notes, retiring colonial officials returned to Britain with furnishings acquired during their period of service in India. These transnational material cultural flows contributed to what Breckenridge (1989: 196) termed the *Victorian ecumene* that mutually constituted 'other' and 'us'. Metropolitan consumers envisioned distant colonies through the lens of their material products at the same time as these products were put to novel uses in the metropole. The preferences of colonial consumers (e.g. their taste in cloth) refigured metropolitan production and in turn metropolitan consumer preference. As such, systematic material histories of these circulations promise to yield rich insights into the relational production of metropoles and colonies.

Genealogically attuned material histories can provide valuable insight into the relationship between colonial policy and practice. It is widely recognized that colonial governmentality involved efforts to materially 'discipline' colonial subjects

(Comaroff and Comaroff 1997; Stoler and Cooper 1997). For example, nineteenth-century British discourses on village life both at home and abroad were simultaneously shaped by a nostalgia for rural life in industrializing Britain and a concern to reconfigure village life in the colonies (Dewey 1972; Breman 1988). Under an encompassing rubric of 'sanitation', wide-ranging reform policies shaped by British conceptualizations of order and accessibility (N. Thomas 1990: 158–166; Stahl 2001: 196–197) were pursued in both the 'urban jungles' of home and in the colonies (Dewey 1972: 293–294; also N. Thomas 1990: 157, 160; Comaroff and Comaroff 1997: 281). Consistent with broader British concerns with 'improvement' (Tarlow 2007; Hicks 2008b), Gold Coast colonial officials pursued a village planning policy from the late nineteenth century in which villagers were 'encouraged' to establish new villages laid out on a grid pattern, with specially defined locations for burying the dead, disposing of refuse, and so on (Stahl 2001: 103–105; see also N. Thomas 1990: 164–166). British colonial administrators idealized a particular form of house and compound arrangement, with implications for the material configuration of domestic living. Though villagers differentially resisted, adapted, or accepted these colonial governmental initiatives, 'the outcome was the modern "traditional" domain, which is as much a product of colonial history as the... [modern domain] to which it has become opposed' (N. Thomas 1990: 151–152). There is considerable potential for archaeological investigation of these processes, to assess first the degree to which policies of village planning were put into practice, and to investigate in specific geographical and temporal contexts the effects on material, culture-making practices.

Genealogical studies of village layout, refuse disposal, and depositional practices provide a means to investigate the differential effects of these policies in relation to practice in both metropolitan and non-metropolitan contexts. Extending beyond the rather shallow histories of formal colonial engagement associated with the production of documentary sources, deeper genealogies of settlement practices promise to inform on the effects of predation and warfare on village configuration in Africa. Though the topic has not been systematically studied, available sources underscore the varied ways in which threats of predation conditioned settlement practices of West African peoples. Under threat of warfare and slaving from the seventeenth through the nineteenth centuries, dispersed settlements gave way to nucleated villages in some areas (Mendonsa 2001: 39–44; Hawthorne 2003: 158), some of which were associated with fortress-like walls (Baum 1999: 93; Hawthorne 1999: 107; Hubbell 2001: 31–32; Swanepoel 2006: 273–276). Others responded to these threats by building expedient structures that could be easily abandoned (Guéye 2003: 54–56). Importantly, these insights draw attention to the dynamic material practices that disappear from view when we assume a stability of village life over time (cf. Breman 1988).

Banda Research Project investigations demonstrate the value of a direct historical approach in which successively earlier sites linked through commonalities in material culture provide genealogical insight into settlement practices (Stahl 2001: 107–214). Following the imposition of colonial rule in 1896, the British pursed a relatively aggressive policy of 'village planning' in the Gold Coast hinterlands (e.g. Boyle 1968: 30–33), with the result that most contemporary Banda villages were established in the period *c.* AD 1916–1922. Features of these 'new' settlements appear consistent with the bureaucratic directives of British colonialism, in that villages were laid out on a grid pattern and houses consist of compounds with limited exterior access and rooms opening on to an interior kitchen courtyard. Walls were durable, of coursed earth ('tauf') construction. The impression that British directives materially reconfigured Banda village life is strengthened— at least at first glance—by archaeological evidence from sites adjacent to the 'new' settlements that were abandoned in the process of village relocation. The houses at these late nineteenth-century sites are quite different in both layout and construction. Instead of the compounds valued by British officials, houses consisted of single or at most double room structures of wattle-and-daub construction. But a deeper genealogy of Banda settlement practice complicates the notion that the British successfully imposed their view of an ideal colonial settlement on Banda peoples. Archaeological investigations corroborate oral historical evidence that late nineteenth-century occupations at sites such as Makala Kataa were reoccupations of sites abandoned in the face of political economic upheaval earlier in that century, associated in part with the British abolition of the trans-Atlantic slave trade (Stahl 2001: 148–214). Warfare and intensified internal slavery ensued after 1807, as captives diverted from the external trade were used to produce and transport agricultural commodities that became the focus of global exchange (Grier 1981; Lovejoy 1983; Haenger 2000). The effects reverberated throughout the interior with significant implications for the character of daily life.

In Banda, the relatively long-lived settlements of the late eighteenth and early nineteenth century were abandoned under pressure of warfare and not reoccupied until late in the nineteenth century, on the eve of British colonization. The small, ephemerally constructed later nineteenth-century houses appear anomalous by comparison with early nineteenth-century building practices, an impression that is strengthened by what we know of sixteenth- and seventeenth-century practices documented at nearby sites. Before the nineteenth-century dislocations, Banda peoples constructed durable, coursed-earth houses comprised of adjoined rooms in an L-shaped configuration that suggests accretionary construction centred on an open kitchen courtyard. Viewed in the context of a longer time scale, the 'new' twentieth-century village looks neither totally new nor anomalous (Stahl 2001: 219–221). Though the grid layout of the village appears as a new element, continuity in the practices of construction and house layout underscore the complexity of material practice in a context of shifting political economic entanglements (Stahl 2002).

CONCLUSIONS: MATERIAL HISTORIES
IN THE PRESENT

The empirically rich case studies highlighted above demonstrate the value of pursuing archaeological variants of what Geschiere (2001: 34–36) terms an 'extended case method'. Comparative analysis of the material practices of daily life (of food ways, dwelling, dress, production, and consumption) in temporally seriated contexts that cross the so-called contact/pre-contact or historic/prehistoric divides provide powerful insight into the material negotiations of colonization (Lightfoot 1995; Stahl 2001; Silliman 2005). But stand-alone culturally specific histories are insufficient for apprehending the saliency of global connections (Chakrabarty 2000: 43; Tsing 2005: 1–5). Rather, we need to enhance our 'extended case studies' with genealogical and biographical perspectives that follow circulations of people and objects if we are to appreciate how colonies and metropoles were relationally produced through practices of production, consumption and governmentality. To achieve this requires that we overcome disciplinary and geographic 'grooves' and instead develop co-ordinated research efforts to better apprehend how life worlds—past and present—were mutually reconfigured through global entanglements.

Material moments like the piecing together of the shattered Vaseline jar bring into view circulations that reshaped practices of production and consumption in the context of changing global entanglements. Analytically, they encourage us to look beyond the 'archived grooves' (Stoler 2001: 863) that highlight circulations within imperial boundaries (e.g. Constantine 1986) and draw attention to ones that transgressed those boundaries (Stoler 2006b: 143). They bring into view the sinewy connections that linked the nineteenth-century life worlds of oil-field workers in Titusville, Pennsylvania and those of Banda villagers whose worlds were simultaneously transformed by their interaction. Apprehending their mutual constitution is enhanced by 'reciprocal comparisons' that explore how findings from 'non-Western' histories might illuminate 'Western' histories (Austin 2007: 3, 18). The material histories produced from such moments problematize what Fabian (1983) termed a 'denial of coevalness'—that obdurate fiction that has long sustained a notion that Africa remains, or remained until recently, aside or apart from the modern world (Achebe 1978; Vaughan 2006; cf. Mitchell 2005). Sustained by forms of historicism that presume 'first in Europe, then elsewhere' it is a fiction that made possible 'completely internalist histories of Europe in which Europe was described as the site of the first occurrence of capitalism, modernity, or Enlightenment' (Chakrabarty 2000: 7). In light of the reconfigured assumptions about materiality outlined above, material histories of global entanglements provide a platform for apprehending the profoundly reciprocal, enmeshed, and mutually entangled quality of our life worlds that appear separate for their distinctive qualities. Contemplate the irony captured by our humble Vaseline jar: that an early twentieth-century Banda villager perhaps experimented with Vaseline as a substitute for the familiar and locally available shea butter that she used to protect her skin against the ravages of the dry season harmattan winds, while shea nuts are one of the only locally available resources that her children's children can today sell for export to be used for shea butter-based cosmetics that are becoming routine components of Western beauty routines (Sylvanus 2007: 203). Material histories bring these processes into view in ways that standard historiographies do not. That these processes are ongoing is abundantly clear (Stoler 2006b), and it is in this regard that these histories are profoundly material to our worlds today.

CHAPTER 6

....

THE MATERIALS
OF STS

....

JOHN LAW

INTRODUCTION

....

Whatever resists trials is real.

The verb 'resist' is not a privileged word. I use it to represent the whole collection of verbs and adjectives, tools and instruments, which together define the ways of being real. We could equally well say 'curdle', 'fold', 'obscure', 'sharpen', 'slide'. There are dozens of alternatives.

Latour (1988b: 158–159)

Matter matters. But how does this happen? This is the issue I explore in this chapter: how science, technology, and society (STS) imagines that matter matters.

Bruno Latour's words above point to the shape of the argument. In STS, materiality is usually understood as relational effect. Something becomes material because it makes a difference, because somehow or other it is detectable. It depends, then, on a relation between that which is detected and that which does the detecting. Matter that does not make a difference does not matter. It is not matter since there *is* no relation. No relation of difference and detection. No relation at all.

Inevitably, there are complications. First, if matter is not given, then neither are relations. They too have to be done. For STS, materiality cannot be prised apart from the enactment of relations or, more generally, the practices that *do* these relations. This leads STS to make a particular methodological proposal: to understand mattering of the material, you need to go and look at practices, and to see *how* they do whatever reals that those practices are doing, relationally. ('Reals' because different realities are being enacted in different practices.) And, a vitally important coda: you don't take any thing for granted.

This leads to a second complication. I've just said: 'you don't take any thing for granted.' This is because relations and the matters that they do may shift in shape. The implication is that if we assume too much about their form we may not be able to detect the character of that shape-shifting, and so will miss the ways in which reals get materialized. But there are two further issues here.

First, in practice, we always and necessarily take all sorts of things for granted. Indeed, more strongly, what we take for granted is mostly invisible, below the waterline. This is a general and inescapable predicament. There is nothing to be done except to be aware of it. Secondly, we may want to say that practices are more or less patterned. If we say this then it follows that materials are *also* more or less patterned: for instance, culturally. They keep on being re-done.

Can we talk, then, of relative stability? Can we talk of relatively stable relations and relatively stable materials? STS researchers are divided on this question. Some say yes, that indeed matters and their practices are relatively stable. This means that modes of mattering extend through time and space. Others are more sceptical. In this second view mattering gets done and redone in ways that shift unpredictably.

The jury is out, and it is most unlikely that a verdict will be returned in the foreseeable future. The division of STS over this issue is my point of departure for this chapter. In exploring the materials of STS, I start with patterned practices and relative stability and show how STS imagines these. Here the story takes two forms—humanist and material semiotic. Then I move to talk about instabilities in practice, and consider the shape-shifting that might be implied in mobile mattering, and the politics that are implied in that mattering. Though my primary aim is to lay out the various STS approaches, I attend in particular to that of material semiotics and in particular to the possibilities and challenges opened up by the move to ontology implied in this approach.

SOCIAL CONSTRUCTION

Imagine a material technology, perhaps one of those explored in STS. It might be an electricity generating plant (Hughes 1971, 1979), a bicycle (Bijker 1995), an electric vehicle (Callon 1980), a print technology (Cockburn 1983, 1999), a missile guidance system (MacKenzie 1990), or a sailing ship (Law 1986a). (For further reading on the study of material technologies in STS, see the edited collections by

Bijker *et al.* 1987; Bijker and Law 1992; MacKenzie and Wajcman 1999.) Then ask, Why does this technology take the form that it does? Common sense suggests an answer. Its form reflects its environment, together with the task for which it is intended. So, the shape of a sailing ship reflects the winds and the sea, the raw materials from which it is built, its environment. It reflects its social environment too—for instance, the skills available in the culture. And then, again socially, it reflects the task for which it is built. Cargo carrying, fighting, or conspicuous consumption—the reason for which it is constructed—is reflected in the built artefact or assemblage. Note that environment and task overlap. Vessels that need to sail close to the shore—or close to the wind—are shaped in one way. Those that don't, in another. And both task and environment may change too. Wood becomes scarce, and steam power gets invented, so the sailing ship gets consigned to history, and is replaced by the steam packet.

The discipline of STS works through case studies. Some of these describe the social shaping of technologies. How did the bicycle come to take the form that it now does? The answer is that it was shaped by economic and social interests, the cultural skills available, and, of course, by the laws of momentum. STS scholar Wiebe Bijker (1995) tells us that the penny-farthing was an excellent bicycle for young men who wanted to display their masculinity, but it wasn't very stable. That, of course, was precisely the point: in the culture of the time in western Europe, stability and virtuoso displays of masculinity were taken to be mutually exclusive. At the same time, this meant that it wasn't suitable for anyone else—and especially for women, constrained in the Victorian period by particular and gendered ideas about modesty. More culture. The regular safety bike with smaller wheels of the same size was much more stable and much more 'suitable' (especially in the version without the crossbar). It therefore had a much larger potential buying public, and was much more profitable. The consequence was that it replaced the penny-farthing. Here's the argument: the bike was shaped (and shaped quite literally) by a combination of economic and social interests and cultural capacities—not to forget the laws of momentum.

This is the social shaping of technology at work. Materials—technologies—are moulded by the intersection of natural and social factors. They are *shaped*. There isn't much difference between this and what is often called the social *construction* of technology. Both phrases are current in STS. If there is a distinction, perhaps it is this. To talk of social shaping draws our attention to the larger factors (economic conditions, cultural assumptions) that pattern materials. By contrast, to talk of social construction differentially draws our attention to the people *doing* the patterning, the act of creating and building, and their uses of culture. But the difference is a nuance and in practice in STS, the terms are used more or less interchangeably.

There is a large body of excellent STS work on the social shaping or the social construction of technologies. It tells us a great deal about particular kinds of materials, and the forms that they take. It is a basic resource in any study of material culture. But its explanatory form runs us into the second complication that I mentioned above. This approach, the idea of the social construction of technology (often known by the acronym SCOT) is certainly relational, but it also makes strong assumptions about the overall shape or pattern taken by those relations. I'll mention three. First, it makes assumptions about people, endowing them with special and creative powers: for instance, the ability to acquire culturally transmitted skills, to design, and to use tools. Secondly, it assumes that the natural world is pretty much a given: that, for instance, the laws of momentum are unlikely to change. And thirdly, it assumes that the social world has a particular, somewhat stable, albeit possibly ultimately revisable, shape too. Ideas about safety, modesty, and the economic interests of bicycle manufacturers, these provide a third part of the explanatory backcloth for the form taken by materials. In SCOT, it is the relations between the three that give shape to the matter at hand: whether the safety bicycle or the sailing ship.

These assumptions reflect a common understanding of the character of proper social science explanation. In part, this is a commitment to theoretical humanism. It is assumed that people are special because they are active agents. They are taken, for instance, to be language users, or they are endowed, as I noted above, with the capacity to use tools and acquire and deploy cultural skills. Probably they count as moral beings too, and appropriately exercise ethical and political judgements. At the same time, as I also mentioned, it is taken for granted that the natural world is relatively stable, and that, at least for the purposes of understanding the shaping of materials, so too is the social and cultural context. This is a metaphysics that generates a particular and highly productive understanding of materiality. In practice, in this way of thinking, the material world acquires its significance in relation to human activity and human purposes or needs. It may do so in the form of an environmental resource where materiality is treated as some kind of standing reserve. Alternatively, materials may be understood as objects that have been given a shape like a tool, something that is of functional use such as a penny-farthing or a safety bicycle, or perhaps to be appreciated aesthetically such as an art object. Materials, then, express, *inter-alia*, sets of cultural practices and prejudices. If we stick with the safety bicycle, these have, for instance, to do with metallurgy and metal working, the organization of labour, and the proper role of women in society. This is material culture at work in the vision offered by SCOT. It is embedded in patterns of working and living, and in the objects that are implicated in such patterns.

Much of STS works this way, but parts do not. 'Material semiotics'—a blanket term that I use in this chapter to cover a range of approaches from so-called actor-network theory (ANT) (Callon 1986a; Law 1992; Latour 1999b), through parts of feminist technoscience studies (Haraway 1989, 1991a, 1991b; Barad 1999), to work in governmentality influenced by the work of Michel Foucault (Barry 2001)—takes none of these categories for granted. In principle in these non-humanist approaches, everything—people, the natural world, and social and cultural con-text—are all shaped in relations. So, what happens to materiality if we think this way?

THE LABORATORY ACCORDING TO THE SOCIOLOGY
OF SCIENTIFIC KNOWLEDGE

Imagine a laboratory, perhaps one of those that have been studied by STS. It might be an historically important laboratory from the English seventeenth century (Shapin and Schaffer 1985), or SLAC (Traweek 1988), the Stanford Linear Accelera-tor, the Salk Laboratory in San Diego (Latour and Woolgar 1986), CERN near Geneva (Knorr-Cetina 1999), or a small laboratory in a provincial British university (Law 1986b). Here is a core question for STS: Why and how do the ideas created in such laboratories take the form that they do?

There are different answers to this question. But if you track and trace the day-to-day work in a scientific laboratory you find a lot of practical work. People are handling objects, instruments, animals, cell lines, and detectors. That's what an experiment is: a whole set of bits and pieces assembled together. You find a series of instruments, from rulers, through scanning electron microscopes, to PCR machines and neutrino detectors. There are lots of texts and inscriptions too. A scientist's desk is covered with notes, papers, books, reports, graphs, photo-graphs, and arrays of figures, electronic or otherwise. And then there is talk. There is gossip, of course, but also science talk, though the two may be impossible to disentangle. So, there are rumours about new experimental results, guesses about what a rival laboratory is up to, and reports of seminar presentations.

STS grew up in debate with philosophers. While epistemologists usually argue that scientific method is philosophically special (though they disagree about how), STS ethnographers and sociologically inclined historians of science are more impressed by the messy mundanity of laboratories. In the STS way of thinking, laboratory work (or science practice in general) often looks more like cookery than cogitation. Or it looks like industry, since some of it is being done in warehouse-sized buildings or tunnels in the ground filled with fancy machinery. Then again, for STS the conduct of science is also a matter of more or less large-scale organiza-tion—both experimental and social (assuming that it is possible to separate the two in the first place). So what should be made of this?

The sociology of scientific knowledge (SSK), in an approach that owes much to the writing of historian of science, Thomas Kuhn (1970), influentially argues that the ideas generated in laboratories reflect the interaction between the natural, social, and cultural environments on the one hand, and the task of solving scientific and technical problems on the other (e.g. Collins 1975; Barnes 1977). It argues that in the laboratory work is messy, practical, and materially heterogeneous. In this way of thinking knowledge may be theoretical, but it is also embodied in skills and ways of seeing, and in the relations between people, machines, and experimental objects. It is shaped or constructed by human beings that deploy cultural and material tools to solve puzzles. Their solutions thus reflect their creativity, those tools, and a relatively stable natural, social, and cultural environment. The argument is similar to that of SCOT—though SSK preceded SCOT, and is much more controversial since it undermines the epistemological version of the scientific method.

THE LABORATORY ACCORDING
TO MATERIAL SEMIOTICS

Material semiotics attends to much the same messy laboratory realities. It starts, like SSK, with a story about the assembly of heterogeneous *materials*. Then it notes, again like SSK, that this is often, indeed perhaps usually, a process beset by *uncertainty*. In most labs and most of the time, at the experimental cutting edge entropy is constantly threatening. Experiments don't work. The signal to noise ratio is too low, a vital input isn't available, the software has crashed, or the experimental rats are anomalous. Then it says (and again this is close to SSK) that laboratory science is all about *ordering* (in) an uncertain environment. It is about lining materials up for long enough to get them to hold in a particular way. It is about creating assemblages that will hold sufficiently well to allow an experiment to take place. But at this point it starts to part company from SSK.

First, and absolutely crucially for any understanding of materiality, it argues that scientific experimenting is about lining heterogeneous components up for long enough to *enact* materials that can be detected, inscribed, and transcribed. Note that: to *enact* materials. This claim of radical relationality represents a substantial break from both SSK and common sense. To repeat, it is being argued that whatever emerges from an experiment is an *effect* of the relations that are assembled and held together in it. Natural, social, and human materials and realities, *all* of these are understood as effects rather than causes. This means that there are no essential or foundational differences between such realities. The differences that there are (and these are often deep) are taken to be consequences, not causes. It also means that they cannot be treated as explanatory resources. The natural, the social, and the human do not explain anything. Rather, it is they that are in need of explanation (Latour 2005a: 1ff).

The STS laboratory ethnographers arrived at this radical position by looking at the messy laboratory practices that generate representations through more or less post-structuralist lenses. What they found is that at the start of a complex and cutting edge experiment, representations, realities, and contexts are usually almost indistinguishable (see Latour and Woolgar 1986; Law 2004). Talk is likely to combine ideas about natural realities, or hints from data sources, with gossip about the reliability of the experimental set-up, the sources of materials, or training of the technicians or the track record of the scientists doing the work. Here methodological concerns, ideas about the natural world and assessments of the social are freely mixed up in the network of relations. The plausibility of a possible empirical result may be inextricably linked to the reputation of a laboratory. Different versions of the real with very short lives are being circulated.

Most putative versions of natural reality never make it past this stage of visibly messy heterogeneity. A few, however, start to become more robust. Doubts about the context in which they were generated, worries about noise in the detectors, or the reliability and integrity of the scientists involved, start to disappear. More data appear because the experimental rig holds together. Then data resonate with a theoretical hunch, or rumours about findings coming from another laboratory. And as this goes on and the network of relations reconfigures itself, particular representations of the real start to lose their qualifications. And if the process goes all the way, then those representations of reality are purified of all their qualifications. They come to stand not for the messy and heterogeneous social-cum-natural-cum-organizational-cum-methodological process out of which they emerged with all the built-in qualifications and doubts. The relations are recon-figured so they come to stand, instead, for a reality that by virtue of this process, has become a feature of the natural world. But only *afterwards*. Only *at the end of the process*.

So material semiotics counter-intuitively assumes that laboratory realities do not exist outside the relations that produce them. But this leads to a second point, for as Mol (2002) has shown, it also distances itself from SSK by insisting that realities and knowledges are not *made* but *done*. Thus in SSK it is usually said that knowledge is 'constructed'. The SSK assumption, perhaps more often tacit than explicit, is that once construction has taken place, 'closure' is achieved and some-thing scientific has been made that achieves a status somewhat like that of the bicycle (see Collins 1975). Once the bits and pieces have been successfully assembled and bolted together, it is taken to have a form and, everything else being equal, it will continue to hold that form. But material semiotics does not share this assumption. Instead it assumes that knowledge and realities are being *continuously* enacted or performed. This talk of performance does not lead us to Goffman (1971), for he assumes that people are resourceful actors on a stage with more or less fixed props. Instead it takes us to the kind of non-humanist and post-structuralist world imagined by Michel Foucault or Judith Butler in which human subjects are being enacted and given form in relational practices just as much as anything else (e.g. Foucault 1977a; Butler 1990). And if the practices stop? Then so do the realities they are performing. For realities only exist in the practices that materialize them. Which leads to a third important consequence. If the realities materialized by science are practice-dependent, then it also follows that they cannot be universal. This means that science and its realities govern, but *only in very specific practices and locations* (Latour and Woolgar 1986; Latour 1988a, 1988b; Law and Mol 2001). And this means in turn that it becomes important to ask geographical questions about *where* the practices materializing realities are located, how they link together, and how materializations circulate—if indeed they do.

All of this is counter-intuitive and controversial, but it is also STS's most distinctive general insight into the character of materiality. And it is what Latour was pointing to in the epigram with which I started this chapter. In saying that the object is to explore 'the whole collection of verbs and adjectives, tools and instruments, which together define the ways of being real', he is pointing to the relational character of materialization, and the way in which this is embedded in practices. In short, in its material semiotic versions, STS is precisely about the processes of *realizing* or *mattering*. And it is telling us that such processes of realizing or mattering do not simply apply at the cutting edge of science—or indeed in the context of technological innovation. Rather it is suggesting that they are ubiquitous. Materializing, inseparable from practices as it is, is being done everywhere.

If this basic insight is correct then it has profound implications for locations and topics that are far removed from experimental science.

PATTERNING

Now we reach a location of debate within material semiotics. This has to do with the patterning of practices. For unless we want to say that practices and the realities that they materialize are utterly idiosyncratic, then we need to attend to how—and the extent to which—those patterns repeat themselves. And even if we ignore sociological theories of practice (on the grounds that they are socially reductionist and therefore don't consider how it is that the social is being redone along with all the other forms of the real), material semiotics has generated at least four different ways of thinking about such patterning (Callon and Latour 1981; Latour 2005a).

First, it has been argued that once practices with specific patterns become established they tend to reproduce themselves and spread. Philosopher and historian of science Ian Hacking catches what is at stake here in the title of his article on 'the self-vindication of the laboratory sciences' (Hacking 1990). His assumption is that the different practices in the laboratory sciences are so inter-linked and mutually dependent that practices and realities at one site are likely to be picked up and incorporated in experimental practice at other sites. In the abstract alternative realities and forms of experimental practice are perfectly conceivable, but in practice they are unlikely. Analogous arguments about what one might think of as the path dependency of scientific practice and its materi-alizations are explored by sociologist of science Andrew Pickering (1993, 1995). Particular versions of the real, particular experimental practices, and particular theories and findings emerge from periodic moments of upheaval in the natural sciences, and then they tend, at least for a time, to become stable. It isn't worth-while—and probably not possible—to articulate alternative sets of practices.

Secondly, and only somewhat differently, it has been argued that practices may be extended but only with considerable effort. So, for instance, Bruno Latour and Steve Woolgar, while arguing like Pickering that it is too expensive, literally and metaphorically, to undermine the interrelated scientific and instrumental practices of materialization, also explore how particular realities and representations may move from site to site in specific material forms that don't get distorted, but rather hold their shape (Latour calls these 'immutable mobiles'). Immutable mobiles may include texts, for instance in the guise of scientific papers or reports, and people such as scientists and technicians who may have particular skills. They also, and possibly in the long run most importantly, include instruments, devices, and technologies that also hold their structure as they are shipped from one location to another. The suggestion is that these get embedded in, and tend to have patterning effects on, other sites of practice (see Latour and Woolgar 1986; Pick-ering 1995). Indeed, Latour has argued that 'technology is society made durable' (Latour 1991). But the argument is a bit tricky—or at least it cannot be applied mechanically. Immutable mobiles may get distorted or lost along the way, and whether they will work, or work in the way that was originally intended when they arrive at their destination, is always an open question. For the argument about immutable mobiles to work, the new site of practice has to reflect the pattern of relations. So, for instance, as Latour shows, to Pasteurize France it was first necessary to reshape French farms as mini-laboratories. It was only then that the vaccines took the proper material form of protecting cattle from disease (Latour 1988a).

The notion of the network is a crucial metaphor in this second version of relational mattering. Scientific practices, and the realities that they enact, only exist within specific sites and networks of relations, and, crucially, it takes a lot of effort to organize these. Latour catches what is at stake when he writes:

We say that the laws of Newton may be found in Gabon and that this is quite remarkable since that is a long way from England. But I have seen Lepetit camemberts in the super-markets of California. This is also quite remarkable, since Lisieux is a long way from Los Angeles. Either there are two miracles that have to be admired together in the same way, or there are none.

Latour (1988b: 227)

The miracle is the creation of networks that carry camemberts or the laws of Newton without melting or otherwise distorting their relational structure.

A third way of thinking about shared patterning attends to *styles* of materialization rather than to specific objects. So, for instance, it is well known that in his writing (surely interpretable as a particular version of material semiotics!) Michel Foucault is preoccupied with the character of epochal epistemes. In particular, he is interested in the way in which what he calls the modern episteme percolated in and through the practices of the social, starting in the late eighteenth century. However, what is the modern episteme? One answer is that it is a particular strategy, often and perhaps usually implicit, that orders the materially heterogeneous relations of the social to generate particular and distinctive patterns of subjectivities and objectivities. Foucault's interest in the processes of decomposition, recomposition, normalization, and self-monitoring that enact modern subjectivities is well known. However, the modern episteme can also be seen as a strategy that tends to generate specific versions of materiality. For, like subjects, objects may also be decomposed, recomposed, and normalized. The rationalization of the subjectivities implied in military drill is only possible if the devices caught up in these practices are also rationalized and standardized. In the absence of a standardized weapon—or industrial machinery—drilling human beings to turn them into docile subjects makes little sense. Perhaps, indeed, it is not even possible. This, then, is a strategy or a style that tends to pattern matter. It is a *mode of mattering*. And it may be that rationalization is not the only style of materialization enacted in the modern episteme. Another that might fit with Foucault's account would be the technologies of surveillance that precede and accompany reflexive self-monitoring. And yet another might be the materializations appropriate to the pleasures embedded in the modern self.

Foucault cannot be claimed for STS, but his work is important because it suggests the possible importance of *styles* in the relational or ontological patterning of practices. Unsurprisingly, some material-semiotic authors have followed his lead. In particular, however, they have suggested that multiple styles or modes of mattering may be practised alongside—or in interaction with—one another (see, for instance, Latour and Venn 2002 on regimes of enunciation, and Boltanski and Thévenot 2006 on *cités* or commonwealths). To take one example, my own work on the ordering processes in a large scientific laboratory argued that managers, man-agement systems, meetings, technologies, and texts all performed a series of differ-ent but recurrent patterns or styles (Law 1994). One of these was 'administrative'. It enacted rational-legal versions of due process in a Weberian mode. This pattern could be found in the laboratory accounting system, in paperwork, such as agendas and minutes, and in versions of management subjectivity that emphasized the importance of rule following. But there was another quite different 'entrepreneurial' mode of ordering. This was carried in a new management accounting system, in publicity materials, and in the organizational insistence on personal responsibility and delivery. The relations between these were contingent. Sometimes they clashed, and on other occasions, they dovetailed together. Both, for instance, were materialized in the design of large-scale scientific instruments that needed to enact both the health and safety regulations (a version of administrative patterning) *and* the needs of possible customers (which reflected a version of entrepreneurial patterning). In these instruments, then, mattering was being done in at least two modes simultaneously—and there was no longer a single ordering episteme, but instead there were several interacting with one another.

But there is a fourth way of thinking of the relations between practices. Instead of looking for common patterns, it is also possible to look for differences and disjunctions. Perhaps Law's emphasis on different modes of ordering or matters starts to do this. But the argument can be made much more emphatically.

Ontological difference

Imagine a set of practices, perhaps one of those that have been studied by STS. They might have to do with an aircraft (Law 2002), or Alzheimer's disease (Moser 2008), or, say, lower limb atherosclerosis (Mol 2002). In this last instance, to take an example, a textbook on atherosclerosis may tell us that changes in the blood, perhaps associated with diet and lack of exercise, lead to disease in the form of atherosclerotic plaques. Then it may tell us that this builds up on the interior walls of blood vessels. If this plaque builds up beyond a certain level then it begins to restrict the flow of blood through the vessel to the extremities of the body—for instance, to the calves and feet. The result is pain on walking because the muscles need more oxygen than they are getting if they are exercised.

Pause for a moment. Lower limb atherosclerosis is a nasty and not uncommon condition. But is it one thing or is it many? The textbook says that it is a single condition. But what happens if we attend to practice rather than to theory? The answer turns out to be surprising. This is because what we discover is a high degree of variability: *mattering is being done in a large number of different ways.* So, for instance, in the doctor's surgery the patient's presenting symptom for the lower limb atherosclerosis is likely to be pain on walking. This is called claudication. In the radiography department the condition appears in the form of an angiogram—that is, as an X-ray that is taken to reveal the position and size of the blood vessels after a radio-opaque dye has been injected into the patient's circulatory system. In an angiogram the narrowing in the patterns that appear on the plate are taken to show stenoses in the blood vessels. In the ultrasound department, the disease appears as an inscription that is assumed to represent the speed of the blood flow. Here the idea is that blood passes more quickly through the diseased and, therefore, constricted parts of a vessel. Blood flow is measured with a device that emits an ultrasound signal and is moved over the gelled skin of the patient following the line of the suspect vessel. The frequency of the signal reflected back into the probe indicates the speed at which the blood is flowing. And then, on the operating table, with the leg opened up and the vessel revealed in a surgical intervention, the disease appears in the form of a thick white paste that may be scraped from the vessel's interior.

So here is the paradox. If we attend strictly to practice, then lower limb atherosclerosis is being materialized in four or five quite different ways, even though everyone also assumes they are dealing with a single body. The issue comes to a head in the practice of the case conference where the professionals meet to decide what to do about a particular patient. Sometimes everything fits together. The different materializations and their practices are successfully co-ordinated to form a consistent whole. Sometimes, then, the textbook account works. But often this is not the case. Perhaps the Doppler investigation doesn't fit with the angiography, or the patient doesn't report claudication even though the angiograph shows precious little blood flow to the leg. This is a major practical problem for healthcare professionals, but is also crucial if we want to understand the character of mattering in practice. The conclusion is that if we consistently attend to practice and how materials are done, then *mattering is multiple*. Mol (2002) indexes this by talking, oxymoronically, of 'the body multiple'.

ONTOLOGY, COMPLEXITY, AND POLITICS

What happens if we take this argument seriously? The first consequence is that mattering becomes complex. A second is that we need to try to find new ways of thinking that complexity. Here the question becomes: How do the multiple realities hold together? But a third is that it opens a new space for what might be called an *ontological politics*.

Mol explores the relations between practices and materializations empirically. Sometimes practices are *consistent* (the nicely running medical case conference about a patient, the character of her condition, and its treatment, where everything fits together). Sometimes they *contradict* one another (the case conference with contraindications). Sometimes practices and their realities are *separate* from one another (epidemiology indicates that physiotherapy may be effective in treating lower limb atherosclerosis, but this reality does not appear at the case conference). Sometimes realities that don't cohere too well are added together in a form of *syncretism* (a single score to test a disease is derived from quite different components). Sometimes one practice is *included* in another (clinical diagnosis indirectly includes epidemiological realities because medical practitioners look for likely conditions, but epidemiological realities conversely include practitioners' clinical observations). But if mattering is empirically complex, then this also suggests a novel way of thinking about politics. Thus if third-wave feminism told us that biology is not destiny, then material semiotics is now telling us that *reality is not destiny*. This is because if we consistently attend to practices, then we start to discover alternative forms of materialization. And if we discover alternative forms of materialization, then it is not surprising that some may be better than others from one point of view or another. And it is this that is the space of an *ontological politics*. The promise of such a politics is being hidden in a widespread assumption of ontological consistency. Most of the time, in theory, the differences between practices are being effaced—which means that matter is being made singular. It is being turned into destiny by sleight of hand. And the textbook is just one example.

So what is the scope of an ontological politics? How might this be done? There can be no general rules. If the general strategy is to bust ontological monopoly, or the appearance of such a monopoly, there are many plausible tactics.

One is to introduce subversive tropes that bend material-semiotic matterings in novel ways. Technoscience writer Donna Haraway works in this way when she mobilizes the radical, anti-racist, feminist trope of the cyborg to interfere with its militaristic and masculinist predecessor project (Haraway 1991a). More recently, she does something similar by re-imagining human–animal relations in her notion of 'companion species'—those species such as dogs that have grown up with humans, interact with the latter, but are nevertheless at the same time always also Other (Haraway 2003, 2008).

Postcolonial STS theorist Helen Verran works, somewhat differently, to soften and multiply reality-enacting practices in her work on encounters between white Australians and Aborigines (Verran 1998; cf. Verran 2001). What is at issue here are the materializations of land in a context of legal disputes about its ownership and use. Is land a fixed reality in a Euclidean space–time box (which is how white people tend to experience and enact it in their practices)? Or is it rather something that is done, and done again, and then done again, within practices and rituals (which would be closer to aboriginal experience)? Verran intervenes to try to undo what she thinks of as the 'hardening of the categories' in white practices and its imagination. Land, she suggests, is being done in legal practices just as much as in

Aboriginal rituals. As a part of this she explores the multiple enactments that are taken for granted in Aboriginal cosmology, which treats the world as a continuing performative expression of practice (cf. Law 2004).

A second strategy is to discover multiplicity within practices that appear to be producing ontological monopoly. This is the tactic adopted by Mol in her work on lower limb atherosclerosis. She might have mounted arguments against the domination of biomedicine and the patriarchal character of the medical profession. No doubt, many such complaints would be justified. But what she actually did was to generate differences and so potential tensions between the practices of different professionals and the materialities that they enact. This is an ontological politics because it makes it possible to propose, for instance, that in particular circumstances, the realities enacted in walking therapy may be better than those of surgery (Mol 1999).

A third related tactic is to discover practices that are materializing alternative but marginalized realities. So, for instance, biomedical enactments of Alzheimer's disease are common and powerful. But there are also alternative non-biomedical enactments of dementia. STS scholar Ingunn Moser describes the Marte Meo method, which is a technique that analyses patterns of interactions between carers and patients to detect and enact otherwise unrecognized competences in the latter. Moser writes that: '[Alzheimer's] is object and relation, and the object is made in and through relations. When the nurses work on the relations of Alzheimer's, they also transform the object. For instance, if they slow down verbal communications and interaction, the person with dementia may be able to act and participate competently' (Moser 2008: 104).

These are practices that materialize dementia quite differently. Moser is showing that biomedical Alzheimer's is not destiny. There are plausible alternatives that matter too.

A fourth option is to attend more carefully to the character of circulation—and to what it is that circulates. How seriously, for instance, should we take Latour's suggestion that technoscientific mattering is co-ordinated in the circulation of immutable mobiles (Latour 1987: 227ff)? That practices are tightly aligned when objects that hold their shape circulate from site to site? The answer is: not necessarily seriously at all. For instance, Marianne de Laet and Annemarie Mol (2000) describe an object that changes its shape as it moves: a water pump that is widely distributed in Zimbabwe. Manufactured in Harare, it is found in many villages. It is mechanically simple and contextually undemanding since it needs a borehole and a concrete platform that are supposedly created by the village collective—but not much else. And the pump itself is flexible, so that when it breaks down it is usually repaired with whatever comes to hand—tree branches or pieces of worn-out tyres. And sometimes it isn't a collective that looks after the pump, but just a few families. Even its manufacturer is agreeably surprised by its degree of flexibility.

The lesson is this. Rather than being immutable, the pump is better understood as a *mutable* mobile, a *fluid* object. It is being materialized in subtly and not so subtly different practices in different locations. And this has a knock-on political consequence, because what we might think of as the 'watering of Zimbabwe' is quite unlike the 'Pasteurization of France' described by Latour. Pasteur set up a rigid network that turned every farm into a laboratory, and located the Institut Pasteur as the central node, the obligatory point of passage. The manufacturer in Harare produces the pump, but once this is done, it drops out of the picture. The fluid materializations of the pump in practice also mean that the centre no longer matters—or, better, that it isn't a centre at all. Explorations of the fluidity of the pump point to the possibility that modes of materialization may be understood topologically as expressions of different spatial systems with different versions of what is to count as a stable object (see Law and Mol 2001; Law and Singleton 2005).

CONCLUSIONS

In this chapter I have explored how STS imagines materials by considering two major story lines. Both take it for granted that objects are relational effects.

The first, SCOT, whose intellectual origins and inspiration are historical and sociological, explores the cultural, social, and human shaping of materiality. It explains why materials take the form that they do by drawing on assumptions about the relative stability of the social, economic, and natural environments on the one hand, and the creative character of human action on the other. Its dominant metaphors talk of construction and the making of materials.

The second, material semiotics, which draws on post-structuralism and post-humanism, treats everything—materials, but also culture, social arrangements, and human subjectivities—as the relationally variable effects of practices. Its metaphors emphasize the enactment and doing of materials or objects. Using verbs rather than nouns, and exploring how it is that processes work, it talks more of mattering or materializing, than of matter or materiality. Since different practices materialize in different ways, its understanding of materiality is complex. How do materials hold together, if they do? This is its analytical and empirical question.

If these two approaches differ analytically, they also differ politically. SCOT identifies social agendas, for instance to do with gender, class, or ethnicity, which are built into or shape materials. It has often been effectively used in the service of social critique. Material semiotics may also explore how social agendas are enacted in practices, but it is distinctive for its sensitivity to the political potential of multiplicity. Its ontological politics talks up and explores different matterings, or modes of mattering. This is a politically performative intervention since it erodes the monopolistic assumption that reality is destiny. It is doubly performative when it is deployed to interfere in particular locations and practices to strengthen or weaken specific materializations or forms of reality.

What we learn in all this work is that in a dozen subtle ways, mattering is simultaneously about the real, what there is in the world, and about the good and the bad, about values and politics. It is sometimes possible and temporarily desirable to tease these apart and talk, for instance, of matters of fact on the one hand, and matters of concern on the other. But they can only be held apart for so long and in particular and specific relations. Again, there can be no general rule. However, such is the complexity and the multiplicity of mattering that located interventions may hold most analytical and political promise. For Helen Verran the questions are: How to go on together? How to go on well? The answers, always enacted anew, will depend on time and place and practice.

PART II

MATERIAL PRACTICES

CHAPTER 7

MATERIAL CULTURE AND THE DANCE OF AGENCY

ANDREW PICKERING

This chapter circles around the discovery of matter. The first section concerns science studies. It emphasizes the importance of a focus on practice and performance as a way of undoing the 'linguistic turn' in the humanities and social sciences. The key concept here is that of a dance of agency. The second section reviews a variety of examples of this dance in fields beyond the natural sciences—civil engineering, pig farming, and convivial relations with dogs, architecture, technologies of the self, biological computing, brainwave music, and a certain hylozoist and Eastern spirituality. A concern here is with contrasting forms that dances of agency and their products can take, depending on the presence or absence of an organizing *telos* of self-extinction. The third and final section reflects on the significance of this contrast for a politics of theory.

THE DISCOVERY OF MATTER; UNDOING THE LINGUISTIC TURN

Given the omnipresence of instruments and machines in science, one might have imagined that science studies as a field would always have centred on a discourse of materiality, but for most of the twentieth century that was not the case. Historians, philosophers, and sociologists instead discussed science as primarily a field of knowledge, in which theory (rather than empirical, factual, knowledge) was always at the centre of attention. Why was that? One can think here of specific trajectories of disciplinary research. Historians tended to focus on the great men of the Scientific Revolution and understood their greatness in terms of their ideas (rather than, say, their virtuosity in the laboratory). In philosophy, the positivism of the Vienna Circle tended to take the empirical dimension of science for granted, preferring instead to explore the structure of scientific knowledge and reasoning, often with normative intent. More broadly, we could think about the Cartesian dualism that, still to a great extent, pervades and defines the disciplines. Matter (nature, machines, instruments) is the stuff of the natural sciences and engineering, but knowledge belongs to us, and is hence the subject matter of the humanities and social sciences.

Backing all of this up, we could think of the linguistic turn taken by the humanities and social sciences in the latter half of the twentieth century. Cartesian dualism elicits profound and disquieting worries about the correspondence between knowledge and its objects, and electing to dwell on just one side, the human, became the favoured way of evading these fears. The model here was Ludwig Wittgenstein's *Philosophical Investigations* (1953), turning aside from putatively undecidable questions of how the world is and focusing instead on something that we might have reliable access to: the world as represented in language, representational knowledge itself, theory. In the humanities, this was the move towards so-called ordinary language philosophy; in the social sciences it lay at the heart of all sorts of social constructivisms that analysed the social structuring of knowledge claims while disdaining any interest in their referents (Hacking 1999); in science studies, it led straight to the aptly named sociology of scientific knowledge (SSK) (Collins 1992; Barnes *et al.* 1996; on SSK and Wittgenstein, Bloor 1983, 1997) and its spin-off, work on the social construction of technology (Pinch and Bijker 1984), as taken to the limit in Steve Woolgar's (1988) 'reflexivity' programme, turning the methods of SSK back on its own knowledge claims.

We could see the linguistic turn as a decisive shift towards *epistemology*—a determined focus on knowledge—and almost a prohibition on thinking about *ontology*—questions of how the world is. The discovery of matter, then, has amounted to a rather patchy and incomplete undoing of the linguistic turn—in science studies and elsewhere. How did that go, and where is it going now?

Many stories could be told. From my own perspective, the key shift was the move from an obsession with knowledge to a sustained interest in practice, in what scientists do as scientists, beginning with questions of what knowledge production actually looks like (see the essays collected in Pickering 1992). Ian Hacking was, and is, the philosopher most interested in contemporary scientific practice, and his 1983 book, *Representing and Intervening*, was a landmark in the transit from traditional epistemology to a more balanced and materialized vision of science. His famous slogan, 'if you can spray it it's real' was a straightforward reflection of his observation that the physicist William Fairbank at Stanford used radioactive sources to change the electric charge of the objects he was experimenting on. Clearly what surfaces here is a notion of material performance and agency: the sources did something in the world that was crucial to experimental practice but that the naked researcher could never have accomplished on his own.

Historians and social scientists went further than Hacking into detailed empirical study of scientific practice. The late 70s and early 80s saw a rash of ethnographic studies of 'laboratory life' (Knorr-Cetina 1981; Lynch 1985a, 1985b; Latour and Woolgar 1986). David Gooding, Trevor Pinch, and Simon Schaffer's edited collection, *The Uses of Experiment: studies in the natural sciences* (1989), was a landmark in the emergence of historical and sociological studies of scientific practice because it made the material culture of science strikingly evident, but the linguistic turn was not entirely undone. Instead, a new bifurcation became evident. A few scholars sought to take seriously the material strata of science, and this is the line I will pursue in this chapter. But it is worth being clear that many did not: many studies of scientific practice fed into a redoing of the old problematics of representation. As brought together, for example, in Michael Lynch and Steve Woolgar's canonical collection *Representation in Scientific Practice* (1990), studies of practice rejuvenated our thinking about the actual mechanics of scientific representation and its epistemological implications while often remaining still faithful to the linguistic turn.

Something of what is at stake here is exemplified in a classic early essay by Bruno Latour, 'Give Me a Laboratory and I Will Raise the World' (1983). Reflecting on Louis Pasteur's work on combating anthrax, Latour offered two rather different accounts of the sources of science's power to move the world. One referred to 'trials of strength' in the laboratory between Pasteur and the microbes. This related directly to the agency of things: things as 'actants'. Pasteur experimented on the microbes, trying out various material procedures in raising and treating them, seeing how they would perform under different conditions, and eventually found a way to 'domesticate' them. The second had to do with scientific strategies of writing and representation, with 'inscription devices', the power of 'immutable mobiles' and so on. Trials of strength appear at several points in Latour's essay, but the analysis of writing dominates his long summary discussion of the power of the laboratory (Latour 1983: 161–165), and this disproportion has echoed down the ages, in Latour's own work and in science and technology studies more generally. And this, in turn, is an aspect of what I meant by saying that the linguistic turn has been only incompletely undone: representation remains a hegemonic obsession, though now construed in new and fascinating ways.

We can return to matter and agency. Early work that focused on these topics seemed to require a surname that ends in 'ing'. I think of the writings of Hacking again (e.g. Hacking 1992) and David Gooding (1992), but I hope they will forgive me if I concentrate on my own perspective here, as summarized in my book, *The Mangle of Practice: time, agency, and science* (Pickering 1995).

METHOD, TIME, AND AGENCY

How can we make matter visible, conceptually, empirically and textually? As far as science is concerned this should be easy. Laboratories are just full of stuff; one can describe it and photograph it. Even the agency of matter is directly visible and describable: 'if you can spray it it's real' (if you can obtain effects by spraying electrons around, then electrons are real: they do things). But in a way this is too easy. The temptation is to say that since materiality is omnipresent like the air we breathe, we can take it for granted, and get back to the old questions of what's really special about science—questions of epistemology or social theory or whatever (see, for example, my debate with Jonathan Harwood: Harwood 2005; Pickering 2005a, 2005b). (A more systematic trick for obscuring the importance of matter is an emphasis in SSK on controversies as the key site for study, e.g. Collins 1992. The argument here is that in controversies, material inputs factor out—the parties have access to the same inputs from nature; therefore something else, namely the social, must structure beliefs. In fact, this argument is erroneous. The parties to controversies seldom if ever refer to identical fields of instrumentation.)

How can we resist this temptation? We could start by paying attention, first, to the fact that much of scientific practice is directed towards fields of machines and instruments and their performance, and, second, to time. Detailed case studies of practice reveal an interesting temporal structure. As the philosopher and medical scientist Ludwik Fleck (1979) suggested many years ago, research practice seems to oscillate between *activity* and *passivity* on the part of the researcher, in which the active phase consists in setting up some material assemblage, and the passive an attentive watching to see what it will do, how it will perform. In the development of the bubble chamber, for example, physicist Donald Glaser put together all sorts of configurations of containers and fluids and each time then stood back with a movie camera in his hand to record their success, or more often failure, in detecting the passage of elementary particles (Pickering 1993, 1995: 37–67).

We can, of course, see this as a prototypical instance of Latour's notion of experimental 'trials', mentioned above, but we can also develop the story further than Latour. This oscillation has more than one step. Glaser did not assemble material configurations at random. Each period of passivity was followed by an active phase informed by the most recent performance of his instrument, in a process that we can describe as 'accommodation' (Pickering 1995): reacting to failures, trying to home in on desirable performances, etc. Further passive phases followed, again seeing what the reconfigured apparatus would do this time, and so on. Moreover, we can symmetrize the picture: passages of human passivity are precisely passages of material activity—which was why Glaser stood back with his camera—and vice versa.

We can thus arrive at an understanding of scientific engagement with the material world as a temporally extended back-and-forth *dance of human and non-human agency* in which activity and passivity on both sides are reciprocally intertwined. (For detailed examples drawn from the history of physics, mathematics, and the workplace, see Pickering 1995.) And these dances of agency are, I think, precisely what we need to focus on empirically and theoretically if we want to grasp the constitutive role of matter and material agency in human culture, scientific and otherwise. I therefore want to make a list of observations about them.

1. Some clarification of how I am using key terms might be appropriate at this point. The social sciences typically define 'agency' as exclusively an attribute of persons. A person has agency precisely to the extent that his or her actions make a difference to other people. It is clear, I hope, that I do not intend my usage of 'agency' to be thus restricted. My idea is that matter has agency too, precisely in the sense that its actions can also make a difference—in respect of human scientists, for example (or all of us in our daily lives). Here I am referring to such actions that make a difference as performances—performances are what agents do, whether human or non-human. My conviction is that we need to move to a performative (rather than representational) idiom for studying and reflecting on science (and on being in general) (Pickering 1995). In this way of talking, 'practice' means 'human performance'.

2. It follows that dances of agency are themselves *performative*, not linguistic, cognitive, or whatever. They have to do with actions, human and non-human, in the material world and the interplay of those. Glaser did something—putting these components together this way, and the assemblage then did something, boiling madly or forming neat strings of bubbles, to which Glaser reacted performatively, and so on. This performative aspect helps us to understand the invisibility of dances of agency within a field of humanities and social sciences fixated on topics of knowledge and representation: they cannot speak about performance in itself. Conversely, attention to performance might be a necessary entering wedge in undoing the linguistic turn.

3. Agency is *emergent* in the brute sense of being unknowable in advance of specific performances. No one could know how Glaser's set-ups would act in advance of their actual performance, and, symmetrically, on the human side, no one could know in advance how Glaser would respond. Much of scientific research, then, consists precisely in *finding out* how the material world (and, in fact, the

human world) will perform in this configuration or that. Again, the classic quest for predictive or causal explanations in both the social and the natural sciences continually acts to obscure this fact.

4. Dances of agency have a *decentred* quality—they are the zones of intersection where the non-human world enters constitutively into the becoming of the human world and vice versa. They cannot be accounted for by focusing either on the human or the non-human alone. If one thinks of 'humanism' as referring to scholarly accounts that centre on purely human variables such as epistemic norms or social structure, and 'antihumanism' as focusing on a nature from which humans have been stripped away (the natural sciences), then the dance of agency has instead to be understood in *posthumanist* terms. (This usage of the word, which emphasizes coupling and embodiment, is more or less the inverse of the sense in which 'posthuman' is used in connection with discussions of 'trans-humanism' as an aspiration to transcend the limitations of the material body: see Hayles 1999.)

5. What is at stake in dances of agency? Everything. Everything one can think of is liable to open-ended transformation here, *mangling* as I called it. I have so far spoken as if dances of agency are purely performative, but this is not the case. Knowledge and representations, for example, often, though not always or necessarily, enter into them. Glaser thought he knew what he was doing and why he was doing it in the course of his development of the bubble chamber. But the important point to note is that his knowledge was itself bound up in the dance of agency, functioning as a retrospective summary of prior experience and as a revisable guide to future practice. His early work drew upon a specific theoretical understanding of bubble-formation, but in the light of the evolving performance of his chambers he eventually switched to a quite different theory. This, then, is how we should think about the domain of knowledge and language in general: not as the sort of cage that the linguistic turn presented us with, but as an integral *part of* practice, just as liable to mangling as the material form and performance of Glaser's chambers.

And the list of cultural elements liable to mangling does not end with knowledge. It is not hard to see that epistemic norms, social structure, and social interests should likewise be understood to be at stake in practice (Pickering 1995). The general point to grasp is that the traditional explanatory and interpretive variables of the humanities and social sciences reappear on this account as just more entries on the list of cultural elements liable to transformation in dances of agency. From another angle, this just reflects the fact that the classic interpretive and explanatory paradigms are humanist, locating all the action in the human sphere, and contriving in various ways to make the mangling of their key terms invisible (Pickering 1995, 2005b).

6. There is one further aspect of the dance of agency that requires a lengthier discussion. My contention is that such dances are visible and indeed ubiquitous

phenomena—the very stuff of our being in the world—and I have already indicated some of the ways in which they have nevertheless largely evaded scholarly attention. Now I need to discuss one further way, which has to do with a certain structure that one often finds imposed on practice.

ASYMMETRIC DUALISM

Glaser undoubtedly engaged in a drawn-out dance of agency with his early bubble chambers, but the *telos* of this work was *to bring the dance to an end*—to arrive at a chamber that would function reliably *on its own* without any continuing back and forth interaction with Glaser—an instrument that could be put to work in further projects by Glaser and others. His success at that was what won him the Nobel Prize in Physics in 1960. Bruno Latour (1987, 1993a) has discussed this *telos* under the headings of black-boxing, purification, and modernity. His idea is that modernity itself is characterized by an impulse somehow to make a clean separation between people and things. This is a very important idea, and I want now to put it in my own terms.

Undoubtedly, this work of purification, as Latour calls it, is central to the modern world. We need here the conception of a *free-standing machine*, using 'machine' in a very generous sense, a material device that performs independently of us (Pickering 2001). The *telos* of much of modern science is to produce free-standing machines and instruments (like a working bubble chamber) and to use them to produce, as it were, free-standing knowledge—this is the heart of scientific objectivity (Daston and Galison 1992). In the realm of technology and engineering, the same object holds (but without any necessary relation to knowledge): cars, TVs, computers, the electricity supply, plumbing—all of these are autonomous machines that take their place in the world precisely as such. My car would be useless if I could not rely on it to perform reliably in taking me from A to B.

So we find ourselves in an almost paradoxical situation—plunged into emergent and decentred dances of agency that aim at and often succeed in extinguishing themselves, in bringing themselves to a point of more or less clear separation between human and non-human agency. What should we make of that? Three points are worth bearing in mind.

First, this telos of purification is important. It has consequences in the world. The evolution of culture—the transformation in time of the made things of science: machines and their performances; bodies of knowledge; social roles and relations—is organized in a certain way around it and is structured and punctuated by it. Modernity, on this line of thought, is substantively characterized by, precisely, the ubiquity of free-standing machines. It is not just a state of mind, a way of thinking or a set of political arrangements as Latour often seems to say.

Secondly, in a technological society it is easy to be dazzled by this sort of punctuation, to focus on its products and their independence from us, and not on the dances of agency that lead up to and away from them. Our made world is saturated with free-standing machines and contemplation of this no doubt contributes to a certain more general ontological appreciation of how the world is. It fosters what I think of as an *asymmetric* or *practical dualism*. Machines confront us immediately with a spectacle of almost overpowering material agency and of a dualist split between people and things: my car and my computer simply do things that I cannot, and vice versa. At the same time, however, a certain backgrounding of material agency can easily take place here, lending a degree of asymmetry to this dualism. My car might be wonderfully powerful, but it was designed and built by humans to serve specific human purposes. It can begin to seem as if human interests and desires somehow bring technological artefacts into existence, as if cars or computers are 'social constructions'. More generally, we can easily arrive at a vision in which humans are active and call all the shots, while the material world is only passive, waiting for us to give it form and purpose. Our made world both *manifests* and *echoes back* to us this sort of asymmetric practical dualism, and this again must be part of the explanation for the disappearance of matter from scholarly discourse.

Thirdly, and obviously, we should not be dazzled by the world of machines. They may punctuate dances of agency, but they do not efface emergence and a posthumanist decentring in the becoming of culture. Dances of agency are what carry us from one moment of punctuation to the next, and their emergent and decentred qualities do not go away at the moment of punctuation—they just more or less pause there for a longer or shorter time.

The upshot of this trip, then, is to leave us where we were before—with dances of agency as the crucial focus for appreciating and grasping the materiality of our culture—but now in the recognition that our dances of agency have a peculiar structure, and that their products can lead us to misapprehend the world we inhabit. An exclusive focus on free-standing machines veils our ontological condition from us.

***

Now I want to change tack. I want to review a range of examples that point to the omnipresence of dances of agency in the world at large. The hope is to show that they are not a special feature of science, but that they are our ontological condition. There is another principle behind the selection of these examples, too, which I can explain as follows.

It is hard work to make dances of agency visible in science studies. One has to read the science against the grain, so to speak. One has continually to resist the temptation to be dazzled by the products of science—powerful and elegant instruments and machines, imposing edifices of knowledge—that emerge at moments of purification and stabilization. We must try instead to take seriously the practices that lead up to and away from them—practices that ceaselessly strive to efface themselves and bury their own traces. Of course, it can easily seem that it has to be this way—so much of our being in the world does indeed seem to be organized around the *telos* of purification and the exploitation of its products, free-standing machines that echo back to us an asymmetric dualist ontology. But, as it happens, it does not have to be that way. Asymmetric dualism is hegemonic, not necessary. In the margins of our culture one can find a quite different set of practices and products that, far from seeking to extinguish the dance of agency, in various ways thematize, exploit, and even revel in it. I find myself especially interested in these, both as sites at which the dance of agency becomes much more readily visible, and as exemplifications of an alternative way to be in the world. I offer several examples below and go on to discuss their political valence in the concluding section (cf. Pickering and Guzik 2008).

THE ENVIRONMENT

Our dealings with the environment are a catalogue of dances of agency writ very large. Sociologist Adrian Franklin's (2008) study of the emergent coupling of eucalypts and fire with Australian identity, desires, and social structures, for example, offers a clear example of a dance of agency with the environment, extending the discussion back into the evolutionary history of the trees themselves. Popular writer John McPhee's *The Control of Nature* (1989) also reviews some richly detailed examples. I have previously discussed his account of the US Army Corps of Engineers' (ACE) struggles to control the Mississippi River elsewhere at some length (Pickering 2008), but briefly the century-long history of these struggles can be understood as an enormous dance of human and non-human agency. In attempts to control flooding and prevent the Mississippi changing course, the ACE has built levees and control structures (especially to limit run-off into a tributary, the Atchafalaya). None of these has ever succeeded in taming the Mississippi—as the levees have risen, so too has the water level in the river (contrary to the best scientific expectations); massive control structures have been eroded and undermined in periodic floods. This history is one of a continual back and forth between the ACE and nature, in which the material form of the river and engineering works around it (as well as the social institutions and relations that depend on its water) have evolved in an emergent and decentred fashion, punctuated most recently, alas, in the tragedy of Hurricane Katrina and the devastation of New Orleans.

I want to make several remarks on this potted history. First, as stated, it exemplifies very nicely the idea of a dance of human and material agency on an enormous scale—now out there in the world, not in the scientific laboratory. Secondly, despite the escape from the laboratory, we have not escaped from the *telos* of dualist purification that characterizes it. The ACE does not enjoy this dance of agency; it would like to get out of it; stretching the usage of the word, it aims to turn the Mississippi and its associated engineering works into a free-standing machine that will act on its own in accordance with human desires. Sociologist Lisa Asplen (2008) refers to this as a command-and-control attitude towards environmental management, and it is surely the paradigmatic and hegemonic approach to engineering in general. Thirdly, we can, nevertheless, make a contrast with laboratory science here. While the development of mainstream sciences like physics is often elegantly punctuated by purifications and stabilizations, the world outside the lab is typically less docile. In instances like this one finds dances of agency that seem liable to continue forever without achieving any rest, and perhaps this is why they are easier to spot and to grasp.

Fourthly, we can turn to the contrast mentioned above. I just described the ACE's stance as paradigmatic of engineering more generally, but there are other ways to relate to the environment. Asplen (2008) describes and analyses approaches to the civil engineering of water that do not seek immediately to impose some dualist *telos*, but that are interested in the dance of agency in itself. 'Adaptive ecological management', for example, is explicitly performative and experimental in its relation to water. Asplen talks about experimental floods on the Colorado River, unleashed from an upstream dam, which have aimed to explore what the river and its ecosystem will do, given the chance. This is a self-consciously posthumanist approach to environmental management, which aims to align human goals with material agency and emergent performances, as well, of course, as vice versa.

This contrast interests me for several reasons. One is just that one can make it. If the dance of agency is everywhere, the dualist *telos* of purification does not have to be. Another is most readily expressed by referring to the philosophy of Martin Heidegger and his famous essay, 'The Question Concerning Technology' (1977). Engineering à la ACE is *enframing* in Heidegger's terms: an attempt to dominate nature and impose a preconceived human plan upon it—this is of a piece with the asymmetric ontological dualism already discussed. Adaptive ecological management is instead an engagement with nature in the mode of *revealing*—an open-ended *finding out* about what the world has to offer us. Put that way, it becomes clear that there is something attractive about adaptive management in contrast to command-and-control (cf. the discussion of the 'urban green' by Whatmore and Hinchliffe this volume, Chapter 19). I will come back to this later under the heading of politics, but for now we could think of the 'danger' that Heidegger associated with enframing. Heidegger himself understood this in existential terms—enframing as a danger to the fibre of our being—but more prosaically, we can see the command-and-control stance as itself precipitating new dangers in the material world. To some degree at least, the disaster of Hurricane Katrina was the nightmarish other side of the dream of enframing the Mississippi (and see Scott 1998 for a whole list of exemplifications of this thought). It is hard to see how engineering in the mode of revealing could generate comparable risks.

Animals

Another excellent site for dance-of-agency spotting is in human relations with animals, and again I want to focus on two contrasting studies. Sociologist Dawn Coppin (2003, 2008) has explored the unglamorous topic of pig farming in the American mid-west. Since World War II this has largely been a quasi-Foucauldian story of confinement: the attempt to raise more and more pigs indoors under controlled conditions. Again, this is a story of a transformative dance of human and non-human agency (capitalists, farmers, pigs, bacteria, chemicals, sunlight). In the process, the very substance of the pig has changed: the animals no longer have enough fat to live outside in winter, and are too pale-skinned to bear the sun in summer, but we can follow Foucault here and focus on architecture as a zone of intersection of human and non-human agency. The form of confinement facilities for pigs has always been and remains a site for performative experimentation, surprise, and emergence. Humans set up the buildings, just like Glaser and his bubble chambers, and then see what happens and how the pigs act, again just like Glaser, in a continuing back and forth of agency. The animals sicken, and the sheds are opened up and reoriented to admit sunlight; the babies die, countered by the introduction of a bit of the wild, a square-foot of sod; the mothers crush the babies, and the bars of the farrowing crates are reconfigured to give the piglets a chance of escape; and so on.

Again then, we find a dance of agency writ large, now in the macro-history of farming. And again too we find the dance structured by a dualist *telos*. This dance too has an aim in which it seeks to extinguish itself but which it never quite achieves, a Heideggerian enframing of the pig, a docile porcine body as a self-acting producer of bacon, ham, and pork chops.

Now we can turn to another way of relating to animals. Coppin speaks of 'nature-cultures' in getting at the coupled becoming of farmers, pigs, and the built environment, taking the phrase from historian, philosopher, and political activist Donna Haraway. Interestingly though, Haraway's focus has shifted from the grim and threatening, if possibly hopeful, figure of the cyborg to relations with dogs, which she evidently relishes (Haraway 2003, 2004). And what fascinates me about this shift is that it elicits a new and mangle-ish conception of *love*. Far from understanding love as a state of mind, Haraway offers us a performative and inherently temporalized vision: love as a process of revealing, of a performative finding out about and accommodation to the other (dogs in this instance, but we could just as well say rivers and the environment, or even other people). Love as reciprocally transformative, decentred, and performative, as openness to emergence and what the world has to offer—a dance of agency for its own stake, structured not by any dualist *telos* but by a self-conscious awareness and appreciation that it is a dance of agency. And again, then, this stance with respect to animals looks very different from the more familiar teleological alternative explored by Coppin.

ARCHITECTURE

Now I want to shift the focus again, remaining in the realm of architecture but leaving the pigs behind, which will enable us to examine the dance of agency from a couple of new angles. Adaptive and interactive architecture is a topic of increasing contemporary interest; here I will focus on just one example, a building called the Fun Palace. As extensively documented by architectural historian Stanley Mathews (2007), the original inspiration for the Fun Palace, to be built in London, came from the radical theatre director and playwright, Joan Littlewood; the principal architect was Cedric Price, and the third major actor in its design was the cybernetician, Gordon Pask (see Pickering 2007, and, on the historical sweep of cybernetics more generally, see Pickering 2010). An enormous amount of planning went into the Fun Palace project in the early and mid-60s, but in the end a site could not be found and it was not built. Nevertheless, certain features of the unrealized design are worth our attention here.

The Fun Palace was intended to be a public space where people could gather in their free time, an antidote to the widely recognized 'leisure problem' that was then expected to result from the automation of production (hard to believe, I know). It was intended to support all sorts of activities—education, sport, theatre, the arts—but beyond that, it was intended to be *reconfigurable* in use. Using a variety of technological means, areas could expand or contract and facilities move around according to their popularity on this day or that. That is the primary sense in which the Fun Palace could be considered an exemplar of *adaptive* architecture, in contrast with the conventional non-adaptive buildings having a fixed shape and layout that surround us all the time (see also Landau 1968, and Sadler 2005 on the Archigram group of architects).

But beyond this, thanks to Pask, the Fun Palace was envisaged as having a further degree of adaptability. Pask imagined an automation of the building's adaptation, and further imagined an adaptive system that would 'get bored' (Pask 1971: 80). Faced with repetitive patterns of use, the building would stop responding, or respond in unpredictable ways, in the hope of eliciting novel responses from its users.

What should we make of this? From one angle, of course, we could see the Fun Palace as yet another instance of dualist enframing, built according to some plan, just like my house or my car, just another free-standing machine in my extended sense. But from another angle, the Fun Palace looks much more interesting and instructive. Its designers were explicit that they could not see the future and that they *did not know* what the building would be used for. If it was a free-standing machine, still it was a revealing not an enframing machine. If conventional architecture seeks to prescribe its own use—homes, prisons, schools, hospitals, museums—the Fun Palace was continually open to finding out what its use would be. It was precisely the kind of architecture one would engage in if one thought of the world as a dance of agency. Especially with Pask's cybernetic input, the building was intended to be lively and emergent, searching through spaces of human agency just as, reciprocally, the human users would search through the spaces of the building's performativity.

As a material object, then, albeit an imagined one, the Fun Palace itself thematized the dance of human and non-human agency. We can grasp it as an exemplary piece of *ontological theatre.* Just as conventional architecture stages for us a sort of asymmetric practical dualism, so the Fun Palace staged an emergent decentred coupling of people and things in a dance of agency. This is one of the new perspectives on the dance of agency that the Fun Palace offers us. In discussing animals and the environment I focused on forms of *practice* that thematize the dance of agency rather than seeking to escape from and conceal it; here instead we have an *object,* a machine, the Fun Palace, which in itself thematized the dance and invited participation in it. It interests me a lot that it is indeed possible to envisage a built environment, a made world, which echoes back to us an ontology of revealing rather than enframing. Such a possibility would be unimaginable if we were to leave the linguistic turn undone, and I will come back to this later. For the moment, I want to comment on one last aspect of the Fun Palace project.

I talked about the Fun Palace as searching through spaces of human agency, and it is interesting to reflect on what that search might have entailed. At the most mundane level, it would involve finding out what sorts of things more or fewer people want to do today—watch television, paint pictures, play football, or whatever. But there was a more visionary line of thought that came down to the Fun Palace from the French Situationist International, via Cedric Price's friend, the Glaswegian writer and radical Alexander Trocchi. This was that certain kinds of built environments and certain kinds of human *selves* hang together. Non-adaptive environments—fixed structures with fixed functions—foster a passive, consumerist self—the bête noir of the 60s counterculture. Conversely, the hope was that a new kind of architecture, exemplified by the Fun Palace, might elicit a *new kind of self*—endlessly creative and emergent. This was never put to the test, but it helps to think here of Foucault again and his notion of *technologies of the self*. Foucault (1988), of course, focused on technologies of the modern self (in a generic sense), practices aimed at forming and controlling, enframing, the self, and we can see much of our built environment as a set of technologies of the modern self—think of Foucault (1977a) on the prison. But just as the Fun Palace thematized emergence in the realm of machines, so the Situationists imagined revealing and the possibility of a thoroughgoing emergence in the domain of the self, and of the coupling of the two (Marcus 1989; Sadler 1998).

Here enormous vistas open up of technologies of the self, running from, for example, new ways of conceptualizing, transforming, and enframing the body and mind (Rose 2007) up to all of those technologies of the self beloved of the counterculture, technologies of revealing and the 'exploration of consciousness'— yoga, meditation, psychedelic drugs, strobes, sensory deprivation tanks (e.g. Huxley 1963; see Pickering 2010 for an overview, and Gomart and Hennion 1999 for a scholarly and insightful sociological discussion of musical and chemical *dispositifs* of self-abandonment). Reflection on these very material technologies of the self, and the sorts of selves they explore, offers us another angle on the coupling of human and non-human agency, but it would take us too far afield to follow this further here.

HYLOZOISM

My last set of examples takes us further into the wild side. Asymmetric dualism and the stance of enframing put all the weight on humanity: as the only genuine agents around, it seems as if we humans call all the shots of history, set all the goals, have to do all the work, and can claim responsibility for everything that happens, for better or for worse. A recognition that we are plunged into decentred and emergent dances of agency takes some of the weight off us and, conversely, promotes a keen appreciation for the agency of matter. My last three examples indicate some of the directions that appreciation can open up.

The first two examples reflect a conviction that, so to speak, *it's all there already*—that instead of engaging in heroic projects of the transformation of matter to bend it to the human will, we might be able to find what we need already in nature. Thus, first, in the late 1950s and early 1960s, two cyberneticians, Stafford

Beer and Gordon Pask pursued an amazingly imaginative project in what one can call *biological computing* (Pickering 2009a, 2010). Their aim was, for example, to replace human factory managers with a certain sort of computing system. But instead of a conventional computing project, which depends upon all sorts of detailed transformations of matter (turning sand and metal into precisely configured silicon chips, and the compilation of long and detailed programs that specify how they should behave), Beer and Pask sought to enrol naturally occurring adaptive systems as controllers of the factory. Their idea was that pond ecosystems, for example, can already adapt to changes in their environment without any help from us, and that if one could only couple a pond to the relevant parameters of a factory, the pond could help the factory to adapt to changes in its environment.

This project went nowhere, of course, but it foundered not on any point of principle, I think, but in practical problems in setting up the necessary couplings—in getting ponds to care about us. We see, nevertheless, the upgraded and thematized appreciation for the agency of matter that such projects exemplify: the pond itself was intended to engage in dances of agency with the factory and its environment just like those of human managers. Another striking example of ontological theatre.

Secondly, we can move from a funny sort of biological engineering to a peculiar kind of music, and an idea of the human brain as just another performative, rather than cognitive, material agent. I think here of the 'brainwave music' that flourished in the 1960s, pioneered by people like Alvin Lucier (Pickering 2010). Now the idea was to use an EEG readout of electrical rhythms in the brain to control a sound-producing system of some sort. Often the system was tuned to the alpha rhythms of the generating brain, completing a sort of biofeedback circuit, in which the mental state of the performer was reciprocally intertwined with the sound output in yet another performative dance of agency. Presumably one does not need to labour the contrast here with more familiar forms of music, entailing the usual cognitive/linguistic detour through composition and notation. As with the earlier examples, we can think of biological computing and brainwave music as evidence that *ontology makes a difference*—that practices and objects that thematize the dance of agency are strikingly different from their more familiar and hegemonic counterparts, which background and aim to efface the dance. And, again, this difference can be caught up as that between revealing and enframing; an exploration of what the world can offer us, as against a determination to impose our will on matter and sound.

My last example takes this line of thought to a sort of limit. The linguistic turn was necessarily a celebration of the specialness of humanity relative to brute matter (to which we were said to have no access). A recognition of material agency and the dance of agency points to a rebalancing of this stance, which has to amount to an upgraded appreciation of matter. And if one thinks of knowledge and language as just a part of the dance, rather than a true description of nature, this rebalancing easily shades into a spiritually charged wonder at the powers of nature that one can call *hylozoism*. And it might therefore be not so surprising, though still striking, that if one explores projects and products that thematize the dance of agency one often finds oneself exploring strange, or at least Eastern and mystically inclined, spiritualities. Stafford Beer, for example, was not only the very successful founder of management cybernetics: he also wrote poems expressing his awe at the extent to which the computational powers of the Irish Sea exceed our own (Blohm *et al.* 1986: 52). Furthermore, any sort of conscious recognition of the dance of agency as decentred and emergent is liable to lead to a decentred understanding of the *self* (as mentioned above) and an awareness of the possibility of its dissolution, a very Eastern and Buddhist conception—the other side of an idea of cosmic unity. One finds this idea in Beer's writings too, as well as in the 'antipsychiatry' of the 1960s, associated with names such as Gregory Bateson and R. D. Laing: schizophrenia as a very confused form of Buddhist enlightenment (e.g. Laing 1967). Beer in fact practised tantric yoga and, as the historian of religion, Mircea Eliade makes very clear in his magisterial *Yoga: Immortality and Freedom* (1969), tantrism is indeed the variety of Eastern spirituality that thematizes material performance and technologies of the self that return to the world in strange performances and magical and alchemical powers.

The point of this last section was not to suggest that an interest in material culture is irrevocably locked together with pond computers, alpha-wave music, or a hylozoist tantrism, it is to suggest that a recognition of the dance of agency can carry us, in general, a long way away from the linguistic turn, in practice as well as theory.

POLITICS

In conclusion, I turn briefly to the politics of theory—the 'so what?' question. This is discussed at greater length in Pickering (2009b), which also notes affinities in what follows with Haraway's discussions of both 'cyborgs' and human relations with companion species (Haraway 2003, 2004). In science and technology studies, the most extensively worked-out discussion of the politics of theory is to be found in Bruno Latour's writings on what he calls a parliament of things (1993a) and the politics of nature (2004b, 2005b). I cannot do justice to the intricacies of Latour's thought here, but a quick summary will help to locate a site of divergence.

First, Latour's politics are situated in a split-level view of the world. At the ground level, we find everyday practices and projects in science and engineering, people struggling with disease, building transportation systems, fighting wars, and so on, and Latour is content to leave these alone and unchanged. In *We Have Never Been Modern*, especially, he expresses his admiration for the processes (though not the self-understandings) of dualist purification that he takes to be definitive of modernity (e.g. Latour 1993a: 132–133, 135, 140), and which I have characterized by the dualist *telos* of extinguishing dances of agency. Against this mundane backdrop, Latour, quite conventionally, locates politics at a meta-level—the space of reflection on the ground level, of talking about real-world projects, deliberating on them, making decisions about them. And this meta-level is where actor-network theory (ANT) finds its political edge. Latour argues that our current political institutions enforce a dualist separation of people and things, with politicians in one place and scientists in another, the former deliberating on human actions, the latter on the state of nature. And Latour's new politics aims precisely and specifically to reform this meta-level, to bring it into line with the non-dualist insights of ANT. Literally or metaphorically this would entail bringing scientists and politicians together under one roof, to deliberate on science and nature as a single topic, with an explicit recognition that decisions about what should be done and about how the world is hang together: science and politics as ANT-in-action.

This is an interesting and possibly viable extension of ANT into politics, but two related features are worth noting. First, this meta-level politics is entirely a matter of the institutional orchestration of talk, thought, deliberation, decision-making. In this sense, it remains securely on the more or less immaterial terrain bequeathed to us by the linguistic turn. Secondly, and obviously, one could go further than Latour and imagine changes at the ground-level, rather than the meta-level, as a further, and less conventional, extension of the politics of theory. This, equally obviously, is what the second part of this chapter has been leading up to, and I can end by elaborating the point.

I have been reviewing examples of the dance of agency in various worldly— ground-level—projects, mainly in an attempt to suggest that the dance of agency is our ontological condition, in science and engineering and our daily lives. However, I have also discussed two forms the dance can take. On the one hand, a hegemonic form organized around a *telos* of dualist purification of people and things, which echoes back to us our specialness and hangs together with the disappearance of matter in the linguistic turn. On the other, a marginal and marginalized form that thematizes dances of agency without pursuing their extinction, which continually reminds us of our entanglements with the agency of matter. Evidently, I find this marginal form attractive. Politically, it offers us an alternative to a hegemonic world of enframing that seems to get grimmer and more hopeless every day. It exemplifies the fact, as Latour's politics does not, that we could indeed try going on in the world at the ground level in another way, in the mode of revealing—of being open to what the world has to offer us instead of always trying to bend it to our will.

My political fantasy, growing out of science and technology studies, is thus that these marginal traditions, sciences, and technologies might grow and become more central to our culture. This would help us to recognize dances of agency as our material condition, rather than veiling this from us, and it would help us to see modernist–dualist projects for what they are: not a necessary way to proceed, but just one option for organizing our action in the world, and an intrinsically risky and dangerous option at that (Scott 1998; Pickering 2008). Heidegger (1981) said that 'only a god can save us', but undoing the linguistic turn in a trip through the materiality of culture and the agency of matter suggests that perhaps we could try looking in the margins of our own culture first.

CHAPTER 8

··

CONSUMPTION

··

MICHAEL DIETLER

INTRODUCTION

···

Consumption is a material social practice involving the *utilization* of objects (or
services), as opposed to their production or distribution. Some scholars, who argue
for the recent development of a distinctive 'consumer society' during the modern
period, would define it even more specifically as the utilization of *commodities* (that
is, objects obtained through exchange, or, yet more narrowly, mass-produced
objects manufactured for commercial exchange), but this seems unnecessarily
restrictive. After many years of surprising neglect, consumption has garnered a
great deal of attention among all the social sciences over the past few decades.
Beginning in the 1970s, but especially from the mid-1980s, consumption suddenly
began to receive increasing recognition as a crucial focus of analysis in a wide
range of disciplines, especially in anthropology (Douglas and Isherwood 1979;
McCracken 1988; Miller 1987, 1995c, 1995d; Howes 1996b; Colloredo-Mansfeld
2005) and sociology (Bourdieu 1984; Campbell 1987, 1995; Bocock 1993; Edgell
et al. 1996; Zukin and Maguire 2004), but also history, geography, economics,
and other fields (Pred and Watts 1992; Brewer and Porter 1993; Jackson and Thrift
1995; Miller 1995a). Indeed, one prominent advocate has even argued that consumption has become 'the vanguard of history' (Miller 1995c: 1) and further
claimed, with perhaps a hint of hyperbole, that the rise of consumption studies
constitutes a fundamental transformation of the discipline of anthropology and
may replace kinship as its core (Miller 1995b, 1995d).

The reasons for this groundswell of interest are several and complex and these will be discussed in greater detail below. However, one may reasonably claim that the surge of engagement with material culture within the social sciences since the 1980s, after decades of languishing in obscurity, is in many ways a by-product of this emergence of consumption as an important research domain. It is the emphasis on the social and symbolic significance of commodities raised by consumption studies that has provoked an interest in material culture more broadly. Consumption was recognized as the social process by which people construct the symbolically laden material worlds they inhabit and which, reciprocally, act back upon them in complex ways. Hence, as interest has grown in consumption as an important arena of agentive social action, symbolic discourse, and cultural transformation, a corresponding realization has emerged of the importance of understanding the long neglected material domain that consumption simultaneously operates within and creates. On the other hand, archaeologists, the one group of specialists for whom the study of material culture has always been a *sine qua non*, have, for different reasons, also recently turned to the study of consumption as something capable of helping to explain material culture and to illuminate ancient societies in novel ways (Deetz 1977; Dietler 1990a, 1990b, 1998, 2006a; Rogers 1990; Mullins 1999). But whatever the relationship between the focus on material culture and the turn to consumption, the promise of consumption studies in the social sciences has stimulated the vigorous development of both cross-disciplinary theoretical discussion and new research strategies and methods.

This chapter offers a brief review of recent studies of consumption, with a particular emphasis on the fields of archaeology and socio-cultural anthropology. It examines the dramatic growth of a general analytical focus on this practice and the relationship to an expanding interest in the study of material culture. By way of example, it then focuses particularly on the possibilities and challenges that the study of consumption presents for anthropological and archaeological analysis of colonialism, while also pointing out more briefly a series of other domains in which consumption studies have been concentrated. Finally, the issue of methodology is briefly assessed, with special reference to the requirements for developing an effective archaeology of consumption.

THE EMERGENCE OF CONSUMPTION STUDIES

Let us first be clear about what is actually new about the recent wave of consumption studies, because it would be misleading to give the impression that consumption, in a very general sense, was completely ignored in the past. Archaeologists, for example, have always been studying the patterns generated most directly by consumption, rather than production or exchange (which are generally another order of inference removed from the archaeological record). This is because, aside from a few cases such as excavations of shipwrecks or production sites (pottery workshops, factories, etc.), consumption is what ultimately determines where most of the objects they excavate are located and in what state they are found. Moreover, the subspecialty of zooarchaeology has been, from the beginning, almost entirely concerned with identifying patterns of food consumption from faunal remains. But, until recently, archaeological treatment of the process of consumption has been largely implicit, accepting it as a transparent epiphenomenon (the end product of production and distribution) rather than as a domain of agentive social action of primary analytical significance.

Economists, as well, have employed a concept of consumption since at least the emergence of marginalist microeconomics in the late nineteenth century; and, indeed, microeconomics might well be described as the study of consumer decision-making. However, economists have tended to treat consumption unproblematically in a very narrow economic sense as simply an aspect of the relationship between supply and demand, the 'marginal propensity to consume' being a response to prices through the rational allocation of resources among alternative wants or preferences. Understanding consumption then becomes a matter of plotting marginal utility and 'indifference' curves for competing commodities and services. But until recently, most economists have shown little interest in the social and cultural dimensions of consumption or the origins, roles, and meaning of consumer preferences; these are simply accepted as background givens and attention is focused narrowly on the process of quantitatively assessing how the preferences of individual consumers are relatively weighted, affected by prices, and satisfied by the allocation of income (see Fine 1995). In contrast, what is novel in the recent turn to consumption is its recognition as an emphatically social and cultural practice that has significant consequences in other domains of social life and that must be explicitly studied and theorized as a distinct field of action.

To be sure, the economist and sociologist Thorsten Veblen (2008) and the sociologist Georg Simmel (1905, 1961) both produced much more explicit *social* analyses of consumption nearly a hundred years ago. However, these studies of newly emerging patterns of consumption among the urban upper-middle classes in America and Germany at the beginning of the twentieth century failed to stimulate a sustained engagement with the analysis of consumption, and they emerged only in the 1980s as re-discovered ancestral precursors of the current consumption literature. Walter Benjamin's early twentieth-century philosophical reflections from the Paris Arcades Project (Benjamin 1999) and, especially, his essay on 'the work of art in the age of mechanical reproduction' (1977) have also been resurrected in recent years to discuss consumption, especially by scholars in the cultural studies and media fields (e.g. Harvey 1989: 346–349; Shields 1992;

Slater 1993: 192–194; Hall 1997: 333–336). Although not focused specifically on consumption, some of Benjamin's musings on themes such as the staging of commodities through retail spectacles and the nature of 'aura' and its role in investing original, singular works of art with forms of value embedded in regressive structures of power and the consequent emancipatory potential of mass reproduction, have been found relevant to issues being explored in the consumption field.

But the development of a serious widespread analytical focus on consumption as a cultural phenomenon and a significant domain of social action really stems from both the rise of mass consumption among the lower middle and working classes in the mid-twentieth century (something beyond the analytical horizons of Veblen and Simmel) and the growing influence of structuralism within the social sciences in the 1960s, as well as the subsequent versions of practice theory that emerged out of a reaction to structuralism. More recently, it has also been greatly stimulated by an interest, in particular among geographers and anthropologists, in the connections between globalization and postmodernity, in which both are understood to involve the development of novel forms of expressive 'consumer culture' in a post-industrial age (e.g. Harvey 1989; Featherstone 1991; Miller 1997; Haugerud et al. 2000). The growth of mass consumption in the United States and Europe since World War II was enabled by the expansion of what Gramsci (1971: 279–322) had earlier labelled 'Fordist' production strategies (i.e. systems of factory production geared toward both the creation of new groups of consumers with increased disposable income from higher wages and the rapid manufacture of inexpensive standardized goods for them to consume). This mass consumption initially elicited a largely negative and pessimistic assessment among scholars on both the political right and left: either elitist disdain or despair about the irresistible, seductive, and destructive power of capitalism and the effects of marketing in determining mass tastes and behaviour. The latter view was heavily indebted to the Frankfurt School's analysis of popular culture (e.g. Marcuse 1964; Horkheimer and Adorno 1972; Adorno 1982), but also to other Marxian traditions in which commoditization was linked to the masking of power relations and the process of alienation. However, by the late 1980s, consumption was increasingly being viewed more optimistically, not as passive acquiescence to a form of capitalist control and distraction of the masses, but as a type of creative resistance and expressive means of constructing identity. It came to be seen as a significant form of agency that resulted in forms of popular culture that were participatory and democratic. This radical transformation in perspective, which has occasionally exhibited an almost neo-Romantic cast (with an elevation of popular culture as a new form of ennobled folk art and a vision of consumption as a kind of individualized heroic aesthetic resistance to capitalism), can be credited in no small part to the influence of structuralism in popularizing a semiotic approach to culture and social action during the 1960s. Early French structuralist analyses of fashion and cuisine, for example, were instrumental in highlighting consumption as a good deal more than the provision of material needs: it was treated as primarily a symbolic domain with a semiotic code to be deciphered (e.g. Barthes 1961, 1967b; Lévi-Strauss 1978). Roland Barthes' (1967b) famous dissection of the fashion industry, for instance, demonstrated the arbitrary quality of signs mobilized in the domain of fashion and the way their naturalization served to assert bourgeois values. The ahistorical, static, and structurally overdetermined aspects of the core research programme of structuralism (that is, searching for hidden 'deep structure' in the surface manifestations of various social and cultural phenomena, such as consumption, myth, and kinship), among other problems, eventually led to a reaction against orthodox structuralism. However, the semiotic and relational forms of analysis that were a hallmark of structuralism were retained as a central feature in the work of anthropologists and sociologists who emerged from the structuralist school and were seminally instrumental in pushing the symbolic analysis of consumption further (e.g. Sahlins 1976; Bourdieu 1984; Baudrillard 1996, 1998).

These analysts viewed consumption as a symbolic process guided by a system of signs that is culturally ordered; but, more than being simply a coded reflection of deep structure, this process was seen to have profound social implications and effects. The early works of Jean Baudrillard and Marshall Sahlins on this theme were primarily interested in explaining the symbolic logic of consumption and asserting a primacy for consumption in shaping the broader political economy, and they operated on a fairly sweeping cultural scale. For instance, Baudrillard, in his *The Consumer Society* (1998), used a somewhat anecdotal approach to evidence from various domains of consumption (media, the body, leisure, etc.) to argue for the idea that consumption as a system of signs had displaced production at the centre of contemporary culture and identity. On the other hand, Pierre Bourdieu, in his *Distinction: a social critique of the judgment of taste* (1984), used a very focused and systematic empirical analysis of French society in the 1960s to apply his general theory of practice (Bourdieu 1990) to the realm of consumption. He was concerned to show the ways in which taste (in things like art, music, literature, home furnishings, etc.) is distributed in highly patterned ways corresponding to positions within fields of social power, and how it both reflects and reinforces those relational positions. Consumption is structured by distinctive sets of aesthetic and moral dispositions that become embodied through life experience within particular class and status positions, and these aspects of a more general 'habitus' also become part of the 'symbolic capital' (or more specifically 'cultural capital') that actively reinforces power relations (Bourdieu 1984: 169–225; 1990: 52–65, 112–121). According to Bourdieu's analysis, the apparently distinctive tastes and consumption patterns of different classes and class fractions must always be viewed in a dynamic relational fashion, such that the dominant aesthetic subtly defines the aesthetic of dominated groups and fractions through a variety of symbolic oppositions, inversions, and imitations. This provides a far more nuanced and flexible basis for analysis than, for example, Veblen's concept of 'conspicuous consumption' (2008: 49–69).

The 1980s witnessed a sudden florescence of concern with consumption within socio-cultural anthropology (especially Anglophone anthropology), influenced by the pioneering studies noted above. But this anthropological engagement with consumption was also influenced by both a growing critique of neo-classical economics and a dissatisfaction with the limitations of traditional anthropological research (particularly the dominant focus on exchange within economic anthropology and the neglect of Western consumer culture as a field of analysis). Anthropologist Mary Douglas and economist Baron Isherwood's co-authored study, *The World of Goods* (1979), was widely influential in stimulating anthropologists to focus on consumption and commoditization, and it directed a clear challenge to the hegemony of economics (as had Sahlins' earlier critique of practical reason [1976]). Anthropologist Arjun Appadurai's equally influential introduction to an edited volume on *The Social Life of Things* (1986b) further opened the field of consumption to anthropologists by deconstructing the entrenched gift/commodity dichotomy and the boundaries between 'traditional' and 'modern' economies that had restricted disciplinary dispositions toward fieldwork. Daniel Miller (1987) was perhaps the most active advocate, pushing anthropologists towards both theorizing consumption in new ways and developing new methods and specific field studies of consumption, but other anthropological approaches to consumption emerged in parallel with his (e.g. Mintz 1985; McCracken 1988; Rutz and Orlove 1989; Friedman 1994). Colin Campbell (1987) played a similar role during this period within sociology.

Much of the growing consumption literature in sociology, geography, and cultural studies since the 1980s has followed Baudrillard's (1998) lead in focusing upon the emergence of a post-modern, post-industrial 'consumer society' in Europe and America, in which the practice of consumption has overtaken class and production-based categories as a means of defining identity (Hebdige 1979; Harvey 1989; Featherstone 1991). While anthropologists have also ventured into this terrain (e.g. Miller 1987, 1998c), a more widespread concern within the recent anthropological literature on consumption has been the flow of commodities across cultural boundaries and the social and cultural consequences of such consumption. This analysis has been directed both back in time, examining the role of consumption in the historical process of colonialism and Western capitalist expansion (e.g. Mintz 1985; Dietler 1990b, 1998, 2005, 2007; Comaroff and Comaroff 1991, 1997; Thomas 1991; Sahlins 1994; Howes 1996a; Mullins 1999), and toward the present, exploring the current process of globalization. Anthropologies of globalization have focused particularly upon the role of consumption in the historically-specific configurations of local/global relations and processes. These have emerged recently in the post-colonial, late-capitalist cultural economy, with their peculiar conjunctures of electronic mass-mediation, mass-migrations, and global capital flows, which have created new forms of diasporic communities and radically new transnational spaces of imagination and identity (e.g. Hannerz 1992; Friedman 1994; Miller 1994, 1997; Appadurai 1996; Haugerud *et al.* 2000).

Archaeologists and historians have made an important contribution in relativizing some of the assumptions of uniqueness for the contemporary situation held by scholars in other fields. As the previous discussion makes clear, most of the consumption literature emerged in the context of an analysis of capitalist mass consumption and the use of industrially produced commodities in the construction of identities in the modern and post-modern eras in the United States and Europe, with the common assertion that there is something qualitatively distinctive about these recent phenomena. This assertion has, however, usually been unsupported by actual empirical analysis of earlier contexts and often rests on little more than conjectural contrasts. There clearly are potential dangers for archaeologists, historians, and historical anthropologists attempting to use theoretical concepts designed to tackle these specific historical situations in order to analyse cases from earlier periods. But these dangers exist only if models are imported as a priori explanatory devices and anachronistically universalized across all cultures and histories; that is, if historians and archaeologists act simply as naive consumers of consumption theory. Instead, they have an opportunity to contribute actively to the development of such theory by examining both similarities and differences between historical cases and thereby contextualizing the modern and postmodern situations that generated much of the early theorizing. Such work serves to temper some of the more radical assertions of uniqueness for modern and postmodern consumption; after all, the widespread circulation and consumption of mass-produced commodities was already a feature of the ancient Mediterranean economy in the first millennium BCE, and styles of consumption already played a major role in the formation of Roman provincial identities within the Empire, to cite but two related examples (see Tchernia 1986; Woolf 1998). Archaeological studies of consumption in past societies can also help to identify and understand genuinely novel aspects of the recent situation by examining simultaneously both continuities and disjunctures, and commonalities and contrasts. In brief, explorations of ancient consumption can serve to counteract tendencies toward both the production of Manichaean conjectural histories of pre-capitalist or pre-modern conditions through simple dichotomous inversion of the present and the facile universalizing of modern Western experience in the way that much social theory has done all too often and easily (e.g. Baudrillard 1996, 1998). In other words, archaeological research, in dialogue with the modern consumption literature, has the potential to develop a more nuanced understanding by demonstrating that modern and postmodern consumption is not unique: since such things as mass consumption of commodities circulating over long distances existed in other earlier contexts. At the same time, however, there are important differences in such things as the organization of commodity chains and the nature of marketing, transport, and media, which prohibit the uncritical generalizing of theory derived from modern Western contexts. This does not make such theory irrelevant to the past: far from it. Rather, it means that archaeology has a role complementary to that of socio-cultural anthropology in helping to 'provincialize' (Chakrabarty 2000) Eurocentric social theory and thereby improve it.

CONSUMPTION, MATERIAL CULTURE, AND COLONIALISM

Studies of consumption have ranged over a wide array of contexts and goods, and one can do little more than point to a selective sampling in a brief review such as this. However, the contribution of consumption studies to the understanding of colonialism will be singled out for somewhat more extensive discussion because, as noted earlier, this has been a particularly productive focus of anthropological research (Dietler 2010). One of its attractions is that, because it is focused on issues of transformation, the field of colonial consumption is one that has emphasized a dynamic view of historical process and avoided a tendency toward somewhat static synchronic visions of consumption that have often characterized analyses of modern Western mass consumption.

A new theoretical interest in consumption within anthropology has accompanied a growing awareness of the significance of material culture and consumption by scholars of colonialism and postcoloniality (e.g. Mintz 1985; Dietler 1990b, 1998, 2005, 2007; Rogers 1990; Comaroff and Comaroff 1991, 1997; Thomas 1991; Sahlins 1992, 1994; Appadurai 1996; Burke 1996; Howes 1996a; Turgeon *et al.* 1996; Turgeon 1998, 2003; Voss 2008b). Consumption in this context has come to be understood as an agentive symbolic activity deeply embedded in, and constitutive of, social relations and cultural conceptions, and is no longer simply an economic product of ends/means calculation (as in neoclassical economics) or a passive reflection of other structures (as in early structuralism). This relational approach to consumption has opened important new vistas for understanding the role of material culture in colonial strategies and processes. In archaeological contexts, it has also provided a way of addressing the issue of agency in colonial situations by revealing patterns of choice and their consequences.

However, while full of promise, one must acknowledge certain dangers in the growing popularity of this consumption work as well. For instance, an exclusive focus on consumption, particularly as exemplified in some of the more semiotically oriented forms of analysis stemming from the early work of Baudrillard, may risk decoupling it from those more traditional, but still important, domains of analysis:

production and exchange. An abstract treatment of consumption as the circulation of pure signs that is divorced from consideration of the relations of power in which they are embedded, or that ignores the crucial material dimension of the objects being consumed, would be particularly dangerous in a colonial context, where the issue of exploitation and the political context of the articulation of production and consumption should be ever-present concerns. Jack Goody (1982), for example, provided a useful critical reminder of what was generally missing from structuralist treatments of foodways as sign systems: an analysis of the structures of colonial power and the patterns of labour exploitation that provided the hidden conditions of possibility for the circulation of exotic foodstuffs in European cuisines (see also Mintz 1985; Cook and Crang 1996).

Nevertheless, with such caveats in mind, one can begin a productive exploration of this relationship between colonialism and consumption with the observation (well supported by the studies noted above) that consumption is *never* simply a satisfaction of utilitarian needs or an epiphenomenon of production. Rather, it is a process of symbolic construction of identity and political relations with important material consequences. Moreover, contrary to certain assumptions of neoclassical economic theory (e.g. see Ghez and Becker 1975; Stigler and Becker 1977; Becker 1996; see Fine 1995 for a critique), anthropological studies of consumption have shown that demand can never be understood as a simple or automatic response to the availability of goods, and particularly not in poly-cultural colonial situations. Consumption is always a culturally specific phenomenon and demand is always socially constructed and historically changing. These features offer, therefore, a good potential starting point for launching an exploration of the role of material culture in colonialism and the operation of agency in colonial encounters.

An approach to colonialism through consumption requires consideration of a few key concepts, not least of which is culture. This is important because, not only is consumption structured by cultural categories and dispositions, but also 'culture is constructed through consumption' (Comaroff 1996: 20). This process of cultural construction through consumption implies two things. In the first place, objects materialize cultural order. They render abstract cultural categories as visible and durable, they aid the negotiation of social interaction in various ways, and they structure perception of the social world (see Douglas and Isherwood 1979; Bourdieu 1984; Baudrillard 1996, 1998). The systems of objects that people construct through consumption serve both to inculcate personal identity and to enable people to locate others within social fields through the perception of embodied tastes and various indexical forms of symbolic capital (Bourdieu 1984). Despite somewhat hyperbolic claims by some scholars about recent revolutionary transformations of such practices (e.g. Miller 1987; Baudrillard 1998), this is by no means something unique to capitalist consumer societies, although it clearly operates in different ways in different contexts. However, more than simply reproducing static systems of cultural categories, consumption constructs culture in a more dynamic sense. This is particularly relevant to the issue of cross-cultural consumption and colonialism. Consumption can thus be understood as a process of structured improvization that continually materializes cultural order by also dealing with alien objects and practices through either transformative appropriation and assimilation or rejection.

To accept this perspective implies a processual understanding of culture that differs fundamentally from the one held by, for example, the older acculturation paradigm that guided earlier analysis of colonialism and culture contact in American anthropology (e.g. Herskovits 1938; Social Science Research Council 1954). Rather than viewing culture as simply an inheritance from the past, a processual approach recognizes that it is, more accurately, a kind of eternal project (Hountondji 1994; Sahlins 1999). In other words, culture is not a fixed, static, homogeneous system of shared beliefs, rules, and traits, but rather sets of embodied categorical perceptions, analogical understandings, and values that structure ways of reasoning, solving problems, and acting upon opportunities. The operation of culture is always a creative process. Among those problems/opportunities to be handled is the ever-present one of dealing with exogenous peoples and objects. This process involves both the selective domestication (or indigenization) of formerly foreign goods, practices and tastes, and the rejection of others. Such selective incorporation operates according to a specific cultural logic, but it also has a continual transformative effect in the reproduction of culture. Moreover, this process, obviously, does not occur through the actions of cultures (seen as reified entities) coming into contact, but rather through the often contradictory actions of individual human beings and social groups located differentially within complex relational fields of power and interest.

This process of selective appropriation and indigenization is not something that is unique to colonial situations. It happens everywhere and continuously, given that societies have never existed in a state of isolation and people must always negotiate their lives in relation to external conditions. This is what Amselle, following Ricoeur's (1992) observation that 'selfhood' is constructed in a permanent relation with alterity, meant in writing about 'originary syncretism' (Amselle 1998: x). Cultures are inherently relational in nature: they have always been both products of fusion and in a ceaseless process of construction through fusion. The distinctive feature of colonial contexts is that the particular configurations of colonial relations of power have a marked influence on the nature and structure of the process. Moreover, precisely because of the significance of consumption to the construction of culture, material culture has repeatedly been used as a tool of colonialism.

Perceiving culture in this way means deconstructing the entrenched Western dichotomy between tradition and change (and the linked dichotomy between static and dynamic societies). It also means understanding that the adoption of foreign goods and practices does not result in 'deculturation', and it does not render cultures inauthentic or incoherent. As Marshall Sahlins (1999: xi) has noted, 'anthropologists have known at least since the work of Boas and his students that cultures are generally foreign in origin and local in pattern'. Moreover, cultural continuity usually consists of the distinctive ways that cultures change (Sahlins 1993: 2). Hence, cross-cultural consumption is a continual process of selective appropriation and creative assimilation according to local logics that is also a way of continually constructing and reconstructing culture (Figure 8.1).

This is not to say that such consumption does not have significant consequences in terms of altering the conditions of cultural reproduction. It clearly does. Moreover, focusing upon the role of consumption in the process of colonial entanglement should underline precisely this feature. However, these effects are often subtle and gradual, and they frequently will not be perceived by the participants as marking a cultural discontinuity (although there will sometimes be generational or gender differences in such perceptions). What is usually perceived by colonized peoples as marked rupture or discontinuity is the imposition of colonial political domination and the forms of colonialism that follow it: that is, the sudden loss of control over the process of cultural reproduction and the imposition of techniques of repression and discipline.

Such considerations argue for a more symmetrical treatment of consumption on both sides of colonial encounters than has usually occurred in the past. The consumption of goods and practices does not flow in one direction only, and the

Fig. 8.1 Local consumption/global circulation: shopping for second-hand European clothes at a rural Kenyan market (Boro, Kenya).

process deserves to be examined in comparable ways in all contexts. For example, consumption of foreign objects and practices by Euro-American societies is rarely credited with provoking sentiments of cultural crisis or inauthenticity in popular consciousness. Europeans and Americans are allowed any number of invented traditions and indigenizations of foreign objects and practices—whether pasta and tomatoes in Italian cuisine, tea in England, or the decoration of American homes with African baskets, Indonesian cloth, Persian rugs, and Japanese furniture, for example—without the suspicion of cultural emulation or incoherence. Yet, similar kinds of adaptations of European or American objects or practices in places such as Africa or the Pacific have often been seen as a flawed mimesis of the West rather than creative, and sometimes subversive, appropriations. Nevertheless, symmetrical analysis of consumption can correct such misperceptions. Jean Comaroff (1996: 31) has used the revealing example of a Tswana chief in South Africa of the 1860s, who had a Western style suit made for himself out of leopard skin, to show that, rather than simply imitating Western goods in a curious way that did not quite get it right, he was creatively playing upon symbols of power from two domains to create an object that doubled its impact.

The case of the Tswana chief underlines the fact that when an object crosses cultural frontiers, it rarely arrives with the same meanings and practices associated with it in its context of origin. If one thinks of the consumption of Coca-Cola, for example, a bottle of this beverage consumed in rural East Africa does not have the same meaning as an identical one consumed in Chicago. In the former context, it may be reserved for serving to distinguished visitors and incorporated into ceremonial commensality in a pattern reminiscent of the use of imported French wine in bourgeois homes in Chicago, where it would be unthinkable to use Coca-Cola in a similar way. Hence, the presence of bottles of Coca-Cola in rural Africa is not a sign of the Americanization of Africa, but rather of the Africanization of Coca-Cola (Dietler 2007). It is crucial to understand the specific contexts of consumption in order to recognize the meaning and significance of goods. After all, it is reported that in Russia Coca-Cola is employed to remove wrinkles, in Haiti it is believed to revive the dead, and in Barbados it is said to transform copper into silver (Pendergrast 1993: 245–247; Howes 1996b: 6). Moreover, Coca-Cola is sometimes valued precisely for its foreign origin (indeed, sometimes for its indexical relationship to an imagined concept of America), while in other contexts it comes to be seen, as Daniel Miller has observed, as a thoroughly local drink without any aura of the exotic (Miller 1994, 1998a).

Obviously, speaking about the Africanization of Coca-Cola does not imply that its consumption is a benign activity without potentially serious economic and cultural consequences. For example, in some contexts, imported soft drinks can come to replace native beverages, and this can have implications for both nutrition and relations of economic dependency (James 1993). Moreover, it is also clear that the availability of Coca-Cola in Africa is driven by strategies of corporate

Fig. 8.2 Coca-Cola advertising in rural Africa (Siaya, Kenya).

executives seeking global market penetration and is enabled by a massive international infrastructure of production and distribution embedded in global geopolitical structures of power. Finally, one must also avoid a romanticized vision of unfettered indigenous agency in which consumption becomes an autonomous form of liberating resistance. There are always both intended and unintended consequences in consuming alien goods, and these consequences ought precisely to be the focus of analysis in understanding the entangling operation of consumption and the subtle transformations of consciousness and identity that result (Dietler 1998, 2007). This is the reason that analysis of consumption should not be simply about the semiotic play of signs, but must be firmly grounded in the material conditions and power relations of the political economy. However, just as clearly, this is not a simple homogeneous, or homogenizing, process of the 'coca-colonization' (Hannerz 1992: 217) of passive peripheral subjects. Whatever the hegemonic schemes of Coca-Cola executives for global market domination, demand for this beverage in Africa, Chicago, Paris, or Trinidad is a product of local desires and tastes generated according to local cultural conceptions and social practices. In order to be desired and used, exotic goods must always be imbued with culturally relevant meaning locally and incorporated into local social relationships. Moreover, these processes of redefinition and reorientation must be contextualized and understood if we are to comprehend the transformative effects of cross-cultural consumption (Figure 8.2).

This approach to consumption also leads to consideration of the significance of material culture in strategies of colonialism, something that has gained increasing recognition among anthropologists in recent years. As Nicholas Thomas has noted, 'material cultures and technologies are central to the transformative work of colonialism' (2002: 182). Given the importance of consumption in constructing culture and social relationships, it should not be surprising that goods have not only been appropriated and indigenized, they have also been used by both parties in exchanges to attempt to control the other—'making subjects by means of objects' (Comaroff and Comaroff 1997: 218). This involved not only attempts to create novel desires for new goods, but also attempts to get people to use imported objects in particular ways, as well as the (usually mistaken) belief that the use of particular objects or technologies would inherently induce certain kinds of desired behaviour. For example, it is clear that clothing played a very important instrumental role in the strategies of European missionaries to colonize the consciousness of indigenous peoples in various parts of the world. Christian missionaries in the Pacific tried to use clothing as a means of transforming Samoan and Tahitian moral consciousness and instilling new concepts of work discipline, temporality, and gender relations (N. Thomas 2002). Similarly, among the Tswana in South Africa, both clothing and architecture served as vehicles for attempts by missionaries to inculcate European concepts of domesticity and bodily discipline; and they became sites of struggle as the Tswana used these new material forms as an expressive language to structure identity in new ways and contest colonial categories and aesthetics (Comaroff and Comaroff 1997). As this case suggests, such strategies to use material objects as vectors of control always have unintended consequences for all the parties concerned.

Anthropological and archaeological studies of consumption guided by this kind of perspective have been instrumental in providing new insights into the operation and consequences of colonialism in a wide variety of colonial and postcolonial (or neocolonial) contexts, ranging from the cases of African and Pacific encounters with Europeans noted above (see also Hansen 1992; Sahlins 1992, 1994; Burke 1996), to European missionary activity in South America (Scaramelli and Tarble de Scaramelli 2005), North American slavery (Mullins 1999), the politics of identity in colonial Ireland (Hartnett 2004), colonial ethnogenesis in eighteenth- and nineteenth-century California (Voss 2008b), and ancient Greco-Roman encounters with indigenous peoples of the Mediterranean (Dietler 1998, 2010).

OTHER FIELDS OF CONSUMPTION

Aside from colonialism, the range of domains of material culture and social action in which consumption research has played a prominent role is extensive. Food, alcohol, and drugs have constituted one obvious area, given that consumption of such 'embodied material culture' (Dietler 2006a: 231–232), transforms goods by ingesting them directly into the body, is so closely linked to the construction and display of social and personal identity. This is also an area where the performative aspects of consumption are closely tied to the creation and maintenance of social relationships and politics. Because of the biological imperatives of nutrition, it is also an area where symbolic action in the domestic sphere is so obviously linked to production and the broader political economy. Hence, it is hardly surprising that this is also an area that attracted the attention of early structuralist analyses (e.g. Barthes 1961; Douglas 1975; Sahlins 1976; Lévi-Strauss 1978) and that has consistently linked social anthropologists, archaeologists, historians, and sociologists in a common dialogue. Subjects of study have ranged from the micro-politics of cuisine in Indian homes to the invention of the restaurant in Europe, the construction of national cuisines, the wine trade in the ancient Mediterranean, the role of alcohol in the construction of gender and class, and the consumption of world cuisine in cosmopolitan cities, to name only a few (e.g. Douglas 1975, 1984, 1987; Appadurai 1981; Goody 1982; Weismantel 1988; Dietler 1990a, 2006a, 2007; Falk 1994; McDonald 1994; Goodman *et al.* 1995; James 1996; Mennell 1996; Counihan and van Esterik 1997; Wilk 1999; de Garine and de Garine 2001; Turgeon 2003; Twiss 2007; Mullins 2008). Most recently, rituals of food and alcohol consumption, called feasts, have attracted particular theoretical and empirical attention, especially by archaeologists, as prominent arenas of political action (e.g. Dietler and Hayden 2001; Bray 2003a; Mills 2004; Wright 2004).

Another domain of consumption closely associated with the body—clothing and dress—has also been a long-term popular theme for researchers from a variety of fields, and has generated an enormous literature. This includes both analysis of fashion (the constantly shifting semiotics of clothing style, especially in Western bourgeois society) and more general treatment of cloth, clothing, jewellery, and other forms of bodily adornment in other contexts (e.g. Hebdige 1979; Turner 1980; Weiner and Schneider 1989; Comaroff 1996; Caplan 2000; Entwistle 2000; Hansen 2000, 2004; N. Thomas 2002; Banerjee and Miller 2003; Allman 2004; Küchler and Miller 2005). Studies of the consumption of media and services have also become increasingly popular, particularly as the former industrial powers of Europe and America move increasingly toward service economies (Morley 1992, 1995; Silverstone and Hirsch 1992; Mazzarella 2003). However, the list of goods and services that have been treated in consumption studies (furniture and other household items, art, music, tourist experiences and memorabilia, automobiles, etc.) is both enormous and expanding daily (Figure 8.3).

For archaeologists and historians, another recent expanding domain of research attention has been the consumption of the past, including concerns about the implication of scholars in this process and the effects it has on both disciplinary practice and society at large (e.g. see Lowenthal 1998; Abu El-Haj 2001; Baram and

Fig. 8.3 Consuming the past: cultural tourism and the use of archaeological objects in popular culture (Murlo, Italy).

Rowan 2004; Dietler 2006b; Silberman 2007). Archaeologists, in particular, have been concerned about the role of the discipline in producing the objects and sites that constitute a material symbolic reservoir for the construction of modern identities. Whether under the banner of 'heritage', which is often linked to nationalizing narratives of the state, or the neo-liberal private commercialization of archaeological sites and artefacts as marketable commodities, entertainment and cultural tourism, or the media-fed integration of archaeology into popular culture under the tropes of mystery, discovery, and adventure, the perceived value of archaeology to consumers plays a major role in the funding and use of research. This fact has a variety of ramifications for archaeological practice that are the subject of a growing body of current research.

METHODS

Analysts of consumption have tended to approach the issue from two directions: focusing either on the symbolic logic and social action of consumers or on the efforts of marketers and vendors to shape and/or follow consumer tastes. The work of early social theorists on consumption was often rather loosely grounded in anecdotal personal impressions and general assumptions (e.g. Baudrillard 1996, 1998). However, the methods used by subsequent analysts vary from detailed ethnographic analysis of communities of consumers or advertising firms (e.g. Comaroff 1996; Mazzarella 2003; Miller 1994), to statistical analysis of consumer tastes and class and status position correlations by sociologists (e.g. Bourdieu 1984), to more text and image-based studies of advertisements, shop windows, and novels by historians and cultural studies scholars (e.g. Leach 1993; Frank 1997), to product biographies tracing the history of the creation, promotion, and reception of particular commodities (e.g. Pendergrast 1993; Parr 1999; Mullins 2008). The demands of consumption studies have also been instrumental in pushing anthropologists and sociologists toward methodological innovation, such as new forms of cooperative 'multi-sited ethnography' (Marcus 1995; Gille and Ó Riain 2002) that are capable, for example, of exploring the social life of classes of objects by following commodity chains or commodity networks (e.g. Mintz 1985; Collins 2000; Hansen 2000, 2002). In this way, the often hidden linkages between the decisions, actions, and effects of consumers and those of transnational corporations, media, bureaucracies, and producers spread around the world can be exposed and analysed.

For archaeologists, the epistemological issues are somewhat different. Historical archaeologists have been able to rely partly on the kind of textual evidence available to historians (archives, advertisements, wills and probate statements, etc.), but supplemented, interwoven with and challenged by the material evidence of consumed objects (Deetz 1977; Mullins 1999; Cochran and Beaudry 2006; Voss 2008b). For those working in periods and areas where textual evidence is scarce or non-existent, the archaeological turn to the study of consumption has required some methodological ingenuity, as older excavations were usually not geared toward the acquisition of data that are useful for detecting consumption patterns.

The kinds of regional distribution maps of objects and limited excavations that have been typical for discussions of trade, and even many typologies of ceramics and other objects that were originally designed for purposes of regional chronologies and culture histories, will often be inadequate for investigating consumption. Moving beyond the limitations of these techniques to study consumption requires examining much more carefully the particular things that were consumed and the ways they were consumed: that is, examining closely the specific *properties* and *contexts* of objects and practices in order to understand the social and cultural logic of the desire for them and the social, economic, and political roles that their consumption played. It is also, of course, necessary to examine the counter-phenomenon—that is, what might be called the logic of indifference and/or rejection. It is necessary to understand what goods and practices were available for appropriation but were ignored or refused, and why a particular pattern of selective consumption emerged from a range of possibilities. In brief, one must seek to discern and explain the *choices* that were made and the consequences of those choices.

This kind of close examination of consumption requires a research strategy geared toward the simultaneous relational analysis, on regional, intra-site and household scales, of several features: the contexts of consumption, the patterns of association among objects consumed, the spatial distribution of objects, the relative quantitative representation of different kinds of objects, and the specific material and functional properties of different objects. Finally, such analysis is most effective when one subjects these patterns to comparative analysis, in both their temporal and spatial dimensions; that is, when there is both a focus on historical process, comparing successive phases at individual sites and within regions, and also an attempt to compare and contrast local patterns with those of adjacent sites and regions. This kind of analysis has, for example, enabled a much richer understanding of the shifting nature of demand for imported wine in Iron Age France, its role in articulating the colonial encounter with Greeks, Etruscans, and Romans over several centuries, and the social and cultural consequences of this consumption (Dietler 1998, 2005, 2010; see also Sanmartí 2009) (Figure 8.4).

This strategy obviously places quite stringent demands upon the archaeological evidence, demands of a kind that cannot always be met adequately by the data from many past and current field research projects. It is clear, for example, that the kind

Fig. 8.4 Studying consumption in the past: open–area excavations necessary to reveal patterns of consumption in multiple contemporary dwellings and neighbourhoods (Lattes, France).

of understanding sought cannot be gleaned from a single site or dwelling in isolation: it requires fairly dense contextual documentation over a regional landscape and over individual sites within that regional landscape (comparing detailed household and funerary data on consumption patterns within and among sites), as well as good chronological control. It is also evident that, by itself, archaeological survey cannot provide an adequate basis for this kind of analysis, because it yields very little *contextual* information. Excavation is therefore essential, but not just any type of excavation. One really needs large-scale, area-extensive excavations that pay very careful attention to the contextual and processual details of domestic and funerary situations, and that record this information in ways that allow fine-grained comparative analysis on a variety of scales. It also requires, for example, classifications of ceramics that are based on functional criteria, rather than on the kinds of decorative elements or fabric types that have been traditionally employed to construct chronologies and trace horizons and trade patterns. Tamara Bray (2003b), for instance, has shown how a major rethinking of ceramic classification was necessary to understand the operation and significance of food consumption rituals of the Inca state (see also Cook and Glowacki 2003; Smith *et al.* 2003).

CONCLUSIONS

Consumption is a material practice that has seen a dramatic increase in research attention in recent decades, and that has had a major impact on the revival of interest in material culture in the social sciences and humanities. Consumption research has stimulated an appreciation of the symbolic significance of the material world and a new analytical focus on the use of objects in the construction of identity and in the politics of daily life. It has also brought about a re-evaluation of popular culture as a domain of consequent agency rather than simply a banal and decadent distraction or a mystification of capitalism.

The pursuit of consumption studies is a vibrant, evolving research frontier that has provoked a good deal of theoretical discussion and methodological innovation. This popularity poses certain dangers, particularly if consumption is studied in isolation or treated in a limited semiotic fashion as an entirely symbolic activity. However, if understood as a social practice with significant material consequences that is intimately entangled in systems of production and distribution, then consumption studies have the potential to serve as a heuristic bridge between various disciplines and fields and to provide novel insights into a variety of phenomena ranging from identity to agency, class, nationalism, colonialism, and globalization. Studies of consumption by archaeologists and socio-cultural anthropologists have a special place in this domain of research because they bring to it a global perspective that ranges widely in time and space. Hence, they offer the crucial ability to relativize and contextualize studies of modern Western consumer culture, which generated most of the early theoretical work on consumption.

CHAPTER 9

FIELDWORK AND COLLECTING

GAVIN LUCAS

INTRODUCTION

Studies of collecting and fieldwork in the disciplines of archaeology and socio-cultural anthropology are relatively undeveloped, but in the past 10–15 years there has been a noticeable rise in interest as part of a broader reflexivity in the practices of these and related disciplines. Collecting, studied from a psychological perspective has a longer history, especially through Freudian interpretations that linked it with the anal retentive stage, thus associating it with certain personality traits (Pearce 1995: 6–8). However, as part of a wider discourse, it is a fairly recent topic of investigation and has been generally approached either in the context of consumer research (Belk 1995) or more commonly, museum studies (Impey and MacGregor 1985; Stocking 1985; Pomian 1990). Susan Pearce's major study *On Collecting: an investigation into collecting in the European tradition* was a landmark volume in a shift over the past two decades from the study of only 'the content of collections' to a focus on 'collecting as a process in itself' (Pearce 1995: vii; cf. Pearce 1992; Elsner and Cardinal 1994). Studies specifically on ethnological collections have also seen a major rise in interest in the past decade (O'Hanlon and Welsch 2000; Gosden and Knowles 2001; Edwards *et al.* 2006), but have a pedigree in George Stocking's seminal volume *Objects and Others: essays on museums and material culture* (Stocking 1985). In parallel with this growing awareness of the practices of collecting, reflexive studies, which examine the nature and practice of anthropological and archaeological fieldwork, have also begun to develop, albeit rather unevenly. In socio-cultural anthropology, a number of recent volumes attest to the growing importance of reflexivity, from George Stocking's *Observers Observed: essays on ethnographic fieldwork* (volume 1 of his seminal *History of Anthropology* series; Stocking 1983a) to more recent collections (Gupta and Ferguson 1997a, 1997b; Amit 1999; cf. Robben and Sluka 2006). In archaeology, similar reflexive studies of fieldwork have developed since the late 1990s, most notably Hodder's *The Archaeological Process*, Lucas' *Critical Approaches to Fieldwork* and Edgeworth's *Acts of Discovery* (Hodder 1999; also see Hodder 1997; Lucas 2001a; Edgeworth 2003).

Contemporary practices of collecting and fieldwork form a key part of material culture research in archaeology and anthropology, but the approaches can vary quite dramatically, depending on the context and the discipline. The most obvious variation relates to the fact that in ethnographic research, material culture is today rarely collected and removed from its context, while this is a central aspect of the archaeological process. This has important consequences for the nature of field-work and its interpretations. This distinction is historical, however, for up until the 1920s, both archaeological and ethnographic or ethnological research shared a similar focus on retrieving and collecting material culture; after this time, the two disciplines diverged. This divergence largely relates to the changing goals of socio-cultural anthropology and its eschewal of material culture studies in favour of direct participant observation. Even since the return of many anthropologists to an interest in material culture, especially from the 1990s (Buchli 2002a), the field has generally maintained this observational rather than interventionist approach to objects. The rest of this chapter presents a review of the history of these practices and the current differences between the treatment of material culture in archaeo-logical and ethnographic fieldwork.

COLLECTING AND THE FIELD

Europeans have been continually exposed to artefacts from other cultures, even back into prehistory. One remarkable example is a bronze statuette of Buddha from northern India found from excavations at the eighth-century Viking trading emporium at Helgö in Sweden (Gyllensvärd *et al.* 2004). Nonetheless, it can be plausibly argued that the Renaissance ushered in a new era of such exotic goods in European history, marked by a sheer increase in scale and variety (Jardine 1996). Such objects initially came from other Old World cultures, especially from the Middle East and Asia, and entered Europe via widespread trade networks, which have been, perhaps misleadingly, named world systems (e.g. Abu-Lughod 1991b;

Frank and Gills 1993). While the connections between Europe and other parts of
the globe before the sixteenth century have without doubt previously been under-
stated by European historians, largely because Europe was usually on the periphery
of these trade systems, as Europe became the core of a truly global system after the
sixteenth century the number of exotic objects—now also from the Americas—
entering its countries also dramatically increased. What emerged at the same time
was a new conception of many of these exotic objects; while many remained
significant items for trade and were inserted into already understood categories
and practices (e.g. spices, jewellery, ceramics), others were constituted as a new
category of 'curiosities' and tied to new and largely elite practices of collecting
(Impey and MacGregor 1985; Pomian 1990).

   One of the most striking aspects of much early collecting is the lack of distinction among objects; curiosities formed a generic group, where items such as fossils,
butterflies, tribal weapons, and antiquities might all jostle side by side in a
collector's cabinet (Figure 9.1). For example, antiquarian researches, such as

Fig. 9.1 Ole Worm's cabinet of curiosities (from Worm 1665: frontispiece).

those of the seventeenth-century Robert Plot, were frequently part of the wider study of natural history, and archaeological remains were discussed alongside flora, fauna, and other aspects of the environment (Schnapp 1993: 198). The gradual development of classification systems was bound up with the emergence of the modern museum and ultimately the emergence of separate disciplines, including archaeology and ethnography (Hooper-Greenhill 1992).

We know very little about the practices that resulted in the primary acquisition of these early ethnographic objects, except that they probably came as random gifts or other items bought by traders, sailors, and travellers, who later donated or sold them on to patrons, dealers, and collectors. In a sense, the 'fieldwork', if one can use that term, of early modern collectors largely involved visiting other collections and dealers, rather than travelling to the source of such curiosities. For example, John Evelyn, the seventeenth-century collector, travelled around Europe visiting other collections and mentions in his diaries a new shopkeeper dealing specifically in curiosities (Hodgen 1964: 114–118). The situation only started to change in the eighteenth and nineteenth centuries, when some collectors started to go into the 'field' to acquire objects themselves. Initially, this happened with ethnologists and naturalists accompanying exploratory or trade voyages, but later, as European colonialism developed, residents such as missionaries and diplomats also built up quite substantial private collections (e.g. Cannizzo 1998; Hasinoff 2006). Similar practices were common in the case of classical antiquities through the rise of international travel among the European elite, whether through the 'Grand Tour' or through official postings (Jenkins 1992). In the case of prehistoric antiquities, however, a tradition of collectors going into the field has, inevitably, a much longer history. This is perhaps unsurprising as such material was often on the collector's 'doorstep', so to speak. This tradition, which included both excavation as well as accidental discovery through other earth-moving activities, was particularly strong in central Europe (Malina and Vašíček 1990: 27; Schnapp 1993). Even in Britain, which was more oriented towards a topographic approach until the nineteenth century, 'fieldwork' was a central component of antiquarianism, where, because it largely involved landscape survey, presence in the field was considered essential—a feature that continues to define British landscape archaeology (Ashbee 1972; Piggott 1976; Johnson 2006).

Although motivations for collections varied, by the nineteenth century collecting practices most commonly remained embedded in commercial transactions and connected to the market; collections were still bought and sold, and individual pieces were obtained in similar ways as before—as gifts or commodities. Yet the fact that collecting antiquities or ethnographic objects was, from the late eighteenth century, increasingly being done by the collector–scientist rather than an intermediary such as a merchant, came to have pivotal consequences for the development of both archaeology and anthropology. Nicholas Thomas' now classic study of early ethnography in the Pacific, *Entangled Objects*, provides invaluable insight into this transition (Thomas 1991). As Thomas shows, the motivations for the acquisition of artefacts by the ethnologist and naturalist Reinhold Forster on Cook's second voyage went little beyond curiosity and an unarticulated sense of aesthetics (Thomas 1991: 130–137) (Figure 9.2). Indeed, there was no attempt at systematic collection or representative samples, but rather what was acquired was largely dictated by what the islanders offered (Thomas 1991: 138). Being in the field did not, then, intrinsically affect the content of collections, as might be expected. The economic nexus in which such artefacts were entangled, however, shows that a new discourse was emerging around collecting, which created a competing set of values. Thomas highlights Forster's irritation over the trade in curiosities carried out by ordinary sailors, who bought items for re-sale back in Europe, knowing their value to collectors. Forster himself clearly purchased items from sailors, but his main grievance was that such trade raised prices and made it more expensive for him to build up scientific collections (Thomas 1991: 140). This story encapsulates the ambiguous status of such objects at the end of the eighteenth century as both commodities and objects of scientific interest. While this ambiguity must have existed since the sixteenth century, it would appear that it was not felt as a problem so long as the collector was at a distant remove in the chain of exchange, but it became problematic once that chain collapsed and there was no mediation between the collector and the original source.

This direct contact between collector and source became a hallmark of scientific authority. Forster quite explicitly criticized those scholars who tried to understand human society solely through their cabinets, which became constituted as second-hand knowledge. Ultimately, presence in the field became the *sine qua non* of proper scientific practice (Thomas 1991: 141; Kuklick 1997: 48), and represented the beginnings of archaeological and anthropological fieldwork. This was by no means an overnight transformation, however, for it was not until the early twentieth century that the modern concept of ethnographic fieldwork emerged, in a process that, ironically, saw a shift of emphasis away from objects, and to which this chapter will return later.

Throughout the nineteenth century, although many ethnologists went into 'the field' to collect artefacts, whether on commissioned expeditions or as resident colonists, many did not. The first-hand reports of these field collectors provided new authenticity for collections. Many of these individuals collected not just for themselves but for museums.

What is interesting about the professionalization of anthropology in the late nineteenth century and its museum phase (Sturtevant 1969) is the fact that fieldwork did not distinguish amateurs from professionals at this time. Museums sent out their staff to collect artefacts, but at the same time purchased material from local collectors; indeed, often it was in the field that the professionals bought collections from amateurs. For example, many of the important museum

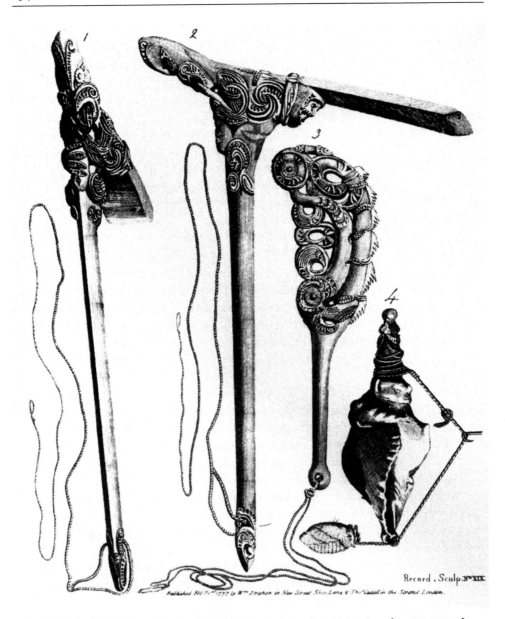

Fig. 9.2 Maori artefacts collected on Cook's second voyage (1772–1775), as illustrated in Plate XVIII in Captain Cook's *A Voyage towards the South Pole and Round the World* . . . (London 1777): (1 and 2) adze, toki pou tangata (Forster 109, PRM 1886.1.1159); (3) knife (Forster 110, PRM 1886.1.1161); (4) shell-trumpet (now in the Cambridge University Museum of Archaeology and Anthropology).

collections of south-west Indian artefacts in North America derive from the practices of one man, Thomas Kearn, who traded and dealt in contemporary and ancient Hopi objects in the last decades of the nineteenth century (Wade 1985). Kearn was well connected to leading anthropologists such as Frank Cushing and Washington Matthews; in 1892, he supplied Jesse Fewkes with over 3,500 objects for $10,000 (Wade 1985: 171). Although Kearn dealt with antiquities, his main influence was on ethnographic collections, while the Wetherill brothers were the master pothunters of the region, excavating Pueblo sites and helping other archaeologists such as Gustaf Nordenskiold and George Pepper (Wade 1985: 175).

Similar practices occurred in Britain, although without institutional backing; the nineteenth century was the great period of barrow diggers—antiquarians who dug into ancient burial mounds, such as the Reverend William Greenwell or the Mortimer brothers (Marsden 1974) (Figure 9.3). Greenwell was a canon at Durham Cathedral who excavated more than 400 barrows all over Britain—often coming into conflict and argument with John Mortimer; Mortimer was a corn merchant from Driffield who, with his brother Robert, excavated about 360 barrows in eastern Yorkshire (Kinnes and Longworth 1985; Giles 2006). Other antiquarians did not solely rely on their own fieldwork to acquire their material, but frequently hired others; James Ruddock, a taxidermist from Pickering, was paid to excavate barrows on behalf of Thomas Bateman, among others. It was also common practice to pay villagers and farmers for bringing in stray finds—the Mortimer brothers, for example, amassed huge numbers of flint tools from east Yorkshire this way, indeed locals referred to flints as 'mortimers' (Sheppard 1911: 186–187).

What is clear from this is that, at least until the late nineteenth century, antiquarians, ethnologists, and museums had no qualms about dealing with and purchasing material from other amateur collectors, so long as they could be trusted. For the emerging profession of anthropology, conducting one's own fieldwork was not essential, so long as a few reliable individuals—whether freelance or museum employees—could safeguard the integrity of collected objects and information. The collection, examined through systems of classification in academic study or the museum gallery, remained the key focus for anthropological practice before a refocusing upon the field and fieldwork in the early twentieth century. Until this change, the dominant concern with universalizing classification and evolutionary typologies meant that fieldwork was viewed primarily as a means of enhancing the collection rather than a concern for understanding the specific cultural context of objects. It is only with a concern for the specific local context—whether this involves participant observation or greater attention to stratigraphy—that presence in the field or on site became important too (Boone 1993: 330; Gupta and Ferguson 1997c: 8).

Fig. 9.3 Barrow digging (from *Gentleman's Magazine* 1852).

THE INVENTION OF FIELDWORK

The modern concept of ethnographic fieldwork is perhaps most firmly associated with the London-based anthropologist Bronislaw Malinowski (Figure 9.4), but this needs some qualification (Jorion 1977; Stocking 1983b; Urry 1984). With the professionalization of British anthropology in the late nineteenth century, the need for greater control over data recovery was initially met by the adoption of the questionnaire. Questionnaires were used by Danish antiquarians at the start of the nineteenth century to assess the extent of antiquities in Denmark and its colonies (Kristiansen 1985: 12), but they became widely used in anthropological sciences in the later nineteenth century. For ethnographic data, questionnaires were sent all over the British Empire and returned a wealth of data on local customs. In Britain, the paradigm of such an approach was the *Notes and Queries on Anthropology* established by the Royal Anthropological Institute, which was issued in various editions between 1874 and 1951 (Urry 1972). One benchmark of the shift away from questionnaires to first-hand fieldwork was the Torres Strait Expedition, which was carried out by a group of Cambridge University-based researchers led by ethnologist A. C. Haddon in 1898. Haddon, along with W. H. R. Rivers (1914), established the critical importance of trained observation in collecting information and the corresponding emphasis on intensive research of a single community (Urry

Fig. 9.4 Bronislaw Malinowski in the Trobriand Islands (1915–1918).

(Source: Archives/Papers of Bronislaw Malinowski, ref. no. LSE_3_18_5; reproduced by kind permission of The Library of the London School of Economics and Political Science)

1984: 44–48; Stocking 1983b). In the subsequent years, Malinowski's approach developed within this context through direct contact with members of this new 'Cambridge School', and was again focused on the anthropology of Melanesia. But what distinguished Malinowski was his ability to communicate what was gained through this method, especially in his seminal work *Argonauts of the Western Pacific* (Malinowski 1922).

During this transitional period from the end of the nineteenth to the early twentieth century, collecting came to be downplayed in British ethnography. From occupying a central role, it became almost peripheral or invisible, ushering in an era of disillusionment around material culture within anthropology that was not revived until decades later, hesitantly at first in the 1960s but only fully in the 1990s (Buchli 2002a). Nonetheless collecting still went on—Malinowski, for example, collected objects, but showed little academic interest in them (Young 2000). Such collecting, however, was increasingly done simply to furnish museum exhibits rather than from an academic interest in objects. Daryll Forde, whose work focused on the anthropology of Africa, was one of the few to keep alive the material dimension of ethnography through his focus on environment and economy (e.g. Forde 1934), but a general abandonment of the study of objects by ethnography took place in the early twentieth century.

In part, this shift related to the complex ethical relations forged by objects themselves between collector (in the field) and donor. Nicholas Thomas' discussion of the tensions between commercial and scientific interests of collectors in the field was mentioned above. Chris Gosden and Chantal Knowles, in a study of the history of ethnographic collecting in Papua New Guinea, highlight further complex meanings and emotions involved around acquiring ethnographic objects (Gosden and Knowles 2001). It is possible that the difficulty in separating the academic value from other meanings by collectors in the field fostered a discomfort with the place of material culture studies within scientific ethnography. Objects may have brought the ethnographers *too* close to their subject. However, the shift can be seen as much in a move towards a new interest in the nature of society, as in a move away from objects. In this context, Radcliffe-Brown, influenced by Durkheimian sociology but also trained by the Cambridge School, played a much greater role in forging the new discipline. Both Malinowski's *Argonauts* and Radcliffe-Brown's *Andaman Islanders*, which were published in the same year (1922), mark the beginning of a new anthropological genre, reflecting this shift: the field monograph.

To further understand the sidelining of collecting in ethnography, it is useful to consider the history of anthropology in North America and, in particular, the role of Franz Boas. Boas began his career as a museum curator in Berlin in the 1880s, and it was while arranging an exhibition of ethnographic objects from the Northwest Coast in British Columbia, Canada, that he found the regional focus of much of his later research (Jacknis 1985). His subsequent fieldwork trips there, especially after his emigration to the States in 1887, resulted in bringing back various collections of material. These he displayed as part of tableaux of native life during a series of museum appointments in the 1890s—first at the Peabody Museum, then the Chicago Field Museum, and finally, the American Museum of Natural History in New York. It is in Boas' arrangements of the objects that one sees the germ of his turning away from museum-based and collection-based ethnography (Jacknis 1985: 77; McVicker 1992). As Ira Jacknis has shown, Boas' rejection of collection-based anthropology in favour of fieldwork stemmed from the tensions that grew between his view of displaying artefacts and the conventions employed by his seniors, particularly Otis T. Mason at the Smithsonian Institution in Washington, DC. Anthropological museum displays of the late nineteenth century were most commonly organized according to typological and evolutionary ideas, whereby artefacts of similar functions but from widely different cultures and periods were juxtaposed. In contrast, Boas wanted the idea of anthropological culture to provide the basis of arranging artefacts, rather than universal schemes of technology. The debate between a typological and a tribal arrangement of artefacts was partially reconciled as Mason started to shift to Boas' views, but it was always limited—simply because insufficient information on provenance and the cultural meanings of objects was available. This of course reflected back on the collecting practices, which subsequently started to become more controlled, especially when they formed part of those expeditions sponsored by the Bureau of American Ethnology (Jacknis 1985: 81). Mason, however, did not substitute the tribal for the typological but merely added it as a complementary method.

Boas continued in museum anthropology until 1905 when he resigned from the American Museum of Natural History after a major disagreement with the administration. At the same time, there was a discernible shift in his thinking. He felt he had reached the 'limitations of the museum method of anthropology', turning instead to a more contextual and psychological approach to other cultures (Jacknis 1985: 108). This is not to say Boas completely left material culture studies behind, for he continued to support its study within archaeology through his students, not least contributing to the development of stratigraphic excavation techniques (Browman and Givens 1996). Nonetheless, within ethnography this shift away from material culture had widespread repercussions for American anthropology, which were evidenced in the work of Boas' students from the 1920s (e.g. Alfred Kroeber, Robert Lowie, Edward Sapir, Fay Cooper-Cole, Leslie Spier, Melville Herskovits) at the same time as the British Social Anthropology of Malinowski and Radcliffe-Brown had become established as the new ethnography. What is clear is that learning from things, both in the United States and Britain, had become a dead end for anthropology by this time, while at the same time, fieldwork became fundamental. Discarding the concept of material culture as a medium for understanding other cultures meant also discarding distance between the anthropologist and the people studied. During the early twentieth century, then, the focus of socio-cultural anthropology in Europe and North America switched from collections to people, their ideas, their beliefs as expressed not through material culture but through their actions. Presence in the field—the ideal of 'participant observation'—came to be an essential element of anyone claiming the title of socio-cultural anthropologist. It was only now that fieldwork became the cornerstone that it remains today within ethnography.

In archaeology, collecting remained and is still a central part of the archaeological method. Nevertheless, just as in ethnography, concerns over trained observation, intensive investigation, and presence in the field developed, and led to the emergence of the professional and a divergence from the amateur. As in anthropology, the professionalization of archaeology was closely linked to institutionalization, and a key part of this transition was related to the changing demands of 'fieldwork' (Hinsley 1976; Levine 1986). Curtis Hinsley's account of the growing distance between the collector Charles Abbott and the museum curator Frederick Ward Putnam during the development of archaeology at the Peabody Museum, Harvard University, encapsulates this transition very well (Hinsley 1985). After nearly a decade of digging in gravel quarries, Abbott expressed his disillusionment over his continued collecting of flints, which seemed to him to say nothing new anymore. In 1878 he wrote to Putnam, asking whether 'in the course of your thoughts from day to day, in archaeological matters, any new question arises, which you think it possible, I may be able to throw some light upon, *by some new style of fieldwork* or otherwise, please let me know' (quoted in Hinsley 1985: 64, emphasis added). The potential for such new methods increasingly preoccupied Putnam, and led to perhaps the first statement on archaeological fieldwork in North America several years later where he argues for greater attention to the depositional structure and stratigraphy of a site (Putnam 1973 [1886]).

Modern archaeological fieldwork—in distinction to the mere field collection of archaeological artefacts—is characterized by one key concern: provenance, and especially the ideas of stratigraphy and stratigraphic context. In relation to collecting artefacts, this entails simply the proper recording of the location of an artefact in relation to the layers of soil. However, an important distinction must be made between stratigraphic *observation* and stratigraphic *excavation*; the former had been established in Europe since the late eighteenth century for Palaeolithic remains but only as a consistent method for archaeology since the mid-nineteenth century (Lucas 2001a). But it is one thing to notice which layer an artefact comes from or even draw sections of the layers, and quite another to excavate the layers themselves with attention to their stratigraphy. The transitional figures in this shift were people like J. J. Worsaae and General Pitt Rivers in Europe or Putnam in North America. Thus it was not until the 1890s that the first steps toward stratigraphic excavations occurred in North America, fully crystallizing in the prehistoric archaeology of the American South-west with Alfred V. Kidder's fieldwork at Pecos Pueblo, near Santa Fe, New Mexico between 1915 and 1927 (Kidder 2000;

Fig. 9.5 Controlled excavation at Maiden Castle by Mortimer Wheeler (1934–1937).
(Source: Wheeler 1943, plate XCVI A; reproduced by kind permission of the Society of Antiquaries)

cf. Browman and Givens 1996; Lyman and O'Brien 1999). A similar development occurred in Britain, where stratigraphy became the key concept driving Mortimer Wheeler's new archaeological field methodologies as laid out in his address to the Royal Society in 1927 (Wheeler 1927) (Figure 9.5).

While early antiquarians and ethnologists helped to constitute the field as an essential, even respectable, location for the practice of ethnography and archaeology (complementing the indoor study of collections), it took a long time for such work carried out in the field to become constituted as 'fieldwork'. However, as we have seen, in both ethnography and archaeology basic principles of a field method were established by the second quarter of the twentieth century. Since that time, although there have been many important developments (see review by Lucas 2001a), the most radical shift has been the emergence of archaeological and anthropological fieldwork as a professional practice, with explicit methods and trained staff. In archaeology, this happened by developing the concept of stratigraphic observation into one of stratigraphic excavation; in ethnography, it happened by replacing questionnaires and indexed collecting with participant observation. In the process, alternative approaches to objects in ethnography and archaeology led to the divergence of the two fields: one retaining its focus on material culture, the other dropping it.

FIELDWORK TODAY

This parting of the ways for anthropology and archaeology has continued into the twenty-first century. Even though in North America, for example, archaeology is still for the most part regarded as part of the four-field division of a wider subject called anthropology (which also includes socio-cultural anthropology, as well as linguistic and physical/biological anthropology), the methods and fieldwork of archaeology remain distinct from those of ethnography. In the past two decades, however, some socio-cultural anthropologists have sought to refocus ethnographic fieldwork upon material culture (Miller and Tilley 1996; Buchli 2002a). Rather than involving collecting, such anthropological material culture studies have generally retained the conventional field methods of ethnography, especially participant observation and the use of questionnaires, sometimes combined with newer concepts borrowed from sociology such as focus group analysis (see discussion by Miller et al. 1998: 53–68).

Nonetheless, there have been recent challenges within socio-cultural anthropology to the concept of fieldwork, which attempt to reconfigure it both spatially and intellectually. Conventional geographical distinctions between 'the field' and 'home', and between participant observation and other modes of research, have been critiqued (Clifford 1990; Gupta and Ferguson 1997a; Amit 1999). Anthropologists no longer need to go to 'exotic' places to conduct research but can choose a locale on their doorstep, for instance in the anthropological study by a team based at University College London of 'shopping, place and identity' at the Brent Cross Shopping Centre (Miller et al. 1998). Today, anthropologists may not even need to meet their subjects face-to-face as other methods such as documentary or archival research are becoming more accepted (e.g. see Amit 1999). These are clearly challenges to the dominant paradigm as established by the Cambridge School and Malinowski, but they are also part of wider developments that involve a blurring of disciplinary boundaries, and a self-awareness of the challenges of defining ethnography in a post-colonial context.

In archaeology, there has been a similar reflexive turn towards rethinking fieldwork in the past decade. However, unlike in anthropology, it has not deconstructed the notion of the 'field' so much as the nature of work done there (Hodder 1999; Lucas 2001a; Edgeworth 2003). Partly this is due to the fact that, although fieldwork remains a strong symbol of what constitutes a 'proper' archaeologist, because archaeology remains wedded to field collection and the study of such collected material—whether fragments of pottery or biological remains such as burnt seeds—still has a central and respectable role in archaeological practice. A researcher can be a fieldworker and a zooarchaeologist, but equally they can be just *one* of these. By and large then, the application of ideas of reflexivity to archaeological fieldwork has involved the application of sociological ideas of the construction of knowledge to field practices, highlighting issues such as the process of on-site interpretation (Hodder 1999; Bender *et al.* 2007) or the challenges of community archaeology (Colwell-Chanthaphonh and Ferguson 2007). Perhaps the most significant development in this context has been the rise of phenomenological approaches to fieldwork, which explore the sensory qualities of the archaeological record in more diverse ways than previously. Features such as visibility and perspective, sound and texture have been explored as a means to understand the role of experiential qualities in structuring the archaeological record (e.g. Tilley 1994, 2004; MacGregor 1999; Watson and Keating 1999; Cummings *et al.* 2002; Cummings and Whittle 2003; Hamilton and Whitehouse 2006). Such studies were initiated within and largely continue to be applied (but not exclusively) to landscape archaeology, especially in Britain, where they were pioneered by Chris Tilley through his seminal work *A Phenomenology of Landscape* (Tilley 1994). They have, however, also been subject to certain criticisms, such as conflating the experience of the archaeologist with that of past people (Brück 2005) or simply being unscientific and overly subjective (Fleming 2005).

Reflexivity has also given rise to the adoption of ethnographic approaches to studying archaeological fieldwork. In the preface to his recent edited volume *Ethnographies of Archaeological Practice*, Matt Edgeworth cites the critical dimension of 'being there' as the criterion for labelling such studies ethnographies (Edgeworth 2006b: xii). Just as socio-cultural anthropologists are deconstructing the traditional notions of fieldwork and field location, it is ironic that archaeologists should adopt such ethnographic approaches to study their own practices. Nonetheless, such studies can reveal important aspects of fieldwork that have tended to be suppressed or unrecognized: the mutually constituting role of people and things (Lucas 2001b; Edgeworth 2003; Yarrow 2003). Archaeologists do not just discover or uncover sites, they also produce them through the physical work of sculpting soil, stones, and other materials, drawing on their sensory properties. Such work also produces the archaeologist and in part, defines their skill and abilities through the exercise of an archaeological sensibility. Archaeology is a materially productive discipline, articulated through the technology, ideology, and organization of fieldwork, while simultaneously, archaeologists and archaeology as a discipline are constituted through this engagement with objects and sites.

Today, the revived interest in materiality in the social sciences presents new challenges for conceptualizing fieldwork in archaeology and anthropology. Chris Gosden has suggested that the changes to the notion of fieldwork in anthropology discussed above may also serve to blur the boundaries with archaeology (Gosden 1999: 61), while some archaeologists have long suggested that archaeology could be redefined as the study of material culture, irrespective of time and space, thus linking it up seamlessly with ethnographic approaches to material culture (Rathje 1981: 52). From one perspective, these comments are certainly important and a lot is to be gained by highlighting similarities; but from another perspective— particularly in terms of fieldwork—such comparisons ignore critical differences. Archaeologists do not engage with material culture in the same way as ethnographers, historians, or sociologists. The archaeological intervention is a material intervention. Despite the important role of non-interventionist fieldwork in archaeology such as landscape survey, or even some archaeologies of the contemporary world that are more ethnographic in their mode of practice (Buchli and Lucas 2001b; McAtackney *et al.* 2007), most archaeology continues to involve collecting objects, pulled from their context in the process of conducting fieldwork (especially but not exclusively through excavation), while an ethnographic approach that focuses on material culture leaves objects in the same state as they were encountered. Ethnographies of archaeological practice demonstrate this difference clearly.

First, archaeological fieldwork, because it is interventionist, is also transformative—or as is usually said, destructive (Lucas 2001b). Secondly, because it continues to collect things—now widened to include not just whole pots but every tiny fragment, and not just artefacts, but seeds, charcoal, animal bone, shells, and so on—it has tended to focus a lot more intensively on the material properties of things, which includes drawing on a panoply of scientific techniques such as compositional or elemental analysis. But what is common to both these elements is the fact that more broadly, archaeology reconstitutes a past material world in the present—albeit in localized and usually small-scale ways. It brings new things— sites and objects—into the world, and it is the power of this *material production* that distinguishes much of archaeology from ethnographic studies of material culture. This is not to deny other correspondences; indeed, all material culture studies, whatever their field methods, perform an act of making materiality 'matter'; i.e. bringing it out of the shadows (Buchli and Lucas 2001b). But while ethnographic fieldwork attempts to understand material things in the presence of other human subjects, for whom these things matter, archaeology (conventionally) has the harder task of doing this in the absence of such subjects.

Of course archaeology, like every discipline, works within a discursive field that is both ethically and emotionally charged; the politics of archaeological fieldwork and collecting reveal that there are multiple and often conflicting interests surrounding archaeological objects (Robson *et al.* 2006). However, it is important to distinguish the processes whereby objects enter the scientific field in the first place, i.e. through being *found* (excavation) or being *given* (exchange). It is as if found objects can be ascribed a null or neutral value *prior to* contemporary claims in a way that is impossible with exchanged objects. This is achieved quite simply through a temporal disengagement: these objects existed before the present, within a different discursive field with no connection to the contemporary one. This recalls Thompson's rubbish theory, which argues that to enable the transition from one value system to another, objects have to pass through a null stage, where they are valueless—i.e. rubbish (Thompson 1979).

The temporal distance which has always been the singular challenge of archaeology ('making the mute stones speak'), has also perhaps been the reason why archaeologists have been able to continue to interact with objects in a way more intimately than any other discipline. The fact that the value and meaning systems of the past society and present archaeologist are so distinct—the fact that crossing this divide is precisely the *problem* for archaeologists—has the advantage of neutralizing any conflict between such systems (but not of course, between the archaeologist and other contemporaries). For ethnography conversely, the fact that the two meaning systems necessarily interact because they occupy the same temporality may enable greater understanding, but it also allows conflict and, in doing so, threatens the detachment and impartiality that ethnographers seek to maintain with their subject. It is this difference that perhaps explains why contemporary material culture studies adopt an ethnographic rather than archaeological methodology. For collecting given objects entails very different ethical consequences from collecting found objects in the context of an academic discipline (or indeed, in any context), which is why collecting remains central to archaeological fieldwork but has largely been abandoned or marginalized in ethnography. Despite the shared reflexive turn in both disciplines towards the nature of their practices, and despite the historical common ground, they remain fundamentally divided in their deontological relation to objects. To what extent this difference has wider epistemological repercussions about the nature of the two disciplines and their interpretation of material culture is an obvious, subsequent question—but one that cannot be pursued here.

CHAPTER 10

GIFTS AND EXCHANGE

HIROKAZU MIYAZAKI

Since the publication of Marcel Mauss' essay, *The Gift: the form and reason for exchange in archaic societies*, in 1923–1924 (Mauss 1990), the relationship between persons and things has been a central subject for the anthropological study of material culture. For Mauss, a gift contains within itself a part of its giver: 'to make a gift of something to someone is to make a present of some part of oneself' (Mauss 1990: 12). Mauss' argument about the intermingled character of persons and things in gifts constitutes his solution to what he viewed as the general problem of reciprocity: that is, the question of how a gift generates an obligation to reciprocate: 'What rule of legality and self-interest, in societies of a backward or archaic type, compels the gift that has been received to be obligatorily reciprocated? What power resides in the object given that causes its recipient to pay it back?' (Mauss 1990: 3).

This chapter traces the trajectories of debates in socio-cultural anthropology that have stemmed from Mauss' solution to the problem of reciprocity, with a view to stepping outside of these trajectories. In the first half of the chapter I seek to demonstrate that the succession of debates following Mauss' essay consists of repeated attempts to rework the relationship between Mauss' original problem and solution. I then turn to Marilyn Strathern's critique of the Maussian formulation of gifts and exchange, set out in her study *The Gender of the Gift: problems with women and problems with society in Melanesia* (1988), and subsequent work, in order to explore the possibility of moving away from what I term the problem–solution framework of Mauss' original essay and ensuing debates in the anthropological study of gifts and exchange. I suggest that the shift will afford an opportunity to reappreciate the relationship between persons and things as neither a problem nor a solution.

Maussian problems and solutions

Mauss' essay, *The Gift*, has generated a long chain of debates. These debates have continually rediscovered the significance of Mauss' insight about the relationship between persons and things. Perhaps the most influential discussion of Mauss' work was Claude Lévi-Strauss' introduction, published in 1950, to a collection of Mauss' essays that included *The Gift* (Lévi-Strauss 2001). Here, Lévi-Strauss suggested that Mauss mistook a Maori theory of *hau*, or the 'spirit of the thing given' (Mauss 1990: 10) for a general theory of exchange. In *The Gift*, Mauss had quoted a statement made by the New Zealander ethnologist Elsdon Best's informant Tamati Ranapiri on the meaning of *hau*:

I will now speak of the *hau* . . . That *hau* is not the *hau* (wind) that blows—not at all. I will carefully explain to you. Suppose that you possess a certain article, and you give that article to me, without price. We make no bargain over it. Now, I give that article to a third person, who, after some time has elapsed, decides to make some return for it, and so he makes me a present of some article. Now, that article that he gives to me is the *hau* of the article I first received from you and then gave to him. The goods that I received for that item I must hand over to you. It would not be right for me to keep such goods for myself, whether they be desirable items or otherwise. I must hand them over to you, because they are a *hau* of the article you gave me. Were I to keep such equivalent for myself, then some serious evil would befall me, even death. Such is the *hau*, the *hau* of personal property, or the forest *hau*. Enough on these points.

Best (1909: 439)

Mauss had interpreted this statement as follows: 'What imposes obligation in the present received and exchanged, is the fact that the thing received is not inactive. Even when it has been abandoned by the giver, it still possesses something of him' (Mauss 1990: 11–12).

In Lévi-Strauss' view, this was nothing but an example of 'mystification, an effect quite often produced in the minds of ethnographers by indigenous people' (Lévi-Strauss 2001: 47). As a result, Lévi-Strauss argued, Mauss was only able to see exchange in terms of the 'three obligations': that is, the obligations 'to give, to receive, [and] to reciprocate' (Mauss 1990: 39). In Lévi-Strauss' view, exchange was the 'primary, fundamental phenomenon . . . which gets split up into discrete operations in social life' (Lévi-Strauss 2001: 47). Instead of approaching exchange as a totality, in other words, Mauss sought to 'reconstruct a whole out of parts; and as that is manifestly not possible, he has to add to the mixture an additional quantity which gives him the illusion of squaring his account. This quantity is *hau*' (Lévi-Strauss 2001: 47). Despite the commonalities between the goals of Mauss' essay and Lévi-Strauss' own project of structural anthropology, which sought to tackle the general sociological problem of how 'to understand social life as a system of relations' (Lévi-Strauss 2001: 50), for Lévi-Strauss, Mauss failed to think in systemic terms to the extent that he found a solution in an indigenous theory, that is, *hau*.

Lévi-Strauss' critique of Mauss subsequently became the starting point of Pierre Bourdieu's effort to construct a theory of practice in which the disjuncture between subjective and objective understandings of exchange was a focus of analysis. In Bourdieu's view, actors' misrecognition of exchange as a discrete act of giving, receiving, or reciprocating, such as in the Maori theory of *hau*, is critical to their strategic manipulations of the timings of giving (Bourdieu 1977: 4–6). In his view, social actors do not approach giving, receiving, and reciprocating as a single chain of related activities that unfolds over time. Such a systemic understanding of exchange only results from an outside observer's objective perspective. The time lag between giving and reciprocating makes it possible for social actors to misrecognize these acts as separate and 'irreversible'. But the temporal lag that enables such 'misrecognition (*meconnaissance*)' also affords social actors space for strategic manipulation, that is, agentive calculation (Bourdieu 1977: 5).

Despite Lévi-Strauss' attempt to background the problem of *hau*, therefore, the quest of what to make of this particular indigenous concept lives on in anthropological debates. In his 1972 essay, 'The Spirit of the Gift', for example, socio-cultural anthropologist Marshall Sahlins pointed out that Lévi-Strauss and other earlier critics of Mauss' rendition of *hau*, such as Raymond Firth (1959) and J. Prytz Johansen (1954), missed the 'true meaning' of *hau* (Sahlins 1972: 153–157). In a way that is characteristic of his attention to historiographical details (e.g. Sahlins 1995), Sahlins closely examined Tamati Ranapiri's above-mentioned statement, proposing to understand *hau* as equivalent to a notion of yield: 'The *hau* in question really means something on the order of "return on" or "product of," and the principle expressed in the text on *taonga* is that any such yield on a gift ought to be handed over to the original donor' (Sahlins 1972: 157).

Sahlins' broader goal here was to unpack the political implications of Mauss' formulation of exchange. Focusing on Mauss' contention that 'to refuse to give, to fail to invite, just as to refuse to accept, is tantamount to declaring war; it is to reject the bond of alliance and commonality' (Mauss 1990: 13), Sahlins contrasted Mauss' essay with Thomas Hobbes' *Leviathan* (1998) in order to 'bring out the almost concealed scheme of *The Gift*' (Sahlins 1972: 171), that is, the idea of the gift as a remedy against the human propensity to war: 'The compulsion to reciprocate built into the *hau* responds to the repulsion of groups built into the society. The force of attraction in things thus dominates the attractions of force among men' (Sahlins 1972: 174). For Sahlins, both Mauss and Hobbes were seeking a solution to the political problem of human nature. In Mauss' terms, according to Sahlins, 'The gift is Reason. It is the triumph of human rationality over the folly of war' (Sahlins 1972: 175). Sahlins thus sought to elevate Mauss' essay to the status of a piece of political philosophy on a par with Hobbes' text.

If Sahlins found a philosophical problem in Mauss' theory of gifts and exchange, Annette Weiner has drawn attention to the problem of social reproduction at the heart of Mauss' discussion of the inalienability of a gift from its giver. In Mauss' terms, a gift's inalienability derives from the fact that it contains within itself a part of its giver and hence demands reciprocation. This led many to make a distinction between gifts and commodities in terms of their respective alienability (see e.g. Gregory 1980, 1982). In contrast, Weiner's argument decoupled the question of alienability from the question of reciprocity. In particular, Weiner focused on the problem of identity and 'inalienable wealth'—those objects that are 'kept rather than given to others' and stay 'out of circulation' (Weiner 1985: 211). For Weiner, what was really at stake in exchange was the problem of 'keeping while giving' (Weiner 1985: 223): that is, the question of how individuals and groups maintain their identity while engaging in acts of giving: 'Keeping things instead of giving them away is essential if one is to retain some measure of one's social identity in the face of potential loss and the constant need to give away what is most valued' (Weiner 1985: 211). Her ethnography highlighted 'a range of solutions to the inherent problem of how one can keep while giving' (Weiner 1985: 211; see also Weiner 1992).

Weiner's (1980) attention to 'inalienable wealth' grew out of her earlier critique of the anthropological preoccupation with the problem of reciprocity, since Bronislaw Malinowski's study of *Crime and Custom in Savage Society* (1926). Weiner (1980: 71) urged anthropologists to 'move beyond traditional approaches that treat reciprocity and generosity as central analytical features or structures in exchange systems' and to move away from 'a Western construct of linear sequences basically concerned with discrete acts of giving and receiving'. Instead, Weiner (1980: 72) proposed a 'cyclical world view in which the processes of reproduction and regeneration are perceived as essential cultural concerns'. Weiner's argument rested on the critical place mortuary exchange occupies in Melanesia as a device for reassembling and re-enacting social relations:

A death must be understood as the moment when huge amounts of re-sorting occur: when all retrievable elements (including the deceased's body and bones) are reordered and redefined by the *dala* [matrilineal lineage and its property] owners. In this respect, death triggers the return of the deceased's body and property to the members of its own *dala*, followed by the concern to make the loss of the deceased (and the loss of social relations) into a positive resource for the regeneration of equivalent social relations.

Weiner (1980: 81)

In this view, '"norms of reciprocity" must be analyzed as part of a larger system—a reproductive system—in which the reproduction and regeneration of persons, objects, and relationships are integrated and encapsulated' (Weiner 1980: 71). Weiner's attention to the central significance of mortuary exchange as a mechanism for reproduction and regeneration in Melanesia leads her to focus on the operation of replacement (of things and persons) as a solution to the general problem of loss and decay (Weiner 1980: 83; see also Foster 1990).

Weiner's revision and renewal of Mauss' thesis of the inalienability of gifts has had a significant impact on subsequent debates about gifts and exchange. Her work has opened up space not only for a series of investigations expanding the scope of analysis beyond instances of reciprocal transaction toward a system of social reproduction (e.g. Turner 1989; Fajans 1993; Godelier 1999) but also for a series of studies drawing attention to the centrality of the problem of materiality in exchange. As Fred Myers has noted, 'subtly but significantly, Weiner's formulation shifted attention from the mechanics of exchange to the movement of objects into or out of different circuits of exchange and control' (Myers 2001: 13). In particular, Myers (2002) has extended Weiner's insights to his study of Australian Aboriginal acrylic paintings and their circulation.

Like Weiner, Jonathan Parry has sought to move away from the dominant emphasis on the problem of reciprocity in the anthropological reading of Mauss' essay. In his essay 'The Gift, the Indian Gift and the "Indian Gift"'(1986), Parry re-examined Mauss' discussion of instances of free and pure religious giving in India. Mauss presented the relationship between persons and things as a 'general principle' (Parry 1986: 457). Mauss' Melanesian and Polynesian examples focused on reciprocal giving, while his Indian examples dealt with un-reciprocal giving. What unites both, in Parry's view, is the problem of 'the absence of any absolute disjunction between persons and things' (Parry 1986: 457). It is precisely because persons and things are not easily separable that conscious effort needs to be made to keep Indian religious giving non-reciprocal (see also Laidlaw 2000):

The gift threatens to cement the two together in a dangerous interdependence; but every attempt is made to sever their bond by insisting on the complete alienation of the thing...While Mauss originally introduced this notion of 'spirit' to explain the inalienability of the object and the necessity of making a return, what it in fact explains in this context is why the gift *must* be alienated, should *never* return, and should endlessly be handed on.

Parry (1986: 461)

Parry effectively reversed the relationship between Mauss' problem and solution. The inseparability of persons and things now became the problem, not the solution, and reciprocal and non-reciprocal gifts became two different solutions to that problem. Parry proceeded to advance a speculative argument concerning the stark contrast between reciprocal and non-reciprocal exchange underlying the dominant reading of Mauss' essay. In Parry's view, Mauss' emphasis on the simultaneously interested and disinterested nature of gifts, and his proposal of a 'new morality' committed to 'a good but moderate blend of reality and the ideal' (Mauss 1990: 69) and a combination of one's 'own interests, and those of society and its subgroups' (Mauss 1990: 70), only made sense as an alternative to the dominant ideological separation of the two: 'Mauss' real purpose here is not to suggest that there is no such thing as a pure gift in *any* society, but rather to show that for many the issue simply cannot arise since they do not make the kinds of distinction that we make' (Parry 1986: 458). Parry's ambitious speculation about the correlation between the ideology of a free and pure gift and the ideologies of the market and of salvation religion makes a radical departure from the tendency to romanticize the idea of the gift that often underlies anthropological studies of gifts, including Sahlins' reinterpretation of the political dimensions of Mauss' essay (cf. Parry and Bloch 1989).

Parry's observations about the work entailed in keeping gifts pure and free in his Indian examples resonates with more recent ethnographic attention to the way actors perceive the precariousness of the boundaries between gift exchange and commodity exchange. For example, Webb Keane's study of Eastern Indonesian exchange focuses on actors' efforts to control the risks of ritual failure through the intricate performance involving the strategic manipulation of ritual objects and words (Keane 1994, 1997): 'In Anakalang, successfully conjoined words and things help portray their transactors as bearing an agency that transcends the physical individuals and temporal moment of the event' (Keane 1994: 606).

One compelling case Keane discusses concerns an episode of marriage negotiation in which an inexperienced spokesman for the bride's side slipped into an informal manner of speaking. The groom's side took advantage of the situation and negotiated for materially favourable terms but, as a result, ill feeling developed between the two sides: 'For Anakalangese, the act of giving without the appropriate verbal exchange resembles a low-status market transaction, an isolated encounter lacking spiritual or social consequences, and underwriting no future memories and obligations' (Keane 1994: 607).

Underlying Keane's analysis is the precariousness of the distinction between gift exchange and commodity exchange (Keane 1994: 623). If not performed properly, an episode of gift giving simply becomes a version of commodity exchange. According to Keane, Anakalang actors deliberately invoke these risks of 'slippage': 'Slippage represents this possibility of denial and shame, and success is conceptualized not in the orderly workings of reciprocity but in the victorious power of one's *dewa*—one's spirit, good fortune and personal relations with the dead—to draw objects towards itself in a flood' (Keane 1994: 620–621). In his later work, Keane has examined the use of money in gift exchange and the problems money poses as a material object of gift exchange, noting that the status of money itself is not entirely stable: in this case it serves as a formal token whose referent is confined to ceremonial exchange, yet it retains the potential for reinterpretation as cash value. In either case it is 'symbolic', but its vulnerability to slippage is a function in part of its irreducible materiality. Even money shares with other objects the property of taking objectual form. Thus it can cross contexts and, being semiotically underdetermined, is subject to reinterpretation.

Keane (2001: 69)

Keane's concern is thus with the instability of material objects. This embrace of the ambiguities of material objects stands in contrast to the durability of material objects that at least implicitly underlies Weiner's earlier attention to inalienable wealth.

Keane's, and to some extent Parry's, ethnographic attention to the conscious efforts human actors make to separate gifts from commodities is particularly interesting in light of the broader emphasis on the blurred boundaries between gifts and commodities in the anthropology of gifts and exchange (Miller 2001c). In his important essay, 'Gifts to Men and Gifts to God', for example, Chris Gregory drew attention to the affinity between sacrificial gifts, that is, gifts to gods, rather than competitive reciprocal gifts, and commodities in terms of their shared alienability (Gregory 1980). Subsequent contributions to the debate inspired by Gregory's later book *Gifts and Commodities* (1982), which sought 'to affirm the coexistence of gifts and commodities in colonial Papua New Guinea' (Gregory 1997: 10), have, however, focused resolutely on the blurred boundaries between gifts and commodities. For example, both Arjun Appadurai's edited volume, *The Social Life of Things* (Appadurai 1986a), and Nicholas Thomas' *Entangled Objects* (1991), pointed to the multiplicity of meanings attributed to a single object in a sequence of transactions. Although these insights have often been contrasted with Mauss' original formulation of gifts (e.g. Lock 2002), as the literary theorist Mark Osteen has pointed out, Mauss' concern with the instability and ambiguity of the gift category anticipated these recent moves to blur the boundaries between gifts and commodities (Osteen 2002).

In contrast to these efforts to point to the blurred boundaries between gifts and commodities, Webb Keane (1994, 1997) paid close ethnographic attention to the labour entailed in demarcating the boundaries of gift exchange. Here the ambiguities inherent in gifts, and material objects more generally, constitute a problem for human actors. The focus of Keane's analysis is on actors' efforts to exert control over those ambiguities.

In my view, Keane's work implies a way out of the problem–solution framework that has hitherto conditioned the debates about the relationship between persons and things because actors can be understood to be deliberately making problems visible in order then to solve them, rather than endlessly seeking to solve universal human problems. I have developed this aspect of Keane's analysis further and have examined the way Fijian gift givers and gift receivers sequentially make appear and disappear their shared concern with the potential inadequacy (and resulting negative effects) of gifts and speeches exchanged (Miyazaki 2000). In the carefully crafted speech presenting gifts, the gift-giving side's spokesman makes explicit his concern with the quality of the gifts as well as that of his speech before asking for the gift-receiving side's forgiveness. The gift-receiving side's spokesman in turn accepts the gifts as plentiful and the speech as respectful. He then declares that the only valuable to be valued is love, that is, God's blessing. In this context, I suggest, the concern with the efficacy of the exchange of gifts and speeches among humans gives rise to a renewed hope for the efficacy of God's ultimate gift (Miyazaki 2004). In both East Indonesian and Fijian cases, therefore, the ritual exchange of valuables and speeches serves as a sequential production and display of problems and solutions. This deliberate display of problems and solutions in turn reminds ritual participants of the human agency and responsibility required for appreciating the enabling quality of supernatural entities' work.

This attention to the delicate work entailed in producing both gifts and exchange constitutes an important innovation in the field. It implicitly builds upon Nancy Munn's analysis of the 'spatiotemporal extension of the self' (Munn 1986: 11) associated with Gawan canoes and pearlshells as part of the *kula* exchange system, set out especially in her classic study, *The Fame of Gawa: a symbolic study of value transformation in a Massim (Papua New Guinea) society* (1986). Here, Munn's focus was on the production and circulation of fame alongside the production and circulation of canoes and shells. One particularly compelling part of Munn's analysis concerns the decoration of canoes and human bodies entailed in Kula exchange (Munn 1986: 138–147; see also Munn 1983): 'a canoe, as the medium *within* which Gawans travel, and in which they first arrive on non-Gawan soil, is itself a resurfacing of the person. Just as men going on kula should decorate themselves and present the best impression possible to seduce their hosts into releasing shells, so also the canoe that carries them should be beautified' (Munn 1986: 147).

Although the Gawan canoe is decorated after the 'image of the ceremonially decorated person, especially a youthful man' (Munn 1986: 138), the construction of a canoe demands a complex process of implicating both male and female elements and substances (Munn 1986: 139–140). In this sense, 'the canoe encodes its producers in itself. From interior to exterior, it is an artifact identified with the human body, which makes it. This production includes inputs of both male and female producers who, through their differential levels of potency create the extended level of Gawan spatiotemporal control embodied in the canoe' (Munn 1986: 147).

As David Graeber has argued, Munn's attention to people's 'investment of … time and energy, intelligence, [and] concern' (Graeber 2001: 45) in the use of material objects in the creation of social relations obviates any a priori dichotomy between gifts and commodities. In doing so, in Graeber's view, Munn's work took a step toward a general theory of value in which material things are implicated. This attention to work, perhaps reminiscent of Marx's labour theory of value, unfolds in a consequentially different direction in Marilyn Strathern's feminist critique of Mauss' work, to which I now turn.

GIFTS AS AESTHETIC CONSTRAINTS

As we have seen, the trajectories of debates deriving from Mauss' original essay have continually redefined and renewed what counts as a Maussian problem. Marilyn Strathern's 1988 study of Melanesian exchange, *The Gender of the Gift*, took a radical departure from the Maussian framework of problems and solutions in at least two different ways.

First, and most concretely, Strathern found Mauss' preoccupation with the relationship between persons and things too narrow. She proposed a much more inclusive scope of inquiry:

> one cannot, out of the workings of Melanesian social action, extract one set of relations as typical of 'gift relations' and another as typical of non-gift relations: the unmediated mode takes its force from the presence of the mediated mode, and vice versa. I therefore use the nomenclature of gift exchange to cover all relations, even though this produces the semantic paradox of there being gift exchange without a gift. The paradox in fact usefully points up the crucial absence (no gift) that characterizes the unmediated mode of symbolization.
>
> Strathern (1988: 179)

Secondly, in a more general sense Strathern moved away from the problem–solution framework of Mauss' original essay and subsequent debates: 'Scholars trained in the Western tradition cannot really expect to find others solving the metaphysical problems of Western thought. Equally absurd, if one thinks about it, to imagine that those not of this tradition will somehow focus their philosophical energies onto issues such as the "relationship" between it [society] and the individual' (Strathern 1988: 3).

Strathern's critique focused on the idea of society in anthropology and the general sociological problem of the relationship between society and individuals; however, the implications of her critique of the problem–solution framework underlying anthropological inquiries are much greater. In what follows, I want to suggest that it is in this context that Strathern's more general focus on aesthetics as 'constraints of form' (M. Strathern 1988: 180–181) needs to be understood.

At first glance, Strathern's critique of Mauss' original framework fits nicely with the general tendency among many other critiques of Mauss' essay to expand the scope of inquiry by adding in other aspects of social and economic life. Unlike Lévi-Strauss' or Annette Weiner's divergent proposals for a more systemic investigation of exchange, Strathern's investigation focused on the specific kind of relationality entailed in Hagen exchange, and its implications in turn for analytical relationality in anthropological knowledge. In other words, Strathern sought to bring to light a range of forms of analytical relationality (between individuals and society, parts and a whole, and so forth) at work, but taken for granted, in Mauss' essay and its subsequent critiques.

Strathern's rejoinder to Annette Weiner's critique of her earlier work, *Women in Between: female roles in a male world* (Strathern 1972), is a useful point of entry into this argument. In her own work, especially *Women of Value, Men of Renown* (1976), Weiner had paid particular attention to the way anthropologists had neglected women's wealth and women's power. Weiner famously indicted Malinowski (1922) for paying virtually no attention to Trobriand women's exchange valuables, such as banana leaf bundles: 'A critical difference between myself and my male predecessors is that I took seemingly insignificant bundles of banana leaves as seriously as any kind of male wealth. I saw Kiriwina women as active participants in the exchange system, and thus I accord them an equal place beside Kiriwina men' (Weiner 1976: 11). In this context, Weiner criticized Strathern's approach in *Women in Between*:

Marilyn Strathern began with a beautiful description of the importance of net bags in dowry exchanges. She then went on to say that 'women's things are divided among women; men are not particularly interested in the netbags' (1972: p. 15). Nevertheless, whether men *say* they are interested, there are many references throughout the book to the distribution of net bags across affinal, consanguineal, and intergenerational lines. But Strathern does not seem to take these transactions seriously and analyze them fully. She therefore falls into the traditional male trap.

Weiner (1976: 13)

In response, Strathern first called attention to a technique Malinowski repeatedly uses in his works, that is, that of the 'straw man' (Strathern 1981: 666) and to the way Weiner uses the same technique in her critique of Malinowski: 'In discarding the chauvinistic past Weiner actually reproduces as analytical technique Malinowski's presentation of his radical view of primitive man' (Strathern 1981: 672).

Strathern proceeded to challenge Weiner's equation of women's wealth with women's power. In Strathern's view, this assumption is unsustainable, at least when it comes to Hagen women's netbags, since in Hagen exchange, transactions, not objects are gendered (Strathern 1981: 679):

In Hagen it is the acts of 'production' and 'transaction' that are given gender, such that the production of wealth in the form of pigs is seen as dependent upon women and its public manipulation and display the prerogative of men ... Hagen women do not publicly transact with netbags, because Hagen women do not publicly transact.

Strathern (1981: 675)

In this sense, since 'women are "in between" the male partners, both fundamental and marginal' (Strathern 1981: 675), 'a proper consideration of Hagen women's roles in exchange would take us from objects over which women have primary control to domains of male activity' (Strathern 1981: 674). Strathern proposed a kind of anthropological knowledge based on the juxtaposition of different analytical aesthetics.

Anthropology cannot really parade as an innocent child of culture. It is true that there seems no way to control the fact that at one point we are satisfied with explanations of one order, and at another tack back to a promontory that will yield a different view. Nevertheless in so far as anthropology is a craft, in the other sense of the word, and in so far as anthropologists are aware of their manufacturing role, certain choices do present themselves. In looking at objects women have at their disposal, various courses are open. In looking at objects women have at their disposal, various courses are open. We may see the predicament of Highlands women as (metonymic) extensions of our own, their netbags self-evident symbols of a continuous femininity; or rather we may see that predicament in an analogous manner, and present the netbags as (metaphorically) standing for an aspect of their position comparable to our own; or we may frame off the experiences of Highlands women and instead juxtapose their artifacts and ours. There is no way to obviate bias . . . But surely we should be reasonably well equipped to perceive at least some of our own symbolic strategies.

                                                                            Strathern (1981: 684)

The language of 'choice' was critical here. Strathern showed how choosing to see from one perspective shifts into the background what can be seen from other perspectives (cf. Strathern 1991). What was at issue was the particular effect of entertaining this relativistic and relativizing stance. If Weiner's problem focused on male bias and her solution rested on careful attention to women's objects, therefore, Strathern here did not seek to 'obviate bias' but instead to obviate the problem–solution framework itself. Thus her goal was to 'learn something about the techniques which, without thinking, we use ourselves' (Strathern 1981: 666).

Strathern's distinctive contribution to the anthropology of gifts and exchange becomes clearer if her analysis of Hagen exchange is contrasted with Andrew Strathern's earlier approach to the same subject. The notion of 'men as transactors' and 'women as producers' appeared prominently in Andrew Strathern's important 1979 paper 'Gender, Ideology and Money in Mount Hagen'. In that paper, however, this ethnographic insight is subsumed under a general problem–solution analytical framework. Andrew Strathern examined the effects of the replacement of pearl shells with money upon gender relations in Hagen exchange. He first draws attention to the particular way Hagen men used to lay claim over pearl shells: 'At public *moka* occasions men laid down rows of shells with great care while women saw to similar rows of pigs tied to stakes' (Strathern 1979: 534). But he also noted this claim was contradicted by the symbolic significance of the colour of pearl shells. Red is symbolically linked to women and consanguineal relations established through the exchange of women:

The men's special admiration for a rich, ruddy colour in pearl shells can itself be seen as a statement that, while men appropriate and control shells, they depend on links made through the exchange of women to obtain them. The statement, if it is such, is made non-verbally, and partially contradicts men's verbal claims that shell 'production' is entirely a male achievement.

                                                                            Strathern (1979: 535)

He then turned to a new problem Hagen men face in the ceremonial presentation of money in place of pearl shells.

Men, after laying out the money in a careful, artistic way, and decorating it further with bright yellow flowers and red leaves (the same colours as the red ochre and the pearl shells), invite their women to come and admire it and 'shake their hands in wonder' (*okli rui*). Women do so, responding well to the rather formal invitation. The men clearly treat this money, ready for *moka*, as theirs, and invite the women to come and view it and praise the men for 'raising' it.... Much of the money has been produced by the women's labour. Yet they seem to have less say in what will happen to the money than they do in the case of pigs which they have reared and which their husbands give to *moka* partners.

Strathern (1979: 538)

Hagen men's problem was defined here in terms of their pursuit of power and prestige: 'Men's problem becomes, then, to obtain the money back from women so as to ensure that they do *not* gain power, and they call on ideological resources and established values in which women share to do this' (Strathern 1979: 539). Andrew Strathern then inserted his problem into a familiar analytical framework of exploitation and mystification, in which

the men were engaged in a remarkable feat of appropriation and mystification, symbolised by their quest for exotic pigs. For home pigs they would be directly dependent on wives... But in taking money and seeking out pigs reared by totally unrelated persons, indeed commercial firms, they assert that even the process of obtaining pigs can now be done independently of women!

Strathern (1979: 544)

Andrew Strathern was aware of the problem–solution framework, which he imposed on his ethnographic data; how his chosen vocabulary, 'the language of intention, strategy, and problem-solving, sharpens up what is in reality a rather more fuzzy perception which people have of their situation' (Strathern 1979: 539). Yet he insisted that Hagen men are also aware of the problem: 'men are in fact at least partially aware of their problem and deliberately act so as to solve it' (Strathern 1979: 539).

The Gender of the Gift presented a very different analysis of gender relations in Hagen exchange. Here the analysis was focused on the production of pigs, which are important exchange items in Hagen exchange.

The Hagen ethnography (e.g. M. Strathern 1972) apparently gives the unfortunate impression that domestic labor is women's labor. It was never the case, of course, that domestic production [of pigs] in Hagen was described as engaging female labor alone. Men and women are both producers; it is in the rhetorical context of evaluating transactions that men distinguish 'male' transaction from 'female' production, thereby feminizing their own productive efforts. *They eclipse their own productive activities as well as women's.*

Strathern (1988: 155; emphasis added)

Andrew Strathern's preoccupation with men's problem of concealing women's labour, contrasts with how Marilyn Strathern drew attention to the way men's solution to their problem eclipses their own contribution to the production of pigs.

The analytical image of eclipse as contrasted with the idea of exploitation was highly significant.

> I use the metaphor 'eclipse' to draw attention to a special feature of this concealment. It is not the case that transforming pigs into gifts re-'produces' them, re-authors them in terms of production. It is not their own (male) labor that is made the basis of their claims . . . the evaluation of Hagen pigs as male wealth entails the apparently paradoxical corollary that female labor as such is not concealed. The creative work of producing pigs is not denied; on the contrary, the work that women do in their gardens and in tending the herds is fully acknowledged.
>
> Strathern (1988: 155)

In distinguishing between two kinds of concealment—exploitation and eclipse— Marilyn Strathern brought to light what different anthropological analytical strategies make 'appear' and 'disappear'. Strathern's attention to familiar anthropological analytical strategies and categories is often regarded as an effort to expose the implicit assumptions of Euro-American anthropological knowledge. But for our present purposes what is more significant is the way she insisted on seeing 'anthropological' and 'Melanesian' analytical strategies or gifts and commodities side by side, as discrete entities. This was a response to a broader tendency in anthropological knowledge towards collapsing such opposed categories as gifts and commodities and 'Euro-American' and 'Melanesian' in the name of historical interdependence and mutual entanglement. While these categories are admittedly 'fictions' (Strathern 1988: 134) in the sense that they are constructed by anthropologists for analytical purposes, the operation of collapsing itself is enabled by these fictional oppositions. Strathern sought to hold the specificity of the character of analytical relations in Euro-American anthropological analysis itself in view and to 'stop ourselves thinking about the world in certain ways' (Strathern 1988: 11). For her, such stoppage requires the relativization of the kind of relationality that unfolds from fictional oppositions such as 'gifts' and 'commodities' (see also Strathern 1990). In other words, Strathern moves away from the propensity to collapse dichotomies. Instead, she seeks to 'make explicit' (and re-appreciate) that propensity itself. In place of collapsing, Strathern deploys a series of juxtapositions across levels of analytical abstraction to hold opposites in view. In other words, Strathern redeploys a series of constructed opposites to hold such unfolding itself.

Through Marilyn Strathern's move, what is made to appear is a different kind of analytical labour: that is, the labour required to sustain the viewing of different analytical strategies, such as exploitation and eclipse, and different analytical categories, such as gifts and commodities, as alternative analytical aesthetics or 'constraints of form' (Strathern 1988: 180–181). Such labour entails resistance to the demand of each analytical strategy or category to unfold itself over time. This resistance in turn has allowed Strathern to circumvent the series of problem– solution sets that have unfolded from Mauss' problem and solution.

EXTENSION VERSUS JUXTAPOSITION

In recalling her ethnographic fieldwork in Hagen, Papua New Guinea, Marilyn Strathern has argued that 'my attention has been transfixed at certain (ethnographic) moments I have never been able—wanted—to shake off' (Strathern 1999: 6), and

> I shall never forget my first sight of mounted pearl shells in Mt Hagen, in 1964, heavy in their resin boards, slung like pigs from a pole being carried between two men, who were hurrying with them because of the weight, a gift of some kind. It was only a glimpse; the men were half-running and their path was almost out of my field of vision. But it belongs to a set of images which have mesmerized me ever since.
>
> Strathern (1999: 8)

She reflects on the way the Hagen aesthetics of exchange have shaped her analytical sensibility.

> I have come to realize the extent to which certain Hagen practices have had enduring effect on my anthropology. These include the gestures and practices of ceremonial exchange by which men, as donors and recipients, alternate their perspectives on one another. What is revealed to the audience on the occasion are the signs of capacity—the properties of persons and things, the substance of body and mind—to which people lay claim; what is simultaneously revealed (to whomever might be paying attention) is the already known fact of the origin of these capacities in other people.
>
> Strathern (1999: 12)

What is significant in this admission of influence and borrowing is not so much the fact that Marilyn Strathern has borrowed the Hagen aesthetics of exchange as her analytical aesthetics, as her insistence on the comparability between the two. This represents a reversal in analytical relationality that dispenses with the familiar problem–solution framework. In other words, she presents the possibility of seeing something other than human actors either solving anthropological problems or solving their own. In order to explore the implications of this move, in this section I want to turn to contrasting efforts to extend theoretical insights of the anthropological studies of gifts and exchange to contemporary issues, such as organ transplants, intellectual property rights, and bureaucratic practices.

Mauss' insights regarding the inseparability between persons and things have been extended both positively and negatively to various forms of giving in the contemporary world (compare with Richard Titmuss' influential 1971 discussion of altruism with reference to blood donation). For example, Margaret Lock (2002) has analysed specific ethical issues at stake in the practices of organ transplantation in Japanese society, which is a well-documented gift economy where a pervasive logic of reciprocity and associated sociality of indebtedness makes altruistic gifts, such as anonymous donations of human organs, almost inconceivable (see also

Ohnuki-Tierney 1994) while making the motivations behind gifts quickly ambiguous (see Befu 1968: 453; Rupp 2003). Here Lock seems to equate Mauss' work with the tendency to romanticize the category of the gift and finds inspiration in efforts, such as those by Appadurai (1986b) and Nicholas Thomas (1991), to blur the boundaries between gifts and commodities. Lock's analysis focuses on the multiple and competing meanings of organs as they are passed on from one person to another. Likewise, Bob Simpson's analysis of various kinds of transaction in body parts and human tissues in Sri Lanka points to a complex field in which local religious conceptions of giving and global discourses of the 'gift of life' generate contradictory and competing meanings of giving (Simpson 2004). In all of these works, Maussian problems (and solutions) have been extended to contemporary forms of giving to the effect of producing a view of complexity.

In contrast, the body of works that apply Marilyn Strathern's critique of the Maussian field of problems and solutions to the study of contemporary issues seem to generate an entirely different effect. I want to focus on two examples of Strathernian analytical juxtaposition: (1) Marilyn Strathern's own discussion of Malanggan, New Ireland sculptures created and disposed of during the course of mortuary exchange, alongside intellectual property rights, and (2) Annelise Riles' juxtaposition of Fijian mats, Fijian women's exchange valuables, and bureaucratic documents some Fijian female bureaucrats and non-governmental organization workers have produced in the context of preparation for a United Nations conference on women. In both studies, the problem–solution framework gives way to a strategy of juxtaposition as well as a particular kind of analytical labour aimed at keeping what is juxtaposed from collapsing into one another.

In her essay, 'The Patent and the Malanggan' (2001), Marilyn Strathern juxtaposes the New Ireland sculptures, Malanggan, with Euro-American intellectual property rights. What prompted this move is Strathern's interest in ownership as a central issue in the relationship between persons and things entailed in Melanesian exchange and Euro-American knowledge practices. Her comparison reveals divergent conceptions of creativity and associated techniques for linking the past to the future.

Strathern draws attention to the ephemeral quality of Malanggan sculptures, which are typically prepared for the final phase of a cycle of mortuary rites and are destroyed or given away to foreigners upon the completion of the cycle of exchanges (Küchler 2002b): 'The moment when the Malanggan is discarded is also the moment at which it or its components may be dispersed to others, the moment people from other localities looking at the sculpture pay for the ability to reproduce the parts of the designs at some time in the future' (Strathern 2001: 6). Strathern considers how Malanggan crystallizes and concentrates dispersed social and property relations following a clansman's death for further future dispersion: 'like technology which combines knowledge, material form and effectiveness, the reproduction of the Malanggan body makes it possible to capture, condense and then release power back into the world' (Strathern 2001: 7).

In going back and forth between Malanggan and the Euro-American notion of the patent, Strathern points to commonalities and differences between the two in the way her analysis 'deliberately echo[es] the New Ireland analysis' (Strathern 2001: 9). For example, Strathern draws attention to the similarity between the two in terms of the role it plays in articulating the past with the future.

The fabrication of Malanggan results in a form which condenses a whole history of interactions, and in the process makes it possible to channel clan powers—the clan and its relationships with others—for future benefit; we might say that the patent results in a form—the potency of information made product—through which technological power is also channeled to the future.

Strathern (2001: 9)

Likewise, Strathern contrasts the ways the Malanggan and the patent imagine the relationship between the origins and the future of knowledge:

Now New Irelanders remake people out of people, so to speak, bodies out of bodies, and the competition is over claims to ancestral power, that is, making claims to what is already specifically identified as theirs. Patent-holders, on the other hand, deal with people in terms of property claims, and instead make their devices out of things, materials and knowledge ultimately part of a 'commons' belonging to everyone and no-one.

Strathern (2001: 16)

Strathern uses the terms of analysis deriving from her analysis of Malanggan to describe the features of the Euro-American intellectual property regime, not the other way around. That is, she is not undertaking a project of applying the Euro-American notion of intellectual property to an analysis of Malanggan with a view to showing the limitations of the parameters of the Euro-American regime of intellectual property rights. Rather, 'the comparison perhaps enables us to grasp some of the imaginative, and ideological, potential of Euro-American intellectual property concepts, one of the many forms which modern rationalities are given' (Strathern 2001: 15).

Strathern's explicit effort to reverse analytical relationality points to what drives these and other modern forms in an analogous fashion to the way Malanggan enables social relations to be renewed again in New Ireland. This is Strathern's long-standing strategy. As in the case of her work in feminist anthropology discussed above (Strathern 1988), the goal is not simply to critique 'Euro-American' anthropological knowledge in light of 'Melanesian' knowledge. Rather, it is to re-appreciate 'Euro-American' knowledge with 'Melanesian materials in mind' (Strathern 2005: 13).

Inspired by Strathern's analytical juxtapositions, the anthropologist and legal scholar Annelise Riles draws attention to an 'aesthetic device' seen both in the way Fijian women handle mats and the way Fijian NGO workers handle bureaucratic documents. Here Riles focuses on the way a sense of infinity is generated in each.

The focus of Riles' attention focuses on the Fijian *vivivi*, a bundle of mats, presented and unfolded in the context of Fijian gift giving.

According to Riles, a *vivivi* is simultaneously both concrete and abstract in that it consists of the concrete number of mats while it also serves as a unit for counting any number of mats in more abstract terms:

> One was never sure at the point of exchange how many mats a *vivivi* contained, as the number of mats in the *vivivi* was concealed in the layering of one mat on the next . . . In it [counting] Fijians came to terms with the potential infinity literally bundled into a *vivivi*— a device, in short that defied the specificity of number.
>
> Riles (1998: 383)

Riles pays particular attention to the way a pattern emerges in layered mats at an exchange event:

> At the moment at which counting stopped, . . . pattern emerged. The turn to pattern was a distinct turn to the visual, as one kind of mental apprehension (counting) gave way to another (seeing). Another way of describing this turn to pattern is that the boundaries of the artifact were no longer foregrounded. Instead, when the mats were laid on the floor of a ceremonial space, the viewer suddenly apprehended a pattern that extended from one mat to the next, from the mats to the plaiting of the walls . . . , or the arrangement of flowers, or the placing of bodies in a ceremonial context, infinitely inward and outward.
>
> Riles (1998: 383–385)

Significantly, 'the pattern of the *vivivi* always anticipated its own disintegration into concreteness' (Riles 1998: 385). Riles finds similar oscillations between concreteness and abstractness, or materiality and pattern, in the negotiation of bureaucratic documents: 'Just as the layered mats brought into view a continuity in pattern from one mat to the next, the organizational pattern of the document also was repeated in the way documents at each level of negotiation mirrored the others in form and function' (Riles 1998: 386). Completed documents are regarded as 'valuable collection items' and 'concrete objects' (Riles 1998: 389). But 'the documents emerged as such objects only after the fact, when the negotiation was complete. During the negotiations, . . . the negotiator's attention was turned only to language and pattern' (Riles 1998: 389). Once again, Riles compares these documents with Fijian mats: 'Like mats layered one upon the next in ceremonial contexts, therefore, documents were entities that at key periods of time faded into patterns replicable at seemingly infinite levels' (Riles 1998: 389).

Riles is not using Fijian women's valuables as a framework for understanding bureaucratic documents that Fijian female bureaucrats and NGO workers negotiated. Rather, in her analysis, both mats and documents entail a similar aesthetic device that she terms 'a figure seen twice' (Riles 1998: 394). More importantly, in a way that is somewhat more methodologically explicit and ethnographically mediated than the way in which Strathern borrows the Hagen aesthetics of switching perspectives, Riles deploys this aesthetic device as her own analytical strategy. As Riles makes mats and documents appear 'seen twice,' she replicates the very oscillation that makes both of these objects generate a sense of infinity and a simultaneous apprehension of different levels of generality (concreteness and abstractness, the local and the global, etc.) to the effect of producing a glimpse of a horizon of new opportunities for ethnographic research beyond the impasse in the anthropology of global forms (see also Riles 2000; Sykes 2005). Thus, Riles' work on exchange is not framed at all in terms of problems and solutions created by persons and things.

CONCLUSIONS

By tracing the trajectories of debates deriving from Mauss' classic essay *The Gift*, I have sought in this chapter to demonstrate how Mauss' original problem and solution have generated a series of efforts to redefine Maussian problems and solutions. I retraced here how these debates led to analytical attention to the labour entailed in producing gifts and exchange. I then sought to demonstrate how Marilyn Strathern's critique of Mauss' theory of gifts and exchange moved away from these trajectories of problems and solutions by performing a different kind of analytical labour. Strathern's insistence on keeping contrasting analytical strategies and categories in view has enabled a view of the relationships between these strategies and categories as a series of oscillations between opposed strategies and categories.

If the shift from the problem of reciprocity to the problem of materiality Weiner and others made replicated the problem–solution framework underlying Mauss' original essay, the Strathernian strategy of juxtaposition offers a view of the relationship between persons and things as neither a problem nor a solution. This in turn has brought to light various aesthetic devices and techniques deployed across different kinds of engagement with persons and things, including the anthropology of gifts and exchange itself.

If attention to the parallel uses of similar aesthetic devices and techniques releases the relationship between persons and things from the confines of the problem–solution framework, such attention to parallel aesthetic devices in turn also makes visible certain aspects of gift giving that have escaped rigorous analytical attention. In my own study of indigenous Fijian mortuary exchange, I have examined the exchange of valuables and speeches and the record keeping of gifts and their amounts as parallel but temporally disjointed processes that are not retroactively accessible once the exchange and the record keeping is complete

(Miyazaki 2006). Likewise, I have shown how the indigenous Fijian urge to extend the protocols of gift giving to touristic encounters parallels the anthropological urge to extend Maussian insights to various contemporary issues. What I have termed the 'hope' Fijians and anthropologists see in the category of the gift derives from the extensibility of the category (Miyazaki 2005).

CHAPTER 11

ART AS ACTION, ART AS EVIDENCE

HOWARD MORPHY

INTRODUCTION: A METHODOLOGICAL PERSPECTIVE ON THE ANTHROPOLOGY OF ART

My aim in this chapter is not to produce another review of the state of studies of art in anthropology and material culture. I have in the past produced two such reviews (Morphy 1994; Morphy and Perkins 2006a) and repetition is in the nature of reviews. There has recently been a tendency in art history as well as anthropology to question the category of 'art' and to replace it with a more general term such as 'visual culture' or 'image', yet the same subset of material culture objects remains as the subject of analysis. I began academic life as a student of material culture and then found myself focusing almost by accident on a subset of objects that fell into many people's ordinary language category of 'art object' (Morphy 1977). I have come to believe in the utility of the concept of art and that the practice and performance of art reflects particular ways of knowing and acting in the world. So this chapter is a strong defence of the idea of 'art' but it also recognizes its complexity and the fact that as a concept, 'art' is fuzzy around the edges. I use a concept of family resemblance and see

I would like to thank Sarah Scott, Roger Ling, and Jeremy Coote for their advice on relevant illustrations and Frances Morphy and Karen Westmacott for their intellectual input and editing skills. The argument has been greatly strengthened by the input of the editors with their perceptive comments and demands for clarification.

art objects as forming polythetic sets. The category contains within it an immense diversity and includes objects that have little in common with each other and require very different methods of analysis. However, at the heart of this concept of art lies a set of loosely connected features or themes around which the idea of art coalesces: art is a form of action, art production is integral to meaning creating processes and requires a sense of form, and art is associated with aesthetic experience. It does not surprise me that, at a very general level, these themes resonate with those of art history and the philosophy of art since European art is equally a part of the family or a member of the set. I define meaning in a very broad way so that it embraces both decorative effect and dense iconographies: meaning merges with meaningful.

I believe art is worth studying for a number of methodological and theoretical reasons. Regarding method, art is often produced in durable and, today, in record-able form. It is analysable from many different perspectives and can become part of the process of interaction between researcher and producer: works of art can be interrogated in their cultural contexts. Many artworks outlast the moment of their making and their maker and hence they are part of the durable record of human action. Unpicking those sequences of action through the analysis of form and connecting form to context are ways in which history can enter anthropology and anthropology can enter history. Works of art enable anthropologists to work with art historians to analyse formal relationships and contextual data that reflect trajectories of change and regional dynamics. Finally, in theoretical terms, if I am right that art production is a significant way in which human beings act in the world—one that reflects emotional and experiential dimensions of being in the world—then art provides us with access to something that is too important to neglect.

Interestingly, if anything in recent years, anthropology has had a greater impact on art history than the other way around. The work of David Freedberg (1989), Hans Belting (2001), and Mariët Westermann (2005) exemplifies the theoretical impact that anthropology has had on some art historians. The impact of art history on anthropology occurred earlier and can be seen to influence anthro-pologists of art from Boas (1927) to the present; but interestingly art history and its findings have had little impact on the discipline of anthropology as a whole. Archaeology's relationship with art history has been both continuous from the early days of the disciplines and contentious (e.g. White 1992; Scott 2006). The contention I believe is located in precisely the same dialectic between a fine art concept of art and a cross-cultural or generic concept of art that has had its impact on art history and anthropology. In anthropology and archaeology, it has resulted historically in a neglect of art as a research resource, and in art history, it underlies the discomfort with the category of art for the analysis of images. This chapter is structured as an argument in which I move from the reasons why non-Western art has been neglected in art history and in anthropology through definitional issues concerning what kind of thing art is, to a methodological perspective that flows out of that definitional prolegomena. Art has to be seen in its full complexity.

ART AND MATERIAL CULTURE

In the 1970s, Peter Ucko led a revival in the study of material culture in Britain. In giving the Curl lecture on the topic of penis sheaths (Ucko 1969) he expressed his surprise that material culture had been long neglected as a source of evidence in anthropology both because of what it could contribute to the study of society as a whole but equally for its intrinsic interest. Ucko's study of material culture was interdisciplinary. It cut across anthropology, archaeology, and art history, and it was inclusive of all categories of artefact from predynastic clay figurines, to house types, to humble and not so humble penis sheaths. In recent years, there has been a consider-able growth in the cross-disciplinary study of material culture. However, in many respects Ucko's original concerns apply as much today as they did then to the study of one branch of material culture studies: the study of art. It is not that art is unstudied, but that its study has remained the province of art historians or other specialists in the study of art (see Heyd 2005: 1 ff. for a relevant discussion). The study of art in other disciplines tends to be quarantined off as the concern of subdisciplinary specialists.

The neglect of the study of art by anthropologists is at first difficult to explain. The societies that anthropologists study—Western and non-Western—all seem to produce works that fit into a broadly defined category of artwork. I will leave matters of definition for the moment. There is great interest in the arts of different cultures: major institutions collect and exhibit it, art is proffered as an arena for cross-cultural discourse and understanding, and art is integral to value creation processes in many different societies. Art ought to be both a source of evidence and a medium for communicating values, knowledge, and ideas cross-culturally. It would seem that in neglecting the audience for art, in standing aside from the spaces for art discourse within the anthropologist's own society, and in failing to capitalize on the interest that students have in Western and non-Western art, anthropologists are missing out on considerable opportunities.

The neglect of art as a source of data is not confined to anthropology and archaeology. The American philosopher Mark Johnson chides his contemporaries for their attitude to art:

Contemporary Anglo American philosophers recognise that the nature of meaning is a pivotal philosophical issue, but they almost never regard art or aesthetics as relevant to this topic. They labour under the illusion of the cognitivist view that meaning is properly only a linguistic phenomenon—a matter of words and sentences. Moreover they tend to think of meaning as involving the truth condition of sentences. . . . [If considered at all] meaning in painting gets reduced to the representational element.

Johnson (2007: 207)

Johnson opposes this to popular attitudes to art in Western society where 'in sharp contrast with this traditional philosophical disparagement of the arts, most people turn to art not just because of its entertainment value, but precisely because it is meaningful and because it helps to understand our human condition' (Johnson 2007: 208). Art has this peculiar characteristic of being highly valued and very visible in contemporary Western society, yet at the same time of being separated as a source of data from general studies of human society and often disregarded as a source of knowledge. Yet if it is accepted that art should be treated as a source of information like any other, the question that then arises is what, if anything, makes art different. My answer will in part be that the very thing that makes art different is what makes it a vital source of data for the study of human society. And here it is necessary to provide a minimal definition of art. It is the production and use of expressive and meaningful forms—aesthetic and representational—for particular purposes. Art objects are usually multifunctional: they can serve an infinity of purposes and need to be treated in the context of the material culture of a society as a whole. Consequently, art as a form of intentional human action can only be understood in the context of the relationships and objectives of human beings acting in the social world.

Alfred Gell in his thought-provoking book, *Art and Agency: an anthropological theory* (1998) appears to oppose an action-oriented theory of art with semantic and aesthetic theories. I will later address other aspects of his theoretical approach to agency and to the overly narrow concept of aesthetics that he adopts. However, at this stage in the development of my argument, it is worth pointing out that the attributes of artworks are precisely what enable them to be used to act in the world and what in some cases enables agency to be attributed to them. As the distinguished archaeologist and art historian Irene Winter has written:

Once the relational nexus surrounding and generating the artwork is seen to function as part of a holistic system, affective properties and meaning intersect with social agency. That is instead of having to choose 'art as a system of action intended to change the world rather than encode symbolic propositions about it' (Gell 1998: 6) one is enjoined to see art both as a system of meaning encoding propositions about the world and as a system of action intended to change the world, precisely because the excitation generated by the art work lies in the interaction between the two.

Winter (2007: 62; see also Layton 2003)

It is important to stress at this point that the art that I am referring to is not the category of Western fine art or high art. Indeed that particular narrowly defined and conceived category of art object is where much of the problem has lain and is in part the source of the neglect of art by anthropologists and to a lesser extent by archaeologists. The Western category of fine art is generally accepted to have developed over the eighteenth and nineteenth centuries. Its history is extremely complex and any generalizations about it are likely to be contested at the level of detail. In essence it is art as a set-apart category of objects viewed independently of their function, housed in institutions of fine art, and appreciated for their aesthetic value, on the basis of disinterested viewing and judgement (see e.g. Winter 2002: 2). Johnson (2007: 210) sees the paradigm shift involving the separation of art from scientific reason as crucial:

The rise of the sciences of human nature during the seventeenth and eighteenth centuries prompted philosophers interested in the arts to change their focus from the nature of art to an almost exclusive concern with how the mind works in aesthetic judgement. By focussing on the faculties of mind that give rise to judgements about beauty—especially the faculties known as imagination and feeling—these philosophers ceased to regard art as a way of worldmaking.

Johnson (2007: 209)

The philosophy of art has tended to collapse aesthetics into beauty (Johnson 2007: 211). Although the concept of beauty associated with Kantian aesthetics is itself highly complex, the association of art with beauty has encouraged some to reject art (and aesthetics for that matter) as a useful category for cross-cultural analysis either on the grounds that it is subjective or that it inevitably involves Western aesthetic evaluations (Overing 1996; Gell 1998). Rather than rejecting the category of aesthetics it is important to disaggregate it from its entanglement with beauty and investigate it in the context of the societies who produced the artworks (see the essays in Coote and Shelton 1992).

There has also been a tendency to associate fine art production with individual creativity. Consequently, connoisseurship in art history has in part been directed to authenticating artworks by identifying the individual hand of the artist, and evaluating them according to qualitative judgements applied to the artist's oeuvre. The focus of this chapter is on the visual arts, but parallel histories can be written for music (see e.g. Goehr 1992).

As sociologist Pierre Bourdieu (1984) demonstrated, fine art is deeply connected to value and status creation processes in Western societies, which are linked in turn to the value of objects in the market (see MacClancy 1988 with reference to the market in 'primitive' art). The value creation processes of the fine art category have been centred on European art history and on the identification of a canon of Western fine art, which provides, at least in part, the skeleton for Western art history. The canon encompasses non-Western and 'ancient' arts to the extent that the latter can be thought to contribute to the historical trajectory of form in Western art. The canon is additive. Connections are traced back in time to Greece, Ancient Egypt, and Mesopotamia. The inclusion of indigenous art occurred after non-Western forms began to influence the development of Western art. Once acknowledged, non-Western art tended to be placed in categories such as Oriental art or primitive art, and occupied spaces in art museums and exhibition calendars reserved for non-Western art. To an extent, non-Western artworks were included not in their own right but as they were 'discovered' and appreciated by Western art worlds. In Jacques Maquet's terms, set out in his book *The Aesthetic Experience: an anthropologist looks at the visual arts* (1986), they were art by metamorphosis, incorporated within the Western framework of fine art. The Eurocentric nature of this 'inclusion' was reflected in the fact that until recently, works by contemporary indigenous artists were in general excluded from the primitive fine art category—primitive art was the art of societies before they were 'contaminated' by outside influence (Price 1989; Errington 1998).

It is certainly important for anthropologists to include 'fine art' as a source of evidence for the analysis of economic and value creation processes in contemporary Western society. This is not only because it encapsulates the ways in which cultural production is caught up in economic and political processes in Western societies but because of the hegemonic nature of the Western fine art category in global processes and its influence on the history of world arts and on contemporary art production. However, in order to understand those very processes and the contemporary challenges to the category of Western fine art, a broader conception of art is required.

The majority of works included in art galleries and museums were not initially produced as works of 'fine' art, but for use in particular contexts—as religious objects, symbols of status, bodily adornments, functional artefacts, embellishments of everyday objects, 'scientific' illustrations, and so on. The status of art by metamorphosis applied as much to medieval and Egyptian art as it did to the arts of Africa or Oceania. Placing works in the original contexts of their production is a main part of the job of art history. Art history is likely to be biased in the direction of the works that are included in art museums—because of the resources that they provide and because of the interest the public has in the works of art they contain. And indeed, art historians and curators do place most works of art included in museums of fine art in the context of their own place and time, researching their history independent of their subsequent recognition as fine art. The iconographic significance of Byzantine icons or Renaissance religious paintings is considered relevant to understanding them as works of art; function and significance is considered relevant to understanding Egyptian or Roman art (Figure 11.1). Even so, as archaeologist Sarah Scott (2006) argues for Roman art, the bias from fine art has had a considerable impact on how they are researched, interpreted, curated, and exhibited. Until recently, this has been even more so in the case of most non-Western art.

Perhaps because so-called 'primitive' art came late to influence Western traditions, perhaps because it was harder to view as antecedent to European traditions, its art history has been largely neglected. In some cases, this omission has been deliberate. For example, art historian and curator William Rubin wrote 'the ethnologists' primary concern—the specific function and significance of each of these objects—is irrelevant to my topic, except in so far as these facts may have been known to the modern artists in question' (2006: 130). Rubin was writing with reference to the 1984 exhibition *Primitivism in Modern Art* that he co-curated with Kirk Varnedoe. The exhibition created considerable controversy precisely

Fig. 11.1 The Westminster Panels. The panels were commissioned by or for George Fascet, Abbot of Westminster from about 1498 to 1500. They depict the Archangel Gabriel and the Virgin standing on plinths, which bear the shield of arms of Westminster Abbey and the Abbot himself. While today they are celebrated as works of fine art, the fact that they are remarkable in part because they survived the destruction of Henry VIII's dissolution of the monasteries signals a quite different history as religious icons. Originally forming the wings of an altarpiece, the oil painted panels represent the high-quality religious artwork available to wealthy medieval Londoners of the time. The Annunciation scene is depicted in glowing colours, with the Archangel Gabriel on the left panel and the Virgin Mary on the right (photo: Museum of London).

because it seemed to subordinate non-European art to Western art (see essays in Morphy and Perkins 2006b: Part II—Primitivism, Art, and Artifacts). The neglect of non-Western art by Western art museums and art historians has tended to create a disjunction between works of art that are treated in their own right and for which information about the context of production and intention of the artist are considered relevant and those for which it is not. As a consequence art historians, with notable exceptions (see e.g. Boone 1986; Blier 1987; McNaughton 1987; Philips 1998), have neglected to study non-Western art in its own contexts of production.

One of the tasks of the anthropology and archaeology of art is simply to provide the equivalent data on non-European artworks that the art historian provides for works in the Western traditions. This does not mean it is assumed that they are the same kind of things.

ART AS A CROSS-CULTURAL CATEGORY

I have argued in detail elsewhere that if anthropologists are to find the concept of art useful, valid or relevant in their research they must employ a cross-cultural and cross-temporal category, one that is distanced dialogically from the concept of art in any particular society (Morphy 2007b). The argument applies equally to archaeologists and art historians. Anthropological categories are derived from cross-cultural comparison and hence are likely to cover great variation in the phenomenon under investigation whether it is religion, gender, aesthetics, or art. Categories are therefore always emergent as understanding of human behaviour across space and time changes. They are reflected as much in the sets of things that people write about as in any substantive definition that they may attribute to them. To an extent, an anthropological category is an intuitive one that attempts to contain the intuitions of people from different cultures. This is why I have argued that the cross-cultural category of artwork is best seen as a polythetic set linked, in Wittgensteinean terms, by 'family resemblance' (Wittgenstein 1953; aphorisms 65–66). Of the things people refer to as games, for example, Wittgenstein wrote 'if you look at them you will not see something that is common to all, but similarities, relationships, and a whole series of them at that' (Wittgenstein 1953; aphorism 66). I would argue that art, like games, is a well worked category, one that has been subject to dialogue in the long term, and that while no single attribute, feature, or essence is going to be a common relatum, 'aesthetic effect broadly defined is likely to be a core feature of the set even if it is not an attribute of every member (artwork)' (Morphy 2007b: 198n12).

In her article on art and archaeologists, Sarah Scott argues that it is important to distance the study of Roman art from the post-Enlightenment aesthetic criteria

Fig. 11.2 Mosaic from Lullingstone Roman villa (4th century AD). Lullingstone Roman Villa is a villa built during the Roman occupation of Britain, situated near the village of Eynsford in north-west Kent, south-eastern England. The mosaic is from the dining room of the villa and represents the abduction of Europa by Jupiter disguised as a bull with two cupids (photo: English Heritage).

with which it has become entangled (Figure 11.2). She shows how criteria associated with Western fine art are applied to Roman art in such a way that Roman art becomes seen and categorized according to the aesthetic judgements of the present: 'we are placing them into an artificial category that has more to do with the development of modern art history and aesthetics than with the contexts for which such objects were originally created' (Scott 2006: 628). Scott is also critical of many of the categories and concepts of art history, terms such as schools and workshops that have been applied directly to what she refers to as ancient arts (2006: 653). The point is not so much that such concepts may not be relevant for cross-cultural analysis. Rather, it is that they should come out of the analysis of the objects in context rather than being imposed on the past as part of an interpretative framework.

The art historian David Freedberg has been equally critical of the constraining nature of the categories of 'fine' art or 'high' art (Freedberg 1989: 22–23). In his analysis of 'realistic' images derived directly from a person's features, he draws connections between, among other things, Roman death masks, the early modern religious sculptures encountered by pilgrims on the climb up the Sacro Monte di Varese in northern Italy, and the wax figures in Madame Tussauds in London. Freedberg notes that in the present day the representations in the wax museum are generally not classified as works of art. Indeed, he argues that we have been taught to see them as not being art. He might also have pointed out that 'sculptures' very similar in their illusionistic realism do have a place as contemporary art.

Duane Hanson's (1925–1996) sculptures of accident victims, American tourists, or a woman pushing a shopping trolley were intended to look like real people, and the 'artist' employed analogous techniques to those used to make the 'non-art' waxwork figures (Figure 11.3). In writing about his work, art museum curators are required to distance it from the craftsmanship of Madame Tussauds, for example,

Fig. 11.3 Duane Hanson, *Tourists*, 1970. Hanson cast his sculptures from life. His sculptures have the appearance of people one might meet outside the gallery, caught unawares. In this case, they are stereotypes of American tourists. The male and female figures were cast separately in the artist's studio and the models never even met. Medium polyester resin and fibreglass, painted in oil, and mixed media. Size of Man 152 × 80.50 × 31 cm; Woman 160 × 44 × 37 cm (National Galleries of Scotland accession no. GMA 2132).

by endowing it with a higher purpose. The website for the exhibition at the Tennis Palace Museum, Helsinki, *Duane Hanson—Sculptures of the American Dream*, asserts that 'Hanson's aim was not to copy real people, but to depict typical humans and humanity in general' (University of Helsinki 2007). The comparison between Madame Tussauds and Hanson's sculptures brings out the diversity of criteria used to separate fine art from its opposite. Philosopher Nick Zangwill, hinting at an institutional definition of art, notes that 'few would think that the waxworks at Madame Tussaud's are works of art. But how are they different from Hanson's sculptures? It seems to be important that Hanson's figures are intended for exhibition in the contexts we normally see sculptures' (Zangwill 2002: 113). The distinction between fine art and non-fine art (or even non-art) in these cases is not helpful either to understanding the particular histories of the works themselves as forms or the impact that they have on the viewer. They are, of course, relevant to understanding the Western fine art category and its articulation within the art market. Freedberg argues for similarities in the ways in which the sculptures at Varese act on the viewer and the impact of images in Madame Tussauds.

Freedberg suggests that if we trace the history of such images back to the Roman period and beyond they can be seen as belonging to the same sequence. The images that he focuses on are ones that create the illusion of the actuality of the person, which make the absent present. They include a great range of different types of images from supposed direct impressions of a person's features as in the case of the Turin shroud, death masks, and wax images. He extends his analysis to include images that are less direct in their representation of the features of a person but which convey attributes of movement or form that are taken to be the person themselves. He argues that a similar range of responses is engendered by such illusionistic representations, irrespective of whether they are or are not classified as 'fine' art. In many respects, they belong to the same set for analytic purposes. Concluding his discussion about wax images, Freedberg notes that 'we need to treat the claim of aesthetic differentiation with caution' (1989: 231). Here Freedberg is arguing for a wider category *than* works of art in order to include the relevant body of data. However, I would argue that this must be seen as a separate issue from a wider definition of the category *of* art. Freedberg argues that we have been taught to see Madame Tussauds as something other than an art gallery and so we remove the works collected within it from the category of *fine art* and displace them from the category of art altogether.

Much of the controversy over the category of art is caused by two factors. One is the collapsing of the broader cross-cultural category of art as a mode of human action into the narrower and relatively recent Western category of fine art as an institutionally defined set of objects. The other is the desire to make the cross-cultural category of art all encompassing and self-contained. All categories of material culture object are defined by or include attributes that they share with other categories of object. It is not a sufficient argument against the category of art that all art objects share some attributes with objects belonging to other categories. Many analytic concepts cross-cut categories defined by other features. Boats, for example, share in common with houses, carriages, and drinking vessels the fact that they are containers. Scott and Freedberg both express unease with the category of art because it is too closely associated with the Western category of fine art. Scott is wary of an aesthetic approach to 'ancient' art objects and Freedberg sees a category wider than fine art as necessary to his analysis of affect, of the power of the works concerned, and hence he subsumes 'art within the history of images' (Freedberg 1989: 23). In Freedberg's case he both gives priority in his definition of art to the category of objects defined as fine art and then sees that many of the objects he has analysed need to be analysed as a part of a wider set. Most of the examples he includes do fit well within the broader concept of art that I have defined. Even if they did not, the fact that a wider set of objects is required to analyse a particular topic—for example, the spiritual power attributed to objects—does not undermine the category of object concerned. Munn's (1986) analysis of value creation processes in Gawa, for example, brings together sets of objects on the basis of criteria such as lightness and heaviness that cross-cut categories of material objects defined on other bases, for example canoes or boundary markers.

Despite its resilience, the issue of developing a substitute term for 'art' is a recurrent theme, so it is worth briefly considering the question of the dissolution of the category of art altogether. There are two main issues: first, whether any of the substitute terms are adequate; secondly, whether or not a cross-cultural category of art can be usefully developed that is free from the biases of Western fine art. Clearly it is possible, as George Kubler (1962: 9) argued, to include artworks under the category of 'the history of things'—his substitute for what he referred to as the 'bristling ugliness of "material culture"'. Others have included art under the more euphonious rubric 'visual culture' (e.g. Mitchell 1986, 2006). And as Jeremy Coote (1992) argues in the case of the 'everyday vision' of cattle-keeping people in southern Sudan it may be more useful to apply a broad concept of aesthetics rather than art. It is also possible to include many artworks under rubrics such as 'images' (Freedberg 1989; Belting 2001) or 'pictures' (Clegg 1987; Mitchell 2006). All of these concepts are relevant ones for cross-cultural analysis. However, I would argue that the former categories are too broad and the latter categories too narrow to encompass the set of objects that are generally brought together under the category of 'art'. In addition, the need to substitute them for art is either because the focus of the study is wider than art or because the definition of art (and in some cases the definition of aesthetics associated with it) is too narrow. In Freedberg's case it was necessary to replace 'art' with 'images' in order to avoid the narrowness of the definition of fine art, while archaeologist John Clegg, like Scott, wishes to escape from overly narrow concepts of the aesthetic.

A central issue is thus to free ourselves from the narrow conception of art associated with Kantian aesthetics and the Western fine art category. By foregrounding fine art, we have been unable to see the family resemblances that connect similar practices across cultures in space and time. The correction is equally relevant to understanding art as a form of action in Western society, bringing together the diversity of practices that intuitively fall into the same broad category, connecting, for example, fine art, with design, craft, decoration, graffiti, and so on. It might be argued that we should encompass art within the broader category of aesthetics rather than arguing for it as a distinct category in its own right (see Coote 1992 for a relevant discussion). Aesthetics, however, while integral to many people's conception of art, is also a much broader category of experience that can be applied equally to features of the natural world as to most areas of human life, whereas 'art' refers specifically to the products and forms of human action. The concept of art emphasizes the connection between aesthetics, representation, and action; art is a way of acting meaningfully in the world. Perhaps it is simply that aesthetics itself has become so closely associated with the idea of disinterested contemplation that it is necessary to reconnect it with purposive action to signify its more general relevance to understanding human history and society.

It is an irony of anthropology and archaeology that by placing objects in the contexts of their own times we are likely to see that they have much in common cross-culturally. It is the narrow Western concept of fine art that has been the distancing mechanism. However, I should stress that the cross-cultural category of art does not correspond to any indigenous or historical category or concept of art any more than it does to Western fine art. Gell's advocacy of 'methodological philistinism' is relevant here. By analogy with agnosticism, as far as other cultures' religious beliefs are concerned, methodological philistinism is 'an attitude of resolute indifference towards the aesthetic value of works of art' (Gell 1992b: 42). There is, however, a distinction that needs to be made between the analyst's own aesthetic response to the object and the aesthetic value it has in the context of the producing society. The matter is more a question of suspending aesthetic judgement rather than adopting a position of philistinism. In his later book *Art and Agency* (Gell 1998), he goes even further than this in criticizing the utility of the concept of aesthetics in cross-cultural analysis. He does so by adopting a very narrow definition of aesthetics, which identifies the aesthetic object with the beautiful (Morphy 2009), and he has been criticized by Winter as reducing the art historians' enterprise by 'employing an old-fashioned definition of aesthetics that demands the work be alienated from its originating context' (Winter 2007: 60).

The absence of terms that can be readily translated into English as 'art' is not a challenge to the idea of a cross-cultural category (see Van Damme 1997 for a relevant discussion). The English category of art is complex and contested and itself comprises a polythetic set: there is no more than a family resemblance among the different things that can be included in the art category. Nonetheless it is an important part of the method of studying non-Western art to analyse the terminologies that apply to 'artworks' and the language that is applied to them.

In approaching the study of visual art in an ethnographic, historic, or archaeological context, the initial approach needs to be pragmatic. Is the material object concerned one that fits into the category of art, or is the analyst's concept of art useful in understanding the object or releasing its potential as evidence for the study of society? Some studies may of course have art as their initial focus: people whose main interest is in studying art, or people who might have a hypothesis about human development or evolutionary psychology or language origins that rests on a concept of art. That does not mean that their research should be restricted only to the body of works they include in the category of art works. Here I would agree with Freedberg that 'no history of art can afford to ignore these lessons of a history of images more widely conceived' (1989: 281). But the fact that it is necessary to place art objects within broader categories and contexts in order to analyse it does not mean that the category is not itself relevant.

METHODOLOGICAL REFLECTIONS ON ART AS A CROSS-CULTURAL CATEGORY

Given the features I see as central to the concept of art, analysis and interpretation will move in the direction of the use of artworks in context, the effect the work has on the observer, and the ways in which it is meaningful to members of the society. On a priori grounds, those questions involve understanding how it is made, how it is used and experienced, how it means, and to whom it means. In the actual research process, it should make little difference whether the works concerned are labelled as art or not. An ethnographically based anthropological study is centred on distinctions that are relevant to the society concerned and understanding the object in the context of the society as a whole. For the anthropologist the most useful thing about the idea of art is that it acts as a flag to signal the kind of thing the object might be. It acknowledges that the semantic and aesthetic dimensions of material culture objects may be integral to their use and places the objects concerned in a broader comparative framework. It directs attention to the form of the object in order to discover what it contributes to the context in which it is used. It requires the researcher to engage with the question of what art, as a form of action, achieves that would not be achieved otherwise.

Thus, my main reason for defending the usefulness of the category of 'art object' is that art is a particular way of acting in the world. If we neglect the art dimension of objects, we fail to understand their significance and overlook a source of data that is often crucial to understanding many aspects of society. As the introduction to Thomas Heyd and John Clegg's book on the aesthetics of rock art suggests, 'If the task of the social scientist is to provide explanations of the forms of life of people in society, neglecting to consider the aesthetics of objects that have aesthetically salient values may lead to the omission of significant sources of information on those societies' (Heyd 2005: 4).

The approach I adopt is in a number of respects almost the antithesis of Alfred Gell's (1992b, 1998). He denies that there is a cross-cultural category of art object but argues for an anthropological approach to objects as agents as the core of a theoretical approach to art. It is certainly important to understand the ways in which material culture objects are integral to social life and to value creation processes, and how in many contexts they stand for, represent, or take the place of human actors and often are endowed with agency by people. However, I am resistant to applying concepts like agency to the objects themselves just as I think that metaphors such as the 'social life of things' (Appadurai 1986a) are overused. And ironically I am cautious precisely because I share Gell's belief that a form of agnosticism lies at the heart of method in anthropology (Gell 1992b). Seeing objects as agents—as persons—collapses theory and ethnography in a way that diverts anthropology from its analytic task. Social relationships are an important focus of anthropological analysis, though I would not quite give them the central role that Gell does. All material objects are entangled in social processes and, clearly, they often do mediate relationships between people and domains of existence, for example, the earthly and the spiritual. And material culture objects can be *believed* to be animate and can be endowed with the attributes of persons and responded to as if they were persons—though it needs to be established in particular cases that this is so. But the analyst who elides the difference between the social relations entailed in the use of objects and the observed belief that some objects are animate, by endowing the objects themselves with agency, cuts too many corners. The agnosticism, the suspension of belief that the anthropologist is required to espouse, is in practice very different from that suggested by Gell. It is necessary to get to see the images in the context of the viewing society and to enter the minds of the makers as much as possible, an exercise that requires an exploration of the cognitive and expressive dimensions of objects, answering the question of how they are seen and how they mean. It is vital that anthropologists acknowledge that certain material culture objects are *thought* to have agency and are *believed* to affect the world. Indeed some do affect the world as a result of the conscious or unconscious agency of people, for example, works that have a performative function, or mark status, or move people emotionally. But the job of the anthropologist, of the analyst, is to determine how they have that impact on people and an effect in the world, how it is that people can believe that objects have agency. As Winter (2007: 43) has written it is important 'to distinguish between agency ascribed by the analyst of a given work from the agency marked by cultural practice, and even grammar, within the originating culture, if we are to fully understand the historical role(s) accorded to artworks . . . to avoid conflating indigenous and analytical perspectives until and unless they can be shown to be congruent'. The work of the anthropologist may begin with the insight that a sculpture is thought to be alive or that death is thought to result from the performance of a dance. Consequently the anthropologist places the questions of what kind of impact a work of art has in context, how it has that impact, how it means or has meaning, at the centre of the analysis of art. Indeed, in many of the analyses that Gell undertakes in *Art and Agency* he exemplifies that method.

The methodological core of an anthropological study of art forms around two sets of questions. The first concerns how the work of art operates in context: the how of meaning and the how of aesthetic effect, 'how . . . intention has been realised' (Wicks 1997: 395). Given the understanding of what art *is*, set out above, 'how' is directly linked to what the object means, what its impact is on the viewer, and what its aesthetic effect is. Indeed analytically 'how' is a prerequisite of understanding what something means even in contexts where we can ask the producers, viewers, or participants. What something means requires analysis. It is seldom reducible to a simple gloss or a particular exegetical interpretation, however useful the latter might be. In archaeological contexts it is essential to the interpretative process: 'how' involves bringing context into the analysis of form.

The second and complementary set of questions centres on the explanation of form itself. Why does the object have the shape it does? Why is it made in the way it is? These questions are clearly interrelated, but each provides an independent perspective on objects. They place them in somewhat different temporal frames.

The first set of questions are centred on the power, meaning, and significance of objects in context, and the second set focuses on their historical trajectory, how they came into being and what technical and cognitive processes are involved in their manufacture. The two come together in the bodies of knowledge that are required to make the objects, in the embodied processes that influence the form of the work, and in the technical skills needed and that may be directly connected to the meaning and significance that the object has to the maker or viewer. The explication of form encourages a journey into the past to trace the histories of designs, techniques, and raw materials. This in turn provides evidence that is essential for a dynamic and historically informed view of the trajectories of regional systems as a whole. The core questions are no different for art than for any other material culture object. The difference lies in what it is necessary to take into consideration in answering them.

The analysis of form is central to both questions of context and questions of process. Form needs to be broadly defined to include all of the material attributes of the objects in addition to shape: the raw materials, their properties such as weight or sheen, colour and texture, and so on. In context, attributes such as

Fig. 11.4 *Kula* canoe setting off on a voyage from Vakuta to Kitava (Papua New Guinea) laden with goods for exchange (photo: Shirley Campbell 1977).

lightness or heaviness, as Nancy Munn (1986) showed in her classic study of *kula* exchange on the island of Gawa, or the quality or composition of the raw material, as Lechtman (1977) demonstrated in the case of Andean gold alloys, are central to understanding the value creation processes associated with art. Such qualities often cross-cut components of form. For example, in the case of the designs on Trobriand canoe prows, the decorated canoes convey a sense of lightness and speed in addition to seductive beauty that is in harmony with the objectives of the voyagers on the *kula* (Campbell 2002) (Figure 11.4). The analysis of details of the form of designs or the different colours or materials used in different contexts provides the basis for asking questions about the structure of systems of meaning and expression. Those questions themselves can only be answered fully by placing the material artwork in the context of action. Nonetheless, if the analyst carries forward information about the diversity of possible forms, and knowledge of the forms that could have been used, he or she is able to view the event more from the perspective of the actor. The wealth of knowledge and experience that the actor brings to the situation, much of which does not find expression in a particular context, in part explains how the object functions in context. Hence part of the method of the study of forms in art must be an initial analysis of the range of material available—museum collections, photographs from the past and observations from the present—to begin to understand the parameters of variation as well as to get a feeling for how the art might work.

Form will also give access to representational processes manifest in the art and to iconographies that may be central to the functioning of a particular system. I find it useful, following Nancy Munn's study, *Walbiri Iconography* (1973), and influenced by semiotic theory, to distinguish broadly between motivated and arbitrary systems of representation, though with a strong note of caution that the boundaries between the two are very fuzzy and that each contains within its ambit great diversity. The attraction of the division is that it acknowledges that most, perhaps all, human societies recognize that some representations are more like their referent than others. They are interpretable at one level by what they resemble. Mimesis falls into this category. In some cases, for example, the many analogues for blood or the hyper-realism of Duane Hanson, or perhaps the Kwakiutl and Haida portrait masks in the theatre of the Potlatch (Rosman and Rubel 1990) (Figure 11.5), the boundary between image and reality merges. And, of course, in representations of the unseen, of the spiritual or imagined, the artwork, the processes involved in art making and the way images enter peoples' lives may in themselves be what makes up the 'real' (see Freedberg 1989: 159). Yet, in many other cases art comprises design elements or schema that are relatively arbitrary or unmotivated in terms of formal resemblance to their referent. The elements are part of systems for encoding meaning that may be limited in their scope to designating particular status categories or may have something of the complexity of verbal languages as a means of conveying information or expressing narratives. Frequently the arbitrary and the motivated are combined within the same overall system. Such systems may be relatively transparent and accessible to those who learn them, and are similar to pictographic writing systems. In some cases, the arbitrary nature of the sign and its uninterpretability out of context or without interpretative guidance is part of what

Fig. 11.5 Haida portrait mask of a dead youth. Masks of this type were used in the winter ceremonial performances of the Haida and other societies of the north-west coast of North America. The rituals included spectacular theatrical performances in which the dead were brought back to life through masquerade. This particular mask of a dead youth is one of a series of four collected by the Reverend Charles Harrison in the 1880s now in the Pitt Rivers Museum. The mask has been attributed to the nineteenth-century Haida artist Simeon Stilthda (photo courtesy of Pitt Rivers Museum, University of Oxford, accession number 1891.49.3).

creates its value. *The capacity of human beings to create representations that take into account the ways they will be interpreted and the effect they will have in context is what makes art a powerful resource for action.*

Methodologically it is important to analyse material form and connect that analysis to contexts of use in order to approach the 'how' of meaning and the 'how' of affect. Posing the question of how something is interpreted, or how it has the effect it does on the participants, places the object in the context of action, enabling the researcher to begin to understand the conditions that enable the work of art to be effective in context. It also ensures that the researcher recognizes that the meaning of the object in its wider sense will depend on who is viewing it and what experience and knowledge they bring to the event or context. Anthropologically we should be in a position to reduce the ambiguity of our interpretations and increase their accuracy through fieldwork. It is self-evident that the same geometric sign can mean completely different things within a culture according to context and that across cultures its meanings may vary even more widely. It is possible to gain an idea of the structural properties of an encoding or representational system through formal analysis, to get an idea of whether or not it is likely to encode meanings in a precise way. However, it is only by gaining additional contextual information, such as access to the range of meanings associated with particular graphic elements and to the information that the interpreter or viewer has in his or her head, that one can begin to see how such systems operate. Similar qualifications apply to expressive aspects of form, since although there may be some similarities in the impact of a design on the senses across cultures, there is likely to be enormous variation in how a particular visual effect is apprehended. In the case of New Guinea Highland body decorations or shields, it is going to depend on factors such as group affiliation or whether one is an aggressor or defender, big man or follower (see O'Hanlon 1995). Thus when interpretations are being sought for representational systems in remote archaeological time, quite different interpretations may be equally plausible.

Reflecting on archaeological contexts, in particular prehistoric ones, is salutary for anthropologists for a number of ironic reasons. Archaeology usually has to deal with limited information and has been forced to come to terms with the limited nature of its contextual data, in the recognition that socio-cultural context is a vital missing ingredient. The evidence that remains is always partial, especially in prehistoric archaeology. This favours certain kinds of representations: rock art and art forms made of durable material, art in burial contexts, and so on. In many cases, nearly all has been lost. Archaeologists need to reconstruct the interpretative context and to reconnect art works to the context of action. Many archaeologists have steered clear of the data from art because of the limited nature of the archaeological record and the difficulties that poses to the interpretative task. This is puzzling in some respects since, in a world that is short of information on qualitative dimensions of the human past, art is a potentially rich source of data. Those archaeologists who have included art among their data have indeed been required to develop hypotheses about the 'how' of meaning in order to begin to develop plausible interpretations that can be tested in their archaeological context.

A major problem in archaeological interpretations of art is that the gap between hypothesis and data is often so great that several hypotheses may be equally plausible. The tendency has been to apply a singular interpretative framework, with one replacing another in sequence. Studies of rock art are particularly salutary in this respect with 'art for art's sake' (Halverson 1987), followed by 'hunting magic', followed by hypotheses about religion and gender (Leroi-Gourhan 1989), art as social communication (Conkey 1982) and boundary maintaining mechanisms (Munn 1986), art as an adjunct to trance (Lewis-Williams 1981), and so on. On reflection, most of these hypotheses are equally tenable or at least contain elements that are worth continuing to apply to the data as they accumulate over time and as the complexities of the forms of the art become better known through analysis. It is vital in case studies of prehistoric art to integrate the analysis of the art within the archaeological data set as a whole, to try to place the art in the context of overall spatio-temporal sequences. Equally important is to develop hypotheses about how the art would have been viewed by placing it in the context of the overall landscape (Tilley 1994; Bradley 1997; A. M. Jones 2006).

Where there are historical data, linguistic evidence and, as we come closer to the present, evidence in the form of film and photography, then that evidence supplements the analysis of the formal properties of objects and needs to be set in dialogue with them. The resources available for analysing and interpreting art from the distant and middle distant past can be considerable. Winter (2007), using the evidence of grammatical structure of early Sumerian texts from 2000 BC, has been able to hypothesize how people responded to images of rulers and how imagery was connected in a nexus of relationships that linked the population to the ruler and with god. And the art historian Sarah Fraser (2004) has been able to use surviving sketches produced by wall painters in Dunhuang, China in the ninth century to reconstruct the performative aspects of the art and link them to Buddhist theology and aesthetics. While the addition of other forms of evidence enriches the analysis of art, the corollary of this is that art in turn provides a form of evidence that can contribute greatly to the understanding of society.

The lesson that should be learnt from the present and applied to the past is that art is likely to be determined in multiple ways and integrated in complex ways with social and cultural processes as a whole. Art is not one way of acting in the world but many ways of acting. Within the same society, different art forms require different interpretative frameworks yet in context they will often combine and can interact. Different representational and expressive systems may be combined in the same complex artwork or performance, gaining coherence through association with an overall theme or set of themes.

As in archaeology, there has been a tendency in anthropology to oppose different attributes of artworks to different effects of artworks, as if they were simple alternatives. In this view, art is either expressive or semantic. Such oppositions are problematic not only because a work of art can be both semantically dense and aesthetically powerful, but also because the very oppositions between the aesthetic—the expressive and the semantic, or between the cognitive and the affective—may be unhelpful oversimplifications. Philosopher Nelson Goodman referred to the dominant dichotomy in Western thought between the cognitive and the emotive:

> On the one side we put sensation, perception, inference, conjecture, all nerveless inspection and investigation, fact and truth; on the other, pleasure, pain, interest, satisfaction, disappointment, all brainless responses liking and loathing . . . [But] the work of art is apprehended through feelings as well as through the senses . . . What we know through art is felt in our bones and nerves and muscles as well as grasped by our minds, that all the sensitivity and responsiveness of the organism participates in the interpretation of symbols.
>
> Goodman (1976: 247–249).

YOLNGU CIRCUMCISION PAINTING

These rather dense methodological points can be explored further through an example from my own research that illustrates the multidimensional nature of form in art and the complex place it can have in world making. The example I want to use derives from ethnographic work among the Yolngu, Australian Aboriginal people from eastern Arnhem Land in northern Australia (see Morphy 1991, 2007b). On the day of his circumcision, a painting is made on the chest of a Yolngu boy. It is made over a period of several hours by men in a shady place. The painting is produced by a number of men working in turn, and their actions are accompanied by songs that relate to the meaning of the painting. The mothers, sisters, and other women relatives sit on the outside of the painting group. They sometimes perform dances that accompany the songs but they tend to look away from the painting itself. When the painting is completed, the child is carried to the place of circumcision on the shoulders of his mother's brother, decorated in parrot feather string ornaments, with a sacred dilly bag under his arm. At this moment, the child is on display and the ritual performance dramatizes his change of status and his separation from his mother (Figure 11.6).

We can understand much about the significance of the painting as an act without considering its form or aesthetics further. Indeed, that is where anthropological analysis of ritual form has often remained. The painting marks the status of the

Fig. 11.6 Boys being painted for a circumcision ceremony at Yirrkala, Arnhem Land, Australia in 1974. Roy Marika, a leader in the Yolngu struggle for land rights, beats his clapping sticks in the foreground. Sacred dilly bags are suspended above the boys representing the baskets carried by Ancestral women (photo: Howard Morphy 1974).

boy. The context of painting reflects the gendered division of Yolngu society. The restriction of the painting marks male control of the sacred and dramatizes the process of inclusion into the male world that the child is undergoing through his change of status. The length of time the painting takes indicates the importance of the occasion and the final, almost triumphal, appearance of the boy on the shoulders of his mother's brother focuses attention on him and makes it his day. All this without referring to the form of the painting. Consideration of the form of the painting requires extending the time of the event and making the event part of the temporal continuity of society.

Fig. 11.7 Body painting at a Yolngu circumcision ceremony at Yilpara, Blue Mud Bay, Arnhem Land, Australia in 2004. The chest painting is in its final stages with lines of cross-hatching being applied by a brush of human hair. The painting belongs to the Djapu clan and the background pattern represents clouds (photo: Howard Morphy).

The painting on the chest is elaborate (Figure 11.7). It combines figurative and geometric motifs and is finished with fine cross-hatching. The design belongs to a set of sacred clan paintings (*likanpuy miny'tji*) associated with *djalkiri* ('foundation') places. The designs are believed to have had their origin in the ancestral past and they encode meanings connected to the ancestral being and events concerned. While sometimes a variant of the same painting may be painted on more than one boy, the number of possible designs is so great that the same design is likely to be repeated only after many years have passed. The painting may be produced in other contexts and on other surfaces, however. A detailed analysis of the overall set of designs reveals an archive of paintings that covers the entire mythological landscape of eastern Arnhem Land (Morphy 1991). The designs are connected to land ownership, mapping the relationships between people and land. By extending the data to include paintings in museum collections and photographs of body paintings over a 60-year period, it is possible to see both continuities in design generation over time and to detect any changes in the usage of the designs and patterns of ownership. In the Yolngu case, the individual painting on a child's chest in a circumcision ceremony is part of the process of the social transmission of religious knowledge over time. This process is deeply connected to the political structure of Yolngu society and clearly contributes to the designs being seen as meaningful objects even if the boy has little idea of the system as a whole. The paintings are decodable and can be interpreted by someone learned in Yolngu art, just as the iconography of Renaissance paintings or Sydney Nolan's Ned Kelly series, which is inspired by the exploits of the renowned Australian bushranger, can be 'decoded' by a knowledgeable person. And the circumcision ceremony is a context in which meaning is built in to the designs through the songs that are sung, the dances that are performed and the ritual process that is taking place. While there are core meanings associated with particular Yolngu designs, the paintings themselves are highly productive semantically and their meaning depends in part on context and on who is viewing them (Morphy 2007a). Some interpretations are restricted, while some depend on individual knowledge and experience.

During the performance of a circumcision ceremony, the experiential and aesthetic dimensions of the painting are what count for most of the participants. Yolngu paintings contain ancestral power that is expressed by the shimmering brilliance of the design produced by the technique of cross-hatching (Morphy 1992). A similar effect is created by the lorrikeet feather decorations and the sheen of the red ochred body. The boy shines with ancestral power, and the effect is augmented by the drama of the ritual as he comes out of the shade fully painted, to be displayed to the assembled company. The aesthetic effect in this context is relatively autonomous of the iconography of the design and can be understood without entering that domain. At the moment of circumcision, the detailed form of the design will surely be irrelevant to the boy. He has lain still for hours in an almost dissociated state as the design on his chest is infilled with the gentle strokes of the *marwat*, the long thin brush of human hair that is drawn across his skin. Experientially the transition from the quiet time of painting to the sharp moment of circumcision is dramatic. But he will remember and be reminded for the rest of his life of the painting that was given to him that day. Yolngu art is something of the moment but it is also a compendium of knowledge that can be acquired through-out a lifetime. Such knowledge is applied in innumerable contexts, in the form of paintings or dances used for particular purposes. The purpose may vary from the transport of the soul of the deceased or the transfer of ancestral power to demon-strations of rights in land. The knowledge contained in paintings in part explains why they can be used to interpret the form of the landscape or to communicate the creative actions of ancestral beings, and how it is that they mark clan identity in ways that can be used to support claims of precedence in political and social life. All of these can be the subject of exegesis and be included in glosses of the meanings of components of paintings. And yet at any moment the practice of art can create a sensation or a transcendent experience, individual or shared, that comes out of the phenomenological experience of the work itself and its effect on the senses, and that gives reality to an idea or a belief. In the Yolngu case, it might be the immanent presence of spiritual power in the world or a feeling of *communitas* at the culmi-nation of a ritual.

CONCLUSIONS: SEEING THE LIGHT

The anthropological study of art as a form of action takes account of the multidi-mensional nature of sets of objects with properties that transcend conventional functional categories and divisions. Art is often deployed in social or religious contexts because it connects the cognitive and affective dimensions of human experience and facilitates complex ways of acting in the world. A work of art may encode meanings precisely, depicting an event, a sequence of action, a religious story, a particular person, or mythic being. Yet, the same work can also point towards ideas that cannot be so easily expressed, creating atmosphere, a sense of personality, or the state of a relationship. Art can 'communicate' through visual codes, the designs of distinctive forms of regalia that mark status, or the patterns that mark clan identity and more mundanely team membership. Visual properties can equally be used aesthetically to convey abstract concepts—time, space, atmosphere, chaos, order, and so on—and colours can be used to convey emotions or, slipping again into the mundane, the appropriate ambience for a kitchen or bathroom. The cognitive and the affective, and the semantic and aesthetic, while relatively autonomous, are in actuality co-present in the form of works of art. The stretching of meaning associated with artworks often happens because some things can be best expressed through aesthetic forms. Such ideas may be expressed through material forms that have a powerful impact on the human body, which create sensations that are almost inescapable—the sensation of the body being filled with light or becoming overwhelmingly heavy. The relationship between physical stimulus and bodily sensation is something all humans experience and art is in part the use of this shared experience to create meaning and to share emotions. In Yolngu art, the brilliance of the design is the ancestral power that is the vital force behind the world. However, similar effects in the context of other societies, while having some synergies, may have quite different significance and be stretching towards very different ideas. The particularities of the meaning of form in context need to be understood before the metaphysics can be appreciated.

While superficially there are elements in common between the approach I adopt to art and that of Alfred Gell's, in that both of us could be interpreted to adopt an action-oriented approach towards art, there are fundamental differences. Gell adopts an explicitly anthropological approach to art in which art as a category more or less disappears. My perspective is centred on art as a particular way of acting in the world that requires an interdisciplinary approach. Aesthetics and semantics are integral to my conception of art but are clearly not confined to art. What is contained under the rubric of art varies widely across cultures and time, but the family resemblance that underlies art objects creates synergies cross-culturally and a sense that certain kinds of things fit within the same broad category. Given the perspective I adopt, then I would advocate that art can profitably be analysed from a similar perspective irrespective of when and where it was produced. A focus on art as action requires that attention is paid to form, to understanding why that kind of object was produced for use in a particular cultural and social context, including of course its impact on and reception by others. And because many artworks are durable, a different set of questions needs to be posed as it is exchanged or traded and outlasts its maker by decades or millennia. On a priori grounds, the same broad range of questions and methods of analysis are going to be relevant to art whether it was produced by hunters in the Upper Palaeolithic, Buddhist wall painters of eighth-century China, Poole pottery painters, Yolngu bark painters, or contemporary graffiti artists. Those questions and methods are going to find that art encompasses many different kinds of things, since what is produced depends on the knowledge and technical accomplishment that goes into it and the purpose for which it is intended. But the archaeologist, the art historian, the anthropologist of art, while they may centre their research on different periods and societies and have access to different sources of data, should be involved in the same overall discourse.

CHAPTER 12

ARCHAEOLOGICAL ASSEMBLAGES AND PRACTICES OF DEPOSITION

ROSEMARY JOYCE
JOSHUA POLLARD

Archaeologists routinely describe sites as composed of assemblages encountered in deposits. But what is actually meant by 'assemblage' and 'deposition'? In this chapter, we explore how these concepts have developed and consider the implications of contemporary understandings of deposition and assemblage that depart significantly from conventional definitions, many still to be found in introductory text books.

We conclude that archaeology, as a result of a long history of employing things associated together in space as a primary basis for interpretation, has developed a set of approaches that if more widely used would fundamentally transform all aspects of our disciplinary practice.

DEFINING TERMS

Conventionally, the term 'assemblage' is applied to a collection of artefacts or ecofacts (animal bones, or seeds, etc.) recovered from a specific archaeological context—a site, an area within a site, a stratified deposit, or a specific feature such as a ditch, tomb, or house. So, an assemblage is a collection of material related through contextual proximity. Inherent in the use of the term in archaeology is the idea that the contextual association makes it possible to interpret the group of materials as evidence for specific events, processes, or practices in the past. Assemblages are often characterized as being open to the assignment of a single date of formation, although the contents of an assemblage may include material of an earlier date recognized as having been curated, recycled, or otherwise moved through time.

In archaeological excavation, the definition of a number of objects as constituting an 'assemblage' rests indissolubly on the identification of delimited deposits whose contents make up the assemblage. Deposition in this sense refers to the process of laying-down or accumulation of sediments and materials to form an archaeological context (see Harris 1989). While early uses of the term assemblage, and most contemporary usage, do not include the bulk sediments that form the 'matrix' of a deposit, some approaches that we discuss further below promote the inclusion in the assemblage of all the contents of a deposit, including sediments.

While not a necessary part of the definition of assemblage, in some instances the association of materials in a deposit is understood to result from intentional actions in the past. For example, tomb assemblages may be considered to be the associated materials resulting from a burial event (Figure 12.1). Even an assemblage that is derived from a context understood as secondary, such as the materials from a cultural fill or from a midden, is interpretable in terms of the human intentions that produced the fill or midden. In fact, this ambivalence is inherent in the use of the term 'assemblage', which references the verb 'assemble', raising the question, who is doing the assembling? While in mid-twentieth-century archaeology that role was clearly assigned to the archaeologist, the association of the term assemblage over the past 25 years with the concept of 'structured deposition' requires active consideration of the likely role of past actors in creating the material remains that the archaeologist describes and interprets.

The concept of 'structured deposition' was originally introduced to demarcate instances when materials were intentionally associated in a patterned fashion (Richards and Thomas 1984). In contemporary practice, the concept is being expanded as a way to recognize the structuring that results from much past human action, whether the structure was consciously intended or an unintended consequence of action, or something in between. The emphasis in the original definition of structured deposition on ritualized or symbolic action has been expanded to include both the structuring effects of everyday pragmatic action, and the phenomenological and experiential qualities of the actions through which structured deposits came into being.

Fig. 12.1 Assemblage and deposition: Early Bronze Age (c.2000–1800 BC) grave goods—ceramic, bone, and stone—associated with a cremation burial from Bulford, near Stonehenge, England.

HISTORIES OF ARCHAEOLOGICAL APPROACHES

The conventional definitions of assemblage and deposition discussed above emerged from geological and processual models of archaeological 'formation processes' that developed from the nineteenth century through the mid-twentieth century (e.g. Schiffer 1976, 1983, 1987; Harris 1989; Rapp and Hill 2006: 4–16; see also Browman and Givens 1996; O'Brien and Lyman 1999). The initial definition of the idea of structured deposition in the early 1980s owes its inspiration to critiques of some of the perspectives of processual archaeology, and especially, to significant concerns with the place of the human actor and human meanings in late processual archaeological models. However, it would be a mistake to conclude that concerns with the phenomena described as 'structured deposition' are exclusively a product of post-processual archaeology.

The main genealogical line for structured deposition can be traced through the work of British prehistorians operating within a functionalist framework during the 1960s to 1970s. Recognition of the unusual context and deliberate juxtaposition of deposits at certain Neolithic sites inspired the identification of these as place-ments of 'ritual rubbish' (e.g. Piggott 1962: 75; Smith 1965: 20; Case 1973: 193–195). Separate Americanist genealogies leading to similar concepts develop from the processual archaeology and site formation processes of Michael Schiffer (1987), and from contemporary archaeology that seeks to bridge the gap between older culture-historical approaches and contemporary archaeologies of practice and meaning (Pauketat 2002). These diverse genealogies for similar concerns with the human structuring of archaeological deposits raise issues of the coherence and compatibility of research that may at first glance seem similar operationally, but is based in different assumptions about the relationships that exist between human action in the past, the material deposits that archaeologists investigate, and the questions that they ask.

Stratigraphic models borrowed from geology were critical to the development of archaeology in the nineteenth century and underlie any archaeological understand-ing of deposition and its interpretation. In particular, the principle of superposi-tion—the idea that the relative vertical position of materials can be read as evidence of the passage of time, with lower positions earlier and higher positions later—became a cornerstone of archaeological practice through the influence of nineteenth-century geology. In the parallel development of geology, the principle of superposition led to a general representation of temporal change as producing a sedimentary layer-cake, with materials embedded in distinct layers being under-stood as typical of the time period when the layer was laid down. Materials found together could be assumed to have the same date—an archaeological inference John Rowe (1962) labelled as the 'principle of association', or 'Worsaae's Law', based on the writing of the Danish archaeologist Jens Worsaae (1849). It is worth quoting Worsaae at length, as his work is generally regarded as critical to the development of ideas in archaeology relating the association of things in space to their associa-tion in time. Worsaae wrote that

we should scarcely have been able to refer... antiquities to three successive periods, if experience had not taught us that objects which belong to different periods are usually found by themselves... It will not be the places where antiquities may be casually met with, but rather our ancient stone structures and barrows, which, with reference to the subject just mentioned, ought to be the subject of a more particular description; for as to the graves themselves we know that, generally speaking, they contain both the bones of the dead, and many of their weapons, implements, and trinkets, which were buried with them. *Here we may therefore, in general, expect to find those objects together which were originally used at the same period.*

Worsaae (1849: 76; emphasis added)

Archaeologists such as John Lubbock also borrowed from geology the idea of characteristic contents of each layer—the 'type fossils' of geology becoming the artefact types of archaeology (Kehoe 1991; O'Brien and Lyman 1999). Archaeolo-gists developed a specialized term for the distinctive materials enclosed in a specific layer of the stratigraphic sequence: the 'assemblage' (Childe 1956: 26–29). John Lubbock, the pioneer British archaeologist, used this collective term without defining it, describing the fauna from stratified cave deposits as an 'assemblage' in the first edition of his landmark book, *Pre-Historic Times* (Lubbock 1865: 305). Succeeding editions used the term 'assemblage' repeatedly for collections of artefacts from individual locations, particularly when his purpose was to compare a collection from one location with that from another (e.g. Lubbock 1865: 11, 107, 377). It appears that Lubbock was drawing on an existing, perhaps recently introduced, term linking geological and archaeological discourse. In 1863, a discussion of the interpretation of collections of stone tools found in geological sediments cited a presentation in 1860 in which Sir R. Murchison wrote that 'whilst the geological geographer who visits the banks of the Somme, and sees such an assemblage of relics beneath great accumulations formed by water . . . is compelled to infer, when such a phenomenon was brought about, the waters . . . had risen in great inundations . . . and swept over the slopes of the chalk in which the primeval inhabitants were fashioning their rude flint instruments' (Royal Anthropological Institute of Great Britain and Ireland 1863: 100). These examples strongly suggest that the term was borrowed from the, by then, widespread use in geological publications of the term 'assemblage' for the group of fossils distinctive of specific geological sediments (e.g. Lyell 1935: 5, 7).

The term 'assemblage' continued to be used as an undefined descriptive term referring to the artefacts collected from a uniform geological sediment in the decades that followed (e.g. Lamplugh 1906; Childe 1943), especially in contrast to other such collections (Moir 1917: 396). By the mid-1940s, the use of the term 'assemblage' in Americanist literature becomes connected to debates about cultural identities based on specific types of artefacts (Griffin 1945; Wedel 1945). But assemblage truly comes into its own as a theoretical concept in the 1950s, possibly as a result of the influence of Gordon Willey and Philip Phillips' book, *Method and Theory in American Archaeology* (1958) and the article that preceded it (Willey and Phillips 1953).

Proposing to place culture-historical archaeology on a solid methodological footing, these authors defined a series of specialized terms to be used by archaeologists. They were particularly concerned not to conflate the descriptive terms proper to living societies with those used for describing the materials recovered by archaeologists. Citing V. Gordon Childe's (1950: 2) definition of the 'archaeological culture' as 'an assemblage of artifacts that recur repeatedly associated together in dwellings of the same kind and with burials of the same rite . . . assumed to be the concrete expressions of the common social traditions that bind together a people', Willey and Phillips (1953: 617) argued that such an 'archaeological culture' was in fact an 'arbitrary division of the space-time-cultural continuum defined by reference to its imperishable content'. This 'imperishable content' of a particular place in the space–time continuum was the archaeological assemblage. Unlike earlier ways of organizing archaeologically recovered materials, in which contextual asso-ciation was not critical, an assemblage was defined by its recovery in context. Assemblages were central to debates in the 1950s about the reality of types (Spauld-ing 1953, 1954; Ford 1954). Artefact assemblages were, for Spaulding (1953: 305), the basic units of analysis and comparison, as they were for many of his contempor-aries. Willey and Phillips (1958: 22–24) saw assemblages, which they understood as the materials in use at one point in time at a particular place by a defined group of people, as the basis for defining site components, which singly or in groups made up their 'phases'. The component was thus for them the abstraction of the activities of people who shared culture at one point in time, represented by the stratigra-phically discrete deposited traces of those activities, or assemblages.

The model of archaeological site formation that went hand-in-hand with the culture-historical method and theory in which assemblages were specifically meaningful was for the most part only lightly changed from the basic geological model of the nineteenth century. Sites were understood to be composed of strata that were the products of occupations, but these occupations were not seen as continuously forming deposits. Rather, an emphasis on superposition and the identification of stratigraphic breaks provided the model of stacked strata that is still taught in most introductory archaeological classes and illustrated repeatedly in museums. Little or no explicit attention was paid to the question of the formation of discontinuities—breaks in deposition, episodes of erosion and the like were encompassed through concepts such as 'reversed stratigraphy' (Hawley 1937). Concepts such as reversed stratigraphy reinforce an overly simple model of depo-sitional history as normally a series of episodes of varying length that produce corresponding differentiated units of deposition (O'Brien and Lyman 1999: 140–147). This geological way of thinking about archaeological stratigraphy corre-sponded to the concept of archaeological cultures as relatively conservative and homogeneous units that changed only through radical breaks, marked by the sharp lines of the nominal stratigraphic profile. When models of past social life changed with the development of processual archaeology, so too did the understanding of deposition, stratigraphy, and the significance of assemblages of contextually associated things.

PROCESSUAL AND POST-PROCESSUAL APPROACHES
TO ASSEMBLAGES AND DEPOSITION

Lewis Binford's initial call to create a new anthropological archaeology included an explicit claim that 'the formal structure of artefact assemblages together with the between element contextual relationships should and do present a systematic and understandable picture of *the total extinct* cultural system' (Binford 1962: 219, original emphasis). Proposing how archaeological research design should change in order to address the systemic processes whose explanation was to be the goal of his new archaeology, Binford (1964: 425) reiterated a geologically based model of deposition that made assemblages natural units of analysis: 'the loss, breakage, and abandonment of implements and facilities at different locations, where groups of variable structure performed different tasks, leaves a "fossil" record of the actual operation of an extinct society'.

Michael Schiffer (1976) later used this passage as key evidence to critique Binford for accepting the so-called 'Pompeii Premise', the idea that archaeologists could recover a largely intact material record of human action. Yet in the same article, Binford recognized the complexity of the depositional histories that created sites, defining a distinction between 'primary' and 'secondary' depositional contexts:

Sites exhibiting primary depositional context have not been altered in their formal properties except through the natural processes of decay of organic material, or the physico-chemical alteration of features and items since the period of occupancy. Sites exhibiting secondary depositional context are those whose formal characteristics, defined in terms of soils, features, and items, have been spatially altered through physical movement or deletion from the loci.

Binford (1964: 431)

The recognition that transformations more continuously affected stratigraphy, rather than the sequence of superimposed deposits resulting from static phases, was a step toward recognizing the need to explore depositional histories. Schiffer (1972, 1987) pursued this goal most systematically, discriminating between the 'systemic context' in which artefacts participated in a living culture, and the 'archaeological context' that they entered after discard, and in which the archaeologist actually encountered them. Schiffer (1975, 1987) developed a taxonomy of 'n-transforms' and 'c-transforms' to describe the 'natural' and 'cultural' processes that in his view always transformed archaeological deposits. There is resonance here in British processual archaeology with D. L. Clarke's call for the development of explicit predepositional and depositional theory—'relating behavioural variability to variability in the record'—as the first subset of a general theory for archaeology (Clarke 1973: 16).

Yet, Schiffer's approach to deposition could still be seen as too closely tied to a notion of static stages in assemblage formation. Binford (1981) suggested that Schiffer's models represented an idealization of selected moments in a continual entropic process through which archaeological deposits were created. Rejecting Schiffer's accusation that he believed in the Pompeii Premise, he contrasted his understanding of deposition as 'slower than the rapid sequencing of events which characterizes the daily lives of living peoples', and stratigraphic deposits as at best 'a massive palimpsest of derivatives from many separate episodes' (Binford 1981: 197).

Processual archaeology productively drew our attention to understanding assemblage formation through deposition; as Schiffer put it, we need to 'view deposits themselves as peculiar artifacts, the characteristics of which must be studied in their own right' (Schiffer 1983: 697). However, these archaeologists ultimately developed what we now see as an untenable separation of human and 'natural' agencies of deposition, requiring archaeologists to adjudicate which depositional events were natural and which cultural. Such concerns lay behind experiments conducted in the United Kingdom during the 1960s to explore the mechanisms by which artefacts entered ditch fills (e.g. Jewell 1963). The underlying models of deposition relied on an assumption that assemblages are the 'fall out' of human action, side stepping questions of human intentions and meanings.

A different perspective on the question of depositional histories was provided by early post-processual work on Neolithic Britain, in which human agency, intentionality, and the symbolically active qualities of material culture were highlighted (Richards and Thomas 1984; Thomas and Whittle 1986; Thomas 1988). At a routine level, even the deposition or disposal of refuse could be seen to play out symbolic structures—ethnoarchaeological work highlighted how semantically different categories of material were treated through deposition in different ways (Hodder 1982a; Moore 1982). Other modes of deposition were seen to draw more actively upon the symbolic qualities and associations of material. Thus, in their study of Durrington Walls, Colin Richards and Julian Thomas (1984: 191) described the assemblages deposited as structured by 'highly formalised, repetitive behaviour' (Figure 12.2), key features for the archaeological identification of ritual (Joyce 2001). These early post-processual studies were heavily influenced by structuralist anthropology, inasmuch as they took as axiomatic an understanding that deposition was structured by and served to reproduce underlying rules or grammars of cultural order.

The idea that some deposits might be highly structured due to the deliberate symbolically charged actions that constituted ritual was actually already accepted in earlier archaeological discussions, even constituting one of the acknowledged cultural depositional processes of behavioural archaeology (Schiffer 1985: 29). But ritual depositional processes were not given substantial attention until after the rise of post-processual archaeology (Walker 1995a, 2002; LaMotta and Schiffer 1999). The recognition that ritual could produce enduring structured deposits automatically required consideration of the intentionality of past human action, not merely the symbolic potential of deposits. In Americanist archaeology, this thread was pursued mostly independently by scholars studying the archaeology of the US Southwestern Pueblos and those working on the city-states of the Classic Maya (Walker and Lucero 2000); while in the United Kingdom the concept was actively explored by prehistorians working on the Neolithic and Iron Age (Richards and

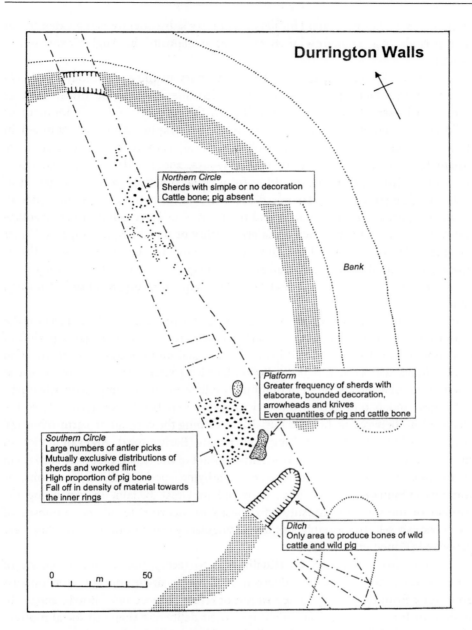

Durrington Walls

Northern Circle
Sherds with simple or no decoration
Cattle bone; pig absent

Bank

Platform
Greater frequency of sherds with
elaborate, bounded decoration,
arrowheads and knives
Even quantities of pig and cattle bone

Southern Circle
Large numbers of antler picks
Mutually exclusive distributions of
sherds and worked flint
High proportion of pig bone
Fall off in density of material towards
the inner rings

Ditch
Only area to produce bones of wild
cattle and wild pig

0   50
ㅣ___ㅣ___ㅣ___ㅣ___ㅣ___ㅣ
       m

Fig. 12.2 Structured deposition in the late Neolithic (*c*.2500 BC) henge enclosure of Durrington Walls, Wiltshire, England. The scheme of depositional patterning identified by Colin Richards and Julian Thomas (based on Richards and Thomas 1984).

Thomas 1984; Thomas 1991a; Hill 1995), its utility subsequently being extended to later periods (e.g. Hamerow 2006 on 'special deposits' in Anglo-Saxon settlements).

William Walker (2002) documented a trajectory in the archaeology of the US Southwest in which specific stratigraphic deposits came to be understood as evidence of past ritual practices, specifically, the burning and abandonment of buildings. He emphasized that 'when these stratigraphic data are examined in detail, they often contain evidence of "impractical" activity that defies pragmatic explanations' (Walker 2002: 160). Walker (1995a, 2002) addressed the particular role of the disposal of refuse resulting from ritual practices in the production of archaeological stratigraphy. He posed the question, 'why not . . . recognize that all behaviors, particularly ritual ones, and the traces they leave behind in archaeological strata are an already ordered material reality of social relationships?' (Walker 2002: 162). Drawing explicitly on British archaeology rooted in the existing literature on structured deposition, Walker (2002: 164) proposed analysis of the differences in strata as evidence of what he called 'sequential organization' of human behaviour.

In the 1980s, with the description of deposits of deliberately broken objects as the residues from termination rituals (Garber 1983), archaeologists began a period of re-examination of the relationships between ritual and depositional practices in Classic Maya sites (Mock 1998). Scholars had long referenced deliberately placed assemblages of artefacts, often in buildings understood to be temples or ballcourts, as 'caches', understood to be dedicatory offerings. Marshall Becker reconsidered the relationships between caches and burials, developing the concept of 'earth-offerings' as a depositional category resulting from rituals (Becker 1993). Re-examination of such deposits emphasized the performative nature of the rituals that produced them (Joyce 1992; Fox 1996). The shift from identifying special facilities, locations, or contents culminated in this area, as it did in Great Britain, in expanding the concept of meaningfully constituted deposits to incorporate others composed of less obviously selective assemblages whose singularity came from the ways they were deposited (Kunen et al. 2002).

The shift from emphasis on ritualization to recognition of intentionality of action as the basis of structured deposition allowed a single concept to encompass everything from the patterned deposition of refuse (Moore 1982; Boivin 2004a) to stylized or formal actions that might owe their deliberate shape to social motivations as compelling as ritual, but distinct from it. Thus depositional structure has more recently been approached from the perspective of material engagements with aesthetic properties (Pollard 2001), as a means of creating social relations (Chapman 2000a), or more generally as evidence of what Brück (2006a: 298) calls 'event-marking'.

The widespread recognition of 'structured deposition'—past action that engaged in a meaningful way with materials leaving what we see today as traces of structure in archaeological deposits—has had a profound effect on methodologies of archaeological excavation, recording, and analysis. While offering a critique of what they see as too much emphasis on intentionality in discussions of structured deposition, Brudenell and Cooper (2008: 31–32) nonetheless accept a framework of analysis that treats deposits as evidence of sequences of events through which human actors positioned materials in relation to each other 'not assuming from the beginning that it was compiled or deposited with any clear purpose' (2008: 31). A reconsideration of the explanation of Neolithic British pit clusters as evidence of structured deposition concludes that the features in question were generated through everyday occupation, but describes these acts of dwelling as deliberate and 'purposeful' (Harding 2006). These shifts from the geological model of stratigraphic accumulation representing an uninterpretable coincidence of materials removed from cultural systems over vast periods of time, to the assumption that deposits can be understood in terms of the temporalities of human lives, are irreversible changes in archaeological perspectives. Contemporary scholarship requires us to set aside artificial distinctions between intentional and unintentional, deliberate and accidental, symbolic and quotidian action, and understand deposition as always the product of practices by differentially knowledgeable actors whose work assembling sediments and worked and unworked things created the contextually associated assemblages we interpret (Joyce 2008a). In part, influence has derived from actor-network theory (Law and Hassard 1999; Latour 2005a) and recent cross-disciplinary studies of materiality (e.g. Miller 2005c; Henare et al. 2007b). These have stressed the imbricated and indissolvable relationship between people and things—how each serves to constitute the other—and the multi-agental nature of networks of practice and effect. Such approaches do not seek to privilege the social (as defined in anthropocentric terms) over the material. Here, there is room to consider 'material effects' as well as conventionally defined social strategies in the study of deposition.

The point can be illustrated by the practice of middening—a midden is defined here as a locus for the deliberate and sequential deposition of refuse (Needham and Spence 1997). A common feature of sedentary and semi-sedentary settlements from later prehistory onwards, middens are the outcomes of numerous depositional actions, many repetitive and largely unconsidered, others more self-conscious and structured (Figure 12.3). Engaging with issues of materiality, practice and temporality, and collapsing distinctions between the symbolic and quotidian and intentional and unintentional, allows us to understand these features (which are both deposit and assemblage) as more than refuse accumulations. While the product of largely prosaic acts of slow accumulation, knowledge of their formation and constitution sometimes transformed the currency of middens, such that they became an index of social and subsistence success, territorial dominance (Needham and Spence 1997: 84–85), and/or of occupational longevity and intergenerational connection—time and group genealogy are worked into the fabric of these structures as much as the

Fig. 12.3 Midden deposits (showing as dark soil) around late Neolithic houses at Durrington Walls, Wiltshire, England (photo: Mike Parker Pearson).

materials from which they are composed. Middens can become definable landmarks, even forms of monumental expression in the case of the massive late Bronze Age–early Iron Age 'black earth' sites of southern central England (McOmish 1996). Neolithic middens near Avebury, Wiltshire, were even incorporated into monumental architecture (Pollard 2005). Thus, the material qualities of middens and the networks of practices and temporalities embroiled in their creation are seen to 'act back' and restructure the possibilities for future social action in a way not envisaged at the outset of their formation.

CONTEMPORARY APPROACHES TO PRACTICES OF DEPOSITION

In the original formulations of structured deposition, the identification of intentional patterns of the placement of materials that might otherwise have been taken simply as accidental refuse was relatively secure because the assemblages came from contexts recognized as likely sites of ritualized action (Richards and Thomas 1984; Thomas and Whittle 1986; Thomas 1988). In the succeeding years, the recognition of structured deposition has expanded greatly. With the broadening from a focus on structure and symbolism, and the idea of deliberate deposits as 'representations' of various kinds, or as the residue of 'ritual action', our analyses now include consideration of the sensuousness of things, phenomenological aspects of the experience of materials, and their agential qualities, as well as broader ways of thinking of signification itself (Pollard 2001; Joyce 2008a). Contemporary scholarship on depositional practices does not just encompass the treatment of those things conventionally defined as material culture; sediments themselves can comprise created deposits of considerable significance (Pauketat and Alt 2003, 2005; Boivin 2004a). Ongoing investigations of Stonehenge and its landscape show how even where the concept of ritualization evident in structured deposits is useful, intentional human action can also be conceptualized in such taken-for-granted aspects of site formation as 'the leaving of posts to decay . . . a process of rotting whose culmination was marked by the digging of a pit to deposit offerings as a "closing" ritual' (Parker Pearson *et al.* 2006: 242). Even structured deposits that closely conform to the original definition of these as assemblages resulting from ritual practice profit from the broader perspectives brought about with a shift from analyses of ritualized or structured deposition to depositional practices.

Depositional practices: the archaeology of Mantecales, Honduras

Archaeological excavations in a number of sites in the lower Ulua River Valley have encountered structured deposits so dramatic that the intentionalities involved cannot be ignored. Rather than simply being encoded in a ritual system, the repetition of episodes of burning incense and deposition of ceramic incense-burning vessels at one of these sites, Mantecales, can be viewed as the product of complex memory work in which humans and non-humans were mutually active. Understanding of this complex deposit illuminates other deposits, burials, caches, and architectural fills, as equally part of memory work, evidence of the historicizing of practice in place.

The Mantecales site, CR-71, is located in northern Honduras, along a tributary of the Ulúa river, the Quebrada Mantecales. This stream today runs in an abandoned course of the ancient Ulúa river that was active during the Late Classic period (*c.* AD 500–800). At that time, along the entire course of this stream, a dense pattern of settlement developed. Most of these settlements were house sites, in which wattle and daub buildings were demolished and reconstructed for generations. These processes of building and rebuilding took place in conjunction with interments and other structured deposition, often associated with the start of rebuilding of houses.

The repeated rebuilding of house sites in place gradually created raised earthen platforms, which were relatively low but quite extensive. Four of these large low platforms were mapped as part of the Mantecales site. As in other such sites, bordering each platform were depressions, likely borrow pits from which sediments were taken to construct the features.

On two of the platforms, the remains of two to three small structures with stone features could be identified on the surface. Investigations begun in 1995 by the Honduran Institute of Anthropology and History recovered an assemblage consistent with the occupation of a small perishable house, including domestic pottery, grinding stones, and chipped stone tools, as well as impressions of the pole structure preserved in its clay covering, on one of the platforms.

A second platform, lacking any visible surface architecture, measuring 40 m by 60 m, was located west of the first platform tested. Excavation of what became a 36-m long north–south trench was carried out by the Honduran archaeological team, which also conducted excavations every 3 m along a perpendicular east–west transect 36 m long. Near the centre of the platform, in an area approximately 14 m by 6 m, these archaeologists encountered remains of clay surfaces, circular patches of carbon and ash, and great quantities of broken ceramics, including complete figural whistles and figurines. Close to the centre of this area, the team recovered a fragment of an unusual green marble vessel. Throughout these excavations, the team encountered ashy deposits, figural artefacts, and broken pottery, along with occasional unusual objects, such as small quartz stones contained in a jar, polished celts, and chipped obsidian bifaces. But while they were able to identify traces of clay surfaces, this platform otherwise lacked the evidence of superstructures found elsewhere, and lacked features that would attest to residential use. Instead, the deposits were composed of surfaces with circles of ash, in some places thicker lenses of ash, alternating with clay, with several dense piles of broken pottery, and in one place, a particular focus of deposition in the form of the cist, green marble vase, and a dense sherd mantle covering this feature.

Later in 1995, a team from Cornell University and Berkeley continued excavation of this central focal deposit (Figure 12.4). These excavations eventually extended to a depth of 1.65 m. The team relocated the stone cist, which formed three sides of a rectangular chamber, open to the north. Here a dense deposit, 90 cm deep, consisted of lenses of burned materials (clay, ash, and carbon) alternating with large portions of unusual pottery vessels. The pottery vessels included polychrome painted serving vessels, red-painted and incised jars, and unslipped jars with handles, forms most likely used to contain and transport liquids. Also present were a number of more specialized vessel forms identified as containers for the burning of local resins. In all, part of at least half a dozen large vessels with modelled decoration, lids placed over burning resin, including two effigies of felines and one standing human figure, were recovered. A minimum of 10 vessels with tubular handles attached to pierced

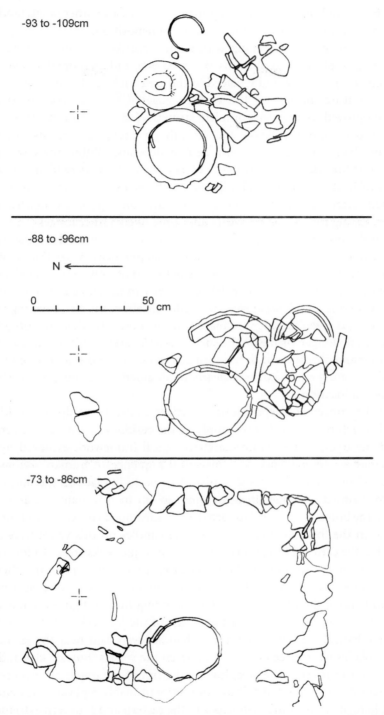

Fig. 12.4 Repetitive deposits of jar necks, sherds, and other materials at Mantecales, Honduras.

shallow bowls for burning resin, and portions of at least 10 other bowls used for this purpose were also included in this sequence of deposition.

All these broken vessels, along with some miscellaneous unusual items (jade beads, obsidian blades, and portions of at least one, and no more than two, mould-made figurines), were carefully placed in the area enclosed by the stone cist. They flanked a feature located on the western edge of the cist, composed of what eventually proved to be seven complete jar necks (28–42 cm in diameter), stacked one on top of another. Below the seventh jar neck, excavations documented alternating layers of clay and dense carbon deposits. Within the cist, two clear stratigraphic breaks, marked by lenses of ash and carbon, were identified between deposits of broken pottery laid adjacent to the stack of jar necks. Based on the associated ceramics, these features were the location of repeated incense-burning episodes, lasting for at least 100 years and quite likely rather longer.

Late in the history of this platform, a major change was made to the use of the area, resulting in marked changes in depositional practices. A clay floor covered the cist, and there is evidence of a clay structure that was constructed and later demolished. About 150 years after the last activity in the stone cist, a dense deposit of pottery serving vessels was placed immediately above the cist, covering the lower half of a carved green marble vase placed almost precisely where the original stack of jar necks, no longer visible on the surface, was located. While the latest use of the place was markedly different in terms of activities (with no evidence of burning of resin), the existing ritual axis was clearly maintained by the people for whom this was a special location.

What the concept of depositional practices allows us to do is consider these unusual structured deposits not simply as the residues of rituals, the ceremonial trash of the updated behavioural archaeological framework explored by Walker (1995a), but as the evidence of a historical sequence of human actions. About AD 600, a visitor to Mantecales set a pair of jar necks in place on the summit of the platform. Painted with red linear designs, 40 cm in rim diameter, and standing 8 cm tall, the bottom jar neck supported a tall, unslipped jar neck with four handles modelled in the form of small animals. The handles on this vessel were carefully oriented to the cardinal directions. Together, these jar necks created a focal axis and a container for the carbon produced when visitors burned resin in other vessels that were then broken and left at the place. Two censer lids, one with modelled spikes and crests, the other supporting a standing human figure holding a bag of resin, were placed north-east and south-east of the jar necks. Broken pieces of at least three hand-held censers with long handles were laid near the jar neck, and obsidian blades were placed carefully between the vessels. Burned clay and carbon was spread over most of the area, leaving the rim of the upper pot exposed.

The actions carried out at this location were probably replicated at many places on the platform at this time. Ash lenses in the eastern and southern extremes of the excavated areas suggest the same ritual actions, but in these other locations, there is no trace of the placement of orienting features like the stacked jar necks. While ash lenses continue to be deposited in these other areas of the platform, they are uncoordinated, and give no hint of the enduring connections between humans over generations that were being produced by the materials used, placed, and remembered at the stacked jar rims. The two stacked jar necks persisted in place, and when later people arrived intent on burning resin, the stacked jar necks oriented them to where to stand to carry out this action. The stack grew with the addition of a new pair of red-painted jar necks. A censer lid with a modelled feline was placed directly to the east of these stacked jar necks, and half a dozen handled censers were used and left to accompany the accumulating body of such vessels, also augmented by portions of at least four other censer lids. While free-form burning continued south and west on the platform, the stacked jar necks and the censers with which they were now connected remained as the core of the place, attracting new visitation.

The painted and incised designs on the red-painted jars, and the polychrome painted designs on plates and cylinders left next to them, show that the repetition of practice persisted over the ensuing generation. While fashions in pottery deco-ration changed, the stacked jar necks remained and structured the repetition of incense burning rituals. The stack grew with the addition of two more jar necks, one from an unslipped jar supporting another red-painted jar neck. Despite the intervening period, and the absence from the immediately visible, most recent, jar stack of the unslipped type, this couple reiterates the original pair of jar necks that established the stack. South-west of these stacked jar necks, another feline censer lid was placed, echoing the preceding deposit.

Up until this point the stacked jar necks alone had provided the central axis to orient the actions of the humans that visited. As part of the third generation of the life of the jar neck stack, selected stones were placed forming an enclosure with the jar necks near the south-west corner, and an opening facing north-east. Sometime after AD 650, a final jar neck was added to the stack. This seventh jar neck, like the second, was from an unslipped jar with four handles. As recovered, these were slightly off cardinal orientation, conforming instead to the axis estab-lished by the U-shaped cist.

The new, expanded focus of ritual action represented by the rectilinear chamber enclosing the stacked jar necks and used censers extended the space occupied by rituals involving burning east, south, and north. Where previously the ashes left behind by such actions had been scattered across the platform, now they were oriented by and to the stacked jar rims. In turn, this focus of action primed the repetition of a sequence of action—burning resin, dumping the residues into the stack, sometimes with jade beads or other small items, and breaking the censers and placing them next to the stack.

Covered over with a clay cap, the stacked jar necks and the censers they drew to them were apparently cut off from active interaction with the new generations of people who followed as occupants and users of the site. Yet, the history of the stacked jar necks was powerful enough that a century later, another group of people was able to precisely place over it a new deposit. The core item in this deposit, the base of a green marble cylindrical vase, at first seems unrelated to the materials that made up the biography of the stack. But like them, it established a vertical axis rooted in the local earth. Spread over this broken vessel, covering it completely, were tens of thousands of sherds from serving dishes. A new network spread out from the place made by the stack, through the participation of the people whose shared meal at this place closed one stage in the network while initiating the next.

Once the first stacked rims were in place, they 'caused' human actors to rebuild the space in ways that preserved the ability of the stacked rims to engage in incense burning rituals with successive generations of humans. What we are seeing in the structured deposition is evidence of the production over time, through the entanglement of people with these things, of a form of depositional practice that was significant, probably meaningful, to those people who repeatedly engaged with the stacked jar rims. In a reflexive reference to incense burning actions by humans, the earliest figural imagery at Mantecales included a censer lid supporting a human being holding a bag of the kind that contained the resins burnt in such vessels. The depositional practices here also connected humans that participated in these rituals with non-human animals. The following episode of growth of the stacked jar necks was accompanied by the deposit of a feline image, likely a jaguar or similar smaller wild cat. Another feline censer lid accompanied the next episode of remodelling.

Even though it is a decisive end to the kind of action previously centred on the jar neck stack, the pavement with smashed pottery covering the green marble vase fragment is still structured by the stack. It is through the use of new materiality that the effects of the orienting stack is changed: from a point-centred series of rituals involving censers and, given the size of the space, a small number of humans, to a horizontal space that perhaps may be the residue of a meal shared among a wider array of humans connected to this multigenerational place of memory.

DISCUSSION

Our emphasis has shifted from specific bounded 'structured deposits' to broader structuring of deposition through which sites as wholes came into being. Pollard and Ruggles (2001: 80) draw our attention to a number of specific features indicative of the structuring of depositional practices at Stonehenge that provide one framework for consideration. They identify repeated emphasis on particular locations, sidedness, concentric spatial divisions, and relationships to external referents as structured by a cosmology that they can perceive through the structuring of the site as a whole. Similarly, research on Cahokia employs concepts of depositional practices to understand everything from the recapitulated creation of postholes to the selection or even production of sediments from which mounds were constructed, in addition to more obvious structured deposits like a cache of axe heads (Pauketat and Alt 2003, 2004, 2005). In discussing the construction of early Neolithic long mounds, Lesley McFadyen (2007a) has sought to collapse the distinction between those materials regarded as deposits (e.g. antler, animal bones, and pottery) and those conventionally labelled as building materials (e.g. soil, chalk, wood, and stone). She highlights how all these substances were implicated in the practice of making architecture, a practice that involved the complex assemblage of things, and that allowed the generation of new material networks fundamental in people's ability to proceed within the world.

Spatial patterning of depositional practices is increasingly understood as evidence of broader structuring principles of spatial organization, including cosmology (Pollard and Ruggles 2001; Boivin 2004a), rather than strictly as evidence of ritual practice. The depositional practices oriented by cosmology can be understood as forms of place-making in which specific materials (some with clear symbolic referents and all probably meaningful) are placed in relation to the expected or intended actions of people (Joyce 1992, 2004, 2007; Pollard and Ruggles 2001; Pauketat et al. 2002; Pauketat and Alt 2003; Boivin 2004a; Woodward and Woodward 2004; Parker Pearson et al. 2006).

Rather than seeking simply to identify structured deposits, contemporary archaeologists are concerned with the processes involved. Fragmentation and accumulation generate the deposits and assemblages we explore today. Rather than simply being matters of association, the production of assemblages makes use of relations such as juxtaposition of materials as an index of other places. While archaeologists encounter structured deposits in an ordered array, our analyses increasingly centre on the actions of display and social performances through which past actors experienced these acts of assemblage, and the participation and employment of deposits in memory work (Jones 2007; Mills and Walker 2008b).

PART III

OBJECTS AND HUMANS

CHAPTER 13

....

TECHNOLOGY AND MATERIAL LIFE

....

KACY L. HOLLENBACK
MICHAEL BRIAN SCHIFFER

INTRODUCTION

....

Humans live in a world of things. From hairpins to computers and cars, we surround ourselves with artefacts. What distinguishes humans from other animals is not that we make and use tools. Rather, it is our total reliance on these objects (Schiffer and Miller 1999), for our lives are shaped by, and in return shape, technologies (Bijker 1995; Chilton 1999). This 'social shaping of technology and the technical shaping of society' (Bijker 1995: 3) has been an increasing focus of research in many disciplines in the past two decades. In archaeology, however, the study of things has been at the heart of the discipline since its inception in the late nineteenth century.

We are grateful to the late Stanley Ahler, Elgin Crowsbreast, Calvin Grinnell, Richard Krause, Paul Picha, and Fern Swenson for their guidance and insights on Mandan–Hidatsa archaeology. Furthermore, we also thank Dana Drake Rosenstein, Brandon Gabler, Robert Jones, David Killick, Katie MacFarland, Elizabeth May, Brian McKee, Caitlin O'Grady, Victoria Phaneuf, William Reitze, and María Nieves Zedeño for reading drafts of this chapter, offering comments, and being generally supportive. Lastly, we would like to acknowledge Christoper I. Roos and Annette Schiffer for always going above and beyond in their support.

The focus of this chapter is on the 'material life' of human beings, and the place of technology within it. We approach this topic from the discipline of archaeology, specifically behavioural archaeology (see Schiffer 2008a), but also draw on research in other fields. Behavioural archaeology strives to understand people–technology interactions at every scale, from individuals to nation states. One of its most important conceptual tools is the life history framework, which aids in structuring research questions and in developing methods for studying material culture. In this chapter, we expand this framework to include the life histories of technologies and associated material practices (but more on this below).

The past 30 years have witnessed debate over what technology is, what role it plays in cultural change, and how technology should be studied. At the outset, we must consider definitions of the terms 'technology' and 'material life'. *Technology* has been an integral part of human life for millennia. It can be defined as the things that humans create. This definition encompasses varied phenomena, from individual artefacts to complex technological systems, but has limitations. An alternative definition, which recognizes three dimensions of 'technology', has been proposed by sociologists (MacKenzie and Wajcman 1985: 3–4; Bijker *et al.* 1987: 4) and archaeologists (Schiffer and Skibo 1987: 595). In this formulation, technology comprises: (1) physical objects or artefacts; (2) activities or processes; and (3) what people know as well as what they can do. By recognizing technology as artefact, technology as practice or process, and technology as knowledge, we gain greater insight into the diversity of technology studies. Material culture studies in archaeology and socio-cultural anthropology tend to focus on only one or two of these dimensions. Different definitions of technology may be appropriate for different research projects. However, using a term with many meanings can lead to confusion and unnecessary debate if researchers do not appreciate that studies of technology can have different foci and goals, depending on the dimension stressed (Killick 2004; Kuhn 2004; Schiffer 2004).

In our view, the concept of *material life* is redundant since it is impossible to imagine a human life that is immaterial. Human interactions, human belief systems, and human cultures require intimate ties to things. Culture is not something that is possessed; rather it is participated in and continuously created (Christensen 1995; Chilton 1999: 1) Artefacts are not just tools for survival; rather, artefact manufacture, use, discard, and reuse are 'constitutive processes' that make culture (Chilton 1999: 1). Socio-cultural anthropologist Merete Christensen (1995), for example, argues that potters' and other artisans' creative reshaping of their physical surroundings through the production and use of material culture is an essential activity in traditional societies. The same processes occur in modern societies, as people structure and arrange their homes and workspaces, filled with the artefacts of everyday activities. Such activities provide contexts for social interaction, the development and transfer of knowledge, as well as produce goods needed for both physical and cultural survival. What makes human life a material life is our total reliance on artefacts.

In this chapter, we contextualize contemporary technology studies, primarily in archaeology, and consider how theoretical concepts from behavioural archaeology and social constructivist studies of technology might be combined. To illustrate the utility of this combined approach we provide two case studies. The first examines the electric car in the United States during the early twentieth century; the second explores the role of ceramic technology in Mandan–Hidatsa society (in present-day North Dakota) before and after smallpox epidemics in the eighteenth and nineteenth centuries.

ARCHAEOLOGICAL STUDIES OF TECHNOLOGY

Multiple theoretical approaches to the study of technology have developed during the past century. In the field of archaeology, the myriad theoretical approaches have different origins, development, and foci (e.g. Killick 2004; Kuhn 2004; Schiffer 2004).

In the late nineteenth century, material culture studies played a central role in anthropology (Conkey 1989: 14). At the time, the discipline was based mainly in museums. The divisions between ethnology and archaeology were not sharp, and there was overlap between the subfields. Scholars in British and American museums, such as the Smithsonian Institution, worked freely across disciplinary boundaries, as they were later developed, by collecting materials and recording production processes from both contemporary and past societies. In the United States, one of the first syntheses of these materials, *The Origins of Invention: a study of industry among primitive peoples*, was written by ethnologist and Smithsonian curator Otis T. Mason (1895). Most nineteenth-century Smithsonian scholars studied both archaeological and ethnographic material culture (Cushing 1886; Fewkes 1891, 1892, 1985 [1903]). Scholars such as John Wesley Powell, the first director of the Bureau of American Ethnology (BAE), collected artefacts copiously, especially among the pueblos of the south-western United States (Powell 1895; Fowler and Fowler 1971). Although many of these early collections obtained for exhibitions or as salvage ethnography were little studied, later researchers and contemporary scholars make extensive use of these unique resources. In England and in continental Europe, early ethnographers were engaged in similar collecting and reporting activities (see Lucas this volume, Chapter 9).

In the early twentieth century, the strength of anthropology rested in its focus on material culture, social organization, and physical anthropology (Pfaffenberger

1992: 491). Indeed, part of the legacy of anthropologist Franz Boas (1858–1942) in North America was to institutionalize a holistic approach to the study of human-kind, built around the concept of culture, which included material culture (Trigger 1989; Willey and Sabloff 1993). Some of the discipline's most prominent Boasians, many of them—like Boas himself—long based in museums, published mono-graphs during the intensive era of 'salvage' ethnography in the first decades of the twentieth century (Wissler 1910; Lowie 1922; Linton 1923; Boas 1927; Gold-enweiser 1931). Ethnographers at this time not only studied living groups, but also documented the suites of technology that these peoples made and used. At the time, archaeologists made strong contributions to anthropology by recording and describing material remains from past human societies, which furnished direct evidence on ancient technologies (Thompson and Parezo 1989). Early efforts in archaeology and cultural anthropology yielded detailed descriptions of artefacts and the techniques employed to create them. The goal of these studies was to identify, characterize, and classify 'cultures'. These endeavours, however, were mainly descriptive.

In the 1940s and 1950s a rift began to form between the subdisciplines in North American anthropology, and included debates over the importance of material culture in human life (Bidney 1944; Hutton 1944). At the core of the debate was disagreement over what 'culture' is, and whether or not technology is a part of culture (Amsbury and Ehrich 1964). Leslie White (1949: 16), for example, included technology in culture as an 'extrasomatic' or 'supra-biological' adaptation. Most socio-cultural anthropologists, however, came to see culture as 'superorganic'. In Kroeber's use of the term, culture is composed of ideas, beliefs, and customs (Kroeber 1917; see also Bidney 1944). Not surprisingly, archaeologists saw material culture as an integral part of culture and what it is to be human (Watson 1995). Unfortunately, the former position, which served to deny the materiality of human life, became dominant in socio-cultural anthropology during the twentieth century, which marginalized studies of material culture and technology. In archaeology, studies of material culture were about to take some interesting turns.

It has been argued that the birth of 'processual' archaeology, also known as 'New Archaeology', in the 1960s further marginalized the study of material culture (Conkey 1989: 17; Stark 1998a: 3–4). New archaeologists saw archaeology as eth-nography of the past (Binford 1962; Longacre 1964; Watson 2007). Employing a systems perspective, which treated society as a set of interdependent subsystems linked by flows of matter, energy, and information, processual archaeologists assumed that 'patterns in . . . archaeological data are coded information about variability in past cultural systems' (Conkey 1989: 17; see Binford 1965; Clarke 1968). Thus, artefacts were studied for what they could tell us about activities and organizations of past cultural systems. The goal of archaeology and anthro-pology was to infer social phenomena, not to understand the complex relation-ships between humans and material culture.

In the 1970s, there was growing dissatisfaction with some of the basic tenets of the New Archaeology, which led to a proliferation of alternative theoretical and methodological approaches. These included behavioural archaeology (Reid *et al.* 1975; Schiffer 1976), neo-Darwinian or evolutionary archaeology (Dunnell 1978, 1980, 1982), and post-processual archaeology (Leone 1977; Hodder 1982c, 1984, 1985; Shanks and Tilley 1987b; Preucel 2006: 122–146), all of which prioritized the study of material culture. These theoretical trends were paralleled by the growing interest in long-term ethnoarchaeology (Longacre and Skibo 1994; David and Kramer 2001) and in experimental archaeology (Schiffer *et al.* 1994b)—research strategies that also emphasized the study of technology.

The 1970s also witnessed the development of science–technology–society studies (STS), which sought new social–scientific approaches to exploring issues and problems relating to modern technology (Bijker 1995: 4–11). Emerging especially from the sociology of science and the history of technology, this approach seeks to understand the relationships between technology and society and to engage issues of socio-technical change (Bijker 1995: 6). STS was highly influential in advocating 'constructivist studies of technology', which originally combined historical and sociological perspectives (Latour and Woolgar 1979; Bijker 1995: 6–7). Today the social construction of technology (SCOT) approach is applied in a number of disciplines, including archaeology (e.g. Killick 2004).

In the late 1970s and 1980s, the rift between archaeology and socio-cultural anthropology began to mend, when a modest interest in material culture reappeared in the latter (Spier 1970; Oswalt 1976; Stott and Reynolds 1987; Conkey 1989; Pfaffenberger 1992). Unlike the detailed descriptions of the early twentieth century, this new research engaged technology as a subject worthy of study in its own right. Two books are often taken to mark this re-emergence: *The World of Goods* (Douglas and Isherwood 1979) and *The Social Life of Things* (Appadurai 1986a). This trend continues today with publications such as the *Journal of Material Culture*.

One reason for the renewed interest in material culture studies was participation in socio-cultural anthropology by archaeologists. Daniel Miller, who trained as an archaeologist at Cambridge under Raymond Allchin, is the most prolific and influential socio-cultural anthropologist studying material culture today. His focus on the material world seems to have come about after his ethnoarchaeological fieldwork in India (Miller 1985). During the late 1980s and 1990s, Miller (1987, 1994, 1998c, 2001b, 2001d) developed ethnographic and theoretical studies of material culture that were focused on consumption processes—how material culture is acquired and used—in the modern world. This work built upon Miller's early training in archaeology, where consumption, along with production, is one of the technological processes that stands out most clearly in the archaeological record. In the United States, some archaeologists were drawn to the study of material culture in socio-cultural anthropology as well. For example, Richard Wilk was trained in Mayan archaeology, behavioural archaeology, and cultural ecology at the University of Arizona in the late 1970s and early 1980s. He has investigated both production and consumption, at various organizational scales, in the field of economic anthropology (Wilk 1989, 2006). In any event, by the late 1980s, studies of technology had achieved legitimacy in both archaeology and cultural anthropology.

At present, the diversity of technology studies in archaeology and anthropology is dizzying (Schiffer 1992, 2001a, 2004; Lemonnier 1993; Lubar and Kingery 1993; Schiffer and Miller 1999; Killick 2004; S. Kuhn 2004; H. M-L. Miller 2007). Each field generates its own methods and theoretical approaches for addressing the dynamic relationships between human society and technology. We believe that archaeology contributes unique elements to this discourse because of the long history of the discipline's engagement with the subject matter and its diachronic perspective. In the rest of this chapter, we discuss perspectives from behavioural archaeology on the study of technology in the hopes of building interdisciplinary bridges and provoking new dialogues.

BEHAVIOURAL ARCHAEOLOGY AND THE STUDY OF TECHNOLOGY

Behavioural archaeology draws together archaeology, material culture studies, and ethnology (Reid *et al.* 1975; Schiffer 1976, 1995a: 1–24). Unlike previous conceptions of archaeology, behavioural archaeology seeks to redefine the discipline as the study of the relationships between human behaviour and material culture (Reid *et al.* 1975; Schiffer 1976: 4; McGuire 1995: 165). In this view, human behaviour can be usefully understood as people–artefact interactions (Walker *et al.* 1995; Schiffer and Miller 1999). Thus, unlike the archaeology of preceding decades, behavioural archaeology privileged material things, such as technology, in the study of human behaviour (Schiffer and Miller 1999).

Behavioural archaeologists investigate interactions between people and artefacts in all times, in all places, and at all scales (Rathje and Schiffer 1982; LaMotta and Schiffer 2001), highlighting the interrelationships between technology and society. While technology is socially constructed, material culture is understood as the medium through which humans interact with and view the world around them. Humans create and shape artefacts, engage with objects, and in turn are shaped by these interactions. This notion is very similar to the contemporary concept of 'materiality' (DeMarrais *et al.* 2004; Meskell 2005b; Miller 2005a).

In the past, practitioners of behavioural archaeology have been criticized for adopting overly utilitarian, capitalist, or Western interpretations of society. Nicholas David and Carol Kramer (2001: 141) have written that aspects of the behavioural framework have set 'forth an unrealistic and ethnocentric image of artisan as engineer-handyman', and Oliver Gosselain (1998: 81) has suggested that behavioural archaeology tends to ignore the cultural dimensions of technological behaviour and to rely on unicausal explanations of technological change. Meanwhile, Randall McGuire (1995: 162) has asserted that behavioural archaeology has created a false opposition between cognitive and materialist views of human society, which has resulted in a failure to explore the dialectical relationship between 'consciousness' or systems of meaning and the material conditions of life (McGuire 1995: 167).

In some instances, these criticisms ring true. A heavy reliance on experimental archaeology and case studies drawn from the past 300 years of Western society has resulted in publications that may seem overly utilitarian or Western. However, behavioural archaeology is not by necessity restricted to such studies, for the framework can investigate systems of meaning as they relate to material culture as well as provide tools useful for studying technology in any society. In the remainder of this chapter we offer insights into a few tools from the 'kit' of behavioural archaeology that we believe may be generally useful for studies of material culture.

In recent years, behavioural archaeologists have demonstrated the analytical utility of the life history framework as well as a focus on people–artefact interactions in activities. From studies of the material dimensions of landscapes (Whittlesey 1998, 2003; Zedeño 1997, 2000; Carroll et al. 2004; Heilen 2005) to explorations of the complex roles of technology in ritual practice (Seymour and Schiffer 1987; Walker 1995a, 1995b, 1998; Walker et al. 2000), behavioural archaeology has offered a framework for studying mechanical, political, social, and ritual meanings, and roles of artefacts. For example, recent research in behavioural archaeology has attended to the ways in which social power is mediated through material culture (Schiffer 2005b; Walker and Schiffer 2006), and examined material choice and technological change in culture contact situations (Griffitts 2006; Margaris 2006).

There is a growing body of literature containing behavioural 'tools'—generalizations and heuristics—for studying technology (Schiffer and Skibo 1987, 1997; LaMotta and Schiffer 2001; Schiffer 2001b, 2002, 2005a, 2008a, 2008b, 2008c; Schiffer et al. 2001; Skibo and Schiffer 2008). These varied tools can be used to study invention and adoption processes, as well as technological change and transfer. Here we concentrate on three concepts: performance characteristics, the life history approach, and behavioural chains.

Performance characteristics

Performance characteristics are the specific behavioural capabilities of objects that come into play in particular interactions and activities (Schiffer and Skibo 1997; Schiffer and Miller 1999: 16–20; Schiffer 2005b: 287). The term, performance characteristic, was originally introduced to archaeology by D. Braun (1983), who used it synonymously with the material properties of artefacts. For behavioural archaeologists, the concept embodies much more than material or formal properties. The claim that behavioural archaeologists adopt overly utilitarian interpretations of technology (e.g. Gosselain 1998: 79) fails to acknowledge the flexibility of the concept of performance characteristic, and overlooks its applications to symbolic and even aesthetic performance. Behavioural archaeologists are well aware that objects have varied and fluid political, ideological, and social functions (Schiffer 1976: 49–53, 1992; Rathje and Schiffer 1982). Indeed, performance characteristics make possible the identification of specific utilitarian, social, and symbolic functions of technologies in specific behavioural contexts. Performance characteristics can relate to mechanical, chemical, and electrical interactions, or economic variables, such as the costs of acquiring, using, and maintaining a technology. Yet, we also emphasize that performance characteristics are the basis of aesthetic and symbolic roles of objects (Mills 2007; Schiffer 2005b; Schiffer and Miller 1999) and are useful for exploring the dialectical relationship between mental and material realms of technology.

The life history approach

An artefact's life history is the sequence of interactions and activities that it goes through during its existence or 'lifetime' (LaMotta and Schiffer 2001: 21). For artefacts, this process begins with the procurement of raw materials, goes through manufacture and use, and ends with deposition in the archaeological record. Life histories also include practices of maintenance and reuse. The most general processes of an artefact's life history, often modelled in a flow chart (e.g. Schiffer 1976), include procurement, manufacture, use, maintenance, reuse, recycling, discard, and post-depositional formation processes (Schiffer 1972). An alternative theoretical approach to objects' life histories in archaeology, which deals mainly with procurement, manufacture, and, more recently, use, comes from the French school of *techniques et culture* or *technologie culturelle*, which has developed especially from the work of Pierre Lemonnier (1986, 1993; see also David and Kramer 2001: 140; Stark 1998a). A central concept in this approach is the *chaîne opératoire* (operational sequence), introduced by André Leroi-Gourhan, which represents 'a series of operations which brings a primary material from its natural state to a fabricated state' (Cresswell 1976: 6, cited by Lemonnier 1986: 181). While the idea of the *chaîne opératoire* has been helpful in examining the interplay of natural constraints and technological choice in the design and production of technology, the life history approach differs in its broader applicability and its inclusion of post-manufacture behaviours such as use, maintenance, reuse, and deposition, and in its concern with design and learning frameworks.

Behavioural chains

The 'behavioural chain' is a heuristic tool applicable to an individual artefact or kind of artefact (LaMotta and Schiffer 2001: 21–24; Schiffer 1995a: 55–66). It describes the entire sequence of interactions and activities that took place during the life history of an object or place, emphasizing types of interactions, social group, frequency, location, archaeological outputs, and conjoined elements or associated artefacts (LaMotta and Schiffer 2001: 24). Evidence for constructing a behavioural chain may include historical documents and ethnographies as well as archaeological materials. Complete behavioural chains are almost impossible to create (LaMotta and Schiffer 2001: 21), and so chain segments pertaining to manufacture, use, or other major processes are developed. Because of their focus on relevant aspects of each activity, behavioural chains are useful for reconstructing particular technologies, and have been employed, for example, to study floral remains such as maize (Schiffer 1976), cotton (Magers 1975), and yucca (Stier 1975).

THE LIFE HISTORY OF TECHNOLOGIES

The life history concept helps us conceptualize and study material practices in relation to objects and technologies. At this point, it is helpful to develop a somewhat different concept for the life histories of technologies, one that does not focus solely on material objects. A technology has a multifaceted life history involving a specific environment with contexts of development and use, and relevant communities of practice and interaction whose members have their own systems of meaning and ways of transferring knowledge. The construction of technology-specific narratives that fully account for historical contingency and social uniqueness offers significant insights for all disciplines that study material culture. However, adopting a generalist perspective designed to understand commonalities among different technologies is also useful. Therefore, the life history approach can be used as an analytical tool for examining the complexities of technologies over time.

For present purposes, a technology's life history can be understood to involve six stages or processes: invention and innovation, experimentation and development, adoption by producers, production, consumption by consumers, and senescence. These processes do not occur in a linear fashion. Rather, they can occur coevally or iteratively with complex overlaps and interrelationships between the different processes and communities of practice that engage with each. By defining and discussing each process, we hope to generate useful heuristic tools for studying technology in relation to material life.

Invention and innovation

Invention is the creation of a new technology through thought and practice. The new technology must possess performance characteristics that differ from those of other technologies in a specific society or area. Invention results in unique artefacts or prototypes, practices, or sets of knowledge. More often than not these 'fail', and are not adopted by a larger community.

Innovation thus represents the process of bringing new methods, ideas, or practices to an existing technology, which substantially modifies an existing technology in a given society, such as the shift to wheel-thrown pottery production from traditional hand-building. Pottery is not a new technology in this case. Nevertheless, a new production technique may represent a change of broader social significance, accompanied by changes in the location of the practice, social organization of production, or changes in associated ritual practices, stories, or beliefs. Innovation is usually based on the recognition and weighting of alternative performance characteristics, which can be ideological, mechanical, political, or economic. Invention is the creation of something new, whereas innovation is the modification of an existing object, practice, or knowledge set that creates something distinct from its immediate predecessor. The process of innovation may result in the proliferation of new varieties, thus leading to technological differentiation (Schiffer 2002).

Experimentation and development

Experimentation takes place when one or more artisans explore specific qualities of the technology (e.g. raw materials, forming techniques, locations of practice, social dynamics, economic variables) to learn which performance characteristics are most desirable for specific applications or activities. It is a process characterized by a high degree of variability in objects, practices, and knowledge. During experimentation (and development), the future 'success' or 'failure' of an invention or innovation may be envisioned. How a technology is 'judged' (i.e. whether its performance characteristics are suitable for specific activities) depends on a society's systems of meaning—including political, economic, social, and ritual systems (Bijker 1995: 7–9)—as well as on environmental and mechanical variables. This process is characterized by producers and users experimenting with a technology.

Development differs from experimentation in that it is usually goal driven and follows the identification of a technology's desired performance characteristics. In striving to achieve these performance characteristics, development involves problem solving to refine the design. Development can occur through trial-and-error experiments, in the context of some kind of intentionality, where communities of practice or an individual seeks to meet specific performance requirements of anticipated activities by applying accumulated knowledge and experience (Schiffer and Skibo 1997). Many would argue that development is a more 'modern' or 'Western' phenomenon, but it need not be limited to these contexts.

Adoption by producers

Differing from previous behavioural conceptions (Schiffer 1996, 2001a, 2008c), adoption is defined here as a process of acceptance and replication of a technology by craftspersons or producers. An example would include the adoption of pottery and pottery production in areas where there had previously been none except through trade with neighbouring regions. Adoption occurs once individuals from a community invest time and energy into acquiring the appropriate knowledge, skills, and materials to replicate the technology. Whether a society has an 'open' or 'closed' system of learning (i.e. learning frameworks) affects the amount of technological variability that occurs at this stage (Wallaert-Pêtre 2001: 482–485). Open systems respond to unstable situations, are highly adaptable, and correspond to trial-and-error training of apprentices (Wallaert-Pêtre 2001: 482). Closed systems are shaped by stable situations, include standardized 'answers to problems', and are associated with observation–imitation types of learning (Wallaert-Pêtre 2001: 482).

Production

Production (also called reproduction or replication) has received the greatest attention in archaeology and anthropology, and is often documented in contemporary social contexts. In archaeology, the *techniques et culture* school, with its *chaîne opératoire* framework, attends mainly to production processes.

Production occurs once a community of producers has adopted a new technology. The production sequence includes the procurement and processing of raw materials, construction or forming, and finishing of the product or artefact. At this point in the technology's life history, there is an established knowledge and code of practice for how, where, when, and why a technology is to be made. An established learning framework with novices and experts, and accompanying sets of practices, characterizes the production stage, which facilitate the transfer of knowledge and practice. This stage also includes associated meanings, rituals, and functions, which are integral parts of the social context.

Consumption and use

In consumption and use, consumers—individuals and groups—have the opportunity to acquire and use the technology. Consumers, who may also be the
producers in some societies, are usually the final arbiters of a technology's success.
How and why a community of users determines whether a technology is 'successful' depends on how consumers evaluate its activity-relevant performance characteristics. A technology may be mechanically or economically sound, but if a
group determines that it lacks relevant political, social, or ritual performance
characteristics, the technology may not be 'consumed'. An alternative scenario is
one in which a technology is not mechanically or economically 'sound' by
Western standards, yet appears to have enjoyed widespread use and importance
in a community because of its acceptable performance in social, ritual, or political
activities.

Senescence

Senescence refers to the 'ageing', replacement, or death of a technology, which we
define as the decline and eventual cessation of production. Use, of course, may
continue long after production ends. There are many causes of senescence, such as
lack of access to raw materials, warfare, epidemic disease, loss of knowledge, or the
judgement that a technology no longer serves a community's utilitarian, social,
political, or ritual purposes. Thus, a technology entering a period of senescence is
characterized by performance characteristics that do not meet the requirements of
a society's activities. During this phase, technologies are usually replaced with
alternative technological systems—or they just seem to 'disappear'. It is possible
for an ageing technology to persist in a society; it may not, however, retain its
original functions or meanings, as for example with vinyl records in contemporary
culture. Records were originally developed for home consumption and music
broadcasting on radio. With the invention of tapes, and later compact discs,
records fell out of favour in mainstream society. A subculture of alternative
collectors and users who used vinyl in performances or in alternative forms of
social signalling soon developed (Plasketes 1992). Today, vinyl records signify
participation in non-mainstream society. This example demonstrates a trend in
processes of senescence where a technology persists with different social meanings
and uses and with significantly altered and diminished production and consumption patterns.

Senescence can also be characterized as the stage in which individuals in a society
give up the adoption or consumption of the technology so that its frequency within
the community declines. For example, consumers may choose to replace a technology with a new one. Senescence can also occur as a result of unforeseen events,

where individuals are forced to give up a technology because of adverse circumstances (e.g. culture contact, warfare, epidemic disease) that cause loss of access to certain resources needed for the technology's production or consumption (e.g. raw materials, craft specialists, or ritual specialists).

Case studies

In order to explore some of the processes discussed above and to demonstrate their usefulness as 'thought-provoking' tools we now provide two case studies. The first explores consumption patterns of the electric car as they relate to gender and socio-economic class in early twentieth-century American society and ties these to the replacement of this technology with gasoline automobiles. This case study demonstrates the utility of using performance characteristics in looking at consumption and senescence stages of a technology's life history. The second explores processes of senescence of ceramic technology in Mandan–Hidatsa society in the eighteenth- and nineteenth-century Northern Plains in the United States. The persistent use of pottery after the introduction of European trade goods was an enigma to archaeologists who did not recognize the social and ideological significance of this traditional technology. The slow decline of pottery production in Mandan–Hidatsa society, however, resulted from outbreaks of epidemic disease and the gradual deterioration of learning frameworks.

What happened to the early electric car?

In the United States, electric automobiles were brought to market by dozens of manufacturers during the period 1894–1920 (Figures 13.1 and 13.2). After 1900, however, these vehicles rapidly lost market share to gasoline cars. As a result of diminished consumption, electric car manufacturers went out of business, merged with each other, or began making other products.

Until recently, automobile historians did not regard the near-total demise of the early electric car industry as a problem needing serious attention. For these scholars, the explanation was obvious: the electric car was a technology defective in critical performance characteristics, such as top speed and range on one charge of the battery, and so could not compete effectively against the ever-improving gasoline car. However, in *Taking Charge: the electric automobile in America*, Michael Schiffer, Tamara Butts, and Kimberly Grimm combined elements of behavioural archaeology and the social construction of technology to demonstrate that the received explanation was simplistic (Schiffer *et al.* 1994a; see Schiffer 1995b, 2000). This example allows us to illustrate an integrated approach to explaining consumption patterns and, finally, the senescence of the early electric car.

Gasoline cars and electric cars did have different performance characteristics, which facilitated different activities. Differences in the activity-related performance characteristics of the two car technologies can be shown in a 'performance matrix',

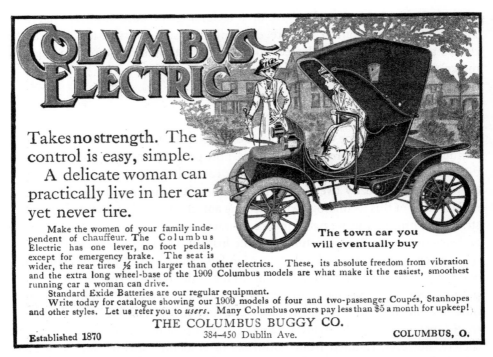

Fig. 13.1 An advertisement promising to liberate the woman driver of a Columbus Electric Automobile (*The Outlook* 27 March 1909).

a tool used by behaviouralists to study adoption processes, particularly among competing technologies (Table 13.1). It is apparent that electric cars were ideal for running errands and travelling to social functions in town. Most of them were all-weather, enclosed vehicles that, after about 1910, could cruise the streets all day long on one charge of the battery (given speed limits of 8–12 mph, geared to the horse). On the other hand, the open-air gasoline car, with its high top speed and essentially unlimited range (gasoline was available in many country stores), was best suited for the activity of touring, which at the time involved travelling long distances in the country. Touring was for the adventurous because gasoline cars broke down frequently and suffered blowouts. Nonetheless, in the first decades of the twentieth century, touring became the *sine qua non* of automobilism (Table 13.1).

Once the activities are identified along with each car's performance characteristics, one can introduce social factors. Indeed, these two sets of activities—touring and travel in town—were highly gendered. Men tended to be tourists and preferred gasoline cars, whereas women drove around town and preferred electric cars. If a family bought only one car, then the activities of either men or women would be

Fig. 13.2 The Detroit Electric's 'Aristocratic Roadster': a roadster style that did not perform like a roadster (*The Literary Digest* 15 June 1912).

Table 13.1 A threshold performance matrix for gasoline and electric automobiles, c.1912.

Activity	Performance Characteristic	Gasoline	Electric
Touring	Range of 100+ miles (T)	+	−
	Top speed of 40–60 mph (T,S)	+	−
	Ease of fuelling, recharging (T)	+	−
	Ruggedness (T)	+	−
	Economy of operation and maintenance (T)	−	−
	Repairability in country (T)	+	−
	Can indicate owner's membership in the group 'tourists' (S)	+	−
	Can indicate owner's wealth (S)	+	+
Running errands in town	Range of 50–100 miles (T)	+	+
	Speed of 12–20 mph (T)	+	+
	Ease of starting (T)	−	+
	East of driving (T)	−	+
	All-weather capability (T)	−	+
	Reliability (T)	−	+
	Economy of operation and maintenance (T)	−	−
	Ease of fuelling, recharging (T)	+	+
	Can indicate owner's wealth (S)	+	+
	Can indicate owner's social position (S)	+	+
Travelling to social functions in town	Range of 50–100 miles (T)	+	+
	Speed of 12–20 mph (T)	+	+
	Ease of starting (T)	−	+
	East of driving (T)	−	+
	All-weather capability (T)	−	+
	Reliability (T)	−	+
	Economy of operation and maintenance (T)	−	−
	Ease of fuelling, recharging (T)	+	+
	Cleanliness of operation (T)	−	+
	Quietness of operation (T,S)	−	+
	Can indicate owner's membership in the 'horsey set' (S)	−	+
	Can indicate owner's wealth (S)	+	+
	Can indicate owner's affinity for 'high culture' (I)	−	+

Entries represent an approximation of how these performance characteristics were judged. A Plus (+) indicates that the car exceeded the threshold value of that performance characteristics; a minus (−) indicates that the car fell short of the threshold value. T=techno-function; S=socio-function; I=ideo-function.

severely compromised because of the almost mutually exclusive sets of perform-ance characteristics.

Although all cars at that time were expensive to purchase and maintain, only members of the elite could afford to buy both gasoline and electric cars. Thus, in the teens, Thomas and Mina Edison had electric cars that Mina drove in town, along with gasoline touring cars that Thomas beat up during summer excursions. Likewise, Henry and Clara Ford had his and hers automobiles, gasoline and electric, respectively.

Middle-class families that could afford to acquire only one car almost uniformly purchased gasoline cars. This seems like a curious choice in view of the gasoline car's limited utilitarian function. However, the gasoline car had a transcendent social function: ownership of a touring car had become a social necessity for middle-class men. Exhibiting their cars to friends, relatives, and acquaintances, or at least talking knowledgeably about them, these men could demonstrate their social competence. Clearly, only in relation to the touring activities of men was the electric car an inferior technology.

The purchase of a gasoline car by middle-class families decisively favoured the leisure activities of men over women's activities. One possible explanation for this consumption pattern is that in the patriarchal middle-class American family, the husband could prevail because he was the 'breadwinner', thus entitled to dictate such a major purchase. Had such families been wealthier or had middle-class women enjoyed greater economic independence—married middle-class women did not work outside the home during those decades—the electric car might have found a market of millions. By combining the elements of behavioural archaeology—activities, artefact functions, and performance characteristics—with elements of the social construction of technology—gender, social class, etc.—one can construct explanations that take advantage of the insights developed by the practitioners of both programmes. By explicitly exploring the consumption stage of this technology's life history, we are able to better explain the electric car's senescence.

Smallpox and Mandan–Hidatsa pottery making

Our second example is drawn from published archaeological and historical accounts of culture contact in the Northern Plains of North America. The senescence of North American indigenous technologies was commonplace after contact with Euro-Americans. This process often resulted from trade, epidemic disease, increased warfare, or most likely, a combination of these factors (Krause 1972). Technological change in ceramics among the Mandan and Hidatsa, two groups of semi-sedentary village horticulturalists from the Missouri River area in North Dakota (Bowers 1992, 2004), provides an interesting case study for exploring the latter stages of a technology's life history. Thanks to detailed accounts of Mandan and Hidatsa society and craft production practices (Wilson 1977; Weitzner 1979; Bowers 1992), the documented impact of eighteenth-century through early twentieth-century smallpox epidemics on demography (Trimble 1985, 1993; Ramenofsky 1987; Chardon 1997 [1932]), and detailed archaeological studies of pre- and post-epidemic villages (Lehmer *et al.* 1978; Ahler 1993; Ahler and Swenson 1993), we can begin to reconstruct the processes of indigenous technological senescence and the relative roles of the adoption of new trade items.

It has been commonly believed that indigenous ceramic production and use ceased at contact in favour of consumption of metal containers. This hypothesis was based on the assumption that European containers (e.g. metal) were functionally superior to those of clay in utilitarian activities. However, this scenario neglects the non-utilitarian performance characteristics of indigenous ceramics related to ritual and social activities. Previous studies have revealed that the Mandan and Hidatsa did not favour European ceramics (Ramenofsky 1998) and indigenous groups attempted to maintain an indigenous production system because of its importance in processes of socialization and ritual practice. In the end, ceramic production ceased because of a loss of craftspersons and their associated knowledge and practices, not because of altered consumption patterns in the society.

To understand technological senescence in the face of epidemic disease, one must be acquainted with social mores concerning illness. In Mandan and Hidatsa society, when a person becomes ill, he or she returns to his or her mother's lodge. Given that smallpox affects the very old and the very young (e.g. craft experts and novices) this would drastically impact upon craft production if knowledge of the practice was transferred within families. Archaeological evidence indicates significant qualitative differences in pre- and post-epidemic pottery from the Northern Plains, including changes in design and 'quality' of pottery (Figure 13.3), which are probably attributable to epidemic disease and colonization and not simply the availability of new technologies (Krause 1972; Lehmer *et al.* 1978). Smallpox

(a)   (b)

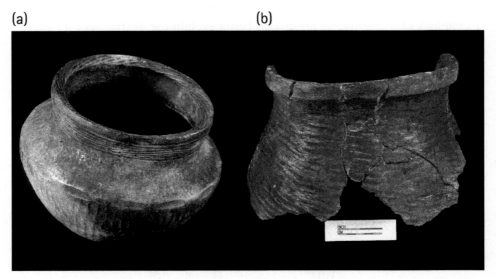

Fig. 13.3 Two ceramic vessels from North Dakota, USA. (a) An example of a pre-epidemic vessel from Alderin Creek (32ME4); (b) an example of a post-epidemic vessel from Amahami (32ME8) (photos courtesy of the Archaeology and Historic Preservation Division, State Historical Society of North Dakota).

resulted in the elimination of entire 'technological lineages'. When sick potters returned to their mothers' lodges they infected or exposed all of the elders who had instructed them in specific kinds of craft practices, as well as the youth they might teach. For the villages, this created a 'technological bottleneck' in material culture, practice, and knowledge.

From ethnohistorical texts, social aspects of Hidatsa pottery production have been reconstructed (Wilson 1977; Weitzner 1979; Bowers 1992). First, the symbolic performance characteristics of ceramic vessels have been documented through their association with sacred bundles and important rituals (Lehmer *et al.* 1978: 182–184; Bowers 1992). Additionally, ceramics played an important role in the maintenance of learning frameworks and processes of socialization. In Mandan and Hidatsa society, older women tend to produce ceramic vessels (Bowers 1992). Women 'purchase' knowledge of pottery production along with the right to practice from older women (e.g. female relatives such as mothers or grand-mothers). Pottery manufacture was a restricted activity (e.g. Wallaert-Pêtre's (2001) closed learning framework). Women secluded themselves in their earth lodges when making vessels, which would have restricted most people from participating in, and possessing knowledge of, production techniques. This seclu-sion made existing mechanisms for the transfer of related knowledge important and imbued the process with sacredness. The teaching and practice of ceramic manufacture was a key part of maintaining Mandan and Hidatsa identity and 'culture'. The technology of ceramic production did not cease when new objects became available. Rather, Mandan and Hidatsa individuals attempted to maintain this tradition in an altered form in the face of catastrophe and chaos.

In this case study, the eventual senescence of ceramic technology after contact was the result of the overwhelming stress of disease, warfare, and colonization, not changes in consumption patterns (as in the electric car case study). These two cases have briefly discussed different processes responsible for senescence—the final stage of a technology's life history.

Conclusions

The simultaneous growth of interest in studying material culture in socio-cultural anthropology, archaeology, and other disciplines since the 1980s furnishes an exciting opportunity for these disciplines to work together. By combining elements from varied theoretical frameworks, such as behavioural archaeology and the social construction of technology, anthropologists in both subdisciplines can pursue new understandings about the material world we create and that, in turn, creates us.

The bare-bones framework presented in this chapter, which includes life histories, activities, performance characteristics, and relevant social actors, explicitly recognizes that human life is a material life. Embedded in systems of meaning and in social networks during its entire cultural existence, material culture is irreducibly material.

To promote a synthesis of material culture studies, we elaborated a six-stage model of the processes in a technology's life history: invention and innovation, experimentation and development, adoption by producers, production, consumption and use, and senescence. Grounded in concrete activities, as favoured by behavioural archaeologists, this approach also directs attention to social contexts, as stressed by social constructivists. By framing research questions in relation to one or more of the six stages, we can seek the specific processes and contingent factors (social, cultural, environmental, etc.) responsible for any technological change.

In the case studies—one on early electric automobiles, the other Mandan and Hidatsa pottery making—we investigated senescence, an oft-neglected stage. The causes of senescence were different in each case, but both contradict simplistic explanations based exclusively on the supposed *technical* superiority of new technologies. The case studies also suggest that different theoretical frameworks—behavioural archaeology and social construction of technology—offer complementary not contradictory formulations for handling both the cultural and the material. It remains to further develop these theoretical synergies and apply them to a wider range of case studies.

....

CHAPTER 14

THE MALICE OF
INANIMATE
OBJECTS

MATERIAL AGENCY

....

A N D R E W   M .   J O N E S
N I C O L E   B O I V I N

That is the only way to get a kettle to boil up the river. If it sees that you are waiting for it and are anxious, it will never even sing. You have to go away and begin your meal, as if you were not going to have any tea at all. You must not even look round at it. Then you will soon hear it sputtering away, mad to be made into tea.

In this review, we have drawn heavily upon discussions and syntheses in our recent Cambridge University Press books, *Material Cultures, Material Minds* (Boivin 2008) and *Memory and Material Culture* (Jones 2007). We acknowledge in these books the many individuals with whom we have discussed and debated our ideas about material culture. We cannot mention all of them here, but would like to acknowledge their contribution and assistance. Boivin would like to thank in particular Richard Bradley and Carl Knappett, while Jones owes a debt of gratitude to Dan Hicks, Josh Pollard, and Laura Watts whose insights, support, and assistance have been particularly relevant to the material discussed here. We would also like to thank Dan Hicks and Mary Beaudry for their invitation to contribute to this volume.

It is a good plan, too, if you are in a great hurry, to talk very loudly to
each other about how you don't need any tea, and are not going to have
any. You get near the kettle, so that it can overhear you and then you
shout out ... Upon which the kettle boils over, and puts the stove out.

Jerome K. Jerome, *Three Men in a Boat* (2004 [1889]: 81)

This excerpt comes from a classic of late Victorian literature. Who has not at one
time or another adopted a similar attitude towards an object, be it car, computer,
or kettle? The capriciousness of things, and their propensity to break down, or
misbehave, just when they are most needed makes the idea of their agency a
crucial component of the comedy and tragedy of human life. Nonetheless, the
very idea of imputing an 'inanimate' object with animacy also appears in many
ways absurd, and explains this passage's inclusion in Jerome's classic of comedy
literature. Is the concept of material agency therefore ridiculous, or do our folk
propensities and real-life engagements with material culture hint at some underlying reality?

The concept of 'material agency', and the attendant concept of materiality, has
been widely adopted in the recent literature in archaeology and anthropology, yet
its meaning has been widely misunderstood. Typical responses treat the concept
as a step too far (Ingold 2007a) or as employed mainly for its shock value rather
than for any higher intellectual purpose (Robb 2004: 131). Accounts such as
Jerome's description of 'the contrariness of tea-kettles' offer a very narrow and
particular view of the material agency of objects acting with their own volition,
often like cranky people or children. This chapter argues that the perceived
problems with the concept of material agency in archaeology and anthropology
derive from similarly narrow conceptions. We want to present a more general
view of the significance of the idea of material agency for archaeology, anthropology, and related disciplines, suggesting that the absurdity of imputing agency
to inanimate objects is an unhelpful product of the Western opposition between
'objects' and 'subjects'. We argue, with Christopher Pinney (2005), for the need to
move beyond this dichotomy.

The chapter begins by outlining the semiotic view of material culture that
emerged during the 1970s and 1980s, and how recent critiques of this view have
prompted scholars to address notions of materiality and material agency. We then
summarize some of the long history of the notion of material agency, in a range of
disciplines from economics to anthropology. The chapter addresses concepts of
material agency in the work of scholars from Karl Marx and Marshall McLuhan to
Anthony Giddens and Alfred Gell. It then discusses differing ontologies of agency,
including animism and fetishism, in which material agency plays a key role.
Beyond locating material agency within these specific ontological frameworks, we
will then expand our discussion to examine the role the concept has played in
science studies and actor-network theory, with particular reference to the work of

Bruno Latour and Michel Callon. Having examined the way in which similar concepts have emerged across a range of disciplines, through two case studies we shall consider what consequences the notion of material agency has for contemporary archaeological and anthropological understandings of material culture.

MEANING, MATERIAL CULTURE, AND THE MODEL OF THE TEXT

Recent suggestions in archaeology and anthropology that artefacts 'have agency' have not been made within an academic vacuum, but rather must be understood as very much the product of, or perhaps more appropriately the response to, a particular academic climate. This climate may be described as a heavily linguistic-oriented one. It is one that came to dominate the social sciences and humanities in the last half of the twentieth century (Rorty 1967; Foucault 1972; Derrida 1978; Rabinow and Sullivan 1979). It owes much to the insights of a Swiss linguist, Ferdinand de Saussure, whose posthumously published teaching notes on the linguistic sign system became highly influential across the humanities and social sciences during the 1980s (de Saussure 1959). Fundamental to de Saussure's argument was the idea that language could serve as a model for understanding other sign systems—this opened the way for a wide variety of phenomena to eventually be demonstrated to be language-like in diverse ways. De Saussure's model also stressed the relational rather than referential properties of language. Thus relationships—or webs of meaning—have become key: words and concepts have been understood not relative to things in the world, but rather through comparison with other words and concepts. Meaning is constructed rather than given. This led to an interest in representation, its power to shape action and thought, and the role of language and discourse in shaping subjectivity, social institutions, and politics (Seidman 1994). Language was increasingly understood less as a neutral medium for representing and understanding the world, and more as a key way through which the world is constructed. Other 'language-like' systems are recognized to share the same partiality.

The 'linguistic turn' fundamentally affected anthropological and archaeological thinking about material culture. In archaeology, it led to an interest in meaning and, in particular, the representational qualities of material culture. The proposition that 'material culture is like a text' (Hodder 1986: 126) became a battle cry that rallied archaeologist Ian Hodder and many of the Cambridge group of students of the late 1970s and early 1980s to develop an entirely new, language-inspired theoretical paradigm for archaeology which came to be known as 'post-processual archaeology' (Hodder 1982a, 1982b, 1985; Miller and Tilley 1984; Shanks and Tilley

1987b). It argued that material culture needed to be understood as 'meaningful' and 'symbolic' (Hodder 1992: 12, 14–15). The textual character of things is clearly highlighted in the concept of 'contextual archaeology'. Hodder defines a context as the 'totality of the relevant environment' of an artefact (Hodder 1992: 14). The concept is developed by Hodder, as he emphasizes the fact that the Latin derivation of context is *contextere*, meaning to weave, join together, and connect (Hodder 1986: 122); from this Hodder develops the idea that in order to understand the meaning of artefacts, a contextual approach is required that involves placing artefacts 'with their texts, con-text' (Hodder 1986: 128). Adopting Paul Ricoeur's (1981) point that human action is best understood in relation to text as opposed to language (Hodder 1986: 155; Moore 1990), he argues that the meaning of archaeological contexts are to be interpreted by examining relations of similarity and difference in the material record.

This new movement was highly critical of the then dominant archaeological models for understanding material culture, which it derided as 'functionalist', 'adaptive', and 'scientistic' (Hodder 1992: 1–7). It critiqued previous attempts to link material culture to social aspects of society, asserting that they portrayed material culture as passive and simply *reflective* of social realities. Material culture, the proponents of the new movement asserted, needed rather to be recognized as *active* in constituting those very realities (Hodder 1982b, 1986, 1992; Shanks and Tilley 1987b; Tilley 1989). It was argued that material culture was a symbolic medium for social practice that was used at times habitually to reproduce social and symbolic structures, and at other times strategically to challenge them. Thus, Hodder studied the domestic material culture of the Ilchamus tribe of Kenya, and argued that women decorated calabashes in order to draw attention to their own important roles in child-rearing and looking after milk (a symbolically important resource) and to challenge their status within a patriarchal society (Hodder 1986). Material culture was strategically used by the Ilchamus during the course of social practice, and did not simply and passively reflect social realities.

Post-processual approaches to material culture have subsequently come to dominate British and some European archaeological traditions and to be increasingly influential in the United States and world-wide. European socio-cultural anthropology, largely through a separate developmental trajectory, also came to take an interest in objects, and their meanings and active employment in human societies (Appadurai 1986a; Lemonnier 1992; Miller 1995a, 1998c; Pfaffenberger 1988, 1992), especially under the rubric of 'material culture studies'.

Increasingly, however, such work has come in for heavy critique as it has been recognized that such approaches often reinforce the distinctions of ideal and material, and of subject and object, that they claim to break down, and in many ways portray material culture in as passive a way as ever. The focus on the representational and meaningful properties of material culture, while a positive and fruitful development in many ways, has also led to an 'etherealisation'

(Jackson 1996) of material culture. Things have been robbed of their solidity, their physicality, and their ability to change our lives. Instead, they have often become mere consequences of our thoughts, actions, and beliefs. They have become things—and things more surface than solid at that—to which our concepts can be attached. Archaeologist Paul Graves-Brown has used the apt analogy of the stage to refer to this view: 'it is as if the material world were merely a stage set in which the props could be made to assume any value chosen by the actors' (Graves-Brown 2000a: 3). Bjørnar Olsen has undertaken even stronger critique, and called specifically for attention to material agency: '[W]e need to relearn to ascribe . . . agency . . . to many more agents than the human subject, as well as to ballast epistemology—and ontology—with a new and unknown actor; the silent thing' (Olsen 2003: 88). A range of archaeologists and anthropologists has begun to call for changes in how we conceive of material culture (see Schiffer 1999; Graves-Brown 2000a; Ingold 2000a; Boivin 2004b; Knappett 2005; Jones 2007; Boivin 2008). Many call for a new emphasis on 'materiality', which in many (but not all) formulations means a focus on the physical properties of things and their role in determining the impacts of material objects and environments on society. These calls to focus upon the material dimension of artefacts have emerged as archaeologists and anthropologists attempt to readdress the fundamental dichotomy that exists in the term 'material culture'.

MATERIAL AGENCY IN HISTORICAL PERSPECTIVE

The view that things have power over humans and their lives is not of course new. Humans have not been unaware of the transformational properties of the things they make and use and, indeed, such beliefs are, and likely long have been, central to many traditional cosmologies. Thirty years ago political scientist Langdon Winner (1977) traced some of the history of notions of material agency in Western culture and academics. He focused on technology in particular, noting that the theme of technology as both out of control and dangerous has a long history in Western culture. Literary creations, such as Mary Shelley's nineteenth-century *Frankenstein*, offer a classic example of such perspectives, illustrating the pervasive notion that human-made machines could develop autonomy and wreak havoc on society. Later in the nineteenth century, the anthropologist Lewis Henry Morgan (1877) developed such folk ideas about technology into a general model of society in which technological changes were viewed as the force behind social progress. His writings were subsequently drawn upon by one of the most notable commentators on the relationship between technology and society, Karl Marx.

Marx's views on the role of technology have been much debated. His historical materialist model can be seen as an argument for the pivotal role of technology in social change. Arguing against the philosophical and political idealism of his time (Winner 1977: 77; W. H. Shaw 1979: 172), Marx asserted that the material conditions of life and their production through human activity were defining features of human life. Productive activity gave form to experience, and created what Marx referred to as a definitive 'mode of life' (Marx and Engels 1977: 42). This view of human beings, life, and activity gave shape to Marx's understanding of how material production—particularly technological production—shapes social, political, and ideological life (Winner 1977: 78). In *The Critique of Political Economy*, Marx stated his general historical principle that 'the mode of production of material life determines the general character of the social, political and spiritual processes of life' (Marx 1964: 51). Subsequently, he divided the mode of production into the forces of production and the relations of production. Marx saw productive forces, understood as human labour power together with the means of production (instruments or technology plus raw materials), as critical in shaping the economic structure of society, and hence the nature of society more generally. Thus, a change in the productive forces would bring about a change in society:

Social relations are closely bound up with productive forces. In acquiring new productive forces men change their mode of production; and in changing their mode of production, in changing the way of earning their living, they change all their social relations. The hand-mill gives you the society with the feudal lord; the steam mill, society with the industrial capitalist.

Marx (1979: 109)

Socio-cultural anthropologists like Julian Steward and Leslie White subsequently drew inspiration from the ideas of both Morgan and Marx to argue for social evolutionary models of society in which material environments and technologies played a significant role in shaping society. The 1950s, 1960s, and 1970s saw a florescence of technology- and ecology-oriented studies in both anthropology and other disciplines (Boivin 2008). For example, the early cultural theorist Marshall McLuhan's work on technology argued that 'the medium is the message' (1964: 1). McLuhan thus sought to emphasize the pivotal role that technological media play in shaping understanding and social relationships—the idea that the medium in which a message is sent is more important than its content. Accordingly, and in characteristic style, McLuhan asserted that '[i]n terms of the way the machine altered our relations to one another and to ourselves, it mattered not in the least whether it turned out cornflakes or Cadillacs' (1964: 7–8). McLuhan's Canadian colleague Harold Innis was similarly interested in the transformative effect of communicative media. He argued that particular media favoured the growth of specific kinds of interests and institutions at the expense of others (Innis 1950, 1951). In this view certain types of media, for example, fostered the growth of empires, encouraged a concern with expansion, and favoured the emergence of secular political authority.

By the end of the 1970s, however, such perspectives started to come under attack, with many calling attention to their often strongly deterministic character. Critiques against determinism, combined with the pull of the linguistic turn, led many scholars in the social sciences and humanities to abandon materialist approaches in favour of idealist models.

Socio-cultural anthropologists interested in the influence of the environment upon human society developed schools of symbolic ecology, historical ecology, and political ecology (Biersack 1999). These drew attention to the social and cultural construction of landscapes and the role of the power relations in structuring human usage of the environment, among other issues. Across the social sciences, Marxists, meanwhile, have since the 1970s been anxious to avoid the 'spectre of technological determinism' (W. H. Shaw 1979: 155), and to demonstrate that Marx was not, as has often been suggested, a technological determinist (MacKenzie 1984; Bimber 1990). The idea that the base (the economy or technology) should determine the super-structure is often dismissed as 'vulgar Marxism', and many Marxists argue for more interaction between base and superstructure, or indeed the relative autonomy of the superstructure. Meanwhile, studies of technology in fields such as history and anthropology have focused on the ways in which technology and technological practices are socially embedded. These studies stress the important place of social and cultural values in technological narratives, and place agency firmly with human beings: '[A]gency . . . is deeply embedded in the larger social structure and culture—so deeply, indeed, as to divest technology of its presumed power as an independent agent initiating change' (Marx and Smith 1994: xiv).

In seeking to demonstrate the interpenetration of technology with social forms and systems of meaning, many anthropologists approached technology as socially constructed (Pfaffenberger 1988: 244). In such social constructionist studies, technology was not understood as an independent variable but, in the words of socio-cultural anthropologist Bryan Pfaffenberger, as 'humanised nature': 'To say that technology is humanised nature is to insist that it is a fundamentally *social* phenomenon: it is a social construction of the nature around us and within us, and once achieved, it expresses an embedded social vision' (Pfaffenberger 1988: 244). This interest in the adoption, use, and transformation of technology as structured by socio-cultural variables was also visible in archaeology. Thus, Heather Lechtman and Bill Sillar examined the various social and cultural factors that led some pre-Columbian technologies to be widely adopted in the Andes, while others, such as metal-working (which had a substantial impact in European and Near Eastern prehistoric societies) remained rather peripheral (Lechtman 1984; Sillar 1996). Sillar emphasized the *philosophical* aspects of technology, which not only imbue techniques with culturally specific meanings, but also influence what people will consider an 'appropriate' technology to apply to a particular problem.

But as we have seen, many now argue that the pendulum has swung too far in the other direction. In particular, critics of technologically deterministic readings of

Marx have been taken to task for producing readings of Marx that while less contentious and more palatable are also less accurate and less interesting (W. H. Shaw 1979; Winner 1986). Philosopher William Shaw, for example, has argued that

to concede, for instance, that the notion of a determining factor in history is incoherent and then to argue that Marx must have meant something else in view is to kill Marx with kindness. Marx was surely concerned to say more than simply that technological factors ought not to be ignored by historians, or that everything is related to everything.

W. H. Shaw (1979: 155–156)

Langdon Winner (1977) has argued against whitewashing Marx, and stressed the need for social scientists to continue to grapple with material culture and technology on their own terms, instead of subsuming them into social frameworks of analysis. Winner and others acknowledge the insights of social constructivist approaches, but decry the way they have drawn scholars away from any interest in or examination of material agency.

EXAMINING AGENCY

But if material artefacts can 'have' agency, then how, if at all, is such agency different from that of humans? Socio-cultural anthropologist Alfred Gell explored this issue in his final work, *Art and Agency: an anthropological theory* (1998), in which he focused in particular on the relationships between social agency and art objects. Gell boldly argued that art objects should be considered as the 'indexes' of social agency. In taking this line, Gell was in many ways following a venerable tradition in anthropology, one that treats things as in some senses person-like, by positioning material objects in the web of social relations normally associated with the person. Such an approach originated with the classic analysis of the gift by Marcel Mauss (1954). This Maussian approach is also evident in the work of anthropologists such as Marilyn Strathern and Roy Wagner, and in particular their work on 'distributed personhood' (Gell 1998: 96–153) in Melanesia (Strathern 1988; Wagner 1991).

Art and Agency was specifically concerned to move the anthropology of art beyond a narrow focus on symbolism and meaning. Gell emphasized that art should be seen as part of a system of action 'intended to change the world rather than encode symbolic propositions about it' (1998: 6). The effects of objects such as artworks, he argued, needed to be accommodated in any discussion of social agency. At points, he generalized this argument to suggest that many other objects, whether a gun, a car, or even a doll, could 'act' as a social agent (Gell 1998: 17–19). However, for Gell art objects and artefacts were not 'primary' but rather, as he described them, 'secondary' agents (Gell 1998: 20–21). In other words, objects can act only as the media of human social agency, which could be distributed through them. For Gell, the facts of intention and will were critical to the definition of real agency, and since material objects obviously lack such characteristics, they were automatically exempted from the status of real agents. Indeed Gell's discussion of the agency of artefacts makes it clear that he actually saw objects as mere passive media for the distribution of human-derived agency. His approach is 'preoccupied with the practical *mediatory* role of art objects in the social process' (1998: 6, our emphasis). While Gell's concerns in *Art and Agency* were of a particular sort, to which his notion of agency was well suited, nevertheless this materialist sympathizer (Gell 1995, 1996a, 1999) shied away from the notion that things themselves could have agency. We shall take up the question of the distribution of agency and the notion of 'secondary agency' below when we examine the contribution of science studies to the debate.

In considering what kind of agency things might have, it is perhaps useful to go back to one of the key discussions of human social agency: Anthony Giddens' formulation of agency and structure under his rubric 'structuration'. The aim of Giddens' sociological model was to overcome the discrepancy between a functionalist approach to society rooted in objectivism on the one hand, and a structuralist account of mind rooted in the pre-eminence of society and subjectivism on the other. Structuration accordingly attempted to provide a coherent approach to society that simultaneously took account of its functional and material conditions alongside its subjective elements. Through structuration, Giddens aimed to overcome the antinomy between the material world and the social world. The following statement, propounded in the early pages of one of his most influential works *The Constitution of Society*, is critical to both our understanding of agency, and material agency: 'In and through their activities agents reproduce the conditions that make these activities possible' (Giddens 1984: 2).

In this view, since the material conditions that enable action are reproduced through subjective social actions, these conditions are then inextricably bound up with the ability to act. Agency can only take place within the framework of material conditions, within the framework of material agencies. Moreover, as Giddens goes on to state, the reflexive monitoring of action by social agents (Giddens 1984: 5) means that those material conditions are much more than a framework: they are also shaped by human action.

Giddens (1984: 174) understood these material conditions as a 'material constraint', arguing that the material world both enables action and acts as a constraint to bodily action. In many senses, here he echoed previous Marxist approaches to the material world (Rowlands 2005). Here we part company with Giddens. We believe he is correct to stress the close relationship between the bodily action of social agents and the physical conditions within which they act. We believe, however, that an approach that promotes the view that people and things exist in a dialectical relationship of mutual self-construction and mutual dependency (which Giddens called structuration, but see also Miller 1987, 2005a: 9) simply serves to re-cast the opposition between subject and object afresh. An acceptance of the concept of agency requires an acceptance of the concept of material agency. One cannot be treated as self-evident, while the other is treated as absurd or bizarre (*pace* Robb 2004). Such a position simply re-enacts the distinction between animate human subjects that exercise agency and inert material objects that are acted upon, a position that no amount of arguments for 'primary agency' exercised by humans and 'secondary agency' exercised by things (Gell 1998; Gosden 2001; Robb 2004) can hope to overcome.

Animism and fetishism: material agency and ontology

In considering alternative ways in which the agency of material things, apart from the constraints upon human social action described by Giddens, might be understood, it is useful to turn to the various broader modes of 'nature–culture' relationships that have been described by anthropologists. Eduardo Viveiros De Castro distinguishes among three modes of the objectification of nature that have been discussed by anthropologists: *totemism* (in which the differences among natural species are used as models for social distinctions); *animism* (in which the 'elementary categories structuring social life' serve to organize the relations between humans and natural species, defining a continuity between the natural and the cultural); and *naturalism* (typified by Western viewpoints that suppose an oppositional duality between nature and culture) (Viveiros De Castro 1998: 473). To this list we would add *fetishism*, which, like animism, uses social categories as an organizational template for the relations among people, presenting a continuity between the natural and the cultural. However, as we shall see, fetishism suggests a quite different ability to act, and intentionality, on the part of the natural world. In the interests of space, our discussion will focus upon animism and fetishism.

Animism

Ethnographic concepts of animism and fetishism are similar in many ways. Historically, both have been the subject of derogatory comment by Western observers of non-Western societies. The belief in the agency of things seen to be 'self-evidently' inanimate, such as trees or rocks, was considered to be a category error to which 'primitive' societies were especially prone (Spyer 1998; Latour 1999c; Harvey 2005).

In *Animism: respecting the living world*, comparative theologist Graham Harvey has brilliantly interrogated this perspective, arguing for a respectful revival of the concept of animism—what he calls a 'new' animism (Harvey 2005: 28). Harvey engages with indigenous and environmental spiritualities in which people celebrate human relationships with significant other-than-human beings. He discusses a variety of religious cultures, including Maori, Ojibwe, Aboriginal Australian, and eco-Pagan, and highlights the diverse ways of being animist. Importantly, taking a theological standpoint on animism, he shifts the argument away from discussions of the epistemological foundations of animism and argues instead for the need to take a respectful stance on animist cultures.

Indeed, in discussing issues such as eco-Paganism and environmentalism, he suggests that a respectful and attentive awareness of the other non-human persons we share our world with in fact offers a potentially important way of addressing some of the ecological problems faced by humankind as a whole. In this, he echoes similar post-humanist concerns related to the role and treatment of companion species in human societies (see Haraway 2008). Haraway is concerned to emphasize the 'entanglements of beings in technoculture that work through reciprocal inductions to shape companion species' (Haraway 2008: 281). Her particular focus is dogs and cats as companion species, although other animals, such as chickens, sheep, wolves, and wombats are also discussed as components in our shared world. The arguments of Harvey and Haraway shift us from an epistemic to an ontological focus. Rather than treating animism as a peculiar world view held by specific cultures, animist relationships are held to relate to a quality of engagement between people and the natural world, an engagement that involves interaction between human and other-than-human persons.

Harvey's arguments demonstrate that taking an animist viewpoint—treating the world as if it were composed of human beings and other-than-human beings and acting accordingly—enables us to overcome many of the inherent problems that arise from the dualisms of modernity, nature and culture, object and subject. For Harvey, rather than being a primitive concept, animism offers an important analytical step forward in re-imagining the links between people and the material and animal worlds (Harvey 2005: 195–212). Animism provides, then, a participatory framework for understanding the place of human beings in the world (by participation is meant the close engagement between humans and other-than-human beings). The participatory nature of Harvey's analysis is something we wish to underline as we go on to consider the type of interaction between things and people known as fetishism, and the ways in which people and things interact as collectives.

Fetishism

As anthropologist Patricia Spyer (1998) notes, the concept of fetishism is peculiar to a particular time and place, although it is a concept with a life and history of its own (Pietz 1985, 1987). Fetishism, as a Western idea, is a hybrid concept that emerged from colonial relations on the Gold Coast of Africa in the sixteenth and seventeenth centuries. The word *feitiço* (and the later derivation *fettiso*) was coined by Portuguese and Dutch merchant-adventurers to describe both a class of objects and an attitude towards them (Pietz 1985, 1987). Whereas animism posits a life force that may occasionally be materialized, for fetishists life force is always materialized. Fetishes are generally materialized as free-standing wooden figurines or as wooden or metal amulets worn around the neck. Fetishes may take many material forms, in fact, almost anything could pass as a fetish object: trees, rocks, bones, animals. The important point, however, is that fetishism was an idea, an idea produced by the interaction between West Africans and Europeans to describe the spiritual relationship of West Africans with the inanimate world. The term 'fetish' and the concept associated with it are not indigenous, but were coined to describe an indigenous relationship with objects that Europeans found peculiar or bizarre (cf. Pels this volume, Chapter 27).

For Europeans, fetishism was felt to describe a confusion of the religious and the economic, a denial of the proper boundaries between things, between animate subjects and inanimate objects (Spyer 1998: 2). In this sense the fetish, and the concept of fetishism (the belief in the fetish), were treated in a derogatory fashion. How is it reasonable, or possible even, to treat material objects as social actors in the same sense as people? Fetishism offered a violation of the naturalism of European cosmologies in which things and people were categorically distinct.

As noted above, there is an important relationship between animism and fetishism; however, there is also an important distinction between the terms. Anthropologist Peter Pels (1998: 94) is quite clear in distinguishing fetishism from animism. Whereas animist belief proposes that spirit resides *in* matter, fetishism posits an assumption of the spirit *of* matter: objects have spirit and are able to act of their own volition to attract or repel people. Thus, fetishes concentrate or localize human experience and belief in the power of objects:

> The fetish is always a meaningful fixation of a singular event; it is above all a 'historical' object, the enduring form and force of a singular event. This object is 'territorialized' in material space (an earthly matrix), whether in the form of a geographical locality, a marked site on the surface of the human body, or a medium of inscription or configuration defined by some portable or wearable thing.
>
> Pietz (1985: 12)

The notion of the fetish highlights some fundamental anthropological problems in dealing with objects. Anthropology and archaeology operate in a conceptual universe where objects have no independent life. If they are made to act or are imputed with meaning, it is assumed that this is through human intentionality; things have no meaning unless meaning is endowed upon them by human agency. But are we always detached from objects in this way? Do we act upon them in a disinterested fashion as and when we choose, or are objects attached to us and as such are they components of what makes us act? These are some of the questions we shall pursue below in our discussion of the treatment of material agency in science studies and actor-network theory, especially in the work of Bruno Latour and Michel Callon.

LESSONS FROM SCIENCE STUDIES
AND ACTOR-NETWORK THEORY

The issue of attachment is central to the re-conceptualization of the relationships between things and people in science studies (Jones 2002a, 2007: 34–35; Olsen 2003). Rather than assuming that the world can be purified into distinct categories named 'object' and 'subject' (see Latour 1993a), or getting caught up in questions of intentionality in relation to object agency (Gell 1998), sociologists of science proceed from the assumption that objects and subjects, people and things are co-mingled and relationally attached (Callon 1991; Latour 1999c). Non-human things have often been assumed to be passive, and therefore possible to bracket off, but as Michel Callon and John Law assert: 'Yes, there are differences between conversations, texts, techniques and bodies. Of course. But why should we start out by assuming that some of these have no active role to play in social dynamics?' (1997: 166). It is therefore not the presence but rather the forms of the attachment between humans and things that requires explanation. Callon (1991: 152–153) describes the processes of social and technical networks as 'heterogeneous'. He begins by describing the way in which people and things are constituted and define one another through their relationships. For Callon, things (whether texts, technical artefacts or abstract values or concepts, such as money or law) act as intermediaries for human action. It is the articulations between actors and their intermediaries that compose networks. Such articulations between people and things effectively 'translate' action and thereby co-ordinate it. These ideas form the core of what has become known as actor-network theory.

Latour (1999b, 2007) has developed Callon's argument further, by noting the way in which people and things are effectively enfolded into one another. Sociology, Latour argues, too often defines the actions of a person as constituted in material or technical form, producing an understanding of a person's actions and intentions as embedded in the technical artefact. In the sociological process, and more widely in modernist thought, the presence of the person is effectively forgotten as it is submerged with, and 'blackboxed' within, the artefact. Blackboxing is here used as a description of the way in which an efficiently running machine focuses attention only on its input and output, not on its technical complexity. Technical complexity provided by the person is then hidden within the smooth working of the machine (Latour 1999b: 304). Through the process of 'blackboxing', the relationship between the person and thing is rendered opaque. However, the constant processes of folding together people and things in networks of activity means that action is distributed between people and things. Attempts to ascribe primary agency to people or secondary agency to things is therefore an impossibility. But to the sociologist, despite the imbrication of people and things, things and people appear distinct. Because agency cannot be directly observed in things, it is assumed to be absent.

The significance of actor-network theory to questions of material agency relates to its critique of the assumption of a pure and essential distinction between things and people, and its replacement with the recognition that people and things are forever entangled with each other. For Latour, this leads to the proposition that we live in collectives of people and things rather than in societies composed only of people (Latour 1999b: 193, 2005a), and that this has always been the case (cf. Gamble 2007). Latour's theoretical model expands the concept of material agency from an absurd notion among a philosophical mindset that assumes the world to be divided into two opposing categories: objects and subjects, or things and people. Moreover, as we have seen, concepts of the agency of things are prevalent in the ontologies and cosmologies of the kind of non-Western or premodern peoples routinely studied by archaeologists and anthropologists, through ideas of animism, totemism, or the fetish.

The question of material agency and its relationship to human agency is also addressed by other science studies scholars, such as Karen Barad (2007). Barad's major area of study is quantum physics, and she is particularly interested in describing the relationship between observed phenomena and observer. Barad argues that materiality is not a given entity, rather it is performed into being. In her account discursive practices are not solely human-based activities but 'specific material (re)configurations of the world through which boundaries, properties, and meanings are differentially enacted' (Barad 2007: 183). Therefore, matter does not have a fixed essence; instead, matter is a substance in its intra-active becoming. Matter is reconceptualized in this account; matter is not a thing, but a doing. Barad's argument is especially important as it addresses the mutual relationship between agency and material agency, and helps us overcome the problem of intentionality. Intentionality does not simply lie on the side of the equation marked 'human agency', instead intentionality is a property of the relationship between people and things: 'discursive practices and material phenomena do not stand in a relationship of externality to each other; the material and discursive are mutually implicated in the dynamics of intra-activity' (Barad 2007: 184).

THE PROBLEM WITH 'MATERIAL CULTURE'

How then, in practice, might we apply ideas of material agency in anthropology and archaeology, which move beyond models of constraint (Giddens) or intentionality (Gell)? Many of the epistemological concerns we have raised with the concept of material agency are neatly encapsulated in that divisive anthropological term 'material culture'.

Like material agency, 'material culture' sutures two opposing ends of the epistemological pole, i.e. the material and the cultural. These two terms, rather than being perfectly combined, sit somewhat uncomfortably side by side. Anthropologist Tim Ingold (2000a: 340) points out that there is a sense in which the 'culture' in material culture studies 'is conceived to hover over the material world but not to permeate it'. Meanings then attach to things and impose themselves or are laid upon things, but are presumed to be distinct from things (Henare *et al.* 2007a: 3). The rise of British anthropological material culture studies, as it emerged from archaeology in the 1980s, tends to perpetuate these distinctions. For example, in his analysis of the significance of Coca-Cola within Trinidadian practices of consumption, Danny Miller discusses Coke as a meta-symbol (Miller 1998a). In discussing the significance of this sweet black drink among African communities in Trinidad, he opposes the consumption of this drink to a comparable sweet red drink traditionally consumed by Indian Trinidadians. The two drinks are discussed as objectifications used to create projects of value for ethnic communities (Miller 1998a). Miller's account gives a detailed picture of the symbolic uses of these drinks, but gives us little flavour of the material properties of the drinks and their sensual appreciation by Trinidadians. A similar approach to material culture is adopted by Chris Tilley in his analysis of Wala canoes in Malekula, Vanuatu (Tilley 1999: 102–132). Tilley employs the concept of material metaphor to discuss the significance of canoes, however—as with Miller's case study discussed above—the emphasis is placed upon the metaphorical (read symbolic) significance of canoes, rather than their material components; while the materials used to build canoes are discussed, it is the symbolic potential of these materials that is emphasized. Arguably, these approaches are immanent in Danny Miller's early account of objectification in *Material Culture and Mass Consumption* (Miller 1987), a text we take to be foundational to the prevailing UCL School of Material Culture.

As anthropologists Amiria Henare, Martin Holbraad, and Sari Wastell observe, the task of this modernist vision of anthropology is the elucidation of social or cultural contexts, as these are used to make sense of social life. An important outcome of this is that the social system becomes the object of knowledge, and 'things' merely serve to illustrate the social system (Henare *et al.* 2007a: 3). Similar problems with the study of artefacts affect archaeological thinking. This is especially true of recent British traditions of interpretative archaeology (Tilley 1993;

Thomas 2000d), which likewise assume a distinction between object and subject, material and culture, person and things, which must be overcome by the analyst. This thinking derives from the particular reception of structuralist, post-structuralist, and hermeneutic thinking in archaeology (Olsen 1990, 2006). One recent example of such an approach might be found in Chris Tilley's *Materiality of Stone* (2004). Here, a nuanced evaluation of the phenomenological experience of encountering megaliths, monuments, and rock art in a variety of European contexts is overlaid with a hermeneutic approach that is focused on meaning. For example, the analysis of the differing qualities of the limestones used to construct the megalithic monuments of Neolithic temples is understood according to the symbolic potentials of these different materials; honeycombed rock formations are therefore symbolically related to honey. In a further symbolic transformation, honey is related to ochre (Tilley 2004: 140–141). Despite the attempt to overcome the nature/culture distinctions that post-processual archaeology recognized as problematic, the adoption of these twin approaches to material and ideas renders the opposition intact.

At the other end of the philosophical spectrum, the focus upon 'material engagement' in those traditions of archaeology influenced by cognitive science often similarly serves to re-enact the distinction between things and people, mind and body, material and cultural, as the concept of engagement still requires there to be two opposing terms to be engaged (Renfrew 2004, 2007; Ingold 2007a; Jones 2007). The presence of these distinctions in contemporary archaeology has been recognized by Julian Thomas (2004) in his analysis of the modernist conditions of archaeology. Thomas argues that despite the prevailing problems with these distinctions, they were also historically a necessary condition for the formation of archaeology as an object of study: 'As part of the structure of modern thought, archaeology seeks clarity, objectivity, and a reduction to law-like or mathematical terms. It demands precision, unambiguous resolution, universality and the transcendence of local conditions. All of this is achieved by declaring the world to be object-like and free of meaning' (Thomas 2004: 247). Thomas' response is to call for the reinsertion of questions of ethics, rhetoric and social relations into a meaningful world, and for the integration of meaning with materiality. It is to this issue that we will now turn.

Some recent approaches within socio-cultural anthropology have shifted away from the dualistic and dialectical approaches encapsulated in anthropological material culture studies (e.g. Miller 2005a) and post-processual archaeology, to explore an approach that gives methodological attentiveness to things: utilizing things as heuristic devices to expose the outlines of disparate ontologies (Wastell 2007; Henare *et al.* 2007a). Such thinking eschews the presumed divisions between objects and subjects and allows the distinctive relationships between people and things to emerge from fieldwork rather than preceding it (Wastell 2007: 68). While being committed to a methodological approach that places the thing at centre stage rather than using things as an illustrative device for social relations or cultural practices, Henare, Holbraad, and Wastell propose a shift away from epistemological concerns to ontological statements. Rather than perceiving ethnographic informants' statements about their beliefs in the material world as simply world views (in the classic cultural relativist sense), they conceive of them as enunciations of different ontological worlds or natures (Henare *et al.* 2007a: 10). One outcome of such a re-conceptualization of things as heuristics is the realization that there may be no useful methodological distinction between concepts and things. Henare *et al.* (2007a) propose a form of radical constructivism, informed by the work of Giles Deleuze, grounded in a shift away from ontological distinction between 'discourse' and 'reality'. For such anthropologists, concepts can be understood to bring about things, because concepts and things are one and the same (Henare *et al.* 2007a: 13). This can lead to 'an artefact-oriented anthropology . . . [that is] not about material culture' (Henare *et al.* 2007a: 1).

This argument echoes some recent developments within archaeology. The pressing need for an artefact-centred approach that draws together the scientific (positivist) and interpretative (constructivist) strands of archaeology is increasingly recognized. Jones' (2002b) analysis of the Late Neolithic settlement of Barnhouse, Orkney, for example, has used an ostensibly 'biographical' approach to trace the production, circulation, and deposition of Late Neolithic Grooved Ware. Grooved Ware vessels of differing categories were produced from different materials in different parts of the settlement at Barnhouse. These materials were related to significant places in the Neolithic landscape. The differing categories of vessels were used differently, and were finally deposited at specific locations within the settlement and at significant locations in the wider landscape, such as the Stones of Stenness and the Quanterness passage grave. Such an approach entrained the use of scientific techniques, including thin-section petrology and gas chromatography alongside interpretative frameworks; by taking an artefact-centred approach the archaeological artefacts in effect become agents in the process of enfolding together disparate strands of archaeological practice.

In a similar sense Boivin (2000, 2004c, 2008) has argued for a mode of analysis that combines a materialist science with the ethnographic awareness of concept. In Boivin's ethnoarchaeological analysis of domestic architecture in rural Rajasthan, India, she has considered the symbolic and material dimensions of the various soils used in the construction and maintenance of houses, and their role in both creating and expressing the temporal cycles of humans and houses. She has analysed these both ethnographically and using the methods of archaeological science. In rural Rajasthan, most houses are traditionally made of mud. These mud-built houses are ephemeral structures that must be constantly maintained through repeated rebuilding and replastering. The ephemeral and malleable nature of houses means that these structures are very fluid, rooms often being added or removed to suit the needs of the developing family. Houses then are highly dynamic entities that manifest various annual, biological, and household group temporalities. This is then further culturally elaborated by coinciding major annual and lifecycle rituals in which attention is drawn to the link between people, houses, and the use of special materials, such as certain soils. Boivin analyses the interleaving of people, houses, and time through the use of specific materials and practices.

These two studies attempt to treat artefacts and materials as both substance and concept, as analysis attends to the way in which materials combine various conceptual realms: the scientific and the interpretative. These examples focus especially on material agency and disciplinary practice, and specifically on the role a materials-based archaeological science may play in addressing the significance of materiality. How does the analysis of material agency affect broader archaeological interpretations?

To discuss this we would like to draw, finally, on the work of archaeologist Lesley McFadyen (2007a). McFadyen is concerned to analyse the constructional histories of Neolithic long barrows in southern England. Her analyses of the sites of Ascott-under-Wychwood (Oxfordshire) and Beckhampton Road (Wiltshire) have demonstrated how important it is to consider the material and structural qualities of the architecture in the practice of building. She has demonstrated that barrows were built 'on the hoof' as it were. The bayed stone and timber architecture of these monuments needed to be propped up during the construction process. McFadyen argues that the material nature of these construction practices engendered particular socialities of participation. 'Practices, previously seen as less tangible, actually created junctions between bodies/animals/plants/material culture that were memorable, and these remembered events, as concrete memories, embedded themselves in the way in which people understood themselves in relation to others' (McFadyen 2007a: 29). Here we have a very clear example of the way in which an attentiveness to the properties of materials in 'material agency' offers a completely fresh perspective on a subject traditionally treated as self-evident. The material qualities of things, and their involvement in social practices, entrain particular modes of being.

CONCLUSIONS

We conclude with the recognition that the concept of material agency not only forces us to think about materiality, but also promotes a rethink of the concept of society (Latour 2005a). 'Material agency' is not then an anachronistic concept to be taken lightly, an absurdity, or a step too far in postmodernist theory. Instead, it is a fundamental concept that allows us to focus upon the way in which people and things are mutually related. Indeed, we would go so far as to suggest that we should rethink the concept of *agency*, rather than material agency. If we consider the perspective of science studies scholar Karen Barad (2007), the mutual relationship between human agency and material agency is critical. Causality does not lie with human agents; rather, in a performative context the subject is not the site of a stable existence prior to the field that it negotiates. Instead it is the reiterative quality of performance that produces agency and causality: agency is a matter of intra-acting, an enactment, it is not possessed by something or someone. Agency cannot be designated as an attribute of either subjects or objects, as neither subjects nor objects pre-exist as fixed entities (Barad 2007: 214).

Focusing our analyses upon material agency enables us to see that the canonical philosophical terms 'subject' and 'object' are rendered problematic when we start to look in detail at the way in which things and people are combined or attached; agency then becomes a diffuse and performative concept, and objects too are participants in courses of action (Latour 2005a: 70). Agency is not then simply a subject-centred ability to act, but instead defines the way in which courses of action are mediated and articulated over time, whether that action is physically carried out by people or by things. As Latour notes (2005a: 46) actors (be they things or people) do not stand alone, rather an 'actor is what is made to act by many others', an actant. Such a perspective enables us to dissolve the pure distinction between agents acting of their own volition and inanimate materials, and to begin to build models of social action and society that recognize the complexity, and challenges, of the worlds that we enact.

CHAPTER 15

....

FROM IDENTITY AND MATERIAL CULTURE TO PERSONHOOD AND MATERIALITY

....

CHRIS FOWLER

INTRODUCTION

....

In recent years a number of studies have focused on one previously overlooked aspect of identity: personhood. Alongside an emerging phenomenological perspective in the social sciences, these studies have proposed new ways to apprehend the material and cultural world. The term 'personhood' refers to the state or condition of being a person. Studies of personhood investigate how persons emerge from specific ways of being in the world, and consider personhood and concepts of the person to be socially and culturally varied. This chapter explores the development of studies of personhood (mainly in anthropology and archaeology) in the context

I would like to thank Mary Beaudry, Dan Hicks, Kevin Greene, Siân Jones, Elizabeth Kramer, Jane Webster, and Rob Young for providing comments on drafts of this chapter.

of previous and ongoing studies of identity and material culture. In so doing it seeks to demonstrate the importance of relationships between personhood and materiality—a term referring to the material character of the world at large, regardless of it being 'cultural' or 'natural'. The chapter begins by outlining the development of studies of social and cultural identity in the nineteenth and twentieth centuries, and explores the role played by material culture in these studies. The second half of the chapter examines personhood as a specific axis of identity, and explores the integral relation between concepts of personhood and conceptions of materiality.

While the study of identity has always been fundamental to the social sciences, 'identity' is in many ways a problematic term due to the complex range of phenomena that it combines. Throughout this piece I will draw out some of the changing definitions and understandings that have been generated to explain what identity 'is'. I will work from the basis that the term *identity* refers to a shared similarity of character for several beings or things—the way in which they are identical—but it also refers to the distinctiveness of any group, being, or thing—its specific identity. Identities therefore consist of relationships, which show up similarities and differences through social interaction. Identity has been considered at many scales, i.e. ethnic group; nation; societal type (e.g. bands, tribes, chiefdoms, and states), social class, the individual, etc. Many features or axes of identity have been studied *across* these scales, i.e. ethnicity, nationalism, complexity, class, gender, etc. The study of personhood is vital to the social sciences as, like the study of gender or ethnicity, personhood, and concepts of the person can be studied at a variety of scales. In common with other aspects of identity, anthropological studies of personhood are concerned with how social relations mediate between similarity and difference at the level of the person. The study of personhood is emphatically not the study of specific individuals, though it may focus on specific individuals as one element of analysis. Individuality is an element of personhood, just as biological sex is a factor in gender. Studying personhood requires an interrogation of the relationship between human beings, objects, animals, substances, and places at a most fundamental level: the boundaries between persons and objects, persons and animals, and persons and divinities can be shown to vary culturally (Fowler 2004a). Specific categories of personhood emerge in specific social and cultural contexts, and it has been argued that recurrent principles, cutting across various cultural contexts, inform the conceptualization of the person and the generation of personhood (Fowler 2004a). Understanding these categories and principles is not only a sociological or anthropological concern, but also a matter fundamental to archaeologists, cultural geographers, and philosophers—indeed to the wider fields of social and cultural studies. Investigating personhood provides a basis for appreciating similarities and differences in what human beings believe it is to be a person and how human societies categorize the relationships between the human and the non-human.

Therefore, studying personhood takes us to the heart of how material things and cultural activities are given value alongside human lives.

MATERIAL CULTURE AND IDENTITY

I will start by exploring various nineteenth- and twentieth-century formulations of the relationship between identity and material culture in archaeology, anthropology, sociology, and cultural studies. The idea of social and cultural identity has a complex history. I will start with Emile Durkheim (1858–1917) because of the wide influence of his formation of society on subsequent concepts of social identity. For Durkheim material things were infrastructural; they were among the 'morphological' features of society that supported the more significant institutionalized trends in action and thinking, and emergent 'social currents' (think, for instance, of the phenomenon of public mourning for Princess Diana in Britain in 1997) (Poggi 2000: 18–21). In Durkheim's view, societies could be classified by type. The form of a society depended on its adaptation within its local ecology. Durkheim did not hold a progressive or teleological view of social evolution (Poggi 2000: 24–27, 37, 47), but he viewed proliferation in the complexity of social identity as a feature of social differentiation, which he saw as an emergent feature of increased sedentism and population density (Poggi 2000: 33–36, 44–57). For Durkheim, personal individualization was a feature of advanced social differentiation: the greater the social differentiation in a society, the more distinct the resultant identities. In the wake of Durkheim, sociology also produced an unhelpful division between modern/state and non- or pre-modern/state societies, which, I will argue later, obscures nuanced comparison of social and cultural identity across contexts. Durkheim's view that material things were infrastructural, that the formation of the physical world gave rise to social patterns, was arguably part of an influential undercurrent in nineteenth- and earlier twentieth-century social thought which also flowed through evolutionary approaches to cultural identity. In the next section, I will explore formulations of the relationship between identity and material culture, before examining how this approach was questioned and replaced by a more sophisticated concept of identity as politically negotiated.

Material reflections of cultural identity

Material culture was so fundamental to the development of both archaeology and anthropology in the late nineteenth and early twentieth century that it was often taken to 'reflect' culture. This was particularly the case for evolutionary approaches to culture and society. For instance, the archaeologist and collector of ethnographic artefacts General Pitt-Rivers (1827–1900), who arranged societies in a progressivist evolutionary continuum based on artefact typology, clearly took simple forms of material culture as an index of a simple culture (cf. Lubbock 1865 or Morgan 1877). Such a stance ignores the fact that, for instance, kinship systems and cosmologies may be extremely complex among mobile hunter-gatherer communities even if the range of artefacts constructed is simple (i.e. streamlined and effective). In a similar way Durkheim's view (*op. cit.*) that increasing sedentism and population density led to social differentiation and proliferating forms of identity ignores the identities accorded to non-human elements of the world, and does not allow for the complex social roles occupied by members of small-scale communities. There were, however, attempts to locate material culture within broader studies of culture: for instance in the study of European prehistory Gordon Childe (1926) and later Colin Renfrew (1987) both attempted to trace a proto-Indo-European language by analysing contemporary and historical languages as well as prehistoric archaeological evidence. Structural and symbolic approaches such as those developed by Claude Lévi-Strauss in the 1960s (e.g. 1964, 1966a, 1966b) recognized that animals, places, natural phenomena and substances could all act as symbols that were organized into meaningful cultural orders. Here culture was perceived to operate in a manner akin to language, representing a means of communication or 'a kind of speech' (Tilley 1989: 187). The application of this view to material culture studies has the strength of recognizing the importance of semantic 'speech acts' and allows us to read material patterns as though they are meaningful texts, but runs the risk of reducing away the qualities that distinguish material culture from spoken and written language. For instance, the way that a song and a conversation work are different, and different again is the way that a room works. While the cultural element of material culture is recognized here, its material aspect requires further theoretical consideration.

A fundamental problem for archaeologists is also instructive for all the social sciences: material culture does *not* simply reflect cultural identity, yet there are observable patterns in the distribution of specific kinds of material culture. Many nineteenth-century studies made inferences about cultural affiliation based on artefact style and not all showed sufficient acknowledgement of this problem. Early twentieth-century culture-historical anthropologists such as Franz Boas (1848–1942) sought to understand the nature of a society in terms of its distinctive cultural character and questioned the existence of identifiable cross-cultural sociological laws of the type proposed by the social evolutionists (e.g. Boas 1938). Material culture was part of a culture's character, which was explained as a result of a combination of environmental factors and historical trends, events, and social and political circumstances. Meanwhile, culture-historical archaeology, exemplified by the work of Vere Gordon Childe (1892–1957; see e.g. Childe 1926) took a similar stance, but here material culture played a more central role in characterizing the culture of a particular society or 'folk', and greater attention was paid to the long-term development and transformations of that culture. An 'archaeological culture' was defined as 'an aggregate of associated elements of material culture' (Piggott 1954: 302) and was taken to relate to a meaningful cultural entity. Childe did not always think that these entities were ethnic groups (see McNairn 1980: 46–73) but the association between the concept of an 'archaeological culture' and a 'culture' has proved difficult to escape.

Culture-historical anthropology and archaeology regarded material culture, alongside language and traditional practices, as a *reflection* of cultural identity. A potter made pots according to a cultural blueprint, following traditional practices and bringing the idea in his or her head into material reality through this cultural lens. The form, the identity, of the potter and the pot were both reflections of cultural precepts: culture was something people did not question, but reiterated as traditional. Cultural historians believed that these styles, these cultural traits, could be mapped out in time and space and grouped together as 'cultures'.

In Childe's view, cultural identities were consistent and traditional, only changing gradually unless a socio-economic crisis or population replacement occurred, allowing a new cultural order to be established in a region. A comparison of the overall assemblages of material culture produced by neighbouring societies would illustrate how cultures were affiliated with and distinguished from one another. While patterns in the distribution of practices and things may coincide with certain socio-cultural boundaries, ethnographic and ethnoarchaeological studies have shown that these rarely represent the boundaries of ethnic groups in the way that culture historians imagined (e.g. Hodder 1982a; Shennan 1982; Jones 1997: 106–127; Lucy 2005; cf. Stark 1998b). This is not to say that identifying clusters of cultural practices and products is without value—as we shall see the identification of such patterns is a vital starting point in analysing the principles structuring practice—but the long-term patterns in material culture studied by culture historians do not always relate to the histories of ethnic groups.

From the 1920s, the functionalist and structural-functionalist schools in anthropology had sought to explain both identities and objects in terms of their practical and social functions. For anthropologists, such as Malinowski, material things were important only as a means to view an overlying and more important social structure. Malinowski (1922: 23) invoked the image of the material and structural bases of a community as its 'skeleton' with daily activities as its 'flesh', and cultural customs as its 'spirit'. Malinowski (1922: 17) paid a great deal of attention to material culture (recorded through photography and the detailed counting of exchange items, for instance), but when he talked of 'concrete manifestations' of cultural phenomena he meant entire observable social events, not the material media mobilized in those events. From the 1950s the functionalist and evolutionary perspectives characteristic of processual or 'New' archaeology focused heavily upon material culture, which is the primary form of archaeological evidence for past societies. While processual archaeology differed from structural-functionalist anthropology in the greater emphasis it placed on the adaptive value of material culture, the archaeologists arguably shared the anthropologists' goal of reconstructing social organization and characterizing cultural forms. The difference was that this had to be achieved by interpreting material culture without the observation of social events.

Processual archaeology adopted a specific definition of culture, which itself provided the basis for understanding material culture. Culture was regarded as 'an extra-somatic mechanism' of adaptation, and 'the functions of culture' were understood as 'to relate man to his environment . . . and relate man to man' (White 1959: 8). Here, culture was understood as the way that human beings extend their influence outside their bodies in order to adapt to changing conditions and fulfil human needs. As a result, material culture was understood in terms of its adaptive function: whether that function operated in environmental, economic, social, ideological, or other spheres of activity. Communities were investigated by examining patterns in material culture, but adaptation was held responsible for the form of social organization. For instance, the emergence of social elites was often explained as an adaptation responding to population increase, increased demand on resources, and increased interaction and competition between local communities (see Brumfiel and Earle 1987: 2). Identities were interpreted as cultural responses to changes in external conditions—they fulfilled human needs and benefited the community. This perspective does not examine how people actively consider or experience their identities or engage in disputes over identity.

While the processual explanation of social stratification oversimplifies the complex political relations involved in its emergence, processual archaeologists did attempt to think further about what identity is and about the social identities that were produced by distinct forms of social relations. Sociologist Ward Goodenough (1965) developed the concept of 'social persona' latent in the work of Durkheim and Mauss, and this was taken up by processual archaeologists Lewis Binford (1971), Arthur Saxe (1970), and Joseph Tainter (1978) in order to discern the rank and status of the deceased from mortuary evidence. Goodenough argued that a social persona was a composite of all the social roles a person occupied within a specific context of interaction. These roles were determined by one person's relationships with others (e.g. mother, daughter, sister, queen) and involved specific social rights and duties. Saxe (1970: 7) argued that all of the aspects of a social persona of a deceased person demanded acknowledgement from the alter egos during the funeral (e.g. her status as mother would be acknowledged by her children). In addition, Binford (1971: 17) hypothesized that the greater the number of social roles composing the social persona the more important the individual would be, the more lavish their funeral, and the more complex the organization of the society to which they belonged. Binford argued that a funeral would reflect the relationship of the greatest scale: i.e. the status of the deceased as a king would dictate the scale of the funeral activity, not his role as a brother. Grave goods, for instance, were evidence of social roles. Social complexity within the community was measured based on social differentiation observed in the constituent features of the mortuary rites, such as the range of equipment in the grave and the amount of energy invested in the mortuary furniture and monument. Far less attention was paid to the negotiation of these roles through the funerary rites, since such roles were taken to reflect the adaptive mechanisms of the cultural group (including the development of social stratification) and therefore to provide an accurate account of the *status quo*. Importantly, Goodenough (1965: 7) is explicit that a social persona is contextual. While Binford, Saxe, and Tainter all recognized this, they paid insufficient attention to mortuary rites as a *specific* context for interaction. Tainter, for instance, follows Saxe in viewing rich infant burials as a reflection of 'social ranking by birth' (Tainter 1978: 106) and does not consider the explicit context in which the distinct social persona of a *deceased* infant arises. Yet mortuary rites transform the dead and may present them in ways which are not typical of other spheres of life, even though statements about the nature of personhood and other features of identity are made through these rituals (Fowler 2004a: 79–100).

In all of these perspectives, the material world reflected culture (cf. Thomas 1996: 11–30; 2004: 202–203, 210–212). Culture was seen either as a mental blueprint followed by practitioners or as an ecological development responding to the infrastructural environment. The conception of identity was normative and epiphenomenal: identity passively reflected more fundamental issues, such as cultural tradition, means of adaptation, or symbolic orders. Interestingly, material culture occupied the same passive position in relation to these major forces. These approaches were not concerned with the individual identities of past people, nor with the conscious generation of identities as a cultural, social, and political issue. Exactly how identities emerge from social and cultural relations was seldom explicitly theorized.

Negotiating the generation of identity and material culture

During the 1970s and 1980s, there was widespread recognition that existing perspectives on identity and on material culture did not satisfactorily account for social and political activity. Firm critiques of normative conceptions of cultural identity were produced, and alternative roles played by material culture in the production of social identities were investigated. One key development lay in critical perspectives on how ethnic identity was negotiated (e.g. Barth 1969a; Bentley 1987; Jones 1997). Socio-cultural anthropologist Fredrik Barth (1969b) argued that ethnic groups were self-defining entities that seek to maintain a sense of ethnic boundedness. However, what is at issue for one community may not be for others: Barth characterized the negotiation of 'boundary objects' and 'boundary subjects' as culturally relative. In other words, some of the practices, objects, and subjects within the experience of an ethnic community become issues by which they define themselves in relation to other ethnic groups at certain times as relations between communities change. Other practices or objects might be shared over large areas and not become boundary objects for any of the communities sharing them. Barth also illustrated how individuals could transcend ethnic boundaries, and how ethnic identities could themselves change. During and after the 1960s it became widely accepted in the social sciences that identities were socially and politically negotiated. This led to the investigation of the role that material culture played in producing, reinforcing, and renegotiating such identities.

For example, some archaeologists adopted Marxist perspectives in conceptualizing how class identities emerge when people come to share the same material conditions of existence and relationships to the means of production, enabling a constrained range of possibilities for them (see McGuire 2006). In this view, people of a particular class inhabit their conditions in similar ways and struggle with other classes that experience a different range of socio-economic possibilities. The tensions between these classes are mediated in various ways. For instance, social institutions exist, which play an ideological role in policing identities and maintaining particular relations between identity groups. From a Marxist perspective, although material culture objectifies the relations that made it, it does not simply reflect a cultural, social, and political order; it is both part of the material conditions of existence and media through which ideological positions are presented and relations are contested. Mortuary practices, for instance, do not passively reflect identities but may be manipulated to make ideological 'masking' or 'naturalizing' statements about identity and social order. Thus, Shanks and Tilley (1982) saw collective burial in Neolithic chambered tombs as projecting an ideology of equality after death that belied inequalities in life, while Shennan (1982) saw early Bronze Age single burials of adorned bodies as naturalizing hierarchy and the institutional power of those buried. Similarly, monument building might mask moments of concern over the security of institutional power or act to enhance the impression of power, rather than reflect the fully established power of elites.

Another key development recognizing the role of material culture in the struggle over identity was in the theorizing of 'objectification'. The key premise is that things embody cultural ideas and that people's identities (and bodies) are shaped as they produce, experience, exchange, and consume those things (see Chapman 1996: 206–210; Miller 1987; Tilley 2007b). The practices by which people make things, live with them, and use them also make those people, so the process of objectification is also a process of personification. Identities are produced out of the ongoing interactions between people and things, not just different groups of people. The dynamics of interaction between what was previously separated out into the cultural and the material (which was seen as taken up and shaped by culture) or into the subject and the object thus come to the fore and illuminate the problems inherent in treating these concepts as real, definitive, and separable categories. To me, the ability to consider this mutual constitution of people and things, materials and cultures, is a prerequisite for any sophisticated analysis of material culture and identity. At the same time, the co-emergence of material worlds and types of identities needs to be placed in the context of social and political interactions. For instance, the sociologist Dick Hebdige (1979) traced the emergence of new cultural identities such as punk alongside the emergence of new material cultures, but situated this clearly within an account of the social and political forces of 1970s Britain. Hebdige used the term 'subcultures' to describe cultural differences in identity that derived from social and political divisions within Britain (i.e. punks and Conservative politicians are all British; the cultural differences lie elsewhere). Equally, working from a theory of objectification, the approach that socio-cultural anthropologist Daniel Miller (1987) developed to material culture and identity placed the emphasis on consumers, who, in using material things, produced their own identities—not in conditions of their making, but in the context of the social, cultural, and political world in which they lived. While the definition of self through consumerism stems from a long historical trajectory where consumption has emerged as a dominant cultural practice (Thomas 2004: 209; Greene 2008), and may therefore not be typical of all human history, the basic idea that personal identities and material worlds are mutually constitutive within the cultural, political, social, and material conditions in which they historically occur has the widest possible appeal.

The idea that 'object and subject are indelibly conjoined in a dialectical relationship' (Tilley 2007b: 61) and that the same practices produce both simultaneously, led to a renewed emphasis on the *practices* that lie behind the formation of such subjects and objects (e.g. Munn 1986; Battaglia 1990; Devisch 1993; Csordas 1999b; Dobres 2000), often drawing on the 'practice theory' of Pierre Bourdieu (1970, 1977) or the 'structuration theory' of Anthony Giddens (1984). These studies concentrated variously upon: productive acts; consumption; bodily comportment; dwelling, inhabitation and the routines of daily life; exchanges or transactions; and special ritual transformations such as rites of passage. Most studies combined several of these spheres of activity to show how the same generative principles are enacted in each sphere, illustrating that dispositions towards certain ways of doing things become carried over from one sphere of practice to others. Bourdieu's notion of *habitus* was frequently employed to describe these 'systems of durable, transposable dispositions' (Bourdieu 1977: 72). It was suggested that the human and non-human elements of the world were all affected equally, so that houses are organized in the same way as bodies, villages, and the landscape, for instance (e.g. Bourdieu 1970; Richards 1996), and often conceptualized as parallel entities. This transferability of organizing principles from one scale and sphere to others frames the possibilities for the kinds of actions that can take place within each context, the ways that meaning can be conveyed and identities formed (e.g. Moore 1986: 75–79). Through such actions, cultural orders, relationships, and identities become sedimented in human bodies and are made manifest in objects, buildings, and landscapes (e.g. a mutual dependence between male and female components of the world: Bourdieu 1970). But cultural orders are not static. People can draw on existing meanings to make new contextual statements, for instance by putting things somewhere other than their normal place or acting atypically, and trends in practices can be altered. For instance, in his 1994 study *Fragments from Antiquity* archaeologist John Barrett illustrated how the process of transformation can be dissected by considering the dynamic relationship between social and political change and material culture. His account of the Neolithic monumental complexes at Avebury and Durrington Walls in southern England demonstrated how the construction sequence of large earthworks—ditched and banked enclosures (henges), burial mounds (barrows), and the exceptional artificial Silbury Hill—involved continuities in practice but also set up new conditions for relations between people. Some were able to claim new social, political, and cultural positions for themselves as a result of their place in the acts of construction and their emergent ability to call on the labour of others (Barrett 1994: 13–32). The act of making a monument also made a community. Rather than seeing material culture as reflecting identity—as in Renfrew's (1973d) reading of these monuments as evidence of 'chiefdoms'—identity depends on social, political, and cultural relationships, which change as individuals and communities interact with one another, including through the enduring media of their world.

The recognition in post-processual archaeology of agents who were able to reflect on the practices they undertook, and to renegotiate the material conditions of their existence through practical engagement, brought an important watershed in the archaeology of identity. Where earlier approaches had left identity in the background, archaeologists used practice theory to make a new connection between trends in practice and forms of identities, but a connection where practices do not 'equal' identities. Rather, similar practices might be taken up by several different identity groups, or an identity group might develop from shared practices that become a means of identification for that group. Structuralist anthropology had already recognized how cultural symbols are manipulated by social agents: Lévi-Strauss (1966a) introduced the concept of *bricolage*, which was foundational to the development of these approaches to cultural identity. The use of practice theory informed a post-structuralist approach to symbolic orders and cultural identities in which these exist only because they are constantly reproduced through practice (e.g. Bentley 1987).

Other post-structuralist approaches influenced studies of identity and material culture from the late 1980s onwards. As Christopher Tilley has argued, we cannot expect to 'read' the material remains of the past as a single 'text' with a single meaning as such texts are always 'written' by multiple agents and may have been interpreted in many different ways in the past—just as they are in the present (Tilley 1989). The relationship between subject-positions, or identities, and material culture may therefore be unstable, and open to question at certain junctures. The proliferation in material culture over the long term of human existence indicates its importance in the constant struggle over social relationships and social identities. For instance, the building of Neolithic chambered tombs in stone not only projected forwards certain relationships between identity groups both living and dead but also generated new relationships; not only proscribed certain experiences of space and interactions within these spaces but also provided future generations with the possibility of altering those relationships (e.g. through architectural embellishment) within new social, political, and cultural contexts unintended and unforeseen by the original builders (Olsen 1990).

Post-structural approaches define identity as something that is continuously deferred, contextual, and inter-referential (e.g. Russell 2004). A number of (broadly post-structural) analyses have paid renewed attention to the relational construction of personal identity: that is, these approaches stress that identity is relative to cultural ideals and to interactions with other agents within specific contexts (e.g. Barth 1969a; Strathern 1988; Butler 1993). Since people mutually constitute each other, and since identities can only be understood in terms of the other identities with which they articulate in specific contexts, identity can therefore only be glimpsed temporarily and partially: we encounter people involved in processes through which they struggle to attain and maintain specific aspects of identity in the eyes of others and in their own minds. This approach differs from the interpretations of 'social persona' mainly in the emphasis on studying a specific context of action—not as indicator of the 'whole' identity, but as providing a distinct arena for the development of particular features of identity. As such, archaeologists do not recover the material remains of complete past identities, but rather the remains of media that people manipulated in the processes and strategies by which they negotiated their identities within specific contexts (Casella and Fowler 2004: 8; Fowler 2004c).

There has therefore been an increase in studies of how material culture is used in negotiating identities. The use of material culture to gain a new perspective on those whose lives are poorly represented in documentary sources, including an emphasis on subaltern voices, has been a particular focus of historical archaeology (Wilkie 2006: 14–15). Such studies in historical archaeology have often identified subordinated and subjugated communities, and have studied their uses of material culture to destabilize the identity politics that surround them (e.g. McGuire and Paynter 1991; Yentsch 1994; Hall and Silliman 2006). Other historical archaeologists have examined the role of material culture in the creation of new identities through processes such as creolization (Ferguson 1992). Historical archaeology can identify particular ethnic groups by name and make strong inferences about class, caste, and other identities in the past, as well as about the processes of change. This is not usually possible in prehistoric archaeology: even where it is clear that certain forms of material culture had particular geographical distributions, and that differing material practices came together at a given time and place, it is seldom possible to identify the nature of the socio-cultural groups that were significant in socio-political interactions. Nonetheless, more sophisticated appreciations of identity politics in the past are emerging, with a strong emphasis on the processes of change.

For instance, one important debate in prehistory concerns the extent to which, or levels on which, a 'Beaker cultural phenomenon' existed across large parts of Europe, and if so, how it relates to past identities and communities (e.g. Needham 2005; Vander Linden 2006). It has long been postulated that a 'cultural package' most recognizable by graves containing Beaker pottery, bodies laying in a crouched position on one side and, sometimes, specific suites of other objects, spread across Europe during the period c.2500–2250 cal BC. Culture-historic approaches had characterized this as a 'Beaker culture' or even 'Beaker folk'. However, there is a lack of an associated unified pattern of settlement or subsistence, and it seems unlikely that this reflects the spread of a particular ethnic group or even 'archaeological culture' (Burgess and Shennan 1976). Instead of seeing 'Beaker people' as an ethnic group we could suggest that the period when this material cultural phenomenon became most widespread was characterized by a loose sense of ethnic boundaries and identities (Vander Linden 2006). In other words, the complex of Beaker material culture and mortuary practices did not always constitute a 'boundary object', at least not at an ethnic level. Indeed, in contrast with views of Beaker burials as statements of individual prestige and social competition, Vander Linden (2006) suggests that a lessening in violence, social tension, and social competition underlie the spread of Beakers in southern France.

This cultural phenomenon was taken up and responded to by different communities in different ways, and the meanings and contextual uses of Beaker pottery changed over time. When Beaker cultural practices and products first appeared in Britain they were not widely integrated into existing practices, and may have existed in tension with the political orientation of other cultural phenomena in some regions (e.g. large ceremonial gatherings at henge monuments in southern England—Thorpe and Richards 1984). Stuart Needham (2005) has illustrated that initially Beaker practices and products may have been adopted by fairly few communities in Britain, transmitted mainly though existing long-distance social relations based on the exchange of other prestigious goods (which may also have involved some long-distance mobility). Then, c.2250 BC, there was more widespread interest in Beaker material culture and burial practices. During c.2250–1950 BC a proliferation of personal objects became associated with those buried with Beakers, and the numbers of Beaker burials increased dramatically. In northern Britain Beaker pottery was contemporaneous with indigenous 'Food Vessel' style ceramics during this period, and the same kinds of material culture were sometimes found in both Food Vessel and Beaker burials. The principles in how bodies with Beakers were laid out in the grave were shared over large areas (e.g. mainly on an east–west orientation in northern England, mainly north–south in central southern England), while the principles for how those buried with Food Vessels (who were also commonly cremated) were laid out sometimes varied locally. In eastern York-shire, Pierpoint (1980: 247–248) argues that the choices in which side of the body males and females were placed in the grave (left or right side) were localized, while the patterns for Beaker burials were more consistent across the region. Furthermore, in Northumberland many Food Vessel burials followed the same principles as Beaker burials during the period, but by 1900 BC both Food Vessel and Beaker burials showed increasing variation in the orientation of the dead in graves and cists (Fowler in press). Bodies were increasingly cremated before deposition, but Beakers were not deposited with cremated remains even though Food Vessels were trans-formed into funerary urns. Indeed, c.1950–1700 BC Beakers became far rarer, and at this point their use in burials was 'nostalgic' (Needham 2005). Beaker burial practices thus followed a complex history in relation with other burial practices and Beakers were understood alongside other forms of material culture as identities were renegotiated at various scales.

Thus, Beaker pottery had many different contextual meanings over several hundred years—it was variously deployed in expressing a distinctive and locally 'alien' identity, in attaining the kudos of the exotic, in social emulation, in developing a ritual arena through specific burial practices, possibly in the creolization of identities over large areas, in new forms of commensality, in rearticulating local social dynamics, and in appealing to vanishing ideas and identities. The extent to which types of identity can be identified with surety in the archaeological record should not therefore be seen as dividing historical and prehistoric archaeologies: An investigation of the changing roles of material culture in relation to identities is vital to both fields. Both fields have continued in a similar direction by considering the extent to which identities are fixed or relational, essential or contextual—or more accurately, by examining *in what ways* identities were contested, contextual and relational (Casella and Fowler 2004: 3).

PERSONHOOD AND MATERIALITY

In this section I bring to the fore one axis of social identity that has been of increasing importance in the social sciences throughout the twentieth and twenty-first centuries: personhood. Tracing its origins to Mauss, I explore the concept of personhood in relation with the emergence of the concept of materiality. These two terms are themselves fairly new to the social sciences, with widespread use mainly from the 1990s onwards, and are involved in a valuable repositioning of the understanding of identity and material culture. I will pursue the development of approaches to personhood and materiality through social and cultural anthropology and prehistoric archaeology, since many studies in these fields were part of that development. Then I will consider the impact of these developments on history and historical archaeology to illustrate the value of comparison between approaches and across different historical and cultural contexts.

Personhood and identity

Social anthropologist Ward Goodenough perceived a division between social identity and personal identity. He argued that social identity is concerned with social rights, duties, and roles while personal identity is an interiorized sense of self that underlies that social identity:

> A social identity is an aspect of the self that makes a difference in how one's rights and duties distribute to specific others. Any aspect of self whose alteration entails no change in how people's rights and duties are mutually distributed, although it affects their emotional orientations to one another and the way they choose to exercise their privileges, has to do with personal identity but not with social identity.
>
> Goodenough (1965: 3–4)

Goodenough's recognition that social identities are defined by social relationships was important, but I do not accept his division between social identity and personal identity: 'social identities' are not a feature distinct from the other aspects that make people who they are and changing social identities very clearly impact on 'emotional orientations'. Therefore, we should consider identity (social, cultural, personal) holistically, considering the relationships between different aspects of identity such as gender, ethnicity, or personhood. These are all heuristic concepts when applied across contexts. We risk leaving a hole at the centre of the concept of identity if what it is to be a person is not considered. Personhood needs to be examined as another heuristic concept, one with fundamental implications for how identity is understood.

A thing may become invested with identity but not be a person: for example, a garment may be gendered or be used to convey an ethnic identity. Identity consists of aspects or axes such as gender, ethnicity, class, age, sexuality, and a host of other phenomena. The idea of *personhood* stands in the same relation to identity as these other phenomena, all of which are investigated in parallel conceptual frames. For instance, we can ask to what extent personhood is a category, to what extent it is natural or naturalized, to what extent it is performed, or to what extent it springs from relationships or practices. The same questions could be asked of gender or ethnicity. In this section, I outline the key features of the sociology and anthropology of personhood as they relate to studies of identity, and in the next section consider the role of materiality in these approaches. It is possible to identify key principles structuring the practices that constitute persons, objects, and places out of bodies and materials. These principles are intertwined with ideas about the relationships between living human beings, animals, substances, the dead, objects, and places. It is my contention that these principles recur in different contexts, playing key roles in shaping distinct modes of personhood. I will therefore illustrate how particular concepts of the person are bound up with specific ways of perceiving the material world and valuing its features.

Nineteenth- and twentieth-century Western discourse often prioritized the individuality and the indivisibility of each person. The person was understood as unique, singular, complete, and contained within and bounded by the body. Across the humanities and social sciences, such a view has been increasingly problematized by approaches that recognize how persons are formed through complex relationships (e.g. Douglas and Ney 1998). Furthermore, cultural diversity in concepts of the person have long been recognized. In his 1938 study of 'The category of the human mind: the notion of the person; the notion of self', Mauss sketched out an area that needed proper interdisciplinary study: concepts of the person (Mauss 1985). Mauss asked whether the cultural conception of the person is the same everywhere and at all times, and whether people emerge as persons in the same ways. Mauss suggested as frames of reference *persona* (a 'mask', an expression of an identity taken on), *personnage* (role or character), *personne* (person), and *moi* (self). For Mauss clans were enduring assemblies of characters (*personnage*), roles that generation after generation of human being would occupy. The role taken on, the *persona*, was like a kind of mask that, given changes in social organization, may then become associated with the individual 'wearing' it so that rights to personhood became identified with the individual rather than the position occupied. His thesis was that frames of reference for personhood have changed throughout time and varied across space so that, for instance, many non-state societies exhibited clear concepts of *personae* and *personnage*, but only with the Romans did this develop into a sense of a priori rights to personhood: '[societies] who have made of the human person a complete entity, independent of all others save God, are rare' (Mauss 1985: 14). Indeed, he argues that the individualistic sense of self we take for granted has emerged from recent European history and is fragile (Mauss 1985: 22–23).

Mauss' legacy is the idea that personhood is relative to socio-cultural context: it is not simply that the terms of reference for personhood vary, but that the very formulation and experience of being a person varies according to distinct cultural ideologies. While we could cast doubt on Mauss' interpretations of the societies he considered, and might replace the terms he developed for categories of the person or question the categories he used, the ideas that personhood has to be 'attained' in many communities and that identities are not accorded on the basis of an a priori individuality have profound implications. The construction of a prehistory and history to the category of the person based largely on using contemporary societies as exemplars for stages in cultural evolution, which other regions of the world had notionally occupied in the past, was deeply problematic, but the idea that we could construct a comparative history of personhood presents a project that contemporary archaeologists, anthropologists, and sociologists can—and, I believe, should—revisit.

An example of the implications of this approach will illustrate the significance of studying personhood compared with simply attending to the lives of specific individuals in a society. Mauss' view that personhood was understood from the basis of cultural mores, cultural ideologies, was adopted by Fortes in his ethnographic work with the Tallensi (Fortes 1987; see LaFontaine 1985 and Carsten 2003: 88). According to Fortes, Tallensi personhood could only be fully achieved once the male life cycle was completed, i.e. after a man had successfully matured, married, procreated, and died, and divination had confirmed the person as an ancestor. The quality necessary for achieving this version of personhood, *yin*, is transmitted along male lines, while, as Carsten (2003: 89–91) relates, *nuor-yin* follows female lines. *Yin* is a relational quality of male lineage, while *nuor-yin* lines distinguish those otherwise of the same *yin* line. Both forces are, however, understood in terms of relationships: ancestral lines of relationships lie at the heart of society and are foundational to each person. Fortes saw personhood as emergent from social relationships, which were negotiated in light of specific moral codes, such as respect for ancestors, and social imperatives, such as the perpetuation of lineages. Crucially, full Tallensi personhood is not accorded to all human beings, yet may be extended to some animals (sacred crocodiles). There are gradations, stages, and types of personhood within Tallensi society, which the anthropologist can study in order to appreciate the Tallensi cultural world.

Thus, individual mortal human beings are not always seen as persons and not always seen as the same type of person. LaFontaine suggests a distinction between individuality and personhood within several small-scale societies:

> ... personhood varies according to social criteria which contain the capacities of the individual within defined roles and categories. Indeed, one might say that where personhood is a status reserved for defined categories of people, parents or men, by implication those who are not persons are individuals and such concepts may be said to distinguish more clearly between these two ideas than most western versions.
>
> LaFontaine (1985: 133)

Throughout the nineteenth and twentieth centuries in the social sciences, the terms *individual* and *individuality* were frequently associated with an indivisible, autonomous, and self-determining person who secondarily enters into social relations. Yet, it would be misleading to take this narrow understanding of personhood to form a useful basis for cultural comparison. While LaFontaine's point that not all human beings are full persons is important, the idea that humans are individuals first and latterly social persons is problematic since the individual is already a social category with a specific history. As social scientists we are interested in studying human beings, whether or not full personhood is accorded to them, but how specific human beings stand with respect to personhood is a crucial issue in understanding their lives. Western concepts of personhood celebrate individuality and see no distinction between the concept of the individual and the person when dealing with human beings (though we might acknowledge the individuality of a pet dog, for instance, without according it the status of a person). Here persons *are* individuals, and individuals are persons by right. However, when operating at an anthropological, sociological, or archaeological level, we would do better to take the analytical perspective that individuality is one aspect of personhood in a loosely similar way that being biologically female would be one aspect of a person's gender. Indeed, persons are composite and may consist of qualities, such as individuality, mind, or personal soul, as well as other features, which may be given cultural priority. Some of these personal qualities may also be recognized in animals, objects, places, and even natural phenomena. Thus, human beings may have qualities (e.g. uniqueness, self-awareness, will, biography) that we would gloss together under the heading of individuality, and be seen as potentially persons, but not be thought of in terms of the Western concept of the individual.

Mauss' work set twentieth-century agendas for interpreting persons according to the social relations from which they emerged, and, from the outset, with Mauss' *Essai sur le Don*, which was published in 1950 (Mauss 1990), material culture was seen as playing a central role in the production of personhood. In *The Gift* Mauss characterized objects and bodies not as owned by autonomous individuals but as owed to others. There are many different ways that persons may be relational, because many different kinds of relationships are evident across human societies. Persons are also 'internally' complex in that as they are generated through their relationships with others each person is a multiply-authored product of those relations. Marriott's (1976) study of social relations, personhood, and the caste system in India illustrated this while adopting Dumont's (1970) stance that while the West champions the individual as the moral and experiential basis on which society rests, India sacralizes society as providing the moral, cultural, spiritual, and social basis for existence, including through the concept of *dharma* (duty). Marriott (1976: 109–110) examined social interactions within relations characterized by social duty: '[v]aried codes of action or codes for conduct (*dharma*) are thought to be naturally embodied in actors and otherwise substantialized in the flow of things that pass among actors'. Central to Marriott's study was the importance of substances in conveying essences or qualities that influenced the internal composition of the person. He argued that '. . . dividual persons absorb heterogenous material substances. They must also give out from themselves particles of their own coded substances—essences, residues, or other active influences—that may then reproduce in others something of the nature of the persons in whom they have originated'

(Marriott 1976: 111). Some of these substances are gross, others more subtle, and each has an impact on the person permeated by it. The ultimate aim of such interactions was to achieve 'power understood as vital energy, substance-code of subtle, homogenous quality, and high, consistent transactional status...' (Marriott 1976: 137).

There are, however, many different strategies through which Indian communities believe such a state can be achieved. The ethos and activities of particular castes, age groups, and cults form the basis for many such strategies. A person's internal composition therefore relates to their exterior relations, and each belongs within specific social networks where certain substances (from 'gross' alcohol and raw meat to 'subtle' grain, money, and knowledge) are exchanged at differing tempos. Materiality is understood in a different way to in Western conceptions here: a different sense of personhood accompanies a different sense of the properties of material and non-material culture. This dividual or composite personhood is also represented in distinctive ways: Pinney (2002: 101) has discussed how central Indian photographic portraits of persons are manipulated to 'set aspects of a person against aspects of that same person' by producing images in which the person depicted appears more than once.

Forms of personhood which stress the relational constitution of the person are not restricted to India or Africa. Nancy Munn's *The Fame of Gawa* argued that persons were generated through an *intersubjective* field of 'social spacetime' (Munn 1986: 14–16). She describes how Gawan practices constitute persons and how persons constitute one another through engaging in those acts that are part of ongoing trends in social practice. She outlines her '...concern with types of practice and their component acts as forming self–other relations and the constructions of self or *aspects* of self that are entailed in these relations' (Munn 1986: 14, italics original). Munn describes how bodies, along with gardens, food, shell goods, and canoes, can be seen as 'qualisigns' of certain types of value, 'that is, they exhibit something other than themselves *in* themselves' (Munn 1986: 74, italics original). This idea is crucial as it enables us to appreciate how qualities such as 'fame', which Gawan persons encapsulate, can be made evident equally in the human body and in other material media. Social practices, such as gift giving, effect 'value transformations' as well as producing and displaying value. At the same time persons are constituted through these practices.

As well as examining a series of expected transformations in the course of ordinary lives, Munn considers an atypical person, the witch, as someone who works against these normative schemes of value production and transformation. While for most Gawans fame, a desirable personal quality, 'is created by a circulation of the identity beyond the physical body via transacted objects that carry with them one's name and the embedment of the self in the reconnaissance of others' witches and witchcraft are '...constituted through the autonomous circulation of the inner, nonrecognizable and unrecognizable component of the person' (Munn 1986: 232). Ordinary persons operate in a known field of relations, which are made manifest in their bodies, objects, buildings, and gardens, while witches attempt to transcend the limits of these forms and normal intersubjective relations through their antisocial activities in which their personhood is extended outside their bodies in unseen ways. Munn (1986: 215–233) further sees the figure of the witch as a psychological construct reinforcing the ethos of Gawan interaction dominating their lives. The concept of the witch and precautions taken against witchcraft provide an avenue through which the conscious reinforcement of that egalitarian ethos occurs in condemning the kind of individualistic will to inequality that the witch represents. That will is there in each Gawan person, but must be negated.

In these examples we can see that social relationships, out of which persons emerge as persons, involve material things so that, as socio-cultural anthropologist Alfred Gell has argued, personhood is routinely distributed outside of human bodies (Gell 1998: 96–154; cf. Hoskins 1998). While we must acknowledge that identities are often contested, we should not implicitly accept that a struggle for individuality and self-benefit is the primary driving force in how identities are negotiated. To take this stance would presume a particular type or feature of personhood as desirable above all others, and implies that, for instance, people care for their individual identities and fates more than they do for those of their families, friends, ancestors, lineages, compatriots, their beliefs, cultural worlds, environments, and so on. It would also overlook the role of socio-cultural ideologies in the formation of personhood, such as the Gawan contrasting of witchcraft and beneficial social interaction (and the figure of the anti-social witch is itself a recurring cultural trend).

It is therefore vital to examine cultural beliefs about personhood and consider the role of material culture compared with human bodies as media through which personhood is negotiated. The formulation of the relationship between personhood and materiality is culturally variable, but certain principles recur in different contexts. At a general level, each person consists of multiple qualities or aspects: for example mind, body, soul or body, breath, image. Difference lies not only in the identification of specific personal aspects, but also in how these features of personhood are distributed in the material world: in other words, how the material world is valued. Marilyn Strathern (1988) considered Marriott's concept of the dividual person in relation to Melanesian communities. She concluded that while Melanesian persons were 'multiply-authored' composites like Indian persons, and therefore could be seen as dividual, they differed in that they were potentially separable into constituent parts or 'partible'. Each person may owe aspects of their person to others for the food that sustains them, the bloodlines that produced them, the relations that nurtured them, and so on. In Melanesia Strathern (1988) argues that the debts people owe to others for their existence are repaid by producing gifts from bodily labour, and these gifts are invested with specific qualities, which are extracted out of the person as conceptualized 'parts'. Thus, although there are also exchanges 'with no gift', where dividual relations are built as substances are conveyed directly from body to body, personal essence can be transferred between bodies through exchange goods. For instance, qualities such as 'image' or 'breath' that persons possess may be variously invested in pigs, taro, or shell goods (Barraud *et al.* 1994). By contrast, Busby (1997) argues that in India coded substances are conveyed through giving gifts such as quantities of food. Such gifts are conceptualized as 'flows' between persons and the qualities associated with these substances transform the internal character of each person. For instance, alcohol makes a person 'hot' and volatile, knowledge is 'cool' and calming. In Melanesia, material gifts, as parts of persons, reflect the character of the person encapsulating them, show them up as certain kinds of persons with certain kinds of qualities. But the value and effect of gifts depends on the context in which they are given. Presenting a gift at an exchange ceremony brings out one aspect of personhood, temporarily stressing one of the many relations that comprises the person (e.g. if the ceremony is a male-dominated sphere the donor may be showing up the part of him that is expressly male when he gives the gift, even if the gift object is the result of joint male and female labour). The gift object might itself be seen as a person in that it is the product of relationships between other persons (Strathern 1988: 134 *inter alia*). It can convey key personal qualities, such as 'image', and bear these to endure beyond the life span of any particular human being. In both of these cases, the community may also be conceptualized as a collective person shaped by the same principles and having the same personal qualities as the singular person—putting into question our presumption that a person can only be an individual human being.

Metaphor is fundamental to the concepts of the person in each context. Melanesian persons (and gifts) are described as grown like the products of the garden economy, the key locus of social productivity in Melanesian communities (Munn 1986; Strathern 1988). We could say that gifts are taken like cuttings from a plant and given to others who absorb these gifts and the qualities they carry, which consequently grow: a horticultural metaphor for personhood is adopted where a person (and a community) is like a garden. By contrast, Busby (1997) and others have argued that Indian persons are like permeable 'vessels' so that each person is both clearly bounded, and also highly permeable to flows of charged essences, the charged or gendered qualities of which are fixed (alcohol always heats and is gross and masculinizing). Persons and their bodies are transformed by mediating flows of substances through them. There is a 'hydraulic' metaphor for personhood where a person (and a community) is like a container for social flows of life-giving essences.

The significance of these anthropological studies is that concepts of the person and conceptions of matter, form, and the efficacy of practice are part of holistic cultural schemes for understanding the world (Fowler 2008b). There are cultural differences in the kinds of qualities that persons are believed to possess and how these qualities are invested in material things as well as the key metaphors for personhood.

The recognition that personhood is relational in non-Western contexts is not to concede to a sociological division of a modern and a pre- or non-modern world, with an attendant dramatic division in social differentiation and forms of identity. Personhood is, to some degree, relational and distributed beyond the human body in contemporary Western cultures too: consider the circulation of personal image in photographs and the publication of personal lives on websites, or the inalienability of heirlooms from families. In all cultural contexts a tension exists between the fixed, individual, and indivisible characteristics of a person and the relational, dividual, and divisible aspects of a person (LiPuma 1998; Fowler 2004a: 33–37). While some research refers to persons as dividual as a shorthand way of pointing out that the relational features of personhood are accentuated in that context, it would be improper to reify one group of persons as 'individual' and another as 'dividual' and more accurate to talk about how the tension between these two features of personhood is resolved. It is partly through the process of dealing with this tension that personhood takes shape, that any Durkheimian process of 'individualization' of persons out of social relations, or more properly, any generation of persons from social relations, occurs. This tension is negotiated in culturally specific ways, but while 'modes of personhood' or ways of generating persons are culturally specific, it has been suggested that some of the key metaphors and principles featured within those modes of personhood recur in unrelated cultural contexts.

For instance it has been suggested that partibility was one of the principles by which persons and objects were interconnected through chains of relationships accentuating their dividual characteristics in historical and contemporary northern Eurasian communities, a range of prehistoric European communities, and pre-contact period Caribbean communities, as well as in contemporary Melanesia (e.g. Chapman 1996, 2000a; Fowler 2004a: 72–76; Harris 2006; Chapman and Gaydarska 2007; Oliver 2009). Equally, the idea of a person permeable to different substances, qualities, and essences has been posited not only for contemporary Indian communities but also for communities from prehistoric, medieval, and early modern Europe (e.g. Harris 2006; Fowler 2008b). But archaeological studies of personhood such as these do not rely on direct analogies with specific present contexts. Some identify recurrent principles or make comparisons with anthropological studies, but all weigh up the precise ways in which relational personhood was mediated through past treatments of human bodies, materials, objects, places, and landscapes (e.g. Fowler 2001, 2004b; Jones 2002a; Whittle 2003: 52–64). Archaeological studies of prehistoric personhood deduce, for instance, the key metaphors for social relations, for the generation of bodies and persons and for the life cycles of bodies, persons, objects, and places, that were materialized in the past (e.g. Brück 2001a, 2004; Fowler 2003, 2008b; cf. Williams 2003). They identify the key cultural conditions and practices foundational to the production of personhood. Investigation extends beyond examining exchanges of objects and the transmission of substances: it also includes analysis of bodily transformations in life and after death, mobility, settlement patterns and daily routines, and architecture, place, and landscape (e.g. Jones 2005; Fowler 2008a).

Archaeological studies throw up new possibilities for how personhood was shaped through cultural practices, by reflecting on comparisons with ethnographic studies. John Chapman and Bisserka Gaydarska (Chapman 2000a; Chapman and Gaydarska 2007) have described how in the Balkan Neolithic, ceramic objects were broken and some of the fragments retained—and embed this in a contextual study of dividual persons. For instance, they point out that some clay figurines were sexually ambiguous (Figure 15.1), and aliken this to the composition of the Melanesian body from male and female elements (Chapman and Gaydarska 2007: 57–70). Displaying only part of such a figurine, or breaking it in half would change the nature of the gendered aspect of personhood that was brought to the fore. Chapman (2000a) suggests that fragments of pots or figurines were a part of the person given away to another in partible relations between dividual persons. The mechanics and effects of this form of relations and personhood were clearly different from that generated through Melanesian prestige goods exchanges (Fowler 2004a: 67–70): in

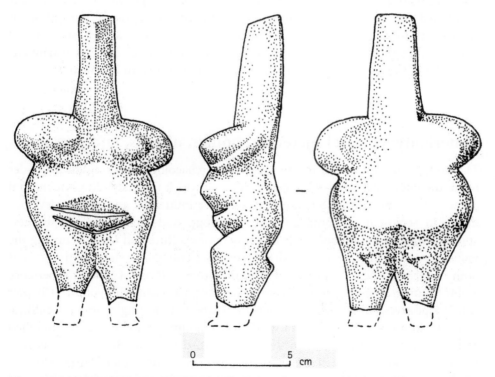

Fig. 15.1 'Androgynous' Hamangia figurine from Neolithic south–east Europe (from Chapman and Gaydarska 2007: 60).

Melanesia partible relations are brought out in the exchange of intact prestigious gift objects not broken objects. This provides a change of perspectives and a reversal of standing from debtor to creditor. Balkan Neolithic practices may have commemorated a shared event and a shared sense of personal composition, rather than a repeated reversal of a mutually interwoven identity as debtor and creditor. However, intact gift objects are also a feature of Balkan prehistory, and these may have been manipulated in claims to partible personhood (Fowler 2008b: 50) or, as Chapman suggests, increasingly in claims to special elite personal identities during the Copper Age, or perhaps a combination of the two in which new categories of persons were emerging. There is more to be said about the role of substance in the composition of persons in Balkan prehistory, but Chapman's research illustrates the interconnectedness not only of personhood and material culture, but also personhood and other features of identity, such as gender.

There may be times and situations during which personhood is particularly at issue and others where it is less so compared with other aspects of identity, or when concepts of the person are narrowly defined and others when these are mutable and less intensively monitored (cf. Schmidt 2004: 79–81). The ways in which personhood comes to be at issue and the media and arenas through which personhood is negotiated have clearly changed through time. In order to appreciate personhood it is necessary to reflect on the value of places, objects, animals, and substances—all of the worldly things that can convey personal qualities, which are also instrumental media in the generation of personhood. I will now turn to these issues.

Materiality: cultural materials, bodies, objects, and persons

The study of personhood in anthropology and archaeology sits alongside a broader phenomenological turn in the social sciences in which understandings of cultural materials, bodies, and objects are at issue. Four influential and related developments in socio-cultural anthropology, sociology, and archaeology led to new approaches to the relationships between material culture and identity during the 1990s and 2000s. First, there were debates over the ambiguous status of the body as both material and cultural and, yet also, the primary locus of human experience and the human subject (Csordas 1999a; Joyce 2005; Crossland this volume, Chapter 16). Perspectives shifted from viewing the body as reflecting dominant cultural concerns to investigating different modes of embodiment and different embodied and experiential engagements in the world (Csordas 1999a: 181–182). Secondly, a phenomenological perspective (variously informed by the work of Hegel, Husserl, Merleau-Ponty, and Heidegger) was adapted to studies of material culture, and particularly to the study of landscape; for instance, by archaeologists such as Chris Gosden (1994), Chris Tilley (1994), and Julian Thomas (1996). Thirdly, the ways in which material culture is valued was reinvestigated, including the different ways that objects have effects, identities (including as personifications), and biographies, and participate in the biographies of human beings (e.g. Appadurai 1986a; Munn 1986; Battaglia 1990; MacKenzie 1991; Chapman 1996; Thomas 1996: 141–182; Hoskins 1998; Brück 2001a). While earlier work suggested that objects in prestige good economies came to have value in a different way from commodities in Western capitalism (e.g. Godelier 1973; Frankenstein and Rowlands 1978), it is arguable that 'prestige' and social competition had been overplayed as the primary principle in gift-giving (Brück 2006b: 74–75, 93). Greater emphasis was therefore placed on the value of things as inalienable from social relations (Strathern 1988; Weiner 1992; cf. Thomas 1996: 141–182). Fourthly, further attention was paid to the constitution of the experiencing subject and the nature of personhood (e.g. Munn 1986; Strathern 1988; Battaglia 1990; Mosko 1992; Chapman 1996; Busby 1997; Fowler 2001, 2002, 2004a). Each of these strands in anthropological and archaeological thought examined how specific configurations of existence are disclosed through embodied engagement in the world. Together, they represented a phenomenological and hermeneutic turn (cf. J. S. Thomas 2007), which challenges us to reflect upon what we mean by material culture.

Structuralist anthropology had brought natural materials into the cultural fold (Lévi-Strauss 1964, 1966b; Douglas 1966, 1973). Thus, Henrietta Moore's (1986) influential ethnography *Space, Text and Gender* discussed goat dung, ash, and chaff as potent cultural materials actively mobilized in the production of identities among the Marakwet in Kenya. Such studies raise the question of whether we should use the term material culture to refer only to artificial things and bring other phenomena (e.g. honey, mud, ash, the sun, the moon, the wind) within culture but not as material culture, or whether we should treat these apparently natural phenomena as material culture, since they are material and invested with cultural meaning. Phenomenological perspectives stress that we experience our world as a whole, and that distinguishing a separate sphere of artificial things is misleading. Instead, I think we are best served by accepting that the whole of the material world, including the medium in which we live (Ingold 2007a: 4)—a combination of air and water—is both natural and cultural to us because aspects of that world can only be grasped through human existence. The distinction between natural and cultural becomes problematic to the point of redundancy, and we are forced to revisit 'material' too. The term *materiality* can be used as an abstract noun to denote the distinctive combination of properties of any thing—the materiality of a copper dagger or a jet necklace or Chesil Beach. 'Materiality' can also refer to 'all of the material world', or a general quality that all material things have: i.e. they are all material so they all possess materiality. Using the term 'materiality' to refer to the entire material world, both cultural objects and natural phenomena, certainly avoids any narrowness associated with the term 'material culture'. But the concept needs further critical reflection (Ingold 2007a). We are best served by considering various properties of a material thing, substance, or medium—its shininess, hardness, brittleness, and so on—in relation to the properties of other media that medium is brought into relation with rather than considering it as having 'materiality'. As Ingold observes, we can then discuss the effects of particular engagements with specific materials through which specific properties emerge. In so doing we apprehend engagements in which human beings are involved with those materials alongside geological processes, animals, the weather, plants, etc. all of which provide relational properties for materials.

[As] the environment unfolds, so the materials of which it is comprised do not *exist*—like the objects of the material world—but *occur*. Thus the properties of materials, regarded as constituents of an environment, cannot be identified as fixed, essential attributes of things, but are rather processual and relational. They are neither objectively determined nor subjectively imagined but practically experienced. In that sense, every property is a condensed story. To describe the properties of materials is to tell the stories of what happens to them as they flow, mix and mutate.

Ingold (2007a: 14)

We therefore move from a view where things are made from natural resources and consumed as cultural, to one where everything in the world can be understood in terms of its contemporary material composition from a myriad of materials through interactions in which certain properties come to light as effective. The forms of things are only ever temporary, though the duration for which they hold that form might be lengthy: we may trace how substances are brought together to compose a thing which draws out certain properties of these combined materials, and then later decays or is further transformed in a way we can compare with other things in that world. I would hold, though, that this understanding of materials could sit well within a duly informed conception of materiality (*pace* Ingold 2007a).

Different cultures appreciate the properties of substances in distinctive ways, so that we might talk of distinct 'materialities', but in each case there are underlying relationships by which materials share properties. These principles guide cultural practices. For instance, among the Merina and the Zafimaniry in Madagascar newness is associated with softness and fluidity and things and persons harden and dry with age: saplings are green, and greenwood is used to build a house for a newly married couple while a couple with descendants will have a house rebuilt with carved hardwood posts; a child is soft and wet but grows firmer with age, and after death the body is buried so the wet flesh can leach into the soil near the village whereas the dried corpse and bones are exhumed and taken to ancestral tombs (Bloch 1982, 1995). Thus, the soft and wet flesh, soil, and greenwood are connected (emergent from funerary practices, house construction etc.) through their equivalent properties; as are the hard and dry bone, uplands, stone tombs, and hardwoods and it is through these interactions that hardwood and stone exhibit properties equated with ancestry, coming to presence ancestors among the living. The relationships between these properties are key to understanding the course of personhood as well as to understanding materiality in this context. Where similar practices relate similar materials, the properties of those materials in relation to one another may also be similar, even in different cultural contexts. The luminosity of some materials might be sometimes associated with vitality or life force, while the durability and longevity of materials that exhibit luminosity, such as shell, metal, glass, and stone, might extend that vitality beyond the human body (see Jones 2002a; Keates 2002). This is not to say that things have 'essential' properties or qualities or that we have to date provided satisfactory and consistent definitions of concepts such as essence or substance (cf. Carsten 2003: 109–135). How properties are invested in materials varies, so that in some cases the properties of things can be fixed in specific substances (as in Marriott's 1976 interpretation of Indian coded substances), while in others it can be more ambiguous (as in Melanesia, where milk and semen may convey the same qualities depending on the context of their transmission). What matters most are the effects of transmitting these substances in specific practices.

Since objects and buildings are composed out of multiple materials, as is the human body, and each may be assembled out of parallel materials according to the same principles, communities reflect upon personhood as they manipulate the materials and forms of their world (Fowler and Cummings 2003; Fowler 2004a: 101–129, 2008a). It has therefore been very productive to think about how specific properties of materials, things, and buildings are brought to the fore through practices which simultaneously generate personhood. An increasing number of studies therefore focus on how worlds are assembled from stone, trees and wood, water, shell, metals, soils, plants, and animal bodies, and how the qualities recognized in human persons are also distributed throughout these worlds (e.g. Strathern and Stewart 2000; Borić 2002, 2003). In socio-cultural anthropology, the appreciation of cultural qualities is largely derived from participant observation. In archaeology, it is derived from inferences based on contextual readings of past configurations of materials and places combined with ethnographic analogies or comparisons drawn with anthropological analyses. While it is difficult for archaeologists to grasp those values, studying patterns in how bodies, objects, and buildings are constituted, reconstituted, and deconstituted from equivalent substances through parallel practices provides archaeologists with a basis from which to interpret modes of personhood in the past (e.g. Brück 2001a; Fowler 2004b, 2008a, 2008b). This has been crucial in considering the effect that inhabiting particular materialities had on people's experiences and understandings of personhood.

While prehistoric studies rely on the comparative treatment of substances, bodies, objects, and architecture to build such interpretations, research into contemporary, proto-historic, and historical societies can field a rich appreciation of the qualities associated with such substances by drawing further on spoken or written sources. In a comparative archaeological analysis of Ancient Egyptian and Classic Mayan bodies and persons, Lynn Meskell and Rosemary Joyce (2003) draw out how bodies are shaped according to predominant concepts of the person and its constituent forces. Among other things, their analysis illustrates the importance of the immaterial aspects of persons in the material techniques by which the body is shaped. For instance, sweat-baths, tooth inlays, and labrets guided the movement of sweat, steam, and breath, each of which conveyed vital aspects of the person (Meskell and Joyce 2003: 29–53). Names and visual representations also conveyed aspects of the person—human beings could be 'consubstantial' with human ancestors and animal spirits or *wayeh* whose presence was made evident in masks and other representations (Figure 15.2) as well as in Mayan composite names (Meskell and Joyce 2003: 49–50, 89–91). While Classic Mayan elite women's bodies

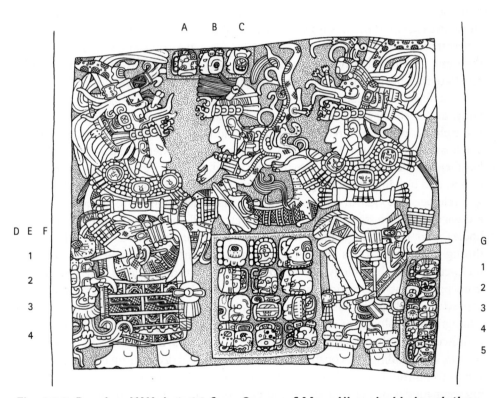

Fig. 15.2 Drawing, YAX: Lnt. 14 from Corpus of Maya Hieroglyphic Inscriptions, Vol. 3, Part 1, Yaxchilan, reproduced courtesy of the President and Fellows of Harvard College. This carved lintel depicts an elite Mayan sister and brother letting blood while a 'wayeh' in the form of a serpent emerges between them, revealing the identity of the woman's future child.

were often depicted swathed in woven textiles emblematic of female productivity, elite male bodies were presented with exposed flesh clad in stone, jade, shell, and animal body parts accentuating male activities, such as hunting and warfare: 'The provision of costumes for warriors made of minimally processed products of the forest, animal skins, bird feathers, and bark cloth strips, demarcated a profound if transitory boundary in personhood between people of the forest and the inhabited towns, where woven cloth was the norm' (Meskell and Joyce 2003: 93–94). Thus, their analysis illustrates how Mayan personhood was materialized at the intersection between the human and the non-human, and alongside gender and status.

Materiality and personhood in historical periods

We can see in the examples cited so far that distinct concepts of the person (and modes of personhood) go hand in hand with specific concepts of materiality (and distinct materialities). These studies have been drawn from social and cultural anthropology and prehistoric archaeology, rather than from history, sociology, or historical archaeology. While the term personhood has been widely adopted in prehistoric archaeology and the archaeology of proto-historic societies, it has not as often been explicitly examined in historical studies or disciplines focused on 'Western' culture, unlike other features of identity. For instance, explorations of race, ethnicity, class, sex, and gender have been integral to historical archaeology (e.g. Gilchrist 1994; Beaudry 1995; Hicks 2000). This does not mean that personhood has not been investigated by historical archaeologists, however, and I want to reflect here on what historical archaeologists have revealed about relationships between personhood and materiality, explicitly *and* implicitly.

One reason why personhood has featured more heavily as an area of study in prehistory than history may be that scholars have felt less inclined to focus on how personhood is itself culturally constructed when there are texts written by individuals about their lives and those of others which allow studies of individual biography to be brought to the fore. Diaries, personal letters, and so on may convince the reader that past people had the same sense of personhood, particularly predicated on individualistic perspectives, as are prevalent in western folk mythology about the person today. Yet, key critical perspectives on personhood and identity in anthropology and sociology are based on studies of known contemporary individuals. Some, such as that of Judith Butler (1993), build upon Foucault's work on the social generation of identities in historical contexts. Foucault (e.g. 1977a) discussed the role of institutions in 'technologies of the self', the remains of which, from prisons and schools to cemeteries, are archaeologically accessible. Indeed, there are sophisticated archaeological studies of social relations within these institutions (e.g. Casella 2000). By and large historical archaeologies that investigate the generation of identity are more likely to draw on the work of sociologists and historians than anthropologists, and thus to work with different terminologies than prehistorians. Nonetheless, similar questions are being asked. Through the research of American historical archaeologists, such as James Deetz and Mark Leone, for instance, it is possible to trace the emergence of a particular form of personhood stressing individual autonomy, consumerism, and personal individualization along with a particular material world and socio-political order (Deetz 1996; Leone 2005). To examine the emergence of a 'possessive individualism' (Leone 2005: 34) is to consider the development of a particular mode of person-hood. Such work, alongside historical studies of manners, etiquette, and the treatments of bodies and their substances (e.g. Rublack 2002), illustrates that it was not only in the postmodern world of the later twentieth century that person-hood became contested, complex, and unstable (cf. Porter 1997).

Historical archaeologists have often attended to the relational nature of past identities in analysing class, sex, gender, or ethnicity. Some investigate historical trajectories in what can usefully be described as personhood and many studies carry important implications for doing so. There are many studies of people's attempts to operate away from or resist an acquisitional and aspirational individu-alism. Such studies focus on community activities and collective identities, and, although these studies are seldom framed in terms of personhood, they effectively produce conclusions about negotiations of personhood in the past. For instance, much work has been done on how slaves generated senses of community identity out of a history of displacement, and attempts to alienate them from their past, and attained personhood in various ways aside from how those who enslaved them did. While pursuing their own 'possessive individualism', slave traders and owners were involved in ongoing attempts to deny, limit, and control the personhood of slaves, who had to struggle for recognition as persons. Leland Ferguson (1991) has used archaeological evidence to illustrate how enslaved African-Americans stressed communal action aside from the individualizing world of white elites through food preparation and consumption, while Ross Jamieson (1995) has examined how archaeological evidence for sixteenth- to mid-nineteenth-century slave funerary practices shows how these often drew on African traditions, including African concepts of the person, death, and ancestry.

Further explicit attention to personhood in studies of historical material worlds in Western contexts might illuminate a series of other issues in the historical past. For instance, the history of the idea of universal human rights and its recognition by nations, and the bearing of such a concept on the material conditions of people's lives in a world of inequality, nations, and corporations could be further compared with the impact of concepts of communal belonging and collective personhood, for instance (cf. Deetz 1996: 256–257). We could also consider the importance of unionization as collective action to resist individualization as a means of social control by State and capitalist institutions. Further research into the relationship between personhood and forms of social organization such as class, caste systems, or clans, and studies comparing special persons such as religious specialists or monarchs supported by 'divine right' with ordinary persons could also be instructive. Julian Thomas (2004: 202–209) has illuminated various understandings of the properties and effects of matter particular to different philosophical and scientific stances in the early modern era, illustrating that different world views attempt to explain the nature of the person according to the same logic by which they explain matter, forms, and relationships. These issues continue to be important. New animals, new technologies, new foods, new groups of people have all appeared throughout each historical period around the world and each translation of these into a community has transformed that community and had an impact on how personhood is understood and negotiated. Such translations and transformations, including those involving contemporary medical technologies and genetic technologies, are very much of interest in anthropology, sociology, philosophy of science, ethics, and cultural studies where the relationships between and understandings of human beings, animals, technology, and environment are pressing topics given the changes occurring in these relationships in our times—history and archaeology together have much to contribute to the debate.

A number of recent studies in historical archaeology have demonstrated the potential of an explicit focus upon personhood as an analytical tool. Archaeologist Jose Oliver (2009) has studied Caribbean Taino concepts of personhood in the precontact and contact periods with particular regard to the role of *cemi* idols, *guaiza* masks, stone ancestral heads, and other special objects, which were imbued with certain qualities of personhood. For instance, *guaiza* masks conveyed the soul and image of *caciques* (chiefs) and were circulated in diplomatic relations (Figure 15.3). *Cemi* idols embodied a supernatural property, 'sweetness', in a personified form that became intimately associated with specific human beings who held them— these *cemi* idols were, Oliver argues, composed as dividual persons with biographies and became inseparable from the human beings who kept them. Oliver's analysis includes insightful discussions of Taino perceptions of Spanish personhood and Spanish perceptions of Taino personhood as well as Taino understandings of personhood in their indigenous world. Among other things, by considering Taino motivations in light of their understanding of personhood his study provides a new perspective on why fifteenth- and sixteenth-century interactions between the Taino and Spanish in the Greater Antilles took the course they did from gift-giving to warfare and the iconoclastic destruction of idols. Oliver's work begs the question of how different understandings of personhood among other indigenous communities and colonial powers have shaped their interactions. Pamela Graves (2008) has explored how English medieval punishments enacted on effigies, including those of saints, indicate that the personal ties people felt with those entities they had petitioned were transformed into feelings of betrayal directed towards effigies of those entities. Graves analyses idols as manifestations of saints' bodies, located in the discourse of a contemporary body culture. She contrasts the defacing and wider

(a)

Fig. 15.3 Two Taino artefacts from the western Caribbean. (a) A side view of a stone pendant depicting a high-ranked personage in seated position and in a state of hallucinatory ecstasy (78 × 44 mm). A guaíza (mask), which only *caciques* (chiefs) had the right to wear is shown sewn into an armband. Museum of History, Anthropology and Art of the University of Puerto Rico (courtesy of José R. Oliver). (b) Two *guaízas* (face masks) made of marine conch shell (*Strombus* spp.) from the Dominican Republic (left specimen approximately 75 mm × 50). Museo Fundación García Arévalo, Santo Domingo (courtesy of José R. Oliver). Both objects derive from the Boca Chica complex of the Chican sub-tradition (AD 800–1500).

(b)

corporal punishment of saints' images with later Protestant acts of iconoclasm, where such personal frustrations were not directed at saints, but at effigies of religious and political figures made for public destruction. Despite religious change, the way that punishment was directed towards heads and hands and the fact that people constructed new kinds of effigies indicates continuity in under-standings of the body, person, and social relations. By placing the punishment of images in the context of late medieval and early modern ritual, legal, and repre-sentational treatments of the body, Graves reveals underlying concepts of the body and the role of these concepts in interpersonal relations. She illustrates the personal and embodied nature of relations between people and saints, and sheds light on how those relations were transferred over to mortal representatives expected to act on the public behalf: while the persons involved in some relations changed (saints, monarchs, politicians) the key modes of relations were relatively enduring as was the role of the body (whether human or effigy).

Both of these studies reach new understandings of past lives, practices, and historical events by considering what treatments of material culture, particularly personified objects, can tell us about underlying trends in personhood. Both situate beliefs about personhood alongside other historical forces. Research like this, taken alongside the ethnographic, prehistoric and protohistoric studies discussed earlier, allows comparison across conventional 'types' of societies to consider the recur-rence of certain trends in ways of relating, and subsequently trends in how personhood is negotiated.

CONCLUSIONS AND OUTLOOK

There are differing schools of thought about the *nature* of culture, material culture, and identity. Many recent approaches have attempted not only to redefine our use of these terms but also to move away from them and head towards a more explicit appreciation of human existence as embedded in a material world. This has suited some fields of study particularly well, such as the archaeology of small-scale prehistoric societies where ways of being in the world can be appreciated at a general level while specific identities and political situations may be far harder to discern. Here, as elsewhere, personhood is only one feature of identity and must be considered alongside others. Investigations of personhood explore cultural bound-aries between persons and objects, humans and animals, the mortal and the divine. In some fields the way that individual identities are constructed in relation to the community has been discussed to excellent effect without explicitly using the term personhood, though I have argued here that making the concept explicit and situating different cultural perspectives on personhood alongside one another affords further dimensions to research. If we are to do away with the alienating dichotomy between modern and non-modern or Western and non-Western societies then a fully comparative investigation of personhood, *as well as* other features of identity, ought to be a key element in this pursuit. Such comparison would necessarily draw on archaeological studies of prehistoric and historical societies, historical research, anthropology, and sociology, and investigate non-industrial and industrialized societies, indigenous, colonial and post-colonial contexts the world over. Comparisons can be based on how materiality is practically manipulated in the social, political, and cultural generation of personhood. It is possible to identify similar features (organizing principles, metaphors, etc.) in how the material world is arranged and understood in distinct cases while also considering differences between those cases. Such an approach emphasizes not the production of strict typologies of societies in a social evolutionary fashion, but an appreciation of types of practices and their effects in differing contexts. This is not to deny the importance of building strong relational analogies where multiple coincidental factors are present in two contexts suggesting that underlying forms of relationships may be similar, or the importance of identifying recurrent bundles of practices and forms of materiality that coexist in many communities. Sometimes it is apparent that societies classified as typologically similar by nineteenth- and twentieth-century scholars *do* exhibit similar kinds of relations, which still deserve further analysis: both similarities and difference need to be appreciated.

There have been some criticisms of the shortcomings of existing approaches to personhood in archaeology. Harris (2006) rightly points out that more attention must be paid to the emotional forces that drive people towards desiring certain forms of personal identities. Chapman and Gaydarska (2007: 54) briefly warn that archaeological studies of personhood need to adequately account for human agency. This warning seems unfounded to me since to study trends in how personhood is constituted is to provide descriptions of forms of agency, as Chapman and Gaydarska go on to illustrate. Studies of personhood appreciate that there are different ways that objectification and personification occur, and different ways that people actively and consciously mobilize the materials of the world, including their own bodies, in making themselves and making other people. For instance, if we consider Marriott's (1976) ethnographic analysis of caste and personhood it is clear that members of different castes exert different forms of agency from one another in their pursuit of a desired form of personhood. These forms of agency, these strategies of identification, are cut across by others adopted by people of a particular age or gender. When we discuss modes of personhood, such agency is therefore already implied because these modes must necessarily be exercised by self-aware, emotive agents. Like 'identity' the term 'agency' by itself is in any case directionless—if the term is to have any value we instead must talk about gendered agency, the agency of children, and so on, or the contexts in which types of agency occur, or outline modes of agency that are constitutive of specific types of person-hood. It equally seems to me unnecessary to create a divide between approaches emphasizing cultural concepts of the body and person and those exploring em-bodied lives (cf. Turner 2003: xvi–xvii). Given sufficient evidence, studies of personhood can clearly attend to concepts of the person and to people's embodied engagements with those concepts through social and cultural practices. To offer a further criticism of existing studies, I would suggest that further work is needed on the relationship between personhood and forms of social differentiation, particu-larly in terms of power relations associated with different concepts of the person in egalitarian, heterarchial, and hierarchial systems. Future projects will need to explore how new types of persons emerge alongside new power relations and new articulations of social relations.

The viewpoints considered in this essay are part of the continuing human reflection on the nature of personhood and on how persons relate to substances, bodies, objects, animals, and forces, as well as to one another. It is clear that debates over the nature of personhood and identity rely on understandings of the material world, and *vice versa*: the two issues are intertwined and inseparable. As social scientists, we can appreciate cultural understandings of person and world, and the effects of those understandings, most effectively by examining routine transforma-tions in bodies, architecture, landscapes, and identifying shifts in the nature of those transformations over time. We can move effectively between cultural com-parison and contextual depth in these studies. Material culture, alongside language, is certain to enjoy a key position in studies of personhood and identity, and all of these concepts are constituents of materiality. Historical trajectories in how mate-riality has been constituted and manipulated provide us with the opportunity to combine archaeology, anthropology, sociology, and many other disciplines in a long-term comparative project to trace the course and variety of forms of person-hood alongside other features of identity.

CHAPTER 16

....

MATERIALITY AND EMBODIMENT

....

ZOË CROSSLAND

INTRODUCTION
....

This chapter considers archaeology's contribution to the interdisciplinary study of materiality and embodiment, focusing especially on the emergence of archaeology of the body since the late 1980s. Human bodies have been a focus of archaeological study since the discipline's antiquarian origins, with two divergent modes of analysis emerging over the course of the twentieth century and acting to constitute separate fields of expertise. On the one hand, the bioarchaeological focus on physical or skeletal remains has tended to address questions of diet, disease, and demography. On the other, a concern with mortuary treatment, grave goods, and figurative representation led to a concern with social roles and identities and ideology (e.g. Binford 1971; Parker Pearson 1982; Shanks and Tilley 1982; Thomas 1991c; Brumfiel 1996; Joyce 1996). The latter included a focus on dress and ornamentation of the body (e.g. Sørenson 1991; Marcus 1993; M. M. Lee 2000), and more recently, the forms of bodily practices that may be inferred from

I'm grateful to Rosemary Joyce and Brian Boyd for taking the time to read through this piece and giving me helpful pointers; also to Terry D'Altroy and the graduate students in his Archaeological Method and Theory class at Columbia University for their commentary on the text; special thanks to Darryl Wilkinson for his close reading. Thanks too to David Bowsher for help with references. Finally, my thanks to Lynn Meskell for her critical feedback on the paper, and to Dan Hicks for his editorial patience and guidance.

representations, such as Timothy McNiven's discussion of gestures of fear and the constitution of masculinity in Athenian Greek art (McNiven 2000), or Miranda Aldhouse-Green's (2004) exploration of the range of bodily gestures portrayed in the European Iron Age. This division of interest reflects a philosophical separation, associated with archaeology's historical emergence as an Enlightenment project of rational and empirical enquiry (Thomas 2004), between the objective material world of fleshy, earthy nature within which 'the body' has been understood to be located, and the subjective world of mind, culture, and representation.

In what follows, I review some of the ways in which archaeologists have attempted to overcome these disciplinary limitations, notably by deploying a range of anti-foundationalist perspectives to theorize the embodied agency of past people. I then explore how questions of materiality have entered into the debates around enbodiment. Finally, I present two case studies. The first considers the use of apotropaic devices (protective objects used to ward off evil) in seventeenth-century England, and the second looks at how the agency of the dead body is portrayed in discourse around contemporary forensic archaeology.

ARCHAEOLOGIES OF EMBODIMENT

The first area of archaeology in which human bodies emerged as a significant focus for archaeological theory was in archaeological studies of gender and sexuality (Conkey and Gero 1991; Walde and Willows 1991; Yates 1993; Kampen 1996; Meskell 1996; Wright 1996). Early gender archaeologies within a social constructionist vein tended to view the physical body as a stable material entity on which gender is inscribed (see reviews by Gilchrist 1999 and Sørenson 2000; additionally Bahrani 2001 and Voss 2008a provide critical perspectives on archaeological approaches to sexuality). The sex/gender distinction, on which social constructionist studies were predicated replicates the dualist partitioning of the naturalized sexed body and the socially constructed, gendered body. Archaeologists Lynn Meskell (1998: 140) and Rosemary Joyce (2005: 142–145) have observed that this has been expressed by an archaeological focus on the surface of the body, whether in terms of dress and adornment or as the focus of artistic representation. Roberta Gilchrist (1999: 6–7) notes, however, that while this focus has dominated in European gender archaeology, in the United States more attention has been paid to the corporeal effects of gender. Christine Hastorf's (1991) study of changing gender relations in relation to shifts in the consumption of food during the intrusion of the Inka state into Sausa social life and politics (in modern-day Peru) illustrates this orientation, as does the pervasive interest in gender hierarchy and differential exposure to disease and bodily life stresses (e.g. Cohen and Bennett 1993; Holliman 2000; Peterson 2000).

Gender archaeology therefore acted as a common node of interest for archaeologists from very different backgrounds and traditions and brought bioarchaeologists and those engaged with more artefact-focused archaeologies into conversation with one another. However, the dominant social constructionist orientation left the body itself somewhat under-theorized, viewing it as a stable biological ground from which gender was elaborated. An early critique of this position within archaeology was made by Nordbladh and Yates (1990), who noted that sex is not the stable and binary biological category that is often assumed (cf. Laqueur 1990; Meskell 1999). This intervention grew from a post-structuralist suspicion of the apparently pre-discursive, empirically verifiable, sexed body that was thought to underwrite gender.

From the late 1990s an emphasis on embodiment and the lived experience of the body emerged in archaeology. This work called the category of 'the body' into question, and developed a focus on the practices and social relations within which bodies are brought into being (e.g. Meskell 1996, 1999; Joyce 1998; Montserrat 1998; Rautman 2000; Hamilakis *et al.* 2002; Fisher and Loren 2003). Archaeologists have explored the production of the lived body and the performance of identity by assembling disparate strands of evidence (e.g. papers in Halperin 2009; Borić and Robb 2008). Thus, Rosemary Joyce (2003) has analysed representations of women as figurines in the Formative period in Mesoamerica, comparing them with grave goods to explore the embodied experience of different life stages, and the transition between them. Brian Boyd (2002) has linked dietary evidence from isotope analysis with the mortuary dress of the dead to explore understandings of pollution and avoidance in the Epipalaeolithic Levant. Another example is provided by Carolyn Nakamura's (2005) account of Neo-Assyrian apotropaic figurines in terms of the sensuous and embodied experience of place.

The turn towards embodiment in archaeology has reflected a broader questioning within the humanities and social sciences of previously unanalysed and naturalized understandings of human bodies (e.g. Turner 1984; Feher 1989; Laqueur 1990; Shilling 1993; Csordas 1994; Bynum 1995; Cohen and Weiss 2003; Shilling 2008; Campbell *et al.* 2009). The conception of 'the body' as a natural and trans-historical entity has been broadly critiqued by these perspectives, which attempt to take account of both the corporeality and sociality of human life, viewing 'the body' as historically contingent and in flux. In its material focus and its long-term perspective, archaeology therefore has much to offer to these broader debates (Meskell and Joyce 2003). Common to all the theories of embodiment drawn upon in archaeology is the critique of the separation of mind and body, subject and object. Such dualisms are conventionally traced to the Cartesian division between the thinking subject (*res cogitans*) and the physical and corporeal world (*res extensa*). Although the emergence of the perceived separation between mind and body did not originate with Descartes and may be situated as part of a dualist tradition, traceable back to Plato and beyond (Loraux 1989; Synott 1992), dualist conceptions of mind and body became increasingly dichotomized during the sixteenth and seventeenth centuries. This shift was part of broader changes bound up with the Protestant Reformation, the expansion of the Renaissance world, and transformations in artistic conventions and scientific knowledge practices (Bordo 1987). In the critique of dualist dichotomies, social and cultural theory has often sought to find ways of re-situating the thinking subject in the world, through its embodiment in the fleshy, living, and breathing body.

The idea of embodiment has emerged from diverse intellectual traditions, most notably phenomenological approaches (Merleau-Ponty 1962, 1968), practice theory (Bourdieu 1977, 1990; Giddens 1984), and feminism and psychoanalytic theory (e.g. Kristeva 1982; Irigaray 1985; Martin 1987; Bordo 1993; Grosz 1994), often influenced by the anthropological work of Mary Douglas (1966). An interrogation of naturalized categories of the body has also characterized those strands of post-structuralist thinking derived from Michel Foucault (e.g. 1973, 1977a), especially as developed by feminist cultural theorist Judith Butler (1990, 1993). As such there are many tensions and incompatibilities in ideas of embodiment as they have entered into archaeological accounts.

Those approaches growing out of a perspective broadly based on the phenomenological writings of Maurice Merleau-Ponty (e.g. Csordas 1990, 1994; Leder 1990; Ihde 2002) aim to start with the pre-reflexive (but, importantly, not pre-cultural) experience of embodied perception, in the act of which consciousness is constituted interactively and intersubjectively, extending into the world and participating in it. Since, as socio-cultural anthropologist Thomas Csordas (1990: 9–10) observed, for Merleau-Ponty there can be no objects prior to perception, the only possible starting point for perception is the body in the world, and as such, the body is privileged as a site for understanding experience, yet without being located as prior to, or separable from that experience.

Phenomenological approaches made their way into the archaeological literature alongside an increased concern with the lived experience of past people, and were first articulated through landscape studies (Tilley 1994; Gosden 1994; Thomas 1996: 11–91). However, philosophers such as Don Ihde (2002) have been critical of the unexamined and implicit body, and its masculine gendering, at the centre of Merleau-Ponty's writings. Such a universal view of the body has characterized much phenomenological archaeology and has been used as the basis for generalizations about past bodies, based on an assumed universality of corporeal experience. The effect has been to narrow the definition of past subjects to healthy individuals of adult height, unburdened by heavy loads, illness, or the distractions of children (Brück 1998), applying twentieth-century categories and assumptions to embodied engagements in the past (Thomas 2001: 181). As Lynn Meskell (1999) has argued, this generalized phenomenological understanding of past individuals has a tendency to obstruct efforts to engage with the specifics of the social and cultural understandings that were involved in people's constitution as embodied persons. The dominant characterization of phenomenology in archaeology has also been accused of over-playing the subjectivity of the interpreter and not adequately emphasizing phenom-enology's attention to things themselves (Olsen 2007).

The widespread use of the 'practice theories' of sociologists Pierre Bourdieu and Anthony Giddens in archaeological interpretation since the 1980s represents a parallel strand in the emergence of archaeologies of embodiment. Critical of what he perceived to be phenomenology's subjectivism, Bourdieu (1990: 25–26) placed more emphasis on the practical interaction between the external structures confronted in day-to-day life and their inculcation and reproduction as *habitus* (Bourdieu 1977). Archaeologists have used Bourdieu alongside Giddens' (1984) theory of structuration to think about the ways in which the material world structures and is structured by embodied practice (e.g. Barrett 1994; Gilchrist 1994; Dietler and Herbich 1998; Nilsson Stutz 2003; Hodder and Cessford 2004). Bourdieu's practice theory has been criticized within anthropology and sociology for relying overly on the concept of *habitus*—durable, transposable dispositions that shape practice and are shaped by it—to conceptualize social practice, thus leaving individual agency, social mobility, and choice inadequately theorized (Jenkins 1982; A. J. Strathern 1996; Shilling 2005; also see Meskell 1999: 27–28). Questions of agency have also been foregrounded in archaeology (Barrett and Fewster 2000; Dobres and Robb 2000b).

Practice theory has been influential in archaeology because it provided a way for archaeologists to consider how human relations were mediated through past material conditions, as John Barrett (1994, 2000) has explored. For the same reasons, Foucault's radical de-centring of the subject has also influenced archaeo-logical accounts (see discussion in Tilley 1990b; Meskell 1999). As part of his critique of phenomenology Foucault elaborated the ways in which embodied subjects are shaped through discursive practices (e.g. Foucault 1970) and through regulatory regimes of surveillance and control (e.g. Foucault 1973). Foucault's countervailing emphasis on the discursive formations within and through which the body is produced acted to disperse the human subject, leading to complaints that he dealt poorly with questions of agency (as for example by sociologist Bryan Turner 1982). Within archaeology Meskell (2000: 16–17) has argued that an over-emphasis on the 'social body', growing in part from practice theory and partly from archaeology's engagement with Foucault, has led to a view of past bodies as 'artefacts', existing in the landscape alongside monuments and other archaeological traces. This she suggests has led to an inadequate consideration of specific forms of embodiment or of the role of individuals.

The influence of Foucault and other post-structuralist thinkers in archaeology has led to a questioning of the biological body's stability and irreducibility, particularly from a gender perspective (Nordbladh and Yates 1990). It has also encouraged a focus on the role of the material world in the production of the lived experience of embodiment, emerging primarily from an engagement with Judith Butler's work on the performance of bodily identities (Meskell 1996, 1999, 2000; Joyce 2000a, 2000b, 2002; J. S. Thomas 2002). However, Judith Butler's emphasis on the materiality of the body as an effect of discourse led her away from a consideration of the corporeal specificities of bodies' compositions, something particularly pertinent to archaeology (Perry and Joyce 2001). Archaeologist Joanna Sofaer (2006a, 2006b) suggests that an emphasis on the materiality and plasticity of the human skeleton can provide a way of thinking through its corporeality more critically. Certainly, the archaeological orientation towards material and substance seems to offer the potential to extend and rework concepts of 'the body' and embodiment as they currently stand. This includes a consideration of the manner in which the body's materiality is constituted and reconstituted, distributed and extended into the world, as will be discussed below.

MATERIALITY AND EMBODIMENT

While the archaeology of embodiment has been characterized by a focus on lived experience (Joyce 2005) new directions in archaeological research are interrogating the implicit limitations that are often assumed to underwrite embodied experience. These developments have grown out of a more general sense of frustration at the lack of engagement with the materiality of archaeological evidence, the inadequacy of textual analogues (e.g. Barrett 1994: 78–79; Buchli 1995), and a sense that the material world has been viewed as secondary to discourse (e.g. Schiffer 1999; Graves-Brown 2000b; Meskell 2004; papers in Meskell 2005b; Knappett 2005; Preucel 2006; Boivin 2008). These approaches have emerged in the context of a broader interdisciplinary concern with materiality and material agency (e.g. Kopytoff 1986; W. J. T. Mitchell 1996; Gell 1998; Brown 2001; Myers 2001; Miller 2005; Henare et al. 2007b), as discussed elsewhere in this volume. The wealth of studies on materiality offers a range of perspectives salient to a development of concepts of embodiment, particularly in relation to the extensions of the body and the body after death. Although theories of embodiment attempt to understand experiences of personhood as situated within and through the body, they also allow for an extended and distributed understanding of self and body, not necessarily bounded by the constraints of the flesh in predictable ways (cf. Bateson 1973; Haraway 1991a, 1991b: 150–155; Latour 1993b; Csordas 1994: 2). An increasingly destabilized and dynamic conception of human bodies has led to a 'post-humanist' concern with bodily boundaries and those sites of transition between human and non-human, whether animals, machines, objects, or otherwise. Donna Haraway (1991a, 1991b) in particular has explored the possibilities of the hybrid body, incorporating technological and non-human elements into its constitution and questioning and challenging the body's accepted boundaries through her conception of the 'cyborg' (cf. Balsamo 1988; Hayles 1999; Featherstone and Burrows 1995). Similarly, the phenomenological focus on the human body in studies of embodiment has been critiqued in socio-cultural anthropology (Hallam *et al.* 1999) and archaeology (e.g. Meskell 1999; Sofaer 2006a) as resting upon an unspoken assumption that self and body are one and the same, and that both are bounded and contained within the skin of a single living and indivisible individual.

Archaeologists have increasingly questioned assumptions about the relationship of the body to an individuated and bounded sense of self (e.g. Houston and Stuart 1998; Gillespie 2001; J. S. Thomas 2002; Fowler 2004a). Marilyn Strathern's (1988) formulation of 'dividual' personhood has been influential in shaping the debate, together with anthropological research on partible, permeable, and distributed conceptions of person in Melanesia (Knauft 1989; Wagner 1991; Mosko 1992; Bird-David 1999 and India (Marriott 1976; Busby 1997, 1999). These understandings of the person challenge assumptions of the one-to-one mapping of self onto the body, and emphasize other more relationally defined possibilities. Dividual personhood is understood to be formed and negotiated through the exchange and circulation of bodily substances and other material extensions of the body. However, it need not be positioned in opposition to the individual (LiPuma 1998), but rather may be viewed as a different inflection or modality of personhood. These ideas have been drawn upon in archaeology to critique the common assumption that personhood is underwritten by a stable, individuated sense of self and body, and to explore other ways to conceptualize personhood in the past (e.g. Chapman 2000a; Thomas 2000b; Brück 2001b; Fowler 2001; Looper 2003; Meskell 2004; Jones 2005).

Concepts of partible, permeable, and distributed personhood have encouraged an archaeological reconsideration of the significance of objects placed in mortuary contexts dating to the Neolithic and Bronze Age in Britain. Recent accounts have re-conceptualized past identities as relational and distributed through an exploration of how grave goods and other curated objects and heirlooms may be endowed with elements of personhood (e.g. Brück 2004; J. S. Thomas 2000a, 2002; Woodward 2002). Recently, Howard Williams also used this perspective to think through the agency of bodies after death in Anglo-Saxon England (Williams 2004). The concept of the distributed person allows an extension of the concept of embodiment so that it does not rest upon a bounded and naturalized physicality, or indeed assume a unified and bounded sense of self, but can be expressed through materials that are distributed and circulated away from the body. It also leads to a focus on the senses and affective states or relationships in the constitution of personhood through the material world (Gosden 2001, 2004a; Hamilakis 2002; cf. Kus 1992), and directs attention to human–animal relations and hybrids

(Philo and Wilbert 2000). Chantal Conneller (2004) has considered red deer remains from the Early Mesolithic site of Star Carr in North Yorkshire, England within this framework. Conneller suggests that red deer antler frontlets were involved in masking practices that acted to reveal hybrid human–deer bodies that took on 'deer effects' through their modification by masking. A focus on human–animal relations has also been used to recast archaeological understandings of the beginnings of domestication and agriculture in Anatolia (Hodder 2006), the Levant (Boyd 2004), and in the Balkans (Borić 2005).

The understanding of the person as distributed rather than confined to the apparent bounds of the body is often characterized as in opposition to liberal humanist perceptions of personhood and individuality (see discussion in Battaglia 1995; also critique in Carsten 2003: 83–108). However, others have generalized the arguments developed within Melanesian ethnography to present broader models of the ways in which humans and objects interact, most markedly in Alfred Gell's (1998) study of *Art and Agency*.

The conception of the distributed person was anticipated in the late nineteenth century by pragmatist philosopher Charles Sanders Peirce, whose semeiotic approach allows a way to think through the lived experience of the body in relation both to the dead and to the phenomenological lifeworld (Peirce 1940a). Peirce rejected the inherited foundationalisms of rationalism and positivism. Instead, he argued that thought takes place through signs, and signs are neither internal mental phenomena nor wholly external objects, but rather relational entities constituted through and within the sensuous world of experience (Peirce 1940d). His approach is distinct from Saussure's semiology, and by convention Peirce's preferred spelling of 'semeiotic' is used to reflect this. Archaeologists have found a Peircean approach useful for thinking through the material and affective dimensions of signs and interpretation (e.g. Preucel and Bauer 2001; Bauer 2002; Preucel 2006; Lele 2006; Watts 2008; Joyce 2008; Crossland 2009b). A Peircean understanding of personhood views it as a shared and social 'outreaching identity' as the anthropologist Milton Singer (1980) has explored. Peirce provides a language and orientation to explore the ways in which personhood emerges relationally through signs. Peirce's conception of person therefore has some commonalities with theories of material engagement (Renfrew 2001, 2004; papers in De Marrais *et al.* 2004; Malafouris 2008a), although he pays more attention to the sensuous semeiosis through which engagement takes place. His semeiotic also allows a consideration of interpretive habits that are neither cognitive in nature, nor restricted to human beings.

Building upon the work of Marcel Mauss (1973) and Leroi-Gourhan (1943, 1945, 1993) an archaeological interest in the relationship of technology to social agency has also led to fruitful avenues of research in relation to embodied social action and the social production of technology (e.g. Lemonnier 1992, 1993; Dobres 2000; Schiffer 2001a; cf. Noland 2009). Archaeological discussions of materiality have also been influenced by recent research in Science and Technology Studies (STS) (e.g. Bloor 1976; Bijker *et al.* 1987), and especially by actor-network theory (ANT) as developed by sociologists of science Michel Callon, John Law, and Bruno Latour (e.g. Callon 1986a; Latour 1987, 1993a, 1999a, 1999b, 2005; Callon and Law 1997; Law and Hassard 1999). Archaeological studies that draw on Latour echo his call for a replacement of the modernist settlement that divides subject from object. Instead, an alternative framework is proposed that focuses on the variety of fluid and constantly changing relationships between non-humans and humans. Rather than assuming the existence of an absolute dividing line demarcating humans from non-humans and culture from nature, all are seen to be entangled in a complex socio-technical assemblage. Humans and non-humans are folded into each other to create distributed but stable networks, which act collectively to achieve certain goals (Olsen 2003; Witmore 2006).

This perspective has been drawn upon to differing degrees to refigure human and non-human relations within archaeology (e.g. Walker 2008; see also Martin 2005 for a use of an earlier strand of Latour). In the view of archaeologist Bjørnar Olsen (2003) the continued primacy afforded to human agency in many accounts of distributed personhood reproduces an unhelpful division between mind and matter. This he argues maintains a focus on dynamic human agents acting on the apparently inert and passive world of things. Olsen makes the case that humans and non-humans might be reconceptualized as entangled hybrids, part of complex socio-technical collectivities that are comprised of mixtures of animals, objects, landscapes, and indeed all material substances, a position reiterated by other authors who subscribe to a broadly Latourian approach (e.g. Witmore 2006, 2007; Shanks 2007; Webmoor 2007). This perspective refuses Gell's characterization of object agency, arguing that his emphasis on the distribution of human agency into objects retains a Cartesian humanism at its core (Olsen 2007; Webmoor 2007: 568; cf. Pels 1998; Meskell 2004: 115). Such an argument moves away from the concept of embodiment, as overly subject-centred and humanistic (Olsen 2003: 101, 2007: 584; cf. Vilaça 2009). It should be noted that there is a theoretical tension between the call to consider the agency of objects and a Latourian view that positions agency as a relational entity distributed throughout the collectivity and not inherent in any particular object or person. This has yet to be adequately addressed in archaeology. A strongly 'symmetrical' approach following Latour (1993a), in which humans and animals may be substituted for one another has come under criticism from within STS for apparently failing to recognize the distinctions between the operations of humans and non-humans (e.g. Pickering 1995; Ihde 2002). This it is argued derives from the influence of structuralist semiotics on ANT (de Saussure 1959; Derrida 1976), encouraging a focus on the dispersed and interchangeable nature of representation, rather than the performative aspects of the agentive acts in which humans and non-humans are involved (but see Hicks 2005 for archaeology). This critique may be situated as part of a wider concern with the erasure of embodiment in the posthumanist literature (Dery 1996; Springer 1996; Hayles 1999; Vint 2007). The posthumanist emphasis on mediation, translation, and transformation demands that we pay attention to the semeiotic links that constitute and maintain hybrids (Latour 1993a, 1999b; Clarke 2008). Arguably, the affective and energetic dimensions of a Peircean semeiotic allow a continuing consideration of embodiment, neither limiting it to the bounds of the flesh, nor eliding the affective, tactile, and corporeal dimensions of meaning. This offers a way to engage with the varied nuances of representation, technical action, and performance. Peirce's semeiotic was influential in Derrida's discussion of the chain of signification and acts as an apposite semeiotic counterpart to theories of distributed and entangled human–non-human entities. Unlike the Saussurean sign his conception of semeiotic meaning is not tied to mental representation, but instead is context-specific and processual, also entailing affective and energetic interpretive responses as much as 'representational' ones (Peirce 1940a). Equally his sign vehicle is not an empty linguistic signifier but is situated in time and place with a variety of characteristics of its own. This opens up possibilities for understanding the materiality and corporeality of the signs of the body on their own terms as much as in relation to other signs.

In order to explore these tensions between embodiment and materiality in archaeology, in the rest of the chapter I shall present two case studies that draw on a Peircean semeiotic. These build upon each other to illustrate the complex ways in which people may be considered to be both bounded and distributed within the framework of Early Modern and Enlightenment thought and Western scientific practices. I start by analysing the spatial boundaries of the body in relation to apotropaic devices in seventeenth-century England, and move on to look at the temporal bounds of embodiment with some discussion of the dead body in present day forensic practice.

Boundaries of the Body: Witch Bottles

A focus on the materiality of the body encourages interrogation of the nature of the collectivity that constitutes the person, accounting for non-humans alongside human beings. It is within this context that I would like to consider early modern apotropaic devices known as 'witch bottles'. The use of witch bottles in seventeenth-century England illustrates the changing perceptions of the body's boundedness at a key period when the mind and matter distinction was being formalized and privileged, and the sense of self interiorized (Bordo 1987). David Canter (2002: 65) notes that the self is an unstable concept, particularly difficult to sustain at times of bodily crisis and violation. He argues that the modes and forms of bodily violation, and responses to them, reveal the techniques through which self is

constructed and the points of potential dislocation and fracture within its constitution. In the context of changing understandings of the constitution of the body
and its relation to the soul and/or mind in seventeenth-century England, apotropaic objects provide striking evidence of the coexistence of different and somewhat
conflicting ways of thinking about the body and its boundaries at moments of
bodily crisis. The practices involved in the use and deposition of 'Bellarmine' witch
bottles provide an example of an Early Modern tradition of embodiment through
objects which were understood to be extensions of the body, and to act and have
agency away from the body. The constitution of the vessels and the elements
contained within them indicate anxieties over bodily integrity and a blurring of
bodily boundaries between 'witch' and victim. At the same time, they show an
increasing concern with the bounded and fragile nature of the body, expressed
through its metaphorical construction as a breakable vessel.

Buried under hearths and thresholds, in ditches and cowsheds, thrown into the
River Thames and retrieved centuries later, witch bottles exert a powerful fascination,
their power to enchant and to capture the imagination apparently still as strong as
ever. Although the use of protective charms has a long history in Britain (Gilchrist
2008), witch bottles appear as part of a distinctive set of new practices in south-east
England in the later sixteenth century, becoming most common in the second half of
the seventeenth century, and persisting until the present day in various forms. The
vessels were often filled with pins and nails, splinters of wood, human hair, nail
parings, and urine, corked tightly, and hidden as a form of protective magic. Initially,
Frechen stoneware Bartman jugs, commonly known as 'Bellarmine' jugs, were used.
These were produced in the Rhineland from the mid-fifteenth century and are
distinctive in their broad belly and narrow neck decorated with a male mask or
face applied in clay before firing (Gaimster 1997: 37) (Figure 16.1). It is usually
suggested that these apparently anthropomorphic vessels were chosen for the task
because of their similarity to the body. I'd like to start with this assumption,
exploring how they are like bodies, and asking why and how the vessel became an
appropriate and common metaphor for the body? Although the vessels were made in
the Rhineland, and traded throughout Europe and beyond, their use as witch bottles
was a peculiarly English practice, found particularly in the south-eastern counties,
but also in North American English colonies (see Merrifield 1987: 174; see also Becker
1978 and Painter 1980 for eighteenth-century examples), and associated with rural
peasants and urban town dwellers alike. Witch bottles can tell us something of the
changing vernacular beliefs about the body through wider society, away from the
learned discourse of royal societies and universities where the emergence of Enlightenment beliefs about the relation of body and soul is usually located. Their appearance prompts the interrogation of the coming into being of a particular set of beliefs
and practices that made these vessels appropriate stand-ins for the body.

The idea of the body as a vessel is a powerful image, one that relies on a
metaphor of containment, which appears to play a key role in organizing our

(a)

Fig. 16.1 Bellarmine jug (a), with (b) contents, comprising brown cloth heart stuck with pins and human hair with nail parings, with cork stopper. Recovered during excavations in Westminster, London in 1904, and donated to the Pitt Rivers Museum by Edward Warren (courtesy of Pitt Rivers Museum, University of Oxford, accession number 1910.18.1).

(b)

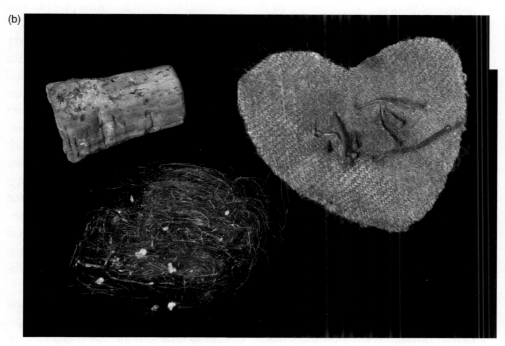

understandings of self and subjectivity (Lakoff and Johnson 1980; Johnson 1987: 21–23). In English, the metaphor finds its expression in language that compares the person to a fragile and breakable vessel, containing fluid and labile emotions (Lupton 1998). It is also articulated in the descriptive terminology and material organization of vessels. Like vessels, people can be *full of joy*; *boiling over with passion*; *brimming with love*; *broken, shattered*; *exploding with anger*. Like people, vessels have feet, bellies, shoulders, necks, lips, and ears. Clearly the concept of person as vessel is deeply embedded in the English language and in the metaphors we use to orient ourselves to the world. Philosopher Mark Johnson (1987) argues that metaphors of containment are fundamental organizing properties of experience, growing out of our material engagement with the world. This may be the case, and indeed, archaeologists commonly find pottery vessels decorated with anthropomorphic motifs in many parts of the world, suggesting that the analogy between vessel and body is one that makes itself felt forcefully in many contexts (e.g. Fowler 2008: 51–56; Joyce 2008b). However, the understanding of fluid emotions as contained within a fragile body has a complex and particular history, one that simultaneously relates to the bounded and individuated sense of self, and also to humoral theories of the body. Viewing the vessel as a natural metaphor for the body masks the difference and variability possible in the metaphor of the body as container. It allows little space to distinguish between seventeenth-century popular understandings of the body as made manifest through apotropaic devices and those that were apparently emerging through Enlightenment scientific practice and foundationalist philosophies.

Archaeologist Ralph Merrifield (1987) collated and synthesized the fragmentary information on witch bottles over the course of his career, bringing the evidence together with documentary sources in his study of *The Archaeology of Ritual and Magic*, one of the very few archaeological studies of folk beliefs in the UK. Brian Hoggard has continued this research, searching for examples hidden in museum and private collections and working towards a synthesis of the available information. Although Merrifield noted that most of the few catalogued examples of witch bottles belonged to the second half of the seventeenth century, Hoggard has subsequently recorded many more English witch bottles. By 2001 his findings indicated that of 187 bottles identified, most (58%) date from before 1700, and that the first examples appear in the mid-sixteenth century (Hoggard 2004: 170), consistent with their documentation in contemporary sources. Although the use of these devices continues until the present day, in general their temporal distribution is consistent with the period of witchcraft accusations from the 1550s to the end of the seventeenth century.

Witch bottles are usually found, often inverted, placed under houses (Merrifield and Smedley 1958), in churchyards and graves (Merrifield 1955: 196), and particularly at thresholds and boundary places. Common locations include under domestic hearths and chimneys (Harvey 1945: 270; Merrifield ibid.), or house doors and walls (e.g. Smedley and Owles 1965: 90), at field boundaries, town ditches, city boundaries (Maloney 1980), and watery places (Allen 1991). Brian Hoggard's (2004: 173) work shows that, although practices vary regionally, the majority of witch bottles have been located under hearths, with others mostly found under walls, floors, and thresholds. The contents are sharp and spiky, with iron nails and brass pins (often bent) and wooden splinters frequently found within them, together with bodily products: urine, hair, and nails. Some of the later seventeenth-century examples have been found containing felt hearts, sometimes pierced through with pins, and they seem to have been stoppered tightly, whether with cork, clay, or wax (Merrifield 1987: 163–165).

The witch bottle seems on first reflection to constitute the body as a bounded and fragile vessel, with a heart at its centre (and clearly an important element of its constitution). Contemporary accounts, such as one by the antiquarian John Aubrey, describe them as defensive in nature, used to attack witches and to protect people and animals from their predations (Aubrey 1696; see Merrifield 1987: 170–171). The vessel works through an extraordinary redundancy of symbolism to effect their sympathetic magic, simultaneously expressing what C. S. Peirce (1940b) would term iconic, indexical, and symbolic relationships with the desired object. Imitative (or iconic) in their similarity to a person (the face mask and maybe the vessel) and contagious (or indexical) in their physical connection (through the inclusion of hair and urine), the devices also include conventional symbolic elements in the form of the felt hearts, which represent the heart without resembling it or having any physical connection with it. They are confusing objects from the perspective of the individuated and indivisible modern body: the Bartmann bottle itself with the often-fearsome bearded mask seems to represent the witch, containing pins and needles to effect injury upon him or her, yet the bodily contents, which are being acted upon by the pins and needles, come from the victim. The manner in which they were understood to affect the witch was explained in a contemporary account:

Another way is to stop the urine of the Patient, close up in a bottle, and put into it three nails, pins or needles, with a little white salt, keeping the urine always warm: if you let it remain long in the bottle, it will endanger the witches life ... The reason ... is because there is part of the vital spirit of the Witch in it, for such is the subtlety of the Devil, that he will not suffer the Witch to infuse any poysonous matter into the body of man or beast, without some of the Witches blood mingled with it ...

Joseph Blagrave's *Astrological Practice of Physick*
(1671: 154–155, quoted in Merrifield 1987: 169–170)

Crucially, in contrast to the individuated and indivisible understanding of vessels and bodies that is common to vessel-metaphors today, both witch *and* victim seem in this account to be represented in the same vessel. As Merrifield (1987: 170) notes, in creating a magical link of sympathy with his or her victim, the witch is left vulnerable to being attacked through the victim's bodily excrescences and secretions. Witch bottles work from the supposition that not only can detached parts of the body (nails, hair, urine) act on another person from far away, but also that the body penetrates into the world through its excised parts and secretions, and in its movements and actions in the world it leaves traces and elements of itself behind. Consequently, witch bottles testify to a very different understanding of the body and its extensions. In this context it is nonsensical to attempt to determine whether the vessel represents witch or patient: it represents both at the same time and their entwined and dependent biographies.

Despite, and perhaps because of, this interpenetration of bodies, the metaphorical deployment of the Bartmann vessel shows a concern with bodily boundaries, a concern that makes a ceramic vessel an appropriate metaphor for the body. However, this seems to be a bounded body that is very different from modern understandings of the body as a vessel for the soul. Another account quoted by Merrifield (1987: 171–172) notes that the efficacy of the device may be improved by heating it until it explodes. The concern with urine and heat, and the stoppering of bodily excretions is in line with theories of bodily humours and temperaments. Within this framework of reference, the fluids and excretions of the body should flow for the continuance of good health: to prevent their egress was dangerous to a person's health and well being. The echoes of this conception remain in present day metaphorical discourses, which emphasize the proper regulation of the flow of emotion (Lupton 1998; Rublack 2002). Here we have a vessel with the heart at its centre (cf. Le Goff 1989) and where the proper circulation of fluids within and through the body is a concern, but where there are also anxieties about bodily boundaries, and the invasion of the body. This tension is negotiated through the gathering of boundaries and their holding in place (cf. Casey 1996: 24–25). Vessels are buried in walls and ditches, marking the edges of place and securing it as a contained and bounded entity, but they are also placed at vulnerable points of transition, particularly at thresholds and chimneys. The buried vessels act to regulate and protect passage into and out of place, mirroring concerns with the regulation of bodily excretions. In passing over thresholds held in place by witch bottles, or in preparing food on hearths under which bottles are buried, thoughts and memories are located in place creating different locales and densities of affective response and meaning within the household and broader community. Diane Purkiss (1995) has suggested that the witch disrupted the boundaries between the house and the exterior world, entering uninvited, and creating domestic disorder. The concern with bodily boundaries was therefore part of a broader concern with the holding of boundaries more generally, simultaneously revealing the place-making activities through which witches were constituted, and through which, as philosopher Edward Casey suggests, modes of containment were composed. To use C. S. Peirce's terminology, the interpretants that the witch bottles elicited were affective as much as they were energetic. This affective recognition of the secured boundaries of the house and of the person informed and maintained the habitual practices that revolved around them, without necessarily entering into any more explicitly discursive realm.

These anxieties about boundaries and flows of excretions are clearly gendered, but space does not permit a detailed analysis here. I should at least note that not only was it mostly women who were accused and convicted in the trials of the sixteenth and seventeenth centuries (Barstow 1994) but witch bottles are often (although not always) found in domestic contexts, and seem to be associated with securing the edges and floor of the house. Historian Laura Gowing (2003: 73–80) has outlined how women's place in the hierarchies of household and community was often defined through the invasion and defence of bodily boundaries, with witches' bodily boundaries problematically masculinized, in that they were understood to be harder, more durable and defended, but also more extended and extendible, out of their houses and communities and into the homes and villages of others (cf. Gilchrist 1999: 109–145).

Witch bottles then have a lot to tell us about the changing understandings of the body in the seventeenth century. In particular, they indicate a concern with the bounded body in popular culture at a moment when the dualist framework of subjective mind and objective body was emerging, while the grotesque and transgressive elements of the medieval body (Bakhtin 1968; see also Stallybrass and White 1986) were increasingly being viewed as problematic and needing containment and regulation. They also emerge at a time when medical discourses on the body were focusing on contagion and its association with sin (Healy 2001: 40–43). Witch bottles therefore point to the incorporation of older conceptions of the body into the dualistic understanding of the body as a bounded vessel for the soul in the Modern period, suggesting that it would come to have such metaphoric power, because the space for its popular acceptance had already been prepared (cf. Healy 2001: 18). In the context of witch bottles we can detect the submerged echoes of the Galenic flows of substances in the metaphors of the emotion-filled body as we use them today (Lupton 1998; cf. Grosz 1994), but tied to an understanding of the body as vessel-like, one that from the eighteenth century onwards no longer needed the iconic elements of the Bellarmine bottle for its force and efficacy. As Deborah Lupton (1998: 97) notes, emotions are viewed as 'problematic in that they tend to dissolve the boundaries between outside and inside'; they relate to Galenic understandings of the body that have been incorporated and bottled in the modern body. The witch bottles seem to speak to a broader anxiety about bodily boundaries in the sixteenth to seventeenth century, one that was being articulated at a popular level through apotropaic devices, as much as through the philosophical discourse of body and soul.

RELATIONSHIPS AFTER DEATH:
FORENSIC ARCHAEOLOGY

Just as the spatial boundaries of the modern embodied self are not firmly delineated, neither are the temporal boundaries. As socio-cultural anthropologists
Elizabeth Hallam, Jenny Hockey, and Glennys Howarth note (1999), the dead
body presents particular challenges for theories of embodiment. Within a liberal
humanist framework, the dead *qua* dead are understood to be body only, with no
agency or mind. Their elision from discussions of embodied experience reveals the
continuing power of the mind–body split that theories of embodiment attempt to
overcome. Archaeologist Sarah Tarlow distinguishes the particular archaeological
focus on the responses of the living to the death of others from the sociological
interest (e.g. Shilling 1993) in personal preparation for one's own anticipated death
(Tarlow 2002: 86). The archaeological focus on those who prepare and dispose of
the body grows from the rationalist conviction that, as matter without mind, the
corpse has no embodied agency and no potential to act. It is clear from the
treatment of the dead body that a concept of the body as a container for the
mind or soul remains a powerful and unspoken metaphorical trope, both within
archaeology and elsewhere. If the body is a container, then the thing it contains
disappears with death, leaving a very different sort of entity behind. This conception of the 'empty vessel' of the body, abandoned after death may seem to have
created the conditions of possibility for the emergence of archaeological exhumation and osteological analysis. However, the sanctioned post-mortem interventions of western science have always drawn on a range of beliefs about the
dead body, including recognition of its continuing agency after death (Ariès 1981:
353–395; Richardson 1987; Tarlow 2008; Crossland 2009a). This calls for a questioning of the archaeological body after death as a naturalized and pre-discursive
category, in the same way that the living body has been questioned. Death may be
viewed as a transformation of embodiment (Boyd 2002: 142) rather than its end,
and the practice of archaeology demands a theory of embodiment that integrates
the dead as well as the lived body. The question of whether 'embodiment' remains an
appropriate term for this conception reveals the degree to which the dead are
positioned as cut off and separate from the living within the framework of analysis
that we currently use.

A theory of embodied experience that moves beyond a Cartesian understanding
of rationality must necessarily acknowledge the materiality and potentiality of the
dead body. In anthropology, studies such as Robert Hertz's (1960) survey of
secondary burial practices have provided illustrations of the ways in which the
dead are commonly understood to have agency, and to continue to embody the
person in some manner after death. This is something that may be recognized

archaeologically in many times and places whether in the Inka customs of feeding and clothing the dead (e.g. Sillar 1992; Salomon 1995), or in secondary burial practices recognized in the Neolithic and elsewhere (e.g. Barrett 1988). Furthermore, an interrogation of the possibilities of embodiment for the dead would not only recognize that feelings or experiences are often attributed to the dead by the living, but would also explore the ways in which the dead body can disrupt and intrude upon human social life (cf. Peirce 1940a). To contribute some notes to this discussion I now turn to the popular discourse of forensic exhumation. This illustrates how, even within the framework of the most apparently empirical and rational of approaches, the agency of individuals is nevertheless understood to persist past death (a more detailed account is given in Crossland 2009b).

The portrayal of human bodies as objectified evidence is fundamental to the discourse of forensic archaeology, used to underwrite truth claims that archaeologists make when testifying in court in the context of criminal proceedings, or in the prosecution of those responsible for human rights abuses. In Foucault and Butler's terms, the status of the corpse as an object is a material effect of its production through discourses of science, law, and archaeology (amongst others). Exploring the ways in which the materiality of the corpse is constituted through acts of excavation and analysis reveals the ways in which the idiom of empiricism marks out the body as dead and as separate from the living. However, somewhat surprisingly, it also reveals recognition of the corpse's agency, elaborated in the language of mass media accounts of forensic practice. In the popular empiricism of these accounts, it is not only facts that speak for themselves, but also the dead. This is made visible in the titles of works such as 'Dead men do tell tales' (Maples and Browning 1994) or 'What the corpse revealed' (Miller 1999). Constantly reiterated is the ability of the corpse to 'speak', to 'reveal', and to 'accuse' (Crossland 2009b: 74–76). These accounts show how the dead are understood as persistently embodied even within a framework that assumes a radical rupture between living and dead. Although the materiality of the corpse is situated within a discursive field that brings it into being as a corpse and as an object that can be excavated and dissected, at the same time elements of the corpse's materiality escape and disrupt this field, contributing to the perception of the corpse as active and 'enminded' (Ingold 2000a: 170–171). The resemblance of the corpse to the living, and the knowledge and memory of human bodies of those who come into the corpse's vicinity, make it difficult, if not impossible to treat as an object. Even cadavers voluntarily donated for medical dissection are covered to hide their shape and features, in this way enabling the disaggregation of the body to take place (Smith and Kleinman 1989). In this sense discursive effects are never complete or totalizing, but are resisted and modified, not through the simple agency of the material world, but through the complex and interactive ways in which material signification emerges. While C. S. Peirce argued that it is in the interruption of the flow of semeiosis that the potential for habit change exists (Peirce 1940c), the ways in which these interruptions and aporiae appear are conditioned by the embodied understanding and memory of past conditions (Peirce 1940d: 230). More generally it shows how the ghostly presence of the dead asserts their continuing agency among the living, both past and present, an appreciation of which extends and complicates an embodied understanding of archaeological practice (Crossland 2002).

This recognition of the agency of the dead simultaneously reveals a foundationalist appeal to the irreducible materiality of the body, creating a solid empirical ground for scientific interpretation, while also acknowledging the power of the dead-as-fetish to destabilize, disrupt, and challenge the representational field that it inhabits. Socio-cultural anthropologist Peter Pels (1998: 91–92) observes that the fetish 'beckon[s] its students to sojourn in the border zones that divide mind and matter, the animate and inanimate', encouraging the questioning of 'boundaries between things and the distinctions they are held to delineate'. The archaeological body indeed attracts attention to its temporal and spatial boundaries, particularly in the crisis moments of permeability and breakdown, illustrating how even the most empirical discourse of forensic science holds at its heart an affective appeal to emotion and 'subjective' experience, one that far from damaging the truth claims it makes, humanizes them and situates them within the ebb and flow of ongoing human relationships. Study of these boundaries calls attention to the relationships between co-inhabitants of the world, providing ways to undercut the Cartesian settlement that has underwritten much of archaeological practice and theory.

CONCLUSIONS

These studies illustrate how the tying together of the literature on embodiment together with that on materiality creates a space for alternate narratives of the coming into being of the bounded body, revealing in the process the complex beliefs about the body that we draw upon and reproduce through the embodied practice of archaeology. Although a focus on the ways in which past human lives were mediated through the material worlds that they inhabited has underwritten much archaeological theory since the 1960s, it is only recently that archaeologists have broadened the scope of their work to consider the ontological groundings of archaeological practice more critically. This opens up a range of possibilities for study, whether in terms of reformulating our understandings of the relationships between humans and non-humans both in the past and in the present; in the problematizing of bodily surfaces and boundaries as something that should be questioned rather than taken as a given (e.g. Looper 2003; Meskell 2004; Joyce

2005); or in rethinking the apparently foundational biological body as something that is continually made and remade through practice (Sofaer 2006a). Peircean approaches encourage a closer attention to the relationships between humans and the material world (Preucel 2006), allowing a refiguring of representation as itself an embodied practice that works to undermine subject–object distinctions. In this way Peirce's semeiotic brings the literatures on materiality and embodiment into productive conversation. In attending to the material world, we can consider the ways in which it can challenge, change, or shape embodied understandings of how to go on, bringing into view the relational emergence of affective response and techniques of the body. These in turn may be situated as interpretants involved in the habitual reproduction of human and non-human worlds. A Peircean orientation therefore provides useful points of intersection with studies of affect and emotion, whether in archaeology (Tarlow 2000; Hamilakis 2002; Gosden 2004a) or elsewhere (e.g. Damasio 2000; Clough and Halley 2007; Thrift 2007) as well as with technology studies (e.g. Lemonnier 1992: 79–103). This opens a space to rethink our tangible engagements with archaeological evidence as forms of representation (Crossland 2009b), as well as considering how past forms of self and person were embodied and constructed through the material world.

CHAPTER 17

MATERIAL CULTURE IN PRIMATES

TATYANA HUMLE

INTRODUCTION: CULTURE AND MATERIAL CULTURE IN NON-HUMAN PRIMATES?

The ascription of culture to non-human animals has been controversial and a source of much debate. Much of this debate hinges on the definition of culture. In 1952, Kroeber and Kluckhohn produced a review of concepts and definitions of culture, compiling 168 definitions, all implying a human prerogative. The classic definition by Tylor (1871: 1) presents culture as 'that complex whole which includes knowledge, belief, art, morals, custom, and any other capabilities and habits acquired by man as a member of society'. However, at the same time, Kawamura (1959: 43) used the terms 'sub-culture' and 'preculture' in his descriptions of potato-washing among Japanese macaques (*Macaca fuscata*) of Koshima Island. The term 'culture' was first used in relation to non-human primates (hereinafter 'primates') by Kummer (1971: 11), although Kroeber, already in 1928, had contemplated the possibility of 'ape culture' (1928: 331).

A clear divide between socio-cultural anthropologists and biologists has prevailed ever since the 1920s concerning what is and what constitutes culture (see McGrew 1992 for further details on this debate). On the one hand, some anthropologists still commonly assume that culture is a unique human characteristic. Indeed, some definitions continue to refer specifically to the human specificity of culture centred on language, symbols, teaching, and imitation (for example, see Carrithers 1990 for reiteration of these themes). These definitions leave little to no room for culture in non-human animals, including early hominids such as *Australopithecus* sp. and *Homo habilis* (McGrew 1992). On the other hand, biologists, including primatologists, generally adhere to more encompassing definitions ranging from basic ones such as culture being 'the way we do things' (McGrew 2003: 433) to more operational ones such as culture constituting 'all group-typical behaviour patterns, shared by members of animal communities, that are to some degree reliant on socially learned and transmitted information' (Laland and Janik 2006: 542).

The perception of culture as 'a system of socially transmitted behaviour(s)' (van Schaik *et al.* 2003a: 102) stimulated a great deal of interest in the study of culture among non-human animals. Many of these studies revealed the prevalence of socially transmitted behavioural variants in a variety of species ranging from insects, fish, and birds to primates, primarily in the domains of foraging and communication (Fragaszy and Perry 2003). These variants among some species of primates concerned an even wider range of domains, including defence, self-maintenance, and social functions, including tool use. The use of tools is, for researchers, the most accessible form of culture among primates. Such elementary technology denotes the knowledgeable use of one or more physical objects as a means to achieve an end, and can be usefully termed 'material culture' if standardized in a collective way that is characteristic of a group of individuals of a same species (McGrew 2004).

Elementary technology among primates concerns predominantly subsistence behaviours, expressed in, often complex, foraging techniques. Elementary technology among wild primates is typically based on natural materials, whether vegetation (most commonly a leaf, leaf midrib, twig, stick, stalk, bark, petiole, stem, shoot, root, or bough) or non-organic matter (such as stones or water). It is rare for non-human primate material culture to include organic matter such as bones or skin. In addition, material culture in primates does not necessarily imply tool modification: stones, sticks, or leaves, for example, may be used without prior modification. Following the distinction made by Oswalt (1976: 14) in his classic study of technology, such unmodified tools may be termed 'naturefacts', as opposed to artefacts that represent rather the end product of a modification process of a raw material to generate a tool. Thanks to the potential rich evidence provided by leftover artefacts, material culture is the most well studied domain of culture among primates.

The capacity to use tools does not necessarily imply material culture. Indeed, a range of animal species, beyond primates, utilize tools (Beck 1980). Examples include woodpecker finches (*Cactospiza pallida*) in the Galapagos Islands utilizing cactus spines as tools to push or lever arthropods out of crevices in bark (Tebbich *et al.* 2001, 2002) or parasitoid digger wasps (*Ammophila* sp.) using pebbles to compact and pound the soil at the entrance of their burrows (Tinbergen 1951). However, these tool use behaviours are innate, genetically based, and thus not reliant on social transmission processes for their acquisition and/or maintenance. These techniques therefore do not qualify as material culture: material culture implies the social transmission of tool use skills, which has so far only ever been witnessed in the wild in capuchin monkeys, orang-utans, chimpanzees, and humans, as well as potentially in some species of macaques.

The processes of transmission
of material culture

Psychologists have focused much attention on determining and defining a range of social learning processes characterizing cultural transmission (Galef 1988; Tomasello *et al.* 1990, 1993; Whiten and Ham 1992). Social learning can be defined as learning that is influenced by the observation of, or interaction with, another animal (typically of the same species) or its products, such as scent marks or excavations (Galef 1988). Different social learning processes identified by psychologists may result in differing levels of fidelity in behavioural transmission (Laland and Kendal 2003). Through *local enhancement*, the behaviour of a knowledgeable individual (A) draws the attention of a second naïve individual (B) to a particular location in the environment (Roberts 1941), while through *stimulus enhancement*, B is more likely to interact with stimuli of the same physical type as those with which A initially interacted with, irrespective of location (Spence 1937). Although local enhancement or even stimulus enhancement may yield group convergence in food choice, neither may necessarily yield high fidelity in the details of how that food is processed.

At the other end of the spectrum, behaviours might be acquired through *imitation* (Thorndike 1911) whereby B reproduces the actions it has observed A perform, such as the processing skills required to gain access to a kernel contained within a hard shell. With imitation, the details of food processing should be consistent throughout the group, regardless of the number of potential variants available. High fidelity in the transmission process should also result from teaching. During teaching, A modifies its behaviour in the presence of B, at some initial cost to itself, so that B can learn more readily (Caro and Hauser 1992). Teaching is expected to be a fast and efficient means of cultural transmission and is, alongside action-level imitation, considered by some as the only mode of cultural transmission in humans (Tomasello 1999).

Evidence for teaching exists in a range of species (e.g. killer whales, *Orcinus orca*: Rendell and Whitehead 2001; meerkats, *Suricata suricatta*: Thornton and McAuliffe 2006). However, active demonstration and assistance in canalizing a young chimpanzee's acquisition of a complex tool use skill have rarely ever been observed (e.g. Boesch 1991), and have so far never been recorded in the context of other complex tool use behaviours in chimpanzees or other primate species. Although local and/or stimulus enhancement is common in primates, the prevalence of action-level imitation remains contentious. Indeed, there is limited evidence for imitation of tool use skills in primates, including in capuchin monkeys (Visalberghi and Frangaszy 2002) and great apes (Whiten *et al.* 2004). The most convincing studies showing that chimpanzees, orang-utans, or capuchins are able to imitate were conducted on '*enculturated*' individuals, i.e. reared by humans in a relatively enriched and stimulating environment. This enculturation process at an early age has been proposed to influence social learning abilities to an extent that is not observed among their wild or non-human reared captive counterparts (Fredman and Whiten 2007; Furlong *et al.* 2008).

Finally, there is a growing consensus that social learning cannot readily be distinguished from asocial (individual) learning processes, and that social learning mechanisms may interact and intermingle in the learning process, thus rendering their distinction in practicality rather tenuous. Indeed, most social learning observed in animals, and primates in general, does not readily fit such clear categories as described above. Learning may thus best be described as *socially biased learning* or socially guided individual learning, a process that is coupled with individual experience and mediated by exposure to the activities and/or behaviours of others (Fragaszy and Visalberghi 2001, 2004). Socially biased learning is therefore distinguished by the context in which learning occurs, and not by distinctive cognitive processes.

In the transmission of material culture, *vertical transmission* (the transmission of behaviour from parent to young, Cavalli-Sforza *et al.* 1982) can affect both *diffusion* (within social units) and *dissemination* (across social units) of cultural variants. Vertical transmission is essential for the intergenerational maintenance of cultural variants within a group. However, it may also promote the spread of the behaviour between groups. Indeed, if the dispersing sex is female, a young adult female integrating a new group or social unit may transfer her skills or knowledge to her offspring who can then later serve as an additional model to other members of the new group. *Horizontal transmission* is between members of the same generation and *oblique transmission* is from non-parental individuals of the parental generation to members of the filial generation or vice versa (Cavalli-Sforza *et al.* 1982). In the context of material culture, these modes of transmission are particularly relevant (1) when a community or group member innovates a tool use behaviour, or (2) when an individual immigrates into a new group carrying with them a set of novel tool use skills within its host community or social unit.

LEVELS OF STUDY

Primate material culture can vary among species, subspecies, populations, and individuals within a community, group, or clan. Interspecific variation in tool use is quite dramatic among primates, and the prevalence of material culture among primates in the wild does not necessarily correlate with evolutionary proximity to humans. Indeed, although material culture is prevalent among great apes, it has also more recently been recognized in capuchin monkeys, a New World primate. Intraspecific variation has also only more recently been documented and studied, as such variation requires longer-term data across multiple individuals. Only now, after practically four decades of fieldwork across a variety of species, can we shed some light on individual variation and how this individual variation relates to culture in general and material culture in relevant species.

CONDITIONS FOR MATERIAL CULTURE

Van Schaik *et al.* (1999) proposed a model suggesting that the explosive expansion of lithic technology among hominin populations was built upon manual, social, and cognitive capacities found among extractively foraging primates. There is indeed growing evidence that wild primate species exhibiting habitual tool use in foraging contexts all share the capacity for extractive foraging, manual dexterity, observational learning, and tolerance for close proximity to skilled demonstrators. Indeed, material culture has thus far been reported in a handful of species, which in spite of their phylogenetic distance, all share these four capacities. I summarize below some of the important, but not always necessary, conditions favouring the emergence, maintenance, diffusion, and dissemination of material culture among primates.

Manual dexterity is a necessary condition for the development of material culture, since all species of primates in which feeding tool use has been observed, whether in the wild or in captivity, have demonstrated dextrous foraging skills in the wild (cf. van Schaik *et al.* 1999). However, not all extractive foragers are necessarily dextrous, and not all dextrous extractive foragers are tool users (van Schaik *et al.* 1999). Another condition, which is shared by all primate species that demonstrate elementary technology in the wild, is slow and delayed maturation or extended juvenility. Considering that young may take several years to learn a tool use skill, such a long period of dependency and tolerated proximity to the mother and other group members favours socially biased transmission whether vertical or oblique (Pereira and Fairbanks 2006).

Whether high levels of social and/or physical cognition are a prerequisite or not to material culture has been the source of much debate (Galef 1992; McGrew 1992; Tomasello 1999). Emergent findings on a range of primate species indicate that imitation or teaching, as in social learning mechanisms requiring higher cognitive abilities, such as 'theory of mind' (the ability to impute knowledge or ignorance to others) or an understanding of the physical properties of objects, may not be necessary conditions for material culture. Indeed, there is little evidence for both in capuchins in captivity (Fragaszy and Visalberghi 2004), although capuchin monkeys in the wild exhibit evidence for material culture.

Social conditions are also among the conditions for material culture. Coussi-Korbel and Fragaszy (1995) suggested that social tolerance and opportunities for close behavioural co-ordination in space and time with group members could explain many of the underlying species differences in their propensity for learning socially. Many studies have shown that social dynamics among group members are more important than cognitive ability or phylogenetic status in predicting social learning. Individuals in more egalitarian and tolerant social groups are more likely to learn socially and exhibit behavioural homogeneity (examples reviewed in Fragaszy and Visalberghi 2004). As an extension to this hypothesis, van Schaik *et al.* (2003a) showed that interpopulational differences in both chimpanzees and orang-utans can also be explained by differential opportunities for *socially biased learning* during ontogeny and variations in social tolerance between populations/ groups or communities. Van Schaik *et al.* (2003b) found support for this hypothesis in explaining intrapopulational differences among orang-utans (*Pongo pygmaeus abelii*) in the Sumatran swamp forest of Suaq Balimbing in their rate of tool use to extract honey, ants, or termites from tree holes and in their level of specialization on tree-hole tool use.

The emergence of tool use also requires favourable *ecological conditions*, especially opportunities for extractive foraging and the availability of raw materials to modify and/or use as tools. Extractive foraging involves locating and/or processing embedded foods, such as underground tubers, roots, and insects or hard-shelled nuts or seeds contained within spiny fruit. Some have suggested that sophisticated techniques for extractive foraging involving elementary technology arose as a result of necessity. The 'necessity hypothesis' implies that increased competition for food resulting from resource scarcity compels an individual to exploit a novel food resource, requiring the invention of a novel extractive foraging technique reliant on the use of tools. Yamakoshi (1998) showed that, when fruits are scarce, the wild chimpanzees of Bossou (Guinea) effectively increase their tool use activities, in order to gain access to otherwise inaccessible food resources and to boost their energy intake. Moura and Lee (2004) also proposed that capuchin monkeys inhabiting a harsh and dry habitat survive food scarcity and foraging time constraints by relying on tool use and exploiting otherwise inaccessible high-energy food resources.

This pattern of reliance on subsistence elementary technology during periods of low food abundance supports the idea that the likelihood of diffusion may depend on the adaptive value of the *innovation*—a process that results in a new or modified learned behaviour that introduces a novel behavioural variant into a group's or social unit's repertoire (van Schaik *et al.* 2006). However, necessity does not always appear to be the mother of invention, and adaptive value does not necessarily ensure diffusion of novel tool use skills. Indeed, patterns of reliance on elementary technology do not always correlate with periods of low availability of primary food resources. Fox *et al.* (2004) showed that among wild orang-utans greater *opportunities for invention* rather than low fruit availability contributed to insect-extraction tool use at Suaq Balimbing. Finally, ecological conditions favouring the emergence of material culture are not always straightforward, although in essence, ecological opportunity for invention appears to be a necessary condition pre-empting the opportunity for socially biased learning, which ensures diffusion of the novel skill.

MATERIAL CULTURE AMONG PRIMATES

Material culture was long thought to be unique to the human species. Before Goodall's observation of termite fishing in chimpanzees at Gombe, Tanzania in 1960 (Goodall 1968, 1986), the evolutionary origins of our material culture were sought in the archaeological records of Plio-Pleistocene hominids, known to use stone tools (lithic technology), as well as probably a variety of organic tools of which little to no evidence remains today. However, it is now accepted that extant primates also make and use tools on a day-to-day basis. Among wild primates, habitual (shown by at least several relevant individuals of the group or social unit) and customary (shown by most or all relevant individuals of the group or social unit) use of tools was for a long time limited to chimpanzees and orang-utans in the wild; however, recent findings on capuchin monkeys are challenging the idea that, beyond humans, material culture belongs only to the great apes.

All species of great apes readily demonstrate the ability to use tools in captivity. However, tool use has rarely been reported among wild bonobos (*Pan paniscus*) (Hohman and Fruth 2003), even though this species exhibits a high propensity for material culture in captivity (e.g. Toth *et al.* 1993). In addition, the first reported observation of tool use among gorillas in the wild took place in 2004 (Breuer *et al.* 2005). Therefore, altogether, it would be presumptuous to rule out the existence of material culture beyond shelter, as in nesting or bed making behaviour, in these two species of great apes. Indeed, there is still scope for observations of elementary technology in both gorillas and bonobos as studies *in situ* continue and more populations are being studied.

Among the great apes, besides humans, all four subspecies of chimpanzee (*Pan troglodytes*) and the Sumatran orang-utan (*Pongo abelii*) have so far been reported to habitually or customarily use and make tools in the wild. The repertoire of elementary technology displayed by these two species is impressive, especially among our closest evolutionary neighbours, the chimpanzee (Whiten *et al.* 1999, 2001). Indeed, four decades of field studies of wild chimpanzees in Africa have revealed substantial differences in behavioural repertoire and elementary technology in particular at the subspecies, population, and community level (Whiten *et al.* 1999, 2001). Tool use in chimpanzees has been observed at all field sites where this species has been studied.

The construction of shelters—nest building or bed making—is a behaviour shared by all great ape species. Fruth and Hohmann (1996: 226) proposed that 'nest building (in great apes) is not only properly placed within the realm of tool use, but it is also the original tool that led to the mental and physical ability to use tools we see today'. Great apes construct beds for resting by day or night by successively bending branches into an interwoven platform. Contrary to other vertebrate species, these nests or beds do not serve to rear young or to store food (Hansell 2005) but rather to rest by night or day. Studies in captivity have demonstrated that observational learning, early experience and practice are essential in ensuring that young acquire nest-building skills (Videan 2006).

Nevertheless, Whiten *et al.* (1999, 2001) ignored nest-building behaviour in chimpanzees in their listing of candidate cultural variants, as they deemed it failed to reveal cross-community variation independent of environmental variations prevalent between sites. Indeed, the majority of studies to date seem to suggest that chimpanzees and other great apes readily adapt their nest-building behaviour to environmental conditions. Population comparisons in nesting behaviour are therefore fraught with difficulties, especially between sites exhibiting wide divergences in habitat types, past and current levels of predation pressure, and climatic conditions. However, all species of great apes show some interpopulational differences in nest-building behaviour (Fruth and Hohmann 1996). Tree species preference for nest building is a good example (e.g. Humle and Matsuzawa 2004). In addition, there is growing evidence that terrestrial nesting in chimpanzees for night-time use is a cultural variant, independent of local meteorological or ecological conditions (Koops *et al.* 2007). Van Schaik *et al.* (2003a) also found several nest building related behavioural variants among wild orang-utans. Finally, the precise function and evolutionary origins of bed building among great apes, the extent of inter- and intrapopulational, as well as species differences, remain still much open for investigation.

Primate material culture also relates to faunivory and herbivory subsistence. Orang-utan tool use in the wild was first reported in 1994 (van Schaik and Fox

1996). Sumatran orang-utans' tool kit concerns primarily the manufacture and/or use of sticks or branches to extract insects, their products (e.g. honey) or water from tree-holes or seeds from the protected *Neesia* fruit (van Schaik *et al.* 2003b). Similarly depending on the community it belongs to, a chimpanzee may use digging sticks and probes to gather honey from stingless bee or honeybee nests; dipping sticks to prey on biting army ants (*Dorylus spp.*) or scoop algae from the surface of ponds; fishing rods or probes to capture subterranean termites or arboreal ants (Figures 17.1–17.3). The tool kit of chimpanzees is ever expanding (e.g. Pruetz and Bertolani 2007; Sanz and Morgan 2007)—chimpanzees at Fongoli (Senegal) manufacture spears that they use to capture galagos (small nocturnal primates), chimpanzees at Goualougo (Republic of Congo) regularly rely on the use of a *tool set* (the compulsory sequential use of two types of tool to attain an objective), for example, to extract underground termites. For further details on the array of the tool kit of chimpanzees and orang-utans see Whiten *et al.* (1999, 2001; Chimpanzee Cultures 2007) for chimpanzees and van Schaik *et al.* (2003a) for orang-utans. Tools used are typically custom-made, with a considerable degree of standardization in length, diameter, raw material selectivity, and end use. Tools are indeed typically well suited to serve their function. However, it remains to be established to what extent inter- and intraspecific and populational differences in tool making and/or tool choice can be attributed to social transmission.

Fig. 17.1 A chimpanzee (*Pan troglodytes verus*) at Bossou, Guinea, West Africa, scooping algae (*Spirogyra* sp.) from the surface of a pond with the aid of a stalk of vegetation, modified for this purpose (photo: Tatyana Humle).

Fig. 17.2 An adult female chimpanzee with her offspring (*Pan troglodytes schwein-furthii*) at Gombe, Tanzania, East Africa, plucking *Macrotermes* termites from a probe she just had inserted into a tunnel in a termite mound (photo: Joshua Leonard).

Fig. 17.3 A chimpanzee (*Pan troglodytes schweinfurthii*) at Mahale, Tanzania, East Africa, inserting a short flexible probe into a small hole up a tree to fish for *Camponotus* ants (photo: Michio Nakamura).

Like chimpanzees, orang-utans also present an array of tool-use behaviours that do not pertain to subsistence but rather self-maintenance and comfort, such as the use of a stick to scratch otherwise unreachable body parts, of a bundle of leaves to wipe latex off the chin or of a branch as a swatter to ward off bees and/or wasps (van Schaik *et al.* 2003a).

Wild capuchin monkeys exhibit several group-specific behavioural traditions whether in the technological domain (Panger *et al.* 2002) or social domain (Perry *et al.* 2003). Capuchin monkeys are well known for their extensive manipulative capabilities, which rival those of great apes, especially chimpanzees. In addition, they exhibit a high degree of social tolerance (Ottoni *et al.* 2005). Until the mid-1980s, evidence for complex tool use and object manipulation, including percussive abilities, among capuchin monkeys came from captive or semi-captive individuals (Beck 1980; Visalberghi 1990). However, since then, there has been an increase in the number of reports of tool use in wild capuchin monkeys, especially *C. apella*, involving cracking nuts, digging tubers, throwing sticks at intruders, and even using leaves to drink (e.g. Moura and Lee 2004).

APPROACHES TO THE STUDY OF MATERIAL CULTURE IN PRIMATES

For animal species that exhibit differences in food processing techniques across study sites, it is difficult to gather the empirical data to show that the young socially learn the technical variants exhibited by their group members. Social learning in animals has primarily been studied in *captive settings*. Studies in captivity have essentially adopted three distinct paradigms. The first is the *demonstrator-naïve individual paradigm*, whereby a naïve individual is given the possibility to observe a demonstrator solving a task. These studies have primarily investigated the ability of primates to reproduce the actions of a skilled demonstrator (human or conspecific) upon observation, i.e. imitation. Some studies have also employed a *two-action design*, whereby a task can be solved in two ways and demonstrators are trained in modelling only one of the two solutions. A second paradigm is the *demonstrator-naïve group paradigm*. The dual action model has also been used with this paradigm to follow the spread of tool-use skills within groups. Finally, a third paradigm is the *diffusion chain paradigm*. In this paradigm, a behaviour is passed from one subject to the next in a linear sequential fashion, similarly to Chinese whispers (e.g. chimpanzees: Whiten *et al.* 2005; Horner *et al.* 2006; capuchin monkeys: Dindo *et al.* 2008). Alternatively, diffusion of the behaviour is first recorded within a group (using the second paradigm), before then being passed on sequentially between groups, mimicking between group transmission of behaviour (chimpanzees: Hopper *et al.* 2007). So far, such kinds of studies have primarily focused on chimpanzees and capuchin monkeys. They have revealed that both species (1) can learn a novel behaviour or skill through observation of skilled conspecifics, and (2) are capable of transmitting behaviour(s) with a relatively high degree of fidelity along a sequential chain of individuals or even between groups.

FIELD OBSERVATIONS AND EXPERIMENTS

In the field, the identification of a cultural variant in non-human animals, including material culture among primates, has typically been established on the basis of a set of indicators. These indicators include: (1) a patchy geographical distribution of the behaviour; (2) its habitual and customary (cf. Whiten *et al.* 1999) occurrence at sites where it has been confirmed; (3) its persistence across generations; (4) the unlikely attribution of its occurrence to ecological or genetic differences between sites (e.g. McGrew *et al.* 1997); and (5) its absence across dispersal barriers (e.g. Boesch *et al.* 1994; van Schaik and Knott 2001). This approach, based on the establishment of geographic variations in behaviour, is known as *the ethnographic method* (Wrangham *et al.* 1994), the *group comparison* (Fragaszy and Perry 2003), or *elimination method* (van Schaik 2003). Whiten *et al.* (1999) thus identified 39 candidate cultural variants in chimpanzees and van Schaik *et al.* (2003a) 24 in orang-utans on the grounds that they occurred sufficiently frequently at one or more site(s) to be consistent with social transmission, yet were absent at one or more other(s) where environmental explanations could be rejected.

In recent years, researchers have adopted supplemental approaches, aimed more specifically at investigating the intergenerational transmission and maintenance of behaviours, including elementary technology, among wild subjects. These include developmental and *in situ* experimental approaches. Thus, Matsuzawa and colleagues have stimulated the occurrence of tool use behaviours in an outdoor laboratory setting (Matsuzawa 1994; Biro *et al.* 2006). In this setting, located within the home range of the chimpanzees of Bossou (Guinea), tool and food availability, distribution, and type can readily be manipulated. When the chimpanzees visit the outdoor laboratory, any occurrence of tool-use, i.e. nut cracking and water drinking in a tree hole, is then video-recorded (Figure 17.4). Consistent data on the same tool-use behaviours can thus be gathered longitudinally year after year. Manipulations can also stimulate the emergence of behavioural innovations, rarely observed first hand in the wild, e.g. the introduction of a novel species of nut. This approach can therefore provide invaluable information on the dynamics of diffusion of novel behaviours

Fig. 17.4 An adult female chimpanzee (*Pan troglodytes verus*) with both her offspring at Bossou, Guinea, West Africa, cracking oil palm nuts (*Elaies guineensis*) using a mobile hammer and anvil stone in the natural outdoor laboratory (photo: Etsuko Nogami).

both between and within a community, beyond what can be gathered by following wild subjects from dawn until dusk. These experiments revealed that adult chimpanzees tolerate close observation by naive young, optimize their interindividual spacing during cracking bouts, show selectivity in their choice of stones for nut cracking and of plant species for water drinking, and a consistent hand preference when using a hammer stone (Biro *et al.* 2006). During these experiments, three chimpanzees were also observed using a third stone as a wedge to keep the surface of the anvil stone flat and stable. The wedge was classified as a *metatool*, i.e. a tool that was used to improve the function of another tool (Matsuzawa 1991).

In spite of the obvious value of this approach, careful and detailed observations of subjects during the course of their daily activities still remain quintessential and provide the most socially and ecologically valid context in which to study material culture in primates. This approach is more laborious and is highly dependent on the natural frequency of occurrence of the focal tool-use skills and level of habituation of the individuals observed. Finally, after decades of studies of chimpanzees in their natural habitat, only recently has such an approach been adopted and shed important light on the learning trajectory of complex tool using skills in young (e.g. Lonsdorf 2005, 2006; Humle *et al.* 2009).

Further insight in behavioural variation in tool use among primates can also be gathered via human replication of tool use aimed at systematically measuring variables otherwise unquantifiable through simple observation or video recording (e.g. simulated chimpanzee ant-dipping behaviour by humans: Humle and Matsuzawa 2002; Möbius *et al.* 2008; Schöning *et al.* 2008). Such an approach has provided convincing evidence that both ecological and cultural processes intermingle in influencing tool length and technique in ant dipping, a tool-use behaviour requiring the use of modified probe of vegetation to capture army ants (*Dorylus spp.*)—both within and between chimpanzee communities.

Some researchers have also made use of archaeological methods to study primate material culture, focusing on the lithic technology used to make stone tools for cracking open nuts, as observed so far in the wild solely among some populations of the West African subspecies of chimpanzee (*Pan troglodytes verus*) and brown or tufted capuchins (*Cebus apella*) (Haslan *et al.* 2009). Mercader and colleagues were the first to apply this approach to a chimpanzee nut-cracking site in the Taï forest, Côte d'Ivoire. Mercader *et al.* (2002) described in detail recent buried remains of unintentionally fractured stone and organic residues resulting from the nut-cracking activities of modern chimpanzees. This study highlighted the potential in applying archaeological methods to the study of material culture among non-human extant primates and in identifying the type of material assemblage that could characterize ancient nut-cracking sites of chimpanzees. Mercader *et al.* (2007) importantly confirmed that chimpanzees and humans share several important elementary technological attributes, including the transport of stones to cracking sites, the optimal combination of locally available raw materials, size, shape, and weight criteria to efficiently crack a given species of nuts, the accumulation and concentration of stones, flake, and shell remains resulting from percussive activities at specific sites within the landscape.

This archaeological approach allows for relatively precise dating of excavated sites by standard archaeometric techniques, e.g. radiocarbon dating. Chimpanzee sites have thus ranged from hundreds (Mercader *et al.* 2002) to thousands (Mercader *et al.* 2007) of years old. No sites of wild capuchins have yet been excavated in this manner. However, emerging data from such sites indicate that capuchin monkeys use hard level surfaces, including large embedded stones or wooden logs, as anvils, and mobile stones as hammers to crack open palm nuts, and transport hammer stones as well as nuts to the anvil sites (Visalberghi *et al.* 2007). Nut cracking in capuchins is a remarkable feat since the hammer stone may weigh on average 1 kg, as in 25–40% of the average body weight for adult males or females (Visalberghi *et al.* 2007) (Figure 17.5). Wild capuchins thus provide an additional reference point for interpreting hominin stone assemblages. Stone-handling during play and stone throwing in Japanese macaques also represent group-specific behavioural traditions, which are shedding some important insights into the evolution of stone technology in hominids (e.g. Leca *et al.* 2007, 2008) (Figure 17.6).

Fig. 17.5 A wild capuchin (*Cebus libidinosus*) in Brazil, South America, cracking a palm nut using a hammer stone and a rock outcrop as an anvil (photo: EthoCebus Research Group).

Fig. 17.6 A Japanese macaque (*Macaca fuscata*) at Arashiyama, Japan, handling stones as a form of play, a possible behavioural precursor of stone technology in hominids (photo: Jean-Baptiste Leca).

The study of inter- and intraspecific variation in environmental and social aspects of tool use among primates, especially in the wild, has the potential to contribute to modelling the conditions that facilitated the evolution of culture and technology (McGrew 1992; van Schaik *et al.* 1999). Indeed, as more empirical data become available across a range of species, modelling studies will become increasingly valuable in helping us formulate or refine predictions and hypotheses (e.g. Laland and Kendal 2003) and understand more generally the interactions between ecology, cognition, and cultural processes.

IMPLICATIONS: MATERIAL CULTURE AND HUMAN UNIQUENESS

Humans rely more on imitation and teaching than other primate species and therefore can exhibit high transmission fidelity of knowledge and information. During hominin evolution, it is likely that socially biased learning abilities, as well as the capacity for innovation were enhanced via natural selection. Since natural selection acts on phenotypes, selection for improved socially biased learning abilities were dependent upon fitness benefits of performing these elementary technologies and the rate of opportunities for socially biased learning. As proposed by van Schaik *et al.* (1999), such conditions are best favoured among tolerant gregarious societies, reliant on extractive foraging and complex foraging skills. Klein (1999) has suggested that these elements may have characterized more savanna-dwelling early *Homo*, with their stone tool-use elementary technology for processing large carcasses, as well as potentially plant foods such as tubers. Such activities likely facilitated social gregariousness, as well as food sharing, and elicited favourable conditions for social tolerance and opportunities for socially biased learning of elementary technology. Ultimately, the ability of humans to invent, transfer, and acquire elementary technology was enhanced by the advent of language: a medium for learning, independent of visual input, favouring horizontal and oblique transmission in the maintenance, diffusion, and dissemination of material culture.

The idea of material culture has often been understood as relating to the existence of cultural regions (McGrew 1992): an approach in which a correlation between geographic distance and variation in material culture is expected (van Schaik and Knott 2001; van Schaik *et al.* 2003a). Van Schaik *et al.* (2003a) and van Schaik and Knott (2001) provided evidence for a correlation between interpopulational variation in material cultural variation and geographical distance in orang-utans, revealing fundamental similarities to human culture. However, nut cracking in chimpanzees long thought to be confined to populations West of Nzo-Sassandra River in Côte d'Ivoire (Boesch *et al.* 1994), has also recently been reported in Cameroon (Morgan and Abwe 2006). Although some studies in chimpanzees have reported the diffusion of behavioural patterns between communities (e.g. Nakamura and Uehara 2004), some have also indicated that transmission of complex tool use behavioural patterns between neighbouring communities do not necessarily correlate with geographical proximity (e.g. Humle and Matsuzawa 2004). These findings raise important questions regarding the respective roles of ecological and social influences and constraints on the process of transmission and maintenance of material culture both within and between communities that no captive study has yet been able to address. Although the loss or extinction of cultures may explain some of the disjointed patterns of geographical distribution, the diffusion of material culture between groups, social units, communities, populations, still remains a poorly understood phenomenon.

A decade ago, Tomasello (1999) proposed the *ratchet effect* as a distinguishing characteristic of human culture. The ratchet effect in material culture implies cumulative modifications and incremental improvements thus resulting in increasingly elaborate technologies. Such a concept, however, has heavily been criticized by anthropologists who deem it simplistic and potentially prejudicial (McGrew 2004). Nevertheless, the ratchet effect may not be as unique to humans as previously suggested, as several primate species (e.g. Japanese macaque, *Macaca fuscata*: Hirata *et al.* 2001; Leca *et al.* 2007), as well as non-primate species (e.g. New Caledonian crow, *Corvus moneduloides*: Hunt and Gray 2003) show evidence of cumulative culture. Since we are now equipped to explore the archaeological lithic technology of chimpanzees and capuchin monkeys (Mercader *et al.* 2007), we will finally be able to more fully explore cumulative culture in primates. In addition, as research at more sites is being carried out, we are beginning to gain a better appreciation for the impressive variability in elementary technology employed by chimpanzees for similar purposes, thus indirectly providing strong evidence for cumulative evolution (e.g. termite fishing; see Sanz and Morgan 2007).

FUTURE PERSPECTIVES

Cultural primatology

As more detailed data are being gathered and compiled across field sites, as new field sites are being established or old ones revived, it has become apparent that we still do not have a complete grasp of the extent of material culture among primates and the processes of cultural transmission. Cultural primatology is still in its infancy and is coming of age. This new field of science is a fusion of elements of fields ranging from comparative experimental psychology, cultural anthropology, archaeology, behavioural ecology, evolutionary biology, and gene culture co-evolution theory. The blending of methods and approaches, and the translocation of approaches, paradigms, and frameworks to new contexts are rapidly helping advance the field of cultural primatology. For example, cladistic methods traditionally applied to evolutionary biology have proved useful in explaining diversity in human material culture. Lycett *et al.* (2007) have recently applied this phylogenetic analytical method to the chimpanzee cultural database to help refute the hypothesis that reported and observed behavioural differences between communities are genetically determined.

Beyond the material, beyond primates

Culture in primates evidently extends beyond the material and tool use. Many candidate cultural variants persist across a wide range of behaviours not necessarily involving subsistence, such as social customs (e.g. grooming variants in chimpanzees, Nakamura and Uehara 2004; social conventions in white-faced capuchins, Perry *et al.* 2003). Social customs have the advantage of being independent of environmental constraints, allowing us to tap into the spread of arbitrary conventions, for which evidence already exists in captive chimpanzees (Bonnie *et al.* 2007), as well as into the prevalence of conformity in primates, topics also relevant to human material culture. R. W. Byrne (2007) has proposed that to enhance our understanding of 'human technological culture' and to model the evolutionary origins of human technology, we should also focus our attention on complex and locally nearly ubiquitous food-processing skills, not requiring the use of tools (e.g. nettle processing in gorillas, R. W. Byrne 2004). Finally, many taxa beyond the great apes and capuchin monkeys (e.g. corvids, Bluff *et al.* 2007; cetaceans, Rendell and Whitehead 2001; callitrichid monkeys—marmosets and tamarins, Snowdon 2001; macaques, Leca *et al.* 2007, 2008) exhibit elements of culture. A broader comparative approach, beyond primates and/or beyond tool use, is likely to yield a more comprehensive understanding of the selective social, ecological, and cognitive factors and evolutionary processes behind culture and material culture in humans.

The survival of culture

We may never understand past changes in human technological culture if we fail to make an urgent, conscientious effort to preserve primate cultures, which represent bits and pieces of the puzzle. Primates are rapidly declining in numbers throughout their habitat range. Species of great apes are no exception; ranging today from endangered to critically endangered (IUCN 2007). Populations, communities, groups, social units, and individuals are increasingly succumbing to the pressures of our own technological evolution, an irony that seems far from being resolved and probably the greatest challenge we face today.

PART IV

LANDSCAPES AND THE BUILT ENVIRONMENT

CHAPTER 18

CULTURAL LANDSCAPES

LESLEY HEAD

THE IDEA OF CULTURAL LANDSCAPES

In considering landscapes, a Handbook of material culture is extending its discussion from objects and buildings to a broader arena that humans have materially transformed, the earth itself. The term 'cultural landscape' is widely recognized as a description of a region of the earth that has been transformed by human action. However, the concept of a cultural landscape has changed over time and evokes a range of contrasting understandings in different regions of the world, different academic disciplines, and different governance contexts. Here, I argue that it is important to understand these differences in order to think clearly about cultural landscapes as a form of material culture.

In this chapter, I examine some moments in the history of the idea of cultural landscapes, focusing on two dichotomies that play in and out of the dominant Anglo-American narratives. The first is the dichotomy between materiality and symbolism; from highly material beginnings in the early twentieth century, writings on cultural landscapes went through periods and contexts where symbolism and ideas were more important. The second is the

This chapter is dedicated to the memory of Val Plumwood, who died during the later stages of its writing. Val was kind enough to let me read her critique of cultural landscapes while it was still in draft form, but she did not get a chance to read my critique of her. She no doubt would have responded, and I'm sure my argument would have been stronger for such engagement.

dichotomy between nature and culture, concepts treated as oppositional for much of this history. I then examine some of the geographic differences, with particular attention to Australian and Scandinavian examples. The next section explores what happens when the cultural landscape idea itself becomes materialized, in the form of land and heritage management frameworks. I will demonstrate that much of the work of the cultural landscape has been oppositional. It puts people and culture into landscapes that had been considered empty and natural. It facilitates a broader context for sites and buildings that have been considered in isolation. Yet it does so in ways that are inherently dichotomous, as entrenched in the term 'cultural landscape' itself. In the final section I discuss a recent critique of the cultural landscape concept, and ask whether it is possible to go beyond the dichotomies, and whether the concept retains any usefulness.

In the anglophone world the idea of the cultural landscape derives especially from the work of American geographer Carl Sauer, who wrote in 1925 that humans had become 'the most important morphologic factor' (Sauer 1965: 341) in the material transformation of natural landscapes. Geographical thought throughout much of the twentieth century, due to the strong influence of the Sauerian tradition, generally distinguished between the natural landscape as a pristine baseline for human life, with the cultural landscape imprinted on top by the transformative activities of human culture. For Sauer (1965: 343), 'the cultural landscape is fashioned from a natural landscape by a culture group. Culture is the agent, the natural area is the medium, the cultural landscape the result.' As has been widely argued, this view of landscape rests on the separation of the natural and the cultural as unproblematic categories. In view of later critique, it is worth remembering what an important role Sauer's work played in having humans and their activities acknowledged as influential landscape actors. The intellectual milieu in which his work was revolutionary was one of environmental determinism.

Nevertheless, geography's 'cultural turn' and associated critique led to a range of studies since the 1980s that, although different in their respective emphases, sought to put forward a much more dynamic view of culture. There were particular challenges to the so-called 'superorganic' view of culture, understood as a total package, with a life of its own operating at a higher level than the individual. Culture was argued to be a more dynamic, multiple, contingent, and contested process, worked out in everyday practice (Jackson 1989; Anderson and Gale 1992). Where landscape was part of these debates, diverse writers argued that the concept of landscape can contain the range of human dimensions encompassed by the terms cultural (and political, and economic) (Cosgrove 1984; Cosgrove and Daniels 1988; Mitchell 1996; Olwig 2002). In other words, that the concept of 'landscape' already contains all the 'culture' it needs. As the titles of their books indicate, Cosgrove and Daniels were particularly influential in drawing attention to the symbolic rather than material dimensions of landscape, as represented for example in iconography and art. The wider cultural turn within the humanities and social sciences also brought more attention to the symbolic and representational dimensions of landscape within archaeology (e.g. Bender 1993; Gosden and Head 1994; Ashmore and Knapp 1999), and the interpretation of these from the material record continues to be a fertile area of debate. By the end of the 1990s, however, there was widespread concern within social and cultural geography that the subdisciplines needed 'rematerialising' (Jackson 2000).

Whatmore argues that both 'old' and 'new' cultural geographies externalized landscapes and cast their making '(whether worked or represented) as an exclusively human achievement'. The big difference in recent work is that it 'shifts the register of materiality from the indifferent stuff of a world "out there", articulated through notions of "land", "nature", or "environment", to the intimate fabric of corporeality' (Whatmore 2006: 602). Whatmore's concept of 'livingness' and her hybrid geographies (Whatmore 2002) have much in common with Ingold's (2000a) discussions of dwelling. Both have been influential in attempts to go beyond the material/symbolic and culture/nature binaries.

Within cultural geography over the last decade or two there has been increasing recognition of the agency of plants, animals, and other parts of the non-human world. These are often referred to as more-than-human geographies (see Braun 2005 for review). Where binarist thinking ultimately forces a choice in terms of 'whodunnit', for writers such as Whatmore, influenced by actor-network theory (ANT), 'the social and the natural are *co-constitutive*' within myriad networks (Castree 2002: 120).

While cultural geographers and others in the humanities were rediscovering the agency of the non-human world, physical geographers and natural scientists were increasingly recognizing culture. On the face of things, the Sauerian concept of a cultural landscape as having been materially transformed by human action was a highly appropriate way of thinking about the fact that humans are inextricably embedded in all earth surface processes, often dominate them and in some cases have done so for many thousands of years. There is an emerging trend in some ecological studies, particularly historical ones, to use the cultural landscape concept to recognize the human presence in the landscape and/or to discuss issues of biodiversity conservation in humanized landscapes, for example traditional agricultural ones (Phillips 1998; Steck *et al.* 2007).

These parallel conversations within the humanities/social sciences and the natural sciences have for the most part gone in opposite directions. The cultural landscape concept in use in the sciences is generally one that retains a conceptually unproblematic distinction between nature and culture (Head 2008). However, there are also grounds for future connections, since in both fields there is increasing recognition of messy networks of agency that are 'multiple, contingent and non-essentialist' (Castree 2002: 121).

Geographic differences in use
of the cultural landscape idea

In this section I illustrate how the cultural landscape idea itself varied geographically. In particular I distinguish between Old World and New World societies. 'Putting culture in' to the landscape was particularly necessary in settler societies, such as Australia, where failure to see and acknowledge the indigenous presence allowed a strong and unproblematic concept of natural landscape to take hold. Importantly for this discussion, what was put in was not just a concept of culture, but one that depended not on material evidence but on oral tradition, stories, and symbolism. On the other hand, use of the cultural landscape concept in relation to indigenous landscape engagements is itself potentially problematic, as it can reinforce a false separation between culture and nature. In Old World contexts such as northern Europe, material cultural influences on the landscape are more self-evident. It is not so much a question of whether culture is absorbed into landscape, but rather whether human activities have been so long-standing as to be absorbed into nature.

Early European settler struggles with an often recalcitrant Australian environment led to themes of emptiness and alienation in cultural engagements with the land. Thus, there is emphasis in art and literature on the 'dead heart' of the desert (Haynes 1998), or the incompatibility of tropical areas with white settlement, particularly by women (Taylor 1940). The harshest parts of the continent, particularly the deserts, have been seen as inimical to culture (just as they are quite literally inimical to agriculture). The agricultural metaphor was central to the colonizing culture's vision of itself and its civilizing presence, and the apparent absence among Aboriginal people of 'tillage' and hence 'culture' was used to justify both physical and conceptual dispossession over the past two hundred years (Head 2000a). To summarize, colonial Australian understandings of nature have either subsumed or rendered invisible the presence of people, particularly indigenous people.

Thus the strongest use of the cultural landscape concept in Australia in the last few decades has been in ways that recognize indigenous presence in and connections to land, that put people back in. The presentation of a place as a cultural landscape implicitly positions it in contrast to a wilderness. This is seen, for example, in the way Australian debates both influenced and utilized the development of the World Heritage category of Associative Cultural Landscapes in the case of Uluṟu-Kata Tjuṯa National Park, a discussion I return to in the next section of the chapter. I have discussed elsewhere in more detail how the process was influenced by academic debates over culture and nature, by the increasing political voices of indigenous and non-Western peoples, and by the practical difficulties of managing inhabited protected areas (Head 2000b).

Nordic geographers, such as Kenneth Olwig (1996, 2002), have been less keen than Anglo-American ones to use the term cultural landscape, arguing that landscape is sufficient. Olwig examines *Landschaft* and related words in the Germanic languages of northern Europe, showing that it has had a broad range of meanings relating to territory and community for the last four or five hundred years: 'When approached in historical and geographical context, it becomes clear that *Landschaft* was much more than "a restricted piece of land". It contained meanings of great importance to the construction of personal, political, and place identity at the time landscape entered the English language' (Olwig 1996: 631). Although Olwig's focus was historical, these themes continue in contemporary Nordic understandings and usages of landscape, especially in relation to landscape management (M. Jones 2006). For example, the Swedish Environmental Protection Agency (Naturvårdsverket) recognizes that one definition of landscape goes back to the territorial units reflected in the names of Swedish provinces (e.g. Halland, Småland). Naturvårdsverket use a concept of landscape that includes 'both natural and cultural phenomena', and is 'defined as the result of the interplay between man, society and nature' (Sporrong 1995: 14).

Jones and Daugstad (1997) show considerable variability in its usage and application. For example, they identify discourses of cultural landscape (e.g. agricultural, nature conservation, cultural heritage, planning) used in land management debates. Thus 'the cultural landscape provides an arena in which different interest groups struggle to influence the formation of our physical surroundings, exemplified in the conflicts that often arise between the production of economic goods and the production of environmental goods' (Jones and Daugstad 1997: 280). The point here is not to argue that 'cultural landscape' is not used in Nordic contexts (see, for example, Naturskyddsföreningen i Skåne 2002), but rather that it is often interchangeable with just 'landscape'. As shown above, the usual usage of this latter concept is inclusive of cultural dimensions. German environmental historians Lekan and Zeller (2005: 3) also emphasize this contrast with New World settler contexts: 'Unlike American environmental culture, which is still dominated by debates about wilderness preservation and the retention of untouched spaces, German landscape perception has long recognized human impacts as part of the "natural" order.' Particular emphasis is placed on the evolution of cultivated and pastoral landscapes over millennia, as the basis for German environmental culture and national identity.

This integration of the cultural dimensions of landscape is also accepted within the European Landscape Convention, whose 'definition of landscape is focused on people' (Rössler 2006: 349).

CULTURAL LANDSCAPES IN LAND
AND HERITAGE MANAGEMENT

The work of Jones and Daugstad, referred to above, is just one example showing how different concepts of, and discourses around, culture and landscapes have material outcomes. They result in maps, fences, legislative and administrative instruments, gates, and boundaries. They keep some people in and some people out. This section provides further examples of these outcomes, and their challenges and dilemmas. I start with discussion of the cultural landscape category within the World Heritage convention, then go on to some contemporary land management examples. The section concludes with consideration of how cultural landscapes have been used in recent archaeological and heritage work.

The World Heritage convention is an arena in which three different categories of cultural landscape are acknowledged (Rössler 2006; UNESCO 2008). Of the 851 properties (660 cultural, 166 natural, and 25 mixed) on the World Heritage list at the end of 2007, 60 were included as cultural landscapes. Other World Heritage cultural property types, such as monuments and sites, would also be considered cultural landscapes in the usual geographic discussion of that term. So indeed would many natural properties that are valued and managed for their beauty, scientific value, or importance for biodiversity conservation. In this section of the discussion, however, I focus on the properties specifically designated as cultural landscapes.

Two particular issues are the degree of material transformation, and the relationship between culture and nature. These categories can also be thought of as being on a continuum of material evidence of human activity; from highly visible to potentially absent.

1. 'The most easily identifiable is the *clearly defined landscape designed and created intentionally by man* (sic)' (UNESCO 2008). These are often garden and parkland landscapes, in which the materiality of the human effort is most obvious.
2. 'The *organically evolved landscape*' (UNESCO 2008). This can be either a relict (fossil) landscape or a continuing one. In either case material form is necessary. In the relict landscape, the distinguishing features are still visible; if continuing, it still exhibits significant material evidence of its evolution over time.
3. 'The *associative cultural landscape*' (UNESCO 2008). In these cases their listing is justified 'by virtue of the powerful religious, artistic or cultural associations of the natural element rather than material cultural evidence, which may be insignificant or even absent' (UNESCO 2008).

Themes of integration and connection between nature and culture are strong in the World Heritage conceptualization of cultural landscapes:

Cultural landscapes are at the interface between nature and culture, tangible and intangible heritage, biological and cultural diversity—they represent a closely woven net of relationships, the essence of culture and people's identity. Cultural landscapes are a focus of protected areas in a larger ecosystem context, and they are a symbol of the growing recognition of the fundamental links between local communities and their heritage, humankind and its natural environment.

Rössler (2006: 334)

While it could be argued that ideas of integration just mix culture and nature together without recognizing that as concepts they may be inherently problematic, it remains the case that the realities of management in most landscapes today involve recognizing and dealing with human actions. The cultural landscape concept appears to be a tool that managers find useful. For example, it is being utilized in coastal New South Wales 'to provide a practical tool whereby Aboriginal community and cultural values can be equitably considered in the future coastal planning, land management, and decision making processes of both state and local government' (Andrews 2006: 1). The approach was developed in recognition that conventional Western systems for assessing landscape significance (e.g. historical, archaeological, anthropological) did not adequately respond to Aboriginal cultural values (Byrne *et al.* 2001; Andrews 2006: 5). Andrews argues that the cultural landscape framework may 'encompass the traditional values [of] Aboriginal peoples regarding their spiritual views of the natural world and associative values in the land, while still being understandable to land and conservation managers whose world views are typically based in Western historical and scientific scholarship' (Andrews 2006: 5). Drawing also on UNESCO definitions of associative cultural landscapes, an Aboriginal cultural landscape is defined as:

A place or area valued by an Aboriginal group (or groups) because of their long and complex relationship with that land. It expresses their unity with the natural and spiritual environment. It embodies their traditional knowledge of spirits, places, land uses, and ecology. Material remains of the association may be prominent, but will often be minimal or absent.

Andrews (2006: 10)

This need to 'put people in' may be particularly strong where the human connections have not transformed the physical landscape, in the Sauerian sense, or at least not to any great extent, and are expressed in intangible values. These are the attachments, which are most difficult to have recognized by other parties and thus protected under management regimes. Rössler (2006: 336) emphasizes that the World Heritage category of 'associative cultural landscape' 'has been crucial in the recognition of intangible values and for the heritage of local communities and indigenous people. The primary difference was the acceptance of communities and their relationship with the environment.' The example in New South Wales is still a work in progress, and it remains to be seen whether it (1) can be operationalized, and

(2) results in different land management strategies than would otherwise be in place. My concern in this discussion is not whether its aims are met or it is an effective tool. Rather it is to highlight the way the cultural landscape concept has been mobilized to, at least in principle, include Aboriginal voices and values in the land management process.

There is increasing recognition by ecologists that the management of 'nature' cannot happen only in protected areas, but must also include landscapes where humans are dominant. For example, Berkes and Davidson-Hunt (2006: 35) argue that 'most of the world's biodiversity is in areas used by people. Hence, to conserve biodiversity, we need to understand how human cultures interact with landscapes and shape them into cultural landscapes.' Berkes and Davidson-Hunt (2006: 43–44) show how the management implications of these types of cultural landscape are a more dynamic engagement than the single use approach. They argue that protected areas managed to maximize conservation, and forestlands managed to maximize timber production, both lead to attempts to fix or freeze the landscape. Management strategies by Anishinaabe people provide at least three mechanisms by which biodiversity can be conserved and enhanced. First, through fire and other kinds of disturbance management, all successional stages are maintained. Secondly, a mosaic landscape with many patches and gaps is maintained. Thirdly, new edges and ecotones are created.

These types of approaches are not confined to hunter-gatherer societies. A related example is found in the traditional agricultural landscapes of northern Europe, where there is widespread recognition among ecologists that traditional management or some replica thereof, is important to biodiversity conservation in the so-called semi-natural grasslands. 'The main reason for restoring these man-made grasslands is their exceptionally high species richness at small spatial scales . . . A prerequisite for keeping high species richness is to continue grazing, as the number of species drastically decline on grasslands when abandoned' (Lindborg 2006: 957). A rather more contested example is when obviously human constructions within the agricultural landscape, such as stone walls, have themselves become sites of biodiversity maintenance. Management strategies might vary considerably depending on whether these are managed for species protection or for cultural heritage. The importance of human activity in maintaining biodiversity in agricultural landscapes is also discussed by Calvo-Iglesias *et al.* (2006) for Spain, and Maurer *et al.* (2005) for the Swiss Alpine grasslands.

It is important to recognize that there are a number of tensions and contradictions in using the cultural landscape concept to recognize indigenous attachments to land in contemporary management regimes. The first is the occasional lack of obvious materiality, discussed above. Secondly, we might consider how well the notion of cultural landscape captures indigenous ideas of the landscape or non-human world itself being sentient, as in the challenging title of Povinelli's (1995) paper 'Do rocks listen?' Along related lines, Rose (2005) has discussed the sentience of other species and of country: 'in this Indigenous system, subjectivity in the form of sentience and agency is not solely a human prerogative but is located throughout other species and perhaps throughout country itself' (Rose 2005: 302). When Aboriginal women such as Biddy Simon and Polly Wandanga call out to country as they approach a hillside to dig for yams (Head *et al.* 2002), they are acknowledging this sentience. To an outsider this can appear to be a symbolic act, but for Biddy and Polly the distinction between symbolism and materiality would itself be a false one.

A third tension is that a highly material landscape, particularly when preserved as World Heritage, can pin in place and time a static understanding of the cultural processes that produced it in the past, and where their descendants might want to be in the present. Archaeologist Denis Byrne tells an evocative story of his visit to the rice terraces of northern Luzon in the Philippines, where the tourist expectation that the 'natural primitiveness of the terraces' be maintained is at odds with the fact that 'the terraces were ephemeral agricultural phenomena that had always been in a state of change ... Outsiders might speak of the terraces as monuments, but they were monuments that never ceased being built' (D. Byrne 2007: 43). Local Ifugao people were also expected to conform to a static external idea of authenticity, for example, when replacing thatch roof on their huts with corrugated roofing iron.

The tension between materiality and meaning, as discussed by Byrne, goes to the nature of archaeology itself. As a discipline constituted by both its attention to material evidence and its pursuit of cultural pasts, archaeology's struggles with landscape are particularly interesting. Within archaeology and some areas of heritage management, the most important work is done by the *landscape* part of the *cultural landscape* concept. In this thinking the landscape is distinguished from the much more specific 'site', such as an excavation pit. This point is made explicitly by archaeologist Robin Torrence (2002: 766): 'important new insights about long-term changes in human behaviour are gained when cultural landscapes rather than focal points of "sites" are studied'. Less attention is given to the way culture is added into the landscape concept, and there is considerable focus on a range of methodologies that allow a fuller reconstruction of the landscape to be elucidated, 'beyond the site'. This can also include consideration of more mobile ways to think through human connections to landscape, such as Snead's (2006) documentation of ancestral Pueblo trails.

Similarly, Taylor and Altenburg (2006) emphasize that an important aspect of the World Heritage Cultural Landscape category is that it puts buildings and monuments into a broader landscape context. Using Asian examples such as Angkor and Borobudur, they argue that a broader physical context would stimulate visitors to look beyond the fabric of the building or complex itself to its landscape setting. Further, there would be emphasis on the living connections that people maintain with these places. Although different in temporal context, a similar sort of work for the landscape end of the concept is implied in Watt *et al.*'s (2004) comparison of laws for endangered species protection and historic preservation. There is a concern to 'expand' to the landscape scale, from the single species, or the single heritage property, in order to manage more effectively.

Two other extensions of the site and indeed the landscape are the concepts of production and the journey, both themes that have been widely written about by archaeologists (e.g. Bradley and Edmonds 1993; Edmonds 1999). Bloxam and Heldal (2007) remind us that the outstanding monuments of pharaonic Egypt, including the pyramids, were dependent on sophisticated production processes of stone quarrying and transport. They describe these ancient quarries and associated constructions (e.g. roads) as Egypt's 'forgotten' archaeological heritage, and argue for their inclusion on the World Heritage list along with the monuments they facilitated. Bloxam and Heldal's focus on the material conditions of production evidenced by the quarry sites does more than link them across the landscape to the pyramids and temples many kilometres away. By providing evidence about the inputs of human labour and associated social organization necessary to produce them, their approach also helps humanize this landscape. For example, what human effort did it take to build and use the quarry road, 2.1 m wide and 11 km long, between Widan el-Faras and Lake Moeris, or the 3,000 stone vessel blanks recorded at the gypsum quarries at Umm es-Sawan (Bloxam and Heldal 2007: 314)? Mobility and the seasonal round are most often commented on for nomadic hunter-gatherer groups (Oetelaar and Meyer 2006), but most patterns of human movement contain seasonal and other rhythms. Some of the patterns identified by Oetelaar and Meyer (or others) will be archaeologically visible, others not. For example, concentrations of sites along waterways attest to their importance as transportation corridors.

In archaeology and heritage studies, as in geography, recent work is grappling with ways to bring together perception and materiality, humans and assorted non-humans, and past and present (e.g. Turner and FairClough 2007).

IS THE CULTURAL LANDSCAPE CONCEPT IRRETRIEVABLY ANTHROPOCENTRIC?

The diversity of uses to which the concept of landscape is put, and the range of meanings attached, leads to regular discussions of whether landscape is a useful concept at all (for a range of recent views see Merriman *et al.* 2008). Rather than rehearse those views here, this section discusses a very specific critique of the cultural landscape concept, by feminist philosopher Val Plumwood (2006). I draw on this example because it seems to me quite different to the more-than-human and dwelling approaches influenced by the work of Whatmore and Ingold. Plumwood argues that the idea in cultural landscape studies of putting humans in has gone too far, merely inverting the arrows of connection and causation found in nature-reductionist science (see also Rose 2006). For her, the concept of cultural landscape

is an example of a concept that invites us to downplay or hide nonhuman agency and to present humans as having a monopoly of creativity and agency in the generation of what are called 'landscapes'... The concept of a cultural landscape has become a key part of an agenda in the humanities of human-centred and eurocentred reductions to culture that is the equal and opposite to the natural sciences reduction of explanation to nature... an unfortunate and unnecessary side-effect of the long overdue recognition of the creativity of indigenous humans has been a denial of creativity to nonhuman species and ecosystems—nature scepticism. This latter denial is unhelpful as well as unnecessary because there is no necessary incompatibility between recognizing indigenous (cultural) agency and recognizing nonhuman (natural) agency.

Plumwood (2006: 119–120)

The type of cultural landscape to which Plumwood (2006) directs her critique is explicitly the Sauerian one (2006: 121) and the landscape concept that she focuses on is a passive one, framed visually (2006: 123). In that respect she is critiquing both early twentieth-century geography and the later cultural turn, and is perhaps less aware of more recent approaches that present dynamic, embodied and less dualistic engagements between humans and non-humans, and attempt to capture these in landscape conceptualizations.

Plumwood (2006: 125) wants to recognize multiple and mixed agencies as shaping material outcomes, 'This means that the outcome of any given landscape is at a minimum biocultural, a collaborative product that its multiple species and creative elements must be credited for.' However, in contrast to more hybrid approaches, which would understand the society–nature dualism as maintaining a misconception 'that entities are "essentially" either social or natural prior to their interaction with one another' (Castree 2002: 118), Plumwood retains and defends the concepts of nature and natural systems. She rejects concepts such as 'naturecultures' that aim to implode the distinction between the two, arguing that rejecting hyperseparation is not to reject difference or distinguishability, 'What is lost when we refuse to acknowledge difference between nature and culture, or when we accept an idealist or social constructionist reduction of nature to culture? There may be a range of situations in which they are hard to separate, but there are an important range of others in which recognizing their difference is crucial...' (Plumwood 2006: 144). Plumwood defends nature as a relevant contrast class precisely because of the current ecological crisis:

There is nothing conceptually absolute, for this kind of collaborative model, about cutting the cast of agents into humans and nature. Doing so will be appropriate in some natural and cultural contexts and inappropriate in others. I think that over the longer term we should aim to decenter the human as a contrast class and draw our distinctions in ways that do not constantly refer back to the human as central. Nevertheless in our present context, the human/nonhuman contrast remains the site of a crucial drama and discourse—that of the decline of natural systems with which this paper began and the need for human attention and action to reverse this situation.

Plumwood (2006: 127)

There are paradoxes in Plumwood's argument here that relate to a form of human chauvinism. Given the human role in recent changes in earth surface processes, particularly climate change, and the need for human action to reverse the situation, there is surely a case for recognition of some strong human agency? (In this I am also taking issue with some relational approaches that give insufficient attention to the power differences between human and non-human others.) On the other hand, the idea that concerted global (human) action is now necessary in order to 'fix' things may be just another example of the anthropogenic conceit.

It follows that there may well be cases where the cultural landscape concept does good work, through for example providing a management context where traditional ecological knowledge is recognized. Further, surely the concept of nature itself must also be removed from the realm of the conceptual absolute? I think Plumwood's defence of nature as an ontological category insufficiently acknowledges sophisticated arguments to the contrary. Her thorough explication of hyperseparation and difference, in the 2006 paper and in earlier work (Plumwood 1993, 2002), are too detailed to discuss here, but provide important and relevant resources for those of us trying to think about relations between nature and culture.

Conclusions

I have sought in this chapter to illustrate some of the ways that materiality plays in and out of the history of the cultural landscape concept, along with ideas about nature and culture. For most of its history, cultural landscape has been a very material concept. It focused first on buildings, fences, and other material human constructions, and later, drawing on techniques from the natural and palaeoecological sciences, on more subtle but very material changes, such as changes in the composition and abundance of forests. If there was a dematerialization throughout the 1980s and 1990s in the attention paid to symbolic, conceptual, and ideational dimensions of landscape, it was relatively brief and appropriately corrective. In the case of indigenous peoples, it provided a means for academic scholarship to acknowledge vital but intangible connections and attachments to land. And, to draw on more recent embodied and hybrid approaches, we might argue that intangible connections have their own materiality, inscribed in bodies, sweat, and the elusive DNA of yam species dug for thousands of years by Aboriginal women.

What are we to do with these geographic, disciplinary, and contextual differences in the kind of work done by the cultural landscape concept? The first thing we should do is recognize the value of the work—all of it has needed to be done at different times and in different places. The political power, albeit limited, that is being given to Aboriginal land managers is a case in point. Amidst the diversity, the main axis of difference is between management contexts that can use the cultural landscape concept as a means of integrated management, also giving expression to values and attachments that do not necessarily have material expression in the landscape, and more academic ones that consider the conceptualization to reinforce rather than remove the binaries. Secondly, we can acknowledge that there is nothing conceptually absolute about a cultural landscape. We should think of it as a historically contingent concept that has played different roles in different times and places. We should also think of the concept as provisional; according to the range of views presented in this chapter it may or may not have outlived its usefulness. *Cultural landscape* is profoundly ambiguous and oppositional even in its linguistic construction.

For me, the demonstrated strength of human power to materially transform earth processes, including the composition of the atmosphere itself, is reason enough to keep the cultural landscape concept alive a while longer. It provides one way to talk about our responsibility for environmental damage and environmental restoration, in language that has strong vernacular resonance. Of course, we do not undertake such transformations alone, but in partnership or conflict with a variety of living and non-living materials—grasses, rocks, rivers, and atmospheric carbon, to name a few.

CHAPTER 19

ECOLOGICAL LANDSCAPES

SARAH WHATMORE
STEVE HINCHLIFFE

INTRODUCTION

This chapter sets out to unsettle some of the most taken for granted co-ordinates of landscapes in general and cities in particular—namely that, if nothing else, we are safe in assuming them to be exclusively human achievements. These co-ordinates are deeply engrained in the primacy so often accorded to the visual in the 'language of landscape' (Spirn 1998), positioning the human first and foremost at one remove from the world in prospect—eyeing it up or taking it in from some unearthly vantage point. They are also underscored by a constellation of spatial narratives and practices in Western societies through which nature has come to be marked out precisely by its distance from human settlement, not least in the enduring current of anti-urbanism that has characterized mainstream environmental thought. We begin by exploring recent geographical thinking about ecological landscapes worked through diverse conversations with other disciplines—notably anthropology, and science and technology studies. Here we highlight developments in the broad areas of phenomenology, affect, and biophilosophy in order to describe some key shifts in cultural geography's handling of materiality. Through this engagement with ecological landscapes and urban natures, our aim is to demonstrate the importance of reconsidering materials less as the passive stuff of which landscapes are made and more as energetic constituents in their fabrication.

We ground this aim in the second part of the chapter, through an exploration of the implications of such perspectives for reworking the antithesis between cities and natures, and informing new urban ecologies and landscaping practices. Here, we address two related themes, illustrating them with examples from original research in the English city of Bristol. The first outlines the concept and practice of *vernacular ecologies* that refigure landscapes as complex assemblages in which people are situated through their practical engagements and affective relations with heterogeneous others, human and non-human. Understanding the lived assemblage of urban natures focuses on the interface between a growing scientific investment in the conservation value of so-called 'recombinant ecology', referring to the biological communities assembled through the dense comings and goings of urban life, and a parallel recognition of its importance to what makes cities liveable and to the attachments of civic identity and association. The second theme picks up the political resonances of refiguring urban ecologies and landscaping practices in this way. This centres on the extent to which this lived ecological fabric is constituted as a public good or urban commons, including: cultivated spaces, such as parks and allotments; feral spaces, such as abandoned railway sidings and derelict land; and remnant spaces, such as waterways and woodlands. Here, we rework the concept of *conviviality* to better understand the gathering political force of the 'urban green'. On this account, to live and live well in cities implies a more-than-human politics of landscap*ing*.

REFIGURING THE HUMAN IN ECOLOGICAL LANDSCAPES: PHENOMENOLOGY, AFFECT, AND BIOPHILOSOPHY

In this section we outline some of the key shifts in recent geographical thinking about landscape as a manifestation of the relationship between human activity and the natural world, beginning with a brief and, necessarily, partial sketch of the long legacy of approaches to landscape with, and against, which these shifts work.

As the landscape geographer Kenneth Olwig (1996) has argued, the etymology of landscape in several north European languages suggests a productive slippage between on the one hand viewing and shaping practices (from the Germanic *skab*, to shape) and, on the other, cultural inhabitation. Elaborating on this theme, cultural geographers and others working in material culture and cultural history traditions have successfully traced the shaping and reshaping of land through human design (Williams 1993). Important here are the everyday routines and practices that accumulate through mass and time to produce habitual or vernacular landscapes (e.g. de Certeau 1984; Jackson 1984). However, most attention has been paid to the more spectacular and planned interventions by nation states and business empires in the scopic regimes of colonies, settlements, estates, parks, and fields (e.g. Macnaghten and Urry 1997). Here, the framing of a view or prospect and the imperatives of a mode of ordering are melded together to produce ideological landscapes. With the invention of perspective and landscape painting in sixteenth- and seventeenth-century Europe and the establishment of some definitive notions of form and aesthetic, the not so strange case of life imitating art has been a common critical trope of work in this area (Cosgrove 1985).

It is not that such work treats landscapes as immaterial but rather that the overriding sense from these accounts is of their formation as first and foremost a cultural accomplishment (see Hinchliffe 2003; Whatmore 2006). Notwithstanding references to sometimes-obvious intransigencies in the stuff of which landscapes are made, any dynamism is the effect of a formative cultural activity. Matter can be obdurate, but not generative. In this way, the material dimensions of the human body and those of the world beyond are brought into landscape studies only on indifferent terms. This anthropocentric tendency to assume the primacy of cultural agency in landscape studies can be understood as an aspect of humanism's legacy, investing the powers of world-making in 'man' instead of 'god'. Over the last decade, there have been a number of resourceful challenges to this legacy that take the stuff of the world seriously as a generative force in the making of landscapes. They share what might be called an *ecological approach* to landscape, which, while rejecting much of the term's problematic baggage, signals recognition of the more-than-human company that goes into making a living and liveable landscape, and the complex relations that make any element of that landscape possible. Three intellectual trajectories that further this project stand out, i.e. phenomenology, affect, and biophilosophy.

Phenomenology

Anthropologist Tim Ingold has done more than most in recent times to unsettle some elements in the anthropocentrism of landscape studies (Ingold 1995, 2000a). In particular his Heidegger-inspired focus on a distinction between building and dwelling has informed a number of attempts to understand landscapes as lived and practised rather than as cultural productions. Ingold sets out to challenge some of the ways in which 'modern' humans and their material constructions are set apart

(a)

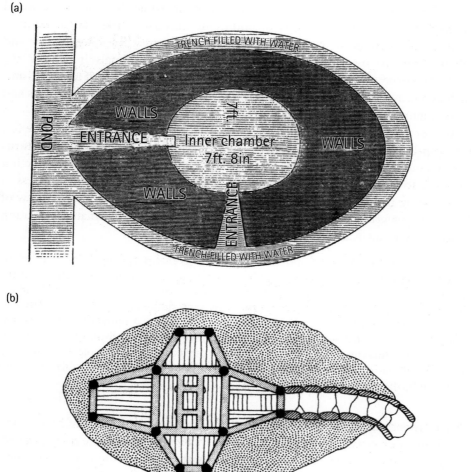

(b)

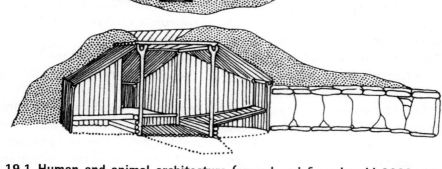

Fig. 19.1 Human and animal architecture (reproduced from Ingold 2000: 174, figure 10.1). (a) Ground plan of beaver lodge (from L. H. Morgan 1868: 142); (b) floor plan and cross-section of Eskimo house, Mackenzie region (from Mauss and Beuchat 1979 [1905]: 4).

from the world, wherein humans are said to build while the rest of the world 'merely' dwells. To build in this dichotomous universe marks out a uniquely human purposefulness, in which conscious design precedes construction and inhabitation. To dwell, by contrast, sees non-human animals inhabiting the world by virtue of what they are, their distinctive *modus operandi* as organisms, such as a beaver constructing its lodge from logs or a bird its nest from twigs and moss (Figure 19.1).

Against this, Ingold argues that when we focus on the practice of landscape (on landscap-ing as a process/verb rather than landscape as an artefact/noun) it turns out that humans and beavers are more alike than the building/dwelling distinction suggests. To landscape involves, or enfolds, all manner of others in the process of constructing that make a difference to what gets produced. This process view of landscaping suggests a dwelling perspective in which people are situated in relation to what makes their fabrications possible. As he expands:

What [a dwelling perspective] means is that the forms that people build, whether in the imagination or on the ground, arise within the current of their involved activity, in the specific relational contexts of their practical engagement with their surroundings. Building, then, cannot be understood as a simple process of transcription, of a pre-existing design of the final product on to a raw material substrate. It is true that human beings—perhaps uniquely among animals—have the capacity to envision forms in advance of their implementation, but this envisioning is itself an activity carried on by real people in a real-world environment, rather than by a disembodied intellect moving in the subjective space delimited by the puzzles it sets out to solve.

Ingold (1995: 76)

This insistence upon the heterogeneity of conduct, and the mixing of human and non-human properties and energies in ways that cannot readily be disaggregated, brings us to the point where the fabric of landscape is understood as an ecological process, what Nigel Thrift calls 'ecologies of place' (Thrift 1999). These ecologies are constituted as much by diverse routines and patterns of everyday inhabitation as by any vision, plan, or grand design.

What Ingold's account suggests is that landscape is always a process involving more than people. In this, he starts to open up a phenomenology of landscaping that promises to disturb the agential apartheid of landscape in terms of the 'who' of the beholder/maker (its subject) and the 'what' of the beheld/made (its object). Nonetheless, his account remains dogged by some of the dangers familiar in its phenomenological antecedents (Hinchliffe 2007). A broad term for a philosophical movement seeking to describe the structures of experience as they present themselves to consciousness, phenomenology is inclined to install an experiencing being as the foundation of agency. Where phenomenological accounts have succeeded in unshackling this agency from a Cartesian cogito, they reproduce a residual Kantian settlement insofar as they continue to divide the world itself against the phenomenological experience of that world. The risk, as the philosopher Graham Harman

(2002) has argued, is that a privileged relation persists through phenomenology's adherence to human being (*Dasein*) as the measure of all things. Identifying Heidegger as that most 'environmental' but, in the end, most anthropological of phenomenological thinkers Harman argues that he

seems to think that human *use* of objects is what gives them ontological depth, frees them from their servitude as mere slabs of present-at-hand physical matter...[Heidegger's approach] wrongly casts Dasein in philosophy's starring role, while preserving the unfortunate belief that the world itself is made up of sheer physical objects: neutral slabs of material accidentally shuffled around or colored by human viewpoints, stable substances volatilized only by an external force.

Harman (2002: 16, 19; original emphasis)

For others, the humanist afterglow that lingers in Ingold's work does not necessarily prevent a phenomenological contribution to the re-distribution of agency in practices of landscaping. Cultural geographers have drawn on Merleau-Ponty's notion of 'the reversibility of the flesh' (see Whatmore 2002) to trace a world in which flesh is a *process* of intertwining and separation, rather than a substance. Here, 'there is no question . . . of an *a priori* thoughtful or competent body-subject whose eyes and hands animate a lumpen materiality, or infuse it with meaningful significance' (Anderson and Wylie 2009: 16; original emphasis). This then is a phenomenology that pushes past Heidegger's affective handling of matter such that all manner of elemental forces take their place alongside those of techno-science as materials party to the uneven historical and geographical processes of sensing and acting *with*. It is this 'being with others' that seems to us a more interesting focus than the 'being there' of certain kinds of phenomenology (see Bingham 2006). Here, phenomenology crosses paths with work in feminist and science studies that has a greater commitment to, and handle on, the co-fabrications invited by this 'with-ness' and to which we now turn.

Affect

The interrogative tense with which a revitalized phenomenology, like that outlined above, addresses the status of subjects and objects resonates with recent reinvestments in the Spinozan notion of 'affect'. Building on the work of feminist scholars and queer theorists who have sought to redress the neglected significance of the body to the conception and practice of thinking and acting, this so-called 'affective turn' (Clough and Halley 2007) calls for a dual focus on emotional states and bodily dispositions, and the myriad encounters through which they are modified. For philosopher and literary theorist Michael Hardt, such work 'illuminate[s] . . . both our power to affect the world around us and our power to be affected by it, along with the relationship between these two powers' (Hardt 2007: ix). He goes on to suggest that affect speaks to the correspondent attributes of mind and body and how, without reducing one to the other, they proceed *in parallel* (an image to which we return below). In the attribute of body, affect structures encounters so that bodies are disposed for action in a particular way. In the attribute of mind, affect structures encounters as a series of modifications arising from relations between ideas. In this, the register of affect takes us further in terms of an ecological approach to landscape by forging connections between the 'bodily capacities to affect and to be affected' and the 'self-feeling of being alive—that is, aliveness or vitality' (Clough 2007: 2). What Patricia Clough points to here, and develops through an engagement with biophilosophical thinking (see below), is that aliveness is a relational condition that extends the company of affectivity beyond both the human and the bodily. To be alive in the world is, unavoidably, to be modified by it.

This correspondence between affecting and being affected, and the kinds of materialities through which it traces a re-distribution of agency, has been elaborated to perhaps greatest effect in the very different arena of science and technology studies, notably in those works loosely grouped under the label of 'actor-network theory' (e.g. Callon 1986b; Law and Hassard 1999; Latour 2005a). Influenced by the Belgian philosopher of science Isabelle Stengers (1997, 2000) and the French historian of science Michel Serres (1980; Serres and Latour 1995) among others, its leading exponent Bruno Latour has most systematically developed this project to underline two key things. First, and consonant with other sociological work on affect (e.g. Cheah 1996), he charts the relationships between knowledge and what Vincianne Despret termed 'learning to be affected' (Despret 2004). For Latour, learning to be moved or set in motion by others (human or non-human) is the condition of embodiment; what makes any particular corporeal arrangement or modification possible. Secondly, and with greater emphasis than work in the humanities on affect, Latour suggests that actor-network theory is remarkable for its treatment of affect as a positive sum game. That is, rather than a body learning to capture the world's energies as it becomes more attuned to and effective in it, body and world *proposition* one another. Where this proposition is successful, the more activity there is from the one (body), the more there is activity from the other (world) (Latour 2004c). Once the body that is learning to be affected becomes articulate in/with a new world of things then both can start to change. To be clear, this is not another constructionist account (still less an idealist one) since articulations and propositions are about co-generating a sensorium in which the more you learn to be affected, the more differences there exist.

Latour uses a metaphor of turbulent flow to suggest the generative dynamics of this intra-active world of affective learning, 'To say that the world is made of articulated propositions is to imagine first *parallel* lines, the propositions, flowing in the same direction in a laminar flow and then, because of some clinamen, generating intersections, bifurcations, splitting, that produce many eddies transforming the laminar flow into a turbulent one' (Latour 2004c: 213). He contrasts this 'rudimentary metaphor' with the more familiar 'face to face' imagery of a subject confronting an object world 'out there'. For the latter, the world is destined to be either misrepresented or accurately represented, with consequent and negative effects on objects or subjects. In contrast, for a world of propositions and articulations in which mind and matter are constitutive parts of a turbulent affective flow then both may gain as differences are sensed. By way of example, we have in mind the co-learning that is generated between Donna Haraway's (2008) 'animal people and their (canine) companions', between horse riders and their mounts (Despret 2004) or elephants and hunters (Lorimer and Whatmore 2008) as their bodies become attuned to the habits of the other, or laboratory and field scientists as they learn to be affected by the materials, microbes, ecologies, and species that they seek to understand (Hinchliffe *et al.* 2005).

Learning to be affected, then, is an achievement *with others*, born of association and practice in which all those enjoined in it can, and do, modify each other (Whatmore 2003). The affective turn as described here moves us outwards from the body-as-organism and away from a phenomenological/physiological divide, or what Whitehead (1978) called the 'bifurcation of nature', towards an understanding of landscapes as lively co-fabrications. Thus freighted with an ecological politics of affect, the conventional 'face off' between subject and object is replaced with a turbulence of articulations that offers a generative account of thinking and acting *with* (Hinchliffe *et al.* 2005). And it is this turbulence, as much as the knot of relations, which is suggestive of a third trajectory for thinking ecological landscapes—biophilosophy.

Biophilosophy

As the preceding sorties into phenomenology and affect suggest, there is more to the matter of landscaping than recalcitrant objects or putty in 'our' (always already human) hands. If these encounters have established heterogeneous materials as generative parties in the turbulent process of landscaping, recent reinvestments in biophilosophy enable us to trace how new configurations of bodies, technologies, and materials redistribute relations between life and earth at the core of landscape concerns.

Biophilosophy departs from a philosophy of biology in that it is interested less in discerning the essence of life, and what distinguishes it from 'inert' matter, than with 'drawing out the network of relations that always takes the living outside itself' (Thacker 2005: 3). In other words, instead of looking for the intrinsic properties of living, it treats life as extrinsic. The impulse is Deleuzian (Deleuze and Guattari 1988; Deleuze 1999), elaborated in inventive and divergent ways in the works of Ansell-Pearson (1999), Parisi (2004), and Thacker (2004), in generating new vitalisms (Fraser *et al.* 2005; Thrift 2005a), informed and conformed materials

(Hinchliffe 2007), and engagements with posthuman (or more-than-human) understandings of life (Braun 2007).

Two general points can be made in relation to the idea of ecological landscapes. First, and in parallel to the other trajectories we have traced, biophilosophy works to 'enliven' the world in ways that attribute generative as well as recalcitrant properties and potentialities to matter and redistribute this liveliness across conventional divisions between bodily ('bio') and earthly ('geo') materialities (Whatmore 2007). This shifts the register of materiality from the indifferent stuff of a world 'out there', articulated through notions of land, nature, or environment, to the intimate fabric of corporeality that includes and redistributes the 'in here' of human being. Secondly, the metaphors by which we conjure the complex causalities and relations between material forces and entities start to change too. Where the classical ecological paradigm relies on homeostatic models of systemic balance and pre-destination to cast external perturbations as risks to default system stability (Cronon 1996; Hinchliffe 2003), recent moves to recast ecological processes as inherently recombinant rely on parasitic and symbiotic models that make differentiation and connectedness intrinsic to default system dynamism (Margulis and Sagan 1986).

A range of images—the germinal (Ansell Pearson 1999); discordance (Botkin 1990); complexity (Clark 2005); the baroque (Kwa 2002); recombinance (Parisi 2004); hybridity (Whatmore 2002)—has been used to start to evoke this shift. What they share in common is a commitment to an ecological imagination that foregrounds the conditional openness or immanence of life such that ecology is less the interaction between pre-figured life forms/material entities than their emergence and transformation in a 'wider field of forces, intensities and durations that give rise to [them]' (Ansell Pearson 1999: 154). Here 'the organism must be rethought as open to information, where information is understood in terms of the event or chance occurrence arising out of the complexity of open systems under far-from-equilibrium conditions of metastability, that is where microstates that make up the metastability are neither in a linear nor deterministic relationship to it' (Clough 2007: 12). In this way, biophilosophy helps to work away from an ecological imagination that casts landscapes as living spaces given shape and form by the activities of pre-constituted bodies, towards one in which both landscapes and bodies are open, interconnected, and material achievements that take, hold, and change their shape through their ongoing relations with others. As geographers and others start to work these ideas through, so the purchase of landscaping is extended to new practices such as those associated with biosecurity and bioterrorism (Braun 2007; Hinchliffe and Bingham 2008), hospitality and disaster (Clark 2005, 2007). Far from presenting a firm ontology of life, biophilosophy provides a means of interrogating essentialisms and received ways of dividing the world up into organism and environment; living and inert; nature and culture; human and non-human (Thacker 2005). As such it presents an invitation to engage with the diverse ontological practices through which worlds and divisions are laboriously made and remade, and thereby to invigorate a politics in which, as the political theorist Jane Bennett (2004: 365) puts it, 'humans are always in composition with nonhumanity, never outside of a sticky web of connections or an ecology'.

These three trajectories and their various intersections provide a range of resources for opening up ecological landscapes as more-than-human achievements (Whatmore 1999). They furnish sensitivities to landscape that can alert us to other ways of inhabiting and other ways of doing ecological politics. In the next section we work through some of their consequences for that most excessively human of landscapes—the city, in order to emphasize some of the possibilities for thinking with the vernacular and convivial practices of such recombinant ecologies, illustrated by reference to empirical work in the English city of Bristol conducted as part of the 'Habitable Cities' Project (Open University 2008).

From Built Environments to Living Cities

Approaches to landscape that cast the human at one remove from the world in prospect are consonant with a categorical displacement of natures from cities writ large in the well practised distinction between natural and built environments. In this part of the chapter we set out to challenge this distinction, working instead towards a more porous understanding of city-scapes as recombinant ecologies assembled through the dense fabric of spatial practices and affective relations generated between all manner of organisms, materials, and elements, as well as people. Understanding urban spaces as 'living cities' rather than 'built environments' requires that these co-habitants are treated as if they matter in, or make a difference to, the co-fabrication of urban ecologies, rather than as background objects upon which human designs can be imposed at will or without consequence.

In this our analytical approach to 'living cities' resonates with a gathering of political energies in the UK around the so-called 'urban green' at the interface between urban policy (e.g. DTLR 2002; ODPM 2002) and biodiversity conservation (DEFRA 2002). Here, in the manner of one of Callon's 'hybrid forums' (Callon et al. 2001: 29–66), the 'urban green' articulates a growing recognition that what makes the green spaces in cities green is less, or at least not only, a matter of the colour-coding conventions of urban design or the public works department of city councils than that they are living ecologies reliant on diverse material, biological and geo-physical processes, and properties to make and sustain them (Hinchliffe et al. 2003). Rather than designated islands of nature in the city, the 'urban green' describes at least three different kinds of forums for ecological co-fabrication between humans and other city inhabitants. These include spaces associated with cultivation, such as allotments, community gardens, and city farms; those associated with land restoration, such as derelict railway, waterfront, or industrial sites; and those associated with conservation, such as remnant woodlands, waterways, and marshes. The purchase of science on these ecological spaces and communities is extended and, not infrequently, troubled by the intimate knowledge of, and passionate enthusiasm for them among city inhabitants, thereby effecting a politically charged redistribution of ecological expertise.

We elaborate on this here in two ways. First, by exploring the ecological knowledges and attachments of city residents honed through practical engagements with the landscapes they inhabit, using the notion of *vernacular ecologies* to amplify the ways in which the intimate interweavings of the life patterns and rhythms of people and other city dwellers refigure the landscapes of everyday life. Secondly, we trace the political consequences of this alignment of ecological energies from an inimical modality that pits cities against natures towards a *politics of conviviality* in which the landscaping practices of the 'urban green' exceed and challenge expert designs. This is an ecological politics that takes seriously the heterogeneous company and dense interconnections of living cities (Hinchliffe and Whatmore 2006: 134).

Vernacular ecologies

In his encyclopaedic *Flora Britannica*, Richard Mabey (1996: 12) argues that 'our vernacular relationships with nature should be taken every bit as seriously' as local or indigenous knowledges in third world countries. But where the latter are now well institutionalized in international development policies, the former are only lately beginning to make their mark in urban and environmental policy circles in the UK. In the context of the nexus of political investments in the 'liveability' agenda, considerable emphasis is currently being placed upon harnessing the ecological knowledges and enthusiasms of 'local citizens' in the creation and management of urban green spaces, even as policy-makers remain unclear about the kinds of knowledge to which they are appealing. At the same time, and as Mabey's argument implies, such 'vernacular relationships' extend political recognition to the more-than-human company of plants, animals, soils, watercourses, and so on that together make cities liveable. It is this nexus of affective knowledge and relations between bodies and elements brought together in the everyday business of city living, and most closely associated with the 'urban green', that we refer to here as *vernacular ecologies*.

By way of illustration we can work these arguments through the landscape of Thingwall Park Allotments, a traditional allotment site amidst an ethnically diverse residential neighbourhood to the east of Bristol city centre. With more than two hundred plots, Thingwall Park is one of the largest of a number of allotment sites owned by the city council. As a result of its size and its proximity to Eastville Park and the River Frome it also forms part of an important wildlife corridor in the city travelled by charismatic creatures such as badgers and foxes, and is inhabited by any number of species of insect, plant, and bird. An association of allotment holders, the Fromeside Allotment Association, manages the site. This is not a landscape that is in prospect but one that is intimately inhabited through cultivation practices and other bodily involvements—watching for wildlife; listening to birds; feeling for weather, soil, and seasonal changes. These routine corporeal engagements involve 'learning to be affected' such that, in Latour's (2004c: 206) words, 'body parts are progressively acquired at the same time that "world counter-parts" are being registered in a new way'. The plot becomes an ecological landscape in which different soil conditions, plant physiognomies, and microclimates are mapped into knowledge by sustained, material interactions. For example, learning what combination of conditions a potato 'likes' in order to thrive, such that a successful crop signals a relational achievement between the demands of the plant, the condition of the soil, and the skills and attentiveness of the gardener (Figure 19.2).

Fig. 19.2 Aerial view of Thingwall Park Allotments, Eastville, Bristol.

As shared spaces or urban 'commons', allotments are forums of association in which people are situated through their practical engagements and affective relations with heterogeneous others. Here, the sights, sounds, and traces of other creatures and awareness of seasonal rhythms in the activity and composition of co-habitants enrich the material register through which the vernacular ecologies of the urban green intensify. As such these are marked out as ecological landscapes in which people's sensibility to being 'always in composition with nonhumanity', to return to Jane Bennett's (2004: 365) phrase, is heightened. In the words of Thingwall allotment holders themselves:

M: I don't necessarily come down here and work all the time. I come down here and sit inside the shed and watch the sun go down for an hour and that is gorgeous. F: And you can hear the birds singing. M: Yes, it's a sanctuary down here as much as anything else. [...] F: I think it becomes part of your life really. You know it's the biggest part of your life, isn't it?
Interview transcript (March 2003, held by authors)

This example of Thingwall Park Allotments fleshes out a sense of ecological co-fabrication in which the life patterns and rhythms of people and other city dwellers are entangled with and against the grain of expert designs. Council regulations for the 'proper' use of the land are challenged and rewritten by the multicultural gardening practices at work in such sites. The priorities of conservation organizations concerned with the protection of rare species of plant and animal are more, and sometimes less, accommodated by the cultivation priorities of the allotment gardeners. The excess of such vernacular ecologies furnishes materialist sensitivities to landscaping central to the appeal of our notion of the 'living city'. As well as challenging the terms of urban analysis, their excess calls for a refigured politics attentive to the heterogeneous company and messy business of living together. It is to these political consequences that we now turn our attention.

Conviviality

The political corollary of the ecological approach to urban landscaping advanced here as a 'politics of conviviality' derives from, and informs, a triangulation of several theoretical impulses that supplement one another in productive ways (Hinchliffe and Whatmore 2006). The first is a reworking of the Deleuzian insistence that the organized spaces (or diagrams) of any prevailing social order are always incomplete such that 'besides the points which social practices connect up, certain relatively free and unbound points, points of creativity, change and resistance are always implicated' (Deleuze and Parnet 1987 [1977]: 66). These *minoritarian* spaces harbour a political capacity produced not by any one social position or political alignment but in the multiplicity of relations through which civic associations and attachments are woven (see Osborne and Rose 1999). The kinds of feral spaces that we are concerned with in which more-than-human attachments and knowledge practices are forged articulate what Cary Wolfe calls 'the materialist promise' of Deleuze's work in that 'it foregrounds the *outside* of any diagram [. . .] as a reservoir of complexity and difference' (Wolfe 1998: 150–151) that actualizes and proliferates creative possibilities. It is this unpredictable mix of civic energies that even policy makers recognize as the political force that makes the difference in the forum of the urban green (DTLR 2002: 71). The second impulse is a feminist insistence on an ethics of social living in which any individual becoming in the world is necessarily and unavoidably conditioned through affective associations with others. This condition of being given in/to others, what Rosalyn Diprose (2002) calls *corporeal generosity*, refigures 'civility' as the practical intercorporeality of civic association in which particular kinds or individuals thrive in combination with others whose capacities and powers enhance their own. Finally, to counter the residual humanism that is differently inflected in both of the foregoing contributions, our notion of a politics of conviviality draws on the work of philosophers of science, like Isabelle Stengers' (1997) *cosmopolitics* to emphasize that politics, like knowledge, is a co-fabrication in which all those (humans and non-humans) enjoined in it can, and do, affect each other in the practice or event of politics.

These arguments can be put to work through the example of Royate Hill, a prominent feature in the landscape of the neighbourhood of Easton in inner city Bristol. This small (four hectare) site is adjacent to a cemetery and amidst a dense mixture of terraced and high rise housing and came into being in the 1870s as part of the Clifton extension to the Midland railway line. With the closure of the line in 1965, trees, shrubs, and grasses that were initially planted by the railway companies on the embankment have since colonized the site. In 1996 it was designated a Local Nature Reserve and is now managed by a local action group with support from the Avon Wildlife Trust. Royate Hill's 'place' in the everyday life of this inner city neighbourhood is best understood as an assemblage of movements, intersections, and criss-crossing paths, rather than as a landscape that prefigures its inhabitation. The viaduct that once provided a passage for trains still functions as such for people and other animals whose tracks mark the ground. Nowadays, Royate Hill is inhabited in various ways: as a shortcut; a play-area; a place to walk the dog; a retreat for both people and wildlife—as an urban green space. In other words, both before and after it became marked out as a 'site' in its transformation into a nature reserve, the fabric and character of this urban green was that of a nexus of energies of all manner of inhabitants on the move (Figure 19.3).

This transformation from derelict railway line to designated nature reserve has been anything but smooth and is the result of the effective mobilization of civic attachments to, and affective knowledge of, the site and its diverse inhabitants to see off the threat of development on more than one occasion. It was in 1986 that local people first became concerned about the future of the viaduct and tried to get it recognized and listed as a historical landmark to enhance its protection under

Fig. 19.3 Local residents campaigning to stop development of Royate Hill Nature Reserve, Easton, Bristol (May 1992).

planning law. In 1990, developers bought the land to construct new housing, prompting sustained local protest and leading to the formation of the Royate Hill Action Group. The first public inquiry in 1991 determined that Royate Hill was not suitable for development because of the site's community and wildlife value and its importance in the daily life of residents. As the Inspector leading that inquiry concluded in his report:

I am in no doubt that residents derive much pleasure from the changing seasonal colours and variety of vegetation on the sites and from the wildlife they support. Whilst trespass does occur, the fact that there is no formal public access to the land does not in my opinion lower materially its visual and emotional value to those who live nearby, pass through or visit the area.

Department of Environment (1991: 5)

Yet, at 6am on 23 May 1992, the Saturday of a bank holiday weekend, bulldozers employed by the developers started to clear the site. Residents spontaneously occupied the site, bodily preventing further work while the City Council obtained an injunction to stop the destruction. Two days later, with about one-third of the site damaged, residents capitalized on the attention of the local media by staging a 'Day of Mourning' for the wildlife lost to the bulldozers. Over 10,000 signatures were collected against the actions of the developers and further development. As the Royate Hill Action Group argued in their evidence to the second public inquiry into development on the site:

The events of that Bank Holiday weekend changed the feeling [of goodwill] to one of determination—most people felt that they would not be bullied out of keeping to their wildlife site. The residents who overlook the part which was totally destroyed were particularly upset: they had lost many beautiful trees and now looked out on what some described as 'scorched earth'.

Department of Environment (1994: 4)

In 1996 the site was acquired by compulsory purchase by Bristol City Council and leased to the Avon Wildlife Trust on a 25-year renewable lease. During the second public inquiry, it was established that the bulldozing of the site had not diminished its wildlife value. Instead, the constituencies opposed to development highlighted the ecological value of disturbed and recolonized land in urban areas. In this, they mobilized the more-than-human inhabitants of the site in its defence, using the scientific protocols of ecological surveys to establish the biodiversity value of Royate Hill. According to the UK government agency responsible for biodiversity and nature conservation at the time (English Nature), the site comprises nine different types of habitat (including rare neutral grassland, woodland, and wetland areas), which are home to a large variety of animals, insects, and birds, and to nearly 200 plant species. The richness of the fauna and flora of Royate Hill is attributed to the unique features that abandoned railway embankments provide, notably the old gravel bed of the former railway that supports so-called 'ballast communities', that is plants that like dry conditions such as rat's tail fescue. Through the campaign to protect the site from development, Royate Hill became one of the best known wildlife sites in the country and continues to be used in a variety of publications as an example of best practice in terms of community action for wildlife (English Nature 1992).

Royate Hill illustrates the diversity of ecological attachments and heterogeneous associations through which the politics of urban landscaping is fabricated. Rather than reading the political ecology of the city off a priori social divisions, the politics of conviviality implicated in our analytical shift towards a 'living city' demands that the more-than-human company assembled in and through urban green spaces be recognized as a key attribute of their political force. Where the affective materialities of a landscape fashioned through diverse rhythms and practices of everyday living gained coherence and expression in the face of commercial designs upon it, the designs failed on several fronts to recognize the ways in which such convivial relations matter.

CONCLUSIONS

We have sought in this chapter to outline a range of conceptual resources for rethinking landscapes as more-than-human achievements and put them to work in refashioning that most excessively human of landscapes—the city. In so doing, the question of how matter comes to matter has been a sustained concern. Another way of framing this rather abstract question, which we have sought to effect through two vignettes of urban landscaping practices in Bristol, is to interrogate the tension between the affective relations between people, other city inhabitants, and the ecological landscapes they fabricate together, and the conventional indifference of urban analysis and policy to this palpable heterogeneity of urban life. Ingold's distinction between 'building' and 'dwelling' perspectives, which we examined earlier, provides a preliminary point of purchase on the problem. Urban theory and planning practice exemplify what he characterizes as a building perspective in which it is assumed that 'the organisation of space cognitively precedes its material expression; built environments are thought before they are built' (Ingold 2000a: 181). Whether market driven or centrally planned, this 'building' perspective projects a remotely sensed urban vision through the devices of surveys, satellite imagery, landscape, and building plans to map what the city is and how it could or should be. The realization of these spatial designs in bricks and mortar is only subsequently inhabited by the appropriate kinds of activities and people. The thoroughly humanist commitments of this perspective are evident both in the genius of the architects/ planners whose visions materialize into the city and in the strictly human terms in which its fabrication and inhabitation are conceived. This is not to suggest that these designs on urban space have not increasingly taken on an environmental hue. Richard (Lord) Rogers' (1999) manifesto for the compact city, for example, precisely allies the building perspective to the rhetoric of sustainable development. There are some important shifts in urban design principles here that are to be welcomed. But the environment enters the 'compact city' in very particular ways, as a contextual resource or constraint to the fabric and order of the city, whether as a thermodynamic system or a landscape aesthetic. The fecund world of creatures and plants as active agents in the making of environments remains firmly outside the city limits and those feral spaces in the city that most sustain them are cast as 'wastelands' ripe for development. Here, too, the designs of architects and planners are allied to the expertise of environmental engineers and scientists, reinforcing the ways in which city inhabitants are disqualified as knowledgeable agents from the building process, even as they are being urged to become 'active citizens'.

In contrast, the 'dwelling perspective' in Ingold's terms, holds on to the sense in which worlds are lived in before they are made. Rather than a simple process of transcribing a pre-existing design on to a raw material substrate, the forms that people build arise within the specific relational contexts of their practical engagement with their surroundings. In this, the dwelling perspective admits affinities between the ways in which humans and other animals make themselves at home in the world through a bodily register of ecological conduct that does not set the city apart. Against the familiar opposition between a purified 'natural environment' tainted by any hint of human presence and a 'built environment' from which all but human relations have been expunged, it shifts attention to the more-than-human agents exercising unbidden, improvised and, sometimes, disruptive energies in the ordering of urban space. Here, the traces and habits of all manner of city dwellers, from trees and ants to foxes and couchgrass, make their presence felt in the urban fabric and networks of social life through strange and familiar encounters.

We have set out to explore some of the implications of the ecological recasting of approaches to landscape outlined above for working towards a mode of urban analysis and design that admits more-than-human energies into the ecological fabric of the city. Our argument has been that cities are inhabited with and against the grain of urban design, that inhabitants are not static beings but entangled in complex processes of becoming, and that attempts to engage with urban heterogeneity requires realignments of people and things, in ways that are responsive to uncertainties and indeterminacies, materialities and passions. What we find at work then in the landscaping practices of living cities are ecological knowledges honed out of 'learning to be affected' and exercised in practical skills and know-hows in the cumulative practice of everyday urban life between human and non-human inhabitants. It is a between-ness that is coming to be recognized by the shifting alliance of wildlife conservation organizations and policy professionals invested in making cities more 'liveable', in terms of the ecological interdependence of the species and spaces of the 'urban green' and the knowledge and enthusiasm of their human inhabitants.

This chapter draws on an Economic and Social Research Council (ESRC) funded research project on 'Habitable Cities: civic spaces and practical ecologies' (R000239283, 2001–2003).

CHAPTER 20

URBAN MATERIALITIES: MEANING, MAGNITUDE, FRICTION, AND OUTCOMES

ROLAND FLETCHER

The cities of the future, rather than being made out of glass and steel as envisioned by an earlier generation of urbanists, are instead largely constructed out of crude bricks, straw, recycled plastic, cement blocks and scrap wood. Instead of cities of light soaring toward heaven, much of the twenty-first-century urban world squats in squalor, surrounded by pollution, excrement and decay.

Davis (2006: 19)

INTRODUCTION

The materiality of urbanism encompasses the words and actions by which we relate ourselves to it, the economics of its creation and maintenance, the impact of the material on the viability of community life, and also the long-term trajectories of urban growth and decline. What interdisciplinary urban studies do not possess is a coherent approach to connecting material phenomena encountered in the built environment across many different temporal and spatial scales. Instead, over the past twenty years particular approaches have come into vogue, such as the emphasis on meaning: through words, discourse, and the 'material as text'. What is not present in these perspectives is the perverse and contrary nature of the material, at odds with its users and their stated opinions and ideologies.

Archaeological approaches to urban materiality tend to focus on how people seek to use the material and also emphasize what the material meant, in verbal terms, to its users. Studying use requires a recognition that the 'material' does not simply correlate to the 'social', especially in the early industrial period as socio-cultural anthropologist Daniel Miller (1998b), to his great credit, has long emphasized. Miller's key point is that people had to learn to be mass consumers because their social behaviour was not in synchrony with the cascade of changes in retail activity that were occurring, especially in large cities. Moreover, while he has approached the key issue of 'why some things matter', Miller has retained a focus that he holds in common with historical archaeologists such as James Symonds, in which 'material culture is identified as playing an active role in the shaping of cultural identities', since 'it both reflects, but also enables, human action' and 'may be regarded as a physical manifestation of discourse, a tangible expression of social attitudes and beliefs' (Symonds 2004: 35; cf. Yentsch and Beaudry 2001).

The same kind of view extended into geography and urban studies in the 1980s and 1990s as Discourse Theory, which seeks the understandings of materiality that are created by discourse, focusing on language change as an index of social change and 'language analysis as a way to understand these phenomena' (Jacobs 1999: 210–211). Peter Jackson's (2000) paper 'Rematerializing social and cultural geography' takes a somewhat different approach by focusing on the relationship between people and things that is different from Chris Philo's (2000: 33) appeal for a more 'thingy' approach. In urban geography and urban studies, a diverse interpretative suite of approaches has developed with varying degrees of focus on actual materiality. Loretta Lees (2002) points out that the urban geographers tend to be sceptical of 'totally dematerialized geographies' but that there is essentially a lack of conceptual coherence. Lees' preference is towards studies that use what she calls an ethnographic approach that moves away from representation and advocates theories of practice (Lees 2002: 107). What is developing in urban geography is a kaleidoscope of positions on materiality and immateriality of abstruse elaboration (Kearnes 2003). Blunt materiality perhaps still needs some more emphasis.

In archaeology, and especially in historical archaeology, the 'meaning' approach to urban materiality—which, to be precise, articulates verbal meaning—continues to be the most overt and vigorously expressed agenda. Even though immense amounts of urban archaeological research on the material data itself are reported world-wide every year, the materiality itself in all its bulk and its rate of development is scarcely discussed and is comprehensively untheorized. To a remarkable degree, we have come to accept that beyond the basics of description the proper way to refer to and comprehend the materiality of urbanism is through the verbalized meanings that observers and users attach to it. Curiously, materials are treated as an epiphenomenon of what people say about it and claim they do with it—as if the words are more 'real' than the actual material. As Philo (2000: 33) has pointed out in geography, 'the bump-into-able, stubbornly there-in-the-world kind of matter' needs to be brought back to our attention. Perhaps that actuality has become marginalized by its sheer magnitude in the industrializing world of the past 150 to 200 years. In sociology and human geography the most urgent concerns, quite correctly, relate to the human issues of how we cope with it all: how we learn to deal with it or fail to do so, how we manipulate its image and the places it creates.

But studies in the archaeology of the modern period remind us that we can also understand this present day, vast phenomenon of urban materiality in larger frames of reference, and that this can provide a perspective on contemporary urban life. We are acutely aware that urban materiality 'matters'. The quantity of garbage and the amount of globally warming gases churned out by cities are clearly having an impact on our world. In themselves, the threats they create have become the concerns of policy that considers potential effects over several centuries. Simultaneously, we are trying to articulate for public awareness, especially in industrialized countries, our own complicity as consumers.

We cannot comprehend the situation unless we bring together the spectrum of perspectives from the immediacy of people's daily lives, what they say and their habits, to the entire, planet-wide history of urbanism. To note that for the first time in the existence of human beings more people live in cities than in the country has an elemental, ominous significance. To contextualize that statement globally requires archaeological knowledge about the genesis, formation, magnitude, and expansion of cities over the past five thousand years and about their place in the evolution of modern human behaviour.

The modern human behavioural repertoire is only apparent even in its most tenuous form within the last 100,000 years. However, in one-twentieth of that time we have generated the material phenomenon of urbanism that is transforming the ecology of the planet. To engage with the materiality of cities that we must not only comprehend what people do, we must also analyse what the material does over

Fig. 20.1 The urban world at night, early twenty–first century AD **(NASA).**

varying time spans. We must recognize the city as an immense, material urban actor without intent, which humans, by default rather than intention, have brought into being (Figure 20.1).

This chapter argues that the study of urban materialities turns on three basic issues about how to deal with the material. First, the issue of words and their relationship to minds, actions, and things. Second, our comprehension of magnitude. Third, the study of material through time: which raises issues of variation and change, the differing degrees of duration through time of different materialities, and the different time spans over which material entities can assert the effects of their existence and generate outcomes, whether fortunate or regrettable for the people they affect.

WORDS, METAPHORS, AND URBAN MATERIALS

In discussing metaphor and the material, Chris Tilley (1999: 6) has remarked that scholars have recognized 'an inherent problem in the precise relationship between a world of words and world of things'. What follows, of course, is not only that we can, do, and indeed must necessarily engage in word play in relation to things, but also that things cannot therefore derive their character or pattern from whatever words may refer to. If there is no essential and inextricable connection between words and things, then things do not specify words and conversely words used by a community cannot specify what or why things it makes and use actually are. Words can only be referential rather than definitive. Therefore, they do not and cannot tell us why the material is the way it is, or about the effects of urban materials. Words may, of course, say something perspicacious about those effects, as Charles Dickens' writing did about the impact of nineteenth-century urbanism on the population of the United Kingdom. But that is not a systematic analysis of the effects and their causes: Dickens' writing simply sought to make his readers pay attention to their and their compatriots' physical situation. For any community, the use of words about materials is not an explanatory referent for the emergence or the nature of the material. Such words are instead the perspicacious way in which the members of the community engage with and seek to comprehend the milieu in which they live.

Words can be used by humans to refer to materiality. When they are, they act as explanatory or analytic tools. They represent the things that a community makes or lives with, and their contexts. But there are several problems with defining, as Tilley does, that mode of representation either as the necessary or the sufficient way to appraise materiality or to explain its form.

There is a continuing tendency to seek explanations of why settlements have particular forms in the words that people use to refer to their residential spaces. Tony Atkin and Joseph Rykwert's book *Structure and Meaning in Human Settlements* (2005) illustrates the approach and is a continuation of the famous anthropological analyses such as Lebeuf's *L'habitation des Fali* (1961) or the often-recounted ideal of the Bororo village by Lévi-Strauss (1936). The problem is that these words may be about the spaces but that does not make them sufficient explanations of the material. This can be seen very clearly in 'ideal' city plans. Steinhardt pointed out in 1999 that Chinese imperial capitals do not conform to the declared urban 'wang cheng' ideal. The nearest correspondence is actually the capital of Dadu built by the Mongols—foreign conquerors of China—to legitimate their claim to power. Similarly in India few, if any, cases are known of a city that conforms to the stated shape and form of the various urban ideals of the Arthaùàs-tra, Smarangåðnasýtradhåra, Mayamata, and Månasåra (see, for example, Chakra-barti's (1997: 257) observation that 'the over-all descriptive pattern remains idealistic'). The nearest may be Sisupalgarh, which Wheeler (1966: 126–127) refers to as distinctive due to its exceptional and unusual, symmetrical square form. The issue of ideals not defining actuality is politically significant and informative. This is because, as in the case of Dadu being built close to the ideal Chinese specification, so likewise Angkor Thom, the late twelfth-century AD walled enclosure at the heart of Angkor is considered by Jacques Gaucher (2004) to follow an ideal Indian model (Figure 20.2), though no specific instance is claimed and the proposition refers to a suite of Indian urban models. The degree to which it did correspond to some external ideal would then have been an index of the degree to which the ruler who instigated its construction, Jayavarman VII, was seeking to be more Indian than the Brahmans of India. 'Degree to which' is, however, the critical qualifier because even this single, well-defined engineering and construction event did not actually produce conformity to an ideal, or even to some ideals. There is partial

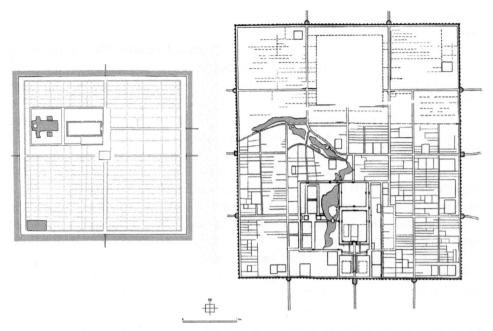

Fig. 20.2 Routeways and enclosures in Da-Du (founded late thirteenth century AD) (after Steinhardt 1999) and Angkor Thom (founded late twelfth century AD) (after Gaucher 2006 and French government diplomatic website).

correspondence but the grid of rectilinear spaces is not symmetrical, nor is the plaza at the centre; and the eastern wall of Angkor Thom has two gates rather than the one, symmetrically located, gate in the centre of the other walls.

We might imagine that the ideal plan is broadly or partially created, but is distorted by circumstances. But once other factors are brought in as explanations some major problems arise. We might consider the undeclared tacit patterning of space that is characteristic of all adult humans, and that is itself community specific (Fletcher 1995: 25–42). Today Angkor Thom may have some Indian-ness, but it is also very obviously a Khmer space (Gaucher 2006) consistent with almost three hundred years of constructions and spaces in Angkor. The overall form of the great low-density urban complex of Angkor does not resemble an Indian pattern or ideal (Figure 20.3). Even in the instance of Angkor Thom, where we can probably concede that one person—Jayavarman VII (AD 1125–1215)—ordered its construction, he and his advisors and engineers had more than one model to follow. The tacit patterning of space has to be included as an influencing factor. In due course we should find its consistencies embedded in the dimensional pattern of the structures, not according to some abstruse, supposedly formal designation of space by distances (see claims of Mannikka 2000 on Angkor Wat), but in a complex constellation of distances and inherent variability (Fletcher 1995: 37–40).

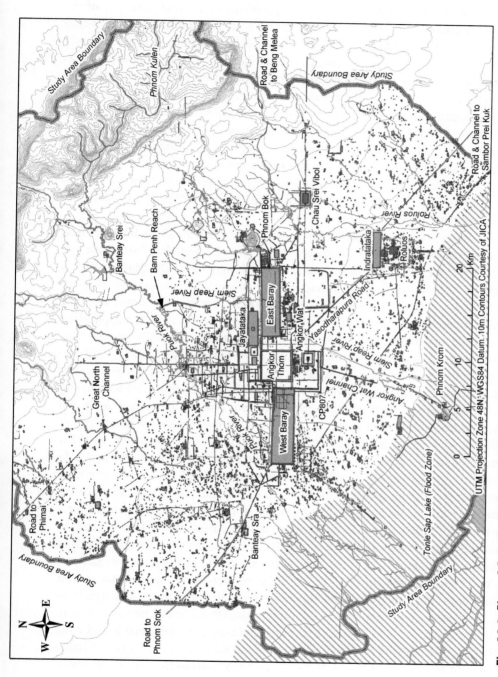

Fig. 20.3 Plan of Greater Angkor, Cambodia ninth to sixteenth century AD (courtesy of C. Pottier and D. Evans).

Once it is apparent that more than one proposition about space can be concurrent, then the 'word picture' ideal becomes problematic as an explanation of the reason why particular forms of space exist. It may seem like common sense to argue that what is said defines what is made, but communities do not have one internally coherent 'world view' or 'mental map'. Different sectors of a community, such as women or lower status people, have different modes of explanation and declared interpretation from, for example, a male elite. Even in small-scale societies, such as the Hopi communities of the North American Southwest, the female 'model' and the male 'model' are not the same (Parsons 1929; see Fletcher 1995: 27–28) so the actual space of the settlement in which they all live cannot be due to what they all say about it. People's words are not a description of the place or a definitive specification of its origin. Instead, they seek to represent the differing human engagement with the space by different sectors of the community. Words are associative referents not determinative indices.

Words cannot suffice to describe the actuality of urban materials because these materials—whether furniture, houses or cities—possess variability. Words are not good at conveying variability and cannot convey it systematically. Mathematics is required to do that. Words tend to refer to types and ideals—propositional forms that are really incompatible with analyses of the transformations that derive from the variability inherent in a class of material phenomena. Types preclude the application of the normal analytic procedures for studying change and variability because they refer to a notional single state that represents a class. The analogy would be with the relationship between the ideal 'horse' as a type and the actuality of a population of horses, which is characterized by variation whether in size, hairiness, leg length, and so on. We can have all sorts of engagement with our notion of a typical horse and produce innumerable illustrations of it. But that will not serve to allow us any way of analysing how present day horses relate to their immediate ancestors, to other mammals, or to life forms in general. Likewise to refer to a 'typical city', as we do repeatedly, is a way of engaging with a type of place. But only by recognizing their diversity, e.g. across the spectrum of high- to low-density cities, can we place the settlement we are analysing in the larger context of transformations through time.

For example, if we define cities as compact, as Westerners and the Chinese tend to do, then we cannot recognize low-density urbanism. And when we do recognize that low-density cities actually exist but view them as an odd characteristic of the past century of industrial growth then we might be inclined to see them as anomalous and for some—hopefully transient. But if we recognize that there were agrarian-based, low-density cities that lasted for centuries, then the assumed necessary link to mechanized transport is broken and the long endurance of industrial low-density cities has to be seriously considered. Furthermore, if we find that the agrarian-based case failed in a very distinctive way, then we should necessarily ask if this was a specifically agrarian condition or if it might be a generic problem of a wide variety of low-density urban settlements past, present, and future.

Metaphor and dualities

The lack of fit between words and materials, described above, has been addressed by writers, such as Chris Tilley, through the idea of metaphor: hence the title of his book *Metaphor and Material Culture* (1999). Such work is part of a tradition of material culture studies in archaeology and anthropology that speaks of the 'social' and the 'material', then talks of correlations or connections between them, or introduces a third element—action or agency—to reconcile the two. But the 'material' covers phenomena ranging from flimsy, small transient objects such as feather head-dresses and paper tissues, which pass rapidly through their use existence to buildings such as nineteenth-century university residences with which the practices and needs of current sociality must negotiate. People do this either through the 'friction' of tolerated inconvenience, or through expensive renovations. Then, beyond the scale and temporal endurance of the buildings are the hundreds of thousands of tons of city infrastructure—intractable and almost immovable—whose wreckage also defines how future tourists perceive us, the builders, whoever we were.

Neither the 'social' nor the 'material' is one class of operator that we can simply contrast with or connect with the other. Instead, each can operate at different rates, at differing magnitudes, and endure for differing lengths of time. In addition, these differing operators are not in simple correspondence. They can and often do clash with each other or generate non-correspondence or friction. Our houses are, in general, not quite what we want and possess characteristics—such as the bicycle necessarily parked in the narrow front hallway—that are a source of irritation and friction. On a larger scale, cities can become too large for the institutions that seek to manage them and infrastructure, such as drainage and water management could become fouled or silted up, creating complex problems that are beyond a resident community's capacity to solve. Once the duality of material–social is removed then we can investigate dissonant or non-correspondent relationships between people and things in terms that systematically incorporate the outcome or outcomes of those collisions (Fletcher 2002, 2004).

MAGNITUDE

The purpose of examining the magnitude of materiality from the entire city to the 'bicycle in the hallway' is to demonstrate that the material has effects at many scales, which impact on sociality. Rather than servicing human social intent, the material can also be lethal, inconvenient, and at odds with peoples wishes. While the lethality on the large scale is well recognized and can be quite easily studied, the

amount of cost, inconvenience, disruption, and friction that the material persistently causes is less tractable. At the locality and household level it has been scarcely
studied in sociology or archaeology, although municipal council records or anecdotal accounts abound with examples. Daily life can be a profoundly frustrating,
endless encounter with inconvenient material facts such as leaking taps, stiff door
locks, foot-trapping carpet rucks, and nasty table corners. We sensibly take these as
given in our daily lives. But they also drop below our intellectual gaze. Perhaps we
should not let them.

Self-inflicted damage in the early industrial city

Cities contain materialities that possess lethal potential which can be released with
devastating effects by external factors. Probably the most comprehensive destruction of a city in the early industrial period of the late nineteenth and early twentieth
century was the demolition of Galveston, Texas, in 1900 by a hurricane. The city
was largely timber-built and a busy trading centre with a population of approximately 42,000 strung out along a sand bar no more than 5.2 feet above the high tide.
It was not protected by a seawall. The hurricane came in over the Gulf of Mexico on
6 and 7 September and hit the waterfront of Galveston about 7.30 pm on Saturday
8 September. During the night the water level rose rapidly to about 20 feet above
normal sea level, and began to smash the waterfront buildings into a gigantic,
floating linear junk pile of broken timber (Larson 2000; Emanuel 2005: 83–90).
Huge dislodged beams became projectiles flung inland by winds of 140 miles per
hour, smashing buildings apart. Then the onshore winds drove the mass of floating
debris across the city and bulldozed 3,600 houses, adding further mass to the pile.
By morning, between 8,000 and 12,000 people were dead. Of one group of about
50 people, who tried to survive by clinging to remnants of their house, only
18 survived. The next day Galveston was a levelled wasteland in which the shells
of a few battered brick and concrete buildings (Figure 20.4) stood like harbingers of
the burned out cities of Japan in 1945.

For centuries, the great agrarian-based capital cities have also been vulnerable to
severe damage—especially from fires. Essentially the cities were packed with the
fuel that could trigger catastrophe for their occupants. An iconic urban fire for
Europeans was the great fire in Rome during Nero's reign, which damaged 10 of the
14 districts in the 18-square kilometre city (Boëthius and Ward-Perkins 1970: 214),
but this pales against the casualties, area of damage, and the proportion of the city
that was destroyed in the fires that afflicted Japanese cities, especially in Edo. Edo,
which covered about 100 square kilometres, was destroyed by fire approximately
every 6 years in the 178-year period from the mid-seventeenth century to the 1830s
(Yazaki 1968: 188–189; Nobuhiko and McClain 1991: 576). In 1657, 107,046 people
lost their lives in a fire that swept through 1,200 streets and destroyed two-thirds of

Fig. 20.4 Galveston, Texas—the morning after the hurricane of AD 1900 (courtesy Rosenberg Library, Galveston, Texas).

the city (Satow and Hawes 1881: 7). Twenty-six thousand died in Nakabashi. One hundred and sixty Daimyo estates, 350 shrines and temples, 750 residential compounds of warriors, and 50,000 commoner houses went up in flames (McClain 1994: 106). Again, in 1668 and in 1698 much of the city was incinerated (Satow and Hawes 1881: 7). The map of the Temmei fire in 1788 in Kyoto shows that all but the outskirts burned out. One hundred and eighty-three thousand 'houses' were said to have been destroyed (Bayrd 1974: 120).

When we come to industrialization, its initial phase produced devastating damage from fires, as for instance in Chicago in 1871 and the fires that followed the San Francisco earthquake in 1906 and the Kanto earthquake in 1923, which burned out much of Tokyo, Edo's successor. Knowledge of these fires was brutally applied to the planned combinations of high explosive bombs to smash tiled roofs and brick walls in European cities, followed by incendiaries so that the contents of the buildings would burn. The apotheosis of aerial bombing in World War II was the application of low-altitude, mass bombing with incendiaries to burn the predominantly timber cities of Japan. In the 5 months up to August 1945, US Army Air Force XXI Bomber Command burned out 65 Japanese cities, destroyed 2.51 million homes, and made 9.2 million people homeless at a cost of US$4 million—twice the cost of developing atomic weapons (Hastings 2007: 342–343). In Tokyo on 9 March they killed over 100,000 people, burned 16 square miles—one-quarter of the city—and dehoused about 1 million of the city's inhabitants (Hastings 2007: 329). By 25 May more than half of Tokyo was a burned out wasteland (Hastings 2007: 335–336). The materiality of cities dominated entire strategic agendas in Europe and the Pacific in 1940s and consumed vast resources whose allocation to civilian slaughter, worker dehousing, and city smashing is now questioned (Keegan 1989: 432–433).

Warfare in industrialized cities

The magnitude of the material fabric of industrial cities also utterly redefined the nature of warfare. Before the mid-nineteenth century, once the defences of a city were breached, it was taken under the control of the attacking force. But the extent and the structure of industrial cities introduced a new ability. A siege could be withstood by fighting a defensive battle in the wreckage of a city. The complex residential and commercial buildings, vast factories and massive storage facilities of a modern city offered numerous defensive opportunities that, in awful additional horror, were further enhanced by the chaotic effects of high explosive bombardment. The epitome of such warfare was the truly pitiless battle for Stalingrad between August 1942 and February 1943. How pitiless it was is indicated by the blunt statistic that the Soviet government shot about 13,500 of their own soldiers for cowardice and desertion (Beevor 1999: xiv).

We should note that the risks of warfare in an industrial city were well known to the Germans in World War II. Even Adolf Hitler balked at direct attacks on major industrial cities. With Leningrad, he opted for a conventional siege, remaining at artillery range away from the city while the German army sought to encircle it and starve the populace. Although this ultimately failed, the point here is that sound military judgements by the German High Command (OKH) and Hitler's opinion, were coincident on what to do about the 250 square kilometres of built area that they confronted. With Kiev in 1941, Hitler again directed that the city be taken by encirclement, initially with two pincer movements by the Sixth Army south and north of the city. Then during 18–19 September, OKH permitted an assault directly into the city as its defences collapsed. Even so, the German army suffered more than a thousand casualties when sabotage using delayed action explosives destroyed the city centre (Conot 1983: 225).

Why the German army fought so vigorously to take Stalingrad is not my concern; nor is the Soviet Union's decision to resist. My focus is upon the character and consequences of a battle in a shattered industrial urban landscape of bent piping, sheared-off reinforcement bars, collapsed girders, tangled wire, smashed glass, thousands of nails, piles of splintered wood, and millions of brick fragments in chaotic landslides of debris between the wrecked buildings (Figure 20.5). You

Fig. 20.5 Stalingrad, late AD 1942 (National Archives, USA).

would not care to walk through it, let alone to run, fight, and dive desperately to the ground for shelter from gunfire. Men fought each other with sharpened spades along wet concrete tunnels; machine gunners hid in cold, dead furnaces firing through the flues and fuel hatches; grenades were thrown into upper floor rooms to collapse the ceilings on the enemy below. Soldiers of both armies held different floors of the same building. A German soldier recounted:

We have fought for fifteen days for a single house with mortars, grenades, machine guns and bayonets. Already by the third day fifty-four German corpses are strewn in the cellars, on the landings and the staircases. The front (line) is a corridor between burnt-out rooms; it is a thin ceiling between two floors. Help comes from neighbouring houses by fire escape and chimney. There is ceaseless struggle from noon to night. From storey to storey, faces black with sweat, we bombed each other with grenades in the middle of explosions, clouds of dust and smoke...And imagine Stalingrad, eighty days and eighty nights of hand-to-hand struggle.

Quoted in Keegan (1989: 230)

A single building, the famous Pavlov house, resisted attack for 58 days (Beevor 1999: 198). The battles for the huge factories were exceptionally brutal and costly. Of 400 German soldiers only 37 men were left alive after 2 weeks of fighting in the Barricades factory (Craig 1973: 155). In the Red October plant 2 days fighting killed 75 per cent of the Soviet defenders (Shaw 1979: 153).

The demolition of Stalingrad made its defence more effective. The battle devolved into teams of a dozen or more men hunting their prey through the ruins. By mid-November the Soviet 62nd Army held ground only a few hundred metres wide along parts of the east bank of the Volga. Shielded by brick and concrete and concealed in a bizarre wasteland a minuscule Russian defence group could hold off their enemy for days, suffering and inflicting awful casualties. In September and October the German 6th Army lost 7,700 men with an additional 31,000 wounded. The Soviet army suffered 80,000 casualties (Shaw 1979: 151–152).

The industrial city has created the landscape for asymmetrical warfare, which the US Army, with professional advice from Australians (Kilcullen 2000), may now be learning to handle in Baghdad. The materiality of cities has started to redefine even the way in which wars are fought. At the other end of the scale of warfare, the magnitude of explosions produced by nuclear weapons matches the scale and durability of the cities that can now be targeted. Aerial bombardment of cities by massed bomber streams of hundreds of aircraft between 1937 and 1945 now seems a curious interlude before the appropriately scaled weapon to deal with industrial cities was developed and used on Hiroshima and Nagasaki in August 1945. The use of nuclear weapons on the planetary surface has no other readily accessible, meaningful target.

The limits of control and the magnitude of agrarian-based capital cities

The capacity for the magnitude of cities to affect sociality is also known from the giant agrarian-based, imperial capitals such as Ming Peking, Tokugawa Edo, or T'ang Chang-an, and Abbasid Baghdad. They reached physical sizes that made them hard to control with urban areas of about 70–100 square kilometres of closely packed buildings, containing about 700,000 to a million people (Fletcher 1995: 203–207). Their sheer magnitude and convoluted spatial structure blunted government control.

In the late fourteenth century AD the President of the Board of War in Ming Peking tried to rid the city of its unregistered inhabitants. Even in the 1500s, the new outer city had a reputation for rowdiness. The day labourers hid themselves and the markets were closed down for days on end. The minister was assaulted in the streets and gave up (Geiss 1979: 173). The Ming dynasty had actually ceased to control Beijing in anything other than formal terms by the mid-sixteenth century. By the early seventeenth century, it only had precarious control, using subsidized grain prices as a pacifier (Geiss 1979: 20).

Just the presence of large numbers of people made rulers uneasy. Harun al-Rashid, the great Abbasid ruler, abandoned al-Khufah as his capital, referring to it as a place of 100,000 potential ambushes (Lassner 1970: 219). Having established Baghdad he then decided to shut the markets out of his central walled Round City and stationed his own troops within the arcades (Rogers 1970: 128). As the population of the Baghdad urban area rose towards a million (Beg 1985: 66) he moved his own palace out of the Round City to a location near the Tigris, controlling the end of the Khurusan road and the bridge of boats across the Tigris (Rogers 1970: 129). If the populace of the capital became aggressive it was dangerous and damaging, whether it unified against its rulers or descended into sectional strife within its convoluted and extensive urban space. The people of Baghdad loathed the 'Turkic' youths, the *ghutams* who al-Mutasim (AD 833–842) had brought in for his army. True, the young men were feckless. They rode their horses with irresponsible abandon in the streets of the city, knocking over bystanders who responded with murder and beatings. When the Caliph's officers arrived, no one had seen anything! (Creswell 1940: 194; al-Janabi 1983: 305). The impression one gains is that al-Mutasim moved his capital to Samarra not to spare the people of Baghdad but to reduce the risks of conflict and to get away from a potentially threatening, huge, and intractable population in an unmanageable metropolis. The social identity of a major city could be a formidable thing.

One indicator was the inability of the state to enforce planning regulations even within a few kilometres of the Imperial palaces. Neither Rome nor Constantinople successfully enforced building regulations. Dangerous multistorey construction, the narrowing of streets and obstructions to neighbours' lights were the main problems. Trajan set a limit of 60 feet on the height of private tenement buildings. Developers are said to have treated it as a minimum (Toynbee 1967: 131). In Constantinople a prohibition issued in AD 450 against buildings more than 10 storeys high suggests a severe problem of construction exceeding safe or permitted heights (surely not much over four to five storeys!) (Çelik 1986: 9). The legislation was re-issued in the reign of Leo VI (886–912) (Toynbee 1967: 162). Nor was regulation any more successful in Istanbul and in Mughal Delhi. In 1558, orders to demolish shops and houses abutting the city wall in Istanbul could not be enforced (Çelik 1986: 26). In Delhi by 1739 just before the Nadir Shah's attack, housing had begun to fill the open spaces and lanes of the city. There were reports of difficulty getting through passageways (Frykenberg 1986: 175).

The same problems affected Tang Ch'ang-an and Tokugawa Edo. Ch'ang-an was managed through thousands of ordinances. At the start of the dynasty, the city was divided into wards. After dusk, the gates into each ward were shut, confining the occupants for the night. Seventy lashes were the penalty for infringing the curfew without permission (Toynbee 1967: 146). Weapons, even rocks used as projectiles, were forbidden. Promulgations on the topic in 737, 778, 792, and 806 (McKnight 1992: 292) perhaps suggest repeated attempts to enforce the unenforceable. Merchants were regulated in guilds. Commercial activity was allocated to two huge, designated markets. Wine shops, pawnshops, and brothels came under government control (Toynbee 1967: 146). Ch'ang-an's social existence was paradoxical. Polyglot in the extreme, with traders from Inner Asia and southern China, its markets held the exotics of Asia yet it was tedious, regimented, and irritating. The intense control was not sustainable. By the late Tang (ninth century AD) the ward system had begun to decline (Benn 2004: 52, 55). One of the official markets had been converted to housing, and shopkeepers could set up business wherever they chose in the commoner city (Elvin 1973: 166). The sheer magnitude of the city and its populace cumulatively overwhelmed the administration by endless, stubborn resistance to constraints. The familiar Chinese city of the twelfth to nineteenth centuries AD was born in the giant early medieval cities whose sheer physical extent and scale allowed the triumph of the ordinary. The great Sung cities, such as Kaifeng, were famous for their open nightlife of restaurants, food stalls, and markets (Heng 1999).

By any account, the Tokugawa regime Japan was one of the more tediously bureaucratized governments on the planet in the seventeenth, eighteenth, and early nineteenth centuries. But its power was limited by the size of the city (Figure 20.6) and its urban populace. Edo was initially laid out with strict social segregation of

Fig. 20.6 View of Edo, Japan: former capital of the Tokugawa state (photo: Felice Beato. Hood Museum of Art, Dartmouth College, Hanover, New Hampshire; purchased through the Julia L. Whittier Fund and a gift from William Sleznick, by exchange).

commoners from the samurai and Daimyo elite areas around the castle, though of course commoners who were retainers lived in row houses around the Daimyo enclosures or even in the interior of the lots (Jinnai 1995: 32). However, even this mixed but well-defined arrangement soon began to break apart. In the early seventeenth century, merchants and artisans moved into Nihonbashi and soon spread around the flanks of the Daimyo area. In 1657, the shogunate ordered all merchants to leave the Edobashi district but in the following decade they moved back in along with the entertainers (McClain and Merriman 1994: 14–15, 28). In the eighteenth century, warriors began to move their residences down into the valleys (Jinnai 1995: 59). Commoner residences infiltrated along the valleys of the High City increasingly mixed up with samurai houses below the Daimyo residences along the ridges.

Even on more particular matters the shogunate's ability to enforce orders was limited. After a severe fire in the mid-seventeenth century the administration wisely decided to create firebreaks (McClain 1994: 107). Large embankments were constructed that had to be kept free of buildings. The Edobashi area was also cleared because it was so near the castle. But land was at a premium in the crowded city. In a short time, the embankments were densely occupied (McClain 1994: 112, 117, 119–120). Such construction put the city at increasing risk of fires and therefore increasingly likely to suffer major catastrophes. Fires became so common and distinctive a part of city life that they were called the 'flowers of Edo'. The increasing magnitude of urban life denied the shogunate the capacity to regulate internal sources of risk, change, and stress. Nonetheless it went on trying even when the orders could no longer be enforced, unable to deal with issues both comprehensively and promptly. This rigorous administration was not always able to rule Edo's million plus populace either very directly or very compellingly. In the eighteenth century, the shogunate no longer defined the nature of the city (Takashi 1994: 41, 42). By the early nineteenth century the proclamations and ordinances of the Shogunate were called 'three-day laws' (Makoto 1994: 404).

Clearly, the physical structure and the magnitude of compact agrarian-based cities had their own distinctive effects on community life. The key implication is that since the even larger and bulkier industrial cities also have their own distinct effects we can expect that varying effects on community life will have occurred at all scales of urban growth. Imperial Rome, for example, was a crowded, dangerous place. Narrow streets were blocked by small shops. From the high wooden balconies you could lean across to shake hands with a neighbour on the other side of the street. Petronius comments on savage street fights fought with butcher's meat hooks and cooking spits. Not surprisingly, from the point of view of professional soldiers, Rome's 90 kilometres of alleyways were too dangerous for troops to enter. In AD 235, even the Praetorian Guard would not go into the alleyways (Whittaker 1995: 9, 22).

Drawing the data together would start to give us a clear perspective on the impact of the expansion, increased magnitude, and increasing durability of urban structure. An important question to ask would be whether the appalling conditions in early industrial cities also had their counterpart in early urban settlements such as Uruk in Mesopotamia in the third millennium BC. We may perhaps misread such early cities as attractive places both because they are relatively small and also because their newness and their art make a favourable impression. What we should note is that by 2900 BC Uruk, with a size of about 5 square kilometres, was about 10 times larger than any settlement in Mesopotamia 500 years or so earlier. For its period, Uruk was proportionately as startling and massive as London was for the United Kingdom in the mid-nineteenth century.

The frictions of daily life

In Rome, Ammianus (AD 325/330 to after AD 391) tells of people living under the bridges, in taverns, and under awnings (Hermansen 1978: 167). Some lived in the mausolea outside the city, which Ulpian (writing AD 211–22) notes were also taken over by brothels and used as lavatories (Whittaker 1995: 11). A little further up the scale of housing standards were the bulk of the population who lived in rented tenements and badly built apartment blocks. Brunt (1966: 13) remarks that 'most of the inhabitants lived in appalling slums' in the Late Republic. In the Empire, Juvenal (late first to early second centuries AD) remarks on 'a city propped up with gimcrack stays and beams . . . the building is permanently in balance like a pack of cards'. Rents could be extortionate, landlords merciless, rooms noisy, airless, and foul smelling (see Mumford 1961: 221; Hammond 1972: 285). A room of 10 square metres might be shared with several other people and rents were three or four times the wages of a poor worker.

Isfahan the capital of the Safavids is often described in eulogies. But Tavernier, in 1667, seems to have actually looked at the city. 'The houses standing at a distance one from the other with everyone a garden, but ill look'd after, not having anything in it perchance but one pitiful tree . . .' (quoted in Curzon 1892: 24). He comments on walls broken by great gaps. The streets were narrow and irregular, filthy with human waste and animal carcasses. Dust filled the streets in summer. In the rain they were a sea of mud. Drains from the houses ran out into the streets. Chardin (1811) says they were cleaned but that was probably near the Maidan and the palaces. Struys is less sanguine about the drains, though not as caustic in his comment as Tavernier (see Stevens 1974: 438).

At the larger end of the scale of ordinary daily engagement with the material structure of city is the cost of maintaining infrastructure. It is well known in archaeology that building a great monument is not very costly (White 1976)—but maintenance is. This is equally applicable to industrial urban development. In the UK, for example, new roadworks in 2000–2001 cost £1.1 billion and new lighting for roads cost £241 million. But maintenance and repair of local roads alone cost about £2 billion, and the associated lighting systems absorbed another £1.3 billion (Graham and Thrift 2007: 17). These figures give some idea of the necessity of maintenance—whose urgency can be seen in a recent estimate that 20 per cent of car breakdowns are considered to be due to potholes in roads (Graham and Thrift 2007: 17, 21). In 2003, 31 per cent of houses in the UK were designated as 'non-decent', and 5 per cent (about 1 million houses) were classed as 'unfit for habitation' (Graham and Thrift 2007: 6). Such observations underline the friction between the material and peoples' daily lives. As Graham and Thrift (2007: 7) note, social theory is conventionally unconcerned with decay, maintenance, and repair. Perhaps short time-span studies can afford to do so, but when the cumulative costs over time, both of repair and the failure to repair material basics are taken into account, then this is clearly a factor that any study with even a moderately long time view cannot afford to ignore. Archaeology in particular needs to rethink its approach to agrarian-based urbanism in terms of the costs of maintenance and the penalties of not doing so. The chronic 'rotting away' of urban fabric has been an underestimated component of their histories. Even in the 1960s, well into industrialization in Britain, Needleman (1965: 191) remarked that 'old buildings are allowed to deteriorate without adequate maintenance and repair, until they become unfit for human habitation, and the operation of the market is inadequate to demolish and replace them'. In particular the historical archaeology of early industrial urbanism will have to attend to this issue, while the focus of the archaeology of twentieth-century urbanism in the developing world must necessarily address the costs, demands, social impact, and consequences of building renovations. Archaeology needs to theorize these matters because conventional tools in social theory and social history do not (Fletcher 2004).

Analysing transformation through time

Not only can we study the short time span of conditions of specific cities, such as the slums of nineteenth-century Sydney (Karskens 2002; Fairbairn 2007) and Melbourne (Mayne and Murray 2001; Murray and Crook 2005) and the highly informative, partial, correspondence between their archaeology and their history, we can also look at larger and longer-term phenomena. We are not limited to studying the topics defined by historical and social theory nor are we constrained to use their methods or conform to their explanatory requirements. Instead, even within historical periods we can assess cross-cultural, long-term phenomena of great consequence for how we understand urbanism and its transformations.

The duration of compact and low-density agrarian-based cities

When the durations of the great compact, agrarian-based Imperial capitals, from their known commencement to their sack or abandonment, are plotted against their areal extent (Fletcher 2004: 127) it is apparent that their duration decreases as their size increases (Figure 20.7). What is also noticeable is that this is only a boundary constraint, as the Interaction–Communication Stress model specifies and relates to the material extent of the city not to its population size (Fletcher 1995: 207–212). Some cities at any size had very short durations and for any given size there is a range of durations that is smaller and smaller the larger the settlements become. Unique histories reside within a boundary constraint that specifies that the larger a compact settlement becomes the less likely it is to persist.

But this temporal constraint does not apply to low-density dispersed urban settlements such as Tikal at about 100 to 200 square kilometres (Webster et al. 2007) and Angkor at about 1,000 square kilometres (Evans et al. 2007). When the known durations for these kinds of settlements are plotted against their approximate extent, it is apparent that they could carry durations far higher than those of the largest compact settlements. Interestingly, the smaller low-density cities, such as Maya Copan (Webster 1999) and Burmese Pagan (Hudson 2000), which are less than 100 square kilometres in extent, conform to the boundary constraint for compact cities, suggesting that perhaps their occupation densities were somewhat higher than we may have supposed, even if still very low.

What is clear is that the compact and dispersed urban settlements had different kinds of histories and endured in different ways and for different reasons. This may be a very non-trivial matter because the current trend of industrial urbanization world-wide is towards low-density dispersed patterns—the conurbation and megalopolies of the industrialized world and the *desakota*—the rapid urbanization of densely populated rural areas—of the industrializing world. One might at first envisage that this could even be desirable in the long term if the industrial dispersed cities like their agrarian-based cousins could endure for much longer spans of time than very extensive compact cities. This would, however, be an unwise assumption for two reasons. First, Konvitz (1990: 1–4) has argued persuasively that the cities of Europe and Japan in the 1940s demonstrate that urban centres have great durability and can recover from extreme damage (1990: 1–4). But this was a characteristic of relatively small and predominantly compact cities. We do not know if it applies at a larger scale and for low-density cities. Secondly, we do know that the demise of the great agrarian-based low-density cities of the Classic Maya period (Sharer 2006) in Mesoamerica, the Anuradhapura, and Pollonaruwa urban centres of Sri Lanka between fourth century BC and late thirteenth century AD (Brohier 1934) and the Angkorian urban centre of Cambodia (Jacques and Freeman 1997), was associated with a long process of regional abandonment. This

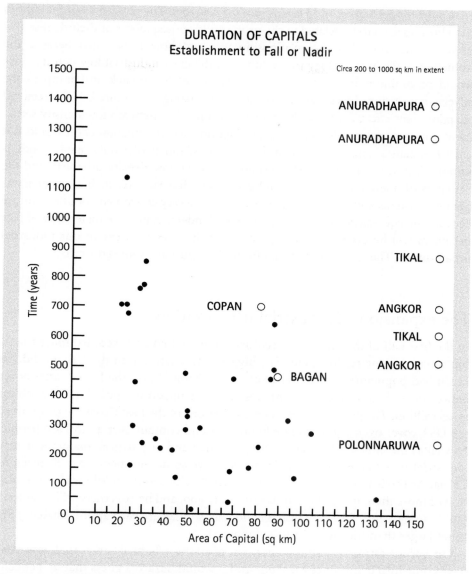

Fig. 20.7 The comparative durations of compact and low-density agrarian-based capitals—third century BC to nineteenth century AD (graph: R. Fletcher).

led to the cultural heartlands of those societies in the central Maya lowlands, the central northern dry zone of Sri Lanka and in central Cambodia on the north side of the Tonle Sap reverting to a sparse distribution of farming villages in extensive regenerated forest. There the great abandoned cities were encountered by European explorers in the nineteenth century (see Sharer 2006 for the Maya; Coningham *et al.* 2007 for Sri Lanka; and Dagens 1995 for Angkor). The physicality of these cities somehow appears to be related to the process and consequences of their demise. We need to find out what the relationship was and how it operated because the immediately obvious analogy to the future of the great industrial low-density cities would be ominous in the extreme. But we cannot legitimately just jump to the adverse conclusion. Investigation not simplistic analogy is required. If the regional abandonment effect derives only from the relationship between low-density settlement patterns and contiguous crop production then the phenomenon would not have any causal applicability to industrial cities, much of whose staple foods is imported. But, if the critical relationship is between low-density urbanism and the demands of maintaining massive and extensive infrastructure, such as water management systems and roadways, then we should be very concerned about our future because the equivalence would be quite close. Understanding the materiality of past urbanism will be essential to comprehending the risks inherent in our industrial urban future. The materiality of that future is a cause for some concern.

The expansion of industrial urbanization

In the first half of the nineteenth century, no inhabited city exceeded more than a 100 square kilometres in extent. The biggest cities, London in the UK and Edo in Japan had populations in the range of 1–1.5 million. Today the largest cities cover between 4 and 7,000 square kilometres and have maximum populations of about 15–25 million. The great low-density conurbations of the East Coast megalopolis of the USA cover over 40,000 square kilometres and contain over 40 million people. As well as the largest cities getting larger in area and population, many more new industrial-based cities and urbanized areas have come into being, e.g. Shenzen in China. As Davis remarks, 'In 1950 there were 86 cities in the world with a population of more than one million; today there are 400, and by 2015 there will be at least 550' (2006: 1), and 'Dhaka, Kinshasa and Lagos today are each approximately *forty* times larger than they were in 1950' (2006: 2).

On a crude estimate, about 90 per cent of all the urbanized areas that now exist have come into being since AD 1800. And, I would hazard a guess that 90 per cent of that new urban space has appeared since the 1950s. An immense, burdensome, and untidy material phenomenon has proliferated across the planet in less than 200 years creating a new material milieu for half the human population, many of whom live in the slums referred to by Davis (*ibid.*). Just as the nineteenth century inflicted appalling conditions of urban habitation on millions of Europeans and created a physical world at odds with the sociality of many of its occupants (Figure 20.8), so likewise that same condition is now expanding worldwide. While Tokyo in 2000 had a population of 20 million—the estimated urban

Fig. 20.8 Squatters along the river: Siem Reap, Cambodia (photo: R. Fletcher 2008).

population of the planet in the late eighteenth century (Davis 2006: 5)—by 2015, Delhi, the capital of India, will have a slum population alone of more than 10 million people (Davis 2006: 18).

We can, of course, quite properly discuss that situation in terms of how people engage with it and utilize the circumstances that are available to them, however bad. Humans are courageous, determined, and resilient—and we should honour and expound those qualities. Cities offer great opportunities and many people can take advantage of what can be gained whether legally or otherwise. But we also now need to focus on the fact that the materiality of vast portions of the contemporary urban landscape is at odds with the social life of its occupants and is directly inimical to a significant number of them. The materiality of the cities, especially their slum areas, is stressing existing sociality to an unprecedented degree and we will see new modes of community life appear from this collision. Amin and Thrift (2005) have already remarked on the need to 'reimagine the urban' including the myriad new opportunities that cities offer and new political practices and configurations they are creating. They also note that the magnitude of cities is rewriting their role in international relations as is to be expected now cities have begun to transgress the boundaries of governance regions such as the provinces and states that form part of modern nation states. I would like to add that the reimagining needs to come to terms with the massive and brutal materiality of industrial urbanism, its capacity to affect paths of social change, and its potential adverse effects on the viability of community life. What is required is to understand and analyse the friction that the materiality generates as well as being aware of its terrible consequences.

CONCLUSIONS

The urban world of the past century and a half is a phenomenon that has never existed before on this scale, and is coming into being at a staggering rate. It is becoming a new milieu, creating conditions of warfare, oppression, resistance, and tragedy that we only partially understand. A mega-scale view, such as that which archaeology can provide, is essential to understanding what is happening at the macro-scale of familiar public milieu and at the micro-scale of personal life. Humans are having to learn, in their daily lives, how to cope with and exploit this new world and its frictions. We are still novices, trying out a myriad strategies to try and learn what we should do and how to do it, just as Daniel Miller (1987) pointed out we did with mass consumption in the late nineteenth and twentieth centuries.

That the issues of scale and comparison are vital is apparent from the debates about industrial low-density urbanism which has usually been regarded by urban planners and historians of urbanism as a uniquely modern pattern of settlements consequent on mechanized transport. Such a perspective might, within its own terms, logically contend that the low-density pattern is an undesirable and transient phenomenon that we should strive to overcome. But once it is apparent that low-density urbanism has a long and diverse past and was created and sustained by several great agrarian-based societies then such propositions may be both unwarranted and may lead to seriously mistaken commitment of effort to rectify a situation in the industrial world that could be highly resistant to change. This is not to make an argument that because there have been earlier, long lasting, low-density cities that they should be simply accepted as desirable. Many common phenomena, such as high infant mortality rates, are not acceptable just because they have been usual. My point is, rather, that it is essential to gain a perspective on the magnitude and potential inertia of low-density urbanism if we should wish to do something about it. And an essential part of that awareness will be the need to comprehend and theorize about the materiality of such places and massive infrastructures in which their occupants' lives can become encased.

What is essential is to develop analytic and conceptual tools to deal with materiality. This is necessary both to understand how and why it has come into being and to deal with what it actually does rather than what people say about it. It is explicitly necessary to move away from notions that verbal sources provide the explanation for why the material is the way it is, towards a richer concept of the verbal as the way in which people seek to articulate their engagement with the material. This shift is also necessary to escape the tendency to assess and perceive the impact of the material and relationship to people in the familiar terms of individual engagement or otherwise with specific technologies. While this, like the verbal declaration approach, are proper parts of a study of the material they are neither necessary nor sufficient. What is required is to engage with the impact of the endless minor physical frictions of daily life, thousands of substandard rooms, ceaseless production of faecal waste by humans and other animals, millions of tons of concrete—the brutally actual, material milieu that can support community life but also stresses, degrades, and ruins it. We need an articulation between new archaeologies, histories, and sociologies of the friction between the material milieu and what people are, and were, striving to do. While we must continue to engage with materials from the perspective of the human actors, we also need new analytic approaches to the materiality of urbanism and its complex and ceaseless effects on human life.

CHAPTER 21

ARCHITECTURE AND CULTURAL HISTORY

CARL R. LOUNSBURY

INTRODUCTION

Buildings tell many stories. They are complex material objects wherein we live, work, worship, socialize, and play. They serve basic functions but also embody culture and express the dynamics of its social, economic, and political fortunes. Good stories always have meanings that aim to tell us something about ourselves, our society, or our place in the universe. Buildings achieve meanings in context. New ones speak of our aspirations and old ones remind us of our past. Although mute, they communicate in different ways. A few are as literal as the sign chiselled above the door to the courthouse in Palymra, Virginia, imploring citizens to 'Obey the Laws', or the words carved over the iron bars of the lockup in Amersham, Buckinghamshire, warning members of the public to 'Commit No Nuisance', below which graffiti answers mockingly. Perhaps these overt references are symbolic of an oppressive political system or a revelation of everyday power relations (Blair 2006: 237). Some buildings are festooned with commonly understood cultural symbols, such as crosses, dollar signs, coats of arms, or names that connote values and functions, patrons, and owners, but the meanings of these signs may be ambiguous or fleeting (Olsen 2006).

Beyond such explicit signs, most buildings have multiple meanings. We can think of them abstractly as ideas, symbols, or elaborations of our imaginations—the idealized vacation home, the perfect court of law, or the phantasmagorical prisons envisioned by eighteenth-century Roman artist Giovanni Piranesi. Buildings also communicate their messages by their unusual forms, gigantic scale, or dramatic settings. The vast majority blend together as unconscious backdrops to daily routines. Yet even as prosaic objects, they have the power to connect the present with the past for they are places where the repetition of everyday activities can become charged with significance, invoking memories of people, events, and other times for individuals, groups, and societies. We have tactile and physiological responses to the physical characteristics of buildings—the feel of materials or the sense of space. There are spaces of intimacy and immensity that are both of the moment and transcendent (Rasmussen 1959; Bachelard 1964; Tilley 1994).

Buildings have life cycles (*sensu* Appadurai 1986a). Date stones celebrate beginnings while commemorative plaques mark past achievements. Like their makers, buildings change over time. Their parts and materials wear out, break, rot, rust, or decay. Structures are refurbished or reconfigured to meet new demands or the latest fashions and are often recycled to serve entirely new functions. Old sweatshops and schools are gutted to accommodate luxury condominiums; medieval churches are converted into art galleries. Most buildings have brief tenures before they are destroyed or fall into ruin. Archaeologists recover the fragmentary remains of long lost structures, which are recontextualized in their resurrected half-life as historic exhibits or as data for scholarly interpretation. Only a very small number of them survive for much longer periods to give an historical dimension to the landscape. The once new and hard edged become worn and venerable. Like their fabric, their stories are mutable and can be read in many different ways.

Constructing meanings from these objects lies in the hands of their interpreters. The study of architecture as material culture today thrives in many branches of the social sciences and the humanities, more specifically among cultural anthropologists, archaeologists, folklorists, geographers, museum curators, architects, art and architectural historians, and social historians who have shaped the epistemological issues and devised the theoretical methodologies that govern our perception of what buildings tell us (Tilley *et al.* 2006: 1). Not surprisingly, the perspectives have varied widely, the voices have been many, and the meanings have been explored in aesthetic, social, cultural, historical, symbolic, environmental, and spiritual terms. Contemporary issues concerning design, the impact of global capitalism on natural resources, and the degradation of historic resources are covered only tangentially in this chapter, which focuses primarily on the ways in which buildings have been studied in the past as sources of design and as cultural artefacts. In order to give some coherence to the issues without appearing too diffuse, much of the scholarship reviewed covers mainly American topics, but the ideas and themes are widely applicable.

Those who work in this broad-based field are heirs to a many-branched lineage. For much of its history, the study of architecture has been conducted outside the academy and has been associated with visual design, antiquarianism, conservation, and commemoration (Upton 1990: 199). It has primarily been an endeavour of Western cultures, though in recent decades with the rise of global interdependence and the decline of colonialism a more transnational perspective has emerged that has challenged many of the old ways of analysing and categorizing buildings (Çelik 2003; Eley 2005; Van Dommelen 2006).

Design sources

The earliest sustained investigation of buildings began more than half a millennium ago when Renaissance scholars and antiquarians examined the architectural ruins of ancient Rome. Their intellectual interests were stimulated by aesthetic considerations and historical curiosity. They systematically recorded the fragmentary remains of classical buildings and codified the rules of design they had observed in their fieldwork in scholarly treatises and more practical building manuals (Onians 1988). This recovery of the ancient rules of design coincided with the rise of the printing press and scores of publications with illustrated images of the classical orders gained wide currency throughout the Western world. These were the first books of architecture that contained information about buildings that were outside most people's everyday experience.

Because of its cultural cachet, classical architecture became the authoritative source for early modern European design. New buildings erected in the manner of or inspired by the antique dominated European and later North American architectural pedagogy for several hundred years. From plans to moulding profiles, architects, and craftspeople cribbed new designs from old models, reassured that their work was grounded in ancient authority. The third American President and author of the Declaration of Independence, Thomas Jefferson, referred to Italian architect Andrea Palladio's *Four Books of Architecture* (1570) as his Bible and carefully considered its strictures on proportion and ornament when he designed Monticello in Western Virginia in the late eighteenth century (Brownell 1992: 212). Architects learned their craft by measuring and sketching old buildings. In the process, they established many of the protocols of field recording that would become one of the hallmarks of architectural research, establishing measured plans, elevations, and sections as integral tools of explication.

From the eighteenth century through the early twentieth century, architects in Europe and America found design precedents in the early buildings of their native lands. The books they published during this time no longer sought to educate their colleagues and workmen or to elucidate the arcane rules of architecture, but were catalogues of a particular style or building type aimed at clients or designers seeking historical inspiration for modern building. They were generated to meet the professional needs of the architect who plumbed the past to appropriate details for new designs. Handsomely illustrated portfolios filled with photographs, plans, and details of Wren churches, old Suffolk farmhouses, or eighteenth-century London townhouses proliferated until the advent of World War II. This long phase of using history in the service of design came to an abrupt end in the second half of the twentieth century with the ascendancy of Modernist design pedagogy, which saw little value in historic buildings. Since then, architectural history (except, ironically, the history of Modernism) has been a marginalized discipline among professionals in design schools (Howard 2002).

BUILDINGS AS ANTIQUITIES

Antiquarians were another early group who studied buildings. Their purpose differed from the practical and aesthetic concerns of architects. Antiquarians sought out ancient castles and churches, old and unusual dwellings, and natural features in the landscape to illuminate aspects of local and national histories. Many of these buildings lay outside the classical tradition and were sometimes seen as embodying national characteristics. The English were among the earliest and most prolific publishers of topographical histories wherein they carefully catalogued and illustrated ancient monuments, great houses, churches, and landscape curiosities. They travelled the countryside to examine and document buildings, using sketches, measurements, and detailed notes to complement or contradict old tales (Sweet 2004). Although much of this antiquarian research was anecdotal at best, some work was more serious and transformed the manner in which buildings were observed. Drawn to the many permutations of Gothic architecture found in the thousands of medieval parish churches, Rickman (1817) observed chronological patterns in the types of tracery and shapes of medieval windows. He recognized distinct periods of medieval window forms that succeeded one another over the course of five centuries. In 1817 he published *An Attempt to Discriminate the Styles of English Architecture from the Conquest to the Reformation*, which provided a framework for the classification of medieval English architecture into stylistic periods with their distinguishing attributes (Rickman 1817).

Rickman's effort to classify medieval architecture was part of the Enlightenment fascination with arranging natural and man-made phenomena into categories of knowledge, of defining hierarchical relationships, and cataloguing things according to observable shared characteristics, a perspective that had informed the methods used in many branches of the natural and social sciences. Generally, these patterns were found to reside in typological and stylistic categories—the way buildings of a certain period shared common characteristics in terms of their composition and details. As Rickman demonstrated from his careful observations, certain features flourished at one period and then were superseded by others.

American antiquarians and architects in the late nineteenth and early twentieth century assumed many of the same attitudes about old buildings as their British predecessors and counterparts. They sought out the primitive and the old in a landscape that was rapidly being transformed by industrial production. A few ventured west to record the lives of Native Americans during a time when traditional patterns were being extinguished. In *Houses and House-Life of the American Aborigines*, Morgan documented an evolutionary sequence of house forms representative of different stages of cultural development (Morgan 1881). In the east, rural crafts, farmsteads, and homes of colonial ancestors held peculiar fascination partly because they were seen to capture some of the values of a simpler society that had largely vanished or continued to exist only in pockets of rural isolation. In the Southern states, decaying plantations held fascination for some as a tangible reminder of a golden era that had disappeared with the American Civil War in the 1860s and the unsettling readjustment of racial and social relations in its aftermath.

In *Early Rhode Island Houses* and *Early Connecticut Houses*, Norman Isham and Albert Brown established many of the lasting methodologies and preoccupations of American architectural scholarship (Isham and Brown 1895, 1900). Like Rickman nearly a century earlier, Isham was a dedicated field recorder interested in framing technology and house forms, which he divided into evolutionary typologies. His biases were inherited from the Arts and Crafts Movement's belief in the superiority of hand craftsmanship and the antiquarian's and ethnographer's fascination with the primitive. Thus, his main interest was in seventeenth-century New England domestic architecture whose irregular forms he associated with Gothic aesthetics (Upton 1990: 201). The same preconceptions appeared in later generations of architectural antiquarians such as Foreman (1934) and Waterman (1946) whose field of interest was the early Chesapeake. More recent works covering the colonial period in the New England and Chesapeake regions shed these notions but retained the functionalist interest in technology (Cummings 1979; Wells 1998).

BUILDINGS AS CULTURE

Many of the same fascinations with the exotic that had motivated early generations of American and European architects and antiquarians to record the early buildings of their own countries informed the work of the emerging discipline of anthropology. Rather than focusing on the past, cultural anthropologists developed the concept of ethnographic fieldwork to explore the structure and material culture of indigenous peoples in Africa, North and South America, Asia, and the Pacific. By the early twentieth century, there was less interest in collecting their material culture for museum displays as the focus shifted to what has become the central role of ethnographic studies—the exploration of the social organization and beliefs of societies (Tilley *et al.* 2006: 2). Therefore, cultural anthropologists rarely featured native building practices until a shift in emphasis in the second half of the twentieth century. At best, early ethnographic studies of architecture focused on functionalist criteria, in particular the impact of climate, technological capabilities, and local building materials on construction practices and house forms.

Daryll Forde's study of housing in West Africa was instrumental in bringing attention to cultural factors in determining the layout and social organization of housing as opposed to purely environmental ones (Forde 1934). It took a later generation to follow this lead (Prussin 1969; Oliver 1997). In *House Form and Culture*, Rapoport (1969) examined patterns of non-Western architecture to argue that socio-cultural factors were far more important in shaping architecture than climate, technology, and materials. This and other works concentrated on the spatial dynamics of building types, which were forged by commonly accepted cultural values. Architectural change occurred with the disruption of local consensus (Rudofsky 1964, 1977; Oliver 1971, 1975, 1987). Recent studies of non-Western and indigenous societies firmly follow this cultural approach of situating traditional domestic architecture within social and symbolic systems (Nabokov and Easton 1989; Waterson 1990). However, the earlier presumption held by Rudofsky and others that traditional architecture is the product of anonymous, untrained builders was challenged by those who emphasized the technological and spatial complexity of many local building forms (Oliver 1997).

THE IMPACT OF THE SOCIAL SCIENCES ON BUILDING HISTORY AND DESIGN

The results from early ethnographic studies may have been meagre, but sociological and anthropological theories became increasingly important in the interpretation of buildings by the middle of the twentieth century among historians, architects, and cultural critics. Along with Marxism, the French *Annales* school of history had a profound influence on the theoretical direction of social history in Western scholarship in the decades following World War II. The *Annales* historians applied concepts from the social sciences wherein they inverted the traditional historical focus on political events and ideas of a particular time to examine the economic and social structure of communities over a long period. They exchanged conventional chronologies for a more challenging framework of the *long durée*, an epochal time in which the *mentalités* (collective attitudes and ways of thinking in a particular culture) of a society were examined through an exploration of social, economic, and cultural topics (Eley 2005: 36–37). In his analysis of dwellings in the early modern era, Braudel emphasized the repetitive and static nature of building where the strength of precedent made itself felt. The structural anthropology of Durkeim and Lévi-Strauss found resonance in Braudel's characterization of a house 'wherever it may be' as 'an enduring thing', which 'bears perpetual witness to the slowness of civilisations, of cultures bent on preserving, maintaining and repeating' (Braudel 1973: 193).

Informed by sociological insights gleaned from the behavioural sciences about the symbiotic relationship between people and their environment, architects and architectural theorists explored the manner in which architecture affected human experience. During World War II, English Prime Minister Churchill epigrammatically observed that 'we shape our buildings, and afterwards our buildings shape us', a perceptive comment about the phenomenological relationship of people to spaces and places (Broad 1972: 301). In the postwar period, architectural writers pursued this insight as they investigated the social dynamics of spatial sensibility and wrote about the perceptual and physiological experience of architectural space (Rasmussen 1959). Newman (1972) used this concept, for example, in his study of the issues of safety in public or council housing in which he argued for the need to create the appropriate kind of communal spaces that would give residents a sense of 'territoriality'—an extension of private responsibility into the public domain.

Architectural critics turned to anthropological theory to reinterpret the role of Western design practices. Structuralism had a powerful impact on Modernists who examined the architectural landscape for timeless patterns and forms that could be extrapolated and applied to contemporary design (Arnheim 1977). Alexander and Rudofsky extended the search for design forms to traditional societies where they saw an architectural process not moulded by architects but by slow patterns of change within 'unselfconscious' cultures. The architectural forms of these pre-industrial cultures were seen as more integrated into their societies and therefore were authentic, less arbitrary models for new design (Alexander 1964; Rudofsky 1964). In turning their backs on the classical tradition, Modernists such as Le Corbusier, one of the pre-eminent theorists of the movement, found inspiration in forms ranging from contemporary automobiles, airplanes, and ships to prehistoric pile dwellings discovered by archaeologists in Switzerland (Frampton 1980). Much of the credo of Modernist pedagogy—the rejection of the past and a belief in the universal applicability of design principles—found support in the synchronic, timeless quality of structuralism. Local materials, traditional technology, and regional building forms found little interest among designers. As a result, the

Modernists' social commitment to ameliorating the plight of the urban poor through better designed housing produced an unrelenting march across the globe of concrete tower blocks from third world slums, Soviet new towns, to urban renewal projects in American inner cities (Wolfe 1981).

Concerns about the depletion and imbalanced exploitation of natural resources, the spoliation of the environment, and the impact of globalization on traditional societies in the past quarter century has renewed interest among architects, cultural critics, and historians of buildings to search for ways of developing sustainable design. Learning from standing structures is often couched in functionalist terms. Since the beginning of the energy crisis in the 1970s, historic preservationists have often pitched conservation lessons that can be gained from the study of traditional building practices. Old houses with operable windows and shutters, high ceilings, shade-providing porches and verandas, and mass walling are cited as more efficient users of energy (Park 1998; Jackson 2005).

This emphasis on finding contemporary solutions in traditional architecture has also encouraged the growing interest in the study of the buildings of non-Western cultures (Oliver 1997; Vellinga *et al.* 2007). Oliver and others have argued that traditional building practices in many parts of the world, though threatened by the legacies of Modernist design principles, the industrialized production of materials, and the assembly of parts on the job site by unskilled labourers, should not be seen as the losing end in the long process of globalization. Old stigmas, which associate traditional materials, plans, and living arrangements as backward or outmoded, need to be redressed so that local building practices might be recognized as contributing to rather than impeding solutions to modern building needs, particularly as demands for housing become increasingly acute in many parts of the world. The message is that the knowledge, skills, and expertise of traditional builders can foster a sense of local identity as well as promote a more sustainable environment (Asquith and Vellinga 2006: 6).

Interpreting buildings
as art and as culture

The diverse ways of conceptualizing the study of buildings have encouraged interdisciplinary approaches, but have also reinforced traditional intellectual and academic boundaries. Inspired by ethnographic methods of anthropologists, social historians have reread documentary evidence 'for means of access to the alien mentalities of a past people' (Isaac 1982: 5). On the other hand, some positivist practitioners of the 'New Archaeology' of the 1960s remained suspicious of historical documents and humanistic topics associated with socio-cultural anthro-pology (Beaudry 1996: 479). Scholarship and design have been uneasy bedfellows. Architects and architectural historians who teach in professional design schools are notorious for their conflicted views of the significance of history and theory. Many architects embrace contemporary theoretical discourse but see little relevance in historical inquiry for their profession (Howard 2002).

These and other divisions cut across the social sciences and the humanities in similar ways. Cultural theories emanating from the social sciences have raised intellectual standards for all those who study buildings as material culture, but the often ponderous prose, the heavy-handed use of evidence to fit universal models of human behaviour, and the consequent downplaying of the importance of chronology, the influence of local forces, and the significance of human agency have soured their reception in some quarters (Carson 1997). An example of the gulf that sometimes exists between intellectual perspectives appears in the work of traditional art historians and those anthropologists and folklorists who appropri-ate the methods used in structural linguistics to study material culture. The former explicate in a few choice buildings the design genius of an individual architect, while the latter strip away the idiosyncrasies of local forms to reveal the underlying principles that have structured building patterns across time.

Art historians have traditionally traced the design pedigree of specific architec-tural forms, locating aesthetic inspiration in the talents of a few designers who consciously created buildings that have achieved canonical status. In the eighteenth and early nineteenth centuries, German scholars were among the first to think of buildings as cultural markers in which their form and aesthetic characteristics or style reflected the spirit of their age. Winckelmann charted the rise and decline of Greek art through an emphasis on the style of an object. The ideas broached in pioneering works of art history were articulated philosophically by Hegel's study of the aesthetics of art. He postulated that aesthetic ideas move through stages of development from the simple to the more complex, finally reaching a plateau from which there is an inevitable falling off or disintegration until new ones rise out of the old and the process begins its dialectical pattern once more. These ideas had a profound influence on the way many art historians in the later nineteenth and twentieth centuries thought of stylistic development as cyclical in nature. These scholars viewed architectural style as part of a broader artistic *zeitgeist* wherein particular characteristics in building such as attenuation of forms could be found in contemporary painting or sculpture and that certain nationalistic traits might be traced in the artistic achievements of a country (Wölfflin 1950).

The concept of style provided art historians with a means of analysing distin-guishing characteristics in the works of individual artists and to give identity and coherence to broad tendencies in art over sustained periods of time. Naturally, they have gravitated toward documenting the most outstanding examples of a given style, excluding most of the built environment or dismissing what they judged to be artistically inferior forms as derivative. 'The term architecture applies only to buildings designed with a view to aesthetic appeal' declared Pevsner, who summarized this scholarly perspective when he observed that 'a bicycle shed is a building; Lincoln Cathedral is a piece of architecture' (Pevsner 1943: 7).

In a popular art history survey, Trachtenberg and Hyman contended that monumental architecture is 'the visual art that is the most sensitive, powerful touchstone of the cultural process . . . We have emphasized great buildings, and the greatest among them are sharply spotlighted, although not without a support cast of lesser works to fill out the historical picture.' They perceived the history of architecture as 'a dynamo of movement, influence, and climatic events. Mainly for this reason, vernacular architecture for the most part has been excluded. The essence of vernacular building is its unchanging quality, having generally come into being in response to the ahistoric conditions of agrarian, backwoods, or primitive societies' (Trachtenberg and Hyman 1986: 41). Harsh words for contemporary social historians and cultural anthropologists who chafe at the elitist focus of such a circumscribed, mainly Western perspective. This point of view, though softened by concerns for social context, urban process, and ritual in recent years, still dominates the discourse of many art history programmes and in particular professional architectural schools (Kostof 1985; Howard 2002).

A different set of social and political values have informed the work of historians and anthropologists who think of buildings as an integral part of common human experience. They have searched for patterns of group behaviour, beliefs, attitudes, and practices that influence the form and functions of buildings. They have elucidated the structure of power in societies, explored gender relationships, and examined ethnic, class, and racial identities within the built environment (Tilley *et al.* 2006). Social historians maintained that their goal was to understand the dynamic of whole societies or *histoire totale*, including 'the material conditions of life' (Eley 2005: 26, 39). Glassie countered the assertions of the art historians by observing that 'important buildings can be interpreted as displays of the values we value—grandeur perhaps, or originality—while unimportant buildings display values that we have not yet learned to appreciate. Neglect is a sign of ignorance.' Trachtenberg and Hyman naturally dismiss 'vernacular architecture', Glassie argued, because it embodies 'values alien to those cherished in the academy' (Glassie 1999: 230). How can non-canonical structures be excluded when they represent geographically and historically the overwhelming majority of the buildings erected over the past two millennia as well as in the world today? (Oliver 2003: 15).

The commonality of vernacular buildings is fundamental to their significance as cultural markers. Where art historians seek out exemplars, folklorists, ethnographers, cultural geographers, historical archaeologists, and social historians have looked for patterns, the underlying principles of design, plan, and function that describe a culture's experience of buildings. Those who work within these disciplines would agree that numbers matter, that counting, classifying, and sorting buildings according to type, function, materials, and siting are fundamental to determining their social, cultural, and symbolic significance.

Buildings have been a means of measuring the social and economic well being of a community, region, or nation. Social historians have used statistical information contained in censuses, tax records, reports, and other documentary sources to gauge building practices, housing standards, habitation patterns, and the distribution of wealth in various places at different periods of time (Burnett 1980; Rilling 2001). From the study of hearth tax records, English historians have a better grasp of housing conditions of that country in the late seventeenth century. As the only national listing of people between medieval poll taxes and nineteenth-century censuses, these records provide a glimpse of the distribution of the country's population, wealth, and housing stock. The tax is a fuzzy snapshot of English society at a particular moment against which the post-medieval housing revolution, the 'great rebuilding' that W. G. Hoskins (1953) postulated in the 1950s from a more informal survey of dated standing buildings, can be measured. These returns illustrate a variety of ways in which buildings and documents can be used together to answer questions about regional variations, the timing, and the level of impact that the great rebuilding had among cottagers, small farmers, and tradesmen in rural and urban areas in the late seventeenth century (Barnwell and Airs 2006). M. H. Johnson (1993) used the hearth taxes as a springboard to ask penetrating questions about the cultural implications of the reconfiguration of the English house in the post-medieval period.

Early twentieth-century cultural geographers took the concept of diffusion to record the movement of groups of people and their material culture across space from their place of origins. In terms of architecture, they identified key characteristics of traditional building in the heartland of a particular group, such as the use of log technology or the circular form of house plans as identifiers, which they could plot spatially to map the spread of their influence beyond their cultural hearth. Beginning with comprehensive windscreen surveys in Louisiana in the 1930s and expanding to encompass much of the eastern half of the United States in the 1960s, Kniffen, who was later joined by Glassie, traced patterns of population movement and settlement through much of the southern and eastern United States through field surveys of building types (Kniffen 1936, 1965; Kniffen and Glassie 1966).

Ethnographers, folklorists, and social historians have argued for more than 40 years that the field of focus needed to be more inclusive of the vast body of people and their buildings that had been ignored in past narratives. Architectural historians who have used the ethnographic approach in their fieldwork recorded the complex spatial arrangements and material lives of contemporary sharecroppers in southern Maryland and subsistence farmers in the mountains of western

North Carolina whose small one- and two-room houses were invariably overlooked by standard architectural surveys except as late exemplars of the crudeness of frontier housing (McDaniel 1982; Williams 1991).

VERNACULAR ARCHITECTURE

Trachtenberg and Hyman's characterization of non-elite architecture as 'vernacular' is problematic as it sets up a dichotomous boundary that is hard to define and lumps too many different types of buildings into a catchall category. The term is very elastic and has been used to describe what others have called indigenous, local, traditional, folk, ordinary, native, primitive, pre-industrial, and popular architecture. It presupposes that there are qualitative differences between canonical buildings and the rest and rather sanctimoniously defines vernacular by what it is not—buildings not erected by architects nor following academic or proscribed rules of design (Upton 1990: 210).

The distinction between polite or academic architecture and vernacular architecture may be a matter of degree (Brunskill 1971: 25). A number of detailed studies of early American architecture have observed a complex interaction between native and outside ideas. They have observed that the dividing line between academic and vernacular is slippery if it exists at all. If it does, then it is only revealed in context. Building types might be linked formally to academic precedents, but the manner in which they are sited in the landscape, their materials, and their construction methods reveal the impact of local conditions. An eighteenth-century log church in low-country South Carolina might be classified as vernacular when set against a nearby brick one with classical detailing and finely executed fittings. Both were fabricated of local materials—logs and brick—but they also contained imported items such as nails, hardware, glass, and, in the case of the larger building, paint. Local craftsmen probably built the two structures with a few simple tools (imported from England). The pulpit design in the brick church was based on a plate from an English architectural book. However, when the masonry church is compared with its ecclesiastical and architectural prototype—a London church designed by Wren—the form and scale of the brick church indicates its regional origins (Upton 1982; Lounsbury 1997).

Despite the difficulty of defining vernacular architecture, several theoretical positions have tried to distinguish its fundamental characteristics. In some instances, the meaning was narrowly applied to a specific building type of a certain social class. Through much of the twentieth century, English historians used it very specifically to connote non-ecclesiastical, sub-manorial medieval and early modern farmhouses and other rural buildings fabricated of local materials (Innocent 1916;

Barley 1961; Wood-Jones 1963; Mercer 1975). Great houses occupied by people of national importance and usually of a size to match the pretentions of their owners were left out of the ranks (Brunskill 1971). Occasionally, urban house forms, if of the same early period (generally pre-1666 fire of London), claimed the attention of medieval historians and members of the Royal Commission on the Historical Monuments who were charged with inventorying the country's ancient buildings (Pantin 1947; O'Neil 1953). Brunskill (1971: 20) admitted industrial buildings within the category as long as they were related to activities in the countryside and manufacturing was of the domestic rather than the commercial scale.

Other views suggest that vernacular should not be regarded as a product or a form, or restricted to the use of native materials, but should be classified as a process, 'which identifies dynamic building traditions that continuously evolve while remaining distinctive to a specific place' (Asquith and Vellinga 2006: 9). Vernacular design is possible because those who participate in the process, from craftsmen to clients, share widely accepted rules about the form, finish, and function of buildings. It is strongest in communities or societies with high degrees of cultural congruence; little needs to be spelled out as most is left to custom (Rapoport 1980; Glassie 1999). Some scholars who think in these terms view building as fundamentally static, or changing slowly only when the cultural equilibrium is disturbed (Rudofsky 1964; Rapoport 1969; Braudel 1973; Glassie 1975). Such a perspective eliminates a large segment of the built environment— all those structures designed by contractors and other non-elite designers that use industrialized building practices and materials. This enormous collection includes shopping malls and other types of commercial structures, offices, warehouses, schools, hospitals, working-class housing, suburban dwellings, and the prosaic buildings associated with roadside commerce, which have become endemic of the modern landscape. Oliver defines such popular buildings as 'the architecture of the people, and by the people, but not for the people'—in other words, not vernacular (Oliver 2003: 15). Common across wide geographic areas, with few local contexts and divorced from local ways of building, popular architecture does not fit the socio-cultural definition of vernacular advocated by many scholars. None-theless, others would contend that they are no less indicative of the cultures that build them than structures considered traditional architecture (Longstreth 1986).

Yet, another approach to defining vernacular is to deny the term any validity as a building form or even as a process. Among folklorists, archaeologists, and archi-tectural historians in the United States, whose work often appears under the aegis of the Vernacular Architecture Forum (established 1980), vernacular architecture has come to mean 'less a kind of building than an approach to looking at buildings. In a literal sense, then, the term is outmoded or inadequate' as it has been expanded 'to include the recording and analysis of structures of every age, form, and function'. According to Wells (1986: 4) the term is an 'unstable and semantically indefensible mixture of evidence, method, and theory'.

SOME RECENT TRENDS IN
ARCHITECTURAL RESEARCH

Studies in architectural history over the past quarter century have moved slowly away from the theoretical constructs that shaped social history and social anthropology for many decades. Ever so gingerly, it has changed with the times, but scholarship in the field is hardly at the forefront of contemporary theoretical discourse. In anthropology, there have been strong critiques of structuralism with its atemporal and overly deterministic and singular reading of culture. With new research and theoretical models comes the dismantling of old verities.

The structuralist model that Glassie (1975) so poetically articulated in *Folk Housing in Middle Virginia*, a study that has been influential among American archaeologists and folklorists since its publication more than 30 years ago, crumbles in the light of new theoretical perspectives and sustained fieldwork in the region. Glassie applied transformational grammar and socio-linguistic theories to construct a geometrical model of the design process that created the small one- and two-storey framed farmhouses found in central Virginia. He borrowed the structuralist model from Lévi-Strauss to define the cultural imperatives that led Virginians to move from house types that were 'open' or irregular in plan with an entrance directly into the principal living space to structures that were 'closed' or symmetrical in form with entry into a buffered area known as a central passage.

Big, encompassing stories founded on the bedrock of structural patterns sometimes founder on small details. As in Rickman's day, architectural research requires a discerning knowledge of the chronological sequence of forms, features, and details. Building historians in the Chesapeake region have paid an extraordinary amount of attention to moulding profiles, carpentry joints, and brick bonding patterns, which may often be the keys in determining periods of construction and alteration (Graham 2003). The devil is in the details, and a misreading of this kind of evidence can sometimes lead to mistaken conclusions. Glassie attributed the transformation of house forms in Virginia to the impact of the republican ideology coming to the fore on the eve of the American Revolution, a very specific event. He interpreted it as a seismic shift in American culture. The irregular facade and open plan of 'the old house belonged to the little community of engagement, of constant and direct exchange'. The symmetrical façade and closed plan of 'the new house belonged to an overarching concept of manifest and self-evident reason—to a political nation as yet unborn' (Glassie 1999: 317).

Unfortunately, his explanation for this change falters with the misreading of his field evidence, ascribing a late eighteenth-century date to structures built 50–75 years after the Revolution (Deetz and Bell 1995). Perhaps even more damaging to his thesis was his self-enclosed methodology that relied entirely on an 'objective' social science model to inform the meaning of his field evidence. He discovered a pattern of architectural design by constructing it according to its own rules of signification, ignoring a reality outside that system. He eschewed 'biased' data from historical records and other architectural histories that would have demonstrated that symmetrical houses with central passages had become a common form among many of the wealthier planters in Tidewater Virginia by the second quarter of the eighteenth century (Waterman 1946; Whiffen 1960). Had he looked at documentary sources, he would have found building contracts with the names of craftsmen and their clients. Rather than recreating the mindset of the anonymous builder, he would have discovered a much messier process of design, one that changed to fit the exigencies of the job and involved craftsmen, labourers, suppliers, and clients in ever-changing roles and responsibilities. The language of those contracts would have revealed how Virginians conceptualized new buildings—from citing neighbourhood precedents for plans and features to their commonly understood notions of acceptable materials and good and workmanlike craftsmanship. These documents range across the social spectrum from the grand gentry's house to the poor tenant's cottage. Recent scholarship has discovered much about the patterns of building in this part of the world, but none resemble the complex, self-contained structural formulations in *Folk Housing* (Upton 1982; Bishir *et al.* 1990). Compelling as the argument once seemed, the field evidence makes the hypothesis untenable and the methodology obscures the work of real people.

New cultural theories have argued for the significance of contingency, individual agency, ambiguity, and the multiplicity of meanings (Tilley *et al.* 2006: 9). The historian Geoff Eley has observed that cultural history has overtaken social history as the leading edge of historical scholarship. He argues that the social history that emerged in the 1960s and 1970s was a product of democratic activism and that recent cultural history has been influenced by contemporary issues such as feminism, questions of subjectivity, and increasing attention to identity, ethnicity, and race (Colomina 1992; Kwolek-Folland 1995; Eley 2005). The search for overarching structure in social history has yielded to microhistories and the cultural construction of social life. An early demonstration of the microhistorical approach to building appeared in Herman's detailed analysis of the social relationships between the protagonists in a court case concerning a 'stolen house' in the state of Delaware. He argued that the actions and interactions of the individuals in this petty drama can be read as an extension 'into the way in which people communicate in a broader landscape and society' (Herman 1992: 3). The challenge in such studies is establishing a solid theoretical bridge from the particular to the general.

These and other perspectives have shaped the direction of architectural research over the last two decades. With various degrees of reflexivity, scholars interrogate the cultural landscape to explore the spatial context of gender, ethnic, class, and racial identities and relations (Bernstein and Torma 1991; Saint George 1998;

Ginsberg 2000; Groth and Wilson 2003). A number of case studies have tried to define the architectural attributes and landscape features associated with ethnic groups and sects as well as to explore the meaning of acculturation into or rejection of the predominant culture (Chappell 1980; Swentzall 1990; Westmacott 1992; Yip 1995). Some have sounded a salutary reminder that the relationship between architectural forms and ethnic and racial identity is sometimes difficult to sort out (Edwards 1994; Upton 1996; Kern 1999).

Slavery has had a commanding presence in the literature of historical archaeology in the United States, in part because of the increasing number of sites that have been excavated in the South over the past 30 years because of the pressures of suburban and coastal development. Yet even with the threat to archaeological resources in the Chesapeake and Carolina low country, trends in social history had precipitated a reassessment of the entire plantation landscape so that national historical sites and museums such as Mt Vernon, the home of George Washington, Jefferson's Monticello, and Williamsburg, the eighteenth-century capital of Virginia, had turned to the archaeological investigation of slave spaces and buildings (Vlach 1993; M. Brown and Samford 1994; Pogue 1994; Sanford 1994). Strongly influenced by socio-cultural theory, many site-specific studies have focused on the spatial dynamics of slavery, architectural and spatial features linked to African forms, artefacts as markers of ethnicity, and the social and spiritual aspects of slave life (Neiman 1978; Ferguson 1992; Singleton 1999; Graham et al. 2007). Some building historians have used documentary evidence and standing structures to recreate the spatial dynamics in which slaves and masters operated. Upton's (1985) analysis of the very different ways in which slaves perceived and moved around a formal plantation landscape and Herman's (2005) explication of the 'invisibility' of slaves in the eyes of white masters in urban settings have provided insights into the manner in which enslaved populations negotiated circumscribed spaces in and between buildings.

Postcolonialism is an umbrella term for ways of dealing with the recent past in many parts of the world where Western colonial influences are now ripe for reinterpretation as well as contemporary issues of globalization (Van Dommelen 2006: 104). While some studies have emphasized the cultural clash between colonizer and colonists, more subtle analyses have recognized the interplay between the two. The concept has featured in recent studies of architectural forms in British India and Africa, but has also been applied to more ancient colonial cultures such as Spanish America (Dean and Liebsohn 2003; Chattopadhyay 2005; Chopra 2007; Harris and Myers 2007). Bailyn and Morgan (1991: 9), historians of early American colonization, have suggested that 'instead of a single, coherent outward thrust by the English, the process should be seen as vastly more complicated, much more double ended, with the colonies playing as dynamic role as the metropolis'. Hybridity, in this sense, has played an integral part in understanding the colonial architecture of early America for several decades (Upton 1986; Lounsbury 2005; Graham et al. 2007).

In recent years cultural landscape studies have explored the fluidity of ethnic and cultural identity and the impact of commemoration, museums, and the historic preservation movement on the shaping of public memories (Small and Eichstedt 2002). This line of scholarship has focused on the role of memory in transmitting knowledge of past events as well as its reverse, cultural amnesia whereby individuals and societies choose to ignore or forget troublesome or traumatic past events or social practices (Lowenthal 1985; Sebald 2003). Cities and regions sometimes remake their public image based on carefully embellished perceptions of their cultural heritage (Van Slyck 1995). In the American Southwest, ethnographers and hucksters came together in the early twentieth century to deliberately recast the image of Santa Fe into a highly romanticized image of pueblo culture. Adobe-inspired museums, hotels, and other structures appeared around the plaza and the accretions of what was considered outside Anglo-American territorial architecture were removed from many of the early buildings, which were restored with more enthusiasm than historical accuracy to accentuate the hybrid style melded from Spanish and Native American traditions. The impact of this repackaging of history has been long lasting. Wilson describes the Santa Fe style as an 'example of inventing a tradition and the ongoing interaction of ethnic identity with tourist image making' (Wilson 1997: 7).

Another American city that refashioned its historic image is Charleston, South Carolina. Yuhl has explored the cultural issues that led to the transformation of the historical perception of Charleston in the 1920s and 1930s. Dismissed earlier as a listless and shabby port town, the city with its old buildings and peculiar customs shrugged off its indolence and provincialism and came to be seen as a charming refutation of modern industrial development. This re-imaging of Charleston was no accident but a conscious effort on the part of a coterie of the city's elite citizens to reshape and redeem a deeply troubling past of slave insurrections, sectional strife, abject defeat, and impoverished fortunes to make it more palatable to a new generation of Americans born after the Civil War. Artists, writers, and preservationists discovered in their heritage a set of conservative values that celebrated family, gentility, and good taste. Through their efforts in historic preservation, painting, literature, and music, they gave material expression to a version of Charleston history that emphasized the continuity of tradition and racial deference. This carefully burnished myth endures today among the tourists who are drawn to the city to gaze at its Spanish-moss draped trees and antebellum mansions and among old white families ensconced in their ancestral homes who find it a reassuring affirmation of their place in the world (Yuhl 2005).

***

Buildings do indeed tell many stories. Recent trends in cultural history have emphasized the ambiguity and malleability of those stories. As the popular architectural images of Santa Fe and Charleston suggest, academics may dominate the professional discourse about the cultural meaning of buildings in classrooms and journals, but their voices sometimes bump up against the hard carapace of public memory where common opinion and myths sometimes trump the findings of scholarly inquiry. Whose stories are the more valid?

CHAPTER 22

HOUSEHOLDS AND 'HOME CULTURES'

VICTOR BUCHLI

INTRODUCTION

The domestic sphere or 'home cultures' as the term is used here is the location of many disciplinary investigations into the home. It is in the domestic sphere that one investigates the key elements of the human condition. It is where family, gender, and the nature of the individual are understood. It is also where the basic elements of cosmology and religious life are lived and perceived and the elemental context for the understanding of political and economic life. Here public and private realms are forged, nature/culture boundaries are created and negotiated. And it is here where power, at the level of the state, community, and family are enacted and most intimately felt. But the domestic sphere as such is an invention as much as any other and with it come many of the problems and issues associated with all human inventions. The invention of the privatized domestic sphere in the Euro-American world is also the invention of domestic violence—where the most problematic aspects of inequality and injustice are perceived, sustained, and masked. What might seem ordinary and unremarkable is in fact deeply fraught and problematic—it is here that the most elemental aspects of social structure and social conflict emerge and are experienced. It is here where the three key topics of the social sciences converge and are forged within; namely, how we characterize mind, body, and environment in the entity that we call the home or more precisely the domestic sphere.

More importantly, the delineation of the domestic sphere itself, as an institution is also a highly politicized act constituting the most fundamental structures of social life and the forms of life that can be identified and sustained or excluded. The domestic sphere as a reified distinct and autonomous sphere is understood as a distinctly nineteenth-century phenomenon (Heynen 2001; Rice 2004; Benjamin 1999). As Walter Benjamin (1999: 220) remarked, 'The nineteenth century like no other century, was addicted to dwelling.' The domestic sphere as it is received and understood in the twentieth- and twenty-first-century context is dependent on this earlier conception as a distinct and separate sphere that produces the contemporary Euro-American individuated self. The dwelling *per se*, however, is as ancient as humanity itself and just as profoundly implicated, but in distinctly different ways in notions of personhood, society, and cosmology in every time and place. It is for this reason that within social and cultural anthropology that the domestic sphere has such an extraordinary importance for understanding how people are actually made up socially and materially.

To explore the role the domestic sphere has taken in the development of anthropology it is worthwhile to consider the wider historical and intellectual conditions in which it has emerged and then consider a number of key problems that have characterized the anthropological study of the domestic sphere.

***

The home is typically how we know the world and know about people who inhabit the world. It is the key point of orientation for members of a given society as it is to its visitors and outsiders. Classical accounts availed themselves of the insights gained through observations of habitations towards categorizing and understanding different peoples and what it means to be human (Vitruvius 2001). It is also the realm we know the least about especially in highly privatized and individuated Western contexts. As socio-cultural anthropologist Daniel Miller (2001e) has noted, no one really knows what goes on behind closed doors. However, the identification of household and home does not necessarily correspond with what we might otherwise call a dwelling. All too often 'bricks and mortar' are considered as homologous to the lived places in which the elemental forms of personhood are forged. The dwelling becomes reified and in fact emerges as an artefact of our intellectual projects that often loses sight of local conditions and meanings and the nature of the wider productive work that dwelling is engaged in.

HOUSE, HOUSEHOLDS, AND THE EMERGENCE OF ANTHROPOLOGY

Notably in the eighteenth century the primacy and distinct quality of the domestic sphere begins to emerge. This is when the discrete nuclear family is thought to arise with its concomitant understandings of gender, privacy, childhood, and domestic life (Jenks 1996: 65). It is also when, in the spirit of enlightenment era encyclopaedists, that the dwelling becomes the means by which to discern the universal qualities of the human condition. Abbé Laugier in his investigations of 'the primitive hut' attempted to delineate the original forms of human habitation, to place the understanding of architecture and domestic space on Descartean principles of rationality where dwelling, selfhood, and the elemental forms of social life could be understood in terms of universal axioms (Laugier 1977; see also Rykwert 1986). Later the rise of the nation state facilitated the emergence of vernacular studies where the home of the nation and its distinctive character could be produced and sustained. When anthropology as a discipline began to emerge into a systematic social science in the nineteenth century, the home, habitations, and dwellings were the key criterion by which people could be understood and the nature of culture and human kind observed. Lewis Henry Morgan's *House and House-life of the American Aborigines*—originally intended to be part of his monumental study *Ancient Society*, a foundational text for social anthropology—clearly situated the analysis of dwellings and 'house-life' as integral to the systematic study of society and social evolution (Morgan 1881; see Bohannan 1965).

In fact, it was the enormous diversity of human social forms and human habitations that motivated the systematic study of 'house-life' by others before him. The pernicious implications of unilineal evolutionary thought associated with Morgan's work and others have long been rehearsed and rightly criticized. It is worth bearing in mind, however, other liberal impulses that motivated such investigations that in the heyday of unilineal evolutionism—before the rise of diffusionist and culture-historical approaches—championed the Enlightenment era notion of the 'psychic unity' of humankind (Trigger 1989: 100; see also Stocking 1995: 180) over various particularized racialist approaches implicated in emergent romantic nationalist ideologies. What was at stake in these investigations was the understanding of the universal features of humankind at all times and in all places as championed by figures such as Tylor and Morgan. The abstraction of dwellings into characteristic features that were integrated into unilineal systems produced the legible terms by which this unity of humankind could be discerned. Such systems made possible universal understandings of what it means to be human that lie behind such contemporary descendants of this enlightenment era legacy, such as the United Nations Universal Declaration of Human Rights, which ensures the right to housing, property, and privacy—in short the right to home and house-life as part of the elemental preconditions of what it is to be human anywhere and at anytime. These nineteenth-century investigations also provided the context for imagining new forms of social life, inclusion, and social reform notably in the work of Frederick Engels (1940 [1884]) in 'Origin of the family, private property and the state', where, quoting Morgan, Engels envisioned a more socially just future that would be 'a revival, in a higher form, of the liberty, equality and fraternity of the ancient gentes' (Engels 1940: 204).

THE TWENTIETH CENTURY AND CHANGING SIGNIFICANCE OF HOUSE-LIFE, ARCHITECTURE, AND THE DOMESTIC REALM

The disenchantment with unilinealism and ethnology that first emerged with the tradition of Franz Boas in the United States and then later within the tradition of British social anthropology in the 1920s, diminished the significance of architectural forms and material culture studies in general. These areas of research were no longer useful for comparative purposes—increasingly bankrupted in terms of unwieldy positions developed with evolutionary schools and the problematic nature of diffusionist positions emphasizing race especially in the construction of nation states. Anthropology would not look at these material forms again as keenly until the post-war period. In the meantime, vernacular studies of dwellings remained in the nationalist ethnological traditions of nation states with the exception of the Soviet Union. There archaeologists and anthropologists were notably preoccupied with dwellings and house-life both ancient and contemporary within the Marxian theoretical tradition, where such evolutionary perspectives found renewed purchase within Marxian social theory (see Childe 1936; Miller 1956; Trigger 1989; Buchli 2000).

This tradition maintained a certain formalist and typological approach towards the study of house-life. Karl Marx's fossil metaphor characterized this approach to material culture in terms of morphology and functional arrangements: 'Relics of bygone instruments of labour possess the same importance for the investigation of extinct economic forms of society, as do fossil bones for the determination of extinct species of animals' (Marx 1986: 78). This echoed sentiments of the mid-nineteenth-century architectural historian and critic Gottfried Semper, who strove, like Cuvier in anatomy, to find the basic morphological types and forms that lay beneath the diversity of architectural and material forms (Hvattum 2004: 123; see Semper 1989).

If we look at Morgan and then consider later post-war twentieth-century figures such as Rapoport (1969, 1982) and Kent (1984, 1990), then it becomes clear how this systematization and formal analysis of the material conditions of human habitation, lies at the basis of a Western liberal understanding of universal humanism, that in the post-war period when Amos Rapoport and Susan Kent were writing were believed to assure the material terms of universal human dignity and life in modernizing and developmental terms—to create as Kent argues 'productive models [which] will aid us in our understanding not only of present uses of space and built environments, but of those of the past and future as well' (Kent 1990: 151). One might question the terms by which such models were created, their accuracy, and validity across times and peoples. However, what was in fact forged within these descriptions was an understanding of a modernizing universal humanism. If it is in fact the dwelling that creates people then this tradition of social scientific investigation into the common principles of human dwelling created our understanding of the universal human—the very problematic and contested understanding of Man at the heart of anthropology. This encyclopaedic tradition is still very much in force with the publication in 1997 of Paul Oliver's magisterial three-volume set: the *Encyclopedia of Vernacular Architecture of the World*. Here the world's vernacular architectural forms are typologized in a multidisciplinary fashion according to environmental, structural, and technical categories, and social forms, continuing an enlightenment era tradition of accounting for the enormous diversity of human built forms towards the rationalizing and humanistic goal of 'wisely managed . . . solutions to the world's housing needs' (Oliver 1997: xxviii).

This problem of the dwelling and the condition of humanity were probably most eloquently summarized within the philosopher Martin Heidegger's highly influential conception of dwelling. Responding to the plight of post-war reconstruction after World War II and the boom in housing construction and population, Heidegger summarized the problem as such: 'The real plight of dwelling is indeed older than the world wars with their destruction, older also than the increase of the earth's population and the condition of the industrial workers. The real dwelling plight lies in this, that mortals ever search anew for the nature of dwelling that they *must ever learn to dwell*' (Heidegger 1978). Rather than seeing this as a final description of the universal terms in which humans emerge within built forms, Heidegger's emphasis is upon the endless and continuous renegotiation of this problem not its resolution. What was at stake here was the process by which dwelling creates people as a process without end. Rather Heidegger notes humankind's essential and defining homelessness: 'What if man's homelessness consisted in this, that man still does not even think of the *real* plight of dwelling as *the* plight? Yet, as soon as man *gives thought* to his homelessness, it is a misery no longer. Rightly considered and kept well in mind, it is the sole summons that *calls* mortals into their dwelling' (Heidegger 1978).

This understanding of dwelling and 'house-life' as 'process' and technique lies at the heart of the two single most important thinkers on the home within anthropology: the French anthropologists Claude Lévi-Strauss and Pierre Bourdieu. These two followed on in a vein of inquiry going back to the anthropologist Marcel Mauss where architecture is 'the archetypal art, as creation par excellence' (Mauss in Schlanger 2006: 131). Mauss argued forcefully against the abstracted morphological account of housing implicated in the establishment of national traditions and the 'almost comic' efforts invoked at the Versailles Peace Conference after World War I that 'such and such nation should extend here or there, on the grounds that we can still find there such or such shape of house' (Mauss in Schlanger 2006: 43). Instead, Mauss argued for the significance of architectural forms as the key technology by which social life and reproduction are made possible. As such, within this emergent tradition, the idiosyncratic problem solving and dynamic qualities of dwelling were emphasized. In this vein Lévi-Strauss characterized the home as a specific problem solving entity as did Bourdieu with his concept of the dwelling as an *opus operatum* establishing the perspective whereby later sociologists of science such as Gieryn who would see architectural spaces such as labs, institutions, and factories as extensions of this *opus operatum* into what Gieryn calls 'walk through machines' for the production of knowledge (Gieryn 2002: 41)—a reprise of the architect Le Corbusier's metaphor of the 'machine for living' (Le Corbusier 1986). Within Lévi-Strauss' (1982: 155) concept of 'house societies', he notes how the house serves as 'the objectification of a relation: the unstable relation of alliance which, as an institution, the house functions to solidify, if only in an illusory form'. The house as such an illusory objectification serves to reconcile social tensions resulting from the competing interests of descent and alliance. Here Lévi-Strauss gives emphasis to the idea of the house as a deliberate 'fetishisation' or misrecognition of a relationship in the spirit of Marx (Carsten and Hugh-Jones 1995: 8). This misrecognition, however, is a productive one that attempts to negotiate, relieve, and overcome existing tensions towards the creation of a particular form of human life, one that is characterized by dynamic processes over static ones (Carsten and Hugh-Jones 1995: 37).

This aspect of the house's work is further emphasized by Pierre Bourdieu in his famous discussion of the Kabyle house of North Africa, where:

> the house, an *opus operatum*, lends itself as such to a deciphering, but only to a deciphering which does not forget that the 'book' from which the children learn their vision of the world is read with the body, in and through the movements and displacements which make the space within which they are enacted as much as they are made by it.
>
> Bourdieu (1977: 90; see Bourdieu 1970)

As a constitutive entity, the dwelling also shapes our understanding of what is understood as the human body itself. As Carsten and Hugh-Jones have noted in relation to Lévi-Strauss, it is difficult to disentangle to what degree the house is a metaphor for the body or the body the metaphor for the house. Both Carsten and Hugh-Jones go further to describe the dynamic 'process' of houses, as animate: 'they are endowed with spirits and souls' (Carsten and Hugh-Jones 1995: 37), and intimately linked with the process of kinship—constantly reworked and rebuilt— where in fact persons and buildings are nearly impossible to disentangle in relation to one another (see Moore 1986; Preston Blier 1987; see also Harris 1999).

In addition to these approaches formed with anthropology, those within archaeology, geography, and the burgeoning field of vernacular architectures studies emphasized the functionalist and mainly environmental aspects of dwellings that are to this day strongly in evidence in the traditions established by Amos Rapoport (1982) and Paul Oliver (1987). In this tradition, house forms were understood in terms of human processes of adaptation to local environments. Daryll Forde, the founder of the University College London Department of Anthropology and who was closely associated with Boas' students Kroeber and Lowie at Berkeley, paid particular attention to the role of architectural forms and wider technologies, which served as adaptive responses to particular environmental conditions (Forde 1934). Other British social anthropologists such as Radcliffe-Brown and his successor at Oxford, E. E. Evans-Pritchard, laid stress on functionalist explanations in terms of social structure for architectural forms. It was this emphasis on functionalism and technological adaptation, notably developed in the neo-evolutionist work of Leslie White (much inspired by Morgan) that laid the foundation within Anglo-American anthropological and archaeological approaches emphasizing adaptive advantages for cultural and technical forms, along with Julian Steward who emphasized the role of the environment (see Trigger 1989: 290).

However, within British archaeology the subsequent impact of the structuralism of Lévi-Strauss and later that of Bourdieu, in ethnography, emphasized the role of cognitive dimensions rather than environmental factors. Notably the British prehistorian Ian Hodder argued for what he called a domus/agrios cognitive opposition that made possible the terms we later understood in which the Neolithic would emerge in the Middle East and Europe. Here particular emphasis was given to the domus or house-life as a product of sedentization. Hodder's thesis suggested a 'deep' cognitive disposition emergent within conditions before the Neolithic revolution that facilitated this distinctive opposition between the wild and the domestic that sedentism and dwelling mediated. As fixed and stabilized entity in time over many generations in one place, the dwelling served as a means of coping with the dangers and instabilities of life: a cognitive and productive technology with which to constitute and control the 'wild' and its conversion into the cultural through the 'domestic', regulating kinship, economy, and cosmology. Thus, the domus becomes the means by which sedentism and then agriculture could be conceived, with the dwelling as the site of this transformation of these unstable entities, both environmentally, reproductively, and cognitively (Hodder 1990: 38, 291; see also Hodder 1994).

Such an approach in relation to what we might understand as the emergence of a home culture or domus in prehistory in Hodder's work is prefigured by earlier attempts to understand technology, including architecture, as an aspect of mind or 'mentalité' deriving from the French tradition of Emile Durkheim and Marcel Mauss. In particular, with Mauss the convergence of praxis and mind are merged in his notion of techniques and his revival of the term habitus (Mauss in Schlanger 2006: 19) latter taken up by Bourdieu. This tradition was particularly important in the development of approaches to mind, cognition, and technique emphasizing the body, cosmology, and architectural form. This aspect of a bodily, architectural, and cognitive technology is further emphasized in British anthropologist Mary Douglas' work regarding protection, notably hygiene and its relation to architectural space (Douglas 1966). However, it is with figures such as M. Griaule (Griaule and Dieterlen 1954), E. T. Hall (1959), Yi-Fu Tuan (1974)—variously inspired by the phenomenological traditions of Martin Heidegger (1978), Christian Norberg-Schulz

(1971), and Gaston Bachelard (1964)—that the notion of embodied consciousness in relation to the material world and in particular the home and the environment emerges. Other figures such as the American folklorist Henry Glassie inspired by the linguistics of Noam Chomsky could conceive of architectural form as a materialization of mind and deep cognitive structures shaping the perception and intervention within the environment (Glassie 1975).

As the dwelling and body are difficult to distinguish and constitutive of one another, so of course are notions of the mind. Bourdieu is particularly clear about this association:

The mind born of the world of objects does not rise as a subjectivity confronting an objectivity: the objective universe is made up of objects which are the product of objectifying operations structured according to the very structures which the mind applies to it. The mind is a metaphor of the world of objects which is itself but an endless circle of mutually reflecting metaphors.

Bourdieu (1977: 91)

This emphasis on mind is particularly prominent in British anthropologist Alfred Gell's work on the anthropology of art, *Art and Agency* (1998). In fact, the New Zealand Maori meeting house at the end of his discussion is the culmination of his argument for an anthropology of art and the final example of how mind, body, and house are inextricably linked: 'the living members of the community, gathered in the house, were so to speak, only "furnishings". They were mobile appurtenances of its solid enduring structure, into which they would eventually be absorbed as "fixtures"' (Gell 1998: 253). And as mere 'fixtures' they were absorbed into what was the expression of the collective mind of the individual lineage as expressed by a lineage's specific meeting house and its various instantiations over time. But more importantly Gell emphasizes the Maori meeting house as an entity composed of multiple bodies distributed over time and space—the ultimate expression of a distributed artefact and agency and of a collective mind. This is not a dwelling where living people lived but where past and future ancestors dwell—a meeting house where ancestry was forged and sustained towards an ever more magnificent but unrealizable future meeting house (Gell 1998: 257)—a profoundly productive misrecognition and 'illusory objectification' but one in which people were collected, moral persons produced, ancestors forged, and a collective mind could be apprehended.

Within this emergent intellectual tradition a number of key problems have emerged which have preoccupied anthropologists considering the domestic sphere in the latter half of the twentieth century and the early years of the twenty-first. These problems mostly focus on the question of gender, consumption, techniques of governance, the impact of new technologies, and new understandings of the body and its sensual capacities and with them new understandings of what it means to experience and create personhood.

GENDER, SEXUALITY, AND CONSUMPTION

As we could see earlier, the dwelling cannot be disentangled from the body, so the gender and sexuality of that body in whichever form it takes is impossible to conceive outside of the nexus of dwelling. The post-war surge in studies in domestic architectural forms within anthropology, sociology, and architectural history coincided with growing feminism to identify the home as a site of oppression hindering the emancipation of women as fully enfranchised subjects and citizens of modern industrialized societies both socialist and capitalist. Studies of the home within the social sciences and in anthropology provided a means of analysing and pathologizing the problem of the particular nexus of female bodies, sexuality, consciousness, and environment that constituted the gendered subject (Hayden 1981; Moore 1986; Spain 1992; Colomina 1992; Valentine 1993; Sanders 1996; Wigley 2001). Alongside this question of gender, the issue of consumerism in the post-war period was seen as inseparable from gender and integral to the understanding of home in post-war societies, particularly as sites of heightened consumption in post-war economies both socialist and capitalist (see Putnam and Newton 1990; Baudriallard 1996; Miller 2001b). At stake within these analyses is the proper role the domestic realm had in relation to human life as a site of consumption and the terms by which subjectivity was forged within these settings, either as dysfunctional responses to consumer society or as the very terms by which authentic forms of personhood were forged (most notably in the tradition championed by Csikszentmihalyi and Rochberg-Halton 1981; Gullestad 1984; McCracken 1989; Chevalier 1997; Cieraad 1999; Miller 2001e).

GOVERNANCE, FOUCAULT,
AND THE NEO-LIBERAL SUBJECT

The shift in analysis from the formal, structural, and environmentally adaptive qualities of dwelling beginning in the nineteenth century moved to a more intimate analysis of the home as ethnographic site and subject especially in terms of the question of consumption and gender. This intimate scale of analysis was further enhanced by the emergent view of the home as a disciplinary space. Michel Foucault's notion of the material dimensions of governmentality had particular significance for emergent analyses of the home as a space for the constitution of disciplined subjects (Foucault 1970, 1977a, 1986). This was especially so in light of his notion of the panopticon, derived from the work of the utilitarian philosopher Jeremy Bentham, that described how architectural spaces could be productive of a particular body, subjectivity, and mind, which became influential for a number of post-modernist and Marxist approaches (Jameson 1984; Gregory and Urry 1985; Soja 1989; McGuire 1991; Markus 1993; de Certeau 1998).

Of particular relevance to our understanding of the domestic sphere, is the sociologist Nikolaus Rose's elaboration of this Foucauldian tradition and his understanding of the 'psy's'. These are the disciplines of psychology, psychiatry, psychoanalysis, and psychotherapy as aspects of neo-liberal governmentality that focus on what we know of as 'lifestyle' and in particular the domestic realm:

> The ethics of the active choosing self can infuse the 'private' domain that for so long appeared essentially resistant to the rationale of calculation and self-promotion. Through this new mechanism, the social field can be governed through an alliance between the powers of expertise and the wishes, hopes and fears of the responsible autonomous family, committed to maximizing its quality of life and to the success of family members.
>
> Rose (1998: 163)

The home as site of lifestyle pursuit in its seemingly banal nature is part of the neo-liberal contract with state power by which self-governing subjects are constituted. This is the key moral site where 'Contemporary individuals are incited to live as if making a project of themselves: they are to *work* on their emotional world, their domestic and conjugal arrangements, their relations with employment and their techniques of sexual pleasure, to develop a "style" of living that will maximize the worth of their existence to themselves' (Rose 1998: 157). The goal is not to conform with social conventions in which to emerge and be recognized to oneself and others in previous settings but rather to fashion the terms of 'personal happiness and an 'improved quality of life' (Rose 1998: 157)—a project of extreme individuation that is complicit with and formed within the terms of the social contract emerging within neo-liberal forms of governance. But the home is just one site in which 'psy' effects shaping subjectivity emerge, following just one of many vectors into 'the configuration of the home, the gym, the analysts' consulting room' (Rose 1998: 194). Immanent within these configurations and settings, new, authentic, and novel forms of human life begin to emerge.

The home more than anywhere else is the nexus where certain 'psy' disciplines that facilitate governance at a distance are territorialized and given spatial expression. And increasingly it is here at this spatialized nexus of 'psy' territoriality that new exclusions emerge where individuals are unable for various reasons to constitute themselves as self-managing individuals worthy of state attention and intervention (see Buchli and Lucas 2001c; Merry 2001; Ong 2006; Das 2007). But this nexus, which traditionally has been implicated in the isomorphic development of space, consciousness, and subjectivity within Foucauldian frameworks of analysis is reconfigured and considerably less localized and spatialized in its disciplining capacity following multiple and divergent lines and scales. If governance at a distance means moving away from the specific site of the body, the site of governance moves to a new configuration and nexus, which works less on bodies *per se*, but as some have observed, on populations instead. Subjectivity emerges as less spatially and physically coincident, but appears instead disaggregated and imbricated in new and shifting scales. The legal scholar Jonathan Simon refers to such forms of governance at a distance as based on the control of variously defined populations through the assessment of risk in relation to actuarial practices. The result is 'Rather than making people up, actuarial practices unmake them' (Simon 1988: 792). Such practices conspire against the sustenance of the sociologist Émile Durkheim's 'moral densities'. Personhood and home emerge at new, attenuated, multiple, and incoherent scales and spaces within this emergent disciplinary nexus. These are the attenuated and incommensurable scales in which migrant transnational families occupy globalized spaces (see Bauman 2000; Sassen 2006; Ong 2006) or where new forms of excluded life emerge that are forsaken by neo-liberal disciplinary structures of juridical and social self-responsibilization and biomedical rationality (see Desjarlais 1997; Das 2000; Merry 2001; Parrot 2005; see also Low 1997). The traditional scale of analysis focused on the dwelling configured as the discrete and reified architectural artefact—a vestige of our nineteenth-century preoccupation with material forms with which to construct a universal 'psychic unit' of humankind—is not well placed to begin to capture the complexity of these new sorts of spaces, networks, and nexuses in which personhood is forged, experienced, and contested.

NEW TECHNOLOGIES

Hilde Heynen (2001) has argued for the home and the dwelling as the central preoccupation of Modernism and in particular its new technologies. Modernism's principles derived from both capitalist and socialist industry and production were focused on the dwelling and served as the key focus for theorizing this realm in which notions of rationalized production such as Fordism, Taylorism, and the implementation of new industrial technologies were directed and thought through to their fullest capacity in relation to the constitution of the human subject. However, Modernism by its very definition is a break with the stabilities of 'rootedness' and dwelling as Heidegger so aptly diagnosed. The home is thus Modernism's central problem—especially the quality of the unhomely or *unheim-lich* (Vidler 1992). Thus, the preoccupation with dwelling is a preoccupation with the inherent 'homelessness' of the modern subject as observed by Heidegger. It is not the built form itself that is problematic, this is merely an effect, a momentary and unstable resolution of the eternal problem of dwelling.

As has been noted in the histories and sociologies of science, the emergence of new technologies reconfigure the terms by which human subjectivities emerge. The impact of the camera obscura in the sixteenth century and print culture created an understanding of mind, space, and subjectivity within a new sensorium: visual, ocular-centric, introspective, and individuated (see Ong 1967; Crary 1992). The introduction of new technologies during the late twentieth and early twenty-first centuries suggests an entirely new sensorium. The philosopher and critic, Frederic Jameson, had famously noted in reference to the emergence of post-modern architectural forms, 'a mutation in object, unaccompanied as yet by any equivalent mutation in the subject' with 'an imperative to expand our sensorium' (Jameson 1984). The philosophers, Gilles Deleuze and Felix Guattari, at a greater level of abstraction speak of the new flows of space and power emergent in the twentieth century (Deleuze and Guattari 1988). They argue for the constant interplay between 'smooth' and 'striated' spaces. What we might know of as the home is suspended in a constant interplay between these technologically mediated experiences of 'smooth' and 'striated' space. The 'smooth' are the horizontal delocalizing dynamics that break up localized and disciplined space characterized by a fixed home with an address in a planned community within a nation state. 'Smooth' unbounded tendencies wrought by telecommunication, the Internet, new globalized flows of labour, migration, capital, and information break up 'striated' spaces. These are the imbrications of scales described by the geographer and urban critic Saskia Sassen, in which we are increasingly seen to 'dwell' (Sassen 2006).

HOME AND THE SENSES

One of the aspects of the study of home long overlooked is the wider sensual aspect in which it emerges. Visualist, ocularcentric forms of knowledge have long privileged a certain hierarchy of sensual knowledge regarding the home, based primarily on visualized formal data. From Morgan onwards the highly sensual realm of the home in terms of smell, touch, vision, temperature, and feel has been sacrificed to the visual or ocularcentric. Recent studies into the anthropology of the senses (Helliwell 1996; Classen 2005; Howes 2005; Edwards *et al.* 2006) have forcefully argued for a shift in sensorial perspectives. A brief look at the representations in almost all of the key texts mentioned here involves an extraordinary mortification and reduction in the sensorial apprehension of these highly sensual spaces. Mostly these contexts are represented schematically by abstracted drawings (the architectural plan, the archaeological site drawing, etc.). The nineteenth century saw the introduction of photography as a means as well, but one poorly suited towards the production of the generalized visualist abstractions our disciplinary structures require. Such generalizable visual abstractions that the typological drawing represents, inhibits highly localized and other sensual engagements beyond the visual. Notably, 'soundscapes' have emerged as significant areas of research (see Helliwell 1996; Tacchi 1998) where sounds become a means of occupying and dwelling in space often at the expense of the exigencies of other material means. The traditional ethnographic contexts in which house and house-life have been described and configured can only begin to describe what these new configurations are—their scales and dimensions and the general outlines of these newly emergent spaces in which persons and house-life are forged. More significantly, work needs to be directed towards understanding the new and unanticipated forms of exclusion that are increasingly being produced within these emergent disciplinary structures.

Concluding thoughts

There is the danger of fetishizing the object of our analyses: the dwelling itself. The architect's and architectural historian's preoccupation with the technologies and histories of buildings as well as the archaeologist's dependence on the survival of architectural traces at the expense of others, might suggest a certain overdetermination of the home. If the home is overdetermined in terms of the constitution of feminine gender in Euro-American contexts and others, while underdetermined in relation to masculinity, then personhood and the making of people might be obscured by a preoccupation with 'bricks and mortar'. The insights of post-structuralist approaches inspired by Foucault, Jameson, Deleuze, and Guattari, and others suggest that the creation of moral persons is not confined to the material dwelling but is implicated in much more complex configurations and imbrications than might conventionally be realized. This connection and isomorphism of different scales has long been noted since Marx and Engels, Lévi-Strauss, and Bourdieu. However, the movements between these scales and their relationship to one another are particularly complex within the conditions of neo-liberal governance and early twenty-first-century life. The noted fluidity of households, migrants, and the generally fluid ontology of Euro-American terms of personhood (Bauman 2000) require an examination of these complex dynamics.

Recent studies have begun to examine these new configurations. Daisy Froud (2004) has shown how new means of experiencing history, identification, and place are forged within a highly mobile labour market that can be seen as responsible for the creation of 'faux' vernacular traditions. Certainly such contexts are 'false' in terms of conventional understandings of place and history, but are most emphatically 'authentic' in terms of facilitating dwelling. Stability, coherence, and dwelling are achieved through a variety of novel means. Julie Botticello (2007) examines how the site for the production of authentic moral personhood shifts from the market spaces inhabited by immigrant Nigerians in London to the domestic realm for their first generation children. While Patrick Laviolette and Julienne Hanson (2007) discuss the imbrications of elderly people's private homes with state-run hospitals through new surveillance technologies, where state institutions, technology, the body, and the architectural space of the home become entangled in novel ways. Jean-Sebastian Marcoux (2004) argues how personhood, gender, and place are forged within the leasing structures of the Montreal property market. And Diana Young describes the fluidity of the London property market where value is achieved through colour namely whiteness, which enhances the fluidity and value of property at the expense of inalienable authentic space. Stability seems to be produced elsewhere through mortgage investment vehicles and life insurance rather than within the material and moral density of the home (Young 2004). While Sarah Pink and Anna Martinez Perez (2006) discuss how earlier forms of commensality forging kinship and home are replaced by taxis and Internet-mediated food exchanges in urban Spain producing novel means by which traditional forms of moral personhood increasingly are achieved.

The home is nonetheless still very much a common object of analysis to which we are rightly committed, but it is increasingly complex, fluid, and unstable. Anthropology's traditional intimacy with its ethnographic subjects, which brought out the significance of the dwelling as the most meaningful ocular of analysis as suggested by Bourdieu's *opus operatum*, is still very relevant and useful for understanding the nature of dwelling and house-life within these increasingly complex emergent settings. As Jonathan Crary (1992) has noted elsewhere, innovations in technology and vision facilitated distinct understandings of the domestic, in relation to cognition and mind when discussing the impact of the stereoscope on the nineteenth-century bourgeois interior. The impacts of current new technologies have yet to begin to describe how this relationship is reconfigured with some notable exceptions just mentioned. House-life also needs to be reconsidered in relation to the impacts of financial instruments used to constitute dwelling, such as mortgages, tax regimes, and actuarial practices. Also yet to be fully appreciated and understood are the impacts of migration, and the increasing fluidity of home occupation and the ways viable human subjects are conceived and sustained within such settings and their attendant concepts of dwelling, which exceed 'bricks and mortar' and their imbrications in new configurations and dimensions.

This issue of the new configurations in which house-life is set must be understood in relation to other sites, spaces, and institutions. This is particularly relevant in terms of the observations made regarding the emerging spaces of techno-science. Historically the spaces of techno-science can be seen to emerge within settings we would otherwise call domestic only to diverge into distinctive and segregated spaces over time. Recent changes collapse and muddle these distinctions once held apart but that were earlier together. Laboratory spaces and hospital spaces developed into specialized spaces of control, docility, and asepsis (Schlich 2007). While increasingly homes emerge equally as similar spaces of control and asepsis through surveillance devices, gated communities, computer-regulated 'smart' homes, and anti-bacterial cleaning regimes. The hospital, laboratory, and home merge, with the introduction of new medical surveillance technologies extending the hospital into the home (Laviolette and Hanson 2007) or the hospital itself becomes a domestic site with living areas, as well as a site for consumption with facilities familiar from shopping malls (Schlich 2007). Telecommuting, home offices, and even home factory production made possible by new technologies such as three-dimensional printing confound those distinctions that once made the domestic a discrete and coherent site.

As the anthropologist Veena Das has noted, there is no point in finding the unified and homologous site of subjectivity which might have been traditionally understood within the context of dwelling, rather, this subjectivity is dispersed 'over various sites, statuses, and positions' (Das 2000: 263, see also Das and Addlakha 2001). This is what Das and Addlakha describe as 'the delicate work of the creation as well as separation of different body selves through which the subject is made and remade' (Das and Addlakha 2001: 529). As the notion of subjectivity can no longer be thought of in any unitary fashion under conditions of post-modernity neither can its homologue of dwelling be understood in similar ways. An overarching language to describe this is not possible; however, a description of the differences and nexuses in which they emerge and are entailed is. Das speaks about 'voice' as lament and testimony to unspoken violence in post-partition India, which provides a means of bridging in an embodied fashion hierarchies of discourse that separate the domestic from the public and state, and thereby offer a momentary coherence (Das 2007). Similarly, Simon speaks to the situated and novel coherences class action suits enable, that counter the 'unmaking' of subjects disaggregated into 'populations' of actuarial control within Western forms of neo-liberal governance (Simon 1988). As the philosopher of science Bruno Latour recently suggested in reference to Heidegger's understanding of the fourfold and the gathering of elements it performs, this gathering needs to be expanded to consider the wider scales and assemblages that produce scientific knowledge (Latour 2007). Similarly, the possibilities of new technologies and regimes of control in relation to the question of dwelling require us to rethink new forms of life and new ways of being emerging in the present.

These understandings do not positionally reject the site of the home nor deny the domestic and the isomorphic understandings of home, place, landscape, and body that we might have understood in the past. There still remains a strong ontological, institutional, and political commitment to this site. However, following Sassen, this site is radically reconfigured within these new nexuses that belie our commonsensical ideas of place and home. The moral and material densities that the site of the home produces through co-presence are refigured in terms of propinquity that denies this conventional material isomorphism. That is, they facilitate nearness spatially, relationally, and socially within new media such as the Internet, mobile telephony, GPS systems etc. as well as within the traditional nexus of 'bricks and mortar' and Heidegger's fourfold of mortals, divinities, earth, and sky, where dwelling begins to emerge in ever new and divergent ways. This is a shift and reconfiguration in our understanding of the Durkheimian 'material densities' that shape our 'moral densities' of social life (Durkheim in Schlanger 2006: 5).

If the thesis of the psychic unity of human beings failed within nineteenth-century universalizing schemas in the face of unwieldy diversity and then nationalist ideologies, then the very fluid, fragile, contingent, and agonistic terms in which human being is shaped within the material circumstances of early twenty-first-century life needs to be reconsidered. Indeed, the very failure of these terms to ever cohere and the eternal dilemma of learning to dwell, established by Heidegger, becomes in fact the possibility by which the universal might be reinvested, not as a norm but as what the philosopher Judith Butler describes as a 'necessary failure' that ensures inclusiveness. As she once noted: 'This failure to fill the place, however, is precisely the futural promise of universality, its status as a limitless and unconditional feature of all political articulation' (Butler 2000: 32).

PART V

STUDYING PARTICULAR THINGS

CHAPTER 23

STONE TOOLS

RODNEY HARRISON

INTRODUCTION: MAKING AS COPYING

The history of stone tool research is linked integrally to the history of archaeology and the study of the human past, and many of the early developments in archaeology were connected with the study of stone artefacts (Odell 2003: 1). The identification of stone tools as objects of prehistoric human manufacture was central to the development of nineteenth-century models of prehistoric change, and especially the Three Age system for Old World prehistory (Stone Age, Bronze Age, Iron Age; see Trigger 1989: 73–79). During the twentieth century, however, a narrow focus upon prehistoric technology meant that the formulation of models that describe the processes by which stone artefacts are produced and discarded has formed the principal goal of stone tool studies. This tradition produced, for example, the analysis of the 'reduction sequences' of the steps through which a tool was created from a stone core and Michael Schiffer's model of five steps in what he termed the 'life cycle of durable elements' such as worked stone: from procurement to manufacture, use, maintenance, and discard (Schiffer 1972: 158; 1976). In Schiffer's terms, once a stone tool was discarded, it moved from 'systemic context' to 'archaeological context', it became inert, and its abandonment as a tool that was no longer functionally useful represented the end of its efficacy or significance (Figure 23.1). While such models have been very important in contributing to a greater understanding of the social and material processes involved in the production of stone tools, they have drawn attention away from any aspects of the efficacy of stone tools that do not relate to their production and use.

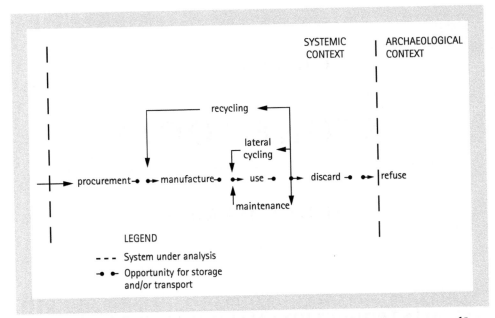

Fig. 23.1 Michael Schiffer's five steps in the life cycle of durable elements (from Schiffer 1972).

In contrast, in this chapter I draw on concepts derived from interdisciplinary material culture studies to consider the role of the artefact *after* discard. I suggest that it is impossible to understand the meaning or efficacy of stone tools without understanding their 'afterlives' following abandonment. Where the concept of *social* agency has recently been mobilized to attempt to explain the efficacy of stone tools, I argue that it is only when we consider stone tools as embodying *material* agency of their own (rather than remaining passive players in a series of social relations that are entirely determined by human actors) that we will develop new understandings of the role of stone tools and other material objects in both the past and present. In doing so, the chapter aims to complement contemporary metrical studies of the identification of stone tools and the description of their production (see Odell 2000, 2001, 2003; Holdaway and Stern 2004; Andrevsky 2005; Clarkson and O'Connor 2006). Such studies make important contributions to archaeological knowledge, but on their own will lead to accounts that focus only upon production, at the expense of consumption, such as those that have been widely discussed in anthropological material culture studies (Douglas and Isherwood 1979; Miller 1987, 1995a, 1998c). Moreover, metrical studies have often tended to privilege a particular attitude to manufacture, in which a mental design is imposed upon the material to create the form of the artefact. Instead of seeing the creation of artefacts as involving the transcription of a design from a previous mental template in this manner, I want to follow the suggestion of anthropologist Tim Ingold that artefact forms 'grow' like organisms, generated from complex interactions between the artefact-maker, their social and natural environment, and the raw materials themselves:

form-making involves a precise co-ordination of perception and action that is learned through copying the movements of experienced practitioners in socially scaffolded contexts. Making, in other words *is* copying; it is not the realisation of a design that has been copied . . . Whatever variations may be introduced in the process lie in the dynamics of the making, not in errors of transmission.

Ingold (2000a: 372)

Moving away from the 'mental template' model of artefact manufacture directs our attention towards the network of both physical and social relationships in which things are bound up, and towards practices of making, copying, and repetition over time. In the case of stone tools, such perspectives may be used to probe those aspects of the life histories of stone artefacts that have been most neglected in archaeology: the ongoing influence of stone artefacts after they cease to be 'functionally' useful, and the material agency of artefacts. After a review of the history of stone artefact studies in archaeology, the chapter draws on insights into the material agency of stone tools from two arenas: cultural heritage management, and the study of museum collections. These two fields allow us to consider the interaction between objects from the past, and people (and other objects) in the present. The survival of objects across time periods is what makes archaeology possible, and stone tools are among the most durable of archaeological materials. However, an awareness of such survival or 'residuality' in the contemporary world has not always been well integrated in archaeological analyses, even by those with an explicit interest in the idea of 'the past in the past' (cf. Bradley 2002). Can the meaning and social role of a stone artefact continue to change not only during the course of its 'life history' with each transformation in its cycle of use, but also after it has been discarded? By working through the changing meanings of prehistoric stone artefacts in the modern world, we may also rethink how we study the meaning and material agency of stone artefacts in the past.

A BRIEF HISTORY OF STONE TOOL STUDIES IN ARCHAEOLOGY

The ability to correctly identify humanly modified stone tools forms a fundamental facet of modern archaeology (Odell 2003: 1). As Gosden (1999, 2004b) notes, the recognition of stone tools as the result of human behaviour was directly linked to the encounters of Europeans with stone artefact using peoples in the early modern period, and the records of colonial encounters with stone artefact producing peoples has become a source for archaeological study in the present (e.g. McBryde 1978; Gould 1980). Stone tools were collected along with other 'curios' in both the Old and New Worlds by amateur collectors, naturalists, and enthusiasts, who were engaged as much as their academic counterparts in the production of a 'historical imagination' (Griffiths 1996: 1), which led to the development of archaeology as a profession. In addition to influencing popular ideas about the human past through their collections, eighteenth- and nineteenth-century antiquarianism can be seen to have contributed to a more sinister uncoupling of Indigenous peoples from the material remnants of their past (Byrne 1998), and concepts of 'otherness', which were integral to the culture of colonialism (Thomas 1994).

The earliest systematic analyses of stone tools were undertaken by antiquarians in the late nineteenth century, such as John Evans in England and France, and William Henry Holmes in the United States (Evans 1872; Holmes 1894; see Lucas 2001a: 67). Evans and Holmes noted the potential of stone tools as chronological markers, and undertook research into the form and function of stone artefacts and their processes of manufacture and use (Andrevsky 2005: 3–4). This early research was dominated by the idea that stone tools represented not only chronological, but also *cultural*, markers that provided evidence for the evolution of increased cultural diversity. Holmes' work was particularly influential in highlighting the process of tool manufacture, especially in his suggestion that crudely shaped bifaces represented tools in earlier stages of the production process rather than simply poorly made tools (Odell 2003: 3). Despite this, it was not until the late 1930s that Alfred Barnes (1939) published the now commonly accepted criteria for distinguishing humanly modified stone artefacts from naturally fractured stone, which derived from his study of the edge angles produced by human processes of stone fracture and a comparison with the edge angles of stone fractured naturally.

An important concept that came to dominate stone tool research throughout the twentieth century was developed by the French archaeologist André Leroi-Gourhan, who was concerned with documenting the chain of processes by which raw materials were selected and transformed into cultural artefacts. A student of anthropologist, Marcel Mauss, during the 1950s he drew on his teacher's discussion of 'techniques' as socially transmitted aspects of the *habitus* and combined them with the work of early archaeologists such as Holmes to suggest a more process-oriented approach to the study of technology. In *La Geste et La Parole*, Leroi-Gourhan (1964: 164) coined the term *chaîne opératoire* and defined it in terms of 'techniques [that] involve both gestures and tools, organised in a chain by a veritable syntax that simultaneously grants to the operational series their fixity and their flexibility' (cf. Schlanger 2005: 27). This process-oriented approach was seen as having major implications for the study not only of individual technologies, but also of societies and technical processes at a variety of spatial and chronological scales. The concept of the *chaîne opératoire* was further developed by Pierre Lemonnier (1986, 1992), who drew a distinction between 'strategic tasks' (fixed operations that cannot be altered in timing or sequence without sabotaging the entire process) and 'technical variants' (flexible choices that are arbitrary in terms of the outcome of the *chaîne opératoire* but that nonetheless have cultural or social implications). The idea of the *chaîne opératoire* was also implicit in the stages of stone tool production suggested by Schiffer in the 1970s and discussed earlier in this chapter.

Research on the *chaîne opératoire* of stone tool manufacture stimulated an interest in the individual mechanical processes involved in the production of particular stone tools in the past. The 1950s and 1960s saw sustained stone tool reproduction experiments by archaeologists such as François Bordes and Don Crabtree, which informed the subsequent development of reduction sequence analysis (e.g. Bradley 1975) and tool refitting research. Taken together, experimental flint knapping and ideas such as the *chaîne opératoire*, reduction sequence analysis, or Schiffer's (1972) stages of production promoted a particular view of the 'life history' of the stone tool, which was related to the manufacture and use of stone tools. The dominant paradigm during this period stressed the close association of stone artefacts' *form* with *function*, allowing the role of a stone tool to be 'read' through the study of its morphological characteristics.

Meanwhile, another area of stone tool studies sought to move beyond purely morphological analyses. Sergei Semenov's 1957 study *Prehistoric Technology*, which was translated into English in 1964, was influential in suggesting that stone tool *morphology* did not always coincide with stone tool *function* (see Semenov 1964). He demonstrated the possibility of the functional analysis of stone tool edges using microscopy through the magnification and recording of the working edges of stone tools, which led to the development of use–wear and residue studies in contemporary archaeology (Andrevsky 2005: 4). The study of microscopic use–wear and residues grew throughout the 1980s and 1990s to become one of the dominant areas of metrical stone tool analysis in archaeology. In an influential paper, George Frison (1968) built on the ideas put forward much earlier by Holmes in relation to Palaeolithic stone axes to suggest that if artefact morphology changed during a stone tool's use life, then stone tool typologies would have to reflect these changes if they are to be useful in determining chronology, site function, and patterns of site use. Frison's work, combined with other developments in the New Archaeology of the 1960s, led to archaeologists perceiving a stone tool's form as dynamic throughout its use. These developments saw a shift away from the correlation of archaeological tool types with prehistoric cultures that characterized culture-historical archaeology, and challenged the widely accepted view that artefact shape was a direct correlate of artefact function (Andrevsky 2005: 5). Odell (2000: 47–48) describes the ways in which this idea influenced the study of projectile points from the Great Basin region in North America during the 1980s and 1990s. Here, the extent to which reworking of broken projectile points can be seen to have given rise to 'new' projectile point forms, which were represented in traditional typological analyses as separate point forms, had been widely debated.

The study of the exchange, rather than simply the production and use, of stone tools has also been a major area of archaeological research since the 1970s. The increasing use of geophysical and geochemical methods in archaeology has led to developments in determining the source of stone used in the manufacture of stone tools. This has then led to a greater understanding of trading networks and the circulation of both stone tools and stone raw materials in prehistory, for example in the study of the wide-ranging trade in obsidian for the production of stone tools in the European Neolithic (e.g. Torrence 1986). Ethnoarchaeological studies have been important both in allowing deeper insights into technological processes of stone tool manufacture (e.g. Gould 1980) as well as the meaning of stone tools within the societies that manufacture them (e.g. Jones and White 1988). For example, Bradley and Edmonds (1993) documented the changing nature and context of the production and exchange of stone axes, which was based on a study of one of the largest sources of raw materials for stone axe manufacture in Britain.

George Odell (2000, 2001) has suggested that the systematic study of stone tools in the last two decades of the twentieth century focused on two main areas, procurement (understanding the pursuit and trade of raw materials) and technology (understanding the various processes that contribute to the production of stone tools). This involved research on the areas of artefact classification (including stone tool typology, debitage analysis, use–wear and residue studies), the study of behavioural processes (including subsistence strategies, risk minimalization, and trade) and conceptual approaches (models that help archaeologists explain their data, including approaches that foreground gender and aspects of design theory). Despite this proliferation of methods and approaches over the 1980s and 1990s it is possible to say that throughout the twentieth century, the formulation of systems that described the *processes* by which stone tools were produced and discarded in the past had formed the fundamental goal of stone tool analysis.

AGENCY AND 'INTERFERENCE'

The emergent interest in symbolism, ideology, and individual choice that accompanied the development of interpretive archaeologies during the 1980s and 1990s (e.g. Shanks and Hodder 1995) stimulated the development of new conceptual approaches and a new-found interest in the symbolic aspects of stone as a raw material (e.g. Ingold 1990; Sinclair 1995; Tilley 2004). About the same time, a new interest in stone tools as markers of gender also emerged (Gero 1991; Sassaman 1992; Dobres 1995). However, due to the widespread adoption of a semiotic approach to emphasize artefacts as a series of signs, critics (e.g. Dobres 2000; Dobres and Robb 2000b; and more generally Thomas 1995, 1996) noted that such approaches tended to downplay the experience of those who made, used, and consumed stone tools. This new focus on meaning produced an effective rift between those studies concerned with the technical aspects of stone tool production and those that focused on stone tools as symbols.

In an attempt to shift the paradigm in stone artefact studies away from the split between symbolic and technical aspects of stone tool manufacture and use, several researchers began to employ the concept of 'social agency'. The relationship between human agency and historical structures was developed by Pierre Bourdieu (1990; see also Robbins 1991) and Anthony Giddens (1982, 1984). Bourdieu argued that practice was conditioned by the *habitus*, a system of historically produced structuring dispositions. The *habitus* varies between individuals, and action mediated by the *habitus* is instinctive and regulated (Robbins 1991). Bourdieu utilizes the metaphor of a sport, where players have a 'feel for the game' that equips them to pursue conscious strategies (see discussion in Last 1995): 'One's feel for the game is not infallible; it is shared out unequally between players, in a society as a team' (Bourdieu 1990: 86).

Anthony Giddens developed the theory of 'structuration' to account for the same problem. The concept of structuration is similar to the *habitus* in that it describes the set of conditions that intervene between structure and practice to allow the reproduction or transformation of that structure. Social practice (or agency) and social structure are linked dialectically. Structures form a medium for practice by both enabling and constraining it, while at the same time they are the outcome of human agency and are reproduced or transformed by it (Shanks and Tilley 1992: 128). It is the high degree of routine in practice that ensures continuity in action. Both change and stability are outcomes of the reproduction of social practice. Agents generate power through being able to mobilize both material and productive resources—power 'is generated in and through the reproduction of structures of dominance' (Giddens 1984: 258). Social change tends to occur at the 'time-space edges' between different sets of routinized structures and practices (Last 1995: 152).

In her study of *Technology and Social Agency*, archaeologist Marcia-Anne Dobres (2000) drew on the work of Anthony Giddens and Pierre Bourdieu to describe the ways in which technologies entail social relationships and engender meaning. For Dobres, it is human agents and their social relations that are central to the everyday reproduction of their social conditions. People experience technology and material culture as physical arenas within which interactions, both material and social, occur as they undertake practical or material action. Hence both people and the material world simultaneously constitute, shape, and are shaped by one another (Dobres 2000: 127).

Technologies are socially constructed practices through which material objects develop their own life histories, taking on a multiplicity of meanings. They are also the means of bodily engagement with the world, and in the process, producers become social products. A recursive process binds together human actors, products, artefacts, landscapes, materials, and meaning—'agency and practice are no less the heart and soul of human technology' (Dobres 2000: 128). Thus, material objects are also involved in the complex web of agency and structure, as conduits through which human actors produce and are produced by their interactions with other agents and the world.

Social agency has been seen as problematic in stone artefact studies, not the least reason being because stone artefacts have often remained apparently static in their form throughout long periods in the past (Wobst 2000; Sassaman 2000). How are we to see the influence of individual social actors and agency faced with an *absence* of change in technology over millennia? Archaeologist Martin Wobst suggests that this stasis itself should actually be seen as quite remarkable, given, for example, the widespread effort to manufacture stylistically identical stone artefacts using raw materials with extremely different flaking properties. For Wobst (2000: 47), such periods of stasis should be seen as the most socially and politically contentious, as they involve the most effort to maintain and control the *habitus* by prehistoric peoples (cf. Wobst 1974).

Thus, Wobst emphasizes the ways in which stone artefacts, like other kinds of material objects, could in the past form reference points in the ways in which humans choose to behave and respond to particular circumstances in the past. The production of artefacts can be thought of as an 'interference' in a particular situation, the intentional insertion of a material object into a circumstance that the artefact maker wished to influence or change by doing so (Wobst 2000: 42). We can think about such interferences as being made with reference to both the physical and social world. Indeed, Wobst (2000: 48) suggests that the development of stone artefacts in the Lower Palaeolithic can be conceptualized as establishing the possibility of forms of interference that stressed and expressed social difference, which have remained unresolved throughout human history.

These various ideas about stone artefacts and social agency establish certain parameters for the study of the life histories of stone artefacts, and in particular their 'afterlives'. I use the term 'afterlife' to define the period after which a stone tool ceases to be functionally useful, after which it would most usually be discarded, but at which point it may also be curated or subsequently lay dormant before being 'rediscovered' at some point in the future. One problem with these studies of social agency in stone tool production and use is that, just like the metrical analyses described above, they tend to focus almost entirely on the experience of production and tool use, rather than on other moments in the life histories of stone tools.

Indeed, the focus on agency in stone tool studies has done little to move beyond the focus on the process of stone tool manufacture, maintenance, and discard embodied in the *chaîne opératoire* and Schiffer's model of the five steps in the life cycle of durable elements. They adopt ideas from the work of Frison and others, which suggest that changes in form relate to different phases in the cycle of stone artefact use. Further, they draw on the work of interpretive archaeologies to suggest that the *meaning* of artefacts can change according to their passing from one context to another. However, these approaches to agency in the study of stone tools have tended to depict stone tools themselves as largely passive—the agency they describe is purely *social agency*. In the rest of the chapter, I want to explore some ideas about *material agency* and the ways in which they might inform our understanding of the relevance of the afterlives of stone tools in both past and contemporary societies.

MATERIAL AGENCY AND THE 'CAPTIVATION' OF STONE TOOLS

In this section, I want to explore the idea of the efficacy of artefacts beyond production and functional use, with reference to social anthropologist Alfred Gell's (1992b, 1996b, 1998) idea of 'captivation' or 'enchantment'. The anthropological perspectives on material culture developed by the late Alfred Gell provide a very useful way of thinking through the social efficacy of artefacts. Gell presents a model in which material objects can mediate the social agency of humans, acting as the 'indexes' of this agency, as 'material entities that motivate inferences, responses, or interpretations' (Thomas 1998: ix). The theory of the 'art nexus' describes the mediation of agency by way of a series of 'agent–patient' relationships that are described according to four main referents that are said to exist in the vicinity of objects: artists, indexes, prototypes, and recipients. For Gell (1998: 26), the social relations that surround artefacts can only exist when they are made manifest in the form of actions. Those people or things that perform social actions are agents with reference to those things on which they perform social action, which are known as patients. Drawing on Marilyn Strathern's (1988) concept of the distributed person in Melanesian anthropology, Gell explains the way in which objects become part of the distributed personhood of the 'artist'—the person who is considered to be responsible in the first instance for the existence of the index, or art object (cf. Wagner 1991). Thus for Gell (1998: 222–223), humans are not confined to a spatial or temporal framework particular to their physical body, 'but consist of a spread of biographical events and memories of events, and a dispersed category of material objects, traces and leavings, which can be attributed to a person and which, in aggregate, testify to agency and patienthood during a biographical career which may, indeed, prolong itself long after biological death'.

Gell distinguishes between the *primary* agency of intentioned and conscious actors, and the *secondary* agency of objects. He uses the gruesome example of the land mines placed by Pol Pot's soldiers (Gell 1998: 20–21), describing them as components both of Pol Pot's personhood, as well as objects that function as secondary agents (in the sense in which they are not sentient, so can only initiate agency with reference to another external agent). Gell sees the land mines as not simply tools used by a soldier, but as part of the material index that defines the soldiers' 'soldier-ness'. The guns and land mines carried by the soldiers are 'a part of' the soldier and act to define the soldier as such. To speak of Pol Pot's soldiers is also to speak of the weapons, military tactics, and their social context. The land mines *themselves* do not initiate happenings or actions 'through acts of will for which they are morally responsible', but nonetheless are 'objective embodiments of the power or capacity to will their use' (Gell 1998: 21).

Discounting an 'aesthetic' model for understanding art and art objects, Gell acknowledges the special kind of agency exhibited by particular art objects, which are:

made with technical expertise and imagination of a high order, which exploit the intrinsic mechanisms of visual cognition with subtle psychological insight, then we are dealing with a canonical form of artistic agency which deserves special discussion ... with artefacts which announce themselves as miraculous creations ... their power rests partly on the fact that their origination is inexplicable except as a magical, supernatural occurrence.

Gell (1998: 68)

Gell (1992b) had previously described the concept of captivation in relation to the efficacy of the prow boards of Trobriand canoes as psychological 'weapons' in ceremonial *kula* exchanges. He argued that the impressive carvings present on prow boards were considered to be magically potent, establishing a sense of inequality between the exchange partners who were viewing the boards for the first time, and the artist(s) who carved them. While 'captivated' by the virtuoso carvings, the trading partners were weakened and engaged in unequal exchanges to the benefit of the artist(s). 'Captivation or fascination—the demoralization produced by the spectacle of unimaginable virtuosity—ensues from the spectator becoming trapped within the index because the index embodies agency which is essentially indecipherable' (Gell 1998: 71).

In *Art and Agency* Gell (1998: 69) describes the 'captivation' of Vermeer's painting *The Lacemaker* as embodied by an inability to conceive of the possibility of producing the artwork. While we can imagine how to mix the paint and move brush over canvas, the technical proficiency of the painting defies our imagination, or more accurately, our ability to conceive a resemblance of our agency to the agency that originated the artwork. This is not simply a case of aesthetic impact (Bolton 2001: 101), but relates to a 'blockage in cognition', which manifests itself at the point when a spectator cannot reconstruct or follow the sequence of steps in an artist's performance. Captivation is 'produced by the spectacle of unimaginable virtuosity' in which the index 'embodies agency which is essentially indecipherable' (Gell 1998: 71). As Bolton (2001: 101) notes, captivation is 'a special kind of agency effected through performance, and embodying indecipherability'.

KIMBERLEY POINTS AS CAPTIVATING OBJECTS

I would like to turn now to how these ideas about the agency of material things, which possess the power to 'captivate' or 'enchant', might be employed to help us to understand the efficacy of stone tools in their afterlives. Figure 23.2 shows a Kimberley Point from the collection of the Pitt Rivers Museum in Oxford, UK. It is labelled with an accession number [1898.75.29], and its accession book entry, dated 1898, identifies it as one of four glass Kimberley Points that were sold to the museum by the collector Emile Clement along with another 109 ethnographic specimens from north-western Australia for which the museum paid £11.0.0. It is one of at least 24 Kimberley spear points, most of them made using glass, which

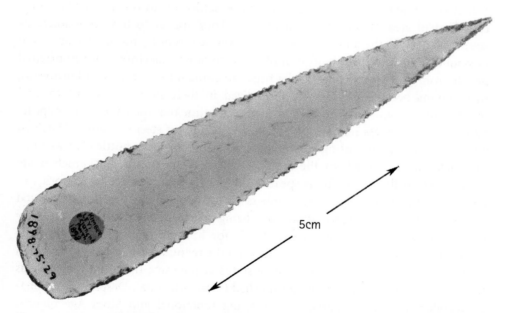

Fig. 23.2 Glass Kimberley Point from the collection of the Pitt Rivers Museum in Oxford, collected by Emile Clement (courtesy of Pitt Rivers Museum, University of Oxford, accession number 1898.75.29).

were obtained by the Pitt Rivers Museum over the period 1898 to 1953. Emile Clement made at least three trips to Western Australia over the period 1895–1900, during which time he amassed a large collection of ethnographic and botanical specimens that he subsequently sold to museums and collectors throughout the UK. We know something of his collecting activities as he published a series of notes and ethnographic observations, along with a catalogue of the objects he collected in a short treatise in 1904 (Clement 1904). While it is possible to understand the social agency involved in the acquisition of glass as a raw material from Europeans within the context of the Australian colonial frontier, the subsequent agency of the toolmaker in producing the tool, and the agency involved in the transactions by which Clement acquired and subsequently sold the point, we might think that its curation within the Pitt Rivers Museum would represent the certain end point of its efficacy as a tool. Lying inert on a dusty museum shelf, surely it cannot be understood to continue to have material or social agency and involve itself in social relations as an actor?

What is clear is that in fact glass Kimberley points *did* continue to have a form of agency after they were collected and removed from their context of manufacture and use. We can use Gell's ideas about the captivation of art objects to help us to interpret the agency of stone and glass spear points from the Kimberley region of Western Australia (Harrison 2006). Bifacially pressure-flaked 'Kimberley' points were a specialized stone tool form, which only began to be manufactured approximately one millennium before Europeans first settled in Australia in a geographically limited area of Australia's north west. They appear to have functioned as spearheads, but in the nineteenth and early twentieth century more often appeared in symbolic gift exchanges and in trade with colonial collectors. After Aboriginal people from north-western Australia began to come into contact with Europeans, these points became increasingly formalized in their shape, grew in size, and became increasingly finely worked at the precise time that their function as spearheads became far less relevant due to the availability of steel and guns (Harrison 2004a). They were increasingly manufactured using European bottle glass as a raw material, which allowed for the manufacture of larger points, but which made them functionally less useful as spearheads. They also appear, contradictorily, to have been made in the greatest numbers on settlements and reserves associated with Europeans, where food rations were being provided, and they would arguably be less necessary as functional spearheads for hunting land game. Within the groups that manufactured them, points (and the manufacture of points) acquired new meanings as symbols of masculine status at the same time that their role as functional spearheads was being diminished (Harrison 2002). Despite the emphasis of collectors and antiquarians on collecting 'functional' and 'Stone Age' objects, these 'replicas' of stone spearheads made using glass were collected widely in colonial Australia, and circulated in large numbers among museums and collectors across the globe. More recently, despite archaeologists' awareness that the form of these particular large, symmetrically pressure flaked bifacial point forms were related more to the demands of a colonial art market than the functional needs of Aboriginal Australians, they have gained an important space in disciplinary self-representations of Australian Aboriginal prehistory. For example, Australian archaeologists have often used images and descriptions of Kimberley Points to represent Australian Aboriginal stone tool technology in general. This is despite the fact that it is widely known that the large invasive bifaces, which were made for trade with Europeans in the late nineteenth and early twentieth century, were largely an invention for the colonial curio market. Elsewhere (2006) I described the use of the generic term 'stone tool' in museum displays of Kimberley Points in Australia. This is despite the fact that this rather specialized form of stone (and more importantly, glass) working technology has relatively little in common with the majority of prehistoric Aboriginal stone tool technology from Australia.

Gell's ideas about the captivation or enchantment of virtuoso objects help to explain the ways in which Kimberley Points acted as agents in distracting and enthralling both colonial collectors and antiquarians in the past, as well as their continued role in captivating archaeologists in the present. Their apparently mysterious method of manufacture and the extremely fine working of these spear points both metaphorically and physically 'dazzled' colonial collectors, but even after their method of manufacture had been discerned, they presented a paradox to antiquarians—a delicately worked glass *objet d'art* manufactured using 'Stone-Age' technologies. This clever contradiction allowed them to find a market among those antiquarians and museums who were primarily interested in 'authentic', 'prehistoric' objects, who might normally have passed them over as souvenirs created for a collector's market. Not only does such an analysis reveal the ingenious engagement of Indigenous Australians with a late nineteenth-century global colonial curio market, but also the ongoing agency of these spear points themselves as they continue to enthral and captivate archaeologists and a museum-going public in the present.

Beyond Social Agency: Heritage, Politics, and the Material Agency of Stone Tools in the Contemporary World

One of the main criticisms of Gell's model of captivation (see Layton 2003) has been the way in which it minimizes the importance of an individual's cultural background in determining their 'reading' of art objects. Indeed, much of the subsequent research that has employed aspects of Gell's model has discussed the ways in which individuals within particular societies are socialized to receive particular kinds of material 'messages' as a starting point (e.g. Campbell 2001; Küchler 2002b). Understanding the ways in which an individual is socially conditioned to receive particular messages from artefacts has largely been understood to form a necessary starting point for any consideration of the efficacy or agency of stone tools (or indeed any material object). This idea is also an integral aspect of the approaches to social agency in stone tools discussed above (e.g. Dobres 2000; Wobst 2000).

A recent critique of Gell's ideas by James Leach (2007) suggests that it is only if we take the direct opposite approach to that suggested by Layton that we could ever allow the sort of *material* agency that appears to be a part of the concept of captivation or enchantment to be understood. Leach argues that it is impossible for objects themselves to have agency if we assume that all objects are necessarily an index of something else. This notion appears in Gell's discussion of the 'abduction' of agency, or the mediation of agency by way of a series of agent–patient relationships as described above. Leach perhaps more helpfully refers to this as the 'artist–author' relationship, in which the creativity embodied by an artwork (or artefact) is assumed to wholly reside within the artist, and not within a distributed network that might involve the materials he or she uses to create the artwork, and the creative tension of the circumstances within which it is made, or within the artwork itself. He suggests that Gell's anthropological theory of art should be seen as essentially flawed, as it places primary agency only in the hands of human actors (or 'artists' in Gell's words) who are seen as the ultimate starting point in the chain of agent–patient relationships he describes. It is only when we effectively admit that an artefact or art object might have primary agency of its own that we can use the distinctive life histories of material objects to generate innovative critical positions and alternate models of the efficacy or agency of stone tools. 'My objection, then, is to the theory of the abduction of agency and the notion that we should treat an object as an index of something else. I point out that questions about what an object is an index of may obscure something that is very important about the object in diverse contexts' (Leach 2007: 184).

Indeed, in my own analysis of glass Kimberley Points recounted here, I was unable to move beyond the primary agency of the Indigenous manufacturers of glass points and the trope by which they dazzled collectors (and its effect on contemporary archaeologists) to develop an argument regarding their material agency, which functioned independently of the intention of their makers. In an attempt to move beyond the limits of the artist–author concept and its constraint on the analysis of material agency, I want to consider the persistence of stone tools in the modern world, returning to Australia as a case study of the contemporary social role of stone artefacts, focusing on the function of stone artefacts in Indigenous heritage discourses. Australia provides an appropriate case study as a place where stone tools have developed new meanings and forms of value for Indigenous people in the context of the politics of post-colonialism and heritage. Indeed, my work with contemporary Indigenous Australians who work in archaeological heritage management suggests that for many Aboriginal people, their encounters with stone artefacts forms the basis for a creative reformulation of identity and self-knowledge as well as poignant tangible objects around which to make concrete various political debates and issues. At the same time, this case study has the potential to relate to other contemporary settler societies such as the United States, Canada, and New Zealand (Lilley 2000), as well as providing insights that can help us understand the agency of stone tools in their afterlives in the more distant past.

After human skeletal remains, stone artefacts have formed the most important nexus for debates around the repatriation of Indigenous cultural remains in Australia. While some of these debates have been public (Murray and Allen 1995), the return of stone artefacts excavated by archaeologists as part of both research and commercial archaeology has now become relatively routine in Australia under circumstances where Indigenous representative bodies request it. Denis Byrne (2003, 2004) has characterized this activity as a form of 'archaeology in reverse' as it often involves the *reburial* of stone artefacts and other archaeological remains excavated by archaeologists.

Labouring on archaeological excavations as untrained field assistants and being involved in field walking surveys to locate archaeological sites is one of the important ways in which Indigenous people in southern, settled Australia[1] gain physical access to stone artefacts and engage in creative encounters with them. It is also a way for Aboriginal people to engage in the cultural 'work' of heritage (after Byrne 2008). Where such work has become more broadly associated with colonialist practices in other countries (e.g. Shepherd 2003), the insistence of Aboriginal people to continue this involvement in archaeological labour has tended to draw it away from criticism in Australia. While criticized by many authors on community archaeology, who have rightly pointed out that the employment of Indigenous community members on archaeological excavations is not a substitute for consultative practices or a collaborative approach to archaeology, the involvement of Indigenous people in the physical work of archaeological heritage management has become a key element of contemporary archaeological heritage management in Australia, as it has in other settler societies such as the United States (Smith and Wobst 2005). For the Aboriginal people to whom I spoke about their involvement in archaeological fieldwork, it was clear that the involvement with artefacts in archaeology provided them with a sense of collective identification as Aboriginal people in the present.

Indeed, when I interviewed Indigenous Australians in settled, south-eastern Australia who work in the field of archaeological heritage management, they appeared to be engaged in a creative re-imagining of their history and culture, which derives from their encounters with stone artefacts in the present. Stone artefacts often hold an intense poignancy for Aboriginal people, not only as symbols but also as physical objects that can provide a material connection with the lives of their ancestors. For example, for descendants of the Muruwari Aboriginal people who used to live on the Dennawan Reserve, a former Aboriginal encampment occupied until the 1930s in western New South Wales, the dead often visit the living in dreams (see further details in Harrison 2003, 2004b, 2005). During site visits, particularly to pre-contact archaeological sites, Muruwari people with whom I worked over the period 2000–2004 would often rub artefacts such as flaked stone artefacts against their skin. Vera Nixon, an Aboriginal woman from western NSW who had been involved in recording archaeological sites with NSW National Parks and Wildlife Service staff, explained: 'when you're rubbing the stones over your skin you can get the feel of ... you sort of get the feeling of the spirits coming into your skin somehow or another. I dunno, it's a strange feeling, but it's a good feeling' (Vera Nixon, 18 November 2001). A belief that an ancestor's spirits are associated with the objects that they used during their lifetimes structures people's interactions with the remains of the former settlement. Josie Byno, Vera's sister explained further: 'When we go and visit the place and see the artefacts that they used to use and the fire there, the oven ... we get very emotional. Not only that, there is a special feeling in the air that surrounds us. We can feel that spiritual feeling wherever we go, and we know that they are with us' (Josie Byno, 18 November 2001). While it is important for people to be able to touch and interact with the artefacts on site, it is considered dangerous to remove them. People who do this are tormented with bad dreams or sickness. In contrast, just being at the site and touching its artefacts is considered to make Muruwari people feel physically healthy. Arthur Hooper (at the time in his seventies), who lived at the site in the 1940s, noted that 'ever since I've been coming out here, doing a little bit of work for people, I've been feeling really great. I'm really happy to see the old place again. And my feelings—inside me it's a very glad feeling, I have no worries about anything else. No aches and pains, I just walk around the place for hours and hours without getting tired' (Arthur Hooper, 18 November 2001). Archaeological sites, such as Dennewan, hold power and fascination for Indigenous Australians as places where local traces and memories persist, challenging and actively assisting in the creation of the past and present. The mutual involvement of people with stone artefacts and other archaeological traces of the past, which both evoke and create collective memories, provide creative opportunities for imagining and connecting oneself with the ancestral past, and building a sense of collective political and social identity in the present. Importantly, Aboriginal people conceptualize these artefacts as having agency of their own, which is independent of that of their makers, allowing them not only to act as a nexus between object and spirit worlds, but also to influence the body and minds of people who encounter them in the present (Figures 23.3 and 23.4).

Many Aboriginal people whom I interviewed about their work in archaeology felt creatively engaged with stone artefacts, and spoke of them as exhibiting their own forms of agency. For example, an Aboriginal woman I interviewed in 2004 who had been working with archaeologists in Armidale, NSW spoke of being able to spot artefacts that the archaeologist couldn't see while they were undertaking a field walking survey as she 'heard the artefacts calling to me'. She had been visiting local archaeological sites for years, not for their traditional associations or to undertake the sort of cultural work that anthropologists would normally identify as the obligations of Aboriginal kinship with the natural world, but to fossick for artefacts with the family and to swim and fish. She spoke of finding a favourite archaeological site that she would often visit. She was driving home one day and it was as 'if the place was calling to her, and when she got out and walked around, it was like being home'. Others spoke of the importance of working with archaeologists and other Aboriginal people as archaeological labourers, and the ways in which this allowed them to develop a sense of identity in spite of their sense of dislocation from their traditional culture.

Fig. 23.3 Arthur Hooper, Vera Nixon, Josey Byno, and Dorothy Kelley on a visit to the archaeological site at the Dennawan Reserve, New South Wales, Australia (photo: R. Harrison 2002).

Fig. 23.4 Josey Byno holding a stone artefact at the Dennawan Reserve, New South Wales, Australia (photo: R. Harrison).

STONE TOOLS AND STRATEGIC ESSENTIALISM

The use of stone tools by contemporary Indigenous Australians to express a sense of collective identity as well as to engage in a creative re-imagining of the past holds problems for those who are interested in the role of archaeology in colonialism and the ongoing influence of colonial discourses in the modern world. One of the major criticisms of archaeology and anthropology during the twentieth century has been the ways in which it has been used to produce stereotyped views of Indigenous people as 'others', views that have subsequently been employed by the state to control them (e.g. Clifford 1988, 1997; Russell 2001). In particular, ideas about the connection between culture and race and the misrepresentation of Aboriginal people as 'living fossils' has been used by the state in Australia to argue for the need for paternalism and control of Aboriginal people (McNiven and Russell 2005), and their position as both non-citizens and wards of the state. It seems problematic that at the same time that archaeology and anthropology has begun to criticize itself for these representations, Indigenous people have begun to rediscover and draw on the power of these same older stereotypes that represent Indigenous Australians by the material traces of their past to objectify themselves. In relation to archaeological heritage, this has been particularly visible in Indigenous self-representations within settler societies in Australia (e.g. Lilley and Williams 2005; Lilley 2006) and elsewhere (Fischer 1999; Kuper 2003; Clifford 2004), where Indigenous people have adopted what might be considered to be a rather conservative or old-fashioned association between race, culture, and material artefacts to represent themselves in the modern world.

The term 'strategic essentialism' was developed by Gayatri Chakravorty Spivak (1996: 214) to describe circumstances under which it may be advantageous for minority groups who hold quite disparate characteristics and ideals to represent their identity as a group in a simplified or stereotypical manner, either as part of a strategy to undermine these same stereotypes by drawing attention to them in a way that deconstructs them, or one that allows people to achieve particular outcomes when grouped in such a manner. Strategic essentialism could be understood as a form of performance in which minority peoples 'play up' to the stereotypes that they have been subject to as part of colonial domination or state control.

As Denis Byrne (2003: 77) notes, Aboriginal people in southern, settled Australia have responded to a sense of being made invisible in a colonized landscape by expressing a sense of fundamental connection to the many thousands of archaeological sites and stone artefacts spread across the country. In doing so, they express a certain level of identification as a group, at the level of an Indigenous 'nation', which would never have been the case in the past. In a sense, such a position is a surprise to Byrne, who notes the awareness of Aboriginal people with the ways in which an identification of 'real' Aboriginal people with stone artefacts and the past has allowed them to be effectively controlled and objectified by the state's programme of archaeological heritage management. Byrne has argued that the emphasis in cultural heritage management in Australia on the protection of archaeological sites has been driven by a desire by settler Australians to disassociate a heroic and authentic 'Aboriginality' from contemporary Aboriginal people. However, the fact the Aboriginal people so closely associate with stone artefacts suggests a strategy. Byrne compares this complicity of Aboriginal people with state-directed archaeological heritage management with Spivak's (1996: 214) notion of 'strategic essentialism'. This complicity has, Byrne (2003: 78) argues, meant that to some extent, Aboriginal people 'have to play up to white expectations and produce performative versions of traditional culture when this is what white people want to see'. He suggests that archaeological sites with physical remains, such as stone artefacts, have been chosen because they are visible places that, at the very least, remind broader settler society of the historical presence of Aboriginal people in a landscape from which they have been excluded.

For the vast majority of contemporary Aboriginal and settler Australians who live in large urban centres, the sense of being dislocated from the past is extreme.

Jeremy Beckett, in commenting on nostalgia and its relationship with place in Indigenous oral historian Myles Lalor's history, notes that for Aboriginal people in southern, settled Australia in the period 1950–1970, 'the emphasis was on the present, while the past was a source of unease and embarrassment rather than empowerment' (Beckett 1996: 321; see Lalor 2000). Beckett suggests that for Lalor and his generation, self-identity, which had traditionally derived from the connections between groups of people and place, had to transform itself in the light of the widespread forced removal and dislocations of Aboriginal people from their homelands. He sees in Lalor's oral history a refusal of nostalgia, in its sense of longing for lost places, by asserting his sense of self and an emergent collective sense of Aboriginality through a narrative that emphasizes social connections over spatial ones. However, the 1970s in Australia saw a changed political climate and the emergence of a revival of the past as a key source for the creation of a collective sense of identity for Aboriginal people. Transformed once again, Aboriginality was expressed through connections to the past, emphasizing the subaltern histories of particular places in the physical Australian landscape and national imaginary. This creation of a national collective Aboriginal identity by Indigenous Australians themselves reclaimed and subverted the State's creation of Aboriginality as a racial, rather than cultural collective. The fragmentary remains of stone artefacts had come to represent a poignant memorial to lives once forgotten, buried, and then subsequently both physically and metaphorically excavated from the dustbin of history.

For many Indigenous people, involvement in archaeological excavations not only allows an active physical engagement with the stone artefacts and other physical traces of their past, but represents a way of performing and realizing Aboriginal identity and community (cf. Anderson 1983; Appadurai 1996, 2001). As Amit and Rapport (2002) note, modern forms of trans-local community are often formed by common interest groups who emphasize their sense of shared experience in preference to their shared histories (cf. Gupta and Ferguson 1997d; Amit 2002). Denis Byrne (2008) points out the cultural 'work' of heritage, in this case the excavation and interaction with stone artefacts through untrained archaeological field labouring, is the 'glue' that people use to create a sense of community and locality in the present. Aboriginal people who are employed on such excavations fill a particular role, as 'consultants' and members of a 'local community' who are being consulted over 'their' heritage. In southern, settled Australia, like many other areas within the major Anglophone settler societies where Indigenous people have largely been denied access to those local places that form their homelands, such radically localizing forms of performed identity provide a rare opportunity for the development of a sense of shared community. While archaeologists have generally perceived the communities with which they are expected to consult as relatively fixed entities, it is clear that they are created dialogically through this process of consultation and the new fields of social relations formed around stone artefacts and other archaeological remains, as much as they exist independently of it. For those Aboriginal Australians involved in this creative engagement with them, stone artefacts have become symbols of local community as well as the (literal) foundation stones for new forms of Aboriginal nationalism in postcolonial Australia (see also Lilley 2006).

CONCLUSIONS

The discussion of the meaning of stone tools in contemporary Australia has demonstrated the latent efficacy of stone tools long after their discard once they have ceased to be functionally 'useful', as well as the importance of understanding the afterlives of stone tools. This has also raised questions about the 'afterlife' of stone tools in the past. The memory of the manufacture of particular stone tool forms, as well as encounters with older, discarded stone tools would potentially have impacted continuously on the production of new stone tools by stone artefact producing peoples in the past. In the same way that stone artefacts exercise a form of material agency in contemporary Australia, which is entirely removed from the agency of the artist/author who produced them, encounters with ancient discarded stone tools in the past must also have enacted forms of material agency. These interventions might have taken the form of the continued production of stone tool forms that were associated with the archaic past in an attempt to maintain the *habitus* as suggested by Wobst (2000), or the creation of new tool forms in reaction against them. However, we should not assume the only interventions were those that derived from people themselves, but instead allow for the possibility that stone artefacts might have generated creative engagements of people and objects, which were entirely independent of those intended by their makers.

This chapter has considered the contribution of interdisciplinary material culture studies to understanding the political power and material agency of stone tools. Drawing on theories of social and material agency and Gell's discussion of the captivation of art objects, I have suggested that the meaning and social role of a stone artefact changes throughout the course of its life history with each transformation in its use cycle, and more importantly, that stone artefacts continue to have material agency and do social 'work' even after they have been discarded. The particular contribution of Gell's work is the way in which it suggests a structure for understanding and conceptualizing the ongoing influence of prehistoric objects both in the past as well as in contemporary social relations. However, we need to go beyond Gell's focus on the primary agency of human author–artists to acknowledge forms of material agency that stone artefacts and other objects might hold, which are independent of them. The challenge for modern stone tool studies is to consider the ways in which we might undertake research in which stone tools and other forms of prehistoric material culture are viewed as embodying material agency rather than remaining passive players in a series of social relations that are entirely determined by human actors.

Note

1. I use this term to refer to Aboriginal people in those parts of Australia who experienced the earliest and greatest disruption by European invasion. The extent and nature of cultural and physical dislocation experienced by Aboriginal people in Australia was extremely variable across the country, but in general terms, Aboriginal people in northern and central Australia were able to maintain a physical presence within their country for much longer, and experience a lesser disruption to their traditional lives than did Aboriginal people in south-eastern Australia.

CHAPTER 24

THE LANDSCAPE GARDEN AS MATERIAL CULTURE: LESSONS FROM FRANCE

CHANDRA MUKERJI

INTRODUCTION

Landscapes or built environments contain distinct lessons about material culture and human life. Land that shows the effects of human activity is material culture, but is often less clearly bounded than other cultural objects and more vividly intertwined with nature. It exists everywhere that the earth and social communities meet: fields opened by deforestation, piles of sludge in the ruins of old manufacturing centres, empty lots in cities, windmills along a ridge, leaking sewer pipes with plants feeding off the effluent, fields of bulbs for commercial sale, trails in national parks, seashores lined with tourist hotels, or grand formal gardens full of sculpture, fountains, and plant collections (Stilgoe 1982, 1983, 1988, 1994; Cronon 1991). These meeting places of nature and human labour are, like other forms of material culture, created for social purposes and designed (at least at the beginning) to have value. Over time, they are either maintained in their original form, or transform (grow, degrade, age) into new ones. In either case, they contain physical memories of human hopes, desires, limits, abilities, and powers.

While most of the examples explored in the following pages are mainly (but not entirely) derived from early modern French landscape history, the principles about the built environment hold for many other places in the Western tradition. Focusing mainly on one site simply helps to demonstrate the local specificities of landscapes and their history, while also pointing to more general patterns of material governance.

THE LANDSCAPE GARDEN AS MATERIAL CULTURE

Studies of the built environment as a form of material culture stand at the intersection of landscape history, colonial history, sociology, political science, and science studies. In landscape history, there have been a number of schools of thought, touching on this issue. Many books analyse the cultural significance of gardens through literature. John Dixon Hunt and Claire Goldstein, among others, have used poetry in particular to address the problem of treating mute landscapes as culturally 'voiced' (Hunt 1986, 1992, 2002; Hunt and Willis 1988; Laird 1999; Goldstein 2000, 2008; Hunt *et al.* 2002). As many gardens were historically de-signed around literary metaphors or were praised in their period in poetry, this approach makes sense, but it also often obscures the complex socio-political relations that allow some people to put poetry into gardens and force other people off the land.

In response to the limitations of this literary tradition, Ann Bermingham famously wrote about the social privilege expressed by English landscape gardens with their rolling lawns, tranquil lakes, and glasshouses full of rare exotics (Bermingham 1986). She argued that these gardens were explicitly 'leisured', expressing the excess wealth of those who did not need to till the land to live. They were gardens of empire, too, with botanical collections that displayed political reach. British leisure was a product of colonial work, and this socio-political reality was embedded in English gardens.

More recently, scholars have tried to blend social and cultural history to explain gardens. Michel Conan at Dumbarton Oaks encouraged this type of work in young scholars, such as Elizabeth Hyde, Mirka Beneš, and Dianne Harris (Conan 2000, 2002; Beneš and Harris 2001; Harris 2003; Conan and Dumbarton Oaks 2005; Hyde 2005). They all treat landscapes as products of the people who commissioned them, developed them, or supplied them with flowers, dreaming cultural dreams but also living in historical moments defined by social relations. Particularly when they draw attention to relationships between houses and gardens, these scholars highlight the continuity of gardens with other forms of material culture.

John Stilgoe and William Cronon have expanded the definition of landscape itself to consider as built environments an array of spaces where land and human communities meet. They draw attention to the subtleties of the interactions between shores and ports, trees and electrical lines, paths and woods, cities and fields, combining documentary history and field studies of places to do so (Stilgoe 1982, 1983, 1988, 1994, 1998; Cronon 1991).

Scholars interested in colonial botany and engineering also have contributed to the study of landscapes as material culture. Londa Schiebinger, Judith Carney, Timothy Mitchell, Richard Drayton, and Kapil Raj look at trade, botany, agriculture, infrastructural engineering, and gardening as material forms that mediate between colonies and colonizing countries, producing distinctive landscapes of power (Drayton 2000; Carney 2001; Mitchell 2002; Schiebinger 2004; Schiebinger and Swan 2005; Raj 2007). Colonial domination, according to these scholars, has not been simply a matter of social domination of people, but also domination of the earth and its flora and fauna. Europeans have often justified colonization as well by their more rational (Western) understandings of nature and more systematic uses of it.

In sociology and political science, Sharon Zukin (1991), James Scott (1998), Patrick Joyce (2003), and Patrick Carroll (2006) have looked at the built environment and its socio-political significance, too. Often using ideas from Foucault as their guide (Burchell *et al.* 1991), they have studied the social practices and significance of built environments from cityscapes to the countryside. Sharon Zukin (1991) famously analysed urban spaces as 'landscapes of power', emphasizing their materiality and the social dynamics that gave them form and that they served. James Scott (1998) studied a set of utopian projects of landscape 'improvement' that had dystopian effects, arguing that engineered landscapes have been active and often destructive parts of political relations. Patrick Joyce (2003) has looked at how the built environment not only symbolizes and facilitates surveillance, but also provides tools of self-governance (with water systems, sewers, and the like) that enrol populations into relations of power. Patrick Carroll (2006) draws attention to the countryside where land reform has been an important political activity, dependent upon and serving science. All these studies point to the centrality of landscapes to power, knowledge, and governance.

Scholars in science studies have added to this intellectual mix by focusing on the importance of 'non-human actants' in social life. Bruno Latour, Michel Callon, Karin Knorr-Cetina, Geof Bowker, and Leigh Star have all studied the power of infrastructures, pointing to the silent, unrecognized and routine ways they can define social reality (Callon 1986a, 1998; Bowker and Star 1999; Knorr-Cetina 1999; Latour 2000b; Knorr-Cetina and Preda 2005). They explain how keys, trains, computer networks, trading markets, and databases—ubiquitous and uncontested elements of material life—construct the order of things. These modest forms of material culture gain their power precisely because they are unquestioned ways of organizing people. This approach to studying infrastructures, common in science studies, has been more often applied to material culture than landscape history (Appadurai 1986a; Mukerji 2003), but has had a powerful influence on some of the work in colonial history and sociology that treats landscape as an important part of social life.

Still, why focus on landscapes? What is to be gained by placing the built environment at the centre of material culture analysis?

The landscape is at the heart of human life—a site of ongoing experiments in survival and betterment. Landscapes are models of human governance of things. They are demonstrations of human power *vis-à-vis* the non-human world. As cultural constructs, serving a range of human hopes, fears, and determinations, they exemplify how we make the earth serve our purposes, how we define what we need, and to what extent we succeed or fail in pursuing material interests. Working on the landscape depends on and is generative of natural knowledge, so landscapes provide evidence of collective knowledge and uses of the earth, and define the logistical bases of collective life (Figure 24.1).

The gardens of Versailles built in the seventeenth century under Louis XIV provide a good example of the socio-cultural importance of landscapes (Adams 1979; Mukerji 1997). The royal garden was a tool of politics, a demonstration of not

Fig. 24.1 Gardens of Versailles: view of the Apollo Fountain and Canal (photo: Becky Cohen).

only the king's glory but also the material techniques of territorial governance. The park was designed to be a microcosm of the kingdom as a whole, suggesting the order and abundance the regime was bringing to all of France. The gardens symbolically joined disparate parts of the realm into an elegant single design, too. They were made up of geometrically formed and organized garden beds and groves of trees each organized around a particular theme (Adams 1979; Hazlehurst 1980). These areas of the garden were like the different provinces of France with boundaries of their own. One was even named the *parterre du Midi*, referencing both the south side of the chateau and the southern region of France. The park, in this way, helped naturalize the centralization of power under this regime with the beauty of the gardens and the wealth of plant life (Mukerji 1997; Hyde 2005; Goldstein 2008) (Figure 24.2).

The park also carried military messages about French power in its engineering. The garden of Versailles had magnificent waterworks, complex terracing, and large bronze statues—all technically difficult engineering used for building fortresses. Terracing was the most important form of military engineering in this period of siege warfare, where fortresses were built with complex systems of raised battlements and deep ditches to arrest invaders. The main terrace behind the chateau at Versailles not only had battlement-style walls, but also contained grand cast bronze statues. These were signed not by the artists who designed them, but the men at the arsenal who cast them. They were symbols of the French ability to cast large metal forms, such as the cannon used by the French army (Mukerji 1997; Goldstein 2008).

Fig. 24.2 Gardens of Versailles: statue of the Rhone River (photo: Becky Cohen).

Fig. 24.3 Gardens of Versailles: North Allée (photo: Becky Cohen).

Other garden areas at Versailles also had military themes. One of the garden groves, for example, the *sal des festins*, had in the centre of a pond a platform built in the shape of a fortress footprint (Mukerji 1997). Other water features had military significance as well. Many represented landscapes that were difficult for soldiers to traverse: swamps, rivers, and lakes. The walks through these places spoke to the French ability to master these environments with technical means—a kind of military expertise that was also being described in print in the period (Mukerji 2002a). The engineering of Versailles, then, carried messages about French military power that were melded with representations of French territorial integration. This was the microcosm standing for the macrocosm of France that was shown to elite visitors to the French court (Mukerji 1997; Beneš and Harris 2001; Goldstein 2008) (Figure 24.3).

Western Gardens as Material
Culture of Power

The garden at Versailles was not unique, but rather part of a turn to gardening and landscape management that developed in the period when territorial engineering was gaining importance in politics. The great gardens of Italy were developed in the period when Renaissance city-states began to make use of the engineering sophistication of the period to improve their economic or strategic situation (Tomasi 1983; Woodward 1996; Mukerji 2002a). Canals were cut through the plains of Lombardy, rivers were 'improved' with locks, and swamps drained for agriculture. It was in this context that members of great families in Italy commissioned gardens with technological marvels (Belidor 1753; Thacker 1979; Hazlehurst 1966; Mariage 1990; Beneš and Harris 2001; Conan 2002).

The formal gardens of France were in part derived from Italian precedents, and similarly, expressed engineered power. With their refined artificiality, both Italian and French gardens emphasized human intervention in the natural world, and the power of engineering. Both types of gardens were organized geometrically, and flowerbeds were set out formally to express the orderliness of nature, as it was becoming known to science. Like the heavens, these earthly paradises followed fundamental mathematical laws, and natural orderliness was associated with intelligent social domination. But in France the royal gardens were public, and stood for France rather than a particular family. And the gardens had more elaborate engineering, demonstrating the efficacy and tools of territorial governance (Belidor 1753; Hazlehurst 1966; Thacker 1979; Mariage 1990; Beneš and Harris 2001; Conan 2002).

English landscape gardens with their rolling lawns and naturalized landscapes eschewed formality, but embodied many of the same social themes. Beautiful English gardens were also 'improved', but not by formal means. They were representations of a poetic, idyllic nature, nature restored not to its underlying mathematical order but its perfect naturalness. These landscape gardens, like their Italian predecessors, gained significance as markers of high rank, but the new eighteenth-century leisure class showed its importance with leisure land (Bermingham 1986; Hunt and Willis 1988; Laird 1999). Glasshouses were the most important area of technological innovation for these gardens both for practical and political reasons (Hix 1974). By helping British gardeners to be good stewards of tender plants from colonial areas, they legitimated colonial domination at the same time that they served botanical and horticultural learning. The controls for heat and humidity in glasshouses were refined to provide adequate shelter for sensitive plants, creating microclimates that often were associated with the geographical sources of plants. As the colonies grew and trade in plants expanded, so did the glasshouses. They became giant glass and steel structures almost reaching the scale of railroad stations, creating worlds unto themselves, and places for people in England to 'travel' to the tropics (Liger d'Auxerre 1706; Bradley 1720; Hix 1974; Bermingham 1986; Hunt 2002) (Figure 24.4).

Even this brief sketch of the history of Western gardens helps show how gardens emerged as an important genre of material culture in Europe. In each case, the gardens were emblems of power, but more than that, too. They not only symbolized but experimented with relationships between Western societies and the natural world.

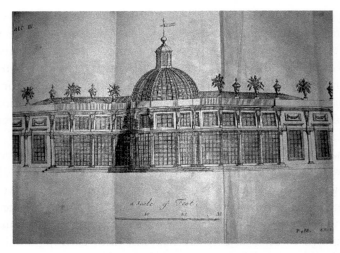

Fig. 24.4 Greenhouse proposed by Louis Liger d'Auxerre for tender trees in northern climates (from Bradley 1720).

LANDSCAPES AND MATERIAL CULTURE STUDIES:
BASIC SIMILARITIES

Studies of material culture generally focus on both the meaning and materiality of things, and landscape studies are no exception. Just as it is not unusual to hear that the vital significance of a chair, for example, does not lie in the wood or plastic used to build it, but rather in our understanding of it as a place to sit, read, write, eat dinner, or play with children, so we hear, too, that gardens are not just collections of trees, shrubs, flowers, and water, but embodiments of poetry and philosophical commitments. Similarly, cities are arrangements of buildings and spaces with histories and purposes, shaped around ideas and ideals of urban design.

Still, a chair is not the same if it is called a throne or a park bench, and it matters whether it is made of granite or from wood from an endangered tree. Things designed by human hands communicate, but like any form of communication, the medium matters. It may not be the message, *per se*, but it makes a difference. The chair—understood through its materials—has significance not only to those who use it, but also to the people who quarry the stone or cut timber in the rain forests of Brazil. Both those who sit on the chair/bench and those who provide raw materials for it are connected culturally by those who fashion chairs or design the parks that need benches. Networks of people are (at least in part) linked through things—including landscapes. As we fashion, use, view, trade, and move material objects, we communicate. Objects embody memories and possibilities for social life. The materiality of social life matters in complex ways, and landscapes help us see it (Appadurai 1986a; Miller *et al.* 1998; Latour and Weibel 2002, 2005).

It is comforting to study material culture like a silver spoon because it can *seem* to be wholly a product of human design. But gardens never hold that illusion—at least for those who do the gardening. Weather affects gardens independently of people, freezing beloved specimens this year, killing others through drought the next. The landscape, then, reveals the centrality of nature to human communities, the desire for government of things, the cultural dreams that shape the countryside, the forms of power exercised over it, the knowledge of nature derived from activity on the earth, and the limits of the environmental controls that people invent.

By looking more closely at the cultural formation of landscapes in France, we can see more precisely, how these general processes have worked out on the ground. France had a geographical location and peculiarities of landscape that influenced its cultural development. At the same time, the accretion of built environments there also installed into the countryside memories, intellectual approaches to land, symbolic forms, and material techniques that provided continuities in both the landscape and culture in France over time.

HOPES AND AMBITIONS

As much as pragmatic considerations may drive people to farm or garden, and devise ways to store the products they grow, desire also plays a part in uses of land. There are powerful utopian cultural threads in the Western world that animate both urbanization and gardening, and have been integral to the formation of modern built environments.

Krzysztof Pawlowski (2003) has described one tradition of material utopianism in the south-west of France. Round enclosures were built there from the first to the tenth century for the collective storage of farm products. These Pawlowski named *circulades Languedociennes*. Originally erected around the rich valleys of the Aude and Hérault Rivers, *circulades* were not narrow towers like silos, but wider and more open spaces—more the size of a plaza—surrounded by a wall with storage space inside. These were not human habitations, but in times of trouble, peasants would join their goods and seek safety behind the defences (Figure 24.5).

The river valleys where the *circulades* were erected were full of good farmland and agricultural goods. During the Roman Empire, this was the heart of the Narbonnaise, a thriving centre of ancient Gaul rich in population, goods, and structures from arenas, bridges, roads, and canals to aqueducts and harbours. The empire fell, but the farming remained vibrant so pirates came to the area expecting to find something to steal. There were no physical barriers from the Mediterranean along these rivers, so raiding was easy (Pawlowski 2003). These valleys also became the sites of an early and major pilgrimage route, connecting the Mediterranean to

Fig. 24.5 Detail of *circulade* storehouse at Bram, Aude, France (photo: C. Mukerji).

Toulouse and the roads to Campostella on the Atlantic Coast of northern Spain. Bandits followed pilgrims into the area, and added to the unusually high flow of traffic through this region that made the farms here both relatively rich and more vulnerable to plunder.

The *circulades* constituted built environments to control the losses of peasants farming the region. They also were designed as perfectly measured circles—important Christian symbols. It would have been easier to make them square or rectangular, so the choice of form was significant. The circle represented perfection, so it was used extensively in Celtic books of the gospel, like the Books of Durrow and Kells, to identify the sacred. The circle was also repeated in medieval maps, where it described Creation as a pure form. To Christians of south-western France at the end of the Roman Empire, putting the gifts of

Fig. 24.6 Street forming part of a *circulade* city at Sorèze, Tarn, France (photo: C. Mukerji).

creation (the harvests of their rich valleys) into a circular walled structure would have made sense on multiple levels. The *circulade* was an Eden for goods given to them by God. People lived *outside* this perfect world, too, in the appropriate place for descendants of Adam and Eve. The *circulades* and their uses enacted sacred truths by giving the landscape its form. They embedded utopian hopes into an engineered place (Figure 24.6).

Eventually, Pawlowski tells us, these structures became sites of habitation. Families decided to stay in them even after threats subsided, perhaps attracted by the conviviality of the settlements. The result was a set of towns with a distinctive form, addressing the problems of living in that particular landscape and protecting it symbolically as well as physically with round walls (Pawlowski 2003).

MORAL REFORM

Another moral constellation became even more important to landscapes in France from the turn of the seventeenth century. It was called *mesnagement* gardening, and was a form of land management designed to restore nature to the perfection of Creation. This philosophy of land reform started to develop during the wars of religion, when towns were multiply sieged, and structures and infrastructures destroyed, leaving them in need of reconstruction (Mukerji 2002c).

Hopes for rebuilding the countryside echoed biblical dreams of restoring Eden—returning the landscape to the perfection of Creation. Good stewardship could bring both prosperity and calm after a period of warfare and poverty. This conception of governance also suited humanist scholars. One of them, the publisher Charles Estienne, wrote one of the early *mesnagement* books, *L'Agriculture et La Maison Rustique* (Estienne 1606). He argued that those willing to approach agriculture with a studious attitude and purposeful discipline could produce the abundance that had sustained the civilizations of the ancients and was implicit in the first act of Creation.

The Huguenot naturalist, ceramicist, and garden writer of the late sixteenth century, Bernard Palissy, connected rational land use practices with moral self-improvement and the exercise of dominion. Working on the land was a way to make the earth more abundant and a spiritual exercise in itself (Palissy 1931, 1988; Palissy and La Rocque 1957). Soul and soil were fundamentally linked.

During the rein of Henri IV, Olivier de Serres not only elaborated land management techniques, but transformed *mesnagement* ideas into a more overt political philosophy. He argued that rational estate development implied making the best use of the existing natural tendencies of a property by deciding through reason and surveys where to plant trees, cultivate gardens, lay roads, and set up mills. Serres described, in other words, ways of constructing a domain to improve the abundance and value of estate lands, and generalized the principle of good governance to the political administration (Serres 1600; Serres and Geffe 1971).

Religious utopianism and belief in human ability and duty to restore nature to a more edenic form, then, gave land improvement a particular Christian significance in Western societies based on the linked ideas of stewardship and dominion. Taming wild nature was a spiritual duty and a utopian goal that was required of princes as well as gentlemen and their labourers.

Natural knowledge

The importance of natural knowledge to French landscapes was illustrated in the gardening books written by these authors. They developed detailed accounts of how to improve soil, bring water to a home or garden, lay out roads, sow seeds, protect melons from frost, and store grain. Drawing on Dutch sources as well as their own experiments in horticulture to explain how to do it, they emphasized the value of growing some of the new species of plants that just in this period were being imported into Europe (Serres 1600; Groen 1669).

The role of knowledge in land management also had a spiritual dimension; working the earth was a way to reveal its secrets, and know the Creator who made it. In stewardship terms, studying the earth was a sacred act, a bond with the Creator. Successful efforts to improve the earth revealed truth, demonstrating an understanding of God's Works. This was possible because God had made men in His image, capable of knowing His design. So, seeking natural knowledge was a spiritual, practical, and intellectual activity (Serres 1600; Palissy 1931).

While some of the knowledge of botany and horticulture affecting French landscapes was recorded in books and used by learned readers to improve their estates, other natural knowledge used in negotiating relations between communities and countryside in the sixteenth and seventeenth centuries was 'tacit knowledge' or 'vernacular knowledge'. Because they worked the land, many peasants developed deep local knowledge of the worlds they lived in. They may not have had the vocabulary to give authority to their understandings, but they still developed conceptions of topography and hydrology, for example, that were locally more sophisticated than formal knowledge of these fields.

Peasant knowledge of the continental divide in Languedoc, for example, was quite complex. Both structures and stories marked the line between watersheds in terms of the movement of water and wind long before the divide was located on maps with geographical measures. For example, the *seuil de Besombes* by Graissens and the *seuil de Naurouze* were both known *points de partage* or places where the waters parted. When it rained at Graissens, people said water flowed in both directions. At Naurouze, the same phenomenon was described in a local legend. The spot was marked with a pile of boulders that, according to myth, had been brought up from the underworld by giants who were doing an errand for the devil. As evil henchmen often were, these giants were clumsy. Somehow, they lost hold of the boulders, and in a fright, dropped them in a pile. Where these evil-saturated stones landed, water fled in both directions. This was the *seuil de Nauruoze* (Mukerji 2002b).

On the Lauragais ridge that rose up from Naurouze, the winds were strong, so windmills dotted the landscape, marking the divide. No geographer was needed here to locate the continental divide by measuring elevations. The wind indicated where the physical impediments were fewest between eastern and western Languedoc, and peasants made note of it when placing their windmills (Figure 24.7).

Surprisingly, the divide was also marked in a spiritual way with Virgin shrines, or small statues of the Virgin over church doors. Apparently, the Virgin had been venerated on this ridge for centuries because the plague had stopped in these hills—a miracle that was attributed to the sympathetic Virgin. Presumably, the plague, carried by rats and notoriously spread in boats, did not cross the divide that

Fig. 24.7 Windmill in Lauragais, France (photo: C. Mukerji).

split watersheds. Plague and miracles as well as windmills, then, marked and characterized the geography of the region, producing a landscape that was deeply cultural and a social life attentive to geographical variations.

Horticultural knowledge
and material technique

The turn toward land management and engineering in early modern France was partly a result of the new interest in ancient Rome. Although histories of the Renaissance usually point to the importance of texts to the revival of the classics, ruins from Rome were numerous and widespread in southern France, and held a fascination for humanists who wanted to improve the present using the wisdom of the past. The famous humanist scholar from Aix-en-Provence, Peiresc, was best known for his exquisite scholarship about ancient texts and extensive correspondence with other humanists, but he also was an avid amateur archaeologist of local

Roman ruins. He sketched famous places like the Pont du Gard, where a three-tiered aqueduct crossed a deep river valley, and some not-so-famous ones at Fréjus where the disbanded soldiers of Caesar's army in Gaul had built their own aqueduct and town. His notebook of sketches added to his knowledge of Roman history and culture. The landscape was for him and other humanists a 'memory palace', containing evidence of classical abilities (P. N. Miller 2000).

Classical ideas about landscape were also put into print in early modern Europe. Authors from the late Empire, many of them of high rank, wrote tomes about estate management and the logistics of farming, construction, gardening, and winemaking that served as models for the later *mesnagement* literature (Long 2001). These authors not only described how to manage a farm, but also how to stabilize the goods it produced, dedicating rooms or outbuildings on their estates to do it. Foodstuffs that would spoil naturally were processed to maintain their nutritional value, and stored in special environments to sustain their usefulness through the winter. Columella even described the proper modes of preparing the floors and walls of a storeroom:

As to the part [of the villa] devoted to the storage of produce, . . . [rooms] on the ground floor may take care of liquid products for the market, such as oil and wine; while dry products, such as grain, hay, leaves, chaff, and other fodder, should be stored in the lofts. [T]he granaries . . . should be reached by ladder and should receive ventilation through small openings on the north side, for that exposure is the coolest and the least humid . . . [The storehouse should have] a vaulted ceiling, [and] its earthen floor, before it is covered over, dug up and soaked with fresh and unsalted lees of oil and packed down with rammers . . . [It should be] overlaid . . . with a pavement of tiles . . . [and] all the joints of the walls and floor built up with a bolstering of tile, for usually when buildings develop cracks in such places they afford holes and hiding places for underground animals.

Columella (1941: 69, 71)

Using estate lands in an informed way was both an intellectual activity and an act of power by powerful men. Domination depended on material management of the landscape, and this remained the case in Western gardens from the Renaissance.

The early plant trade in Europe provided another stimulus for gardening experiments. New materials were imported from afar, addressing and furthering interest in botany, horticulture, pharmacology, and gardening. The importation of tender species necessitated the design of new built environments to protect rare and vulnerable plant materials. Although seeds and bulbs were relatively stable commodities, imported plants posed massive problems of transport and warehousing.

Market gardeners, plant collectors, and nurserymen alike in the early modern period experimented with microclimates to raise seedlings and bulbs. Sometimes they simply covered garden beds with cloth and lath structures to protect delicate, tender seedlings outdoors. They also made cold frames, glass lanterns, and hot houses, experimenting with different types of 'housing' for plants to force vegetables and fruits to grow out of season, or to allow foreign plants to survive on

European soil. The result was a model of governance in the garden with micro-climates and specialized housing for plants (Groen 1669; Hyde 2005; Liger d'Aux-erre 1706; van Oosten 1703; de la Quintinie 1692; Stearn 1961).

Gentlemen collectors also often sought out exotics, and became particularly concerned about acclimatizing and propagating new plants. They had orangeries to fill with tender trees, and experimented with hothouses and cold frames. Collectors had the money for construction and land for building microclimates. So they experimented with sunken gardens, surrounding a planting area with stone retain-ing walls that functioned as solar collectors. Some covered their beds in sunken gardens with lath and fabric to impede pests and retain heat. Most used cloth rather than glass (except at Versailles) because the latter was too expensive and rare for many nurserymen, market gardeners and individual collectors (Groen 1669; Quintinie 1692; Liger d'Auxerre 1706; van Oosten 1703; Stearn 1961; Hyde 2005).

With these inventions, gardens and estates had new structures to use for taming wild nature and exercising dominion. They had ways to control pests, ways to force plants in the spring, ways to disperse or collect heat, and ways to create built environments more favourable to their desires.

TERRITORIAL GOVERNANCE

The result of all this moral, social, and material experimentation in the countryside was a distinct form of land management, a way to rule over the earth to serve human ends. During the seventeenth and eighteenth centuries, then, French royal gardens drew on these traditions, making landscapes crucial elements of French political culture just as state territoriality became the goal of government.

While fortresses were constructed around the perimeter of France and forests were being surveyed for reform, formal gardens were laid out at Versailles and other royal residences as symbols of territorial domination and exemplars of orderly land management. They demonstrated and experimented with the French capacity to control natural resources and use them for advantage. In this context, the collec-tion and display of rare and exotic plants took on strategic significance. Colonial botany became embroiled in state politics, too, as finding exotic species, learning their uses, collecting their various names, sending them to France, displaying them in botanical gardens, and comparing them systematically constituted practices of power as well as of natural history (Paskvan 1971; Mukerji 2005).

Imported plants had a small but important role in the military articulation of state boundaries as well. Trees were needed for fortress construction and shipbuild-ing, so they were essential for defending state borders. Need for timber was the impetus for forest reform, and why importations of new species of trees and the development of techniques for transferring large specimens into French gardens became exercises in military management as well as horticulture. The botanist Pierre Belon brought plane trees into France, and Jacques Cornuti sent tree specimens from Canada to the *Jardin du Roi* that he thought might be useful for the reforestation of France (Cornuti 1635; Paskvan 1971).

These traditions of land use provided material techniques and moral rationales for the park at Versailles, giving the grand park enormous cultural power and political significance. Promenades in the gardens became important to the king because they were effective diplomatic vehicles, displaying his power as a wonder to behold. He wrote the itineraries, choreographies of experience, defining where the visitors should go, where they should look, how they should turn and walk, and what they should see (Thacker 1972). The garden was meant to impress visitors as much as the coliseum in Rome or the Pont-du-Gard arches, demonstrating a superhuman power over the earth.

The gardens also made the valley behind the chateau at Versailles aesthetically French. The gardens resembled the interior of the house, marking the landscape with political signs and defining it as the material culture of the state. The garden beds were made to look like oriental carpets, and the cloths worn by courtiers were embroidered with parterre designs. The land of France and French nobles were aesthetically aligned through the garden, and met there in *divertissements* orchestrated by the king.

The fountains of Versailles also helped to convey the spiritual legitimacy of the regime's material order. Most had circular reflecting pools that brought images of the heavens down to the earth. They contrasted with Italian fountains that tended to have a pyramid of nested reservoirs that drew the eyes of visitors from the lowest reservoir up to smaller ones and then the heavens. In contrast, the fountains at Versailles mainly sat on the earth, using circular forms to frame images of the sky as icons of perfection (Mukerji 1997) (Figure 24.8).

The statues in the centre of these pools also spoke to the peace and abundance brought to earth in this reign. For example, the fountains of the seasons depicted spring laden with flowers, autumn was full of wheat, and winter rich with shellfish. These were the fruits of proper land and resource management. They spoke to the material efficacy of the regime and legitimated the state's intervention into the French countryside. They also mirrored in art the natural abundance of the garden beds and forest rooms that were carefully kept that way by royal gardeners.

Landscape in this context was both a form of material culture and a place of power that was modified to produce a more powerful regime. These gardens showcased the traditions of knowledge, cultural purposes, and political requirements of the period, embodying the human purposes and natural processes of the world beyond. 'Improved' landscapes on both sides of the garden walls showed the efficacy of period methods of material governance.

Fig. 24.8 Gardens of Versailles: Fountain of Summer (Ceres) (photo: Becky Cohen).

The example of French gardens helps to make the point that the landscape itself was enrolled into social relations, and made a powerful form of material culture. It did not just express or symbolize power, but demonstrated the techniques of making the material serve social life. The garden of Versailles was cultivated with the techniques used on country farms; it was a genealogical inheritor of the *mesnagement* tradition of material governance, using land more productively to serve God and men. The garden of Versailles was a land of leisure, so the earth did not need to grow food, but France was presented in statuary as a golden land of abundance to legitimate the king with symbols of his good stewardship.

MATERIAL ORDER

Social regimes are material and political orders—built on landscapes as well as social hierarchies. The countryside they incorporate provides evidence of the technical, cultural, and political stakes and tools that define regimes (and their weaknesses). The landscape gardens in France dramatized and illustrated a material order, legitimating human domination over nature with ideas of human dominion over the earth and its creatures. Dominion, of course, was never realized on the ground, yet its pursuit and representations were made enduring techniques of power.

The gardens of Versailles were not only demonstrations of political might, but also repositories of historically cultivated ways of living in the natural world. In this, the royal park was like most forms of material culture. But it was a laboratory, too, for experiments in using nature to serve a socio-political order. It explored as well as demonstrated how to use the earth more productively, or make it politically more effective. Human powers were formalized on the ground under refined and controlled circumstances that could never be fully generalized, but nonetheless became an inspiration in Western culture that has, since that time, served to direct and plague our relations to the natural world.

CHAPTER 25

BUILT OBJECTS

DOUGLASS BAILEY
LESLEY McFADYEN

INTRODUCTION

This chapter presents two bodies of work, both of which take an interdisciplinary approach to the study of buildings from Neolithic Europe. The first connects archaeology to theories in architectural history, while the second creates links between archaeology and art. Our intention is not an extensive review of Neolithic architectural studies. Instead, we work through four ideas about architecture that we offer as disconnected propositions. There is no easy narrative for this chapter, just as there is none for the living built environment of the past or the present. Our proposal is that archaeologists step away from accepted and comfortable knowledges of architectural form and interpretation.

The aim of this chapter is to work through four case studies from our work on prehistoric European architecture. The case studies illuminate four propositions, which are offered as provocations for further work on architecture by archaeologists but also by anthropologists and other social scientists and humanities scholars whose work engages architecture. If there is a common theme to the

Lesley McFadyen would like to thank Douglass Bailey and Mark Knight for encouragement and help with her part of the chapter. She gratefully acknowledges Don Benson and Alasdair Whittle for permission to reproduce material in this chapter. Douglass Bailey acknowledges the support of a Research Leave Grant from the Arts and Humanities Research Council which he held while writing this chapter. Portions of Proposition 4 appear in Bailey (2005b).

chapter then it is dissatisfaction with the ways that archaeologists have responded to the record of the architectural past that they discover. The propositions and case studies are shared efforts not only to disable current thinking about architecture but also to provide examples of more exciting ways that architecture can be engaged.

The chapter begins with an examination of long barrows from Neolithic Britain (from the fourth millennium cal BC), investigates building as practice, and then argues that we will benefit from thinking about such ancient architecture in terms of 'quick architecture'. The second case study shifts the investigation to eastern Europe and the early Neolithic (6000–5000 cal BC) practice of making and using pit dwellings. The argument redefines these features by focusing attention not on their potential functions (be they economic or ritual) but on the processes of cutting surfaces and intervening into the landscape. The third case study looks again at the British Neolithic record and examines the role that gaps and disjunctions play in the sequences of evidence and phases of activity. The proposal is that interruptions and breaks in sequences have an equal (and perhaps greater) importance to architectural continuities than do more obvious stratigraphic continuities. In the final case study, again from south-eastern Europe, we propose that much traditional archaeological analysis of buildings has been misdirected, having paid greatest attention to microdetails of construction technique and records of activity. The alternative that we argue for is that we step back and try to see buildings as specific objects, particularly in ways similar to those of some Minimalist artists of the 1960s and 1970s who worked through issues of meaning and unintended consequence. Together, these apparently disparate case studies provide an argument for an alternative to the traditional study of architecture by archaeologists, but also by anthropologists and other social scientists.

Proposition 1

Architecture is often seen as the most significant piece of material culture in archaeology and anthropology because it is considered to be grounded in context and rooted to the spot. It is treated as a super artefact: architecture is understood as the social blueprint by which societies organize themselves (Buchli 2002b). Plan drawings are often implicitly read as blueprints in archaeology. Architecture in these archaeological accounts is depicted as one thing, as one clear-cut built object. It is drawn and written as a thing that is thought about as an idea, that idea then being translated into material form, that material form then being used.

The contradiction is that excavation often reveals the fact that architectures have several phases of construction and that these cannot be understood in sequential terms.

Neolithic long barrows, building as practice and quick architecture

One of us (Lesley) has focused most of her research on Neolithic long barrow sites in southern England questioning the idea of treating such monuments as a straightforward architectural object—the remains of *a building* that existed in the Neolithic, and that needs to be explained today. The overall excavation plan of the long barrow at Ascott-under-Wychwood, Oxfordshire is presented in Figure 25.1. The plan aims to show a Neolithic design process, in which a barrow was constructed in a series of rectangular bays on either side of an axial alignment, as a one-off. The plan depicts the infilling of a structural framework with material from quarries or flanking ditches, and then the subsequent use of the building as a tomb for the dead (Benson and Clegg 1978; Darvill 2004; Benson and Whittle 2007).

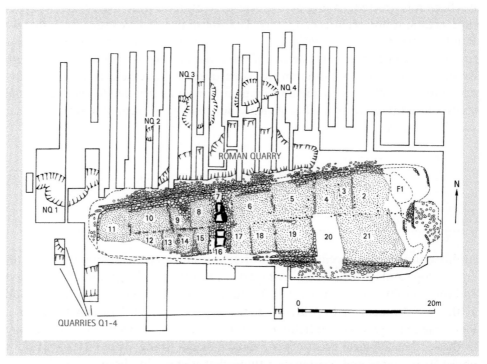

Fig. 25.1 Excavation plan of the Ascott-under-Wychwood long barrow, Oxford-shire (from Benson and Whittle 2007).

The plan conveys a concept of architecture that exists as one object, even when its form should be described and understood to have come about through several phases of activity. The primary phase of barrow construction was in 3760–3700 cal BC. The secondary phase of barrow construction was in 3745–3670 cal BC, but what is important is that the deposition of human remains occurred from the initial phases of construction onwards. The dead were incorporated into a construction site and not a finished tomb; there is no straightforward or sequential story here of construction and then use, contrary to the architectural object portrayed in the plan.

The call is for some critical questions. In the early Neolithic, did people build a hardbound architectural object with clear-cut conceptual parameters in mind, which were based on the presumptions of a trajectory from design (with its beginnings in thought) to an end product (finishing in a physical object)? Did they understand architecture as some thing that was made only once, that was built for a reason, and that it was used or occupied for that purpose (Rendell, 1998, has critiqued this simple and straightforward story of the built word within architectural history)? This object-led view ignores the fact that it is difficult to differentiate among kinds of practice at long barrow sites (for example, between the ways in which evidence for occupation and barrow construction are intertwined) and that it is difficult to pinpoint when the construction of a long barrow starts. Construction events extended over several generations. We might therefore think of the dead being incorporated not into finished buildings but into building sites. Thus, the point that archaeologists continue to recognize as the end product in these site histories should be best understood as the point at which they were abandoned, when they were no longer effective as a medium (McFadyen 2007b).

Our intention here is to show how a focus on practices-of-making engages the material and historical conditions of early Neolithic life in a better way, how such a focus wrestles with the variability of the evidence (and remains open to changes in a site's ongoing history), and how this focus gives architecture its context.

Architectural historians such as Diane Agrest (1991), Beatriz Colomina (1988), Jonathan Hill (1998, 2003), and Jane Rendell (1998) have sought to reveal the key elements and structure (and weaknesses) of the traditional story of architecture by presenting a more complex, changing, and non-linear account of architecture as practice. For example, Hill (1998) has written of the use of a building as a creative activity and as a form of construction itself. Such work questions the conventional focus in architectural history upon the actions of architects. It questions the idea that only architects make buildings, and it demonstrates how an object does not become any one end product or take any final form.

This thinking in architectural history holds significant potential to inform the interpretation of prehistoric monuments. It demonstrates how accounts of architecture might begin after a building was built, exploring the ways in which structures are occupied (Hill 2003). What is important about these writings is their emphasis on architectures as spaces that are always in the process of being made. For example, Jane Rendell (1998) has described how the top floor of a terraced house in Clapham, London was dramatically changed through home improvement plans and Do-It-Yourself projects. This work unbalances our understanding of the one-sided nature of architecture–user relations, which assume that buildings are used only in one preconceived way, as if architects freeze their original building plans. In addition, this work describes a more flexible practice of building that does not have any single fixed point of inspiration. Rendell describes how her partner undid the compartmental ordering of the house's rooms, each of which had been assigned a distinct activity such as sleeping, cooking, or having a bath.

The bath sat in the centre of the roof space. The roof space was bedroom, workroom and living room, and many other places all at once. From the bath you could look up into the sky, and down into the toilet, or directly onto the stove, beyond it to those eating at the table, and further through the window into the street.

Rendell (1998: 240)

In such accounts, the conventional story of order is undone and the knowledge of architecture is understood through a different kind of assembly, where building work is ongoing and open to the rhythms and routines of occupation. The distinctive thing about this work, and perhaps its most useful link to archaeology, is that is focuses upon material things, rather than architects' ideas.

The focus upon the ongoing nature of building practice in such architectural studies is significant for archaeologists seeking to account for those parts of the evidence that, on the face of things, simply do not make logical sense. Parts of the construction process at long barrow sites were very complex—more so than was necessary for structural soundness. This kind of practice can be described as 'quick architecture' (McFadyen 2006, 2007a, 2007b). This means that if you write about the physical practice of building, and think about the speed of different building techniques, then you can engage with what this does to people as they build.

At Ascott-under-Wychwood, high up in the build of the upcast mound of the barrow (i.e. not set in the ground but used in the upper levels of the unstable matrix of mounded material), people started to use large, thin stone slabs, turned up on to their sides. For example, between what the excavation report provisionally termed Bays 9 and 13 (Benson and Whittle 2007: 97–100), the axial alignment was made up of a double row of stones (slabs that were 0.40 m long, 0.03 m wide and 0.50 m high) (see context 60 in Figure 25.2). 'Bays' are traditionally considered to be stone walls that supply the structural framework in barrow building, but what we hope to show is that these 'bays' do not stand up and that they are dependent on the materials that are dumped on either side of the stone. These slabs were not set in another feature, and were not fixed steadfast, but were propped up, one after the other, and then almost immediately pinned on either side by dumps of yellow sand with small limestone rubble to the north (context 17) and larger limestone rubble in a sandy matrix to the south (context 40). Upon excavation, the sand and rubble were found to have been directly pressed up against the stones, and from the

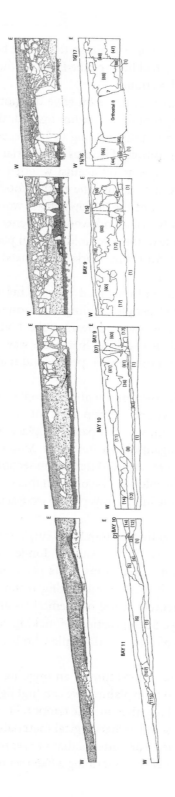

Fig. 25.2 Longitudinal section through the Ascott-under-Wychwood long barrow, Oxfordshire (from Benson and Whittle 2007).

contours of these dumps of material (the shape that these held in the section), it was possible to deduce that they had been pushed against the stonework on either side, concurrently from both directions.

This technique of setting pieces of stone on edge did not create a partition or structural element from which to build out from; instead, the stones would have been precarious and unstable and thus needing to be placed, propped, and then held in place with the rapid deposition of dumps of material on either side (Figure 25.2). Many of the pieces of stone were set against wooden panels, but the panels were not tied to wooden stakes that cut into the earth. Wood had not been used as shoring or scaffolding in this part of the build; instead, wood was as precariously pitched, as was the stone. Both stone and wood elements would have required dumps of material on either side of them to hold them in place. Setting stones and wood on edge created the need for future work; if that need went unsatisfied then the whole project would collapse.

We can imagine the intense and entwined movements of people and things, propping each other up: some people holding the stonework in place, others packing sand and rubble around them, smearing the bodies of those acting as props. Before the sand and rubble could act in a stable way on the build (and thus leading to materials standing on their own), people and materials were caught up in the matrix of construction.

This way of working had its own momentum. People could not stop and put things down. People would have had to prop up stonework with their bodies and hands, or would have had to jam wooden panels in place with their bodies while other materials were dumped against those junctions. Momentarily, people became labour and scaffolding at the same time. Material connections between people and things became evident when people were involved in this kind of building practice. While constructing and building in this way, people were acutely aware of how they were making their world.

To build in such a way, by setting materials on edge, was to employ a building technique that changed matter. Stone was no longer solid and structurally independent; instead, it became precarious in its placement and dependent on other materials and people's help. These building techniques also affected the builder; they made people acutely aware of themselves and their relations with other people and other things. Such practices of making created very demanding and very direct articulations of things and people who became caught up in each other.

By understanding Neolithic architecture as an ongoing practice, rather than a completed object that needs to be explained, we can highlight the dynamic ways in which materials are assembled together and the temporality of that practice that are of importance. We can understand archaeological materials as a medium of action in the past, rather than as objects or patterns that are set in a record, and to focus upon practices of building rather than ascribing a fixed set of traits to a built object.

This approach brings us close to approaches within material culture studies that focus upon 'thinking through things', describing the close relationships between things and concepts (Henare *et al.* 2007b). A focus upon Neolithic practice does not just yield new and different understandings of architecture; it suggests new dimensions to thinking about people as they build, and about the construction of their identities.

PROPOSITION 2

In the archaeological study of prehistoric architecture, a routine differentiation distinguishes durable, substantial structures, built on top of the land surface from short-term, small, dwellings that are constructed by digging a pit into the ground. Interpretations of group mobility, economy, and social complexity follow this distinction. The proposal made here is that archaeologists could refine (perhaps even transform) their understandings of pit houses and of the place of pit houses in prehistoric communities if they thought about pits not in terms of function or economy, but in terms of the particular processes involved in pit digging (i.e. of cutting and intervening in surfaces, and of negative space), especially as these processes were engaged in the late 1960s by some Land Artists.

Neolithic pits in south-eastern Europe

One of the most secure components in the classic definition of the Neolithic in south-eastern Europe is the establishment of a sedentary life-style based on the adaptation of walled built environments, from 6500 cal BC in northern Greece and somewhat later to the north in temperate eastern Europe. This is a vital checklist item for the culture-historian and the generalizing prehistorian; it is also a source of much (productive and welcome) thinking about the social and political significances of buildings, houses, and villages in early agricultural communities (see overviews by Tringham 1991a, 1991b, 1994, 1995; Stevanović 1997; Bailey 2000, 2005a). Overshadowed by the more substantial studies that reconstruct the architectural materials and methods of Neolithic houses and villages are the investigations of pit houses and pit dwellings. Pit houses are most often read as evidence for emerging sedentism and a shift from mobility (Figure 25.3). There has been little critical attention directed at these pit features. One of us (Doug) naively assumed in his earlier writings (Bailey 1999, 2000) that pit features represented pit houses

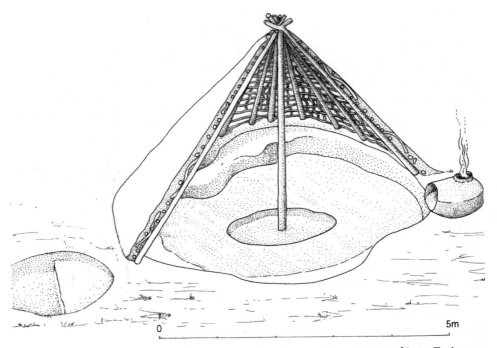

Fig. 25.3 Reconstruction of Neolithic pit hut at Podgoritsa-platoto (from Todorova and Vajsov 1993).

and that there was little room for discussion (see the criticisms of such approaches in the contributions to Bailey *et al.* 2005, 2008).

However, John Chapman asked important new questions about the intentions of Neolithic pit diggers and pit users (Chapman 2000a, 2000b), and about our interpretations of prehistoric pits, most usefully through the concept of 'structured deposition', which has been a significant theme in the study of west European prehistory for the past 25 years (Richards and Thomas 1984; Pollard 1995, 2001; Brown 1991; Harding 2006; see Joyce with Pollard this volume, Chapter 12). In general, however, the assumption remains that in the early Neolithic people dug small pits into the ground and used them for shelter or for rubbish deposition (or, sequentially, for both). Based on this assumption, research agendas for the study of the Neolithic have focused on reconstructing social life from these pits and their contents. Rather than seeing 'pit dwellings' as a simple marker of a step in a logical sequence from mobility to sedentism in one part of the world during one particular period, a potentially fruitful alternative is to recognize these 'pit features' as widespread beyond chronological, geographic, or cultural boundaries, from the Upper Palaeolithic to the European Middle Ages, the prehistory of Japan, and the American Southwest. In broadening the range of our thinking, we may find that existing reconstructions (such as those popular in the study of the Neolithic), which focus on economy or degrees of mobility, represent only one possible understanding of this record of activity.

What if the pit dwellings' primary, secondary, tertiary, or later uses and purposes are not their only, nor even their primary, significant dimension? Undoubtedly, these pit features had primary functions—as rubbish pits, houses, shelters, ritual depositories, building material sources—and the people who dug out these pits, placed objects into them, filled them in, and covered them over did so with very particular intentions. Nevertheless, we could understand pit dwellings/structures as interventions (the pit) into surfaces (the ground). The consequence would be that we would need to examine the act of digging as an act of intervention into the ground in terms of the consequences of adjusting ground surface and of creating negative space. This focus would raise different questions from those of conventional archaeological studies: not 'How should we describe the material assemblages that a pit contains' or 'What can these assemblages tell us about ancient activities?', but 'What are the unintended consequences for Neolithic people of digging, using, experiencing, filling, forgetting (or remembering) such features?' The shift in approach would be from a search for a social meaning to a consideration of the affordance that comes from digging-as-intervention.

Archaeological questions usually seek information about the number of flint scrapers in a pit, or about the type of economy, or the degree of community mobility, or the ratio of wild cattle to domestic pig bone. Such questions seek patterns in evidence that can be read as proxies for patterns of prehistoric behaviour. In this tradition, standard (and entirely valid) questions guide professional and rigorous research strategies: How can the material contained in each pit help us to determine community mobility/sedentism? What is the lifetime of a pit feature (a year, a season, a month, a week, a day, an afternoon)? Did people 'live' here in one place for one season, for two, or for many? Were these pits used at the same time (and do they thus represent a set of contemporary activities that were carried out by a sizeable group of people)? Does each pit and its contents represent a single set of spatially and socially restricted activities, and thus is each pit chronologically distinct from all others? Similar types of questions seek to understand patterns of deposition and taphonomy: Are there any stable relationships between pit contents and primary actions? Is the record-as-excavated nothing more than a jumble of secondary and tertiary (and beyond) traces of intentional activities or are they the unintended consequences of disconnected events? All of these questions are legitimate and important and need to be asked and answered. Though they are the accepted basis of the archaeological project, they follow a traditional relational logic and seek the answers that make us the most comfortable. An alternative is to set aside those questions, and in doing so, to open up fresh ground in which we can tackle record and behaviour.

Double negative

In winter 1969–1970, Michael Heizer and a team of workers used heavy construction corers, dynamite, backhoes, and bulldozers to excavate a quarter of a million
tons of rock and sand from the edge of Virgin Mesa near Overton in the state of
Nevada in the American Southwest (Figure 25.4). The trench that they dug was 500
m long, 10 m wide, and 15 m deep. Running along the edge of the mesa, it cut a long
rectangle of empty space across a small canyon. The resulting intervention into the
landscape, *Double Negative*, was one of many works by Heizer (and others) that art
historians now group under the category Land Art (Heizer 1991; cf. Crone 1982;
Brown 1984; Whitney 1990; Celant 1997). *Double Negative* was created out in the
open, away from the built environment, far from cities and populations, and
specifically beyond the reach of museums, galleries, collectors, and auction houses,
as was most Land Art (Andrew Dickinson White Museum of Art 1970; Kastner and
Wallis 1998; Beardsley 2006). Works such as Heizer's *Double Negative* stimulate us
to think about two issues that are critical to the archaeology of pit features and pit
dwellings: the human physical engagement with ground and its surface, and the
paradoxes of creating negative space.

In *Double Negative*, as in much of his work, Michael Heizer was drawn to the
ground and to its surface. Heizer's medium is the earth and he works this medium
as if it were a membrane (Celant 1997: xvii). As Heizer himself put it, 'My personal

Fig. 25.4 Michael Heizer's *Double Negative* (1969–1970), earth and air, The
Museum of Contemporary Art, Los Angeles.

associations with dirt are very real. I really like it, I really like to lie in the dirt' (Tomkins 1972: 48). Heizer is the son of the late Robert Heizer, an archaeologist who taught at University of California at Berkeley, but there are no clear references to the archaeological in *Double Negative*, although in other works, such as *Elevated, Surface, Depressed* and *Displaced/Replaced Mass*, Michael Heizer played with the ideas and consequences of moving stone from its source to distant places of consumption (Dietz 1984: 77).

This active relationship with ground is the link between Heizer and other provocative Land Artists (e.g. Richard Long, Dennis Oppenheim, Robert Smithson, Robert Morris, William Bennett) as well as other people who were wrestling from the late 1960s to the present with similar concepts, such as surface and perforation (e.g. Gordon Matta-Clark and his building dissections). As Germano Celant advises, once we have thought through these works by Heizer and his contemporaries, we recognize the inadequacies (or the inaccuracies) of speaking about human behaviour in the context of landscapes (Celant 1997: xxiv), and we meet a freshness of perspective for thinking about ground. In thinking with Land Art, we can come to recognize the limitations of restricting our archaeological discussions to terms of function, economy, and sedentism.

Through the transformation of the ground surface, Land Art manipulates and releases our perspectives on ground and thus on one of the primary dimensions along which we measure our existence. Ground is that relationship providing the most authoritative sense of who we are, where we are, and what is our position relative to others (Kastner and Wallis 1998: 12–13). In creating new elevations, forms, and locations, works of Land Art, such as *Double Negative*, change the potential, weight, impact, and presence of existing landforms. As Kastner (1998) argues, this process adjusts one's perceptions of the panorama, where panorama is taken in its traditional sense (i.e. the visual) but also with respect to other fields (the political, social, cosmological, temporal, and corporeal). Adjustment of field (of the viewed and the viewer) relative to panorama has significant effects on people (doing, digging, looking, touching, inhuming, and exhuming). A good example is Maya Lin's Vietnam Veteran's Memorial on the Mall in Washington, DC. In designing the monument, Lin specifically played with ideas about appropriate relationships between people and ground. By placing the monument below ground surface, Lin achieved several things. First, she adhered to the design brief: that the monument provides a refuge from the noise and distractions (of traffic, tourists, and city) of the National Mall. Secondly, she intensified the intimacy of the encounter of mourner and monument (and thus of the mourned). Thirdly, and unintentionally (one assumes), she stimulated a debate/outcry from those who implicitly assigned negative and dishonourable values with below-ground positions.

In this way we begin to think about the parameters of visual (and auditory, olfactory) sensory reference of person to ground, and particularly of the position of spectator/listener/smeller relative to panorama: to raise/lower the ground or to raise/lower the spectator is to manipulate and adjust relationships. Critical issues emerge: of distinguishing a view from above (a totalizing panoptic gaze, a sense of looking at something) from a view from below or from ground level (an invitation to participation and to community) (Kastner and Wallis 1998: 30). These are sensory relationships of power and hierarchy. The physical adjustment of the characters and the conditions of these relationships has important, often unintentional, consequences. What are the unintended consequences of new perspective(s) and panorama(s)? Do consequences unbalance existing relationships? Is this unbalancing abrupt or is it subtle? Does the creation of new panoramas undermine the authority of a mono-perspectival understanding of being? Are alternative, potentially conflicting perspectives thus brought into play? By manipulating, altering, perforating, and transforming ground surface, works of Land Art, such as Heizer's *Double Negative*, cut into the never absent connection of person to his or her environment. In these terms, the affective potential of Land Art is substantial: it transgresses, attacks (Kastner and Wallis 1998: 72), perforates, punctuates, dissects, cuts, refashions, and overturns a fundamental dimension of our being.

By thinking with Land Art, we begin to confront pit dwellings in unusual ways; significance rests in their potential to transform ground and thus to adjust relationships of people, objects, and places. Yes, early Neolithic pit features were used as source pits for building material, as shelters, as storage facilities, and as refuse depositories. As important as these functions were however, the proposal here is that the most significant consequences of digging, using, and filling any of those pits are in terms of their subtle alterations in Neolithic senses of being via the ground.

Relations to ground and adjustments or alterations of panorama and perspective are potent characteristics of Land Art. While with *Double Negative* Heizer offers an example of these characteristics, he also works with another theme, which is at the core of much Land Art and is of relevance for our attention to Neolithic pit activity: the paradox of creating negative space. By dissecting the ground surface, by subtracting and removing mass, weight, and density, with *Double Negative* Heizer created a transparent and invisible structure. Heizer defined a space in the ground, which had a power and a force that was disproportionate to its emptiness (Celant 1997: xxi). Kastner calls *Double Negative* a monument to displacement, a sculpture that is created not by solid mass but by void. There is nothing there but it is still sculptural (Kastner and Wallis 1998: 29, 54). This sort of work has implications that move well past function and economy; *Double Negative* engages the metaphysical and mingles with the impossible: the literal impossibility of a double negative (i.e. a positive produced by negation) (Kastner and Wallis 1998: 228). To push these paradoxes even further, *Double Negative* has been called the 'presence of an absence that is the absence of presence' (Taylor 1991: 17). By removing and creating emptiness, Heizer has provided a stimulus to thought in a most unusual and complex manner: something that comes from nothing.

By thinking through Land Art like Heizer's *Double Negative*, we are forced to think beyond the usual conclusions and interpretations both of art as cultural product and of pit features as shelter or rubbish site: the former is artistic work that cannot be bought, owned, collected, exhibited, and sold; the latter is a hole into which people dumped the leftover bits of their meals, or defecated/urinated, or placed (with precision) intentionally fractured fine-ware vessels. We are forced to consider the potential for the unintentional consequences of pits when we understand them as interventions into life's essential surfaces.

To move forward in our thinking we need to address the act of digging as a physically intimate collaborative effort, as a physical event, in many ways like the 'quick architecture' of long barrows described above, as well as an opportunity (perhaps not otherwise possible) for conversation, shared experience, and argument. We must think about the consequences of inserting a break (the pit) in an otherwise continuous surface (the ground). It is also important for us to consider the potential that such an adjustment and alteration provides for new panoramas: of looking down from 'old' ground level on to people and objects resting/standing on a 'new' ground, of looking up and out from the former to the latter, or of bringing people together into the (new) shared perspective (located down-and-in or up-and-out). Finally, we will benefit from thinking around the deeper metaphysical levels of manipulating our fundamental physical connection with the world, from thinking through the consequences of altering our literal grounding of bodies to place.

So, how can we understand the Neolithic pit features that we excavate in southeastern Europe? As semi-subterranean dwellings? There is no reason that they could not have served as short-term shelter. As storage or rubbish pits? Quite possibly, though it is just as likely that they served other functions. As pits dug to access materials needed for building, potting, or body painting? Certainly, though this may only relate to a single event within more complex use-lives. However, regardless of the intended functions of these pit features, archaeology is also capable of attending to the unintended consequences of intervening into ground and or creating, and eventually closing, negative space. Thinking in these ways would not produce the comfortable answers that can find easy support in quantifications of pit contents or stratigraphic matrices of depositional units. Among other things, the answers will bring us face-to-face with an unintended reconsideration of the practice of archaeology as a protocol for its own pit digging—the trench, sondage, and excavation unit—and with its own modern justification for intervening into ground and for creating negative space.

PROPOSITION 3

Excavation often shows that prehistoric architectures have several phases of construction and that these cannot be understood in sequential terms. In this proposition, we engage with some of this evidence in order to write about the gaps and disjunctions between phases of activity, and the implications of signs of transformation over time.

Time, practice, and disjuncture

The relationships between time and practice also require examination. In the opening proposition, we discussed the speed of the practice of building and the idea of 'quick architecture'. But practices do not just make time, they can also interrupt time. The architecture and work of Bernard Tschumi is of particular importance here. In 1982 Tschumi won a competition to construct Parc de la Villette in Paris, one of the *Grand Projêts* initiated by President Mitterand. Later, in his architectural writing Tschumi described how he approached the competition by seeking to create 'a structure without centre or hierarchy, a structure that would negate the simplistic assumption of a causal relationship between a programme and the resulting architecture' (Tschumi 1996: 193). The Parc de la Villette project was not composed of parts in a seamless arrangement, but involved a practice of making in which three autonomous and unpredictable fragments reacted with each other and thus created disjuncture.

It is at this point that we want to lay some groundwork for Proposition 4 (see below) where we suggest that archaeologists have been transfixed by the internal details, the composition, of Neolithic houses. We want to foreshadow this alternative proposition that houses are only of interest when we start to think about them in terms of external relations (i.e. to think of the object's articulation of space), but here we want to look at the temporality of Neolithic practice. There has been much debate in prehistoric studies about early Neolithic occupation in southern Britain, in particular when dealing with the relatively ephemeral evidence for timber structures. Prehistorians have sought to define the number and location of timber structures on particular sites, variously describing structures as timber halls or as rather less substantial structures of postholes (Darvill and Thomas 1996; Armit *et al.* 2003). These approaches focus on the structural details (what we call the internal details) of a Neolithic house as a thing that constitutes a particular physical location, and as a thing that is fixed in time in a static contemporaneity. An alternative is to explore the different temporalities that emerge from the longer activity at a site, but understood as a relationship where activities are autonomous and unpredictable fragments that react with each other, rather than as ordered series of event after event.

At Ascott-under-Wychwood, there is evidence for a connection between the occupation of timber structures and the construction of the barrow. The archaeological record shows how timber structures and a midden feature became entwined with the construction of the barrow (McFadyen 2007b: 348–349). There were two timber structures at Ascott-under-Wychwood 3980–3810 cal BC before the barrow construction 3760–3700 cal BC (Figure 25.5), and these were a part of a larger area of occupation, which was indicated by the distribution of worked flint (Benson and Whittle 2007: figure 2.7), characteristic of general 'domestic' activity (Cramp *et al.* 2007: 310). A concentration of cores, knives, scrapers, retouched blades, and burnt pieces was recovered from the midden (Benson and Whittle 2007: figures

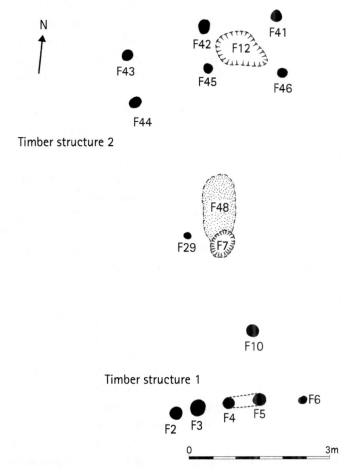

Fig. 25.5 Plan of timber structures at the Ascott-under-Wychwood long barrow, Oxfordshire (after Benson and Whittle 2007).

2.10–2.13) indicating perhaps a propensity for the pick up of tools during the second half of the fortieth century cal BC or the thirty-ninth century cal BC. There was a series of hearths, one of which had been cut by a pit. The pit had been backfilled with large parts of young pigs, a large number of burnt flakes, and unburnt sherds of pottery (McFadyen 2007b: 350).

The stratigraphical sequence indicates that there was an accumulation of midden material around the timber structures, which seems to have been contemporary with the occupation of these structures. There was then a gap in activity (after the structures had gone out of use), followed by the formation of a large accumulation of midden material over the features. In both phases of midden formation, a large number of flint tools as well as abraded fragments of pottery and animal bone was present. The material was 'more typical of pots which had been broken elsewhere, or which had suffered some further disturbance (perhaps trampling) before being partially collected for deposition' (Barclay and Case 2007: 278) rather than representing the *in situ* breakage of a vessel. Most of the animal bone was highly abraded, and was recorded as 'rolled' or 'weathered' (Mulville and Grigson 2007: 240). The post-breakage histories of the pottery and animal bone suggest that there may have been other gaps in the occupation of this site.

Bernard Tschumi (1996: 212) has argued that 'event' and 'disjunction' are both a part of architecture: 'In architecture such disjunction implies that at no moment can any part become a synthesis or self-sufficient totality; each part leads to another, and every construction is off-balance, constituted by the traces of another construction.' Tschumi's argument is significant in our interpretation of the archaeological sequence at Ascott-under-Wychwood, which indicates that there was a period of activity, a gap, and then another period of activity. Such gaps were a material record of people who were no longer present. They were a central part of the architectural process: a part of the way in which people built and occupied the site of Ascott-under-Wychwood. It would be wrong to understand the contexts in which these actions took place as simply a series of progressive activities that produced construction events that were separated by gaps.

Time was not marked out simply as a clear succession of events but instead was interrupted by significant gaps and delays that were then followed by practices of making. Early practices generated time-gaps between events in constructions; thus, we need to consider what these conditions might be saying about mobility and how these people went about living their lives. If people were living mobile (rather than sedentary) lives at this time, as Alasdair Whittle (1990) and Joshua Pollard (2005) have argued, then should not these various and non-continuous activities be considered as a part of architecture? If disjunction is also a part of that practice, then these kinds of sites always have a disconnection and an elsewhere. The force of action goes out and on in the world; this is how space comes to be distributed. We need to develop an approach to these sites that is created through departure and dispersal (Deleuze and Guattari 1977: 113), as well as one that considers the nested quality of a location and staying put (Ingold 2000a).

Alex Gibson (2003) has argued that the concept of Neolithic settlement should look beyond the evidence for built structures, that we can no longer afford to fix our sights on house plans, and that we must study all evidence for how Neolithic people went about living their lives. One might add to Gibson's argument the observation that the nature of this wider range of evidence is also telling us something about a distributed practice in the Neolithic. What this means is that we are not dealing with the distribution of a series of independent homes, defined in terms of their number and location: these sites have to be understood in the way in which they connect together. For a mobile population, occupation lies in the relationship between sites and not in the sites in themselves. Living in the Neolithic was on a scale that cannot be confined to the level of the site. The temporal gaps and practices described above were also a part of other long barrows and pit sites, as well as the fills of pits at causewayed enclosures.

How did Neolithic people feel about living in this way? Traditionally, prehistorians have argued about what is (or is not) a house by comparing plan upon plan (for example, Darvill and Thomas 1996), and argued that these homes have always been structured around centres. Here a Neolithic house is viewed as a thing that constitutes a particular physical location, and as a thing that is fixed in time in a static contemporaneity. An alternative to this approach is to start to think about sites as fragments of distributed practice, and engage with the decentred nature of the evidence. At times, people took with them everyday things (e.g. flint nodules, pots, and animals), thus making themselves at home through objects. Within this set of conditions, the location is not fixed but the objects that people live with are. A framework through which to understand this way of living is that of the 'mobile home'. At other times their practices of making involved leaving things behind or not clearing things away (e.g. flint tools, broken pots, and fragments of animal bone, as was the case with the material in the back-filled pit and the midden at Ascott-under-Wychwood). So sometimes life was characterized by the things people did not carry with them: this kind of dynamic generates the possibility of return. In the Neolithic, rather than people understanding house and home as a building in a central place, perhaps people were constantly pulling the inside out. Therefore, at Ascott-under-Wychwood the abandonment both of wooden structures (which would be the focus for a later phase of midden deposition) and of ceramics and animal bone (left to weather on the ground) is of significance. In both cases, the interrupted and non-continuous fragments of activity are parts of the conditions of living a mobile life in the Neolithic. Event and disjunction make the Neolithic home mobile.

PROPOSITION 4

The archaeological study and interpretation of architectural form from the prehistoric past remain central parts of how the distant past is understood and how social organization and structures are reconstructed. Almost without exception, analysis focuses on ever increasingly refined details of architecture, from macroscopic analysis of wall paintings to micromorphological investigations of floor-plastering sequences to chemical description of mortar recipes to DNA analysis of cereal grains perservered in oven remains. The proposal here is to step back from this increasingly tight focus on individual elements of architectural structure and its contents, and, as an alternative, to think about buildings as coherent objects themselves, especially with the intellectual stimulus of particular works of late twentieth-century Minimalist Art.

Neolithic houses in southeastern Europe

Archaeological studies of Neolithic houses in southeastern Europe have avoided two fundamental questions: Why are these buildings similar in appearance (Figure 25.6)? Why do these buildings occur in aggregations? Instead, archaeologists have looked at building and settlement composition, and the material and political interiors, of Neolithic sites. Increasingly fine-grained and minute internal details of Neolithic houses and villages have been traced: we have sought answers in the precise patterns of artefacts, residues, traces, and social contexts.

But what if none of what we have discovered about Neolithic houses matters? Perhaps it is unimportant what happened inside Neolithic houses, how a Neolithic house was built, abandoned, or destroyed, or whether a Neolithic house represents a social unit such as a household? And what if Neolithic building morphology and aggregation are interesting only when we see them as uninteresting? Perhaps Neolithic buildings are of interest only when we step away from the accepted questions and methods that seek compositional interpretation or explanation; Neolithic architecture becomes interesting only when we stop focusing on the building itself and on its internal components; Neolithic buildings are only of interest when we start to think about them in terms of external relations, from the eyes of the spectator?

Primary structures

In spring 1966, *Primary Structures: younger American and British sculpture* opened at the Jewish Gallery in New York. The show gathered together work made by a group of artists who shared a common approach to material objects and to space,

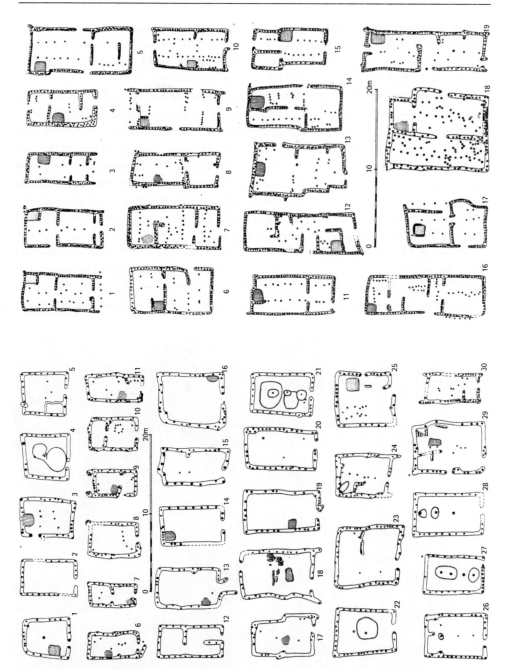

Fig. 25.6 Assorted house plans from the late Neolithic of Bulgaria.

and a common philosophical commitment to the abstract, anti-compositional material object (Meyer 2001: 13–30). *Primary Structures* contained seminal Minimalist pieces including important work by Donald Judd, Sol LeWitt, Robert Smithson, Robert Morris, Dan Flavin, among others.

Robert Morris showed two identical, grey, three-dimensional L-shaped forms (*Untitled, 2 L-Beams*; 1965–1967) (Figure 25.7): extravagantly large objects with arms over two metres long, making the pieces taller than most visitors to the installation. *2 L-Beams* was a strangely stimulating piece. Morris had placed the two L-shapes in conflicting positions: the first securely on the floor with its long arm running along the ground and its short arm standing straight up perpendicular to the floor; the outside tip of the right angle of the second pointed upwards, with the ends of the two arms of the L pointing down like legs, supporting the teetering shape with only a small area touching the ground.

Although identical in size, form, and colour, the objects' different positionings made them appear as different forms: one L was solid and stable; the other was balanced precariously, ready to topple. Viewers were faced with a paradox: two objects that were the same but which appeared not to be. The result was a tension

Fig. 25.7 Robert Morris' *Untitled (2 L-Beams)* (1965–1967). Installation from Primary Structures, 27 April–12 June 1966. The Jewish Museum, New York, NY, USA. Photo Credit: The Jewish Museum, NY/Art Resource, NY. Art © Judd Foundation. Licensed by VAGA, New York.

between the two pieces (same or different; different or same) and between the pieces and the gallery visitor (I see the same thing but in different ways). Minimalists were especially successful in creating and positioning identical three-dimensional objects in ways that confronted viewers with apparent contradictions: for Morris' *Ls*, the implicit contradiction was, 'it is the same but it is not the same'.

The *Ls* stimulated the spectator through the contradiction emerging from the repetition of a right-angled, three-dimensional L-shape, as well as through the objects' size and positioning; they forced spectators to consider things and places beyond the pieces displayed. Like the pieces of many of his colleagues, Morris' *Ls* were environmental: they focused the viewer's eye not on the object itself but on the object's articulation of space. Where traditional sculpture was self-contained and attracted the viewer's gaze towards it and then into its component (usually representational) parts, Minimalist art activated the space beyond and around the piece itself.

Minimalist art's environmental stimulation and activation of extra-object space brings the spectator and the piece of work into a shared space; powerful perceptual relationships emerge across and within the space that traditionally separated spectator and object. Critically, the meaning that emerges out of Minimalist art rests not in a formal analysis of object contents or their internal relationships. The only meaning available comes from each spectator's experience with each object. Thus, Minimalist art does not engage the viewers in the same way as traditional representational art engages them (LeWitt 1969).

Looking at traditional representational art (e.g. a sculpture bust), spectators make series of rational decisions about what is depicted, and meaning comes from those decisions: this is a nose and not an arm, this is a man's face and not a woman's. We are trained to approach Neolithic houses in a similar manner: this is a rectilinear, two-room structure and not an oval pit. This house has walls made with 10 cm diameter wooden posts (and not stone or mudbrick), the walls are covered with 17 layers of alternating white and red plaster (and not with 54 layers of brown and black plaster). The structure in the corner of the inner room is a grain silo (and not an oven); the silo is in the inner room (and not the outer room). And so on, and so on, until we understand the house within our understanding of the Neolithic.

American artist Sol LeWitt suggested another way of putting parts together, and thus of making objects engage spectators; it was a way that followed a *logical*, as opposed to a *rational*, sequence of decisions, in which each part was dependent on the previous one. In LeWitt's terms, a sequence has a logic to it and if a spectator engages that logic, then there is no need for decisions, questions, or answers. This logic is non-rational and viewers do not need to think; it is not even a way of thinking. Logical things just are (Colpitt 1990: 58).

Minimalist art was logical. It offered sequences of visual and physical stimuli that did not need thinking about. If viewers did start to think about a Minimalist object or sequence in a rational way, then they became lost. If they started asking questions, they became frustrated: when they think that they have located a possible answer, they are angry because there is no way of determining the potential accuracy of their answer. A good example of this logic is Carl Andre's *Lever* (1966), a sequence of 137 firebricks placed in a line along the floor. People who read this work in a rational way, quickly become irritated: if they ask rational questions about each brick (seeking answers before moving on to the next brick), they find that there are no decisions to be made: no questions and no answers. People who approach Minimalist art expecting a rational experience end up asking the minimalistically most futile questions. What does it mean? I can't see that it means anything. Why can't I understand this work? They end up with a traditional answer: because it isn't art.

In the wake of the suggestions that LeWitt's works made about the logical sequence of Minimalist art, there follows the rejection of the rational reference and representationality that is at home in traditional art and that seeks answers in internal elements and their composition. Thinking with Minimalism, we reject the importance of internal composition and its rational decisions, and we are forced to focus on the object and on notions of objecthood. Minimalist artists created objects that were non-representational, which offered no illusions of rational representation, but which, at the same time, were real and palpable, that occupied space. For Minimalists, objecthood was three-dimensionality without the illusion that accompanies representation. Minimal art is not imitation; there is no illusion to a something else, or a somewhere else. The work sought to be non-referential.

The critical thing is not what a Minimalist object alludes to: it is its shape. The shape is the object; it is the whole thing and there is nothing else. Minimalist objects are simple and single, but also repetitive and modular shapes that have no internal meanings or rational relationships (Judd 1965). Thus, the cube became the ultimate, basic, and most standard empty shape. It has no referential components to distract spectators: by looking inside, one finds nothing to be seen but the inside of the cube; looking outside finds only the cube. There is nothing there. Furthermore, a cube is solid and stationary; it does not go anywhere and thus does not take the spectator anywhere with it. Environmentally, the cube might push the spectator away from the object, but the cube itself remains immobile and does not accompany the viewer. Of all shapes, it is the most basic, the most standard; the only thing that a cube represents is . . . well . . . a cube, and if that is all then it is not representational at all.

For Minimalism, the cube is interesting as an object simply because it is uninteresting. The cube is empty of anything but itself. Hollow and empty, it directs the spectator outwards and away from itself. If there is meaning, then it is somewhere else. It might be in the person looking at the cube. It might be in the relationship between the position of the cube and the spectator. It might be anywhere else but it will not be in the cube. Even more importantly, the cube has the extraordinary power of making explicit its empty hollowness. By surrounding empty space with solid areas, the cube creates emptiness, surrounding but not filling the space within. Thus, in a sensationally, apparently contradictory, physical fashion, the cube creates negative volume, an emptiness that is environmental, a manifestation of emptiness that pushes the spectator away into thinking about anything and everything except the cube itself.

With Minimalist objects we become interested not in the thing itself, but in the external arrangements, repetitions, and series orchestrated by the artist. With Carl Andre's linear series of bricks on the floor (e.g. *Lever*, 1966), the interesting thing is not the bricks as identical objects, but the way that Andre arranged and repeated the identical units. Arranging identical units in logical series Andre (and Morris *inter alia*) imposed an order that operated beyond each physical object itself. Along with the environment, repetition of form, and attention to the specific object, the serial ordering of objects was a powerful tool of the Minimal artists. The imposition of a serial order to specific-object arrangement was more than a method; it was an attitude that subsumed a work under the order and the repetition of form (Bochner 1967).

The perception of serial work has important consequences for spectators. Without internal relationships, content, or sets of rational decisions, viewers consume Minimalist objects more easily. Less perceptual work is required. Where rational work had to be chewed over, through sequences of decisions, questions, and answers, Minimal work slides right down in one logical gulp. Such simplicity brings an unexpected impact to the spectators' role(s). Identical-forms-in-series may have been more easily taken in, but they do not sequentially reveal the object or its meaning. In fact they do the opposite, pushing the spectator away, to think and look elsewhere; they frustrated meaning. Thus, Minimalist work increased the spectators' workload: there is no easy visual path to understanding or meaning. In fact, there was no particular meaning at all, only sets of tensions and the stimuli to think. Among these tensions is the realization that the individual specific objects are less important than the systems within which they exist and are arranged. The individual objects do not really matter at all; the important entities are the ordered sets of objects. Arrangement becomes the end; individual form becomes nothing more than the means.

Minimalist art and Neolithic houses

Thinking about Minimalist art helps us with our investigations of Neolithic houses, of the formal similarities of the Neolithic built environment, and of the aggregation of Neolithic buildings into villages. There follow three proposals. First, we should think about Neolithic buildings as anti-compositional and non-referential. Their importance lies not only in what they contain or in how each building in a village was constructed. If we accept this, then most interpretations of Neolithic buildings and building morphology—ours included (Bailey 1990, 1999, 2000)—only offer a portion of a full understanding of a building. In fact, we may wish to reject (as the anti-thesis of meaning) our existing schemes and attitudes about the Neolithic built environment. The second proposal is that we should think about Neolithic buildings as empty spaces, as negative volumes, and as the manifestations of hollowness. The third proposal is that we should think about Neolithic buildings as environmental, in the Minimalist sense.

In these terms, therefore, Neolithic buildings positioned people in space, not simply in as architecture choreographing movement or social relations, but in the sense of specific objects pushing spectator/villager/visitor away from the building and its contents. By working from these perspectives, one consequence is that we turn Neolithic spectators away from the individual components of a particular building design or form; Neolithic people find themselves looking at and living among logical series where repetition of a common form pushes them to think away from the house and its contents. Critically for our understanding of the past, the importance of Neolithic buildings may not rest only with their interiors and our analysis of their contents. These buildings were/are specific objects: physical, palpable but not representational or illusory. Their shape is their meaning, but only when their shape is taken as a specific object. They are anti-compositional (and not rational); thus, they will not repay rational investigation based on rational questions seeking rational answers.

What was a Neolithic building during the Neolithic? It was an object that forced people to think externally about themselves in relations to others, which slid down without chewing, like a Big Mac, something that was accepted without thinking. Furthermore, the meaning of aggregations of Neolithic buildings may not be found in the sum contents of individual structures. We can now ask another question: What is a Neolithic village from a Neolithic perspective? In the terms proposed here, the answer is that a Neolithic village is both a serial order of specific objects and a single specific object. At yet a further step away, a Neolithic village is just one specific object within a longer serial order of villages across a landscape, up a river valley, across a region, and through a sequence running for hundreds and sometimes thousands of years.

The value to be found in using terminology and ways of thinking that comes from Minimalist Art may not be that they present us with new information or that they reveal new meanings. We are not suggesting that they do. Ideas such as serial order, the specific object, serial repetition, and environmental engagements between spectator and work push us away from the search for a single, closed meaning of the Neolithic built environment. This is/not a house. This is/not a household. This is/not a place of shelter. This is/not evidence of privacy and social inequality. This is/not a village. The challenge will be to see if the perspective elaborated here can work alongside the current knowledges, methods, and accumulated understandings of Neolithic buildings and villages that we have become so proficient in developing. This is the provocation, but so, we suggest, were the houses and villages of the Neolithic.

Conclusions

Our four propositions present diverse arguments. Proposition 1 uses a direct engagement with the archaeological evidence in order to present a critique of the idea of architecture-as-object rather than archaeology-as-practice, and to put forward the idea of 'quick architecture'. In contrast, Proposition 2 uses analogies with Land Art to move away from the internal details of the archaeological evidence, in order to explore how to work with what the past is not, with absences, and with the negative. Proposition 3 focuses on the nature of the archaeological evidence in order to consider the forms of time that emerge from tracing archaeological sequences. Proposition 4 uses ideas from Minimalist Art to call for thinking through the range of external relations to the archaeological record.

Regardless of these differences in focus, together these propositions seek to disrupt the widely accepted archaeological understanding of Neolithic buildings as straightforward projects, both in the prehistoric past and in the interpretive present. In Propositions 1 and 2, we focus on Neolithic architecture as a physical practice: as quick architecture or as interventions into surfaces. Proposition 3 looks at how architecture can be constituted through disjuncture as well as through practice, exploring what the gaps in archaeological sequences might tell us about mobile life in the early Neolithic of southern Britain. Proposition 4 looks at houses as objects that are bound up in external relations, using analogies with modern art to explore the consequences of looking through the eyes of the spectator and of the environmental impact of serial, specific objects, where 'environment' is understood in the terms of the Minimalist artist.

Together, our four propositions call for the unlearning of how we look at archaeological evidence of houses, building, and architecture, and our case studies seek to explore this potential in practice, to assist archaeologists in getting closer to an affective understanding of how past peoples understood their worlds. We hope that these four propositions from the European Neolithic will offer to scholars of different periods, regions, and disciplines, examples of unexpected alternatives to the traditional investigation of architecture and the built environment.

CHAPTER 26

CERAMICS (AS CONTAINERS)

CARL KNAPPETT

LAMBROS MALAFOURIS

PETER TOMKINS

INTRODUCTION

What makes 'ceramics' a particular category of thing worthy of special attention? For an archaeologist, two different answers might normally come to mind. One is purely pragmatic: ceramics are very often one of the most abundant categories of archaeological find, for example in the later prehistory of the Near East and Mediterranean, and thus any archaeological analysis of material culture is bound to encounter ceramics sooner or later. A second answer is more conceptual: ceramics are considered a key feature of human material culture because of what they are taken to represent in economic, technological, and evolutionary terms. The innovation of taking the plastic medium of clay and marrying it with pyro-technology to create irreversibly a resilient object—usually in the form of a container, but also sometimes in other forms, such as figurines—has frequently been assumed to mark a revolutionary (Neolithic) stage in the development of modern human thought and practice, forming with agriculture and sedentism a trinity of epoch-changing innovations (e.g. Childe 1936, 1942: 43–61; Renfrew 2003; see Gamble 2007: 10–32).

Neither of these answers, though, is particularly satisfactory. Quantity alone is unconvincing as a motivation for academic study. Equally, the traditional idea of a Neolithic/pottery revolution is no longer sustainable in view both of the deep pre-Neolithic history of ceramic production among mobile hunter-gatherers *c.*12300–7200 BC (e.g. Jordan and Zvelebil 2010) and the long delay in the Near East between the development of agriculture and the adoption of pottery (Hoopes and Barnett 1995: 4–5).

Even more tellingly, material culture is not just for archaeologists. How might a socio-cultural anthropologist, for example, react to the idea that ceramics constitute a notable category of material culture? Or a sociologist or geographer? We suspect that the response would be quite different and not altogether positive (e.g. Leach 1973). In an ethnographic setting, why should a pot be marked out for special attention, rather than a basket, a mat or a stone tool or, for that matter, a can of coke or pair of jeans? Would it not be more worthwhile in such a context to examine categories of practice, perhaps 'cooking', 'containing', or 'sheltering'? In such a framework, the focus would fall on ceramics as containers, first and foremost, to be considered alongside other kinds of containers such as baskets, gourds, and metal vessels.

We are inclined to adopt this approach for two reasons. First, we believe that to treat 'ceramics' as containers first, and as a technology of fired clay second, actually offers a rather different perspective on the innovation of pottery in Europe and Asia during the early Holocene, and indeed on its subsequent trajectories during the Neolithic and Bronze Age (see Gamble 2007). Secondly, it is in line with the spirit of the present volume to see the territory of 'material culture studies' as spanning both past and present, and hence not the privilege of any particular discipline. Thus our perspective draws upon ideas from socio-cultural anthropology and elsewhere concerning the category of 'containers' and practices of 'containing' while also adopting an archaeological approach that is long term and 'developmental'. We begin by reviewing ideas from cognitive psychology on the role of the body in providing metaphors of 'containing', with the work of George Lakoff and Mark Johnson, as well as Ed Hutchins, featuring prominently. While material culture does play some role in their thinking, our approach demands more explicit attention to artefacts and the qualities of the material world as experienced by the human body; for this we turn to the work of anthropologists Tim Ingold and Jean-Pierre Warnier. Further theoretical development is provided from the 'material engagement' perspective within archaeology (Renfrew 2001; Malafouris 2004), as well as related work in archaeology by John Chapman (2000a) and Clive Gamble (2007). Armed with a theoretical framework for approaching containment, we consider some of the evidence for the earliest ceramic containers from the Mesolithic and Neolithic of the east Mediterranean, as well as continuing the story of the development of containers through to the Bronze Age. What this approach allows us is a more dynamic perspective on human practices of containing, one that acknowledges the constitutive role of material culture itself in changing notions of what it means to contain, literally and metaphorically.

BODY AS CONTAINER

What does it mean to contain? From where does this idea derive? Despite containers being one of the most abundant categories of archaeological find, and thus arguably the chief focus for study, the concepts they objectify have rarely preoccupied archaeological thinking, with a few recent exceptions (e.g. Tilley 1999; Gamble 2007). 'Containment' may well be the 'function' offering archaeology one of the most important sources of archaeological data and windows into the prehistoric mind, society, and culture; but very little is known about the cognitive, experiential, and evolutionary grounding of the concepts embodied in each and every container. Naturally, as we said, ceramics as a category encompass more than just containers, and containers can certainly be found outside the category of ceramics. Yet, one cannot fail to notice that once ceramics were first introduced, with the advent of sedentism in Europe and the Near East, they become associated with two major forms of 'containment'. The first form is of course that of a pot or a vessel. Here the association with containment is obvious at the functional level. The second is that of clay figurines. Here the association with containment is less direct but equally powerful, realized through the semiotic relation of these objects with the human and animal body, i.e. the biological container par excellence. Although these two major categories of artefact, pots and figurines, often receive different archaeological treatment, the first as belonging to the realm of the functional and mundane and the latter to that of representation and symbolism, we suggest that a more focused view may reveal that they are more closely related than is often assumed. We argue it is not simply the knowledge about the properties of clay and fire that link these objects but a new way of thinking about the body that these objects bring forth. And it is this new understanding, i.e. *the body as container*, that the many examples of anthropomorphic vessels from that period exemplify (e.g. see Gimbutas 1989: 22, 52, 191; Perlès 2001: 264–267). In what follows we shall be arguing that there is more to this blending of pots and bodies than meets the eye, and that in addition to the usual archaeological assumptions about the social and symbolic role of Neolithic containers as a new technology of meaning in the construction and communication of social identity (e.g. Thomas 1996; Tilley 1996), containment may have a more basic and to a large extent neglected role in the shaping of human intelligence.

To make our case more clearly in this chapter we stress that in speaking about 'containment' we are not just concerned with or referring to the physical capacity of a clay vessel to contain, e.g. to hold a liquid, but rather with the interactive properties, possibilities, or affordances that emerge because of the vessel's ability to contain (Knappett 2004). Containers are not simply vessels but action possibilities that bring forth new forms of mediated action, agency, and material engagement, both in terms of use and manufacture (Knappett and Malafouris 2008b). It is precisely at this elementary level of mind–body–world interaction that the significance of containment can be found. Containers, very simply, are important because they introduce 'a different topology—*a surface around a void*' (Read and van der Leeuw 2008: 1965). Put in terms of the embodied mind and conceptual metaphor theory (CMT) that we shall turn to discuss now, containers are important because they afford the enactive realization of the container 'image-schema'. That is, of an image-schema that consists of (1) a boundary that demarcates (2) an interior from (3) an exterior. This may seem a trivial observation to a modern observer surrounded by and moving in and out of containers, perhaps hundreds of times each day, but it was certainly not trivial when ceramic technologies were first introduced in the Neolithic.

But let us take one step at a time, and start by taking a closer look at what the embodied mind theory is all about.

EMBODIED MIND AND METAPHOR THEORY

The *embodied mind* and *conceptual metaphor theory*, developed especially by cognitive psychologists such as George Lakoff and Mark Johnson (1999), maintains that the body is not just a passive container for the mind but is an active component in its formation. A focus upon embodied cognition treats human conceptual categories as, to a large extent, dependent on 'the bodily nature of the people doing the categorizing' (Lakoff 1987: 371), rather than corresponding to inherent objective properties of an external reality. Concepts are constructed on the basis of 'interactional' rather than objective properties (Lakoff and Johnson 1980); they derive from 'our interactions as part of our physical and cultural environments given our bodies and cognitive apparatus' (Lakoff 1987: 51). This view also finds support in neurobiological research (e.g. Gallese 2005; Gallese and Lakoff 2005).

In embodied mind theory, 'the very structures on which reason is based emerge from our bodily sensorimotor experiences' (Lakoff 1987: 386). The implications of such a position are far-reaching, shaking the heart of the objectivist foundation of traditional cognitive science. From such a stance, embodiment is the condition for meaningfulness (Lakoff and Johnson 1999). This point is crucial for our purposes here and, as such, it is worth raising two further related questions. The first question concerns the exact nature of these preconceptual bodily experiences that define the way humans make sense of the world. The second relates to how abstract or higher-level cognitive operations can be explained in terms of this preconceptual structure.

Addressing the first question, George Lakoff and Mark Johnson jointly introduced the notion of 'image schema' (cf. Lakoff 1987: 459–461; Johnson 1987: 19–21). An image schema is a recurring dynamic pattern of our perceptual interactions and motor programmes that gives coherence and structure to our experience. In particular, according to Lakoff and Johnson, image schemas: (a) are *directly meaningful preconceptual* structures, which arise from, or are grounded in, human recurrent bodily movements through space, perceptual interactions, and material engagement, and (b) integrate information from multiple senses and operate *beneath* conscious awareness, prior to and independently of other concept modalities. Thus image schemas should have the following qualifications: they must be: (a) pervasive in experience; (b) well understood and well structured; and (c) emergent and well demarcated (Lakoff 1987: 278).

Tackling the second question, concerning the relationship between preconceptual 'image schematic' structure and 'higher-level' cognitive processing, embodied mind theory suggests that in domains where no preconceptual structure is directly available on the basis of experience, humans import such structure by way of metaphor (Johnson 1987; Lakoff 1987; Fauconnier and Turner 1998). As various experimental studies in cognitive psychology have revealed (especially Turner 1987, 1991; Lakoff and Turner 1989), an extensive system of metaphorical mappings underlies human thought processes, structuring some of the most basic categorizations that humans conventionally employ in conceptualizing the world. Based on these observations, embodied mind theorists have situated metaphor at the very centre of human cognition, especially since George Lakoff and Mark Johnson's study *Metaphors We Live By* (1980).

For CMT the word *metaphor* refers to *a cross-domain mapping in the human conceptual system*, that constitutes the *basis* of understanding and meaning construction (Johnson 1987). More simply, metaphor is the crucial vehicle that enables the human mind to apprehend the many 'domains of experience that do not have a pre-conceptual structure of their own' (Lakoff 1987: 303). In other words, abstract conceptual structures that, in contrast to image-schematic structures are not directly meaningful, become meaningful through their association with meaningful image-schematic structures; that is, employing metaphorical projections from concrete to abstract domains.

FROM BODIES TO ARTEFACTS

How can the ideas of embodied mind theory and CMT help with answering our initial question about containment? Where does the notion of containment come from? Given what we discussed above the answer that immediately comes to mind is deceptively simple: the human body. In particular, the idea of containment, like many metaphors through which humans understand the world around us, stems from the body and from the basic experience of being.

As the human body not only has a longer ancestry than the manufacture and use of containers, but also can be directly experienced and understood in itself as a container (with the skin as the boundary between inside and outside), the primacy of the 'body container' over the 'artefact container' would seem beyond doubt. Grounded upon our image-schematic understanding of what it means to live through a human body, it seems perfectly reasonable that, starting with the experience of the human body, interiors will be mapped on to interiors, exteriors on to exteriors, and boundaries on to boundaries. This is a basic assumption implicit in the work of Lakoff and Johnson (1980), and adopted by most archaeologists working on this theme, such as Chris Tilley (1999) and Clive Gamble (2007). For example, as Tilley characteristically remarks in his *Ethnography of the Neolithic*:

A connection between pots and bodies is clear in the occurrence of face pots, or pots with eyes, at the tombs. Smashing a pot with a face is metaphorically like smashing and destroying a human body, or more specifically another container, the skull. It is the rim or orifice area of the pots that are particularly elaborated through decoration and a major context for the deposition of these pots is in the entrances, or orifices, to the dolmens and passage graves. The pot is a container of fluids and substances which enter it and flow out of it, with the decoration on its surface, acting as a skin...The symbolic parallels I have drawn out between pots and bodies may not have been unnoticed by Neolithic populations.

Tilley (1996: 318)

By the same token Clive Gamble in his *Origins and Revolutions* (2007), although explicitly emphasizing the 'material basis of human identity' when discussing his proposed division of the material world into 'instruments' and 'containers', overlooks the ways in these objects themselves shape rather than reflect a new understanding of human experience.

Although the above suggestions make good sense of many cultural manifestations of the phenomenon of containment, we should not deny the possibility that artefact containers, rather than just the body, may themselves be the source domain of metaphorical mappings, rather than the target. Human thought is not only embodied, but also situated in a complex material environment with which the human body constantly engages. To illustrate this more fully, we need to highlight an important drawback that lies at the heart of the embodied cognition framework and metaphor theory.

The embodied mind theory of Lakoff and Johnson, by grounding cognition in bodily experience, has undoubtedly made a successful step towards resolving the unhelpful mind–body dichotomy. Nevertheless, what this step implies for the proponents of embodied mind theory is simply an expansion of the ontological boundaries of thought (*res cogitans*) rather than the dissolution of those boundaries altogether (Malafouris 2004, 2008a). In this approach, material reality remains external and epiphenomenal to the cognitive structure. This has two major implications for our understanding of the relation between embodiment and material culture as well as the nature of metaphorical projections as these can be seen to operate beyond the linguistic realm.

The first implication is that the active role of material culture in mediating and enacting metaphorical projection is neglected; artefacts are not considered integral to the cognitive process. The second is that the various means for intervening in the environment, like language, artefact, gesture or ritual, etc., are homogenized, rather than allowing for their quite different properties and possibilities for metaphorical and integrative projections. Chris Tilley made note of this misconception in his *Metaphor and Material Culture*. He distinguished between the operational properties of metaphor in matter and metaphor in language, observing that 'solid metaphor cannot be reduced to a series of linguistic metaphors' as they are not materialized substitutes for them (Tilley 1999: 270). Nonetheless, Tilley maintains the internal/external dualism found in the work of Lakoff and Johnson, from whom much of his approach to metaphor derives.

Materially enacted metaphors present no text-like propositionality as in the case of their linguistic expressions. They do not simply communicate meaning but, actively doing something, they objectify sets of ontological correspondences. Instead, Tilley suggests that

> the artefacts work as prompts to perform processes of conceptual mapping between them. Perhaps the most common case is the perception of shared parts or elements such as bodies and pots and houses having openings or orifices or being containers, thus permitting them to be linked, or shared aspects of physical structure . . . sharing the same shape or form.
>
> Tilley (1999: 268)

Once we accept this, the most interesting questions, as Tilley observes, are those to do with the way in which human cognition 'becomes articulated to produce particular kinds of metaphorical links within historically determinant and determined social circumstances' (Tilley 1999: 35). Indeed if metaphor is, as CMT would argue, 'as much a part of our functioning as our sense of touch' (Lakoff and Johnson 1980: 239), and if preconceptual structure is to be accepted as the experiential foundation of an embodied human mind, then both metaphor and preconceptual structure have to be placed and analysed upon the concrete support of material culture. In fact, it can be argued that none of the 'image schematic structures' (discussed above) can be experienced outside some context of material engagement. In such contexts of situated action, though, the boundaries of the embodied mind are not determined solely by the physiology of the body, but also from the available constraints and affordances of the material reality with which it is constitutively intertwined (Knappett 2004, 2006; Malafouris 2004, 2008a, 2008b). Thus, we need to develop an approach to containment that builds upon the insights of embodied mind theory and related perspectives, but which moves out into the material world and includes it as part and parcel of the processes of cognitive metaphor. We can achieve this by drawing on recent work in both anthropology by Jean-Pierre Warnier and Tim Ingold and in archaeology by Clive Gamble and John Chapman.

SITUATED METAPHOR: BRINGING MATERIAL CULTURE IN

As socio-cultural anthropologist Jean-Pierre Warnier asks, 'is not material the indispensable and unavoidable mediation or correlate of all our motions and motor habits? Are not all our actions, without any exception whatsoever, propped up by or inscribed in a given materiality?' (Warnier 2001: 6). Warnier's perspectives are significant here because he does not only link the body and material culture: he also develops a consistent and insistent focus on the meshing of the *techniques* and *gestures* of the body with material culture (Warnier 2001, 2006). This concern comes from a long French anthropological tradition focusing on gestures (see also de Beaune 2000) that can be traced back through Leroi-Gourhan (1964) to the work of Marcel Mauss on the cultural specificity of bodily techniques (Mauss 1973; originally Mauss 1936). There are all kinds of gestures through which human identity is performed and constituted, and most involve movement, except perhaps for some static gestures, like holding one's breath (Warnier 2006). Movement demands perception, which takes place through the seven senses: the five familiar ones, to which are added proprioception and the vestibular sense of gravitation and spatial orientation (Warnier 2006: 186; see also Berthoz 1997). To movement and perception, Warnier adds a third dimension: using neuroscientist Antonio Damasio's study of *The Feeling of What Happens* (2000), Warnier asserts that no sensorimotor conduct exists without desires and emotions.

So we have the *sensori-affectivo-motor* conducts (Warnier 2006: 187) of the subject as key, and Warnier takes the significant step of adding material culture to the equation; though he is quick to point out that integrating material culture in this way was a step already taken in the 1920s by Schilder, with his concept of the 'bodily schema'. Taken together, this creates a schema of 'sensori-affectivo-motor conducts geared to material culture' (Warnier 2006: 187). This he dubs 'praxeology'. This fits with a much broader 'enactive' theory of perception (e.g. Noë 2004), and is also consistent with the 'embodied mind' perspective already outlined; however, it does emphasize the integration of movement, gesture, and material culture rather more explicitly. The emphasis in Warnier's approach of movement, technique, and gesture can serve to avoid the division of the material world into basic categories, such as 'artefacts' and 'landscapes' (Gosden 1999: 152).

Warnier's discussion of containers requires a fluidity that allows for the shifting of scales between the human body, clothing, pottery, houses, and even whole kingdoms. Ingold's (2007a: 45) use of Gibson's tripartite scheme of medium, substance, and surface is similarly fluid (Gibson 1979). For example, we can readily see how containers have *surfaces* that can exclude some *media* (e.g. air), while containing others (e.g. liquids). Furthermore, containers might be made of various kinds of *substances* that can achieve containment in a range of ways; compare, for example, skin, basketry, clay, metal, and plastic. The different technologies of containment may enable or constrain different kinds of practices, and, in this chapter, we should of course consider the particular affordances and constraints of pottery as a technology of containment.

Thus, we need to look at the particular ways in which certain gestures and materials come to express ideas of containment. Even though the human skin is sometimes depicted in psychology and psychiatry as the 'arch-container' (Anzieu 1995; Warnier 2006: 187), the variety of practices and technologies of containment suggest the human body might experience containment in ways not derived purely from the body. Warnier enumerates a basic repertoire of practices, including feeding, breathing, defecating, and being held, that 'develop at one and the same time both the sensorimotor and the psychic components of containment and its correlates' (Warnier 2006: 188). The performance of such activities means that the concept of the body as container is dynamically constituted by universal processes; and yet significant cultural differences can exist in how these processes are performed. In practice the human body frequently supplements itself with other kinds of surfaces that 'contain', working outwards from clothing, to objects to dwellings. These too are likely to be comprehended using bodily metaphors: the opening of a building will be understood in relation to the orifices of the body, and the wrapping of the body in garments will relate to the conception of the skin as a surface (see Blier 1987, 2006: 241; Gamble 2007: 98–99). But this is not simply one-way traffic outwards from the body: practices and gestures performed on buildings, pots, and clothing may act back on the body, changing ideas and practices of bodily containment in the process. The variable character of technologies of containment from one society to another underlines this sense of a two-way process back and forth between the body and the environment. Part of the complexity of this relationship means, however, that we cannot gloss it as solely 'social'; bodily gestures and technologies are psychologically and biologically grounded too. Mauss described 'l'homme total' as a bio-psycho-social phenomenon (Mauss 1973).

Therefore, the image-schematic structure of containment, far from a fixed and universal embodied experience, presents a variety of forms and cultural instantiations. Although there may be a tendency in cognitive and social science to grant primacy to the human body, the idea of the body as a container may well be the emergent product of human interaction with containers and the bodily practices that surround them. This would mean that a deeply entrenched metaphor of the body as container might have originated in the extensive engagement of humans with the use and manufacture of containers, ceramic and otherwise. In other words, it can be argued that the relatively unstructured target domain of the human body becomes experientially grounded via containing technologies. Thus a body can be understood as the metaphorical container of a soul or spirit; a mental category can be understood as the container for an idea; and even mathematical relations like those of the Venn diagrams may take on meaning in the same way (Lakoff and Núñez 2000). From such a perspective, one can see how such macro-scale events as sedentism might have significant implications in terms of their capacity to restructure central aspects of human experience and by extension human conceptual architecture.

Accepting the idea that different cultural instantiations exist, we need to give fuller attention to the role of different containing technologies. These include technologies of the body, such as scarification and tattooing, as well as clothing, textiles, basketry, wood, clay, stone, metal, and plastic containers. The various practices of skin and beyond skin have been approached recently in archaeology in slightly different though complementary ways. John Chapman (2000a; Chapman and Gaydarska 2007) has differentiated between 'accumulation' and 'enchainment' as two technological means that humans employ in their use of material culture, with different spatio-temporal reaches. This has been critiqued and adapted slightly by Knappett (2006) who differentiates instead between layering and networking as two ways that humans extend beyond the body. Gamble, in a similar vein, and drawing on both of these approaches, talks of 'sets' and 'nets'; as technologies move further away from the body and what is proximate, that which is accumulated or layered close by in 'sets' may easily become fragmented and separated, finding itself distributed or enchained in 'nets' (Gamble 2007: 139–152). These approaches highlighting the varying levels of connection between the human body and material culture can all be seen as part of the broader inquiry into the various ways in which humans engage with their material worlds, encapsulated in what has been termed 'material engagement' (Malafouris 2004; see also the idea of 'tectonoetic awareness' in Malafouris 2008a). Thinking in such terms helps us to understand the enactive role of material culture in human practices and identity in broad terms, but we need to work through specific examples to push the debate forward—and here we will examine the role specifically of pottery containers. There is certainly scope for pursuing these ideas in ethnographic contexts, which is precisely Warnier's (2007) approach as he examines the role of pots and bodies as containers in the expression of kingship in Cameroon. However, we shall focus here upon archaeological material, addressing the development of technologies of containment over the long term.

CONTAINERS IN THE MESOLITHIC AND NEOLITHIC

In considering the first appearances of pottery in the Near East and south-east European Mesolithic and Neolithic, we might assume that pottery is a revolutionizing invention: an engine of social evolution, transforming people's capabilities and propelling them towards the modern world. This view lies at the heart of social evolutionary models of adoption that emphasize the superior performance of ceramic containers for storing, cooking, or serving food, and how these properties transform adaptive potential and create the possibility for socio-economic growth (e.g. Childe 1942: 44–45; Brown 1989; O'Brien et al. 1994; Hayden 1995; Rice 1999: 2–14). Such models exhibit a preoccupation with rational economy, retrodicting pottery as a fully formed technological complex in the assumption that its properties and potentials would have been as accessible and compelling to people of the past as they are to a modern materials scientist. A characteristic assumption made by such approaches is that once pottery appears other, older containment technologies become marginalized or disappear (e.g. Childe 1942: 45).

An alternative approach would view the relationship between technology and people in more dialectical terms, as a process of mutual determination, in which technology reacts to rather than revolutionizes its social context. Innovation is a multistage process, beginning with invention in discrete centres of origin, followed by a wider dispersal along existing social networks (Edgerton 2006; Knappett and van der Leeuw nd). Usually, therefore, the decision to innovate is a straightforward question of adopting or resisting externally sourced bodies of knowledge and practice. In the case of the earliest ceramic containers, the decision to adopt or resist will not simply depend on the advantages perceived as accruing to this particular form of containment technology, but on wider sets of contextual criteria.

While the archaeological record has long been understood to be but a fragment of the totality of the past (e.g. Childe 1956: 12), the temptation to allow it to structure archaeological enquiry has often proved hard to resist. Pottery is invariably treated as a separate material category and its study has become a disciplinary specialization within archaeology. Exploration of the context in which pottery was made, used, and discarded generally proceeds along temporal and spatial lines. However, if we extend our understanding of context across surfaces and between substances, a much broader and more complex universe of containers in leather, basketry, wood, stone, and metal, comes into view alongside the ceramic. However dimly perceived and poorly represented in the archaeological record, the usage of non-ceramic containers stretches back millennia before the inception of pottery and continues alongside it up to the present-day (Gamble 2007: 194–204). Occasionally ceramic studies have broken free to acknowledge the existence of metaphorical links with a wider non-ceramic container context, usually in obvious cases where the surfaces and forms of ceramic containers are recognized as mimicking those in other substances, a phenomenon known as skeuomorphism (e.g. Childe 1956: 12–14; Vickers and Gill 1994: 105–153; Hodder 1998: 64–69). Rarely, however, does the recognition of these linkages impact upon how pottery is contextualized and understood (but see, for example, Vickers and Gill 1994). This is a pity, a missed opportunity even, because the interplay of metaphor between container substances is far more profound and, at times, subtle than the current focus on the more literal skeuomorphs might imply. The plasticity of clay imbues ceramic technology with a Protean ability to take on the appearance and form of any container, while the physical and chemical changes wrought by firing grant it a durability in the archaeological record. Through this unique combination of plasticity and durability, pottery allows us glimpses into the non-ceramic container worlds of the archaeological past, albeit through a ceramic lens or filter. A challenge for archaeological ceramic studies, but one all too infrequently met, is to find ways of adequately exploring the broader context of container usage and explaining the contingent nature of the metaphorical links between different container substances.

Our earliest window on to this world of containers comes with the first appearance of ceramic containers, produced by hunter-gatherers in eastern Russia, China, and Japan around 12300 BC (Kuzmin 2006; Jordan and Zvelebil 2010). Once viewed as an independent centre of origin, unconnected with the origins of pottery in the West (e.g. Moore 1995: 40–46), more recently East Asia has emerged as the origin point in a westward chain of successive pottery adoptions, which reached the Near East in the late eighth millennium BC (Jordan and Zvelebil 2010). Thereafter its dispersal into Europe becomes entangled with that of agriculture: an entanglement highlighted in conventional models of the European Neolithic.

Early pottery contexts within this east–west dispersal are characterized by a wide variety of forms and sizes, but share the same production sequence and often similar technological features, such as a preference for organic tempering (Jordan and Zvelebil 2010). From a purely ceramic perspective, where the typology and technology of early pottery is viewed as a discrete techno-complex evolving under its own internal logic, this pattern poses certain problems of interpretation. Where did the typological variability exhibited by early pottery originate? How can the successive westward adoption of pottery be understood as a dispersal, when its form and usage in neighbouring regions often seems so utterly different (e.g. Kuzmin 2006: 368–389)?

The earliest pottery in the Aegean region of the Mediterranean is typical of this trend in manifesting a range of different forms from its first appearance (*c*.6500/ 6400 BC; e.g. Evans 1964: 196). Such typological complexity has been conventionally explained by postulating the existence of an earlier, simpler stage of ceramic invention and typological development, which has then been placed either locally in the poorly documented Initial Neolithic phase that precedes pottery use (*c*.7000–6500 BC) (e.g. Vitelli 1995: 60–61; Perlès 2001: 64–97) or externally in one or more underexplored regions further east (e.g. Evans 1921: 35; Evans 1968: 271; Weinberg 1970: 583). However, the continued absence of evidence to support the existence of such an experimental stage makes this a highly unsatisfactory explanation.

If, however, one approaches the problem from a broader container perspective, it becomes possible to decouple typology from technology. The dispersal of early pottery can thus be recast, more simply, as the dispersal of a technology or body of technical knowledge and practice, while early typological complexity and variability may be understood in terms of the influence of pre-existing traditions of non-ceramic container usage and variation between these traditions through space. For example, the forms adopted by the earliest pottery from the site of Knossos (Crete) appear to have been entirely determined by two separate, pre-existing container typologies in wood and basketry, each with specific sets of perceived properties and meanings (see Tomkins 2007a). Thus the dark polished surfaces, thinner walls, and flat bases of a range of small- to medium-sized bowl types imitate a class of wooden (tableware) containers suitable for the serving of food and drink (Figure 26.1). The deliberate use of non-calcareous dark-firing slips, polishing techniques that simulate wood grain, and a series of carved handle-types are more specific indicators of wood skeuomorphism (Figure 26.2). In addition, the relatively long and heavy wishbone handle type, found on a type of dipper or ladle, presupposes structural properties that are present in wood but absent in ceramic, where such handles consistently break at their narrow point of attachment. Conversely, a second group of medium to large ceramic vessels, characterized by globular, semi-closed forms, rounded bases, strap handles, and, occasionally, corded decoration would appear to imitate a class of basket containers, intended for use on an uneven surface and suitable for storage, transportation, and cooking (Figure 26.3; Wengrow 2001: 171–178, for similar such examples from the Near East).

Recognition of the influence of this wider world of non-ceramic containers also helps us to understand certain other aspects of early pottery use. During the earliest phase of ceramic use in the Aegean (*c*.6500/6400–6000 BC; Perlès 2001: 98–112;

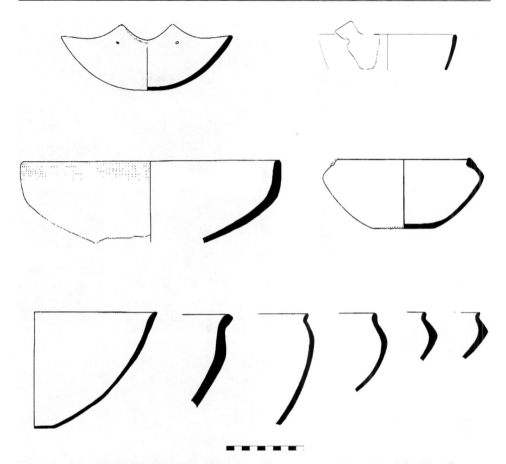

Fig. 26.1 Ceramic tableware forms skeuomorphing wooden containers, Early and Middle Neolithic Knossos (Knossos Stratigraphical Museum) (Tomkins 2007: figs. 1.3, 7–13, 14, 27; 1.4, 4).

Tomkins 2007b: 21–23), ceramic containers were consumed in very small quantities with rates of deposition estimated at about five to twenty-five vessels per year (Vitelli 1993: 210; Perlès 2001: 214; Tomkins 2007a: 181). Given evidence for the importance of curation (e.g. drilled mend-holes; Tomkins 2007a: 182) such low rates of deposition imply a production output that was lower still. Technological studies of early pottery in Mediterranean Eurasia have consistently noted high interest (measured in investment of time, energy, and skill) in the forming and especially finishing of containers (e.g. Vitelli 1995: 60), but have generally failed to find clear evidence for the deliberate manipulation of ceramic properties to enhance efficiency, output, or performance (Björk 1995; Le Mière and Picon 1999). Put simply, the quantities and qualities of early ceramic containers suggest they were specifically created to

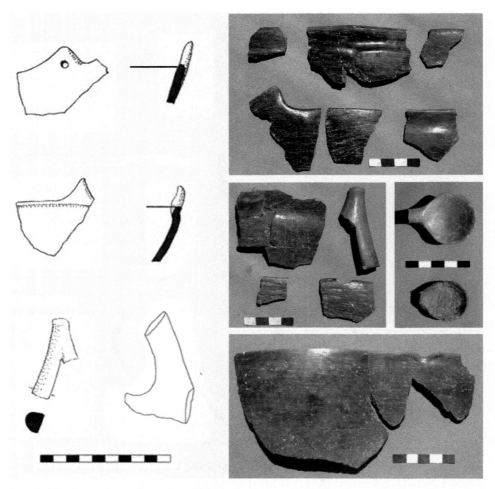

Fig. 26.2 Ceramic surfaces and forms skeuomorphing wooden containers, Early and Middle Neolithic Knossos (Knossos Stratigraphical Museum) (Tomkins 2007: figs. 1.3, 24; 1.4, 11–12, 22; photos p, Tomkins).

be used only on a restricted, probably ritual basis, as high-value versions of a range of non-ceramic containers whose superior resistance to stress continued to recommend them as the daily containers of preference.

Consideration of the role of early ceramic containers in exchange adds further to this picture. A series of petrographic studies in the Near East, Aegean, and west Mediterranean have independently demonstrated that early pottery, especially finewares, was widely exchanged, with some vessels travelling distances of more than 200 km from their original place of production (Le Mière and Picon 1987; Barnett 1990; Tomkins et al. 2004). Comparative analyses of form and finish support these conclusions; with large zones of stylistic similarity the rule for the

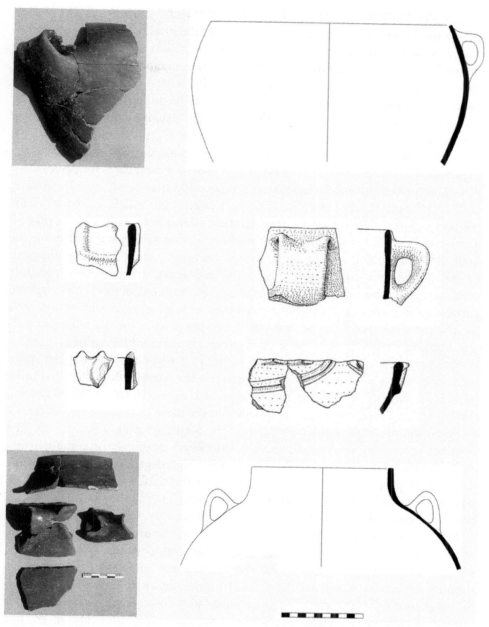

Fig. 26.3 Ceramic forms skeuomorphing basketry, Early and Middle Neolithic Knossos (Knossos Stratigraphical Museum) (Tomkins 2007: figs. 1.3, 1–2; 1.4, 1–2; photos P. Tomkins).

earliest phases of ceramic use in the Aegean (e.g. Weinberg 1970: 584). The scale of these long-distance interactions is far in excess of the local networking required to ensure demographic viability and would appear to reflect a deliberate and highly energetic social strategy, in which distance (social, geographical, cosmological; see Helms 1993; Barrett 1998) is a key resource in the negotiation of status. Distant social relationships and their entangled objects may be understood in terms of the accumulation of 'symbolic capital' that might be deployed in order to define identity and negotiate status (Bourdieu 1977: 171–183; Appadurai 1986b: 29–31). The choice to adopt pottery may well have been bound up with this process, the high value of ceramic containers making them obvious candidates for deployment in such networking. Nevertheless, analogous networks may be envisaged stretching back into the pre-ceramic past, involving non-ceramic containers and tools (Gamble 2007: 97–110). More than passive signifiers of meaning, such objects play an active role in enacting metaphorical projection, serving as material proxies for the body (Warnier 2006: 193–194; Gamble 2007: 107–109), which, when exchanged, extend bodies and identities through time and space. In the case of ceramic containers, the centrality of their role in ritualized occasions of food consumption, above all group commensality, meant that they were an especially effective vehicle for the conversion of distance into status, serving as cues for the telling of self-aggrandizing stories of acquisition or illustrious container biographies (Tomkins 2004: 48–50; 2007a: 192–193). In this way it may be suggested that the key factor mediating in favour of an adoption of pottery in the late Mesolithic and Neolithic periods in the Old World was not a far-sighted appreciation of the long-term revolutionizing potential of its technology, but the more immediate and unthreatening appeal of its more basic properties. The plasticity of its substance ensured continuity, allowing traditional, socially sanctioned categories of container and container consumption to be reproduced with a high degree of conformity, while its different properties in relation to other container substances defined it as a separate and more valuable container category, which might then be deployed as a means of negotiating value in people and practices.

The burnished or polished monochrome surfaces that are such a notable feature of the very earliest pottery to appear in the Near East, Anatolia, and the Aegean, would seem to reflect a fairly literal rendering of the surfaces of containers, in substances such as wood and basketry. However, in each region this phase is followed by one where certain ceramic forms start to carry a heavier decorative burden of painted or incised motifs. From the late seventh millennium BC, this explosion in decoration represents the exploitation of another property of ceramic containers, namely the ease and effectiveness with which their surfaces may be altered in order to represent additional layers of meaning or emphasis. In many such cases, the forms and decorative elements continue to reference containers in other substances. For example, David Wengrow (2001: 171–181) has argued that Halaf and Samarran painted pottery in the Near East draws heavily upon traditions

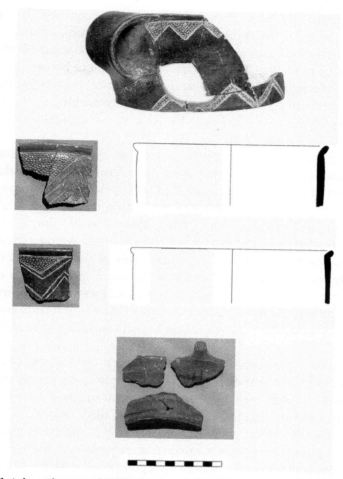

Fig. 26.4 Flat-based mugs, Middle and Late Neolithic I Knossos (Knossos Stratigraphical Museum; Herakleion Museum) (top: Furness 1953: pl. 30, c; remainder: P. Tomkins).

of decorated basketry. In other cases, however, forms and motifs suggest a new source domain, that of the human body. For example, at Knossos the transition to the Middle Neolithic (c.6000 BC; Tomkins 2007b: 23–27) witnessed the appearance of a new tableware form, the flat-based mug, usually decorated with incised triangular motifs filled with punctuated dots or *pointillé* (Figure 26.4). Incised and/or punctuated decoration also appears on some ceramic figurines, usually female if gender is explicit, and has been interpreted as representing clothing, tattooing, or scarification (Ucko 1968: 329–330; Mina 2008: 121–130). A metaphorical link with the body is reinforced by rare examples of flat-based mugs that have the upper torso and head of a figurine moulded on to their rim (Figure 26.4; Evans

1964: 226, fig. 60.6–7). The decoration on these ceramic containers and figurines is incised using a similar tool, probably a class of bone needles, and filled with white and more rarely red colorants, raw quantities of which also occur (Evans 1964: 236, 238; fig. 61.11, 13; pl. 60.1–2). The links in tool and technique between a specific type of ceramic container, ceramic figurines, and the (female) body imply that material inscription paralleled corporeal inscription, probably marking moments of transition in the female life cycle when new identity or status was achieved (cf. Wengrow 2001: 174–177, for the Near East).

More specifically, cases where flat-based mugs form the lower part of the upper torso and head of a figurine seem to suggest that the form of such vessels referenced the lower part of the female torso, specifically the pelvic region and womb, as the source and container of human life. Further hints in this direction are the preference for an incised triangular motif filled with (pointillé) dots on the exterior surface of flat-based mugs and the use of incised triangles to render female genitalia on figurines. More speculatively, the white colour of the calcareous residue that is frequently encrusted on the interiors of flat-based mugs, but no other vessel form, may carry with it a reference to semen. In this way a series of metaphorical links are made between the surfaces and form of ceramic figurines and flat-based mugs, on the one hand, and, on the other, the skin and form of the female human body.

In this example, the decorative explosion in early pottery may be connected with an extension to the range and complexity of the ontological correspondences that are objectified by ceramic containers, shifting from the purely artefactual to the human body and from more literal renderings of single sets of correspondences (skeuomorphism) to a freer, more complex layering or mixing of metaphors. The flat-based mug form represents a mixture of metaphorical linkages to different container source domains, combining a dark polished, flat-based (tableware) form, suggestive of wooden tableware, with strap handles, suggestive of basketry, and forms of adornment and inscription that reference the female body, particularly the pelvic region.

Stepping back from this point, the implications of a broader container-based perspective to pottery extend in different chronological directions and into different domains of archaeological practice. Looking backwards it becomes clear that we need to engage more actively with earlier, pre-ceramic phases of container use, such as the Mesolithic and aceramic Neolithic (Gamble 2007: 110). One way of doing this is to take a fresh look at archaeological typologies of early pottery, which, though created primarily to answer questions of chronology and cultural affiliation, have the potential to serve as windows on a wider and older world of containers and its intersection with the ceramic. Such effort is necessary, if only to prevent us from mistakenly spinning a surge in the *visibility* of technologies of containment, occasioned by the adoption of ceramic technology, into a 'container revolution' or, in Warnier's (2006: 193–194) words, a major shift in the 'domestic technology of containment'. Looking forwards, we would prefer to reserve such language for contexts where regimes of production are of sufficient intensity, quality, and output, and levels of ceramic use and discard are sufficiently high as to suggest that pottery has encroached upon or even replaced other container technologies in daily consumption. Such conditions would appear to have been first met in the Aegean during the Bronze Age, when pottery comes under the influence of new regimes of value and consumption and a new range of containers in metal and stone.

CONTAINERS IN THE BRONZE AGE

Although a wide range of container types are employed in the Neolithic, those in ceramic are foremost in quantity and diversity. Ceramic containers facilitated further changes, principally through extensive 'enchainment' in assemblages across space and time; as prehistorian Clive Gamble (2007: 272) puts it, 'this form of container had in turn the almost infinite potential for further divisibility and reproduction, just by making more pots'. We can follow the story through into the Bronze Age, charting this substantial growth of ceramic assemblages, the continuing significance of inter-media associations (skeuomorphism), and hence the impossibility of understanding ceramics in isolation from the broader range of material culture.

From the beginning of the Bronze Age in the Aegean (c.3100/3000 BC; Warren and Hankey 1989; Manning 1995), we see the addition of metal and stone to the repertoire of container technologies. Although copper and silver objects first appeared during the later Neolithic, these were not containers, but, in Gamble's (2007) terms, instruments, such as adornments (e.g. pins, beads, pendants) or tools (e.g. awls, axes) (Zachos 2007). In the case of Crete, evidence for ceramic skeuomorphism of sheet metal vessels, in the form of rivets, tubular loop handles, and grey and red polished surfaces, began in EB I (3100/3000–2650 BC). But it is not until EB II in the Aegean that the use of silver and bronze containers really took off, part of what has been called 'Metallschock' (Schachermeyr 1955; Renfrew 1972: 338; Nakou 2007). Although stone vessels were very occasionally made during the Neolithic, their incidence increases significantly from the start of the Early Bronze Age (Bevan 2004).

Metal and stone introduced new properties and hence new possibilities for socio-material expression. Metal has the plasticity and solidity of ceramics (varying with the involvement of heat), but could also be recycled by being melted down, thus enabling it to function as a form of currency and an index of wealth in a pre-monetary economy. Furthermore, metal, and to a lesser extent stone, differs profoundly from clay in the extremely uneven distribution of their raw material sources. Whereas clay is more or less ubiquitous, sources of specific stone types and metal were very restricted: Crete, famously, has no metal resources to speak of. Metal and stone are also more resistant to shock than pottery. These properties mean that metal or stone containers (or instruments, for that matter) are much more likely to have impressive 'back stories' in terms of their production and circulation. All of which factors served to define metal and stone containers as new high-value container categories, thus usurping the previously unassailable position enjoyed by pottery during the Neolithic.

Relegated to the middle register in a hierarchy of container substances, Bronze Age pottery developed in two different directions. One involved taking on containers in stone and metal, not only by skeuomorphing these vessels (Knappett 2002, 2008; Nakou 2007), but also by developing increasingly complex and technically demanding *chaînes opératoires*, both of which come together in high-value pottery styles, such as the polychrome painted Kamares Ware, produced on Crete during the Middle Bronze Age (Figure 26.5; Walberg 1976; Faber *et al.* 2002; Day *et al.* 2006). At the same time the quality, output, intensity, and efficiency of pottery production was increased to the point that pottery was able to rival traditional daily technologies of containment, such as wood and basketry. In this regard one might single out the use of the wheel for manufacturing an increasingly wide range of pottery vessels during the Middle Bronze Age (Knappett 1999), and the

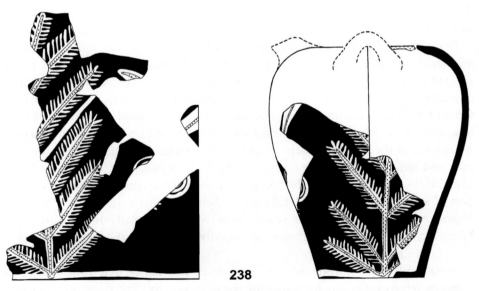

238

Fig. 26.5 A polychrome 'Kamares' jar, Middle Minoan IB Knossos (Macdonald and Knappett 2007, fig. 3.8).

Fig. 26.6 Minoan conical cups, Late Minoan I, from Kastri on Kythera (see Bevan et al. 2002; photo C. Knappett).

development of the conical cup in the latter part of that period as a mass-produced vessel used in a whole variety of settings, both domestic and cultic (Figure 26.6; Gillis 1990). Unsurprisingly, pottery continues also to skeuomorph containers in basketry and wood, for example (Knappett 2002, 2008).

We might also look at particular categories of container that emerge in the early Bronze Age and remain in use, more or less, throughout its duration. One of these categories—a storage vessel known as a 'pithos' (Figure 26.7)—is found almost exclusively in ceramic form, while another—a 'ceremonial' vessel with two openings known as a 'rhyton'—occurs principally in ceramic, metal, and stone, the ceramic examples frequently skeuomorphing the form and decoration of the latter two substances. These can be seen as two particular technologies of containment, the former aimed at containing large quantities over relatively long periods, and the latter was designed for containing small quantities over short periods. The pithos is a type that had its origins in the ceramic storage vessels of the later Neolithic, increased notably in size during the Bronze Age and has continued in one form or another up to the present day (Cullen and Keller 1990). A recent typological study of Minoan pithoi has identified 122 different forms (Christakis 2005). The majority (60%) of those treated in Christakis' study are from storage areas in palaces and houses, and many are capable of holding hundreds of litres of solid or liquid commodities. What is of further interest, given our earlier discussion of the metaphorical connections with the body, is that in 30% of known cases, pithoi are used for burials (Christakis 2005: 55). Again, as with their use for storing

Fig. 26.7 Minoan pithos (height 87 cm), Middle Minoan II, from Quartier Mu, Malia (see Poursat and Knappett 2005, pl. 7, 123).

agricultural produce, we can see how pithoi were destined for long-term storage of one kind or another.

The rhyton, however, clearly works on quite different timeframes: containment is inevitably followed very quickly by release. The 'flow' of liquids rather than their static containment is key, and the Greek word 'rhyton' itself comes from the verb 'rhein', 'to flow' (Koehl 2006: 5). The vessel has in common with many vessels a primary opening, but then has a smaller, secondary opening, often a perforation in the base of the vessel (Figure 26.8; or in the muzzle in the case of animal rhyta). This suggests that a user would have filled the vessel with a finger over the narrow opening, and then in a particular gesture (perhaps in a ritual setting) would have released the finger thus allowing the contents to flow out of the container. The earliest rhyta belong to Early Minoan II and the latest to the end of the Bronze Age. Though less long-lived than pithoi, they are far more diverse morphologically. Some of the earliest are anthropomorphic and zoomorphic, in the form of birds or bulls in particular (Koehl 2006), thereby further emphasizing the connection between bodies and vessels as containers (albeit containers allowing matter to flow freely both in and out). Rhyta are also found in a wide range of materials, in contrast to pithoi: they occur in ceramic of course, but also various kinds of metal (silver, gold) and stone (e.g. serpentine, chlorite, limestone, breccia), as well

Fig. 26.8 Minoan rhyton (base with pierced hole facing up), Middle Minoan IIIA, from Akrotiri, Thera (Knappett and Nikolakopoulou 2008, fig. 21).

as ostrich eggshell, faience, and various composite types combining some of the above materials (Koehl 2006).

CONCLUSIONS

The pithos and the rhyton are just two categories of container from the Aegean Bronze Age. We might also have chosen a number of others, such as tripod cooking pots, conical cups, or beaked jugs, all of which are extensively used as containers, in their differing ways and with their distinct affordances. The technologies and assemblages of containment in the Bronze Age are complex and varied, but we should resist the temptation to interpret pottery in isolation from other container substances. There is always a wider container context that is just within reach if we look for references to it in the form and appearance of ceramic containers. Judged from this perspective the history of pottery use is characterized not by revolutions, either at the beginning of the Bronze Age or indeed at the onset of pottery use in the Neolithic, so much as continuity in the ever-present intersection of different materials and technologies, and of different tendencies towards 'accumulation' or 'enchainment' (Chapman 2000a; Gamble 2007). These intersections and tendencies are not so strongly materialistic that human identity is entirely moulded by them; but neither are they merely the by-products of an overarching quest for human identity that is predominantly cognitive. What we are seeking is an intermediary perspective that pays full attention to material properties, and the particular affordances of ceramic and other technologies, while also attuned to the importance of human relationships in mobilizing these technologies.

We find that the praxeology perspective developed by Warnier (2001, 2006, 2007), when set within the broader context of 'embodied mind' and 'enactive' approaches (Malafouris 2007, 2008a, 2008b), is a very promising way forward for material culture studies. Taking the techniques and gestures of the body as central allows a more dynamic approach to material culture. Rather than being mired in arguments over ceramics as a category, we can start thinking much more fruitfully about what and how ceramics mean and do. Hence by focusing on technologies of containing and containment we seek to avoid an essentializing perspective that makes 'pottery' or 'ceramics' primary, and to allow ourselves, in this case, a much more dynamic and indeed human perspective on the material culture of the Neolithic and Bronze Age Aegean, one that can begin to provide more satisfactory explanations of both continuity and change over space and time.

CHAPTER 27

MAGICAL THINGS: ON FETISHES, COMMODITIES, AND COMPUTERS

PETER PELS

When are things magical? From a sceptical secularist point of view, they are never magical by themselves: they require the intervention of human intentions, since something material only becomes wonderful or out-of-the-ordinary *for* human beings. Yet, things are also only perceived as magical when they exert agency beyond or against human intentions—when, rather than being passive, inert, and merely material, they *do* something to us. This, in a nutshell, is the problematic of magical things, taken as comprising fetishes, amulets, charms, icons, relics, commodities, and a host of other objects that behave themselves as subjects. On the one hand, a modernist way of thinking argues that such things ought not to move people, since authentic and rational human beings, instead of being controlled by things, are supposed to be in control of themselves and the matters around them. On the other, the need for concepts like 'commodity fetishism' indicates that everyday life in modern societies is often determined by the contrary: by people losing control of themselves through being swayed by the things their society offers. Thus, while magical things themselves are of all ages and cultures, the *problematic* of magical things seems to be a typically modern one.

This chapter focuses on this problematic, for without this focus we cannot reach an understanding of magical things—or the relationship between magic and materiality—in general. My aim is to use three modern categories of artefact— the fetish, the commodity, and the technology—to understand our (modern) uses of 'magic' in relation to materiality. To do so, I will start in the nineteenth century to outline how magic became divorced from materiality in Euro-American thought. This brief theoretical diversion will then allow me to use the fetish as an exemplification of the modern European understanding of magical things—as objects that, as agents, are not supposed to exist, and that fall under a regime of simultaneous fascination and iconoclasm. The understanding reached by the impossibility of the fetish can be extended to our own everyday lives by zooming in on the magic of the commodity (or 'commodity fetishism')—to show that a certain fear of the object that behaves as a subject is both affirmed as well as denied in consumer society. Lastly, I hope to show through a reflection on the early popularization of the computer how the modern problematic of magical things plays out even in contexts where people embrace rather than fear the autonomous- ly acting object. Throughout, I focus, by diverse means, on folk theories current in modern life, in a largely anthropological effort to show that our attempts towards understanding materiality may be better served by an adequate recognition of folk theory on magic than by some, often illusory, academic striving towards theoretical rupture with our often enchanted everyday lives.

Magic and materiality

Modernist discourse—especially as it emerged in the 'academic science of magic' during the Victorian period (Hanegraaff 1998)—has positioned magic in three dominant and mutually contradictory ways: first, it portrayed magic as the antith- esis and supplement of modernity, defining the latter in the process; secondly, it delineated certain typically modern objects and routines as magical, raising doubts about the extent to which they are properly 'modern'; and thirdly, it denied the materiality of magic by implicitly but exclusively focusing the problematic of magic on problems of human subjectivity (Pels 2003: 4–5, 31). This explains why mod- ernist discourse on magic never defined it in any satisfactory sense: if 'modernity' needed 'magic' as a supplement, defining itself by what it was not (and vice versa), the closure of a definition was impossible to achieve. At the same time, it shows why the vast majority of attempts to define magic concentrated on abnormal or marginal subjectivities: if modernity was to be characterized by the rational calculation of the value of material goods or facts of nature—by capitalism and/or science—then the definition of magic had to derive from some non-rational form of valuation. Some of the sources of such modern valuations—the church, religious belief—were embattled but powerful presences in modern life. Hence, magic was mostly defined and modernized by relatively young and secular modes of subjectivity like psychology and poetics.

This historical moment is best illustrated by the 'fathers' of the science of magic, the anthropologists Edward Tylor and James Frazer, who both thought that magic ought to be explained primarily as mistaken belief—an error of psychology. (Other, more sociological dematerializations of magic occurred later, but cannot be dealt with here—see below.) Their social–evolutionist dismissal of magic as a previous stage of human development that did not properly belong in modern society—a 'survival'—was ambivalent. While Tylor sometimes allowed for a universal mytho-poetic or 'analogic' consciousness to exist next to archaic survivals of magic, he was also worried that the latter survivals would turn out to be 'revivals' within modern Victorian society—as the hype of the spiritualist séance seemed to suggest. Frazer worried that Victorian civilization would turn out to be merely a thin crust easily rent by the slumbering savage forces of human nature, and his work did, against his intentions, indeed stimulate a number of occultist revivals in the late nineteenth and early twentieth century (see Frazer 1911: 235–6; Hanegraaff 1998; Pels 2003: 9–11; Tylor quoted in Stocking 1971: 90). The modernist effort to define and dismiss magic defeated itself by, first, having to define magic in universalist (because modernist) psychological or poetic terms, and secondly, then having to explain why this universalism did not apply to modern society—or, when it did apply, having to admit that modern magic exists but to deny that it characterizes modernity. Contemporary currents of Victorian 're-enchantment' such as the celebration of the 'magic of monarchy', the discovery of the unconscious in art, literature, and psychology, and the emergence of spiritualism and modern occult-ism compounded this conundrum.

In retrospect, what stands out in this period of European thought is the tendency not to think of magic in terms of material items, except in classifications that reduced objects to exotic items of display in ethnographic museums, where they still exerted the fascination that Western people had long felt for fetishes and rarities (but as items of horror more than of awe or wonder). This tendency became particularly dominant after Tylor, in particular, redefined primitive reli-gion away from 'fetishism' (which made explicit that primitives held certain untranscended materials in awe—Comte 1840) towards 'animism' (in which even primitive religion started from the primacy of the spiritual). The tendency to downplay the materiality of magical items was not significantly changed in the twentieth century, because the intellectualist and functionalist theories that de-scribed magic and witchcraft were relatively uninterested in magical matters, while the more relativist theories that drew these theories in doubt around the 1970s were still predominantly spiritual or idealist. While a marginal anthropologist like Alfred

Wallace could, around 1870, still argue that certain material manifestations (such as a hopping table) proved that the spirits of the séance were real (Wallace 1896 [1874]), even self-confessed magicians in the twentieth century (such as Aleister Crowley) claimed that magic was a primarily (voluntaristic) psychic phenomenon (Crowley 1987 [1904]). While such psychological dematerializations of magic passed into popular culture, a certain 'sociological dematerialization' of magic took place in the early twentieth century under the influence of functionalist theory (Malinowski 1935, 1948; Evans-Pritchard 1937; Mauss and Hubert 1972). Especially Mauss' and Malinowski's more pragmatic approaches introduced interesting and important novelties in the modernist theorizing of magic, but did not (yet) result in more appreciation for magic's materiality (for an overview, see Pels 2003). An approach that would do justice to the materiality of magic could only start to appear at the end of the second millennium, and it required, both literally and figuratively, a return of the fetish.

Fetishes

While the 1980s and 1990s saw a broader resurgence of anthropological interest in fetishism (Ellen 1988; Apter and Pietz 1993; Spyer 1998), some of the most profound insights into the magic of materiality and the materiality of magic came from a series of path-breaking essays by cultural historian William Pietz (1985, 1987, 1988, 1993, 1999). His analysis takes us several steps back from Victorian modernism. Pietz's writings demonstrate that the fascination that the fetish has exerted on people since the seventeenth century is, at least in part, rooted in the mercantile alienation of objects from their contexts that characterized this period of 'scientific revolution', yet has endured into the nineteenth century and (I would add) into the popular culture of the twentieth and twenty-first century. From its emergence in the context of Protestant capitalism and the hegemony of the rational calculation of the value of things, the fetish was subsequently marginalized by Enlightenment taxonomies, becoming an anomaly in nineteenth-century anthropology and religious studies, its ethnographic museums, and later psychological reasoning. Throughout, however, the fetish retained a position of significant otherness out of proportion to the relevance modern people allotted to it for their own lives and practices—a position based on the fact that it defined a subject from whom the modern self wanted to strictly differentiate itself. Part of the argument of this section will therefore be that the fetish cannot be understood unless we position it against the background of the history of modern object categories—not a history of things, but a history of the (proper) definition of things. We shall see that the fetish emerged as a thing compelling worship from deluded people, signifying a form of agency that the Victorian reformulations of magic referred to above subsequently denied.

One might summarize Pietz's genealogy of the fetish—and the novelty of his approach—by saying that he described the fetish as a novel category of objects expressing a material trade relationship between Europeans and Africans that emerged on the West African coast, that was subsequently turned into the definition of an irrational state of mind exclusively characterizing Africans. The novel category of objects designated by the pidgin word *fetisso* emerged in Portuguese West African trade and probably referred to a (subsection of a) group of objects that comprised both Christian objects (such as rosaries) as well as African amulets, and that identified the wearer of these objects as a middleman in that trade. Since these middlemen did not leave an account of their work, the process can only be reconstructed on the basis of the ethnographies left by their successors: the Dutch Protestant traders who ousted the Portuguese from the 'Gold Coast' in the course of the sixteenth century. These ethnographies suggest that *fetisso* referred to something radically different from the Portuguese *feitiço* ('charm')—the word from which it was derived. Removed from the medieval Christian doctrine of idolatry, which treated material objects as merely passive media for the relationships between spiritual agents (the context of *feitiço*), *fetisso* could raise 'the essential problem of the fetish': that of the social and personal value of material objects themselves (Pietz 1987: 35). When Dutch merchants such as Pieter de Marees and Willem Bosman witnessed the use of *fetissos* as, for example, means to take oaths that ensured permanent and reliable trade relationships between relative strangers, the political and economic importance of *fetissos* added to the already existing confusion about value in a situation where, for example, gold was exchanged for 'trifles' such as beads (Pietz 1987).

These Dutch merchants turned their confusion about the proper value of objects in West African trade into a judgement on the basis of the Protestant, mercantile valuation of normal and abnormal exchange. The *fetisso* was generalized into the 'fetish', defined as an object valued by Africans' (quasi-Catholic) 'capricious fancy' and opposed to the rational (Protestant) merchant's appreciation of technological and commercial value (de Marees 1987 [1602]: 39; Bosman 1967 [1705]: 154; Pietz 1988: 111). Anything that took Africans' fancy or struck them as out of the ordinary—from a stone on the road or a cheap bead to a piece of gold or an elaborate piece of marine technology—could, according to this early modern theory, become a fetish. Moreover, the worship of 'fetish', in this theory, also implied an assessment of African politics, because such generalized caprice could only be tamed by the fear of the fetish, fed by a class of 'fetish priests' who had similar if perverted interests in mind as did the European traders themselves (Pietz 1987: 39–42; 1988: 117). Bosman's (1967 [1705]) representation of African life in his *New and Accurate Description of the Coast of Guinea* reached a broad audience in Europe, and was modified by its translation into the European doctrine of 'fetishism'—a material-istic cult incommensurable with Christian categories, conceived 'as the worship of haphazardly chosen material objects believed to be endowed with purpose, inten-tion, and a direct power over the material life of both human beings and the natural world' (Pietz 1988: 106)—especially by Charles de Brosses' *Du culte des dieux fétiches* (1998 [1760]).

While the career of the fetish since its emergence and popularization was, as we shall see, highly complex and contradictory, two things stand out in most circum-stances in which we find it. First, the fetish usually poses the problem of the agency of the material object—the object behaving as subject. Secondly, its emergence is usually and paradoxically accompanied by the alienation and desecration of objects. The problem and its origin in alienation are related through the Protestant ethic, which assumed that the value of a human being is defined by his radical distinction from and superiority over material goods (Keane 2002). Even a worship *through* material goods smacked of Catholic Popery—let alone a worship *of* objects—and this condemnation of the material side of religion betrayed the Protestant dogma that all material goods should be subject to human intention and/or manufacture (see Latour 2002). This iconoclastic mentality appeared in the emergence of the fetish when Pieter de Marees, for example, declared that the things that some of his African trading partners valued so highly were, in actual fact, 'trinkets' (*cramerye*)—worthless trifles (de Marees 1987 [1602]: 72; Pietz 1987: 41).

They were, of course, trifles only in relation to commodities with a higher exchange value. The 'facticity' on which De Marees and Bosman built their iconoclasm was capitalist; it was rooted in the alienation of objects from their contexts of origin by global trade. But global trade produced other alienated objects as well, including some more familiar ones that also threatened the Protes-tant primacy of the human mind over material objects. The rarity, for example, despite the fact that it is often regarded as the prototype of the museum object, can perhaps be better compared with the fetish and (strangely enough) to the positivist, modern fact. Sixteenth-century Europeans collected rarities because of the sense of wonder they called up in the viewer, but their quality of being marvellous was precisely as systematic as the 'capricious fancy' that the Protestant merchants perceived in the Africans' selection of fetishes. Fetish and rarity are so much alike that it is not difficult to see that European folk theory implicitly posited the latter as a positive version of the former—and indeed, *minkisi* (the so-called 'nail fetishes' from Congo) were, like modern fetishes, often included in European collections of rarities (Pels 1998: 110—see the conclusion). That implied, however, that rarities, while inspiring the Scientific Revolution's anti-scholastic sense of factuality on the one hand (Daston 1994: 261–2), could, like fetishes, also call up the fear of the Protestant for unruly and undomesticated material goods on the other. Insofar as mercantile aesthetics appreciated the rarity positively, it also allowed such objects to act as subjects, doing things to people.

It comes as no surprise, therefore, that such unruly early modern objects had to be domesticated further—had to become 'facts *for*' a more encompassing modern understanding—first by the Enlightenment's taxonomic fervour (epitomized by Linnean botany) and then by the nineteenth-century's preoccupation with evolutionary or developmental order, both, in the end, being materialized by the emergence of the modern museum (see also Poovey 1998). Never mind that the fetish and the rarity were some of the first manifestations of the ways in which modernity produces its own magical things: taxonomic classification and developmental order (not to forget the valuation of self-possessed labour—see below) soon marginalized them in the leisurely space of consumption (and the '*fancy*-fair') or in the educational shrines of the museum. Or so it seemed: for even in the serene isolation of the museum halls—those temples to the Protestant primacy of mind over matter—the fetish could still exert some of its unruly magicality, and subject people to its influence.

The fetish stirred trouble even under the regime of European taxonomy and evolution or progress. In European popular culture, the classification of the fetish as magical and hence irrational, and the evolutionary argument (already embryonic in the Protestant merchants' work) that magicians use fetishes for fraud, were derived from nineteenth-century anthropology—but always against the

Fig. 27.1 'Kill the white man! Him violated fetish!' The fetish in modern European popular culture: Hergé, *Kuifje in Afrika*, 1947 [1931] pp. 25 and 27 (Dutch edition). © Hergé/Moulinsart. The comic strip Tintin has long been regarded as racist despite the fact that the author toned down its colonial character in the 1947 edition.

background of alienation and desecration, whether of the missionary or the museological kind (Figures 27.1 and 27.2). It pays off, however, to look at some missionary and museological examples more closely. When, for example, the fetish reappears in a context seemingly most hostile to it—the pages of a Roman Catholic missionary journal published in the Netherlands in 1951—one discovers a strange agency. The photographs of the 'king' or *grand-feticheur* and the 'fetish hut', made by a missionary in Senegal, are somewhat drab and unremarkable, and need a caption to bring out their interest (Figure 27.3). They are situated, however, in a remarkable way: they do not illustrate the message of the text, but seem to have been included as if they carry an interest or fascination by themselves (a common procedure with exotic photographs, at least in Dutch Catholic journals: Pels 1999: 55–66). This can be rationalized, of course, by the fact that the missionary journal

Fig. 27.2 The fetish in modern European popular culture: Hergé, *Het Gebroken Oor*, 1945 [1937], p. 3 (Dutch edition). © Hergé/Moulinsart.

zegen met het Allerheiligste gaf stroom-
de de kerk leeg. Dat hadden zij niet
meer nodig. Dat zei hen niets. Zij hadden iets gezien. Een theater. Daar kan
een Lof niet tegen aan. Druk pratend
en gesticulerend trokken zij af. Ik wist
niet wie ik meer moest betreuren. De
pastoor of de gelovigen. Waarschijnlijk
beter allebei.

Dat is nu Amazonas op zijn best.
Alles uiterlijkheid. Grote processies en
veel vuurwerk. Alles ter ere van de
heiligen. Drinken en dansen ter ere
Gods. Tot zij er bij neer vallen. Als
ik zo iets meemaak denk ik altijd aan
die priester van het Heilig Hart, die in
het scholasticaat een missielezing gaf
over de Indianen van de Vaupesmissie
in Columbia. „En dan feesten ze maar
twee dagen en twee nachten en dat om
de veertien dagen". En die goede pater
herhaalde dat minstens elke vijf minu-
ten, zodat ik tenslotte meer medelijden
had met de pater, die maar niet van zijn
thema kon afstappen, dan met de Indianen, die zo hopeloos verslaafd zijn aan
drank en dans.

Goed en kwaad gaat hand in hand.
Je kunt dit zien en horen. Op alle ogen-
blikken en bij alle gelegenheden.

In de kajuit van de commandant van
de rivierschepen, die op onze post aan-
leggen, zijn het totaal naakte figuren
naast het beeld van O.L. Vrouw. Op
de blote borsten van het scheepsvolk
hangen grote en dure medailles en veel
kruisjes, terwijl zij de grootste bandie-
ten zijn, die de Kerk met hun Vrij-
metselarij geducht afbreuk doen.

Om te werken op Zondag of om te

Pater Henk Govers, C.S.Sp., is met zijn foto-
apparaat terecht gekomen bij de nog zeer
primitieve mensen in het gebied van Oussoye
(Senegal, A.O.F.). Zijn missiegebied zit nog
vol fetichisme en andere primitieve praktijken.

1. De Koning van Oussoye; men zou het hem
zo niet aanzien dat hij ook chef-tovenaar
en groot-feticheur van de streek is.

2. Een begraafplaats van fetichen te Oussoye.
Pater Govers vond reeds tientallen van deze
hutten.

3. Een fetichen-hut, die varkenskaken en palm-
wijnpotten als beschermstukken herbergt,
naast andere hier onnoembare voorwerpen.

166

Fig. 27.3 The fetish in missionary propaganda. Page 166 from the *Bode van de Heilige Geest* ('Holy Ghost Messenger') the propaganda journal of the Congregation of the Holy Ghost in the Netherlands (vol. 47, no. 12 [1951]). The caption reads 'Father Henk Govers, C.S.Sp. has arrived, together with his camera, among the still very primitive people in the Oussoye area (Senegal, A.O.F.). His mission area is still full of fetishism and other primitive practices. (1) The King of Oussoye; one can hardly judge from his looks that he is also head-magician and grand-feticheur of the area. (2) A burial-ground of fetishes in Oussoye. Father Govers has already found scores of these huts. (3) A hut of fetishes, that accommodates pigs' jaws and palm-wine pots, apart from other objects that we cannot mention here.' Note that the text of the article next to the photographs is unrelated: it is an account of the Holy Ghost Fathers' mission in Amazonas, Brazil.

was 'both pulpit and collecting-bag' (Pels 1989: 35) and that such pictures were meant to attract paying customers by playing on a less elevated fascination than their Christian sentiments. That, however, only displaces the question of agency to another level, where the fetish exerts fascination on the paying audience despite this audience's conscious subordination to the regime of a civilizing mission.

This can be generalized: the iconoclasm that we commonly associate with the undoing of the magicality of a magical thing more often than not pays such things an amount of attention wholly out of proportion to the missionary iconoclast's judgement that these things are trifles or have no intrinsic value (Corbey 2000: 61–70). The magical swords or knives known as *kris* that Dutch colonialists brought from the Indies not only fetched prizes out of proportion to the value of their constituent elements or aesthetic appeal (indicating that their history as magical things also appealed to prospective buyers), they also attracted a worshipful audience when on display in a Dutch colonial museum, and even continue to haunt their Dutch owners when passed from one to the other long after arrival in the Netherlands (Wiener 2007). Thus, if the fetish first emerged as a magical thing that was defined in order to be denounced as a magical thing, we see that it retained at least the power to hit back, in an 'iconoclash' that also seems characteristic of other ways in which modern people digest the Protestant heritage (Latour 2002). The fetish, therefore, epitomizes the modern problematic of magic, as a thing that should not but in fact does move people in mysterious ways.

COMMODITIES

If the previous section argued that the early modern attempt to conjure the fetish away met with limited success, its nineteenth-century redefinition as a category for the discussion of the magic of commodities and capital—understood as something negative, a misplaced devotion—further boosted its career. Critiques of consumption could range from the general fear (rooted in, among other things, the Protestant anxiety to put mind over matter) that the materialism evoked by the fetishized commodity would inhibit people's moral and spiritual development. Such inhibitions were most famously epitomized by the miser Scrooge of Charles Dickens' *Christmas Carol* (see Dickens 1971 [1843] and below). Beyond such ('spiritual') folk theory, critiques of consumption extended to the materialist argument that the commodity concealed the physical work that went into its manufacture, making relations between people appear as relations between things (most famously argued by Karl Marx (1974 [1867]: 86) in the first chapter of

Capital. These imaginations posited the materiality of the commodity as both magical and suspect, capable of leading people astray. Interestingly, however, after the materiality of things in general was brought back to anthropological attention in the 1980s—coinciding with Pietz's rehabilitation of early modern folk theory's emphasis on the fetish's untranscended materiality—the critical idea of commodity fetishism was sometimes completely dropped. For example, socio-cultural anthropologist Daniel Miller's later studies of consumption and commodities (e.g. Miller 1995d) came to mention fetishism only as 'an academic and colloquial prejudice' about consumption (Miller 1998c: 128), despite his earlier acknowledgement that an 'obsessive concern' with material goods 'describes an actual condition in modern life' (Miller 1987: 204). In contrast, rather than dropping or downplaying the notion of commodity fetishism, this section of my argument asks whether such prejudices and obsessions do not indicate that the magic of commodities takes up a more distinct, elaborate, and complex place or phase in modern tournaments of value than Miller's celebration of consumer choice allows.

Today, the most persistent modern labour to turn commodities into independent agents occurs in advertising. But commodity fetishism was, of course, older than that. It came out, for example, when in 1843 Charles Dickens made the Ghost of Christmas Present show Scrooge the contrast between the enjoyment of Christmas consumption and the children of Want and Ignorance (Figure 27.4):

> The poulterers' shops were still half open, and the fruiterers' were radiant in their glory. There were great round, pot-bellied baskets of chestnuts, shaped like the waist-coats of jolly old gentlemen, lolling at the doors, and tumbling out into the streets in their apoplectic opulence. There were ruddy, brown-faced, broad-girthed Spanish onions, shining in the fatness of their growth like Spanish friars; and winking from their shelves in wanton slyness at the girls as they went by, and glanced demurely at the hung-up mistletoe.
>
> Dickens (1971 [1843]: 89–90)

And so on. In *A Christmas Carol*—that early Victorian charter for capitalist sociability—the fetishized commodity emerges in all its still-life seduction. However, it does so only to be tempered by devotion and familial love, both symbolized by the unselfish generosity that, in the end, Scrooge the miser learns to extend to family and employee alike. Dickens thereby epitomized the folk theory that the fetishized commodity may be enjoyed innocently—but only when joined by its opposite: the gift that expects no return. The Dickensian magic of the commodity emerges in the context of a specific cultural sequence, one based on the expectation of the consumer that the acquisition of the commodity will lead to a phase in which s/he can direct its disposal beyond individual consumption—turning it, for example, into a gift to others. Two decades before Marx identified the commodity in terms of its capacity to conceal the agency of the labouring subject, Dickens set the magic of commodities to work to reveal the consumer's sovereignty to decide on enjoying them himself or turning them into gifts for other, sometimes more needy,

Fig. 27.4 Commodity fetishism in early Victorian Britain: John Leech's drawing of the Ghost of Christmas Present for the first (1843) edition of Charles Dickens' *A Christmas Carol*.

consumers. The magic of the commodity—the agency it exerts on humans—may well be indulged in, but above all (says Dickens) when its capacity to transform a bundle of social relationships, of redefining the subject as both consumer, family member, and philanthropist, is maximized. The crux is that advertising—rather than merely enhancing the aura of the product—tries to maximize the capacity of things to transform social relationships. What haunts every form of modern advertising is that it is dependent on a choice that is both social (conformist, materialist) and antisocial (individuating, spiritualist) at the same time.

In other words, while the commodity's magic relies, on the one hand, on alienation (i.e. its capacity to appear divorced from human relationships at the moment of its purchase), it also depends on the various ways in which it can be deployed by a 'sovereign' consumer on the other. Like people, commodities have histories; like people, they do some things better than others; like people, their performance changes from one situation to another. In advertising, this implies that the ingredients of the social relationship in which magical capacity is being maximized—the product, its performance, and the subject desiring either or both—change in relation to each other. Turning to popular culture again, we see, for example, that in Dorothy L. Sayers' *Murder must Advertise* (1959 [1933]), the relationship between product and performance initially takes centre stage. Most discussions among the employees of the advertising company in which Lord Peter Wimsey tries to solve a murder revolve around the best words to describe margarine ('better than butter and half the price') or sedatives ('Nerves need Nutrax'). Even more, the *discrepancy* between product and performance is what boosts sales (dyspeptic Mr Copley is best at selling foodstuffs, while Miss Meteyard is good at writing copy for anything but women's goods); yet it makes advertising 'an awfully immoral job' at the same time. Later in the novel, however, Lord Wimsey devises the Whifflet Campaign, boosting a cigarette brand through handing out coupons for Whifflet weddings, Whifflet houses, or Whifflet holidays ('If that's what you want, you can Whiffle for it'): a 'brand' image more usually associated with the advertising of the second half of the twentieth century. Then again, Miss Sayers drew on her extensive advertising experience when she indicated that in Pym's Publicity, all sexual innuendo in advertising texts was declared taboo—an impossible suggestion in, for example, the United States of the 1950s (as we shall see).

Perhaps an even more important difference between the magic of pre- and post-World War II advertising lies in the definition of the desiring subject. For Miss Sayers in 1933, 'the wealthy . . . buy only what they want when they want it': the desires of Lord Peter Wimsey and his fellow Oxbridge colleagues at Pym's Publicity are based on 'plain' use values. The 'vast superstructure' of the advertising industry, as she argues, was not built on them, 'but on those who, aching for a luxury beyond their reach and for a leisure for ever denied them, could be bullied or wheedled into spending their few hardly won shillings on whatever might give them, if only for a moment, a leisured and luxurious illusion' (Sayers 1959 [1933]: 136). Advertising gave rationality for the upper class and 'phantasmagoria' and 'Cloud Cuckooland' for the workers. How different this is from the subject imagined by the advertisers denounced in Vance Packard's *The Hidden Persuaders* (1958), who 'see us as bundles of daydreams, misty hidden yearnings, guilt complexes, irrational emotional blockages' and, not least, sexual yearnings (1958: 4). In Packard's book—one of the great US bestsellers of 1958—the class opposition of pre-war British advertising has vanished, and is replaced by a conspiracy of (middle-class) social scientists, psychologists, and advertisers against the (equally middle-class) American public. Together with science fiction novels, such as *The Space Merchants* (Pohl and Kornbluth 1953), it even helped generate the urban legend of subliminal advertising (the myth that movies and other advertising channels were laced with hidden messages, subconsciously urging people to consume)—a paranoid vision of consumerism very much at home in the atmosphere of the Cold War.

Packard's 1950s advertisers thought they needed to generate a product that was not so much determined by 'product benefits' as by the needs with which it could be associated. This implied a disdain for the consumer as a conscious agent: as the journal *Advertising Age* put it, '[i]n very few instances do people really know what they want, even when they say they do' (quoted in Packard 1958: 8). It also implied that the material use-values of the product became less important: 'The cosmetic manufacturers are no longer selling lanolin, they are selling hope . . . We no longer buy oranges, we buy vitality. We do not just buy an auto, we buy prestige' (Packard 1958: 5), 'What makes this country great is the creation of wants and desires, the creation of dissatisfaction with the old and outmoded' (Packard 1958: 16). Among the professional anthropologists (talking 'symbols') and psychologists (talking 'motivation') who wrought this magic of modernity, Ernest Dichter, a pupil of both Sigmund Freud and Paul Lazarsfeld before the war, stands out as having boosted the idea of the 'personality' or 'image' of the product appealing to the 'hidden desires and urges' of the consumer. Dichter's 'soul of things' was a decidedly vulgar Freudianism, as his explanation of the success of the 1950s Esso (later Exxon) campaign 'Put a Tiger in your Tank' shows:

A gas tank is mysterious and dark like a womb. It can be fertile or sterile. The hose of the gas pump resembles you-know-what. Rational? Who cares? The symbol of power, of virility, of strength, goes through the oddly shaped nozzle into the receptive womb and gives it power and strength. It worked practically around the world.

Ernest Dichter (quoted in Bennett 2005: 53)

This fine example of propaganda for sexual fetishism signifies—together with the scandal caused by Packard's book—less a scientific discovery of hidden dimensions of consumption as the successful popularization of a psychoanalytic (and somewhat paranoid) culture, as David Bennett (2005: 23) argues in his essay on Dichter. Equally interesting is the fact that even the advertising 'agent' doesn't really understand what he is doing, for as Dichter continues: 'I want you to realize that I am as amazed as the infidels are. How can such a contrived mixture between sexual allegories, mysticism, and caveman symbolism result in millions of dollars of very unmysterious cash through increased sales?' (quoted in Bennett 2005: 13). I recall that, as a Dutch 5-year-old, I was indeed excited when my mother pulled up next to the Esso pump, but on my part that most likely had more to do with the Esso Tiger's combination of strength and cuddliness than with any premature sexual identification with an oddly shaped nozzle. This may remind us of the fact that the consumer's 'obsession' takes diverse forms, and that the materiality of the Tiger's (or the nozzle's) image was a polyvalent bundle whose meanings were not exhausted by the subject of sexual desire. It may be even more important to note that this turns the magic of commodity into something not completely comprehensible even to modern sorcerer/scientists such as Dichter—something that they may have in common with their non-modern colleagues (see Taussig 2003 and below).

Even during the 1950s, the triangular network between product, performance, and consuming subject characterized by Dichter's psychoanalysis already contained the seeds of a new phase in the magic of advertising, perhaps best symbolized by Dichter's campaign for Mattel's Barbie doll—who was never sold as a doll but as a person, in the hope that both daughter and mother would mould the former's personality on Barbie herself (Bennett 2005: 16). Through the intervention of the 'counterculture' in the 1960s, marketing strategy shifted yet again, away from the psychoanalytic subject haunted by repressed desires, towards the 'cool' consumer exemplified by the happily unmarried adolescents of whom Barbie was an early ancestor. Norman Mailer's 1957 juxtaposition of the young 'hip' hedonist to the all-too-adult 'square' provided the template for such an 'infantilization' of the consumer (Mailer quoted in Frank 1997: 12; Barber 2007). The countercultural desire to set oneself against a dull, materialist, or politically suspect generation was hijacked by business culture and mainstreamed into 'an essentially agnostic cult of style worship' characterized by the brand (Andrew Ross quoted by Frank 1997: 30). The brand marks the magical capacity of 'the construction of consumer subjectivity' *as such*: the desire to be different, rather than the desire to be different through using a specific product. The 'Pepsi Generation' that was created in the 1960s was, as Thomas Frank puts it, the 'ur-segmentation' of identity focused on youth that preceded all subsequent attempts to fuse being and having in a single (often textual or visual) symbol of 'being different' (Frank 1997: 24). The Nike Air Pegasus sold in 1995 exemplifies the political economy of product and performance in this brand image: $10 materials, $1.66 labour costs, and $2.82 overhead leave a more than $45 margin of profit and advertising costs on the retail price of $70 (*The Observer*, quoted in Vreeswijk 2001: 79). A Dutch advertiser wistfully stated that 'people in America' have killed for a Nike shoe, showing that a brand 'can take on the size of a religion' (Vreeswijk 2001: 63). 'Performance' costs have definitely outstripped 'product' costs in this example.

If in 1930 Pym's Publicity tried to enchant products, in 1950 Ernest Dichter enchanted the needs of the car owner, and in 1988 Nike's *Just do it* campaign enchanted the shoe wearer's personality, what does the magic of the commodity actually consist of? If Pepsi Cola carries a kind of magic, is it the mostly forgotten fact that when Caleb Bradham registered the name in 1903, it referred to the product's capacities of relieving dyspepsia? Is it the moment of Pepsi's first major advertising success, the radio jingle 'Nickel Nickel' of 1940 celebrating its 5-cent price? Or is it the rise of the prototype of niche identity marketing, the 'Pepsi Generation' campaign launched in 1963 (and enhanced in the twenty-first century by buying the collaboration of major celebrities)? The possible points where the commodity can find purchase on people vary: the use value of curing an upset stomach, the exchange value of being cheap, and the value of being different (or famous), have all contributed to the magic of Pepsi. Reduced to a—perhaps crude—trichotomy of value, we can say that the modern magic of the commodity relies on: (1) a reification of use value (such as curing dyspepsia); (2) a reification of exchange value (such as the price—but more generally, such as the sovereign consumer's capacity, celebrated by Dickens, to decide on how, when, and by whom the commodity may be enjoyed); and (3) a reification of consumer subjectivity (such as being a member of the Pepsi generation; or being like Beyoncé or Britney Spears). All may work in tandem. Also, all rely on the capacity of the commodity to conceal certain aspects of its production while revealing this reified aspect—via a kind of mythical multiplication that starts with the fact that the product (something that cures dyspepsia) has to be made to *perform* as itself (something *presented* as curing dyspepsia, whether it does so or not). This multiplication—first theorized as modern 'myths' by Roland Barthes in 1957 (Barthes 1972 [1957])—can then proceed further by adding, for example, a reification of exchange value ('Good for your tummy, and only a nickel!') or of subjectivity ('Be your own Beyoncé or Britney self!').

However, nothing truly 'magical' or agentive adheres to the modern commodity unless coupled to a moment of alienation on the one hand, and an iconoclastic moment of denying the object's inherent value on the other (the fetish, in other words, remains our prototype). This is brought out by Dickens, since the enjoyment of alienated and fetishized Christmas goods is perfectly all right as long as the consumer retains the capacity to nullify the consumer values they present in an unselfish gift. It also remains true in advertising circles: the admiration of marketers for a successfully magico-religious brand, such as Nike or Pepsi, is often contextualized by a theory of communication, which ('iconoclastically') denies images and things their autonomous capacity for powerful communication. As Bram Vreeswijk has observed through participant observation in a large Amsterdam advertising firm, marketers try to reduce this capacity to 'tricks' they use to communicate a message about the product to prospective buyers to the advantage of their clients (Vreeswijk 2001: 83). This is not surprising given the fact that marketers have to continue to believe their work has some effect in the real world. The frequency with which marketers acknowledge their own lack of understanding of successful marketing processes (as Dichter himself acknowledged) is only surprising when we forget that magicians in general forge their self-understanding on the basis of an oscillation of faith *and* scepticism (Taussig 2003). Both magicians and marketers play with our credulity, but they only do so because we allow them to—because we *like* them to do so. We will understand much more about the magic of things once we realize, on the basis of the previous discussion, that the concealment of the social relations they effect is not just a denial of the labour relations that went into their production (as Marx would have it) or a denial of the trading relations that brought them to their point of purchase (which Marx failed to stress)—but more importantly, that it is a denial of the social relationships and the history that turned them into *positive* representations of a certain product capacity, need, or subjectivity. Thus, the magic of commodities cannot simply be subsumed under the generalized human trait of realizing cultural being through things (as argued by Miller 1998c: 169). There is more involved, if only because the object *points to* (or reveals) something for somebody just as much as it *points away from* (or conceals) something else. (More about this indexical aspect below.) This can, finally, be understood once we look at modern things in a context where their agency is celebrated, rather than being subject to fear—computer technophilia.

TECHNOLOGIES

Computer technology is one of the few and most important social fields in which the term 'magic' is consistently applied to modern innovations that were hitherto associated with its opposite: rational technology. This departs from most modern conceptions of magic in two important ways. Understandably, computer aficionados rarely use 'magic' to refer to their favourite pastime in a derogatory way, as based on mistaken or irrational beliefs. Equally self-evident, their uses of 'magic' are focused on a material thing—a box wired with gadgets, chips, and batteries. This understanding of the magic of the computer is itself part of a folk theory—one suspiciously close to a techno-deterministic and hence fetishized way of looking at the world. Its comparison of magic with technology may provide us with an alternative to earlier theories—equally modern, if sometimes less 'folk'—that points the way to more profound understanding of magic and materiality in general.

Steven Levy's *Hackers: heroes of the computer revolution* (2001) first appeared in 1984, the same year that the science-fiction writer William Gibson coined the word 'cyberspace' and provided hackers with their first fictional hero in his widely acclaimed *Neuromancer* (Gibson 1984). Both books can be seen as charters of the computer revolution in the 1980s, providing it with myths of origin as well as with an image of a future to which the new technology could be attuned (although Gibson's future is far bleaker than Levy's). Like radio and television in previous eras (the 1920s and the early 1950s, respectively), this was a technology that had not yet settled as a new social form (cf. R. Williams 2002 [1974]: 32). Marketers were still trying to determine how the personal computer, catapulted on to the market by the Altair in 1975, the IMSAI in 1976, and the Sol in 1977, could best be turned into a consumer electronic, and hesitated to proclaim openly the goal for which these machines, joined by the Apple II, were now predominantly used: for hobbyists fiddling with their own computer languages and writing their own programs, and above all for the rapidly booming computer game industry (Haddon 1988). Levy's book was one of the publications that turned hackers into heroes by providing them with a 'hackers' ethic' and outlining three path-breaking generations to mark the stages of technological innovation (as in any heroic history of technology)—until the 1980s, when 'Computer Liberation' (as an influential book of the early 1970s had it) was subverted by marketers and commerce (Levy 2001: 424). Written on the cusp of a peculiar moment in the history of the technology—just before the popularization of the graphics user interface by the Apple Macintosh in 1985, and the spread of the World Wide Web in the early 1990s—Levy's book is a good medium through which to analyse this technology's folk theory of 'magic'.

Levy did, indeed, varnish his heroic stories with the metaphors of magic and wizardry, and although he provided many of these glosses himself, the number of quotes from his heroes indicate that this was not just his own gloss, but a sense of wonder shared by the different generations of computer aficionados that he describes. The words 'magic' (or 'magician', or 'magical') and 'wizard/ry' recur throughout the book: on average on every sixth page.[1] As Levy (2001: 129) described the 'Golden Age' of computer hacking at the MIT artificial intelligence lab in the 1960s, 'Art, science and play had merged into the magical activity of programming, with every hacker an omnipotent master of the flow of information within the machine.' This shows the two most prominent tropes by which the computer was linked to magic. First, the wonder at the impossible capacities of the 'magic machine that had intelligence', as hacker Steven Dompier put it, and whose agency turned programming into a 'magical activity'. Secondly, the heroic image of the computer hacker as the 'omnipotent master of the flow of information' who could therefore be seen as a 'wizard'. Both tropes are united by the image of the computer as a machine for 'protean magic' (Levy 2001: 433), a shape-changing tool generating worlds of its own, and they thereby highlight the mediating role of this machine. But they also play upon two somewhat contradictory registers of magic:

the imagery of omnipotence and wizardry, emphasizing control; and the imagery of wonder and amazement, emphasizing lack or loss of control in the face of the powers of the machine. Even more confusing, the two registers sometimes seem to coincide.

The appellation 'master magicians' or 'wizards' most often seems to apply to the world produced by computer software or those proficient in its manipulation. It generates something akin to the Romantic deification of the creative genius, admiring the fact that machines have been created that 'can make you do anything you can think of' (programmer Margot Tommervik, quoted in Levy 2001: 309), or celebrating that 'by manipulating a world inside a computer, people realized that they were capable of making things happen by their own creativity. Once you had that power, you could do anything' (game designer Ken Williams, quoted in Levy 2001: 337). The finished software product alone could generate such feelings. Showing the Sol, one of the earliest personal computers, on a television show, the TV host Ted Snyder (a 'technical illiterate') was completely hooked by the 'feeling of *power*' that playing a shooting-aliens game gave, and it gave him a sense of what it would mean when you could use such a machine 'to actually create' (Snyder quoted in Levy 2001: 243). 'Wizardry' in computing, therefore, was not far removed from the omnipotence experienced in the computer game itself, that allowed one, as the sales line of Richard Garriot's immensely popular game Ultima 2 put it, to 'travel throughout the solar system', 'be seduced in a bar', 'meet prominent people within the computer industry', 'cast magical spells at evil creatures', and 'grow to wield the most powerful magic known to man' (Garriot quoted in Levy 2001: 381).

In contrast, those command-line and hardware hackers and computer aficionados who created the possibilities for the materialization of that separate realm, or who discerned a kind of liberation in spreading computer literacy beyond the world of the expert 'wizard', tend to emphasize—at least in Levy's book—a more humble way of realizing human potential *vis-à-vis* the computer. Even at MIT, hacker Peter Samson's view that the 'magical appeal' of programming lies in the fact that your effort to 'fix a behavioral problem' results in 'exactly an image of what you meant' one discerns the awe at the capacity of this machine that allows you to do just that. This ambivalence is also apparent in Levy's celebration of the 'magic machine' that could produce an early game like Spacewar, that first provided the space in which later software hackers would locate their omnipotence (Levy 2001: 58, 65, 142, 296).[2] Countercultural hackers or their promoters saw, in the computer, a 'magic box' that, miraculously, made 'weird-type people sit in kitchens and basements and places all hours of the night, soldering things to boards to make machines go flickety-flock' to become 'adventurers in a new land' just like the early American pioneers (in the words of Les Solomon, the editor of *Popular Electronics*, who first publicized the Altair PC). Steve Dompier, hacker of the Sol PC, was flabbergasted by 'that first magic where this machine talks back to you and does mathematics incredibly fast' and recorded everybody's awe towards it 'for the first four of five months until they understood it really wasn't intelligent' (Dompier quoted in Levy 2001: 190–3). 'Magic' was the only word that these hackers and promoters of hacking could think of when imagining a future in which, in Ted Nelson's words '[T]he dinky computers are working magic enough. They will bring about changes in society as radical as those brought about by the telephone or the automobile' (Nelson quoted in Levy 2001: 267).

The retrospective truth of Nelson's prediction does not, of course, deny that this is technodeterminism in its everyday guise (and it should not make us forget that, despite the view of computer aficionados, there are many modern people who criticize it). It is based on a form of fetishization that is quite close to that of modern magical objects discussed previously (Pfaffenberger 1988: 242). In relation to the problematic of magical things in modernity, the crucial point to make is that, in relation to the computer, we find little trace of the 'fear of objects supplanting people' (Miller 1998c: 169). Instead, in the case of computer technology, the fetishism is *welcomed*. In our discussion of modern magical objects, we come, in a sense, full circle. The fetish is the stereotype of the modern magical thing: it denies that objects can behave as subjects, but is haunted by this prospect as a result. The commodity stands in a painful relation to the fetish, being constantly threatened by it, but—as Dickens and the twentieth-century marketers discussed above bring out—often building on its capacity to transform social relationships at the same time. Finally, the technology is more often allowed to exert its magical transformations on us, showing the full extent of modern magic—but reminding us at the same time that the neglect of the materiality of magic has often blinded us to the fact that the more profound understanding we can gain of magical things in general might not come from the, so-called pre-modern, fetish, but from the modern engagement with technology instead.

CONCLUSIONS

Let us end, therefore, with a (supposedly) non-modern magical thing. Socio-cultural anthropologist Alfred Gell recorded an interpretation of the *nkisi*, the famous Congo 'nail-fetish' that brings out its material being. The *nkisi* can act as an arbiter in judicial procedure, punishing those who lie on oath by the power that it has accumulated. The power partly comes from the actions of an occult expert, who has helped to ingest the (memory of) power of a proficient hunter into a tree; the power from the tree, subsequently turned into sculpture, is activated when a nail is driven into it, to initiate a judicial procedure. The nail-fetish thereby becomes 'the visible knot which ties together an invisible skein of relations'. It is not a symbol, 'for these relations have produced this particular thing in its concrete, factual presence; and it is because these relations exist(ed) that the fetish can exercise its judicial role' (Gell 1998: 62). In this interpretation, it is the visible presence of the abductions of agency that give the nail-fetish its power that allows it to be an agent in the first place. In other words, the distributed agency of which all magical things are an indication or index is here not denied or feared, but put to an explicitly acknowledged use (just as some hackers transfer human agency to the computer). Magical things, therefore, seem to become all the more magical in modernity precisely because such a distribution of agency is ruled out as a possibility—as the result of a series of reworkings of, among other things, a Protestant intellectual heritage. The modern assessment of materiality may become less magical and painful, and probably make us feel more akin to those who use nail-fetishes or their equivalent, once this distribution of agency is accepted as a normal aspect of human life and its engagement with artefacts and technologies. I do not think, however, that that will fully 'undermine magic as an analytic' as Wiener (2007: 46) hopes, for how else will we continue to discuss our experience of objects behaving as subjects?

NOTES

1. Using the 'search inside' facility on Amazon, one finds 34 entries for magic, one for magician, nine for magical, 30 for wizard, and 10 for wizardry: 84 items across 464 pages. I thank the editors for enhancing my weak skills with numbers.
2. Spacewar spread from MIT to the Stanford Artificial Intelligence laboratory, where even the food-vending machine was named after a bar in that paradigm of magic, J. R. R. Tolkien's Middle Earth, and cloned the Tolkien-inspired 'Adventure' game in the process (for its earliest celebration, see Brand 1972).

CHAPTER 28

AFTERWORD: *FINGS AIN'T WOT THEY USED T' BE*: THINKING THROUGH MATERIAL THINKING AS PLACING AND ARRANGEMENT

NIGEL THRIFT

Placing Vases: Depending on the style of the vase, set it on a Japanese table of appropriate size, using bronze in the winter or spring, porcelain for the summer and winter. Vases for the reception hall should be large; those for the studio should be small. Value bronze or ceramic, and hold gold and silver cheap, avoiding those with ring handles or which come in pairs. Flowers should be emaciated and curious; they should not be over-complicated. If using a cut branch, then it must be selected to be curious and antique. If there are two then their relative heights must be suitable. It is particularly important to have no more than one or two varieties, since too many gives the appearance of a wine shop. This does not apply to a small vase with an arrangement of autumn flowers. In placing flowers do not burn incense with the windows closed, lest the smoke blight the petals. This is particularly the case with narcissi. Nor should flowers be placed on a painting table.

From Wen Zhenheng's *Treatise on Superfluous Things* (1620–1627), cited by Clunas (1997: 44)

INTRODUCTION

In 1762 Oliver Goldsmith (2006 [1762]) used the figure of an imaginary Chinese mandarin traveller, Lien-chi Altangi, to parody the customs and mores of eighteenth-century London. Prominent among the mandarin's epistolary observations was Londoners' obsession with the getting of goods (and his susceptibility to their methods of selling them). Clearly, Goldsmith was not writing with much in the way of knowledge of Chinese culture since, if he had been, he would have realized that Chinese culture was similarly preoccupied.[1] Since the latter part of the Ming dynasty, consumer goods had been circulating among not just the elite but many other segments of society, often in much the same way as in the supposed heartlands of the consumer revolution like England and the Netherlands. In a masterly series of works, Clunas (1991, 1997, 2007) and Brook (1998) show that market mechanisms and networks of information were in place to allow a growth of mundane and luxury consumption that in places was on a par with that of Europe: brushes from Anhui province, ceramics from the great potteries of Jingdexhen, books compiled in many locations. Here was a proto-consumer culture that had moved a long way beyond the bazaar.

As if to underline the main tenet of Dipesh Chakrabarty's *Provincializing Europe* (2000), a unitary historical time simply serves to underline Western notions of the centrality of 'modernity' that the historical record immediately belies. For the historical record shows that in most places at most times there is a fascination with goods, at least on the evidence of trade routes that we now realize to have been more extensive at an earlier date than had heretofore been understood (e.g. Cunliffe 2008). In other words, people have always been intent on adding use and magic to their lives by acquiring goods. In a later period in which the economic formation commonly called capitalism holds sway, diagnoses of the desire to acquire have been legion. Marxists like to talk of commodity fetishism. Eco-moralists like to talk, simply and straightforwardly, of greed and waste. But there are other accounts. For example, inspired by the practice of potlatch, Bataille wanted to account for the power of excess energy through the notion of 'general economy', arguing that this excess energy was channelled into lavish expenditure. The lack of scarcity is a theme taken up by more recent authors too. For example, Sloterdijk (2007: 346), reverses Gehlen's emphasis on lack of means, arguing instead that we now occupy a time of excess in which waste 'is the primary civic duty'. But the need to condemn almost always returns. Thus, Sloterdijk, along with authors, such as Zizek and Bauman, is convinced we have transited to a time in which we inhabit a public form of privacy that will drag us down into mediocrity, able to choose consumer obsessions but not much else, thus echoing the standard critique of the ultimate venality of consumerism.

But, though I would certainly not want to argue the case for unlimited expansion of the acquisition of goods, not least because of the catastrophic environmental consequences, I would want to argue for the assertion of a basic aesthetic impulse in human being that drives our love of things as much as the self-milling mill of production: aesthetics as a biologically endowed proclivity, an evolved species characteristic. Of course, things are useful means of getting things done. But even the simplest of tools often turns out to have many ways of being produced—they are ordered to at least certain aesthetic norms, which are often abstract and abstracted. One thinks of Gell's famous paper on the fish trap: was this device a matter of art or utility? One thinks of all the forms of plaiting, binding, and knitting, and the way these lattices produce contrasting forms: 'for example, in Baroque emblem construction as well as the wrapped funerary effigies of New Ireland in the Pacific Ocean where the body emerges from the fretwork' (Stafford 2007: 21). And one thinks of the power of the bare line, repeated over and over again on so many goods (Ingold 2007c). People delight in looking at things, in touching things, and generally in getting to grips with them. That contact makes them *feel* good. Their enjoyment is real and it is not derived from some other source. It is not epiphenomenal. It follows that people want to enhance their sensory surroundings, to shape time and space by populating them with objects, whether this be in the form of the decoration of temples or the most mundane of domestic spaces. This basic aesthetic impulse—aesthetics as a behaviour—has been written about at length by many writers from different disciplines in varied ways. But one thing we do know, it is not a one-sided relationship in which we simply project our concerns on to things. Things draw and hold us too. They become a means through which we gain not only sustenance but also comfort, whether it be from CD collections, vintage Fisher Price toys, or stamps (Miller 2008). And, in turn, we can see this quality of what might be called the craft (and sometimes it really is a craft) of generalized connoisseurship, mixed with sometimes selective, sometimes all but random accumulation of all kinds of goods, as an aspect of evolution just as important as other putatively critical milestones like tool-use:

> along with gaining better control of the means of subsistence by the use of material technology, humans took an additional remarkable and unprecedented evolutionary step. They gilded the lily, making sure that their technology 'worked' by deliberately reinforcing it with emotionally satisfying special elaborations and shaping. Thus, in the history of the human species, it is not only the development of language or the invention of technological 'means of production' that has made us anomalous or unique. Our invention and application of what might be called the 'means of enhancement' or 'means of refinement'—for an infinity of possible objects and occasions—is equally impressive and equally deeply engrained in human nature.
>
> Dissanayake (1993: 95)

In other words, perhaps our relationship to things has what might be called a musical quality, which we forget at our peril. Music has, of course, routinely been degraded as evolutionarily peripheral and even non-adaptive (Pinker 1997) but it keeps stubbornly reappearing as a quality we cannot reduce to something else, including in the history of evolution (cf. Mithen 2005). Perhaps the aesthetic quality of things has the same kind of resonance, one that can be ignored but only with dire consequences for the power of our explanations. Things may not just talk to us, sometimes they sing.

Material culture regnant

This Handbook demonstrates how the study of material culture has come of age. From being the preserve of a few hardy souls working in disconnected island communities—the social and economic history of consumption, ethnographies of contemporary consumption, the anthropology of goods, such as clothing and pottery, material culture studies in archaeology—it has become the stamping ground of many. Why that should be is, I think, entirely understandable. To begin with, there is the sheer profusion of things in many contemporary societies. We live in the culture of Novalis' self-milling mill where things populate the world in ways undreamt of in earlier cultures. For example, the number of passenger vehicles in the world is currently estimated at 622 million, up from 500 million in 2000 and a mere 53 million in 1950, and still climbing year on year. In turn, the profusion of such things generates its own population ecologies. Five come immediately to mind. To begin with, there is the domain of the second-hand. And it is a vast domain, ranging from used car yards through charity shops to a considerable part of the economy of poorer communities. Then, there is repair and maintenance (Graham and Thrift 2007). Cars, for example, need repair and maintenance and this repair and maintenance is carried out in culturally specific ways, from the vast repair shops run by some car dealerships to the large number of small repair shops to the kind of informal operations exemplified by Australian Walpiri bush mechanics. And, this is before we get to the general practice of tinkering with objects that typifies so much human life. Then, there is waste. The spectacular sight of barges of rubbish moving up the rivers or of ships loaded with metals for recycling is but the tip of an iceberg of waste dumping and recycling, which is truly global in nature, connecting American computer users with Indian villagers, and vice versa. Finally, there is an ecology of litter to be reckoned with. Litter has become an integral part of the landscapes of many countries, populating roadside verges, blowing along the street, migrating across the oceans. It is hardly a new phenomenon. Even in 1950, the British propensity for littering was rampant: the *Manchester Guardian* decried 'the accumulation of cartons and large rags of newspaper and miscellaneous wrappings, which lie about for days on end' (R. Lee 2000). At the time, it was reckoned that about half a million bus tickets were dropped on the streets every day. The nature of the detritus may have changed but, otherwise, plus ça change.

But this is not all. Things have now become a key part of worlds. That was always true in the sense that the layout of things has always been a powerful pointer to a culture's propensities and dispositions. But what has changed is that landscapes are now fashioned by things in much more active ways. This is not some new version of commodity fetishism but rather what the Italian operaismo Marxists call 'worlding', a situation in which the determinate relationship between subjects and objects is replaced by a set of spatio-temporal sequences, hybrid networks, which distribute subjects and objects in knowing ways so as to harness affective flow. In a sense, everything becomes furniture bent to this task. In the same spirit, these worlds are predicated upon producing continuous engagement with various things so that the commodity appears increasingly as a process rather than a thing that is fixed in time (Thrift 2005b, 2007; Lash and Lury 2007; Klingman 2007). Often they depend upon the granting of a good deal of freedom to the consumer in order to produce new forms of affective energy—and new products. Consider only the enormous artefactual-cum-affective force produced by the public intimacy of Western 'women's culture' in all its forms, a culture that uses commodities to fuel practices, such as giving and loving and complaining and being in pain, which is both a commercial colossus and a resource, an unfinished event that has all kinds of 'juxtapolitical' possibilities (Berlant 2008).

Finally, and relatedly, we have become knowing about things in unparalleled ways. The outbreak of reflexivity concerning material practices in the academic sphere, in which all manner of methods allow the erstwhile savant to knowingly observe the knowing—sometimes in ways that seem to mimic the self-absorption to be found in so many blogs and facebook entries—is simply an echo of the corporate and consumer practices of 'knowing capitalism' in which expertise about things is sought out and incorporated into the process of commodity production (Thrift 2005b, 2007; Savage and Burrows 2007). Even archaeological methods are being transferred into the present as investigators increasingly treat material culture as the deposition of an instant (Buchli and Lucas 2001b).

No doubt it is possible to argue about the effects that the sheer profusion of things has had on us. We certainly don't need to overdramatize it. As Cohen (2006) points out, quantity of things is no guide to how they are used: contrast what to us seems like the clutter of many Victorian homes with the spare quasi-modernist mien pursued in the homes of many consumers today, all around the globe (Jacobs and Cairns 2008). Rather, the move to prioritizing the material in material culture 'explicitates'[2] a series of processes by formalizing knowledge that was formerly informal. I will pull out just three of these processes of expli-citation to produce the outline of a body of knowledge, which seems to me to be central to any 'thing talk'. They are not exhaustive or exclusive but hopefully they make the point that, to use the title of the old Lionel Bart musical, 'fings ain't wot they used t' be'.

THREE PROCESSES OF EXPLICITATION

First off, social and cultural theory is taking things into account in a way that it only did sporadically before, as many papers in this collection attest. To begin with, the idea of a divide between humans and things now looks like a relict. Things do not need to be chaperoned by human beings to have presence or force (Harman 2005). Many accounts have emphasized this point, dating from before phenomenology. But it has now become something of an orthodoxy. So, at the very least, things are counted as material prostheses to the human body, extensions that allow human beings to become more alive. One thinks of the long line of devices that have extended the representational functions of the hand, for example: stylus, brush, pen, keyboard, mouse, touchscreen, and so on, and the new languages that have arisen from their deployment such as writing and software, sometimes still replete with deictic traces. Equally, one thinks of all the devices that have extended the human capacity for movement: shoe, wheel, cart, coach, train, car, plane. Then things can have their own force, which acts back. Things come alive, prodding us into action in unforeseen ways. One thinks, for example, of the way in which stage props like the handkerchief, the skull, the fan, and the gun are gradually acknowledged as actors in their own right, able not just to haunt the imagination but do things that are pivotal to action (Sofer 2003). Or, on a more dramatic level, one thinks of the case of barbed wire, wonderfully elicited by Netz (2004). Netz shows how barbed wire, intended as a controlling technology meant to guarantee territory by inflicting pain on animals, allowed a massive extension of the means of violence by producing new means of territorialization premised on the ability to construct proxy landscapes in which motion could be prevented. Then, things increasingly think, in however a rudimentary fashion, increasingly blurring the boundary between live and not live, or at least producing a new psychological category (Turkle 2008). They do not think in the same way as humans, but after over 50 years of the quest for non-biological intelligence, it is difficult to say that the increased understanding of intelligence that has followed in the wake of a sometimes quixotic attempt to build artificial intelligence has brought forth no fruit, just not the fruit that were expected (Ekbia 2008). In particular, it has produced remarkable evidence of how intelligent behaviour is consequent on the interactions between humans and machines, which do not fix the category of either human or machine. This art of effective arrangement of powers and responsibilities in functioning gestalts is, of course, at the heart of actor-network theory and more general theories of distributed cognition. Finally, things have lives of their own. As Harman (2005) argues, there is no reason to believe that things exist just to bolster the absorption of our lives. They may have biographies but this itself is too human-centred a description of their existence. Rather, one might say that things are a carnival which, to some extent, will always elude our senses, a world 'packed full with objects that generate their own private lives and both welcome and resist our attempts to garner information' (Harman 2005: 238).

Then, theory is changing its style to cope with this upwelling of interest. To begin with, it is clear that writing, especially the restricted code of alphabetic writing, is unequal to the task of portraying things by itself. In a world in which things have voice, new means of logographic representation become not just necessary but vital in order to locate the penumbra of things. Consider objects as not just marking time and space in each register of the senses but making them. That must mean making objects that precisely show this quality, which means working in many media other than print (Clarke *et al.* 2007). Thus, installation art often seems to provide insights missing from the material culture literature about disposition (Bishop 2005). Equally, literature is becoming replete with means of communication, which can better take the heft of things into account (Schwenger 2006). One thinks of photographs, maps, comic book formats, and all manner of other logographic possibilities. And this is before we reach the domain of the moving picture, itself an archive for considering how things work, whether in anthropological films or Hollywood movies, but now moving into new dimensions as a result of the addition of a digital domain that offers on-line museum archives alongside collectors' forums alongside experiments in performance, which allow things to cast new shadows. The idea of simply writing about things will, I suspect, become increasingly alien: it is no surprise that disciplines that have spent so much time working with things—anthropology, archaeology, art and performance, ge-ography—now seem so peculiarly fitting to the times. For they redefine the empirical in ways that have become increasingly pressing for all disciplines, moving towards both natural science and arts models simultaneously.

Then again, things are producing a politics that had been little thought of or practised before. Once things are granted symmetry as elements of gestalt networks, then it becomes interesting to think about how the art of politics needs to be defined in a non-reductive way. This is not just a case of understanding the ways in which things (like meters) allow different modes of engagement with issues, such as sustainability and green living, important as these undoubtedly are. Rather it is about turning object-centred practices into sites of public involvement. In turn, that allows all manner of questions to be asked. What is a democracy of hybrid networks? What gets to vote and how? Indeed, can 'humans' vote? How would a parliament of things be constituted? And so on.

Secondly, the fact that things inflect cultures in very different ways has become more and more explicit. It hardly needs me to document the vast explosion of work that has set out the very different use of things in different cultures and the way that this use inflects everyday life (Brewer and Trentmann 2006). This book provides ample evidence of that proposition over and over again. But there is more to it than that: the motivating principles and dilemmas and the dreams of different cultures are often constituted through the clash of things and their dispositions. Let me expand.

To begin with, think of the religious landscape of Reformation England and the force of an iconoclastic aesthetic made flesh through a very different form of visual culture, one that swept away the old visual culture of late medieval Catholicism (Duffy 1997). Think of the elaborate decoration and the complex sounds and smells that made up so much of what constituted the liturgy for ordinary people up to that time—the conventions and contents of lay prayer; the relation of orthodox religious practice and magic; the Mass and the cult of the saints; and the lay belief about death and the afterlife—all expressed through objects nostalgically recalled in the years after the destruction of so much of this way of life. Equally, think of the ascetic aesthetic of modernism and its impact on popular taste which still exists in muted form in the domestic spaces of so many people, yet alone in large-scale architectural projects that seem unable to escape its spell. Yet this aesthetic varies from culture to culture in both its reception and practice, and in turn, these practices can travel back and forth, producing new subjectivities (Bayart 2007).

Such contemplation leads, in turn, to the general issue of how things are described in different cultures. For what seems clear is that the weight of descrip-tion of things varies among different cultures in radical ways. The prose of things varies according to the means of description available and the emphasis placed on particular elements of these means. Note that I am not suggesting that all descrip-tion has to pass through spoken and written language (which can, in any case, vary massively in its content and syntax). Description can also take place simply through the work of imposing form on materials and the ways materials resist that embrace, as authors as different as Simondon, Flusser (1999), and Stiegler have pointed out. (Indeed, so far as Stiegler is concerned, this process explains our consciousness of time.) And it can also arise out of the ways in which objects are placed in hybrid networks so as to give them more or less power and 'objectivity' (Daston and Galison 2007). In turn, description can undergo sea changes. Consider Wall's account of the transformation of description in eighteenth-century England in which the rewriting of descriptions of things signals a whole new attitude to what counts as acceptable description:

> experientially, to technologically new ways of seeing and appreciating objects in the ordinary world, through the popular prostheses of microscope, telescope and technical analysis; economically, to the expansion of consumer culture in the increasing presence and awareness of things on the market, in the house, in daily life; epistemologically, to the changing attitudes toward the general and particular, the universal and the individual; and, narratively, to the perception and representation of domestic space.
>
> Wall (2006: 2)

To round the account of this second process off, it is also possible to think about how persons can be thought of as things by different cultures. Putting it this way can sound as though one is sanctioning a reduction of the human to a cipher, with all the consequences that became clear over the course of the blighted twentieth century. But there is another way to think this issue through, the kind of approach championed by authors such as Roach (2007) and Marilyn Strathern (2004a). For example, Roach shows how Western embodiment is constructed from a confusion of 'surfaces' (itself a problematic nomenclature), which vary historically and have all kinds of implications. Bodies are the sum of a series of surface characteristics, often summed up in a brief glance: the flash of a hat, dark glasses, and a particular bodily stance may be what we see and how we come to judgement. This makes these living effigies' clothes and accessories, hairstyle[3] and the skin, and all manner of other characteristics that occupy the boundaries of the body, into powerful supplemental but still telling cultural signposts, which have the look and feel of things: props that are themselves performances. Thus Roach shows how modern charismatic celebrity is often simply an aggregation of these surfaces, a kind of living/not-living brand. But the point is more general than the name, the face, and the scandal of celebrity. These surfaces vary enormously among cultures and it might be better to treat them as things, rather than falling back on standard humanist motifs.

Thirdly, and relatedly, there is the continuing explicitation of things as existing in many registers at once as well as the processes that become possible because of this both simple and complex fact. To begin with, and most simply, we can think of things as communicating not just in the visual register but across every sense (understanding that the senses are themselves cultural-biological amalgams). Thus, as Smith (2007) and many others have pointed out, we communicate with things in many registers at once, an insight that is only heightened by the advent of 'intelligent' materials that can respond much more subtly to users (Küchler 2008), materials that are able to feel personalized and personalize feel, whether these be surfaces, sounds, smells, or what have you: each individual can exist in an increasingly modulated environment. But this is surely a subset of a larger development that I have already referred to as worlding, the production of environments (or atmospheres as Sloterdijk would have it) that can catch and modulate affect. I wrote earlier of the musical side of things, which is wrapped up with their ability to trap or generate affect through a certain extravagance that we are biologically constituted to respond to. Producers now play to these moods by constructing carefully designed climatizations that perform object desires. One thinks of modern malls and shops as the primary instruments of object desires, carefully edited spaces within which attention can be focused on things through the medium of things by playing to minor affects, such as envy, and major affects, such as love, using increasingly sophisticated knowledges of the spatial disposition of things. But that is but a small part of the affective grip of things. Think only of the immense emotional investments now made in the home as a space for depositing goods. Recent industry-oriented books on the home act as primers for amplifying passions: home is literally where the heart is. Homes, and the things that constitute them, are about addressing basic emotional needs.[4] Bathing, for example, becomes a key sensuous moment, akin to that found in the true bathing cultures of the world: the Turkish bath, the Japanese *onsen*, the Scandinavian sauna. And bathing is a good metaphor for what is being aimed at.

To bolster this statement and to understand the general aim of this process more fully, let me move to another kind of bathing experience, that provided by the garden. Chandra Mukerji (this volume, Chapter 24) takes as her example gardens that have an iconic status, those gardens with explicit messages to impart. But such gardens are few and far between, even the most formal of them. Only a few landscape gardens and almost no domestic gardens[5] contain truly iconographic programmes and 'even those are frequently meant to be evocative or polysemic rather than programmatic' (Elkins 2008: 70). Rather, gardens' effects are ambiguous and largely semiconscious, based on a different kind of grip that oft times resists the illusion of an observing subject: 'the object isn't bound by our attention: it binds us' (Elkins 2008: 69). To put it another way: 'If I step into a bath I am going to warm up: and perhaps gardens have that kind of control over our responses. On the other hand, it might be better to say that the reverie of gardens is only an inducement to a kind of thought that is often dormant in our professional prose' (Elkins 2008: 71). The mention of the semiconscious refers us immediately to the work of writers, such as Gabriel Tarde, whose geography of mimetics has, as I have argued elsewhere, more significance than it has often been given credit for. Spaces are increasingly designed as trails of statements laid out in the form of dispositions of things, rather like a form of music, making statements that we feel and respond to through long and involved chains of semiconscious mimesis, which constantly echo back and forth. This diagramming of emotions through the medium of things is now moving from being an art to becoming a science.

CONCLUSIONS

Let me end where I began—with China. It is a truism that China has been passing through a moment of binge consumerism. What sometimes looks like a middle class orgy of brands and a general consumer boosterism seems to be going on apace, one which to listen to most commentators has been invented anew by consumer naifs. But look deeper, and we can see something much more interesting. First, and most obviously, the history of China shows an alternative timeline in which the early invention of printing, minutely modularized production, and sophisticated consumer knowledges produced an early consumer sensibility among a part of the population: the primer of Wen Zhenheng could have come from the pages of *House and Garden*. Secondly, it is quite clear that the Chinese have forged their own consumer sensibility, as the work of Davis, Schein, and others shows only too well, one that engages with what we might stereotypically call a Western formation of desire but only in the broadest and most nuanced sense (see Rofel 2007). Thirdly, and most importantly, the per(re)ception of goods still carries elements of an older tradition of thinking about materiality, which is becoming better and better known—through a general interest in Eastern philosophy, through Heidegger's appropriation of Eastern thinking, and through the uncanny echoes between certain Eastern and Western traditions of thought, as found in writers as diverse as Leibniz, Whitehead, and Latour. In particular, there is the absence of clarity and distinctiveness in Chinese thinking about the empirical. In contrast to many other traditions, Chinese thinking is—absolutely, if you like—relational, intent on pursuing a logic of influence through 'the eternal silence of processes' (Jullien 2007: 151) without the massive investments and reinvestments in meaning typical of the Western tradition. When Roland Barthes arrived back from China, he argued that he had found a society with no signs but what he was actually witnessing was a cultural emphasis on the potential, the virtual, the in-between, and on process generally that can be realized in a great number of ways, in a great range of concrete objects (Jullien 2000, 2007a, 2007b). It seems to me that it is towards this vision of a kind of nourishment of and by things as they unfold in time that we are now all heading, each in our own ways: a transformation of description that takes up a model of something like music, one might even say.

NOTES

1. Goldsmith does mention the shops of Pekin and Chinese governance in a way that shows he had more than just a passing knowledge of China. At the time, the general appetite for things Chinese, for Chinoiserie, objects made in China specifically for the European market, for things that mimicked Chinese style, such as chairs and clocks, and for books such as Olfert Dapper's *Atlas Chinensis* (1671) (a style bible full of elaborate observations by an author who, nonetheless, had never been to China) must have sensitized him to that country's culture (see Markley 2006).

2. I take the term from the work of Peter Sloterdijk.

3. I have tried to show the enormous reach of consumer industries, such as hairstyling, in modern economies in Thrift (2008).

4. Equally, we could dip further into the vast edifice of women's culture: a circulation of dreams and things that has been brought into existence since the nineteenth century (Berlant, 2008).

5. Incidentally, gardens have become one of the great consumer industries on a world-wide scale (see Lees 2002).

REFERENCES

ABC 2007. Police clamp down on shipwreck 'looting'. *ABC News* 24 January www.abc.net. au/news/stories/2007/01/24/1832419.htm (accessed 17 November 2008).

ABU EL-HAJ, N. 2001. *Facts on the Ground: archaeological practice and territorial self-fashioning in Israeli society.* Chicago: University of Chicago Press.

ABU-LUGHOD, J. L. 1991a. Writing against culture. In R. G. Fox (ed.) *Recapturing Anthropology: working in the present.* Santa Fe: School of American Research, pp. 137–162.

ABU-LUGHOD, J. L. 1991b. *Before European Hegemony: the world system AD 1250–1350.* Oxford: Oxford University Press.

ACHEBE, C. 1978. An image of Africa. *Research in African Literatures* 9(1): 2–15.

ADAMS, W. H. 1979. *The French Garden, 1500–1800.* New York: Braziller.

ADORNO, T. W. 1982 [1938]. On the fetish character in music and the regression of listening. In A. Arato and E. Gebhardt (eds) *The Essential Frankfurt School Reader.* New York: Continuum, pp. 270–299.

AGREST, D. 1991. *Architecture from Without: theoretical framings for a critical practice.* Cambridge, MA: MIT Press.

AGYEMAN, J. and NEAL, S. (eds) 2006. *The New Countryside? Ethnicity, nation and exclusion in contemporary rural Britain.* London: Policy Press.

AHLER, S. 1993. Architecture and settlement change in the Upper Knife-Heart region. In T. Thiessen (ed.) *The Phase I Archeological Research Program for the Knife River Indian Villages National Historic Site, Part IV: Interpretation of the Archeological Record.* Lincoln, NE: National Park Service Midwest Archeological Center, pp. 33–55.

AHLER, S. and SWENSON, F. 1993. KNRI and Upper Knife-Heart Region Pottery. In T. Thiessen (ed.) *The Phase I Archeological Research Program for the Knife River Indian Villages National Historic Site, Part III: Analysis of the physical remains.* Lincoln, NE: National Park Service Midwest Archeological Center, pp. 1–171.

AL-JANABI, T. 1983. Islamic archaeology in Iraq: recent excavations at Samarra. *World Archaeology* 14(3): 305–327.

ALDHOUSE-GREEN, M. 2004. *An Archaeology of Images: iconology and cosmology in Iron Age and Roman Europe.* London: Routledge.

ALEXANDER, C. 1964. *Notes on the Synthesis of Form.* Cambridge, MA: Harvard University Press.

ALEXANDER, E. P. 1983. Artur Hazelius and Skansen: The Open Air-Museum. In E. P. Alexander (ed.) *Museum Masters, Their Museums, and Their Influence.* Nashville: American Association for State and Local History, pp. 239–275.

ALLEN, D. 1991. Four bellarmine stoneware 'witch bottles' from Abbotts Ann, Hampshire. In E. Lewis (ed.) *Custom and Ceramics. Essays presented to Kenneth Barton.* Wickham: APE, pp. 147–156.

ALLMAN, J. (ed.) 2004. *Fashioning Power: clothing politics and African identities.* Bloomington: Indiana University Press.

ALPERN, S. B. 1995. What Africans got for their slaves: a master list of European trade goods. *History in Africa* 22: 5–43.

AMIN, A. and THRIFT, N. J. 2005. Citizens of the world: seeing the city as a site of international influence. *Harvard International Review* 27: 14–17.

AMIT, V. (ed.) 1999. *Constructing the Field: ethnographic fieldwork in the contemporary world.* London: Routledge.

AMIT, V. 2002. Reconceptualizing community. In V. Amit (ed.) *Realizing Community: concepts, social relationships and sentiments.* London: Routledge, pp. 1–20.

AMIT, V. and RAPPORT, N. 2002. *The Trouble with Community: anthropological reflections on movement, identity and collectivity.* London: Pluto Press.

AMSBURY, C. and EHRICH, R. 1964. Ehrich–Amsbury correspondence concerning 'material culture'. *American Anthropologist* 66(4): 900–903.

AMSELLE, J-L. 1998. *Mestizo Logics: anthropology of identity in Africa and elsewhere.* Stanford: Stanford University Press.

ANDERSON, B. 2007. Hope for nanotechnology: anticipatory knowledge and the governance of affect. *Area* 39(2): 156–165.

ANDERSON, B. R. O'G. 1983. *Imagined Communities: reflections on the origin and spread of nationalism.* London: Verso.

ANDERSON, B. and TOLIA-KELLY, D. 2004. Matter(s) in social and cultural geography. *Geoforum* 35(6): 669–674.

ANDERSON, B. and WYLIE, J. 2009. On geography and materiality. *Environment and Planning A* 41(2): 318–335.

ANDERSON, B., KEARNES, M. and DOUBLEDAY, R. 2007. Geographies of nano-technoscience. *Area* 39(2): 139–142.

ANDERSON, K. and GALE, F. 1992. Introduction. In K. Anderson and F. Gale (eds) *Inventing Places: studies in cultural geography.* Melbourne: Longman Cheshire, pp. 1–14.

ANDERSON, P., CARVALHO, M. and TOLIA-KELLY, D. 2001. Intimate distance: fantasy islands and English lakes. *Ecumene* 8(1): 112–119.

ANDREVSKY, A. 2005. *Lithics: macroscopic approaches to analysis* (second edition). Cambridge: Cambridge University Press.

ANDREW DICKSON WHITE MUSEUM OF ART. 1970. *Earth Art.* Ithaca, NY: Cornell University Press.

ANDREWS, G. 2006. Aboriginal Cultural Landscape Planning of the NSW Coastal Zone. Paper on behalf of the Department of Natural Resources/Department of Planning Coastal Aboriginal Cultural Landscape Planning Project Team. http://www.eurocoast. nsw.gov.au/coastal/coastalconpapers/AboriginalCulturalLandscape.pdf (Accessed 26 September 2008).

ANON 1952. Seminars on the Folk Culture of the Pennsylvania Dutch County. *Pennsylvania Dutchman* 4: 1.

ANSELL PEARSON, K. 1999. *Germinal Life. The difference and repetition of Deleuze.* London: Routledge.

ANZIEU, D. 1995. *Le Moi-peau.* Paris: Dunod.

APPADURAI, A. 1981. Gastropolitics in Hindu South Asia. *American Ethnologist* 8: 494–511.

APPADURAI, A. (ed.) 1986a. *The Social Life of Things: commodities in cultural perspective.* Cambridge: Cambridge University Press.

APPADURAI, A. 1986b. Introduction: commodities and the politics of value. In A. Appadurai (ed.) *The Social Life of Things: commodities in cultural perspective*. Cambridge: Cambridge University Press, pp. 3–63.

APPADURAI, A. 1996. *Modernity at Large: cultural dimensions of globalization*. Minneapolis: University of Minnesota Press.

APPADURAI, A. 2001. The globalisation of archaeology and heritage: a discussion with Arjun Appadurai. *Journal of Social Archaeology* 1(1): 35–49.

APTER, E. and Pietz, W. (eds) 1993. *Fetishism as Cultural Discourse*. Ithaca, NY: Cornell University Press.

ARDENER, E. 1985. Social anthropology and the decline of modernism. In J. Overing (ed.) *Reason and Morality*. London: Tavistock (ASA Monographs 24), pp. 47–70.

ARIÈS, P. 1981. *In The Hour of Our Death*. New York: Alfred A. Knopf.

ARMIT, I., MURPHY, E., NELIS, E. and SIMPSON, D. (eds) 2003. *Neolithic Settlement in Ireland and Western Britain*. Oxford: Oxbow Books.

ARMSTRONG, R. P. 1971. *The Affecting Presence: An Essay in Humanistic Anthropology*. Urbana: University of Illinois Press.

ARNHEIM, R. 1977. *The Dynamics of Architectural Form*. Berkeley: University of California Press.

ASCHER, R. 1961. Analogy in archaeological interpretation. *Southwestern Journal of Anthropology* 17: 317–326.

ASCHER, R. 1962. Ethnography for archeology: a case from the Seri Indians. *Ethnology* 1(3): 360–369.

ASCHER, R. 1968. Time's arrow and the archaeology of a contemporary community. In K. C. Chang (ed.) *Settlement and Archaeology*. Palo Alto, CA: National Press, pp. 43–52.

ASCHER, R. 1974a. Tin*Can archaeology. *Historical Archaeology* 8: 7–16.

ASCHER, R. 1974b. How to build a time capsule. *Journal of Popular Culture* 8(2): 241–253.

ASHBEE, P. 1972. Field archaeology: its origins and development. In P. J. Fowler (ed.) *Archaeology and the Landscape*. London: John Baker, pp. 38–74.

ASHMORE, W. and Knapp, A. B. (eds) 1999. *Archaeologies of Landscape: contemporary perspectives*. Oxford: Blackwell (Studies in Social Archaeology).

ASPLEN, L. 2008. Going with the flow: living the mangle through environmental management practice. In A. Pickering and K. Guzik (eds) *The Mangle in Practice: science, society and becoming*. Durham, NC: Duke University Press, pp. 163–184.

ASQUITH, L. and VELLINGA, M. 2006. *Vernacular Architecture in the Twenty-first Century: theory, education and practice*. London: Taylor and Francis.

ATELJEVIC, I. and DOORNE, S. 2004. Cultural circuits of tourism: commodities, place and re-consumption. In A. Lew, C. M. Hall and A. Williams (eds) *A Companion to Tourism*. Oxford: Blackwell, pp. 291–302.

ATKIN, T. and RYKWERT, J. (eds) 2005. *Structure and Meaning in Human Settlements*. Philadelphia: University of Pennsylvania Museum of Archaeology and Anthropology.

ATTFIELD, J. 2000. *Wild Things*. Oxford: Berg.

AUBREY, J. 1696. *Miscellanies upon the Following Subjects*. London: printed for Edward Castle.

AUSTIN, G. 2007. Reciprocal comparison and African history: tackling conceptual Eurocentrism in the study of Africa's economic past. *African Studies Review* 503: 1–28.

BACHELARD, G. 1964. *The Poetics of Space* (trans. M. Jolas). New York: Orion Press.

BAHRANI, Z. 2001. *Women of Babylon: gender and representation in Mesopotamia*. New York: Routledge.

BAILEY, D. W. 1990. The living house: signifying continuity. In R. Samson (ed.) *The Social Archaeology of Houses.* Edinburgh: Edinburgh University Press, pp. 19–48.

BAILEY, D. W. 1999. Pit-huts and surface-level structures: the built environment in the Balkan Neolithic. *Documenta Praehistorica Ljubljana* 25: 15–30.

BAILEY, D. W. 2000. *Balkan Prehistory: exclusion, incorporation and identity.* London: Routledge.

BAILEY, D. W. 2005a. *Prehistoric Figurines: representation and corporeality in the Neolithic.* London: Routledge.

BAILEY, D. W. 2005b. Beyond the meaning of Neolithic houses: specific objects and serial repetition. In D. W. Bailey, A. Whittle and V. Cummings (eds) *unsettling the Neolithic.* Oxford: Oxbow, pp. 95–106.

BAILEY, D. W., WHITTLE, A. and CUMMINGS, V. (eds) 2005. *Unsettling the Neolithic.* Oxford: Oxbow.

BAILEY, D. W., WHITTLE, A. and HOFMANN, D. (eds) 2008. *Living Well Together: sedentism and mobility in the Balkan Neolithic.* Oxford: Oxbow.

BAILYN, B. and MORGAN, P. (eds) 1991. *Strangers in the Realm: cultural margins of the first British Empire.* Chapel Hill: University of North Carolina Press.

BAKER, F. and THOMAS, J. S. (eds) 1990. *Writing the Past for the Present.* Lampeter: St David's University College.

BAKHTIN, M. 1968. *Rabelais and his World* (trans. H. Iswolsky). Cambridge, MA: MIT Press.

BAKKER, K. and BRIDGE, G. 2006. Material worlds? Resource geographies and the 'matter of nature'. *Progress in Human Geography* 30(1): 5–27.

BALFOUR, H. 1893. *Evolution of Decorative Art.* London: Rivington, Percival and Co.

BALSAMO, A. 1988. *Technologies of the Gendered Body. Reading cyborg women.* Durham: Duke University Press.

BANERJEE, M. and MILLER, D. 2003. *The Sari.* New Delhi: Roll Books.

BAPTY, I. and YATES, T. (eds) 1990. *Archaeology After Structuralism.* London: Routledge.

BARAD, K. 1999. Agential realism: feminist interventions in understanding scientific practices. In M. Biagioli (ed.) *The Science Studies Reader.* New York: Routledge, pp. 1–11.

BARAD, K. 2007. *Meeting the Universe Halfway: quantum physics and the entanglement of matter and meaning.* Durham, NC: Duke University Press.

BARAM, U. and ROWAN, Y. (eds) 2004. *Marketing Heritage: archaeology and the consumption of the past.* Walnut Creek, CA: AltaMira Press.

BARBER, B. 2007. *Consumed: how markets corrupt children, infantilize adults, and swallow citizens whole.* New York: W. W. Norton.

BARCLAY, A. and CASE, H. 2007. The Early Neolithic pottery and fired clay. In D. Benson and A. Whittle (eds) *Building Memories: the Neolithic Cotswold long barrow at Ascott-under-Wychwood, Oxfordshire.* Oxford: Oxbow Books, pp. 263–282.

BARLEY, M. 1961. *The English Farmhouse and Cottage.* London: Routledge and Kegan Paul.

BARNES, A. S. 1939. The difference between natural and human flaking on prehistoric flint implements. *American Anthropologist* 41: 99–112.

BARNES, B. 1977. *Interests and the Growth of Knowledge.* London: Routledge and Kegan Paul.

BARNES, B., BLOOR, D. and HENRY, J. 1996. *Scientific Knowledge: a sociological analysis.* Chicago: University of Chicago Press.

BARNES, T. 2006. Situating economic geographical teaching. *Journal of Geography in Higher Education* 30(3): 405–409.

BARNETT, C. and LAND, D. 2007. Geographies of generosity: beyond the 'moral turn'. *Geoforum* 38(6): 1065–1075.

BARNETT, W. K. 1990. Production and distribution of early pottery in the west Mediterranean. In D. W. Kingery (ed.) *The Changing Roles of Ceramics in Society: 26,000 B. P. to the present.* Westerville, OH: American Ceramic Society Ceramics and Civilization (volume 5), pp. 137–157.

BARNWELL, P. and AIRS, M. (eds) 2006. *Houses and the Hearth Tax: the later Stuart house and society.* York: Council for British Archaeology.

BARRAUD, C., DE COPPET, D., ITEANU, A. and JAMOUS, R. 1994. *Of relations and the dead: four societies viewed from the angle of their exchanges.* Oxford: Berg.

BARRETT, J. 1987a. Contextual archaeology. *Antiquity* 61: 468–473.

BARRETT, J. 1987b. Fields of discourse: reconstituting a social archaeology. *Critique of Anthropology* 7(3): 5–16.

BARRETT, J. C. 1988. The living, the dead and the ancestors: Neolithic and Early Bronze Age mortuary practices. In J. C. Barrett and I. A. Kinnes (eds) *The Archaeology of Context in the Neolithic and Bronze Age.* Sheffield: Department of Archaeology and Prehistory, pp. 30–41.

BARRETT, J. C. 1994. *Fragments from Antiquity: an archaeology of social life in Britain, 2900–1200.* Oxford: Blackwell (Studies in Social Archaeology).

BARRETT, J. C. 1998. The politics of scale and the experience of distance: the Bronze Age world system. In L. Larsson and B. Stjernquist (eds) *The World-View of Prehistoric Man.* Stockholm: Almquist and Wiksell, pp. 13–25.

BARRETT, J. C. 2000. A thesis on agency. In M-A. Dobres and J. Robb (eds) *Agency in Archaeology.* London: Routledge, pp. 61–68.

BARRETT, J. C. and FEWSTER, K. 2000. Intimacy and structural transformation: Giddens and archaeology. In C. Holtorf and H. Karlsson (eds) *Philosophy and Archaeological Practice.* Gothenburg: Bricoleur Press, pp. 25–33.

DE BARROS, P. L. 2001. The effect of the slave trade on the Bassar ironworking society, Togo. In C. DeCorse (ed.) *West Africa during the Atlantic Slave Trade. Archaeological perspectives.* London: Leicester University Press, pp. 59–80.

BARRY, A. 2001. *Political Machines: governing a technological society.* London: The Athlone Press.

BARRY, A., BORN, G. and WESZKALNYS, G. 2008. Logics of interdisciplinarity. *Economy and Society* 37(1): 20–49.

BARSTOW, A. L. 1994. *Witchcraze: a new history of the European witch hunts.* San Francisco: HarperCollins.

BARTH, F. (ed.) 1969a. *Ethnic Groups and Boundaries.* Boston: Little Brown.

BARTH, F. 1969b. Introduction. In F. Barth (ed.) *Ethnic Groups and Boundaries.* Boston: Little Brown, pp. 9–38.

BARTHES, R. 1961. Vers une psycho-sociologie de l'alimentation moderne. *Annales. Économies, Sociétés, Civilisations* 5: 977–986.

BARTHES, R. 1967a. *Elements of Semiology* (trans. A. Lavers and C. Smith). New York: Hill and Wang.

BARTHES, R. 1967b. *The Fashion System* (trans. M. Ward and R. Howard). Berkeley: University of California Press.

BARTHES, R. 1972 [1957]. *Mythologies* (trans. A. Lavers; orig. published 1957). New York: Hill and Wang.

BARTHES, R. 1977. Image-Music-Text (trans. S. Heath). London: Fontana.

BÅSK, K. 1990. The present in the rear-view mirror: reflections on the 75th anniversary celebrations of the folklife archive in Lund. *Ethnologia Scandinavica* 20: 140–144.

BATESON, G. 1973. *Steps to an Ecology of Mind.* London: Granada Press.

BATTAGLIA, D. 1990. *On the Bones of the Serpent: person, memory and mortality in Sabarl society.* Chicago: Chicago University Press.

BATTAGLIA, D. 1995. Problematizing the self: a thematic introduction. In D. Battaglia (ed.) *Rhetorics of Self-making.* Berkeley: University of California Press, pp. 1–15.

BAUDRILLARD, J. 1983. Simulations (trans. P. Foss, P. Patton and P. Beitchman). New York: Semiotext(e).

BAUDRILLARD, J. 1996. *The System of Objects* (trans. J. Benedict). London: Verso.

BAUDRILLARD, J. 1998. *The Consumer Society: myths and structures* (trans. G. Ritzer). London: Sage.

BAUER, A. A. 2002. Is what you see all you get? Recognizing meaning in archaeology. *Journal of Social Archaeology* 2(1): 37–52.

BAUM, R. M. 1999. *Shrines of the Slave Trade: Diola Religion and Society in Precolonial Senegambia.* Oxford: Oxford University Press.

BAUMAN, Z. 2000. *Liquid Modernity.* Cambridge: Polity Press.

BAUSINGER, H. 1990. *Folk Culture in a World of Technology* (trans. Elke Dettmer). Bloomington: Indiana University Press.

BAYART, F. 2007. *Global Subjects. A political critique of globalization.* Cambridge: Polity Press.

BAYERISCHER VOLKSFEST 2008. The Story of the Bayerischer Volksfest Verein. http://www.philadelphia-bavarian-club.com/history/ (Accessed 15 December 2008).

BAYRD, N. 1974. *Kyoto.* New York: Newsweek.

BBC NEWS 2007a. Crane barges sail to Napoli's aid. *BBC News* 25 January 2007 http://news.bbc.co.uk/1/hi/england/6297767.stm (Accessed 17 November 2008).

BBC NEWS 2007b. Looting victim visits Napoli site. *BBC News* http://news.bbc.co.uk/1/hi/england/devon/6687659.stm (Accessed 17 November 2008).

BEARDSLEY, J. 2006. *Earthworks and Beyond: contemporary art in the landscape* (fourth edition). New York: Abbeville.

BEAUDRY, M. C. 1995. Review essay: exploring gender relations in historical America. *American Anthropologist* 97(3): 587–589.

BEAUDRY, M. C. 1996. Reinventing Historical Archaeology. In L. A. De Cunzo and B. Herman (eds) *Historical Archaeology and the Study of American Culture.* Winterthur, DE: Winterthur Museum, pp. 473–97.

DE BEAUNE, S. 2000. *Pour une archéologie du geste.* Paris: CNRS Editions.

BECK, B. B. 1980. *Animal Tool Behaviour.* New York: Garland STPM.

BECKER, G. S. 1996. *Accounting for Tastes.* Cambridge, MA: Harvard University Press.

BECKER, M. J. 1978. A witch-bottle excavated in Chester County, Pennsylvania: archaeological evidence for witchcraft in the mid-eighteenth century. *Pennsylvania Archaeologist* 48(1–2): 1–11.

BECKER, M. J. 1993. Earth offering among the Classic Period lowland Maya: burials and caches as ritual deposits. In M. J. I. Ponce de León and F. L. Perramon (eds) *Perspectivas Antropológicas en el Mundo Maya.* Girona: Sociedad Española de Estudios Mayas (Publicaciones de la S. E. E. M. No. 2), pp. 45–74.

BECKETT, J. 1996. Against nostalgia: place and memory in Myles Lalor's 'Oral History'. *Oceania* 66(4): 312–322.

BECKFORD, M. 2007. Going, going, gone from eBay website. *Daily Telegraph* 24 January http://www.telegraph.co.uk/news/uknews/1540386/Going-going-gone-from-eBay-website.html (Accessed 20 November 2008).

VAN BEEK, G. 1989. The object as subject: new routes to material. *Critique of Anthropology* 9: 91–99.

BEEVOR, A. 1999. *Stalingrad: the fateful Siege 1942–43*. London: Penguin.

BEFU, H. 1968. Gift-giving in a modernizing Japan. *Monumenta Nipponica* 23(3/4): 445–456.

BEG, M. A. J. 1985. Historic cities of Asia: an overview. In M. A. J. Beg (ed.) *Historic Cities of Asia: an introduction to Asian cities from Antiquity to Pre-Modern times*. Percetakan Ban Huat Seng: Malaysia, pp. 13–122.

BELIDOR, B. F. DE 1753. *Architecture Hydraulique seconde partie qui comprend l'Art de diriger les eaux des la Mer and des Rivieres à l'avantage de la défense des places, du Commerce and de l'Agriculture par M. Belidor, Colonel d'Infanterie*. Paris: Jombert.

BELK, R. 1995. *Collecting in a Consumer Society*. London: Routledge.

BELL, C. 1992. *Ritual Theory, Ritual Practice*. Oxford: Oxford University Press.

BELTING, H. 2001. *Bild-Anthropologie: Entwürfre für eine Bildwissenschaft*. Munich: Wilhelm Fink.

BENDER, B. (ed.) 1993. *Landscape: politics and perspectives*. Oxford: Berg.

BENDER, B., HAMILTON, S. and TILLEY, C. (with contributions from ANDERSON, E., HARRISON, S., HERRING, P., WALLER, M. WILLIAMS, T. and WILMORE, M.) 2007. *Stone Worlds: narrative and reflexivity in landscape archaeology*. Oxford: Berg.

BENDIX, R. 1988. Folklorism: the challenge of a concept. *International Folklore Review* 6: 5–14.

BENEŠ, M. and HARRIS, D. S. 2001. *Villas and gardens in early modern Italy and France*. Cambridge: Cambridge University Press.

BENJAMIN, W. 1977. The work of art in the age of mechanical reproduction. In W. Benjamin *Illuminations* (ed. H. Arendt; trans. H. Zohn). New York: Schocken Books.

BENJAMIN, W. 1999. *The Arcades Project* (trans. H. Eiland and K. McLaughlin). Cambridge, MA: Belknap Press.

BENN, C. D. 2004. *China's Golden Age: everyday life in the Tang Dynasty*. Oxford: Oxford University Press.

BENNET, D. 2005. Getting the id to go shopping: psychoanalysis, advertising, Barbie dolls, and the invention of the consumer unconscious. *Public Culture* 17(1): 1–25.

BENNETT, J. 2001. *The Enchantment of Modern Life: attachments, crossings and ethics*. Princeton: Princeton University Press.

BENNETT, J. 2004. The force of things: steps to an ecology of matter. *Political Theory* 32/3: 347–372.

BENSON, D. and CLEGG, I. 1978. Cotswold burial rites? *Man* 13: 134–137.

BENSON, D. and WHITTLE, A. (eds) 2007. *Building Memories: the Neolithic Cotswold long barrow at Ascott-under-Wychwood, Oxfordshire*. Oxford: Oxbow Books.

BENSON, P. and FISCHER, E. 2007. Broccoli and desire. *Antipode* 39(5): 800–820.

BENTLEY, G. 1987. Ethnicity and practice. *Comparative Studies in Society and History* 29: 24–55.

BERGER, P. 1967. *The Scared Canopy: Elements of a Sociological Theory of Religion*. Garden City, NY: Doubleday.

BERKES, F. and DAVIDSON-HUNT, I. J. 2006. Biodiversity, traditional management systems, and cultural landscapes: examples from the boreal forest of Canada. *International Social Science Journal* 58: 35–47.

BERLANT, L. 2008. *The Female Complaint: the unfinished business of sentimentality in American culture*. Durham, NC: Duke University Press.

BERMINGHAM, A. 1986. *Landscape and Ideology: the English rustic tradition, 1740–1860*. Berkeley: University of California Press.

BERNARD, H. R. 2005. *Research Methods in Anthropology: qualitative and quantitative approaches* (fourth edition). Walnut Creek, CA : AltaMira Press.

BERNSTEIN, R. and TORMA, C. 1991. Exploring the role of women in the creation of vernacular architecture. In T. Carter and B. Herman (eds) *Perspectives in Vernacular Architecture* (volume 4). Columbia: University of Missouri Press, pp. 64–72.

BERTHOZ, A. 1997. *The Brain's Sense of Movement* (trans. G. Weiss). Cambridge, MA: Harvard University Press.

BEST, E. 1909. Maori forest lore: being some account of native forest lore and woodcraft, as also of many myths, rites, customs, and superstitions connected with the flora and fauna of the Tuhoe or Ure-wera District (Part III). *Transactions of the New Zealand Institute* 42: 433–481.

BEVAN, A. 2004. Emerging civilized values? The consumption and imitation of Egyptian stone vessels in EM II–MM I Crete and its wider eastern Mediterranean context. In J. C. Barrett and P. Halstead (eds) *The Emergence of Civilisation Revisited*. Oxford: Oxbow (Sheffield Studies in Aegean Archaeology 6), pp. 107–126.

BEVAN, A. KIRIATZI, E., KNAPPETT, C., KAPPA, E., and PAPACHRISTOU, S. 2002. Excavation of Neopalatial deposits at Tholos (Kastri), Kythera. *Annual of the British School at Athens* 97: 55–96.

BICKERSTAFF, K. and WALKER, G. P. 2003. The place(s) of matter: matter out of place—public understandings of air pollution. *Progress in Human Geography* 27(1): 45–67.

BIDNEY, D. 1944. On the concept of culture and some cultural fallacies. *American Anthropologist* 46(1): 30–44.

BIERSACK, A. 1999. Introduction: from the 'New Ecology' to the new ecologies. *American Anthropologist* 10: 5–18.

BIJKER, W. E. 1995. *Of Bicycles, Bakelite and Bulbs: toward a theory of sociotechnical change*. Cambridge, MA: MIT Press (Inside Technology series).

BIJKER, W. E. and LAW, J. (eds) 1992. *Shaping Technology, Building Society: studies in sociotechnical change*. Cambridge, MA: MIT Press.

BIJKER W. E., HUGHES, T. P. and PINCH, T. J. (eds) 1987. *The Social Construction of Technological Systems: new directions in the sociology and history of technology*. Cambridge, MA: MIT Press.

BIMBER, B. 1990. Karl Marx and the three faces of technological determinism. *Social Studies of Science* 20: 333–351.

BINFORD, L. R. 1962. Archaeology as anthropology. *American Antiquity* 28(2): 217–225.

BINFORD, L. R. 1964. A consideration of archaeological research design. *American Antiquity* 29: 425–441.

BINFORD, L. R. 1965. Archaeological systematics and the study of culture process. *American Antiquity* 31(2): 203–210.

BINFORD, L. R. 1971. Mortuary practices: their study and potential. In J. Brown (ed.) *Approaches to the Social Dimensions of Mortuary Practices*. Washington DC: Society for American Archaeology (Memoirs of the Society for American Archaeology 25), pp. 6–29.

BINFORD, L. R. 1973. Interassemblage variation: the Mousterian and the 'functional' argument. In A. C. Renfrew (ed.) *The Explanation of Culture Change*. London: Duckworth, pp. 227–254.

BINFORD, L. R. 1978. *Nunamiut Ethnoarchaeology*. New York: Academic Press.

BINFORD, L. R. 1981. Behavioral archaeology and the Pompeii premise. *Southwestern Journal of Anthropology* 37: 195–208.

BINFORD, L. R. 1983. *In Pursuit of the Past: decoding the archaeological record*. London: Thames and Hudson.

BINGHAM, N. 2006. Bees, butterflies, and bacteria: biotechnology and the politics of nonhuman friendship. *Environment and Planning A* 38: 483–498.

BIRD-DAVID, N. 1999. Animism revisited: personhood, environment, and relational episte-mology. *Current Anthropology* 40 (Supplement): 67–92.

BIRO, D., SOUSA, C. and MATSUZAWA, T. 2006. Ontogeny and cultural propagation of tool use by wild chimpanzees at Bossou, Guinea: case studies in nut cracking and leaf folding. In T. Matsuzawa, M. Tomonaga and M. Tanaka (eds) *Cognitive Development in Chimpanzees*. New York: Springer, pp. 476–508.

BISHIR, C., BROWN, C., LOUNSBURY, C. and WOOD, E. 1990. *Architects and Builders in North Carolina: a history of the practice of building*. Chapel Hill: University of North Carolina Press.

BISHOP, C. 2005. *Installation Art. A Critical History*. London: Tate.

BJÖRK, C. 1995. *Early Pottery in Greece. A technological and functional analysis of the evidence from Neolithic Achilleion Thessaly*. Studies in Mediterranean Archaeology. Vol. CXV. Jonsered: Paul Åströms Förlag.

BLAIR, S. 2006. Vernacular architecture. In C. Tilley, W. Keane, S. Küchler, M. Rowlands and P. Spyer (eds) *Handbook of Material Culture*. London: Sage, pp. 230–253.

BLIER, S. P. 1987. *The Anatomy of Architecture: ontology and metaphor in Batammaliba architectural expression*. Cambridge: Cambridge University Press.

BLIER, S. P. 2006. Vernacular architecture. In C. Tilley, W. Keane, S. Küchler, M. Rowlands and P. Spyer (eds) *Handbook of Material Culture*. London: Sage, pp. 230–253.

BLOCH, M. E. F. (ed.) 1975. *Marxist Analyses and Social Anthropology*. London: Malaby Press (ASA Studies 2).

BLOCH, M. E. F. 1982. Death, women and power. In M. E. F. Bloch and J. Parry (eds) *Death and the Regeneration of Life*. Cambridge: Cambridge University Press, pp. 211–230.

BLOCH, M. E. F. 1995. Questions not to ask of Malagasy carvings. In I. Hodder, M. Shanks, A. Alexandri, V. Buchli, J. Carman, J. Last and G. Lucas (eds) *Interpreting Archaeology: finding meaning in the past*. London: Routledge, pp. 212–215.

BLOCH, M. E. F. 1998. *How We Think They Think*. Boulder, CO: Westview Press.

BLOCH, M. L. B. 1953. *The Historian's Craft* (trans. P. Putnam). New York: A. A. Knopf.

BLOHM, H., BEER, S. and SUZUKI, D. 1986. *Pebbles to Computers: the thread*. Toronto: Oxford University Press.

BLOOR, D. 1976. *Knowledge and Social Imagery*. London: Routledge.

BLOOR, D. 1983. *Wittgenstein: a social theory of knowledge*. London: Macmillan.

BLOOR, D. 1997. *Wittgenstein, Rules and Institutions*. London: Routledge.

BLOXAM, E. and HELDAL, T. 2007. The industrial landscape of the Northern Faiym Desert as a World Heritage Site: modeling the 'outstanding universal value' of third millennium BC stone quarrying in Egypt. *World Archaeology* 39: 305–323.

BLUFF, L. A., WEIR, A. A. S., RUTZ, C., WIMPENNY, J. H. and KACELNIK, A. 2007. Tool-related cognition in New Caledonian crows. *Comparative Cognition and Behavior Reviews* 2: 1–25.

BLUNT, A., BONNERJEE, J., LIPMAN, C., LONG, J. and PAYNTER, F. 2007. My home: text, space and performance. *Cultural Geographies* 14: 309–318.

BOAS, F. 1927. *Primitive Art*. Oslo: H. Ashehoug and Co.

BOAS, F. 1938. Introduction. In F. Boas (ed.) *General Anthropology*. New York: D. C. Heath and Company, pp. 1–6.

BOAST, R. 1996. A small company of actors: a critique of style. *Journal of Material Culture* 2 (2): 173–198.

BOCHNER, M. 1967. The serial attitude. *Artforum* 6: 73–77.

BOCOCK, R. 1993. *Consumption*. London: Routledge.

BOESCH, C. 1991. Teaching among wild chimpanzees. *Animal Behaviour* 41: 530–532.

BOESCH, C., MARCHESI, P., MARCHESI, N., FRUTH, B. and JOULIAN, F. 1994. Is nut-cracking in wild chimpanzees a cultural behaviour? *Journal of Human Evolution* 26: 325–338.

BOËTHIUS, A. and WARD-PERKINS, J. B. 1970. *Etruscan and Roman architecture.* Harmondsworth: Penguin.

BOHANNAN, P. 1965. Introduction. In L. H. Morgan *Houses and House Life of the American Aborigines.* Chicago: University of Chicago Press, pp. v–xxi.

BOIVIN, N. 2000. Life rhythms and floor sequences: Excavating time in rural Rajasthan and Neolithic Çatalhöyük. *World Archaeology* 31: 367–388.

BOIVIN, N. 2004a. Landscape and cosmology in the South Indian Neolithic: new perspectives on the Deccan Ashmounds. *Cambridge Archaeological Journal* 14: 235–257.

BOIVIN, N. 2004b. Mind over matter? Collapsing the mind–matter dichotomy in material culture studies. In E. DeMarrais, C. Gosden and A. C. Renfrew (eds) *Rethinking Materiality: the engagement of mind with the material world.* Cambridge: McDonald Institute for Archaeological Research, pp. 63–72.

BOIVIN, N. 2004c. Geoarchaeology and the goddess Laksmi: Rajasthani insights into geoarchaeological methods and prehistoric soil use. In N. Boivin and M. A. Owoc (eds) *Soils, Stones and Symbols: cultural perceptions of the mineral world.* London: UCL Press, pp. 165–186.

BOIVIN, N. 2008. *Material Cultures, Material Minds: the impact of things on human thought, society, and culture.* Cambridge: Cambridge University Press.

BOLTANSKI, L. and THÉVENOT, L. 2006. *On Justification: economies of worth.* Princeton: Princeton University Press.

BOLTON, L. 2001. What makes *Singo* different: North Vanuatu textiles and the theory of captivation. In C. Pinney and N. Thomas (eds) *Beyond Aesthetics: art and the technologies of enchantment.* Oxford: Berg, pp. 97–116.

BONNIE, K. E., HORNER, V., WHITEN, A. and DE WAAL, F. B. M. 2007. Spread of arbitrary conventions among chimpanzees: a controlled experiment. *Proceedings of The Royal Society B-Biological Sciences* 274(1608): 367–372.

BOONE, E. H. 1993. Collecting the Pre-Columbian past: historical trends and the process of reception and use. In E. H. Boone (ed.) *Collecting the Pre-Columbian Past.* Washington, DC: Dumbarton Oaks, pp. 315–350.

BOONE, S. 1986. *The Radiance from the Waters.* New Haven: Yale University Press.

BOOTH, M. 1996. *Opium: a history.* London: Simon and Schuster.

BORDES, F. 1973. On the chronology and the contemporaneity of different Palaeolithic cultures in France. In A. C. Renfrew (ed.) *The Explanation of Culture Change.* London: Duckworth, pp. 217–226.

BORDO, S. 1987. *The Flight to Objectivity. Essays on Cartesianism and culture.* New York: State University of New York Press.

BORDO, S. 1993. *Unbearable Weight: feminism, Western culture, and the body.* Berkeley: University of California Press.

BORIĆ, D. 2002. Apotropaism and the temporality of colours: colourful Mesolithic-Neolithic seasons in the Danube Gorges. In A. Jones and G. MacGregor (eds) *Colouring the Past: the significance of colour in archaeological research.* Oxford: Berg, pp. 23–43.

BORIĆ, D. 2003. 'Deep time' metaphor: mnemonic and apotropaic practices at Lepenski Vir. *Journal of Social Archaeology* 3(1): 46–74.

BORIĆ, D. 2005. Body metamorphosis and animality: volatile bodies and boulder artworks from Lepenski Vir. *Cambridge Archaeological Journal* 15(1): 35–69.

Borić, D. and Robb, J. 2008. *Past Bodies: body-centered research in Archaeology*. Oxford: Oxbow Books.

Bosman, W. 1967 [1705]. *A New and Accurate Description of the Coast of Guinea* (fourth English edition, ed. J. R. Willis, J. D. Fage and R. E. Bradbury). London: Cass.

Botkin, D. 1990. *Discordant Harmonies*. Oxford: Oxford University Press.

Botticello, J. 2007. Lagos in London: finding the space of home. *Home Cultures* 4(1): 7–23.

Bourdieu, P. 1970. The Berber house or the world reversed. *Social Science Information* 9: 151–70.

Bourdieu, P. 1977. *Outline of a Theory of Practice* (trans. R. Nice). Cambridge: Cambridge University Press.

Bourdieu, P. 1984. *Distinction: a social critique of the judgement of taste* (trans. R. Nice). Cambridge, MA: Harvard University Press.

Bourdieu, P. 1990. *The Logic of Practice* (trans. R. Nice). Cambridge: Polity Press.

Bowerman, D. 2007. Suitcase sent to Africa washed up on shore Branscombe. *Sidmouth Herald* 3 February 2007.

Bowers, A. 1992. *Hidatsa Social and Ceremonial Organization*. Lincoln: University of Nebraska Press.

Bowers, A. 2004. *Mandan Social and Ceremonial Organization*. Lincoln: University of Nebraska Press.

Bowker, G. C. and Star, S. L. 1999. *Sorting Things Out: classification and its consequences*. Cambridge, MA: MIT Press.

Boyd, B. 2002. Ways of eating/ways of being in the Later Epipalaeolithic (Natufian) Levant. In Y. Hamilakis, M. Pluciennik and S. A. Tarlow (eds) *Thinking Through the Body: archaeologies of corporeality*. New York: Kluwer/Plenum, pp. 137–152.

Boyd, B. 2004. Agency and landscape: abandoning the nature/culture dichotomy in interpretations of the Natufian and the transition to the Neolithic. In C. Delage (ed.) *The Last Hunter-Gatherer Societies in the Near East*. Oxford: Archaeopress (British Archaeological Reports, International Series 1320), pp. 119–136.

Boyle, L. 1968. *Diary of a Colonial Officer's Wife*. Oxford: Alden.

Bradley, R. 1720. *The gentleman and gardener's kalendar directing what is necessary to be done every month in the kitchen-garden, fruit-garden, nursery, management of forest-trees, green-house, and flower-garden*. London: W. Mears.

Bradley, R. J. 1975. Lithic reduction sequences: a glossary and discussion. In E. Swanson (ed.) *Stone Tool Use and Manufacture*. The Hague: Mouton Press, pp. 5–14.

Bradley, R. J. 1997. *Rock Art and the Prehistory of Atlantic Europe: signing the land*. London: Routledge.

Bradley, R. J. 2002. *The Past in Prehistoric Societies*. London: Routledge.

Bradley, R. J. and Edmonds, M. 1993. *Interpreting the Axe Trade: production and exchange in Neolithic Britain*. Cambridge: Cambridge University Press (New Studies in Archaeology).

Brand, S. 1972. Spacewar: fanatic life and symbolic death among the computer bums. *Rolling Stone* 7 December 1972: 50–58.

Braudel, F. 1973. *Capitalism and Material Life, 1400–1800* (trans. M. Kochan). London: Weidenfeld and Nicolson.

Braudel, F. 1981. *The Structures of Everyday Life: the limits of the possible* (trans. M. Kochan, revised S. Reynolds). London: Collins.

Braun, B. 2005. Environmental issues: writing a more-than-human urban geography. *Progress in Human Geography* 29, 635–650.

Braun, B. 2007. Biopolitics and the molecularization of life. *Cultural Geographies* 14: 6–28.

BRAUN, D. 1983. Pots as tools. In A. Keene and J. Moore (eds) *Archaeological Hammers and Theories*. New York: Academic Press, pp. 107–134.

BRAY, T. L. (ed.) 2003a. *The Archaeology and Politics of Food and Feasting in Early States and Empires*. New York: Kluwer Academic/Plenum Publishers.

BRAY, T. L. 2003b. To dine splendidly: imperial pottery, commensal politics, and the Inca state. In T. L. Bray (ed.) *The Archaeology and Politics of Food and Feasting in Early States and Empires*. New York: Kluwer Academic/Plenum Publishers, pp. 93–142.

BRECKENRIDGE, C. A. 1989. The aesthetics and politics of colonial collecting: India at world fairs. *Comparative Studies in Society and History* 312: 195–216.

BREMAN, J. 1988. *The Shattered Image: construction and deconstruction of the village in colonial Asia*. Dordrecht: Foris Publications.

BRESSEY, C. 2009. The legacies of 2007: remapping the black presence in Britain. *Geography Compass* 3(3): 903–917.

BREUER, T., NDOUNDOU-HOCKEMBA, M. and FISHLOCK, V. 2005. First observation of tool use in wild gorillas. *PLoS Biology* 3(11): 2041–2043.

BREWER, J. and TRENTMANN, F. (eds) 2006. *Consuming Cultures, Global Perspectives*. Oxford: Berg.

BREWER, J. and PORTER, R. (eds) 1993. *Consumption and the World of Goods*. London: Routledge.

BRIDGE, G. and SMITH, A. 2003. Intimate encounters: culture—economy—commodity. *Environment and Planning D: Society and Space* 21(3): 257–268.

BRIGGS, A. 1988. *Victorian Things*. London: Batsford.

BROAD, L. 1972. *Winston Churchill: the years of achievement*. Westport, CT: Greenwood Press.

BROHIER, R. L. 1934. *Ancient irrigation works in Ceylon*. Colombo: Ceylon Government Press.

BROOK, T. 1998. *The Confusions of Pleasure. Commerce and culture in Ming China*. Berkeley: University of California Press.

BROOK, T. 2007. *Vermeer's Hat: the seventeenth century and the dawn of the global world*. New York: Bloomsbury Press.

DE BROSSES, C. 1998 [1760]. *Du culte des dieux fétiches*. Paris: Fayard.

BROWMAN, D. L. and GIVENS, D. R. 1996. Stratigraphic excavation: the first 'new archaeology'. *American Anthropologist* 98: 80–95.

BROWN, A. 1991. Structured deposition and technological change among flaked stone artefacts from Cranbourne Chase. In J. Barrett, R. J. Bradley and M. Green (eds) *Papers on the Prehistoric Archaeology of Cranbourne Chase*. Oxford: Oxbow Books, pp. 101–133.

BROWN, B. 2001. Thing theory. *Critical Inquiry* 28(1): 1–22.

BROWN, B. 2003. *A Sense of Things: the object matter of American Literature*. Chicago: University of Chicago Press.

BROWN, C. A. 1996. Testing the boundaries of marginality: twentieth-century slavery and emancipation struggles in Nkanu, Northern Igboland, 1920–29. *Journal of African History* 372: 51–80.

BROWN, J. (ed.) 1984. *Michael Heizer: sculpture in reverse*. Los Angeles, CA: Museum of Contemporary Art.

BROWN, J. A. 1989. The beginnings of pottery as an economic process. In S. E. van der Leeuw and R. Torrence (eds) *What's New? A Closer Look at the Process of Innovation*. London: Unwin Hyman, pp. 203–224.

BROWN, M. and SAMFORD, P. 1994. Current archaeological perspectives on the growth and development of Williamsburg. In P. Shackel and B. Little (eds) *Historical Archaeology of the Chesapeake*. Washington, DC: Smithsonian Institution Press, pp. 231–245.

BROWNELL, C. 1992. Monticello, First House. In C. Brownell, C. Loth, W. Rasmussen, and R. Wilson (eds) *The Making of Virginia Architecture*. Richmond: Virginia Museum of Fine Arts, pp. 212–213.

BRÜCK, J. 1998. In the footsteps of the ancestors. A review of Christopher Tilley's 'A Phenomenology of Landscape: places, paths, monuments'. *Archaeological Review from Cambridge* 15: 23–36.

BRÜCK, J. 2001a. Body metaphors and technologies of transformation in the English Middle and Late Bronze Age. In J. Brück (ed.) *Bronze Age Landscapes: Tradition and Transformation*. Oxford: Oxbow, pp. 149–160.

BRÜCK, J. 2001b. Monuments, power and personhood in the British Neolithic. *Journal of the Royal Anthropological Institute* 7(4): 649–667.

BRÜCK, J. 2004. Material metaphors. The relational construction of identity in Early Bronze Age burials in Ireland and Britain. *Journal of Social Archaeology* 4(3): 307–333.

BRÜCK, J. 2005. Experiencing the past? The development of a phenomenological archaeology in British prehistory. *Archaeological Dialogues* 12(1): 45–72.

BRÜCK, J. 2006a. Fragmentation, personhood and the social construction of technology in Middle and Late Bronze Age Britain. *Cambridge Archaeological Journal* 16: 297–315.

BRÜCK, J. 2006b. Death, exchange and reproduction in the British Bronze Age. *European Journal of Archaeology* 9(1): 73–101.

BRUDENELL, M. and COOPER, A. 2008. Post-middenism: depositional histories on later Bronze Age settlements at Broom, Bedfordshire. *Oxford Journal of Archaeology* 27(1): 15–36.

BRUMFIEL, E. M. 1996. Figurines and the Aztec state. Testing the effectiveness of ideological domination. In R. P. Wright (ed.) *Gender and Archaeology*. Philadelphia: University of Pennsylvania Press, pp. 143–166.

BRUMFIEL, E. M. 2003. It's a material world: history, artifacts, and anthropology. *Annual Review of Anthropology* 32: 205–223.

BRUMFIEL, E. M. and EARLE, T. 1987. Specialization, exchange and complex societies: an introduction. In E. M. Brumfiel and T. Earle (eds) *Specialization, Exchange and Complex Societies*. Cambridge: Cambridge University Press, pp. 1–9.

BRUNSKILL, R. 1971. *Illustrated Handbook of Vernacular Architecture*. London: Faber and Faber.

BRUNT, P. A. 1966. The Roman mob. *Past and Present* 35: 3–27.

BUCHLI, V. 1995. Interpreting material culture: the trouble with text. In I. Hodder, M. Shanks, V. Buchli, J. Carman, J. Last and G. Lucas (eds) *Interpreting Archaeology: finding meaning in the past*. London: Routledge, pp. 181–193.

BUCHLI, V. 1999. *An Archaeology of Socialism*. Oxford: Berg.

BUCHLI, V. 2000. Constructing utopian sexualities: the archaeology and architecture of the early Soviet state. In R. Schmidt and B. Voss (eds) *Archaeologies of Sexuality*. London: Routledge, pp. 236–249.

BUCHLI, V. 2002a. Introduction. In V. Buchli (ed.) *The Material Culture Reader*. Oxford: Berg, pp. 1–22.

BUCHLI, V. 2002b. Architecture and the domestic sphere. In V. Buchli (ed.) *The Material Culture Reader*. Oxford: Berg, pp. 207–213.

BUCHLI, V. 2002c. Towards an archaeology of the contemporary past. *Cambridge Archaeological Journal* 12(1): 131–150.

BUCHLI, V. 2004. Material culture: current problems. In L. Meskell and R. Preucel (eds) *Companion to Social Archaeology*. Oxford: Blackwell, pp. 179–194.

BUCHLI, V. and LUCAS, G. 2001a. The absent present: archaeologies of the contemporary past. In V. Buchli and G. Lucas (eds) *Archaeologies of the Contemporary Past*. London: Routledge, pp. 3–18.

BUCHLI, V. and LUCAS, G. (eds) 2001b. *Archaeologies of the Contemporary Past*. London: Routledge.

BUCHLI, V. and LUCAS G. 2001c. The archaeology of alienation: a late twentieth-century British council flat. In V. Buchli and G. Lucas, *Archaeologies of the Contemporary Past*. London: Routledge, pp. 158–167.

BURBACK, B. 1984. *Ivory and its Uses*. Rutland, VT: Charles E. Tuttle.

BURCHELL, G., GORDON, C. and MILLER, P. 1991. *The Foucault effect: studies in governmentality: with two lectures by and an interview with Michel Foucault*. Chicago: University of Chicago Press.

BURGESS, C. and SHENNAN, S. 1976. The Beaker phenomenon: some suggestions. In C. Burgess and R. Miket (eds) *Settlement and Economy in the Third and Second Millennia BC*. Oxford: British Archaeological Reports (British Archaeological Reports, British series 33), pp. 309–331.

BURKE, T. 1996. *Lifeboy Men, Lux Women: commodification, consumption, and cleanliness in modern Zimbabwe*. Durham, NC: Duke University Press.

BURNETT, J. 1980. *A Social History of Housing 1815–1970*. London: Methuen.

BURNS, E. 2007. *The Smoke of the Gods: a social history of tobacco*. Philadelphia: Temple University Press.

BUSBY, C. 1997. Permeable and partible persons: a comparative analysis of gender and the body in a fishing community in South India and Melanesia. *Journal of the Royal Anthropological Institute* 3(2): 261–278.

BUSBY, C. 1999. Agency, power and personhood: discourses of gender and violence in a fishing community in south India. *Critique of Anthropology* 19(3): 227–248.

BUTLER, J. 1990. *Gender Trouble: feminism and the subversion of identity*. New York: Routledge.

BUTLER, J. 1993. *Bodies That Matter: on the discursive limits of 'sex'*. New York: Routledge.

BUTLER, J. 1998. Merely cultural. *New Left Review* I (227): 33–44.

BUTLER, J. 2000. Restaging the universal: hegemony and the limits of formalism. In J. Butler, E. Laclau, S. Žižek (eds) *Contingency, Hegemony, Universality: contemporary dialogues on the left*. London: Verso, pp. 11–43.

BUTLER, T. 2006. A walk of art: the potential of the sound walk as practice in cultural geography. *Social and Cultural Geography* 7(6): 889–908.

BUTLER, T. 2007. Memoryscape: how audio walks can deepen our sense of place by integrating art, oral history and cultural geography. *Geography Compass* 1(3): 360–372.

BYNUM, C. W. 1995. Why all the fuss about the body? A medievalist's perspective. *Critical Inquiry* 22(1): 1–33.

BYRNE, D. 1998. Deep nation: Australia's acquisition of an indigenous past. *Aboriginal History* 20: 82–107.

BYRNE, D. 2003. The ethos of return: erasure and reinstatement of Aboriginal visibility in the Australian historical landscape. *Historical Archaeology* 37(1): 73–86.

BYRNE, D. 2004. Archaeology in reverse. In N. Merriman (ed.) *Public Archaeology.* London: Routledge, pp. 240–254.

BYRNE, D. 2007. *Surface Collection. Archaeological travels in Southeast Asia.* Lanham, MD: Altamira Press.

BYRNE, D. 2008. Heritage as social action. In G. Fairclough, R. Harrison, J. Schofield and J. Jameson (eds) *The Heritage Reader.* London: Routledge; pp. 149–173.

BYRNE, D., BRAYSHAW, H. and IRELAND, T. 2001. *Social Significance: a discussion paper.* Hurstville, NSW: NSW National Parks and Wildlife Service.

BYRNE, R. W. 2004. The manual skills and cognition that lie behind hominid tool use. In A. E. Russon and D. R. Begun (eds) *The Evolution of Thought: evolutionary origins of great intelligence.* Cambridge: Cambridge University Press, pp. 31–44.

BYRNE, R. W. 2007. Culture in great apes: using intricate complexity in feeding skills to trace the evolutionary origin of human technical prowess. *Philosophical Transactions of the Royal Society B-Biological Sciences* 362(1480): 577–585.

CALLAWAY, H. 1992. Dressing for dinner in the bush: rituals of self-definition and British Imperial authority. In R. Barnes and J. B. Eicher (eds) *Dress and Gender: making and meaning in cultural contexts.* New York: Berg.

CALLON, M. 1980. The state and technical innovation: a case study of the electric vehicle in France. *Research Policy* 9: 358–376.

CALLON, M. 1986a. Some elements of a sociology of translation: domestication of the scallops and the fishermen of Saint Brieuc Bay. In Law, J. (ed.) *Power, Action and Belief: a new sociology of knowledge?* London: Routledge and Kegan Paul (Sociological Review Monograph 32), pp. 196–233.

CALLON, M. 1986b. The sociology of an Actor-Network: the case of an electric vehicle. In M. Callon, J. Law and A. Rip (eds) *Mapping the Dynamics of Science and Technology.* London: Macmillan, pp. 19–34.

CALLON, M. 1991. Techno-economic networks and irreversibility. In J. Law (ed.) *A Sociology of Monsters: essays on power, technology and domination.* London: Routledge, pp. 132–164.

CALLON, M. 1998. *The laws of the markets edited by Michel Callon.* Oxford: Blackwell.

CALLON, M. and LATOUR, B. 1981. Unscrewing the Big Leviathan: how actors macrostructure reality and how sociologists help them to do so. In K. D. Knorr-Cetina and A. V. Cicourel (eds) *Advances in Social Theory and Methodology: toward an integration of micro- and macro-sociologies.* London: Routledge and Kegan Paul, pp. 277–303.

CALLON, M. and LAW, J. 1997. After the individual in society. Lessons on collectivity from science, technology and society. *Canadian Journal of Sociology* 22(2): 165–182.

CALLON, M., LASCOUMES, P. and BARTHE, Y. 2001. *Agir dans un monde incertain: essaie sure la démocratie technique.* Paris: Éditions du Seuil.

CALVO-IGLESIAS, M. S., CRECENTE-MASEDA, R. and FRA-PALEO, U. 2006. Exploring farmer's knowledge as a source of information on past and present cultural landscapes. A case study from NW Spain. *Landscape and Urban Planning* 78: 334–343.

CAMPBELL, C. 1987. *The Romantic Ethic and the Spirit of Modern Consumerism.* Oxford: Blackwell.

CAMPBELL, C. 1995. The sociology of consumption. In D. Miller (ed.) *Acknowledging Consumption: a review of new studies.* London: Routledge, pp. 58–95.

CAMPBELL, S., MEYNELL, L. and SHERWIN, S. (eds) 2009. *Embodiment and Agency.* University Park, PA: Pennsylvania State University Press.

CAMPBELL, S. F. 2001. The captivating agency of art: many ways of seeing. In C. Pinney and N. Thomas (eds) *Beyond Aesthetics: art and the technologies of enchantment.* Oxford: Berg, pp. 117–135.

CAMPBELL, S. F. 2002. *The Art of the Kula.* Oxford: Berg.

CANDEA, M. 2007. Arbitrary locations: In defence of the bounded field-site. *Journal of the Royal Anthropological Institute* 13(1): 167–184.

CANNIZZO, J. 1998. Gathering souls and objects: missionary collections. In T. Barringer and T. Flynn (eds) *Colonialism and the Object: Empire, material culture and museum.* London: Routledge, pp. 153–166.

CANNSTATTER VOLKSFEST 2008. Cannstatter Volksfest: History. http://www.cannstatter-volksfest.de/index.php?id=50andL=1 (Accessed 1 December 2008).

CANT, S. and MORRIS, N. 2006. Geographies of art and the environment. *Social and Cultural Geography* 7(6): 857–861.

CANTER, D. 2002. The violated body. In S. T. Sweeney and I. Hodder (eds) *The Body.* Cambridge: Cambridge University Press, pp. 57–74.

CAPLAN, J. (ed.) 2000. *Written on the Body: the tattoo in European and American history.* London: Reaktion Books.

CARNEY, J. A. 2001. *Black Rice: the African origins of rice cultivation in the Americas.* Cambridge, MA: Harvard University Press.

CARO, T. and HAUSER, M. D. 1992. Is there teaching in non-human animals? *The Quarterly Review of Biology* 67: 151–171.

CAROLAN, M. 2007. Introducing the concept of tactile space: creating lasting social and environmental commitments. *Geoforum* 38(6): 1264–1275.

CARRIER, J. G. and MILLER, D. (eds) 1998. *Virtualism: a new political economy.* Oxford: Berg.

CARRITHERS, M. 1990. Why humans have cultures. *Man* 25: 189–206.

CARROLL, A., ZEDEÑO, M. and STOFFLE, R. 2004. Landscapes of the ghost dance: a cartography of Numic ritual. *Journal of Archaeological Method and Theory* 11(2): 127–156.

CARROLL, P. 2006. *Science, Culture, and Modern State Formation.* Berkeley: University of California Press.

CARSON, B. 1990. *Ambitious Appetites: dining, behavior and patterns of consumption in Federal Washington.* Washington, DC: American Institute of Architects Press.

CARSON, C. 1997. Material culture history: the scholarship nobody knows. In A. S. Martin and R. Garrison (eds) *American Material Culture: the shape of the field.* Winterthur, DE: Winterthur Museum, pp. 401–428.

CARSTEN, J. 2003. *After Kinship.* Cambridge: Cambridge University Press.

CARSTEN, J. and HUGH-JONES, S. 1995. Introduction. In J. Carsten and S. Hugh-Jones (eds) *About the House: Lévi-Strauss and beyond.* Cambridge: Cambridge University Press, pp. 1–46.

CASE, H. 1973. A ritual site in north-east Ireland. In G. Daniel and P. Kjaerum (eds) *Megalithic Graves and Ritual.* Aarhus: Jutland Archaeological Society, pp. 173–196.

CASELLA, E. 2000. 'Doing trade': a sexual economy of nineteenth century Australian female convict prisons. *World Archaeology* 32(2): 209–221.

CASELLA, E. and FOWLER, C. 2004. Beyond identification: an introduction. In E. Casella and C. Fowler (eds) *The Archaeology of Plural and Changing Identities: beyond identification.* Kluwer Academic/Plenum Press, pp. 1–8.

CASEY, E. 1996. How to get from space to place in a fairly short stretch of time. In S. Feld and K. Basso (eds) *Senses of Place.* Santa Fe: SAR Press, pp. 13–52.

CASTREE, N. 2002. False antitheses? Marxism, nature and actor-networks. *Antipode* 34: 111–146.

CASTREE, N. 2004. The geographical lives of commodities: problems of analysis and critique. *Social and Cultural Geography* 5(1): 21–35.

CAVALLI-SFORZA, L. L., FELDMAN, M. W., CHEN, K. H. and DORNBUSCH, S. M. 1982. Theory and observation in cultural transmission. *Science* 218: 19–27.

CELANT, G. 1997. *Michal Heizer.* Milan: Fondazionetion Prada.

ÇELIK, Z. 1986. *The remaking of Istanbul: portrait of an Ottoman city in the nineteenth century.* Seattle: University of Washington Press.

ÇELIK, Z. 2003. Editor's Concluding Notes: teaching the history of architecture: a global inquiry. *Journal of the Society of Architectural Historians* 62(1): 121–124.

DE CERTEAU, M. 1984. *The Practice of Everyday Life* (trans. S. Rendall). Berkeley: University of California Press.

DE CERTEAU, M. 1998. *The Practice of Everyday Life. Volume 2: Living and cooking* (trans. T. J. Tomasik). Minneapolis: University of Minnesota Press.

CHAKRABARTI, D. K. 1997. *The Archaeology of Ancient Indian Cities.* Oxford: Oxford University Press.

CHAKRABARTY, D. 1994. The difference-defferal of a colonial modernity: public debates on domesticity in British India. *Subaltern Studies* 8: 50–88.

CHAKRABARTY, D. 2000. *Provincializing Europe: postcolonial thought and historical difference.* Princeton, NJ: Princeton University Press (Princeton Studies in Culture/Power/History).

CHAPMAN, J. 1996. Enchainment, commodification, and gender in the Balkan Copper Age. *Journal of European Archaeology* 4: 203–242.

CHAPMAN, J. 2000a. *Fragmentation in Archaeology: people, places and broken objects in the prehistory of south eastern Europe.* London: Routledge.

CHAPMAN, J. 2000b. Pit-digging and structured deposition in the Neolithic and Copper Age of central and eastern Europe. *Proceedings of the Prehistoric Society* 66: 61–88.

CHAPMAN, J. and GAYDARSKA, B. 2007. *Parts and Wholes: fragmentation in prehistoric context.* Oxford: Oxbow.

CHAPPELL, E. 1980. Acculturation in the Shenandoah Valley: rhenish houses of the Massanutten settlement. *Proceedings of the American Philosophical Society* 124(1): 55–89.

CHARDIN, J. 1811. *Voyages du Chevalier Chardin, en Perse et Autres Lieux de l'Orient* (ed. L. Langlès), Volumes VII–VIII. Paris.

CHARDON, F. 1997 [1932]. *Chardon's Journal at Fort Clark, 1834–1839.* Lincoln: University of Nebraska Press.

CHATTOPADHYAY, S. 2002. Goods, chattels and sundry items. Constructing 19th-century Anglo-Indian domestic life. *Journal of Material Culture* 7(3): 243–271.

CHATTOPADHYAY, S. 2005. *Representing Calcutta: modernism, nationalism, and the colonial uncanny.* London: Routledge.

CHEAH, P. 1996. Mattering. *Diacritics* 26: 108–139.

CHEVALIER, S. 1997. From woolen carpet to grass carpet: bridging house and garden in an English suburb. In D. Miller (ed.) *Material Cultures: why some things matter.* London: UCL Press, pp. 47–71.

CHILDE, V. G. 1925. *The Dawn of European Civilisation.* London: Kegan Paul, Trench, Trubner and Co.

CHILDE, V. G. 1926. *The Aryans: a study of Indo-European origins.* London: Kegan Paul.

CHILDE, V. G. 1936. *Man Makes Himself.* London: Watts and Co.

CHILDE, V. G. 1942. *What Happened in History.* Harmondsworth: Penguin.

CHILDE, V. G. 1943. The Mesolithic and Neolithic in northern Europe. *Man* 43: 34–36.

CHILDE, V. G. 1950. *Prehistoric Migrations in Europe*. Oslo: Aschehoug.

CHILDE, V. G. 1956. *Piecing Together the Past: the interpretation of archaeological data*. London: Routledge and Kegan Paul.

CHILTON, E. 1999. Material meanings and meaningful materials: an introduction. In E. Chilton (ed.) *Material Meanings: critical approaches to the interpretation of material culture*. Salt Lake City: University of Utah Press, pp. 1–6.

CHIMPANZEE CULTURES 2007. Chimpanzee Cultures. http://biologybk.st-and.ac.uk/cultures3/ (Consulted 10 March 2009).

CHOPRA, P. 2007. Reconfiguring the colonial city: recovering the role of local inhabitants in the construction of colonial Bombay, 1854–1918. *Buildings and Landscapes: Journal of the Vernacular Architecture Forum* 14: 109–125.

CHRISTAKIS, K. 2005. *Cretan Bronze Age Pithoi: traditions and trends in the production and consumption of storage containers in Bronze Age Crete*. Philadelphia, PA: INSTAP Academic Press (Prehistory Monographs 18).

CHRISTENSEN, M. 1995. In the beginning was the potter: material culture as mode of expression and anthropological object. *Folk* 37: 5–24.

CIERAAD, I. (ed.) 1999. *At Home: an anthropology of domestic space*. Syracuse: Syracuse University Press.

CLARK, J. G. D. 1961. *World Prehistory: an outline*. Cambridge: Cambridge University Press.

CLARK, N. 2005. Ex-orbitant globality. *Theory, Culture and Society* 22: 165–185.

CLARK, N. 2007. Living through the tsunami: vulnerability and generosity on a volatile earth. *Geoforum* 38: 1127–1139.

CLARKE, A. 1998. Window Shopping at Home: Catalogues, classifieds and new consumer skills. In D. Miller (ed.) *Material Cultures: why some things matter*. London: Routledge (Consumption and Space), pp. 73–99.

CLARKE, B. 2008. *Posthuman Metamorphosis: narrative and systems*. New York: Fordham University Press.

CLARKE, D. L. 1968. *Analytical Archaeology*. London: Methuen.

CLARKE, D. L. 1973. Archaeology: the loss of innocence. *Antiquity* 47: 6–18.

CLARKE, D. L. (ed.) 1977. *Spatial Archaeology*. London: Academic Press.

CLARKE, L. B., GOUGH, R. and WATT, D. (eds) 2007. Special Issue: Objects. *Performance Research* 12(4).

CLARKSON, C. and O'CONNOR, S. 2006. An introduction to stone artefact analysis. In J. Balme and A. Paterson (eds) *Archaeology in Practice: a student guide to archaeological analyses*. Oxford: Blackwell, pp. 159–206.

CLASSEN, C. (ed.) 2005. *The Book of Touch*. Oxford: Berg.

CLEGG, J. 1987. Style and tradition at Sturt's Meadow. *World Archaeology*, 199: 2, 236–255.

CLEMENT, E. 1904. Ethnographical notes on the western Australian Aborigines: with a descriptive catalogue of a collection of ethnographical objects from Western Australia by J. D. E. Schmeltz. *Internationales Archiv für Ethnographie* 16(1–2): 1–29.

CLIFFORD, J. 1988. *The Predicament of Culture: twentieth-century ethnography, literature and art*. Cambridge, MA: Harvard University Press.

CLIFFORD, J. 1990. Notes on (Field)notes. In R. Sanjek (ed.) *Fieldnotes: the makings of anthropology*. Ithaca, NY: Cornell University Press, pp. 47–70.

CLIFFORD, J. 1997. *Routes: travel and translation in the late twentieth century*. Cambridge, MA: Harvard University Press.

CLIFFORD, J. 2004. Looking several ways: anthropology and native heritage in Alaska. *Current Anthropology* 45(1): 5–30.

CLIFFORD, J. and MARCUS, G. (eds) 1986. *Writing Culture: the poetics and politics of ethnography*. Berkeley: University of California Press.

CLOKE, P., COOK, I., CRANG, P., GOODWIN, M., PAINTER, J. and PHILO, C. 2004. *Practising Human Geography*. London: Sage.

CLOUGH, P. T. 2007. Introduction. In P. T. Clough and J. Halley (eds) *The Affective Turn*. Durham, NC: Duke University Press, pp. 1–33.

CLOUGH, P. T. and HALLEY, J. (eds) 2007. *The Affective Turn: theorizing the social*. Durham, NC: Duke University Press.

CLUNAS, C. 1991. *Superfluous Things. Material culture and social status in early modern China*. Cambridge: Polity Press.

CLUNAS, C. 1997. *Pictures and Visuality in Modern China*. London: Reaktion.

CLUNAS, C. 2007. *Empire of Great Brightness. Visual and material cultures of Ming China, 1368–1644*. London: Reaktion.

CNN 2007. Woman pleads for return of belongings. *CNN.com* 23 January 2007. http://cnn.hu/2007/WORLD/europe/01/23/ship.wreck/index.html (Accessed 17 November 2008).

COCHRAN, M. and BEAUDRY, M. C. 2006. Material culture studies and historical archaeology. In D. Hicks and M. C. Beaudry (eds) *The Cambridge Companion to Historical Archaeology*. Cambridge: Cambridge University Press, pp. 191–204.

COCKBURN, C. 1983. *Brothers: male dominance and technological change*. London: Pluto.

COCKBURN, C. 1999. The material of male power. In D. MacKenzie and J. Wajcman (eds) *The Social Shaping of Technology* (second edition). Buckingham: Open University Press, pp. 177–198.

COE, S. D. and COE, M. D. 1996. *The True History of Chocolate*. London: Thames and Hudson.

COHEN, D. 2006. *Household Gods. The British and their possessions*. New Haven, CT: Yale University Press.

COHEN, J. J. and WEISS, G. (eds) 2003. *Thinking the Limits of the Body*. Albany: State University of New York Press.

COHEN, M. N. and BENNETT, S. 1993. Skeletal evidence for sex roles and gender hierarchies in prehistory. In B. Miller (ed.) *Sex and Gender Hierarchies*. Cambridge: Cambridge University Press, pp. 273–296.

COHN, B. 1996. *Colonialism and its Forms of Knowledge: The British in India*. Princeton: Princeton University Press.

COLCHESTER, C. (ed.) 2003. *Clothing the Pacific*. Oxford: Berg.

COLLINGWOOD, R. G. 1946. *The Idea of History*. Oxford: Oxford University Press.

COLLINS, H. M. 1975. The seven sexes: a study in the sociology of a phenomenon, or the replication of experiments in physics. *Sociology* 9: 205–224.

COLLINS, H. M. 1992. *Changing Order: replication and induction in scientific practice* (second edition). Chicago: University of Chicago Press.

COLLINS, J. L. 2000. Tracing social relations in commodity chains: the case of grapes in Brazil. In A. Haugerud, M. P. Stone and P. D. Little (eds) *Commodities and Globalization: Anthropological Perspectives*. Boulder, CO: Rowman and Littlefield, pp. 97–112.

COLLOREDO-MANSFELD, R. 2003. Introduction: matter unbound. *Journal of Material Culture* 83(3): 245–254.

COLLOREDO-MANSFELD, R. 2005. Consumption. In J. G. Carrier (ed.) *A Handbook of Economic Anthropology*. Northampton, MA: Edwar Elgar, pp. 210–225.

COLLS, R. 2004. 'Looking alright, feeling alright': emotions, sizing and the geographies of women's experiences of clothing consumption. *Social and Cultural Geography* 5: 583–596.

COLLS, R. 2006. Outsize/outside: bodily bigness and the emotional experiences of British women shopping for clothes. *Gender, Place and Culture* 13(5): 529–545.

COLLS, R. 2007. Materialising bodily matter: intra-action and the embodiment of 'Fat'. *Geoforum* 38: 353–365.

COLOMINA, B. 1988. Introduction: on architecture, production and reproduction. In B. Colomina (ed.) *Architectureproduction.* New York: Princeton Architectural Press, pp. 7–23.

COLOMINA, B. (ed.) 1992. *Sexuality and Space.* New York: Princeton Architectural Press.

COLPITT, F. 1990. *Minimal Art: the critical perspective.* Seattle, WA: University of Washington Press.

COLUMELLA, L. J. M. 1941. *On Agriculture* (Volume I, Book I; trans. H. Boyd Ash). Cambridge, MA: Harvard University Press.

COLWELL-CHANTHAPHONH, C. and FERGUSON, T. (eds) 2007. *Collaboration in Archaeological Practice: engaging descendant communities.* New York: AltaMira Press.

COMAROFF, J. 1996. The Empire's old clothes: fashioning the colonial subject. In D. Howes (ed.) *Cross-Cultural Consumption: global markets, local realities.* Routledge, London, pp. 19–38.

COMAROFF, J. and COMAROFF, J. L. 1991. *Of Revelation and Revolution: christianity, colonialism, and consciousness in South Africa* (Volume 1). Chicago: University of Chicago Press.

COMAROFF, J. L. and COMAROFF, J. 1997. *Of Revelation and Revolution,* Volume 2: *The dialectics of modernity on a South African frontier.* Chicago: University of Chicago Press.

COMTE, A. 1840. First theological phase: Fetichism. In H. Martineau (ed.; transl.) *The Positive Philosophy of Auguste Comte.* New York: Eckler, pp. 545–561.

CONAN, M. (ed.) 2000. *Environmentalism in Landscape Architecture.* Washington, DC: Dumbarton Oaks Research Library and Collection.

CONAN, M. (ed.) 2002. *Bourgeois and Aristocratic Cultural Encounters in Garden Art, 1550–1850.* Washington, DC: Dumbarton Oaks Research Library and Collection.

CONAN, M. and DUMBARTON OAKS. 2005. *Baroque garden cultures: emulation, sublimation, subversion.* Washington, DC: Dumbarton Oaks Research Library and Collection.

CONINGHAM, R., GUNAWARDHANA, P., MANUEL, M., ADIKARI, G., KATUGAMPOLA, M., YOUNG, R., SCHMIDT, A., KRISHNAN, K., SIMPSON, I., MCDONNELL, G. and BATT, C. 2007. The state of theocracy: defining an early medieval hinterland in Sri Lanka. *Antiquity* 81(313): 699–719.

CONKEY, M. 1982. Ritual communication, social elaboration and the variable trajectories of Palaeolithic material culture. In T. D. Price and J. A. Brown (eds) *Prehistoric Hunter-Gatherers: the emergence of social and cultural complexity.* London: Academic Press, pp. 299–333.

CONKEY, M. 1989. The place of material culture in contemporary anthropology. In A. Hedlund (ed.) *Perspectives on Anthropological Collections from the American Southwest: Proceedings of a Symposium.* Tempe: Arizona State University (Arizona State University Anthropological Research Papers No. 40), pp. 13–31.

CONKEY, M. 2006. Style, design and function. In C. Tilley, W. Keane, S. Küchler, M. J. Rowlands and P. Spyer (eds) *Handbook of Material Culture.* London: Sage, pp. 355–372.

CONKEY, M. W. and GERO, J. M. (eds) 1991. *Engendering Archaeology: women and prehistory.* London: Blackwell (Studies in Social Archaeology).

CONNELLER, C. 2004. Becoming deer: corporeal transformations at Star Carr. *Archaeological Dialogues* 11(1): 37–56.

CONOT, R. E. 1983. *Justice at Nuremberg.* New York: Harper and Row.

CONSTANTINE, S. 1986. *Buy and Build: the advertising posters of the Empire Marketing Board.* London: Her Majesty's Stationery Office.

COOK, A. G. and GLOWACKI, M. 2003. Pots, politics, and power: Huari ceramic assemblages and imperial administration. In T. L. Bray (ed.) *The Archaeology and Politics of Food and Feasting in Early States and Empires.* New York: Kluwer Academic/Plenum Publishers, pp. 173–202.

COOK, I. and CRANG, P. 1996. The world on a plate: culinary culture, displacement and geographical knowledges. *Journal of Material Culture* 1(2): 131–153.

COOK, I. and HARRISON, M. 2003. Cross over food: re-materialising postcolonial geographies. *Transactions of the Institute of British Geographers* 28(3): 296–317.

COOK, I. and HARRISON, M. 2007. Follow the thing: 'West Indian hot pepper sauce'. *Space and Culture* 10(1): 40–63.

COOK et al., I. 2000. Social sculpture and connective aesthetics: Shelley Sacks' 'Exchange Values'. *Ecumene* 7(3): 338–344.

COOK et al., I. 2004. Follow the thing: papaya. *Antipode* 36(4): 642–664.

COOK, I., EVANS, J., GRIFFITHS, H., MORRIS, R. and WRATHMELL, S. 2007. 'It's more than just what it is': defetishising commodities, expanding fields, mobilising change . . . *Geoforum* 38(6): 1113–1126.

COOK, J. 1777. *A Voyage towards the South Pole and Round the World: performed in His Majesty's Ships Resolution and Adventure, in the years 1772, 1773, 1774, and 1775.* London: W. Strahan and T. Cadell.

COOPER, F. and STOLER, A. L. (eds) 1997. *Tensions of Empire: colonial cultures in a bourgeois world.* Berkeley: University of California Press.

COOTE, J. 1992. The marvels of everyday vision. In J. Coote and A. Shelton (eds) *Anthropology, Art and Aesthetics.* Oxford: Clarendon Press, pp. 245–273.

COOTE, J. and SHELTON, A. 1992. *Anthropology, Art and Aesthetics.* Oxford: Clarendon Press.

COPPIN, D. 2003. Foucauldian hog futures: the birth of mega-hog farms. *Sociological Quarterly* 44: 597–616.

COPPIN, D. 2008. Crate and mangle: questions of agency in confinement livestock facilities. In A. Pickering and K. Guzik (eds) *The Mangle in Practice: Science, Society and Becoming.* Durham, NC: Duke University Press, pp. 46–66.

CORBEY, R. 2000. *Tribal Art Traffic. A chronicle of taste, trade and desire in colonial and post-colonial times.* Amsterdam: Royal Tropical Institute.

CORNUTI, J-P. H. 1635. *Canadensium Plantarum Historia de J.-PH. Cornuti.* Paris.

COSGROVE, D. 1984. *Social Formation and Symbolic Landscape.* London: Croom Helm.

COSGROVE, D. 1985. Prospect, perspective and the evolution of the landscape idea. *Transactions of the Institute of British Geographers* 10: 45–62.

COSGROVE, D. and DANIELS, S. (eds) 1988. *The Iconography of Landscape.* Cambridge: Cambridge University Press.

COUNIHAN, C. and VAN ESTERIK, P. (eds) 1997. *Food and Culture: a reader.* London: Routledge.

COUSSI-KORBEL, S. and FRAGASZY, D. M. 1995. On the social relation between social dynamics and social learning. *Animal Behaviour* 50: 1441–1453.

CRAIG, W. 1973. *Enemy at the Gates: the Battle for Stalingrad.* New York: Penguin.

CRAMP, K., CASE, H. and NIMMO, K. 2007. The flint. In D. Benson and A. Whittle (eds) *Building Memories: the Neolithic Cotswold long barrow at Ascott-under-Wychwood, Oxfordshire*. Oxford: Oxbow Books, pp. 289–314.

CRANG, M. A. and COOK, I. 2007. *Doing ethnographies* (new edition). London: Sage.

CRANG, P. 2005. The geographies of material culture. In P. Cloke, P. Crang and M. Goodwin (eds) *Introducing Human Geographies* (second edition). London: Arnold, pp. 168–181.

CRARY, J. 1992. *Techniques of the Observer: on vision and modernity in the nineteenth century.* Cambridge, MA: MIT Press.

CRESSWELL, R. 1976. Avant-propos. *Techniques et culture* 1: 5–6.

CRESWELL, K. A. C. 1940. *Early Muslim Architecture* (Volume 2). Oxford: Oxford University Press.

CREWE, L. 2008. Ugly beautiful? Counting the cost of the global fashion industry. *Geography* 93(1): 25–33.

CREWE, L. and GREGSON, N. 2003. *Second-hand cultures.* Oxford: Berg.

CRONE, R. 1982. Prime objects in art: scale, shape, time: creations by Michael Heizer in the deserts of Nevada. *Perspecta: The Yale Architectural Journal* 19: 14–35.

CRONON, W. (ed.) 1996. *Uncommon Ground: rethinking the human place in nature.* New York: W. W. Norton.

CRONON, W. 1991. *Nature's Metropolis: Chicago and the Great West.* New York: W. W. Norton.

CROSSLAND, Z. 2002. Violent spaces: conflict over the reappearance of Argentina's disappeared. In J. Schofield, C. Beck and W. G. Johnson (eds) *Matériel Culture: the archaeology of 20th century conflict.* London: Routledge, pp. 115–131.

CROSSLAND, Z. 2009a. Acts of estrangement. The post-mortem making of self and other. *Archaeological Dialogues* 16(1): 102–125.

CROSSLAND, Z. 2009b. Of clues and signs: the dead body and its evidential traces. *American Anthropologist* 111(1): 69–80.

CROWLEY, A. 1987 [1904]. *Liber al vel Legis (The Book of the Law).* Boston: Weiser Books.

CRUZ, M. D. 2003. Shaping Quotidian Worlds: Ceramic Production and Consumption in Banda, Ghana c. 1780–1994. Unpublished Ph.D. dissertation, Department of Anthropology, State University of New York at Binghamton, Binghamton, NY.

CSIKSZENTMIHALYI, M. and ROCHBERG-HALTON, E. 1981. *The Meaning of Things: domestic symbols and the self.* Cambridge: Cambridge University Press.

CSORDAS, T. 1999a. The body's career in anthropology. In H. Moore (ed.) *Anthropological Theory Today.* Cambridge: Polity Press, pp. 172–205.

CSORDAS, T. 1999b. Embodiment and cultural phenomenology. In G. Weiss and H. Faber (eds) *Perspectives on Embodiment: the intersections of nature and culture.* London: Routledge, pp. 143–162.

CSORDAS, T. J. 1990. Embodiment as a paradigm for anthropology. *Ethos* 18(5): 5–47.

CSORDAS, T. J. 1994. *Embodiment and Experience.* Cambridge: Cambridge University Press.

CULLEN, T. and KELLER, D. 1990. The Greek pithos through time: multiple functions and diverse imagery. In W. D. Kingery (ed.) *The Changing Roles of Ceramics in Society: 26,000 B. P. to the Present.* Westerville, OH: American Ceramics Society, pp. 183–207.

CUMMINGS, A. 1979. *The Framed Houses of Massachusetts Bay, 1625–1725.* Cambridge, MA: Harvard University Press.

CUMMINGS, V. and WHITTLE, A. 2003. Tombs with a view. Landscape, monuments and trees. *Antiquity* 77: 255–266.

CUMMINGS, V., JONES, A. and WATSON, A. 2002. Divided places. Phenomenology and asymmetry in the monuments of the Black Mountains, southeast Wales. *Cambridge Archaeological Journal* 12: 57–70.

CUNIN, O. 2007. The Bayon: an archaeological and architectural study. In J. Clark (ed.) *Bayon: new perspectives*. Bangkok: River Books, pp. 136–229.

CUNLIFFE, B. 2008. *Europe Between the Oceans, 9000 BC–AD 1000*. New Haven, CT: Yale University Press.

CURZON, G. N. 1892. *Persia and the Persian Question*. London: Longmans, Green and Co.

CUSHING, F. 1886. *A Study of Pueblo Pottery as Illustrative of Zuñi Culture Growth*. Washington, DC: US Government Printing Office (Fourth Annual Report of the Bureau of Ethnology to the Secretary of the Smithsonian Institution).

DAGENS, B. 1995. *Angkor, Heart of an Asian Empire*. London: Thames and Hudson.

DALGLISH, C. 2003. *Rural Society in the Age of Reason: an archaeology of the emergence of modern life in the south Scottish Highlands*. Cambridge: Cambridge University Press.

DAMASIO, A. 2000. *The Feeling of What Happens: body and emotion in the making of consciousness*. London: Vintage.

DANIEL, E. V. 1998. The limits of culture. In N. B. Dirks (ed.) *In Near Ruins: cultural theory and the end of the century*. University of Minnesota Press, pp. 67–92.

DANIELS, S. 1993. *Fields of Vision: landscape imagery and national identity in England and the United States*. Cambridge: Polity.

DARBY W. J. 2000. *Landscape and Identity*. Oxford: Berg.

DARNELL, G. 1977. History of anthropology in historical perspective. *Annual Review of Anthropology* 6: 399–417.

DARVILL, T. C. 2004. *Long Barrows of the Cotswolds and Surrounding Areas*. Stroud: Tempus.

DARVILL, T. C. and THOMAS, J. S. (eds) 1996. *Neolithic Houses in Northwest Europe and Beyond*. Oxford: Oxbow.

DAS, V. 2000. The practice of organ transplants: networks, documents, translations. In M. Lock, A. Cambrosio and A. Young (eds) *Living and Working with the New Medical Technologies*. Cambridge: Cambridge University Press, pp. 263–287.

DAS, V. 2007. *Life and Words: violence and the descent into the ordinary*. Berkeley: University of California Press.

DAS, V. and ADDLAKHA, R. 2001. Disability and domestic kinship in public citizenship. *Public Culture* 13(3): 511–531.

DASTON, L. 1994. Marvelous facts and miraculous evidence in early Modern Europe. In J. Chandler, A. I. Davidson and H. Harootunian (eds) *Questions of Evidence*. Chicago: Chicago University Press, pp. 243–274.

DASTON, L. and GALISON, P. 1992. The image of objectivity. *Representations* 40: 81–128.

DASTON, L. and GALISON, P. 2007. *Objectivity*. New York: Zone Books.

DAVID, N. and KRAMER, C. 2001. *Ethnoarchaeology in Action*. Cambridge: Cambridge University Press.

DAVIS, M. 2006. *Planet of Slums*. London: Verso.

DAY, P. M., RELAKI, M. and FABER, E. 2006. Pottery making and social reproduction in the Bronze Age Mesara. In M. H. Wiener, J. L. Warner, J. Polonsky and E. E. Hayes (eds) *Pottery and Society: The Impact of Recent Studies in Minoan Pottery. Gold Medal Colloquium in Honor of Philip P. Betancourt*. Boston: Archaeological Institute of America, pp. 22–72.

DEAN, C. and LIEBSOHN, D. 2003. Hybridity and its discontents: considering visual culture in colonial Spanish America. *Colonial Latin American Review* 12(1): 5–35.

DEETZ, J. F. 1967. *Invitation to Archaeology.* Garden City, NY: Natural History Press.

DEETZ, J. F. 1972. Archaeology as a social science. In M. P. Leone (ed.) *Contemporary Archaeology: a guide to theory and contributions.* Carbondale, IL: Southern Illinois University Press, pp. 108–117.

DEETZ, J. F. 1977. *In Small Things Forgotten: the archaeology of early American life.* Garden City, NY: Anchor Books.

DEETZ, J. F. 1991. Introduction: archaeological evidence of sixteenth- and seventeenth-century encounters. In L. Falk (ed.) *Historical Archaeology in Global Perspective.* Washington, DC: Smithsonian Institution Press, pp. 1–9.

DEETZ, J. F. 1996. *In Small Things Forgotten: an archaeology of early American life* (Revised and expanded 2nd edition). New York: Anchor Books.

DEETZ, J. F. and BELL, A. 1995. 'Folk housing' revisited. *Louisa County Historical Magazine* 26(2): 59–71.

DEFERT, D. 1982. The collection of the world: accounts of voyages from the sixteenth to eighteenth centuries. *Dialectical Anthropology* 7: 11–20.

DEFRA (DEPARTMENT OF ENVIRONMENT, FOOD AND RURAL AFFAIRS). 2002. *Biodiversity Strategy.* London: HMSO.

DELEUZE, G. 1999. *Foucault.* London: Continuum.

DELEUZE, G. and GUATTARI, F. 1977. *Anti-Oedipus: capitalism and schizophrenia* (trans. R. Hurley, M. Seem and H. R. Lane). New York: Viking Press.

DELEUZE, G. and GUATTARI, F. 1988. *A Thousand Plateaus: capitalism and schizophrenia* (trans. B. Massumi). London: Athlone.

DELEUZE, G. and PARNET, C. 1987 [1977]. *Dialogues* (trans. H. Tomlinson and B. Habberjam). London: Athlone Press.

DEMARRAIS, E., GOSDEN, C. and RENFREW, A. C. (eds) 2004. *Rethinking Materiality: the engagement of mind with the material world.* Cambridge: McDonald Institute for Archaeological Research.

DEPARTMENT OF ENVIRONMENT 1991. *Report of the Public Enquiry into the Proposed Development of Royate Hill, Bristol.* Inspector's summary. London: HMSO.

DEPARTMENT OF ENVIRONMENT 1994. *Report of the Public Enquiry into the Proposed Compulsory Purchase of Royate Hill, Bristol.* Written evidence submitted by the Royate Hill Action Group. London: HMSO.

DERRIDA, J. 1976. *Of Grammatology* (trans. G. C. Spivak). Baltimore: Johns Hopkins University Press.

DERRIDA, J. 1978. *Writing and Difference* (trans. A. Bass). Chicago: University of Chicago Press.

DERY, M. 1996. *Escape Velocity: cyberculture at the end of the century.* New York: Grove.

DESILVEY, C. O. 2006. Observed decay: telling stories with mutable things. *Journal of Material Culture* 11(3): 318–338.

DESILVEY, C. O. 2007. Salvage memory: constellating material histories on a hardscrabble homestead. *Cultural Geographies* 14(3): 401–424.

DESJARLAIS, R. 1997. *Shelter Blues: sanity and selfhood among the homeless.* Philadelphia: University of Pennsylvania Press.

DESPRET, V. 2004. The body we care for: figures of anthropo-zoo-genesis. *Body and Society* 10: 111–134.

DEVISCH, R. 1993. *Weaving the Threads of Life: the Khita gyn-eco-logical healing cult among the Yaka.* Chicago: University of Chicago Press.

DEWEY, C. 1972. Images of the village community: a study in Anglo-Indian ideology. *Modern Asian Studies* 6(3): 291–328.

DICKENS, C. 1971 [1843]. A Christmas Carol. In C. Dickens, *The Christmas Books, vol. 1.* Harmondsworth: Penguin, pp. 38–134.

DIETLER, M. 1990a. Driven by drink: the role of drinking in the political economy and the case of Early Iron Age France. *Journal of Anthropological Archaeology* 9: 352–406.

DIETLER, M. 1990b. Exchange, Consumption, and Colonial Interaction in the Rhône Basin of France: A Study of Early Iron Age Political Economy. Unpublished Ph.D. dissertation, University of California, Berkeley.

DIETLER, M. 1998. Consumption, agency, and cultural entanglement: theoretical implications of a mediterranean colonial encounter. In J. Cusick (ed.) *Studies in Culture Contact: Interaction, Culture Change, and Archaeology.* Carbondale: Southern Illinois University (Center for Archaeological Investigations Occasional Paper 25), pp. 288–315.

DIETLER, M. 2005. *Consumption and Colonial Encounters in the Rhône Basin of France: a study of Early Iron Age political economy.* Lattes: Association pour le Développement de l'Archéologie en Languedoc-Roussillon (CNRS, Monographies d'Archéologie Méditerranéenne 21).

DIETLER, M. 2006a. Alcohol: anthropological/archaeological perspectives. *Annual Review of Anthropology* 35: 229–249.

DIETLER, M. 2006b. Celticism, celtitude, and celticity: the consumption of the past in the age of globalization. In S. Rieckhoff (ed.) *Celtes et Gaulois dans l'histoire, l'historiographie et l'idéologie moderne. Actes de la table ronde de Leipzig, 16–17 juin 2005,* (Bibracte 12/1). Glux-en-Glenne, France: Bibracte Centre Archéologique Européen, pp. 237–248.

DIETLER, M. 2007. Culinary encounters: food, identity, and colonialism. In K. C. Twiss (ed.) *The Archaeology of Food and Identity.* Carbondale: Center for Archaeological Investigations, Southern Illinois University, pp. 218–242.

DIETLER, M. 2010. *Archaeologies of Colonialism: consumption, entanglement, and violence in ancient Mediterranean France.* Berkeley: University of California Press.

DIETLER, M. and HAYDEN, B. (eds) 2001. *Feasts: archaeological and ethnographic perspectives on food, politics, and power.* Washington, DC: Smithsonian Press.

DIETLER, M. and HERBICH, I. 1998. Habitus, techniques, style: an integrated approach to the social understanding of material culture and boundaries. In M. T. Stark (ed.) *Archaeology of Social Boundaries.* Washington, DC: Smithsonian Institution Press, pp. 232–263.

DIETZ, P. 1984. Downtown in the desert. In J. Brown (ed.) *Michael Heizer: sculpture in reverse.* Los Angeles: Museum of Contemporary Art, pp. 76–95.

DINDO, M., THIERRY, B. and WHITEN, A. 2008. Social diffusion of novel foraging methods in brown capuchin monkeys (*Cebus apella*). *Proceedings of the Royal Society B-Biological Sciences* 275(1631): 187–193.

DIPROSE, R. 2002. *Corporeal generosity: on giving with Nietzsche, Merleau-Ponty and Levinas.* New York: State University of New York Press.

DIRKS, N. B. 2001. *Castes of Mind: colonialism and the making of modern India.* Princeton, NJ: Princeton University Press.

DISSANAYAKE, E. 1993. *Homo Aestheticus: where art comes from and why.* Riverside, NJ: Free Press.

DOBRES, M-A. 2000. *Technology and Social Agency: outlining a practice framework for archaeology.* Oxford: Blackwell (Studies in Social Archaeology).

DOBRES, M-A. 1995. Gender and prehistoric technology. *World Archaeology* 27(1): 25–49.

DOBRES, M-A. and ROBB, J. E. 2000a. Agency in archaeology: paradigm or platitude? In M-A, Dobres and J. E. Robb (eds) *Agency in Archaeology*. London: Routledge, pp. 1–17.

DORST, J. D. 1989. *The Written Suburb: an American site, an ethnographic dilemma*. Philadelphia: University of Pennsylvania Press.

DOUBLEDAY, R. 2007. Organizing accountability: co-production of technoscientific and social worlds in a nanoscience laboratory. *Area* 39(2): 166–175.

DOUGLAS, M. 1966. *Purity and Danger: an analysis of concepts of pollution and taboo*. London: Routledge and Kegan Paul.

DOUGLAS, M. 1973. *Natural Symbols*. New York: Vintage.

DOUGLAS, M. 1975. Deciphering a meal. *Daedalus* 101: 61–82.

DOUGLAS, M. 1984. Standard social uses of food: introduction. In M. Douglas (ed.) *Food in the Social Order*. New York: Russell Sage, pp. 1–39.

DOUGLAS, M. (ed.) 1987. *Constructive Drinking: perspectives on drink from anthropology*. Cambridge: Cambridge University Press.

DOUGLAS, M. and ISHERWOOD, B. 1979. *The World of Goods: towards an anthropology of consumption*. London: Routledge.

DOUGLAS, M. and NEY, S. 1998. *Missing Persons: a critique of personhood in the social sciences*. Berkeley: University of California Press.

DRAYTON, R. H. 2000. *Nature's Government: science, imperial Britain, and the 'improvement' of the world*. New Haven: Yale University Press.

DRESCH, P. 1992. Ethnography and general theory or people versus humankind. *Journal of the Anthropological Society of Oxford* 23: 17–36.

DRIVER, F., NASH, C., PRENDERGAST, C. and SWENSON, I. (eds) 2002. *Landing: eight collaborative projects between artists and geographers*. London: Royal Holloway, University of London.

DTLR (DEPARTMENT OF TRANSPORT, LOCAL GOVERNMENT AND THE REGIONS). 2002. *Green Spaces, Better Places*. Report of the Urban Green Spaces Task Force. London: HMSO.

DUFFY, F. 1997. *The New Office*. London: Conran Octopus.

DU GAY, P., HALL, S., JANES, L., MACKAY, H. and NEGUS, K. 1997. *Doing Cultural Studies: the story of the Sony Walkman*. London: Sage.

DUMONT, L. 1970. The individual as an impediment to sociological comparison and Indian history. In L. Dumont (ed.) *Religion/Politics and History in India: collected papers in Indian sociology*. Paris: Mouton, pp. 133–150.

DUNDES, A. 1965. Editorial notes prefacing C. W. von Sydow 'Folktale Studies and Phililogy: Some Points of View'. In A. Dundes (ed.) *Fields of Folklore*. Englewood Cliffs, NJ: Prentice Hall, pp. 219–242.

DUNNELL, R. 1978. Style and function: a fundamental dichotomy. *American Antiquity* 43(2): 192–202.

DUNNELL, R. 1980. Evolutionary theory and archaeology. In M. B. Schiffer (ed.) *Advances in Archaeological Method and Theory* (vol. 3). New York: Academic Press, pp. 35–99.

DUNNELL, R. 1982. Science, social science, and common sense: the agonizing dilemma of modern archaeology. *Journal of Anthropological Research* 38(1): 1–25.

DURKHEIM, E. and MAUSS, M. 1963 [1903]. *Primitive Classification* (trans. R. Needham). Chicago: University of Chicago Press.

EDENSOR, T. and KOTHARI, U. 2006. Extending networks and mediating brands: stallholder strategies in a Mauritian market. *Transactions of the Institute of British Geographers* 31(3): 323–336.

EDGELL, S., HETHERINGTON, K. and WARDE, A. (eds) 1996. *Consumption Matters: the production and experience of consumption.* Oxford: Blackwell.

EDGERTON, D. 2006. *The Shock of the Old: technology and global history since 1900.* Oxford: Oxford University Press.

EDGEWORTH, M. 1990. Analogy as practical reason: the perception of objects in excavation practice. *Archaeological Review from Cambridge* 9(2): 243–252.

EDGEWORTH, M. 2003. *Acts of Discovery: an ethnography of archaeological practice.* Oxford: Archaeopress (British Archaeological Reports 1131).

EDGEWORTH, M. (ed.) 2006a. *Ethnographies of Archaeological Practice: cultural encounters, material transformations.* Lanham, MD: Altamira Press, pp. 1–19.

EDGEWORTH, M. 2006b. Preface. In M. Edgeworth (ed.) *Ethnographies of Archaeological Practice: cultural encounters, material transformations.* Lanham, MD: Altamira Press, pp. ix–xvi.

EDMONDS, M. 1999. *Ancestral Geographies of the Neolithic: landscapes, monuments and memory.* London: Routledge.

EDWARDS, E., GOSDEN, C. and PHILLIPS, R. (eds) 2006. *Sensible Objects: colonialism, museums and material culture.* Oxford: Berg.

EDWARDS, J. 1994. The origins of Creole architecture. *Winterthur Portfolio* 29(2/3): 155–189.

EKBIA, H. R. 2008. *Artificial Dreams. The quest for non-biological intelligence.* Cambridge: Cambridge University Press.

ELEY, G. 2005. *A Crooked Line: from cultural history to the history of society.* Ann Arbor: University of Michigan Press.

ELIADE, M. 1969. *Yoga: immortality and freedom.* Princeton, NJ: Princeton University Press.

ELKINS, J. 2008. Writing moods. In R. Z. DeLue and J. Elkins (eds) *Landscape Theory.* London, Routledge, pp. 69–86.

ELLEN, R. 1988. Fetishism, *Man* (n.s.) 23: 213–235.

ELSNER, J. and CARDINAL, R. (eds) 1994. *The Cultures of Collecting.* Cambridge, MA: Harvard University Press.

ELVIN, M. 1973. *The Pattern of the Chinese Past.* Stanford: Stanford University Press.

EMANUEL, K. A. 2005. *Divine Wind: the history and science of hurricanes.* Oxford: Oxford University Press.

ENGELS, F. 1940. *The Origin of the Family, Private Property and the State.* London: Lawrence and Wishart Ltd.

ENGELS, F. 1999 [1892]. *Socialism: utopian and scientific.* Broadway, New South Wales: Resistance Books.

ENGLISH NATURE 1992. *The Flowering of the Cities—the natural flora of urban commons.* Peterborough: English Nature.

ENTWISTLE, J. 2000. *The Fashioned Body: fashion, dress and modern social theory.* Cambridge: Polity Press.

EPSTEIN, A. L. (ed.) 2002. *The Craft of Social Anthropology* (second edition). Piscataway, NJ: Transaction.

ERIXON, S. 1937. Nordic open-air museums and Skansen. *Proceedings of the Scottish Anthropological and Folklore Society* 2(3): 31–45.

ERIXON, S. 1945. *Svenska kulturalnser och kulturprovinser.* Stockholm: Lantbruksfolrbundets tidskrift.

ERIXON, S. 1953. *Byggnaskulter.* Stockholm: Bonnier.

ERIXON, S. 1999. *Svensk folklivsforskning: uppsatser 1929–1965,* ed. Karl-Olov Arnstberg. Stockholm: Carlssons.

ERRINGTON, S. 1998. *The Death of Authentic Primitive Art and other Signs of Progress.* Berkeley: University of California Press.

ESCHER, W., LIEBL, E. and NIEDIRER, A. 1995. *Atlas der Schweizerischen Volkskunde: Register zu den Kommentaren, Sachregister, und Wortregister.* Basel: Schweitzerische Gesellschaft für Volkskunde.

ESTIENNE, C. 1606. *Maison Rustique or The Country Farme.* Compiled in the French tongue by Charles Stevens and John Liebault, Doctors of Physicke. And translated into English by Richard Surflet Practioner in Physicke (trans. R. Surflet). London: Arnold Hatsfield for John Norton and John Bill.

EVANS, A. J. 1921. The Neolithic stage in Crete. In A. J. Evans *The Palace of Minos* (Volume I). London: Macmillan, pp. 32–55.

EVANS, D., POTTIER, C., FLETCHER, R., HENSLEY, S., TAPLEY, I., MILNE, A. and BARBETTI, M. 2007. A comprehensive archaeological map of the world's largest pre-industrial settlement complex at Angkor, Cambodia. *Proceedings of the National Academy of Sciences of the United States of America* 104(36): 14277–14282.

EVANS, E. E. 1930. The Pyrenees: a geographical interpretation of their role in human times. In I. C. Peate (ed.) *Studies in Regional Consciousness and Environment: essays presented to H. J. Fleure.* Oxford: Oxford University Press, pp. 45–68.

EVANS, E. E. 1942. *Irish Heritage: the landscape, the people, and their work.* Dundalk: Dundalgan Press.

EVANS, E. E. 1957. *Irish Folk Ways.* London: Routledge and Kegan Paul.

EVANS, E. E. 1959. A Pennsylvania folk festival. *Ulster Folklife* 5: 14–19.

EVANS, J. 1872. *Prehistoric Stone Implements, Weapons, and Ornaments of Great Britain.* London: Longmans.

EVANS, J. D. 1964. Excavations in the Neolithic Settlement at Knossos, 1957–60. *Annual of the British School at Athens* 59: 132–240.

EVANS, J. D. 1968. Knossos Neolithic, Part II, summary and conclusions. *Annual of the British School at Athens* 63: 267–276.

EVANS-PRITCHARD, E. E. 1937. *Witchcraft, Oracles and Magic among the Azande.* Oxford: Clarendon Press.

EVANS-PRITCHARD, E. E. 1950. Social Anthropology: past and present. *Man* 50: 118–124.

Exmouth Herald 2007. Napoli reaches Irish shipyard. *Exmouth Herald* 17 August 2007.

Exmouth Journal 2007a. Napoli will be tugged along our coastline. *Exmouth Journal* 10 August 2007.

Exmouth Journal 2007b. Police are left powerless as looters swoop. *Exmouth Journal,* 26 January 2007.

Exmouth Journal 2007c. Napoli will be tugged along our coastline. *Exmouth Journal* 10 August 2007.

Express and Echo 2007. Village exhibition tells of effects of the grounding of holed container ship. *Express and Echo* 22 October 2007.

FABER, E. W., KILIKOGLOU, V., DAY, P. M. and WILSON, D. E. 2002. A technological study of Middle Minoan polychrome pottery from Knossos, Crete. In V. Kilikoglou, A. Hein and

Y. Maniatis (eds) *Modern Trends in Scientific Studies on Ancient Ceramics. Papers Presented at the 5th European Meeting on Ancient Ceramics, Athens, 1999.* Oxford: Archaeopress (British Archaeological Report, International Series 1011), pp. 129–141.

FABIAN, J. 1983. *Time and the Other: how anthropology makes its object.* New York: Columbia University Press.

FAHLANDER, F. and OESTIGAARD, T. 2004. Introduction: material culture and post-disciplinary sciences. In F. Fahlander and T. Oestigaard (eds) *Material Culture and Other Things: post-disciplinary studies in the 21st century.* Gothenburg: Department of Archaeology, University of Gothenburg (Gotarc series C, number 61), pp. 1–19.

FAIRBAIRN, A. 2007. Seeds from the slums: archaeobotanical investigations at Mountain Street, Ultimo, Sydney, New South Wales. *Australian Archaeology* 64: 1–8.

FAJANS, J. (ed.) 1993. *Exchanging Products: producing exchange.* Sydney: University of Sydney Press (Oceania Monograph 43).

FALK, P. 1994. *The Consuming Body.* London: Sage.

FARDON, R. 1990. General introduction. Localising strategies: the regionalisation of ethnographic accounts. In R. Fardon (ed.) *Localising Strategies: regional traditions of ethnographic writing.* Edinburgh: Scottish Academic Press, pp. 1–35.

FAUCONNIER, G. and TURNER, M. 1998. Conceptual integration networks. *Cognitive Science* 22(2): 133–187.

FEATHERSTONE, M. 1991. *Consumer Culture and Postmodernism.* London: Sage.

FEATHERSTONE, M. and BURROWS, R. (eds) 1995. *Cyberspace/Cyberbodies/Cyberpunk. Cultures of technological embodiment.* London: Sage.

FEHER, M. 1989. *Fragments for a History of the Human Body,* Parts 1–3. New York: Zone.

FENTON, W. N. 1974. The advancement of material culture studies in modern anthropological research. In Miles Richardson (ed.) *The Human Mirror: material and spatial images of man.* Baton Rouge: Louisiana State University Press, pp. 15–36.

FERGUSON, J. and GUPTA, A. 2002. Spatializing states: toward an ethnography of neoliberal governmentality. *American Ethnologist* 29(4): 981–1002.

FERGUSON, L. (ed.) 1977. *Historical Archaeology and the Importance of Material Things.* Columbia, SC: Society for Historical Archaeology.

FERGUSON, L. 1991. Struggling with pots in colonial South Carolina. In R. McGuire and R. Paynter (eds) *The Archaeology of Inequality.* Oxford: Blackwell, pp. 28–39.

FERGUSON, L. 1992. *Uncommon Ground: archaeology and Early African America, 1650–1800.* Washington, DC: Smithsonian Institution Press.

FERME, M. C. 2001. *The Underneath of Things: violence, history, and the everyday in Sierra Leone.* Berkeley: University of California Press.

FEWKES, J. 1891. *A Journal of American Ethnology and Ethnography,* Volume 1. Boston: Houghton, Mifflin and Company. .

FEWKES, J. 1892. *A Journal of American Ethnology and Ethnography,* Volume 2. Boston: Houghton, Mifflin and Company.

FEWKES, J. 1985 [1903]. *Hopi Katcinas.* New York: Dover Publications, Inc.

FINE, B. 1995. From political economy to consumption. In D. Miller (ed.) *Acknowledging Consumption: a review of new studies.* London: Routledge, pp. 127–163.

FIRTH, R. 1959. *Economics of the New Zealand Maori.* Wellington: R. E. Owen, Government Printer.

FIRTH, R., HUBERT, J. and FORGE, A. 1970. *Families and Their Relatives: kinship in a middle-class sector of London.* London: Routledge and Kegan Paul.

FISCHER, E. F. 1999. Cultural logic and Maya identity: rethinking constructivism and essentialism. *Current Anthropology* 40(4): 473–499.

FISHER, G. and LOREN, D. D. 2003. Introduction: embodying identity in archaeology. *Cambridge Archaeological Journal* 13: 225–230.

FLECK, L. 1979. *Genesis and Development of a Scientific Fact*. Chicago: University of Chicago Press.

FLEMING, A. 2005. Megaliths and post-modernism: the case of Wales. *Antiquity* 79: 921–932.

FLETCHER, R. J. 1995. *The Limits of Settlement Growth. A theoretical outline*. Cambridge: Cambridge University Press.

FLETCHER, R. J. 2002. The hammering of society: Non-correspondence and modernity. In J. Schofield, W. G. Johnson and C. Beck (eds) *Materiél Culture: the archaeology of 20th century conflict*. London: Routledge (One World Archaeology 44), pp. 303–311.

FLETCHER, R. J. 2004. Materiality, space, time and outcome. In J. L. Bintliff (ed.) *The Blackwell Companion to Archaeology*. Oxford: Blackwell, pp. 110–140.

FLUSSER, W. 1999. *The Shape of Things. A philosophy of design*. London, Reaktion.

FORD, J. A. 1954. Comment on A. C. Spaulding, 'Statistical Techniques for the Discovery of Artifact Types'. *American Antiquity* 19: 390–391.

FORDE, C. D. 1934. *Habitat, Economy and Society: a geographical introduction to ethnology*. London: Methuen.

FOREMAN, H. C. 1934. *Early Manor and Plantation Houses of Maryland*. Easton, MD: privately printed.

FORGE, A. 1973a. Introduction. In A. Forge (ed.) *Primitive Art and Society*. London: Oxford University Press for Wenner-Gren Foundation for Anthropological Research, pp. xiii–xxii.

FORGE, A. 1973b. Style and meaning in Sepik art. In A. Forge (ed.) *Primitive Art and Society*. London: Oxford University Press for Wenner-Gren Foundation for Anthropological Research, pp. 169–192.

FORTES, M. 1987. The concept of the person. In M. Fortes (ed.) *Religion, Morality and the Person: essays in Tallensi religion*. Cambridge: Cambridge University Press, pp. 247–286.

FOSTER, K and LORIMER, H. 2007. Some reflections on art-geography as collaboration. *Cultural Geographies* 14(3): 425–432.

FOSTER, R. 1990. Value without equivalence: exchange and replacement in a Melanesian society. *Man* (n.s.), 25(1): 54–69.

FOSTER, R. 2006. Tracking globalisation: commodities and value in motion. In C. Tilley, W. Keane, S. Küchler, M. J. Rowlands and P. Spyer (eds) *Handbook of Material Culture*. London: Sage, pp. 285–302.

FOUCAULT, M. 1970. *The Order of Things: an archaeology of the human sciences* (trans. A. Sheridan Smith). New York: Random House.

FOUCAULT, M. 1972. *The Archaeology of Knowledge* (trans. A. Sheridan Smith). New York: Harper and Row.

FOUCAULT, M. 1973. *The Birth of the Clinic: an archaeology of medical perception* (trans. A. Sheridan). New York: Pantheon Books.

FOUCAULT, M. 1977a. *Discipline and Punish: the birth of the prison* (trans. A. Sheridan). New York: Pantheon Books.

FOUCAULT, M. 1977b. Questions on geography. In *Power/Knowledge. Selected interviews and other writings, 1972–1977* (trans. C. Gordon). New York: Pantheon Books.

FOUCAULT, M. 1986. Space, knowledge, and power. In P. Rabinow (ed.) *The Foucault Reader: an introduction to Foucault's thought*. London: Harmondsworth.

FOUCAULT, M. 1988. *Technologies of the Self: a seminar with Michel Foucault* (eds L. H. Martin, H. Gutman and P. H. Hutton). Amherst, MA: University of Massachusetts Press.

FOUCAULT, M. 1991. Governmentality. In G. Burchell, C. Gordon and P. Miller (eds) *The Foucault Effect: studies in governmental rationality*. Hemel Hempstead: Harvester Wheat-sheaf, pp. 87–104.

FOUCAULT, M. and RABINOW, P. 1984. Space, knowledge, and power (trans. C. Hubert). In P. Rabinow (ed.) *The Foucault Reader*. London: Penguin, pp. 239–256.

FOWLER, C. 2001. Personhood and social relations in the British Neolithic with a study from the Isle of Man. *Journal of Material Culture* 6: 137–163.

FOWLER, C. 2002. Body parts: personhood and materiality in the Manx Neolithic. In Y. Hamilakis, M. Pluciennik and S. A. Tarlow (eds) *Thinking Through the Body: archae-ologies of corporeality*. London: Kluwer/Academic Press, pp. 47–69.

FOWLER, C. 2003. Rates of (ex)change: decay and growth, memory and the transformation of the dead in early Neolithic southern Britain. In H. Williams (ed.) *Archaeologies of Remembrance: death and memory in past societies*. New York: Kluwer Academic/Plenum Press, pp. 45–63.

FOWLER, C. 2004a. *The Archaeology of Personhood: an anthropological approach*. London: Routledge.

FOWLER, C. 2004b. In touch with the past? Bodies, monuments and the sacred in the Manx Neolithic. In V. Cummings and C. Fowler (eds) *The Neolithic of the Irish Sea: materiality and traditions of practice*. Oxford: Oxbow, pp. 91–102.

FOWLER, C. 2004c. Identity politics: personhood, kinship, gender and power in Neolithic and Early Bronze Age Britain. In E. Casella and C. Fowler (eds) *The Archaeology of Plural and Changing Identities: beyond identification*. New York: Kluwer, pp. 109–134.

FOWLER, C. 2008a. Landscape and personhood. In B. David and J. S. Thomas (eds) *Handbook of Landscape Archaeology*. Walnut Creek, CA: Left Coast Press, pp. 291–299.

FOWLER, C. 2008b. Fractal bodies in the past and present. In D. Borić and J. Robb (eds) *Past Bodies*. Oxford: Oxbow, pp. 47–57.

FOWLER, C. In press. Change and continuity in Early Bronze Age mortuary rites: a case study from Northumberland. In R. Brandt, H. Ingvaldsen and M. Prusac (eds) *Ritual Changes and Changing Rituals: function and meaning in ancient funerary practices*. Exeter: Exeter University Press.

FOWLER, C. and CUMMINGS, V. 2003. Places of transformation: building monuments from water and stone in the Neolithic of the Irish Sea. *Journal of the Royal Anthropological Institute* 9: 1–20.

FOWLER, D. and FOWLER, C. (eds) 1971. *Anthropology of the Numa: John Wesley Powell's manuscripts on the Numic peoples of western North America 1868–1880*. Washington, DC: Smithsonian Institution Press.

Fox, C. 1923. *The Archaeology of the Cambridge region: a topological study of the Bronze, Early Iron, Roman and Anglo-Saxon Ages, with an introductory note on the Neolithic Age*. Cambridge: Cambridge University Press.

Fox, C. 1932. *The Personality of Britain*. Cardiff: National Museum of Wales.

Fox, C. and RAGLAN, F. R. S. 1951. *Monmouthshire Houses: a study of building techniques and smaller house plans in the fifteenth to the seventeenth centuries*. Part I: *Medieval houses*. Cardiff: National Museum of Wales and the Welsh Folk Museum.

Fox, C. and Raglan, F. R. S. 1953. *Monmouthshire Houses: a study of building techniques and smaller house plans in the fifteenth to the seventeenth centuries*. Part II: *Sub-Medieval houses, c. 1550–1610*. Cardiff: National Museum of Wales and the Welsh Folk Museum.

Fox, C. and Raglan, F. R. S. 1954. *Monmouthshire Houses: a study of building techniques and smaller house plans in the fifteenth to the seventeenth centuries*. Part III: *Renaissance houses, c. 1590–1714*. Cardiff: National Museum of Wales and the Welsh Folk Museum.

Fox, E. A., van Schaik, C. P., Sitompul, A. and Wright, D. N. 2004. Intra- and interpopulational differences in orangutan (*Pongo pygmaeus*) activity and diet: implications for the invention of tool use. *American Journal of Physical Anthropology* 125(2): 162–174.

Fox, J. G. 1996. Playing with power: ballcourts and political ritual in southern Mesoamerica. *Current Anthropology* 37: 483–509.

Fragaszy, D. M. and Perry, S. E. (eds) 2003. *The Biology of Traditions: models and evidence*. Cambridge University Press.

Fragaszy, D. M. and Visalberghi, E. 2001. Recognizing a swan: socially-biased learning. *Psychologia* 44: 82–98.

Fragaszy, D. M. and Visalberghi, E. 2004. Socially biased learning in monkeys. *Learning and Behavior* 32(1): 24–35.

Frampton, K. 1980. *Modern Architecture: a critical history*. New York: Oxford University Press.

Frank, A. G. and Gills, B. K. (eds) 1993. *The World System: five hundred years or five thousand?* London: Routledge.

Frank, B. E. 1993. Reconstructing the history of an African ceramic tradition: technology, slavery and agency in the region of Kadiolo Mali. *Cahiers d'Études Africaines* 33/131: 381–401.

Frank, T. 1997. *The Conquest of Cool. Business culture, counterculture, and the rise of hip consumerism*. Chicago: The University of Chicago Press.

Frankenstein, S. and Rowlands, M. 1978. The internal structure and regional context of Early Iron Age society in south-western Germany. *Bulletin of the Institute of Archaeology* 15: 73–112.

Franklin, A. 2008. A choreography of fire: a posthumanist account of Australians and Eucalypts. In A. Pickering and K. Guzik (eds) *The Mangle in Practice: Science, Society, and Becoming*. Durham, NC: Duke University Press, pp. 17–45.

Fraser, M., Kember, S. and Lury, C. 2005. Inventive life: approaches to the new vitalism. *Theory, Culture and Society* 22: 1–14.

Fraser, S. E. 2004. *Performing the Visual: Buddhist wall painting practice in China and Central Asia, 618–960*. Stanford, CA: Stanford University Press.

Frazer, J. 1911. *The Golden Bough. A study in magic and religion* (third edition). London: Macmillan.

Fredman, T. and Whiten, A. 2007. Observational learning from tool using models by human-reared and mother-reared capuchin monkeys (*Cebus apella*). *Animal Cognition* 11(2): 295–309.

Freedberg, D. 1989. *The Power of Images: studies in the history and theory of response*. Chicago: University of Chicago Press.

Freidberg, S. 2003. Editorial. Not all sweetness and light: new cultural geographies of food. *Social and Cultural Geography* 4(1): 3–6.

Freidberg, S. 2005. French beans for the masses: a modern historical geography of food in Burkina Faso. In J. Watson and M. Caldwell (eds) *The Cultural Politics of Food and Eating: a reader*. Oxford: Blackwell, pp. 21–41.

Friedman, J. 1974. Marxism, structuralism, and vulgar materialism. *Man* (n.s.) 9(3): 444–69.

FRIEDMAN, J. 1975. Tribes, states and transformations. In M. E. F. Bloch (ed.) *Marxist Analyses and Social Anthropology*. London: Malaby Press (ASA Series 2), pp. 161–202.

FRIEDMAN, J. (ed.) 1994. *Consumption and Identity*. Chur, Switzerland: Harwood Academic Publishers.

FRISON, G. C. 1968. A functional analysis of certain chipped stone tools. *American Antiquity* 33: 149–55.

FROUD, D. 2004. Thinking beyond the homely: countryside properties and the shape of time. *Home Cultures* 1(3): 211–233.

FRUTH, B. and HOHMANN, G. 1996. Nest building behavior in the great apes: the great leap forward? In W. C. McGrew, L. F. Marchant and T. Nishida (eds) *Great Ape Societies*. Cambridge: Cambridge University Press, pp. 225–240.

FRYKENBERG, R. E. 1986. *Delhi through the ages: essays in urban history, culture, and society*. Oxford: Oxford University Press.

FURLONG, E. E., BOOSE, K. J., BOYSEN, S. T. 2008. Raking it in: the impact of enculturation on chimpanzee tool use. *Animal Cognition* 11: 83–97.

FURNESS, A. 1953. The Neolithic pottery of Knossos. *Annual of the British School at Athens* 48: 94–134.

GAILEY, A. 1984. *Rural Houses of the North of Ireland*. Edinburgh: John Donald.

GAILEY, A. 1990. Obituary: Emyr Estyn Evans (1905–1989). *Folklore* 101(2): 231–232.

GAIMSTER, D. R. M. 1997. *German Stoneware 1200–1900: archaeology and cultural history*. London: British Museum Press.

GALEF, B. G. 1988. Imitation in animals: history, definitions and interpretation of the data from the psychological laboratory. In T. R. Zentall and B. G. J. Galef (eds) *Social Learning: psychological and biological perspectives*. Hillsdale: Erlbaum, pp. 3–28.

GALEF, B. G. 1992. The question of animal culture. *Human Nature* 3: 157–178.

GALLESE, V. 2005. Embodied simulation: from neurons to phenomenal experience. *Phenomenology and the Cognitive Sciences* 4: 23–48.

GALLESE, V. and LAKOFF, G. 2005. The brain's concepts: the role of the sensory-motor system in reason and language. *Cognitive Neuropsycholology* 22: 455–479.

GAMBLE, C. 2007. *Origins and Revolutions: human identity in earliest prehistory*. Cambridge: Cambridge University Press.

GARBER, J. F. 1983. Patterns of jade consumption and disposal at Cerros, northern Belize. *American Antiquity* 48: 800–807.

GARFINKEL, H. 1967. *Studies in Ethnomethodology*. Englewood Cliffs: Prentice-Hall.

DE GARINE, I. and DE GARINE, V. (eds) 2001. *Drinking: anthropological approaches*. New York: Berghahn.

GARROW, D. and SHOVE, E. 2007. Artefacts between disciplines. The toothbrush and the axe. *Archaeological dialogues* 14(2), 117–131.

GAUCHER, J. 2006. Ville et archeologies, une approche globale: Angkor Thom, capital du Cambodge ancient (X^e–XVIe siecles). In X. Chen and M. Bussotti (eds) *Decouvertes archeologiques et reconstitution de l'histoire*. Beijing and Paris: Sinologie Francaise (XI EFEO), pp. 267–294.

GAUCHER, J. 2004. Angkor Thom, une utopie réalisée? Structuration de l'espace et modèle d'urbanisme ancien dans le Cambodge ancien. *Arts Asiatiques* 59: 58–86.

GEERTZ, C. 1973. *The Interpretation of Cultures*. New York: Basic Books.

GEISS, J. 1979. Peking under the Ming, 1368–1644. Unpublished Ph.D. dissertation, Princeton University.

GELL, A. 1986. Newcomers to the world of goods: consumption among the Muria Gonds. In A. Appadurai (ed.) *The Social Life of Things*. Cambridge: Cambridge University Press, pp. 110–138.

GELL, A. 1992a. Inter-tribal commodity barter and reproductive gift exchange in old Melanesia. In C. Humphrey and S. Hugh-Jones (eds) *Barter, Exchange and Value*. Cambridge: Cambridge University Press, pp. 142–168.

GELL, A. 1992b. The technology of enchantment and the enchantment of technology. In J. Coote and A. Shelton (eds) *Anthropology, Art and Aesthetics*. Oxford: Clardendon Press (Oxford Studies in Social and Cultural Anthropology), pp. 40–63.

GELL, A. 1995. The language of the forest: landscape and phonological iconism in Umeda. In E. Hirsch and M. O'Hanlon (eds) *The Anthropology of Landscape: perspectives on place and space*. Oxford: Clarendon Press, pp. 232–254.

GELL, A. 1996a. Language is the essence of culture: against the motion. In T. Ingold (ed.) *Key Debates in Anthropology*. London: Routledge, pp. 159–164.

GELL, A. 1996b. Vogel's net: traps as artworks and artworks as traps. *Journal of Material Culture* 1(1): 15–38.

GELL, A. 1998. *Art and Agency: an anthropological theory*. Oxford: Clarendon.

GELL, A. 1999. *The Art of Anthropology: essays and diagrams* (London School of Economics Monographs on Social Anthropology 67). London: Athlone Press.

GEOGHEGAN, H. in press. Museum geography: some reflections on museums, collections and museum practice. *Geography Compass*.

GERO, J. M. 1991. Genderlithics: women's roles in stone tool production. In J. M. Gero (ed.) *Engendering Archaeology: women in prehistory*. Oxford: Blackwell (Studies in Social Archaeology), pp. 163–193.

GESCHIERE, P. 2001. Historical anthropology: questions of time, method and scale. *Interventions* 3(1): 31–39.

GHEZ, G. R. and BECKER, G. S. 1975. *The Allocation of Time and Goods over the Life Cycle*. New York: Columbia University Press.

GIBSON, A. 2003. What do we mean by Neolithic settlement? Some approaches, 10 years on. In I. Armit, E. Murphy, E. Nelis and D. Simpson (eds) *Neolithic Settlement in Ireland and Western Britain*. Oxford: Oxbow, pp. 136–145.

GIBSON, J. J. 1979. *The Ecological Approach to Visual Perception*. Hillsdale, NJ: Lawrence Erlbaum.

GIBSON, W. 1984. *Neuromancer*. New York: Ace Books.

GIDDENS, A. 1976a. *New Rules of Sociological Method: a positive critique of interpretive sociologies*. Cambridge: Polity Press.

GIDDENS, A. 1976b. Hermeneutics, ethnomethodology, and problems of interpretative analysis. In L. A. Coser and O. N. Larsen (eds) *The Uses of Controversy in Sociology*. New York: Free Press, pp. 315–328.

GIDDENS, A. 1979. *Central Problems in Social Theory*. London: Macmillan.

GIDDENS, A. 1981. *A Contemporary Critique of Historical Materialism*. London: Macmillan.

GIDDENS, A. 1982. *Profiles and Critiques in Social Theory*. London: Macmillan.

GIDDENS, A. 1984. *The Constitution of Society: outline of the theory of structuration*. Berkeley: University of California Press.

GIERYN, T. 2002. What buildings do. *Theory and Society* 31: 35–74.

GILCHRIST, R. L. 1994. *Gender and Material Culture: the archaeology of religious women*. London: Routledge.

GILCHRIST, R. L. 1999. *Gender and Archaeology: contesting the past*. London: Routledge.

GILCHRIST, R. L. 2004. Archaeology and the life course: a time and age for gender. In L. Meskell and R. Preucel (eds) *Companion to Social Archaeology*. Oxford: Blackwell, pp. 142–160.

GILCHRIST, R. L. 2008. Magic for the dead? The archaeology of magic in later medieval burials. *Medieval Archaeology* 52: 119–159.

GILES, M. 2006. Collecting the past, constructing identity: the antiquarian John Mortimer and the Driffield Museum of Antiquities and Geological Specimens. *Antiquaries Journal* 86: 279–316.

GILLE, Z. and Ó RIAIN, S. 2002. Global ethnography. *Annual Review of Sociology* 28: 271–295.

GILLESPIE, S. 2001. Personhood, agency, and mortuary ritual: a case study from the ancient Maya. *Journal of Anthropological Archaeology* 20: 73–112.

GILLIS, C. 1990. *Minoan Conical Cups. Form, function and significance*. Gothenburg: Paul Åström.

GILROY, P. 1991. *'There ain't no Black in the Union Jack': the cultural politics of race and nation*. Chicago: University of Chicago Press.

GIMBUTAS, M. 1989. *The Language of the Goddess*. London: Thames and Hudson.

GINSBERG, R. 2000. 'Come in the Dark': domestic workers and their rooms in apartheid-era Johannesburg, South Africa. In S. McMurry and A. Adams (eds) *People, Power, Places: perspectives in vernacular architecture VIII*. Knoxville, TN: University of Tennessee Press, pp. 83–100.

GLASSIE, H. 1969. *Pattern in the Material Folk Culture of the Eastern United States*. Philadelphia: University of Pennsylvania Press.

GLASSIE, H. 1975. *Folk Housing in Middle Virginia: a structural analysis of historic artifacts*. Knoxville, TN: University of Tennessee Press.

GLASSIE, H. 1976. *All Silver and No Brass: an Irish Christmas mumming*. Bloomington: Indiana University Press.

GLASSIE, H. 1977. Archaeology and folklore: common anxieties, common hopes. In L. Ferguson (ed.) *Historical Archaeology and the Importance of Material Things*. Columbia, SC: Society for Historical Archaeology (Special Publication 2), pp. 23–35.

GLASSIE, H. 1982. *Passing the Time in Ballymenone: culture and history of an Ulster community*. Philadelphia: University of Pennsylvania Press.

GLASSIE, H. 1993. *Turkish Traditional Art Today*. Bloomington: Indian University Press.

GLASSIE, H. 1997. *Art and Life in Bangladesh*. Bloomington: Indiana University Press.

GLASSIE, H. 1999. *Material Culture*. Bloomington: Indiana University Press.

GLASSIE, H. and MAHMUD, F. 2000. *Contemporary Traditional Art of Bangladesh*. Dhaka: Bangladesh National Museum.

GLEN, C. 2007. Human cargo. *Art Monthly* (November 2007).

GLUCKMAN, M. 1961. Ethnographic data in British social anthropology. *Sociological Review* 9: 5–17.

GODELIER, M. 1973. *Horizon: Trajets Marxiste en Anthropologie* (trans. R. Brain). Paris: Maspero.

GODELIER, M. 1975. Modes of production, kinship and demographic structures. In M. E. F. Bloch (ed.) *Marxist Analyses and Social Anthropology*. London: Malaby Press (ASA Studies 2), pp. 3–27.

GODELIER, M. 1977. *Perspectives in Marxist Anthropology* (trans. R. Brain). Cambridge: Cambridge University Press.

GODELIER, M. 1986. *The Mental and the Material* (trans. M. Thom). London: Verso.

GODELIER, M. 1999. *The Enigma of the Gift* (trans. N. Scott). Chicago: University of Chicago Press.

GOEHR, L. 1992. *The Imaginary Museum of Musical Works: an essay in the philosophy of music*. Oxford: Clarendon Press.

GOFFMAN, E. 1971. *The Presentation of Self in Everyday Life*. Harmondsworth: Penguin.

GOFFMAN, E. 1974. *Frame Analysis: an essay on the organisation of experience*. New York: Harper and Row.

GOLDENWEISER, A. 1931. *Robots or Gods: an essay on craft and mind*. New York: Knopf.

GOLDSMITH, O. 2006 [1762]. *The Citizen of the World*. Dublin: Nonsuch.

GOLDSTEIN, C. 2000. Building the grand siècle: the context of literary transformations from Vaux-Le-Vicomte to Versailles (1656–1715). Unpublished Ph.D. dissertation, University of Pennsylvania.

GOLDSTEIN, C. 2008. *Vaux and Versailles: the appropriations, erasures, and accidents that made modern France*. Philadelphia: University of Pennsylvania Press.

GOMART, E. and HENNION, A. 1999. A sociology of attachment: music amateurs, drug users. In Law, J. and J. Hassard (eds) *Actor Network Theory and After*. Oxford: Blackwell, pp. 220–247.

GOMBRICH, E. 1979. *The Sense of Order: a study in the psychology of decorative art*. London: Phaidon Press.

GOODALL, J. 1968. The behaviour of free-living chimpanzees in the Gombe Stream Reserve. *Animal Behaviour Monographs* 1: 161–311.

GOODALL, J. 1986. *The Chimpanzees of Gombe*. Cambridge: Belknap Press.

GOODENOUGH, W. 1965. Rethinking 'status' and 'role': towards a general model of the cultural organization of social relationships. In M. Blanton (ed.) *The Relevance of Models to Social Anthropology*. London: Tavistock, pp. 1–24.

GOODING, D. 1992. Putting agency back into observation. In A. Pickering (ed.) *Science as Practice and Culture*. Chicago: University of Chicago Press, pp. 65–112.

GOODING, D., PINCH, T. J. and SCHAFFER, S. (eds) 1989. *The Uses of Experiment: studies in the natural sciences*. Cambridge: Cambridge University Press.

GOODMAN, J., LOVEJOY, P. E. and SHERRATT, A. G. (eds) 1995. *Consuming Habits: drugs in history and anthropology*. London: Routledge.

GOODMAN, N. 1976. *The Languages of Art: an approach to a theory of symbols*. Indianapolis: Hackett.

GOODY, J. 1982. *Cooking, Cuisine and Class: a study in comparative sociology*. Cambridge: Cambridge University Press.

GOODY, J. 1995. *The Expansive Moment: the rise of social anthropology in Britain and Africa, 1918–1970*. Cambridge: Cambridge University Press.

GOSDEN, C. 1994. *Social Being and Time*. Blackwell: Oxford (Studies in Social Archaeology).

GOSDEN, C. 1999. *Anthropology and Archaeology: a changing relationship*. London: Routledge.

GOSDEN, C. 2001. Making sense: archaeology and aesthetics. *World Archaeology* 33(2): 163–167.

GOSDEN, C. 2004a. Aesthetics, intelligence and emotions: implications for archaeology. In E. DeMarrais, C. Gosden and A. C. Renfrew (eds) *Rethinking Materiality: the engagement of mind with the material world*. Cambridge: McDonald Institute for Archaeological Research, pp. 33–40.

GOSDEN, C. 2004b. *Archaeology and Colonialism: cultural contact from 5000 BC to the present*. Cambridge: Cambridge University Press.

GOSDEN, C. 2005. What do objects want? *Journal of Archaeological Method and Theory* 12(3): 193–211.

GOSDEN, C. 2006. Material culture and long-term change. In C. Tilley, W. Keane, S. Küchler, M. J. Rowlands and P. Spyer (eds) *Handbook of Material Culture*. London: Sage, pp. 425–441.

GOSDEN, C. and HEAD, L. 1994. Landscape—a usefully ambiguous concept. *Archaeology in Oceania* 29: 113–116.

GOSDEN, C. and KNOWLES, C. 2001. *Collecting Colonialism: material culture and colonial change*. Oxford: Berg.

GOSDEN, C. and LARSON, F. 2007. *Knowing Things: exploring the collections at the Pitt Rivers Museum 1884–1945*. Oxford: Oxford University Press.

GOSDEN, C. and MARSHALL, Y. 1999. The cultural biography of objects. *World Archaeology* 31(2): 169–178.

GOSS, J. 2004. The souvenir: conceptualising the object(s) of tourist consumption. In A. Lew, C. M. Hall, and A. Williams (eds) *A Companion to Tourism*. Oxford: Blackwell, pp. 327–336.

GOSS, J. 2006. Geographies of consumption: the work of consumption. *Progress in Human Geography* 30(2): 237–249.

GOSSELAIN, O. 1998. Social and technical identity in a clay crystal ball. In M. Stark (ed.) *The Archaeology of Social Boundaries*. Washington, DC: Smithsonian Institution Press, pp. 78–106.

GOSSELAIN, O. P. 2000. Materializing identities: an African perspective. *Journal of Archaeological Method and Theory* 7(3): 187–217.

GOULD, R. A. (ed.) 1978. *Explorations in Ethnoarchaeology*. Albuquerque: University of New Mexico Press.

GOULD, R. A. 1980. *Living Archaeology*. Cambridge: Cambridge University Press.

GOULD, R. A. and SCHIFFER, M. B. (eds) 1981. *Modern Material Culture: the archaeology of us*. New York: Academic Press.

GOWING, L. 2003. *Common Bodies. Women, touch and power in 17th century England*. New Haven: Yale University Press.

GRAEBER, D. 2001. *Toward an Anthropological Theory of Value: the false coin of our own dreams*. New York: Palgrave.

GRAHAM, S. and THRIFT, N. J. 2007. Out of order: understanding repair and maintenance. *Theory, Culture and Society* 24(3): 1–25.

GRAHAM, W. 2003. Preindustrial framing in the Chesapeake. In A. Hoagland and C. Breisch (eds) *Constructing Image, Identity, and Place: perspectives in vernacular architecture IX*. Knoxville, TN: University of Tennessee Press, pp. 179–196.

GRAHAM, W., HUDGINS, C., LOUNSBURY, C., NEIMAN, F. and WHITTENBURG, J. 2007. Adaptation and innovation: archaeological and architectural perspectives on the seventeenth-century Chesapeake. *William and Mary Quarterly* 3rd ser. 64(3): 451–522.

GRAMSCI, A. 1971. *Selections from the Prison Notebooks of Antonio Gramsci* (trans. Q. Hoare and G. N. Smith). New York: International Publishers.

GRANT, I. F. 1924. *Every-Day Life on an Old Highland Farm, 1769–1782*. London: Longman, Green and Co.

GRANT, I. F. 1961. *Highland Folk Ways*. London: Routledge and Kegan Paul.

GRAVES-BROWN, P. M. 2000a. Introduction. In P. M. Graves-Brown (ed.) *Matter, Materiality and Modern Culture*. London: Routledge, pp. 1–30.

GRAVES-BROWN, P. M. (ed.) 2000b. *Matter, Materiality, and Modern Culture*. London: London: Routledge.

GRAVES, P. 2008. From an archaeology of iconoclasm to an anthropology of the body: images, punishment and personhood in England, 1500–1660. *Current Anthropology* 49(1): 35–57.

GREENE, K. 2008. Learning to consume: consumption and consumerism in the Roman Empire. *Journal of Roman Archaeology* 21: 64–82.

GREGORY, C. A. 1980. Gifts to men and gifts to God: gift exchange and capital accumulation in contemporary Papua. *Man* (n.s.) 15(4): 626–652.

GREGORY, C. A. 1982. *Gifts and Commodities*. London: Academic Press.

GREGORY, C. A. 1997. *Savage Money: the anthropology and politics of commodity exchange*. Amsterdam: Harwood Academic Publishers.

GREGORY, D. and URRY, J. 1985. Introduction. In D. Gregory and J. Urry (eds) *Social Relations and Spatial Structures*. Basingstoke: Macmillan, pp. 1–8.

GREGSON, N. and CREWE, L. 1997. Performance and possession: rethinking the act of purchase in the light of the car boot sale. *Journal of Material Culture* 2(2): 241–263.

GREGSON, N. and CREWE, L. 2003. *Second-hand cultures*. Oxford: Berg.

GREGSON, N. and BEALE, V. 2004. Wardrobe matter: the sorting, displacement and circulation of women's clothing. *Geoforum* 35(6): 689–700.

GREGSON, N., METCALFE, A. and CREWE, L. 2007a. Moving things along: the conduits and practices of divestment in consumption. *Transactions of the Institute of British Geographers*, 32(2): 187–200.

GREGSON, N., METCALFE, A. and CREWE, L. 2007b. Identity, mobility and the throwaway society. *Environment and Planning D: Society and Space* 25(4): 682–700.

GREGSON, N. ALEXANDER, C., AMIN, A., BICKERSTAFF, K., CRANG, M., DUBOW, J., HUDSON, R., JACKSON, P., MILLER, D. and NORRIS, L. nd. *Waste of the World: strand 1—waste economies value and spatial divisions of labour* (ESRC programme). http://www.thewasteoftheworld.org/html/strand1.html (Accessed 2 January 2009).

GRIAULE, M. and DIETERLEN, G. 1954. The Dogon of the French Sudan. In C. D. Forde (ed.) *African Worlds*. London: Oxford University Press, pp. 83–110.

GRIER, B. 1981. Underdevelopment, modes of production, and the state in colonial Ghana. *African Studies Review* 24(1): 21–47.

GRIFFIN, J. B. 1945. An interpretation of Siouan Archaeology in the Piedmont of North Carolina and Virginia. *American Antiquity* 10: 321–330.

GRIFFITHS, H. 2004. *Funky Geography: Paulo Freire, critical pedagogy and school geography*. Unpublished MSc thesis, School of Geography, Earth and Environmental Sciences, University of Birmingham. http://makingtheconnectionresources.files.wordpress.com/2008/08/helens-msc-thesis.pdf (Accessed 14 February 2009).

GRIFFITHS, T. 1996. *Hunters and Collectors: the antiquarian imagination in Australia*. Cambridge: Cambridge University Press.

GRIFFITTS, J. 2006. Bone Tools and Technological Choice: Change and Stability on the Northern Plains. Unpublished Ph.D. Dissertation, Department of Anthropology, University of Arizona.

GROEN, V. de 1669. *Jardinier hollandais*. Amsterdam: Marc Doornick.

GROSZ, E. A. 1994. *Volatile Bodies: toward a corporeal feminism*. Bloomington: Indiana University Press.

GROTH, P. and WILSON, C. (eds) 2003. *Everyday America: cultural landscape studies after J. B. Jackson*. Berkeley: University of California Press.

GUÉYE, A. 2003. The Impact of the Slave Trade on Cayor and Baol: Mutations in Habitat and Land Occupancy. In S. A. Diouf (ed.) *Fighting the Slave Trade: West African Strategies*. Athens, OH: Ohio University Press, pp. 50–61.

GULLESTAD, M 1984. *Kitchen Table Society: a case study of family and friendships of young working-class mothers in urban Norway*. Oslo: Universitetsfrolaget.

GUPTA, A. 2001. History, rule, representation: scattered speculations on 'of revelation and revolution Volume II'. *Interventions* 3(1): 40–46.

GUPTA, A. and FERGUSON, J. (eds) 1997a. *Anthropological Locations: boundaries and grounds of a field science*. Berkeley: University of California Press.

GUPTA, A. and FERGUSON, J. (eds) 1997b. *Culture, Power, Place: explorations in critical anthropology*. Durham, NC: Duke University Press.

GUPTA, A. and FERGUSON, J. 1997c. Discipline and practice: 'the field' as site, method and location in anthropology. In A. Gupta and J. Ferguson (eds) *Anthropological Locations: boundaries and grounds of a field science*. Berkelery: University of California Press, pp. 1–46.

GUPTA, A. and FERGUSON, J. 1997d. Culture, power, place: ethnography at the end of an era. In A. Gupta and J. Ferguson (eds) *Culture, Power, Place: explorations in critical anthropology*. Durham, NC: Duke University Press, pp. 1–21.

GYLLENSVÄRD, B., HARBISON, P., AXBOE, M., LAMM, J. P., ZACHRISSON, T. and REISBORG, S. 2004. *Excavations from Helgö XVI: exotic and sacral finds from Helgö*. Stockholm: Almqvist and Wiksell.

HAAS, J. 1996. Power, objects, and a voice for anthropology. *Current Anthropology* 37 (Supplement): S1–S22.

HACKING, I. 1983. *Representing and Intervening*. Cambridge: Cambridge University Press.

HACKING, I. 1990. *The Taming of Chance*. Cambridge: Cambridge University Press.

HACKING, I. 1992. The self-vindication of the laboratory sciences. In A. Pickering (ed.) *Science as Practice and Culture*. Chicago: University of Chicago Press, pp. 29–64.

HACKING, I. 1999. *The Social Construction of What?* Cambridge, MA: Harvard University Press.

HADDON, A. C. 1895. *Evolution in Art: as illustrated by the life-histories of designs*. London: Walter Scott.

HADDON, A. C. 1900. A classification of the stone-clubs of British New Guinea. *Journal of the Anthropological Institute of Great Britain and Ireland* 30: 221–250.

HADDON, L. 1988. The home computer: the making of a consumer electronic. *Science as Culture* 2: 7–51.

HAENGER, P. 2000. *Slaves and Slave Holders on the Gold Coast: towards an understanding of social bondage in West Africa* (trans. C. Handford; ed. J. J. Shaffer and P. E. Lovejoy). Basel: P. Schlettwein Publishing.

HALL, E. T. 1959. *The Silent Language*. Greenwich, CT: Fawcett Publications.

HALL, M. 1993. The archaeology of colonial settlement in Southern Africa. *Annual Review of Anthropology* 22: 177–200.

HALL, M. 2001. Social archaeology and the theatres of memory. *Journal of Social Archaeology* 1: 50–61.

HALL, M. and SILLIMAN, S. (eds) 2006. *Historical Archaeology*. Oxford: Blackwell.

HALL, S. 1996. The West and the rest: discourse and power. In S. Hall, D. Held, D. Hubert and K. Thompson (eds) *Modernity: An Introduction to Modern Societies*. Oxford: Blackwell, pp. 184–227.

HALL, S. 1997. *Representation: cultural representations and signifying practices*. London: Sage.

HALL, S. 1999. Whose heritage?: unsettling 'the heritage', re-imagining the post-nation. *Third Text* 49: 3–13.

HALLAM, E. and HOCKEY, J. 2001. *Death, Memory and Material Culture*. Oxford: Berg.

HALLAM, E., HOCKEY, J. and HOWARTH, G. 1999. *Beyond the Body: death and social identity*. London: Routledge.

HALPERIN, C. T. 2009. *Mesoamerican Figurines: small-scale indices of large-scale social phenomena*. Gainesville: University Press of Florida.

HALVERSON J. 1987. Art for art's sake in the Paleolithic (with Comments and Reply). *Current Anthropology* 28(1): 63–89.

HAMEROW, H. 2006. 'Special deposits' in Anglo-Saxon settlements. *Medieval Archaeology* 50: 1–30.

HAMILAKIS, Y. 2002. The past as oral history: towards an archaeology of the senses. In Y. Hamilakis, M. Pluciennik and S. A. Tarlow (eds) *Thinking Through the Body: archaeologies of corporeality*. New York: Kluwer/Plenum, pp. 121–134.

HAMILAKIS, Y., PLUCIENNIK, M. and TARLOW, S. A. (eds) 2002. *Thinking Through the Body: archaeologies of corporeality*. New York: Kluwer/Plenum.

HAMILTON, S. and WHITEHOUSE, R. 2006. Phenomenology in practice: towards a methodology for a 'subjective' approach. *European Journal of Archaeology* 9(1): 31–71.

HAMMOND, M. 1972. *The City in the Ancient World*. Cambridge, MA: Harvard University Press.

HANEGRAAFF, W. 1998. The emergence of the academic science of magic: The Occult Philosophy in Tylor and Frazer. In A. L. Molendijk and P. Pels (eds) *Religion in the Making: the emergence of the sciences of religion*. Leiden: Brill, pp. 253–275.

HANNERZ, U. 1992. *Cultural Complexity: studies in the social organization of meaning*. New York: Columbia University Press.

HANSELL, M. H. 2005. *Animal Architecture*. Oxford: Oxford University Press.

HANSEN, K. T. (ed.) 1992. *African Encounters with Domesticity*. New Brunswick, NJ: Rutgers University Press.

HANSEN, K. T. 2000. *Salaula: the world of secondhand clothing and Zambia*. Chicago: University of Chicago Press.

HANSEN, K. T. 2002. Commodity chains and the international secondhand clothing trade: *Salaula* and the world of consumption in Zambia. In J. Ensminger (ed.) *Theory in Economic Anthropology*. Walnut Creek, CA: Altamira Press, pp. 221–236.

HANSEN, K. T. 2004. The world in dress: anthropological perspectives on clothing, fashion, and culture. *Annual Review of Anthropology* 33: 369–392.

HARAWAY, D. J. 1988. Situated knowledges: the science question in feminism and the privilege of a partial perspective. *Feminist Studies* 14(3): 575–600.

HARAWAY, D. J. 1989. *Primate Visions: gender, race and nature in the world of modern science*. London: Routledge and Chapman Hall.

HARAWAY, D. J. 1991a. A cyborg manifesto: science, technology and socialist feminism in the late twentieth century. In D. J. Harawary *Simians, Cyborgs and Women: the reinvention of nature*. London: Routledge, pp. 149–181. London: Free Association Books. Also available at http://www.stanford.edu/dept/HPS/Haraway/CyborgManifesto.html (Accessed 1 November 2008).

HARAWAY, D. J. 1991b. *Simians, Cyborgs and Women: the reinvention of nature*. London: Free Association Books.

HARAWAY, D. J. 1997. *Modest_Witness@Second_Millennium. FemaleMan©_Meets_Onco-Mouse*[tm]. London: Routledge.

HARAWAY, D. J. 2003. *The Companion Species Manifesto: dogs, people, and significant otherness.* Chicago: Prickly Paradigm Press.

HARAWAY, D. J. 2004. A manifesto for cyborgs: science, technology, and socialist-feminism in the 1980s. In *The Haraway Reader.* New York: Routledge, pp. 7–45.

HARAWAY, D. J. 2008. *When Species Meet.* Minneapolis: University of Minnesota Press.

HARDING, J. 2006. Pit-digging, occupation and structured deposition on Rudstone Wold, Eastern Yorkshire. *Oxford Journal of Archaeology,* 25(2): 109–126.

HARDT, M. 2007. Foreword: What affects are good for. In P. T. Clough and J. Halley (eds) *The Affective Turn.* Durham and London: Duke University Press, pp. ix–xiii.

HARMAN, G. 2002. *Tool-being: Heidegger and the metaphysics of objects.* Chicago, IL: Open Court.

HARMAN, G. 2005. *Guerilla Metaphysics. Phenomenology and the Carpentry of Things.* Chicago, IL: Open Court.

HARRIS, D. S. 2003. *The Nature of Authority: villa culture, landscape, and representation in eighteenth-century Lombardy.* University Park, PA: Pennsylvania State University Press.

HARRIS, E. C. 1989. *Principles of Archaeological Stratigraphy* (second edition). London: Academic Press.

HARRIS, M. 1968. *The Rise of Anthropological Theory.* New York: Crowell.

HARRIS, N. 1999. *Building Lives: constructing rites and passages.* New Haven: Yale University Press.

HARRIS, O. 2006. Identity, Emotion and Memory in Neolithic Dorset. Unpublished Ph.D. thesis, Cardiff University.

HARRIS, R. and MYERS, G. 2007. Hybrid housing: improvement and control in late colonial Zanzibar. *Journal of the Society of Architectural Historians* 66(4): 476–493.

HARRISON, R. 2002. Archaeology and the colonial encounter: Kimberley spear points, cultural identity and masculinity in the north of Australia. *Journal of Social Archaeology* 2(3): 352–377.

HARRISON, R. 2003. The archaeology of 'lost places': ruin, memory and the heritage of the Aboriginal diaspora in Australia. *Historic Environment* 17(1): 18–23.

HARRISON, R. 2004a. Kimberley points and colonial preference: new insights into the chronology of pressure flaked point forms from the southeast Kimberley, Western Australia. *Archaeology in Oceania* 39(1): 1–11.

HARRISON, R. 2004b. *Shared Landscapes.* Sydney: University of New South Wales Press.

HARRISON, R. 2005. 'It will always be set in your heart': archaeology and community values at the former Dennawan Reserve, northwestern NSW, Australia. In N. Agnew and J. Bridgeland (eds) *Of the Past, For the Future: integrating archaeology and conservation.* Los Angeles: Getty Conservation Institute, pp. 94–101.

HARRISON, R. 2006. An artefact of colonial desire? Kimberley points and the technologies of enchantment. *Current Anthropology* 47(1): 63–88.

HARRISON, S., MASSEY, D. and RICHARDS, K. 2006. Complexity and emergence (another conversation). *Area* 38(4): 465–471.

HARRISON, S., MASSEY, D., RICHARDS, K., MAGILLIGAN, F. J., THRIFT, N. J. and BENDER, B. 2004. Thinking across the divide: perspectives on the conversations between physical and human geography. *Area* 36(4): 435–442.

HARRISON, S., PILE, S. and THRIFT, N. J. (eds) 2004. *Patterned Ground: entanglements of nature and culture.* London: Reaktion.

HARTNETT, A. 2004. The politics of the pipe: clay pipes and tobacco consumption in Galway, Ireland. *International Journal of Historical Archaeology* 8(2): 133–147.

HARTWICK, E. 1998. Geographies of consumption: a commodity-chain approach. *Environment and planning D: Society and Space* 16(4): 423–437.

HARTWICK, E. 2000. Towards a geographical politics of consumption. *Environment and Planning A* 32(7): 1177–1132.

HARVEY, D. 1989. *The Condition of Postmodernity: an inquiry into the origins of cultural change*. Oxford: Blackwell.

HARVEY, D. 2003. 'National' identities and the politics of ancient heritage: continuity and change at ancient monuments in Britain and Ireland, *c.* 1675–1850. *Transactions of the Institute of British Geographers* 28: 473–487.

HARVEY, G. 2005. *Animism: respecting the living world*. London: Hurst.

HARVEY, K. (ed.) 2009. *History and Material Culture: a student's guide to approaching alternative sources*. London: Routledge.

HARVEY, N. 1945. Some further notes on Suffolk folklore. *Folklore* 56(2): 269–270.

HARWOOD, J. 2005. Comments on Andy Pickering's Paper. *Perspectives on Science* 13: 411–415.

HASINOFF, E. 2006. Christian trophies or Asmat ethnografica? *Journal of Social Archaeology* 6(2): 147–174.

HASLAM, M., HERNANDEZ-AGUILAR, A., LING, V., CARVALHO, S., DE LA TORRE, L., DE STEFANO, A., DU, A., HARDY, B., HARRIS, J., MARCHANT, L., MATSUZAWA, T., McGREW, W., MERCADER, J., MORA, R., PETRAGLIA, M., ROCHE, H., VISALBERGHI, E., WARREN, R. 2009. Primate Archaeology. *Nature* 460: 339–344.

HASTINGS, M. 2007. *Nemesis: the battle for Japan, 1944–45*. London: Harper Press.

HASTORF, C. 1991. Gender, space and food in prehistory. In J. Gero and M. Conkey (eds) *Engendering Archaeology*. Oxford: Blackwell (Studies in Social Archaeology), pp. 132–159.

HAUGERUD, A., STONE, M. P. and LITTLE, P. D. (eds) 2000. *Commodities and Globalization: anthropological perspectives*. Boulder, CO: Rowman and Littlefield.

HAWKES, C. 1954. Archeological theory and method: some suggestions from the Old World. *American Anthropologist* 56(2): 155–168.

HAWLEY, R. 1937. Reversed stratigraphy. *American Antiquity* 2: 297–299.

HAWTHORN, G. 1972. Review of R. Firth, J. Hubert and A. Forge 'Families and their relatives: kinship in a middle-class sector of London'. *American Journal of Sociology* 77(5): 996–998.

HAWTHORNE, W. 1999. The production of slaves where there was no state: the Guinea-Bissau region, 1450–1815. *Slavery and Abolition* 20(2): 97–124.

HAWTHORNE, W. 2003. Strategies of the decentralized: defending communities from slave raiders in Coastal Guinea-Bissau, 1450–1815. In S. A. Diouf (ed.) *Fighting the Slave Trade: West African Strategies*. Athens, OH: Ohio University Press, pp. 152–169.

HAYDEN, B. 1995. The Emergence of Prestige Technologies and Pottery. In W. Barnett and J. W. Hoopes (eds) *The Emergence of Pottery. Technology and Innovation in Ancient Societies*. Washington, DC: Smithsonian Institution Press, pp. 257–265.

HAYDEN, D. 1981. *The Grand Domestic Revolution: A History of Feminist Designs for American Homes, Neighborhoods, and Cities*. Cambridge, MA: MIT Press.

HAYLES, N. K. 1999. *How We Became Posthuman. Virtual bodies in cybernetics, literature and informatics*. Chicago: University of Chicago Press.

HAYNES, R. D. 1998. *Seeking the Centre: the Australian desert in literature, art and film*. Cambridge: Cambridge University Press.

HAZLEHURST, F. H. 1966. *Jacques Boyceau and the French formal garden*. Athens: University of Georgia Press.

HAZLEHURST, F. H. 1980. *Gardens of Illusion: the genius of André Le Nostre*. Nashville: Vanderbilt University Press.

HEAD, L. 2000a. *Second Nature. The history and implications of Australia as Aboriginal landscape*. Syracuse: Syracuse University Press.

HEAD, L. 2000b. *Cultural Landscapes and Environmental Change*. London: Arnold.

HEAD, L. 2008. Is the concept of human impacts past its use-by date? *The Holocene* 18: 373–377.

HEAD, L., ATCHISON, J. and FULLAGAR, R. 2002. Country and garden: ethnobotany, archaeobotany and Aboriginal landscapes near the Keep River, northwestern Australia. *Journal of Social Archaeology* 2: 173–191.

HEALY, M. 2001. *Fictions of Disease in Early Modern England: bodies, plagues and politics*. New York: Palgrave.

HEBDIGE, D. 1979. *Subculture: the meaning of style*. London: Methuen.

HEDBLOM, F. 1961. The Institute for Dialect and Folklore research at Uppsala, Sweden. *The Folklore and Folk Music Archivist*, Indiana University 3(4): 1–2.

HEIDEGGER, M. 1971 [1949]. The thing. In *Poetry, Language, Thought* (trans. A. Hofstadter). Lonon: Harper and Row, pp. 163–184.

HEIDEGGER, M. 1977. The question concerning technology. In *The Question Concerning Technology and Other Essays* (trans. W. Lovitt). New York: Harper and Row, pp. 3–35.

HEIDEGGER, M. 1978. Building, dwelling, thinking. In *Basic Writings* (ed. D. F. Krell). London: Routledge, pp. 347–363.

HEIDEGGER, M. 1981. 'Only a God Can Save Us': the *Spiegel* interview (1966). In T. Sheehan (ed.) *Heidegger: The Man and the Thinker*. Chicago: Precedent Publishing, pp. 45–67.

HEILEN, M. 2005. An Archaeological Theory of Landscapes. Unpublished Ph.D. dissertation, Department of Anthropology, University of Arizona.

HEIZER, M. 1991. *Double Negative: sculpture in the land*. New York: Rizzoli.

HELLIWELL, C. 1996. Space and sociality in a Dayak Longhouse. In M. Jackson (ed.) *Things as they are: new directions in phenomenological anthropology*. Bloomington: Indiana University Press, pp. 128–148.

HELMS, M. 1993. *Craft and the Kingly Ideal: art, trade and power*. Austin: University of Texas Press.

HENARE, A. 2005a. *Museums, Anthropology and Imperial Exchange*. Cambridge: Cambridge University Press.

HENARE, A. 2005b. Nga Aho Tipuna (Ancestral Threads): Maori Cloaks from New Zealand. In D. Miller and S. Küchler (eds) *Clothing as Material Culture*. Oxford: Berg, pp. 121–138.

HENARE, A., HOLBRAAD, M. and WASTELL, S. 2007a. Introduction: thinking through things. In A. Henare, M. Holbraad and S. Wastell (eds) *Thinking Through Things: theorising artefacts ethnographically*. Routledge: London, pp. 1–31.

HENARE, A., HOLBRAAD, M. and WASTELL, S. (eds) 2007b. *Thinking Through Things: theorising artefacts ethnographically*. London: Routledge.

HENG, C. K. 1999. *Cities of Aristocrats and Bureaucrats: The development of medieval Chinese cities*. Honolulu: University of Hawai'i Press.

HERMAN, B. L. 1992. *The Stolen House*. Charlottesville: University Press of Virginia.

HERMAN, B. L. 2005. *Town House: architecture and material life in the early American city, 1780–1830*. Chapel Hill: University of North Carolina Press.

HERMANSEN, G. 1978. The population of Imperial Rome: the Regionaries. *Historia* 27(1): 129–68.

HERSKOVITS, M. 1938. *Acculturation: the study of culture contact.* New York: J. J. Augustin.

HERTZ, R. 1960. *Death and the Right Hand* (trans. R. and C. Needham). Aberdeen: Cohen and West.

HETHERINGTON, K. 2004. Secondhandedness: consumption, disposal, and absent presence. *Environment and Planning D: Society and Space* 22(1): 157–173.

HEWISON, R. 1987. *The Heritage Industry: Britain in a climate of decline.* London: Methuen.

HEYD, T. 2005. Aesthetics and rock art: an introduction. In T. Heyd and John Clegg (eds) *Aesthetics and Rock Art.* Aldershot: Ashgate, pp. 1–17.

HEYNEN, H. 2001. *Architecture and Modernity: a critique.* Cambridge, MA: MIT Press.

HICKS, D. 2000. Ethnicity, 'race', and the archaeology of the Atlantic slave trade. *Assemblage* 5. http://www.assemblage.group.shef.ac.uk/5/hicks.html (Accessed 1 October 2008).

HICKS, D. 2003. Archaeology unfolding: diversity and the loss of isolation. *Oxford Journal of Archaeology* 22(3): 315–329.

HICKS, D. 2005. 'Places for thinking' from Annapolis to Bristol: situations and symmetries in 'world historical archaeologies'. *World Archaeology* 37(3): 373–391.

HICKS, D. 2007a. Historical archaeology in Britain. In D. M. Pearsall (ed.) *Encyclopedia of Archaeology.* San Diego: Academic Press, pp. 1318–1327.

HICKS, D. 2007b. *The Garden of the World: an historical archaeology of sugar landscapes in the eastern Caribbean.* Oxford: Archaeopress (British Archaeological Reports international series 1632).

HICKS, D. 2008a. Review of T. Rowley 'The English Landscape in the 20th Century'. *Landscapes* 9(1): 86–90.

HICKS, D. 2008b. Improvement: What kind of archaeological object is it? A review article. *Journal of Field Archaeology* 33: 111–116.

HICKS, D. 2009. Review of B. Bender, S. Hamilton and C. Tilley 'Stone worlds: narrative and reflexivity in landscape archaeology'. *American Antiquity* 74(3): 590–591.

HICKS, D. and MCATACKNEY, L. 2007. Introduction: landscapes as standpoints. In D. Hicks, L. McAtackney and G. Fairclough (eds) *Envisioning Landscape: situations and standpoints in archaeology and heritage.* Walnut Creek, CA: Left Coast Press (One World Archaeology 52), pp. 13–29.

HICKS, D. and BEAUDRY, M. C. (eds) 2006a. *The Cambridge Companion to Historical Archaeology.* Cambridge: Cambridge University Press.

HICKS, D. and BEAUDRY, M. C. 2006b. Introduction: the place of historical archaeology. In D. Hicks and M. C. Beaudry (eds) *The Cambridge Companion to Historical Archaeology.* Cambridge: Cambridge University Press, pp. 1–9.

HICKS, D. and HORNING, A. J. 2006. Historical archaeology and buildings. In D. Hicks and M. C. Beaudry (eds) *The Cambridge Companion to Historical Archaeology.* Cambridge: Cambridge University Press.

HIGHLAND FOLK MUSEUM, 2008. Dr Isabel Frances Grant: Founder of the Highland Folk Museum. http://www.highlandlandfolk.com/kingussie-founder.php (Accessed 1 December 2008).

HIGHMORE, B. 2002. Introduction: questioning everyday life. In B. Highmore (ed.) *The Everyday Reader.* London: Routledge, pp. 1–34.

HILL, D. and MATTHEWS, S. 2004. Cyril Fox on Tour 1927–1932: Two of Sir Cyril's Note-books Describing Minor Earthworks of the Welsh Marches and Visits to Four Welsh

Museums, with Two Other Unpublished Papers. Oxford: Archaeopress (British Archaeological Reports 364).

HILL, J. 2007. The story of the amulet: locating the enchantment of collections. *Journal of Material Culture* 12(1): 65–87.

HILL, J. D. 1995. *Ritual and Rubbish in the Iron Age of Wessex: a study on the formation of a specific archaeological record.* Oxford: British Archaeological Reports 242.

HILL, J. M. (ed.) 1998. *Occupying Architecture. Between the architect and the user.* London: Routledge.

HILL, J. M. 2003. *Actions of Architecture. Architects and creative users.* London: Routledge.

HINCHLIFFE, S. 2003. Inhabiting—landscapes and natures. In K. Anderson, M. Domosh, S. Pile and N. J. Thrift (eds) *The Handbook of Cultural Geography.* London: Sage, pp. 207–226.

HINCHLIFFE, S. 2007. *Geographies of Nature.* London: Sage.

HINCHLIFFE, S. and BINGHAM, N. 2008. Securing life: the emerging practices of biosecurity. *Environment and Planning A* 40(7): 1534–1552.

HINCHLIFFE, S. and WHATMORE, S. 2006. Living cities: towards a politics of conviviality. *Science as Culture* 15/2: 123–138.

HINCHLIFFE, S., KEARNES, M., DEGEN, M. and WHATMORE, S. 2005. Urban wild things: a cosmopolitical experiment. *Environment and Planning D: Society and Space* 23: 643–658.

HINCHLIFFE, S., WHATMORE, S., DEGEN, M. and KEARNES, M. 2003. *Living Cities: a new agenda for urban natures.* http://www.open.ac.uk/socialsciences/habitable-cities/ (Accessed 11 January 2009).

HINSLEY, C. M. 1976. Amateurs and professionals in Washington anthropology, 1879 to 1903. In J. V. Murra (ed.) *American Anthropology: the early years.* St Paul, Minnesota: West Publishing, pp. 36–68.

HINSLEY, C. M. 1985. From shell-heaps to stelae: early anthropology at the Peabody Museum. In G. W. Stocking (ed.) *Objects and Other: essays on museums and material culture.* Madison, WI: University of Wisconsin Press, pp. 49–74.

HIRATA, S., WATANABE, K. and KAWAI, M. 2001. 'Sweet-potatoe washing' revisited. In T. Matsuzawa (ed.) *Primate Origins of Human Cognition and Behavior.* Tokyo: Springer-Verlag, pp. 487–508.

HIX, J. 1974. *The Glass House.* London: Phaidon.

HOAD, G. 2007. Human Cargo. *Interface.* http://interface.a-n.co.uk/reviews/single/390419 (Accessed 17 November 2008).

HOBBES, T. 1651 [1998]. *Leviathan* (ed. J. C. A. Gaskin). Oxford: Oxford University Press.

HOBHOUSE, L. T., WHEELER, G. C. and GINSBERG, M. 1915. *The Material Culture and Social Institutions of the Simpler Peoples.* London: Chapman and Halls.

HODDER, I. 1978a. Simple correlations between material culture and society: a review. In I. Hodder (ed.) *The Spatial Organisation of Culture.* London: Duckworth, pp. 3–24.

HODDER, I. 1978b. The spatial structure of material 'cultures': a review of some of the evidence. In I. Hodder (ed.) *The Spatial Organisation of Culture.* London: Duckworth, pp. 93–111.

HODDER, I. 1981. Towards a mature archaeology. In I. Hodder, G. Isaac and N. Hammond (eds) *Pattern of the Past: studies in honour of David Clarke.* Cambridge: Cambridge University Press, pp. 2–13.

HODDER, I. 1982a. *Symbols in Action: ethnoarchaeological studies of material culture.* Cambridge: Cambridge University Press (New Studies in Archaeology).

HODDER, I. (ed.) 1982b. *Symbolic and Structural Archaeology.* Cambridge: Cambridge University Press (New Directions in Archaeology).

HODDER, I. 1982c. Theoretical archaeology: a reactionary view. In I. Hodder (ed.) *Symbolic and Structural Archaeology.* Cambridge: Cambridge University Press (New Directions in Archaeology), pp. 1–16.

HODDER, I. 1984. Archaeology in 1984. *Antiquity,* 58: 25–32.

HODDER, I. 1985. Postprocessual archaeology. In M. B. Schiffer (ed.) *Advances in Archaeological Method and Theory* (Volume 8). New York: Academic Press, pp. 250–269.

HODDER, I. 1986. *Reading the Past: current approaches to interpretation in archaeology.* Cambridge: Cambridge University Press.

HODDER, I. (ed.) 1987a. *Archaeology as Long-Term History.* Cambridge: Cambridge University Press.

HODDER, I. (ed.) 1987b. *The Archaeology of Contextual Meanings.* Cambridge: Cambridge University Press.

HODDER, I. (ed.) 1989. *The Meanings of Things: material culture and symbolic expression.* London: Unwin Hyman (One World Archaeology 6).

HODDER, I. 1989. This is not an article about material culture as text. *Journal of Anthropological Archaeology* 8: 250–269.

HODDER, I. 1990. *The Domestication of Europe.* Oxford: Blackwell (Studies in Social Archaeology).

HODDER, I. 1991a. Archaeological theory in contemporary European societies: the emergence of competing traditions. In I. Hodder (ed.) *Archaeological Theory in Europe: the last three decades.* London: Routledge, pp. 1–24.

HODDER, I. 1991b. Post-modernism, post-structuralism and post-processual archaeology. In I. Hodder (ed.) *The Meanings of Things.* London: Routledge (One World Archaeology 6), pp. 64–78.

HODDER, I. 1991c. *Reading the Past: current approaches to interpretation in archaeology* (second edition). Cambridge: Cambridge University Press.

HODDER, I. 1992. *Theory and Practice in Archaeology.* London: Routledge.

HODDER, I. 1994. Architecture and meaning: the example of Neolithic houses and tombs. In M. Parker Pearson and C. Richards (eds) *Architecture and Order.* London: Routledge, pp. 73–86.

HODDER, I. 1997. Always momentary, fluid and flexible: towards a self-reflexive excavation methodology. *Antiquity,* 71: 691–700.

HODDER, I. 1998. Creative thought. A long-term perspective. In S. Mithen (ed.) *Creativity in Human Prehistory and Evolution.* London: Routledge, pp. 61–77.

HODDER, I. 1999. *The Archaeological Process: an introduction.* Oxford: Blackwell.

HODDER, I. 2004. Dialogical archaeology and its implications. In *Archaeology Beyond Dialogue.* Salt Lake City: University of Utah Press (Foundations of Archaeological Enquiry), pp. 1–7.

HODDER, I. 2006. *The Leopard's Tale. Revealing the mysteries of Çatalhöyük.* London: Thames and Hudson.

HODDER, I. and CESSFORD, C. 2004. Daily practice and social memory at Çatalhöyük. *Amercican Antiquity* 69: 17–40.

HODDER, I., LEONE, M. P., BERNECK, R., SHANKS, M., TOMÁŠKOVÁ, S., MCANANY, P. A., SHENNAN, S. and RENFREW, A. C. 2007. Revolution fulfilled? 'Symbolic and structural archaeology' a generation on. *Cambridge Archaeological Journal* 17: 199–228.

HODDER, I., SHANKS, M., ALEXANDRI, A., BUCHLI, V., CARMAN, J., LAST, J. and LUCAS, G. (eds) 1995a. *Interpreting Archaeology: finding meaning in the past.* London: Routledge.

HODDER, I., SHANKS, M., ALEXANDRI, A., BUCHLI, V., CARMAN, J., LAST, J. and LUCAS, G. (eds) 1995b. Introduction. In I. Hodder, M. Shanks. A. Alexandri, V. Buchli, J. Carman, J. Last and G. Lucas (eds) *Interpreting Archaeology: finding meaning in the past.* London: Routledge, pp. 1–2.

HODGEN, M. 1964. *Early Anthropology in the Sixteenth and Seventeenth Centuries.* Philadelphia: University of Pennsylvania Press.

HOESCHLER, S. and ALDERMAN, D. H. 2004. Memory and place: geographies of a critical relationship. *Social and Cultural Geography* 5(3): 347–356.

HOGENDORN, J. and JOHNSON, M. 1986. *The Shell Money of the Slave Trade.* Cambridge: Cambridge University Press.

HOGGARD, B. 2004. The archaeology of counter-witchcraft and popular magic. In O. Davies and W. de Blécourt (eds) *Beyond the Witch Trials: witchcraft and magic in Enlightenment Europe.* Manchester: Manchester University Press, pp. 167–186.

HOHMANN, G. and FRUTH, B. 2003. Culture in Bonobos? Between-species and within-species variation in behavior. *Current Anthropology* 44(4): 563–571.

HOLDAWAY, S. and STERN, N. 2004. *A Record in Stone: the study of Australia's flaked stone artefacts.* Canberra: Aboriginal Studies Press.

HOLLANDER, G. 2003. Re-naturalising sugar: narratives of place, production and consumption. *Social and Cultural Geography* 4(1): 59–74.

HOLLIMAN, S. E. 2000. Sex, health, and gender roles among the Arikara of the northern plains. In A. E. Rautman (ed.) *Reading the Body. Representations and remains in the archaeological record.* Philadelphia: University of Pennsylvania Press, pp. 25–37.

HOLLOWAY, S. L. 2003. Outsiders in rural society?: Constructions of rurality and nature–society relations in the racialisation of English Gypsy-Travellers, 1869–1934. *Environment and Planning D: Society and Space* 21: 695–715.

HOLLOWAY, S. L. 2004. Rural roots, rural routes: discourses of rural self and travelling other in debates about the future of Appleby New Fair, 1945–1969. *Journal of Rural Studies* 20: 143–156.

HOLLOWAY, S. L. 2005. Articulating otherness? White rural residents talk about gypsy-travellers. *Transactions of the Institute of British Geographers* 30: 351–367.

HOLLOWAY, S. L. 2007. Burning issues: whiteness, rurality and the politics of difference. *Geoforum* 38: 7–20.

HOLMES, W. H. 1894. Natural history of flaked stone implements. In C. S. Wake (ed.) *Memoirs of the International Congress of Anthropology.* Chicago: Schulte, pp. 120–139.

HOLTORF, C. 2002. Notes on the life-history of a pot sherd. *Journal of Material Culture* 7(1): 49–71.

HOLTORF, C. and H. WILLIAMS 2006. Landscapes and memories. In D. Hicks and M. C. Beaudry (eds) *The Cambridge Companion to Historical Archaeology.* Cambridge: Cambridge University Press, pp. 235–254.

HOOPER-GREENHILL, E. 1992. *Museums and the Shaping of Knowledge.* London: Routledge.

HOOPES, J. W. and BARNETT, W. 1995. The shape of early pottery studies. In W. Barnett and J. W. Hoopes (eds) *The Emergence of Pottery. Technology and innovation in ancient societies.* Washington: Smithsonian Institution Press, pp. 1–7.

HOPPER, L., SPITERI, A., LAMBETH, S. P., SCHAPIRO, S. J., HORNER, V. and WHITEN, A. 2007. Experimental studies of traditions and underlying transmission processes in chimpanzees. *Animal Behaviour* 73(6): 1021–1032.

HORKHEIMER, M. and ADORNO, T. W. 1972. The culture industry: enlightenment as mass deception. In *Dialectic of Enlightenment*. New York: Seabury, pp. 120–167.

HORNER, V., WHITEN, A., FLYNN, E. and DE WAAL, F. B. M. 2006. Faithful replication of foraging techniques along cultural transmission chains by chimpanzees and children. *Proceedings of the National Academy of Sciences of the United States of America* 103(37): 13878–13883.

HORST, H. and MILLER, D. 2006. *The Cell Phone: an anthropology of communication*. Oxford: Berg.

HOSKINS, G. 2007. Materialising memory at Angel Island Immigration Station, San Francisco. *Environment and Planning A* 39: 437–445.

HOSKINS, J. 1998. *Biographical Objects: how things tell the stories of people's lives*. London: Routledge.

HOSKINS, W. G. 1953. The rebuilding of rural England, 1570–1640. *Past and Present* 4: 44–59.

HOSKINS, W. G. 1955. *The Making of the English Landscape*. London: Hodder and Stoughton.

HOUNTONDJI, P. 1994. *Culture and development in Africa: lifestyles, modes of thought and forms of social organization*. Paper presented at World Commission on Culture and Development, June 8. Paris (UNESCO, CCD-IV/94REG/INF. 9).

HOUSTON, S. D. and STUART, D. 1998. The ancient Maya self: personhood and portraiture in the Classic period. *RES* 33: 73–101.

HOWARD, D. 2002. Teaching architectural history in Great Britain and Australia: local conditions and global perspectives. *Journal of the Society of Architectural Historians* 61(3): 346–354.

HOWES, D. (ed.) 1996a. *Cross-Cultural Consumption: global markets, local realities*. London: Routledge.

HOWES, D. 1996b. Introduction: commodities and cultural borders. In D. Howes (ed.) *Cross-Cultural Consumption: global markets, local realities*. London: Routledge, pp. 1–16.

HOWES, D. 2005. (ed.) *Empire of the Senses*. Oxford: Berg.

HUBBELL, A. 2001. A view of the slave trade from the margin: Souroudougou in the late nineteenth-century slave trade of the Niger Bend. *Journal of African History* 42: 25–47.

HUDSON, B. 2000. The origins of Bagan: new dates and old inhabitants. *Asian Perspectives* 40(1): 48–74.

HUGHES, A. 2000. Retailers, knowledges and changing commodity networks: the case of the cut flower trade. *Geoforum* 31(2): 175–190.

HUGHES, E. C. 1971. *The Sociological Eye: selected papers on work, self and the study of society*. Chicago: Aldine Atherton.

HUGHES, T. P. 1979. The electrification of America: the system builders. *Technology and Culture* 20: 124–161.

HUMAN CARGO 2007a. Educators' Notes, Contemporary Art Responses: Human Cargo: The Transatlantic Slave Trade, its Abolition and Contemporary Legacies in Plymouth and Devon. Plymouth City Museum and Art Gallery, 22 September–24 November 2007. http://www.humancargo.co.uk/HC_ContemporaryArt.pdf (Accessed 17 November 2008).

HUMAN CARGO 2007b. Human Cargo: Educators' notes on Contemporary Art Responses. Plymouth: Plymouth City Museum and Art Gallery. http://www.plymouth.gov.uk/human_cargo_contemporary_art_educators_notes.pdf (Accessed 25 January 2010).

HUMLE, T. and MATSUZAWA, T. 2002. Ant dipping among the chimpanzees of Bossou, Guinea, and comparisons with other sites. *American Journal of Primatology* 58: 133–148.

HUMLE, T. and MATSUZAWA, T. 2004. Oil palm use by adjacent communities of chimpanzees at Bossou and Nimba Mountains, West Africa. *International Journal of Primatology* 25: 551–581.

HUMLE, T., SNOWDON, C. T. and MATSUZAWA, T. 2009. Social influences on ant-dipping acquisition in the wild chimpanzees (Pan Troglodytes verus)of Bossou, Guinea, West Africa. *Animal Cognition*. DOI 10.1007/510071-009-0272-6.

HUMPHREY, C. 1974. Inside a Mongolian yurt. *New Society* 31(629): 13–15.

HUMPHREY, C. 1988. No place like home in anthropology: the neglect of architecture. *Anthropology Today* 4(1): 16–18.

HUNT, G. R. and GRAY, R. D. 2003. Diversification and cumulative evolution in New Caledonian crow tool manufacture. *Proceedings of the Royal Society B-Biological Sciences* 270(1517): 867–874.

HUNT, J. D. 1986. *Garden and Grove: the Italian Renaissance garden in the English imagination, 1600–1750*. Princeton: Princeton University Press.

HUNT, J. D. 1992. *Gardens and the Picturesque: studies in the history of landscape architecture*. Cambridge, MT: MIT Press.

HUNT, J. D. 2002. *The Picturesque Garden in Europe*. New York: Thames and Hudson.

HUNT, J. D. and WILLIS, P. (eds) 1988. *The Genius of the Place: the English landscape garden 1620–1820*. Cambridge, MA: MIT Press.

HUNT, J. D., CONAN, M. and GOLDSTEIN, C. (eds) 2002. *Tradition and Innovation in French garden Art: chapters of a new history*. Philadelphia: University of Pennsylvania Press.

HUTTON, J. H. 1944. The place of material culture in the study of anthropology. *Journal of the Royal Anthropological Institute of Great Britain and Ireland* 74(1/2): 1–6.

HUXLEY, A. 1963. *The Doors of Perception, and Heaven and Hell*. New York: Harper and Row.

HVATTUM, M. 2004. *Gottfried Semper and the Problem of Historicism*. Cambridge: Cambridge University Press.

HYDE, E. 2005. *Cultivated Power: flowers, culture, and politics in the reign of Louis XIV*. Philadelphia: University of Pennsylvania Press.

HYMES, D. 1964. *Language in Culture and Society: a reader in linguistics and anthropology*. New York: Harper and Row.

IHDE, D. 2002. *Bodies in Technology*. Minnesota: University of Minnesota Press.

IMPEY, O. and MacGREGOR, A. (eds) 1985. *The Origins of Museums: the cabinet of curiosities in sixteenth and seventeenth century Europe*. Oxford: Clarendon Press.

INGOLD, T. 1990. Society, nature and the concept of technology. *Archaeological Review from Cambridge* 9: 5–17.

INGOLD, T. 1993. The temporality of the landcape. *World Archaeology* 25(2): 152–174.

INGOLD, T. 1995. Building, dwelling, living—How animals and humans make themselves at home in the world. In M. Strathern (ed.) *Shifting Contexts: transformations in anthropological knowledge*. London: Routledge, pp. 57–80.

INGOLD, T. 2000a. *The Perception of the Environment of the Environment: essays on livelihood, dwelling and skill*. London: Routledge.

INGOLD, T. 2000b. Making culture and weaving the world. In P. M. Graves-Brown (ed.) *Matter, Materiality and Modern Culture*. London: Routledge, pp. 50–71.

INGOLD, T. 2005. Comments on C. Tilley 'The materiality of stone: explorations in landscape phenomenology'. *Norwegian Archaeological Review* 38(2): 122–126.

INGOLD, T. 2007a. Materials against materiality. *Archaeological Dialogues* 14(1): 1–16.

INGOLD, T. 2007b. Comment. *Journal of Iberian Archaeology* 9/10 (Special Issue: 'Overcoming the Modern Invention of Material Culture'): 313–317.

INGOLD, T. 2007c. *Lines: a brief history*. London: Routledge.

INGOLD, T. 2007d. A response to my critics. *Archaeological Dialogues* 14(1): 31–38.

INGOLD, T. 2007e. Archaeology is *not* ethnography. *Proceedings of the British Academy* 154: 69–92.

INGOLD, T. 2008. When ANT meets SPIDER: social theory for arthropods. In C. Knappett and L. Malafouris (eds) *Material Agency: towards a non-anthropocentric approach*, New York: Spinger, pp. 209–216.

INIKORI, J. E. 2002. *Africans and the Industrial Revolution in England: a study in international trade and economic development*. Cambridge: Cambridge University Press.

INNIS, H. A. 1950. *Empire and Communications*. Toronto: University of Toronto Press.

INNIS, H. A. 1951. *The Bias of Communication*. Toronto: University of Toronto Press.

INNOCENT, C. 1916. *The Development of English Building Construction*. Cambridge: Cambridge University Press.

INSOLL, T. 2006. Shrine franchising and the Neolithic in the British Isles: some observations based upon the Tallensi, northern Ghana. *Cambridge Archaeological Journal* 16(2): 223–238.

IRIGARAY, L. 1985. *This Sex Which is Not One*. Ithaca, NY: Cornell University Press.

ISAAC, R. 1982. *The Transformation of Virginia, 1740–1790*. Chapel Hill: University of North Carolina Press.

ISHAM, N. and BROWN, A. 1895. *Early Rhode Island Houses*. Providence, RI: Preston and Rounds.

ISHAM, N. and BROWN, A. 1900. *Early Connecticut Houses*. Providence, RI: Preston and Rounds.

IUCN (INTERNATIONAL UNION FOR THE CONSERVATION OF NATURE). 2007. *IUCN Red List of Threatened Species*. Switzerland: Gland.

JACKNIS, I. 1985. Franz Boas and exhibits: on the limitations of the museum method of anthropology. In G. W. Stocking (ed.) *Objects and Others: Essays on Museums and Material Culture*. Madison, WI: University of Wisconsin Press, pp. 75–111.

JACKSON, J. B. 1984. *Discovering the Vernacular Landscape*. New Haven, CT: Yale University Press.

JACKSON, M. (ed.) 2005. Sustainability and preservation. *Association for Preservation Technology Bulletin* 36(4): 2–54.

JACKSON, M. D. 1996. Introduction. Phenomenology, radical empiricism, and anthropological critique. In M. D. Jackson (ed.) *Things as They Are: new directions in phenomenological anthropology*. Bloomington IN: University of Indiana Press, pp. 1–50.

JACKSON, P. 1989. *Maps of Meaning: an introduction to cultural geography*. London: Unwin Hyman.

JACKSON, P. 1999. Commodity cultures: the traffic in things, *Transactions of the Institute of British Geographers*, 24(1): 95–108.

JACKSON, P. 2000. Rematerializing social and cultural geography. *Social and Cultural Geography* 1(1): 9–14.

JACKSON, P. 2002. Commercial cultures: transcending the cultural and the economic. *Progress in Human Geography* 26(1): 3–18.

JACKSON, P. and THRIFT, N. J. 1995. Geographies of consumption. In D. Miller (ed.) *Acknowledging Consumption: a review of new studies*. London: Routledge, pp. 204–237.

JACOBS, J. M. 2006. A geography of big things. *Cultural Geographies* 13: 1–27.

JACOBS, J. M. and CAIRNS, S. 2008. The modern touch: interior design and modernisation in post-independence Singapore. *Environment and Planning A* 40: 572–595.

JACOBS, K. 1999. Conclusion. *Urban Studies* 36(1): 203–213.

JACQUES, C. and FREEMAN, M. 1997. *Angkor: cities and temples.* London: Thames and Hudson.

JAFFEE, D., KLOPPENBURG, J. and MONROY, M. 2004. Bringing the 'moral charge' home: fair trade within the North and within the South. *Rural sociology* 69(2): 169–196.

JAMES, A. 1996. Cooking the books. Global and local identities in contemporary British food cultures. In D. Howes (ed.) *Cross-Cultural Consumption: global markets, local realities.* London: Routledge, pp. 77–92.

JAMES, J. 1993. *Consumption and Development.* New York: St Martin's Press.

JAMESON, F. 1984. Postmodernism, or the cultural logic of late capitalism. *New Left Review* 146: 53–92.

JAMIESON, R. 1995. Material culture and social death: African-American burial practices. *Historical Archaeology* 29(4): 39–58.

JARDINE, L. 1996. *Wordly Goods: a new history of the Renaissance.* London: Papermac.

JAYA 2007. Port city: on exchange and mobility. *Mute: culture and politics after the net* http://www.metamute.org/en/port_city_on_exchange_and_mobility (Accessed 20 November 2008).

JAZEEL, T. 2005. Nature, nationhood and the poetics of meaning in Rahuna (Yala) National Park, Sri Lanka. *Cultural Geographies* 12(2): 199–227.

JENKINS, I. 1992. *Archaeologists and Aesthetes in the Sculpture Galleries of the British Museum 1800–1939.* London: British Museum Press.

JENKINS, L. 2002. Geography and architecture: 11, rue du Conservatoire and the permeability of buildings. *Space and Culture* 5(3): 222–236.

JENKINS, R. 1982. Pierre Bourdieu and the reproduction of determinism. *Sociology* 16(2): 270–281.

JENKS, C. 1996. *Childhood.* London: Routledge.

JEROME, J. K. 2004 [1889]. *Three Men in a Boat.* Whitefish, MT: Kessinger Publishing.

JEWELL, P. A. 1963. *The Experimental Earthwork at Overton Down, Wiltshire, 1960.* London: British Association for the Advancement of Science.

JINNAI, H. 1995. *Tokyo: a spatial anthropology* (trans by Kimiko Nishimura). Berkeley: University of California Press.

JOHANSEN, J. P. 1954. *The Maori and His Religion in Its Non-ritualistic Aspects.* København: I kommission hos E. Munksgaard.

JOHNSON, M. H. 1993. *Housing Culture: traditional architecture in an English landscape.* London: UCL Press.

JOHNSON, M. H. 1996. *The Archaeology of Capitalism.* Oxford: Blackwell (Studies in Social Archaeology).

JOHNSON, M. H. 2006. *Ideas of Landscape.* Oxford: Blackwell.

JOHNSON, M. L. 1987. *The Body in the Mind: the bodily basis of meaning, imagination and reason.* Chicago: University of Chicago Press.

JOHNSON, M. L. 2007. *The Meaning of the Body: the aesthetics of human understanding.* Chicago: University of Chicago Press.

JOHNSON, N. C. 2000. Historical geographies of the present. In B. J. Graham and C. Nash (eds) *Modern Historical Geographies.* Harlow: Prentice Hall, pp. 251–272.

JOHNSON, N. C. 2004. Heritage landscapes, geographical imaginations and material cultures: tracing Ulster's past. In T. Mels (ed.) *Reanimating Places: a geography of rhythms.* London: Ashgate, pp. 227–239.

JOINT, L. 2007. Villagers record Napoli experiences. BBC Devon 27 November www.bbc.co.uk/devon/content/articles/2007/09/18/branscombe_project_napoli_feature.shtml   (Accessed 17 November 2008).

JONES, A. M. 2002a. *Archaeological Theory and Scientific Practice.* Cambridge: Cambridge University Press.

JONES, A. M. 2002b. A biography of colour: colour, material histories and personhood in the early Bronze Age of Britain and Ireland. In A. Jones and G. MacGregor (eds) *Colouring the Past: the significance of colour in archaeological research.* Oxford: Berg, pp. 159–174.

JONES, A. M. 2005. Lives in fragments? Personhood and the European Neolithic. *Journal of Social Archaeology* 5: 193–224.

JONES, A. M. 2006. Animated images: agency and landscape in Kilmartin, Argyll, Scotland. *Journal of Material Culture* 11(1–2): 211–225.

JONES, A. M. 2007. *Memory and Material Culture.* Cambridge: Cambridge University Press.

JONES, A. M. 2009. Into the future. In B. Cunliffe, C. Gosden and R. A. Joyce (eds) *The Oxford Handbook of Archaeology.* Oxford: Oxford University Press, pp. 89–114.

JONES, A. M. and MacGregor, G. (eds) 2002. *Colouring the Past: the significance of colour in archaeological research.* Oxford: Berg.

JONES, D. D. 1951. Preface. In C. Fox and F. R. S. Raglan *Monmouthshire Houses: a study of building techniques and smaller house plans in the fifteenth to the seventeenth centuries.* Part I: *Medieval houses.* Cardiff: National Museum of Wales and the Welsh Folk Museum, pp. 1–3.

JONES, D. D. 1953. Preface. In C. Fox and F. R. S. Raglan *Monmouthshire Houses: a study of building techniques and smaller house plans in the fifteenth to the seventeenth centuries.* Part II: *Sub-Medieval houses, c. 1550–1610.* Cardiff: National Museum of Wales and the Welsh Folk Museum, p. 3.

JONES, M. 2006. Landscape, law and justice—concepts and issues. *Norsk Geografisk Tidsskrift* 60: 1–14.

JONES, M. and DAUGSTAD, K. 1997. Usages of the 'cultural landscape' concept in Norwegian and Nordic landscape administration. *Landscape Research* 22(3): 267–281.

JONES, R. and FOWLER, C. 2008. *Placing the Nation: Aberystwyth and the reproduction of Welsh nationalism.* Cardiff: University of Wales.

JONES, R. and WHITE, N. 1988. Point blank: stone tool manufacture at the Ngilipitji quarry, Arnhem Land, 1981. In B. Meehan and R. Jones (eds) *Archaeology with Ethnography: an Australian perspective.* Canberra: Australian National University (Research School of Pacific Studies Occasional Papers in Prehistory 15), pp. 51–87.

JONES, S. 1997. *The Archaeology of Ethnicity: a theoretical perspective.* London: Routledge.

JORDAN, P. and ZVELEBIL, M. 2010. *Ceramics before Farming: the Origins and Dispersal of Pottery among Hunter-Gatherers of Northern Eurasia from 16000BP.* Walnut Creek: Left Coast Press.

JORION, P. 1977. Anthropological fieldwork: forerunners and inventors. *Cambridge Anthropology* 3(2): 22–25.

JOYCE, P. 2003. *The Rule of Freedom: liberalism and the modern city.* London: Verso.

JOYCE, R. A. 1992. Ideology in action: the rhetoric of Classic Maya ritual practice. In A. S. Goldsmith, S. Garvie, D. Selin and J. Smith (eds) *Ancient Images, Ancient Thought: the archaeology of ideology. Papers from the 23rd Chacmool Conference*. Calgary: Department of Archaeology, University of Calgary, pp. 497–506.

JOYCE, R. A. 1996. The construction of gender in Classic Maya monuments. In R. Wright (ed.) *Gender in Archaeology: essays in research and practice*. Philadelphia: University of Pennsylvania Press, pp. 167–195.

JOYCE, R. A. 1998. Performing the body in prehispanic Central America. *RES* 33: 147–165.

JOYCE, R. A. 2000a. Girling the girl and boying the boy: the production of adulthood in ancient Mesoamerica. *World Archaeology* 31(3): 473–483.

JOYCE, R. A. 2000b. *Gender and Power in Prehispanic Mesoamerica*. Austin: University of Texas Press.

JOYCE, R. A. 2001. Ritual and symbolism, archaeology of. In N. J. Smelser and P. B. Baltes (eds) *International Encyclopedia of the Social and Behavioral Sciences* volume 20. Oxford: Elsevier, pp. 13371–13375.

JOYCE, R. A. 2002. Beauty, sexuality, body ornamentation and gender in ancient Meso-America. In S. M. Nelson and M. Rosen-Ayalon (eds) *In Pursuit of Gender: worldwide archaeological approaches*. Walnut Creek, CA: Altamira Press, pp. 81–91.

JOYCE, R. A. 2003. Making something of herself: embodiment in life and death at Playa de los Muertos, Honduras. *Cambridge Archaeological Journal* 13(2): 248–261.

JOYCE, R. A. 2004. Unintended consequences? Monumentality as a novel experience in formative Mesoamerica. *Journal of Archaeological Method and Theory* 11: 5–29.

JOYCE, R. A. 2005. Archaeology of the body. *Annual Review of Anthropology* 34: 139–158.

JOYCE, R. A. 2007. Building houses: the materialization of lasting identity in formative Mesoamerica. In R. Beck (ed.) *The Durable House: house society models in archaeology*. Carbondale: Southern Illinois University (Center for Archaeological Investigations, Occasional Paper No. 35), pp. 53–72.

JOYCE, R. A. 2008a. Practice in and as deposition. In B. J. Mills and W. H. Walker (eds) *Memory Work: archaeologies of material practice*. Sante Fe, NM: School for Advanced Research Press, pp. 25–39.

JOYCE, R. A. 2008b. When the flesh is solid but the person is hollow inside: formal variation in hand-modelled figurines from Formative Mesoamerica. In D. Borić and J. Robb (eds) *Post Bodies. Body-centered research in archaeology*. Oxford: Oxbow Books, pp. 37–45.

JOYCE, R. A. and LOPIPARO, J. 2005. PostScript: doing agency in archaeology. *Journal of Archaeological Method and Theory* 12(4): 365–374.

JUDD, D. 1965. Specific objects. *Arts Yearbook* 8: 74–82.

JULLIEN, F. 2000. *Detour and Access*. New York: Zone Books.

JULLIEN, F. 2007a. *In Praise of Blandness*. New York: Zone Books.

JULLIEN, F. 2007b. *Vital Nourishment. Departing from happiness*. New York: Zone Books.

JURASSIC COAST nd. *South West Coast Path*. http://www.jurassiccoast.com/281/category/south-west-coast-path-149.html (Accessed 17 November 2008).

KAMENETSKY, C. 1972. Folklore as political in Nazi Germany. *Journal of American Folklore* 85: 221–236.

KAMPEN, N. B. (ed.) 1996. *Sexuality in Ancient Art: Near East, Egypt, Greece and Italy*. Cambridge: Cambridge University Press.

KARSKENS, G. 2002. Small things, big pictures: new perspectives from the archaeology of Sydney's Rocks neighbourhood. In A. Mayne and T. Murray (eds) *The Archaeology of Urban Landscapes: explorations in slumland*. Cambridge, Cambridge University Press, pp. 69–85.

KASTNER, J. 1998. Preface. In J. Kastner and B. Wallis (eds) *Land and Environmental Art.* London: Phaidon.

KASTNER, J. and WALLIS, B. (eds) 1998. *Land and Environmental Art.* London: Phaidon.

KAUFMANN, E. 1998. Naturalizing the nation: the rise of naturalistic nationalism in the United States and Canada. *Comparative Studies in Society and History* 40(4): 666–695.

KAWAMURA, S. 1959. The process of sub-cultural propagation among Japanese macaques. *Primates* 2: 43–60.

KAZIM, H. 2007. The night of the treasure hunters. *Spiegel online* (23 January) www.spiegel.de/international/0,1518,461595,00.html (Accessed 1 October 2008).

KEANE, W. 1994. The value of words and the meanings of things in Eastern Indonesian Exchange. *Man* (n.s.) 29(3): 605–629.

KEANE, W. 1997. *Signs of Recognition: powers and hazards of representation in an Indonesian society.* Berkeley: University of California Press.

KEANE, W. 2001. Money is no object: materiality, desire, and modernity in an Indonesian society. In F. R. Myers (ed.) *The Empire of Things: Regimes of Value and Material Culture.* Santa Fe: School of American Research Press, pp. 65–90.

KEANE, W. 2002. Sincerity, 'modernity' and the Protestants. *Cultural Anthropology* 17(1): 65–92.

KEANE, W. 2003. Semiotics and the social analysis of material things. *Language and Communication* 23: 408–425.

KEARNES, M. B. 2003. Geographies that matter: the rhetorical deployment of physicality? *Social and Cultural Geography* 4(2): 139–152.

KEARNES, M. B. 2007. (Re)making matter: design and selection. *Area* 39(2): 143–155.

KEATES, S. 2002. The flashing blade: copper, colour and luminosity in north Italian Copper Age society. In A. Jones and G. MacGregor (eds) *Colouring the Past: The significance of colour in archaeological research.* Oxford: Berg, pp. 109–127.

KEEGAN, J. 1989. *The Second World War.* London: Pimlico.

KEHOE, A. B. 1991. The invention of prehistory. *Current Anthropology* 32: 467–476.

KENT, S (ed.) 1990. *Domestic Architecture and the Use of Spaces: an interdisciplinary cross-cultural study.* Cambridge: Cambridge University Press.

KENT, S. 1984. *Analyzing Activity Areas: an ethnoarchaeological study of the use of space.* Albuquerque: University of New Mexico Press.

KERN, S. 1999. Where did the Indians sleep? An archaeological and ethnohistorical study of mid-eighteenth-century Piedmont Virginia. In M. Franklin and G. Fesler (eds) *Historical Archaeology, Identity Formation, and the Interpretation of Ethnicity.* Williamsburg: Colonial Williamsburg Foundation, pp. 31–46.

KIDDER, A. V. 1932. *The Artifacts of Pecos.* New Haven: Yale University Press (Phillips Academy, Papers of the Southwestern Expedition 6).

KIDDER, A. V. 2000. *An Introduction to Southwestern Archaeology* (new edition). New Haven: Yale University Press.

KILCULLEN, D. J. 2000. The political consequences of military operations in Indonesia 1945–99: a fieldwork analysis of the political power-diffusion effects of guerilla conflict. Unpublished Ph.D. dissertation, Australian Defence Force Academy, University of New South Wales.

KILLICK, D. 2004. Social constructionist approaches to the study of technology. *World Archaeology* 36(4): 571–578.

KINDON, S., PAIN, R. and KESBY, M. (eds) 2008. *Participatory Action Research Approaches and Methods: connecting people, participation and place.* London: Routledge.

KINMAN, E. and WILLIAMS, J. 2007. Domain: collaborating with clay and cartography. *Cultural Geographies* 14(3): 433–444.

KINNES, I. A. and LONGWORTH, I. H. 1985. *Catalogue of the Excavated Prehistoric and Romano-British Material in the Greenwell Collection.* London: British Museum Press.

KLEIN, R. G. 1999. *The Human Career: Human Biological and Cultural Origins.* Chicago: University of Chicago Press.

KLIMT, A. 1989. Returning 'home': Portuguese migrants notions of temporariness, permanence, and commitment. *New German Critique* 46 (Winter): 47–70.

KLIMT, A. 2000. Enacting national selves: authenticity, adventure, and disaffection in the Portuguese diaspora. *Identities* 11(2): 513–550.

KLIMT, A. and LEAL, J. 2005. Introduction: the politics of folk culture in the Lusophone world. *Etnográfica* 9(1): 5–17.

KLINGMANN, A. 2007. *Brandscapes. Architecture in the experience economy.* Cambridge, MA: MIT Press.

KNAPPETT, C. 1999. Tradition and innovation in pottery forming technology; wheel-throwing at Middle Minoan Knossos. *Annual of the British School at Athens* 94: 101–129.

KNAPPETT, C. 2002. Photographs, skeuomorphs and marionettes: some thoughts on mind, agency and object. *Journal of Material Culture* 7(1): 97–117.

KNAPPETT, C. 2004. The affordances of things: a post-Gibsonian perspective on the relationality of mind and matter. In E. DeMarrais, C. Gosden and A. C. Renfrew (eds) *Rethinking Materiality: the engagement of mind with the material world.* Cambridge: McDonald Institute for Archaeological Research, pp. 43–51.

KNAPPETT, C. 2005. *Thinking Through Material Culture.* Philadelphia: University of Pennsylvania Press.

KNAPPETT, C. 2006. Beyond skin: layering and networking in art and archaeology. *Cambridge Archaeological Journal* 16(2): 239–251.

KNAPPETT, C. 2008. Protopalatial Crete: the material culture. In C. Shelmerdine (ed.) *The Cambridge Companion to the Aegean Bronze Age.* Cambridge: Cambridge University Press, pp. 121–139.

KNAPPETT, C. and MALAFOURIS, L. 2008a. Material and nonhuman agency: an introduction. In C. Knappett and L. Malafouris (eds) *Material Agency: towards a non-anthropocentric approach.* New York: Springer, pp. ix–xix.

KNAPPETT, C. and MALAFOURIS, L. (eds) 2008b. *Material Agency: towards a non-anthropocentric approach.* New York: Springer.

KNAPPETT, C. and NIKOLAKOPOULO, I. 2008. Colonialism without colonies? A Bronze Age case study from Akrotiri, Thera. *Hesperia* 77: 1–42.

KNAPPETT, C. and VAN DER LEEUW, S., nd. Innovation as distributed cognition: archaeological and inter disciplinary perspectives (manuscript currently under review).

KNAUFT, B. M. 1989. Bodily images in Melanesia: cultural substance and natural metaphors. In M. Feher (ed.) *Fragments for a History of the Human Body 3.* New York: Zone, pp. 192–279.

KNIFFEN, F. 1936. Louisiana house types. *Annals of the Association of American Geographers* 26: 179–193.

KNIFFEN, F. 1965. Folk housing: key to diffusion. *Annals of the Association of American Geographers* 55: 549–577.

KNIFFEN, F. 1986 [1965]. Folk housing: key to diffusion. In D. Upon and J. M. Vlach (eds) *Common Places: reading in American vernacular architecture*. Athens, GA: University of Georgia Press, pp. 3–26.

KNIFFEN, F. and GLASSIE, H. 1966. Building in wood in the Eastern United States: a time–place perspective. *Geographical Review* 56: 40–66.

KNORR-CETINA, K. D. 1981. *The Manufacture of Knowledge: an essay on the constructivist and contextual nature of science*. Oxford: Pergamon.

KNORR-CETINA, K. D. 1999. *Epistemic Cultures: how the sciences make knowledge*. Cambridge, MA: Harvard University Press.

KNORR-CETINA, K. D. and PREDA, A. 2005. *The Sociology of Financial Markets*. Oxford: Oxford University Press.

KOEHL, R. B. 2006. *Aegean Bronze Age Rhyta*. Prehistory Monographs 19. Philadelphia, PA: INSTAP Academic Press.

KONVITZ, J. W. 1990. Why cities don't die. *Invention and Technology* 5(3): 58–63.

KOOPS, K., HUMLE, T., STERCK, E. H. M. and MATSUZAWA, T. 2007. Ground-nesting by the chimpanzees of the Nimba Mountains, Guinea: environmentally or socially determined? *American Journal of Primatology* 69: 1–13.

KOPYTOFF, I. 1986. The cultural biography of things: commoditization as a process. In A. Appadurai (ed.) *The Social Life of Things*. Cambridge: Cambridge University Press, pp. 64–91.

KOSTOF, S. 1985. *A History of Architecture: settings and rituals*. New York: Oxford University Press.

KOTHARI, U. and LAURIE, N. 2005. Different bodies, same clothes: an agenda for local consumption and global identities. *Area* 37(2): 223–227.

KRAMER, C. (ed.) 1979. *Ethnoarchaeology*. Albuquerque: University of New Mexico Press.

KRAMER, C. 1985. Ceramic ethnoarchaeology. *Annual Review of Anthropology* 14: 77–102.

KRAUSE, R. 1972. *The Leavenworth Site: archaeology of an historic Arikara community*. Lawrence: University of Kansas (University of Kansas Publications in Anthropology 3).

KRISTEVA, J. 1982. *Powers of Horror: an essay on abjection*. New York: Columbia University Press.

KRISTIANSEN, K. 1985. A short history of Danish archaeology. In K. Kristiansen (ed.) *Archaeological Formation Processes*. Copenhagen: National Museum, pp. 12–34.

KROEBER, A. L. 1917. The superorganic. *American Anthropologist* 19(2): 163–213.

KROEBER, A. L. 1928. Sub-human culture beginnings. *Quarterly Review of Biology* 3: 325–342.

KROEBER, A. L. and C. KLUCKHOHN. 1952. Culture: a critical review of concepts and definitions. *Papers of the Peabody Museum of American Archaeology and Ethnology* 47: 1–223.

KUBLER, G. 1962. *The Shape of Time: remarks on the history of things*. New Haven: Yale University Press.

KÜCHLER, S. 2002a. The anthropology of art. In V. Buchli (ed.) *The Material Culture Reader*. Oxford: Berg, pp. 57–62.

KÜCHLER, S. 2002b. *Malanggan: art, memory and sacrifice*. Oxford: Berg.

KÜCHLER, S. 2008. Technological materiality: beyond the dualist paradigm. *Theory, Culture and Society* 25(1): 101–120.

KÜCHLER, S., and MILLER, D. (eds) 2005. *Clothing as Material Culture*. Oxford: Berg.

KUHN, S. 2004. Evolutionary perspectives on technology and technological change. *World Archaeology* 36(4): 561–570.

KUHN, T. S. 1970. *The Structure of Scientific Revolutions*. Chicago: Chicago University Press.

KUKLICK, H. 1997. After Ishmael: the fieldwork tradition and its future. In A. Gupta and J. Ferguson (eds) *Anthropological Locations: boundaries and grounds of a science.* Berkeley: University of California Press, pp. 47–65.

KUMMER, H. 1971. *Primate Societies: group techniques of ecological adaptation.* Chicago: Aldine.

KUNEN, J. L., GALINDO, M. J. and CHASE, E. 2002. Pits and bones: identifying Maya ritual behavior in the archaeological record. *Ancient Mesoamerica* 13: 197–211.

KUPER, A. 2003. The return of the native. *Current Anthropology* 44(3): 389–402.

KURATH, H. 1939. *Handbook of the Linguistic Geography of New England.* 3 vols. Providence: Brown University Press.

KURATH, H. 1949. *A Word Geography of the Eastern United States.* Ann Arbor: University of Michigan Press.

KURLANSKY, M. 1997. *Cod: a biography of the fish that changed the world.* New York: Walker.

KURLANSKY, M. 2002. *Salt: a world history.* London: Jonathan Cape.

KUS, S. 1992. Towards an archaeology of body and soul. In J-C. Gardin and C. Peebles (eds) *Representations in Archaeology.* Bloomington: Indiana University Press, pp. 168–177.

KUZMIN, Y. V. 2006. Chronology of the earliest pottery in East Asia: progress and pitfalls. *Antiquity* 80: 362–371.

KWA, C. 2002. Romantic and baroque conceptions of complex wholes in the sciences. In J. Law and A. Mol (eds) *Complexities: social studies of knowledge practices.* Durham, NC: Duke University Press, pp. 23–52.

KWOLEK-FOLLAND, A. 1995. Gender as a category of analysis in vernacular architecture studies. In E. Cromley and C. Hudgins (eds) *Gender, Class, and Shelter: perspectives in vernacular architecture V.* Knoxville, TN: University of Tennessee Press, pp. 3–10.

DE LAET, M. and MOL, A. 2000. The Zimbabwe Bush Pump: mechanics of a fluid technology. *Social Studies of Science* 30(2): 225–263.

LAFONTAINE, J. S. 1985. Person and individual: some anthropological reflections. In M. Carrithers, S. Collins and S. Lukes (eds) *The Category of the Person: anthropology, philosophy, history.* Cambridge: Cambridge University Press, pp. 123–140.

LAIDLAW, J. 2000. A free gift makes no friends. *Journal of the Royal Anthropological Institute* (n.s.) 6(4): 617–634.

LAING, R. D. 1967. *The Politics of Experience.* New York: Pantheon.

LAIRD, M. 1999. *The Flowering of the Landscape Garden: English pleasure grounds, 1720–1800.* Philadelphia: University of Pennsylvania Press.

LAKOFF, G. 1987. *Women, Fire, and Dangerous Things: what categories reveal about the mind.* Chicago: University of Chicago Press.

LAKOFF, G. and JOHNSON, M. L. 1980. *Metaphors We Live By.* Chicago: University of Chicago Press.

LAKOFF, G. and JOHNSON, M. L. 1999. *Philosophy in the Flesh: the embodied mind and its challenge to Western thought.* New York: Basic Books.

LAKOFF, G. and TURNER, M. 1989. *More than Cool Reason: a field guide to poetic metaphor.* Chicago: University of Chicago Press.

LAKOFF, G. and NÚÑEZ, R. 2000. *Where Mathematics Comes From: how the embodied mind brings mathematics into being.* New York: Basic Books.

LALAND, K. N. and KENDAL, J. R. 2003. What models say about social learning. In D. M. Fragaszy and S. Perry (eds) *The Biology of Traditions: models and evidence.* Cambridge: Cambridge University Press, pp. 33–55.

LALAND, K. N. and JANIK, V. M. 2006. The animal cultures debate. *Trends In Ecology and Evolution* 21(10): 542–547.

LALOR, M. 2000. *Wherever I go: Myles Lalor's 'oral history'* (ed. J. Beckett). Carlton South: Melbourne University Press.

LaMOTTA, V. and SCHIFFER, M. B. 2001. Behavioral archaeology: toward a new synthesis. In I. Hodder (ed.) *Archaeological Theory Today*. Oxford: Blackwell, pp. 14–64.

LaMOTTA, V. M. and SCHIFFER, M. B. 1999. Formation processes of house floor assemblages. In P. Allison (ed.) *The Archaeology of Household Activities*. London: Routledge, pp. 19–29.

LAMPLUGH, G. W. 1906. Notes on the occurrence of stone implements in the Valley of the Zambesi around Victoria Falls. *Journal of the Anthropological Institute of Great Britain and Ireland* 36: 159–169.

LANDAU, R. 1968. *New Directions in British Architecture*. London: Studio Vista.

LANE, P. 2006. Present to past: ethnoarchaeology. In C. Tilley, W. Keane, S. Küchler, M. J. Rowlands and P. Spyer (eds) *Handbook of Material Culture*. London: Sage, pp. 402–424.

LAQUEUR, T. W. 1990. *Making Sex: body and gender from the Greeks to Freud*. Cambridge, MA: Harvard University Press.

LARSON, E. 2000. *Isaac's Storm: a man, a time, and the deadliest hurricane in history*. New York: Vintage.

LASH, S. and LURY, C. 2007. *Global Culture Industry: the mediation of things*. Cambridge: Polity Press.

LASSNER, J. 1970. *Topography of Baghdad in the Early Middle Ages: texts and studies*. Detroit, MI: Wayne State University Press.

LAST, J. 1995. The nature of history. In I. Hodder, M. Shanks, A. Alexandri, V. Buchli, J. Carman, J. Last and G. Lucas (eds) *Interpreting Archaeology: finding meaning in the past*. London: Routledge, pp. 141–157.

LATHAM, A. and McCORMACK, D. 2004. Moving cities: rethinking the materialities of urban geographies. *Progress in Human Geography* 28(6): 701–724.

LATOUR, B. 1983. Give me a laboratory and I will raise the world. In K. D. Knorr-Cetina and M. Mulkay (eds) *Science Observed: perspectives on the social study of science*. Beverly Hills: Sage, pp. 141–170.

LATOUR, B. 1987. *Science in Action: how to follow scientists and engineers through society* (trans. C. Porter). Cambridge, MA: Harvard University Press.

LATOUR, B. 1988a. Part One: War and peace of microbes. In *The Pasteurization of France* (trans. A. Sheridan and J. Law). Cambridge, MA: Harvard University Press, pp. 3–150.

LATOUR, B. 1988b. Part Two: Irréductions. In *The Pasteurization of France* (trans. A. Sheridan and J. Law). Cambridge, MA: Harvard University Press, pp. 153–236.

LATOUR, B. 1991. Technology is society made durable. In J. Law (ed.) *A Sociology of Monsters? Essays on power, technology and domination*. London: Routledge (Sociological Review Monograph 38), pp. 103–131.

LATOUR, B. 1992. Where are the missing masses? the sociology of a few mundane artefacts. In W. Bijker and J. Law (eds) *Shaping Technology*. Cambridge, MA: MIT Press, pp. 225–258.

LATOUR, B. 1993a. *We Have Never Been Modern* (trans. C. Porter). Cambridge, MA: Harvard University Press.

LATOUR, B. 1993b. On technical mediation. *Common Knowledge* 3(2): 29–64.

LATOUR, B. 1999a. On recalling ANT. In J. Law and J. Hassard (eds) *Actor-Network Theory and After*. Oxford: Blackwell.

LATOUR, B. 1999b. *Pandora's Hope: essays on the reality of science studies.* Cambridge, MA: Harvard University Press.

LATOUR, B. 1999c. Factures/fracture: from the concept of network to the concept of attachment. *RES* 36: 20–31.

LATOUR, B. 2000a. When things strike back: a possible contribution of 'science studies' to the social sciences. *British Journal of Sociology* 51(1): 107–123.

LATOUR, B. 2000b. The Berlin key or how to do things with words. In P. Graves-Brown (ed.) *Matter, Materiality and Modern Culture.* London: Routledge, pp. 10–21.

LATOUR, B. 2002. What is Iconoclash? Or is there a world beyond the image wars? In B. Latour and P. Weibel (eds) *Iconoclash.* Karlsruhe and Cambridge, MA: ZKM/MIT Press, pp. 13–38.

LATOUR, B. 2004a. Why has critique run out of steam? From matters of fact to matters of concern. *Critical Inquiry* 30: 225–248.

LATOUR, B. 2004b. *The Politics of Nature: how to bring the sciences into democracy* (trans. C. Porter). Cambridge, MA: Harvard University Press.

LATOUR, B. 2004c. How to talk about the body? The normative dimension of science studies. *Body and Society* 10: 205–229.

LATOUR, B. 2005a. *Reassembling the Social: an introduction to Actor-Network Theory.* Oxford: Oxford University Press.

LATOUR, B. 2005b. From realpolitik to dingpolitik or how to make things public. In B. Latour and P. Weibel (eds) *Making Things Public—Atmospheres of Democracy.* Cambridge, MA: MIT Press, pp. 4–31.

LATOUR, B. 2007. Can we get our materialism back, please? *Isis* 98(1): 138–142.

LATOUR, B. and VENN, C. 2002. Morality and technology: the end of the means. *Theory, Culture and Society* 19(5–6): 247–260.

LATOUR, B. and WEIBEL, P. (eds) 2002. *Iconoclash: beyond the image wars in science, religion and art.* Cambridge, MA: MIT Press.

LATOUR, B. and WEIBEL, P. (eds) 2005. *Making Things Public: atmospheres of democracy.* Cambridge, MA: MIT Press.

LATOUR, B. and WOOLGAR, S. 1979. *Laboratory Life: the construction of scientific facts.* Beverly Hills: Sage.

LATOUR, B. and WOOLGAR, S. 1986. *Laboratory Life: the construction of scientific facts* (second edition). Princeton, Princeton University Press.

LAUGIER, M-A. 1977. *An Essay on Architecture.* Los Angeles: Hennessy and Ingalls.

LAUWERS, P., SIMONI-AUREMBOU, M-R. and SWIGGERS, P. 2002. *Géographie Linguistique et Biologique du Langage: Autour de Jules Gilliéron.* Dudley, MA: Peeters Publishers.

LAVIOLETTE, P. and HANSON, J. 2007. Home is where the heart stopped: panopticism, chronic disease, and the domestication of assistive technology. *Home Cultures* 4(1): 1–20.

LAW, J. 1986a. On the methods of long distance control: vessels, navigation and the Portuguese route to India. In J. Law (ed.) *Power, Action and Belief: a new sociology of knowledge?* London: Routledge and Kegan Paul (Sociological Review Monograph 32), pp. 234–263.

LAW, J. 1986b. Laboratories and texts. In M. Callon, J. Law and A. Rip (eds) *Mapping the Dynamics of Science and Technology: sociology of science in the real world.* London: Macmillan, pp. 35–50.

LAW, J. 1992. Notes on the theory of the actor-network: ordering, strategy and heterogeneity. *Systems Practice* 5: 379–393.

LAW, J. 1994. *Organizing Modernity.* Oxford: Blackwell.

LAW, J. 2002. *Aircraft Stories: decentering the object in technoscience.* Durham, NC: Duke University Press.

LAW, J. 2004. *After Method: mess in social science research.* London: Routledge.

LAW, J. and MOL, A. 2001. Situating technoscience: an inquiry into spatialities. *Society and Space* 19: 609–621.

LAW, J. and HASSARD, J. (eds) 1999. *Actor-Network Theory and After.* Oxford: Blackwell.

LAW, J. and SINGLETON, V. 2005. Object lessons. *Organization* 12(3): 331–355.

LAWRENCE, S. (ed.) 2003. *Archaeologies of the British: explorations of identity in Great Britain and its colonies 1600–1945.* London: Routledge (One World Archaeology 46).

LAYTON, R. 1981. *The Anthropology of Art.* St Albans: Granade.

LAYTON, R. 1991. The political use of Australian Aboriginal body painting and its archaeological implications. In I. Hodder (ed.) *The Meanings of Things.* London: Routledge (One World Archaeology 6), pp. 1–11.

LAYTON, R. 2003. Art and agency: a reassessment. *Journal of the Royal Anthropological Institute* (n.s.) 9(3): 447–464.

LAYTON, R., SHENNAN, S. and STONE, P. 2006. Introduction. In P. J. Ucko, R. Layton, S. Shennan and P. G. Stone (eds) *A Future for Archaeology.* London: Routledge Cavendish, pp. 1–6.

LE BILLON, P. 2006. Fatal transactions: conflict diamonds and the (anti)terrorist consumer. *Antipode* 38(4): 778–801.

LE CORBUSIER 1986. *Towards a New Architecture.* New York: Dover Publications.

LE GOFF, J. 1989. Head or heart? The political use of body metaphors in the Middle Ages. In M. Feher (ed.) *Fragments for a History of the Human Body.* New York: Zone, pp. 12–26.

LE MIÈRE, M. and PICON, M. 1987. Productions Locales et Circulation des Céramiques au VIe millénaire, au Proche-Orient. *Paléorient* 13(2): 133–147.

LE MIÈRE, M. and PICON, M. 1999. Les Débuts de la Céramique au Proche-Orient. *Paléorient* 24(2): 5–26.

LEACH, E. 1961. *Rethinking Anthropology.* London: Athlone Press.

LEACH, E. 1973. Concluding address. In A. C. Renfrew (ed.) *The Explanation of Culture Change: models in prehistory.* London: Duckworth, pp. 761–771.

LEACH, E. 1977. A view from the bridge. In M. Spriggs (ed.) *Archaeology and Anthropology.* Oxford: British Archaeological Reports (BAR supplementary series 19), pp. 161–176.

LEACH, E. 1978. Does space syntax really constitute the social? In D. Green, C. Haselgrove and M. Spriggs (eds) *Social Organisation and Settlement.* Oxford: British Archaeological Reports (International Series 47: ii), pp. 343–385.

LEACH, J. 2007. Differentiation and encompassment: a critique of Alfred Gell's theory of the abduction of agency. In A. Henare, S. Wastell and M. Holbraad (eds) *Thinking Through Things: theorising artefacts ethnographically.* London: Routledge, pp. 167–188.

LEACH, J. W. and LEACH, E. (eds) 1983. *The Kula: new perspectives on Massim exchange.* Cambridge: Cambridge University Press.

LEACH, W. R. 1993. *Land of Desire: merchants, power, and the rise of a new American culture.* New York: Pantheon Books.

LEBEUF, J-P. 1961. *L'Habitation des Fali, montagnards du Cameroun septentrional: Technologie, sociologie, mythologie, symbolisme.* Paris: Hachette.

LECA, J. B., NAHALLAGE, C. A. D., GUNST, N. and HUFFMAN, M. A. 2008. Stone-throwing by Japanese macaques: form and functional aspects of group-specific behavioral tradition. *Journal of Human Evolution* 55: 989–998.

LECA, J. B., GUNST, N. and HUFFMAN, M. A. 2007. Japanese macaque cultures: Inter- and intra-troop behavioural variability of stone handling patterns across 10 troops. *Behaviour* 144: 251–281.

LECHTMAN, H. 1977. Style in technology: some early thoughts. In H. Lechtman and R. Merrill (eds) *Material Culture: styles, organization and dynamics of technology. Proceedings of the American Ethnological Society for 1975.* St Paul: West Publishing Company, 3–20.

LECHTMAN, H. 1984. Andean value systems and the development of prehistoric metallurgy. *Technology and Culture* 15: 1–36.

LEDER, D. 1990. *The Absent Body.* Chicago: University of Chicago Press.

LEE, M. M. 2000. Deciphering gender in Minoan dress. In A. E. Rautman (ed.) *Reading the Body. Representations and remains in the archaeological record.* Philadelphia: University of Pennsylvania Press, pp. 111–123.

LEE, R. 2000. Shelter from the storm? Geographies of regard in the worlds of horticultural consumption and production. *Geoforum* 31: 137–157.

LEES, L. 2002. Rematerializing geography: the 'new' urban geography. *Progress in Human Geography* 26(1): 101–112.

LEFEBVRE, H. 1991. *The Production of Space* (trans. D. Nicholson-Smith). Oxford: Blackwell.

LEHMER, D., WOOD, W. and DILL, C. 1978. The Knife River Phase. Unpublished Manuscript on file at Midwest Archaeological Center, National Park Service, Lincoln, Nebraska.

LEKAN, T. and ZELLER, T. 2005. The landscape of German environmental history. In T. Lekan and T. Zeller (eds) *Germany's Nature. Cultural landscapes and environmental history.* New Brunswick: Rutgers University Press, pp. 1–16.

LELE, V. P. 2006. Material habits, identity, semeiotic. *Journal of Social Archaeology* 6(1): 48–70.

LEMONNIER, P. 1986. The study of material culture today: toward an anthropology of technical systems. *Journal of Anthropological Archaeology* 5: 147–186.

LEMONNIER, P. 1992. *Elements for an Anthropology of Technology.* Michigan: University of Michigan (Museum of Anthropology, Anthropological Paper No. 88).

LEMONNIER, P. (ed.) 1993. *Technological Choices. Transformation in material cultures since the Neolithic.* London: Routledge.

LEONE, M. P. 1972. Issues in Contemporary Archaeology. In M. P. Leone (ed.) *Contemporary Archaeology: a guide to theory and contributions.* Carbondale, IL: Southern Illinois University Press, pp. 14–27.

LEONE, M. P. 1977. The new Mormon Temple in Washington D.C. In L. Ferguson (ed.) *Historical Archaeology and the Importance of Material Things.* Tucson, AZ: Society for Historical Archaeology, pp. 43–61.

LEONE, M. P. 1982. Commentary: Childe's offspring. In I. Hodder (ed.) *Structural and Symbolic Archaeology.* Cambridge: Cambridge University Press, pp. 179–184.

LEONE, M. P. 2005. *The Archaeology of Liberty in an American Capital: excavations in Annapolis.* Berkeley: University of California Press.

LEROI-GOURHAN, A. 1943. *Evolution et Techniques: L'homme et la matière.* Paris: Albin Michel.

LEROI-GOURHAN, A. 1945. *Evolution et Techniques: milieu et techniques.* Paris: Albin Michel.

LEROI-GOURHAN, A. 1964. *Le Geste et la Parole* (two volumes). Paris: Albin Michel.

LEROI-GOURHAN, A. 1989. *The Hunters of Prehistory* (trans. C. Jacobson). New York: Atheneum.

LEROI-GOURHAN, A. 1993. *Gesture and Speech* (trans. A. Bostock Berger). Cambridge, MA: MIT Press.

LESLIE, D. and REIMER, S. 1999. Spatializing commodity chains. *Progress in Human Geography* 23(3): 401–420.

LÉVI-STRAUSS, C. 1936. Contribution a l'Etude de l'Organisation Sociale des Indiens Bororo. *Journal de la Societe des Americanistes* 28: 269–304.

LÉVI-STRAUSS, C. 1963. *Structural Anthropology* (volume 1) (trans. C. Jacobson and B. Grundfest Schoepf). New York: Basic Books.

LÉVI-STRAUSS, C. 1964. *Totemism* (trans. R. Needham). London: Merlin Press.

LÉVI-STRAUSS, C. 1966a. *The Savage Mind.* Chicago: Chicago University Press.

LÉVI-STRAUSS, C. 1966b. *The Raw and the Cooked: introduction to a science of mythology 1.* London: Penguin.

LÉVI-STRAUSS, C. 1978. *The Origin of Table Manners* (trans. J. Weightman and D. Weightman). Chicago: University of Chicago Press.

LÉVI-STRAUSS, C. 1982. *The Way of the Masks* (trans. S. Modelski). Seattle: University of Washington Press.

LÉVI-STRAUSS. C. 2001. *An Introduction to the Work of Marcel Mauss* (trans. F. Baker). London: Routledge.

LEVINE, P. 1986. *The Amateur and the Professional: antiquarians, historians and archaeologists in Victorian England, 1836–1886.* Cambridge: Cambridge University Press.

LEVY, S. 2001. *Hackers: heroes of the computer revolution* (2nd edition). Harmondsworth: Penguin Books.

LEWIS-WILLIAMS, D. J. 1981. *Believing and Seeing: symbolic meanings in southern San Rock painting.* London: Academic Press.

LeWITT, S. 1969. Sentences on conceptual art. *Art-Language* 1: 11–13.

LEYSHON, A., LEE, R. and WILLIAMS, C. (eds) 2003. *Alternative economic spaces.* London: Sage.

LIGER D'AUXERRE, L. 1706. The compleat florist or, The universal culture of flowers, trees and shrubs. In F. Gentil (ed.) *Le jardinier solitaire: the solitary or Carthusian gard'ner, being dialogues between a gentleman and a gard'ner.* London: Printed for Benj. Tooke (unpaginated).

LIGHTFOOT, K. G. 1995. Culture contact studies: redefining the relationship between prehistoric and historic archaeology. *American Antiquity* 60: 199–217.

LIGHTFOOT, K. G. 2006. Missions, furs, gold, and manifest destiny: rethinking an archaeology of colonialism for western North America. In M. Hall and S. W. Silliman (eds) *Historical Archaeology.* Oxford: Blackwell, pp. 272–292.

LILLEY, I. 2000. Professional attitudes to indigenous interests in the Native Title era: settler societies compared. In I. Lilley (ed.), *Native Title and the Transformation of archaeology in a Postcolonial World.* Sydney: Oceania Publications, pp. 99–120.

LILLEY, I. 2006. Archaeology, diaspora and decolonization. *Journal of Social Archaeology* 6(1): 28–47.

LILLEY, I. and WILLIAMS, M. 2005. Archaeological significance and indigenous knowledge: a view from Australia. In C. Mathers, T. Darvill and B. Little (eds) *Heritage of Value, Archaeology of Renown: reshaping archaeological assessment and significance.* Gainesville: University of Florida Press, pp. 227–257.

LINDBORG, R. 2006. Recreating grasslands in Swedish rural landscapes—effects of seed sowing and management history. *Biodiversity and Conservation* 15: 957–969.

LINTON, R. 1923. *The Material Culture of the Marquesas Islands.* Honolulu, HI: Bishop Museum Press (Memoirs of the Bernice Pauahi Bishop Museum 8, number 5).

LiPuma, E. 1998. Modernity and forms of personhood in Melanesia. In M. Lambek and A. J. Strathern (eds) *Bodies and Persons: comparative views from Africa and Melanesia*. Cambridge: Cambridge University Press, pp. 53–79.

Lock, M. 2002. The social life of human organs. In *Twice Dead: organ transplants and the reinvention of death*. Berkeley: University of California Press, pp. 315–346.

Löfgren, O. 1997. Scenes from a troubled marriage: Swedish ethnology and material culture studies. *Journal of Material Culture* 2(1): 95–113.

Long, P. O. 2001. *Openness, Secrecy, Authorship Technical Arts and the Culture of Knowledge from Antiquity to the Renaissance*. Baltimore: Johns Hopkins University Press.

Longacre, W. 1964. Archeology as anthropology: a case study. *Science* 144(3625): 1454–1455.

Longacre, W. and Skibo, J. (eds) 1994. *Kalinga Ethnoarchaeology: expanding archaeological method and theory*. Washington, DC: Smithsonian Institution Press.

Longstreth, R. 1986. Compositional types in American commercial architecture. In C. Wells (ed.), *Perspectives in Vernacular Architecture II*. Columbia: University of Missouri Press, pp. 12–23.

Lonsdorf, E. V. 2005. Sex differences in the development of termite-fishing skills in the wild chimpanzees, *Pan troglodytes schweinfurthii*, of Gombe National Park, Tanzania. *Animal Behaviour* 70: 673–683.

Lonsdorf, E. V. 2006. What is the role of mothers in the acquisition of termite-fishing behaviors in wild chimpanzees (*Pan troglodytes schweinfurthii*)? *Animal Cognition* 9(1): 36–46.

Looper, M. G. 2003. From inscribed bodies to distributed persons: contextualizing Tairona figural images in performance. *Cambridge Archaeological Journal* 13: 25–40.

Loraux, N. 1989. Therefore Socrates is immortal. In M. Feher (ed.) *Fragments for a History of the Human Body Part One*. New York: Zone Books, pp. 12–45.

Loren, D. D. 2001. Social Skins: Orthodoxies and practices of dressing in the early colonial Lower Mississippi Valley. *Journal of Social Archaeology* 1: 172–189.

Lorimer, J. and Whatmore, S. 2009. After the 'king of the beasts': historical geographies of elephant hunting in mid-nineteenth century Ceylon. *Journal of Historical Geography* 35: 668–689.

Lounsbury, C. 1997. The dynamic of architectural design in eighteenth-century Charleston and the Lowcountry. In A. Adams and S. McMurry (eds) *Exploring Everyday Landscapes: perspectives in vernacular architecture VII*. Knoxville, TN: University of Tennessee Press, pp. 58–72.

Lounsbury, C. 2005. *The Courthouses of Early Virginia*. Charlottesville: University Press of Virginia.

Lovejoy, P. E. 1983. *Transformations in Slavery: a history of slavery in Africa*. Cambridge: Cambridge University Press.

Lovejoy, P. E. and Richardson, D. 2003. Anglo-Efik relations and protection against illegal enslavement at Old Calabar, 1740–1807. In S. A. Diouf (ed.) *Fighting the Slave Trade: West African strategies*. Athens, OH: Ohio University Press, pp. 101–118.

Low, S. 1997. Urban fear: building the fortress city. *City and Society* 9(1): 53–71.

Lowenthal, D. 1985. *The Past is a Foreign Country*. Cambridge: Cambridge University Press.

Lowenthal, D. 1998. *The Heritage Crusade and the Spoils of History*. Cambridge: Cambridge University Press.

Lowie, R. 1922. *The Material Culture of the Crow Indians*. New York: American Museum of Natural History.

LUBAR, S. and KINGERY, W. (eds) 1993. *History from Things: essays on material culture.* Washington, DC: Smithsonian Institution Press.

LUBBOCK, J. 1865. *Pre-Historic Times: as illustrated by ancient remains and the manners and customs of modern savages.* London: Williams and Norgate.

LUCAS, G. 2001a. *Critical Approaches to Fieldwork: contemporary and historical archaeological practice.* London: Routledge.

LUCAS, G. 2001b. Destruction and the rhetoric of excavation. *Norwegian Archaeological Review,* 34(1): 35–46.

LUCAS, G. 2008. Time and the archaeological event. *Cambridge Archaeological Journal* 18(1): 59–65.

LUCY, S. 2005. Ethnic and cultural identities. In M. Diaz-Andreu, S. Lucy, S. Babić and D. Edwards (eds) *The Archaeology of Identity: approaches to gender, age, status, ethnicity and religion.* London: Routledge, pp. 86–109.

LUPTON, D. 1998. Going with the flow. Some central discourses in conceptualizing and articulating the embodiment of emotional states. In S. Nettleton and J. Watson (eds) *The Body in Everyday Life.* London: Routledge, pp. 82–99.

LYCETT, S. J., COLLARD, M. and McGREW, W. C. 2007. Phylogenetic analyses of behavior support existence of culture among wild chimpanzees. *Proceedings of the National Academy of Sciences of the United States of America* 104(45): 17588–17592.

LYELL, C. 1935. The Bakerian Lecture: on the proofs of a gradual rising of the land in certain parts of Sweden. *Philosophical Transactions of the Royal Society of London* 12: 1–38.

LYMAN, R. and O'BRIEN, M. 1999. Americanist stratigraphic excavation and the measurement of culture change. *Journal of Archaeological Method and Theory,* 6: 55–108.

LYNCH, M. 1985a. Discipline and the material form of images: an analysis of scientific visibility. *Social Studies of Science* 15: 37–66.

LYNCH, M. 1985b. *Art and Artifact in Laboratory Science: a study of shop work and shop talk in a research laboratory.* London: Routledge and Kegan Paul.

LYNCH, M. and WOOLGAR, S. (eds) 1990. *Representation in Scientific Practice.* Cambridge, MA: MIT Press.

LYONS, C. L. and PAPADOPOULOS, J. K. (eds) 2002. *The Archaeology of Colonialism: issues and debates.* Los Angeles, CA: Getty Publications.

MABEY, R. 1996. *Flora Britannica.* London: Sinclair and Stevenson.

MACA, A., REYMAN, J. and FLOAN, W. (eds) 2009. *Prophet, Pariah and Pioneer: Walter W. Taylor and dissension in American archaeology.* Boulder, CO: University Press of Colorado.

McATACKNEY, L., PALUS, M. and PICCINI, A. (eds) 2007. *Contemporary and Historical Archaeology in Theory.* Oxford: Archaeopress (British Archaeological Reports International Series 1677).

McBRYDE, I. 1978. *Records of times past: ethnohistorical essays on the culture and ecology of the New England tribes.* Canberra: Australian Institute of Aboriginal Studies.

McCLAIN, J. L. and MERRIMAN, J. M. 1994. Edo and Paris: cities and power. In J. L. McClain, J. M. Merriman and U. Kaoru (eds) *Edo and Paris: urban life and the state in the early modern era.* Ithaca: Cornell University Press, pp. 3–38.

McCLAIN, J. L. 1994. Edobashi: power, space and popular culture in Edo. In J. L. McClain, J. M. Merriman and U. Kaoru (eds) *Edo and Paris: urban life and the state in the early modern era.* Ithaca: Cornell University Press, pp. 105–131.

MacCLANCY, J. 1988. A natural curiosity: the British market in primitive art. *RES* 15: 563–576.

MacCLANCY, J. 1995. Brief Encounter: the meeting, in Mass-Observation, of British surrealism and popular anthropology. *Journal of the Royal Anthropological Institute* 1(3): 495–512.

McCracken, G. 1989. Homeyness. In E. Hirschman (ed.) *Interpretive Consumer Research*. Provo, UT: Association for Consumer Research, pp. 168–183.

McCracken, G. D. 1988. *Culture and Consumption: new approaches to the symbolic character of consumer goods and activities*. Bloomington: Indiana University Press.

McDaniel, G. 1978. Review of Henry Glassie 'Folk housing in middle Virginia: a structural analysis of historic artifacts'. *Journal of American Folklore* 91(361): 851–853.

McDaniel, G. 1982. *Hearth and Home: preserving a people's culture*. Philadelphia: Temple University Press.

MacDonald, C. F. and Knappett, C. 2007. *Knossos: Protopalatial deposits in Early Magazine A and the South-west Houses*. London: British School at Athens Supplementary Volume no. 41.

McDonald, M. (ed.) 1994. *Gender, Drink and Drugs*. Oxford: Berg.

McFadyen, L. 2006. Building technologies, quick and slow architectures and early Neolithic long barrow sites in southern Britain. *Archaeological Review from Cambridge* 21(1): 115–34.

McFadyen, L. 2007a. Neolithic architecture and participation: practices of making at long barrow sites in southern Britain. In J. Last (ed.) *Beyond the Grave: new perspectives on barrows*. Oxford: Oxbow Books, pp. 22–29.

McFadyen, L. 2007b. Making Architecture. In D. Benson and A. Whittle (eds) *Building Memories. The Neolithic Cotswold long barrow at Ascott-under-Wychwood, Oxfordshire*. Oxford: Oxbow, pp. 348–354.

McGowan, A. S. 2005. 'All that is rare, characteristic or beautiful': design and the defense of tradition in colonial India, 1851–1903. *Journal of Material Culture* 10(3): 263–287.

MacGregor, G. 1999. Making sense of the past in the present. A sensory analysis of carved stone balls. *World Archaeology* 31: 258–271.

McGrew, W. C. 1992. *Chimpanzee Material Culture: implications for human evolution*. Cambridge: Cambridge University Press.

McGrew, W. C. 2003. Ten dispatches from the chimpanzee culture wars. In F. B. M. de Waal and P. L. Tyack (eds) *Animal Social Complexity. Intelligence, culture and individualized societies*. Cambridge, MA: Harvard University Press, pp. 419–439.

McGrew, W. C. 2004. *The Cultured Chimpanzee: Reflections on Cultural Primatology*. New York: Cambridge University Press.

McGrew, W. C., Ham, R. M., White, L. J. T., Tutin, C. E. G. and Fernandez, M. 1997. Why don't chimpanzees in Gabon crack nuts? *International Journal of Primatology* 18: 353–374.

McGuire, R. H. 1991. Building power in the cultural landscape of Broome County, New York, 1880–1940. In R. H. McGuire and R. Paynter (eds) *The Archaeology of Inequality*. Oxford: Blackwell, pp. 102–124.

McGuire, R. H. 1995. Behavioral archaeology: reflections of a prodigal son. In J. Skibo, W. Walker and A. Nielsen (eds) *Expanding Archaeology*. Salt Lake City: University of Utah Press, pp. 162–177.

McGuire, R. H. 2006. Marxism and capitalism in historical archaeology. In D. Hicks and M. C. Beaudry (eds) *The Cambridge Companion to Historical Archaeology*. Cambridge: Cambridge University Press, pp. 123–142.

McGuire, R. H. and Paynter, R. (eds) 1991. *The Archaeology of Inequality*. Oxford: Blackwell.

McIntosh, A. 1952. *An Introduction to a Survey of Scottish Dialects*. London: Thomas Nelson (Linguistic Survey of Scotland, Monographs 1).

McKendrick, N., Brewer, J. and Plumb, J. 1983. *The Birth of a Consumer Society*. London: Hutchinson.

MacKenzie, D. 1984. Marx and the machine. *Technology and Culture* 25: 473–502.

MacKenzie, D. 1990. *Inventing Accuracy: a historical sociology of nuclear missile guidance.* Cambridge, MA: MIT Press.

MacKenzie, D. and Wajcman, J. (eds) 1985. *The Social Shaping of Technology: how the refrigerator got its hum.* Milton Keynes: Open University Press.

MacKenzie, D. and Wajcman, J. (eds) 1999. *The Social Shaping of Technology* (second edition). Milton Keynes: Open University Press.

MacKenzie, M. 1991. *Androgynous Objects: string bags and gender in central New Guinea.* London: Routledge.

McKnight, B. E. 1992. *Law and Order in Sung China.* Cambridge: Cambridge University Press.

McLuhan, M. 1964. *Understanding Media.* London: Routledge and Kegan Paul.

McNairn, B. 1980. *The Method and Theory of V. Gordon Childe.* Edinburgh University Press.

Macnaghten, P. and Urry, J. 1997. *Contested Natures.* London: Routledge.

McNaughton, P. 1987. *The Mande Blacksmith: knowledge, power and art in West Africa.* Bloomington: University of Indiana Press.

McNiven, I. and Russell, L. 2005. *Appropriated Pasts: indigenous peoples and the colonial culture of archaeology.* Walnut Creek: AltaMira Press.

McNiven, T. J. 2000. Fear and gender in Greek art. In A. E. Rautman (ed.) *Reading the Body. Representations and remains in the archaeological record.* Philadelphia: University of Pennsylvania Press, pp. 124–131.

McOmish, D. 1996. East Chisenbury: ritual and rubbish at the British Bronze Age–Iron Age transition. *Antiquity,* 70: 68–76.

McPhee, J. 1989. *The Control of Nature.* New York: Farrar, Straus, Giroux.

McVicker, D. E. 1992. The matter of Saville: Franz Boas and the anthropological definition of archaeology. In J. E. Reyman (ed.) *Rediscovering Our Past: essays on the history of American archaeology.* Aldershot: Avebury, pp. 145–160.

Magers, P. 1975. The cotton industry at Antelope House. *Kiva* 41(1): 39–47.

Makoto, T. 1994. Festivals and fights: the law and the people of Edo. In J. L. McClain, J. M. Merriman and U. Kaoru (eds) *Edo and Paris: urban life and the state in the early modern era.* Ithaca: Cornell University Press, pp. 384–406.

Malafouris, L. 2004. The cognitive basis of material engagement: where brain, body and culture conflate. In E. DeMarrais, C. Gosden and A. C. Renfrew (eds) *Rethinking Materiality: the engagement of mind with the material world.* Cambridge: McDonald Institute for Archaeological Research, pp. 53–62.

Malafouris, L. 2007. Before and beyond representation: towards an enactive conception of the Palaeolithic Image. In A. C. Renfrew and I. Morley (eds) *Image and Imagination: a global history of figurative representation.* Cambridge: McDonald Institute for Archaeological Research, pp. 289–302.

Malafouris, L. 2008a. Between brains, bodies and things: *tectonoetic* awareness and the extended self. *Philosophical Transactions of the Royal Society of London B* 363: 1993–2002.

Malafouris, L. 2008b. At the potter's wheel: an argument for material agency. In C. Knappett and L. Malafouris (eds) *Material Agency: towards a non-anthropocentric approach.* New York: Springer, pp. 19–36.

Malan, P. 2007. 'Best tea set' goes to looters. *Die Burger,* 23 January 2007 http://www.news24.com/News24/South_Africa/News/0,,2-7-1442_2058762,00.html (accessed 17 November 2008).

MALINA, J. and VAŠÍČEK, Z. 1990. *Archaeology Yesterday and Today: the development of archaeology in the sciences and humanities*. Cambridge: Cambridge University Press.

MALINOWSKI, B. K. 1922. *Argonauts of the Western Pacific: an account of native enterprise and adventure in the archipelagoes of Melanesian New Guinea*. London: George Routledge and Sons.

MALINOWSKI, B. K. 1926. *Crime and Custom in Savage Society*. London: Kegan Paul.

MALINOWSKI, B. K. 1935. *Coral Gardens and their Magic* (Volume 1). London: George Allen and Unwin.

MALINOWSKI, B. K. 1948 [1926]. *Magic, Science and Religion and Other Essays* (selected and with an introduction by R. Redfield). Glencoe, IL: Free Press.

MALONE, A. 2008. Branscombe one year on: a village torn apart by greed. *Daily Mail* 24 January 2007.

MALONEY, C. 1980. A witch-bottle from Dukes Place, Aldgate. *Transactions of the London and Middlesex Archaeological Society* 31: 157–158.

MANNIKKA, E. 2000. *Angkor Wat: time, space, and kingship*. Honolulu: University of Hawaii Press.

MANNING, S. W. 1995. *The Absolute Chronology of the Aegean Early Bronze Age*. Sheffield: Sheffield Academic Press.

MANSFIELD, B. 2003. 'Imitation crab' and the material culture of commodity production. *Cultural Geographies* 10(2): 176–195.

MAPLES, W. R. and BROWNING, M. 1994. *Dead Men Do Tell Tales: the strange and fascinating cases of a forensic anthropologist*. New York: Doubleday.

MAQUET, J. 1986. *The Aesthetic Experience: an anthropologist looks at the visual arts*. New Haven, CT: Yale University Press.

MARCOUX, J.-S. 2004. Body exchanges: material culture, gender and stereotypes in the making. *Home Cultures* 1(1): 51–60.

MARCUS, G. 1989. *Lipstick Traces: a secret history of the twentieth century*. Cambridge, MA: Harvard University Press.

MARCUS, G. E. 1995. Ethnography in/of the world system: the emergence of multi-sited ethnography. *Annual Review of Anthropology* 24: 95–117.

MARCUS, G. E. 2000. The twistings and turnings of geography and anthropology in winds of millennial transition. In I. Cook, D. Crouch, S. Naylor and J. R. Ryan (eds) *Cultural Turns/Geographical Turns: perspectives on culture geography*. Harlow: Prentice Hall, pp. 13–25.

MARCUS, G. E. and D. CUSHMAN 1982. Ethnographies as texts. *Annual Review of Anthropology* 11: 25–69.

MARCUS, M. 1993. Incorporating the body: adornment, gender and social identity in Ancient Iran. *Cambridge Archaeological Journal* 3(2): 157–178.

MARCUSE, H. 1964. *One Dimensional Man: studies in the ideology of advanced industrial society*. Boston, MA: Beacon Press.

MAREES, P. DE 1987 [1602]. *Description and Historical Account of the Gold Kingdom of Guinea* (ed. and trans. A. Van Dantzig and A. Jones). Oxford: Oxford University Press.

MARGARIS, A. 2006. Alutiiq Engineering: The Mechanics and Design of Skeletal Technologies in Alaska's Kodiak Archipelago. Unpublished Ph.D. dissertation, Department of Anthropology, University of Arizona.

MARGULIS, L. and SAGAN, D. 1986. *Microcosmos: four billion years of evolution from our microbial ancestors*. New York: Summit.

MARIAGE, T. 1990. *L'univers de Le Nostre: les origines de l'aménagement du territoire*. Brussels: P. Mardaga.

MARKLEY, R. 2006. *The Far East and the English Imagination 1600–1730*. Cambridge: Cambridge University Press.

MARKUS, T. 1993. *Buildings and Power*. London: Routledge.

MARRIOTT, M. 1976. Hindu transactions: diversity without dualism. In B. Kapferer (ed.) *Transaction and Meaning: directions in the anthropology of exchange and symbolic behaviour*. Philadelphia, PA: Institute for the Study of Human Issues, pp. 109–137.

MARSDEN, B. M. 1974. *The Early Barrow Diggers*. Park Ridge, NJ: Noyes Press.

MARTIN, A. 2005. Agents in inter-action: Bruno Latour and agency. *Journal of Archaeological Method and Theory* 12(4) Agency: Methodologies for Interpreting Social Reproduction, Part 2, pp. 283–311.

MARTIN, E. 1987. *The Woman in the Body: a cultural analysis of reproduction*. Boston: Beacon Press.

MARX, K. 1964. *Selected Writings in Sociology and Social Philosophy* (trans. T. B. Bottomore). London: McGraw-Hill.

MARX, K. 1974 [1867]. *Das Kapital: Kritik der Politischen Ökonomie*. Vol. 1. Berlin: Dietz Verlag.

MARX, K. 1979. *The Poverty of Philosophy*. New York: International Publishers.

MARX, K. 1986. *Karl Marx: a reader* (ed. Jon Elstner). Cambridge: Cambridge University Press.

MARX, K. and ENGELS, F. 1977. *The German Ideology*. London: Lawrence and Wishart.

MARX, L. and SMITH, M. R. 1994. Introduction. In M. R. Smith and L. Marx (eds) *Does Technology Drive History? The dilemma of technological determinism*. Cambridge, MA: MIT Press, pp. 2–26.

MASON, O. 1895. *The Origins of Invention: a study of industry among primitive peoples*. New York: Charles Scribner's Sons.

MASSEY, D. 2006. Landscape as provocation: reflections on moving mountains. *Journal of Material Culture* 11(1–2): 33–48.

MATHEWS, S. 2007. *From Agit-Prop to Free Space: the architecture of Cedric Price*. London: Black Dog.

MATLESS, D. 1998. *Landscape and Englishness*. London: Reaktion.

MATSUZAWA, T. 1991. Nesting cups and metatools in chimpanzees. *Behavioural and Brain Sciences* 14(4): 570–571.

MATSUZAWA, T. 1994. Field experiments on use of stone tools by chimpanzees in the wild. In R. W. Wrangham, W. C. McGrew, F. B. M. de Waal and P. G. Heltne (eds) *Chimpanzee Cultures*. Cambridge, MA: Harvard University Press, pp. 351–370.

MAURER, K., WEYAND, A., FISCHER, M. and STÖCKLIN, J. 2005. Old cultural traditions, in addition to land use and topography, are shaping plant diversity of grasslands in the Alps. *Biological Conservation* 130: 438–446.

MAUSS, M. 1936. Les techniques du corps. *Journal de Psychologie* 32: 271–293.

MAUSS, M. 1954. *The Gift: forms and functions of exchange in archaic societies* (trans. I. Cunnison). Glencoe: The Free Press.

MAUSS, M. 1973. Techniques of the body (trans. B. Brewster). *Economy and Society* 2(1): 70–88.

MAUSS, M. 1985. A category of the human mind: the notion of the person; the notion of the self (trans. W. D. Hall). In M. Carrithers, S. Collins and S. Lukes (eds) *The Category of the Person: anthropology, philosophy, history*. Cambridge: Cambridge University Press, pp. 1–25.

MAUSS, M. 1990. *The Gift: the form and reason for exchange in archaic societies* (new trans. By W. D. Hall). New York: Norton.

MAUSS, M. and BEUCHAT, H. 1979 [1905]. *Seasonal Variations of the Eskimo* (trans. J. J. Fox). London: Routledge.

MAUSS, M. and HUBERT, H. 1972 [1902]. *A General Theory of Magic* (translation from French original). London: Routledge and Kegan Paul.

MAYNE, A. and MURRAY, T. (eds) 2001. *The Archaeology of Urban Landscapes: explorations in slumland.* Cambridge: Cambridge University Press.

MAZZARELLA, W. 2003. *Shoveling Smoke: advertising and globalization in contemporary India.* Durham, NC: Duke University Press.

MEILLASSOUX, C. 1972. From reproduction to production. *Economy and Society* 1: 93–105.

MENDONSA, E. L. 2001. *Continuity and Change in a West African Society: globalization's impact on the Sisala of Ghana.* Durham NC: Carolina Academic Press.

MENNELL, S. 1996. *All Manners of Food: eating and taste in England and France from the Middle Ages to the present* (second edition). Urbana: University of Illinois Press.

MERCADER, J., BARTON, H., GILLESPIE, J., HARRIS, J., KUHN, S., TYLER, R. and BOESCH, C. 2007. 4,300-year-old chimpanzee sites and the origins of percussive stone technology. *Proceedings of the National Academy of Sciences of the United States of America* 104(9): 3043–3048.

MERCADER, J., PANGER, M. and BOESCH, C. 2002. Excavation of a chimpanzee stone tool site in the African rainforest. *Science* 296: 1452–1455.

MERCER, E. 1975. *English Vernacular Houses: a study of traditional farmhouses and cottages.* London: HMSO.

MERLEAU-PONTY, M. 1962. *Phenomenology of Perception* (trans. C. Smith). London: Routledge and Kegan Paul.

MERLEAU-PONTY, M. 1968. *The Visible and the Invisible* (ed. C. Lefort, trans. A. Lingis). Illinois: Northwestern University Press.

MERRIFIELD, R. 1955. Witch bottles and magical jugs. *Folklore* 66(1): 195–207.

MERRIFIELD, R. 1987. *The Archaeology of Ritual and Magic.* London: Batsford.

MERRIFIELD, R. and SMEDLEY, N. 1958. Two witch-bottles from Suffolk. *Proceedings of the Suffolk Institute of Archaeology* 28: 97–100.

MERRIMAN, P., REVILL, G., CRESWELL, T., LORIMER, H., MATLESS, D., ROSE, G. and WYLIE, J. 2008. Landscape, mobility and practice. *Social and Cultural Geography* 9(2): 191–212.

MERRY, S. E. 2001. Spatial Governmentality and the New Urban Social Order: Controlling Gender Violence through Law. *American Anthropologist* 103(1): 16–29.

MESKELL, L. M. 1996. The somatisation of archaeology: institutions, discourses, corporeality. *Norwegian Archaeological Review* 29(1): 1–16.

MESKELL, L. M. 1998. The irresistible body and the seduction of archaeology. In D. Montserrat (ed.) *Changing Bodies, Changing Meanings: studies on the human body in antiquity.* London: Routledge: 139–61.

MESKELL, L. M. 1999. *Archaeologies of Social Life: age, sex and class in ancient Egypt.* Oxford: Blackwell.

MESKELL, L. M. 2000. Writing the body in archaeology. In A. E. Rautman (ed.) *Reading the Body: representations and remains in the archaeological record.* Philadelphia: University of Pennsylvania Press, pp. 13–21.

MESKELL, L. M. 2004. *Object Worlds in Ancient Egypt: material biographies past and present.* Oxford: Berg.

MESKELL, L. M. 2005a. Introduction: object orientations. In L. Meskell (ed.) *Archaeologies of Materiality.* Oxford: Blackwell, pp. 1–17.

MESKELL, L. M. (ed.) 2005b. *Archaeologies of Materiality.* Oxford: Blackwell.

MESKELL L. M and JOYCE, R. M. 2003. *Embodied Lives: figuring ancient Maya and Egyptian experience.* London: Routledge.

MESSENGER, J. 1989. *Inis Beag Revisited: the anthropologist as observant participator.* Salem: Sheffield Publishing Company.

MEYER, J. 2001. *Minimalism: art, and polemics in the sixties.* New Haven: Yale University Press.

MILLER, D. 1980. Archaeology and development. *Current Anthropology* 21(6): 709–726.

MILLER, D. 1982a. Artefacts as products of human categorisation processes. In I. Hodder (ed.) *Symbolic and Structural Archaeology.* Cambridge: Cambridge University Press, pp. 17–25.

MILLER, D. 1982b. Explanation and social theory in archaeological practice. In A. C. Renfrew, M. J. Rowlands and B. Abbott Seagraves (eds) *Theory and Explanation in Archaeology: the Southampton Conference.* New York: Academic Press, pp. 83–95.

MILLER, D. 1982c. Structures and strategies: an aspect of the relationship between social hierarchy and cultural change. In I. Hodder (ed.) *Symbolic and Structural Archaeology.* Cambridge: Cambridge University Press, pp. 89–98.

MILLER, D. 1983. Things ain't what they used to be. *Royal Anthropological Institute News* 59: 5–7.

MILLER, D. 1984. Modernism and suburbia as material ideology. In D. Miller and C. Tilley (eds) *Ideology, Power and prehistory.* Cambridge: Cambridge University Press, pp. 37–49.

MILLER, D. 1985. *Artefacts as Categories: a study of ceramic variability in central India.* Cambridge: Cambridge University Press (New Studies in Archaeology).

MILLER, D. 1987. *Material Culture and Mass Consumption.* Oxford: Blackwell (Studies in Social Archaeology).

MILLER, D. 1988. Appropriating the State on the Council Estate. *Man* 23: 353–372.

MILLER, D. 1989. The limits of dominance. In D. Miller, C. Tilley and M. Rowlands (eds) *Domination and Resistance.* London: Routledge (One World Archaeology 3), pp. 63–79.

MILLER, D. 1990. Persons and blue jeans: beyond fetishism. *Etnofoor* 3: 97–111.

MILLER, D. 1994. *Modernity: an ethnographic approach. Dualism and mass consumption in Trinidad.* Oxford: Berg.

MILLER, D. (ed.) 1995a. *Acknowledging Consumption. A review of new studies.* London: Routledge.

MILLER, D. 1995b. Consumption studies as the transformation of anthropology. In D. Miller (ed.) *Acknowledging Consumption: a review of new studies.* London: Routledge, pp. 264–295.

MILLER, D. 1995c. Consumption as the vanguard of history: a polemic by way of an introduction. In D. Miller (ed.) *Acknowledging Consumption: a review of new studies.* London: Routledge, pp. 1–57.

MILLER, D. 1995d. Consumption and commodities, *Annual Review of Anthropology* 24: 141–161.

MILLER, D. 1997. *Capitalism: an ethnographic approach.* Berg, Oxford.

MILLER, D. 1998a. Coca-Cola: a black sweet drink from Trinidad. In D. Miller (ed.) *Material Cultures: why some things matter.* London: Routledge (Consumption and Space), pp. 169–188.

MILLER, D. 1998b. Why some things matter. In D. Miller (ed.) *Material Cultures: why some things matter.* London: Routledge (Consumption and Space), pp. 3–21.

MILLER, D. 1998c. *A Theory of Shopping.* Cambridge: Polity Press.

MILLER, D. 2000. Virtualism: the culture of political economy. In I. Cook, D. Crouch, S. Naylor and J. R. Ryan (eds) *Cultural Turns/Geographical Turns: perspectives on cultural geography.* Harlow: Prentice Hall, pp. 196–213.

MILLER, D. 2001a. Possessions. In D. Miller (ed.) *Home Possessions.* Oxford: Berg, pp. 107–122.

MILLER, D. (ed.) 2001b. *Home Possessions.* Oxford: Berg.

MILLER, D. 2001c. Alienable gifts and inalienable commodities. In F. R. Myers (ed.) *The Empire of Things: regimes of value and material culture.* Santa Fe: School of American Research Press, pp. 91–115.

MILLER, D. (ed.) 2001d. *Consumption: critical concepts in the social sciences.* New York: Routledge.

MILLER, D. 2001e. Behind closed doors. In D. Miller (ed.) *Home Possessions.* Oxford: Berg, pp. 1–19.

MILLER, D. 2002. Abstract for 'Materiality' session, American Anthropological Association annual meeting 2002. http://sca.culanth.org/news/news1002.htm (Accessed 12 December 2008).

MILLER, D. 2003. Could the internet defetishise the commodity? *Environment and Planning D: Society and Space* 21: 359–372.

MILLER, D. 2005a. Materiality: an introduction. In D. Miller (ed.) *Materiality.* Durham: Duke University press, pp. 1–50.

MILLER, D. 2005b. Reply to Michel Callon. *European Newsletter for Economic Sociology* 6(3): 3–13.

MILLER, D. (ed.) 2005c. *Materiality.* Durham, NC: Duke University Press.

MILLER, D. 2006a. Consumption. In C. Tilley, W. Keane, S. Küchler, M. J. Rowlands and P. Spyer (eds) *Handbook of Material Culture.* London: Sage, pp. 341–354.

MILLER, D. 2006b. Conclusion: a theory of virtualism. In J. G. Carrier and D. Miller (eds) *Virtualism: a new political economy.* Oxford: Berg, pp. 187–215.

MILLER, D. 2007. Stone Age or plastic age? *Archaeological Dialogues* 14(1): 23–27.

MILLER, D. 2008. *The Comfort of Things.* Cambridge: Polity Press.

MILLER, D. and TILLEY, C. (eds) 1984. *Ideology, Power and Prehistory.* Cambridge: Cambridge University Press.

MILLER, D. and TILLEY, C. 1996. Editorial. *Journal of Material Culture,* 1: 5–14.

MILLER, D. and SLATER, D. (eds) 2000. *The Internet: an ethnographic approach.* Oxford: Berg.

MILLER, D. and WOODWARD, S. 2007. Manifesto for a study of denim. *Social Anthropology* 15: 335–351.

MILLER, D., JACKSON, P., THRIFT, N. J., HOLBROOK, B. and ROWLANDS, M. 1998. *Shopping, Place and Identity.* London: Routledge.

MILLER, H. 1999. *What the Corpse Revealed: murder and the science of forensic detection.* New York: St Martin's Press.

MILLER, H. M-L. 2007. *Archaeological Approaches to Technology.* London: Academic Press.

MILLER, M. O. 1956. *Archaeology in the USSR.* London: Atlantic Press.

MILLER, P. N. 2000. Peiresc's Europe: learning and virtue in the seventeenth century. New Haven: Yale University Press.

MILLS, B. J. (ed.) 2004. *Identity, Feasting, and the Archaeology of the Greater Southwest.* Boulder, CO: University of Colorado Press.

MILLS, B. J. 2007. Performing the feast: visual display and suprahousehold commensalism in the Puebloan southwest. *American Antiquity* 72(2): 210–239.

MILLS, B. J. and WALKER, W. H. 2008a. Memory, materiality, and depositional practice. In B. J. Mills and W. H. Walker (eds) *Memory Work: archaeologies of depositional practice.* Santa Fe, NM: School of Advanced Research Press, pp. 3–24.

MILLS, B. J. and WALKER, W. H. (eds) 2008b. *Memory Work: archaeologies of material practices.* Santa Fe, NM: School of Advanced Research Press.

MINA, M. 2008. Figurin' Out Cretan Neolithic society: anthropomorphic figurines, symbolism and gender dialectics. In V. Isaakidou and P. Tomkins (eds) *Escaping the Labyrinth. New perspectives of the Neolithic of Crete.* Oxford: Oxbow Books, pp. 115–135.

MINTZ, S. 1985. *Sweetness and Power: the place of sugar in modern history.* New York: Viking.

MITCHELL, D. 1996. *The Lie of the Land: migrant workers and the California landscape.* Minneapolis: University of Minnesota Press.

MITCHELL, P. 2005. *African Connections: archaeological perspectives on Africa and the wider world.* Walnut Creek, CA: AltaMira Press.

MITCHELL, T. 2002. *Rule of experts: Egypt, techno-politics, modernity.* Berkeley: University of California Press.

MITCHELL, W. J. T. 1986. *Iconology: image, text, ideology.* Chicago: University of Chicago Press.

MITCHELL, W. J. T. 1996. What do pictures really want? *October 77:* 71–82.

MITCHELL, W. J. T. 2006. *What do Pictures Want? The lives and loves of images.* Chicago: University of Chicago Press.

MITHEN, S. 2005. *The Singing Neanderthals. The origins of music, language, mind and body.* London: Weidenfeld and Nicolson.

MITZKA, W. 1950. Die Methodik des Deutschen Sprachatlas und des Deutschen Volkeskundeatlas. *Hessische Blätter für Volkeskunde,* 41: 134–149.

MIYAZAKI, H. 2000. Faith and its fulfillment: agency, exchange and the Fijian aesthetics of completion. *American Ethnologist* 27(1): 31–51.

MIYAZAKI, H. 2004. *The Method of Hope: anthropology, philosophy, and Fijian knowledge.* Stanford: Stanford University Press.

MIYAZAKI, H. 2005. From sugar cane to 'swords': hope and the extensibility of the gift in Fiji. *Journal of the Royal Anthropological Institute* (n.s.) 11(2): 277–295.

MIYAZAKI, H. 2006. Documenting the present. In A. Riles (ed.) *Documents: artifacts of modern knowledge.* Ann Arbor: University of Michigan Press, pp. 206–225.

MÖBIUS, Y., BOESCH, C., KOOPS, K., MATSUZAWA, T. and HUMLE, T. 2008. Cultural differences in army ant predation by West African chimpanzees? A comparative study of microecological variables. *Animal Behaviour* 76(1): 37–45.

MOCK, S. B. (ed.) 1998. *The Sowing and the Dawning: termination, dedication, and transformation in the archaeological and ethnographic record of mesoamerica.* Albuquerque: University of New Mexico Press.

MOERAN, B. 1987. Review of D. Miller 'Artefacts as categories: a study of ceramic variability in central India'. *Bulletin of the School of African and Oriental Studies* 50(3): 578–579.

MOIR, J. R. 1917. On some human and animal bones, flint implements, etc., discovered in two ancient occupation-levels in a small valley near Ipswich. *The Journal of the Royal Anthropological Institute of Great Britain and Ireland,* 47: 367–412.

MOL, A. 1999. Ontological politics: a word and some questions. In J. Law and J. Hassard (eds) *Actor Network Theory and After.* Oxford: Blackwell, pp. 74–89.

MOL, A. 2002. *The Body Multiple: ontology in medical practice.* Durham, NC: Duke University Press.

MONTELIUS, O. 1903. *Die typologische Methode; die älteren Kulturperioden im Orient und in Europa.* Stockholm: self published.

MONTSERRAT, D. (ed.) 1998. *Changing Bodies, Changing Meanings: studies on the human body in antiquity*. London: Routledge.

MOORE, A. M. T. 1995. The inception of potting in Western Asia and its impact on economy and society. In W. Barnett and J. W. Hoopes (eds) *The Emergence of Pottery. Technology and innovation in ancient societies*. Washington: Smithsonian Institution Press, pp. 39–53.

MOORE, H. L. 1982. The interpretation of spatial patterning in settlement residues. In I. Hodder (ed.) *Symbolic and Structural Archaeology*. Cambridge: Cambridge University Press, 74–79.

MOORE, H. L. 1986. *Space, Text and Gender: an anthropological study of the Marakwet of Kenya*. Cambridge: Cambridge University Press.

MOORE, H. L. 1990. Paul Ricoeur: Action, meaning and text, in Tilley, C. (ed.) *Reading Material Culture*. Oxford: Blackwell (Studies in Social Archaeology), pp. 85–120.

MORGAN, B. J. and ABWE, E. E. 2006. Chimpanzees use stone hammers in Cameroon. *Current Biology* 16(16): R632–R633.

MORGAN, L. H. 1868. *The American Beaver and his Works*. New York: Burt Franklin.

MORGAN, L. H. 1877. *Ancient Society or Researches in the Lines of Human Progress from Savagery through Barbarism to Civilization*. London: MacMillan.

MORGAN, L. H. 1881. *Houses and House-Life of the American Aborigines*. Washington, DC: US Government Printing Office.

MORLEY, D. 1992. *Family Television: cultural power and domestic leisure*. London: Comedia.

MORLEY, D. 1995. Theories of consumption in media studies. In D. Miller (ed.) *Acknowledging Consumption: a review of new studies*. London: Routledge, pp. 296–328.

MORPHY, H. 1977. Schematisation, meaning and communication in Toas. In P. J. Ucko (ed.) *Form in Indigenous Art: schematisation in the art of Aboriginal Australia and prehistoric Europe*. Canberra: Australian Institute of Aboriginal Studies, pp. 77–90.

MORPHY, H. 1991. *Ancestral Connections: art and an aboriginal system of knowledge*. Chicago: University of Chicago Press.

MORPHY, H. 1992. From dull to brilliant: the aesthetics of spiritual power among the Yolngu. In Coote, J. and A. Shelton (eds) *Anthropology, Art and Aesthetics*, Oxford: Clarendon Press, pp. 181–208.

MORPHY, H. 1994. The anthropology of art. In T. Ingold (ed.) *Companion Encyclopaedia to Anthropology*. London: Routledge, pp. 648–685.

MORPHY, H. 2007a. Anthropological theory and the multiple determinacy of the present. In D. Parkin and S. Ulijaszek (eds) *Holistic Anthropology: emergence and convergence*. Oxford: Berghahn, pp. 148–181.

MORPHY, H. 2007b. *Becoming Art: exploring cross-cultural categories*. Oxford: Berg.

MORPHY, H. 2009. Art as a Mode of Action: some problems with Gell's art and agency. *Journal of Material Culture* 14(1): 5–27.

MORPHY, H. and PERKINS, M. 2006a. The anthropology of art: a reflection on its history and contemporary practice. In H. Morphy and M. Perkins (eds) *The Anthropology of Art: a reader*. Oxford: Blackwell, pp. 1–32.

MORPHY, H. and PERKINS, M. (eds) 2006b. *The Anthropology of Art: a reader*. Oxford: Blackwell.

MORRIS, S. 2007. Fears grow for heritage coast as salvage of wreck likely to last a year. *The Guardian* 24 January 2007.

MORRIS, W. 1973 [1878]. The Lesser Arts. In A. L. Morton (ed.) *Political Writings of William Morris*. New York: International Publishers, pp. 31–57.

MOSER, H. 1962. Vom Folklorismus in unserer Zeit. *Zeitschrift für Volkskunde* 58: 177–209.

MOSER, I. 2008. Making Alzheimer's disease matter: enacting, interfering and doing politics of nature. *Geoforum* 39: 98–110.

MOSKO, M. 1992. Motherless sons: 'divine kings' and 'partible persons' in Melanesia and Polynesia. *Man* 27: 697–717.

MOURA, A. C. D. and LEE, P. C. 2004. Capuchin stone tool use in Caatinga dry forest. *Science* 306(5703): 1909.

MOXHAM, R. 2003. *Tea: addiction, exploitation and empire*. London: Constable.

MUDIMBE, V. Y. 1988. *The Invention of Africa: gnosis, philosophy, and the order of knowledge*. Bloomington, IN: Indiana University Press.

MUDIMBE, V. Y. 1994. *The Idea of Africa*. Bloomington, IN: Indiana University Press.

MUKERJI, C. 1989. Review of D. Miller 'Material culture and mass consumption'. *American Journal of Sociology* 94(6): 1462–1464.

MUKERJI, C. 1997. *Territorial Ambitions and the Gardens of Versailles*. Cambridge: Cambridge University Press.

MUKERJI, C. 2002a. Engineering and French formal gardens in the Reign of Louis XIV. In J. D. Hunt, M. Conan and C. Goldstein (eds) *Tradition and Innovation in French Garden Art: chapters of a new history*. Philadelphia: University of Pennsylvania Press, pp. 22–43.

MUKERJI, C. 2002b. Entrepreneurialism, land management and cartography during the age of Louis XIV. In P. H. Smith and P. Findlen (eds) *Merchants and Marvels: commerce, science, and art in early modern Europe*. London: Routledge, pp. 248–276.

MUKERJI, C. 2002c. Material practices of domination and techniques of Western power. *Theory and Society* 31: 1–31.

MUKERJI, C. 2003. Intelligent uses of engineering and the legitimacy of state power. *Technology and Culture* 44: 655–676.

MUKERJI, C. 2005. Dominion, demonstration, and domination: religious doctrine, territorial politics and French plant collection. In L. L. Schiebinger and C. Swan (eds) *Colonial Botany: science, commerce, and politics in the early modern world*. Philadelphia: University of Pennsylvania Press, pp. 19–33.

MULLINS, P. R. 1999. *Race and Affluence: an archaeology of African America and consumer culture*. New York: Kluwer Academic/Plenum Publishers.

MULLINS, P. R. 2008. *Glazed America: a history of the doughnut*. Gainesville: University Press of Florida.

MULVILLE, J. and GRIGSON, C. 2007. The animal bones. In D. Benson and A. Whittle (eds) *Building Memories: the Neolithic Cotswold long barrow at Ascott-under-Wychwood, Oxfordshire*. Oxford: Oxbow, pp. 237–254.

MUMFORD, L. 1961. *The City in History: its origins, its transformations, and its prospects*. New York: Harcourt, Brace and World.

MUNN, N. 1973. *Walbiri Iconography: graphic representation and cultural symbolism in a central Australian society*. Ithaca: Cornell University Press.

MUNN, N. 1983. Gawan Kula: spatiotemporal control and the symbolism of influence. In J. W. Leach and E. R. Leach (eds) *The Kula: new perspectives on Massim exchange*. Cambridge: Cambridge University Press, pp. 277–308.

MUNN, N. 1986. *The Fame of Gawa: A symbolic study of value transformation in a Massim (Papua New Guinea) Society*. Cambridge: Cambridge University Press.

MURDOCH, J. 1997. Towards a geography of heterogenous associations. *Progress in Human Geography* 21(3): 321–337.

MURRAY, T. and ALLEN, J. 1995. The forced repatriation of cultural properties to Tasmania. *Antiquity* 69: 871–874.

MURRAY, T. and CROOK, P. 2005. Exploring the archaeology of the modern city: Melbourne, Sydney and London in the 19th century. *International Journal of Historical Archaeology* 9: 89–109.

MYERS, F. R. 2001. Introduction: the empire of things. In F. R. Myers (ed.) *The Empire of Things: regimes of value and material culture.* Santa Fe: School of American Research Press, pp. 3–61.

MYERS, F. R. 2002. *Painting Culture: the making of an Aboriginal high art.* Durham: Duke University Press.

MYRES, J. L. 1911. *The Dawn of History.* London: Williams and Norgate (Home University Library of Modern Knowledge 29).

NABOKOV, P. and EASTON, R. 1989. *Native American Architecture.* Oxford: Oxford University Press.

NAKAMURA, C. 2005. Mastering matters: magical sense and apotropaic figurine worlds of Neo-Assyria. In L. Meskell (ed.) *Archaeologies of Materiality.* Oxford: Blackwell, pp. 18–45.

NAKAMURA, M. and UEHARA, S. 2004. Proximate factors of different types of grooming hand-clasp in mahale chimpanzees: Implications for chimpanzee social customs. *Current Anthropology* 45(1): 108–114.

NAKOU, G. 2007. Absent presences: metal vessels in the Aegean at the end of the third millennium. In P. M. Day and R. C. P. Doonan (eds) *Metallurgy in the Early Bronze Age.* Oxford: Oxbow Books (Sheffield Studies in Aegean Archaeology 7), pp. 224–244.

NASH, C. 2005. Geographies of relatedness. *Transactions of the Institute of British Geographers* 30: 449–462.

NATURSKYDDSFÖRENINGEN I SKÅNE 2002. *Det skånska kulturlandskapet* [The cultural landscape of Skåne]. Lund: Författarna och Naturskyddsföreningen i Skåne.

NEEDHAM, S. 2005. Transforming beaker culture in north-west Europe: processes of fusion and fission. *Proceedings of the Prehistoric Society* 71: 171–218.

NEEDHAM, S. and SPENCE, T. 1997. Refuse and the formation of middens. *Antiquity,* 71: 77–90.

NEEDLEMAN, L. 1965. *The Economics of Housing.* London: Staples.

NEIMAN, F. 1978. Domestic architecture at the Clifts Plantation: the social context of early Virginia buildings. *Northern Neck of Virginia Historical Magazine* 28: 3096–3128.

NETZ, R. 2004. *Barbed Wire. An ecology of modernity.* Middletown, CT: Wesleyan University Press.

NEWMAN, O. 1972. *Defensible Space: crime prevention through urban design.* New York: Macmillan.

NIELSON, A. E. 2008. The materiality of ancestors. Chullpas and social memory in the late prehispanic history of the South Andes. In B. J. Mills and W. H. Walker (eds) *Memory Work: archaeologies of depositional practice.* Santa Fe, NM: School of Advanced Research Press, pp. 207–231.

NILSSON STUTZ, L. 2003. *Embodied Rituals and Ritualized Bodies. Tracing ritual practices in Late Mesolithic burials.* Lund: Wallin and Dahlholm Boktryckeri AB (Acta archaeologica Lundensia 46).

NOBUHIKO, N. and McCLAIN, J. L. 1991. Commercial change and urban growth in early modern Japan. In J. W. Hall (ed.) *The Cambridge History of Japan, Volume 4: Early modern Japan.* Cambridge: Cambridge University Press, pp. 519–595.

NOË, A. 2004. *Action in Perception.* Cambridge, MA: MIT Press.

NOLAND, C. 2009. *Agency and Embodiment: performing gestures/producing culture.* Cambridge, MA: Harvard University Press.

NORBERG-SCHULZ C. 1971. *Existence, Space and Architecture.* London: Studio Vista.

NORDBLADH, J. and YATES, T. 1990. This perfect body, this virgin text. In I. Bapty and T. Yates (eds) *Archaeology After Structuralism.* London: Routledge, pp. 222–237.

NYLANDER, J. C. 1993. *Our Own Snug Fireside: images of the New England home, 1760–1860.* New York: Knopf.

O'BRIEN, M., and LYMAN, R. L. 1999. *Seriation, Stratigraphy, and Index Fossils: the backbone of archaeological dating.* New York: Kluwer Academic/Plenum.

O'BRIEN, M. J., HOLLAND, T. D., HOARD, R. J. and FOX, G. L. 1994. Evolutionary implications of design and performance characteristics of prehistoric pottery. *Journal of Archaeological Method and Theory* 1: 259–304.

O'HANLON, M. 1995. Communication and affect in New Guinea art. *Journal of the Royal Anthropological Institute* 1(4): 832–833.

O'HANLON, M. and WELSCH, R. (eds) 2000. *Hunting the Gatherers: ethnographic collectors, agents and agency in Melanesia, 1870s–1930s.* Oxford: Berghahn Books.

O'NEIL, B. 1953. Some seventeenth-century houses in Great Yarmouth. *The Antiquaries Journal* 33: 141–180.

ODELL, G. H. 2000. Stone tool research at the end of the millennium: procurement and technology. *Journal of Archaeological Research* 8(4): 269–331.

ODELL, G. H. 2001. Stone tool research at the end of the millennium: classification, function, and behaviour. *Journal of Archaeological Research* 9(1): 45–100.

ODELL, G. H. 2003. *Lithic Analysis.* New York: Kluwer Academic.

ODPM (OFFICE OF THE DEPUTY PRIME MINISTER). 2002. *Living Places, Cleaner, Greener, Safer.* London: HMSO.

OETELAAR, G. A. and MEYER, D. 2006. Movement and Native American landscapes: a comparative approach. *Plains Anthropologist* 51: 355–374.

OGBORN, M. 2004. Archives. In S. Harrison, S. Pile and N. J. Thrift (eds) *Patterned Ground: entanglements of nature and culture.* London: Reaktion, pp. 240–242.

OGUNDIRAN, A. 2002. Of small things remembered: beads, cowries, and cultural translations of the Atlantic experience in Yorubaland. *International Journal of African Historical Studies* 35: 427–457.

OGUNDIRAN, A. and FALOLA, T. (eds) 2007. *Archaeology of Atlantic Africa and the African Diaspora.* Bloomington: Indiana University Press.

OHNUKI-TIERNEY, E. 1994. Brain death and organ transplantation: cultural bases of medical technology. *Current Anthropology* 35(3): 233–254.

OLIVER, J. 2009. *Caciques and Cemi Idols: the web spun by Taino rulers between Hispanola and Boriquén.* Tuscaloosa: University of Alabama Press.

OLIVER, P. (ed.) 1971. *Shelter in Africa.* London: Barrie and Jenkins.

OLIVER, P. (ed.) 1975. *Shelter, Sign and Symbol.* London: Barrie and Jenkins.

OLIVER, P. 1987. *Dwellings: the house across the world.* Oxford: Phaidon.

OLIVER, P. (ed.) 1997. *Encyclopedia of Vernacular Architecture of the World.* Cambridge: Cambridge University Press.

OLIVER, P. 2003. *Dwellings: the vernacular house world wide.* London: Phaidon.

OLIVIER, L. 2001. Duration, memory and the nature of the archaeological record. In H. Karlsson (ed.) *It's about Time: the concept of time in archaeology.* Göteborg: Bricoleur Press, pp. 61–70.

OLSEN, B. 1990. Roland Barthes: from sign to text, in Tilley, C. (ed.) *Reading Material Culture*. Oxford: Blackwell (Studies in Social Archaeology), pp. 63–205.

OLSEN, B. 2003. Material culture after text: re-membering things. *Norwegian Archaeological Review* 36(2), 87–104.

OLSEN, B. 2006. Scenes from a troubled engagement: post-structuralism and material culture studies. In C. Tilley, W. Keane, S. Küchler, M. J. Rowlands and P. Spyer (eds) *Handbook of Material Culture*. London: Sage, pp. 85–103.

OLSEN, B. 2007. Keeping things at arm's length. A genealogy of asymmetry. *World Archaeology* 39(4): 579–588.

OLWIG, K. 1996. Recovering the substantive nature of landscape. *Annals of the Association of American Geographers* 86: 630–653.

OLWIG, K. 2002. *Landscape, Nature, and the Body Politic*. Madison, WI: University of Wisconsin Press.

ONG, A. 2006. *Neoliberalism as Exception: mutations in citizenship and sovereignty*. Durham, NC: Duke University Press.

ONG, W. 1967. *The Presence of the Word*. New Haven: Yale University Press.

ONIANS, J. 1988. *Bearers of Meaning: the classical orders in Antiquity, the Middle Ages, and the Renaissance*. Princeton, NJ: Princeton University Press.

VAN OOSTEN, H. 1703. *The Dutch gardener or, the compleat florist. Containing, the most successful method of cultivating all sorts of flowers; . . . Together with a particular account of the nursing of lemon and orange trees in northern climates*. Written in Dutch, by Henry Van Oosten, . . . and made English. London: D. Midwinter and T. Leigh.

OPEN UNIVERSITY 2008. *Habitable Cities: civic spaces and ecological practices*. http://www.open.ac.uk/socialsciences/habitable-cities/ (Accessed 1 February 2009).

ORTNER, S. 1984. Theory in anthropology since the sixties. *Comparative Studies in Society and History* 26(1): 126–166.

ORTON, H. and WRIGHT, N. 1974. *A Word Geography of England*. London: Seminar Press.

OSBORNE, T. and ROSE, N. 1999. Governing cities: notes on the spatialisation of virtue. *Environment and Planning D: Society and Space* 17: 737–760.

OSTEEN, M. (ed.) 2002. *The Question of the Gift: essays across disciplines*. London: Routledge.

OSWALT, W. 1976. *An Anthropological Analysis of Food-Getting Technology*. New York: Wiley.

OTTONI, E. B., DE RESENDE, B. D. and IZAR, P. 2005. Watching the best nutcrackers: what capuchin monkeys (*Cebus apella*) know about others' tool-using skills. *Animal Cognition* 8(4): 215–219.

OVERING, J. 1996. Is aesthetics a cross-cultural category? Against the motion. In Tim Ingold (ed.) *Key Debates in Anthropology*. London: Routledge, pp. 260–266.

PACKARD, V. 1958. *The Hidden Persuaders*. New York: Pocket Books.

PAGE, B. 2005. Paying for water and the geography of commodities. *Transactions of the Institute of British Geographers* 30(3): 293–306.

PAGLEN, T. 2006. Late September at an undisclosed location in the Nevada Desert. *Cultural geographies* 13, 293–300.

PAIN, R. and BAILEY, C. 2004. British social and cultural geography: beyond turns and dualisms? *Social and Cultural geography* 5(2), 319–329.

PAINTER, F. 1980. An early 18th century witch bottle. *The Chesopiean* 18(3–6): 62–71.

PALISSY, B. 1931. *A Delectable Garden* (trans. F. H. Morgenthau). Peekskill, NY: Watch Hill Press.

PALISSY, B. 1988. *Recepte Veritable: Volume 359* (trans. K. Cameron). Geneva: Droz.

PALISSY, B. and LA ROCQUE, A. 1957. *Admirable Discourses*. Urbana: University of Illinois Press.

PALMER, A. 1993. *Glass in Early America: selections from the Henry Francis du Pont Winterthur Museum*. Winterthur, DE: Henry Francis du Pont Winterthur Museum.

PANGER, M. A., PERRY, S., ROSE, L. M., GROS-LOUIS, J., VOGEL, E., MACKINNON, K. C. and BAKER, M. 2002. Cross-site differences in foraging behavior of white-faced capuchins (*Cebus capucinus*). *American Journal of Physical Anthropology* 119(1): 52–66.

PANTIN, W. 1947. The development of domestic architecture in Oxford. *The Antiquaries Journal* 27: 120–150.

PARISI, L. 2004. *Abstract Sex: philosophy, biotechnology and the mutations of desire*. London: Continuum.

PARK, S. 1998. Sustainable design and historic preservation. *CRM* 2: 13–16.

PARKER PEARSON, M. 1982. Mortuary practices, society and ideology: an ethnoarchaeological study. In I. Hodder (ed.) *Symbolic and Structural Archaeology*. Cambridge: Cambridge University Press, pp. 89–98.

PARKER PEARSON, M., POLLARD, J., RICHARDS, C., THOMAS, J., TILLEY, C., WELHAM, K. and ALBARELLA, U. 2006. Materializing Stonehenge: The Stonehenge Riverside Project and new discoveries. *Journal of Material Culture*, 11: 227–261.

PARKER, J. 2004. Witchcraft, anti-witchcraft and trans-regional ritual 1889–1910. *Journal of African History* 45: 393–420.

PARKER, J. 2006. Northern gothic: witches, ghosts and werewolves in the Savanna hinterland of the Gold Coast, 1900s–1950s. *Africa* 76(3): 352–380.

PARR, J. 1999. *Domestic Goods: the material, the moral, and the economic in the postwar years*. Toronto: University of Toronto Press.

PARROT, F. 2005. It's not forever. *Journal of Material Culture* 10(3): 245–262.

PARRY, J. 1986. The gift, the Indian gift and the 'Indian gift.' *Man* (n.s.) 21(3): 453–473.

PARRY, J. and BLOCH, M. E. F. (eds) 1989. *Money and the Morality of Exchange*. Cambridge: Cambridge University Press.

PARSONS, E. C. 1929. The social organisation of the Tewa of New Mexico. *Memoirs of the American Anthropological Association* 36: 7–309.

PARSONS, T. 1937. *The Structure of Social Action: a study in social theory with special reference to a group of recent European writers*. New York: McGraw-Hill.

PASK, G. 1971. A comment, a case history and a plan. In J. Reichardt (ed.), *Cybernetics, Art, and Ideas*. Greenwich, CT: New York Graphics Society, pp. 76–99.

PASKVAN, R. F. 1971. The Jardin Du Roi: the growth of its plant collection (1715–1750). Unpublished Ph.D. thesis, University of Minnesota.

PATERSON, M. 2009. Haptic geographies. *Progress in Human Geography* 33(6): 766–788.

PATTERSON, T. C. 2003. *Marx's Ghost: conversations with archaeologists*. Oxford: Berg.

PAUKETAT, T. R. 2002. Practice and history in archaeology. *Anthropological Theory* 1: 73–98.

PAUKETAT, T. R. 2008. Founders' cults and the archaeology of Wa-kan-da. In B. J. Mills and W. H. Walker (eds) *Memory Work: archaeologies of depositional practice*. Sante Fe, NM: School of Advanced Research Press, pp. 61–80.

PAUKETAT, T. R. and ALT, S. M. 2003. Mounds, memory, and contested Mississippian history. In R. Van Dyke and S. Alcock (eds) *Archaeologies of Memory*. Oxford: Blackwell, pp. 151–179.

PAUKETAT, T. R. and ALT, S. M. 2004. The making and meaning of a Mississippian axe-head cache. *Antiquity*, 78: 779–797.

PAUKETAT, T. R. and ALT, S. M. 2005. Agency in a postmold? Physicality and the archaeology of culture-making. *Journal of Archaeological Method and Theory* 12(3): 213–236.

PAUKETAT, T. R., KELLY, L. S., FRITZ, G. J., LOPINOT, N. H., ELIAS, S. and HARGRAVE, E. 2002. The residues of feasting and public ritual at Early Cahokia. *American Antiquity* 67: 257–279.

PAWLOWSKI, K. 2003. *Circulades languedociennes de l'an mille: naissance de l'urbanisation européenne.* Montpellier: Nouvelles Presses du Languedoc.

PEARCE, S. 1992. *Museums, Objects and Collections.* Leicester: Leicester University Press.

PEARCE, S. 1995. *On Collecting: an investigation into collecting in the European tradition.* London: Routledge.

PEATE, I. C. 1933. *Y Crefftwr yng Nghymru.* Cardiff: National Museum of Wales.

PEATE, I. C. 1944. *The Welsh House: a study in folk culture.* Liverpool: H. Evans and Sons, the Brython Press.

PEATE, I. C. 1957. Editorial notes. *Gwerin* 1(3): 97–98.

PEATE, I. C. 1963. Editorial notes. *Folklife* 1: 3–4.

PEIRCE, C. S. 1940a. The principles of phenomenology. In J. Buchler (ed.) *The Philosophy of Peirce: selected writings.* London: Kegan Paul, pp. 74–97.

PEIRCE, C. S. 1940b. Logic as semiotic: the theory of signs. In J. Buchler (ed.) *The Philosophy of Peirce: selected writings.* London: Kegan Paul, pp. 98–119.

PEIRCE, C. S. 1940c. The fixation of belief. In J. Buchler (ed.) *The Philosophy of Peirce: selected writings.* London: Routledge and Kegan Paul, pp. 5–22.

PEIRCE, C. S. 1940d. Some consequences of four incapacities. In J. Buchler (ed.) The Philosophy of Peirce: selected writings. London: Kegan Paul, pp. 228–250.

PELS, P. 1989. Africa Christo! The use of photographs in Dutch Catholic Mission Propaganda, 1946–1960. *Critique of Anthropology* 9(1): 33–47.

PELS, P. 1997. The anthropology of colonialism: culture, history, and the emergence of Western governmentality. *Annual Review of Anthropology* 26: 163–183.

PELS, P. 1998. The spirit of matter: on fetish, rarity, fact and fancy. In P. Spyer (ed.) *Border Fetishisms. Material objects in unstable spaces.* London: Routledge, pp. 91–121.

PELS, P. 1999. *A Politics of Presence. Contacts between missionaries and Waluguru in Late Colonial Tanganyika, 1925–1960.* Chur/Reading: Harwood Academic Publishers.

PELS, P. 2003. Introduction: magic and modernity. In B. Meyer and P. Pels (eds) *Magic and Modernity. Interfaces of revelation and concealment.* Stanford: Stanford University Press, pp. 1–38.

PENDERGRAST, M. 1993. *For God, Country and Coca-Cola: the unauthorized history of the great American soft drink and the company that makes it.* Toronto: Maxwell Macmillan.

PENNSYLVANIA DUTCHMAN. 1952. Seminars on the folk-culture of the Pennsylvania Dutch Country. *Pennsylvania Dutchman* 4(1): 2.

PENNSYLVANIA DUTCHMAN. 1956. Table of Contents. *Pennsylvania Dutchman* 8(1): ii.

PENNSYLVANIA FOLKLIFE. 1963 Program: 14th Annual Pennsylvania Dutch Folk Festival. *Pennsylvania Folklife* 13(3): 28–31.

PEREIRA, M. E. and FAIRBANKS, L. A. (eds) 2006. *Juvenile Primates: life history, development and behavior.* Chicago: University of Chicago Press.

PERLÈS, C. 2001. *The Early Neolithic in Greece: the first farming communities in Europe.* Cambridge: Cambridge University Press.

PERRY, E. M. and JOYCE, R. A. 2001. Interdisciplinary applications: providing a past for 'Bodies That Matter': Judith Butler's impact on the archaeology of gender. *International Journal of Sexuality and Gender Studies* 6(1–2): 63–76.

PERRY, S., BAKER, M., FEDIGAN, L., GROS-LOUIS, J., JACK, K., MacKINNON, K. C., MANSON, J. H., PANGER, M., PYLE, K. and ROSE, L. 2003. Social conventions in wild white-faced capuchin monkeys—Evidence for traditions in a neotropical primate. *Current Anthropology* 44(2): 241–268.

PETERSON, J. D. 2000. Labor Patterns in the Southern Levant in the Early Bronze Age. In A. E. Rautman (ed.) *Reading the Body. Representations and remains in the archaeological record*. Philadelphia: University of Pennsylvania Press, pp. 38–54.

PEVSNER, N. 1943. *An Outline of European Architecture*. Harmondsworth: Penguin Books.

PFAFFENBERGER, B. 1988. Fetishised objects and human nature: towards an anthropology of technology. *Man* (n.s.) 23: 236–252.

PFAFFENBERGER, B. 1992. Social anthropology of technology. *Annual Review of Anthropology* 21: 491–516.

PHILIPS, R. 1998. *Trading Identities: the souvenir in Native American art from the Northeast, 1700–1900*. Seattle: University of Washington Press.

PHILLIPS, A. 1998. The nature of cultural landscapes—a nature conservation perspective. *Landscape Research* 23: 21–38.

PHILO, C. 2000. More words, more worlds: reflections on the cultural turn and human geography. In I. Cook, D. Crouch, S. Naylor and J. Ryan (eds) *Cultural Turns/Geographical Turns: perspectives on cultural geography*. Harlow: Prentice Hall, pp. 26–53.

PHILO, C. and WILBERT, C. (eds) 2000. *Animal Spaces, Beastly Places: new geographies of human–animal relations*. London: Routledge.

PICKERING, A. (ed.) 1992. *Science as Practice and Culture*. Chicago: University of Chicago Press.

PICKERING, A. 1993. The mangle of practice: agency and emergence in the sociology of science. *American Journal of Sociology* 99: 559–589.

PICKERING, A. 1995. *The Mangle of Practice: time, agency, and science*. Chicago: University of Chicago Press.

PICKERING, A. 2001. Science as alchemy. In Joan W. Scott and Debra Keates (eds) *Schools of Thought: twenty-five years of interpretive social science*. Princeton, NJ: Princeton University Press, pp. 194–206.

PICKERING, A. 2005a. Decentring sociology: synthetic dyes and social theory. *Perspectives on Science* 13: 352–405.

PICKERING, A. 2005b. From Dyes to Iraq: A Reply to Jonathan Harwood. *Perspectives on Science* 13: 416–425.

PICKERING, A. 2007. Science as theatre: Gordon Pask, cybernetics and the arts. *Cybernetics and Human Knowing* 14(4): 43–57.

PICKERING, A. 2008. New ontologies. In A. Pickering and K. Guzik (eds) *The Mangle in Practice: science, society and becoming*. Durham, NC: Duke University Press, pp. 1–14.

PICKERING, A. and GUZIK, K. (eds) 2008. *The Mangle in Practice: science, society and becoming*. Durham, NC: Duke University Press.

PICKERING, A. 2009a. Beyond design: cybernetics, biological computers and hylozoism. *Synthese* 3: 469–491.

PICKERING, A. 2009b. Producing another world, with some thoughts on Latour. *Journal of Cultural Economy* 2(1/2): 197–212.

PICKERING, A. 2010. *The Cybernetic Brain: Sketches of Another Future*. Chicago: University of Chicago Press.

PICKETT, L. 2003. The material turn in Victorian studies. *Literature Compass* 1: 1–5.

PIERPOINT, S. 1980. *Social Patterns in Yorkshire Prehistory 3500–750 BC.* Oxford: British Archaeological Reports (BAR British Series 74).

PIETZ, W. 1985. The problem of the fetish, I. *RES* 9: 5–17.

PIETZ, W. 1987. The problem of the fetish, II. The origin of the fetish. *RES* 13: 23–45.

PIETZ, W. 1988. The problem of the fetish, IIIa: Bosman's Guinea and the Enlightenment theory of fetishism. *RES* 16: 105–123.

PIETZ, W. 1993. Fetishism and materialism: the limits of theory in Marx. In E. Apter and W. Pietz (eds) *Fetishism as Cultural Discourse.* Ithaca: Cornell University Press, pp. 119–151.

PIETZ, W. 1999. The fetish of civilization. Sacrificial blood and monetary debt. In P. Pels and O. Salemink (eds) *Colonial Subject: essays in the practical history of anthropology.* Ann Arbor: University of Michigan Press, pp. 53–81.

PIGGOTT, S. 1954. *Neolithic Cultures of the British Isles.* Cambridge University Press.

PIGGOTT, S. 1962. *The West Kennet Long Barrow Excavations 1955–56.* London: Her Majesty's Stationery Office.

PIGGOTT, S. 1976. *Ruins in a Landscape: essays in antiquarianism.* Edinburgh: Edinburgh University Press.

PINCH, T. J. and BIJKER, W. 1984. The social construction of facts and artefacts: or how the sociology of science and the sociology of technology might benefit each other. *Social Studies of Science* 14: 399–441.

PINK, S. and PEREZ, A. M. 2006. A fitting social model: culturally locating Telemadre.com. *Home Cultures* 3(1): 63–86.

PINKER, S. 1997. *How the Mind Works.* New York, Norton.

PINNEY, C. 2002. Photographic portraiture in Central India in the 1980s and 1990s. In V. Buchli (ed.) *The Material Culture Reader.* Oxford: Berg, pp. 87–104.

PINNEY, C. 2005. Things happen: or from what moment does that object come? In D. Miller (ed.) *Materiality.* Durham, NC: Duke University Press, pp. 256–272.

PINNEY, C. 2006. Four types of visual culture. In C. Tilley, W. Keane, S. Küchler, M. J. Rowlands and P. Spyer (eds) *Handbook of Material Culture.* London: Sage, pp. 131–144.

PITT RIVERS, A. H. L. F. 1875. On the evolution of culture. *Proceedings of the Royal Anthropological Institute* 7: 496–520.

PITT RIVERS, A. H. L. F. 1891. Typological museums, as exemplified by the Pitt Rivers Museum at Oxford, and his provincial museum at Farnham, Dorset. *Journal of the Society of the Arts* 40: 115–122.

PLASKETES, G. 1992. Romancing the record: the vinyl de-evolution and subcultural evolution. *Journal of Popular Culture* 26(1): 109–122.

PLATTDEUTCHE VOLKSFEST 2008. Plattdeutche Volksfest Verein History. http://www.volksfest.org/PVV_History.htm (Accessed 5 December 2008).

PLUMWOOD, V. 1993. *Feminism and the Mastery of Nature.* London: Routledge.

PLUMWOOD, V. 2002. *Environmental Culture: the ecological crisis of reason.* London: Routledge.

PLUMWOOD, V. 2006. The concept of a cultural landscape: nature, culture and agency in the land. *Ethics and the Environment* 11: 115–150.

PLYMOUTH CITY COUNCIL 2007. Major exhibition considers past and present legacies of the Transatlantic Slave Trade. http://www.plymouth.gov.uk/textonly/museumsnewsitem?newsid=148200 (Accessed 17 November 2008).

POCIUS, G. L. 1991. *A Place to Belong: community order and everyday space in Calvert, Newfoundland.* Athens: University of Georgia Press.

POGGI, G. 2000. *Durkheim.* Oxford: Oxford University Press.

POGUE, D. 1994. Mount Vernon: transformation of an eighteenth-century plantation system. In P. Shackel and B. Little (eds) *Historical Archaeology of the Chesapeake*. Washington, DC: Smithsonian Institution Press, pp. 101–114.

POHL, F. and KORNBLUTH, C. M. 1953. *The Space Merchants*. New York: Ballantine.

POLANYI, K. 1957. The economy as instituted process. In K. Polanyi, C. M. Arensberg and H. W. Pearson (eds) *Trade and Market in the Early Empires: economies in history and theory*. Glencoe, IL: The Free Press, pp. 243–270.

POLLARD, J. 1995. Inscribing space: formal deposition at the Later Neolithic Monument of Woodhenge, Wiltshire. *Proceedings of the Prehistoric Society* 61: 137–156.

POLLARD, J. 2001. The aesthetics of depositional practice. *World Archaeology* 33(2): 315–333.

POLLARD, J. 2004. The art of decay and the transformation of substance. In C. A. Renfrew, C. Gosden and E. DeMarrais (eds) *Substance, Memory, Display: archaeology and art*. Cambridge: McDonald Institute for Archaeological Research, pp. 47–62.

POLLARD, J. 2005. Memory, monuments and middens in the Neolithic landscape. In G. Brown, D. Field and D. McOmish (eds) *The Avebury Landscape: aspects of the field archaeology of the Marlborough Downs*. Oxford: Oxbow Books, pp. 103–114.

POLLARD, J. 2008. Deposition and material agency in the Early Neolithic of Southern Britain. In B. J. Mills and W. H. Walker (eds) *Memory Work: archaeologies of depositional practice*. Santa Fe, NM: School of Advanced Research Press, pp. 41–60.

POLLARD, J. and RUGGLES, C. 2001. Shifting perceptions: spatial order, cosmology, and patterns of deposition at Stonehenge. *Cambridge Archaeological Journal*, 11: 69–90.

POMIAN, K. 1990. *Collectors and Curiosities: Paris and Venice, 1500–1800*. Cambridge: Polity Press.

POOVEY, M. 1998. *A History of the Modern Fact: problems of knowledge in the sciences of wealth and society*. Chicago: Chicago University Press.

PORTER, R. (ed.) 1997. *Rewriting the Self: histories from the Renaissance to the present*. London: Routledge.

POURSAT, J-C. and KNAPPETT, C. 2005. Le Quartier Mu IV. *La Poterie du Minoen Moyen II: Production et Utilisation*. Paris: Etudes Crétoises 33.

POVINELLI, E. 1995. Do rocks listen? The cultural politics of apprehending Australian Aboriginal labor. *American Anthropologist* 97(3): 505–518.

POWELL, J. 1895. *Canyons of the Colorado*. Meadville, PA: Flood and Vincent.

PRATT, A. 2004. The cultural economy: a call for spatialised 'production of culture' perspectives. *International Journal of Cultural Studies* 7(1): 117–128.

PRED, A. and WATTS, M. J. 1992. *Reworking Modernity: capitalism and symbolic discontent*. New Brunswick, NJ: Rutgers University Press.

PREDA, A. 1999. The turn to things: arguments for a sociological theory of things. *Sociological Quarterly* 40(2): 347–366.

PRESTHOLDT, J. 2004. On the global repercussions of East African Consumerism. *American Historical Review* 109(3): 755–780.

PRESTON BLIER, S. 1987. *The Anatomy of Architecture: ontology and metaphor in Batammaliba architectural expression*. Cambridge: Cambridge University Press.

PREUCEL, R. W. 2006. *Archaeological Semiotics*. Oxford: Blackwell.

PREUCEL, R. W. and BAUER, A. (2001). Archaeological pragmatics. *Norwegian Archaeological Review* 34(2): 85–96.

PRICE, S. 1989. *Primitive Art in Civilized Places*. Chicago: University of Chicago Press.

PRIGOGINE, I. and STENGERS, I. 1984. *Order out of Chaos: man's new dialogue with nature*. London: Heinemann.

PRUDAMES, D. 2005. Artist puts message in a pebble for coastal erosion project. *24-Hour Museum* 16 November 2007. http://www.24hourmuseum.org.uk/nwh_gfx_en/ART25904. html (Accessed 20 November 2008).

PRUETZ, J. D. and BERTOLANI, P. 2007. Savanna chimpanzees, *Pan troglodytes verus*, hunt with tools. *Current Biology* 17(5): 412–417.

PRUSSIN, L. 1969. *Architecture in Northern Ghana: a study of forms and functions*. Berkeley: University of California Press.

PURKISS, D. 1995. Women's stories of witchcraft in early modern England: the house, the body, the child. *Gender and History* 7(3): 408–432.

PUTNAM, F. W. 1973 [1886]. On Methods of Archaeological Research in America. In S. Williams (ed.) *The Selected Archaeological Papers of Frederic Ward Putnam*. New York: AMS Press Inc, pp. 1–4.

PUTNAM, T. and NEWTON, C. (eds) 1990. *Household Choices*. London: Middlesex Polytechnic and Futures Publications.

QUIMBY, I. M. G. (ed.) 1978. *Material Culture and the Study of American Life*. New York: W. W. Norton.

DE LA QUINTINIE, J. 1692. *Instructions pour les jardins fruitiers et potagers*. Amsterdam: Henri Desbordes.

RABINOW, P. and SULLIVAN, W. M. (eds) 1979. *Interpretive Social Science: a reader*. Berkeley: University of California Press.

RADCLIFFE-BROWN, A. R. 1922. *The Andaman Islanders*. Cambridge: Cambridge University Press.

RADCLIFFE-BROWN, A. R. 1941. The study of kinship systems. *Journal of the Royal Anthropological Society of Great Britain and Ireland* 71(1/2): 1–18.

RAHMAN, M. and WITZ, A. 2003. What really matters? The elusive quality of the material in feminist thought. *Feminist Theory* 4: 243–261.

RAJ, K. 2007. *Relocating Modern Science: circulation and the construction of knowledge in South Asia and Europe, 1650–1900*. Basingstoke: Palgrave Macmillan.

RAMENOFSKY, A. 1987. *Vectors of Death: the archaeology of European contact*. Albuquerque: University of New Mexico Press.

RAMENOFSKY, A. 1998. Evolutionary theory and the native record of replacement. In J. Cusick (ed.) *Studies in Culture Contact: Interaction, Culture Change, and Archaeology*. Occasional Paper 25. Carbondale: Center for Archaeological Investigations, Southern Illinois University, pp. 77–93.

RAPOPORT, A. 1969. *House Form and Culture*. Engelwood Cliffs, NJ: Prentice-Hall.

RAPOPORT, A. 1980. Vernacular architecture and the cultural determinants of form. In A. King (ed.), *Buildings and Society*. London: Routledge and Kegan Paul, pp. 283–305.

RAPOPORT, A. 1982. *The Meaning of the Built Environment: a non-verbal communication approach*. Beverly Hills, CA: Sage.

RAPP, G. R. and HILL, C. L. 2006. *Geoarchaeology: The earth-science approach to archaeological interpretation*. Princeton, NJ: Princeton University Press.

RASMUSSEN, S. 1959. *Experiencing Architecture*. New York: John Wiley and Sons.

RATHJE, W. L. 1979. Modern material culture studies. In M. B. Schiffer (ed.) *Advances in Archaeological Method and Theory* (volume 2). New York: Academic Press, pp. 1–37.

RATHJE, W. 1981. A manifesto for modern material culture studies. In M. B. Schiffer and R. Gould (eds) *Modern Material Culture Studies: the archaeology of us*. New York: Academic Press.

RATHJE, W. and SCHIFFER, M. B. 1982. *Archaeology*. San Diego: Harcourt Brace Jovanovich.

RATHJE, W. H. 2001. Integrated archaeology: a garbage paradigm. In V. Buchli and G. Lucas (eds) *Archaeologies of the Contemporary Past*. London: Routledge, pp. 63–76.

RATZEL, F. 1896. *The History of Mankind* (trans. A. Butler) (volume 1). London: Macmillan.

RATZEL, F. 1897. *The History of Mankind* (trans. A. Butler) (volume 2). London: Macmillan.

READ, D. and VAN DER LEEUW, S. 2008. Biology is only part of the story . . . *Philosophical Transactions of the Royal Society B* 363(1499): 1959–1968.

REHNBERG, M. 1957. *The Nordiska Museet and Skansen: an introduction to the history and activities of a famous Swedish museum*. Stockholm: Nordiska Museet.

REID, A. and LANE, P. 2004. African historical archaeologies: an introductory consideration of scope and potential. In A. M. Reid and P. J. Lane (eds) *African Historical Archaeologies*. New York: Kluwer Academic/Plenum Publishers, pp. 1–32.

REID, J., SCHIFFER, M. B. and RATHJE, W. 1975. Behavioral archaeology: four strategies. *American Anthropologist* 77(4): 864–869.

REIMER, S. and LESLIE, D. 2008. Design, national imaginaries, and the home furnishings commodity chain. *Growth and Change* 39(1): 144–171.

RENDELL, J. 1998. Doing it, undoing it, overdoing it yourself: rhetorics of architectural abuse. In J. Hill (ed.) *Occupying Architecture. Between the architect and the user*. London: Routledge, pp. 229–246.

RENDELL, L. and WHITEHEAD, H. 2001. Culture in whales and dolphins. *Behavioral and Brain Sciences* 24: 309–382.

RENFREW, A. C. 1972. *The Emergence of Civilisation. The Cyclades and the Aegean in the third millennium BC*. London: Methuen.

RENFREW, A. C. 1973a. *Before Civilization: the radiocarbon revolution and prehistoric Europe*. London: Cape.

RENFREW, A. C. 1973b. *Social Archaeology. An inaugural lecture delivered at the university, 20th March 1973*. Southampton: University of Southampton.

RENFREW, A. C. (ed.) 1973c. *The Explanation of Culture Change: models in prehistory*. London: Duckworth.

RENFREW, A. C. 1973d. Monuments, mobilisation and social organisation in Neolithic Wessex. In A. C. Renfrew (ed.) *The Explanation of Culture Change*. London: Duckworth, pp. 539–558.

RENFREW, A. C. 1987. *Archaeology and Language: the puzzle of Indo-European origins*. London: Jonathan Cape.

RENFREW, A. C. 2001. Symbol before concept, material engagement and the early development of society, in I. Hodder (ed.), *Archaeological Theory Today*. Cambridge: Polity Press, pp. 122–140.

RENFREW, A. C. 2003. *Figuring it Out: What are we? Where do we come from? The parallel visions of artists and archaeologists*. London: Thames and Hudson.

RENFREW, A. C. 2004. Towards a theory of material engagement. In E. DeMarrais, C. Gosden and A. C. Renfrew (eds) *Rethinking Materiality: the engagement of mind with the material world*. Cambridge: The McDonald Institute for Archaeological Research, pp. 23–31.

RENFREW, A. C. 2007. *The Prehistory of the Mind*. London: Weidenfeld and Nicholson.

VAN REYBROUCK D. V. 2000. Beyond ethnoarchaeology? A critical history on the role of ethnographic analogy in contextual and post-processual archaeology. In A. Gramsch (ed.) *Vergleichen als archäologische Methode: Analogien in den Archäologien*. Oxford: Archaeopress (BAR International Series 825), pp. 39–51.

REYNOLDS, B. 1983. The relevance of material culture to anthropology. *Journal of the Anthropological Society of Oxford* 2: 63–75.

RICE, C. 2004. Rethinking histories of the interior. *Journal of Architecture* 9(3): 275–288.

RICE, P. M. 1999. On the origins of pottery. *Journal of Archaeological Method and Theory* 6 (1): 1–54.

RICHARDS, C. 1996. Life is not that simple: architecture and cosmology in the Balinese house. In T. Darvill and J. S. Thomas (eds) *Neolithic Houses in Northwest Europe and Beyond*. Oxford: Oxbow, pp. 173–184.

RICHARDS, C. and THOMAS, J. S. 1984. Ritual activity and structured deposition in Later Neolithic Wessex. In R. J. Bradley and J. Gardiner (eds) *Neolithic Studies: a review of some recent work*. Oxford: British Archaeological Reports (BAR British Series 133), pp. 189–218.

RICHARDSON, D. 1979. West African consumption patterns and their influence on the eighteenth-century English slave trade. In H. A. Gemery and J. S. Hogendorn (eds) *The Uncommon Market: essays in the economic history of the Atlantic slave trade*. New York: Academic Press, pp. 303–330.

RICHARDSON, L. 2000. Writing: a method of inquiry. In N. Denzin and Y. Lincoln (eds) *The Handbook of Qualitative Research* (second edition). London: Sage, pp. 923–948.

RICHARDSON, R. 1987. *Death, Dissection and the Destitute*. London: Routledge and Kegan Paul.

RICKMAN, T. 1817. *An Attempt to Discriminate the Styles of English Architecture from the Conquest to the Reformation*. London: Longman, Hurst.

RICOEUR, P. 1981. *Hermeneutics and the Human Sciences*. Cambridge: Cambridge University Press.

RICOEUR, P. 1992. *Oneself as Another*. Chicago: University of Chicago Press.

RIGGINS, S. H. 1994. Introduction. In S. H. Riggins (ed.) *The Socialness of Things: essays on the socio-semantics of objects*. Berlin: Mouton de Gruyter, pp. 1–6.

RILES, A. 1998. Infinity within the brackets. *American Ethnologist* 25(3): 378–398.

RILES, A. 2000. *The Network Inside Out*. Ann Arbor: University of Michigan Press.

RILLING, D. 2001. *Making Houses, Crafting Capitalism: builders in Philadelphia 1790–1850*. Philadelphia: University of Pennsylvania Press.

RITT, K. 2001. The idea of German cultural regions in the Third Reich: the work of Franz Petri. *Journal of Historical Geography* 27(2): 241–58.

RIVERS, W. H. R. 1914. *The History of Melanesian Society*. Cambridge: Cambridge University Press.

ROACH, J. 2007. *It*. Ann Arbor: University of Michigan Press.

ROBB, J. 2004. The extended artefact and the monumental economy: a methodology for material agency. In E. DeMarrais, C. Gosden and A. C. Renfrew (eds) *Rethinking Materiality: the engagement of mind with the material world*. Cambridge: McDonald Institute Monographs, pp. 131–140.

ROBBEN, A. and SLUKA, J. (eds) 2006. *Ethnographic Fieldwork: an anthology*. Oxford: Blackwell.

ROBBINS, R. 1991. *The Work of Pierre Bourdieu: recognising society*. London: Open University Press.

ROBERTS, D. 1941. Imitation and suggestion in animals. *Bulletin of Animal Behaviour* 1: 11–19.

ROBERTS, G. 2007. Branscombe barmaid saw her case wash up on beach. *The Independent* 27 January 2007.

ROBERTS, R. 1996. West Africa and the Pondicherry Textile Industry. In T. Roy (ed.) *Cloth and Commerce: textiles in colonial India*. Walnut Creek, CA: AltaMira Press, pp. 142–174.

ROBERTS, Y. 2008. The bay of the jackals. *Sunday Times* 20 January http://www.timesonline.co.uk/tol/news/uk/article3196943.ece (Accessed 17 November 2008).

ROBSON, E., TREADWELL, L. and GOSDEN, C. (eds) 2006. *Who Owns Objects? The ethics and politics of collecting cultural artifacts*. Oxford: Oxbow Books.

ROCKSBOROUGH SMITH, E. 2001. From the holiday to the academy: implications for physical geography in higher education arising from popular field-based geography in Dorset. *Journal of Geography in Higher Education* 25(2): 241–248.

ROFEL, L. 2007. *Desiring China. Experiments in neoliberalism, sexuality, and public culture*. Durham, NC: Duke University Press.

ROGERS, D. 1990. *Objects of Change: the archaeology and history of Arikara contact with Europeans*. Washington, DC: Smithsonian Institution Press.

ROGERS, J. M. 1970. Samarra: a study in medieval town planning. In A. Hourani and S. Stern (eds) *The Islamic City: a colloquium*. Oxford: Cassirer, pp. 119–156.

ROGERS, R. 1999. *Manifesto for the Compact City*. London: Design Press.

RORTY, R. (ed.) 1967. *The Linguistic Turn: essays In philosophical method*. Chicago: University of Chicago Press.

ROSE, D. B. 2005. An indigenous philosophical ecology: situating the human. *The Australian Journal of Anthropology* 16(3): 294–305.

ROSE, G. and BROOK, C. 2008. Preface. In N. Clark, D. Massey and P. Sarre (eds) *Material Geographies: a world in the making*. London: Sage, pp. vii–ix.

ROSE, M. 2006. Gathering 'dreams of presence': a project for the cultural landscape. *Environment and Planning D: Society and Space* 24: 537–554.

ROSE, N. 1998. *Inventing Our Selves: psychology, power, and personhood*. Cambridge: Cambridge University Press.

ROSE, N. 2007. *The Politics of Life Itself: biomedicine, power, and subjectivity in the twenty-first century*. Princeton, NJ: Princeton University Press.

ROSMAN, A. and RUBEL, P. G. 1990. Structural patterning in Kwakiutl art and ritual. *Man* 25(4): 620–639.

RÖSSLER, M. 2006. World Heritage Cultural Landscpes: A UNESCO Flagship Programme 1992–2006. *Landscape Research* 31: 333–353.

ROWE, J. H. 1962. Worsaae's law and the use of grave lots for archaeological dating. *American Antiquity* 28: 129–137.

ROWLANDS, M. 1983. Material culture studies at British universities: University College London. *Royal Anthropological Institute Newsletter* 59: 15–16.

ROWLANDS, M. 1998. Remembering to forget: sublimation as sacrifice in war memorials. In A. Forty and S. Küchler (eds) *The Art of Forgetting*. Oxford: Berg, pp. 129–145.

ROWLANDS, M. 2004. Relating anthropology and archaeology. In J. Bintliff (ed.) *A Companion to Archaeology*. Oxford: Blackwell, pp. 473–489.

ROWLANDS, M. 2005. A materialist approach to materiality. In D. Miller (ed.) *Materiality*. Durham, NC: Duke University Press, pp. 72–87.

ROWLANDS, M. and GLEDHILL, J. 1976. The relation between archaeology and anthropology. *Critique of Anthropology* 2: 23–37.

ROYAL ANTHROPOLOGICAL INSTITUTE OF GREAT BRITAIN AND IRELAND. 1863. Notes on the antiquity of Man. *Anthropological Review*, 1: 60–106.

RUBIN, W. 2006. Modernist primitivism: an introduction. In H. Morphy and M. Perkins (eds) *The Anthropology of Art: a reader.* Oxford: Blackwell, pp. 129–146.

RUBLACK, U. 2002. Fluxes: the early modern body and the emotions. *History Workshop Journal* 53(1): 1–16.

RUDOFSKY, B. 1964. *Architecture without Architects: an introduction to nonpedigree architecture.* New York: Museum of Modern Art.

RUDOFSKY, B. 1977. *The Prodigious Builders.* New York: Harcourt Brace Jovanovich.

RUPP, K. 2003. *Gift-Giving in Japan: cash, connections, cosmologies.* Stanford: Stanford University Press.

RUSSELL, L. 2001. *Savage Imaginings: historical and contemporary constructions of Australian Aboriginalities.* Kew (Vic): Australian Scholarly Publishing.

RUSSELL, L. 2004. Resisting the production of dichotomies: gender race and class in the pre-colonial period. In E. Casella and C. Fowler (eds) *The Archaeology of Plural and Changing Identities: beyond identification.* New York: Kluwer, pp. 33–51.

RUSTEN, G. and BRYSON, J. 2007. The production and consumption of industrial design expertise by small- and medium-sized firms: some evidence from Norway. *Geografiska annaler* 89B(S1): 75–87.

RUTZ, H. J. and ORLOVE, B. S. (eds) 1989. *The Social Economy of Consumption.* Lanham, MD: University Press of America.

RYDELL, R. W. 1993. A cultural frankenstein? The Chicago World's Columbian Exposition of 1893. In N. Harris, W. de Wit, J. Gilbert, and R. W. Rydell (eds) *Grand Illusions: Chicago's World's Fair of 1893.* Chicago: Chicago Historical Society, pp. 141–170.

RYKWERT, J. 1986. *On Adams House in Paradise: the idea of the primitive hut in architectural history.* Cambridge, MA: MIT Press.

SABC NEWS 2007. Shipwreck forces Volkswagen SA to cut back. *SABC News*, 25 January 2007. http://www.sabcnews.com/south_africa/general/0,2172,142583,00.html (Accessed 17 November 2008).

SADLER, S. 1998. *The Situationist City.* Cambridge, MA: MIT Press.

SADLER, S. 2005. *Archigram: architecture without architecture.* Cambridge, MA: MIT Press.

SAHLINS, M. D. 1972. *Stone Age Economics.* London: Routledge.

SAHLINS, M. D. 1976. *Culture and Practical Reason.* Chicago: University of Chicago Press.

SAHLINS, M. D. 1992. The economics of develop-man in the Pacific. *Res* 21: 12–25.

SAHLINS, M. D. 1993. Goodbye to tristes tropes: ethnography in the context of modern world history. *Journal of Modern History* 65: 1–25.

SAHLINS, M. D. 1994. Cosmologies of capitalism. The trans-Pacific sector of 'The World System'. In N. B. Dirks, G. Eley, and S. B. Ortner (eds) *Culture/Power/History: a reader in contemporary social history.* Princeton, NJ: Princeton University Press, pp. 412–455.

SAHLINS, M. D. 1995. *How 'Natives' Think: about Captain Cook, for example.* Chicago: University of Chicago Press.

SAHLINS, M. D. 1999. What is anthropological enlightenment? Some lessons of the twentieth century. *Annual Review of Anthropology* 28: i–xxiii.

SAID, E. W. 1978. *Orientalism.* New York, NY: Pantheon.

SAINT GEORGE, R. B. 1998. *Conversing by Signs: poetics of implication in colonial New England culture.* Chapel Hill: University of North Carolina Press.

SALDANHA, A. 2007. *Psychedelic white: Goa trance and the viscosity of race.* Minneapolis: University of Minnesota Press.

SALOMON, F. 1995. The beautiful grandparents. Andean ancestor shrines and mortuary ritual as seen through colonial records. In T. Dillehay (ed.) *Tombs for the Living: Andean mortuary practices*. Washington, DC: Dumbarton Oaks, pp. 315–353.

SANDERS, J. (ed.) 1996. *Stud*. New York: Princeton Architectural Press.

SANFORD, D. 1994. The archaeology of plantation slavery in Piedmont Virginia: context and process. In P. Shackel and B. Little (eds) *Historical Archaeology of the Chesapeake*. Washington, DC: Smithsonian Institution Press, pp. 115–130.

SANMARTÍ, J. 2009. Colonial relations and social change in Iberia (seventh to third centuries BC). In M. Dietler and C. López-Ruiz (eds) *Colonial Encounters in Ancient Iberia: Phoenician, Greek, and indigenous relations*. Chicago: University of Chicago Press, pp. 49–88.

SANZ, C. M. and MORGAN, D. B. 2007. Chimpanzee tool technology in the Goualougo Triangle, republic of Congo. *Journal of Human Evolution* 52(4): 420–433.

SASSAMAN, K. E. 1992. Lithic technology and the hunter-gatherer sexual division of labour. *North American Archaeologist* 13: 249–262.

SASSAMAN, K. E. 2000. Agents of change in hunter-gatherer technology. In M. A. Dobres and J. Robb (eds) *Agency in Archaeology*. London: Routledge, pp. 148–168.

SASSEN, S. 2006. *Territory, Authority, Rights: from medieval to global assemblages*. Princeton, NJ: Princeton University Press.

SATOW, E. M. and HAWES, L. A. G. S. 1881. *Handbook for Travellers in Central and Northern Japan*. Yakohama: Kelly and Co.

SAUER, C. O. 1965. The morphology of landscape. In J. Leighly (ed.) *Land and Life: a selection from the writings of Carl Ortwin Sauer* (second edition). Berkeley: University of California Press, pp. 315–350.

SAUNDERS, N. J. 1999. Biographies of brilliance: Pearls, transformations of matter and being, c. AD 1492. *World Archaeology* 31(2): 243–257.

DE SAUSSURE, F. 1959 [1916]. *Course in General Linguistics* (eds C. Bally and A. Reidlinger; trans. W. Baskin). New York: Philosophical Library.

SAVAGE, M. and BURROWS, R. 2007. The coming crisis of empirical sociology. *Sociology* 41: 885–899.

SAVILL, R. 2007a. Beachcombers make the most of sea harvest. *Daily Telegraph* 24 January 2007.

SAVILL, R. 2007b. Strange case of the photos that made a return trip via Napoli. *Daily Telegraph* 27 January 2007.

SAXE, A. 1970. Social Dimensions of Mortuary Practices. Unpublished Ph.D. thesis, University of Michigan.

SAYERS, D. 1959 [1933]. *Murder must Advertise*. London: New English Library.

SCALWAY, H. 2006. A patois of pattern: pattern, memory and the cosmopolitan city. *Cultural Geographies* 13: 451–457.

SCARAMELLI, F. and TARBLE DE SCARAMELLI, K. 2005. The roles of material culture in the colonization of the Orinoco, Venezuela. *Journal of Social Archaeology* 5(1): 135–168.

SCHACHERMEYR, F. 1955. *Die ältesten Kulturen Griechenlands*. Stuttgart: Kohlhammer.

VAN SCHAIK, C. P. 2003. Local traditions in orangutans and chimpanzees: social learning and social tolerance. In D. Fragaszy and S. E. Perry (eds) *The Biology of Traditions: models and evidence*. Cambridge: Cambridge University Press, pp. 297–328.

VAN SCHAIK, C. P. and Fox, E. A. 1996. Manufacture and use of tools in wild Sumatran orangutans. *Naturwissenschaften* 83: 186–188.

VAN SCHAIK, C. P. and KNOTT, C. D. 2001. Geographic variation in tool use on Neesia fruits in orangutans. *American Journal of Physical Anthropology* 114(4): 331–342.

VAN SCHAIK, C. P., DEANER, R. O. and MERRILL, M. Y. 1999. The conditions for tool use in primates: implications for the evolution of material culture. *Journal of Human Evolution* 36(6): 719–741.

VAN SCHAIK, C. P., ANCRENAZ, M., BORGEN, G., GALDIKAS, B., KNOTT, C. D., SINGLETON, I., SUZUKI, A., SUCI UTAMI, S. and MERRILL, M. 2003a. Orangutan cultures and the evolution of material culture. *Science* 299(5603): 102–105.

VAN SCHAIK, C. P., FOX, E. A. and FECHTMAN, L. T. 2003b. Individual variation in the rate of use of tree-hole tools among wild orangutans: implications for hominin evolution. *Journal of Human Evolution* 44: 11–23.

VAN SCHAIK, C. P., VAN NOORDWIJK, M. A. and WICH, S. A. 2006. Innovation in wild Bornean orangutans (*Pongo pygmaeus wurmbii*). *Behaviour* 143: 839–876.

SCHAMA, S. 1995. *Landscape and memory*. London: Harper Collins.

SCHIEBINGER, L. L. 2004. *Plants and empire: colonial bioprospecting in the Atlantic world*. Cambridge, MA: Harvard University Press.

SCHIEBINGER, L. L. and SWAN, C. (eds) 2005. *Colonial Botany: science, commerce, and politics in the early modern world*. Philadelphia: University of Pennsylvania Press.

SCHIFFER, M. B. 1972. Archaeological context and systemic context. *American Antiquity* 37(2): 156–165.

SCHIFFER, M. B. 1975. Archaeology as behavioral science. *American Anthropologist* 77: 836–848.

SCHIFFER, M. B. 1976. *Behavioral Archeology*. New York: Academic Press.

SCHIFFER, M. B. 1983. Toward the identification of formation processes. *American Antiquity* 48: 675–706.

SCHIFFER, M. B. 1985. Is there a 'Pompeii premise' in archaeology? *Journal of Anthropological Research* 41: 18–41.

SCHIFFER, M. B. 1987. *Formation Processes of the Archaeological Record*. Albuquerque: University of New Mexico Press.

SCHIFFER, M. B. 1992. *Technological Perspectives on Behavioral Change*. Tucson, AZ: University of Arizona Press.

SCHIFFER, M. B. 1995a. *Behavioral Archaeology: first principles*. Salt Lake City: University of Utah Press.

SCHIFFER, M. B. 1995b. Social theory and history in behavioral archaeology. In J. Skibo, W. Walker, and A. Nielsen (eds) *Expanding Archaeology*. Salt Lake City: University of Utah Press, pp. 22–35.

SCHIFFER, M. B. 1996. Some relationships between behavioral and evolutionary archaeologies. *American Antiquity* 61(4): 643–662.

SCHIFFER, M. B. 1999. *The Material Life of Human Beings: artifacts, behavior, and communication*. London: Routledge.

SCHIFFER, M. B. 2000. Indigenous theories, scientific theories and product histories. In P. Graves-Brown (ed.) *Matter, Materiality and Modern Culture*. London: Routledge, pp. 72–96.

SCHIFFER, M. B. (ed.) 2001a. *Anthropological Perspectives on Technology*. Albuquerque: University of New Mexico Press.

SCHIFFER, M. B. 2001b. The explanation of long-term technological change. In M. Schiffer (ed.) *Anthropological Perspectives on Technology*. Albuquerque: University of New Mexico Press, pp. 215–235.

SCHIFFER, M. B. 2002. Studying technological differentiation: the case of eighteenth-century electrical technology. *American Anthropologist* 104(4): 1148–1161.

SCHIFFER, M. B. 2004. Studying technological change: a behavioral perspective. *World Archaeology* 36(4): 579–585.

SCHIFFER, M. B. 2005a. The devil is in the details: the cascade model of invention processes. *American Antiquity* 70(3): 485–502.

SCHIFFER, M. B. 2005b. The electric lighthouse in the nineteenth century: aid to navigation and political technology. *Technology and Culture* 46(2): 275–305.

SCHIFFER, M. B. 2008a. Behavioral archaeology. In D. Pearsall (ed.) *Encyclopedia of Archaeology* (Volume 2). New York: Elsevier, pp. 909–919.

SCHIFFER, M. B. 2008b. Transmission processes: a behavioral perspective. In M. O'Brien (ed.) *Cultural Transmission and Archaeology: issues and case studies.* Washington, DC: Society for American Archaeology, pp. 102–111.

SCHIFFER, M. B. 2008c. *Power Struggles: scientific authority and the creation of practical electricity before Edison.* Cambridge, MA: MIT Press.

SCHIFFER, M. B. and SKIBO, J. 1987. Theory and experiment in the study of technological change. *Current Anthropology,* 28(4): 595–622.

SCHIFFER, M. B. and SKIBO, J. 1997. The explanation of artefact variability. *American Antiquity* 62(1): 27–50.

SCHIFFER, M. B. and MILLER, A. 1999. *The Material Life of Human Beings: artefacts, behavior, and communication.* London: Routledge.

SCHIFFER, M. B., BUTTS, T. and GRIMM, K. 1994a. *Taking Charge: the electric automobile in America.* Washington, DC: Smithsonian Books.

SCHIFFER, M. B., SKIBO, J., BOELKE, T., NEUPERT, M. and ARONSON, M. 1994b. New perspectives on experimental archaeology: surface treatments and thermal response of the clay cooking pot. *American Antiquity* 59(2): 197–217.

SCHIFFER, M. B., SKIBO, J., GRIFFITTS, J., HOLLENBACK, K. and LONGACRE, W. 2001. Behavioral archaeology and the study of technology. *American Antiquity* 66(4): 729–738.

SCHLANGER, N. (ed.) 2006. *Marcel Mauss, Techniques, Technology and Civilisation.* Oxford: Berghahn.

SCHLANGER, N. 2005. The chaîne opératoire. In A. C. Renfrew and P. Bahn (eds) *Archaeology: the key concepts.* London: Routledge; pp. 35–41.

SCHLERETH, T. J. 1981. Material culture studies in America, 1876–1976. In T. Schlereth (ed.) *Material Culture Studies in America.* Nashville: American Association for State and Local History, pp. 1–75.

SCHLICH, T. 2007. Surgery, science and modernity: operating rooms and laboratories as spaces of control. *History of Science* 45: 231–256.

SCHMIDT, P. R. 1983. An alternative to a strictly materialist perspective: a review of historical archaeology, ethnoarchaeology, and symbolic approaches in African Archaeology. *American Antiquity* 48(1): 62–79.

SCHMIDT, R. 2004. The contribution of gender to personal identity in the southern Scandinavian Mesolithic. In E. Casella and C. Fowler (eds) *The Archaeology of Plural and Changing Identities: beyond identification.* New York: Kluwer, pp. 79–108.

SCHNAPP, A. 1993. *The Discovery of the Past. The origins of archaeology.* London: British Museum Press.

SCHÖNING, C., HUMLE, T., MÖBIUS, Y. and McGREW, W. C. 2008. The nature of culture: technological variation in chimpanzee predation on army ants revisited. *Journal of Human Evolution* 55(1): 48–59.

SCHWENGER, P. 2006. *The Tears of Things. Melancholy and physical objects.* Minneapolis: University of Minnesota Press.

SCOTT, D. 1995. Colonial governmentality. *Social Text* 43: 191–220.

SCOTT, J. 1998. *Seeing Like a State: how certain schemes to improve the human condition have failed.* New Haven, CT: Yale University Press.

SCOTT, S. 2006. Art and the archaeologist. *World Archaeology* 38(4): 628–643.

SEBALD, W. G. 2003. *On the Natural History of Destruction.* New York: Alfred A. Knopf.

SEIDMAN, S. (ed.) 1994. *The Postmodern Turn: new perspectives on social theory.* Cambridge: Cambridge University Press.

SEKULA, A. 2003. *Fish Story.* Düsseldorf: Richter Verlag.

SEMENOV, S. A. 1964. *Prehistoric Technology: an experimental study of the oldest tools and artefacts from traces of manufacture and wear.* London: Cory, Adams and Mackay.

SEMPER, G. 1989. *The Four Elements of Architecture and Other Writings.* Cambridge: Cambridge University Press.

SERRES, M. 1980. *Le Parasite.* Paris: Grasset and Fasquelle.

SERRES, M. and LATOUR, B. 1995. *Conversations in Science, Culture and Time.* Ann Arbor, MI: University of Michigan Press.

SERRES, O. DE 1600. *Le theatre d'agricvltvre et mesnage des champs.* Paris: I. Métayer imprimeur ordinaire du roy.

SERRES, O. DE and GEFFE, N. 1971. *The Perfect Vase of Silk-wormes, Volume 345.* Amsterdam: Theatrum Orbis Terrarum and Da Capo Press.

SEYMOUR, D. and SCHIFFER, M. B. 1987. A preliminary analysis of pithouse assemblages from Snaketown, Arizona. In S. Kent (ed.) *Method and Theory for Activity Area Research: an ethnoarchaeological approach.* New York: Columbia University Press, pp. 549–603.

SHANKS, M. 1990. Reading the signs: responses to 'Archaeology After Structuralism'. In I. Bapty and T. Yates (eds) *Archaeology After Structuralism.* London: Routledge, pp. 294–310.

SHANKS, M. 1998. The life of an artefact in an interpretive archaeology. *Fennoscandia Archaeologica* 15: 15–42.

SHANKS, M. 2007. Symmetrical archaeology. *World Archaeology* 39(4): 589–596.

SHANKS, M. and McGUIRE, R. H. 1996. The craft of archaeology. *American Antiquity* 61(1): 75–88.

SHANKS, M. and TILLEY, C. 1982. Ideology, symbolic power and ritual communication: a reinterpretation of Neolithic mortuary practices. In I. Hodder (ed.) *Symbolic and Structural Archaeology.* Cambridge: Cambridge University Press, pp. 129–154.

SHANKS, M. and TILLEY, C. 1987a. *Re-Constructing Archaeology.* London: Routledge.

SHANKS, M. and TILLEY, C. 1987b. *Social Theory and Archaeology.* Cambridge: Polity.

SHANKS, M. and TILLEY, C. 1989. Preface to the second edition. In M. Shanks and C. Tilley *Re-Constructing Archaeology* (second edition). London: Routledge, pp. xvii–xxiv.

SHANKS, M. and TILLEY, C. 1992. *Re-Constructing Archaeology: theory and practice* (second edition). London: Routledge.

SHANKS, M. and HODDER, I. 1995. Processual, post-processual and interpretive archaeologies. In I. Hodder, M. Shanks, A. Alexandri, V. Buchli, J. Carman, J. Last and G. Lucas (eds) *Interpreting Archaeology: finding meaning in the past.* London: Routledge, pp. 3–29.

SHAPIN, S. and SCHAFFER, S. 1985. *Leviathan and the Air Pump: Hobbes, Boyle and the Experimental Life*. Princeton: Princeton University Press.

SHARER, R. J. 2006. *The Ancient Maya* (6th edition). Stanford: Stanford University Press.

SHAW, J. 1979. *Red Army Resurgent*. Chicago: Time-Life Books.

SHAW, R. 2002. *Memories of the Slave Trade: ritual and historical imagination in Sierra Leone*. Chicago: University of Chicago Press.

SHAW, W. H. 1979. 'The handmill gives you the feudal lord': Marx's technological determinism. *History and Theory* 18: 155–176.

SHELLER, M. and URRY, J. 2006. The new mobilities paradigm. *Environment and Planning A* 38(2): 207–226.

SHENNAN, S. 1982. Ideology, change and the European Early Bronze Age. In I. Hodder (ed.) *Symbolic and Structural Archaeology*. Cambridge: Cambridge University Press, pp. 155–161.

SHEPHERD, N. 2003. 'When the hand that holds the trowel is black...': Disciplinary practices of self-representation and the issue of 'native' labour in archaeology. *Journal of Social Archaeology* 3(2): 334–352.

SHEPPARD, T. 1911. John Robert Mortimer. *The Naturalist* (May 1911): 186–191.

SHERRATT, A. G. 1989. V. Gordon Childe: archaeology and intellectual history. *Past and Present* 125: 151–185.

SHIELDS, R. (ed.) 1992. *Lifestyle Shopping: the subject of consumption*. London: Routledge.

SHILLING, C. 1993. *The Body and Social Theory*. London: Sage.

SHILLING, C. 2005. *The Body in Culture, Technology and Society*. London; Thousand Oaks, CA: Sage.

SHILLING, C. 2008. *Changing Bodies: habit, crisis and creativity*. Los Angeles; London: Sage.

Sidmouth Herald 2007a. So why did they risk our beautiful beaches? *Sidmouth Herald* 26 January 2007.

Sidmouth Herald 2007b. Fate of birds caught in oil. *Sidmouth Herald* 25 June 2007.

Sidmouth Herald 2007c. Portrayed as thieves. *Sidmouth Herald* 26 January 2007.

Sidmouth Herald 2007d. Arrest warning. *Sidmouth Herald*, 23 January 2008.

Sidmouth Herald 2007e. Eager to return Napoli photographs. *Sidmouth Herald*, 28 June 2007.

Sidmouth Herald 2007f. Plague of locusts descended on us. *Sidmouth Herald*, 26 January 2007.

Sidmouth Herald 2007g. Adois Napoli. *Sidmouth Herald* 25 May 2007.

Sidmouth Herald 2007h. Now for scrappers. *Sidmouth Herald* 27 July 2007.

Sidmouth Herald 2007i. Europe's biggest sea crane will help to remove the stranded Napoli. *Sidmouth Herald* 2 November 2007.

Sidmouth Herald 2007j. Napoli reaches Irish shipyard. *Sidmouth Herald* 17 August 2007.

Sidmouth Herald 2007k. Reliving plunder emotions. *Sidmouth Herald* 1 June 2007.

Sidmouth Herald 2007l. Town's business boom. *Sidmouth herald* 3 February 2007.

Sidmouth Herald 2007m. For the moment, it's the Swag Inn of York Street! *Sidmouth Herald* 26 January 2007.

SILBERMAN, N. A. 2007. 'Sustainable' heritage? Public archaeological interpretation and the marketed past. In Y. Hamilakis and P. Duke (eds) *Archaeology and Capitalism: from ethics to politics*. Walnut Creek, CA: Left Coast Press (One World Archaeology 54), pp. 179–193.

SILLAR, B. 1992. The social life of the Andean dead. *Archaeological Review from Cambridge* 11: 107–124.

SILLAR, B. 1996. The dead and the drying: techniques for transforming people and things in the Andes. *Journal of Material Culture* 1: 259–289.

SILLIMAN, S. W. 2005. Culture contact or colonialism? Challenges in the archaeology of Native North America. *American Antiquity* 70(1): 55–74.

SILVERSTONE, R. and HIRSCH, E. 1992. *Consuming Technologies: media and information in domestic spaces*. London: Routledge.

SIMMEL, G. 1905. Fashion. *International Quarterly* 10: 130–155.

SIMMEL, G. 1961 [1903]. *Metropolis and Mental Life* (trans. H. H. Gerth and C. Wright Mills). Chicago: University of Chicago Press.

SIMON, J. 1988. The ideological effects of actuarial practices. *Law and Society Review* 22(4): 771–800.

SIMPSON, B. 2004. Impossible gifts: bodies, buddhism and bioethics in contemporary Sri Lanka. *Journal of the Royal Anthropological Institute* (n.s.) 10(4): 839–859.

SINCLAIR, A. 1995. The technique as symbol in late glacial Europe. *World Archaeology* 27(1): 50–62.

SINGER, M. 1980. Signs of the self: an exploration in semiotic anthropology. *American Anthropologist* (n.s.) 82(3): 485–507.

SINGLETON, T. A. (ed.) 1985. *The Archaeology of Slavery and Plantation Life*. NY: Academic Press.

SINGLETON, T. A. (ed.). 1999. *'I Too am America': archaeological studies of African-American life*. Charlottesville: University Press of Virginia.

SKIBO, J. and SCHIFFER, M. B. 2008. *People and Things: a behavioral approach to material culture*. New York: Springer.

SLATER, D. and MILLER, D. 2006. Moments and movements in the study of consumer culture: a discussion between Daniel Miller and Don Slater. *Journal of Consumer Culture* 7(1): 5–23.

SLATER, D. R. 1993. Going shopping: markets, crowds and consumption. In C. Jenks (ed.) *Cultural Reproduction*. London: Routledge, pp. 188–209.

SLOTERDIJK, P. 2007. What happened in the twentieth century? En route to a critique of extremist reason. *Cultural Politics* 3: 327–356.

SMALL, S. and EICHSTEDT, J. 2002. *Representations of Slavery: race and ideology in Southern plantation museums*. Washington, DC: Smithsonian Institution Press.

SMEDLEY, N. and OWLES, E. 1965. More Suffolk witch-bottles. *Proceedings of the Suffolk Institute of Archaeology* 30: 88–93.

SMITH, A. C. and KLEINMAN, S. 1989. Managing emotions in medical school: students' contacts with the living and the dead. *Social Psychology Quarterly* 52(1): 56–69.

SMITH, C. and WOBST, H. M. (eds) 2005. *Indigenous Archaeologies: decolonising theory and practice*. London: Routledge.

SMITH, I. F. 1965. *Windmill Hill and Avebury: excavations by Alexander Keiller 1925–1939*. Oxford: Clarendon Press.

SMITH, M. 2007. *Sensory History*. Oxford: Berg.

SMITH, M. E., WHARTON, J. B. and OLSON, J. M. 2003. Aztec feasts, rituals, and markets: political uses of ceramic vessels in a commercial economy. In T. L. Bray (ed.) *The Archaeology and Politics of Food and Feasting in Early States and Empires*. New York: Kluwer Academic/Plenum Publishers, pp. 235–268.

SNEAD, J. E. 2006. Ancestral Pueblo trails and the cultural landscape of the Pajarito Plateau, New Mexico. *Antiquity* 76: 756–765.

SNOWDON, C. T. 2001. Social process in communication and cognition in callitrichid monkeys: a review. *Animal Cognition* 2: 247–257.

SOCIAL SCIENCE RESEARCH COUNCIL 1954. Acculturation: an exploratory formulation (Social Science Research Council Summer Seminar on Acculturation, 1953). *American Anthropologist* 56: 973–1000.

SOFAER, J. R. 2006a. *The Body as Material Culture*. Cambridge: Cambridge University Press.

SOFAER, J. R. 2006b. Gender, bioarchaeology and human ontogeny. In R. Gowland and C. Knüsel (eds) *Social Archaeology of Funerary Remains*. Oxford: Oxbow Books, pp. 155–167.

SOFER, A. 2003. *The Stage Life of Props*. Ann Arbor: University of Michigan Press.

SOJA, E. 1989. *Postmodern Geographies: the reassertion of space in critical social theory*. London: Verso.

SOUTH, S. 1979. Historic site content, structure, and function. *American Antiquity* 44(2): 213–237.

SØRENSON, M-L. 1991. Construction of gender through appearance. In D. Walde and N. D. Willows, (eds) *The Archaeology of Gender: Proceedings of the Twenty-Second Annual Conference of the Archaeological Association of the University of Calgary*. Calgary: University of Calgary Archaeological Association, pp. 121–129.

SØRENSON, M-L. 2000. *Gender Archaeology*. Cambridge: Polity Press.

SPAIN, D. 1992. *Gendered Spaces*. Chapel Hill: University of North Carolina Press.

SPAULDING, A. C. 1953. Statistical techniques for the discovery of artifact types. *American Antiquity* 18: 305–313.

SPAULDING, A. C. 1954. Reply to Ford. *American Antiquity* 19: 391–393.

SPENCE, K. W. 1937. Experimental studies of learning and higher mental processes in infra-human primates. *Psychological Bulletin* 34: 806–850.

SPIER, R. 1970. *From the Hand of Man: primitive and preindustrial technologies*. Boston: Houghton Mifflin.

SPIRN, A. W. 1998. *The Language of Landscape*. New Haven: Yale University Press.

SPIVAK, G. C. 1996. *The Spivak Reader*. Donna Landry and Gerald MacLean (ed.). New York: Routledge.

SPORRONG, U. 1995. *Swedish Landscapes*. Stockholm: Swedish Environmental Protection Agency.

SPRINGER, C. 1996. *Electronic Eros: bodies and desire in the postindustrial age*. Austin: University of Texas Press.

SPYER, P. 1998. (ed.) *Border Fetishisms: material objects in unstable spaces*. London: Routledge.

STAFFORD, B. M. 2007. *Echo Objects. The cognitive work of images*. Chicago: University of Chicago Press.

STAHL, A. B. 2001. *Making History in Banda: anthropological visions of Africa's past*. Cambridge: Cambridge University Press.

STAHL, A. B. 2002. Colonial entanglements and the practices of taste: an alternative to logocentric approaches. *American Anthropologist* 104(3): 827–845.

STAHL, A. B. 2007. Entangled lives: the archaeology of daily life in the Gold Coast Hinterlands, AD 1400–1900. In A. Ogundiran and T. Falola (eds) *Archaeology of Atlantic Africa and the African Diaspora*. Bloomington: Indiana University Press, 49–76.

STAHL, A. B. 2008a. Dogs, pythons, pots and beads: the dynamics of shrines and sacrificial practices in Banda, Ghana, AD 1400–1900. In B. Mills and W. Walker (eds) *Memory Work: the materiality of depositional practice*. Santa Fe, NM: School of Advanced Research, pp. 159–186.

STAHL, A. B. 2008b. The slave trade as practice and memory. What are the issues for archaeologists? In C. M. Cameron (ed.) *Invisible Citizens: captives and their consequences*. Salt Lake City: University of Utah Press, pp. 25–56.

STAHL, A. B. and STAHL, P. W. 2004. Ivory production and consumption in Ghana in the early second millennium AD. *Antiquity* 78: 86–101.

STALLYBRASS, P. and WHITE, A. 1986. *The Politics and Poetics of Transgression*. London: Methuen.

STARK, M. 1998a. Technical choices and social boundaries in material culture patterning: an introduction. In M. Stark (ed.) *The Archaeology of Social Boundaries*. Washington, DC: Smithsonian Institution Press, pp. 1–11.

STARK, M. (ed.) 1998b. *The Archaeology of Social Boundaries*. Washington, DC: Smithsonian Institution Press.

STEARN, W. T. 1961. *Early Leyden Botany*. Van Gorcum-Assen: Universitaire Per Leiden.

STECK, C. E., BURGI, M., COCH, T. and DUELLI, P. 2007. Hotspots and richness pattern of grasshopper species in cultural landscapes. *Biodiversity and Conservation* 16: 2075–2086.

STEINER, C. 1985. Another image of Africa: toward an ethnohistory of European cloth marketed in West Africa 1873–1960. *Ethnohistory* 32(2): 91–110.

STEINER, C. 1994. *African Art in Transit*. Cambridge: Cambridge University Press.

STEINHARDT, N. S. 1999. *Chinese Imperial City Planning*. Honolulu: University of Hawaii Press.

STENGERS, I. 1997. *Cosmopolitiques*. Paris, La Découverte/Poche.

STENGERS, I. 2000. *The Invention of Modern Science* (trans. D. W. Smith). Minneapolis: University of Minnesota Press.

STEVANOVIĆ, M. 1997. The Age of Clay: the social dynamics of house destruction. *Journal of Anthropological Archaeology* 16(4): 334–395.

STEVENS, R. 1974. European visitors to the Safavid court. *Iranian Studies* 7: 421–457.

STEWART, S. 1993. *On Longing: narratives of the miniature, the gigantic, the souvenir, the collection*. Durham, NC: Duke University Press.

STIER, F. 1975. Behavioral chain analysis of Yucca remains at Antelope House. *Kiva* 41(1): 57–64.

STIGLER, G. and BECKER, G. S. 1977. De gustibus non est disputandum. *American Economic Review* 67(2): 76–90.

STILGOE, J. R. 1982. *Common Landscape of America, 1580 to 1845*. New Haven: Yale University Press.

STILGOE, J. R. 1983. *The Metropolitan Corridor: railroads and the American scene*. New Haven: Yale University Press.

STILGOE, J. R. 1988. *Borderland: origins of the American suburb, 1820–1939*. New Haven: Yale University Press.

STILGOE, J. R. 1994. *Alongshore*. New Haven: Yale University Press.

STILGOE, J. R. 1998. *Outside Lies Magic: regaining history and awareness in everyday places*. New York: Walker and Co.

STOCKING, G. W. 1971. Animism in theory and practice: E. B. Tylor's Unpublished 'Notes on Spiritualism'. *Man* (n.s.) 6: 88–104.

STOCKING, G. W. (ed.) 1983a. *Observers observed. Essays on ethnographic fieldwork*. Madison, WI: University of Wisconsin Press.

STOCKING, G. W. 1983b. The ethnographer's magic: fieldwork in British anthropology from Tylor to Malinowski. In G. W. Stocking (ed.) *Observers Observed: essays on ethnographic fieldwork*. Madison, WI: University of Wisconsin Press, 70–120.

STOCKING, G. W. 1985. Essays on museums and material culture. In G. W. Stocking (ed.) *Objects and Others: essays on museums and material culture*. Madison, WI: University of Wisconsin Press, pp. 3–14.

STOCKING, G. W. 1987. *Victorian Anthropology*. New York: Free Press.

STOCKING, G. W. 1995. *After Tylor*. Madison, WI: University of Wisconsin Press.

STOCKING, G. W. 2001. *Delimiting Anthropology: occasional inquiries and reflections*. Madison, WI: University of Wisconsin Press.

STOLER, A. L. 1989. Rethinking colonial categories: European Communities and the boundaries of rule. *Comparative Studies in Society and History* 31: 134–161.

STOLER, A. L. 2001. Tense and tender ties: the politics of comparison in North American history and post colonial studies. *Journal of American History* 88(3): 829–865.

STOLER, A. L. 2006a. Intimidations of Empire: predicaments of the tactile and unseen. In A. L. Stoler (ed.) *Haunted by Empire: geographies of intimacy in North American history*. Durham, NC: Duke University Press, pp. 1–22.

STOLER, A. L. 2006b. On degrees of imperial sovereignty. *Public Culture* 18(1): 125–146.

STOLER, A. L. and COOPER, F. 1997. Between metropole and colony: rethinking a research agenda. In F. Cooper and A. L. Stoler (eds) *Tensions of Empire: colonial cultures in a bourgeois world*. Berkeley: University of California Press, pp. 1–56.

STOLLER, P. 1997. *Sensuous Scholarship*. Philadelphia: University of Pennsylvania Press.

STOTT, M. and REYNOLDS, B. 1987. Material anthropology: contemporary approaches to material culture. In B. Reynolds and M. Stott (eds) *Material Anthropology: contemporary approaches to material culture*. Lanham, MD: University Press of America, pp. 1–12.

STRATHERN, A. J. 1979. Gender, ideology and money in Mount Hagen. *Man* (n.s.) 14(3): 530–548.

STRATHERN, A. J. and STEWART, P. 2000. Dangerous woods and perilous pearl shells: the fabricated politics of a longhouse in Pangia, Papua New Guinea. *Journal of Material Culture* 5: 69–89.

STRATHERN, A. J. 1996. *Body Thoughts*. Ann Arbor: University of Michigan Press.

STRATHERN, M. 1972. *Women in Between; female roles in a male world: Mount Hagen, New Guinea*. London: Seminar Press.

STRATHERN, M. 1981. Culture in a netbag: the manufacture of a subdiscipline in anthropology. *Man* (n.s.) 16(4): 665–688.

STRATHERN, M. 1987. The limits of auto-anthropology. In A. Jackson (ed.) *Anthropology at Home*. London: Tavistock Publications (ASA Monographs 25), pp. 16–37.

STRATHERN, M. 1988. *The Gender of the Gift: problems with women and problems with society in Melanesia*. Berkeley: University of California Press.

STRATHERN. M. 1990. Artefacts of history: events and the interpretation of images. In J. Siikala (ed.) *Culture and History in the Pacific*. Helsinki: Finnish Anthropological Society, pp. 24–44.

STRATHERN, M. 1991. *Partial Connections*. ASAO Special Publications No. 3. Savage, MD: Rowman and Littlefield.

STRATHERN, M. 1996. Cutting the network. *Journal of the Royal Anthropological Institute* 2: 517–535.

STRATHERN, M. 1999. *Property, Substance and Effect. Anthropological essays on persons and things*. London: Athlone Press.

STRATHERN, M. 2001. The patent and the Malanggan. *Theory, Culture and Society* 18(4): 1–26.

STRATHERN, M. 2004a. *Partial Connections* (updated edition). Walnut Creek, CA: Altamira.

STRATHERN, M. 2004b. *Commons and Borderlands*. Wantage: Sean Kingston.

STRATHERN, M. 2005. *Kinship, Law and the Unexpected: relatives are always a surprise.* Cambridge: Cambridge University Press.

STRUM, S. and LATOUR, B. 1987. Redefining the social link: from baboons to humans. *Social Science Information* 26(4): 783–802.

STURCKE, J. and MORRIS, S. 2007. Salvage boats refloat Napoli cargo ship. *The Guardian*, 9 July 2007.

STURTEVANT, W. 1969. Does anthropology need museums? *Proceedings of the Biological Society of Washington* 82: 619–650.

STYLES, O. 2007. French barrel maker loses over 100k in Napoli grounding. *Decanter* 26 January http://www.decanter.com/news/107468.html?aff=rss (Accessed 17 November 2008).

SUMNER, W. G. 1906. *Folkways: a study of the sociological importance of manners, customs, mores and morality.* Boston: Ginn.

SWANEPOEL, N. 2006. Socio-political change on a slave-raiding frontier: war, trade and 'big men' in nineteenth century Sisalaland, Northern Ghana. In T. Pollard and I. Banks (eds) *Past Tense: studies in the archaeology of conflict.* Leiden: Brill, pp. 265–293.

SWEET, R. 2004. *Antiquaries: the discovery of the past in eighteenth-century Britain.* London: Hambledon.

SWENTZALL, R. 1990. Conflicting landscape values: Santa Clara Pueblo day school. *Places* 7: 19–27.

SYKES, K. 2005. *Arguing With Anthropology: an introduction to critical theories of the gift.* London: Routledge.

SYLVANUS, N. 2007. The fabric of Africanity: tracing the global threads of authenticity. *Anthropological Theory* 7(2): 201–216.

SYMONDS, J. 2004. Historical archaeology and the recent urban past. *International Journal of Heritage Studies* 10(1): 33–48.

SYNOTT, A. 1992. Tomb, temple, machine and self: the social construction of the body. *British Journal of Sociology* 43(1): 79–110.

TACCHI, J. 1998. Radio textures: between self and others. In D. Miller (ed.) *Material Cultures: why some things matter.* Chicago: University of Chicago Press, pp. 25–46.

TAINTER, J. 1978. Mortuary practices and the study of prehistoric social systems. *Advances in Archaeological Method and Theory* 1: 105–139.

TAKASHI, K. 1994. Governing Edo. In J. L. McClain, J. M. Merriman and U. Kaoru (eds) *Edo and Paris: urban life and the state in the early Modern Era.* Ithaca: Cornell University Press, pp. 41–67.

TARLOW, S. A. 2000. Emotion in archaeology. *Current Anthropology* 41(5): 713–746.

TARLOW, S. A. 2002. The aesthetic corpse in the nineteenth century. In Y. Hamilakis, M. Pluciennik and S. A. Tarlow (eds) *Thinking Through the Body: archaeologies of corporeality.* New York: Kluwer, pp. 85–97.

TARLOW, S. A. 2007. *The Archaeology of Improvement in Britain, 1750–1850.* Cambridge: Cambridge University Press.

TARLOW, S. A. 2008. The extraordinary history of Oliver Cromwell's head. In D. Borić and J. Robb (eds) *Past Bodies. Body-centered research in archaeology.* Oxford: Oxbow books, pp. 69–78.

TARLOW, S. A. and WEST, S. (eds) 1999. *The Familiar Past? Archaeologies of later historical Britian.* London: Routledge.

TAUSSIG, M. 2003. Viscerality, faith and skepticism. Another theory of magic. In B. Meyer and P. Pels (eds) *Magic and Modernity. Interfaces of revelation and concealment*. Stanford: Stanford University Press, pp. 272–306.

TAYLOR, K. and ALTENBURG, K. 2006. Cultural landscapes in Asia-Pacific: potential for filling World Heritage gaps. *International Journal of Heritage Studies* 12: 267–282.

TAYLOR, M. C. 1991. Rendering. In M. Heizer (ed.) *Double Negative: sculpture in the land*. New York: Rizzoli, pp. 12–22.

TAYLOR, T. G. 1940. *Australia: a study of warm environments and their effect on British settlement*. London: Methuen.

TAYLOR, W. 1948. A study of Archaeology. Washington, DC: American Anthropological Association (American Anthropological Association Memoir 69).

TAYLOR, W. 1972. Old wine and new skins: a contemporary parable. In M. P. Leone (ed.) *Contemporary Archaeology*. Carbondale: Southern Illinois University Press, pp. 28–33.

TCHERNIA, A. 1986. *Le vin de l'Italie romaine: essai d'histoire économique d'après les amphores*. Paris: Boccard.

TEBBICH, S., TABORSKY, M., FESSL, B. and DVORAK, M. 2002. The ecology of tool-use in the woodpecker finch (*Cactospiza pallida*). *Ecology Letters* 5: 656–664.

TEBBICH, S., TABORSKY, M., FESSL, B. and BLOMQVIST, D. 2001. Do woodpecker finches acquire tool-use by social learning? *Proceedings of the Royal Society B-Biological Sciences* 268 (1482): 2189–2193.

TERRAY, E. 1972. *Marxism and 'Primitive' Societies* (trans. M. Klopper). New York: Monthly Review Press.

TERRAY, E. 1975. Classes and class consciousness in the Abron Kingdom of Gyaman (trans. A. Bailey). In M. E. F. Bloch (ed.) *Marxist Analyses and Social Anthropology*. London: Malaby Press (ASA Studies 2), pp. 85–136.

THACKER, C. 1972. Le manière de montrer les jardins de Versailles. *Journal of Garden History* 1: 49–69.

THACKER, C. 1979. *The History of Gardens*. Berkeley: University of California Press.

THACKER, E. 2004. *Biomedia*. Minneapolis: University of Minnesota Press.

THACKER, E. 2005. Biophilosophy for the 21st century. *CTheory* http://www.ctheory.net/articles.aspx?id=472 (Accessed 18 January 2009).

THOMAS, J. S. 1988. The social significance of Cotswold-Severn burial practices. *Man* (n.s.) 23: 540–559.

THOMAS, J. S. 1990. Same, other, analogue: writing the past. In F. Baker and J. S. Thomas (eds) *Writing the Past in the Present*. Lampeter: St David's University College, Lampeter, pp. 18–23.

THOMAS, J. S. 1991a. *Rethinking the Neolithic*. Cambridge: Cambridge University Press (New Studies in Archaeology).

THOMAS, J. S. 1991b. Reading the Neolithic. *Anthropology Today* 7(3): 9–11.

THOMAS, J. S. 1991c. Reading the body: beaker funerary practice in Britain. In P. Garwood, D. Jennings, R. Skeates and J. Toms (eds) *The Sacred and the Profane. Proceedings of a Conference on Archaeology, Ritual and Religion, Oxford 1989*. Oxford: Oxford University Committee for Archaeology, pp. 33–42.

THOMAS, J. S. 1993. The hermeneutics of megalithic space. In C. Tilley (ed.) *Interpretative Archaeology*. Oxford: Berg, pp. 73–98.

THOMAS, J. S. 1995. Reconciling symbolic significance with being-in-the-world. In I. Hodder, M. Shanks, A. Alexandri, V. Buchli, J. Carman, J. Last and G. Lucas (eds) *Interpreting Archaeology: finding meaning in the past*. London: Routledge, pp. 210–211.

THOMAS, J. S. 1996. *Time, Culture and Identity: an interpretive archaeology*. London: Routledge.

THOMAS, J. S. 1999. An economy of substances in Earlier Neolithic Britain. In J. Robb (ed.) *Material Symbols: culture and economy in prehistory*. Carbondale: Southern Illinois University Press, pp. 70–89.

THOMAS, J. S. 2000a. Death, identity and the body in Neolithic Britain. *Journal of the Royal Anthropological Institute* (n.s.) 6: 653–668.

THOMAS, J. S. 2000b. Reconfiguring the social, reconfiguring the material. In M. B. Schiffer (ed.) *Social Theory in Archaeology*. Salt Lake City: University of Utah Press, pp. 143–155.

THOMAS, J. S. 2000c. Introduction: the polarities of post-processual archaeology. In J. S. Thomas (ed.) *Interpretive Archaeology: a reader*. Leicester: Continuum, pp. 1–18.

THOMAS, J. S. (ed.) 2000d. *Interpretative Archaeology: a reader*. Leicester: Leicester University Press.

THOMAS, J. S. 2001. Archaeologies of place and landscape. In I. Hodder (ed.) *Archaeological Theory Today*. London: Polity Press, pp. 165–186.

THOMAS, J. S. 2002. Archaeology's humanism and the materiality of the body. In Y. Hamilakis, M. Pluciennik and S. A. Tarlow (eds) *Thinking Through the Body: archaeologies of corporeality*. New York: Kluwer/Plenum, pp. 29–45.

THOMAS, J. S. 2004. *Archaeology and Modernity*. London: Routledge.

THOMAS, J. S. 2006. Phenomenology and material culture. In C. Tilley, W. Keane, S. Küchler, M. J. Rowlands and P. Spyer (eds) *Handbook of Material Culture*. London: Sage, pp. 43–59.

THOMAS, J. S. 2007. The trouble with material culture. *Journal of Iberian Archaeology* 9/10: 11–23.

THOMAS, J. S. and WHITTLE, A. 1986. Anatomy of a tomb: West Kennet revisited. *Oxford Journal of Archaeology* 5: 129–154.

THOMAS, N. 1990. Sanitation and seeing: the creation of state power in early colonial Fiji. *Comparative Studies in Society and History* 32: 149–170.

THOMAS, N. 1991. *Entangled Objects: Exchange, Material Culture, and Colonialism in the Pacific*. Cambridge, MA: Harvard University Press.

THOMAS, N. 1994. *Colonialism's Culture: anthropology, travel and government*. Princeton, NJ: Princeton University Press.

THOMAS, N. 1998. Foreword. In A. Gell *Art and Agency*. Oxford: Clarendon Press, pp. vii–xiii.

THOMAS, N. 1999. The case of the misplaced ponchos. Speculations concerning the history of cloth in Polynesia. *Journal of Material Culture* 4: 5–20.

THOMAS, N. 2000. Technologies of conversion: cloth and Christianity in Polynesia. In A. Brah and A. E. Coombes (eds) *Hybridity and its Discontents: politics, science, culture*. London: Routledge, pp. 198–215.

THOMAS, N. 2002. Colonizing cloth: interpreting the material culture of nineteenth-century Oceania. In C. Lyons and J. Papadopoulos (eds) *The Archaeology of Colonialism*. Los Angeles: Getty Research Institute, pp. 65–95.

THOMAS, N. J. 2007. Embodying empire: dressing the Vicereine, Lady Curzon 1898–1905. *Cultural Geographies* 14(3), 369–400.

THOMPSON, M. 1979. *Rubbish Theory: the creation and destruction of value*. Oxford: Oxford University Press.

THOMPSON, R. and PAREZO, N. 1989. A historical survey of material culture studies in anthropology. In A. Hedlund (ed.) *Perspectives on Anthropological Collections from the American Southwest: Proceedings of a Symposium*. Tempe: Department of Anthropology, Arizona State University (Anthropological Research Papers 40), pp. 33–65.

THORNDIKE, E. L. 1911. *Animal Intelligence*. New York: MacMillan.

THORNTON, A. and MCAULIFFE, K. 2006. Teaching in wild meerkats. *Science* 313(5784): 227–229.

THORPE, I. J. and RICHARDS, C. 1984. The decline of ritual authority and the introduction of beakers into Britain. In R. J. Bradley and J. Gardiner (eds) *Neolithic Studies*. Oxford: British Archaeological Reports (BAR British series 133), pp. 67–84.

THRIFT, N. J. 1985. Bear and mouse or bear and tree? Anthony Giddens' reconstitution of social theory. *Sociology* 19(4): 609–623.

THRIFT, N. J. 1999. Steps to an ecology of place. In D. Massey, J. Allen and P. Sarre (eds) *Human Geography Today*. Cambridge: Polity Press, pp. 295–322.

THRIFT, N. J. 2000. Introduction. Dead or alive? In I. Cook, D. Crouch, S. Naylor and J. R. Ryan (eds) *Cultural Turns/Geographical Turns: perspectives on culture geography*. Harlow: Prentice Hall, pp. 1–6.

THRIFT, N. J. 2005a. From born to made: technology, biology and space. *Transactions of the Institute of British Geographers* 30: 463–476.

THRIFT, N. J. 2005b. *Knowing Capitalism*. London: Sage.

THRIFT, N. J. 2007. *Non-Representational Theory. Space/politics/affect*. London: Routledge.

THRIFT, N. J. 2008. The material practices of glamour. *Journal of Cultural Economy* 1: 9–23.

TILLEY C. 1994. *A Phenomenology of Landscape*. Oxford: Berg.

TILLEY, C. 1981. Conceptual frameworks for the explanation of sociocultural change. In I. Hodder, G. Isaac and N. Hammond (eds) *Pattern of the Past*. Cambridge: Cambridge University press, pp. 363–386.

TILLEY, C. 1982. Social formation, social structures and social change. In I. Hodder (ed.) *Symbolic and Structural Archaeology*. Cambridge: Cambridge University Press, pp. 26–38.

TILLEY, C. 1989. Interpreting material culture. In I. Hodder (ed.) *The Meanings of Things: material culture and symbolic expression*. London: Unwin Hyman (One World Archaeology 6), pp. 185–194.

TILLEY, C. (ed.) 1990a. *Reading Material Culture: structuralism, hermeneutics and post-structuralism*. Oxford: Blackwell (Studies in Social Archaeology).

TILLEY, C. 1990b. Michel Foucault: towards an archaeology of archaeology. In C. Tilley (ed.) *Reading Material Culture: structuralism, hermeneutics and post-structuralism*. Oxford: Blackwell (Studies in Social Archaeology), pp. 281–347.

TILLEY, C. 1991. *Material Culture and Text: the art of ambiguity*. London: Routledge.

TILLEY, C. 1993. Introduction: interpretation and a poetics of the past. In C. Tilley (ed.) *Interpretative Archaeology*. Oxford: Berg, pp. 1–27.

TILLEY, C. 1994. *A Phenomenology of Landscape: places, paths, and monuments*. Oxford: Berg.

TILLEY, C. 1996. *An Ethnography of the Neolithic: early prehistoric societies in southern Scandinavia*. Cambridge: Cambridge University Press.

TILLEY. C. 1998. Archaeology: the loss of isolation. *Antiquity* 72: 691–693.

TILLEY, C. 1999. *Metaphor and Material Culture*. Oxford: Blackwell.

TILLEY, C. 2002. Metaphor, materiality and interpretation. In V. Buchli (ed.) *The Material Culture Reader*. Oxford: Berg, pp. 23–26.

TILLEY, C. 2004. *The Materiality of Stone: explorations in landscape phenomenology.* Oxford: Berg.

TILLEY, C. 2006a. Editorial. *Journal of Material Culture Studies* 11/12: 5–6.

TILLEY, C. 2006b. Introduction. In C. Tilley, W. Keane, S. Küchler, M. J. Rowlands and P. Spyer (eds) *Handbook of Material Culture.* London: Sage, pp. 1–6.

TILLEY, C. 2006c. Introduction: identity, place, landscape and heritage. *Journal of Material Culture* 11/12: 7–32.

TILLEY, C. 2007a. Materiality in materials. *Archaeological Dialogues* 14(1): 16–20.

TILLEY, C. 2007b. Objectification. In C. Tilley, W. Keane, S. Küchler, M. Rowlands and P. Spyer (eds) *Handbook of Material Culture.* London: Sage, pp. 60–73.

TILLEY, C., KEANE, W., KÜCHLER, S., ROWLANDS, M. and SPYER, P. (eds) 2006. *Handbook of Material Culture.* London: Sage.

TINBERGEN, N. 1951. *The Study of Instinct.* Oxford: Oxford University Press.

TITMUSS, R. M. 1972 [1971]. *The Gift Relationship: from human blood to social policy.* New York: Vintage Books.

TODOROVA, H. and VAJSOV, I. 1993. *Novo-kamennata Epokha v Bulgariya.* Sofia: Nauka i Izkustvo.

TOLIA-KELLY, D. 2004a. Locating processes of identification: studying the precipitates of re-memory through artefacts in the British Asian home. *Transactions of the Institute of British Geographers* 29(3): 314–329.

TOLIA-KELLY, D. 2004b. Materializing post-colonial geographies: examining the textural landscapes of migration in the South Asian home. *Geoforum* 35(6): 675–688.

TOLIA-KELLY, D. 2007. Fear in paradise: the affective registers of the English Lake District landscape re-visited. *Senses and Society* 2(3): 329–351.

TOMASELLO, M. 1999. *The Cultural Origins of Human Cognition.* Cambridge, MA: Harvard University Press.

TOMASELLO, M., CALE KRUGER, A. and HORN RATNER, H. 1993. Cultural learning. *Behavioural and Brain Sciences* 16: 495–552.

TOMASELLO, M., PARKER, S. T. and GIBSON, K. R. 1990. *Cultural Transmission in the Tool Use and Communicatory Signalling of Chimpanzees?* Cambridge: Cambridge University Press, pp. 274–311.

TOMASI, L. 1983. Projects for botanical and other gardens: a 16th-century manual. *Journal of Garden History* 2: 1–34.

TOMKINS, C. 1972. Onward and upward with the arts: maybe a quantum leap. *The New Yorker* 15 February: 48.

TOMKINS, P. 2004. Filling in the 'Neolithic background': social life and social transformation in the Aegean before the Bronze Age. In J. C. Barrett and P. Halstead (eds) *The Emergence of Civilisation Revisited.* Oxford: Oxbow Books, pp. 38–63.

TOMKINS, P. 2007a. Communality and competition. The social life of food and containers at Aceramic and Early Neolithic Knossos, Crete. In C. Mee and J. Renard (eds) *Cooking Up the Past. Food and culinary practices in the Neolithic and Bronze Age Aegean.* Oxford: Oxbow Books, pp. 174–199.

TOMKINS, P. 2007b. Neolithic: Strata IX–VIII, VII–VIB, VIA–V, IV, IIIB, IIIA, IIB, IIA and IC Groups. In N. Momigliano (ed.) *Knossos Pottery Handbook: Neolithic and Bronze Age (Minoan).* London: British School at Athens (British School at Athens Studies no. 14), pp. 9–48.

TOMKINS, P., DAY, P. M. and KILIKOGLOU, V. 2004. Knossos and the Early Neolithic Landscape of the Herakleion Basin. In G. Cadogan, E. Hatzaki and A. Vasilakis (eds) *Knossos: Palace, City, State. Proceedings of the Conference in Herakleion in November 2000.* London: British School at Athens, pp. 51–59.

TORRENCE, R. 1986. *Production and Exchange of Stone Tools: prehistoric Obsidian in the Aegean.* Cambridge: Cambridge University Press.

TORRENCE, R. 2002. Cultural landscapes on Garua Island, Papua New Guinea. *Antiquity* 76: 766–777.

TOTH, N., SCHICK, K. D., SAVAGE-RUMBAUGH, E. S., SEVCIK, R. A. and RUMBAUGH, D. M. 1993. Pan the tool-maker—investigations into the stone tool-making and tool-using capabilities of a bonobo (*Pan paniscus*). *Journal of Archaeological Science* 20(1): 81–91.

TOYNBEE, A. J. 1967. *Cities of Destiny.* London: Thames and Hudson.

TRACHTENBERG, M. and HYMAN, I. 1986. *Architecture: from prehistory to post-modernism.* New York: Prentice Hall/Abrams.

TRAWEEK, S. 1988. *Beamtimes and Lifetimes: the world of high energy physics.* Cambridge, MA: Harvard University Press.

TRIGGER, B. G. 1984. Archaeology at the crossroads: what's new? *Annual Review of Anthropology* 13: 275–300.

TRIGGER, B. 1989. *A History of Archaeological Thought* (first edition). Cambridge: Cambridge University Press.

TRIGGER, B. G. 2006. *A History of Archaeological Thought* (second edition). Cambridge: Cambridge University Press.

TRIMBLE, M. 1985. Epidemiology on the Northern Plains: A Cultural Perspective. Unpublished Ph.D. dissertation, Department of Anthropology, University of Missouri-Columbia.

TRIMBLE, M. 1993. Infectious disease and the Northern Plains horticulturists: a human-behavior mode. In T. Thiessen (ed.) *The Phase I Archeological Research Program for the Knife River Indian Villages National Historic Site, Part II: Ethnohistorical Studies.* Lincoln, NE: National Park Service Midwest Archeological Center, pp. 75–129.

TRINGHAM, R. 1991a. Men and women in prehistoric architecture. *Traditional Dwellings and Settlements Review* 3(1): 9–28.

TRINGHAM, R. 1991b. Households with faces: the challenge of gender in prehistoric architectural remains. In J. Gero and M. Conkey (eds) *Engendering Archaeology: women and prehistory.* Oxford: Blackwell (Studies in Social Archaeology), pp. 93–131.

TRINGHAM, R. 1994. Engendered places in prehistory. *Gender, Place and Culture* 1(2): 169–203.

TRINGHAM, R. 1995. Archaeological houses, households, housework and the home. In D. Benjamin and D. Stea (eds) *The Home: words, interpretations, meanings, and environments.* Aldershot: Avebury Press, pp. 79–107.

TROUILLOT, M. R. 1995. *Silencing the Past: power and the production of history.* Boston: Beacon Press.

TROUILLOT, M-R. 2003. *Global Transformations: anthropology and the modern world.* London: Palgrave Macmillan.

TSCHUMI, B. 1996. *Architecture and Disjunction.* Cambridge, MA: MIT Press.

TSING, A. L. 2005. *Friction: an ethnography of global connection.* Princeton, NJ: Princeton University Press.

TUAN, Y.-F. 1974. *Topophilia.* Englewood Cliffs, NJ: Prentice Hall.

TURGEON, L. (ed.) 1998. *Les entre-lieux de la culture.* Quebec: Presses de l'Université Laval.

TURGEON, L. 2003. *Patrimoines métissés. Contextes coloniaux et postcoloniaux.* Paris: Maison des Sciences de l'Homme.

TURGEON, L., DELÂGE, D. and OUELLET, R. (eds) 1996. *Transferts culturels et métissages, Amérique/Europe XVIe–XXe siècle.* Quebec: Presses de l'Université de Laval.

TURKLE, S. (ed.) 2008. *Falling for Science. Objects in mind.* Cambridge, MA: MIT Press.

TURNER, B. 2003. Foreword. In L. Meskell and R. Joyce (eds) *Embodied lives: figuring Ancient Mayan and Egyptian experience.* London: Routledge, pp. xiii–xx.

TURNER, B. S. 1982. The government of the body: medical regimens and the rationalization of diet. *British Journal of Sociology* 33(2): 254–269.

TURNER, B. S. 1984. *The Body and Society.* Oxford: Blackwell.

TURNER, M. 1987. *Death Is the Mother of Beauty: mind, metaphor, criticism.* Chicago: Chicago University Press.

TURNER, M. 1991. *Reading Minds: the study of English in the age of cognitive science.* Princeton: Princeton University Press.

TURNER, S. and FAIRCLOUGH, G. 2007. Common culture: time-depth and landscape character in European Archaeology. In D. Hicks, L. McAtackney and G. Fairclough (eds) *Envisioning Landscape: situations and standpoints in archaeology and heritage.* Walnut Creek, CA: Left Coast Press (One World Archaeology 52), pp. 120–145.

TURNER, T. 1980. The social skin. In J. Cherfas and R. Lewin (eds) *Not Work Alone: a cross-cultural view of activities superfluous to survival.* Beverly Hills: Sage, pp. 112–140.

TURNER, T. S. 1989. A commentary [on T. O. Beidelman's 'Agnostic Exchange: Homeric Reciprocity and the Heritage of Simmel and Mauss']. *Cultural Anthropology* 4(3): 260–264.

TURNER, V. 1967. *The Forest of Symbols: aspects of Ndenbu ritual.* Ithaca: Cornell University Press.

TURNER, V. 1975. Symbolic studies. *Annual Review of Anthropology* 4: 145–161.

TWISS, K. C. (ed.) 2007. *The Archaeology of Food and Identity.* Carbondale: Center for Archaeological Investigations, Southern Illinois University (Occasional Paper 34).

TYLOR, E. B. 1871. *Primitive Culture: researches into the* development of mythology, philosophy, religion, art and custom. London: Murray.

TYLOR, E. B. 1896. Preface. In F. Ratzel *The History of Mankind* (trans. A. Butler) (volume 1). London: Macmillan, pp. i–xxiv.

UCKO, P. J. 1968. *Anthropomorphic Figurines of Predynastic Egypt and Neolithic Crete with Comparative Material from the Prehistoric Near East and Mainland Greece.* London: Szmidla.

UCKO, P. J. 1969. Penis sheaths: a comparative study. *Proceedings of the Royal Anthropological Institute of Great Britain and Ireland* 2: 27–67.

UCKO, P. J. 1987. *Academic Freedom and Apartheid: the story of the World Archaeological Congress.* London: Duckworth.

UCKO, P. J. 1995. Archaeological interpretation in a world context. In P. J. Ucko (ed.) *Archaeological Theory: a world perspective.* London: Routledge, pp. 1–27.

ULRICH, L. T. 2001. *The Age of Homespun: objects and stories in the creation of an American myth.* New York: Vintage.

UNESCO 2008. World Heritage Cultural Landscapes http://whc.unesco.org/en/cultural landscape/ (Accessed 3 March 2008).

UNESCO nd. *Dorset and East Devon Coast.* http://whc.unesco.org/en/list/1029 (Accessed 17 November 2008).

University of Helsinki 2007. *Duane Hanson—Sculptures of the American Dream.* http://www.helsinki.fi/en/index/taidejakulttuuri/nayttelyt/taidemuseossa_nyt_072007.html (Accessed 23 September 2008).

University of Sussex 2005. *Geography Inspires Artist to Put Love on the Rocks.* University of Sussex press release, 20 January 2005. http://www.sussex.ac.uk/press_office/media/media457.shtml (Accessed 20 November 2008).

Upton, D. 1982. Vernacular domestic architecture in eighteenth-century Virginia. *Winterthur Portfolio* 17: 95–119.

Upton, D. 1985. White and black landscapes in eighteenth-century Virginia. *Places* 2(2): 59–72.

Upton, D. 1986. *Holy Things and Profane: Anglican Parish Churches in Colonial Virginia.* Cambridge, MA: MIT Press.

Upton, D. 1990. Outside the academy: a century of vernacular architecture studies, 1890–1990. In E. B. MacDougall (ed.), *The Architectural Historian in America.* Washington, DC: National Gallery of Art, pp. 199–213.

Upton, D. 1996. Ethnicity, authenticity, and invented traditions. *Historical Archaeology* 30(2): 1–7.

Upton, D. 1998. *Architecture in the United States.* Oxford: Oxford University Press.

Upton, D. 2008. *Another City: urban life and urban spaces in the new American Republic.* New Haven, CT: Yale University Press.

Urry, J. 1972. Notes and queries on anthropology and the development of field methods in British Anthropology 1870–1920. *Proceedings of the Royal Anthropological Institute for 1972*: 45–57.

Urry, J. 1984. A history of field methods. In R. F. Ellen (ed.) *Ethnographic Research: a guide to general conduct.* San Diego, CA: Academic Press, pp. 35–61.

Usbourne, S. 2008. Local heroes: Mark Hix reveals his Britain's finest independent producers. *The Independent* 15 November, http://www.independent.co.uk/life-style/food-and-drink/features/local-heroes-mark-hix-reveals-his-britains-finest-independent-producers-1015339.html (accessed 20 November 2008).

Valentine, G. 1993. (Hetero)sexing space: lesbian perceptions and experiences of everyday spaces. *Environment and Planning D: Society and Space* 11(4): 395–413.

Van Damme, W. 1997. Do non-Western cultures have words for art? An epistemological prolegomenon to the comparative studies of philosophies of art. In E. Benitez (ed.) *Proceedings of the Pacific Rim Conference in Transcultural Aesthetics.* Sydney: Sydney University, pp. 6–113.

Van Dommelen, P. 2000. Material concerns and boundless diversity. *European Journal of Archaeology* 3(3): 409–416.

Van Dommelen, P. 2006. Colonial matters: material culture and postcolonial theory in colonial situations. In C. Tilley, W. Keane, S. Keuchler, M. Rowlands and P. Spyer (eds) *Handbook of Material Culture.* London: Sage, pp. 104–124.

Van Slyck, A. 1995. Mañana, Mañana: racial stereotypes and the anglo rediscovery of the Southwest's vernacular architecture, 1890–1920. In E. Cromley and C. Hudgins (eds) *Gender, Class, and Shelter: perspectives in vernacular architecture V.* Knoxville, TN: University of Tennessee Press, pp. 95–108.

Vander Linden, M. 2006. For whom the bell tolls: social hierarchy vs social integration in the Bell beaker culture of Southern France. *Cambridge Archaeological Journal* 16(3): 317–332.

Vaseline 2008. History of Vaseline. http://www.vaseline.co.uk/Carousel.aspx?Path=Consumer/AboutUs/History (Accessed 22 April 2008).

VAUGHAN, M. 2006. Africa and the birth of the modern world. *Transactions of the Royal Historical Society* 16: 143–162.

VEBLEN, T. 2008 [1912]. *The Theory of the Leisure Class.* Oxford: Oxford University Press.

VELLINGA, M., OLIVER, P. and BRIDGE, A. (eds) 2007. *Atlas of Vernacular Architecture of the World.* London: Taylor and Francis.

VERRAN, H. 1998. Re-imagining land ownership in Australia. *Postcolonial Studies* 1(2): 237–254.

VERRAN, H. 2001. *Science and an African Logic.* Chicago: Chicago University Press.

VICKERS, M. and GILL, D. 1994. *Artful Crafts. Ancient Greek silverware and pottery.* Oxford: Clarendon Press.

VIDEAN, E. N. 2006. Bed-building in captive chimpanzees (*Pan troglodytes*): The importance of early rearing. *American Journal of Primatology* 68(7): 745–751.

VIDLER, A. 1992. *The Architectural Uncanny.* Cambridge, MA: MIT Press.

VILAÇA, A. 2009. Bodies in Perspective: a critique of the embodiment paradigm from the point of view of Amazonian ethnography. In H. Lambert and M. McDonald (eds) *Social Bodies.* New York: Bergahn Books, pp. 129–147.

VINT, S. 2007. *Bodies of Tomorrow. Technology subjectivity, science fiction.* Toronto: University of Toronto Press.

VISALBERGHI, E. 1990. Tool use in Cebus. *Folia Primatologica* 54(3–4): 146–154.

VISALBERGHI, E. and FRAGASZY, D. 2002. Do monkeys ape? Ten years after. In K. Dautenhahn and C. L. Nehaniv (eds) *Imitation in Animals and Artifacts.* Cambridge, MA: MIT Press, pp. 471–499.

VISALBERGHI, E., FRAGASZY, D., OTTONI, E., IZAR, P., DE OLIVEIRA, M. G. and ANDRADE, F. R. D. 2007. Characteristics of hammer stones and anvils used by wild bearded Capuchin monkeys (*Cebus libidinosus*) to crack open palm nuts. *American Journal of Physical Anthropology* 132(3): 426–444.

VITELLI, K. D. 1993. *Franchthi Neolithic Pottery: classification and Ceramic Phases 1 and 2.* Excavations at Franchthi Cave, Greece, fasc. 8. Bloomington and Indianapolis: Indiana University Press.

VITELLI, K. D. 1995. Pots, potters and the shaping of the Greek Neolithic. In W. K. Barnett and J. W. Hoopes (eds) *The Emergence of Pottery: technology and innovation in ancient societies.* Washington: Smithsonian Institution Press, pp. 55–64.

VITRUVIUS, P. 2001. *The Ten Books on Architecture.* Cambridge: Cambridge University Press.

VIVEIROS DE CASTRO, E. 1998. Cosmological deixis and Amerindian perspectivism. *Journal of the Royal Anthropological Institute* 4(3): 469–488.

VLACH, J. 1993. *Back of the Big House: the architecture of plantation slavery.* Chapel Hill: University of North Carolina Press.

VOIGT, V. 1980. Folklore and 'folklorism' today. In V. J. Newall (ed.) *Folklore Studies in the Twentieth Century: Proceedings of the Centenary Conference of the Folklore Society.* Totowa, NJ: Rowman and Littlefield, pp. 419–424.

VON SYDOW, C. W. 1977 [1948]. Geography and folktale oicotypes. In L. Bødker (ed.) *Selected Papers on Folklore.* New York: Arno Press.

VOSS, B. L. 2008a. Sexuality studies in archaeology. *Annual Review of Archaeology* 37: 317–336.

VOSS, B. L. 2008b. *The Archaeology of Ethnogenesis: race and sexuality in colonial San Francisco.* Berkeley: University of California Press.

VREESWIJK, B. 2001. Krachtige communicatie. Magie, religie en reclame. Unpublished MA thesis, Social Anthropology, University of Amsterdam.

WADE, E. L. 1985. The Ethnic Art Market in the American Southwest, 1880–1980. In G. W. Stocking (ed.) *Objects and Others: essays on museums and material culture.* Madison, WI: University of Wisconsin Press, pp. 167–191.

WAGNER, R. 1991. The fractal person. In M. Godelier and M. Strathern (eds) *Big Men and Great Men: personifications of power in Melanesia.* Cambridge: Cambridge University Press, pp. 159–173.

WALBERG, G. 1976. *Kamares: a study of the character of palatial Middle Minoan pottery.* Uppsala: University of Uppsala (Acta Universitatis Upsaliensis 8).

WALDE, D. and WILLOWS, N. D. (eds) 1991. *The Archaeology of Gender: Proceedings of the Twenty-Second Annual Conference of the Archaeological Association of the University of Calgary.* Calgary: University of Calgary Archaeological Association.

WALKER, W. H. 1995a. Ceremonial trash? In J. Skibo, W. Walker, and A. Nielsen (eds) *Expanding Archaeology.* Salt Lake City: University of Utah Press, pp. 67–79.

WALKER, W. H. 1995b. Ritual prehistory: a Pueblo case study. Unpublished Ph.D. dissertation, Department of Anthropology, University of Arizona.

WALKER, W. H. 1998. Where are the witches of prehistory? *Journal of Archaeological Method and Theory,* 5(3): 245–308.

WALKER, W. H. 2002. Stratigraphy and practical reason. *American Anthropologist* 104: 159–177.

WALKER, W. H. 2008. Practice and nonhuman social actors. The afterlife histories of witches and dogs in the American Southwest. In B. J. Mills and W. H. Walker (eds) *Memory Work. Archaeologies of material practice.* Santa Fe: School for Advanced Research Press, pp. 137–157.

WALKER, W. H. and LUCERO, L. J. 2000. The depositional history of ritual and power. In M-A. Dobres and J. Robb (eds) *Agency in Archaeology.* New York: Routledge, pp. 130–147.

WALKER, W. H. and SCHIFFER, M. B. 2006. The materiality of social power: the artifact-acquisition perspective. *Journal of Archaeological Method and Theory* 13(2): 67–88.

WALKER, W. H., SKIBO, J. and NIELSEN, A. 1995. Introduction: expanding archaeology. In J. Skibo, W. Walker and A. Nielsen (eds) *Expanding Archaeology.* Salt Lake City: University of Utah Press, pp. 1–12.

WALKER, W. H., LaMOTTA, V. and ADAMS, E. 2000. Katsinas and Kiva abandonment at Homol'ovi: a deposit oriented perspective on religion in southwestern prehistory. In M. Hegmon (ed.) *The Archaeology of Regional Interaction: religion, warfare, and exchange across the American Southwest and beyond.* Boulder, CO: University Press of Colorado, pp. 341–360.

WALL, C. S. 2006. *The Prose of Things: transformations of description in the eighteenth century.* Chicago: Chicago University Press.

WALLACE, A. 1986 [1874]. *Miracles and Modern Spiritualism* (3rd revised edn). London: George Redway.

WALLAERT-PÊTRE, H. 2001. Learning how to make the right pots: apprenticeship strategies and material culture, a case study in handmade pottery from Cameroon. *Journal of Anthropological Research* 57(4): 471–493.

WALLERSTEIN, I. 1974. *The Modern World System* (Volume 1). New York: Academic Press.

WARNIER, J.-P. 2001. A praxeological approach to subjectivation in a material world. *Journal of Material Culture* 6(1): 5–24.

WARNIER, J.-P. 2006. Inside and outside: surfaces and containers. In C. Tilley, W. Keane, S. Küchler, M. Rowlands and P. Spyer (eds) *Handbook of Material Culture.* London: Sage, pp. 186–195.

WARNIER, J.-P. 2007. *The Pot-King: the body, material culture and technologies of power.* Leiden: Brill.

WARREN, P. and HANKEY, V. 1989. *Aegean Bronze Age Chronology.* Bristol: Bristol Classical Press.

WASTELL, S. 2007. The 'legal thing' in Swaziland: res judicata and divine kingship. In A. Henare, M. Holbraad and S. Wastell (eds) *Thinking Through Things: theorising artefacts ethnographically.* London: Routledge, pp. 68–92.

WATERMAN, T. 1946. *The Mansions of Virginia 1706–1776.* Chapel Hill: The University of North Carolina Press.

WATERSON, R. 1990. *The Living House: an anthropology of architecture in South-East Asia.* Oxford: Oxford University Press.

WATSON, A. and KEATING, D. 1999. Architecture and sound. An acoustic analysis of megalithic monuments in prehistoric Britain. *Antiquity* 73: 325–336.

WATSON, P. J. 1995. Archaeology, anthropology, and the culture concept. *American Anthropologist* 97(4): 683–694.

WATSON, P. J. 2007. The new archaeology and after. In J. Skibo, M. Graves, and M. Stark (eds) *Archaeological Anthropology: perspectives on method and theory.* Tucson: University of Arizona Press, pp. vii–x.

WATT, L. A., RAYMOND, L. and ESCHEN, M. L. 2004. Reflections on preserving ecological and cultural landscapes. *Environmental History* 9: 620–647.

WATTS, C. M. 2008. On mediation and material agency in the Peircean semeiotic. In C. Knappett and L. Malafouris (eds) Material Agency. Towards a non-anthropocentric approach. New York: Springer, pp. 187–207.

WEATHERILL, L. 1989. Review of D. Miller 'Material Culture and Mass Consumption'. *Journal of Historical Geography* 15(4): 438–439.

WEATHERILL, L. 1996. *Consumer Behavior and Material Culture in Britain 1660–1760* (Second Edition). London: Routledge.

WEBMOOR, T. 2007. What about 'one more turn after the social' in archaeological reasoning? Taking things seriously. *World Archaeology* 39(4): 563–578.

WEBMOOR, T. and WITMORE, C. 2008. Things are us! A commentary on human/things relations under the banner of a 'social' archaeology. *Norwegian Archaeological Review* 41(1): 53–70.

WEBSTER, D. L. 1999. The archaeology of Copan, Honduras. *Journal of Archaeological Research* 7: 1–53.

WEBSTER, D., MURTHA, T., STRAIGHT, K. D., SILVERSTEIN, J., MARTINEZ, H., TERRY, R. E. and BURNETT, R. 2007. The Great Tikal Earthwork revisited. *Journal of Field Archaeology* 32: 41–64.

WEDEL, W. R. 1945. On the Illinois Confederacy and Middle Mississippian Culture in Illinois. *American Antiquity* 10: 383–386.

WEINBERG, S. S. 1970. The Stone Age in the Aegean. In I. E. S. Edwards, C. J. Gadd and N. G. L. Hammond (eds) *Cambridge Ancient History. Volume I. Part 1. Prolegomena and Prehistory* (3rd Edition). Cambridge: Cambridge University Press, pp. 557–618.

WEINER, A. 1976. *Women of Value, Men of Renown: new perspectives in Trobriand exchange.* Austin: University of Texas Press.

WEINER, A. 1980. Reproduction: a replacement for reciprocity. *American Ethnologist* 7(1): 71–85.

WEINER, A. 1985. Inalienable wealth. *American Ethnologist* 12(2): 210–227.

WEINER, A. 1992. *Inalienable Possessions: the paradox of keeping-while-giving.* Berkeley: University of California Press.

WEINER, A. and SCHNEIDER, J. (eds) 1989. *Cloth and the Human Experience.* Washington, DC: Smithsonian Institution Press.

WEISMANTEL, M. 1988. *Food, Gender, and Poverty in the Ecuadorian Andes.* Philadelphia: University of Pennsylvania Press.

WEISS, R. 1946. *Volkskunde der Schweiz, Grundreiss.* Erlenbach-Zürich: E. Rentsch.

WEISS, R. and GEIGER, P. 1950–1979. *Atlas der schweizerischen Volkskunde.* Basel: Schweizer-ischen Gesellschaft für Volkskunde.

WEITZNER, B. 1979. Notes on the Hidatsa Indians Based on Data Recorded by the Late Gilbert L. Wilson. *Anthropological Papers of the American Museum of Natural History* 56(2): 181–322.

WELLS, C. (ed.) 1986. *Perspectives in Vernacular Architecture II.* Columbia: University of Missouri Press.

WELLS, C. 1998. The multi-storied house: twentieth-century encounters with the domestic architecture of colonial Virginia. *Virginia Magazine of History and Biography* 106: 353–418.

WENGROW, D. 2001. The evolution of simplicity: aesthetic labour and social change in the Neolithic Near East. *World Archaeology* 33(2): 168–188.

WESTERMANN. M. 2005. Introduction. In M. Westermann (ed.) *Anthropologies of Art.* Williamstown, MA: Sterling and Francine Clark Art Institute, pp. vii–xxxi.

WESTMACOTT, R. 1992. *African-American Gardens and Yards in the Rural South.* Knoxville, TN: University of Tennessee Press.

WHATMORE, S. 1999. Hybrid geographies. Rethinking the 'human' in human geography. In D. Massey, J. Allen and P. Sarre (eds) *Human Geography Today.* Cambridge: Polity Press, pp. 24–39.

WHATMORE, S. 2002. *Hybrid Geographies: natures, culture, spaces.* London, Sage.

WHATMORE, S. 2003. Generating materials. In M. Pryke, G. Rose and S. Whatmore (eds) *Using Social Theory: thinking through research.* London, Sage, pp. 105–121.

WHATMORE, S. 2006. Materialist returns: practicing cultural geographies in and for a more-than-human world. *Cultural Geographies,* 13/4: 600–610.

WHATMORE, S. 2007. Between earth and life: re-figuring property through bio-resources. In H. Clout (ed.) *Land, Property, Resources.* London: UCL Press, pp. 84–95.

WHEELER, M. 1966. *Civilisations of the Indus Valley and Beyond.* New York: McGraw-Hill.

WHEELER, R. E. M. 1927. History by excavation. *Journal of the Royal Society of Arts* 75: 812–835.

WHEELER, R. E. M. 1954. *Archaeology from the Earth.* Oxford: Clarendon Press.

WHIFFEN, M. 1960. *The Eighteenth-century Houses of Williamsburg.* Williamsburg, VA: Colonial Williamsburg Foundation.

WHITE, J. P. 1976. *The Past Is Human.* London: Angus and Robertson.

WHITE, L. A. 1949. *The Science of Culture.* New York: Farrar, Strauss.

WHITE, L. A. 1959. *The Evolution of Culture: the development of civilization to the fall of Rome.* New York: McGraw-Hill.

WHITE, R. 1992. Beyond art: towards an understanding of the origins of material representation in Europe. *Annual Review of Anthropology* 21: 537–564.

WHITEHEAD, A. N. 1978 [1929]. *Process and Reality* (corrected edition). New York: The Free Press.

WHITEN, A. and R. HAM. 1992. On the nature and evolution of imitation in the animal kingdom: reappraisal of a century of research. *Advances in the Study of Behavior* 21: 239–283.

WHITEN, A., GOODALL, J., McGREW, W. C., NISHIDA, T., REYNOLDS, V., SUGIYAMA, Y., TUTIN, C. E. G., WRANGHAM, R. W. and BOESCH, C. 1999. Cultures in chimpanzees. *Nature* 399(6737): 682–685.

WHITEN, A., GOODALL, J., McGREW, W. C., NISHIDA, T., REYNOLDS, V., SUGIYAMA, Y., TUTIN, C. E. G., WRANGHAM, R. W. and BOESCH, C. 2001. Charting cultural variation in chimpanzees. *Behaviour* 138: 1481–1516.

WHITEN, A., HORNER, V. and DE WAAL, F. B. 2005. Conformity to cultural norms of tool use in chimpanzees. *Nature* 437(7059): 737–740.

WHITEN, A., HORNER, I., LITCHFIELD, C. A. and MARSHALL-PESCINI, S. 2004. How do apes ape? *Learning and Behavior* 32(1): 36–52.

WHITNEY, D. 1990. *Michael Heizer*. London: Waddington Galleries.

WHITTAKER, C. R. 1995. Do theories of the ancient city matter? In T. J. Cornell and K. Lomas (eds) *Urban Society in Roman Italy*. London: University College London Press, pp. 9–26.

WHITTLE, A. 1990. A model for the Mesolithic–Neolithic transition in the Upper Kennet Valley, North Wiltshire. *Proceedings of the Prehistoric Society* 56: 101–10.

WHITTLE, A. 2003. *The Archaeology of People: dimensions of Neolithic life*. London: Routledge.

WHITTLESEY, S. 1998. Archaeological landscapes: a methodological and theoretical discussion. In S. Whittlesey, R. Ciolek-Torrello and J. Altschul (eds) *Vanishing River: Landscapes and Lives of the Lower Verde Valley*. Tucson, AZ: SRI Press, pp. 17–28.

WHITTLESEY, S. 2003. *Rivers of Rock*. Tucson, AZ: SRI Press.

WICKS, R. 1997. Dependent beauty as the appreciation of teleological style. *Journal of Aesthetics and Art Criticism* 55: 387–400.

WIENER, M. 2007. The magical life of things. In P. ter Keurs (ed.), *Colonial Collections Revisited*. Leiden: CNWS Publications, pp. 45–70.

WIESSNER, P. 1984. Reconsidering the behavioral basis for style: a case study among the Kalahari San. *Journal of Anthropological Archaeology* 3: 190–234.

WIGLEY, M. 2001. *White Walls, Designer Fashion: The Fashioning of Modern Architecture*. Cambridge, MA: MIT Press.

WILK, R. 1999. 'Real Belizean food': building local identity in the transnational Caribbean. *American Anthropologist* 101: 244–255.

WILK, R. R. (ed.) 1989. *The Household Economy: reconsidering the domestic mode of production*. Boulder, CO: Westview.

WILK, R. R. 2006. *Home Cooking in the Global Village: Caribbean food from buccaneers to ecotourists*. Oxford: Berg.

WILK, R. R. and CLIGGETT, L. C. 2007. *Economies and Cultures: foundations of economic anthropology* (2nd edition). Boulder, CO: Westview Press.

WILKIE, L. A. 2003. *The Archaeology of Mothering: an African-American midwife's tale*. London: Routledge.

WILKIE, L. A. 2005. Inessential archaeologies: problems of exclusion in Americanist archaeological thought. *World Archaeology* 37: 337–351.

WILKIE, L. A. 2006. Documentary archaeology. In D. Hicks and M. C. Beaudry (eds) *The Cambridge Companion to Historical Archaeology*. Cambridge: Cambridge University Press, pp. 13–33.

WILLEY, G. R. and PHILLIPS, P. 1953. Method and theory in American archaeology: an operational basis for culture-historical integration. *American Anthropologist* 55: 615–633.

WILLEY, G. R. and PHILLIPS, P. 1958. *Method and Theory in American Archaeology*. Chicago: University of Chicago Press.

WILLEY, G. R. and SABLOFF, J. 1993. *A History of American Archaeology* (3rd edition). New York: W. H. Freeman and Company.

WILLIAMS, C. 2007. Branscombe shipwreck: eBay flogfest begins. *The Register* 23 January 2007. http://www.theregister.co.uk/2007/01/23/branscombe_ebay/ (Accessed 20 November 2008).

WILLIAMS, H. 2004. Death warmed up. The agency of bodies and bones in Early Anglo-Saxon cremation rites. *Journal of Material Culture* 9(3): 263–291.

WILLIAMS, M. 2003. Growing metaphors: the agricultural cycle as metaphor in the Later Prehistoric Period of Britain and north-western Europe. *Journal of Social Archaeology* 3: 223–255.

WILLIAMS, M. A. 1991. *Homeplace: the social use and meaning of the folk dwelling in Southwestern North Carolina*. Athens: University of Georgia Press.

WILLIAMS, R. 1958. *Culture and Society, 1780–1950*. London: Chatto and Windus.

WILLIAMS, R. 1993 [1975]. *The Country and the City*. London: Hogarth Press.

WILLIAMS, R. 2002 [1974]. Technology and society. In K. Askew and R. Wilk (eds) *The Anthropology of Media: a reader*. Oxford: Blackwell, pp. 27–40.

WILLIAMS, R., CUROY, J., DORNBUSCH, U. and MOSES, C. 2005. *Longshore Drift on the Sussex, Kent and Picardie Coasts: preliminary notes on the BAR natural and resin tracer experiments*. Brighton: University of Sussex BAR (English Scientific Geomorphology Reports), www.geog.susx.ac.uk/BAR/Publish/Phase-1-final-drift%20experiments.pdf (Accessed 20 November 2008).

WILSON, C. 1997. *The Myth of Santa Fe: creating a modern regional tradition*. Albuquerque: University of New Mexico Press.

WILSON, G. 1977. Mandan and Hidatsa pottery making. *Plains Anthropologist* 22(76): 97–105.

WILSON, W. 1976. *Folklore and Nationalism in Modern Finland*. Bloomington: Indiana University Press.

WINNER, L. 1977. *Autonomous Technology: technics-out-of-control as a theme in political thought*. Cambridge, MA: MIT Press.

WINNER, L. 1986. *The Whale and the Reactor*. Chicago: University of Chicago Press.

WINTER, I. 2002. Defining 'aesthetics' for non-Western studies: the case for Ancient Mesopotamia. In M. A. Holly and K. Moxey (eds) *Art History, Aesthetics and Visual Studies*. Williamstown, MA: Sterling and Francine Clark Art Institute, pp. 3–28.

WINTER, I. 2007. Agency marked, agency ascribed: the affective object in Ancient Mesopotamia. In R. Osborne and J. Tanner (eds) *Art's Agency and Art History*. Oxford: Blackwell, pp. 42–69.

WISSLER, C. 1910. *Material Culture of the Blackfoot Indians*. New York: Trustees of the American Museum of Natural History (Anthropological Papers of the American Museum of Natural History 5, Part 1).

WITMORE, C. 2006. Vision, media, noise and the percolation of time: symmetrical approaches to the mediation of the material world. *Journal of Material Culture* 11(3): 267–292.

WITMORE, C. 2007. Symmetrical archaeology: excerpts of a manifesto. *World Archaeology* 39(4): 546–562.

WITTGENSTEIN, L. 1953. *Philosophical Investigations* (trans. G. E. M. Anscombe). New York: Macmillan.

WOBST, H. M. 1974. Boundary conditions for palaeolithic social systems: a simulation approach. *American Antiquity* 39: 149–178.

WOBST, H. M. 1977. Stylistic behaviour and information exchange. In C. E. Cleland (ed.) *Research Essays in honour of James B. Griffin*. Ann Arbor: University of Michigan Press (Research Papers of the University of Michigan 61), pp. 317–342.

WOBST, H. M. 2000. Agency in (spite of) material culture. In M. A. Dobres and J. Robb (eds) *Agency in Archaeology*. London and New York: Routledge, pp. 40–50.

WOLF, E. R. 1982. *Europe and the People without History*. Berkeley: University of California Press.

WOLFE, C. 1998. *Critical Environments*. Minneapolis: University of Minnesota Press.

WOLFE, T. 1981. *From Bauhaus to Our House*. New York: Farrar Straus Giroux.

WÖLFFLIN, H. 1950. *Principles of Art History*. New York: Dover.

WOOD-JONES, R. 1963. *Traditional Domestic Architecture of the Banbury Region*. Manchester: Manchester University Press.

WOODWARD, A. 2002. Beads and beakers: heirlooms and relics in the British Early Bronze Age. *Antiquity* 76: 1040–1047.

WOODWARD, D. 1996. *Maps as Prints in the Italian Renaissance: makers, distributors and consumers*. London: British Library.

WOODWARD, P. and WOODWARD, A. 2004. Dedicating the town: urban foundation deposits in Roman Britain. *World Archaeology*, 36: 68–86.

WOOLF, G. 1997. Beyond Romans and natives. *World Archaeology* 28: 339–350.

WOOLF, G. 1998. *Becoming Roman: the origins of provincial civilization in Gaul*. Cambridge: Cambridge University Press.

WOOLGAR, S. 1988. *Science: the very idea*. London and New York: Tavistock.

WORM, O. 1655. *Museum Wormianum*. Amsterdam: Ludovicum and Danielem Elzevirio.

WORSAAE, J. J. A. 1849. *Primeval Antiquities of Denmark: translated and applied to the illustration of similar remains in England by William J. Thoms*. London: John Henry Parker.

WRANGHAM, R. W., DE WAAL, F. B. M. and McGREW, W. C. 1994. The challenge of behavioral diversity. In R. W. Wrangham, W. C. McGrew, F. B. M. de Waal, P. G. Heltne and L. A. Marquardt (eds) *Chimpanzee Cultures*. Cambridge, MA: Harvard University Press, pp. 1–18.

WRIGHT, J. C. (ed.) 2004. *The Mycenaean Feast*. Athens: American School of Classical Studies at Athens (Supplement to *Hesperia: the Journal of the American School of Classical Studies at Athens* 73(2)).

WRIGHT, R. P. (ed.) 1996. *Gender and Archaeology*. Philadelphia: University of Pennsylvania Press.

WYLIE, J. 2005. A single day's walking: narrating self and landscape on the South West Coast Path. *Transactions of the Institute of British Geographers* 30(2): 234–247.

WYLIE, J. in press. Non-representational subjects (all I ever wanted was to be taken seriously as a writer . . .). In B. Anderson and P. Harrison (eds) *Taking place: non-representational theories and geography.* London: Ashgate.

YAMAKOSHI, G. 1998. Dietary responses to fruit scarcity of wild chimpanzees at Bossou, Guinea: possible implications for ecological importance of tool-use. *American Journal of Physical Anthropology* 106: 283–295.

YARROW, T. 2003. Artefactual persons: the relational capacities of persons and things in the practice of excavation. *Norwegian Archaeological Review,* 36(1): 65–73.

YARROW, T. 2008. In context: meaning, materiality and agency in the process of archaeological recording. In C. Knappett and L. Malafouris (eds) *Material Agency: towards a non-anthropocentric approach,* pp. 121–138.

YATES, T. 1993. Frameworks for an archaeology of the body. In C. Tilley (ed.) *Interpretive Archaeology.* Oxford: Berg, pp. 31–72.

YAZAKI, T. 1968. *Social change and the city in Japan: from earliest times through the Industraial Revolution.* Tokyo: Japan Publications.

YENTSCH, A. 1994. *A Chesapeake Family and their Slaves: a study in historical archaeology.* Cambridge: Cambridge University Press.

YENTSCH, A. and BEAUDRY, M. C. 2001. American material culture in mind, thought and deed. In I. Hodder (ed.) *Archaeological Theory Today.* Cambridge: Polity Press, pp. 214–240.

YEUNG, G. and MOK, V. 2006. Regional monopoly and interregional and intra-regional competition: the parallel trade in Coca-Cola between Shanghai and Hangzhou in China. *Economic Geography* 82(1): 89–109.

YIP, C. 1995. Association, residence, and shop: an appropriation of commercial blocks in North American Chinatowns. In E. Cromley and C. Hudgins (eds) *Gender, Class, and Shelter: perspectives in vernacular architecture, V.* Knoxville, TN: University of Tennessee Press, pp. 109–17.

YODER, D. 1961. *Pennsylvania Spirituals.* Lancaster: Pennsylvania Folklife Society.

YODER, D. 1963. The Folklife Studies Movement. *Pennsylvania Folklife* 13(3): 43–56.

YODER, D. 1981. Foreword. In L. L. St. Clair and A. B. Govenar, *Stoney Knows How: life as a tattoo artist.* Lexington, KY: University Press of Kentucky, i–xxxii.

YODER, D. 2003. *Groundhog Day.* Mechanicsburg, PA: Stackpole Books.

YODER, D. and GRAVES, T. E. 1989. *Hex Signs: Pennsylvania Dutch barn symbols and their meaning.* New York: E. P. Dutton.

YODER, D., BOYER, W. E. and BUFFINGTON, A. F. (eds) 1951. *Songs Along the Mahantongo, Pennsylvania Folksongs.* Lancaster, PA: Pennsylvania Dutch Folklore Center.

YOUNG, D. 2004. The material value of colour: the estate agent's tale. *Home Cultures* 1(1): 5–22.

YOUNG, M. 2000. The careless collector: Malinowksi and the antiquarians. In M. O'Hanlon and R. Welsch (eds) *Hunting the Gatherers: Ethnographic Collectors, Agents and Agency in Melanesia, 1870s–1930s.* New York: Berghahn Books, pp. 181–202.

YOUNG, R. J. C. 2007. *The Idea of English Ethnicity.* Oxford: Blackwell.

YUHL, S. 2005. *A Golden Haze of Memory: the making of historic Charleston.* Chapel Hill: University of North Carolina Press.

ZACHOS, K. 2007. The Neolithic background: a reassessment. In P. M. Day and R. C. P. Doonan (eds) *Metallurgy in the Early Bronze Age.* Sheffield Studies in Aegean Archaeology 7. Oxford: Oxbow Books, pp. 168–206.

ZANGWILL, N. 2002. Are there counterexamples to aesthetic theories of art? *Journal of Aesthetics and Art Criticism* 60(2): 111–118.

ZEDEÑO, M. 1997. Landscapes, land use, and the history of territory formation: an example from the Puebloan Southwest. *Journal of Archaeological Method and Theory* 4(1): 67–103.

ZEDEÑO, M. 2000. On what people make of places: a behavioral cartography. In M. B. Schiffer (ed.) *Social Theory in Archaeology*. Salt Lake City: University of Utah Press, pp. 97–111.

ZUKIN, S. 1991. *Landscapes of power: from Detroit to Disney World*. Berkeley: University of California Press.

ZUKIN, S. and MAGUIRE, J. S. 2004. Consumers and consumption. *Annual Review of Sociology* 30: 173–197.

INDEX